The Thomas Guide®

Santa Clara County
street guide

TELL US WHAT YOU THINK
comment card on last page

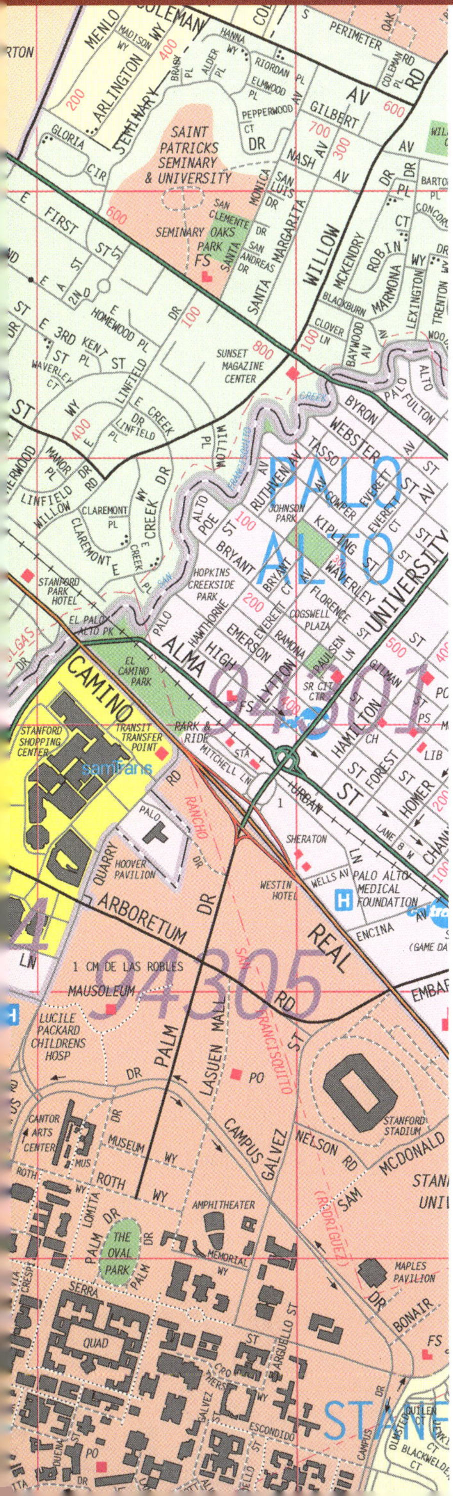

Contents

Introduction

Maps

Lists and Indexes

PageFinder™ Map U.S. Patent No. 5,419,586
Canadian Patent No. 2,116,425
Patente Mexicana No. 188186

Published in U.S.A. Printed in Canada.

RAND McNALLY
Rand McNally Consumer Affairs
P.O. Box 7600
Chicago, IL 60680-9915
randmcnally.com
For comments or suggestions, please call
(800) 777-MAPS (-6277)
or email us at:
consumeraffairs@randmcnally.com

Legend

- Freeway
- Interchange/ramp
- Highway
- Primary road
- Secondary road
- Minor road
- Restricted road
- Alley
- Unpaved road
- Tunnel
- Toll road
- High occupancy vehicle lane
- Stacked multiple roadways
- Proposed road
- Proposed freeway
- Freeway under construction
- One-way road
- Two-way road
- Trail, walkway
- Stairs
- Railroad
- Rapid transit
- Rapid transit, underground

- Ferry
- City boundary
- County boundary
- State boundary
- International boundary
- Military base, Indian reservation
- Township, range, rancho
- River, creek, shoreline
- 98607 ZIP code boundary, ZIP code
- 5 Interstate
- 5 Interstate (Business)
- 3 U.S. highway
- 1 4 8 9 State highways
- Carpool lane
- A Street list marker
- Street name continuation
- Street name change
- Station (train, bus)
- Building (see List of Abbreviations page)
- Building footprint
- Public elementary school
- Public high school

- Private elementary school
- Private high school
- Fire station
- Library
- Mission
- Campground
- H Hospital
- Mountain
- Section corner
- Boat launch
- Gate, locks, barricades
- Lighthouse
- Major shopping center
- Dry lake, beach
- Dam
- Intermittent lake, marsh
- 29 Exit number
- Caltrain Caltrain Station
- samTrans samTrans Transfer/ Park n Ride Centers
- VTA VTA Light Rail Station/ Park n Ride Lot
- ACE, Amtrak-Capital Corridor

we've got you COVERED

Rand McNally's broad selection of products is perfect for your every need. Whether you're looking for the convenience of write-on wipe-off laminated maps, extra maps for every car, or a Road Atlas to plan your next vacation or to use as a reference, Rand McNally has you covered.

Street Guides

Alameda County
Alameda & Contra Costa Counties
Bay Area Metro
Contra Costa County
Marin & Sonoma Counties
Monterey Bay
Napa & Solano Counties
Napa & Sonoma Counties
Sacramento County
Sacramento & Solano Counties
San Francisco & Marin Counties
San Francisco & San Mateo Counties
Santa Clara County
Santa Clara & San Mateo Counties
San Francisco/ Northern Peninsula Cities
San Francisco Bay Area Regional
San Jose/ Silicon Valley
San Mateo/ Redwood City
Santa Cruz/ Watsonville
Santa Rosa/ Sonoma

Folded Maps

EasyFinder® Laminated Maps

California
Concord/ Walnut Creek
Marin County
Monterey/ Carmel
North Bay & the Wine Country
Northern California
Oakland/ Berkeley
Peninsula Cities
San Francisco
San Francisco Bay Area Regional
San Jose/ Santa Clara
Silicon Valley

Paper Maps

California
Citrus Heights/ Carmichael
Concord/ Antioch/ Walnut Creek/ Danville
Fremont/ Hayward
Livermore/ Pleasanton
Marin County
Monterey/ Carmel/ Salinas
Napa/ Fairfield
Oakland/ Berkeley/ Richmond

Wall Maps

Bay Area to Sacramento Regional
California Arterial

Road Atlases

California Road Atlas
Road Atlas
Road Atlas & Travel Guide
Large Scale Road Atlas
Midsize Road Atlas
Deluxe Midsize Road Atlas
Pocket Road Atlas

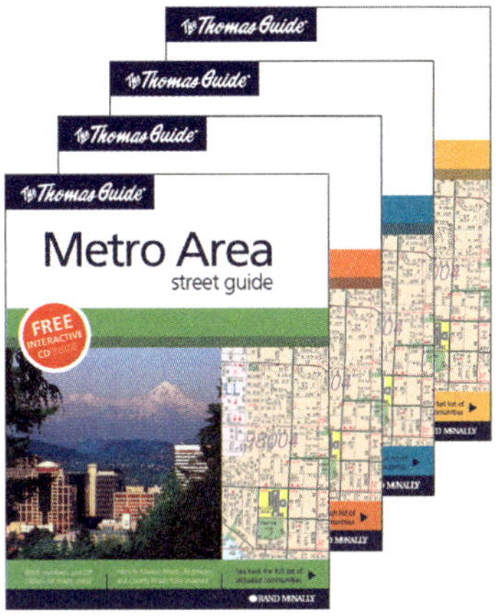

Wherever Rand McNally products are sold or at
www.randmcnally.com

Downtown San Jose

Points of Interest

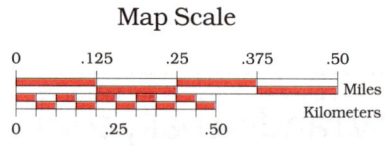

1	California Theatre	F5
2	Center for the Performing Arts	E6
3	Children's Discovery Museum	E6
4	City Hall	F4
5	Civic Auditorium	F5
6	Civic Center	D2
7	County Administration Bldg	D2
8	County Courthouse	E4
9	County Sheriff's Office	D1
10	Crowne Plaza San Jose	E6
11	Fairmont Hotel	F5
12	Hotel De Anza	E5
13	HP Pavillion	D5
14	Hyatt Sainte Claire	F5
15	Martin Luther King Jr Library	F4
16	Montgomery Theater	F5
17	Museum of Art	F5
18	Norman Y. Mineta San Jose International Airport	B1
19	Parkside Hall	E5
20	Peralta Adobe	E4
21	Rosicrucian Egyptian Museum & Planetarium	A5
22	San Jose McEnery Convention Center	F6
23	San Jose Hilton & Towers Hotel	F6
24	San Jose Marriott	F5
25	San Jose State University	G5
26	Santa Clara County Service Center	E5
27	The Tech Museum of Innovation	F5
28	US Army Reserve Center	C2
29	Visitors Bureau	F6

Map Scale

0 .125 .25 .375 .50 Miles

0 .25 .50 Kilometers

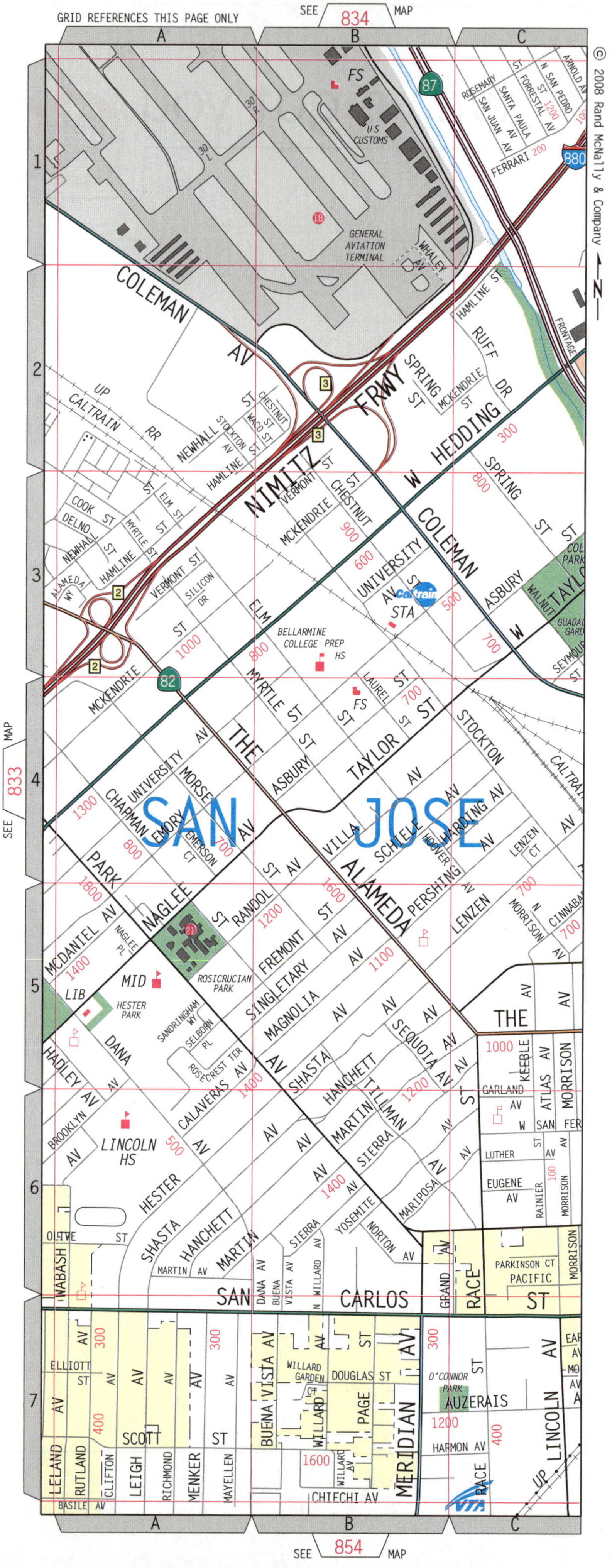

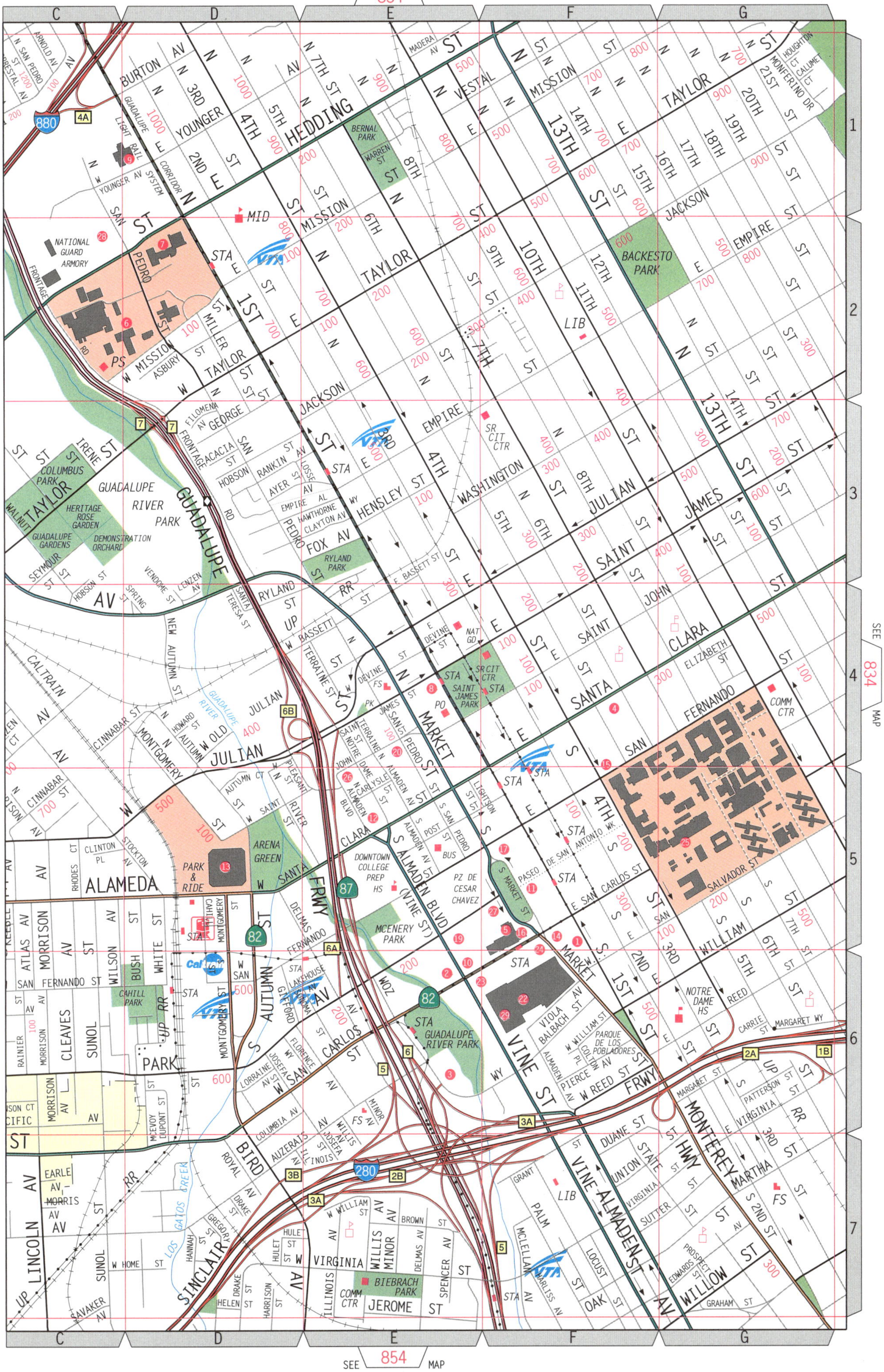

SEE 834 MAP
C
D
E
F
G
© 2008 Rand McNally & Company
1
2
3
4
5
6
7
SEE 834 MAP
HEDDING
TAYLOR
JACKSON
EMPIRE
WASHINGTON
JULIAN
SAINT JAMES
SAINT JOHN
SANTA CLARA
SAN FERNANDO
SAN CARLOS
WILLIAM
REED
VIRGINIA
JEROME ST
WILLOW ST
MONTEREY HWY
VINE ST
ALMADEN BLVD
MARKET ST
GUADALUPE FRWY
ALAMEDA
PARK AV
BIRD AV
SINCLAIR FRWY
LINCOLN AV
AUTUMN ST
MONTGOMERY ST
DELMAS AV
13TH ST
BACKESTO PARK
BERNAL PARK
COLUMBUS PARK
GUADALUPE RIVER PARK
HERITAGE ROSE GARDEN
GUADALUPE GARDENS
DEMONSTRATION ORCHARD
RYLAND PARK
SAINT JAMES PARK
ARENA GREEN
PARK & RIDE
DOWNTOWN COLLEGE PREP HS
PZ DE CESAR CHAVEZ
MCENERY PARK
CAHILL PARK
BIEBRACH PARK
NOTRE DAME HS
NATIONAL GUARD ARMORY
COMM CTR
SR CIT CTR
LIB
STA
PS
FS
PO
MID
BUS
CALTRAIN
LOS GATOS CREEK
GUADALUPE RIVER
880
280
87
82
SANTA CLARA CO.
SEE 854 MAP

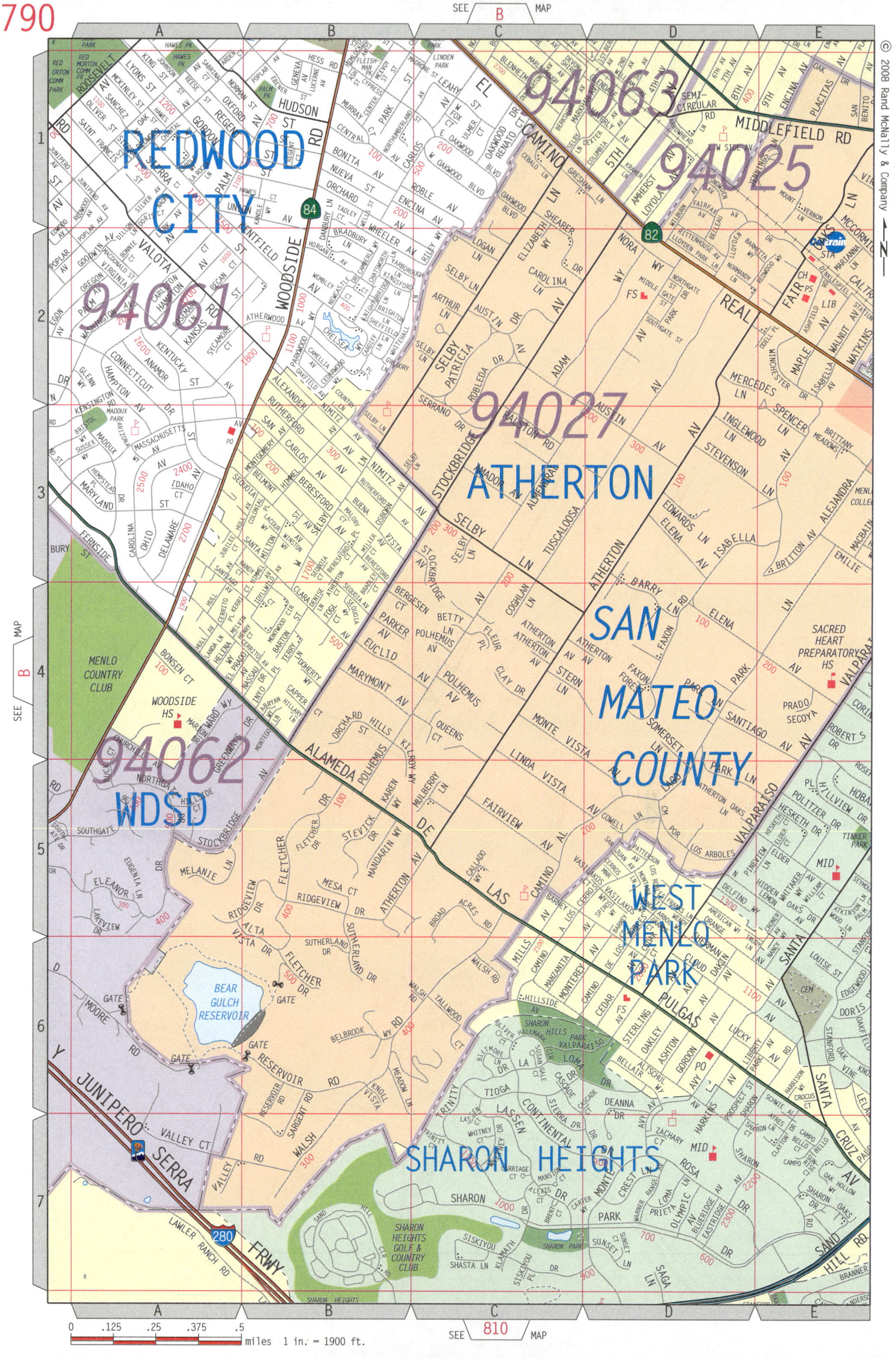
SEE B MAP
REDWOOD CITY
94061
94063
94025
94027
ATHERTON
SAN MATEO COUNTY
94062
WDSD
WEST MENLO PARK
SHARON HEIGHTS
MENLO COUNTRY CLUB
WOODSIDE HS
BEAR GULCH RESERVOIR
SHARON HEIGHTS GOLF & COUNTRY CLUB
SACRED HEART PREPARATORY HS
MIDDLEFIELD RD
EL CAMINO REAL
WOODSIDE RD
ALAMEDA DE LAS PULGAS
JUNIPERO SERRA FRWY
SAND HILL RD
SANTA CRUZ AV
VALPARAISO AV
ATHERTON AV
STOCKBRIDGE AV
SELBY LN
FLETCHER DR
RESERVOIR RD
SHARON PARK DR
FERNSIDE ST
LAWLER RANCH RD
SEE 810 MAP
0 .125 .25 .375 .5 miles 1 in. = 1900 ft.
SANTA CLARA CO.

SEE B MAP

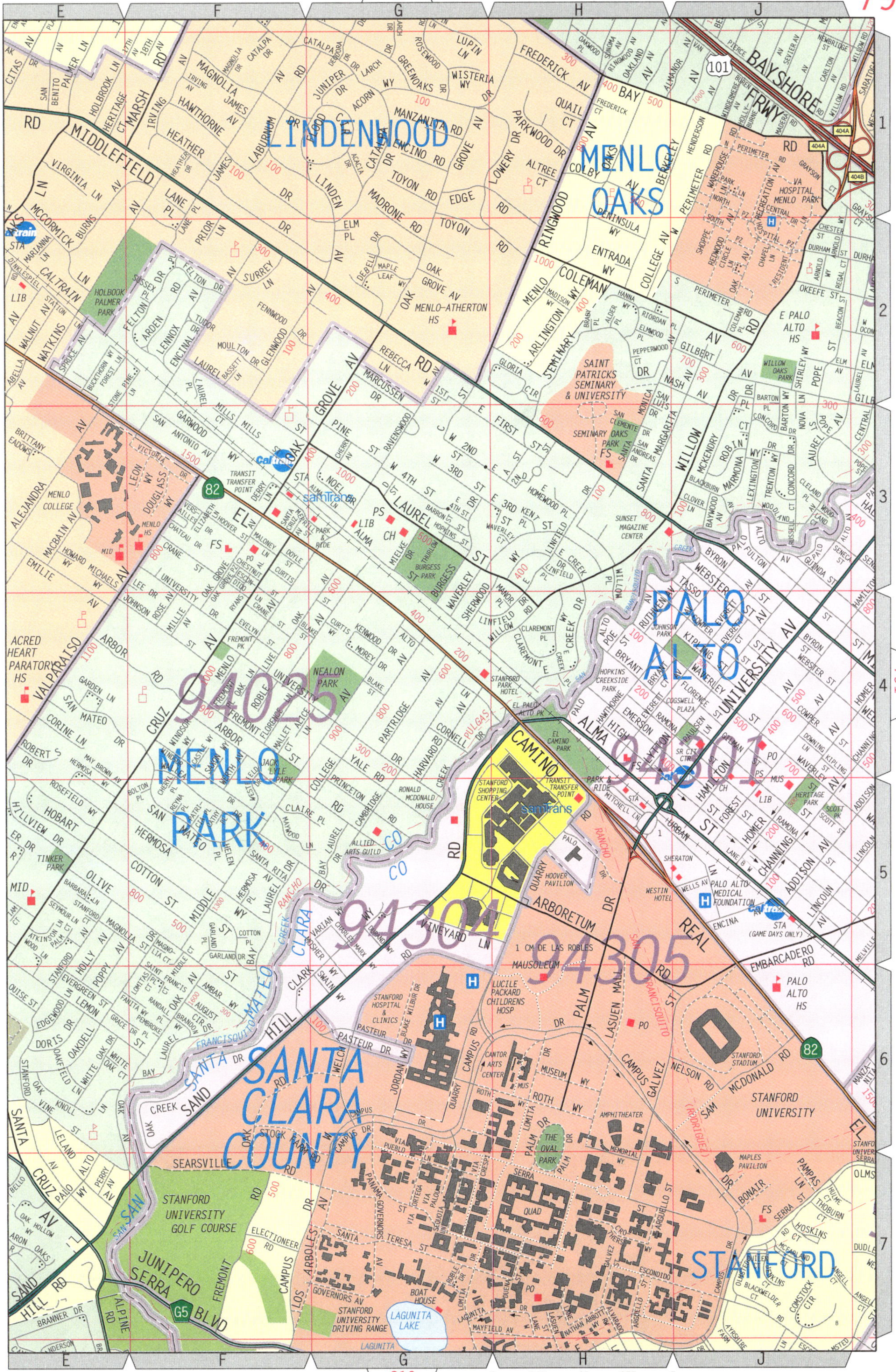

SEE 791 MAP

SEE 810 MAP

0 .125 .25 .375 .5 miles 1 in. = 1900 ft.

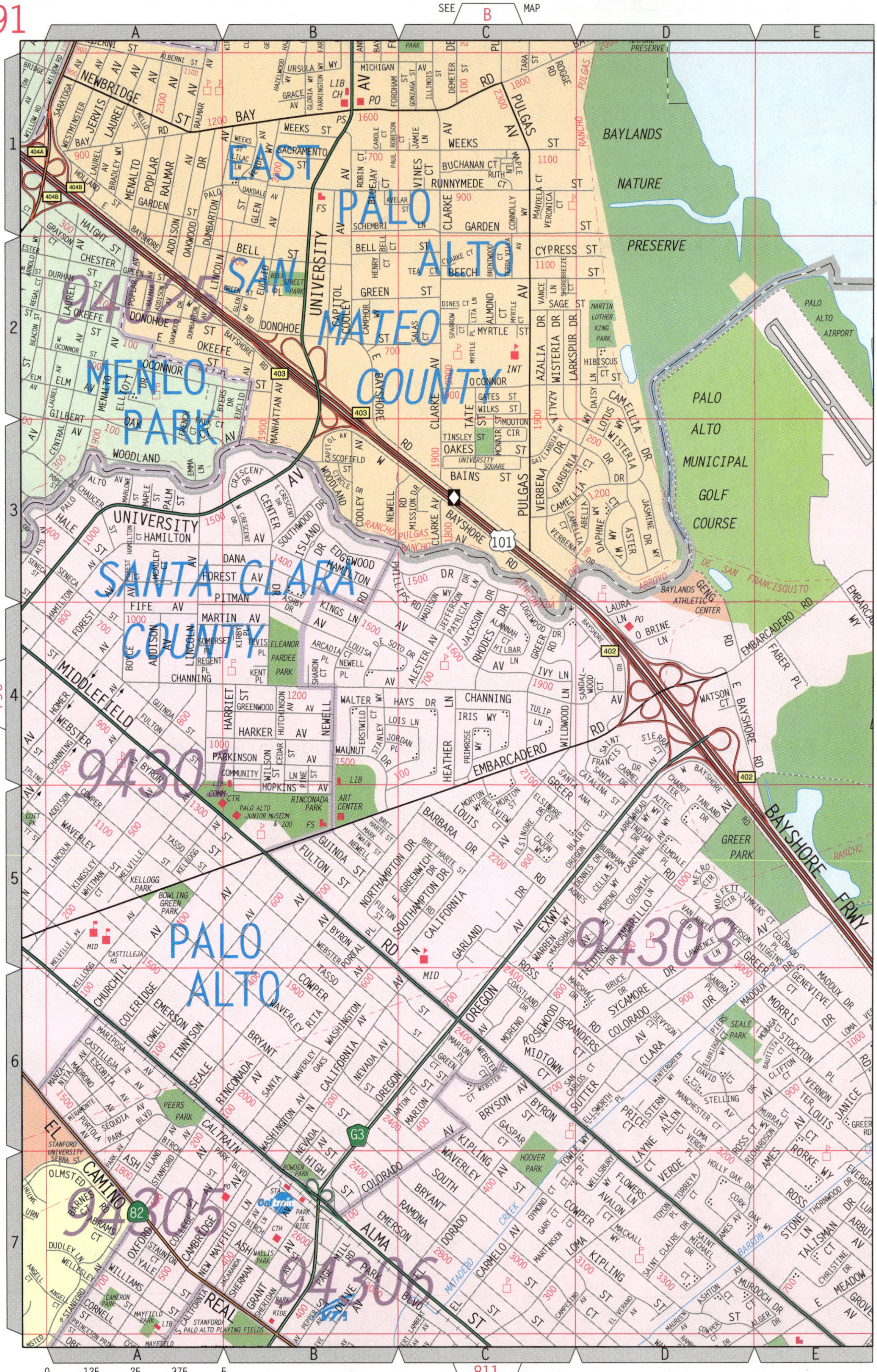

SEE B MAP
A
B
C
D
E
1
2
3
4
5
6
7
EAST PALO ALTO
SAN MATEO COUNTY
MENLO PARK
SANTA CLARA COUNTY
PALO ALTO
94025
94301
94303
94305
94306
BAYLANDS NATURE PRESERVE
PALO ALTO AIRPORT
PALO ALTO MUNICIPAL GOLF COURSE
BAYSHORE FRWY
EMBARCADERO RD
UNIVERSITY AV
MIDDLEFIELD RD
EL CAMINO REAL
ALMA ST
OREGON EXWY
GREER PARK
HOOVER PARK
PEERS PARK
SEALE PARK
ELEANOR PARDEE PARK
RINCONADA PARK
PALO ALTO JUNIOR MUSEUM & ZOO
ART CENTER
BAYLANDS ATHLETIC CENTER
SEE 790 MAP
SEE 811 MAP
0 .125 .25 .375 .5 miles 1 in. = 1900 ft.

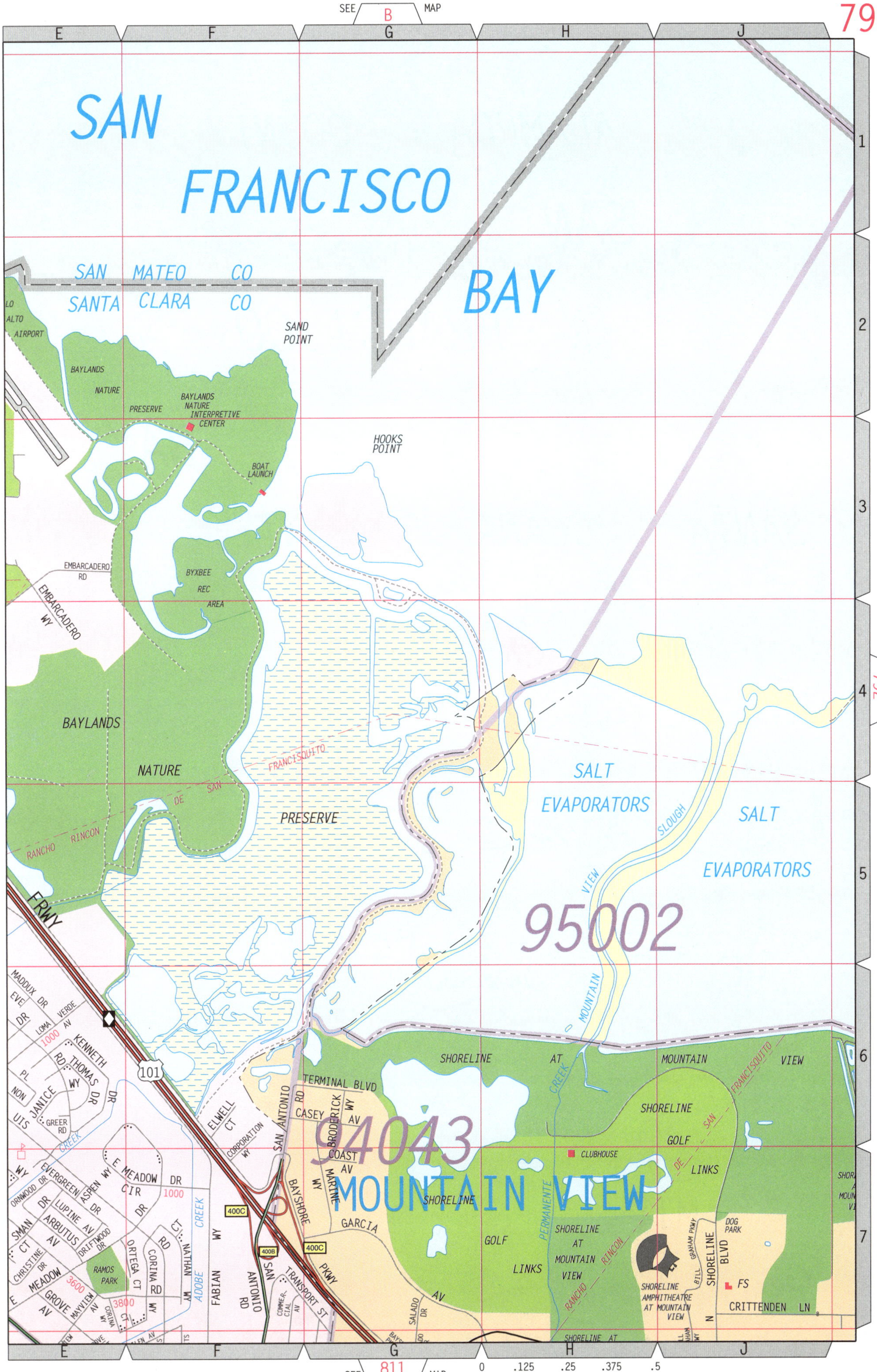
SEE B MAP
E
F
G
H
J
1
2
3
4
5
6
7
SAN FRANCISCO BAY
SAN MATEO CO
SANTA CLARA CO
LO ALTO AIRPORT
SAND POINT
BAYLANDS NATURE PRESERVE
BAYLANDS NATURE INTERPRETIVE CENTER
HOOKS POINT
BOAT LAUNCH
EMBARCADERO RD
EMBARCADERO WY
BYXBEE REC AREA
BAYLANDS NATURE PRESERVE
RANCHO RINCON DE SAN FRANCISQUITO
SALT EVAPORATORS
SALT EVAPORATORS
MOUNTAIN VIEW SLOUGH
95002
SEE 792 MAP
FRWY
101
MADDUX DR
EVE DR
LOMA VERDE AV
1000
KENNETH DR
THOMAS DR
JANICE WY
GREER RD
CREEK
ELWELL CT
CORPORATION WY
SAN ANTONIO RD
TERMINAL BLVD
CASEY AV
BRODERICK WY
COAST AV
MARINE WY
BAYSHORE PKWY
94043
MOUNTAIN VIEW
SHORELINE AT MOUNTAIN VIEW
SHORELINE GOLF LINKS
CLUBHOUSE
PERMANENTE CREEK
SHORELINE AT MOUNTAIN VIEW
SHORELINE GOLF LINKS
GARCIA AV
EVERGREEN DR
ASPEN WY
MEADOW CIR
DR
LUPINE AV
ARBUTUS AV
DRIFTWOOD DR
ORTEGA CT
CORINA WY
NATHAN WY
ADOBE CREEK
FABIAN WY
SAN ANTONIO RD
TRANSPORT ST
COMMERCIAL
RAMOS PARK
MEADOW GROVE AV
3600
3800
400C
400B
400C
SALADO DR
SHORELINE AMPHITHEATRE AT MOUNTAIN VIEW
GRAHAM PKWY
BILL GRAHAM PKWY
SHORELINE BLVD
DOG PARK
FS
CRITTENDEN LN
SHORELINE AT
SEE 811 MAP

SANTA CLARA CO.

0 .125 .25 .375 .5 miles 1 in. = 1900 ft.

SEE B MAP
A
B
C
D
E
1
2
3
4
5
6
7
94555
ALAMEDA
COUNTY
DON EDWARDS
SAN FRANCISCO BAY
NATIONAL WILDLIFE
REFUGE
SAN
SANTA CLARA CO
ALAMEDA CO
CALAVERAS PT
FRANCISCO
COYOTE CREEK
BAY
SANTA
CLARA
COUNTY
95002
GUADALUPE SLOUGH
SEE 791 MAP
SALT
EVAPORATORS
SALT
EVAPORATOR
94089
SHORELINE AT MOUNTAIN VIEW
CRITTENDEN LN
MTVW
MOFFETT FEDERAL AIRFIELD
RD
ZOOK
AMES RESEARCH CENTER
94043
SUNNYVALE
RANCHO POSOLMI
MARRIAGE RD
94035
MOFFETT FIELD GOLF COURSE
0 .125 .25 .375 .5
miles 1 in. = 1900 ft.
SEE 812 MAP

SANTA CLARA CO.

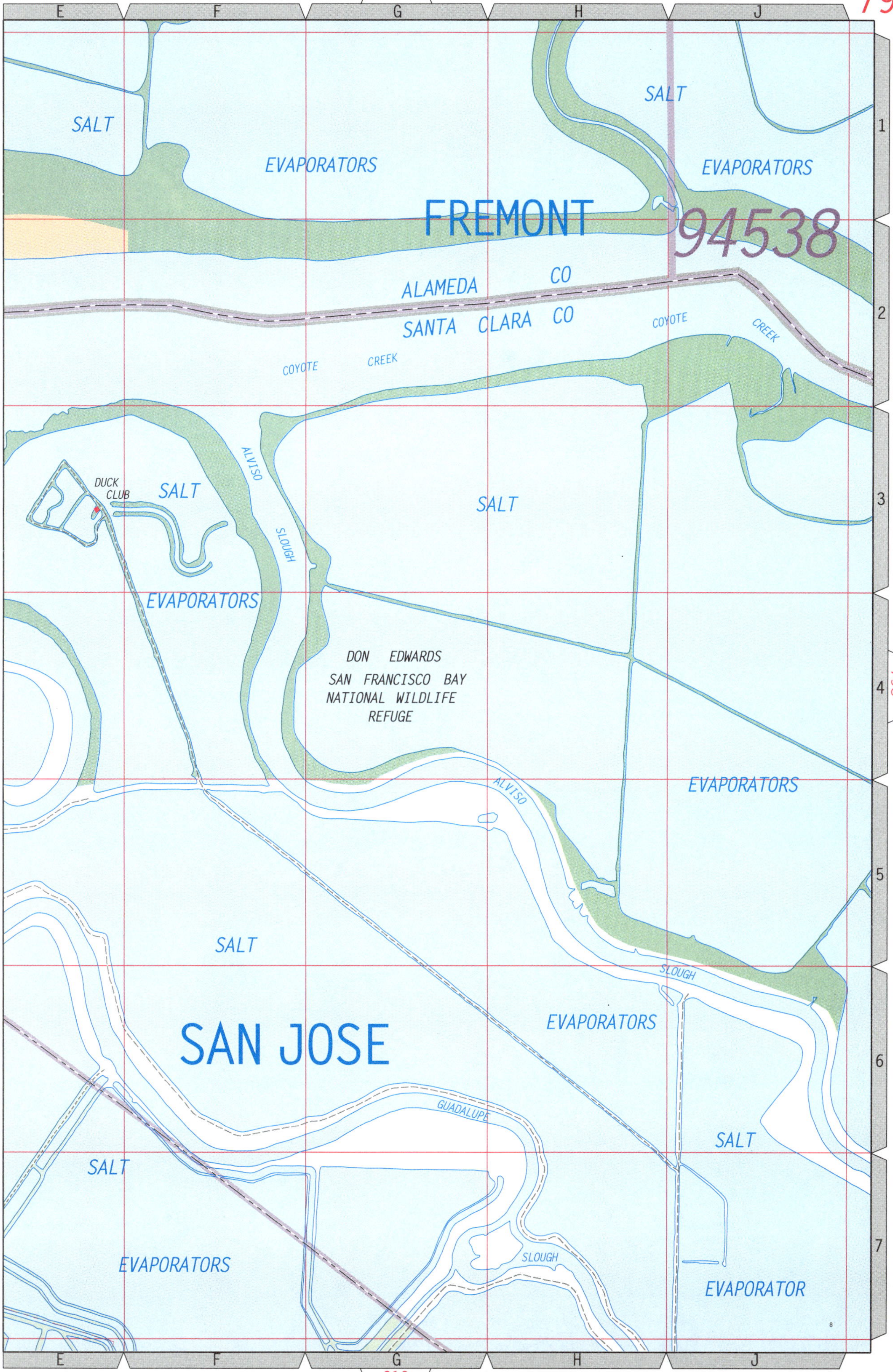
SEE B MAP
E
F
G
H
J
SALT
EVAPORATORS
SALT
EVAPORATORS
FREMONT
94538
ALAMEDA CO
SANTA CLARA CO
COYOTE CREEK
COYOTE CREEK
ALVISO SLOUGH
DUCK CLUB
SALT
SALT
EVAPORATORS
DON EDWARDS SAN FRANCISCO BAY NATIONAL WILDLIFE REFUGE
ALVISO SLOUGH
EVAPORATORS
SALT
EVAPORATORS
SAN JOSE
GUADALUPE SLOUGH
SALT
SALT
EVAPORATORS
EVAPORATOR
1
2
3
4
5
6
7
SEE 793 MAP
SEE 812 MAP
0 .125 .25 .375 .5 miles 1 in. = 1900 ft.

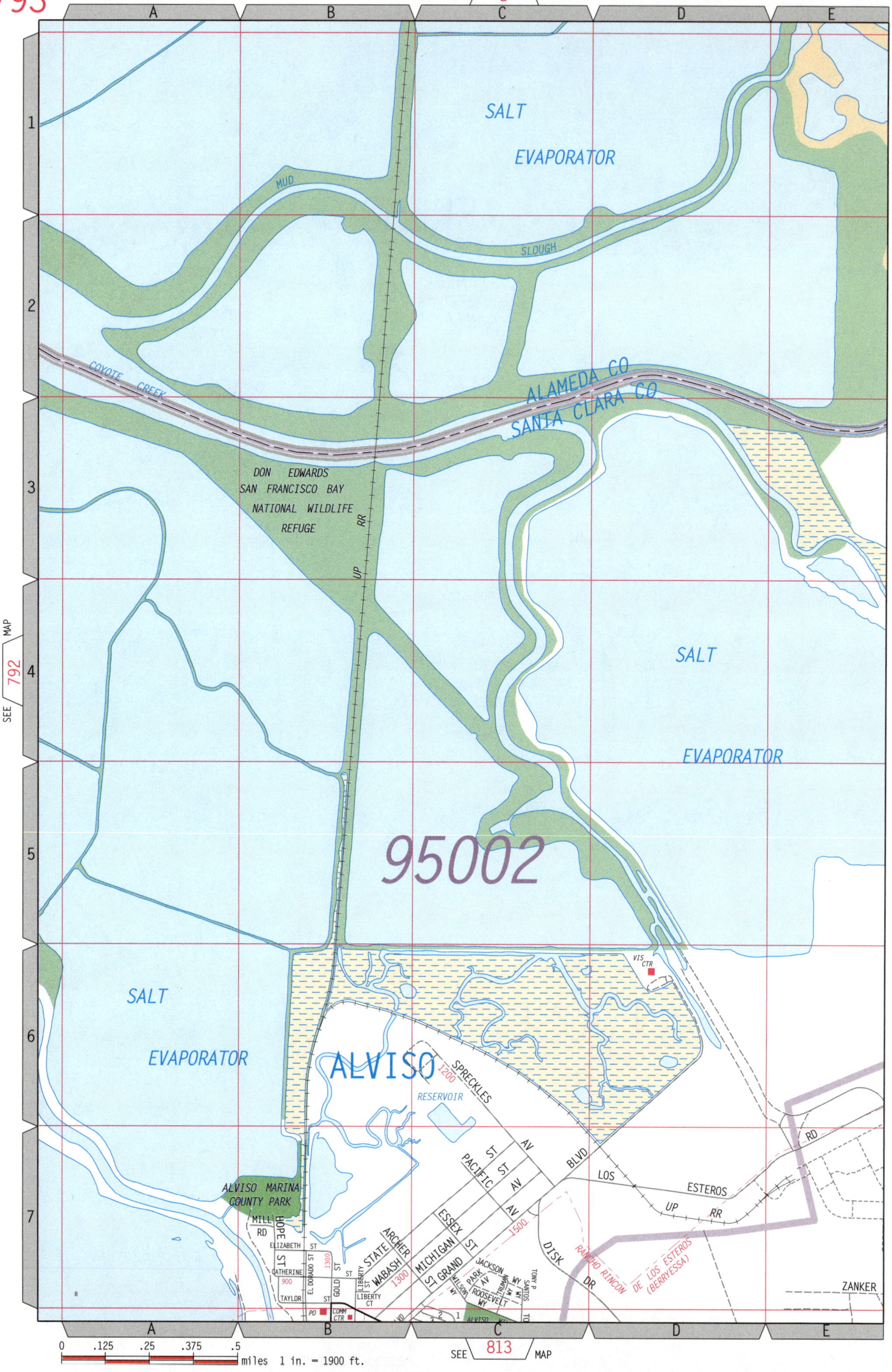

SEE B MAP
SALT
EVAPORATOR
MUD
SLOUGH
COYOTE CREEK
ALAMEDA CO
SANTA CLARA CO
DON EDWARDS
SAN FRANCISCO BAY
NATIONAL WILDLIFE
REFUGE
UP RR
SALT
EVAPORATOR
95002
SALT
EVAPORATOR
VIS CTR
ALVISO
SPRECKLES
RESERVOIR
ALVISO MARINA
COUNTY PARK
MILL RD
HOPE ST
ELIZABETH ST
CATHERINE
TAYLOR
EL DORADO ST
GOLD ST
LIBERTY ST
LIBERTY CT
STATE
WABASH
ARCHER
MICHIGAN
GRAND ST
ESSEX ST
PACIFIC AV
BLVD
LOS ESTEROS RD
UP RR
DISK DR
RANCHO RINCON DE LOS ESTEROS (BERRYESSA)
ZANKER
SANTA CLARA CO.
SEE 792 MAP
SEE 813 MAP
miles 1 in. = 1900 ft.

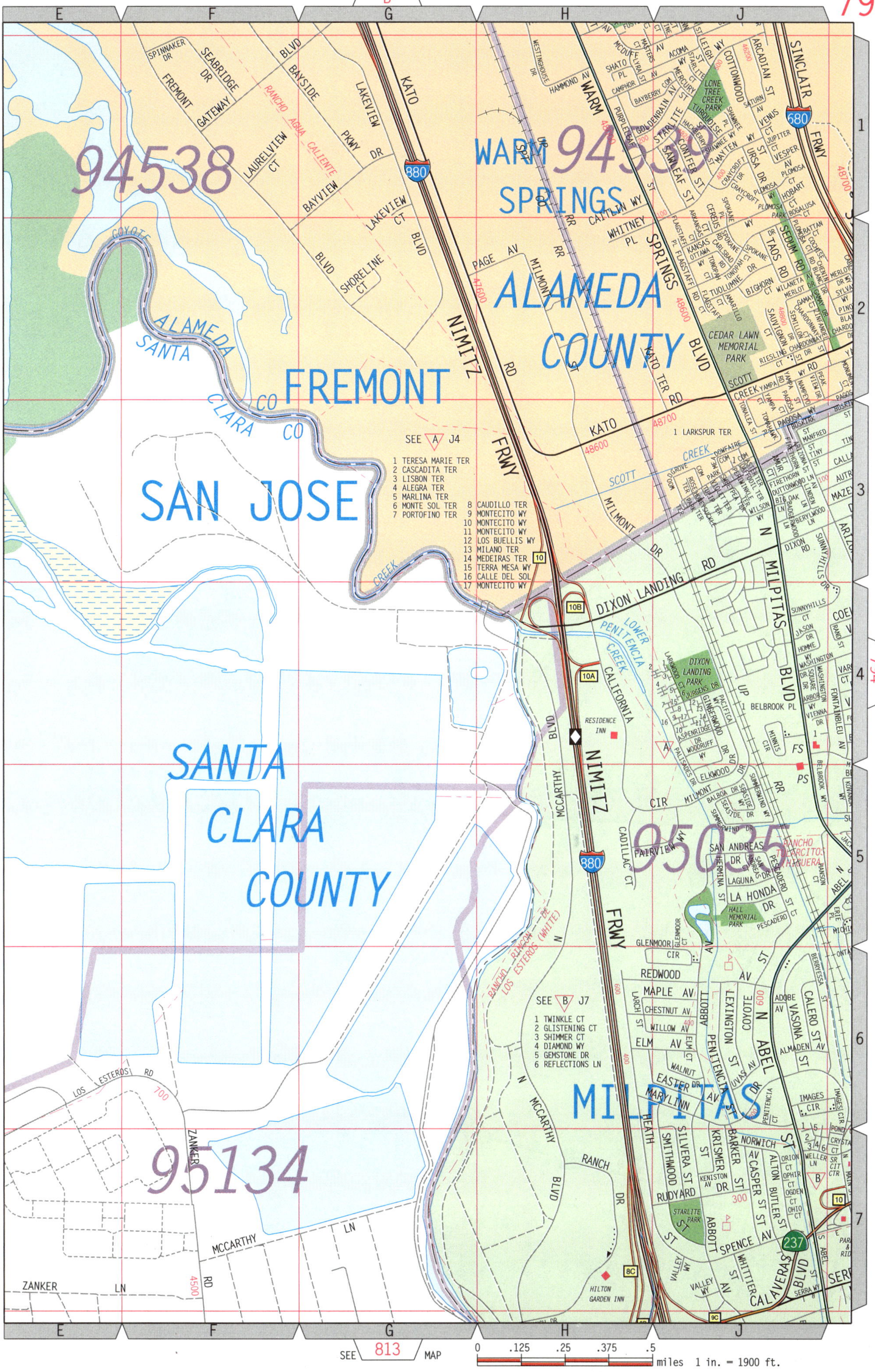
SEE B MAP
94538
94539
WARM SPRINGS
ALAMEDA COUNTY
FREMONT
SAN JOSE
SANTA CLARA COUNTY
95035
MILPITAS
95134
SEE A J4
1 TERESA MARIE TER
2 CASCADITA TER
3 LISBON TER
4 ALEGRA TER
5 MARLINA TER
6 MONTE SOL TER
7 PORTOFINO TER
8 CAUDILLO TER
9 MONTECITO WY
10 MONTECITO WY
11 MONTECITO WY
12 LOS BUELLIS WY
13 MILANO TER
14 MEDEIRAS TER
15 TERRA MESA WY
16 CALLE DEL SOL
17 MONTECITO WY
SEE B J7
1 TWINKLE CT
2 GLISTENING CT
3 SHIMMER CT
4 DIAMOND WY
5 GEMSTONE DR
6 REFLECTIONS LN
NIMITZ FRWY
DIXON LANDING RD
CEDAR LAWN MEMORIAL PARK
DIXON LANDING PARK
HALL MEMORIAL PARK
STARLITE PARK
LONE TREE CREEK PARK
RESIDENCE INN
HILTON GARDEN INN
SEE 794 MAP
SEE 813 MAP
0 .125 .25 .375 .5 miles 1 in. = 1900 ft.
SANTA CLARA CO.

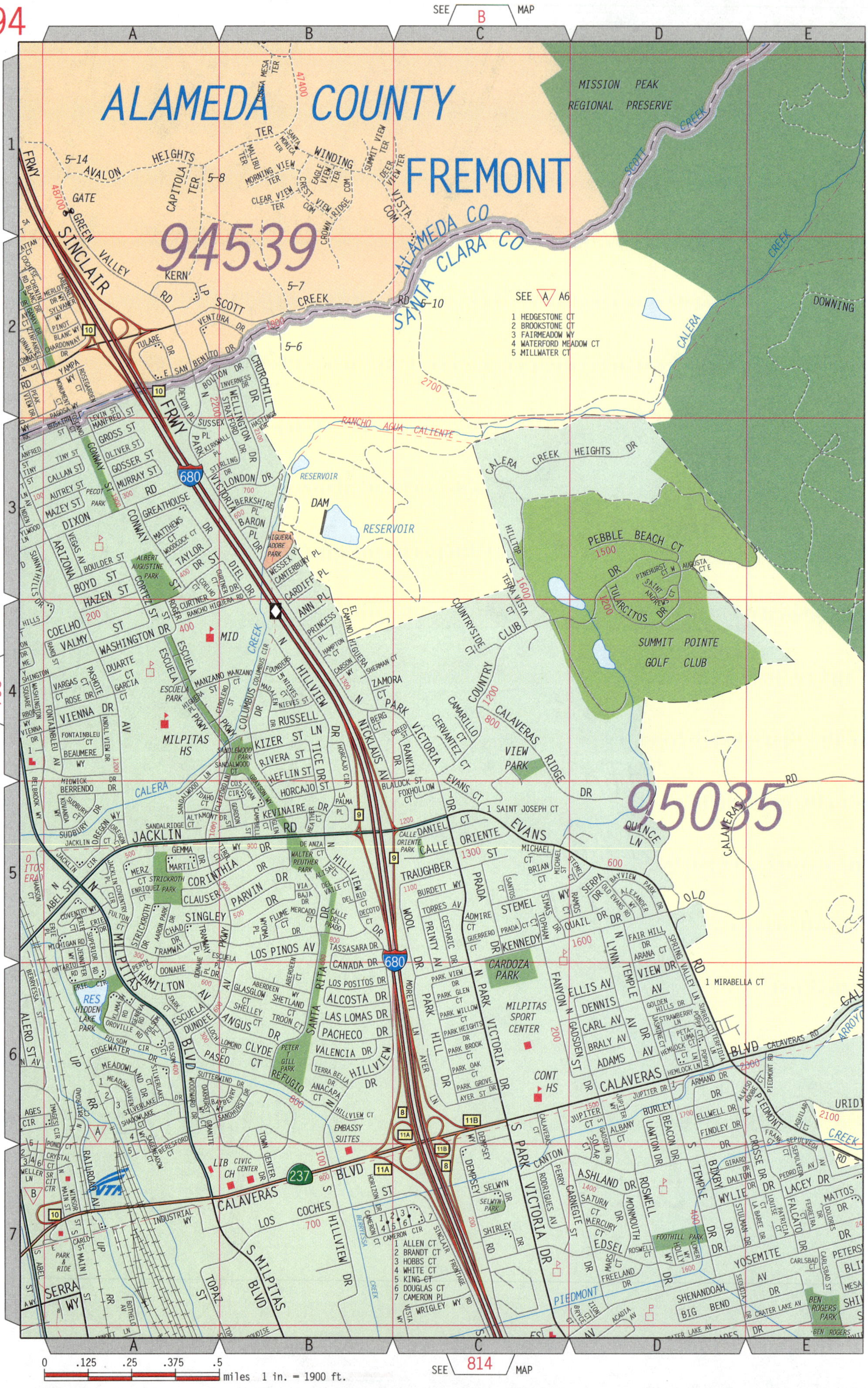
SEE B MAP
SEE 793 MAP
SEE 814 MAP
SANTA CLARA CO.
ALAMEDA COUNTY
FREMONT
94539
95035
MISSION PEAK REGIONAL PRESERVE
ALAMEDA CO
SANTA CLARA CO
SEE A6
1 HEDGESTONE CT
2 BROOKSTONE CT
3 FAIRMEADOW WY
4 WATERFORD MEADOW CT
5 MILLWATER CT
SCOTT CREEK
CALERA CREEK
RANCHO AGUA CALIENTE
RESERVOIR
DAM
CALERA CREEK HEIGHTS DR
PEBBLE BEACH CT
SUMMIT POINTE GOLF CLUB
VIEW PARK
CALAVERAS RIDGE DR
1 SAINT JOSEPH CT
1 MIRABELLA CT
MILPITAS HS
MID
JACKLIN RD
EVANS RD
MILPITAS BLVD
CALAVERAS BLVD
CARDOZA PARK
MILPITAS SPORT CENTER
CONT HS
EMBASSY SUITES
CIVIC CENTER
1 ALLEN CT
2 BRANDT CT
3 HOBBS CT
4 WHITE CT
5 KING CT
6 DOUGLAS CT
7 CAMERON PL
HIDDEN LAKE PARK
PETER GILL PARK
FOOTHILL PARK
BEN ROGERS PARK
PIEDMONT
SINCLAIR FRWY
680
237
0 .125 .25 .375 .5 miles 1 in. = 1900 ft.

SEE B MAP

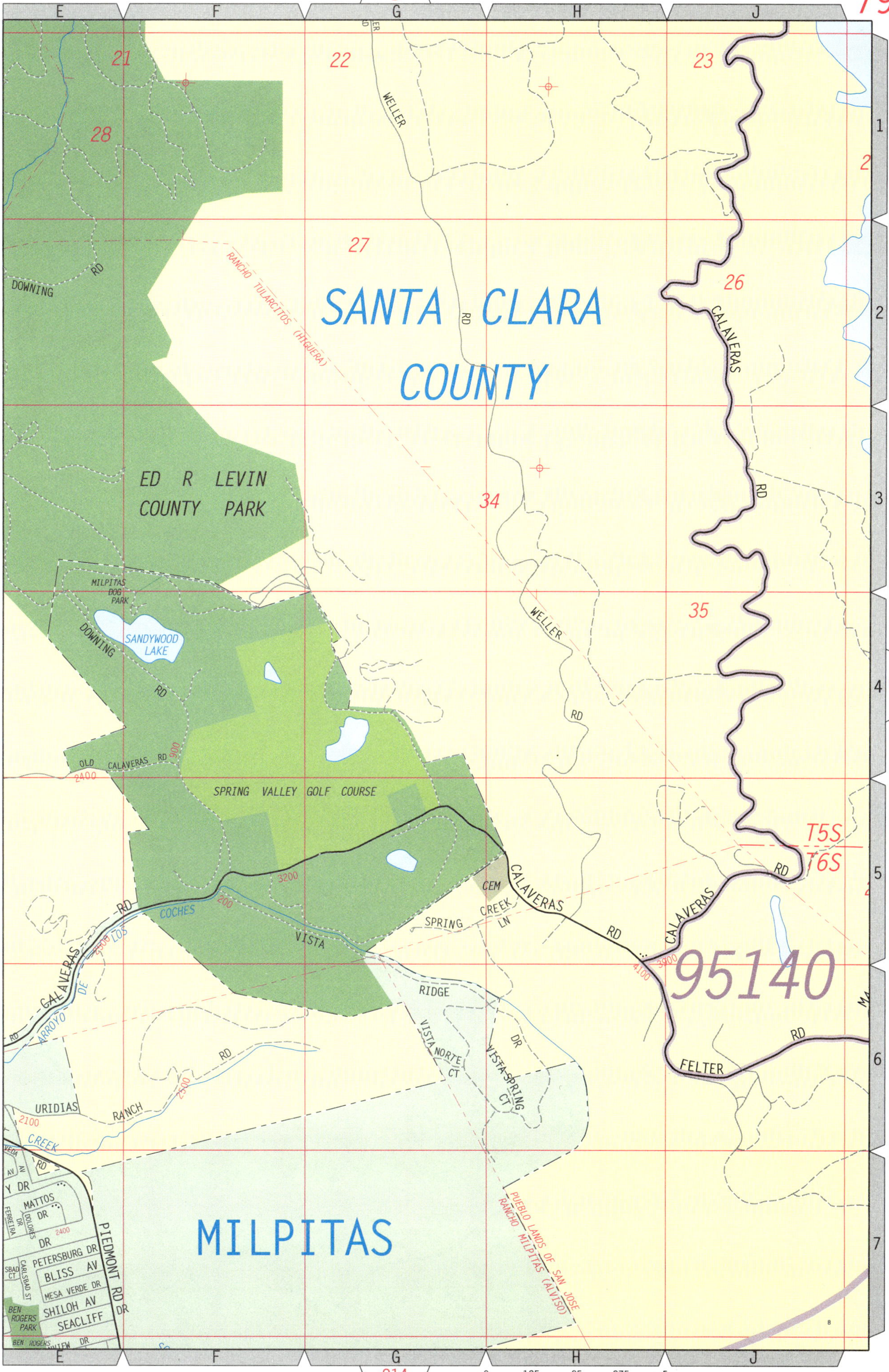

SEE 814 MAP

0 .125 .25 .375 .5 miles 1 in. = 1900 ft.

SEE 790 MAP

SEE B MAP

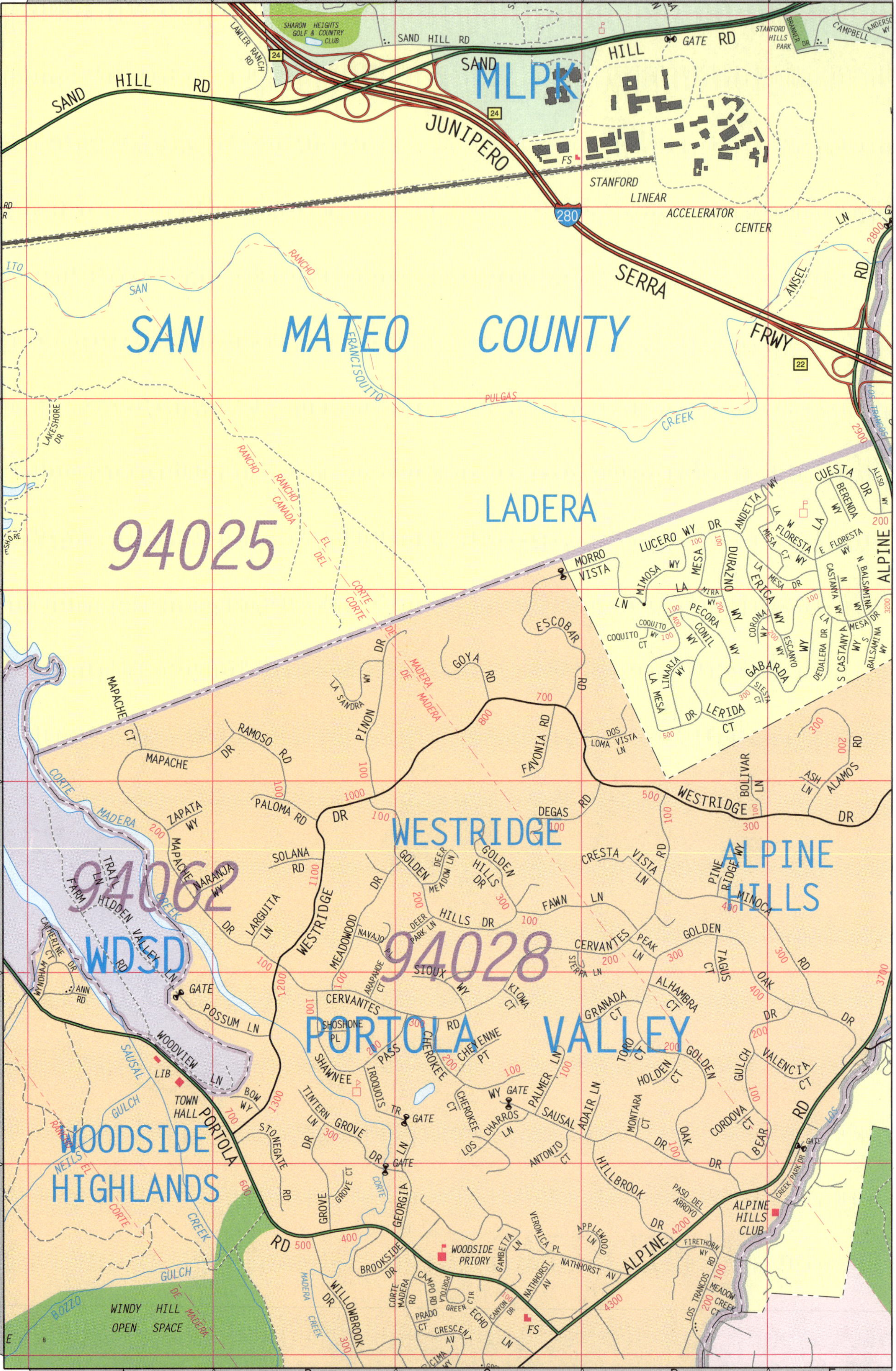

0 .125 .25 .375 .5 miles 1 in. = 1900 ft.

SEE 830 MAP

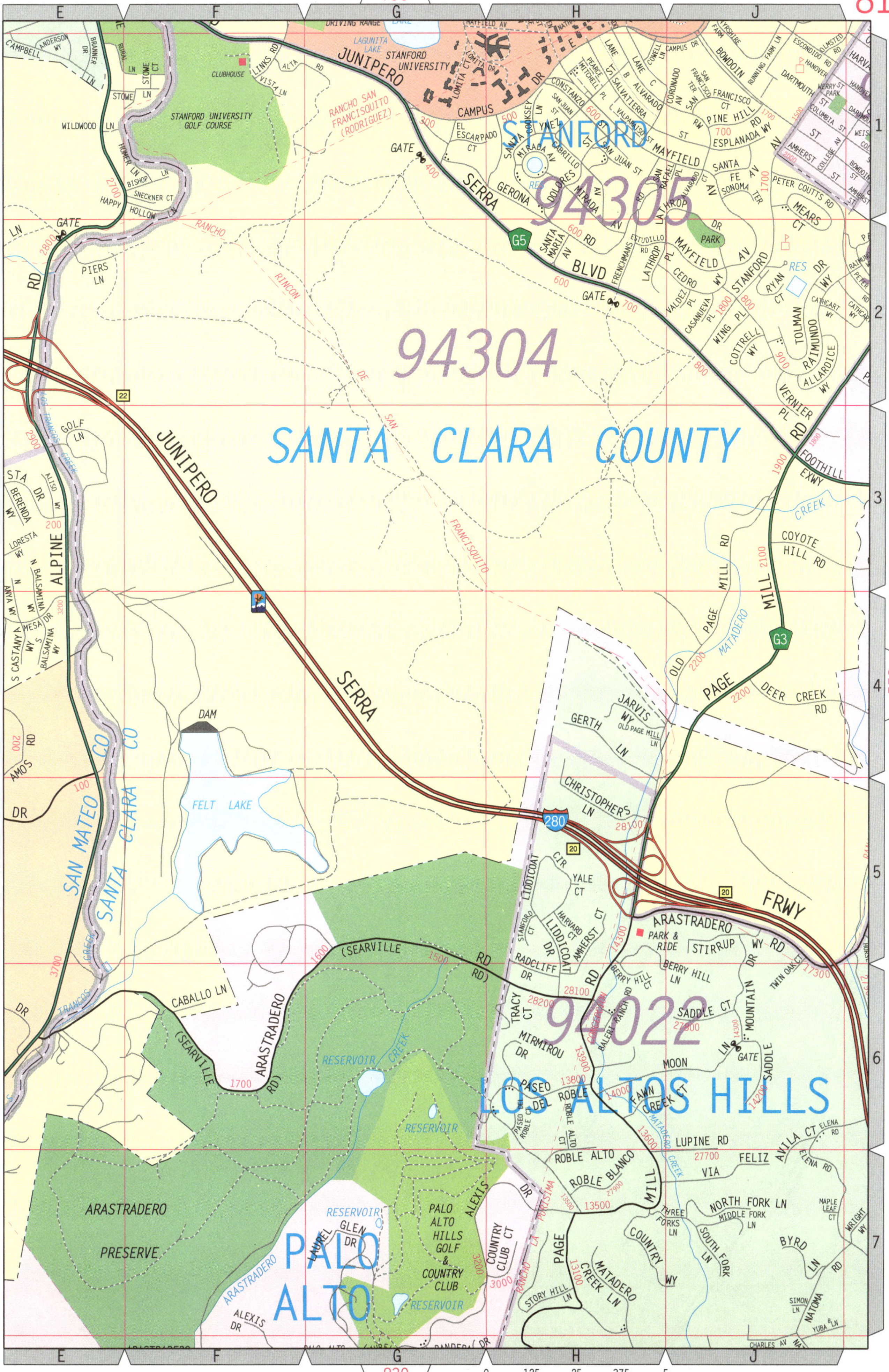
SANTA CLARA COUNTY
STANFORD
94305
94304
94022
LOS ALTOS HILLS
PALO ALTO
STANFORD UNIVERSITY
STANFORD UNIVERSITY GOLF COURSE
JUNIPERO SERRA BLVD
JUNIPERO SERRA FRWY
FELT LAKE
DAM
ARASTRADERO PRESERVE
PALO ALTO HILLS GOLF & COUNTRY CLUB
PAGE MILL RD
FOOTHILL EXWY
ARASTRADERO RD
ALPINE RD
SAN MATEO CO
SANTA CLARA CO
RANCHO SAN FRANCISQUITO (RODRIGUEZ)
SEE 790 MAP
SEE 811 MAP
SEE 830 MAP
0 .125 .25 .375 .5 miles 1 in. = 1900 ft.

SEE 791 MAP

SANTA CLARA CO.

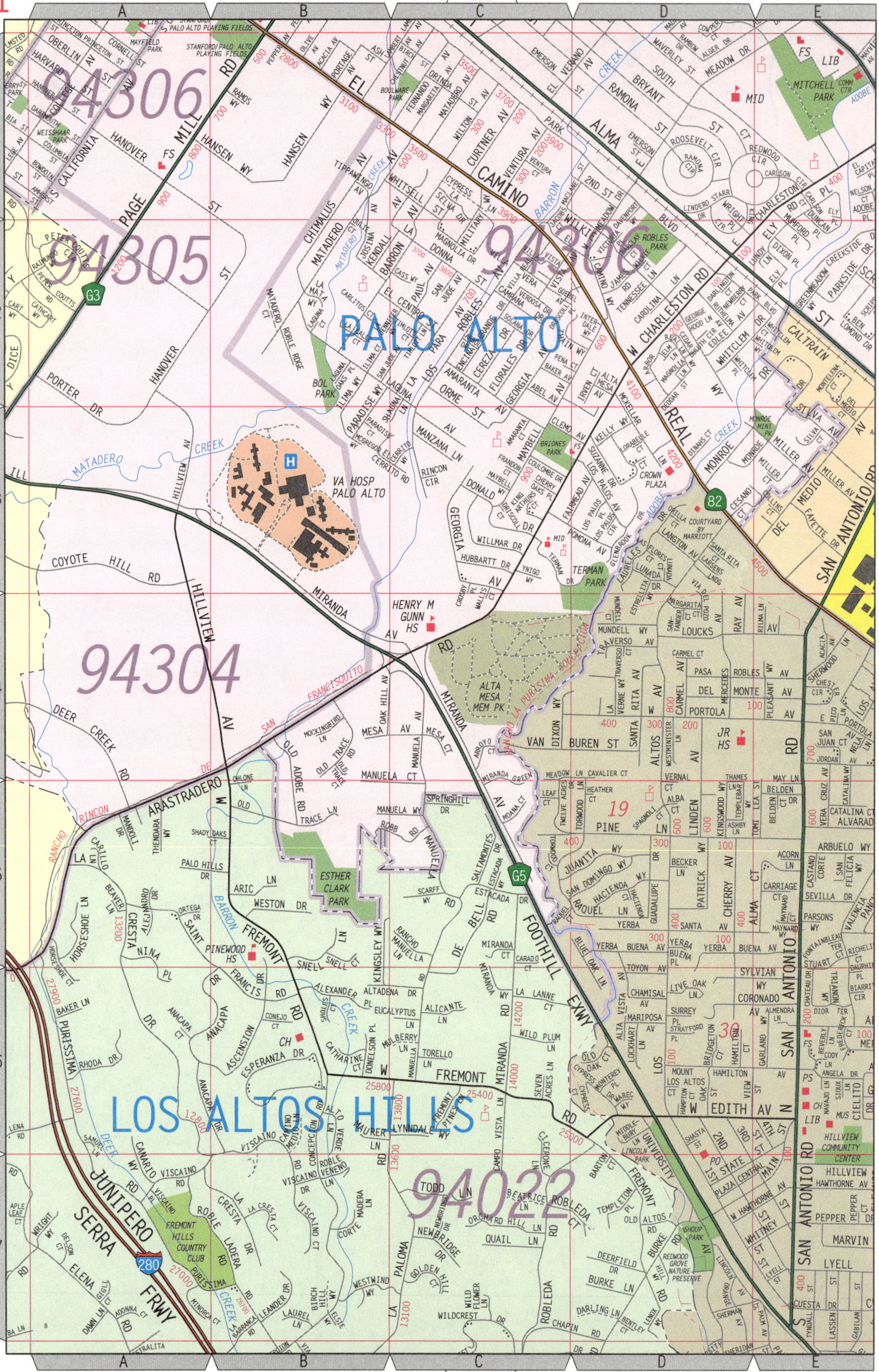

SEE 810 MAP

SEE 831 MAP

0 .125 .25 .375 .5 miles 1 in. = 1900 ft.

SEE 791 MAP

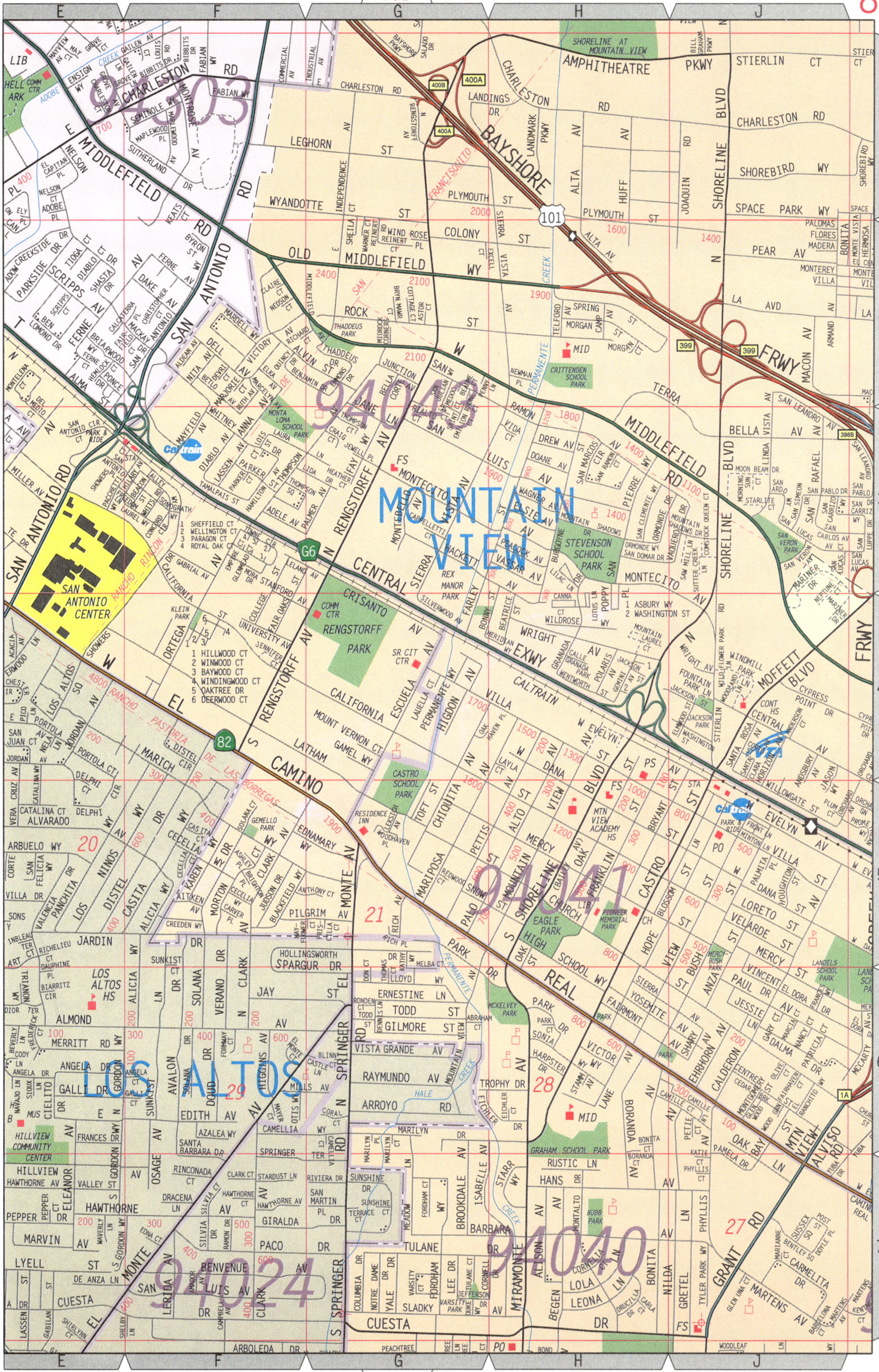

SEE 812 MAP

SEE 831 MAP

0 .125 .25 .375 .5 miles 1 in. = 1900 ft.

SANTA CLARA CO.

SEE 792 MAP

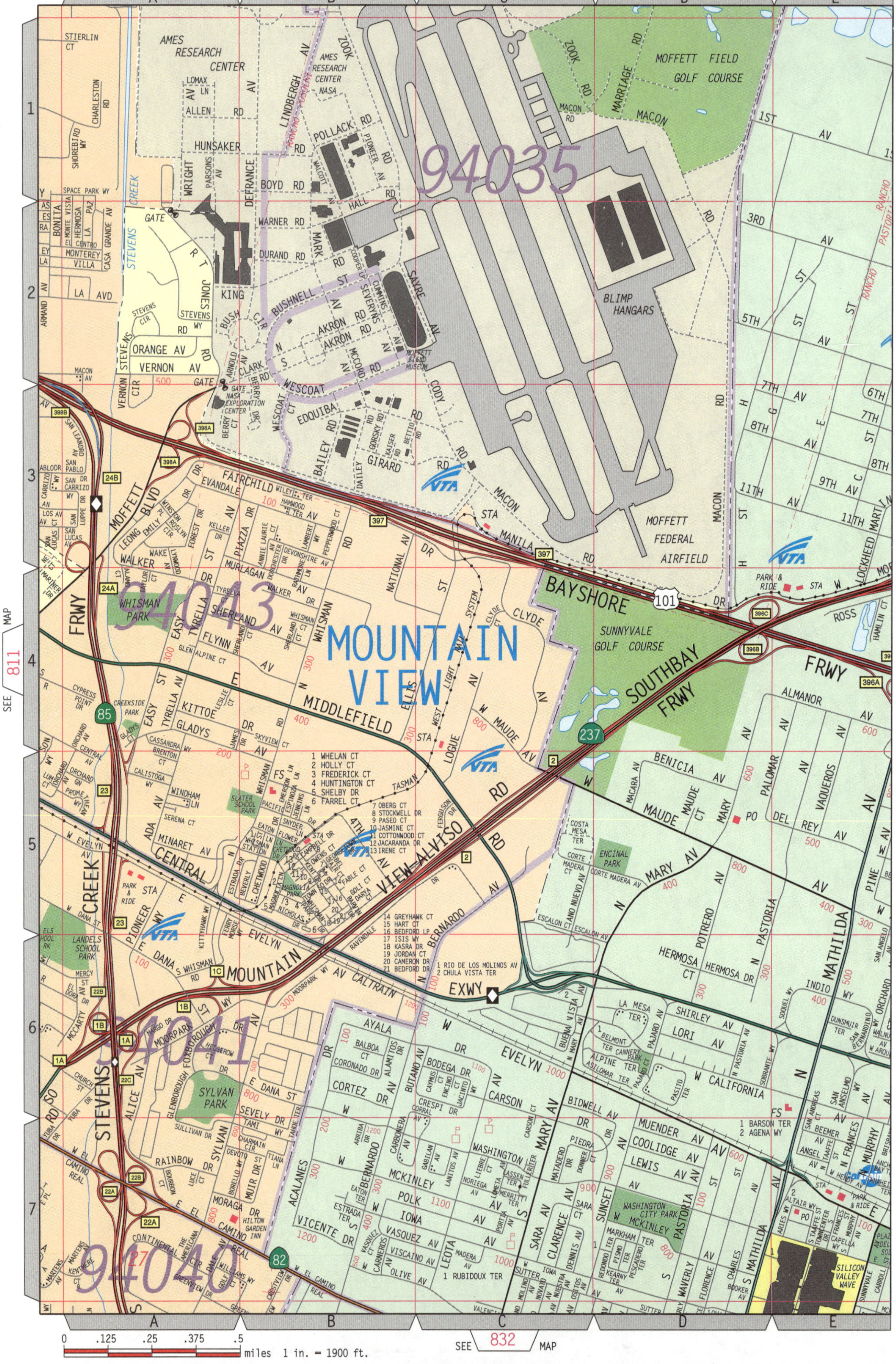
A
B
C
D
E
1
2
3
4
5
6
7
AMES RESEARCH CENTER
AMES RESEARCH CENTER NASA
MOFFETT FIELD GOLF COURSE
94035
BLIMP HANGARS
MOFFETT FEDERAL AIRFIELD
94043
MOUNTAIN VIEW
94041
94040
WHISMAN PARK
SUNNYVALE GOLF COURSE
BAYSHORE FRWY
SOUTHBAY FRWY
MOFFETT BLVD
MIDDLEFIELD RD
CENTRAL EXWY
CALTRAIN
STEVENS CREEK FRWY
MOUNTAIN VIEW-ALVISO RD
EL CAMINO REAL
W EVELYN AV
MATHILDA AV
N PASTORIA AV
W MAUDE AV
N MARY AV
SYLVAN PARK
ENCINAL PARK
WASHINGTON CITY PARK
SLATER SCHOOL PARK
LANDELS SCHOOL PARK
SILICON VALLEY WAVE
MOFFETT FIELD MUSEUM
NASA EXPLORATION CENTER
HILTON GARDEN INN
1 WHELAN CT
2 HOLLY CT
3 FREDERICK CT
4 HUNTINGTON CT
5 SHELBY DR
6 FARREL CT
7 OBERG CT
8 STOCKWELL DR
9 PASEO CT
10 JASMINE CT
11 COTTONWOOD CT
12 JACARANDA DR
13 IRENE CT
14 GREYHAWK CT
15 HART CT
16 BEDFORD LP
17 ISIS WY
18 KASRA DR
19 JORDAN CT
20 CAMERON DR
21 BEDFORD DR
1 RIO DE LOS MOLINOS AV
2 CHULA VISTA TER
1 BARSON TER
2 AGENA WY
101
237
85
82
SEE 811 MAP
0 .125 .25 .375 .5 miles 1 in. = 1900 ft.

SEE 832 MAP

SANTA CLARA CO.

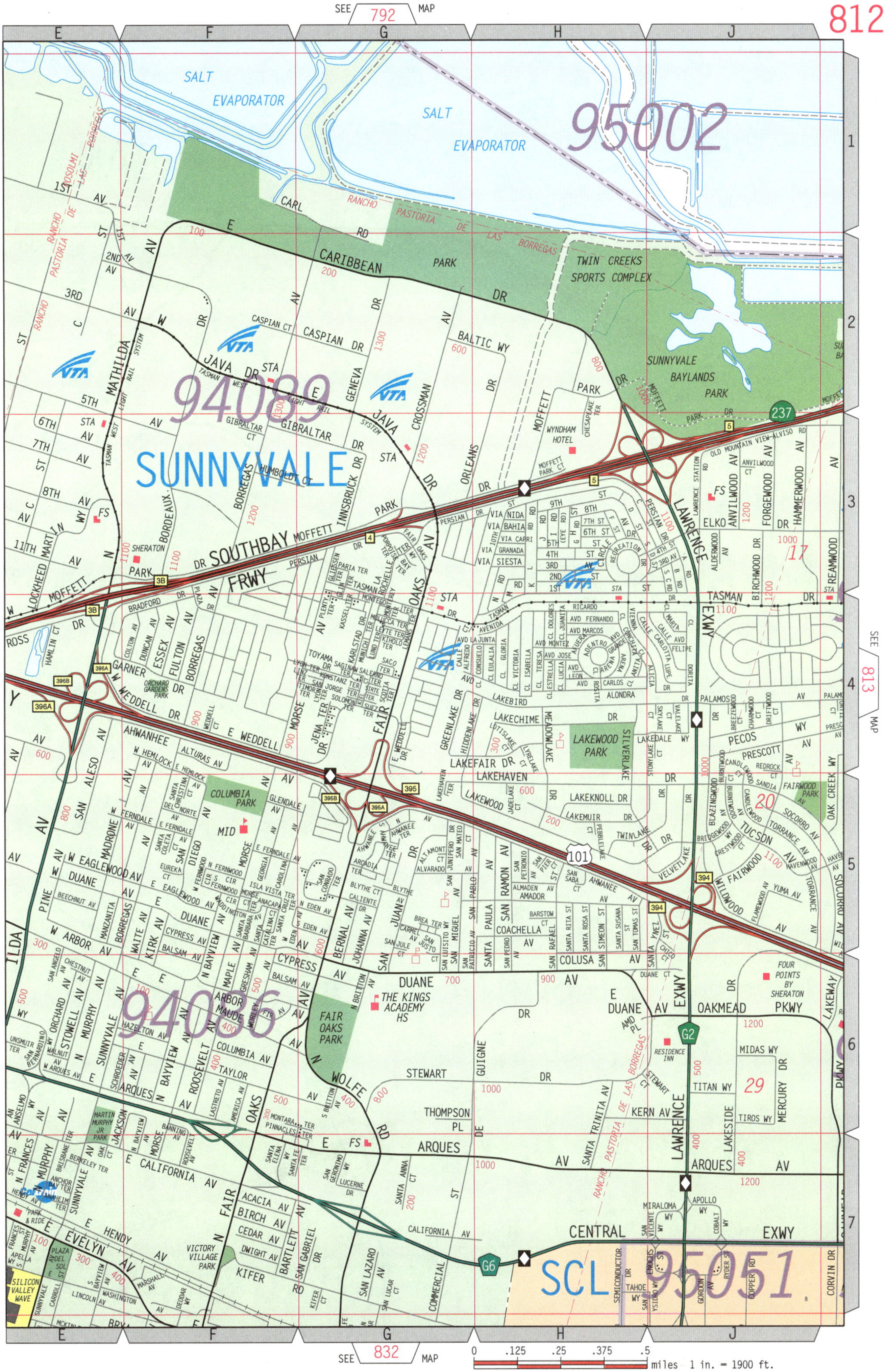

SEE 792 MAP
SEE 832 MAP
SEE 813 MAP
E F G H J
1 2 3 4 5 6 7
SALT EVAPORATOR
SALT EVAPORATOR
95002
94089
94086
95051
SUNNYVALE
SCL
TWIN CREEKS SPORTS COMPLEX
SUNNYVALE BAYLANDS PARK
LAKEWOOD PARK
COLUMBIA PARK
FAIR OAKS PARK
ORCHARD GARDENS PARK
MARTIN MURPHY JR PARK
VICTORY VILLAGE PARK
FAIRWOOD PARK
RANCHO PASTORIA DE LAS BORREGAS
E CARIBBEAN DR
CASPIAN DR
JAVA DR
GIBRALTAR DR
SOUTHBAY FRWY
MOFFETT PARK DR
LAWRENCE EXWY
CENTRAL EXWY
TASMAN DR
E WEDDELL DR
DUANE AV
OAKMEAD PKWY
STEWART DR
ARQUES AV
CALIFORNIA AV
E EVELYN AV
E HENDY AV
KIFER RD
N FAIR OAKS AV
N MATHILDA AV
BORREGAS AV
N WOLFE RD
THE KINGS ACADEMY HS
WYNDHAM HOTEL
SHERATON
FOUR POINTS BY SHERATON
RESIDENCE INN
SILICON VALLEY WAVE
237
101
G2
G6
0 .125 .25 .375 .5 miles 1 in. = 1900 ft.

SEE 793 MAP

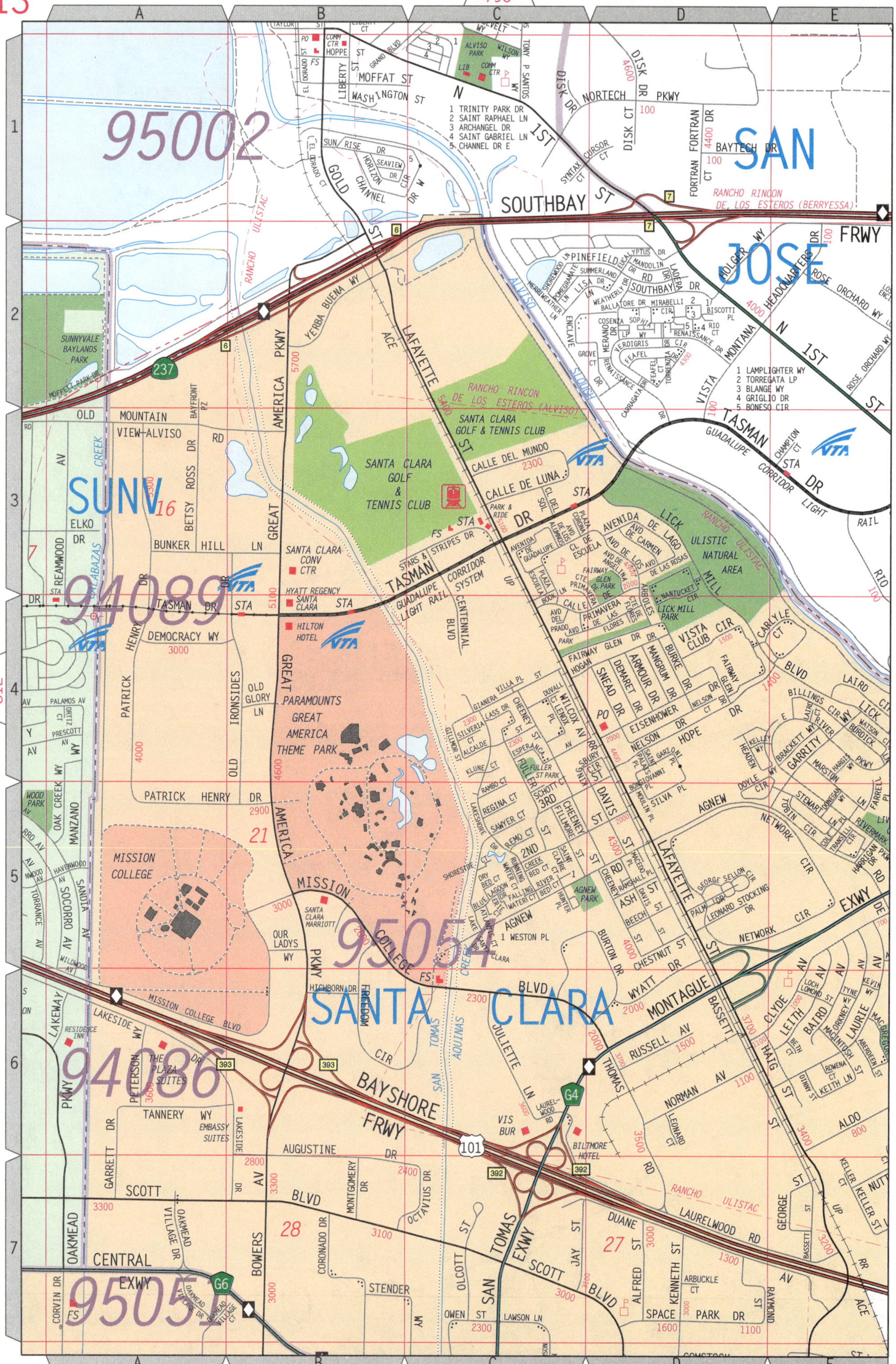

0 .125 .25 .375 .5 miles 1 in. = 1900 ft.

SEE 812 MAP

SEE 833 MAP

SEE 793 MAP

SANTA CLARA CO.

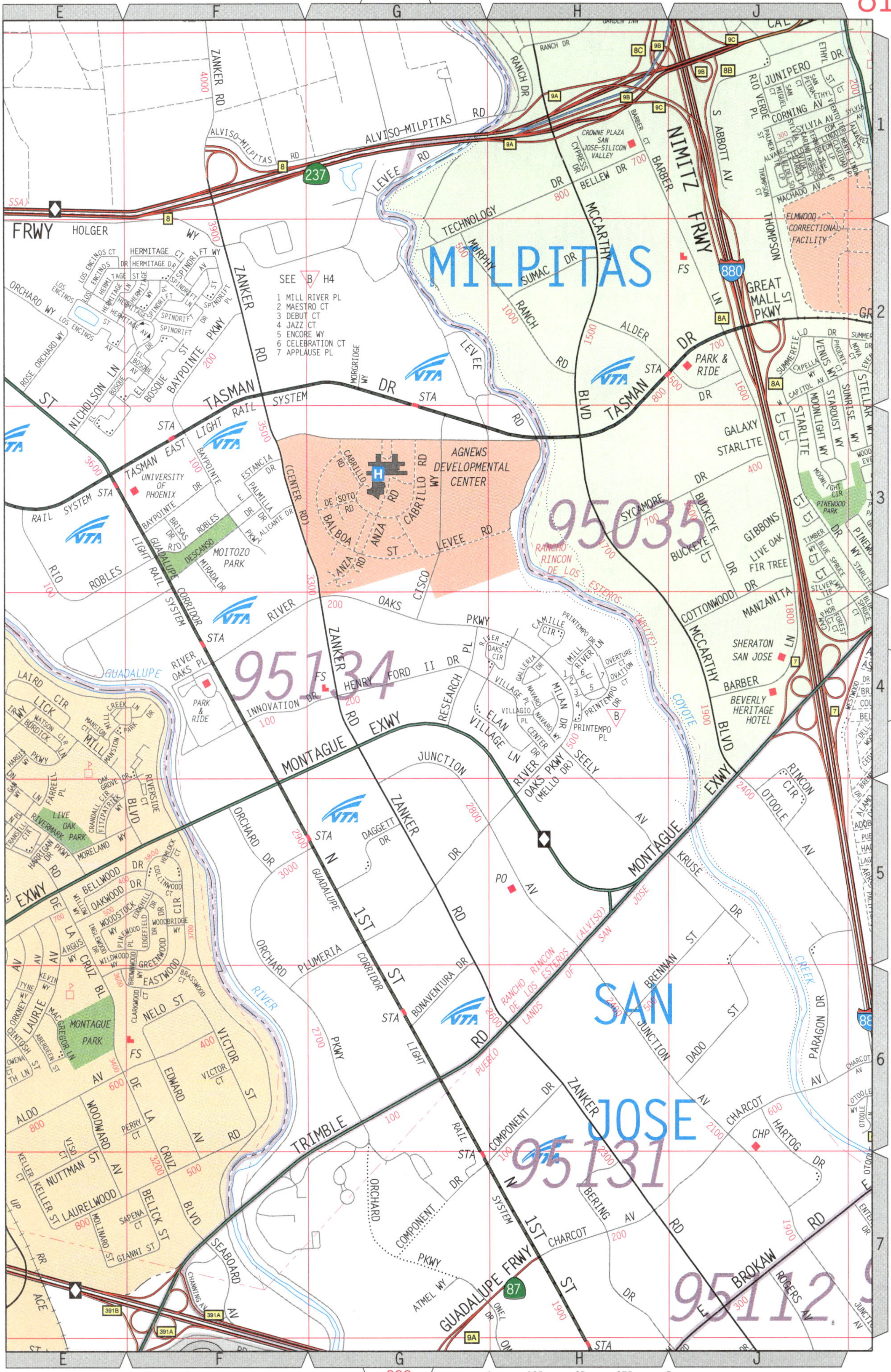
MILPITAS
SAN JOSE
95035
95134
95131
95112
ALVISO-MILPITAS RD
237
880
87
NIMITZ FRWY
TASMAN DR
MONTAGUE EXWY
TRIMBLE RD
BROKAW RD
GUADALUPE FRWY
ZANKER RD
N 1ST ST
MCCARTHY BLVD
BARBER LN
RIVER OAKS PKWY
AGNEWS DEVELOPMENTAL CENTER
ELMWOOD CORRECTIONAL FACILITY
UNIVERSITY OF PHOENIX
MOITOZO PARK
MONTAGUE PARK
LIVE OAK RIVERMARK PARK
PINEWOOD PARK
CROWNE PLAZA SAN JOSE-SILICON VALLEY
SHERATON SAN JOSE
BEVERLY HERITAGE HOTEL
GUADALUPE RIVER
COYOTE CREEK
RANCHO RINCON DE LOS ESTEROS
SEE B H4
1 MILL RIVER PL
2 MAESTRO CT
3 DEBUT CT
4 JAZZ CT
5 ENCORE WY
6 CELEBRATION CT
7 APPLAUSE PL
SEE 814 MAP

SEE 833 MAP

0 .125 .25 .375 .5 miles 1 in. = 1900 ft.

SEE 794 MAP

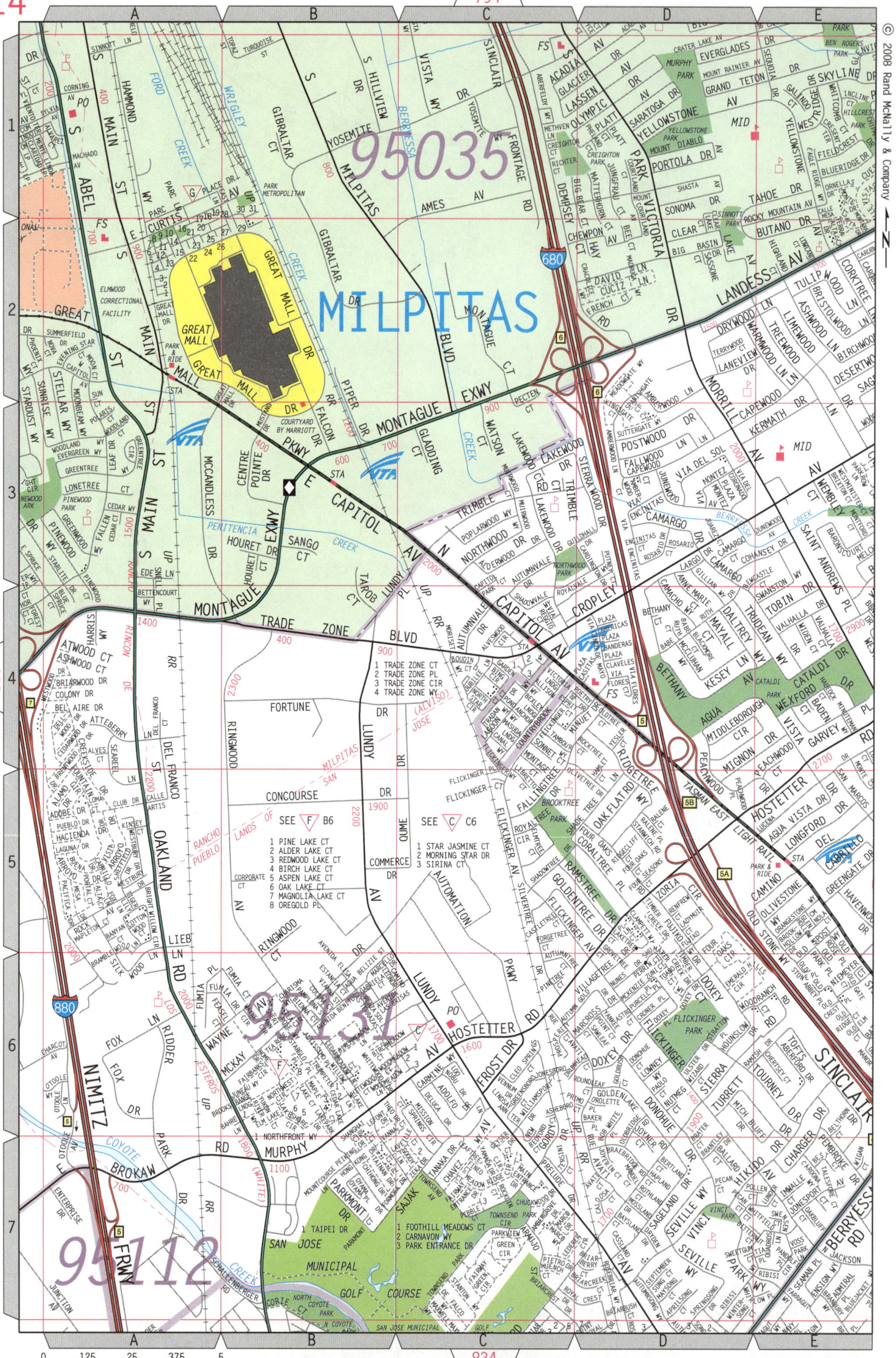

MILPITAS
95035
95131
95112
GREAT MALL
ELMWOOD CORRECTIONAL FACILITY
MONTAGUE EXWY
CAPITOL AV
LANDESS AV
GREAT MALL PKWY
TRADE ZONE BLVD
S MAIN ST
S ABEL ST
N MILPITAS BLVD
SINCLAIR FRWY
NIMITZ FRWY
OAKLAND RD
LUNDY AV
HOSTETTER RD
BROKAW RD
MURPHY AV
BERRYESSA RD
SAN JOSE MUNICIPAL GOLF COURSE
FLICKINGER PARK
BETHANY
SEE F B6
1 PINE LAKE CT
2 ALDER LAKE CT
3 REDWOOD LAKE CT
4 BIRCH LAKE CT
5 ASPEN LAKE CT
6 OAK LAKE CT
7 MAGNOLIA LAKE CT
8 OREGOLD PL
SEE C C6
1 STAR JASMINE CT
2 MORNING STAR DR
3 SIRINA CT
1 TRADE ZONE CT
2 TRADE ZONE PL
3 TRADE ZONE CIR
4 TRADE ZONE WY
1 TAIPEI DR
1 FOOTHILL MEADOWS CT
2 CARNAVON WY
3 PARK ENTRANCE DR
1 NORTHFRONT WY
SEE 813 MAP

0 .125 .25 .375 .5 miles 1 in. = 1900 ft.

SEE 834 MAP

SEE 794 MAP

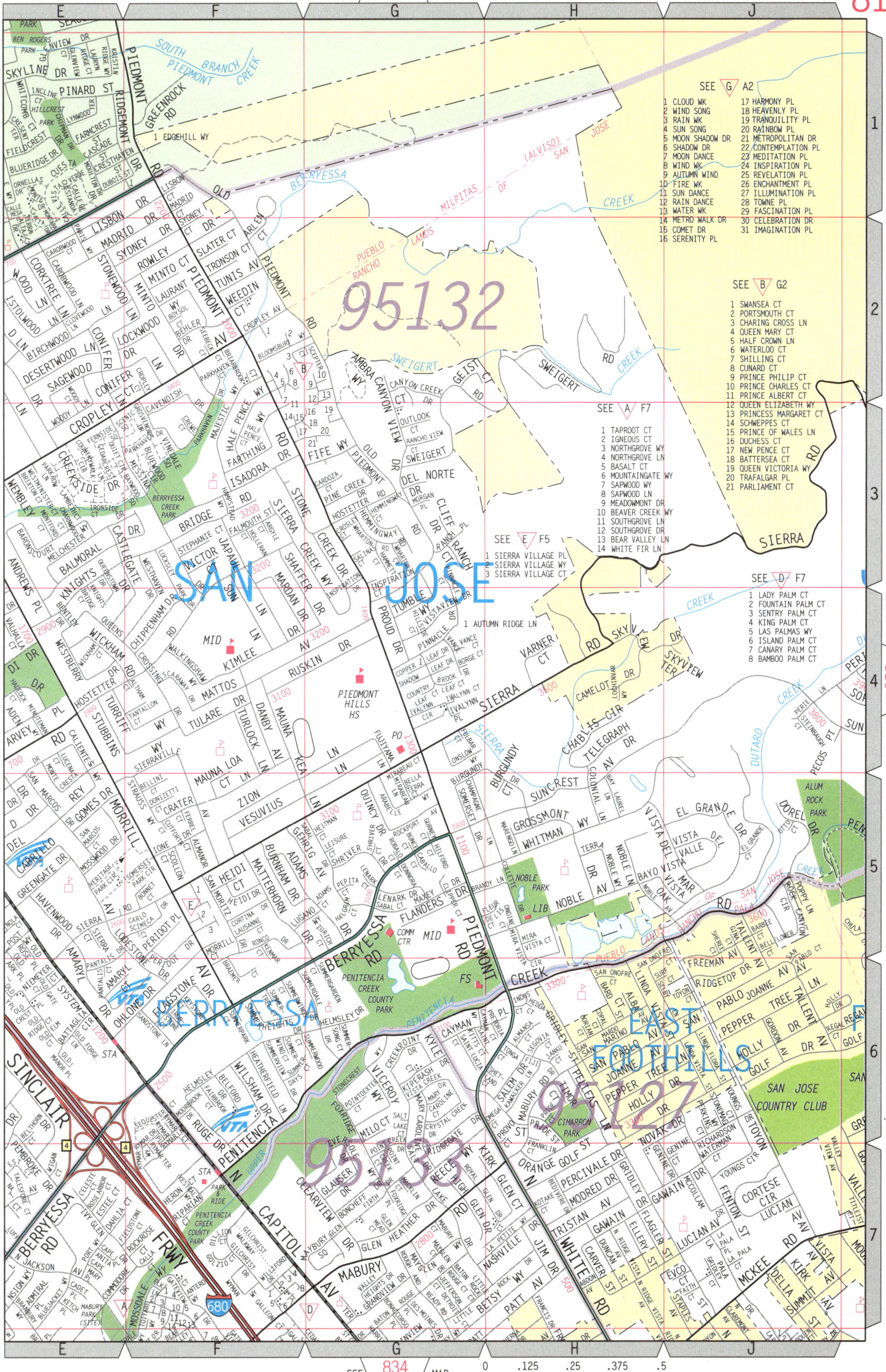
E F G H J
1 2 3 4 5 6 7
SAN JOSE
BERRYESSA
EAST FOOTHILLS
95132
95127
95133
SEE G A2
1 CLOUD WK
2 WIND SONG
3 RAIN WK
4 SUN SONG
5 MOON SHADOW DR
6 SHADOW DR
7 MOON DANCE
8 WIND WK
9 AUTUMN WIND
10 FIRE WK
11 SUN DANCE
12 RAIN DANCE
13 WATER WK
14 METRO WALK DR
15 COMET DR
16 SERENITY PL
17 HARMONY PL
18 HEAVENLY PL
19 TRANQUILITY PL
20 RAINBOW PL
21 METROPOLITAN DR
22 CONTEMPLATION PL
23 MEDITATION PL
24 INSPIRATION PL
25 REVELATION PL
26 ENCHANTMENT PL
27 ILLUMINATION PL
28 TOWNE PL
29 FASCINATION PL
30 CELEBRATION DR
31 IMAGINATION PL
SEE B G2
1 SWANSEA CT
2 PORTSMOUTH CT
3 CHARING CROSS LN
4 QUEEN MARY CT
5 HALF CROWN LN
6 WATERLOO CT
7 SHILLING CT
8 CUNARD CT
9 PRINCE PHILIP CT
10 PRINCE CHARLES CT
11 PRINCE ALBERT CT
12 QUEEN ELIZABETH WY
13 PRINCESS MARGARET CT
14 SCHWEPPES CT
15 PRINCE OF WALES LN
16 DUCHESS CT
17 NEW PENCE CT
18 BATTERSEA CT
19 QUEEN VICTORIA WY
20 TRAFALGAR PL
21 PARLIAMENT CT
SEE A F7
1 TAPROOT CT
2 IGNEOUS CT
3 NORTHGROVE WY
4 NORTHGROVE LN
5 BASALT CT
6 MOUNTAINGATE WY
7 SAPWOOD WY
8 SAPWOOD LN
9 MEADOWMONT DR
10 BEAVER CREEK WY
11 SOUTHGROVE LN
12 SOUTHGROVE DR
13 BEAR VALLEY LN
14 WHITE FIR LN
SEE E F5
1 SIERRA VILLAGE PL
2 SIERRA VILLAGE WY
3 SIERRA VILLAGE CT
SEE D F7
1 LADY PALM CT
2 FOUNTAIN PALM CT
3 SENTRY PALM CT
4 KING PALM CT
5 LAS PALMAS WY
6 ISLAND PALM CT
7 CANARY PALM CT
8 BAMBOO PALM CT
1 EDGEHILL WY
1 AUTUMN RIDGE LN
PIEDMONT RD
SIERRA RD
BERRYESSA RD
CAPITOL AV
SINCLAIR FRWY
PIEDMONT HILLS HS
PENITENCIA CREEK COUNTY PARK
SAN JOSE COUNTRY CLUB
ALUM ROCK PARK
NOBLE PARK
CIMARRON PARK
BERRYESSA CREEK PARK
PUEBLO RANCHO OF SAN JOSE
MILPITAS (ALVISO)
680
SEE 815 MAP

SEE 834 MAP

0 .125 .25 .375 .5 miles 1 in. = 1900 ft.

SANTA CLARA CO.

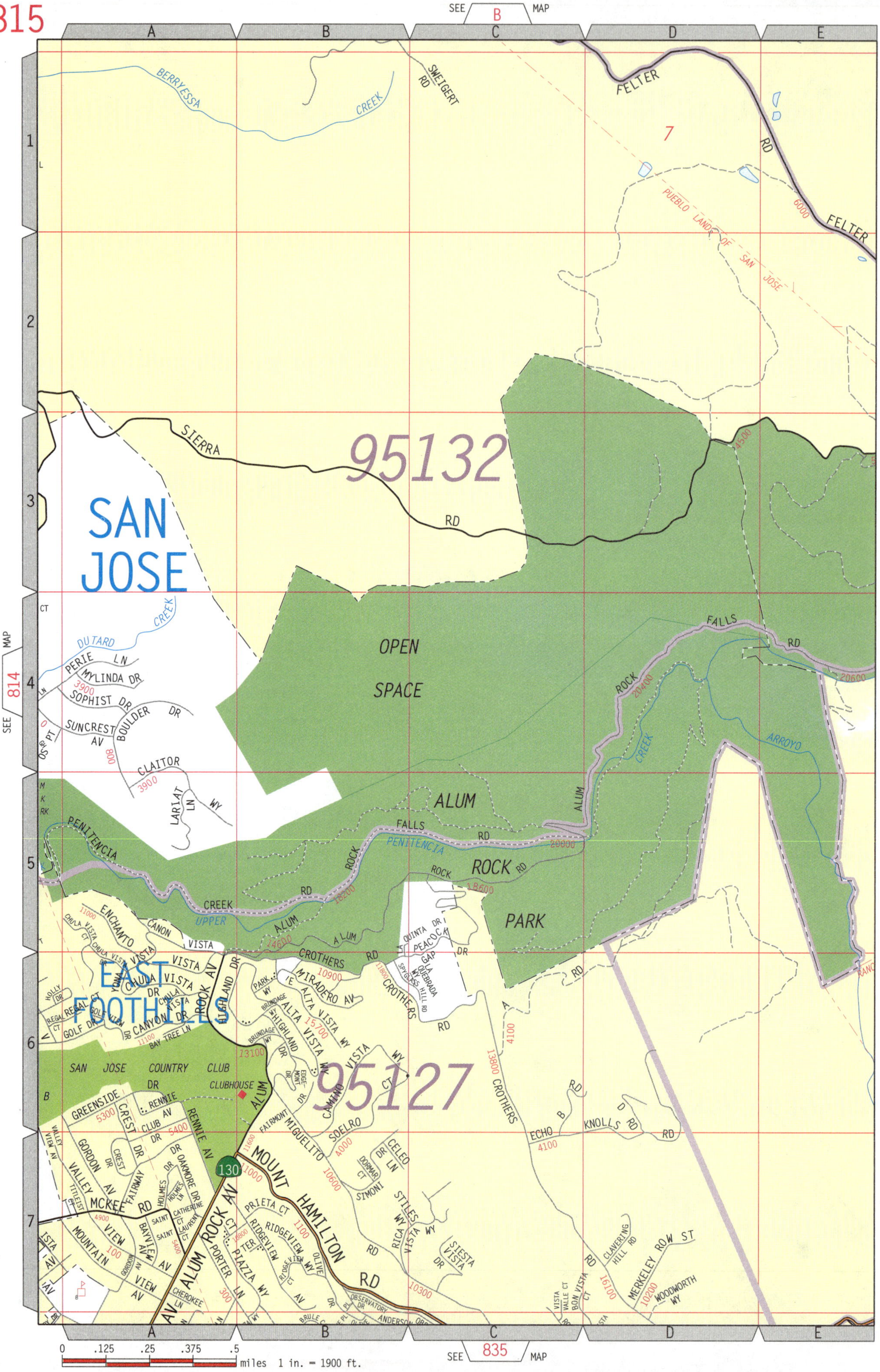
SEE B MAP
SEE 814 MAP
SEE 835 MAP
A
B
C
D
E
1
2
3
4
5
6
7
SAN JOSE
EAST FOOTHILLS
95132
95127
OPEN SPACE
ALUM ROCK PARK
PUEBLO LANDS OF SAN JOSE
7
BERRYESSA CREEK
SWEIGERT RD
FELTER RD
6000
SIERRA RD
4500
DUTARD CREEK
PERIE LN
MYLINDA DR
3900
SOPHIST DR
BOULDER DR
SUNCREST AV
800
CLAITOR WY
3900
LARIAT LN
PENITENCIA CREEK
UPPER PENITENCIA CREEK
ALUM ROCK FALLS RD
20600
20400
20000
18600
18200
14600
ARROYO CREEK
ENCHANTO VISTA
CANON VISTA
CHULA VISTA
11000
ALUM ROCK AV
HIGHLAND DR
CROTHERS RD
10900
MIRADERO AV
ALTA VISTA WY
15700
13100
PEACOCK GAP
QUINTA DR
SPYGLASS HILL RD
11800
13800 CROTHERS RD
4100
GOLF DR
CANYON DR
BAY TREE LN
SAN JOSE COUNTRY CLUB
CLUBHOUSE
GREENSIDE DR
RENNIE AV
5300
CLUB DR
5400
CREST DR
130
11600
11000
MOUNT HAMILTON RD
MIGUELITO RD
SOELRO AV
4000
10600
CAMINO VISTA CT
CELEO LN
SIMONI DR
STILES RD
ECHO RD
4100
KNOLLS DR
CLAVERING HILL RD
MERKELEY ROW ST
10200
16100
WOODWORTH WY
10300
GORDON AV
VALLEY VIEW AV
MCKEE RD
4900
MOUNTAIN VIEW AV
100
FAIRWAY DR
OAKMORE DR
BAYVIEW AV
CATHERINE CT
PRIETA CT
1100
RIDGEVIEW WY
OLIVE DR
PORTER LN
PIAZZA WY
CHEROKEE LN
300
OBSERVATORY DR
ANDERSON
0
.125
.25
.375
.5
miles 1 in. = 1900 ft.

SEE B MAP

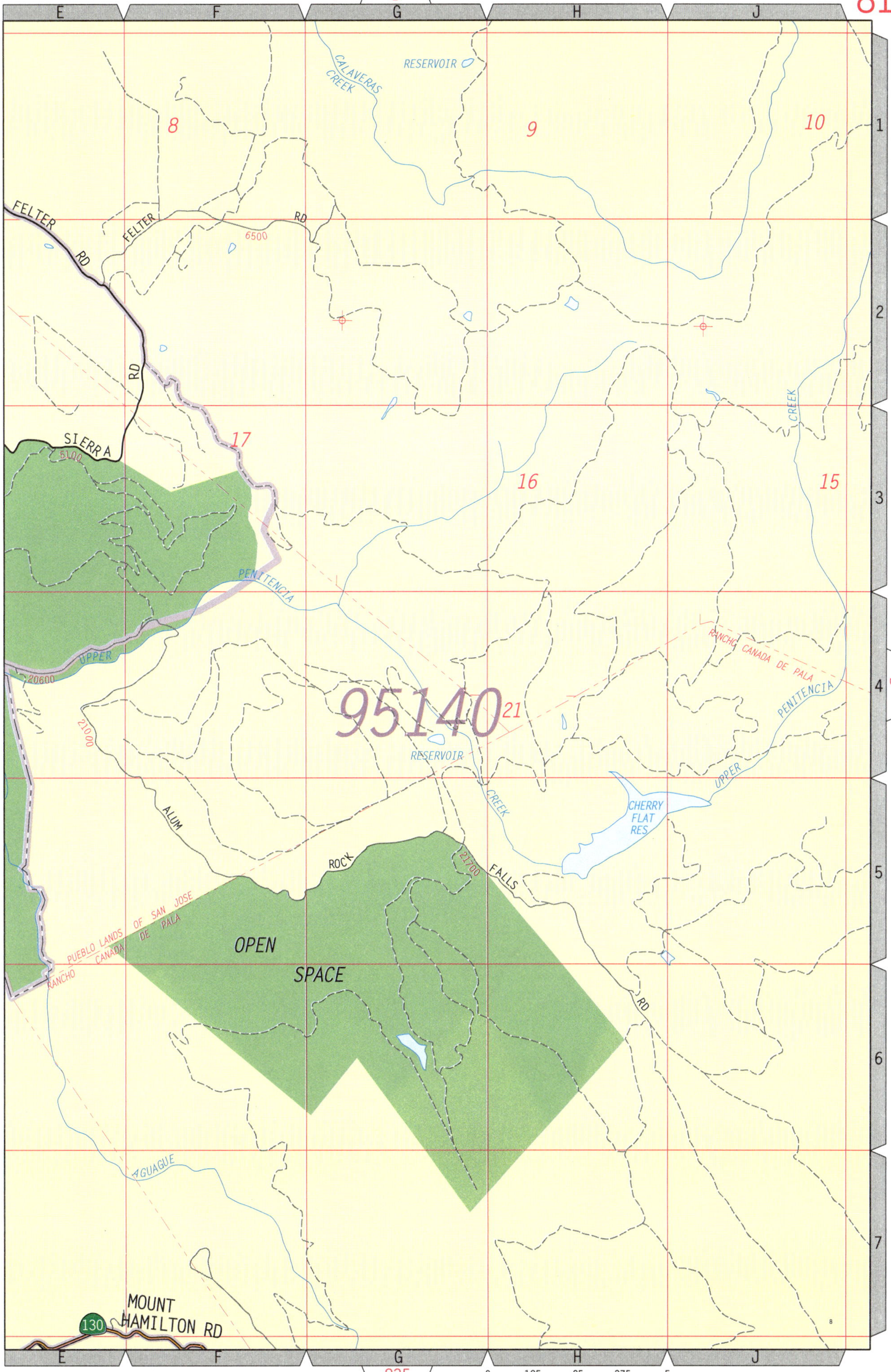

SEE B MAP

SEE 835 MAP

0 .125 .25 .375 .5 miles 1 in. = 1900 ft.

SEE 810 MAP

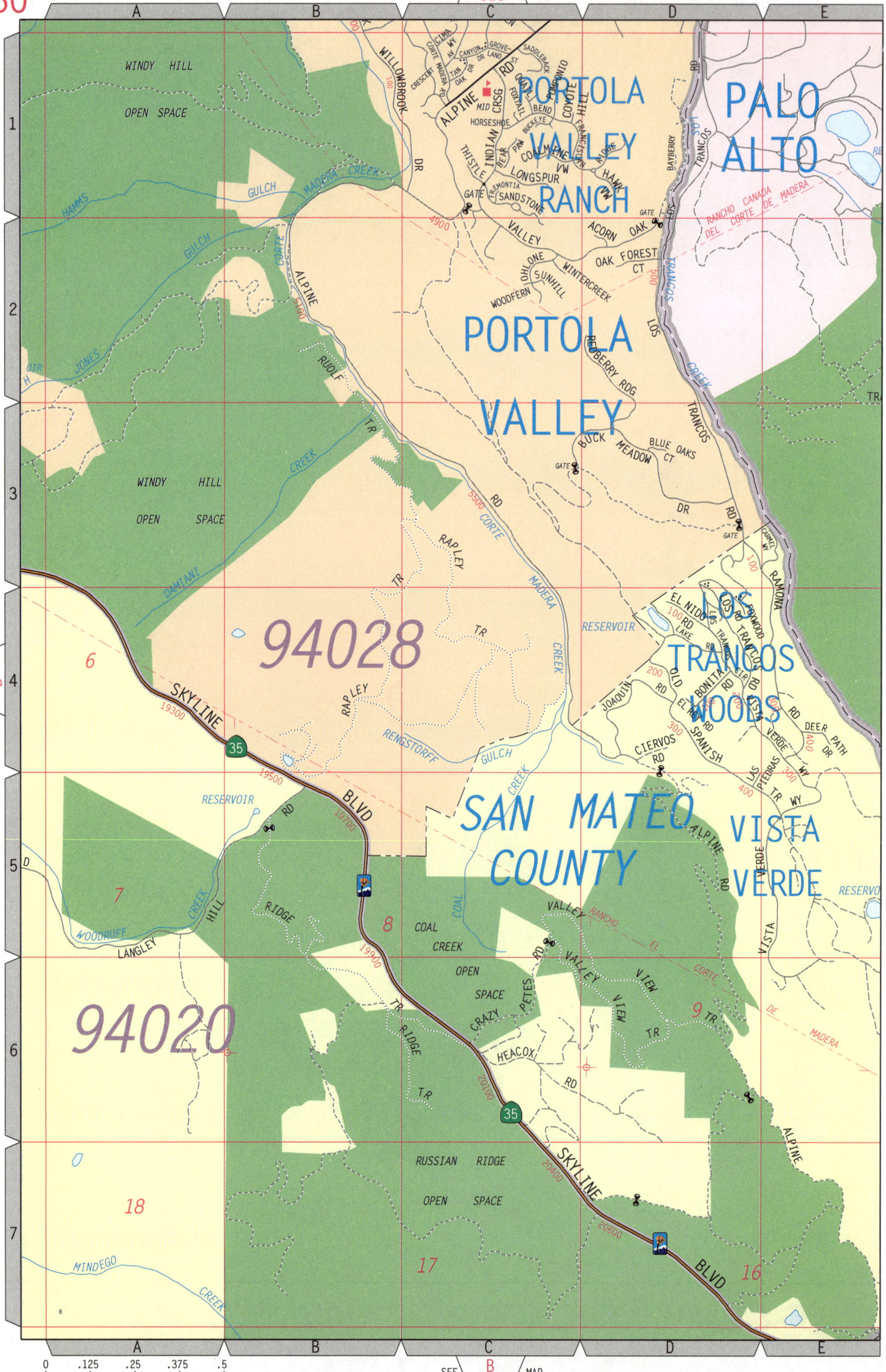

WINDY HILL OPEN SPACE
PORTOLA VALLEY RANCH
PALO ALTO
PORTOLA VALLEY
LOS TRANCOS WOODS
SAN MATEO COUNTY
VISTA VERDE
94028
94020
SKYLINE BLVD
35
ALPINE RD
CORTE MADERA CREEK
LOS TRANCOS RD
LOS TRANCOS CREEK
WILLOWBROOK DR
RANCHO CANADA DEL CORTE DE MADERA
HAMMS GULCH
JONES
DAMIANI CREEK
RUOLF TR
RAPLEY TR
RESERVOIR
RENGSTORFF GULCH
WOODRUFF CREEK
LANGLEY HILL RIDGE
COAL CREEK OPEN SPACE
RUSSIAN RIDGE OPEN SPACE
MINDEGO CREEK
VALLEY VIEW TR
CRAZY PETES RD
HEACOX RD
RIDGE TR
ACORN
OAK FOREST CT
WINTERCREEK
SUNHILL
OHLONE
WOODFERN
REDBERRY RDG
BUCK MEADOW DR
BLUE OAKS CT
GATE
SANDSTONE
LONGSPUR
THISTLE
INDIAN CRSG
HORSESHOE BEND
COALMINE VW
COYOTE HILL
HAWK VW
BAYBERRY
JOAQUIN RD
CIERVOS RD
SPANISH RD
EL NIDO RD
RAMONA
DEER PATH DR
LAS PIEDRAS TR
VISTA VERDE WY
6
7
8
9
16
17
18
SANTA CLARA CO.
© 2008 Rand McNally & Company

SEE B MAP

0 .125 .25 .375 .5 miles 1 in. = 1900 ft.

SEE 810 MAP

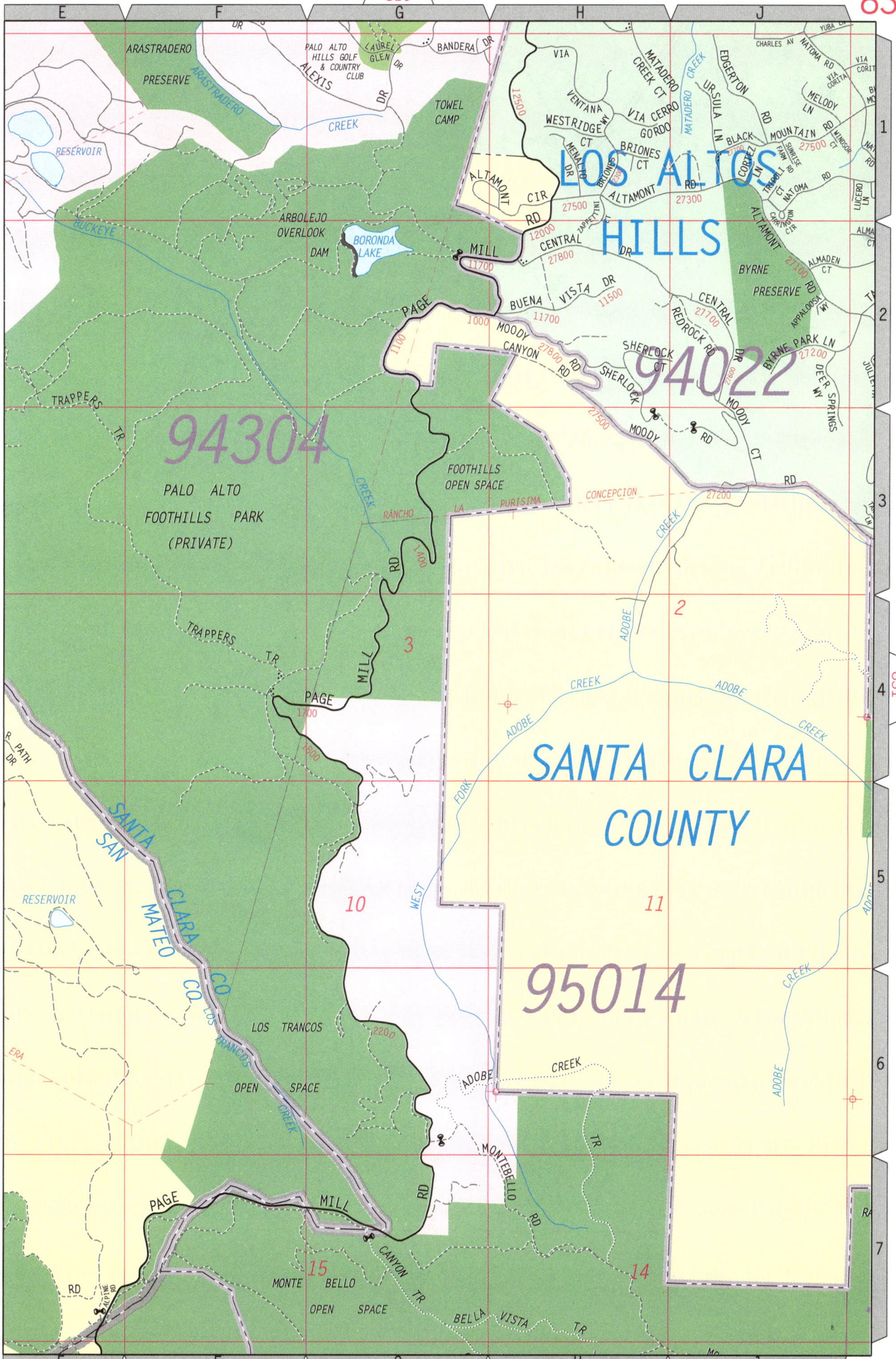

SANTA CLARA CO.

SEE B MAP

0 .125 .25 .375 .5 miles 1 in. = 1900 ft.

SEE 811 MAP

SANTA CLARA CO.

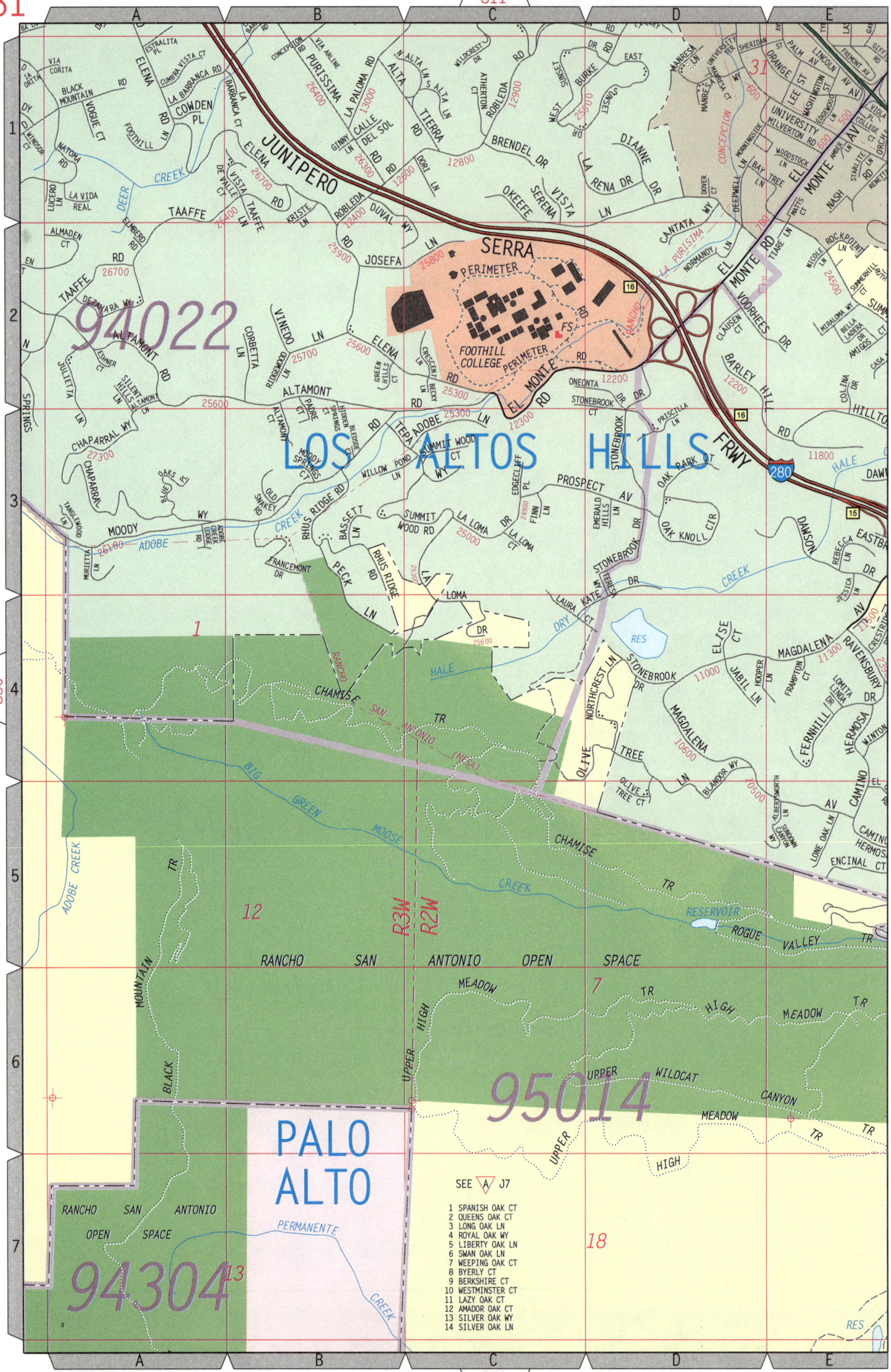

SEE 830 MAP

SEE 851 MAP

0 .125 .25 .375 .5 miles 1 in. = 1900 ft.

SEE 811 MAP

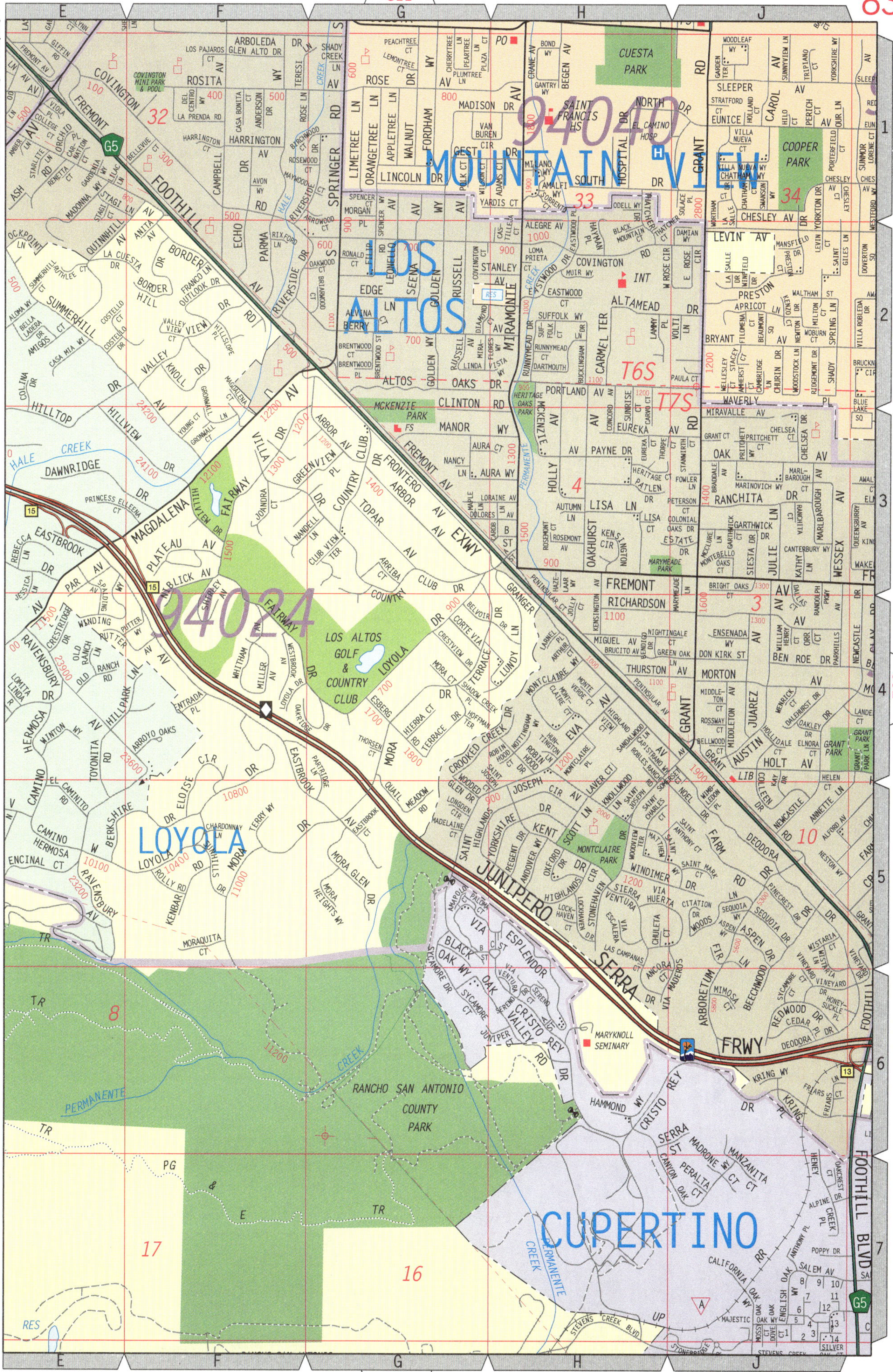

SEE 832 MAP

SEE 851 MAP

SEE 812 MAP

SANTA CLARA CO.

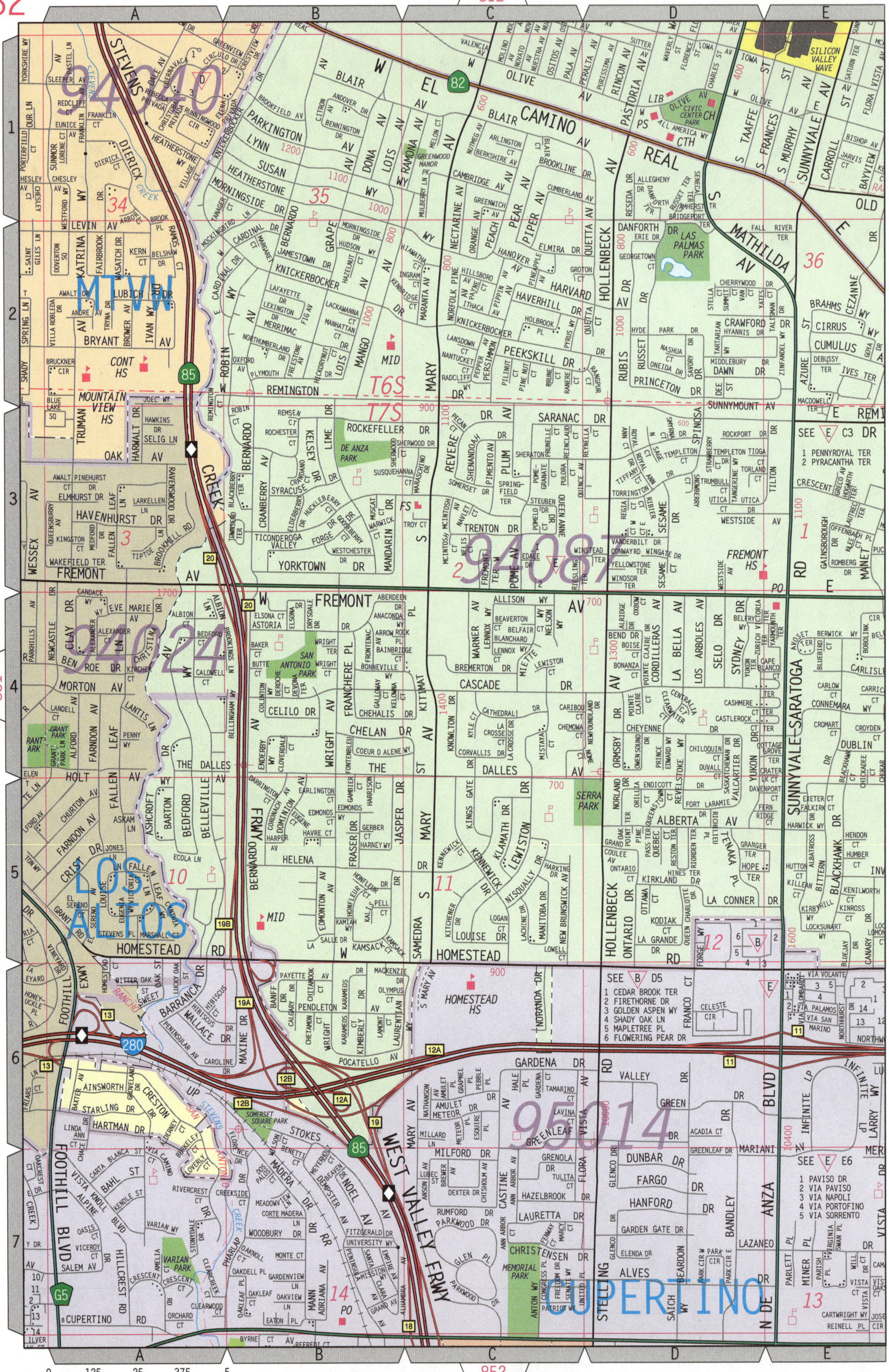

SEE 831 MAP

0 .125 .25 .375 .5 miles 1 in. = 1900 ft.

SEE 852 MAP

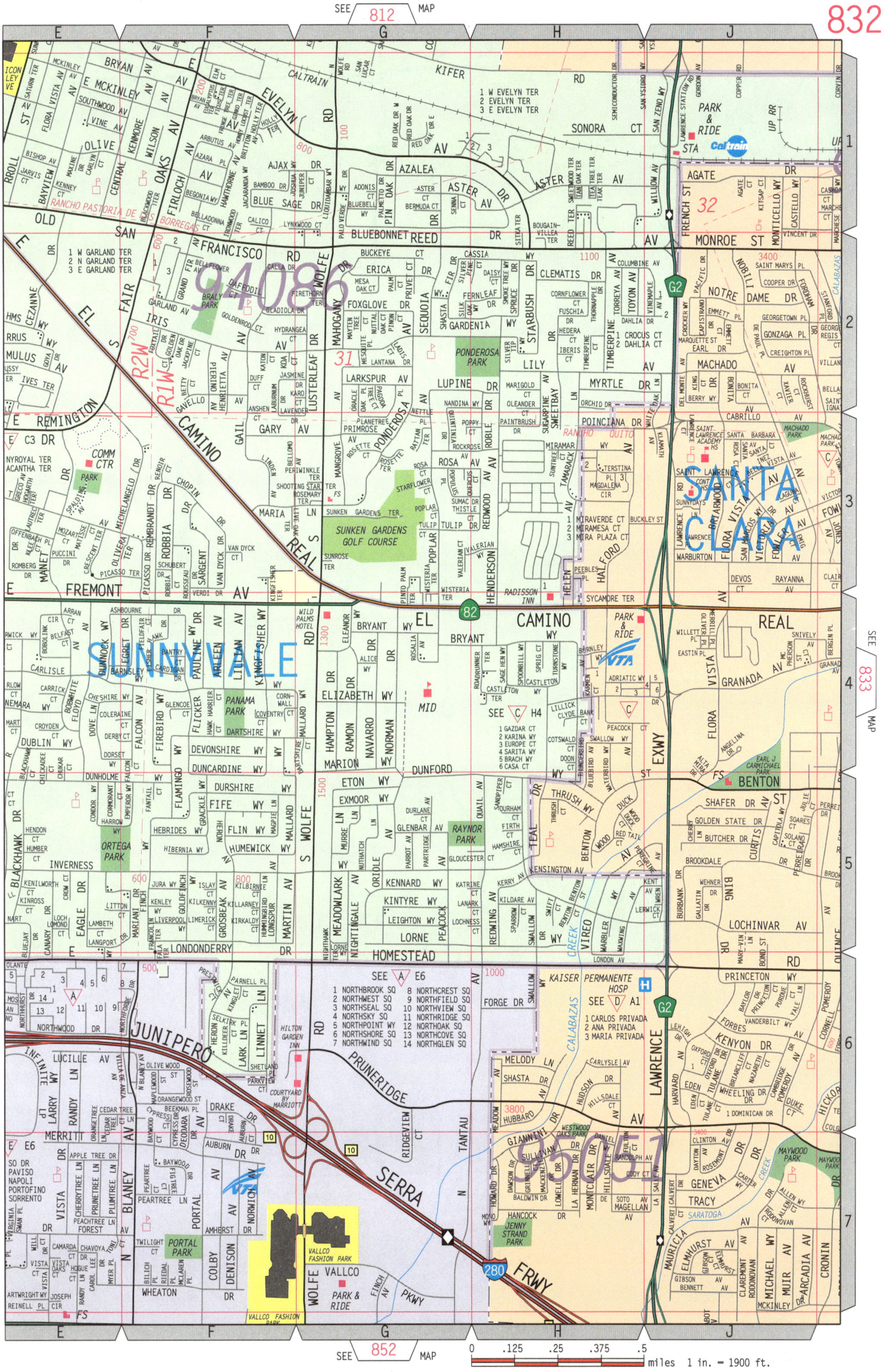
SEE 812 MAP
SEE 833 MAP
SEE 852 MAP
SUNNYVALE
SANTA CLARA
94086
95051
CALTRAIN
EVELYN AV
KIFER RD
SONORA CT
AZALEA AV
ASTER AV
MONROE ST
OLD SAN FRANCISCO RD
BLUEBONNET DR
REED AV
WOLFE RD
S FAIR OAKS AV
E REMINGTON DR
CAMINO REAL
E FREMONT AV
EL CAMINO REAL
BRYANT WY
BRAVY PARK
PONDEROSA PARK
SUNKEN GARDENS GOLF COURSE
COMM CTR
PARK
PANAMA PARK
ORTEGA PARK
RAYNOR PARK
DUNFORD WY
BENTON ST
HOMESTEAD RD
LONDONDERRY DR
LOCHINVAR AV
LAWRENCE EXWY
KAISER PERMANENTE HOSP
JUNIPERO SERRA FRWY
PRUNERIDGE AV
TANTAU AV
HILTON GARDEN INN
COURTYARD BY MARRIOTT
VALLCO FASHION PARK
VALLCO PKWY
PARK & RIDE
JENNY STRAND PARK
PORTAL PARK
MAYWOOD PARK
EARL J CARMICHAEL PARK
CALABAZAS CREEK
SARATOGA CREEK
MACHADO PARK
SAINT LAWRENCE ACADEMY HS
RADISSON INN
WILD PALMS HOTEL
MID
RANCHO PASTORIA DE LAS BORREGAS
RANCHO QUITO
R2W
R1W
280
82
G2
E
F
G
H
J
1
2
3
4
5
6
7
0 .125 .25 .375 .5 miles 1 in. = 1900 ft.

SEE 813 MAP

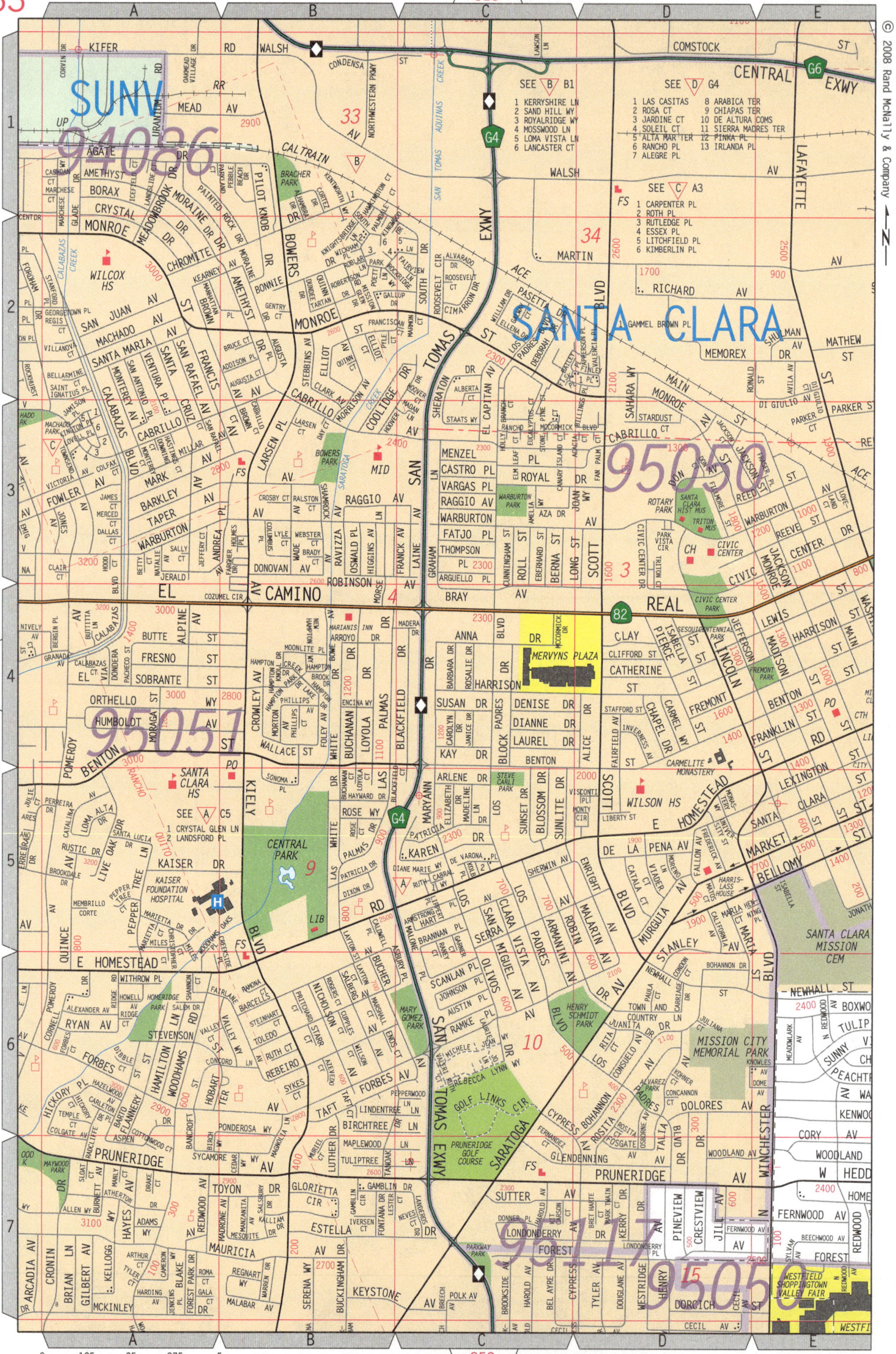

SEE 832 MAP

0 .125 .25 .375 .5 miles 1 in. = 1900 ft.

SEE 853 MAP

SEE 813 MAP

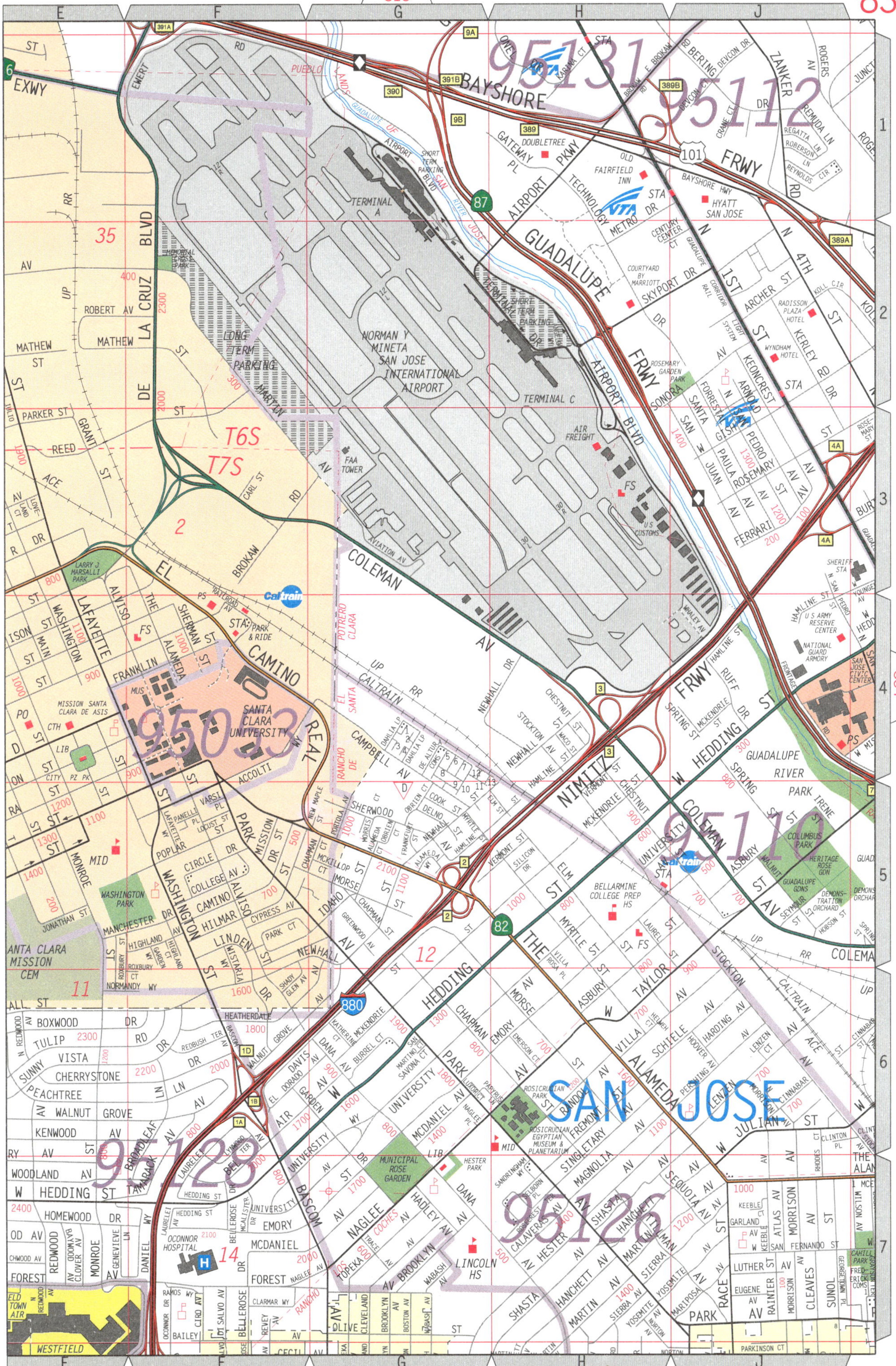

SEE 834 MAP

SANTA CLARA CO.

SEE 853 MAP

See Page F for Downtown Map

0 .125 .25 .375 .5 miles 1 in. = 1900 ft.

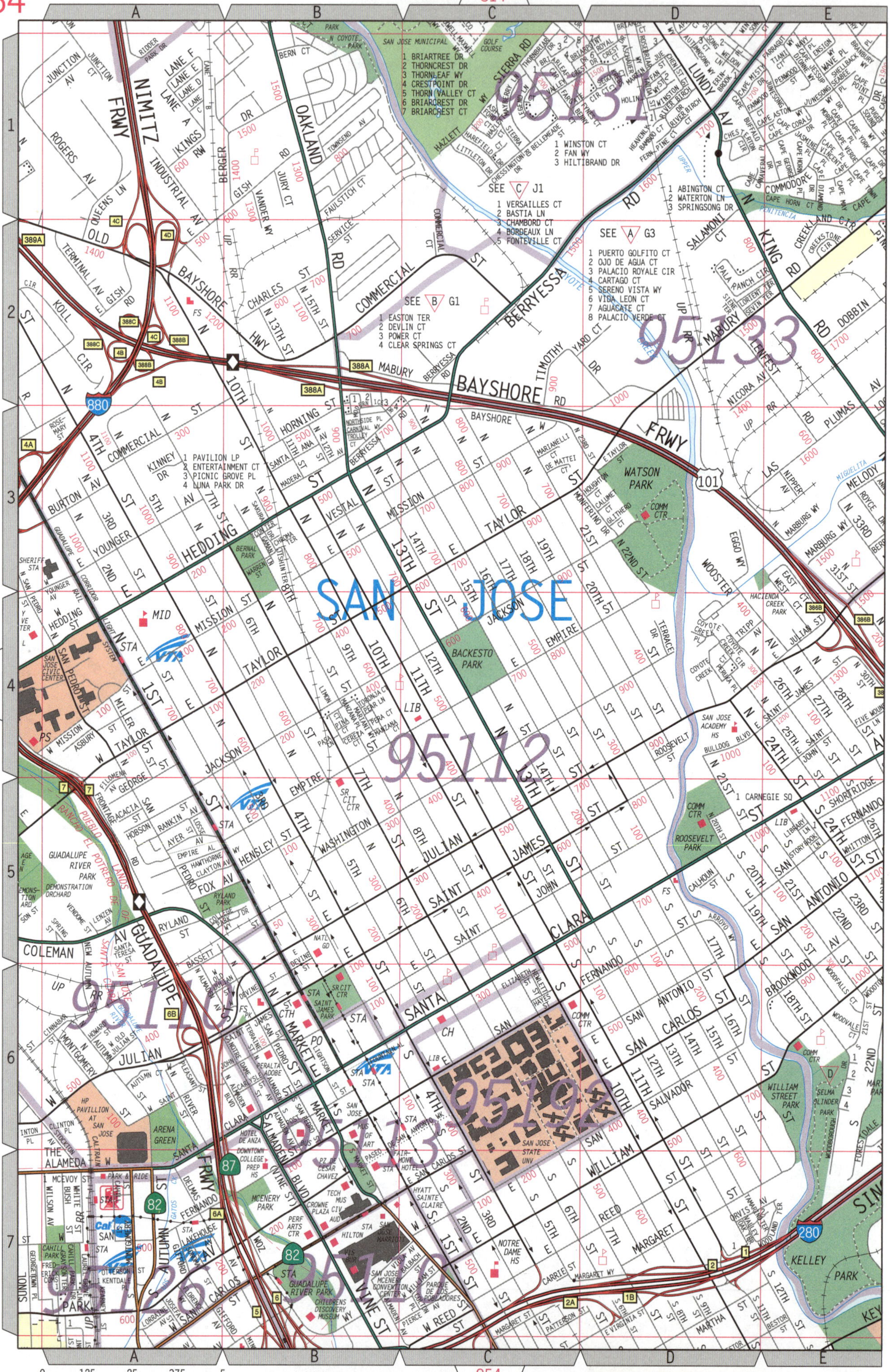
SEE 814 MAP
SEE 833 MAP
SEE 854 MAP
SANTA CLARA CO.
© 2008 Rand McNally & Company
SAN JOSE
95131
95133
95112
95110
95113
95192
95126
NIMITZ FRWY
BAYSHORE FRWY
OAKLAND RD
BERRYESSA RD
HEDDING ST
TAYLOR ST
JULIAN ST
SANTA CLARA ST
SAN CARLOS ST
SAN SALVADOR ST
WILLIAM ST
REED ST
KEYES ST
MABURY RD
KING RD
COLEMAN AV
THE ALAMEDA
GUADALUPE FRWY
WATSON PARK
BACKESTO PARK
ROOSEVELT PARK
KELLEY PARK
WILLIAM STREET PARK
GUADALUPE RIVER PARK
SAN JOSE STATE UNIV
SAN JOSE MUNICIPAL GOLF COURSE
SEE C J1
1 VERSAILLES CT
2 BASTIA LN
3 CHAMBORD CT
4 BORDEAUX LN
5 FONTEVILLE CT
SEE A G3
1 PUERTO GOLFITO CT
2 OJO DE AGUA CT
3 PALACIO ROYALE CIR
4 CARTAGO CT
5 SERENO VISTA WY
6 VIDA LEON CT
7 AGUACATE CT
8 PALACIO VERDE CT
SEE B G1
1 EASTON TER
2 DEVLIN CT
3 POWER CT
4 CLEAR SPRINGS CT
1 BRIARTREE DR
2 THORNCREST DR
3 THORNLEAF WY
4 CRESTPOINT DR
5 THORN VALLEY CT
6 BRIARCREST DR
7 BRIARCREST CT
1 WINSTON CT
2 FAN WY
3 HILTIBRAND DR
1 ABINGTON CT
2 WATERTON LN
3 SPRINGSONG DR
1 PAVILION LP
2 ENTERTAINMENT CT
3 PICNIC GROVE PL
4 LUNA PARK DR
1 CARNEGIE SQ
0 .125 .25 .375 .5 miles 1 in. = 1900 ft.
See Page F For Downtown Map

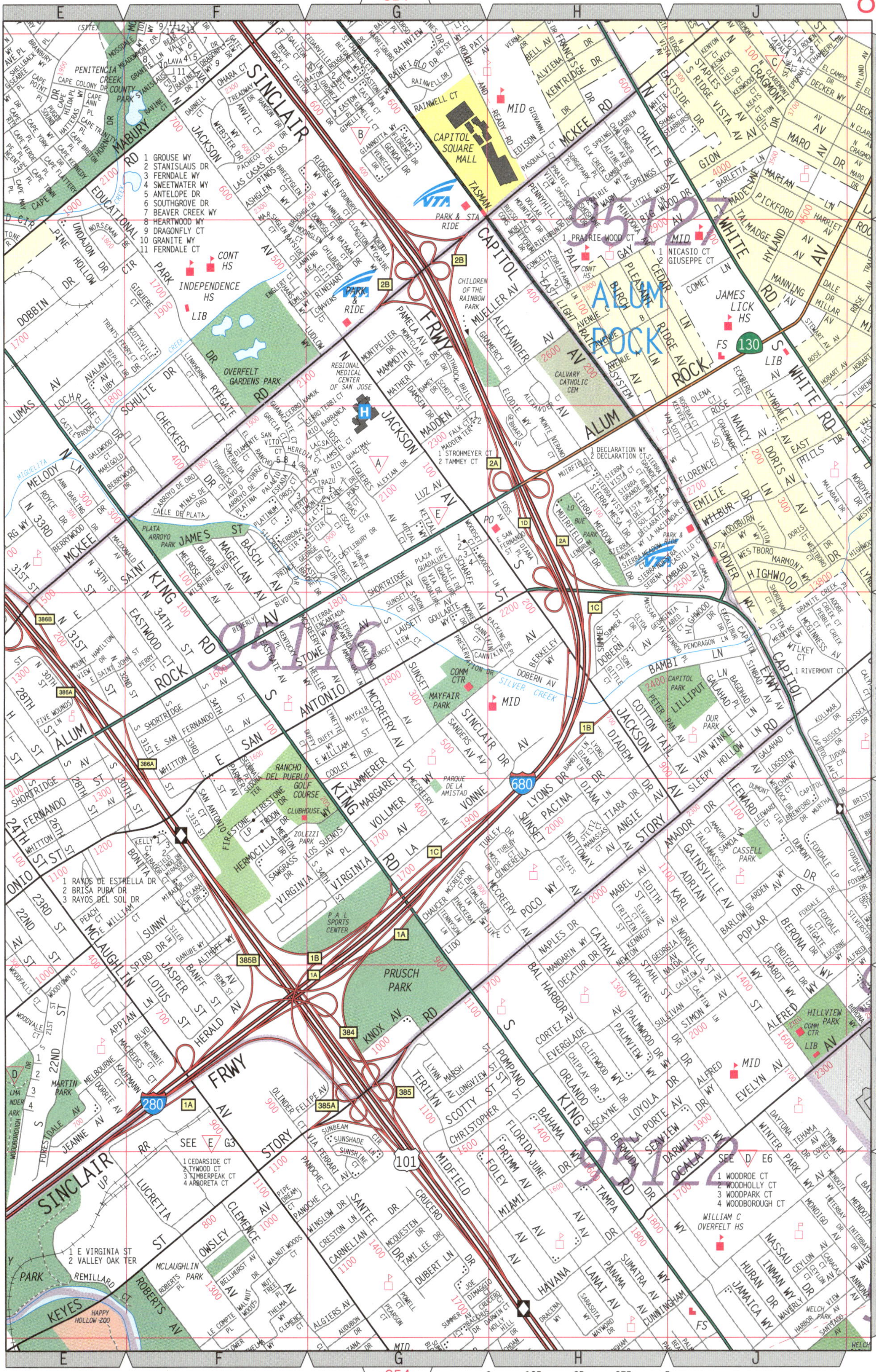

SEE 814 MAP
SEE 835 MAP
SEE 854 MAP
SANTA CLARA CO.
© 2008 Rand McNally & Company
CAPITOL SQUARE MALL
PARK & RIDE
INDEPENDENCE HS
OVERFELT GARDENS PARK
REGIONAL MEDICAL CENTER OF SAN JOSE
CALVARY CATHOLIC CEM
ALUM ROCK
JAMES LICK HS
MAYFAIR PARK
RANCHO DEL PUEBLO GOLF COURSE
PRUSCH PARK
P A L SPORTS CENTER
CAPITOL PARK
HILLVIEW PARK
CASSELL PARK
MARTIN PARK
HAPPY HOLLOW ZOO
WILLIAM C OVERFELT HS
95127
95116
95122
SINCLAIR FRWY
CAPITOL EXWY
STORY RD
KING RD
TULLY
0 .125 .25 .375 .5 miles 1 in. = 1900 ft.

SEE 815 MAP

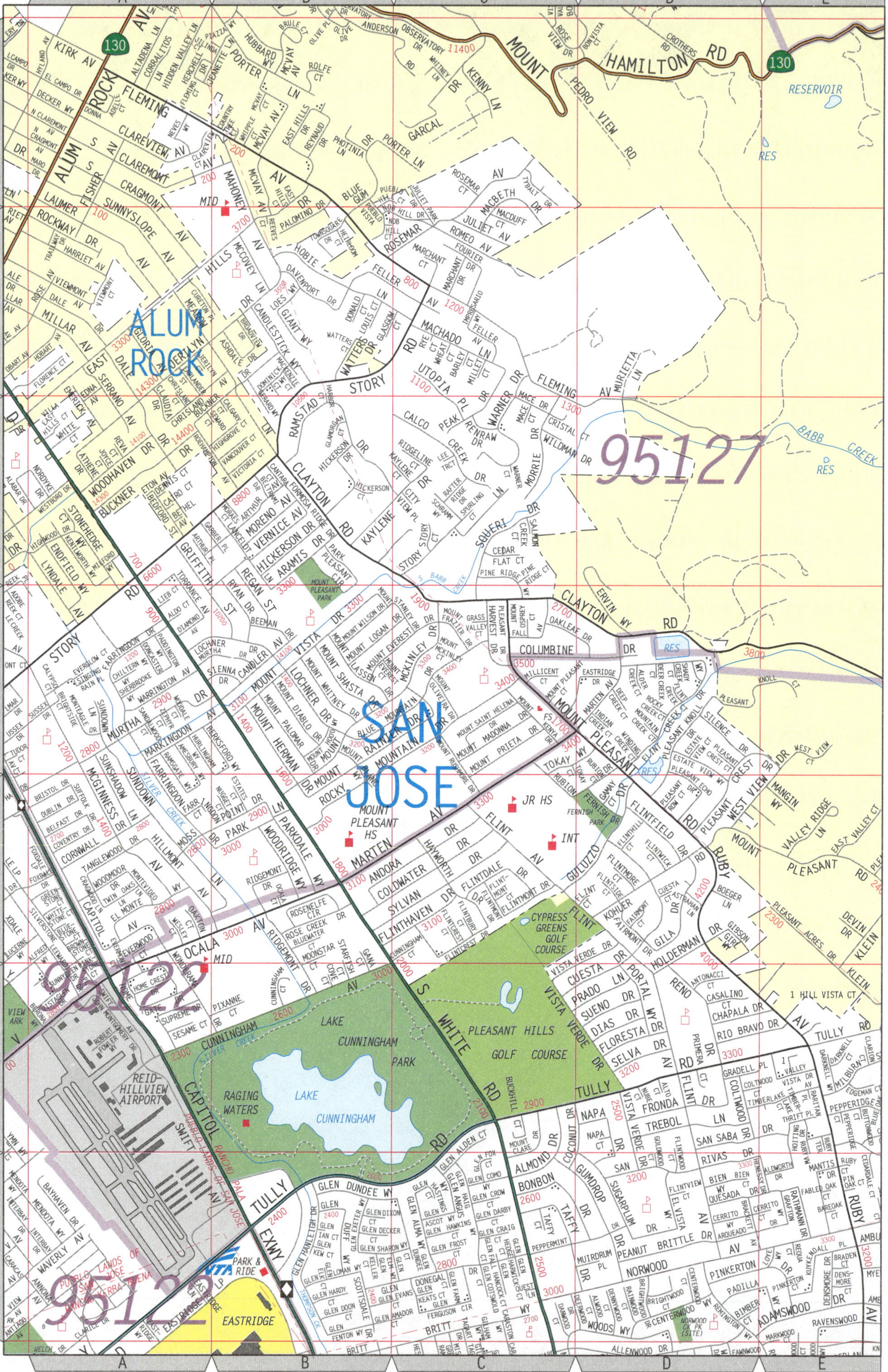

0 .125 .25 .375 .5
miles 1 in. = 1900 ft.

SEE 834 MAP

SEE 855 MAP

SEE 815 MAP

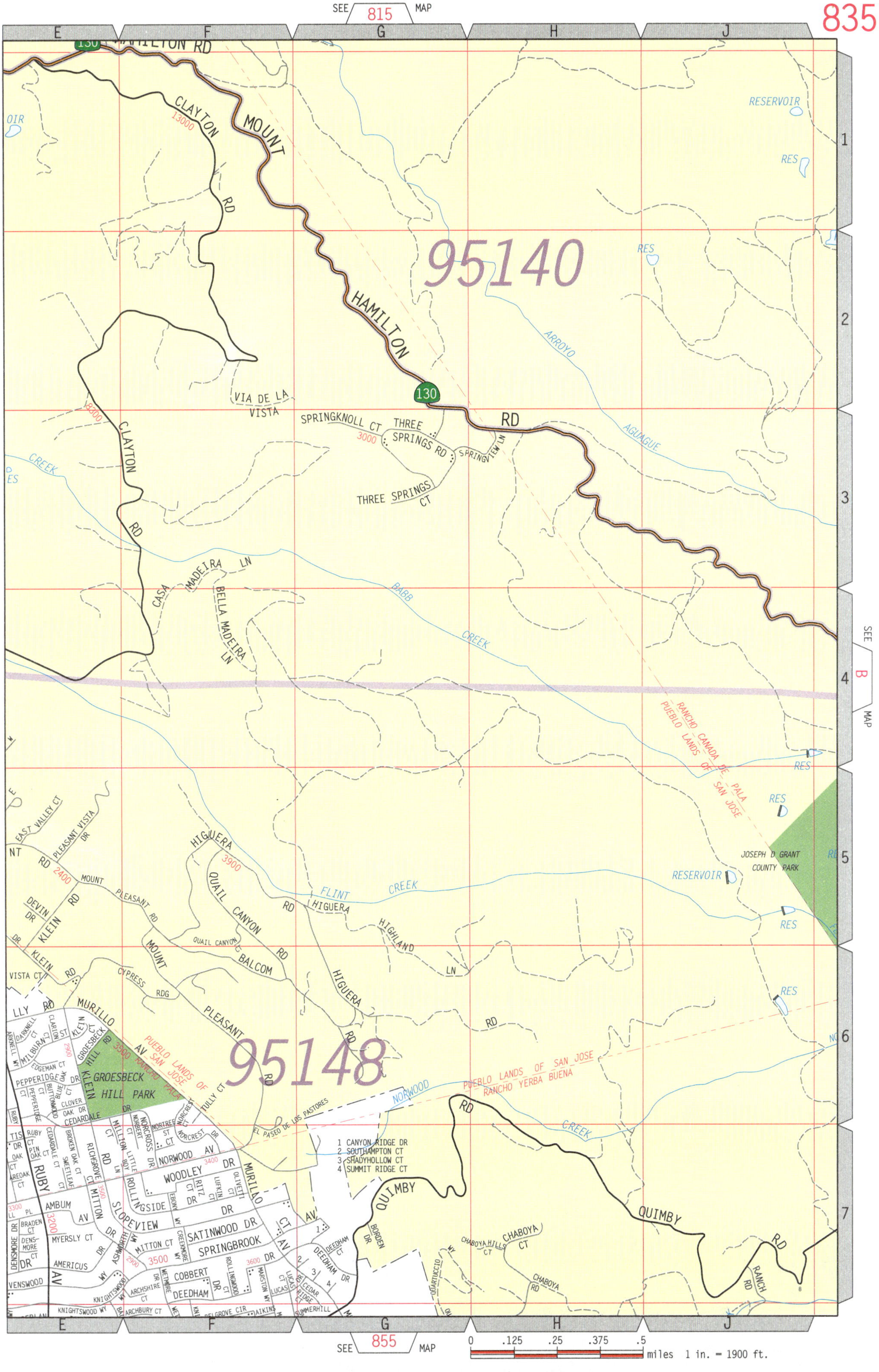
95140
95148
MOUNT HAMILTON RD
130
CLAYTON RD
13000
8300
VIA DE LA VISTA
SPRINGKNOLL CT
THREE SPRINGS RD
THREE SPRINGS CT
SPRINGVIEW LN
3000
CASA MADEIRA LN
BELLA MADEIRA LN
BABB CREEK
ARROYO AGUAGUE
CREEK
RESERVOIR
RES
RANCHO CANADA DE PALA
PUEBLO LANDS OF SAN JOSE
JOSEPH D GRANT COUNTY PARK
EAST VALLEY CT
PLEASANT VISTA DR
MOUNT PLEASANT RD
2400
DEVIN DR
KLEIN RD
HIGUERA RD
3900
QUAIL CANYON RD
QUAIL CANYON CT
BALCOM RD
FLINT CREEK
HIGHLAND LN
CYPRESS RDG
VISTA CT
MURILLO AV
GROESBECK HILL PARK
PUEBLO LANDS OF SAN JOSE
RANCHO PALA
TULLY CT
EL PASEO DE LOS PASTORES
NORWOOD CREEK
PUEBLO LANDS OF SAN JOSE
RANCHO YERBA BUENA
1 CANYON RIDGE DR
2 SOUTHAMPTON CT
3 SHADYHOLLOW CT
4 SUMMIT RIDGE CT
QUIMBY RD
RANCH RD
CHABOYA CT
CHABOYA HILLS CT
CHABOYA RD
BORDEN DR
DEEDHAM DR
DEEDHAM CT
RUBY AV
AMBUM AV
SLOPEVIEW DR
SATINWOOD DR
SPRINGBROOK AV
NORWOOD AV
WOODLEY DR
COBBERT DR
MITTON CT
MYERSLY CT
AMERICUS DR
KNIGHTSWOOD WY
ARCHSHIRE CT
ARCHBURY CT
BELGROVE CIR
SUMMERHILL
PEPPERIDGE DR
CEDARDALE DR
MILBURN ST
CLAYTON CT
EDGEMAN CT
3500
3400
3200
3300
3600
2900
E F G H J
1 2 3 4 5 6 7
SANTA CLARA CO.
SEE B MAP
0 .125 .25 .375 .5 miles 1 in. = 1900 ft.

SEE 855 MAP

SEE 831 MAP

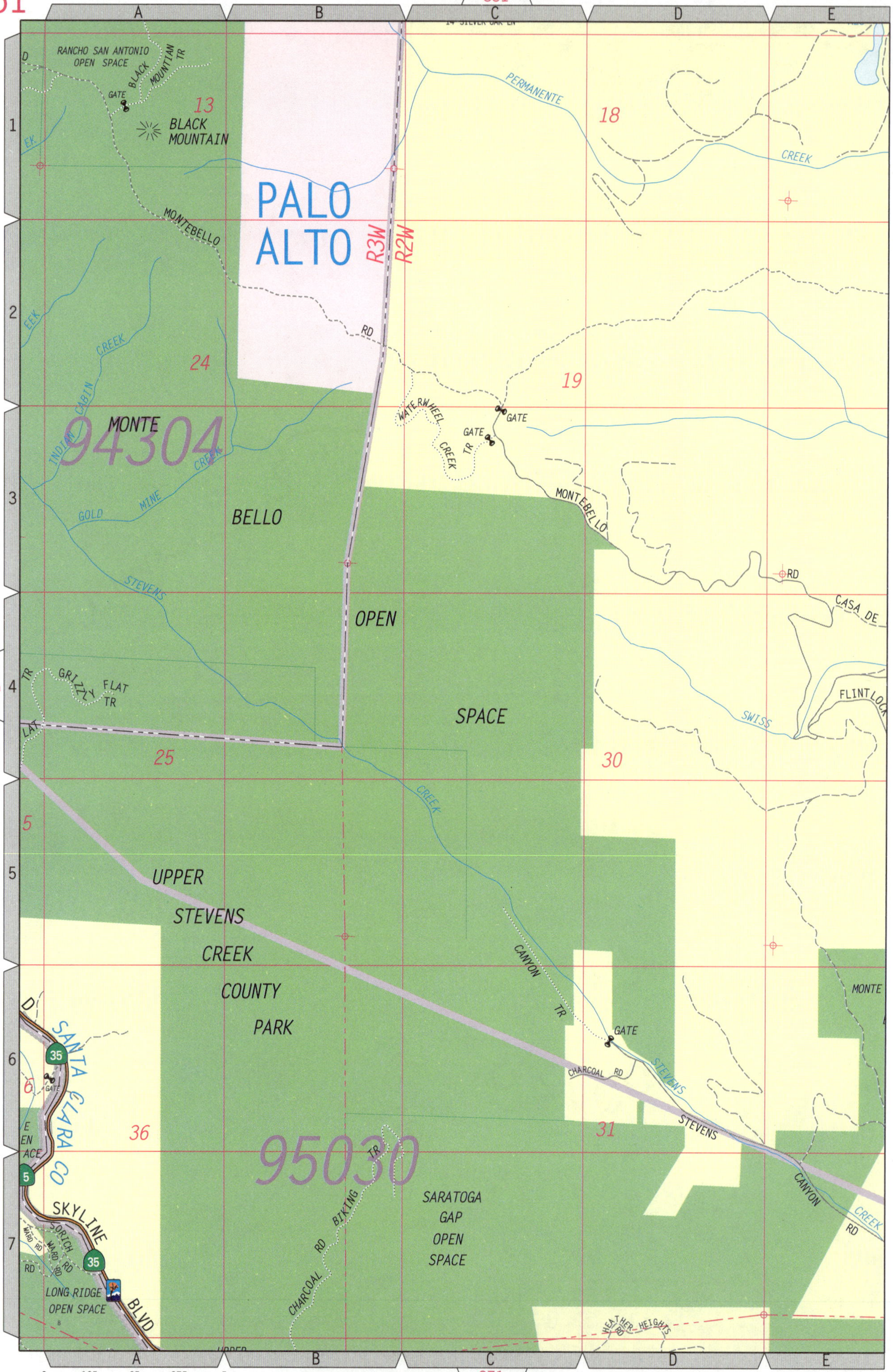

SEE B MAP

SEE 871 MAP

0 .125 .25 .375 .5 miles 1 in. = 1900 ft.

SANTA CLARA CO.

SEE 831 MAP

SANTA CLARA CO.

SEE 852 MAP

SEE 871 MAP

0 .125 .25 .375 .5 miles 1 in. = 1900 ft.

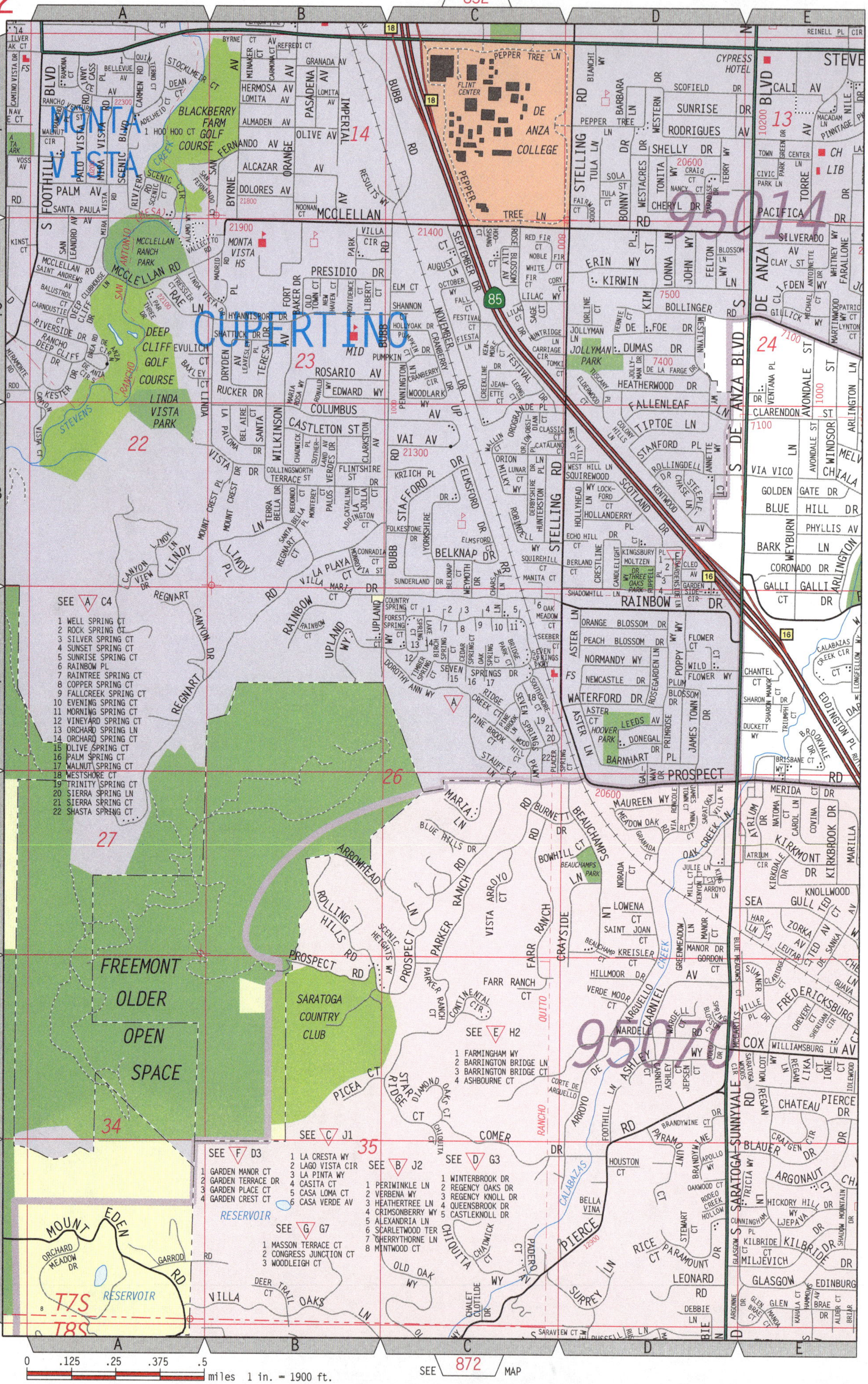
SEE 832 MAP
SEE 851 MAP
SEE 872 MAP
SANTA CLARA CO.
MONTA VISTA
CUPERTINO
DE ANZA COLLEGE
FLINT CENTER
BLACKBERRY FARM GOLF COURSE
MCCLELLAN RANCH PARK
DEEP CLIFF GOLF COURSE
LINDA VISTA PARK
MONTA VISTA HS
JOLLYMAN PARK
HOOVER PARK
BEAUCHAMPS PARK
FREEMONT OLDER OPEN SPACE
SARATOGA COUNTRY CLUB
RESERVOIR
MOUNT EDEN RD
95014
95070
T7S
T8S
MCCLELLAN RD
PROSPECT RD
RAINBOW DR
STELLING RD
DE ANZA BLVD
S SARATOGA SUNNYVALE RD
FOOTHILL BLVD
BUBB RD
PIERCE RD
SEE A C4
1 WELL SPRING CT
2 ROCK SPRING CT
3 SILVER SPRING CT
4 SUNSET SPRING CT
5 SUNRISE SPRING CT
6 RAINBOW PL
7 RAINTREE SPRING CT
8 COPPER SPRING CT
9 FALLCREEK SPRING CT
10 EVENING SPRING CT
11 MORNING SPRING CT
12 VINEYARD SPRING CT
13 ORCHARD SPRING LN
14 ORCHARD SPRING CT
15 OLIVE SPRING CT
16 PALM SPRING CT
17 WALNUT SPRING CT
18 WESTSHORE CT
19 TRINITY SPRING CT
20 SIERRA SPRING LN
21 SIERRA SPRING CT
22 SHASTA SPRING CT
SEE E H2
1 FARMINGHAM WY
2 BARRINGTON BRIDGE LN
3 BARRINGTON BRIDGE CT
4 ASHBOURNE CT
SEE F D3
1 GARDEN MANOR CT
2 GARDEN TERRACE DR
3 GARDEN PLACE CT
4 GARDEN CREST CT
SEE C J1
1 LA CRESTA WY
2 LAGO VISTA CIR
3 LA PINTA WY
4 CASITA CT
5 CASA LOMA CT
6 CASA VERDE AV
SEE B J2
1 PERIWINKLE LN
2 VERBENA WY
3 HEATHERTREE LN
4 CRIMSONBERRY WY
5 ALEXANDRIA LN
6 SCARLETWOOD TER
7 CHERRYTHORNE LN
8 MINTWOOD CT
SEE D G3
1 WINTERBROOK DR
2 REGENCY OAKS DR
3 REGENCY KNOLL DR
4 QUEENSBROOK DR
5 CASTLEKNOLL DR
SEE G G7
1 MASSON TERRACE CT
2 CONGRESS JUNCTION CT
3 WOODLEIGH CT
0 .125 .25 .375 .5
miles 1 in. = 1900 ft.

SEE 832 MAP

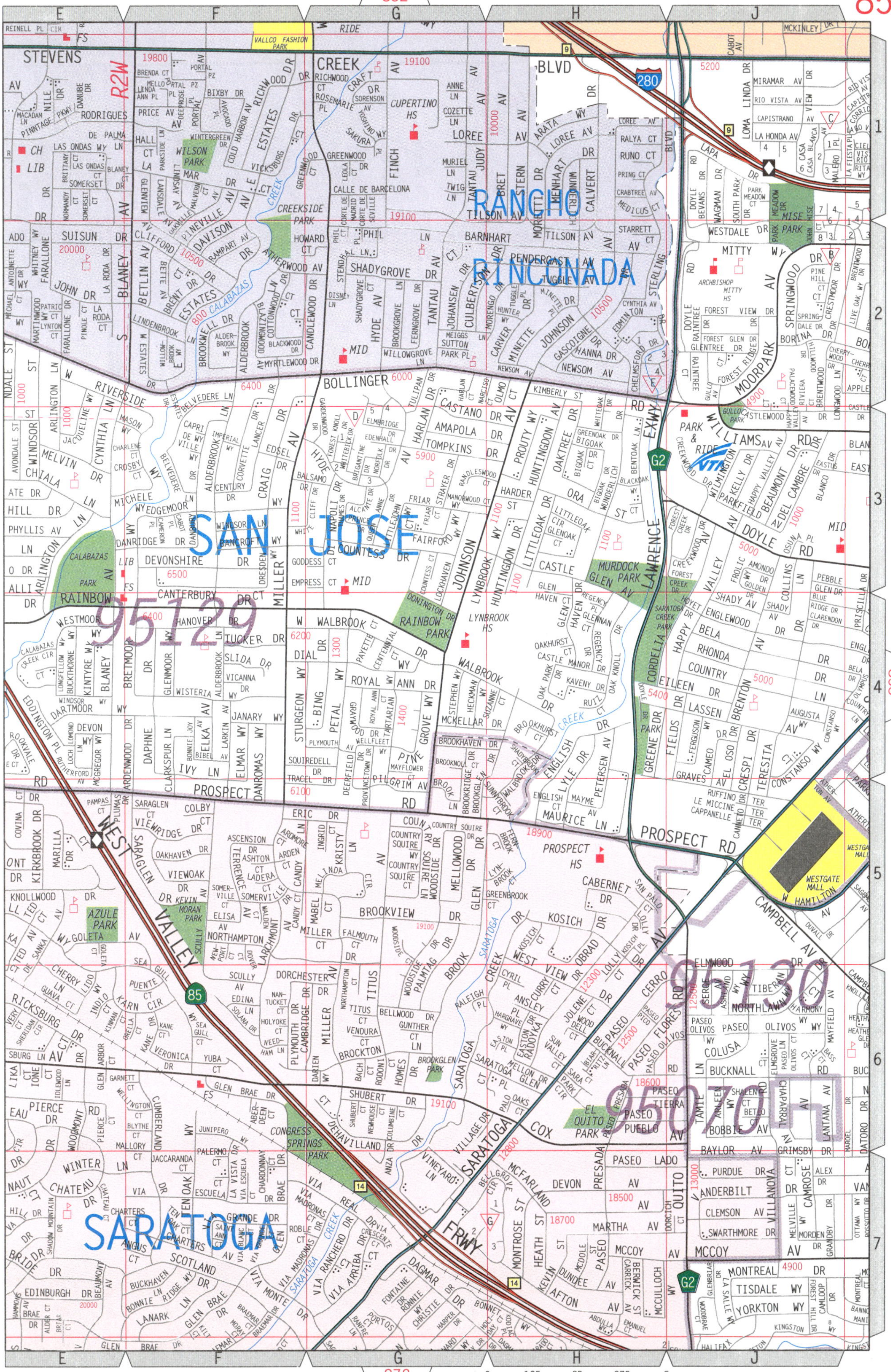

SEE 853 MAP

SEE 872 MAP

0 .125 .25 .375 .5 miles 1 in. = 1900 ft.

SEE 833 MAP

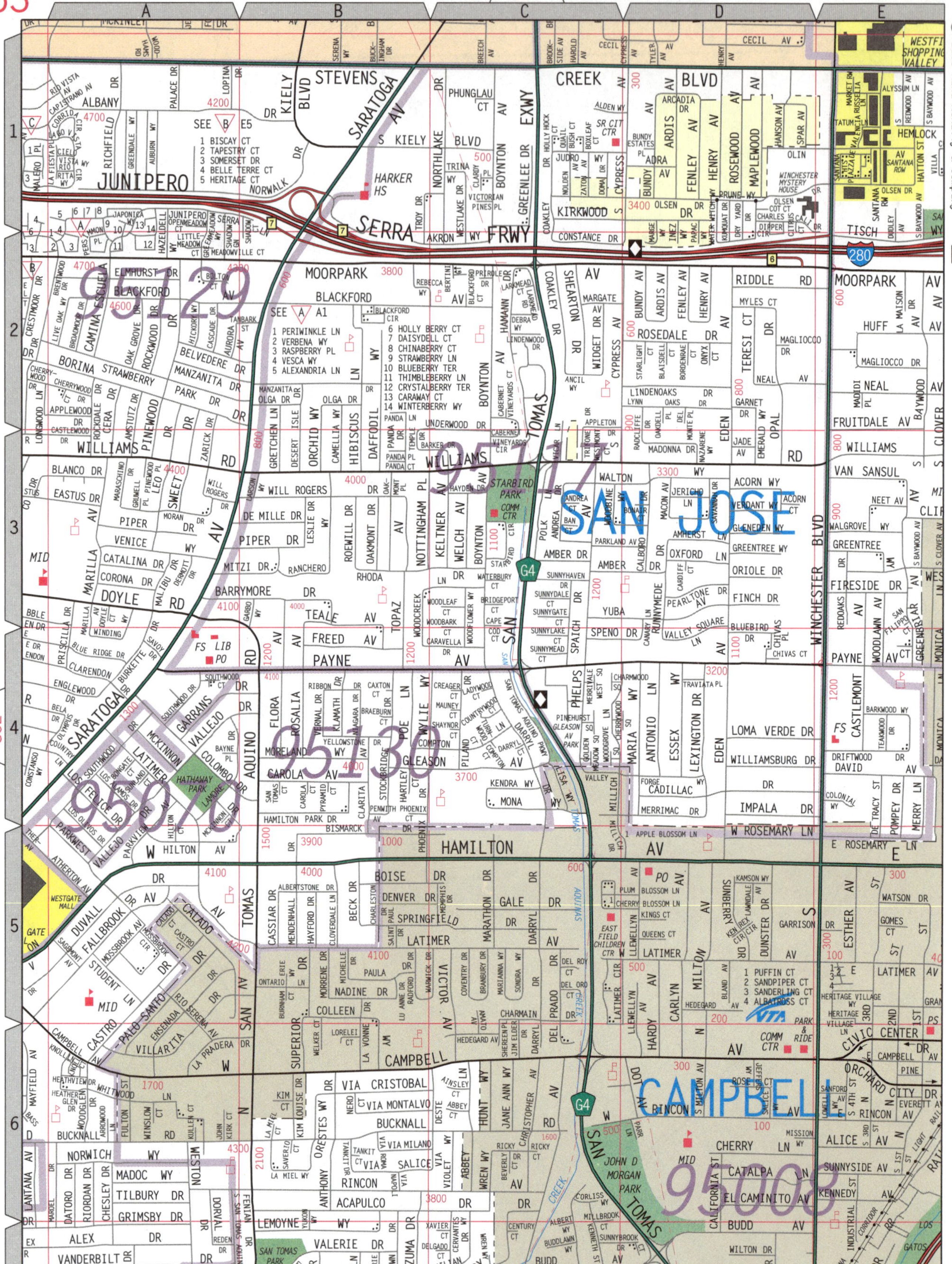

0 .125 .25 .375 .5 miles 1 in. = 1900 ft.

SEE 873 MAP

SEE 833 MAP

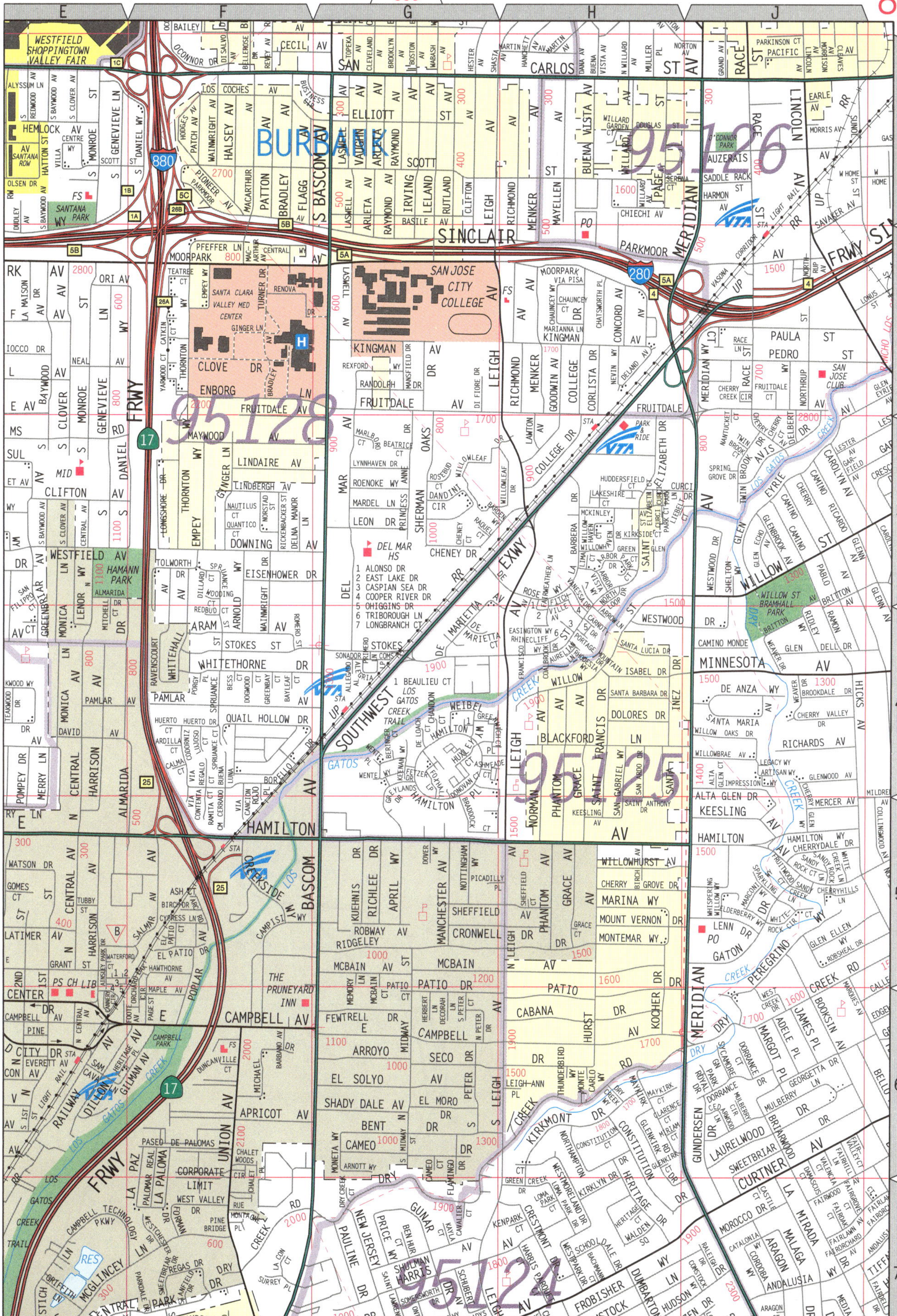

SEE 854 MAP

SANTA CLARA CO.

SEE 873 MAP

0 .125 .25 .375 .5 miles 1 in. = 1900 ft.

SEE 834 MAP

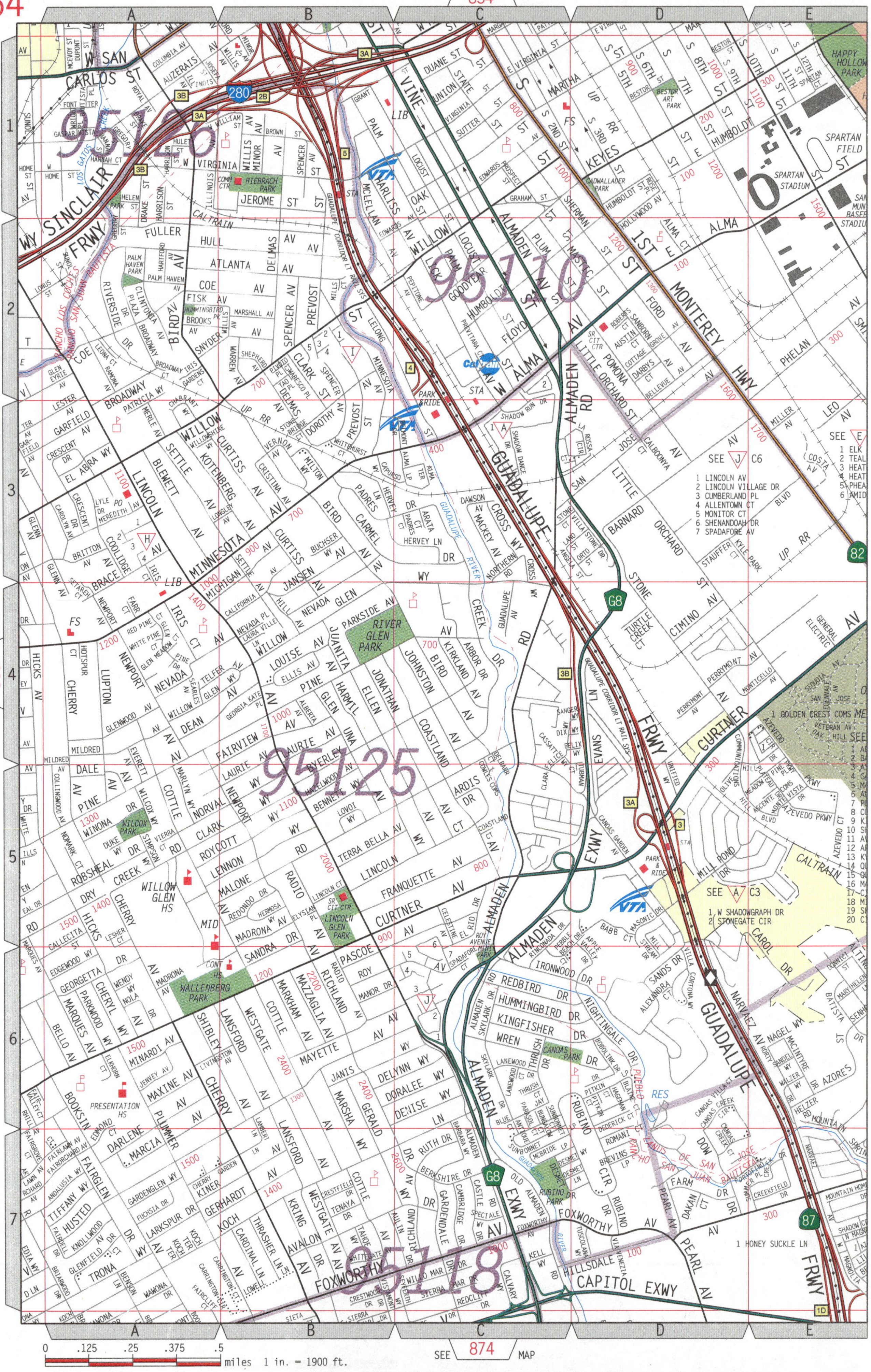
95126
95110
95125
95118
W SAN CARLOS ST
SINCLAIR FRWY
CALTRAIN
GUADALUPE FRWY
ALMADEN EXWY
CAPITOL EXWY
MONTEREY HWY
CURTNER AV
FOXWORTHY AV
MINNESOTA AV
WILLOW ST
LINCOLN AV
BROADWAY
HICKS AV
CHERRY AV
MERIDIAN AV
ALMA AV
KEYES ST
VIRGINIA ST
HUMBOLDT ST
SPARTAN STADIUM
SPARTAN FIELD
HAPPY HOLLOW PARK
BIEBRACH PARK
RIVER GLEN PARK
WILCOX PARK
LINCOLN GLEN PARK
WALLENBERG PARK
CANOAS PARK
RUBINO PARK
WILLOW GLEN HS
PRESENTATION HS
GUADALUPE RIVER
SANTA CLARA CO.
0 .125 .25 .375 .5 miles 1 in. = 1900 ft.

SEE 853 MAP

SEE 874 MAP

SEE 834 MAP

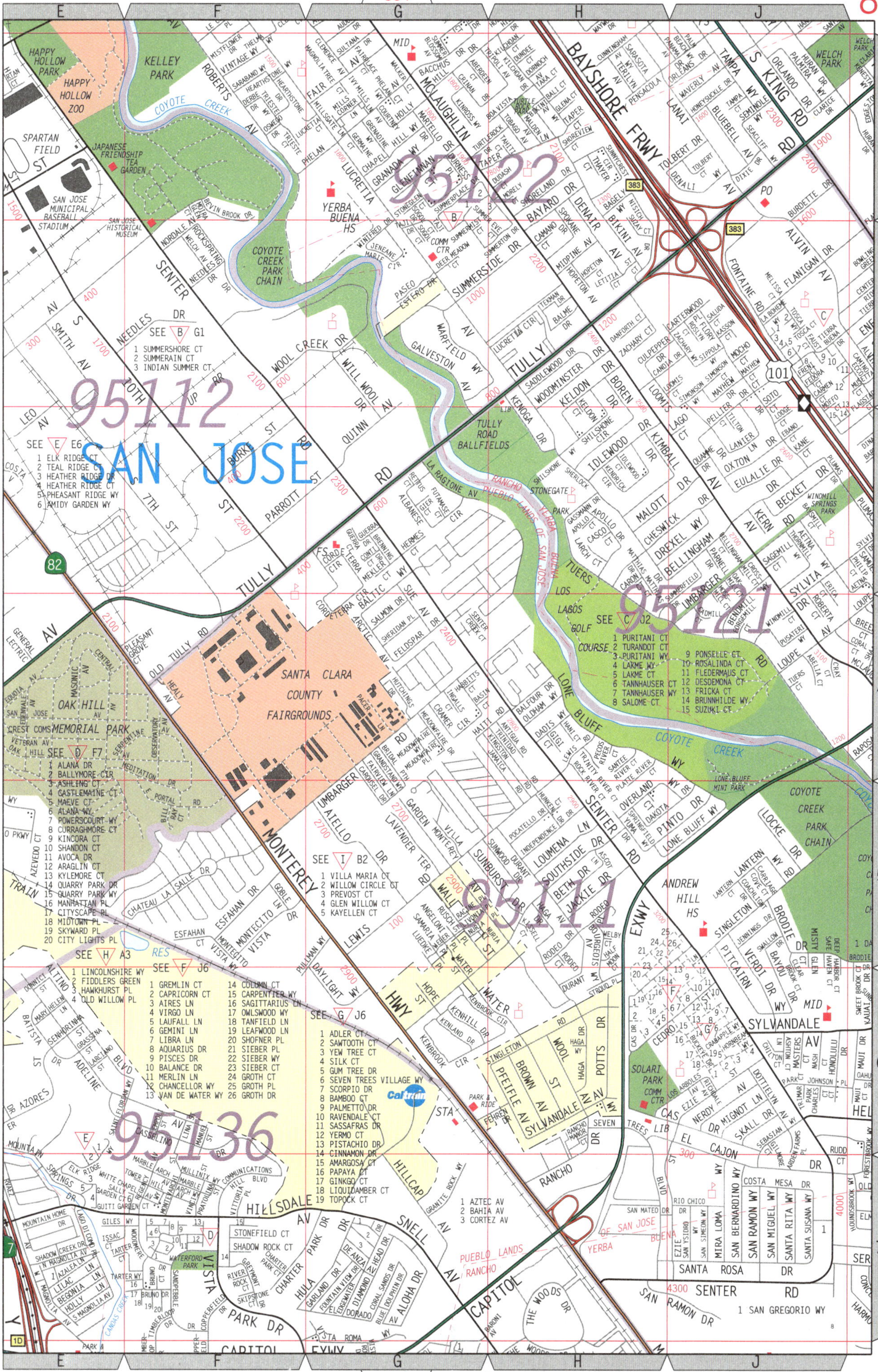

E
F
G
H
J
1
2
3
4
5
6
7
HAPPY HOLLOW PARK
HAPPY HOLLOW ZOO
KELLEY PARK
COYOTE CREEK
SPARTAN FIELD
JAPANESE FRIENDSHIP TEA GARDEN
SAN JOSE MUNICIPAL BASEBALL STADIUM
SAN JOSE HISTORICAL MUSEUM
COYOTE CREEK PARK CHAIN
YERBA BUENA HS
95122
95112
SAN JOSE
95121
95111
95136
BAYSHORE FRWY
101
383
82
WELCH PARK
S KING RD
TULLY RD
TULLY ROAD BALLFIELDS
SENTER RD
MONTEREY HWY
CAPITOL EXWY
SANTA CLARA COUNTY FAIRGROUNDS
OAK HILL MEMORIAL PARK
LOS LAGOS GOLF COURSE
RANCHO PUEBLO LANDS OF SAN JOSE
LONE BLUFF MINI PARK
ANDREW HILL HS
SOLARI PARK
SYLVANDALE AV
HILLSDALE AV
SNELL AV
EL CAJON DR
STONEGATE PARK
WINDMILL SPRINGS PARK
SEE B G1
1 SUMMERSHORE CT
2 SUMMERAIN CT
3 INDIAN SUMMER CT
SEE E E6
1 ELK RIDGE CT
2 TEAL RIDGE CT
3 HEATHER RIDGE DR
4 HEATHER RIDGE CT
5 PHEASANT RIDGE WY
6 AMIDY GARDEN WY
SEE C J2
1 PURITANI CT
2 TURANDOT CT
3 PURITANI WY
4 LAKME WY
5 LAKME CT
6 TANNHAUSER CT
7 TANNHAUSER WY
8 SALOME CT
9 PONSELLE CT
10 ROSALINDA CT
11 FLEDERMAUS CT
12 DESDEMONA CT
13 FRICKA CT
14 BRUNNHILDE WY
15 SUZUKI CT
SEE D F7
1 ALANA DR
2 BALLYMORE CIR
3 ASHLING CT
4 CASTLEMAINE CT
5 MAEVE CT
6 ALANA WY
7 POWERSCOURT WY
8 CURRAGHMORE CT
9 KINCORA CT
10 SHANDON CT
11 AVOCA DR
12 ARAGLIN CT
13 KYLEMORE CT
14 QUARRY PARK DR
15 QUARRY PARK WY
16 MANHATTAN PL
17 CITYSCAPE PL
18 MIDTOWN PL
19 SKYWARD PL
20 CITY LIGHTS PL
SEE I B2
1 VILLA MARIA CT
2 WILLOW CIRCLE CT
3 PREVOST CT
4 GLEN WILLOW CT
5 KAYELLEN CT
SEE H A3
1 LINCOLNSHIRE WY
2 FIDDLERS GREEN
3 HAWKHURST PL
4 OLD WILLOW PL
SEE F J6
1 GREMLIN CT
2 CAPRICORN CT
3 AIRES LN
4 VIRGO LN
5 LAUFALL LN
6 GEMINI LN
7 LIBRA LN
8 AQUARIUS DR
9 PISCES DR
10 BALANCE DR
11 MERLIN LN
12 CHANCELLOR WY
13 VAN DE WATER WY
14 COLUMN CT
15 CARPENTIER WY
16 SAGITTARIUS LN
17 OWLSWOOD WY
18 TANFIELD LN
19 LEAFWOOD LN
20 SHOFNER PL
21 SIEBER PL
22 SIEBER WY
23 SIEBER CT
24 GROTH CT
25 GROTH PL
26 GROTH DR
SEE G J6
1 ADLER CT
2 SAWTOOTH CT
3 YEW TREE CT
4 SILK CT
5 GUM TREE DR
6 SEVEN TREES VILLAGE WY
7 SCORPIO DR
8 BAMBOO CT
9 PALMETTO DR
10 RAVENDALE CT
11 SASSAFRAS DR
12 YERMO CT
13 PISTACHIO DR
14 CINNAMON DR
15 AMARGOSA CT
16 PAPAYA CT
17 GINKGO CT
18 LIQUIDAMBER CT
19 TOPOCK CT
1 AZTEC AV
2 BAHIA AV
3 CORTEZ AV
1 SAN GREGORIO WY

SEE 855 MAP

SEE 874 MAP

0 .125 .25 .375 .5 miles 1 in. = 1900 ft.

SEE 835 MAP

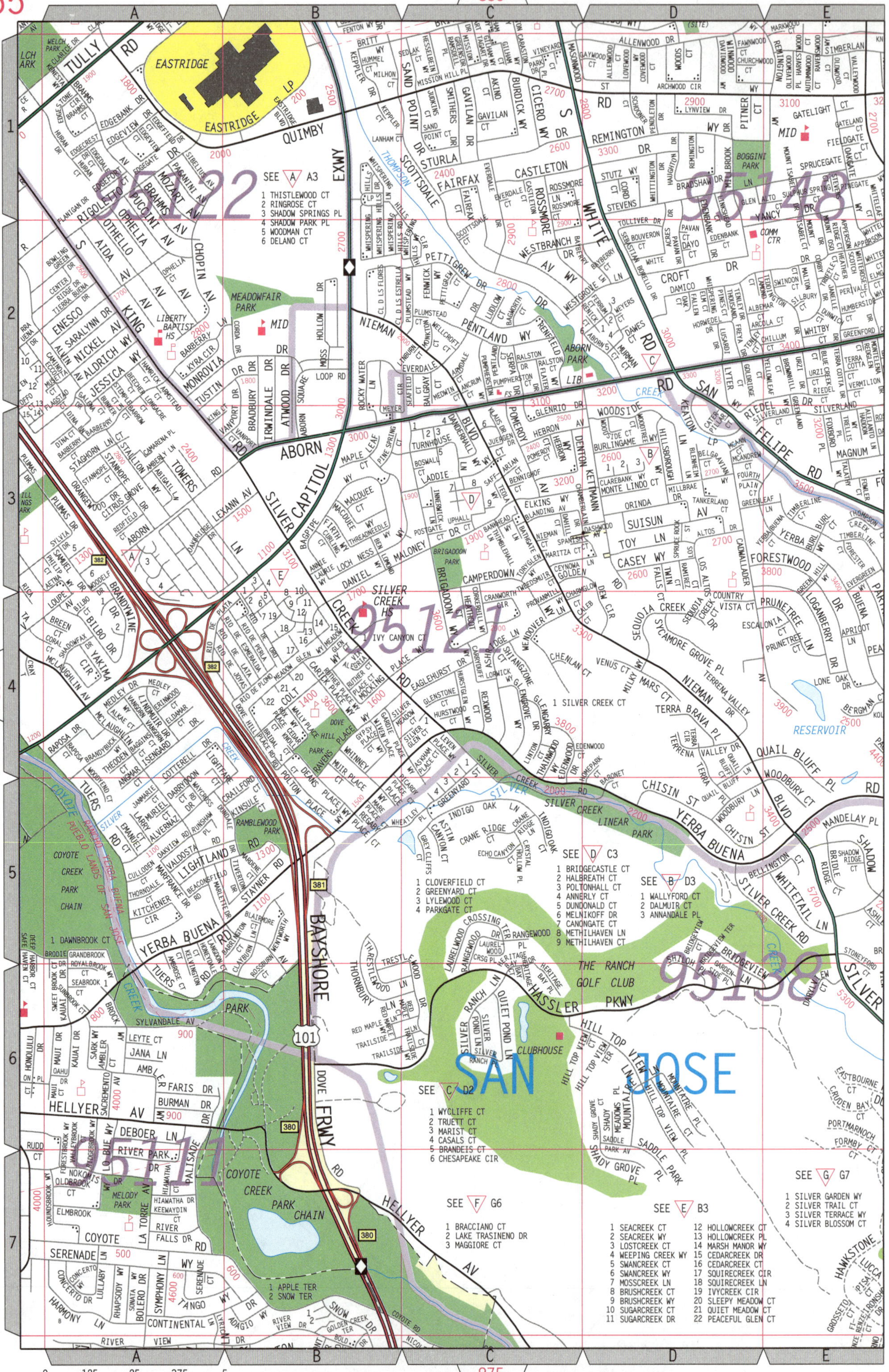
SANTA CLARA CO.
A
B
C
D
E
1
2
3
4
5
6
7
SAN JOSE
95122
95148
95121
95138
95111
EASTRIDGE
QUIMBY RD
TULLY RD
CAPITOL EXWY
ABORN RD
KING RD
STORY RD
WHITE RD
SAN FELIPE RD
YERBA BUENA RD
SILVER CREEK RD
NIEMAN BLVD
HELLYER AV
BAYSHORE FRWY
101
380
381
382
COYOTE CREEK PARK CHAIN
MEADOWFAIR PARK
BOGGINI PARK
ABORN PARK
BRIGADOON PARK
RAMBLEWOOD PARK
DOVE HILL PARK
MELODY PARK
SILVER CREEK LINEAR PARK
THE RANCH GOLF CLUB
CLUBHOUSE
RESERVOIR
HASSLER PKWY
SILVER CREEK HS
LIBERTY BAPTIST HS
SEE A A3
1 THISTLEWOOD CT
2 RINGROSE CT
3 SHADOW SPRINGS PL
4 SHADOW PARK PL
5 WOODMAN CT
6 DELANO CT
SEE D C3
1 BRIDGECASTLE CT
2 HALBREATH CT
3 POLTONHALL CT
4 ANNERLY CT
5 DUNDONALD CT
6 MELNIKOFF DR
7 CANONGATE CT
8 METHILHAVEN LN
9 METHILHAVEN CT
1 CLOVERFIELD CT
2 GREENYARD CT
3 LYLEWOOD CT
4 PARKGATE CT
SEE B D3
1 WALLYFORD CT
2 DALMUIR CT
3 ANNANDALE PL
SEE C D2
1 WYCLIFFE CT
2 TRUETT CT
3 MARIST CT
4 CASALS CT
5 BRANDEIS CT
6 CHESAPEAKE CIR
SEE F G6
1 BRACCIANO CT
2 LAKE TRASINENO DR
3 MAGGIORE CT
SEE E B3
1 SEACREEK CT
2 SEACREEK WY
3 LOSTCREEK CT
4 WEEPING CREEK WY
5 SWANCREEK CT
6 SWANCREEK WY
7 MOSSCREEK LN
8 BRUSHCREEK CT
9 BRUSHCREEK WY
10 SUGARCREEK CT
11 SUGARCREEK DR
12 HOLLOWCREEK CT
13 HOLLOWCREEK PL
14 MARSH MANOR WY
15 CEDARCREEK CT
16 CEDARCREEK DR
17 SQUIRECREEK CIR
18 SQUIRECREEK LN
19 IVYCREEK CIR
20 SLEEPY MEADOW CT
21 QUIET MEADOW CT
22 PEACEFUL GLEN CT
SEE G G7
1 SILVER GARDEN WY
2 SILVER TRAIL CT
3 SILVER TERRACE WY
4 SILVER BLOSSOM CT
1 1 SILVER CREEK CT
1 DAWNBROOK CT
1 APPLE TER
2 SNOW TER
SEE 854 MAP

0 .125 .25 .375 .5 miles 1 in. = 1900 ft.

SEE 875 MAP

SEE 835 MAP

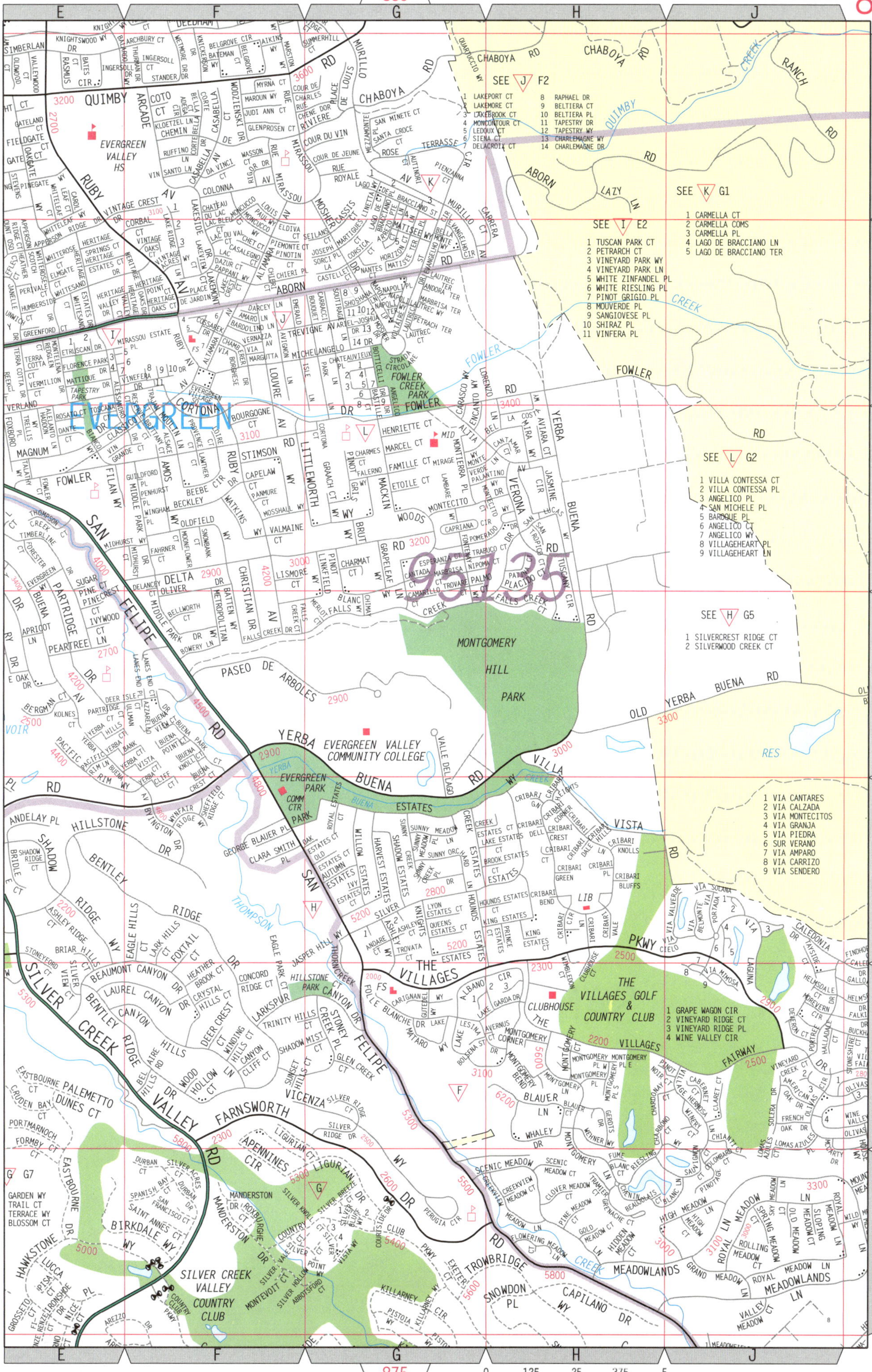
SEE J F2
1 LAKEPORT CT
2 LAKEMORE CT
3 LAKEBROOK CT
4 MONCONTOUR CT
5 LEDOUX CT
6 SIENA CT
7 DELACROIX CT
8 RAPHAEL DR
9 BELTIERA CT
10 BELTIERA PL
11 TAPESTRY DR
12 TAPESTRY WY
13 CHARLEMAGNE WY
14 CHARLEMAGNE DR
SEE K G1
1 CARMELLA CT
2 CARMELLA COMS
3 CARMELLA PL
4 LAGO DE BRACCIANO LN
5 LAGO DE BRACCIANO TER
SEE I E2
1 TUSCAN PARK CT
2 PETRARCH CT
3 VINEYARD PARK WY
4 VINEYARD PARK LN
5 WHITE ZINFANDEL PL
6 WHITE RIESLING PL
7 PINOT GRIGIO PL
8 MOUVERDE PL
9 SANGIOVESE PL
10 SHIRAZ PL
11 VINFERA PL
SEE L G2
1 VILLA CONTESSA CT
2 VILLA CONTESSA PL
3 ANGELICO PL
4 SAN MICHELE PL
5 BAROQUE PL
6 ANGELICO CT
7 ANGELICO WY
8 VILLAGEHEART PL
9 VILLAGEHEART LN
SEE H G5
1 SILVERCREST RIDGE CT
2 SILVERWOOD CREEK CT
1 VIA CANTARES
2 VIA CALZADA
3 VIA MONTECITOS
4 VIA GRANJA
5 VIA PIEDRA
6 SUR VERANO
7 VIA AMPARO
8 VIA CARRIZO
9 VIA SENDERO
SEE G G7
GARDEN WY
TRAIL CT
TERRACE WY
BLOSSOM CT
EVERGREEN
95135
EVERGREEN VALLEY HS
MONTGOMERY HILL PARK
EVERGREEN VALLEY COMMUNITY COLLEGE
EVERGREEN PARK
FOWLER CREEK PARK
THE VILLAGES GOLF & COUNTRY CLUB
SILVER CREEK VALLEY COUNTRY CLUB
THE VILLAGES
QUIMBY RD
CHABOYA RD
ABORN RD
FOWLER RD
YERBA BUENA RD
OLD YERBA BUENA RD
SAN FELIPE RD
SILVER CREEK VALLEY RD
FARNSWORTH DR
VILLAGES PKWY
RUBY AV
RES
E F G H J
1 2 3 4 5 6 7

SEE 875 MAP

SEE 856 MAP

SANTA CLARA CO.

0 .125 .25 .375 .5 miles 1 in. = 1900 ft.

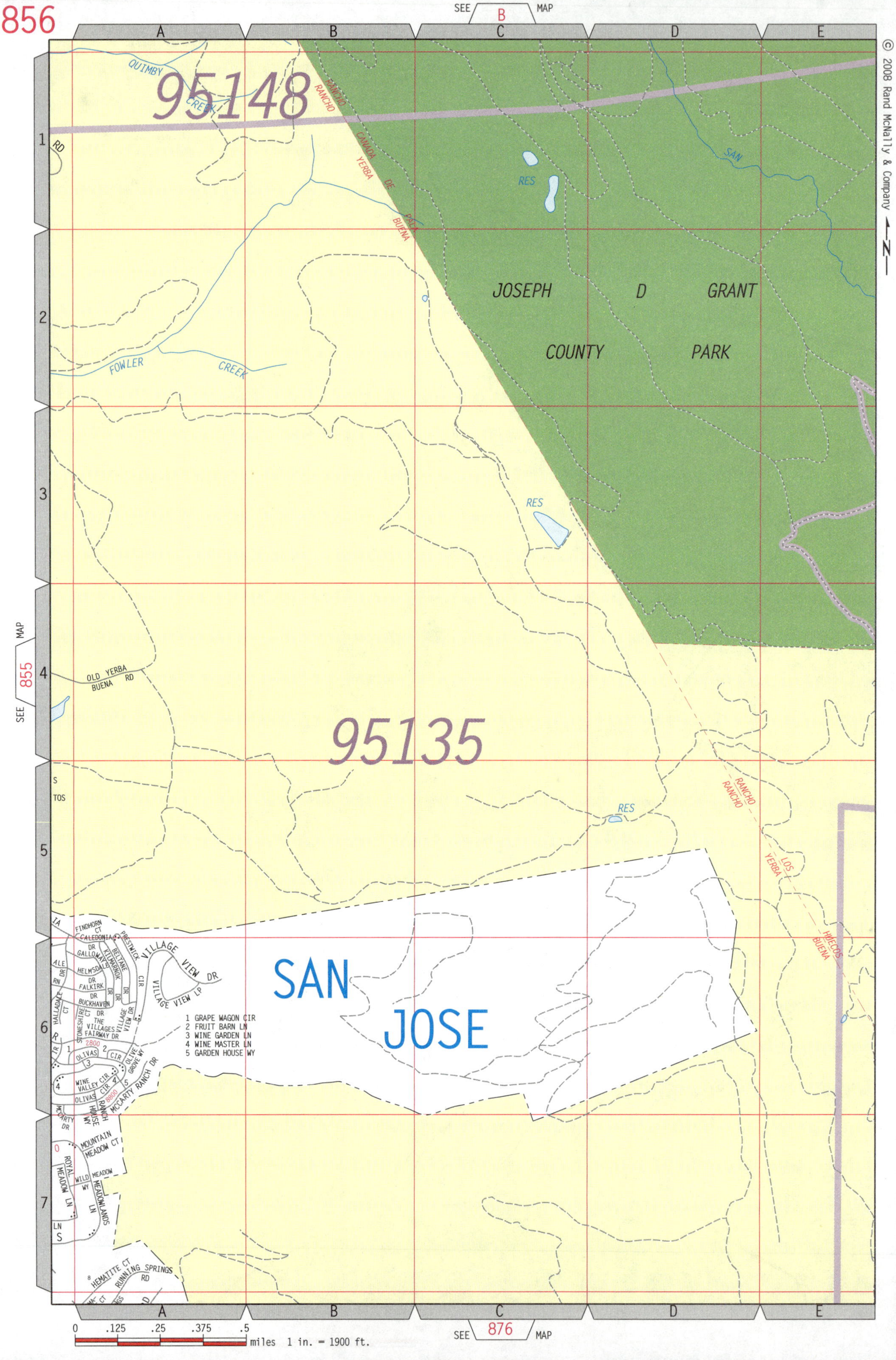

SEE B MAP
95148
QUIMBY CREEK
RANCHO CANADA DE YERBA BUENA
RD
SAN
RES
JOSEPH D GRANT COUNTY PARK
FOWLER CREEK
SANTA CLARA CO.
SEE 855 MAP
OLD YERBA BUENA RD
95135
RANCHO YERBA BUENA
RANCHO LOS HUECOS
RES
SAN JOSE
FINDHORN CT
CALEDONIA
GALLOWAY DR
HELMSDALE DR
FALKIRK DR
BUCKHAVEN DR
HALLADALE CT
STONESHIRE CT
THE VILLAGES FAIRWAY DR
PRESTWICK CIR
BELTANE DR
KILMARNOCK DR
VILLAGE VIEW DR
VILLAGE VIEW LP
1 GRAPE WAGON CIR
2 FRUIT BARN LN
3 WINE GARDEN LN
4 WINE MASTER LN
5 GARDEN HOUSE WY
OLIVAS CIR
OLIVE GROVE WY
WINE VALLEY CIR
MCCARTY RANCH DR
RANCH HOUSE WY
MCCARTY DR
MOUNTAIN MEADOW CT
ROYAL MEADOW LN
WILD MEADOW WY
MEADOWLANDS LN
HEMATITE CT
RUNNING SPRINGS RD
0 .125 .25 .375 .5 miles 1 in. = 1900 ft.
SEE 876 MAP

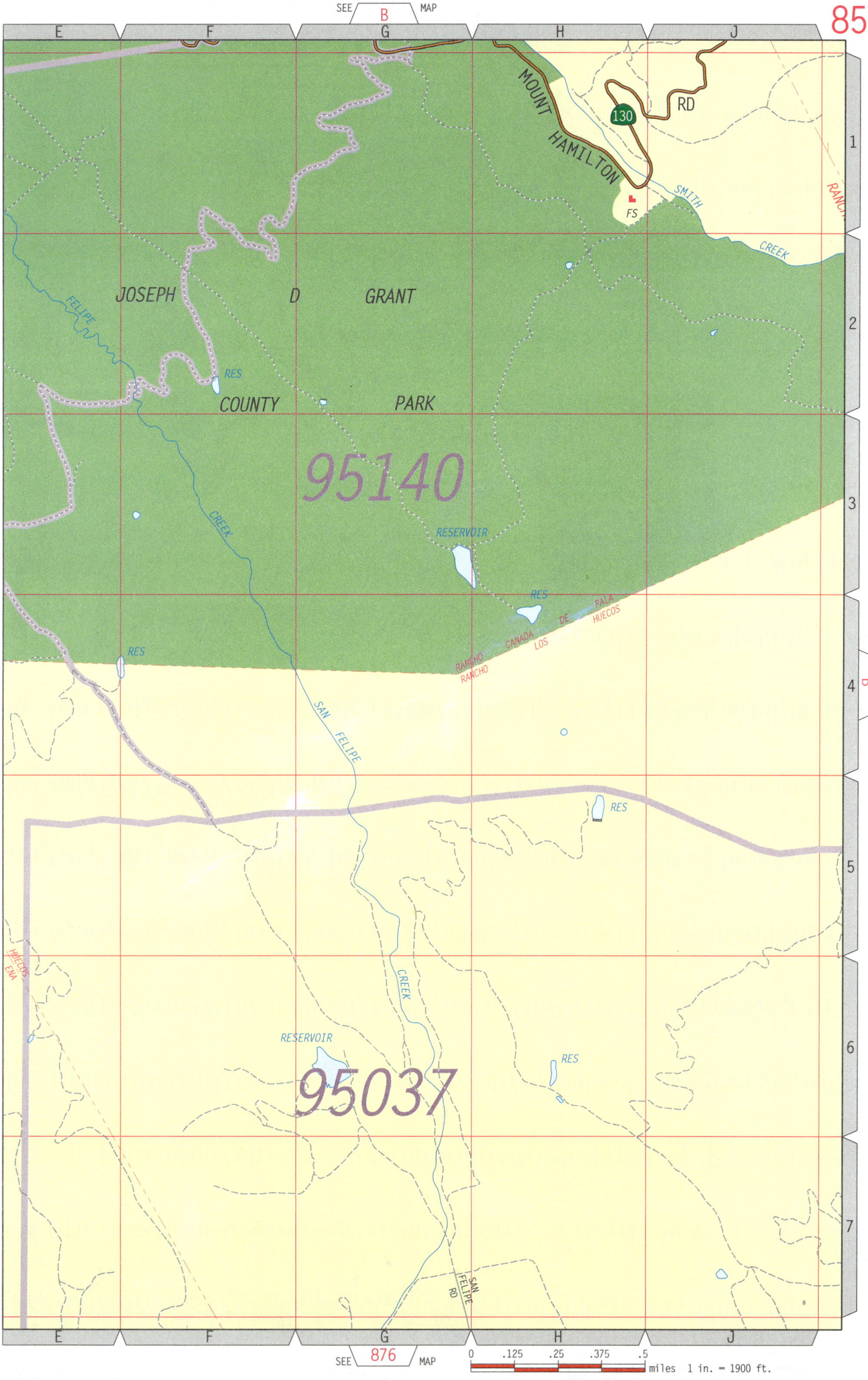
SEE B MAP
E
F
G
H
J
MOUNT HAMILTON RD
130
SMITH CREEK
FS
RANCH
JOSEPH D GRANT COUNTY PARK
FELIPE CREEK
RES
95140
RESERVOIR
RANCHO CANADA DE LOS PALA HUECOS
RANCHO
SEE B MAP
SAN FELIPE CREEK
HUECOS
ENA
RESERVOIR
95037
SAN FELIPE RD
1
2
3
4
5
6
7
SEE 876 MAP
0 .125 .25 .375 .5 miles 1 in. = 1900 ft.

SEE 851 MAP

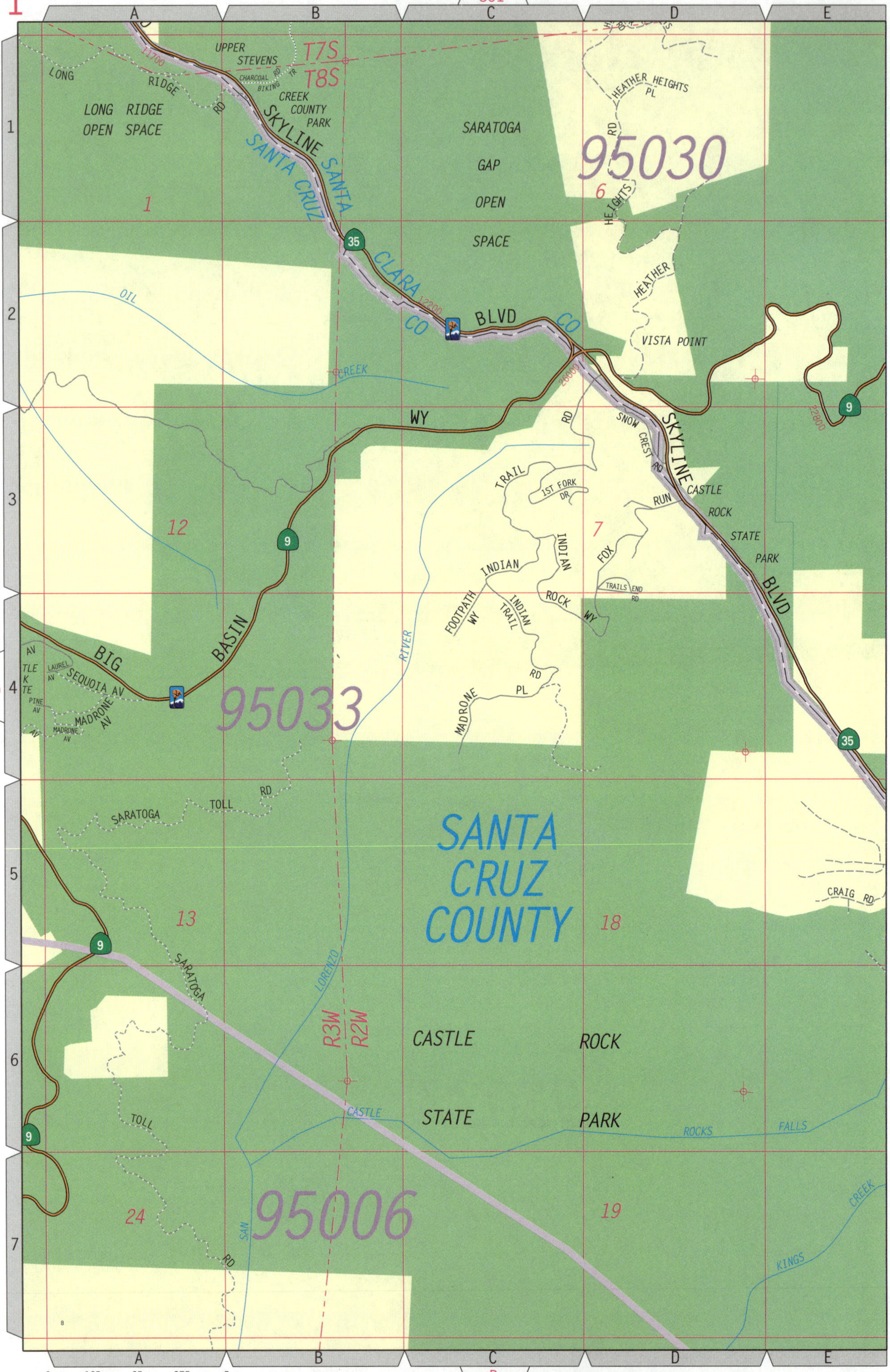

SEE B MAP

0 .125 .25 .375 .5 miles 1 in. = 1900 ft.

© 2008 Rand McNally & Company

N

SANTA CLARA CO.

A B C D E

LONG

UPPER STEVENS

T7S
T8S

CHARCOAL RD
BIKING

CREEK
COUNTY
PARK

RIDGE

LONG RIDGE
OPEN SPACE

SKYLINE SANTA

SANTA CRUZ

1

SARATOGA

GAP

OPEN

SPACE

HEATHER HEIGHTS
PL

95030

6

RD

1

2

OIL

35

CLARA

CO

CREEK

BLVD

CO

HEATHER

VISTA POINT

HEIGHTS

9

WY

SKYLINE

SNOW CREST RD

RD

TRAIL

1ST FORK
DR

CASTLE

RUN

ROCK

3

12

INDIAN

FOX

7

STATE

PARK

BLVD

INDIAN

FOOTPATH WY

ROCK

WY

TRAILS END
RD

INDIAN

TRAIL

AV

BIG

BASIN

TLE KTE

LAUREL
AV

RD

MADRONE

AV

PL

PINE
AV

SEQUOIA AV

MADRONE
AV

MADRONE AV

9

95033

CASTLE

ROCK

4

35

SARATOGA

TOLL

RD

SANTA

CRUZ

COUNTY

CRAIG RD

5

9

13

STATE

18

SARATOGA

PARK

R3W R2W

CASTLE

ROCK

6

TOLL

CASTLE

9

ROCKS

FALLS

24

SAN

95006

RD

19

KINGS

CREEK

7

A B C D E

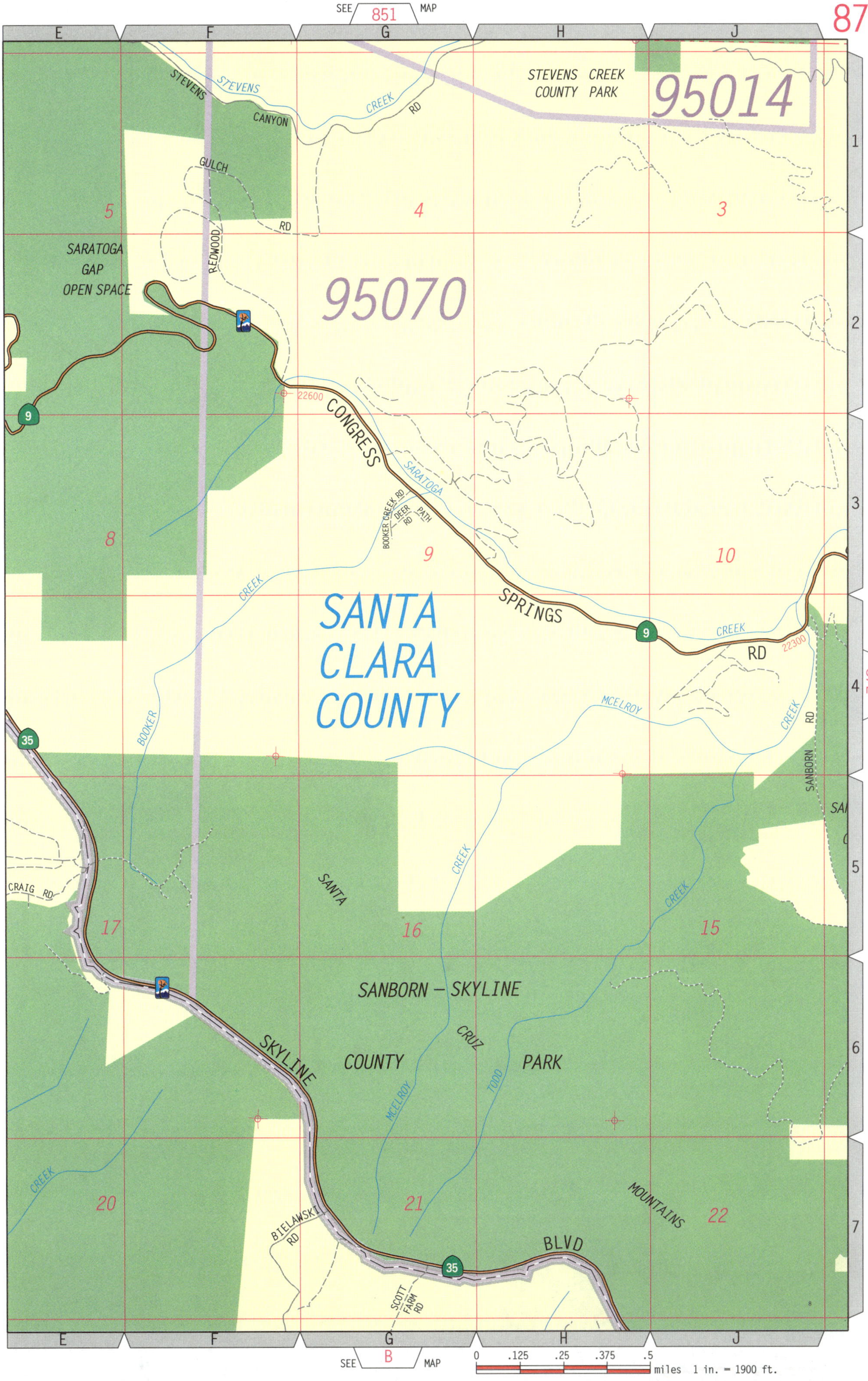
SEE 851 MAP
E
F
G
H
J
1
2
3
4
5
6
7
95014
95070
STEVENS CREEK COUNTY PARK
STEVENS CANYON RD
STEVENS CREEK
GULCH RD
REDWOOD
SARATOGA GAP OPEN SPACE
9
22600
CONGRESS SPRINGS RD
SARATOGA
BOOKER CREEK RD
DEER PATH
BOOKER
CREEK
SANTA CLARA COUNTY
22300
MCELROY
SANBORN RD
35
CRAIG RD
SANTA CRUZ MOUNTAINS
SANBORN – SKYLINE COUNTY PARK
SKYLINE BLVD
MCELROY
TODD
BIELAWSKI RD
SCOTT FARM RD
5
4
3
8
9
10
17
16
15
20
21
22
SEE 872 MAP
SEE B MAP
0 .125 .25 .375 .5 miles 1 in. = 1900 ft.

SEE 852 MAP

© 2008 Rand McNally & Company

—N—

95070

T8S

A B C D E

1
2
3
4
5
6
7

MOUNT EDEN RD

PIERCE RD

CALABAZAS CREEK

SARATOGA

CONGRESS SPRINGS RD

SARATOGA CREEK

SANBORN SKYLINE COUNTY PARK

RESERVOIR

SANBORN RD

BOHLMAN RD

CONGRESS SPRINGS

WILDCAT CREEK

VILLA MONTALVO

VILLA MONTALVO ARBORETUM

STUART CAMP

SAN TOMAS

EL SE OPEN S

BIG BASIN WY

SARATOGA

SARATOGA-SUNNYVALE RD

HAKONE GARDENS

MADRONIA CEM

SARATOGA HS

HERRIMAN AV

KITTRIDGE RD

SANBORN SKYLINE COUNTY PARK

LAKE RANCH RD

AMBROSE RD

MCGILL RD

BAY SPRINGS RD

SEE A D1
1 MAGNOLIA CT
2 MINA WY
3 PETUNIA CT
4 VERDE CT

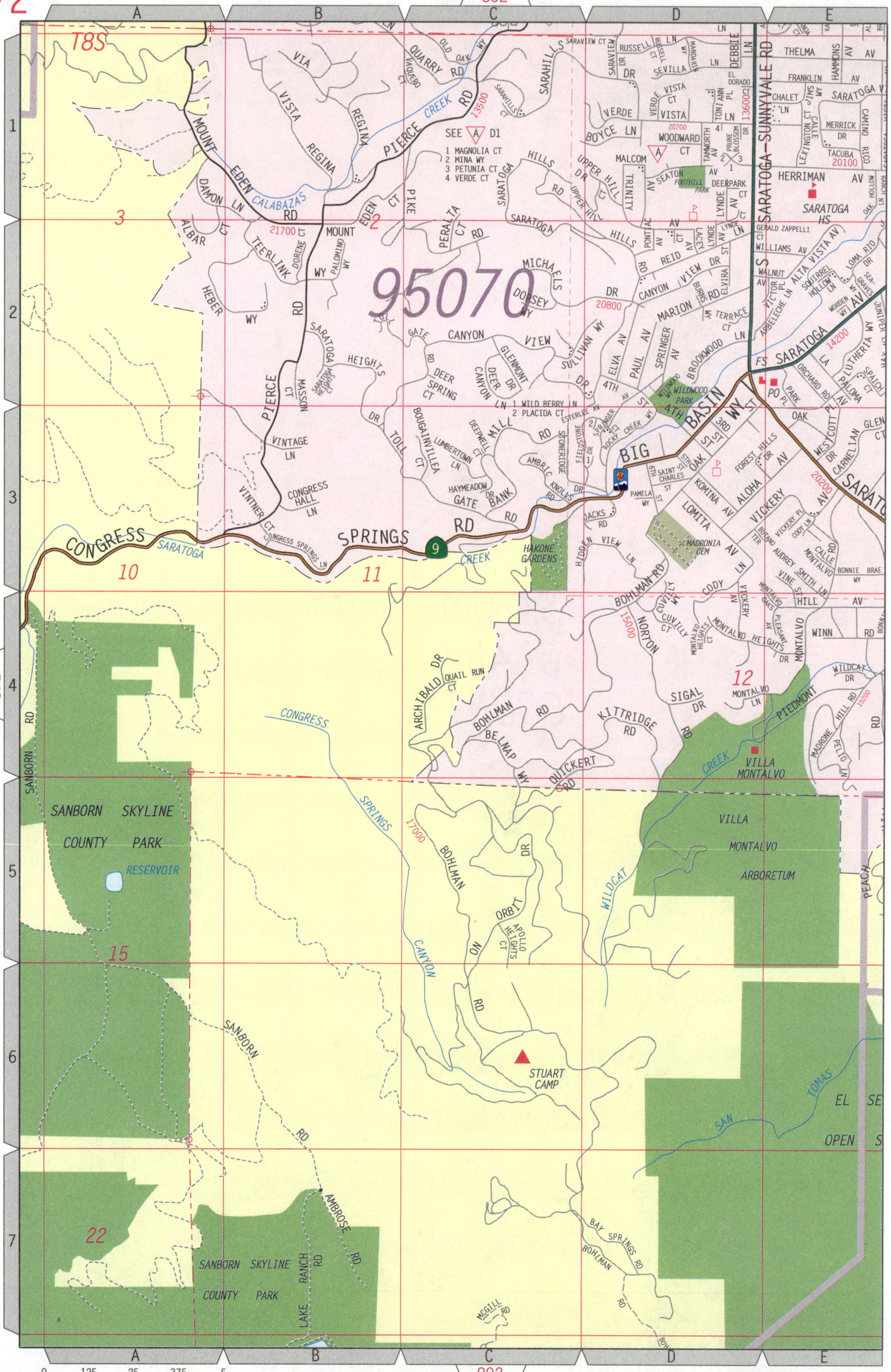

SEE 871 MAP

SEE 892 MAP

0 .125 .25 .375 .5 miles 1 in. = 1900 ft.

9 10 11 12 15 22

SEE 852 MAP

SANTA CLARA CO.

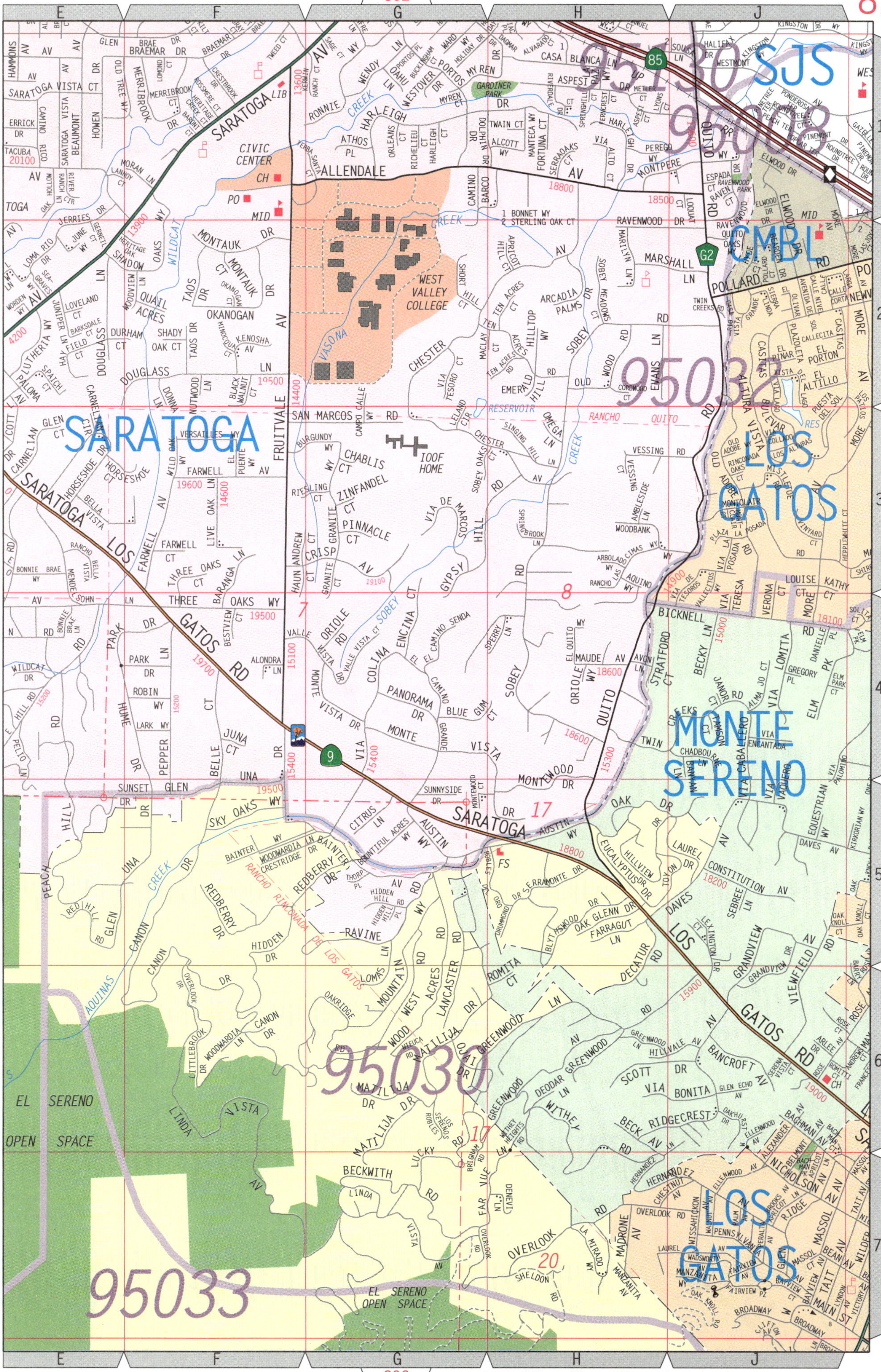

SEE 873 MAP

SEE 892 MAP

0 .125 .25 .375 .5 miles 1 in. = 1900 ft.

SEE 853 MAP

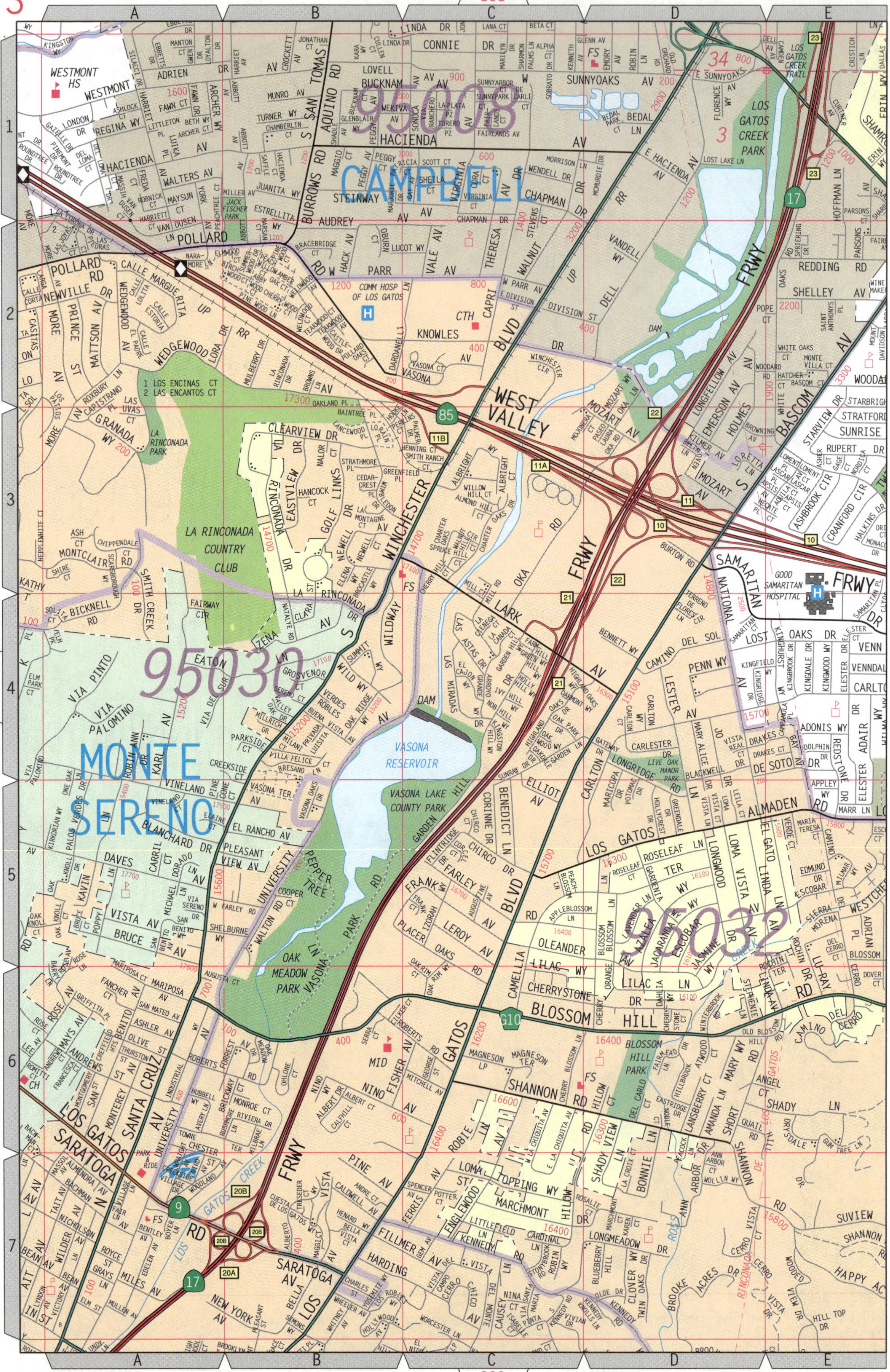

SEE 872 MAP

SEE 893 MAP

0 .125 .25 .375 .5 miles 1 in. = 1900 ft.

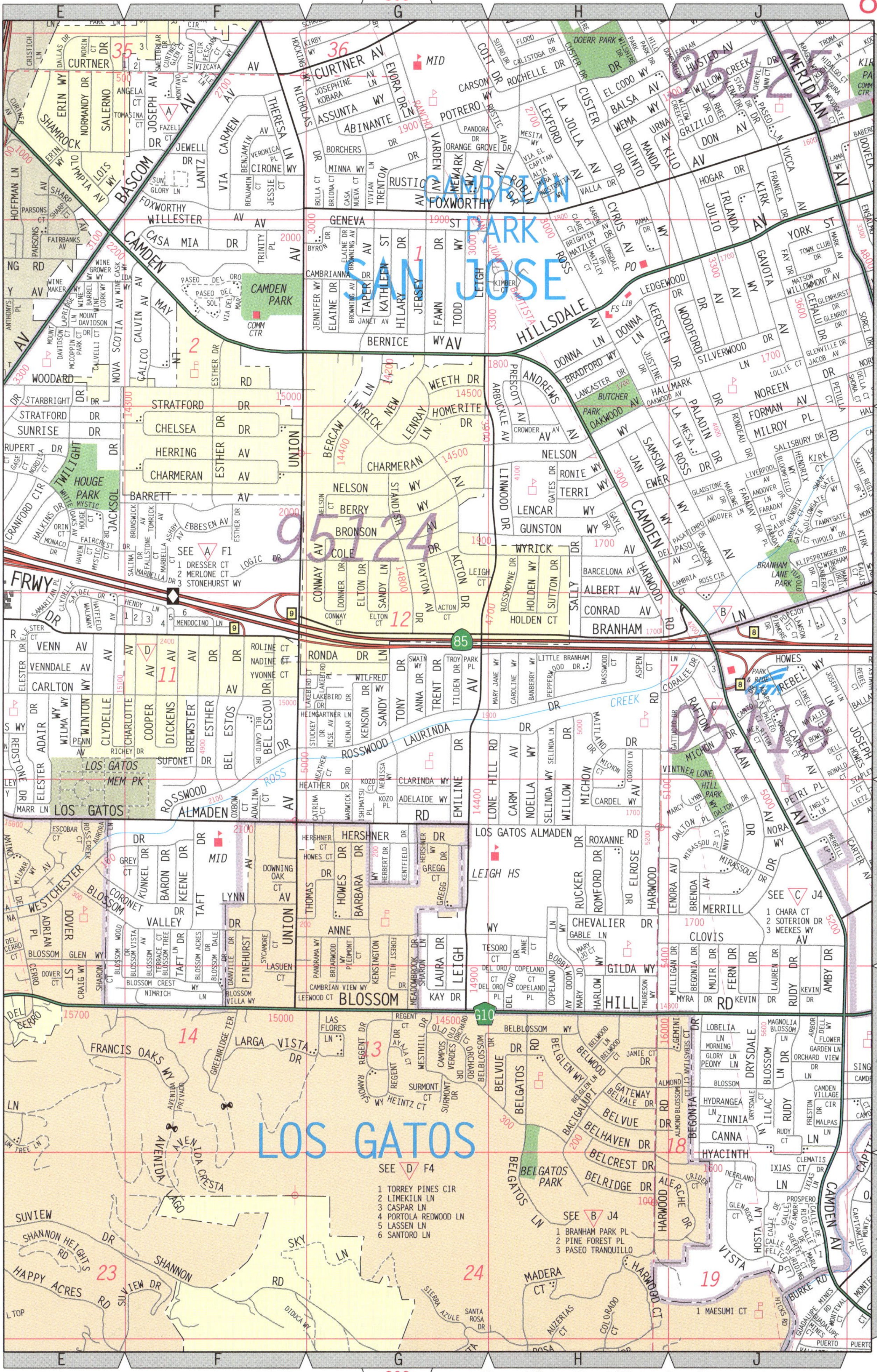
SEE 853 MAP
SEE 893 MAP
SEE 874 MAP
SANTA CLARA CO.
© 2008 Rand McNally & Company
E F G H J
1 2 3 4 5 6 7
SAN JOSE
CAMBRIAN PARK
LOS GATOS
95124
95125
95118
CAMDEN PARK
HOUGE PARK
LOS GATOS MEM PK
BUTCHER PARK
BRANHAM LANE PARK
VINTNER LONE HILL PARK
DOERR PARK
BELGATOS PARK
LEIGH HS
85
G10
9
8
CAMDEN AV
BASCOM AV
HILLSDALE AV
MERIDIAN AV
UNION AV
LOS GATOS ALMADEN RD
BLOSSOM HILL RD
BRANHAM LN
CURTNER AV
FOXWORTHY AV
CAMDEN AV
SEE A F1
1 DRESSER CT
2 MERLONE CT
3 STONEHURST WY
SEE C J4
1 CHARA CT
2 SOTERION DR
3 WEEKES WY
SEE D F4
1 TORREY PINES CIR
2 LIMEKILN LN
3 CASPAR LN
4 PORTOLA REDWOOD LN
5 LASSEN LN
6 SANTORO LN
SEE B J4
1 BRANHAM PARK PL
2 PINE FOREST PL
3 PASEO TRANQUILLO
1 MAESUMI CT
0 .125 .25 .375 .5 miles 1 in. = 1900 ft.

SEE 854 MAP

SANTA CLARA CO.

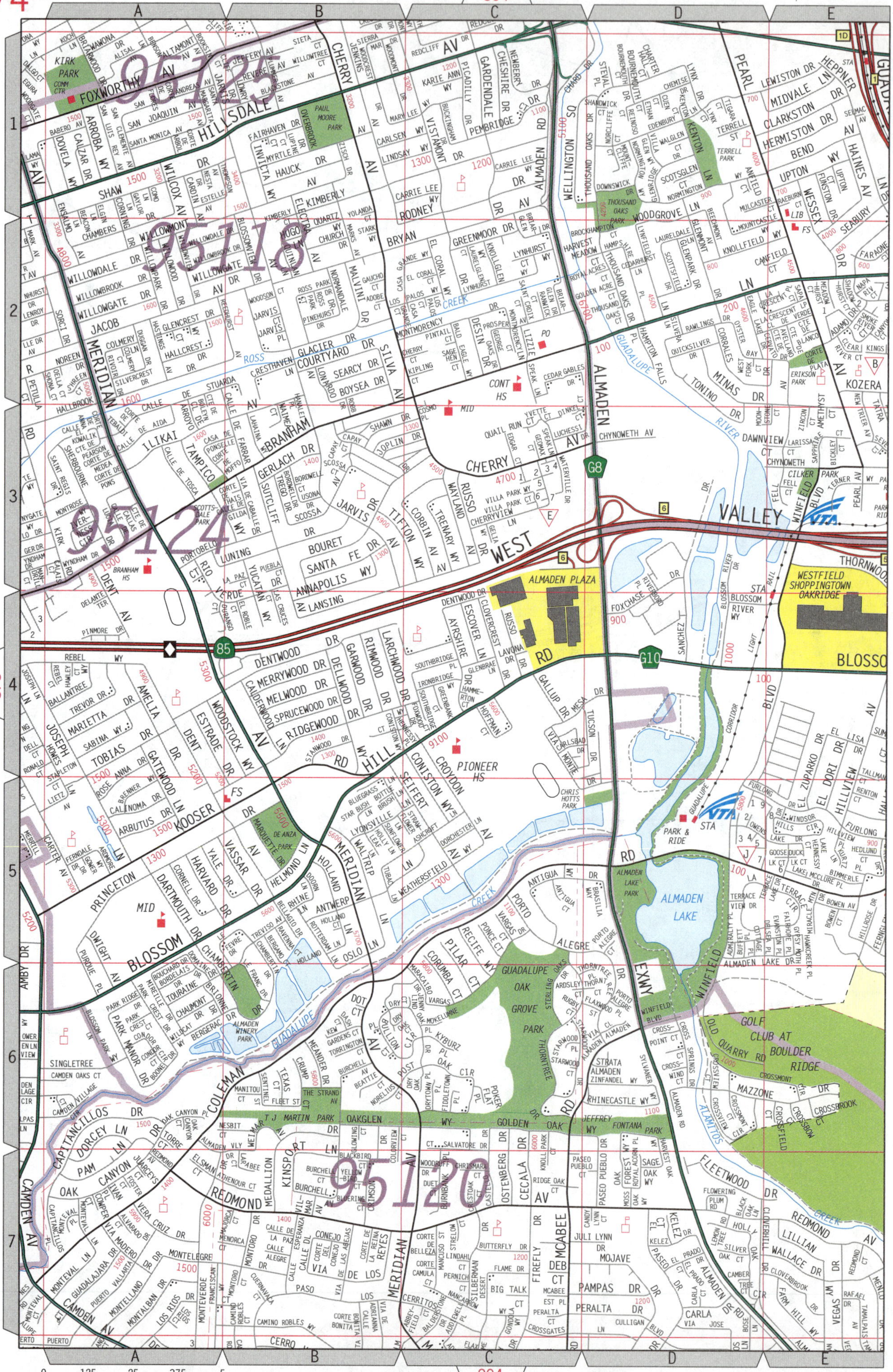

0 .125 .25 .375 .5 miles 1 in. = 1900 ft.

SEE 894 MAP

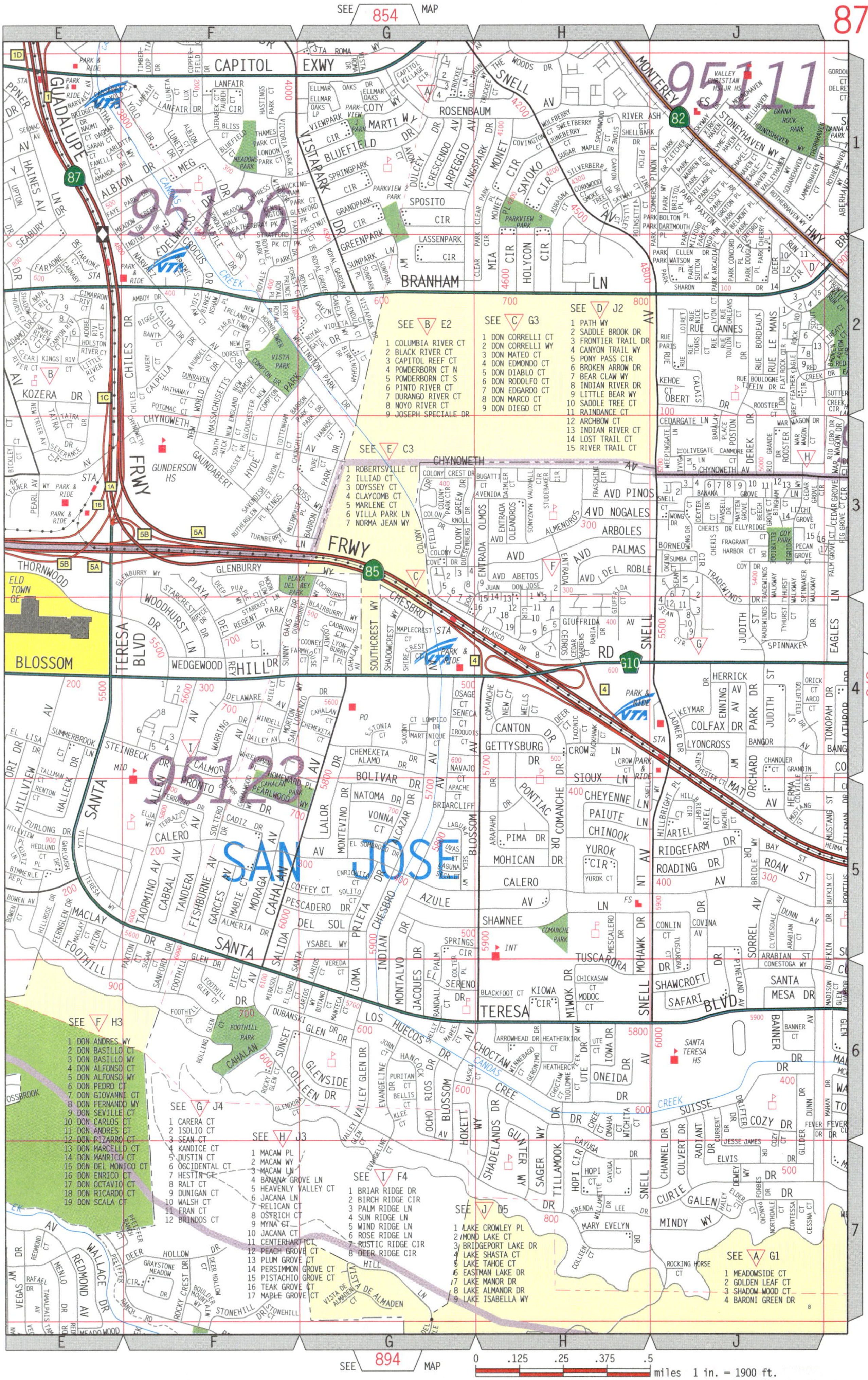
SEE 854 MAP
SEE 875 MAP
SEE 894 MAP
95111
95136
95123
SAN JOSE
CAPITOL EXWY
MONTEREY HWY
GUADALUPE FRWY
BRANHAM LN
CHYNOWETH AV
BLOSSOM HILL RD
SANTA TERESA BLVD
SNELL AV
FRWY
SEE B E2
1 COLUMBIA RIVER CT
2 BLACK RIVER CT
3 CAPITOL REEF CT
4 POWDERBORN CT N
5 POWDERBORN CT S
6 PINTO RIVER CT
7 DURANGO RIVER CT
8 NOYO RIVER CT
9 JOSEPH SPECIALE DR
SEE C G3
1 DON CORRELLI CT
2 DON CORRELLI WY
3 DON MATEO CT
4 DON EDMONDO CT
5 DON DIABLO CT
6 DON RODOLFO CT
7 DON EDGARDO CT
8 DON MARCO CT
9 DON DIEGO CT
SEE D J2
1 PATH WY
2 SADDLE BROOK DR
3 FRONTIER TRAIL DR
4 CANYON TRAIL WY
5 PONY PASS CIR
6 BROKEN ARROW DR
7 BEAR CLAW WY
8 INDIAN RIVER DR
9 LITTLE BEAR WY
10 SADDLE TREE CT
11 RAINDANCE CT
12 ARCHBOW CT
13 INDIAN RIVER CT
14 LOST TRAIL CT
15 RIVER TRAIL CT
SEE E C3
1 ROBERTSVILLE CT
2 ILLIAD CT
3 ODYSSEY CT
4 CLAYCOMB CT
5 MARLENE CT
6 VILLA PARK LN
7 NORMA JEAN WY
SEE F H3
1 DON ANDRES WY
2 DON BASILLO CT
3 DON BASILLO WY
4 DON ALFONSO CT
5 DON ALFONSO WY
6 DON PEDRO CT
7 DON GIOVANNI CT
8 DON FERNANDO WY
9 DON SEVILLE CT
10 DON CARLOS CT
11 DON ANDRES CT
12 DON PIZARRO CT
13 DON MARCELLO CT
14 DON MANRICO CT
15 DON DEL MONICO CT
16 DON ENRICO CT
17 DON OCTAVIO CT
18 DON RICARDO CT
19 DON SCALA CT
SEE G J4
1 CARERA CT
2 ISDLIO CT
3 SEAN CT
4 KANDICE CT
5 DUSTIN CT
6 OCCIDENTAL CT
7 HESTIN CT
8 RALT CT
9 DUNIGAN CT
10 WALSH CT
11 FRAN CT
12 BRINDOS CT
SEE H J3
1 MACAW PL
2 MACAW WY
3 MACAW LN
4 BANANA GROVE LN
5 HEAVENLY VALLEY CT
6 JACANA LN
7 PELICAN CT
8 OSTRICH CT
9 MYNA CT
10 JACANA CT
11 CENTERHART CT
12 PEACH GROVE CT
13 PLUM GROVE CT
14 PERSIMMON GROVE CT
15 PISTACHIO GROVE CT
16 TEAK GROVE CT
17 MAPLE GROVE CT
SEE I F4
1 BRIAR RIDGE DR
2 BIRCH RIDGE CIR
3 PALM RIDGE LN
4 SUN RIDGE LN
5 WIND RIDGE LN
6 ROSE RIDGE LN
7 RUSTIC RIDGE CIR
8 DEER RIDGE CIR
SEE J D5
1 LAKE CROWLEY PL
2 MONO LAKE CT
3 BRIDGEPORT LAKE DR
4 LAKE SHASTA CT
5 LAKE TAHOE CT
6 EASTMAN LAKE DR
7 LAKE MANOR DR
8 LAKE ALMANOR DR
9 LAKE ISABELLA WY
SEE A G1
1 MEADOWSIDE CT
2 GOLDEN LEAF CT
3 SHADOW WOOD CT
4 BARONI GREEN DR
0 .125 .25 .375 .5
miles 1 in. = 1900 ft.

SANTA CLARA CO.

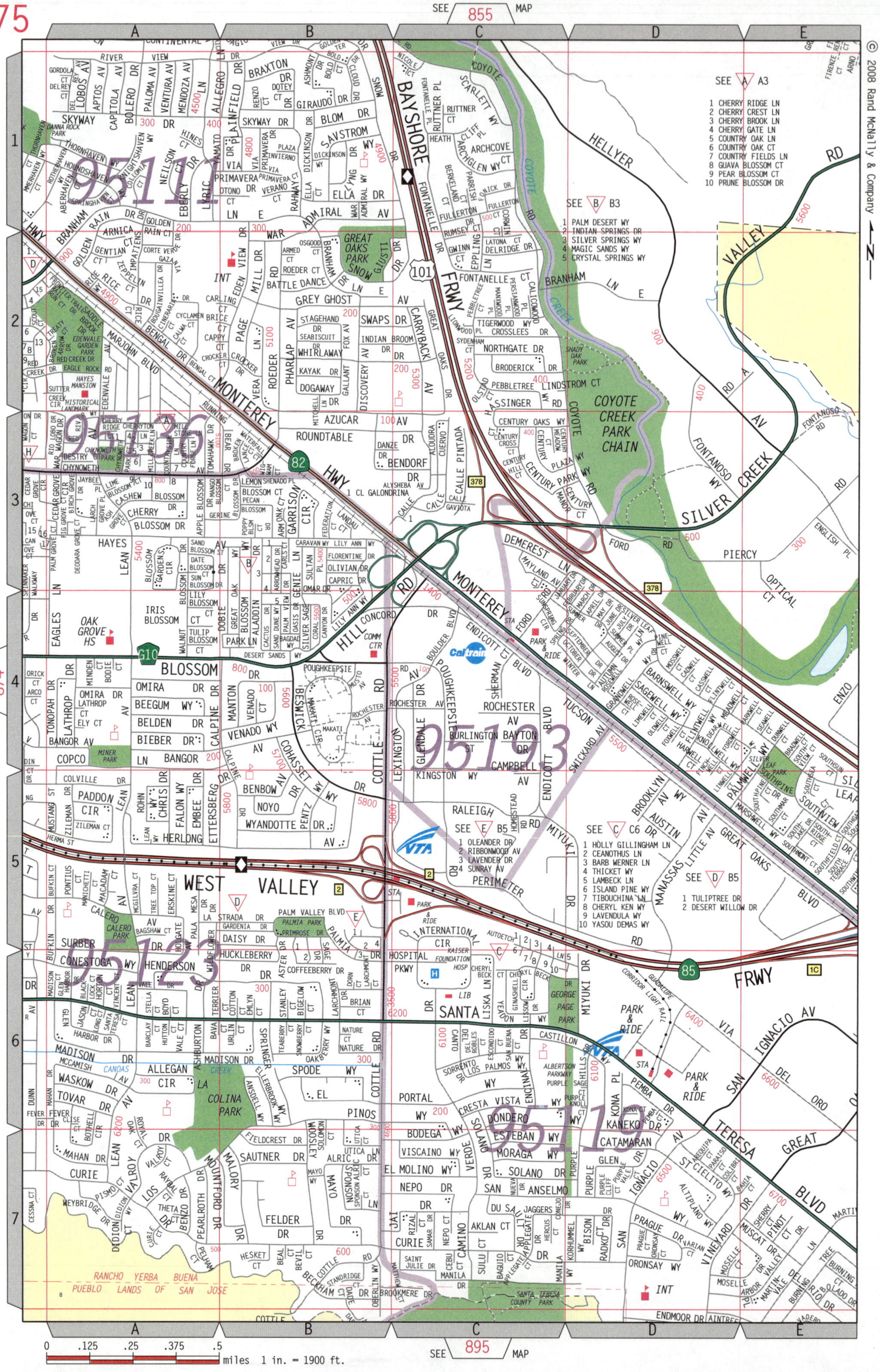
SEE 855 MAP
SEE 874 MAP
SEE 895 MAP
A
B
C
D
E
1
2
3
4
5
6
7
SEE A A3
1 CHERRY RIDGE LN
2 CHERRY CREST LN
3 CHERRY BROOK LN
4 CHERRY GATE LN
5 COUNTRY OAK LN
6 COUNTRY OAK CT
7 COUNTRY FIELDS LN
8 GUAVA BLOSSOM CT
9 PEAR BLOSSOM CT
10 PRUNE BLOSSOM DR
SEE B B3
1 PALM DESERT WY
2 INDIAN SPRINGS DR
3 SILVER SPRINGS WY
4 MAGIC SANDS WY
5 CRYSTAL SPRINGS WY
SEE E B5
1 OLEANDER DR
2 RIBBONWOOD AV
3 LAVENDER DR
4 SUNRAY AV
SEE C C6
1 HOLLY GILLINGHAM LN
2 CEANOTHUS LN
3 BARB WERNER LN
4 THICKET WY
5 LAMBECK LN
6 ISLAND PINE WY
7 TIBOUCHINA LN
8 CHERYL KEN WY
9 LAVENDULA WY
10 YASOU DEMAS WY
SEE D B5
1 TULIPTREE DR
2 DESERT WILLOW DR
95111
95136
95193
95123
95119
BAYSHORE FRWY
MONTEREY HWY
FRWY
HELLYER
VALLEY
SILVER CREEK
BLOSSOM
WEST VALLEY
SANTA TERESA BLVD
SAN IGNACIO AV
BRANHAM LN E
COYOTE CREEK PARK CHAIN
GREAT OAKS PARK SNOW
HAYES MANSION
OAK GROVE HS
MINER PARK
CALERO PARK
LA COLINA PARK
GEORGE PAGE PARK
SANTA TERESA COUNTY PARK
RANCHO YERBA BUENA
PUEBLO LANDS OF SAN JOSE
INTERNATIONAL CIR
KAISER FOUNDATION HOSP
PARK & RIDE
COMM CTR
101
82
85
378
G10
0 .125 .25 .375 .5
miles 1 in. = 1900 ft.

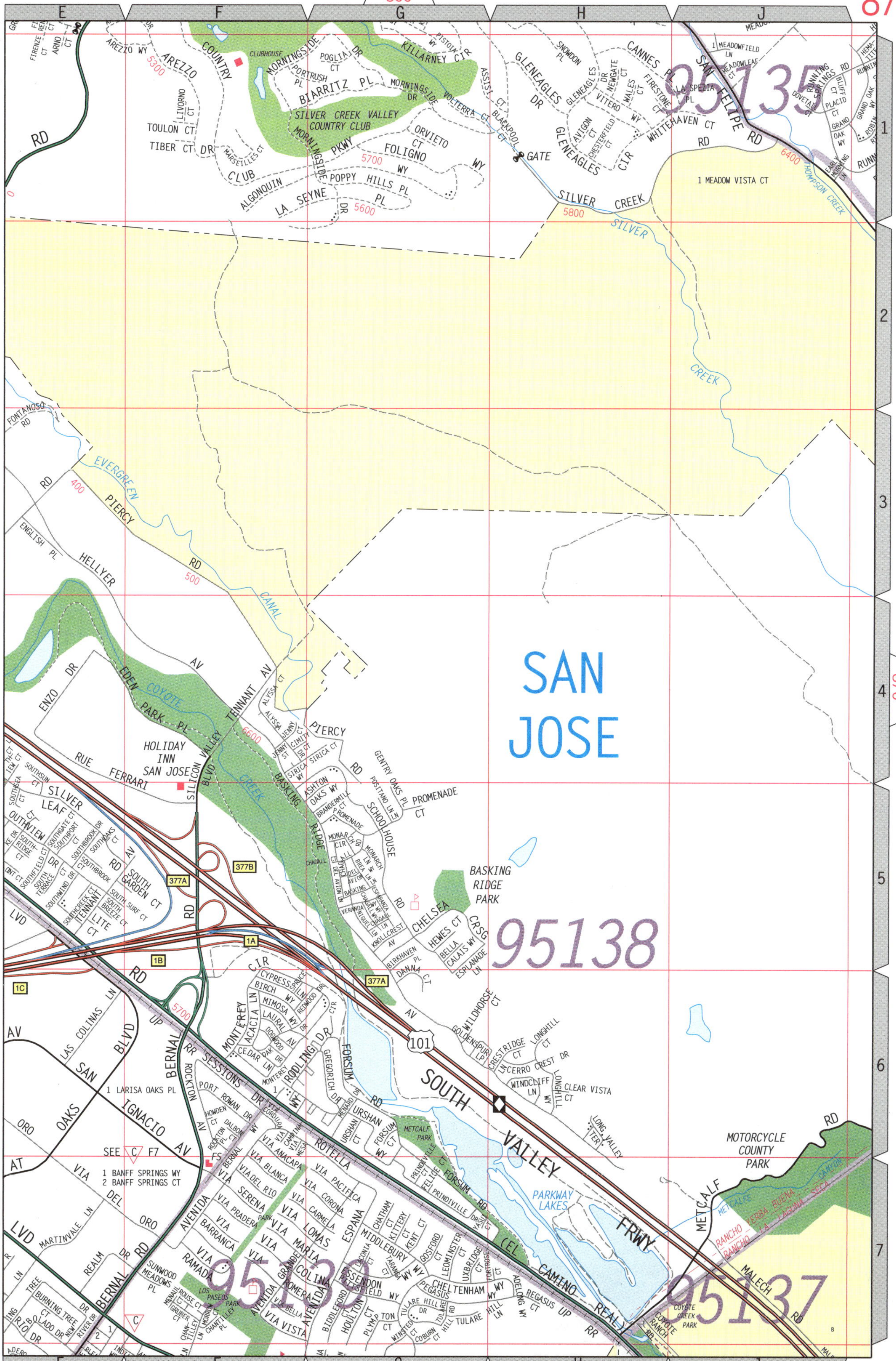
875
SEE 855 MAP
SEE 876 MAP
SEE 895 MAP
SANTA CLARA CO.
© 2008 Rand McNally & Company
SAN JOSE
95135
95138
95139
95137
SILVER CREEK VALLEY COUNTRY CLUB
CLUBHOUSE
GATE
SILVER CREEK RD
SAN FELIPE RD
1 MEADOW VISTA CT
THOMPSON CREEK
SILVER CREEK
EVERGREEN CANAL
FONTANOSO RD
PIERCY RD
HELLYER AV
ENGLISH PL
COYOTE CREEK
EDEN PARK PL
ENZO DR
HOLIDAY INN SAN JOSE
RUE FERRARI
SILICON VALLEY BLVD
TENNANT AV
BASKING RIDGE
BASKING RIDGE PARK
SCHOOLHOUSE RD
PROMENADE CT
GENTRY OAKS PL
CHELSEA CRSG
101
SOUTH VALLEY FRWY
MONTEREY RD
BERNAL RD
SAN IGNACIO AV
OAKS
1 LARISA OAKS PL
1 BANFF SPRINGS WY
2 BANFF SPRINGS CT
SEE C F7
METCALF PARK
METCALF RD
MOTORCYCLE COUNTY PARK
PARKWAY LAKES
COYOTE CREEK PARK
COYOTE RANCH
RANCHO YERBA BUENA
RANCHO LA LAGUNA SECA
MALECH RD
CAMINO REAL
FORSUM RD
ROTELLA
SESSIONS DR
377A
377B
1A
1B
1C
0
.125
.25
.375
.5
miles 1 in. = 1900 ft.

SEE 856 MAP

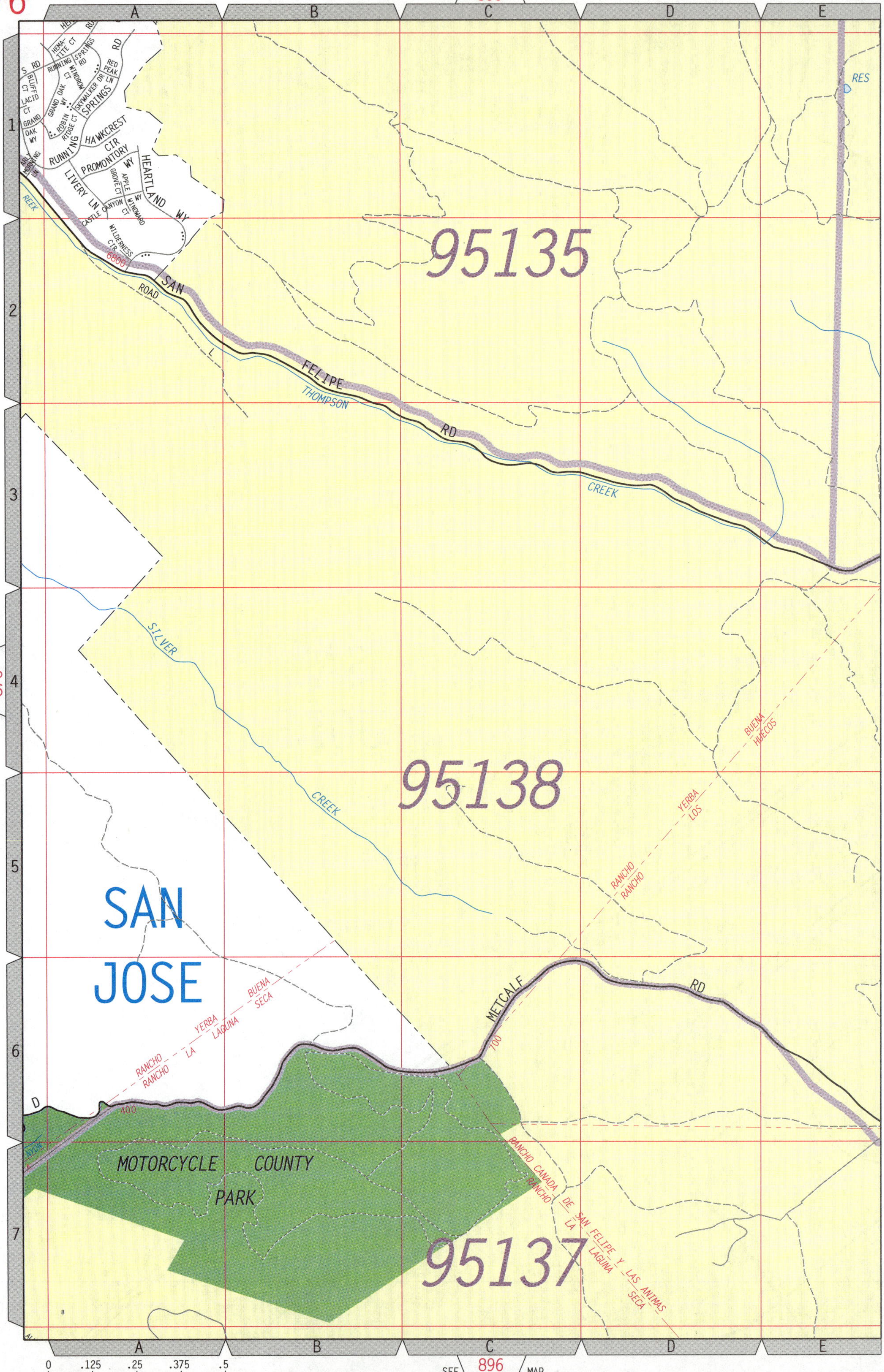

SEE 875 MAP

SANTA CLARA CO.

0 .125 .25 .375 .5 miles 1 in. = 1900 ft.

SEE 896 MAP

SEE 856 MAP

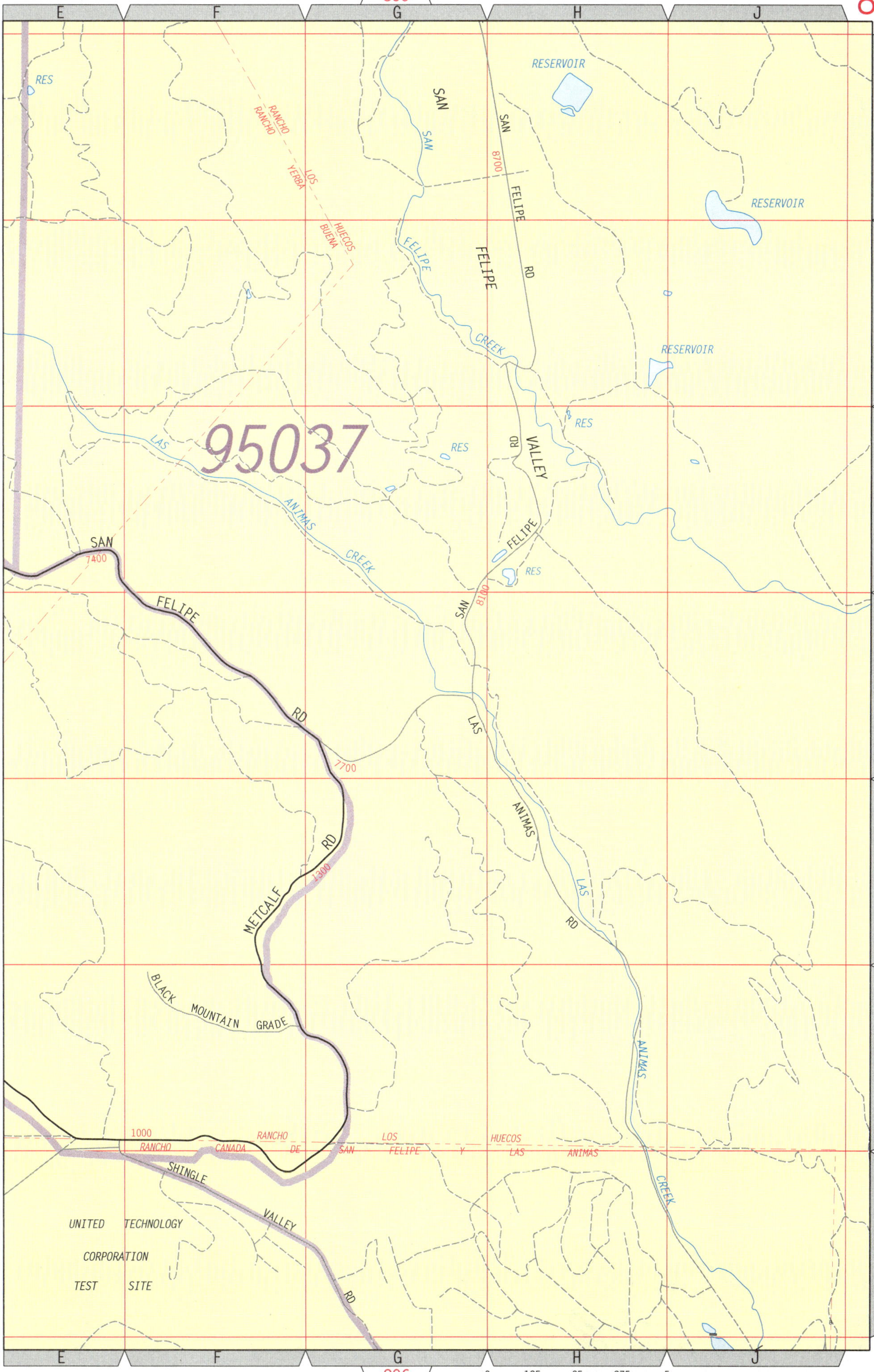

SEE B MAP

SEE 896 MAP

0 .125 .25 .375 .5 miles 1 in. = 1900 ft.

SEE 872 MAP

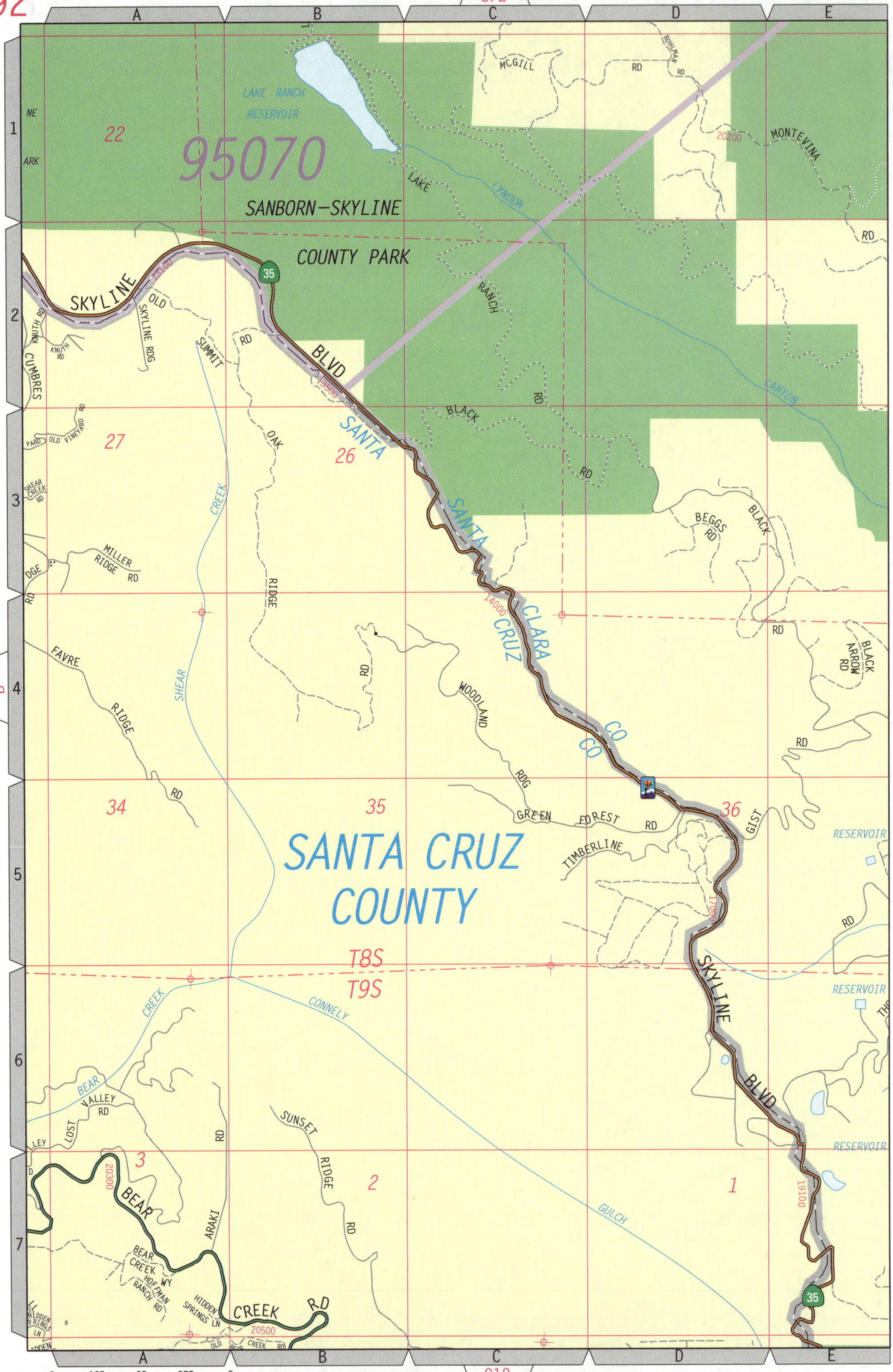

SEE B MAP

0 .125 .25 .375 .5 miles 1 in. = 1900 ft.

SEE 912 MAP

SEE 872 MAP

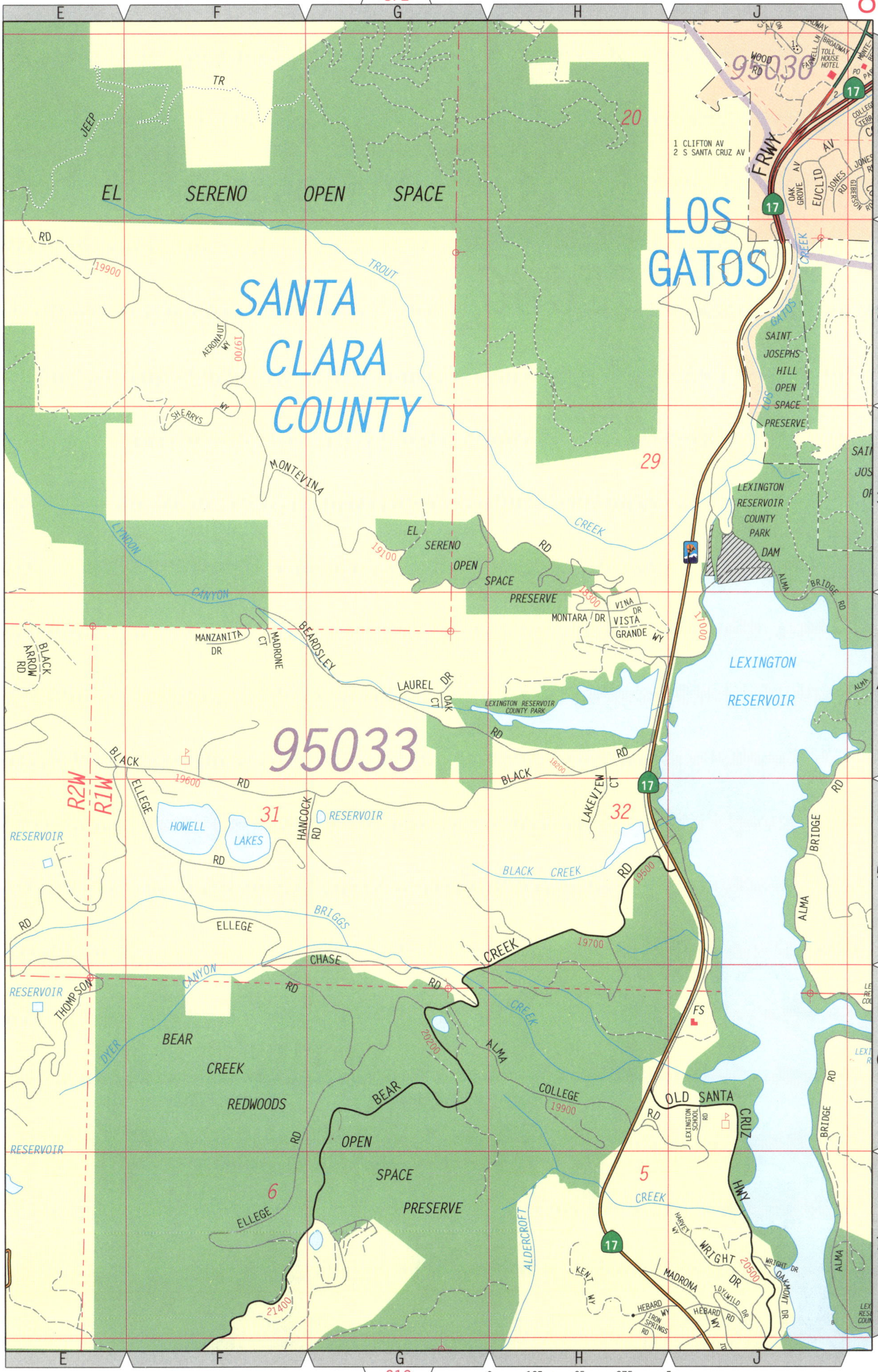

SEE 893 MAP

SEE 912 MAP

© 2008 Rand McNally & Company

N

SANTA CLARA CO.

E F G H J

95030
WOOD
RD
FRWY
17

1 CLIFTON AV
2 S SANTA CRUZ AV

BROADWAY
TOLL HOUSE HOTEL
FARWELL LN
CANYON
MOTEL
PO

COLLEGE TERR
OAK GROVE AV
EUCLID AV
JONES AV
JONES RD
GIBSON CT

1

LOS GATOS

TR

JEEP

EL SERENO OPEN SPACE

RD

19900

SANTA
CLARA
COUNTY

TROUT

SAINT
JOSEPHS
HILL
OPEN
SPACE
PRESERVE

LOS GATOS CREEK

2

AERONAUT WY

19700

SHERRYS WY

MONTEVINA

CREEK

29

LEXINGTON
RESERVOIR
COUNTY
PARK

SAIN
JOS
OF

3

LYNDON

CANYON

19100

EL
SERENO
OPEN
SPACE
PRESERVE

RD

18300

17000

DAM

ALMA

BRIDGE RD

MANZANITA DR
MADRONE CT
BEARDSLEY

VINA DR
MONTARA DR
VISTA
GRANDE WY

BLACK
ARROW
RD

LAUREL DR
OAK CT

LEXINGTON RESERVOIR
COUNTY PARK

RD

**LEXINGTON
RESERVOIR**

4

95033

R2W R1W

BLACK

19600

RD

31

HOWELL
LAKES

HANCOCK RD

RESERVOIR

BLACK

18600

RD

LAKEVIEW CT

32

17

ELLEGE

RESERVOIR

RD

BRIGGS

ELLEGE

CHASE

RD

CREEK

BLACK CREEK RD

19700

19500

ALMA

BRIDGE RD

5

THOMPSON

RESERVOIR

DYER

BEAR

CREEK

REDWOODS

CANYON

RD

BEAR

20000

RD

ALMA

COLLEGE

19900

FS

OLD SANTA

LEXINGTON SCHOOL
RD

BRIDGE RD

6

RESERVOIR

ELLEGE

OPEN

SPACE

PRESERVE

6

ALDERCROFT

CREEK

5

CREEK

SANTA
CRUZ
HWY

RD

WRIGHT DR

HARVEY WY

OAKMONT DR

ALMA

7

21400

17

KENT WY

MADRONA

HEBARD
IRON
SPRINGS
RD

HEBARD WY

IDYLWILD DR

WRIGHT DR

20500

LEX
RES
COU

0 .125 .25 .375 .5 miles 1 in. = 1900 ft.

SEE 873 MAP

SEE 892 MAP

SANTA CLARA CO.

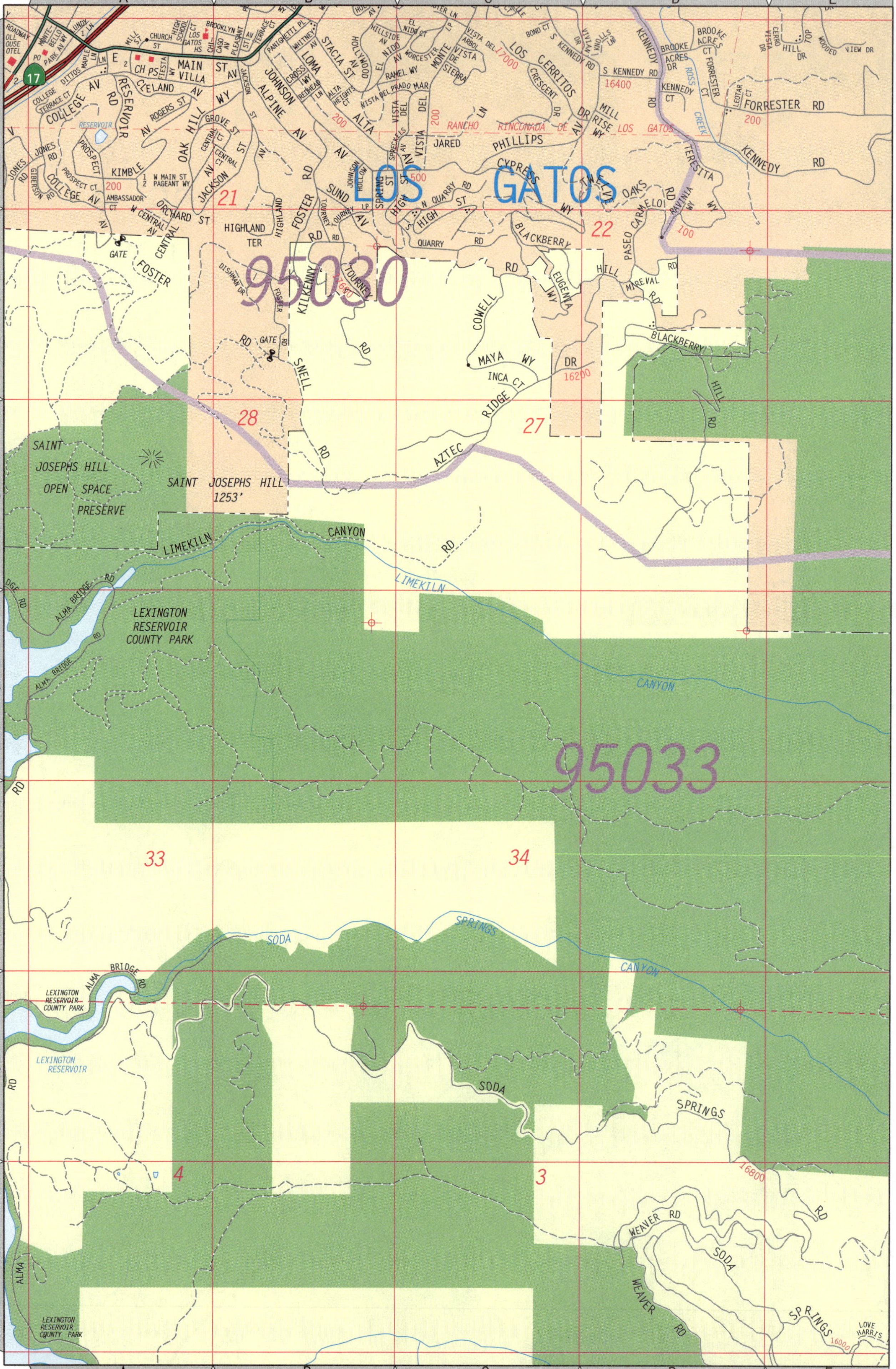

0 .125 .25 .375 .5 miles 1 in. = 1900 ft.

SEE 913 MAP

SEE 873 MAP

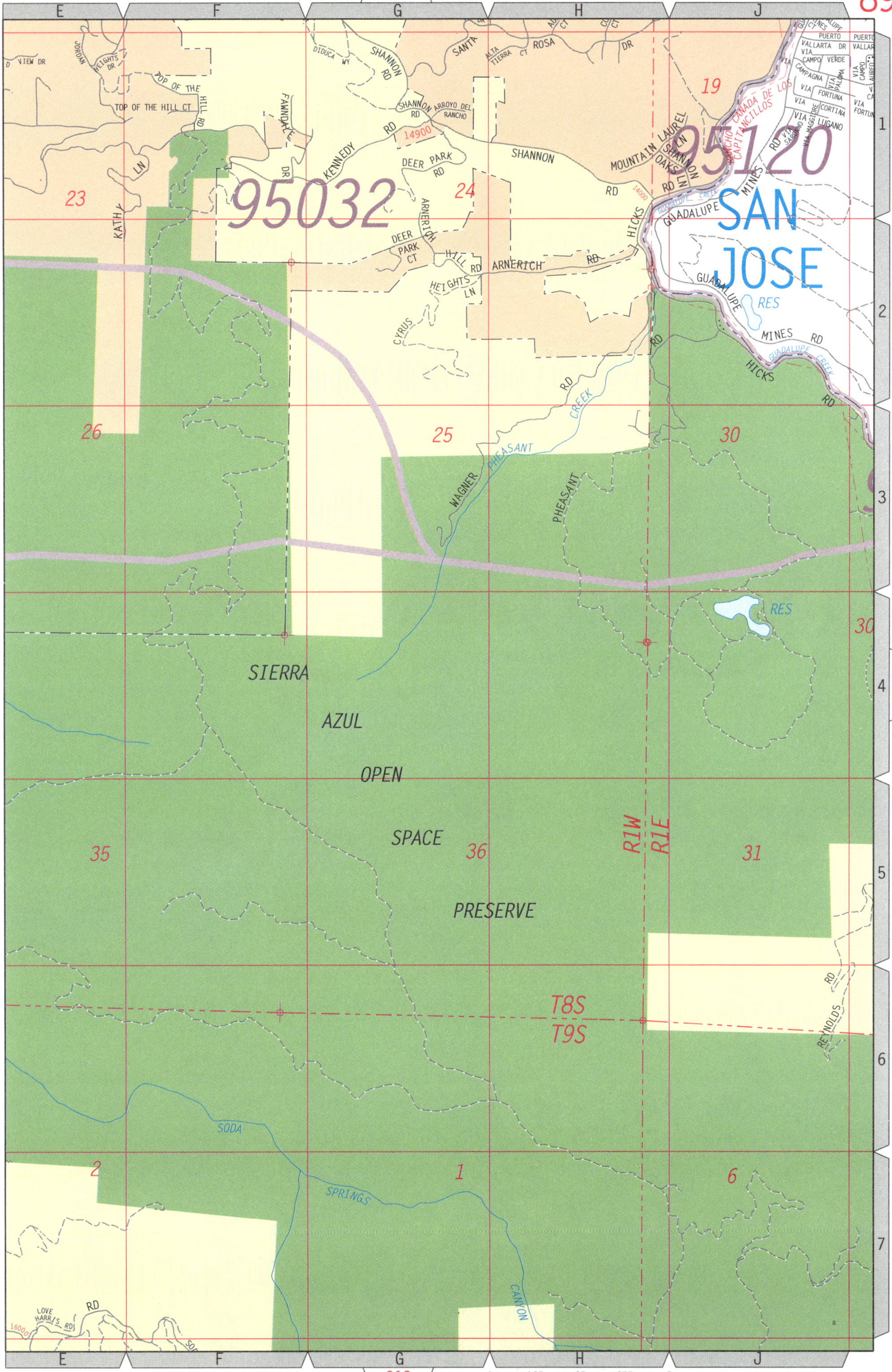

SEE 894 MAP

SEE 913 MAP

0 .125 .25 .375 .5 miles 1 in. = 1900 ft.

SANTA CLARA CO.

SEE 874 MAP

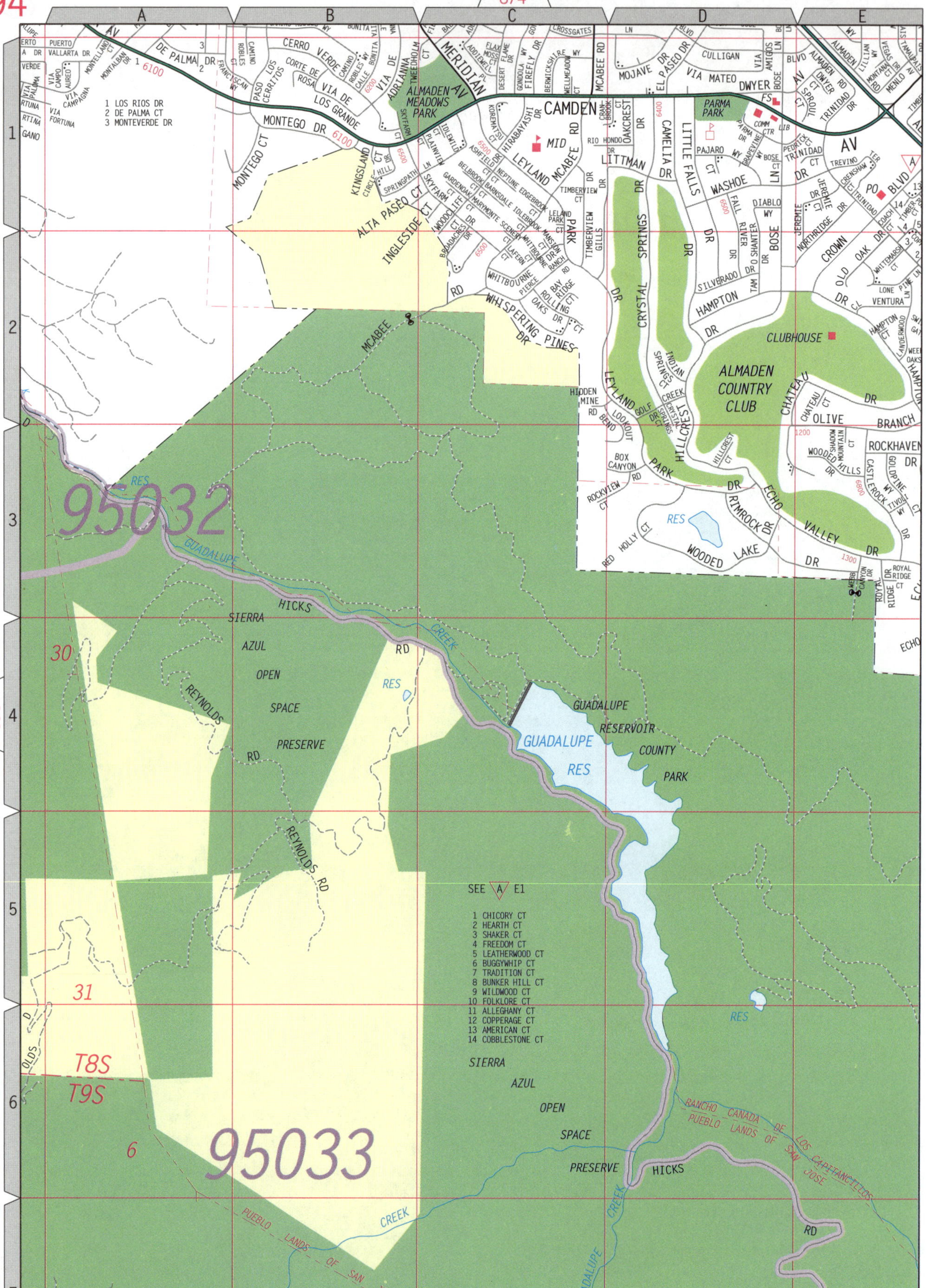
A
B
C
D
E
1
2
3
4
5
6
7
CAMDEN AV
MERIDIAN AV
ALMADEN MEADOWS PARK
PARMA PARK
ALMADEN COUNTRY CLUB
CLUBHOUSE
MID
DE PALMA DR
CERRO VERDE
MONTEGO DR
MONTEGO CT
LOS GRANDE
KINGSLAND CIRCLE
ALTA PASEO CT
INGLESIDE CT
SKYFARM
LEYLAND PARK
MCABEE RD
WHISPERING PINES DR
LITTMAN DR
CRYSTAL SPRINGS DR
CAMELIA DR
LITTLE FALLS DR
WASHOE DR
DWYER
VIA MATEO
MOJAVE DR
EL PASEO DR
CULLIGAN
HAMPTON DR
CROWN
OLD OAK DR
VENTURA
CHATEAU DR
OLIVE BRANCH
ROCKHAVEN DR
ECHO VALLEY DR
RIMROCK DR
WOODED LAKE DR
HILLCREST
LOOKOUT BEND
HIDDEN MINE RD
BOX CANYON RD
ROCKVIEW CT
RED HOLLY CT
ROYAL RIDGE CT
1 LOS RIOS DR
2 DE PALMA CT
3 MONTEVERDE DR
95032
95033
RES
GUADALUPE CREEK
HICKS RD
SIERRA AZUL OPEN SPACE PRESERVE
REYNOLDS RD
GUADALUPE RES
GUADALUPE RESERVOIR COUNTY PARK
SEE A E1
1 CHICORY CT
2 HEARTH CT
3 SHAKER CT
4 FREEDOM CT
5 LEATHERWOOD CT
6 BUGGYWHIP CT
7 TRADITION CT
8 BUNKER HILL CT
9 WILDWOOD CT
10 FOLKLORE CT
11 ALLEGHANY CT
12 COPPERAGE CT
13 AMERICAN CT
14 COBBLESTONE CT
30
31
6
5
T8S
T9S
RANCHO CANADA DE LOS CAPITANCILLOS
PUEBLO LANDS OF SAN JOSE
RINCON CREEK
WOOD RD
SEE 893 MAP

0 .125 .25 .375 .5 miles 1 in. = 1900 ft.

SEE 914 MAP

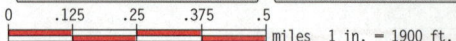

SEE 874 MAP

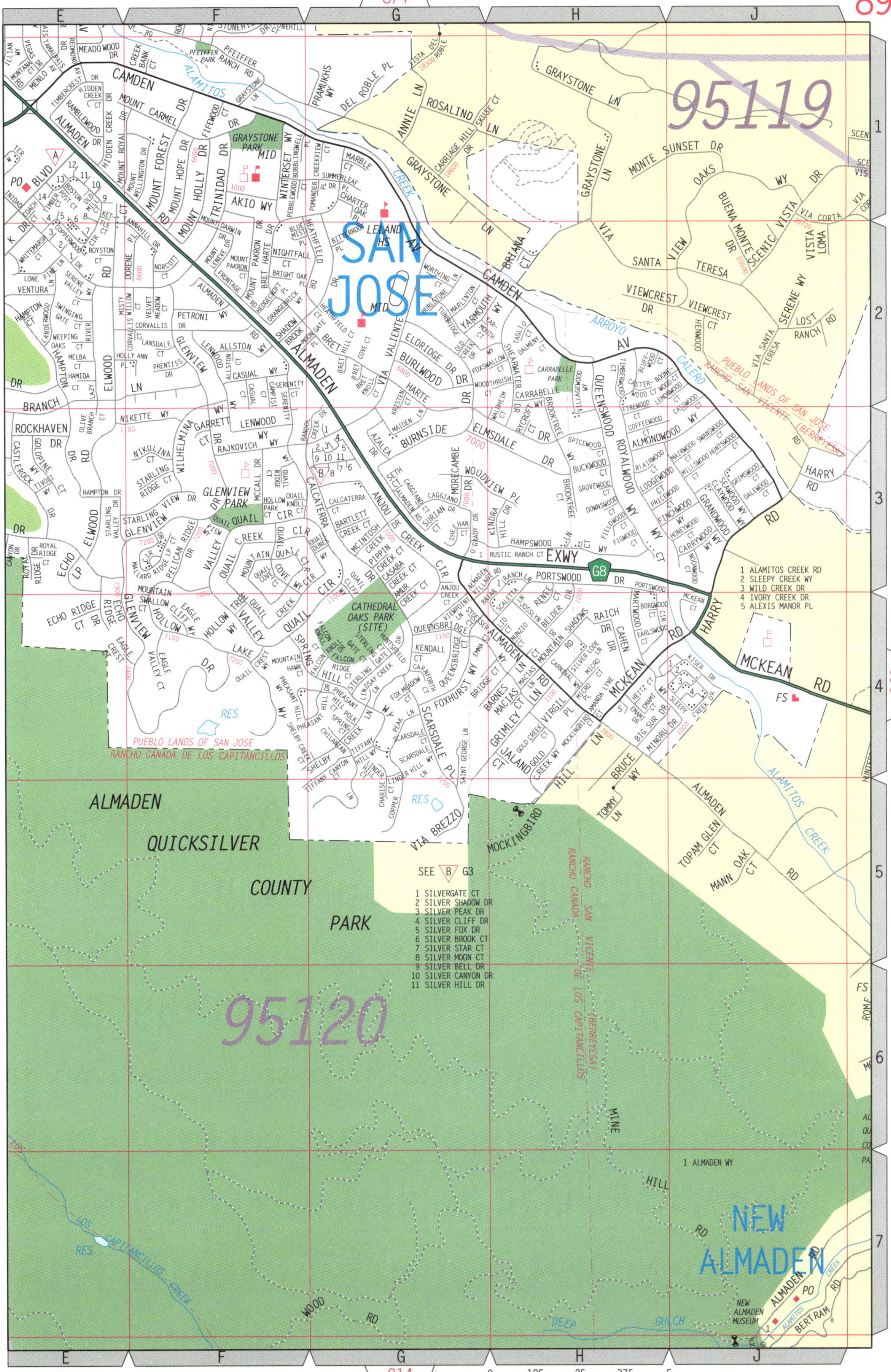

E F G H J
1 2 3 4 5 6 7
95119
95120
SAN JOSE
NEW ALMADEN
ALMADEN QUICKSILVER COUNTY PARK
CAMDEN AV
ALMADEN EXWY
G8
MCKEAN RD
HARRY RD
GRAYSTONE LN
GRAYSTONE PARK
CATHEDRAL OAKS PARK (SITE)
GLENVIEW PARK
CARRABELLE PARK
LELAND HS
ALAMITOS CREEK
ARROYO CALERO
PUEBLO LANDS OF SAN JOSE
RANCHO SAN VICENTE (BERREYESA)
RANCHO CANADA DE LOS CAPITANCILLOS
LOS CAPITANCILLOS CREEK
DEEP GULCH
MINE HILL RD
WOOD RD
MOCKINGBIRD
VIA BREZZO
TOPAM GLEN CT
MANN OAK CT
NEW ALMADEN MUSEUM
SEE B G3
1 SILVERGATE CT
2 SILVER SHADOW DR
3 SILVER PEAK DR
4 SILVER CLIFF DR
5 SILVER FOX DR
6 SILVER BROOK CT
7 SILVER STAR CT
8 SILVER MOON CT
9 SILVER BELL DR
10 SILVER CANYON DR
11 SILVER HILL DR
1 ALAMITOS CREEK RD
2 SLEEPY CREEK WY
3 WILD CREEK DR
4 IVORY CREEK DR
5 ALEXIS MANOR PL
1 ALMADEN WY
RES
FS
PO

SEE 895 MAP
SEE 914 MAP

0 .125 .25 .375 .5 miles 1 in. = 1900 ft.

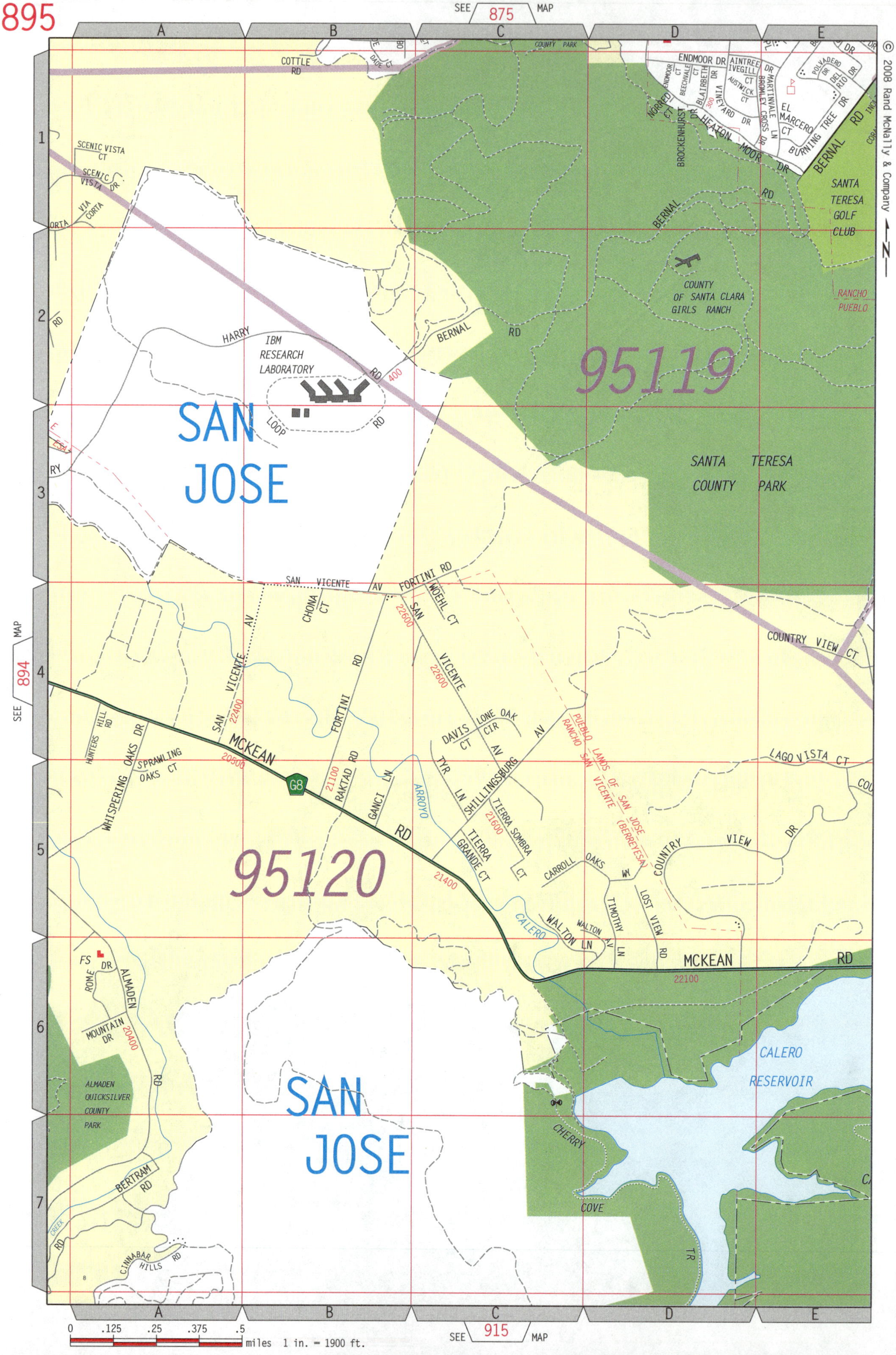
SEE 875 MAP
SEE 894 MAP
SEE 915 MAP
SANTA CLARA CO.
A
B
C
D
E
1
2
3
4
5
6
7
COTTLE RD
SCENIC VISTA CT
SCENIC VISTA DR
VIA CORTA
ENDMOOR DR
AINTREE
IVEGILL
AUSTWICK CT
BEECHVALE CT
BLAIRBETH DR
VINEYARD DR
MARTINVALE LN
BROMLEY CROSS DR
NORWED CT
BROCKENHURST DR
HEATON MOOR DR
EL MARCERO CT
BURNING TREE DR
BERNAL RD
SANTA TERESA GOLF CLUB
RANCHO PUEBLO
COUNTY OF SANTA CLARA GIRLS RANCH
HARRY RD
IBM RESEARCH LABORATORY
LOOP RD
400
95119
SAN JOSE
SANTA TERESA COUNTY PARK
SAN VICENTE AV
FORTINI RD
CHONA CT
WOEHL CT
22600
COUNTRY VIEW CT
HUNTERS HILL RD
WHISPERING OAKS DR
SPRAWLING OAKS CT
MCKEAN RD
20500
22400
G8
21100
RAKTAD RD
GANCI LN
ARROYO
DAVIS CT
LONE OAK CIR
AV
TYR LN
SHILLINGSBURG AV
TIERRA SOMBRA CT
21600
TIERRA GRANDE CT
PUEBLO LANDS OF SAN JOSE
RANCHO SAN VICENTE (BERREYESA)
LAGO VISTA CT
COUNTRY VIEW DR
95120
21400
CARROLL OAKS WY
CALERO
WALTON LN
WALTON AV
TIMOTHY LN
LOST VIEW RD
MCKEAN RD
22100
FS
ROME DR
ALMADEN RD
MOUNTAIN DR
20400
ALMADEN QUICKSILVER COUNTY PARK
CALERO RESERVOIR
CHERRY
COVE
TR
BERTRAM RD
CREEK
CINNABAR HILLS RD
0 .125 .25 .375 .5 miles 1 in. = 1900 ft.

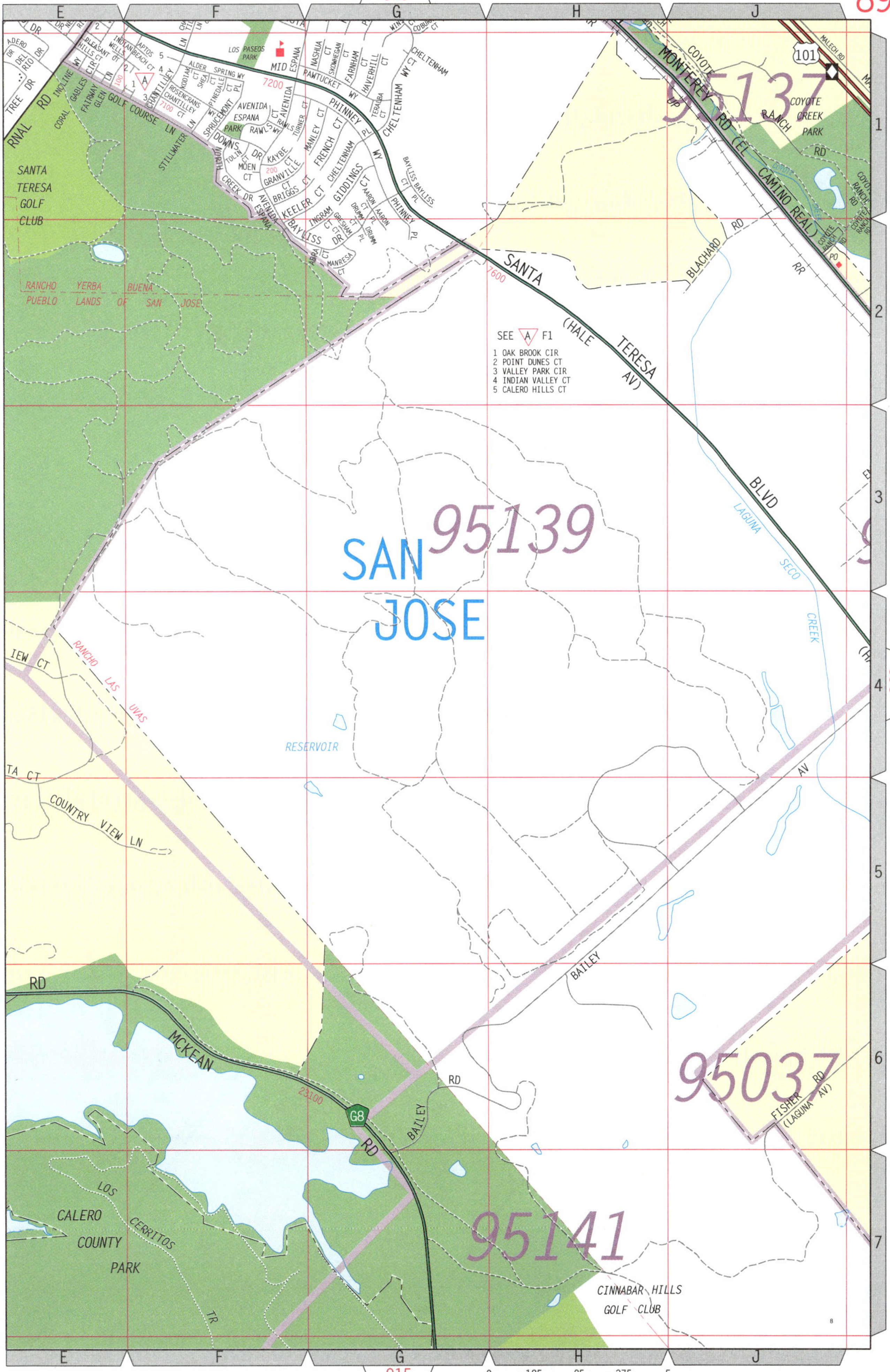
SEE 875 MAP
SEE 915 MAP
SEE 896 MAP
SANTA CLARA CO.
SAN JOSE
95139
95137
95037
95141
SANTA TERESA GOLF CLUB
RANCHO YERBA BUENA
PUEBLO LANDS OF SAN JOSE
RANCHO LAS UVAS
RESERVOIR
SANTA TERESA BLVD
(HALE AV)
MONTEREY RD (EL CAMINO REAL)
COYOTE CREEK PARK
BLACHARD RD
LAGUNA SECO CREEK
BAILEY AV
BAILEY RD
COUNTRY VIEW LN
MCKEAN RD
CALERO COUNTY PARK
LOS CERRITOS TR
CINNABAR HILLS GOLF CLUB
FISHER RD (LAGUNA AV)
G8
101
SEE A F1
1 OAK BROOK CIR
2 POINT DUNES CT
3 VALLEY PARK CIR
4 INDIAN VALLEY CT
5 CALERO HILLS CT
0 .125 .25 .375 .5 miles 1 in. = 1900 ft.

SEE 876 MAP

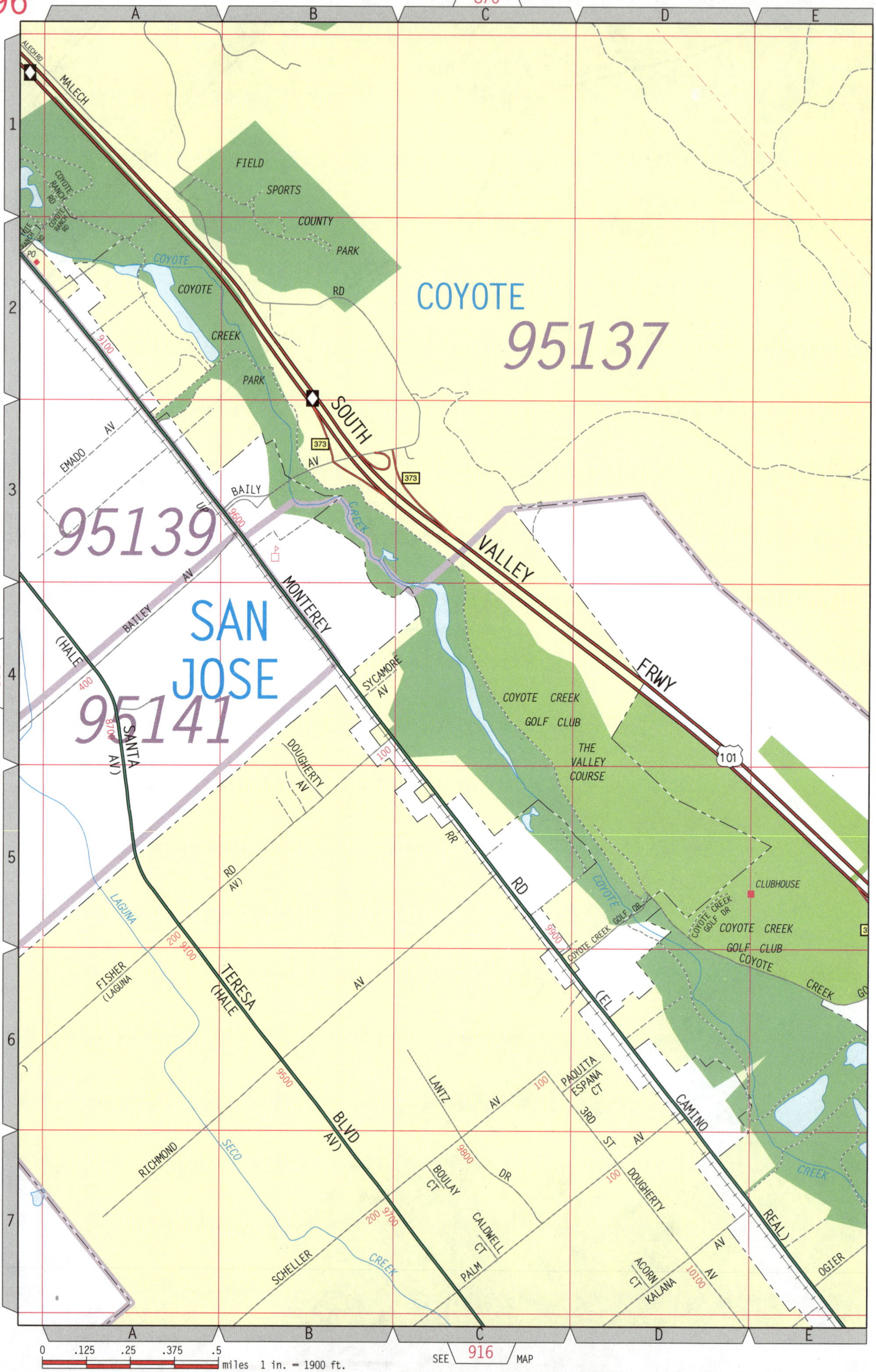

0 .125 .25 .375 .5 miles 1 in. = 1900 ft.

SEE 895 MAP

SEE 916 MAP

SANTA CLARA CO.

SEE 876 MAP

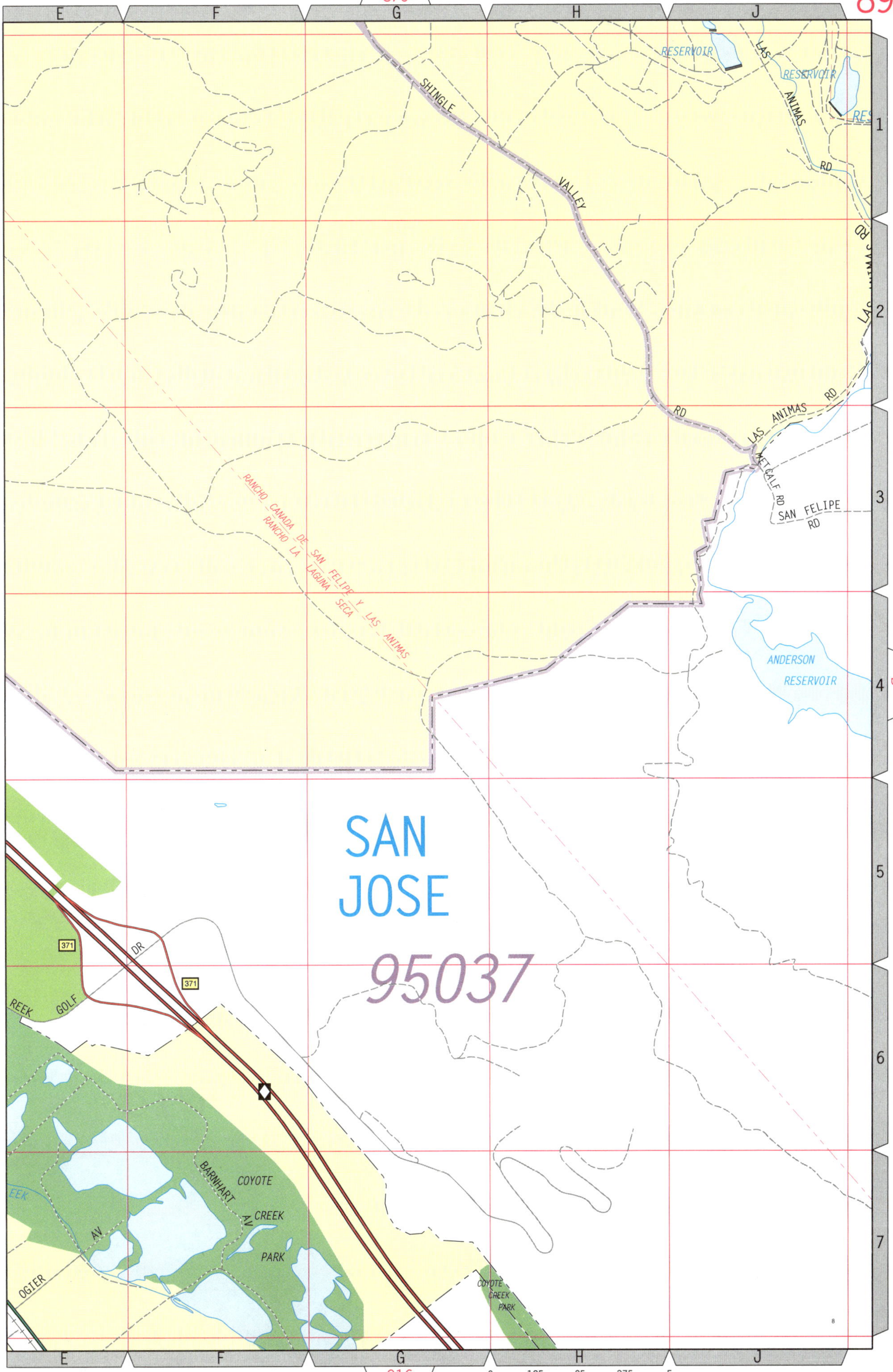

SEE B MAP

SEE 916 MAP

0 .125 .25 .375 .5 miles 1 in. = 1900 ft.

SEE 892 MAP

SANTA CLARA CO.

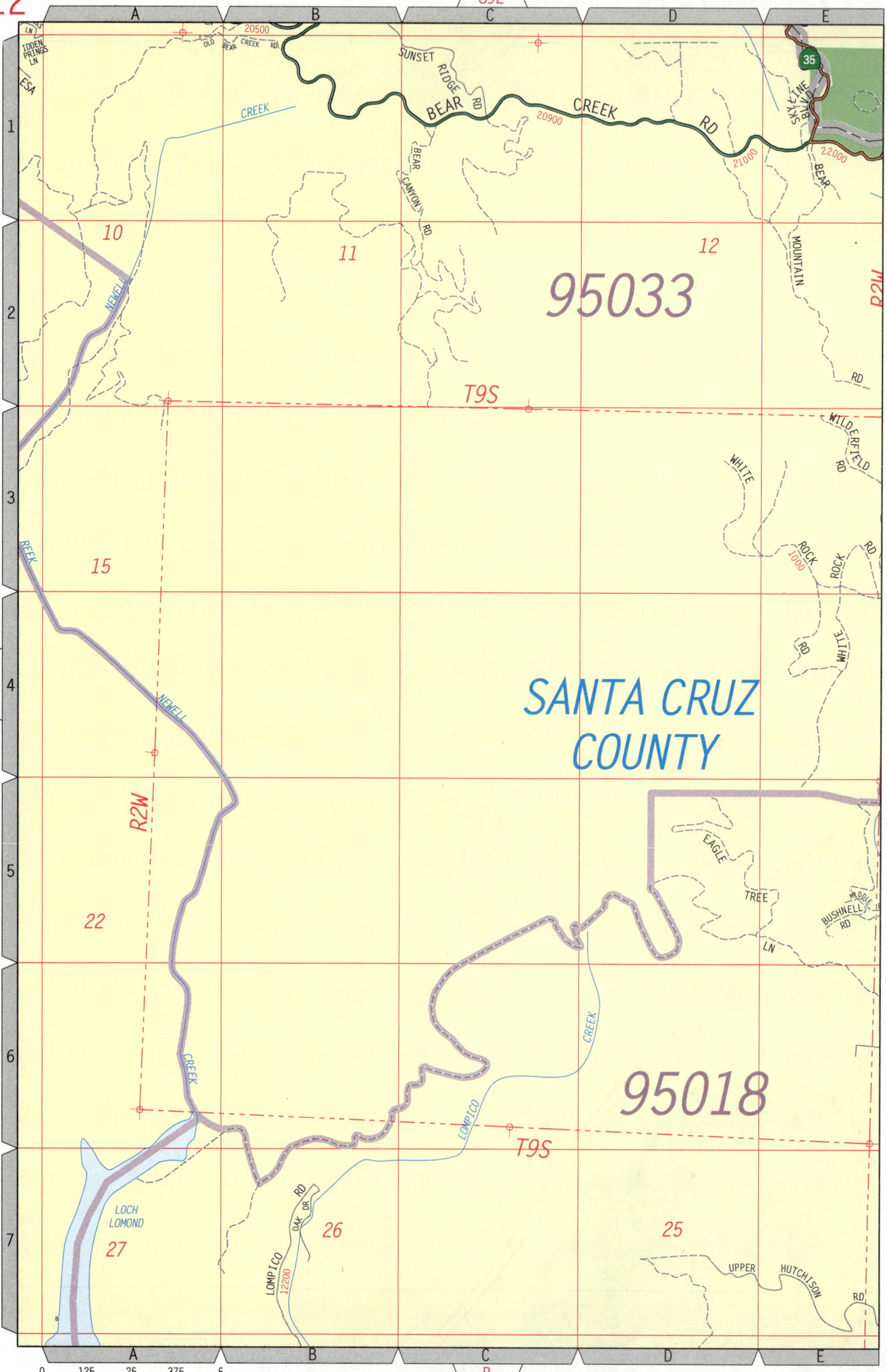

SEE B MAP

0 .125 .25 .375 .5 miles 1 in. = 1900 ft.

SEE B MAP

SEE 892 MAP

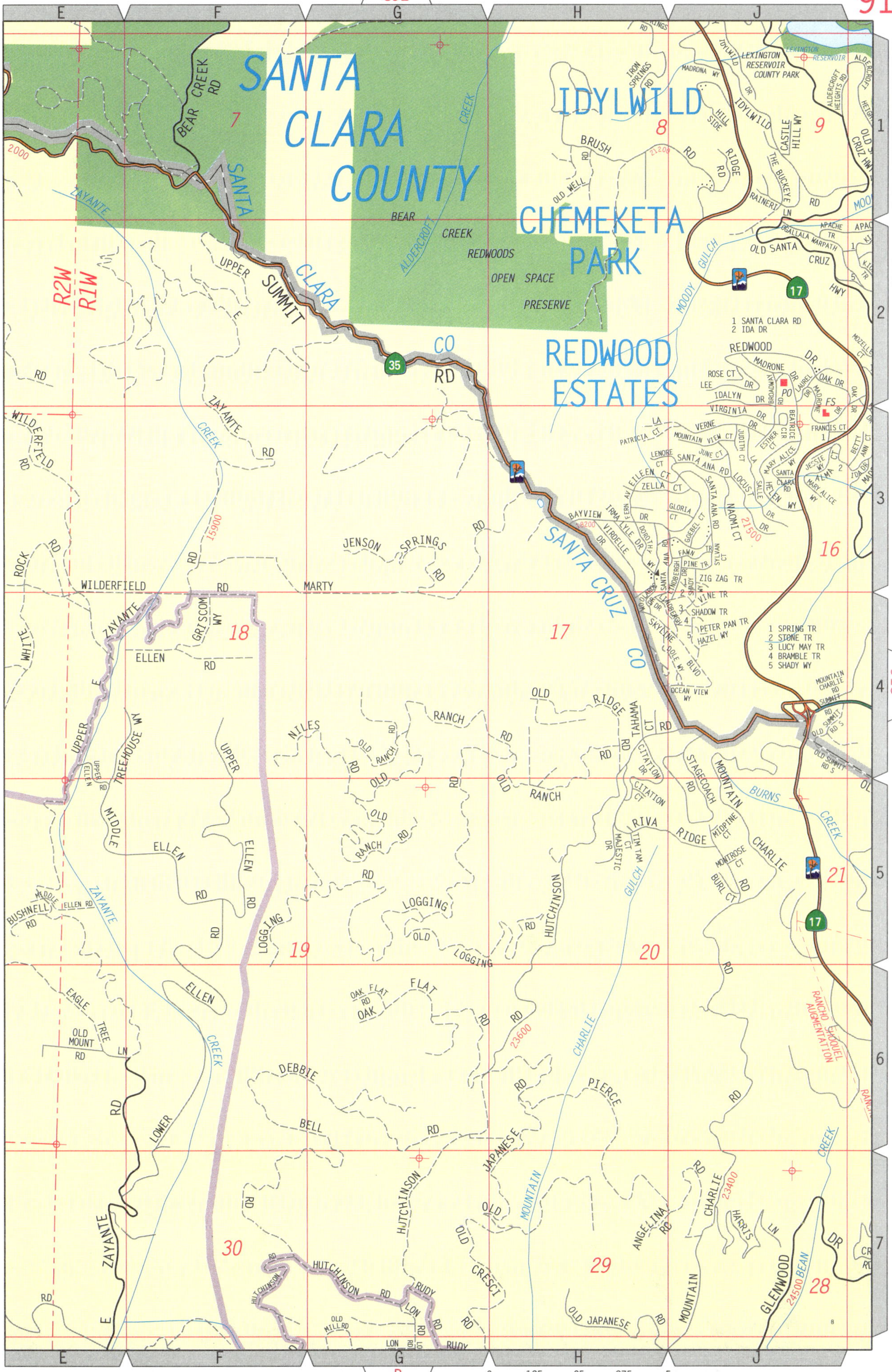

SEE 913 MAP

SEE B MAP

0 .125 .25 .375 .5 miles 1 in. = 1900 ft.

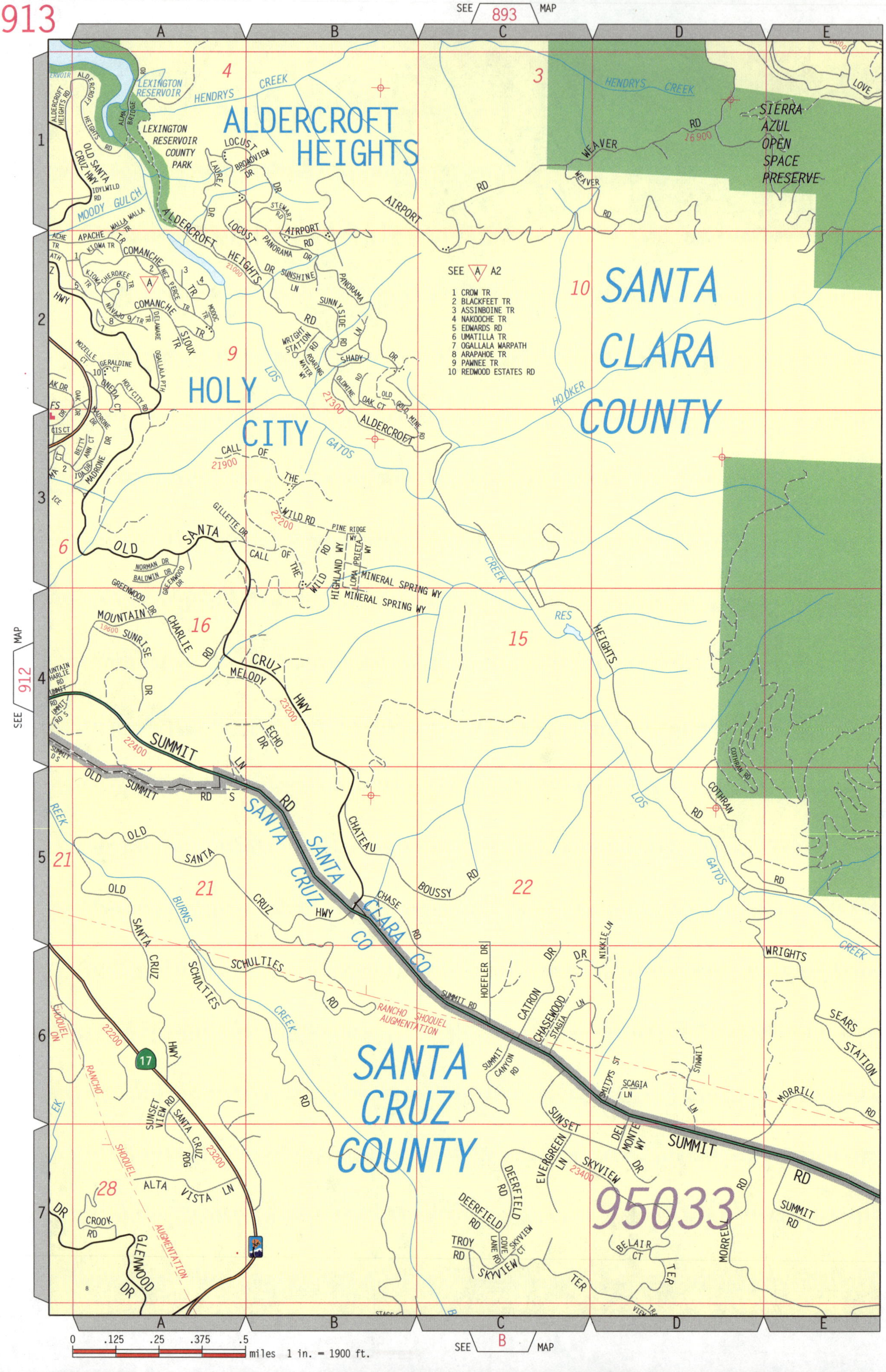

SEE 893 MAP
SEE 912 MAP
SEE B MAP
ALDERCROFT HEIGHTS
HOLY CITY
SANTA CLARA COUNTY
SANTA CRUZ COUNTY
SIERRA AZUL OPEN SPACE PRESERVE
LEXINGTON RESERVOIR
LEXINGTON RESERVOIR COUNTY PARK
HENDRYS CREEK
MOODY GULCH
LOS GATOS CREEK
HOOKER
BURNS CREEK
RANCHO SHOQUEL AUGMENTATION
SEE A A2
1 CROW TR
2 BLACKFEET TR
3 ASSINBOINE TR
4 NAKOOCHE TR
5 EDWARDS RD
6 UMATILLA TR
7 OGALLALA WARPATH
8 ARAPAHOE TR
9 PAWNEE TR
10 REDWOOD ESTATES RD
WEAVER RD
AIRPORT RD
OLD SANTA CRUZ HWY
SANTA CRUZ HWY
SUMMIT RD
OLD SUMMIT RD
MINERAL SPRING WY
SUMMIT RD
SCHULTIES RD
ALTA VISTA LN
GLENWOOD DR
CROOK RD
WRIGHTS STATION RD
SEARS STATION
MORRILL RD
SKYVIEW DR
DEERFIELD RD
95033
miles 1 in. = 1900 ft.
0 .125 .25 .375 .5

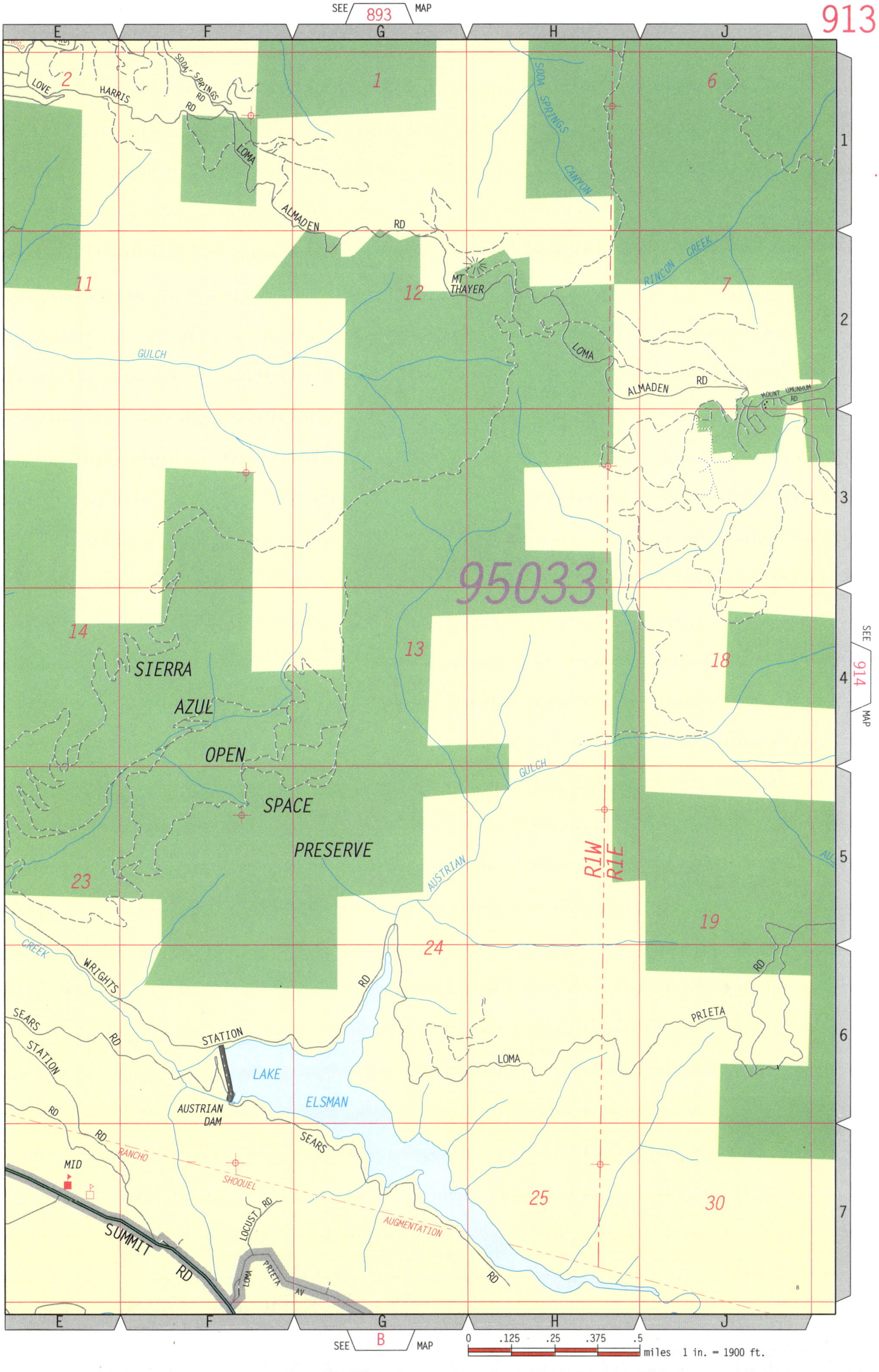
SEE 893 MAP
E
F
G
H
J
1
2
3
4
5
6
7
LOVE
HARRIS
SODA SPRINGS RD
RD
LOMA
ALMADEN
RD
SODA SPRINGS
CANYON
MT THAYER
RINCON CREEK
LOMA
ALMADEN
RD
MOUNT UMUNHUM RD
GULCH
95033
SIERRA
AZUL
OPEN
SPACE
PRESERVE
GULCH
AUSTRIAN
R1W
R1E
CREEK
WRIGHTS
SEARS
RD
STATION
RD
STATION
LAKE
ELSMAN
AUSTRIAN DAM
RD
LOMA
PRIETA
RD
RD
RANCHO
SEARS
MID
SHOQUEL
LOCUST
RD
AUGMENTATION
SUMMIT
RD
LOMA
PRIETA
AV
RD
SEE 914 MAP
SANTA CLARA CO.
SEE B MAP
0 .125 .25 .375 .5 miles 1 in. = 1900 ft.

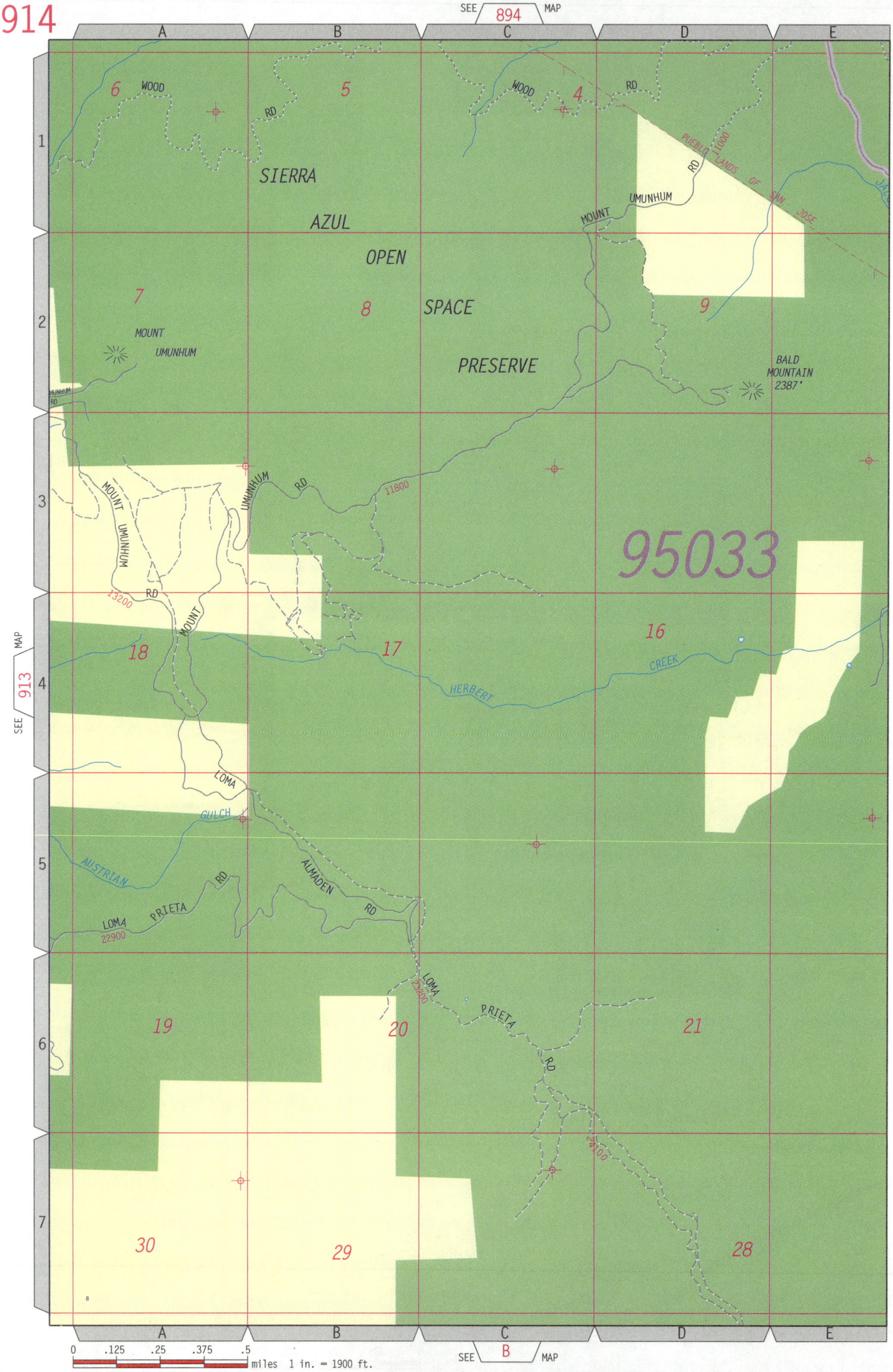
SEE 894 MAP
A
B
C
D
E
1
2
3
4
5
6
7
SEE 913 MAP
SIERRA
AZUL
OPEN
SPACE
PRESERVE
WOOD
RD
MOUNT
UMUNHUM
RD
PUEBLO 11000 LANDS OF SAN JOSE
MOUNT
UMUNHUM
BALD
MOUNTAIN
2387'
11800
13200
95033
HERBERT
CREEK
LOMA
GULCH
AUSTRIAN
ALMADEN
RD
LOMA
PRIETA
RD
22900
23800
24100
6
5
4
7
8
9
18
17
16
19
20
21
30
29
28
0
.125
.25
.375
.5
miles 1 in. = 1900 ft.
SEE B MAP

SEE 894 MAP

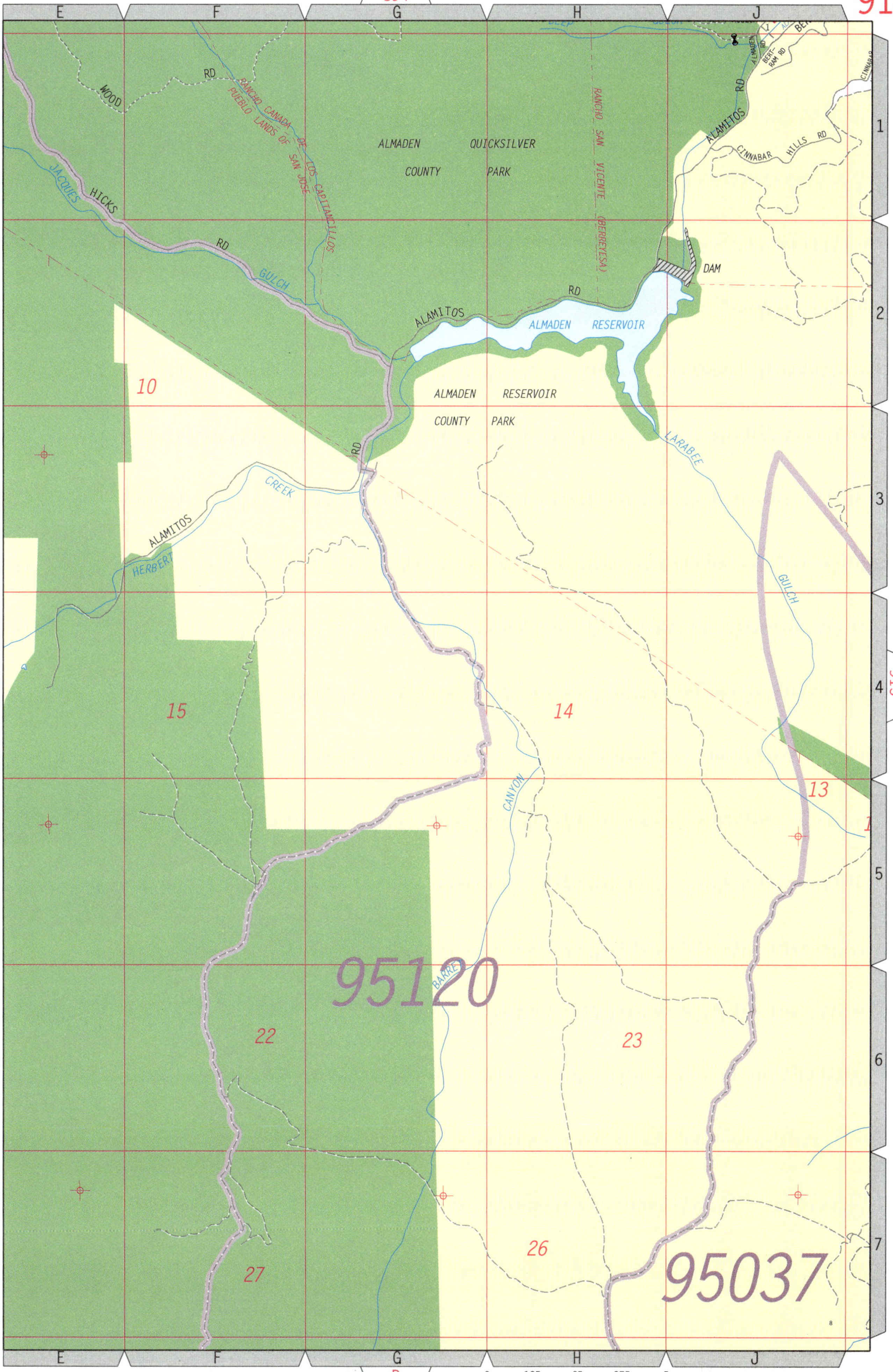

SEE 915 MAP

SEE B MAP

0 .125 .25 .375 .5 miles 1 in. = 1900 ft.

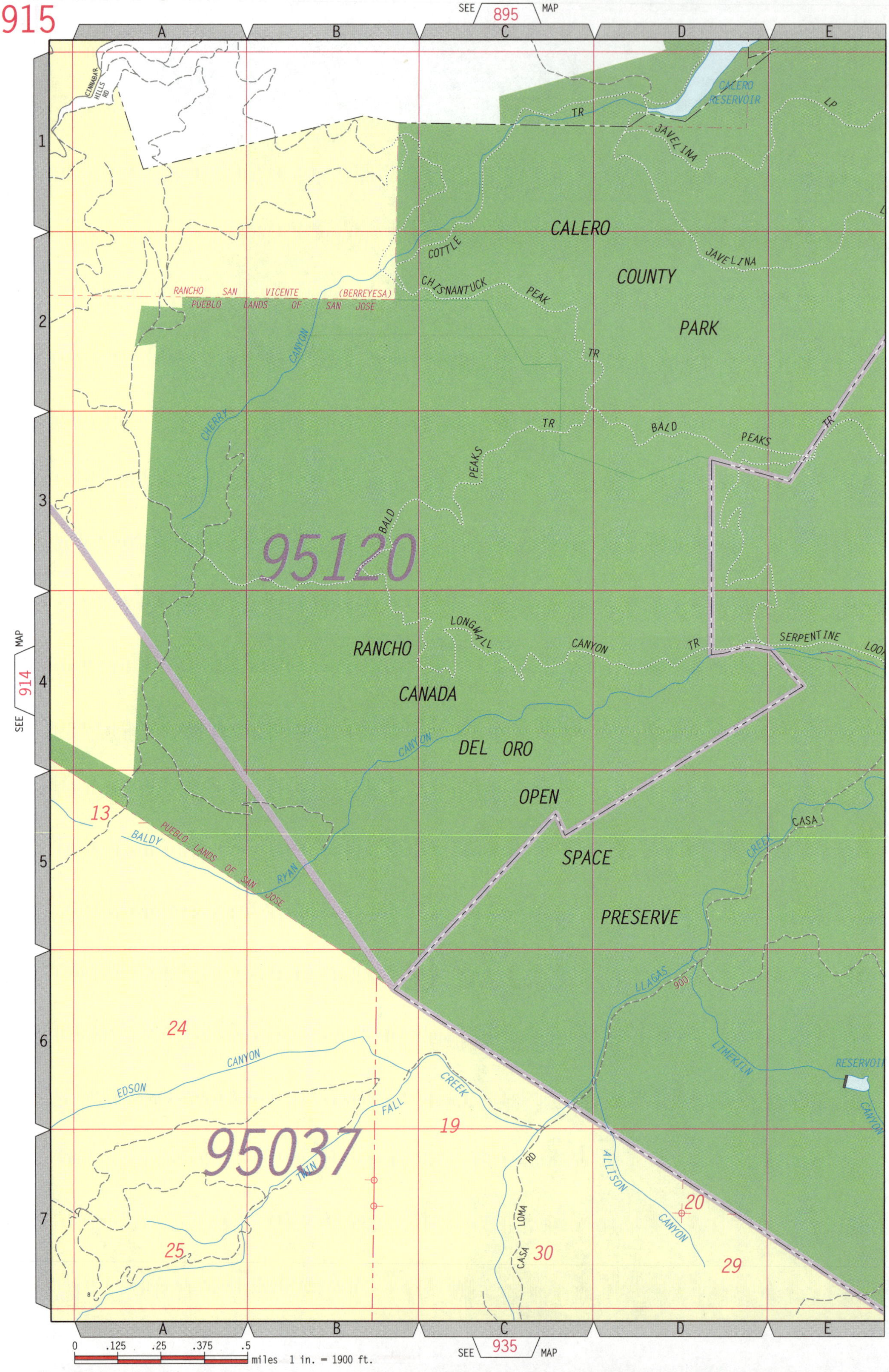
SEE 895 MAP
SEE 914 MAP
SEE 935 MAP
A
B
C
D
E
1
2
3
4
5
6
7
CINNABAR HILLS RD
CALERO RESERVOIR
TR
LP
JAVELINA
CALERO COUNTY PARK
COTTLE
CHISNANTUCK PEAK TR
RANCHO SAN VICENTE (BERREYESA)
PUEBLO LANDS OF SAN JOSE
CHERRY CANYON
BALD PEAKS TR
95120
LONGWALL CANYON TR
SERPENTINE LOOP
RANCHO CANADA DEL ORO OPEN SPACE PRESERVE
CANYON
13
BALDY RYAN
PUEBLO LANDS OF SAN JOSE
CASA
CREEK
LLAGAS
900
LIMEKILN
RESERVOIR
CANYON
24
EDSON CANYON
CREEK
FALL
19
95037
TWIN
RD
LOMA
CASA
ALLISON CANYON
20
25
30
29
0 .125 .25 .375 .5 miles 1 in. = 1900 ft.

SEE 895 MAP

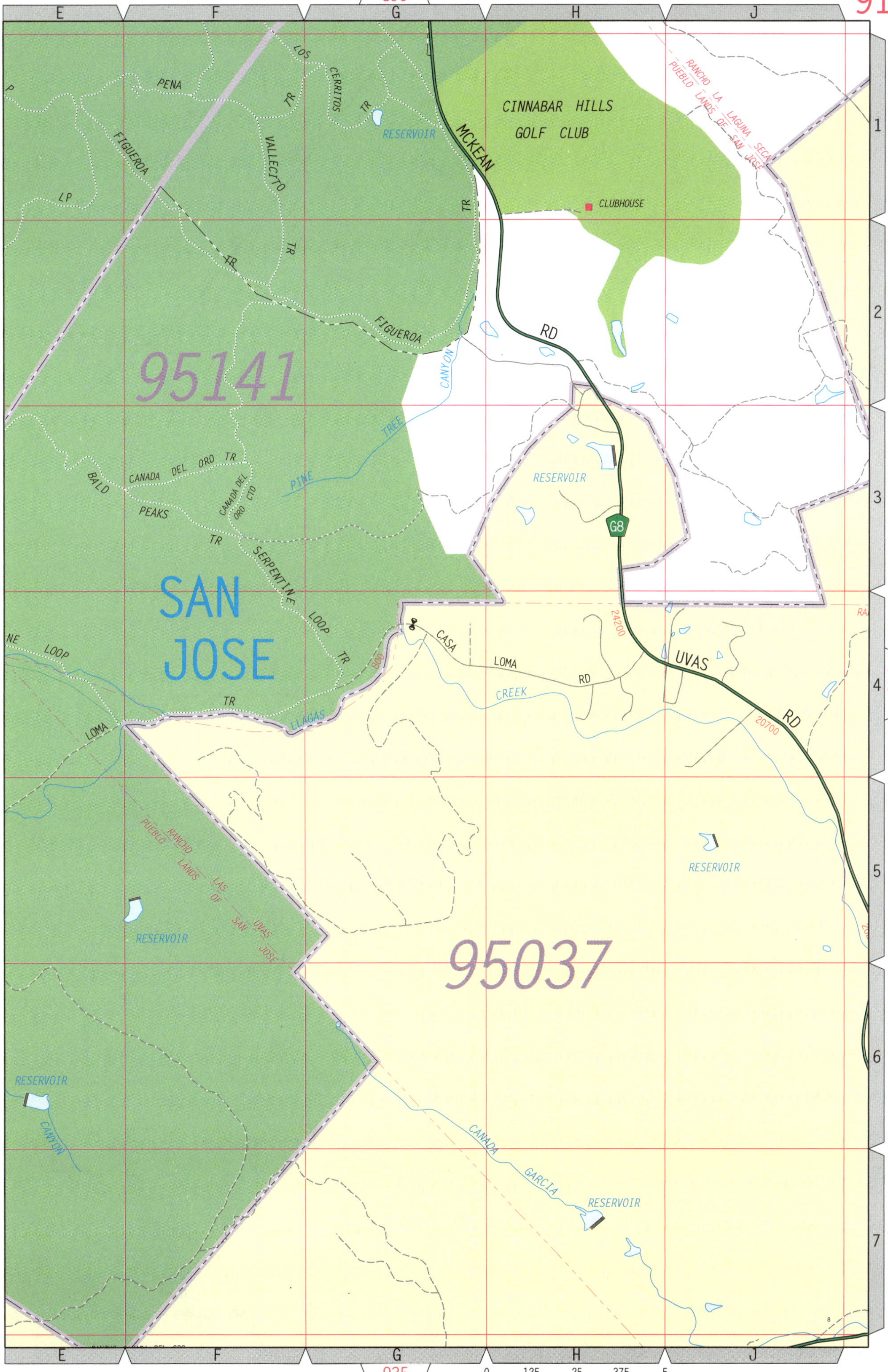

SEE 916 MAP

SEE 935 MAP

0 .125 .25 .375 .5 miles 1 in. = 1900 ft.

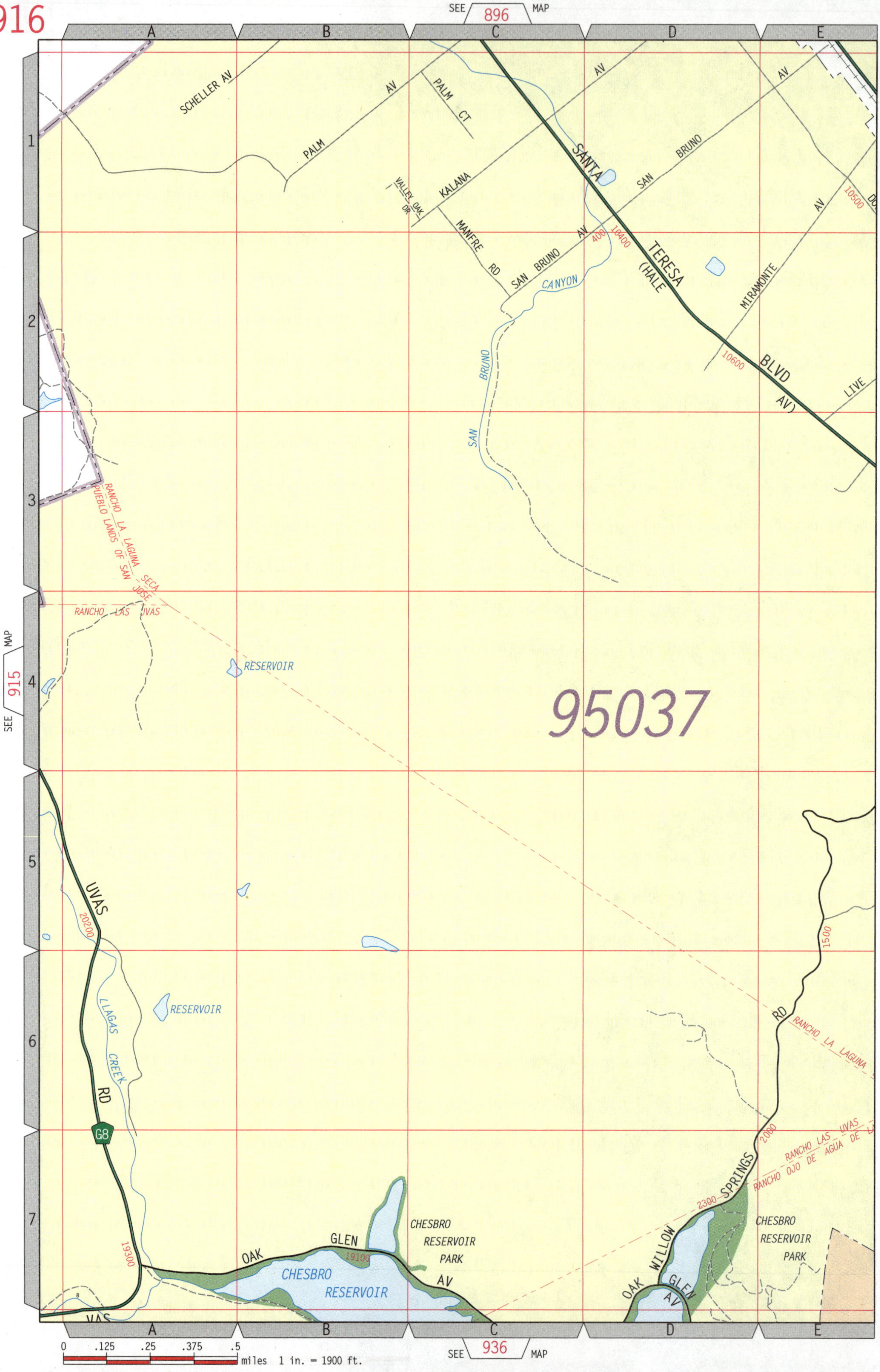
SEE 896 MAP
A
B
C
D
E
1
2
3
4
5
6
7
SEE 915 MAP
SCHELLER AV
PALM AV
PALM CT
VALLEY OAK DR
KALANA
MANFRE RD
SAN BRUNO AV
SAN BRUNO AV
SANTA TERESA (HALE AV) BLVD
MIRAMONTE AV
LIVE
DO
10500
10400
406
10600
SAN BRUNO CANYON
RANCHO LA LAGUNA SECA
PUEBLO LANDS OF SAN JOSE
RANCHO LAS UVAS
RESERVOIR
RESERVOIR
95037
UVAS RD
20200
LLAGAS CREEK
G8
19300
OAK GLEN AV
19100
CHESBRO RESERVOIR
CHESBRO RESERVOIR PARK
CHESBRO RESERVOIR PARK
OAK GLEN AV
WILLOW SPRINGS RD
1500
2000
2300
RANCHO LA LAGUNA
RANCHO LAS UVAS
RANCHO OJO DE AGUA DE LA
VAS
0 .125 .25 .375 .5
miles 1 in. = 1900 ft.
SEE 936 MAP

SEE 896 MAP

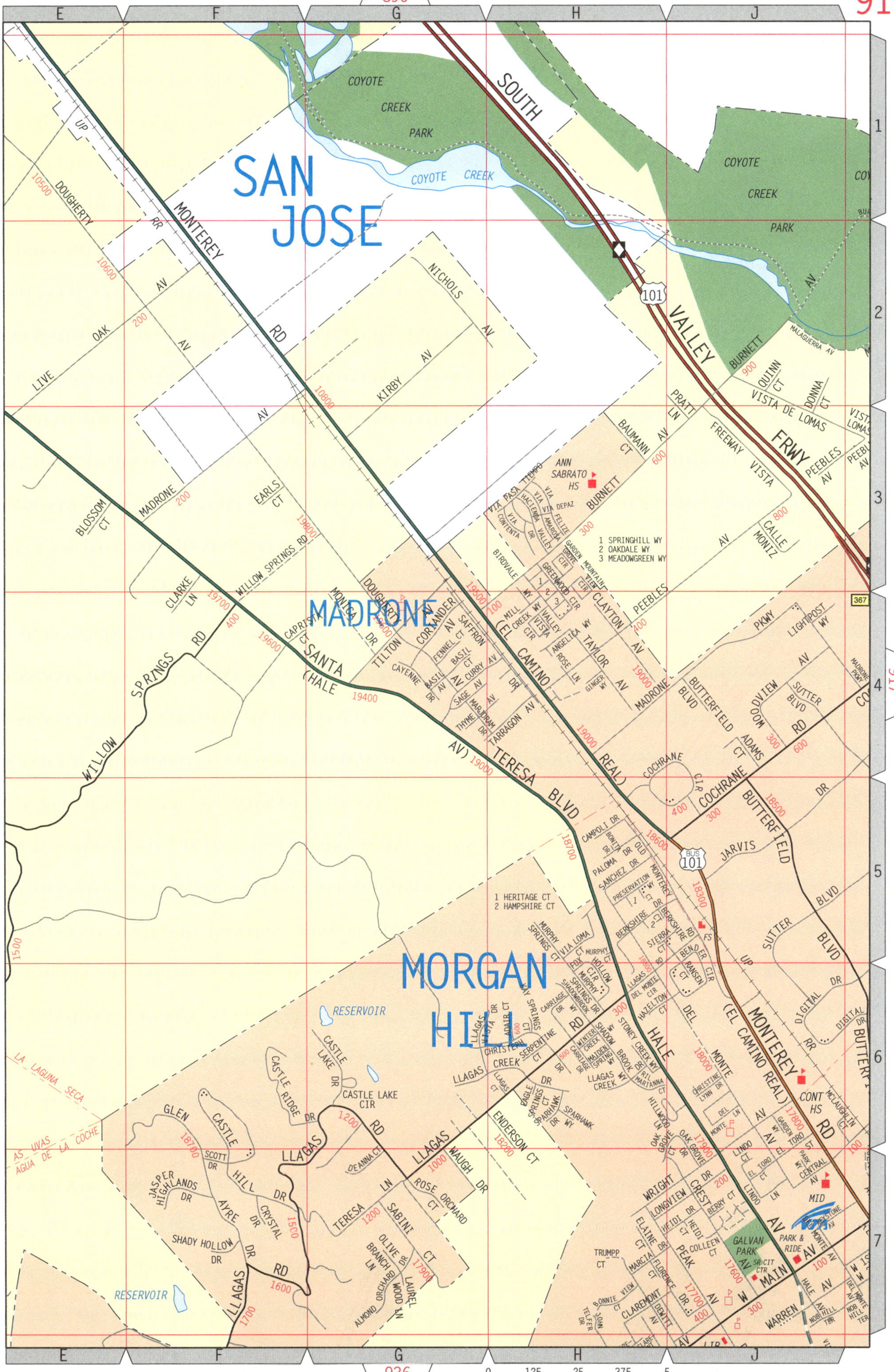

SEE 917 MAP

SEE 936 MAP

0 .125 .25 .375 .5 miles 1 in. = 1900 ft.

SEE B MAP

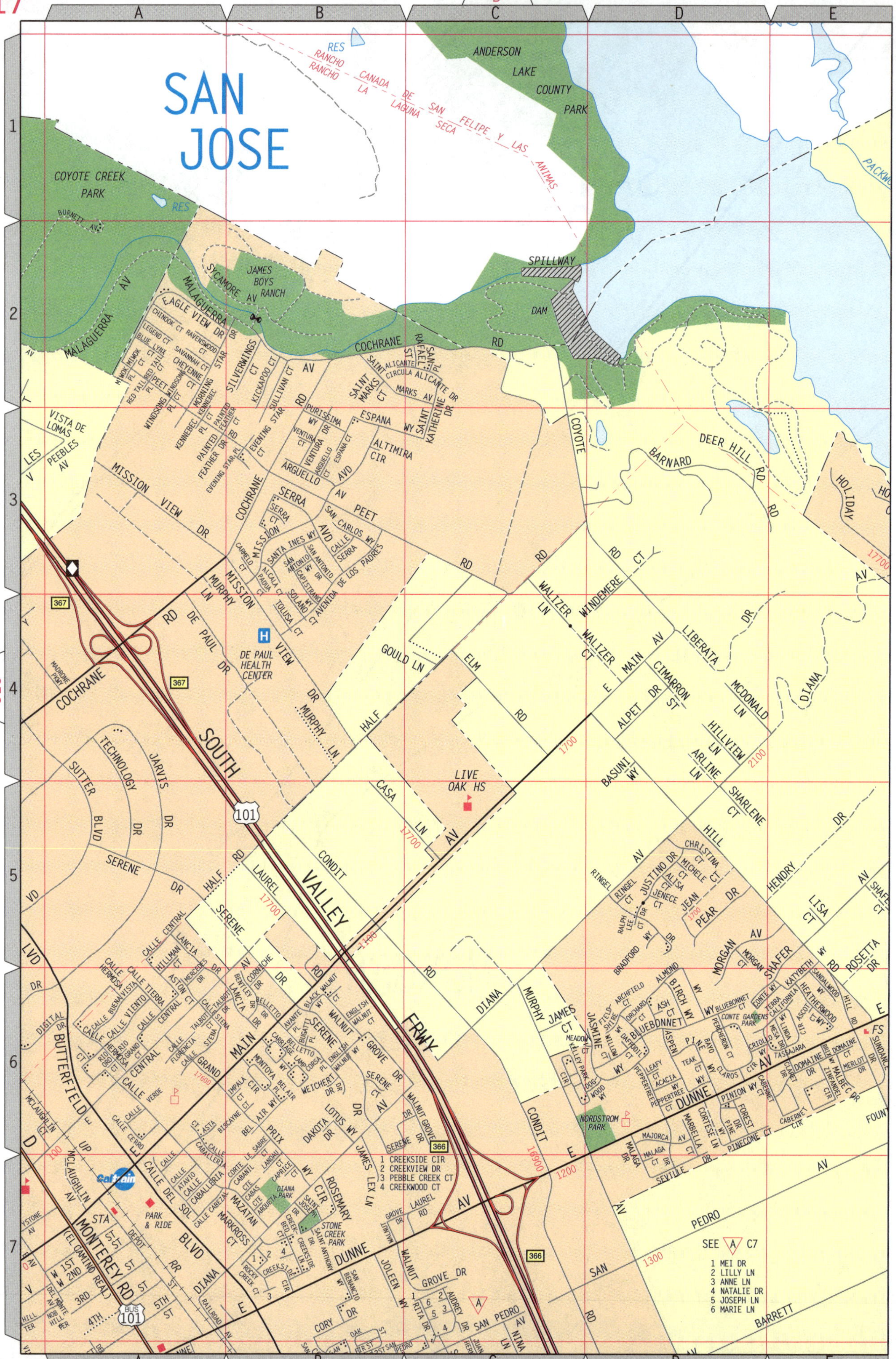

SEE 916 MAP

0 .125 .25 .375 .5 miles 1 in. = 1900 ft.

SEE 937 MAP

SEE B MAP
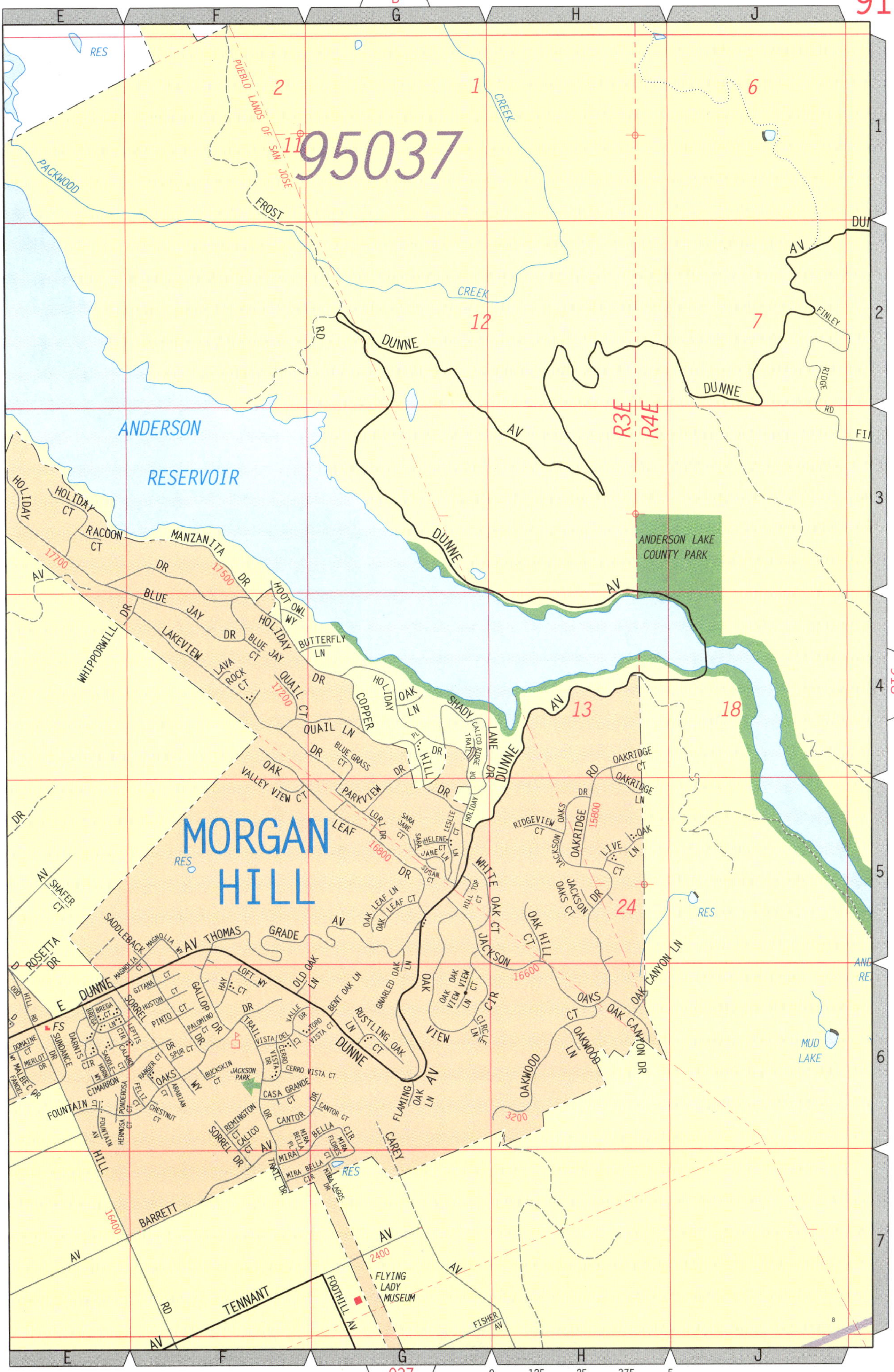

SEE 918 MAP
SEE 937 MAP
0 .125 .25 .375 .5 miles 1 in. = 1900 ft.

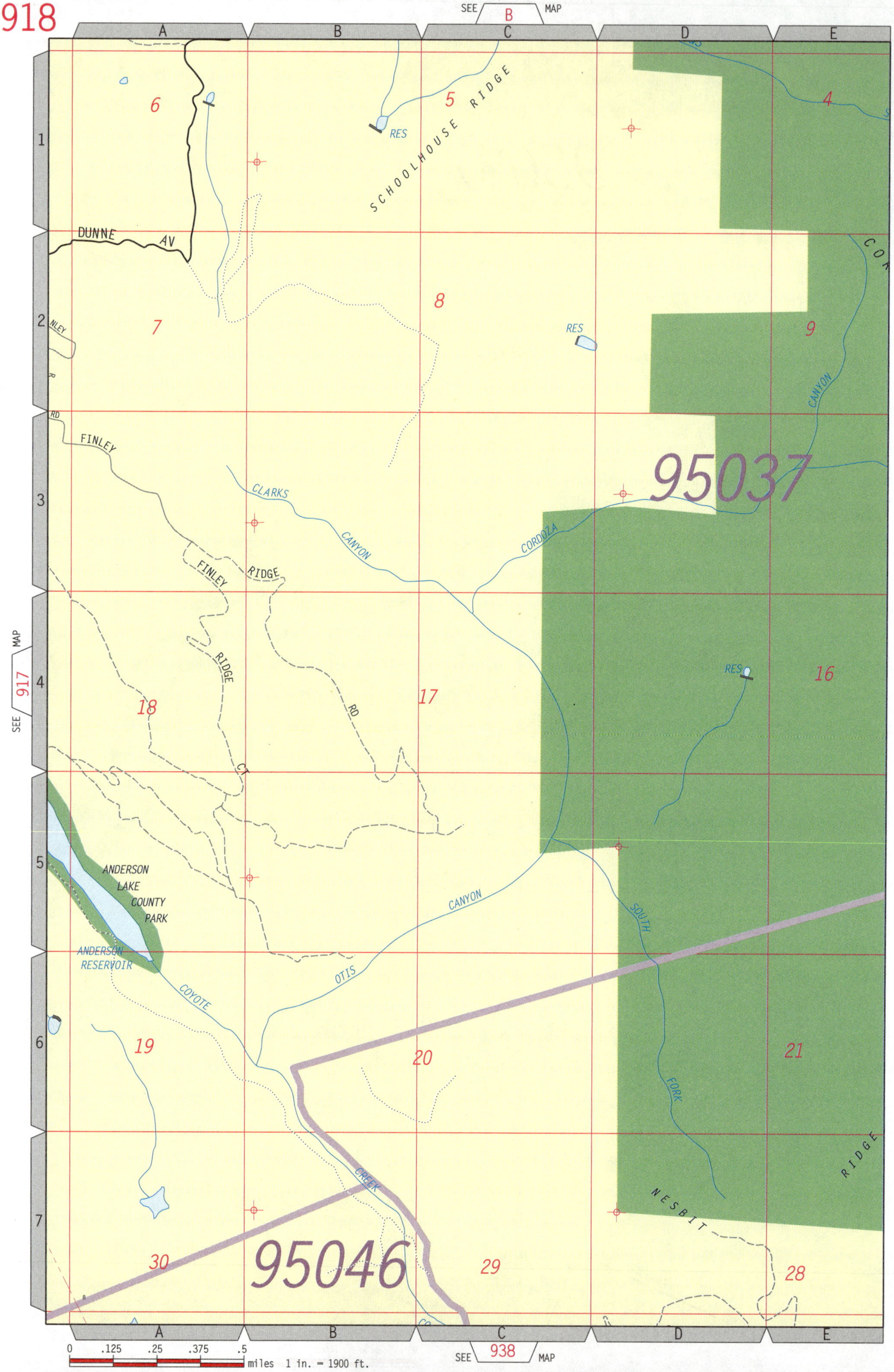

SEE B MAP
SEE 938 MAP
SEE 917 MAP
A
B
C
D
E
1
2
3
4
5
6
7
DUNNE AV
SCHOOLHOUSE RIDGE
RES
FINLEY RD
FINLEY RIDGE
FINLEY RIDGE CT
RD
CLARKS CANYON
CORDOZA CANYON
OTIS CANYON
SOUTH FORK
COYOTE CREEK
ANDERSON LAKE COUNTY PARK
ANDERSON RESERVOIR
NESBIT RIDGE
95037
95046
4
5
6
7
8
9
16
17
18
19
20
21
28
29
30
0 .125 .25 .375 .5 miles 1 in. = 1900 ft.

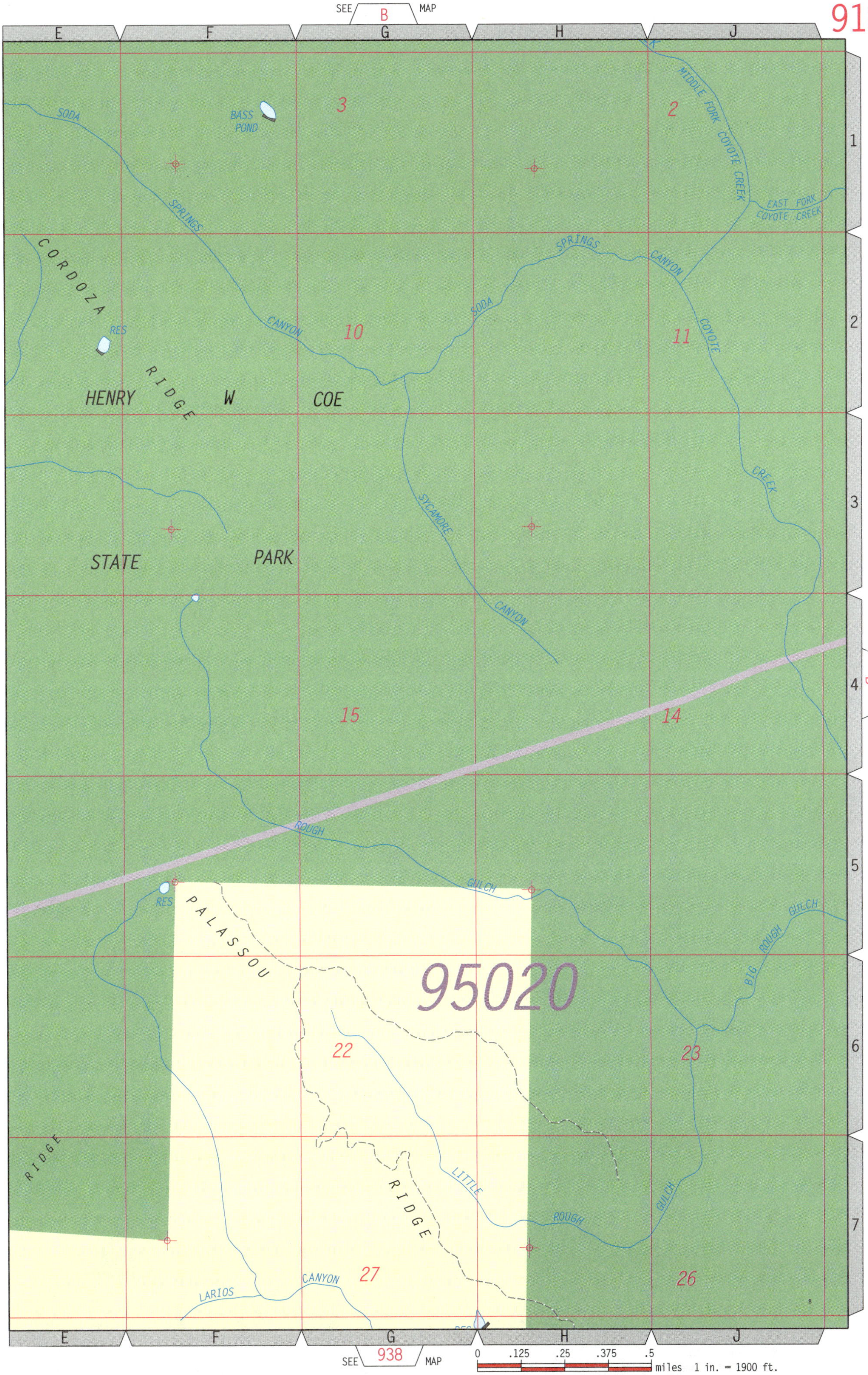

SEE B MAP
E
F
G
H
J
1
2
3
4
5
6
7
SEE B MAP
SODA
SPRINGS
CANYON
BASS POND
3
2
MIDDLE FORK COYOTE CREEK
EAST FORK COYOTE CREEK
SPRINGS
CANYON
SODA
CORDOZA
RIDGE
RES
10
11
COYOTE
HENRY
W
COE
CREEK
SYCAMORE
CANYON
STATE
PARK
15
14
ROUGH
GULCH
RES
PALASSOU
95020
BIG ROUGH GULCH
22
23
RIDGE
RIDGE
LITTLE
ROUGH
GULCH
27
26
LARIOS
CANYON
SEE 938 MAP
0 .125 .25 .375 .5 miles 1 in. = 1900 ft.

SEE 915 MAP

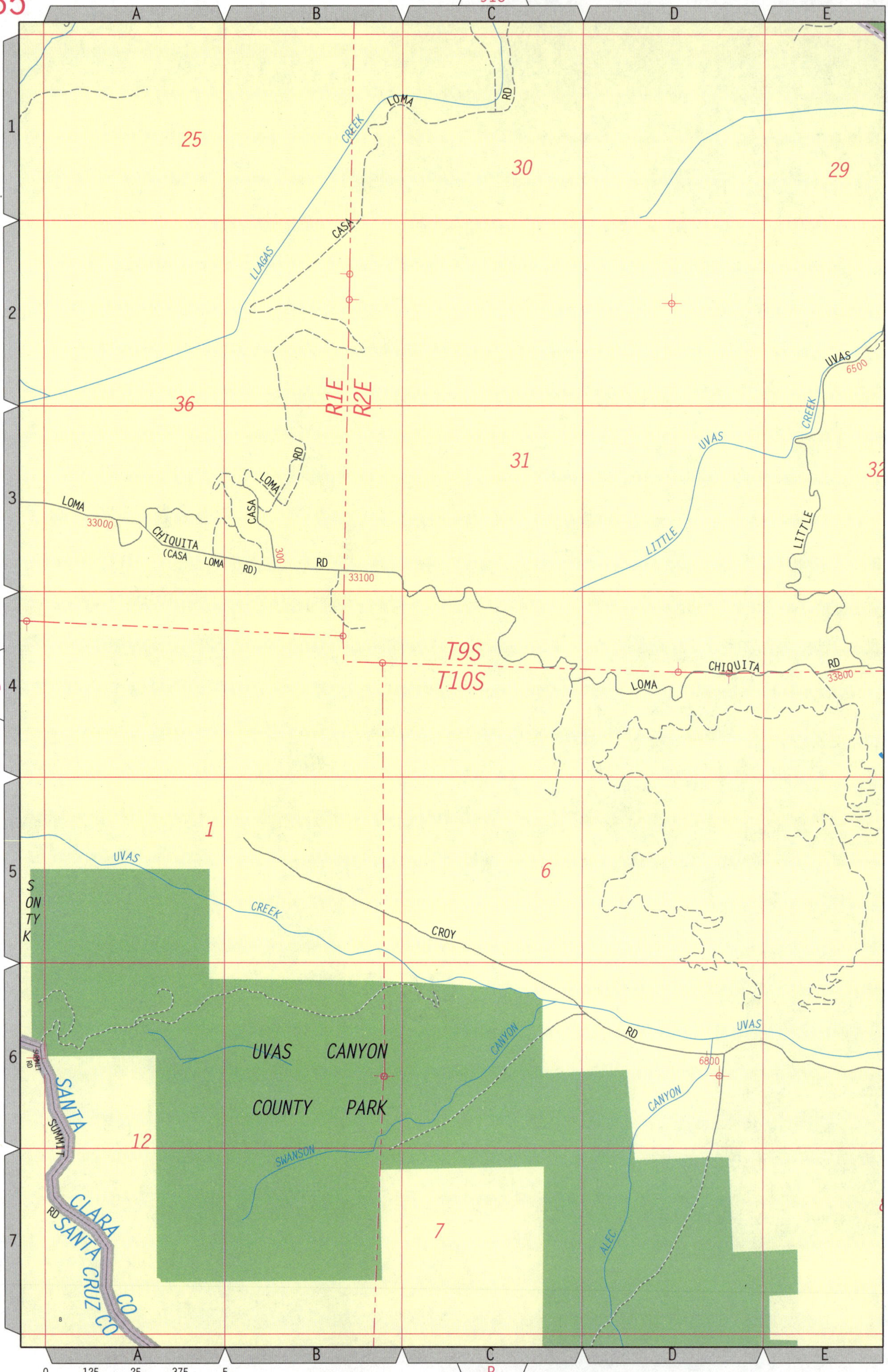

SANTA CLARA CO.

SEE B MAP

SEE B MAP

0 .125 .25 .375 .5 miles 1 in. = 1900 ft.

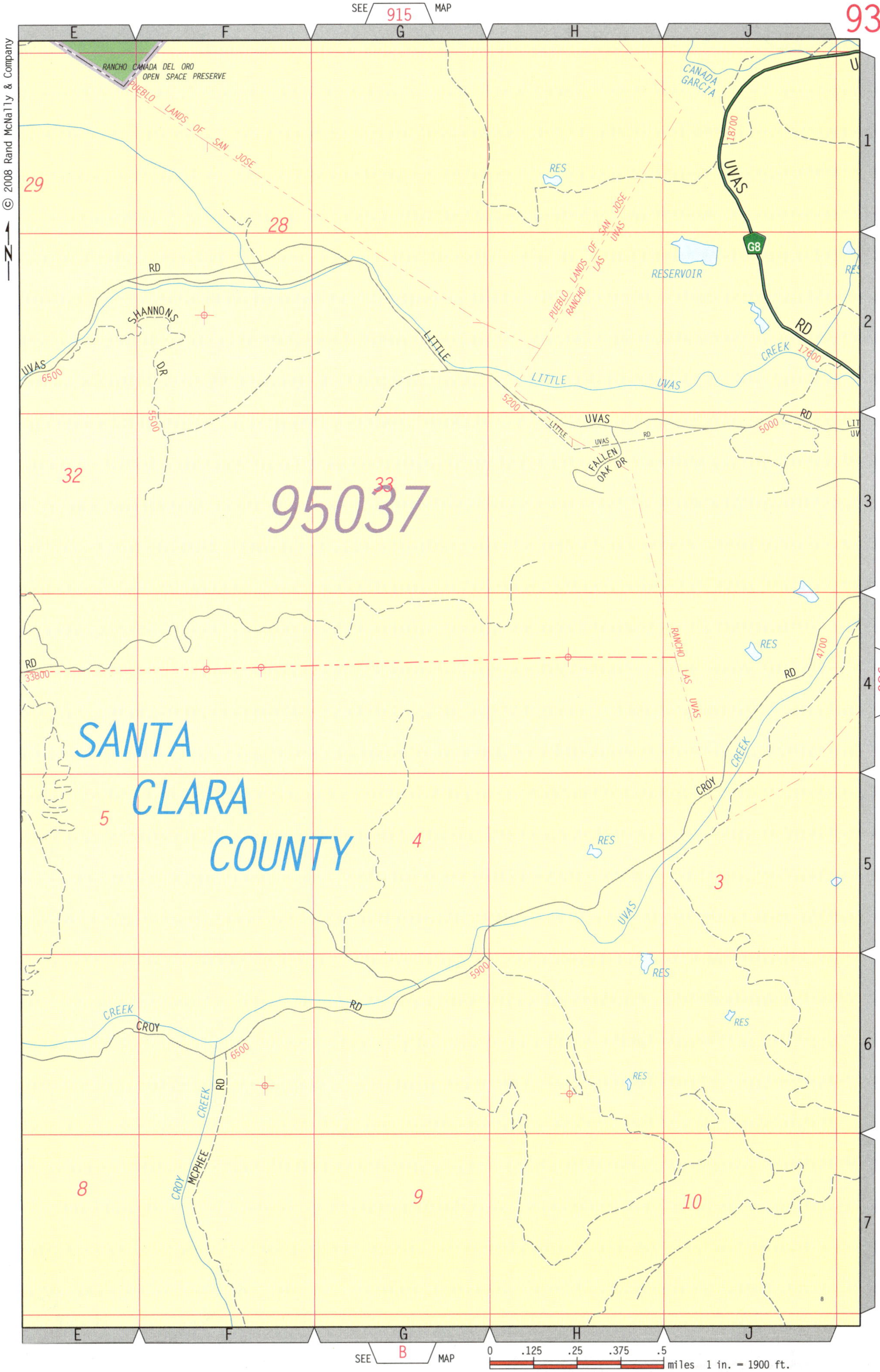
SEE 915 MAP
E
F
G
H
J
1
2
3
4
5
6
7
SEE 936 MAP
SEE B MAP
RANCHO CANADA DEL ORO
OPEN SPACE PRESERVE
PUEBLO LANDS OF SAN JOSE
CANADA GARCIA
UVAS RD
18700
17600
G8
RES
RESERVOIR
PUEBLO LANDS OF SAN JOSE
RANCHO LAS UVAS
29
28
RD
SHANNONS DR
UVAS
6500
5500
LITTLE
LITTLE UVAS CREEK
5200
UVAS RD
5000
LITTLE UVAS RD
FALLEN OAK DR
32
33
95037
RD
33800
RANCHO LAS UVAS
4700
RD
CROY
UVAS CREEK
SANTA CLARA COUNTY
5
4
3
5900
CREEK
CROY
RD
6500
MCPHEE CREEK RD
CROY
8
9
10
0 .125 .25 .375 .5
miles 1 in. = 1900 ft.

SEE 916 MAP

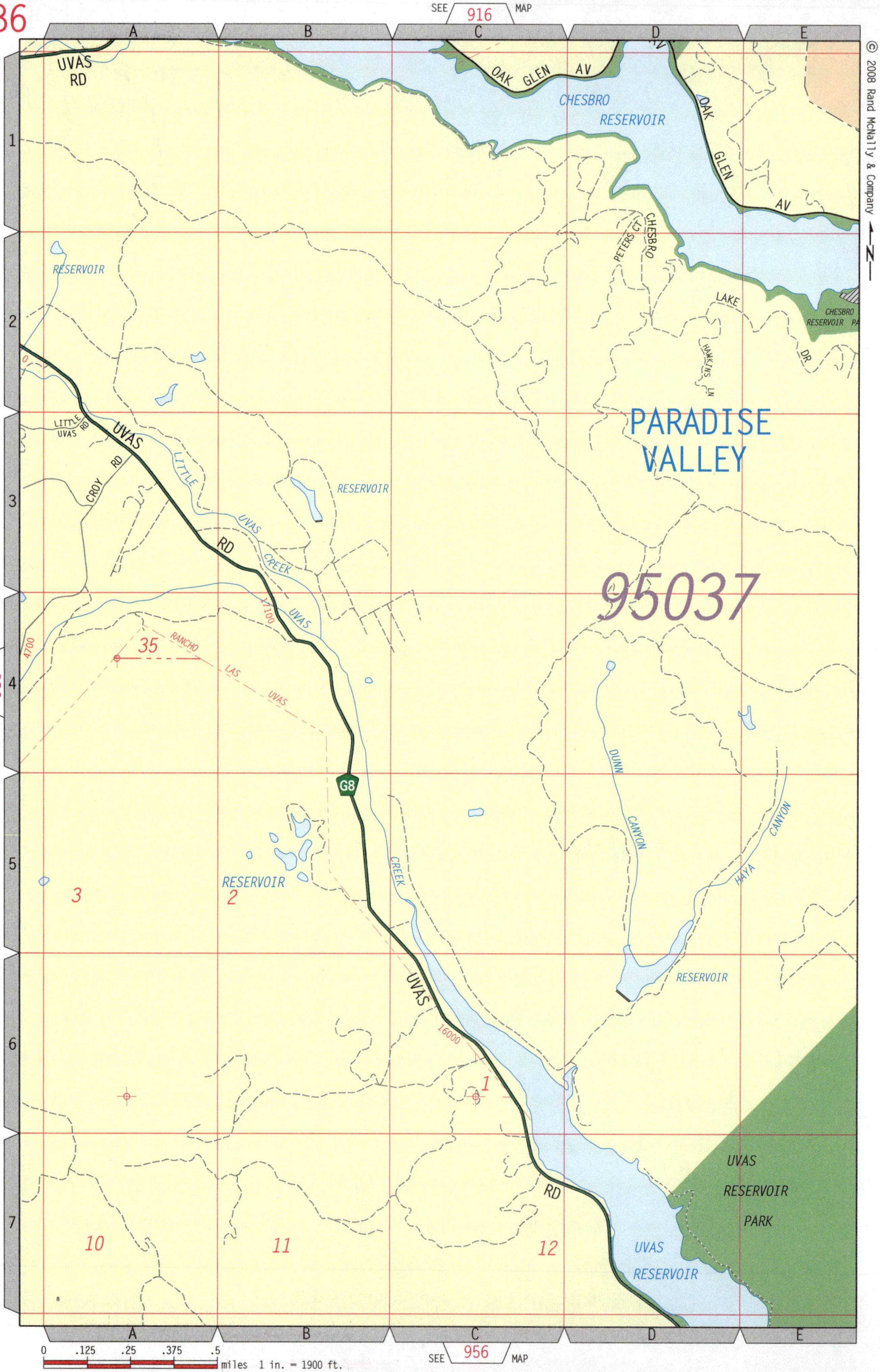

SEE 935 MAP

SANTA CLARA CO.

0 .125 .25 .375 .5 miles 1 in. = 1900 ft.

SEE 956 MAP

SEE 916 MAP

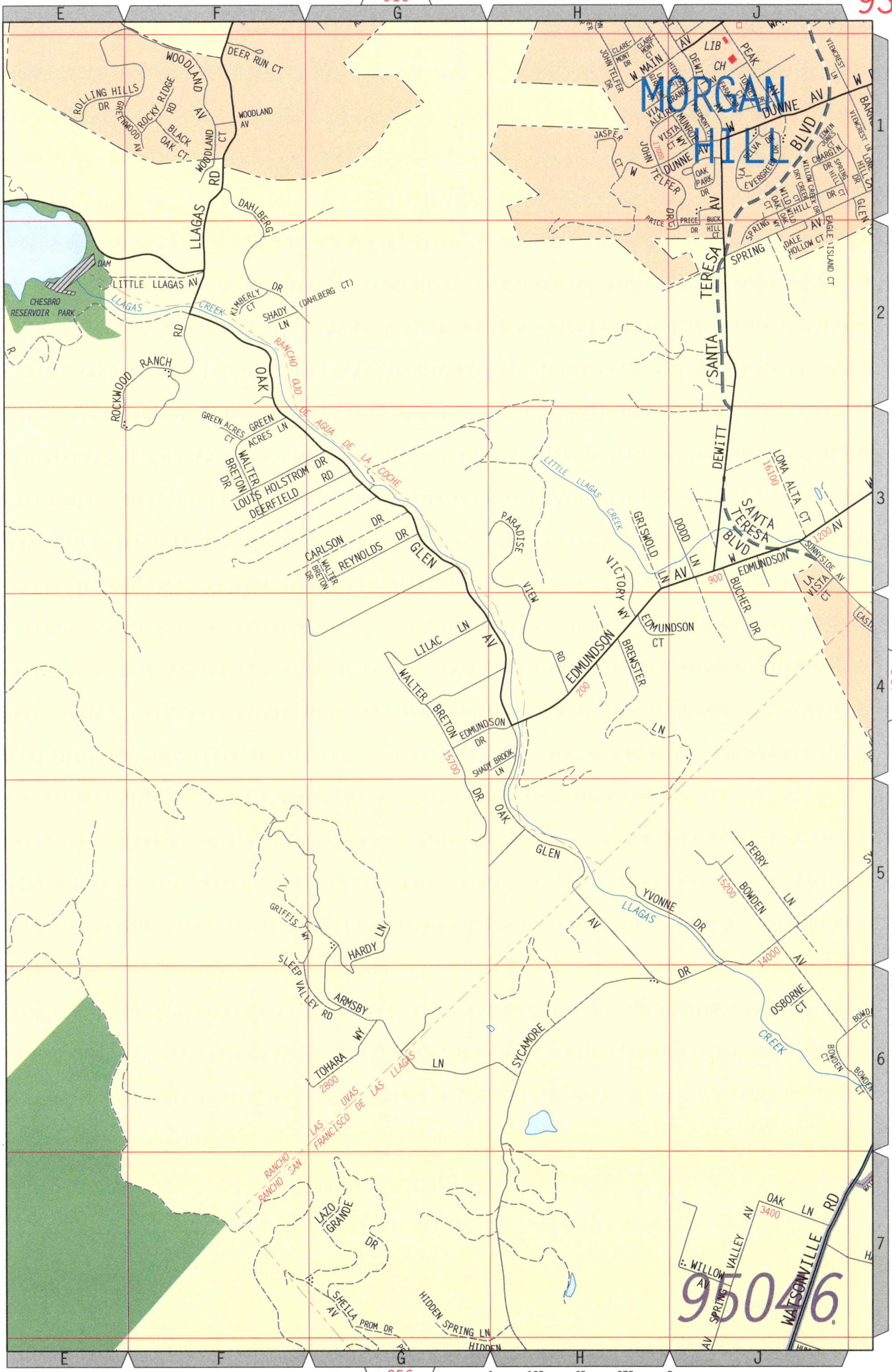

SEE 937 MAP

SEE 956 MAP

SEE 917 MAP

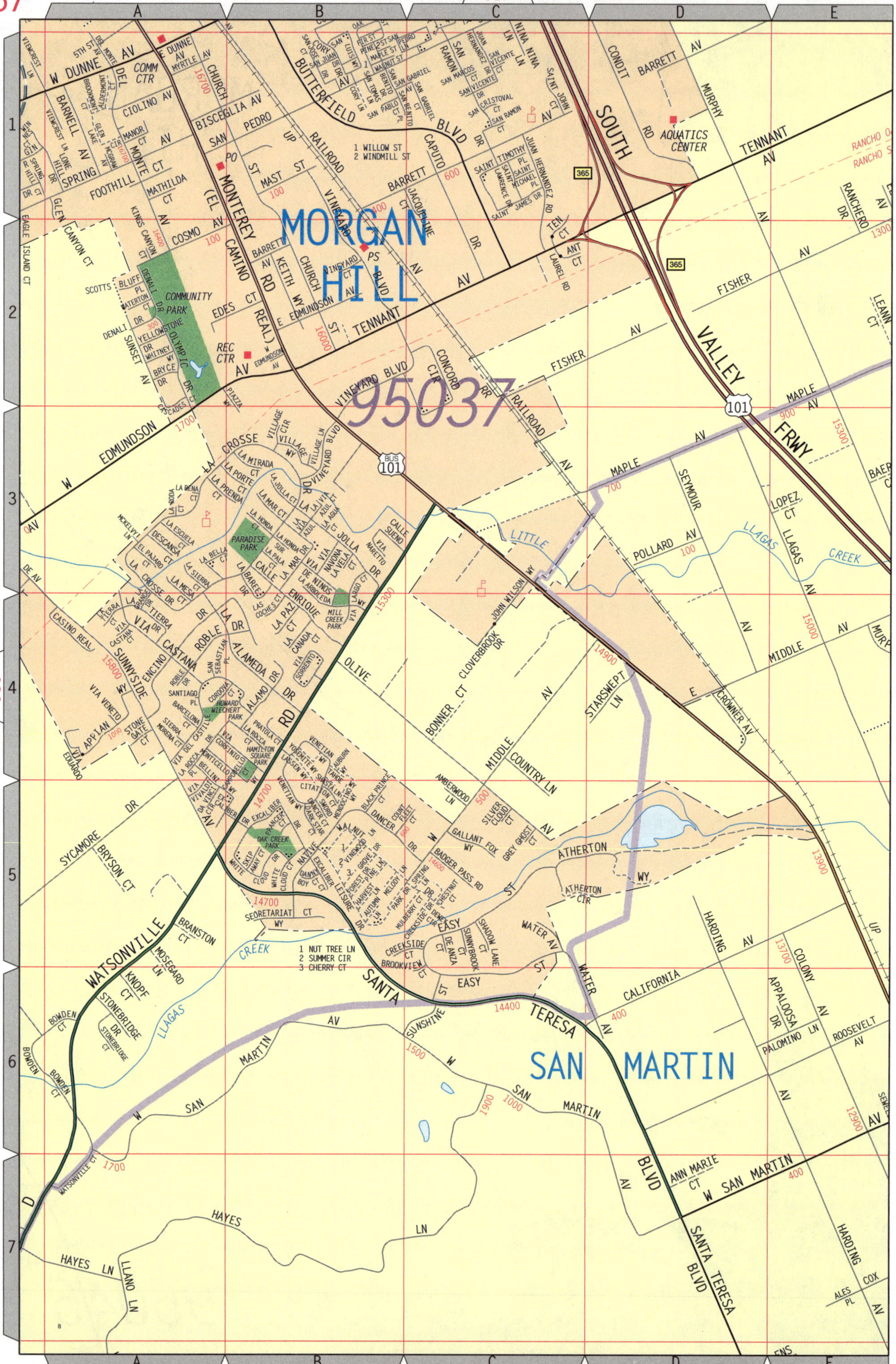

0 .125 .25 .375 .5
miles 1 in. = 1900 ft.

SEE 936 MAP

SEE 957 MAP

SEE 917 MAP

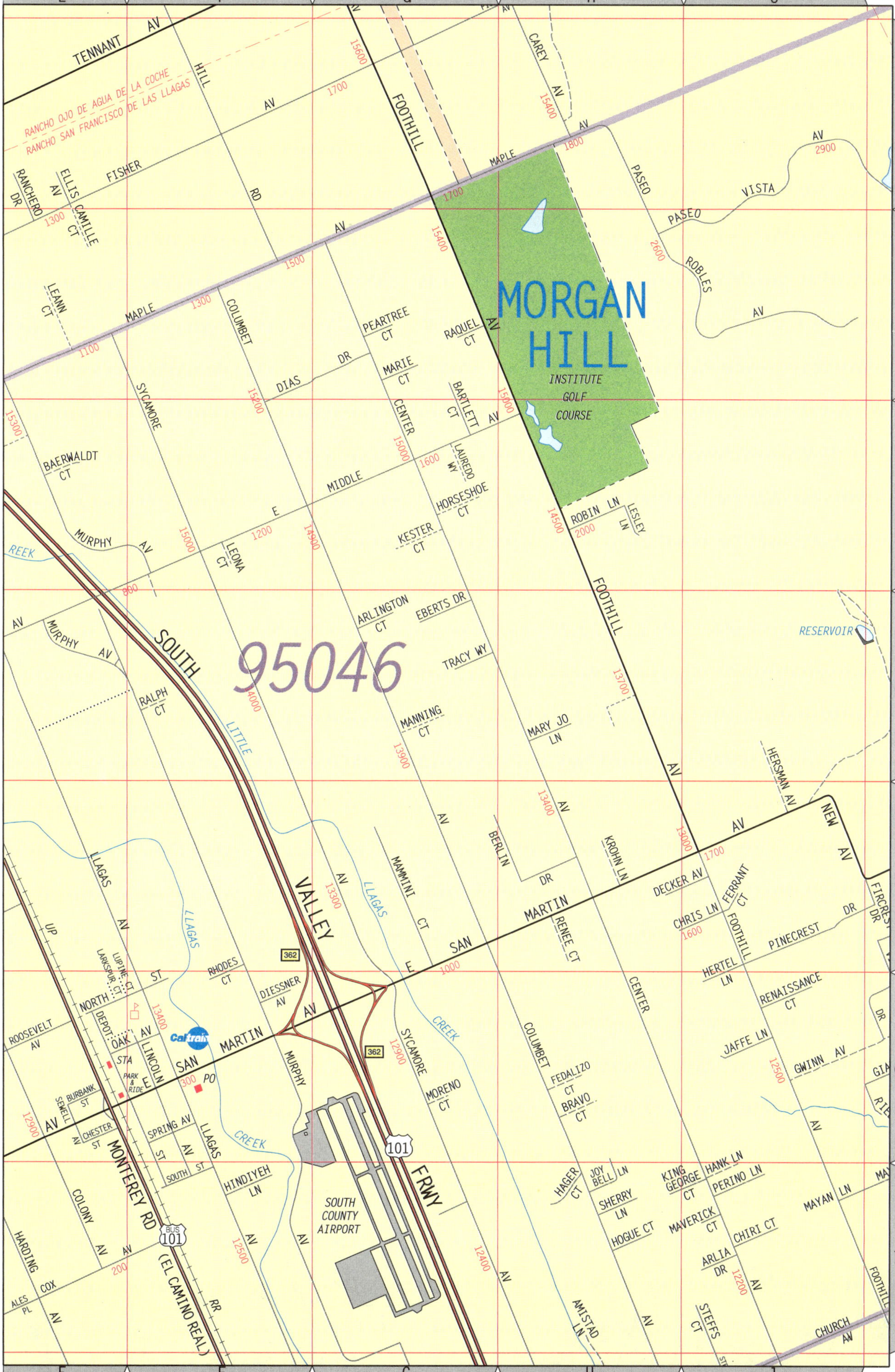

SEE 938 MAP

SEE 957 MAP

0 .125 .25 .375 .5 miles 1 in. = 1900 ft.

© 2008 Rand McNally & Company

N

SANTA CLARA CO.

E F G H J

TENNANT AV

RANCHO OJO DE AGUA DE LA COCHE
RANCHO SAN FRANCISCO DE LAS LLAGAS

CAREY AV

1

FOOTHILL

HILL

AV

RD

FISHER

RANCHERO DR
ELLIS
CAMILLE AV
1300

1700

MAPLE

1800

PASEO

VISTA
2900

AV

1500

15400

2

LEANN CT

MAPLE 1300

COLUMBET

1100

SYCAMORE

DIAS DR

PEARTREE CT

MARIE CT

15600

CENTER

RAQUEL CT

BARTLETT CT

MORGAN
HILL

INSTITUTE
GOLF
COURSE

PASEO

ROBLES
2600

AV

15300

BAERWALDT CT

15200

E

MIDDLE

15000

1600

LAUREDO WY

AV

19000

3

MURPHY AV

15000

LEONA CT

1200

14900

KESTER CT

HORSESHOE CT

14500

ROBIN LN
2000

LESLEY LN

REEK

SOUTH

800

ARLINGTON CT

EBERTS DR

TRACY WY

FOOTHILL

RESERVOIR

4

AV

MURPHY AV

RALPH CT

4000

LITTLE

95046

MANNING CT

13900

MARY JO LN

13700

HERSMAN AV

AV

13400

AV

VALLEY

LLAGAS

LLAGAS

AV

13300

LLAGAS

MAMMINI CT

BERLIN DR

SAN

MARTIN

AV

KROHN LN

DECKER AV

NEW AV

1700

FIRCREST DR

5

LLAGAS

UP

ST

LARKSPUR CT
LUPINE CT

13400

RHODES CT

DIESSNER AV

362

E

1000

CHRIS LN
1600

FERRANT CT

FOOTHILL

PINECREST DR

NORTH

DEPOT

OAK AV

CalTrain

MURPHY AV

SYCAMORE

CREEK

COLUMBET

HERTEL LN

RENAISSANCE CT

DR

6

ROOSEVELT AV

STA

LINCOLN

SAN MARTIN

362

MORENO CT

FEDALIZO CT

BRAVO CT

JAFFE LN

GWINN AV
12500

GIA

RIE

BURBANK ST
SEWELL AV
12500 AV
CHESTER ST

PARK & RIDE

E

300

PO

12900

HAGER CT

JOY
BELL LN

KING
GEORGE CT

HANK LN

PERINO LN

SPRING AV

LLAGAS ST

CREEK

SHERRY LN

MAVERICK CT

ARLIA DR

CHIRI CT

MAYAN LN

7

MONTEREY RD

COLONY AV

SOUTH ST

HINDIYEH LN

SOUTH COUNTY AIRPORT

12500

12400

HOGUE CT

12200

AV

HARDING AV
COX AV
200

ALES PL

RR

BUS 101

FRWY

101

(EL CAMINO REAL)

AMISTAD AV

STEFFS CT

CHURCH AV

E F G H J

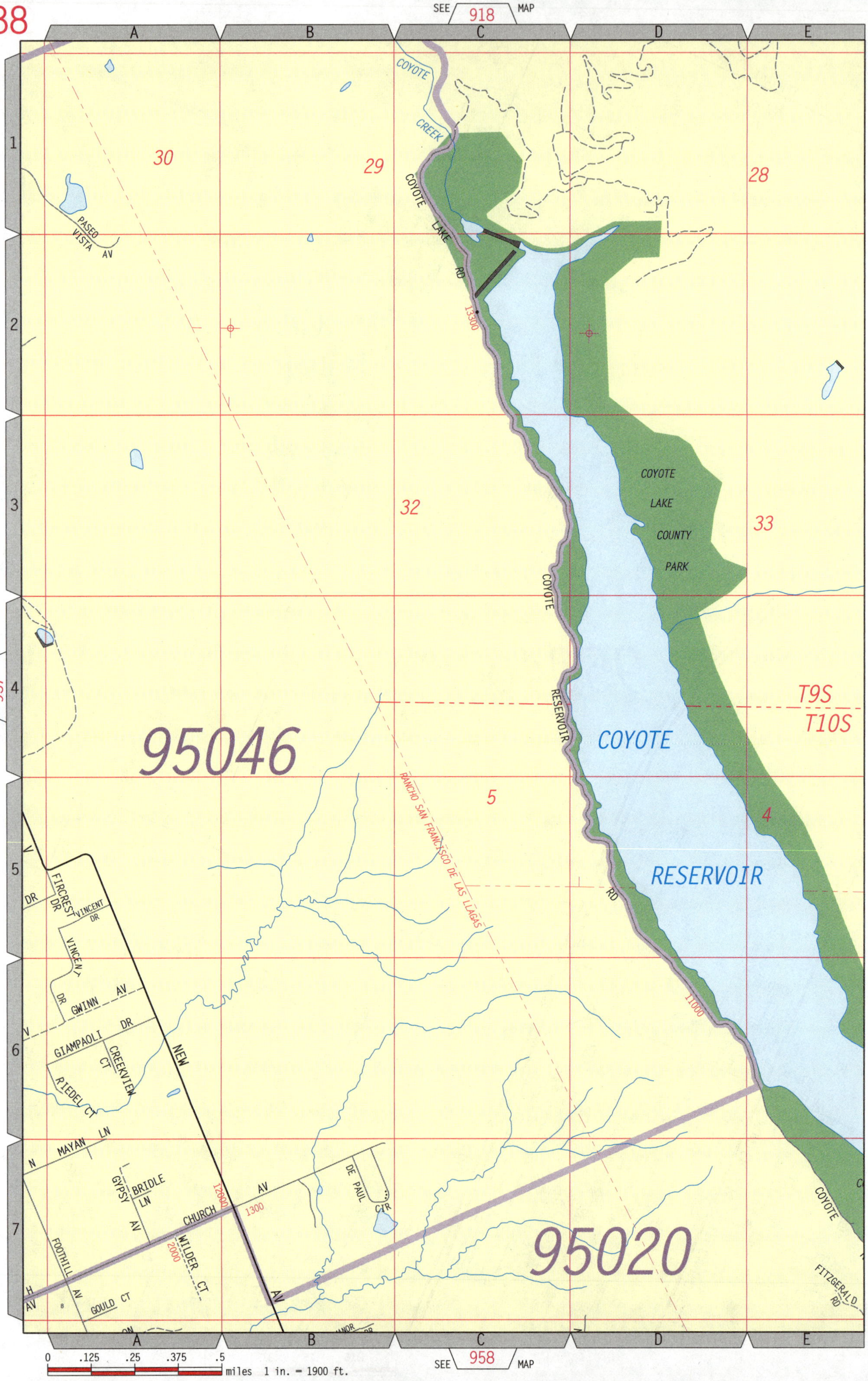
SEE 918 MAP
A
B
C
D
E
1
2
3
4
5
6
7
SEE 937 MAP
COYOTE CREEK
30
29
28
32
33
5
4
COYOTE LAKE RD
13300
PASEO VISTA AV
COYOTE LAKE COUNTY PARK
COYOTE RESERVOIR RD
COYOTE RESERVOIR
T9S
T10S
95046
95020
RANCHO SAN FRANCISCO DE LAS LLAGAS
11000
FIRCREST DR
VINCENT DR
VINCENT DR
GWINN AV
DR
GIAMPAOLI DR
CREEKVIEW CT
RIEDEL CT
NEW AV
MAYAN LN
GYPSY AV
BRIDLE LN
CHURCH AV
12900
1300
2000
WILDER CT
DE PAUL CIR
FOOTHILL AV
GOULD CT
COYOTE
FITZGERALD RD
SEE 958 MAP
0 .125 .25 .375 .5
miles 1 in. = 1900 ft.

SEE 918 MAP

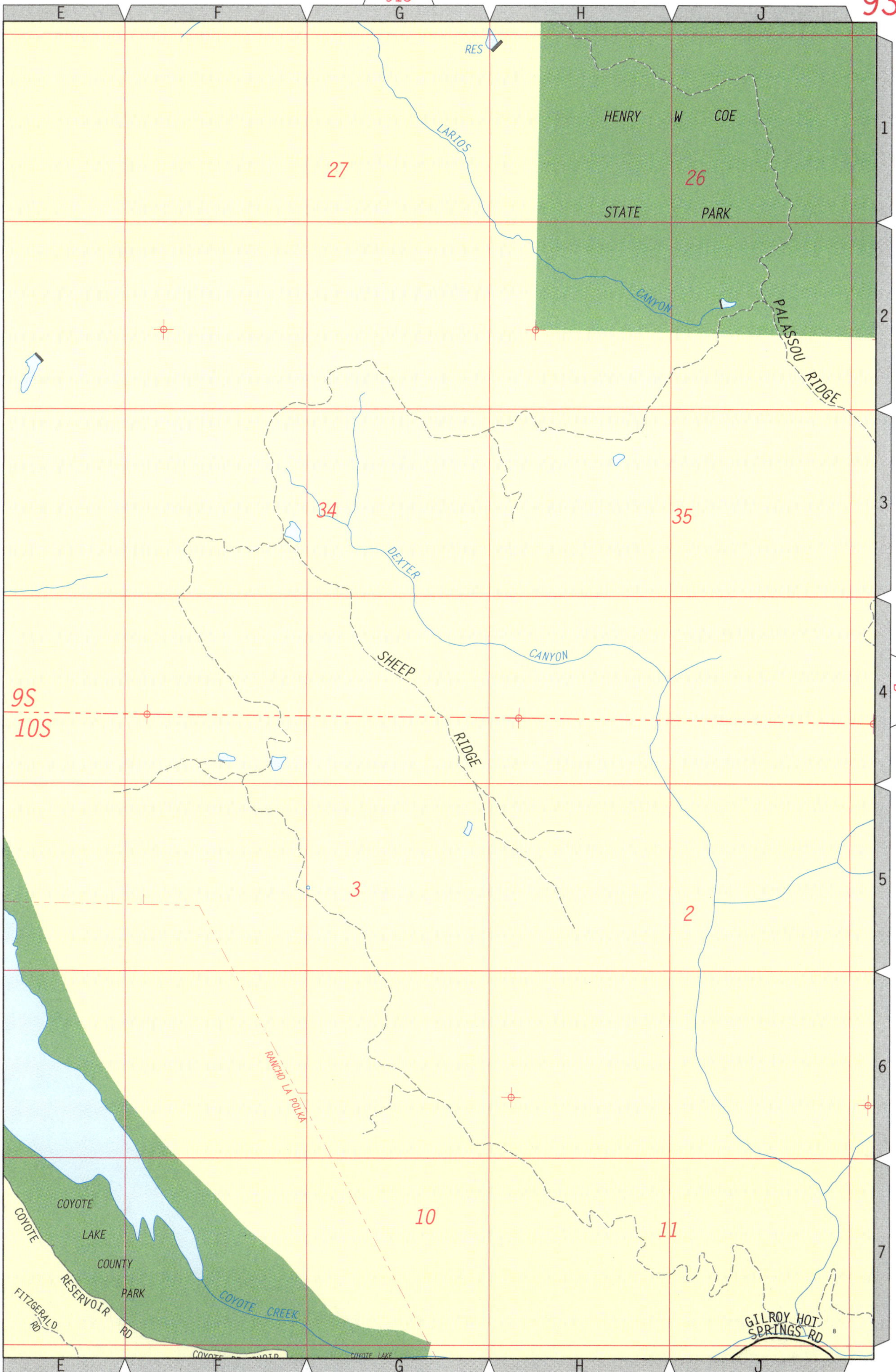

SEE B MAP

SEE 958 MAP

0 .125 .25 .375 .5 miles 1 in. = 1900 ft.

SEE 936 MAP

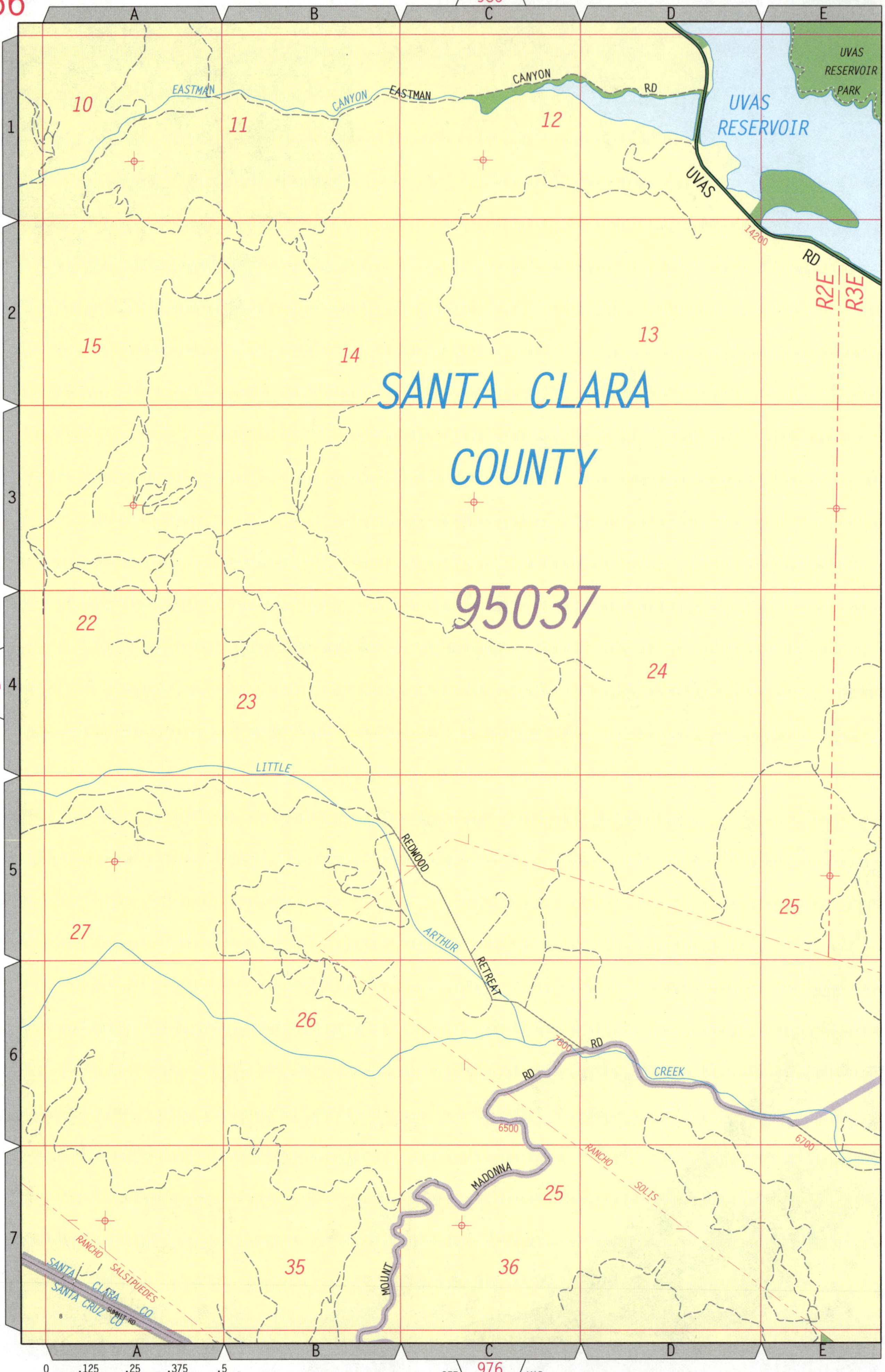

SEE B MAP

SEE 976 MAP

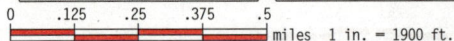

0 .125 .25 .375 .5 miles 1 in. = 1900 ft.

SANTA CLARA CO.

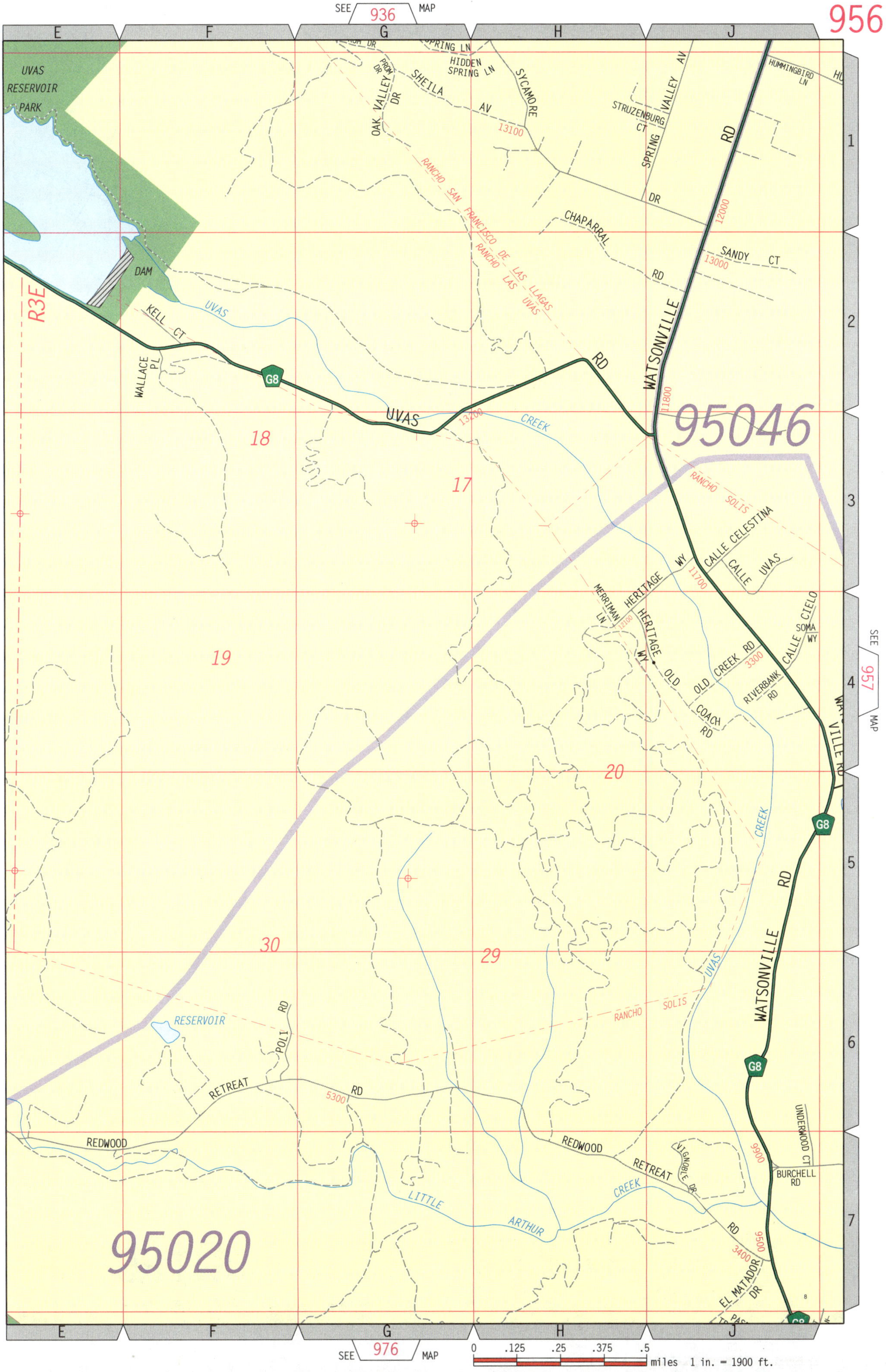
SEE 936 MAP
E
F
G
H
J
1
2
3
4
5
6
7
UVAS RESERVOIR PARK
DAM
R3E
UVAS
KELL CT
WALLACE PL
G8
UVAS
13200
CREEK
RD
WATSONVILLE
11800
95046
OAK VALLEY DR
PROM DR
SHEILA
AV
13100
HIDDEN SPRING LN
SYCAMORE
STRUZENBURG CT
SPRING VALLEY AV
DR
RD
12000
CHAPARRAL
RD
SANDY CT
13000
HUMMINGBIRD LN
RANCHO SAN FRANCISCO DE LAS LLAGAS
RANCHO LAS UVAS
18
17
19
20
30
29
RANCHO SOLIS
CALLE CELESTINA
CALLE UVAS
11700
HERITAGE WY
MERRIMAN LN
12100
HERITAGE WY
OLD OLD COACH RD
CREEK RD
3300
RIVERBANK RD
CALLE SOMA WY
CIELO
WATSONVILLE RD
CREEK
G8
WATSONVILLE RD
UVAS
RANCHO SOLIS
RESERVOIR
POLI RD
RETREAT
5300
RD
REDWOOD
REDWOOD
RETREAT
RD
VIGNOBLE DR
CREEK
LITTLE
ARTHUR
9900
UNDERWOOD CT
BURCHELL RD
3400
9500
EL MATADOR DR
95020
SEE 957 MAP
SEE 976 MAP
0 .125 .25 .375 .5 miles 1 in. = 1900 ft.

SEE 937 MAP

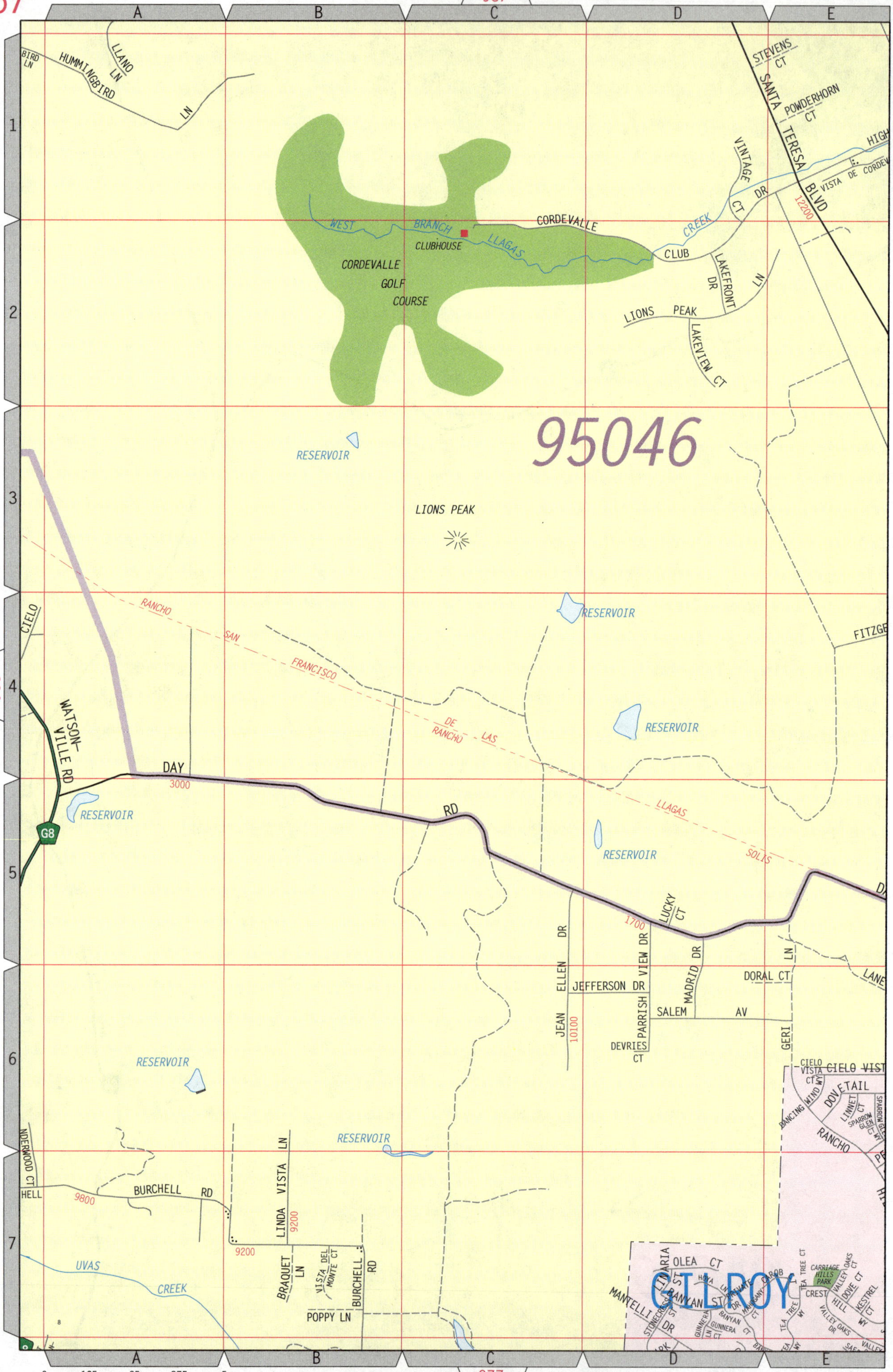

SEE 956 MAP

0 .125 .25 .375 .5 miles 1 in. = 1900 ft.

A B C D E

1

BIRD LN
HUMMINGBIRD LN
LLANO LN

STEVENS CT
SANTA TERESA BLVD
POWDERHORN CT
VINTAGE DR CT
VISTA DE CORDEV
12200

WEST BRANCH LLAGAS
CORDEVALLE
CLUBHOUSE
CORDEVALLE GOLF COURSE
CLUB
CREEK
LAKEFRONT DR
LAKEVIEW CT
LIONS PEAK
LN

2

RESERVOIR

95046

3

LIONS PEAK

RESERVOIR

FITZGE

CIELO
RANCHO SAN FRANCISCO
DE RANCHO LAS

RESERVOIR

4

WATSON-VILLE RD
DAY
3000
RESERVOIR
G8

RESERVOIR

RD
LLAGAS SOLIS
RESERVOIR
LUCKY CT
1700
DA

5

ELLEN DR
JEAN
10100
JEFFERSON DR
PARRISH VIEW DR
DEVRIES CT
SALEM AV
MADRID DR
DORAL CT
GERI
LANE

6

RESERVOIR

CIELO VISTA
VISTA CIELO VIST
DOVETAIL
DANCING WIND
LINNET
SPARROW GLEN
RANCHO
CT

NDERWOOD CT
HELL
9800
BURCHELL RD
LINDA VISTA LN
9200
RESERVOIR

7

UVAS CREEK
BRAQUET LN
VISTA DEL MONTE CT
BURCHELL RD
9200
POPPY LN

OLEA CT
CARRIAGE HILLS PARK
GILROY
MANTELLI

8

SEE 977 MAP

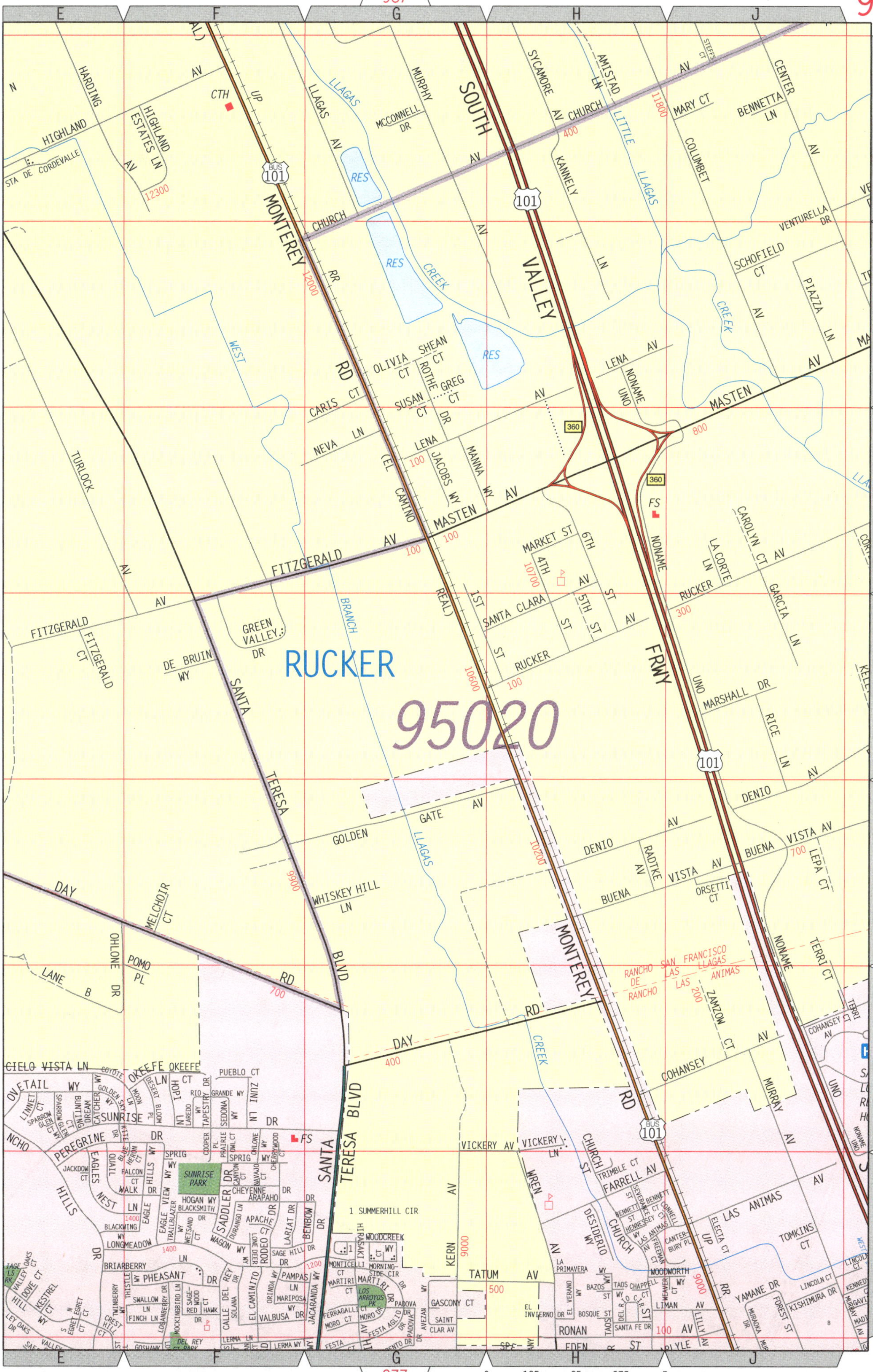
RUCKER
95020
MONTEREY RD
SOUTH VALLEY FRWY
SANTA TERESA BLVD
MASTEN AV
FITZGERALD AV
DAY RD
GOLDEN GATE AV
DENIO AV
BUENA VISTA AV
CHURCH AV
SANTA CLARA CO.
SEE 958 MAP
RANCHO SAN FRANCISCO DE LAS LLAGAS
RANCHO LAS ANIMAS
SUNRISE PARK
© 2008 Rand McNally & Company

SEE 938 MAP

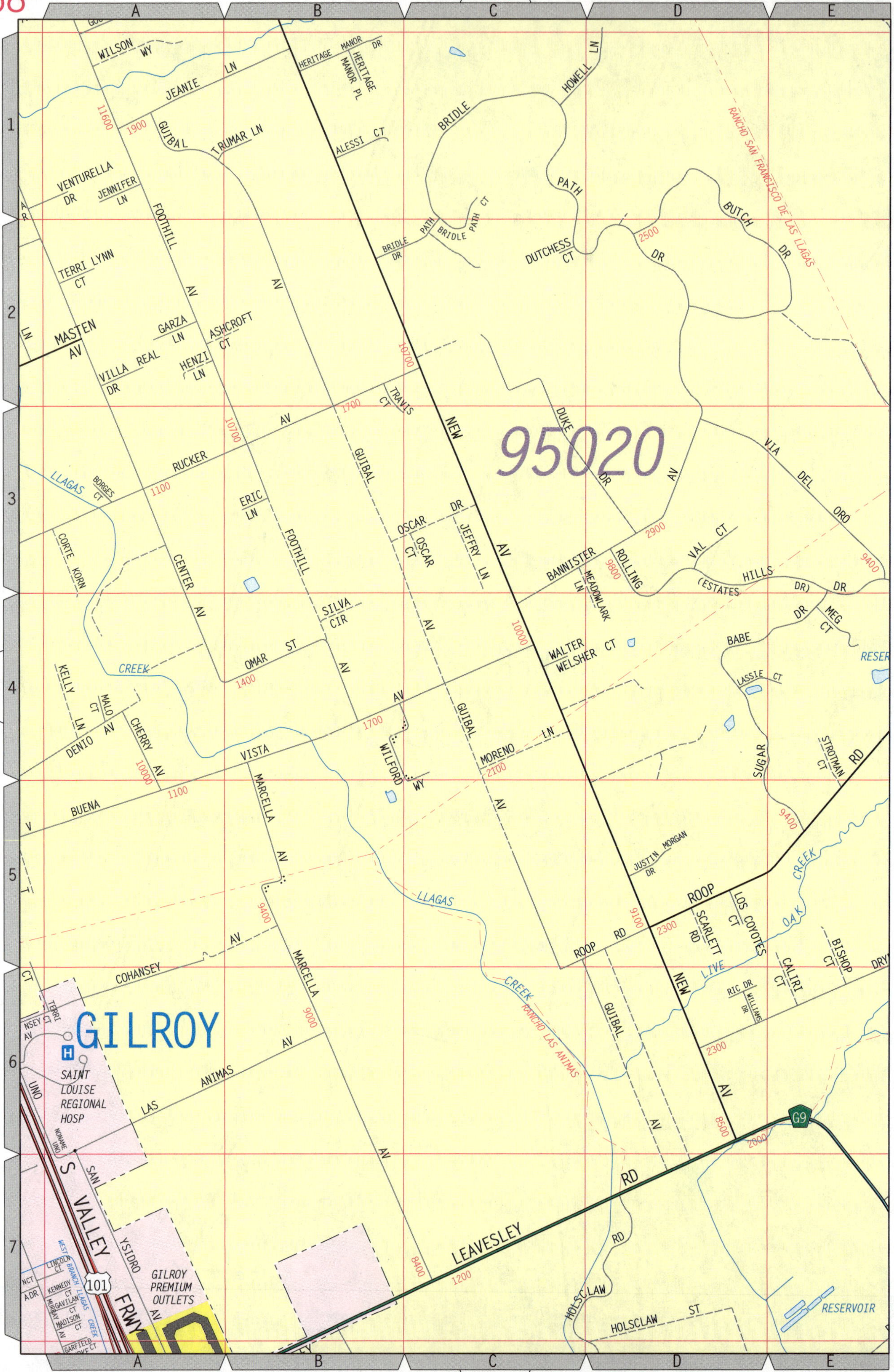

SEE 957 MAP

SEE 978 MAP

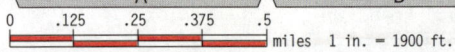

0 .125 .25 .375 .5 miles 1 in. = 1900 ft.

SEE 938 MAP

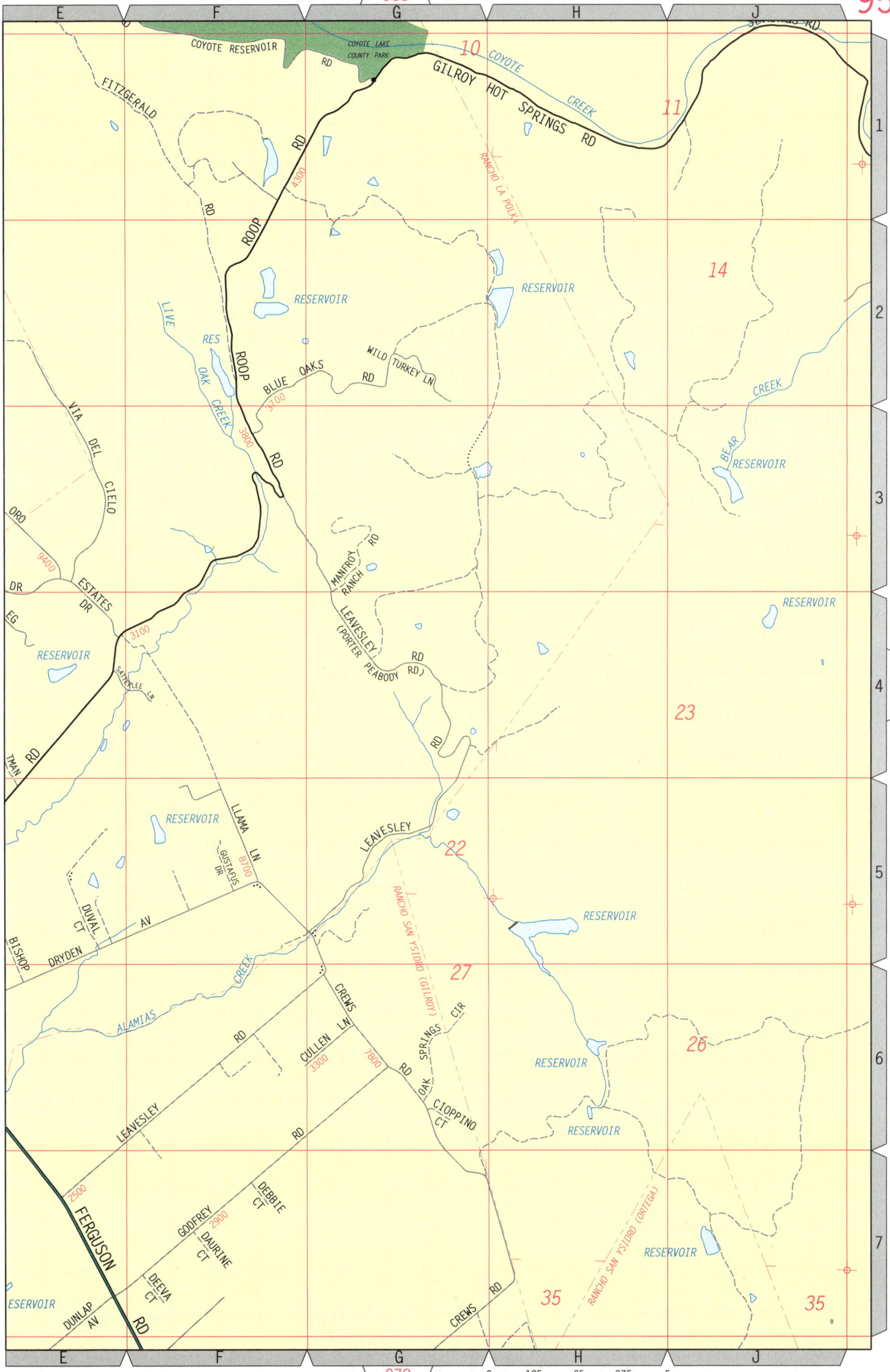

SEE B MAP
SEE 978 MAP

© 2008 Rand McNally & Company

N

COYOTE RESERVOIR

COYOTE LAKE COUNTY PARK

RD

10

COYOTE

GILROY HOT SPRINGS RD

CREEK

11

SPRINGS RD

FITZGERALD

ROOP RD

4300

RANCHO LA POLKA

14

1

LIVE

RES

OAK CREEK

ROOP RD

3700

3800

BLUE OAKS

RESERVOIR

WILD TURKEY LN

RD

RESERVOIR

BEAR

CREEK

RESERVOIR

2

VIA DEL CIELO

ORO

9400

DR

EG

RESERVOIR

ESTATES DR

3100

SATTERLEE LN

MANFRO RANCH RD

LEAVESLEY (PORTER PEABODY RD)

RD

RD

RESERVOIR

3

TMAN RD

RESERVOIR

LLAMA LN

8700

GUSTAFS DR

DUVAL CT

AV

LEAVESLEY

23

22

RESERVOIR

4

BISHOP

DRYDEN

CREEK

ALAMIAS

CREWS

CULLEN LN

3300

RD

7800

RD

RANCHO SAN YSIDRO (GILROY)

OAK SPRINGS CIR

27

RESERVOIR

26

5

6

LEAVESLEY

RD

CIOPPINO CT

RESERVOIR

DEBBIE CT

GODFREY CT

2900

DAURINE CT

FERGUSON

2500

DEEVA CT

ESERVOIR

DUNLAP AV

RD

CREWS RD

CREWS RD

35

RANCHO SAN YSIDRO (ORTEGA)

RESERVOIR

35

7

0 .125 .25 .375 .5 miles 1 in. = 1900 ft.

E F G H J

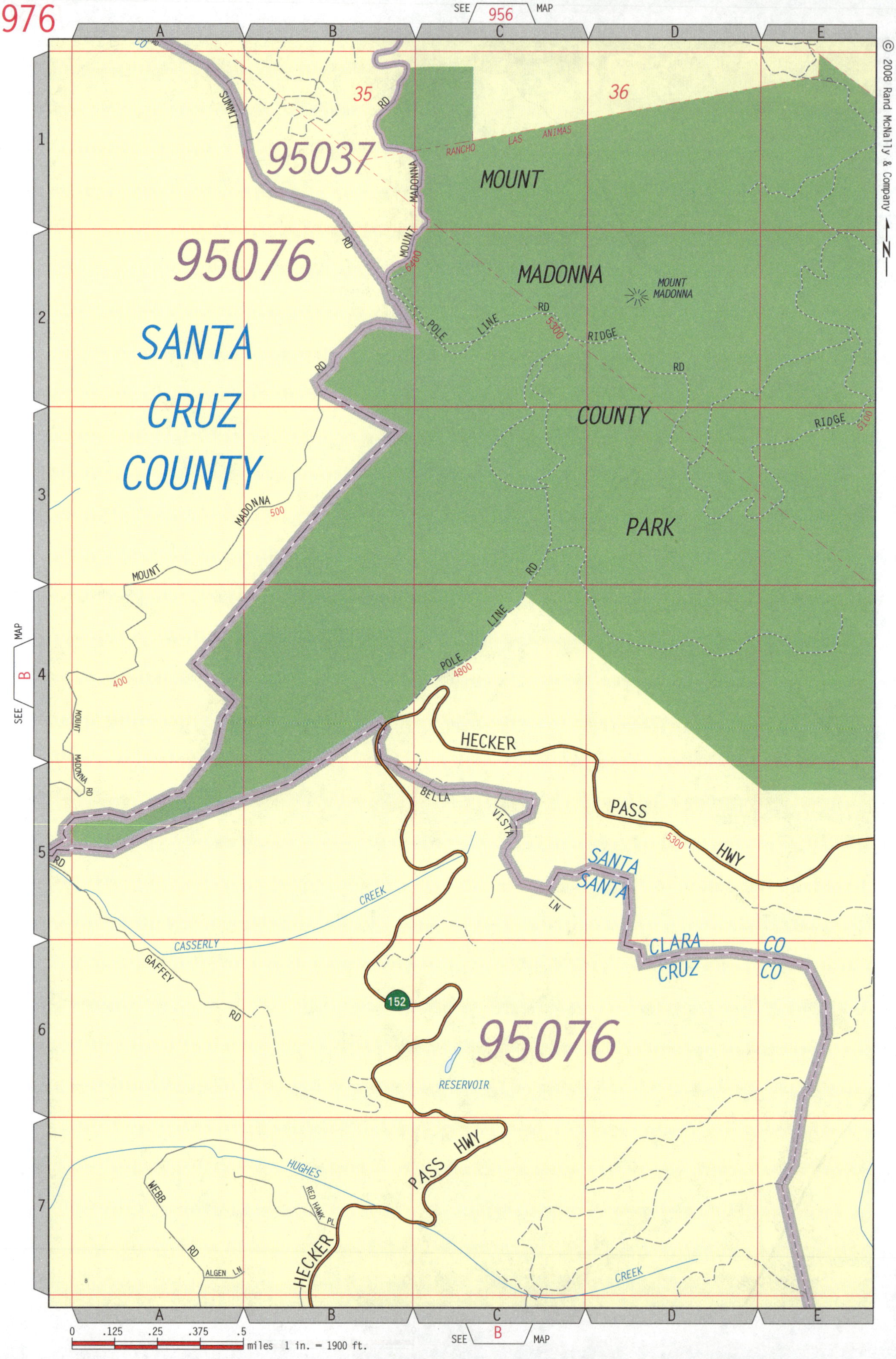
SEE 956 MAP
SEE B MAP
SEE B MAP
A
B
C
D
E
1
2
3
4
5
6
7
95037
95076
95076
SANTA CRUZ COUNTY
MOUNT MADONNA COUNTY PARK
MOUNT MADONNA
35
36
RANCHO LAS ANIMAS
SUMMIT RD
MOUNT MADONNA RD
POLE LINE RD
RIDGE RD
HECKER PASS HWY
152
BELLA VISTA LN
SANTA CLARA CO
SANTA CRUZ CO
CASSERLY CREEK
GAFFEY RD
RESERVOIR
HUGHES CREEK
WEBB RD
RED HAWK PL
ALGEN LN
6400
5300
5100
4800
500
400
0 .125 .25 .375 .5
miles 1 in. = 1900 ft.

SEE 956 MAP

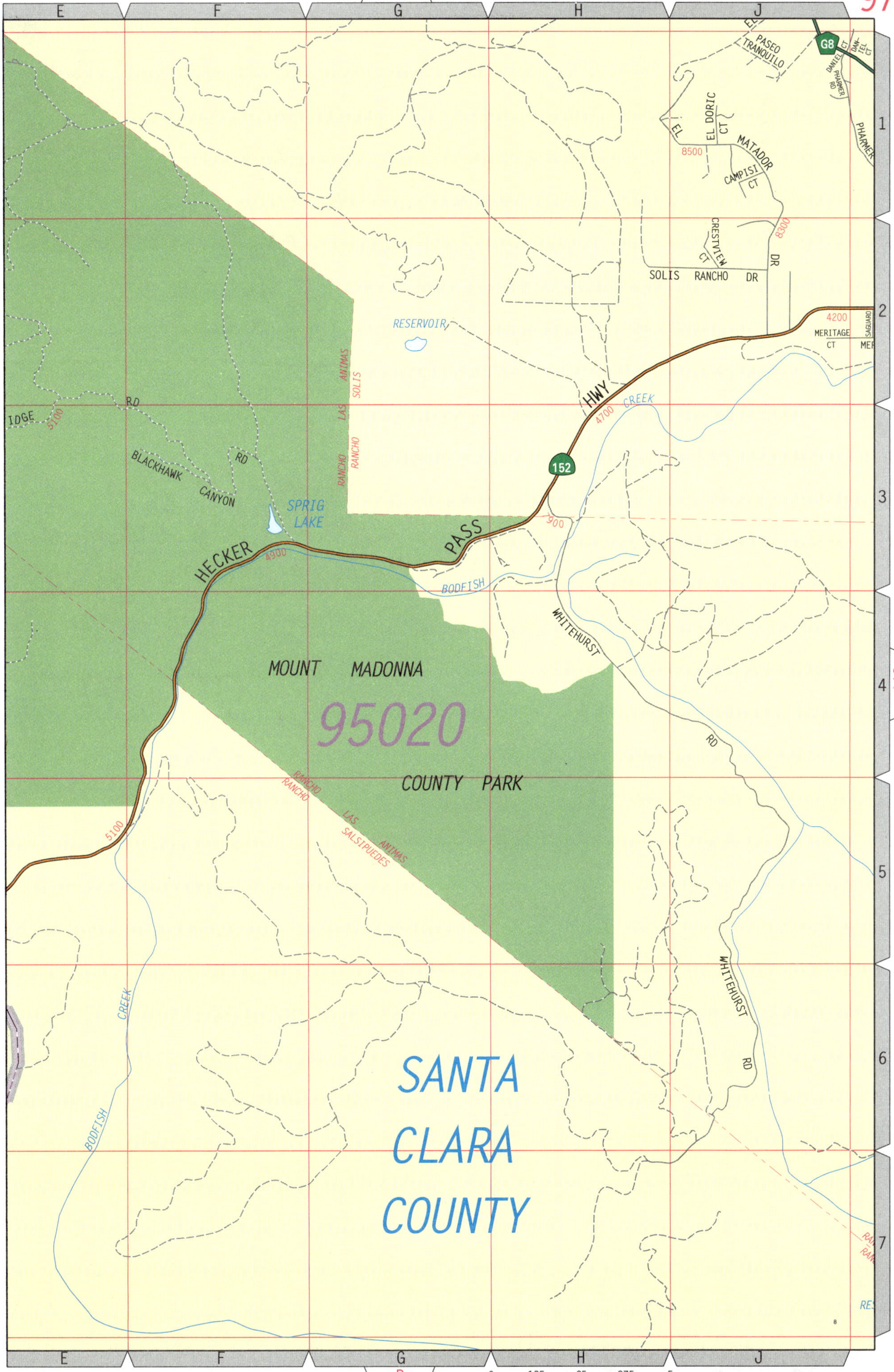

SEE 977 MAP
SEE B MAP
0 .125 .25 .375 .5 miles 1 in. = 1900 ft.

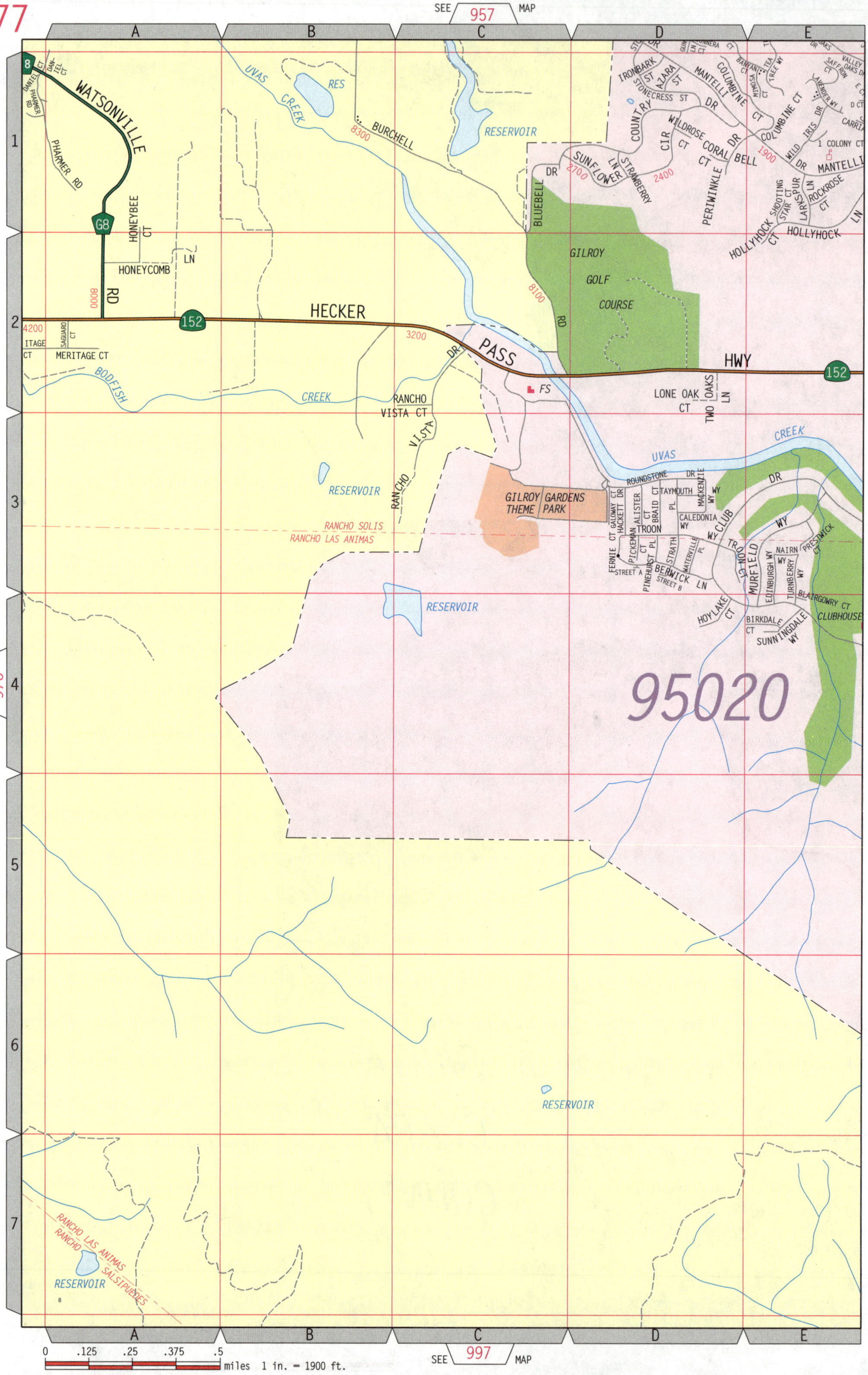
SEE 957 MAP
SEE 997 MAP
SEE 976 MAP
A
B
C
D
E
1
2
3
4
5
6
7
WATSONVILLE
RD
G8
PHARMER RD
HONEYBEE CT
HONEYCOMB
LN
8000
HECKER
PASS
HWY
152
4200
3200
MERITAGE CT
BODFISH
CREEK
UVAS
CREEK
RES
BURCHELL
8300
RESERVOIR
BLUEBELL
DR
8100
RD
GILROY
GOLF
COURSE
IRONBARK
ST
AZARA
STONECRESS ST
COUNTRY
CIR
WILDROSE
CT
CORAL
DR
BELL
SUNFLOWER
LN
STRAWBERRY
2700
2400
1900
PERIWINKLE
COLUMBINE
MANTELLI
DR
HOLLYHOCK
SHOOTING STAR CT
LARKSPUR
ROCKROSE
FS
LONE OAK CT
TWO OAKS LN
RANCHO VISTA CT
VISTA
RANCHO
GILROY GARDENS THEME PARK
ROUNDSTONE
TAYMOUTH
CALEDONIA WY
TROON
CLUB
MURFIELD
EDINBURGH WY
NAIRN
PRESTWICK
BERWICK LN
HOYLAKE CT
BIRKDALE CT
SUNNINGDALE WY
CLUBHOUSE
RANCHO SOLIS
RANCHO LAS ANIMAS
RANCHO SALSIPUEDES
95020
0
.125
.25
.375
.5
miles 1 in. = 1900 ft.

SEE 957 MAP

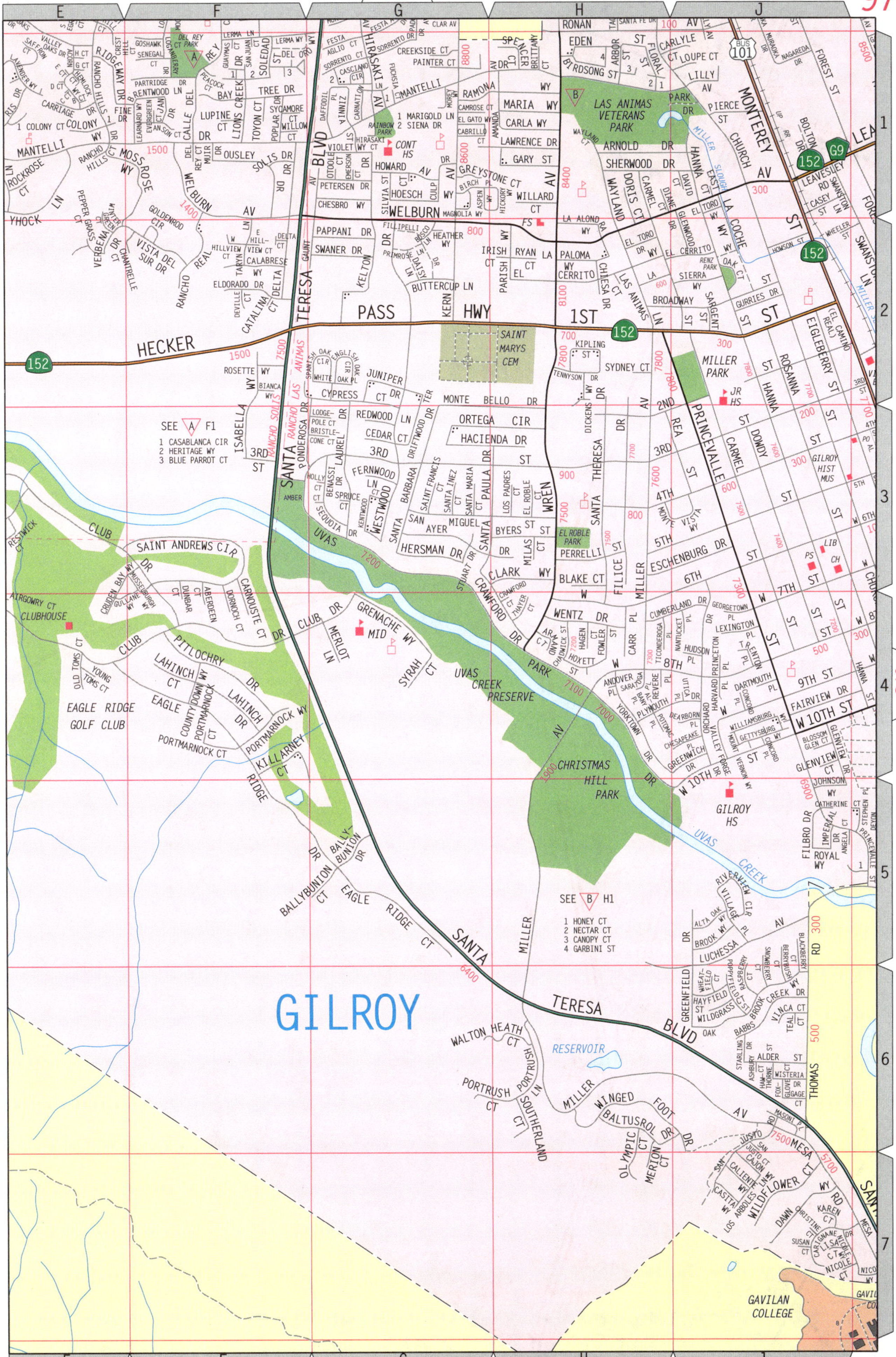

SEE 978 MAP

SEE 997 MAP

0 .125 .25 .375 .5 miles 1 in. = 1900 ft.

SEE 958 MAP

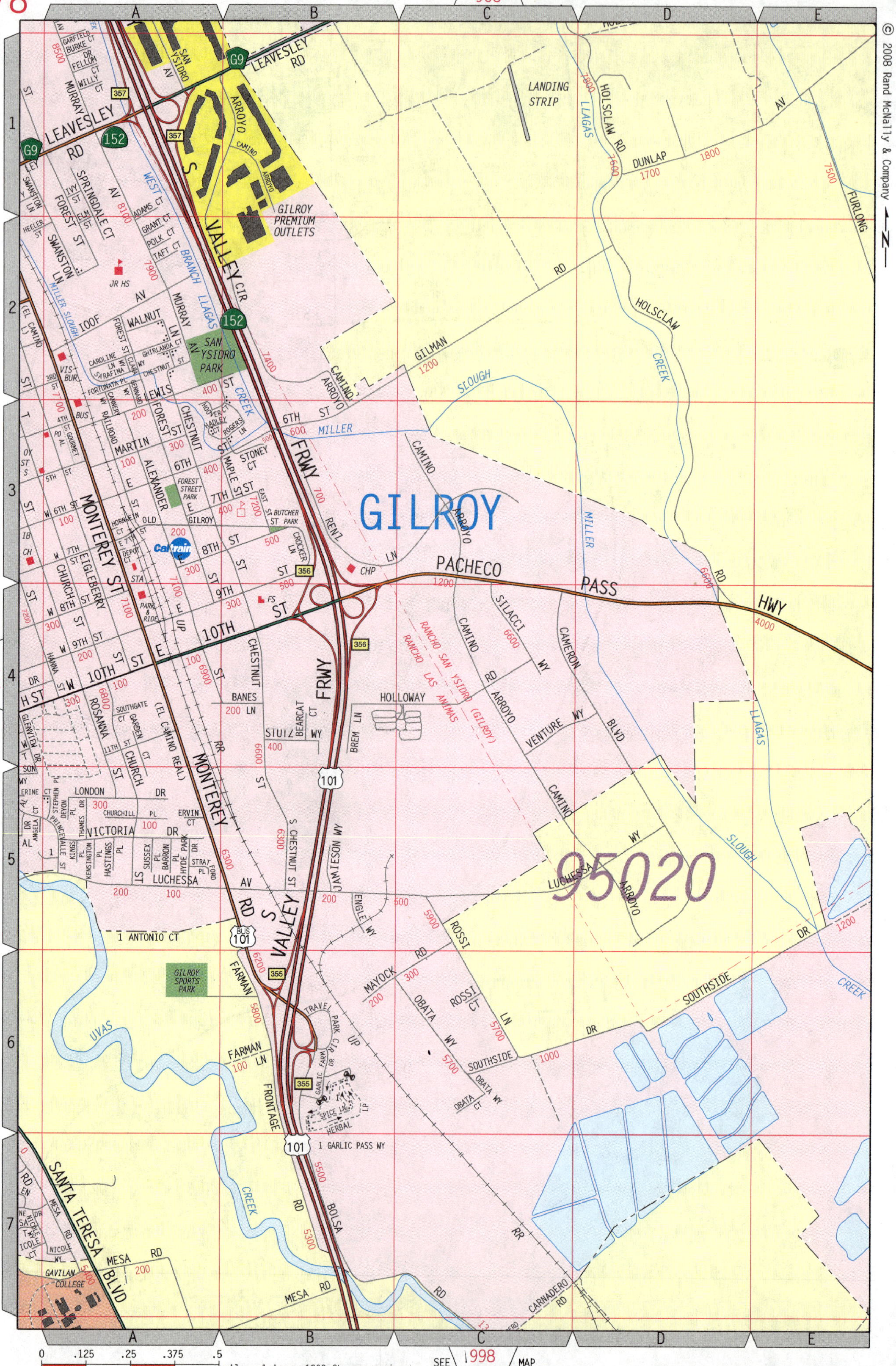

SEE 977 MAP

SEE 998 MAP

0 .125 .25 .375 .5
miles 1 in. = 1900 ft.

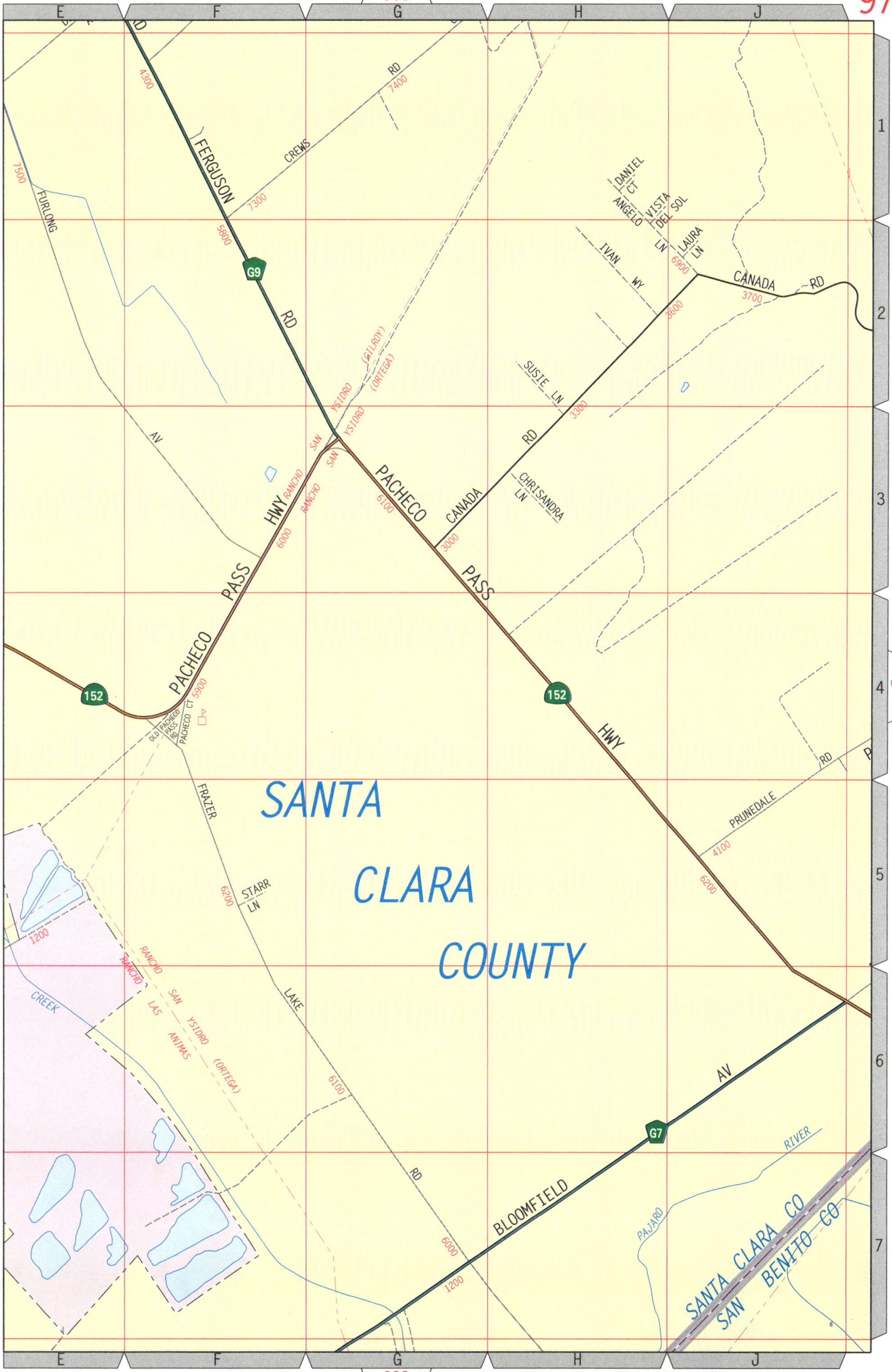
SEE 958 MAP
E
F
G
H
J
1
2
3
4
5
6
7
SANTA CLARA CO.
FERGUSON
RD
CREWS
RD
FURLONG
AV
G9
DANIEL CT
ANGELO LN
VISTA DEL SOL
LAURA LN
IVAN WY
CANADA RD
SUSIE LN
CHRISANDRA LN
CANADA RD
PACHECO PASS HWY
RANCHO SAN YSIDRO
(GILROY)
(ORTEGA)
152
OLD PACHECO PASS RD
PACHECO CT
FRAZER LAKE RD
STARR LN
PRUNEDALE RD
SANTA CLARA COUNTY
CREEK
RANCHO LAS ANIMAS
RANCHO SAN YSIDRO (ORTEGA)
BLOOMFIELD AV
G7
PAJARO RIVER
SANTA CLARA CO
SAN BENITO CO
SEE B MAP
SEE 998 MAP
0 .125 .25 .375 .5 miles 1 in. = 1900 ft.

SEE 977 MAP

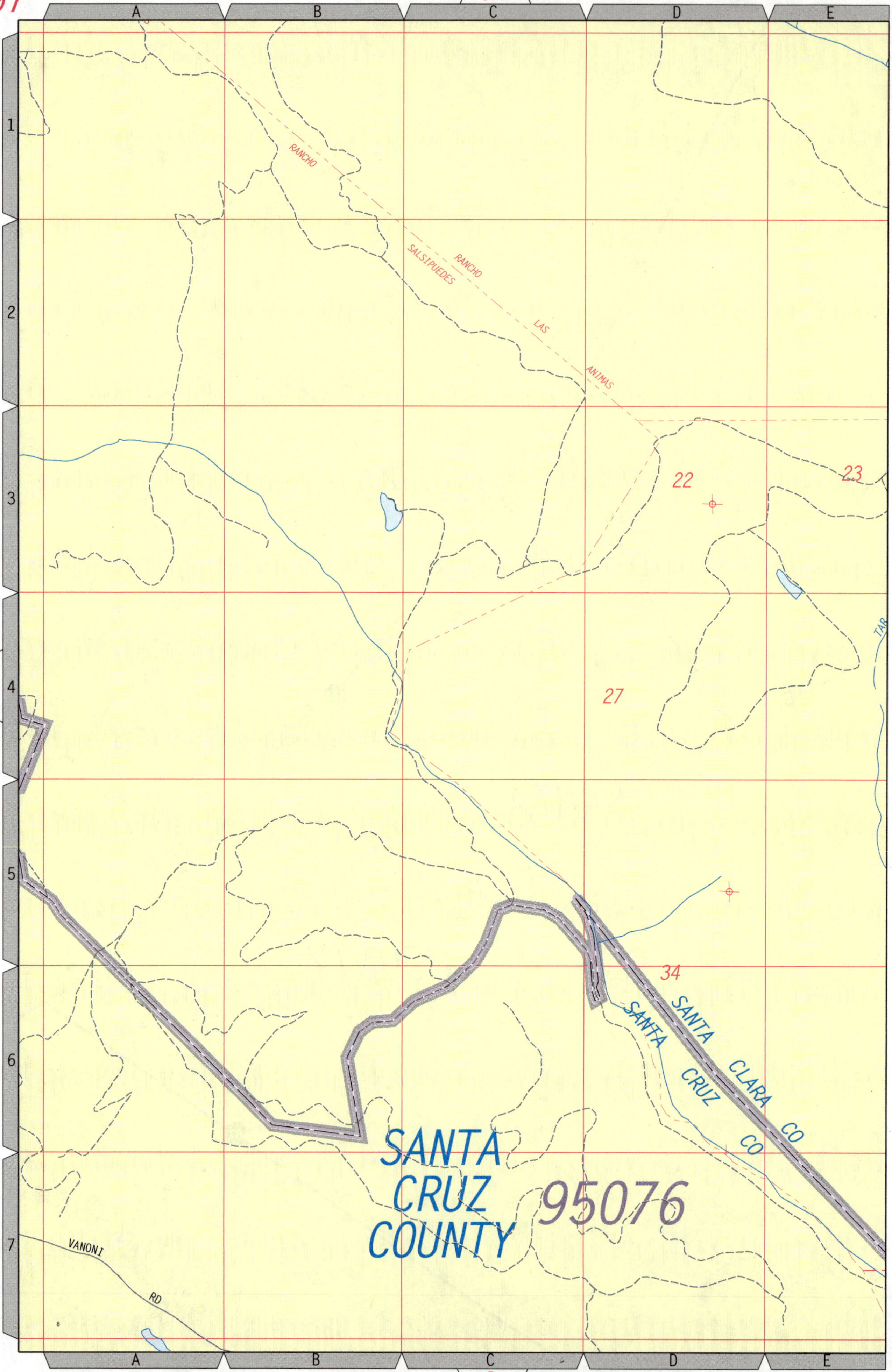

SEE B MAP

SEE B MAP

0 .125 .25 .375 .5 miles 1 in. = 1900 ft.

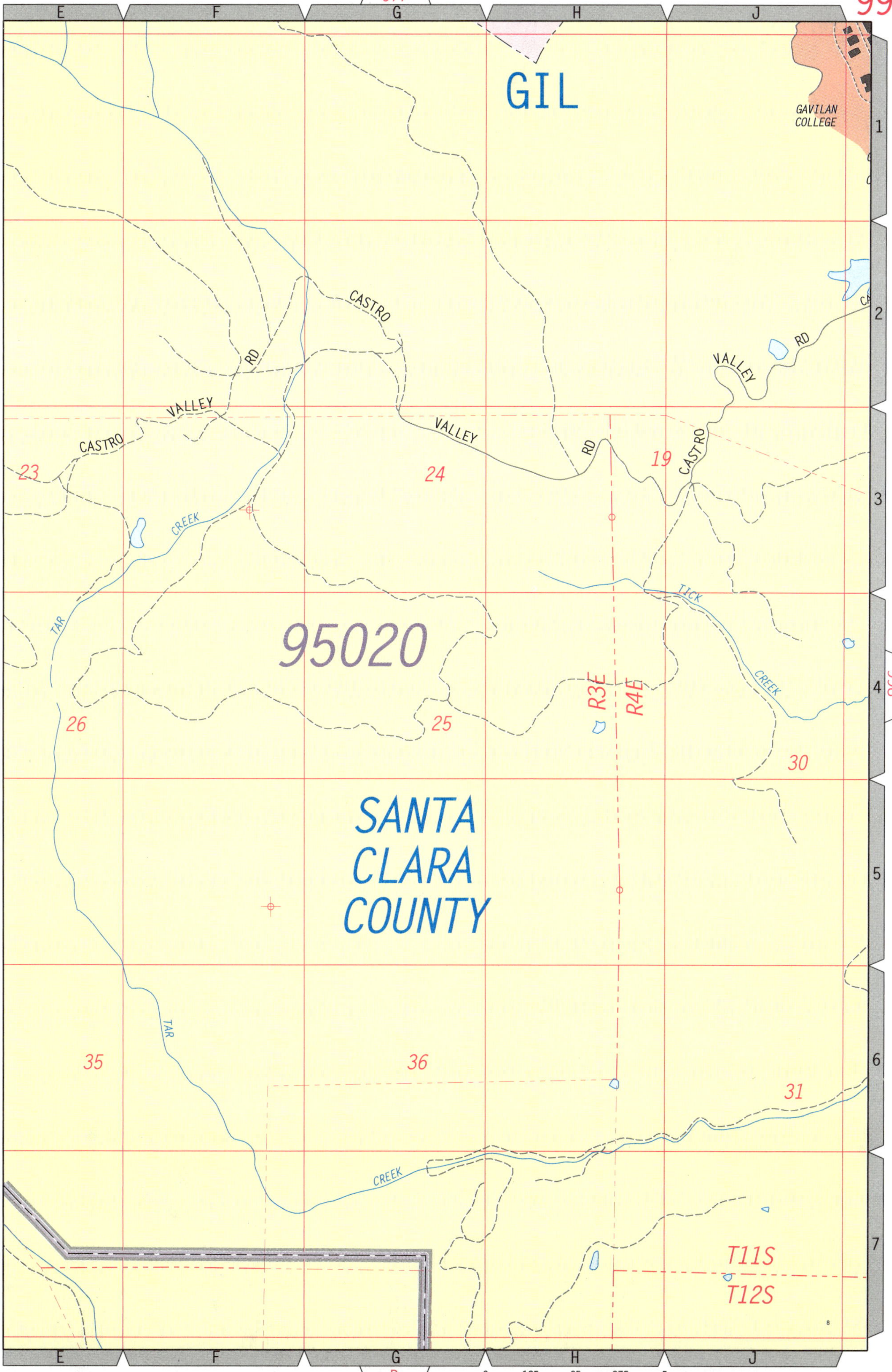
SEE 977 MAP
E
F
G
H
J
GIL
GAVILAN
COLLEGE
CASTRO
RD
VALLEY
CASTRO
VALLEY
RD
19
CASTRO
VALLEY
RD
CA
23
24
CREEK
TAR
95020
TICK
CREEK
R3E
R4E
26
25
30
SEE 998 MAP
SANTA
CLARA
COUNTY
TAR
35
36
31
CREEK
T11S
T12S
1
2
3
4
5
6
7
SEE B MAP
0 .125 .25 .375 .5
miles 1 in. = 1900 ft.
SANTA CLARA CO.

SEE 978 MAP

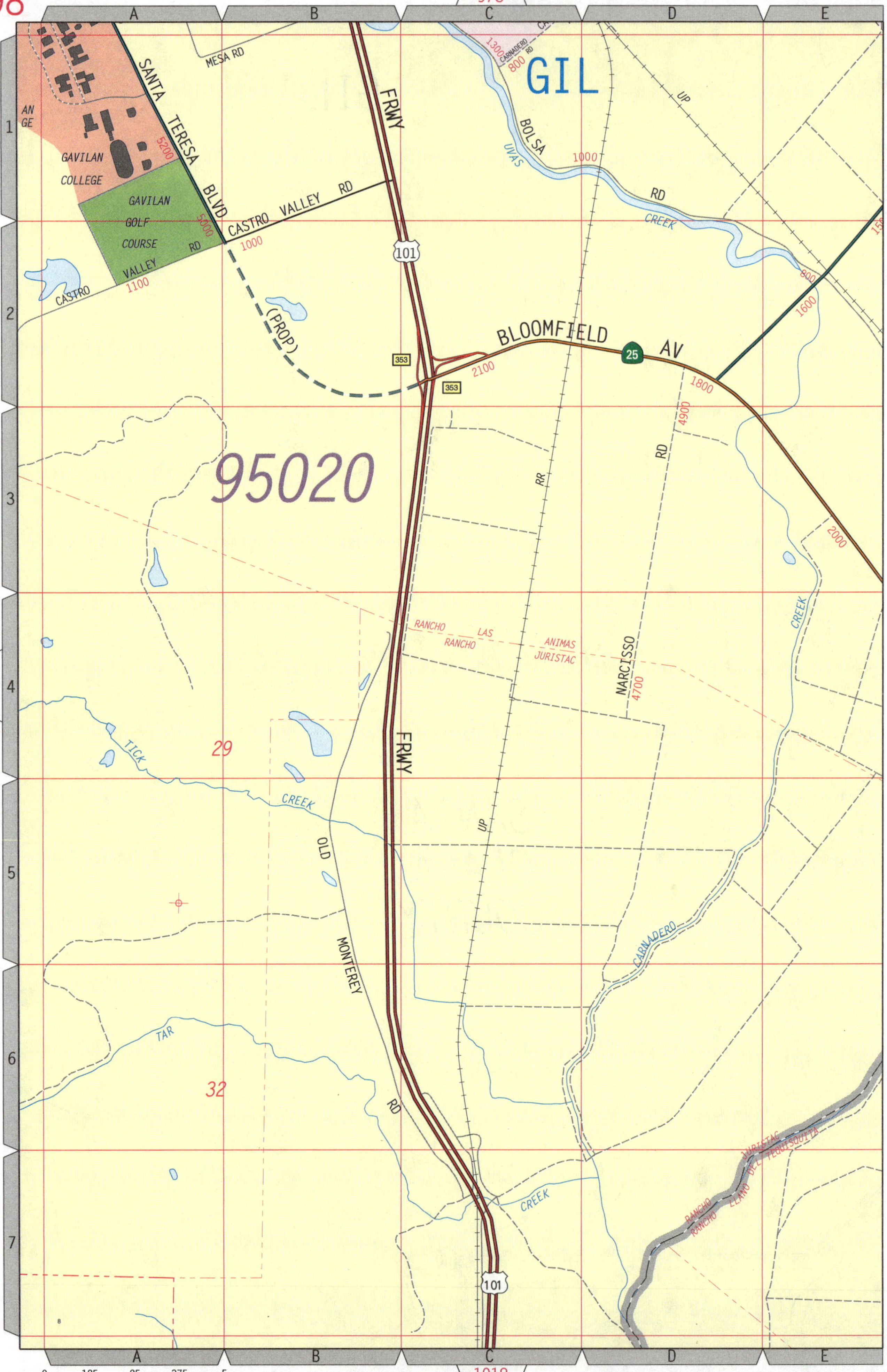

SEE 997 MAP

SEE 1018 MAP

0 .125 .25 .375 .5 miles 1 in. = 1900 ft.

SEE 978 MAP

SANTA CLARA CO.

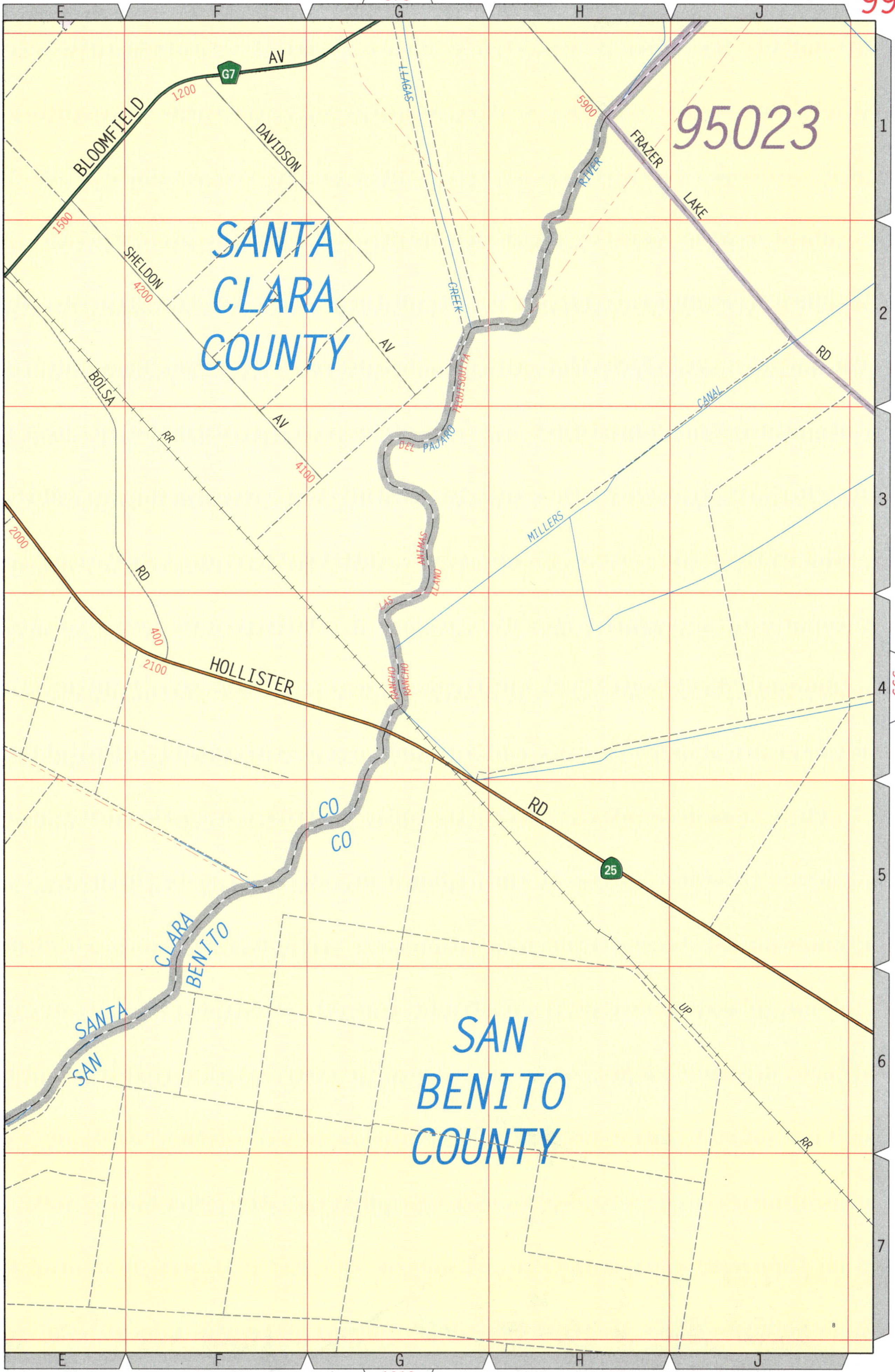

SEE 999 MAP

SEE 1018 MAP

0 .125 .25 .375 .5 miles 1 in. = 1900 ft.

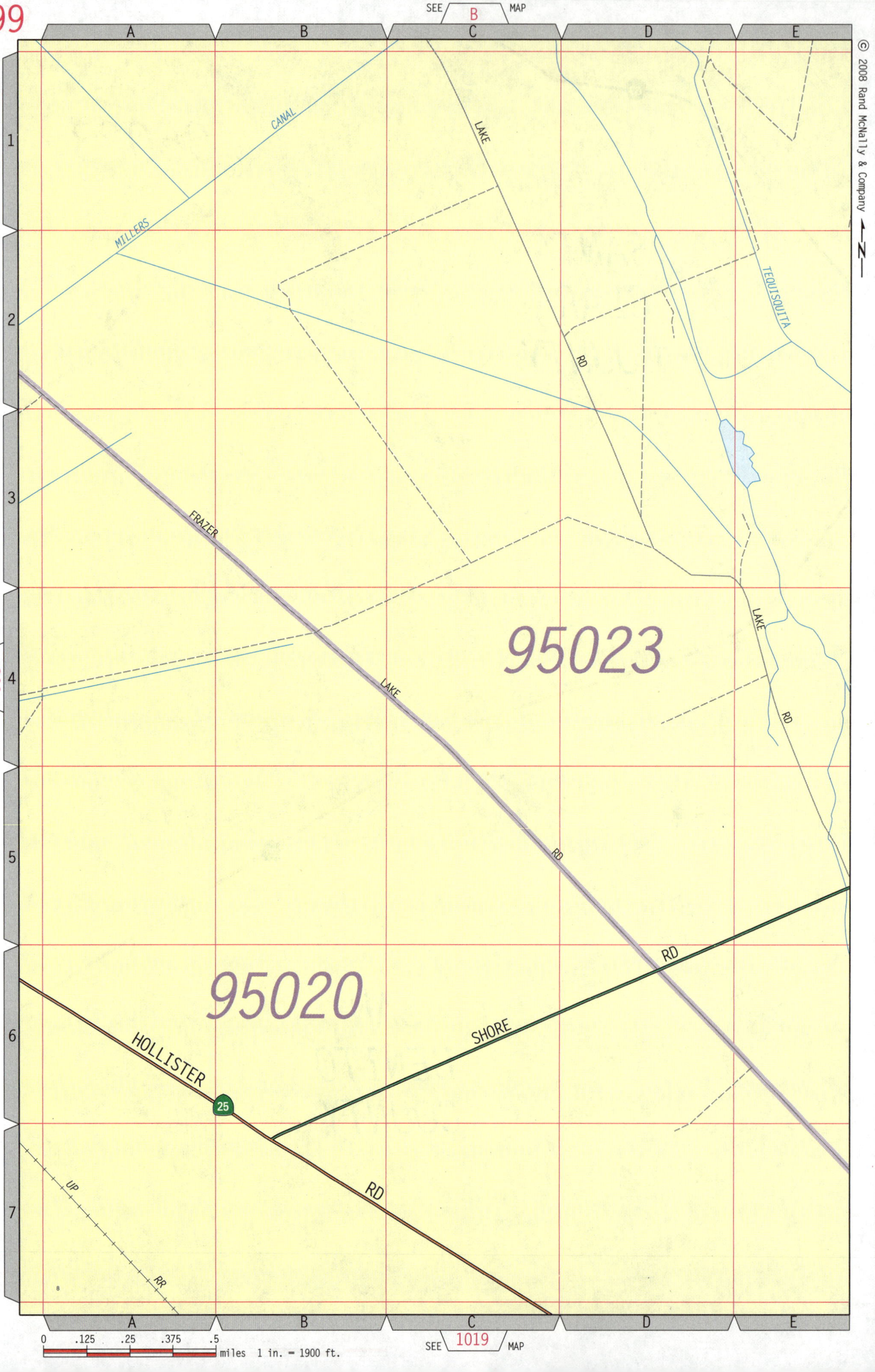
SANTA CLARA CO.
SEE B MAP
A
B
C
D
E
1
2
3
4
5
6
7
SEE 998 MAP
SEE 1019 MAP
MILLERS
CANAL
LAKE
RD
TEQUISQUITA
FRAZER
LAKE
RD
LAKE
RD
95023
95020
HOLLISTER
RD
25
SHORE
RD
UP
RR
0 .125 .25 .375 .5
miles 1 in. = 1900 ft.

SEE B MAP

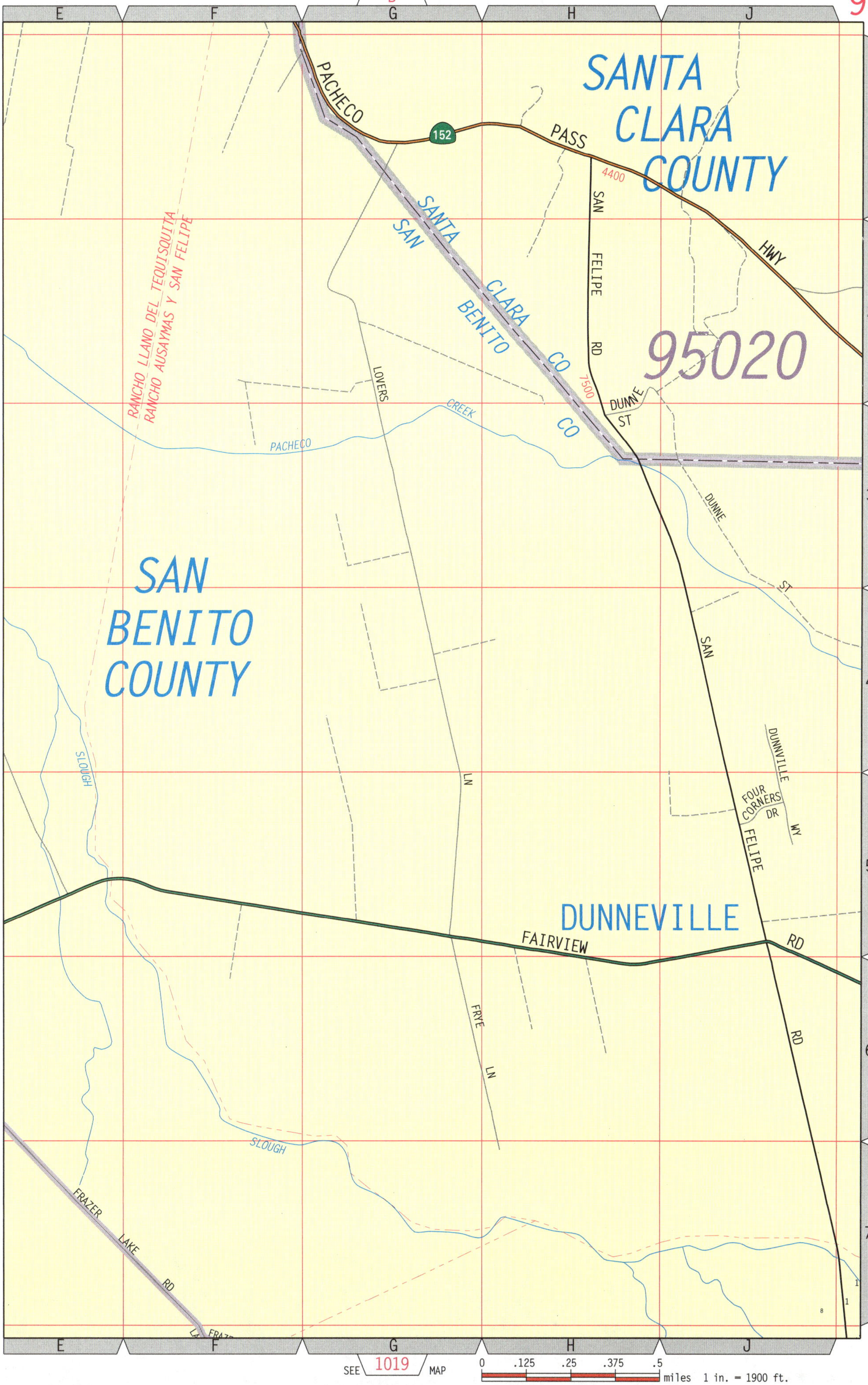
SANTA CLARA COUNTY
SAN BENITO COUNTY
95020
DUNNEVILLE
PACHECO PASS HWY
152
4400
SAN FELIPE RD
7500
SANTA CLARA CO
SAN BENITO CO
DUNNE ST
LOVERS LN
PACHECO CREEK
RANCHO LLANO DEL TEQUESQUITA
RANCHO AUSAYMAS Y SAN FELIPE
SLOUGH
FOUR CORNERS DR
DUNNVILLE WY
FAIRVIEW RD
FRYE LN
FRAZER LAKE RD
E F G H J
1 2 3 4 5 6 7
0 .125 .25 .375 .5 miles 1 in. = 1900 ft.

SEE 1000 MAP

SEE 1019 MAP

SEE B MAP

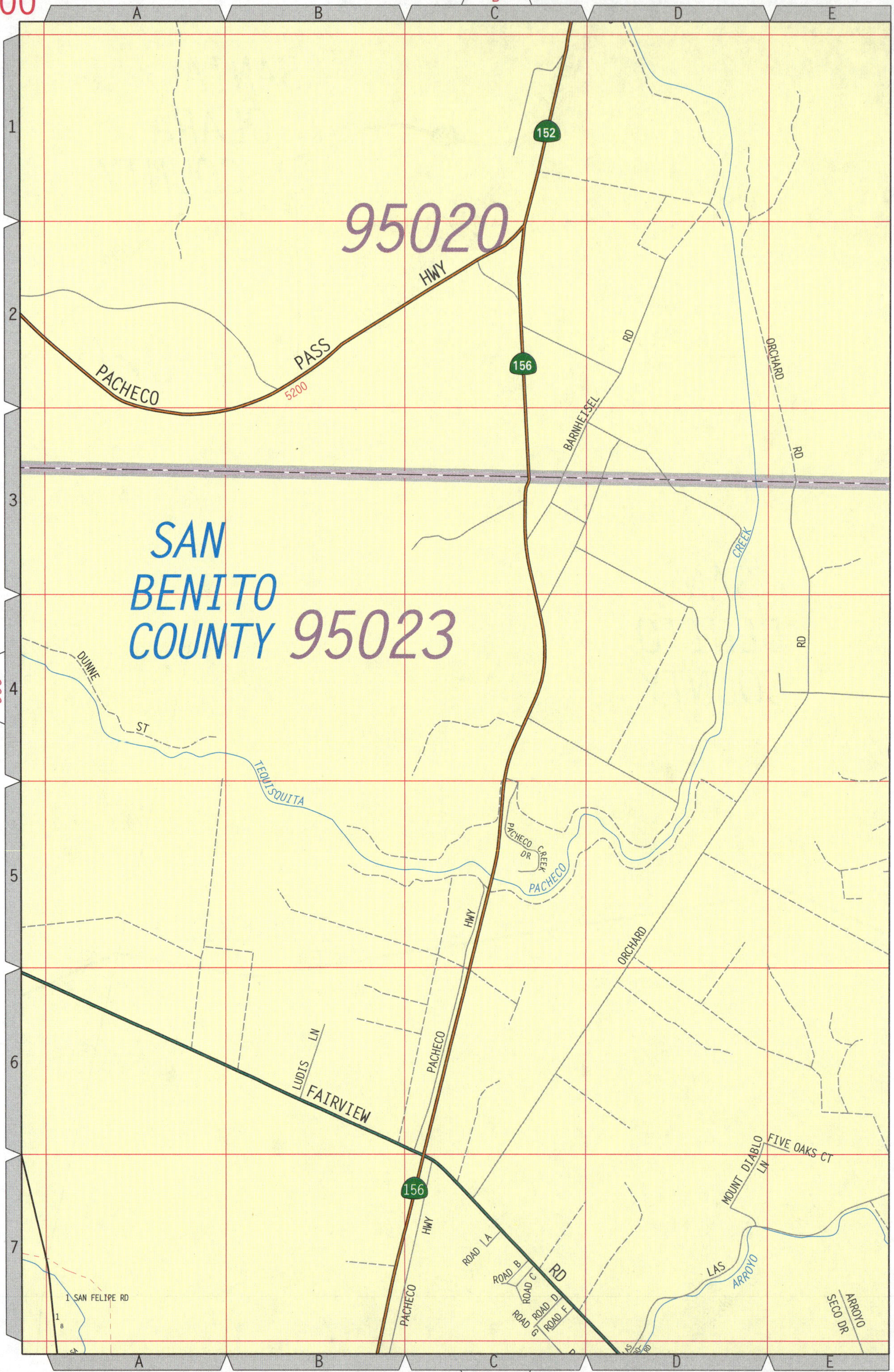

SEE 999 MAP

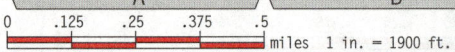

SEE 1020 MAP

0 .125 .25 .375 .5 miles 1 in. = 1900 ft.

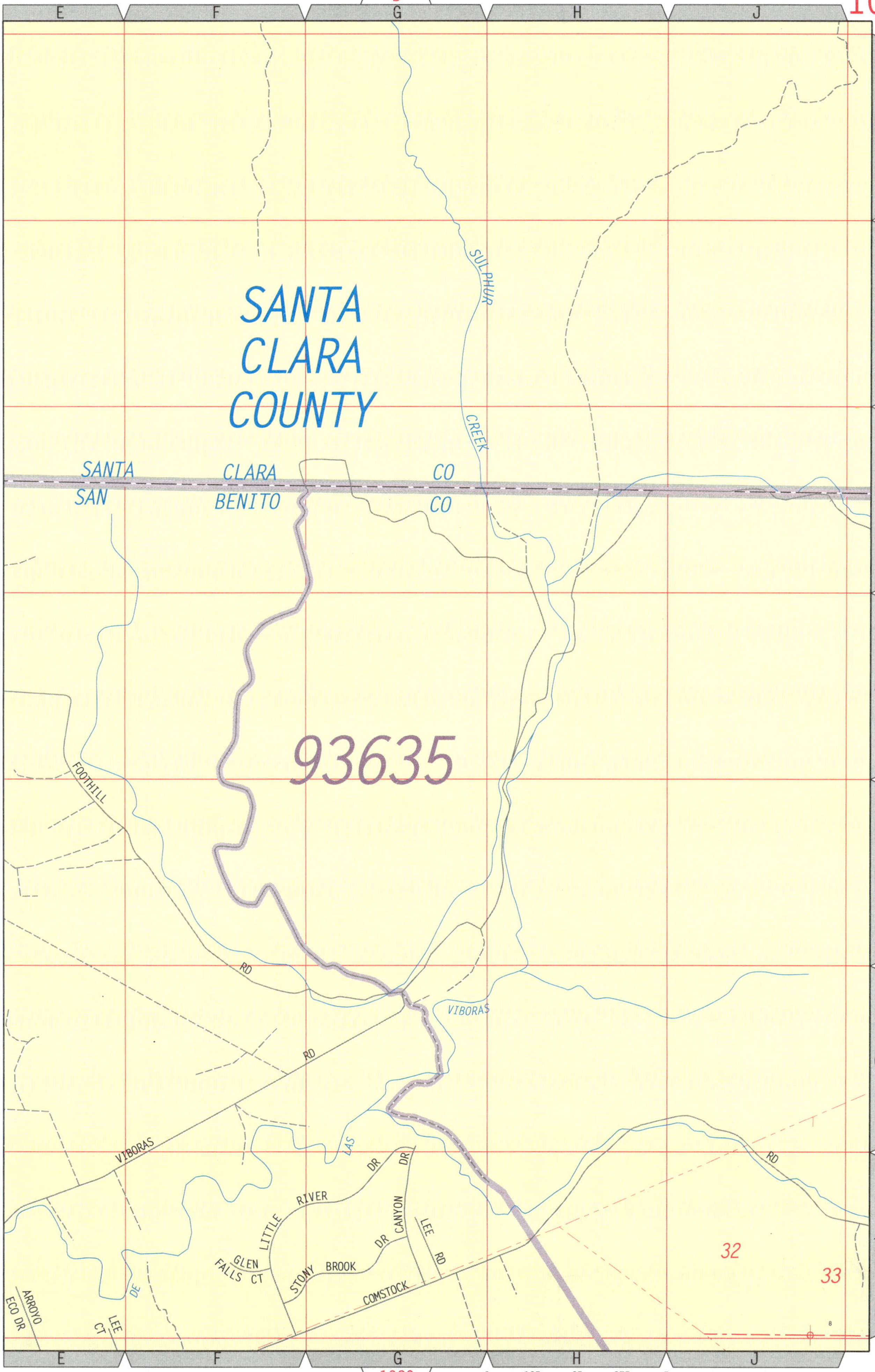
SEE B MAP
E
F
G
H
J
1
2
3
4
5
6
7
SEE B MAP
SANTA CLARA COUNTY
SULPHUR
CREEK
SANTA
SAN
CLARA
BENITO
CO
CO
93635
FOOTHILL
RD
VIBORAS
RD
VIBORAS
LAS
RD
RIVER
DR
DR
LITTLE
CANYON
LEE
RD
DR
GLEN
FALLS CT
STONY
BROOK
COMSTOCK
ARROYO
ECO DR
LEE
CT
DE
32
33
SEE 1020 MAP
0 .125 .25 .375 .5
miles 1 in. = 1900 ft.
N

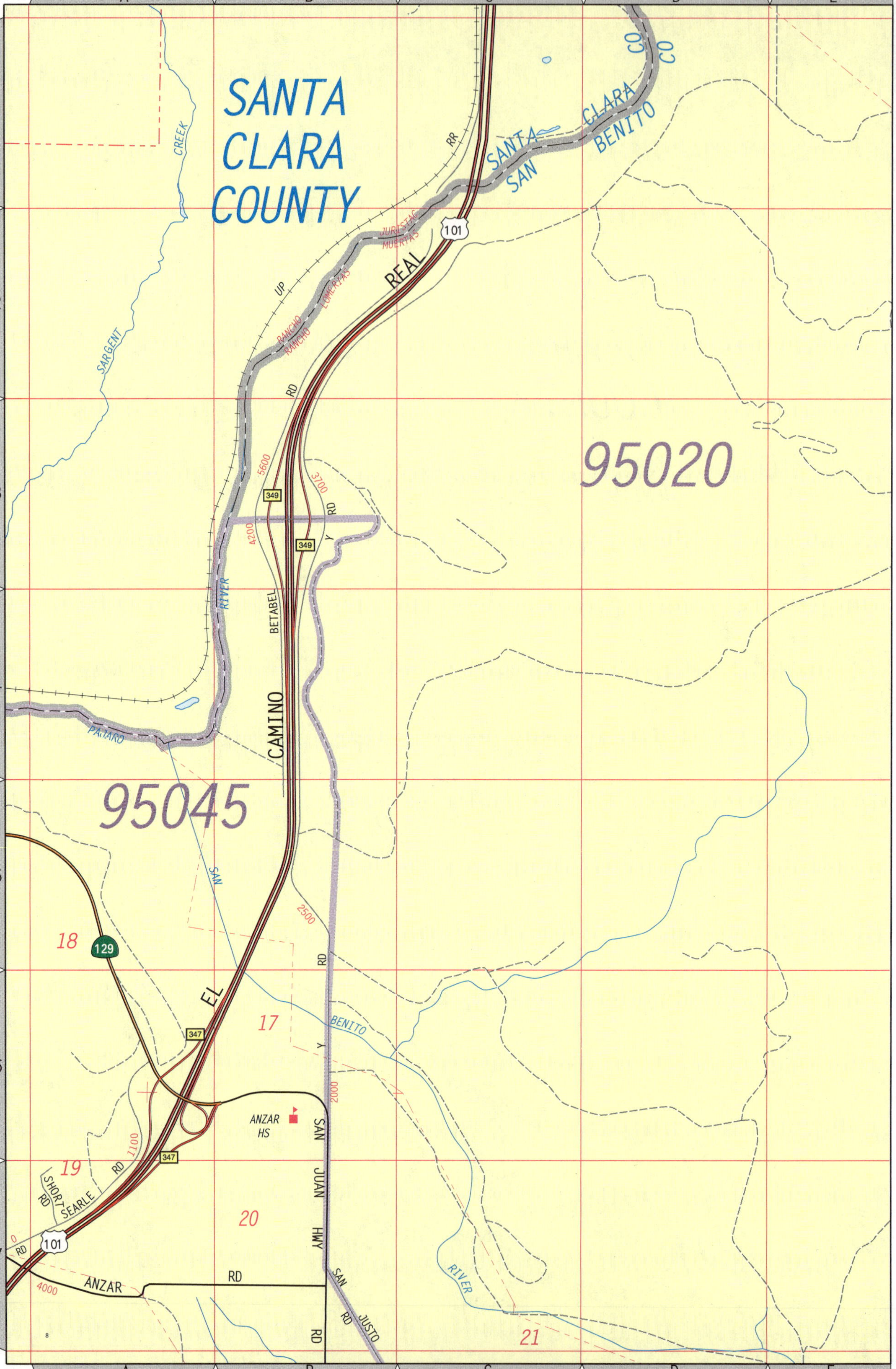

A B C D E
1 2 3 4 5 6 7

0 .125 .25 .375 .5 miles 1 in. = 1900 ft.

SEE 1038 MAP

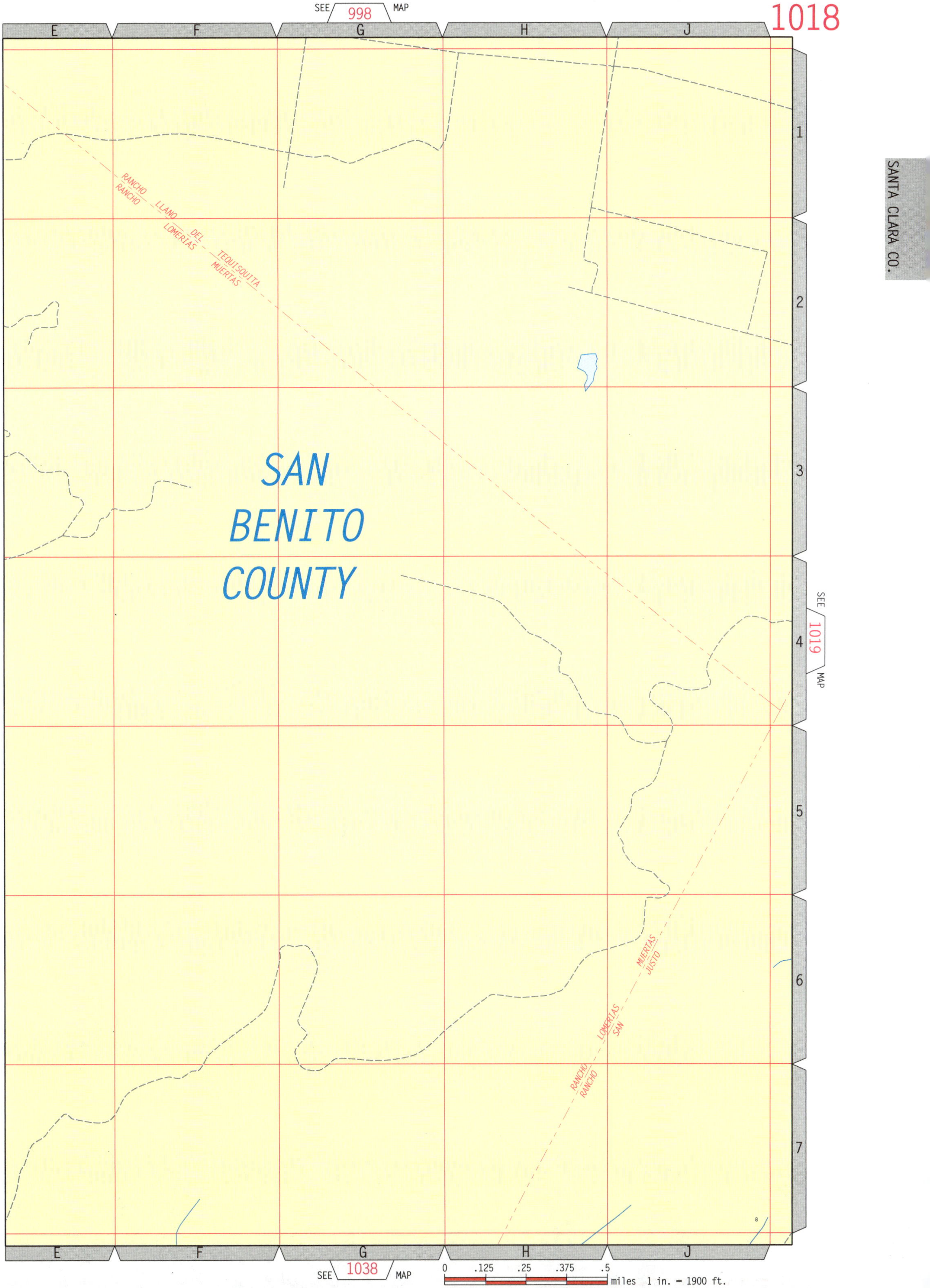
SEE 998 MAP
E
F
G
H
J
1
2
3
4
5
6
7
SEE 1019 MAP
RANCHO LLANO DEL TEQUISQUITA
RANCHO LOMERIAS MUERTAS
SAN BENITO COUNTY
RANCHO LOMERIAS MUERTAS
RANCHO SAN JUSTO
SEE 1038 MAP
SANTA CLARA CO.
0 .125 .25 .375 .5 miles 1 in. = 1900 ft.

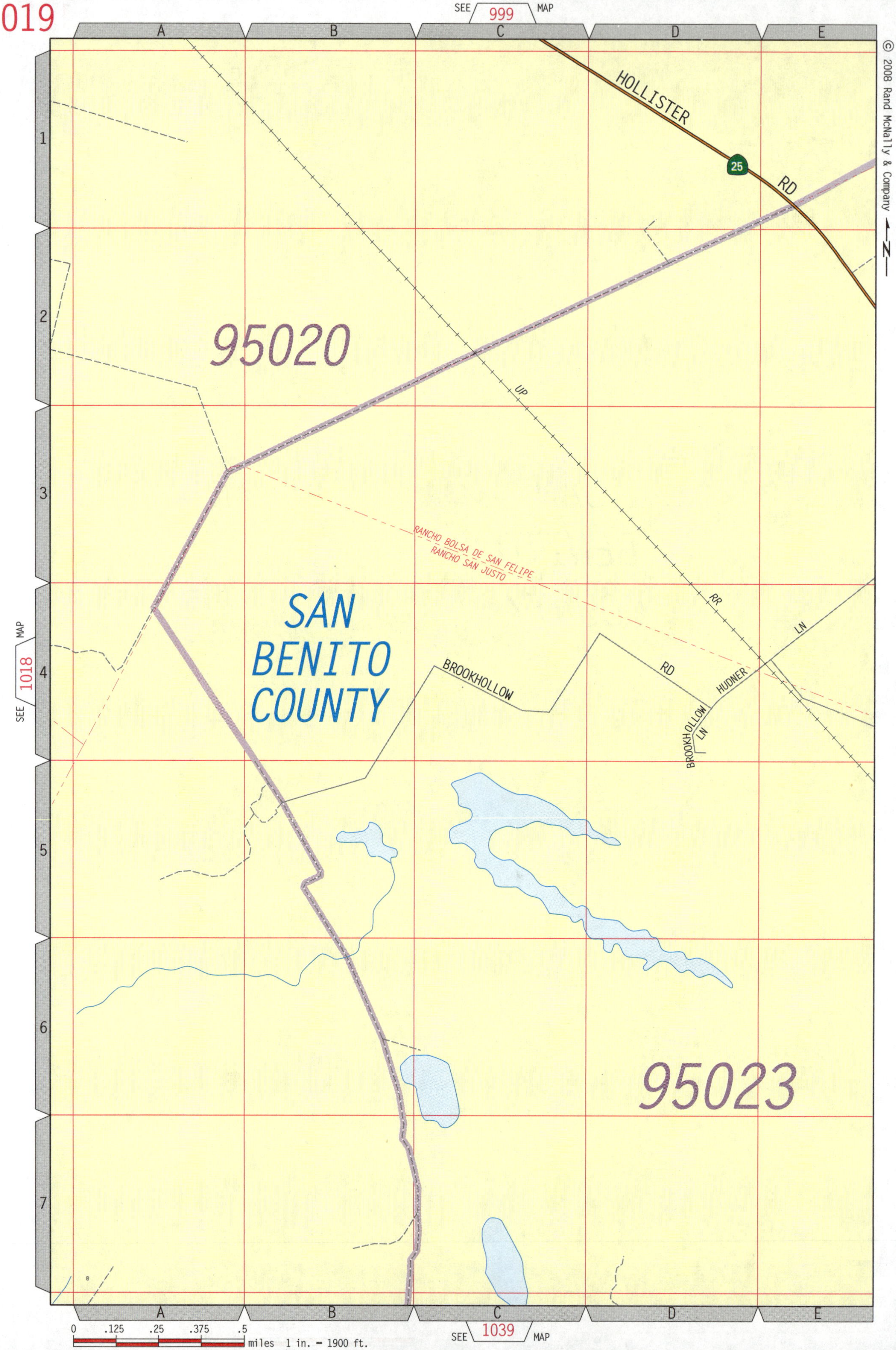
SEE 999 MAP
A
B
C
D
E
1
2
3
4
5
6
7
SANTA CLARA CO.
SEE 1018 MAP
HOLLISTER
25
RD
95020
UP
RANCHO BOLSA DE SAN FELIPE
RANCHO SAN JUSTO
RR
SAN BENITO COUNTY
BROOKHOLLOW
RD
LN
HUDNER
BROOKHOLLOW LN
95023
0 .125 .25 .375 .5
miles 1 in. = 1900 ft.
SEE 1039 MAP

SEE 999 MAP

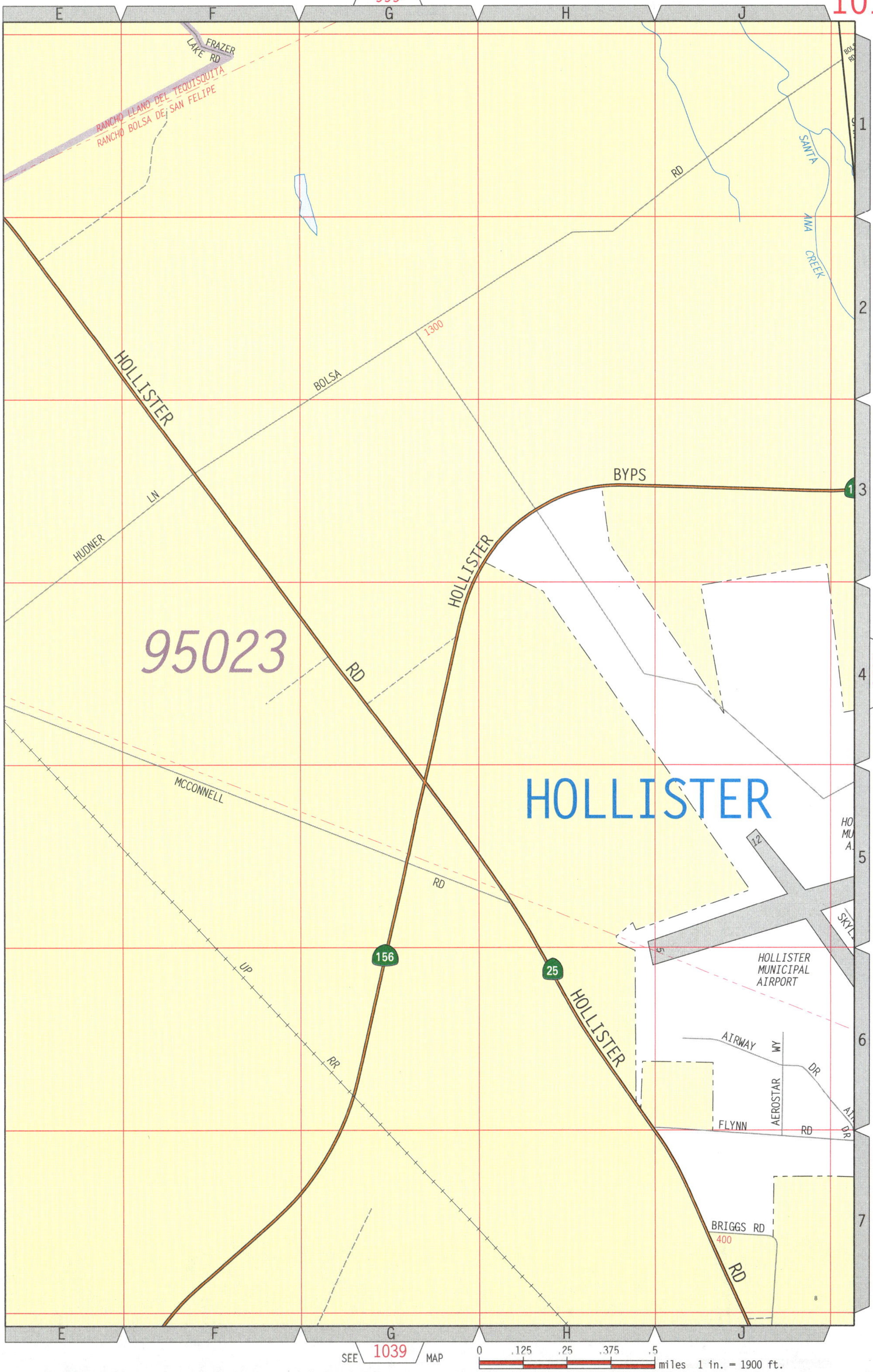
E
F
G
H
J
1
2
3
4
5
6
7
FRAZER LAKE RD
RANCHO LLANO DEL TEQUISQUITA
RANCHO BOLSA DE SAN FELIPE
RD
1300
BOLSA
HUDNER LN
HOLLISTER RD
SANTA ANA CREEK
BYPS
HOLLISTER
95023
HOLLISTER
MCCONNELL RD
UP RR
156
25
HOLLISTER RD
12
HOLLISTER MUNICIPAL AIRPORT
AIRWAY DR
WY
AEROSTAR
FLYNN RD
BRIGGS RD
400
RD
0 .125 .25 .375 .5 miles 1 in. = 1900 ft.

SEE 1020 MAP
SEE 1039 MAP

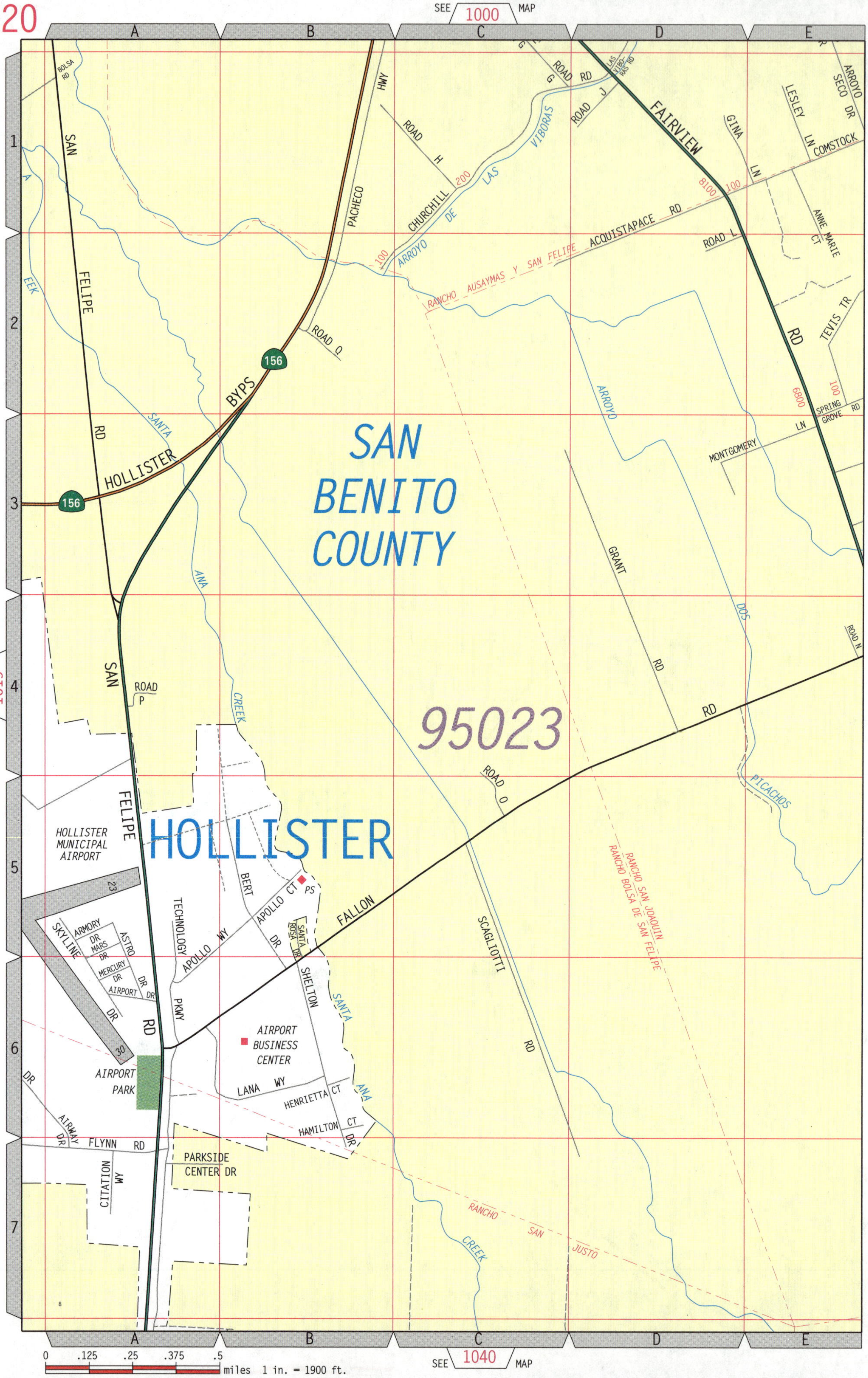
SEE 1000 MAP
SEE 1040 MAP
SEE 1019 MAP
A
B
C
D
E
1
2
3
4
5
6
7
SAN BENITO COUNTY
HOLLISTER
95023
SAN FELIPE RD
BOLSA RD
HOLLISTER BYPS
156
PACHECO HWY
ROAD Q
ROAD H
ROAD G
ROAD J
CHURCHILL
ARROYO DE LAS VIBORAS
FAIRVIEW RD
GINA LN
LESLEY LN
ARROYO SECO DR
COMSTOCK
ACQUISTAPACE RD
ROAD L
ANNE MARIE CT
RANCHO AUSAYMAS Y SAN FELIPE
TEVIS TR
SPRING GROVE RD
MONTGOMERY LN
ARROYO DOS PICACHOS
GRANT RD
ROAD N
ROAD P
ROAD O
SANTA ANA CREEK
FALLON RD
SCAGLIOTTI RD
RANCHO SAN JOAQUIN
RANCHO BOLSA DE SAN FELIPE
HOLLISTER MUNICIPAL AIRPORT
SKYLINE DR
ARMORY DR
MARS DR
MERCURY DR
ASTRO DR
AIRPORT DR
TECHNOLOGY PKWY
APOLLO WY
APOLLO CT
BERT DR
SANTA ROSA DR
PS
SHELTON DR
AIRPORT BUSINESS CENTER
LANA WY
HENRIETTA CT
HAMILTON CT
AIRPORT PARK
AIRWAY DR
FLYNN RD
CITATION WY
PARKSIDE CENTER DR
RANCHO SAN JUSTO
CREEK
100
200
8100
6800
23
30
8
0 .125 .25 .375 .5 miles 1 in. = 1900 ft.

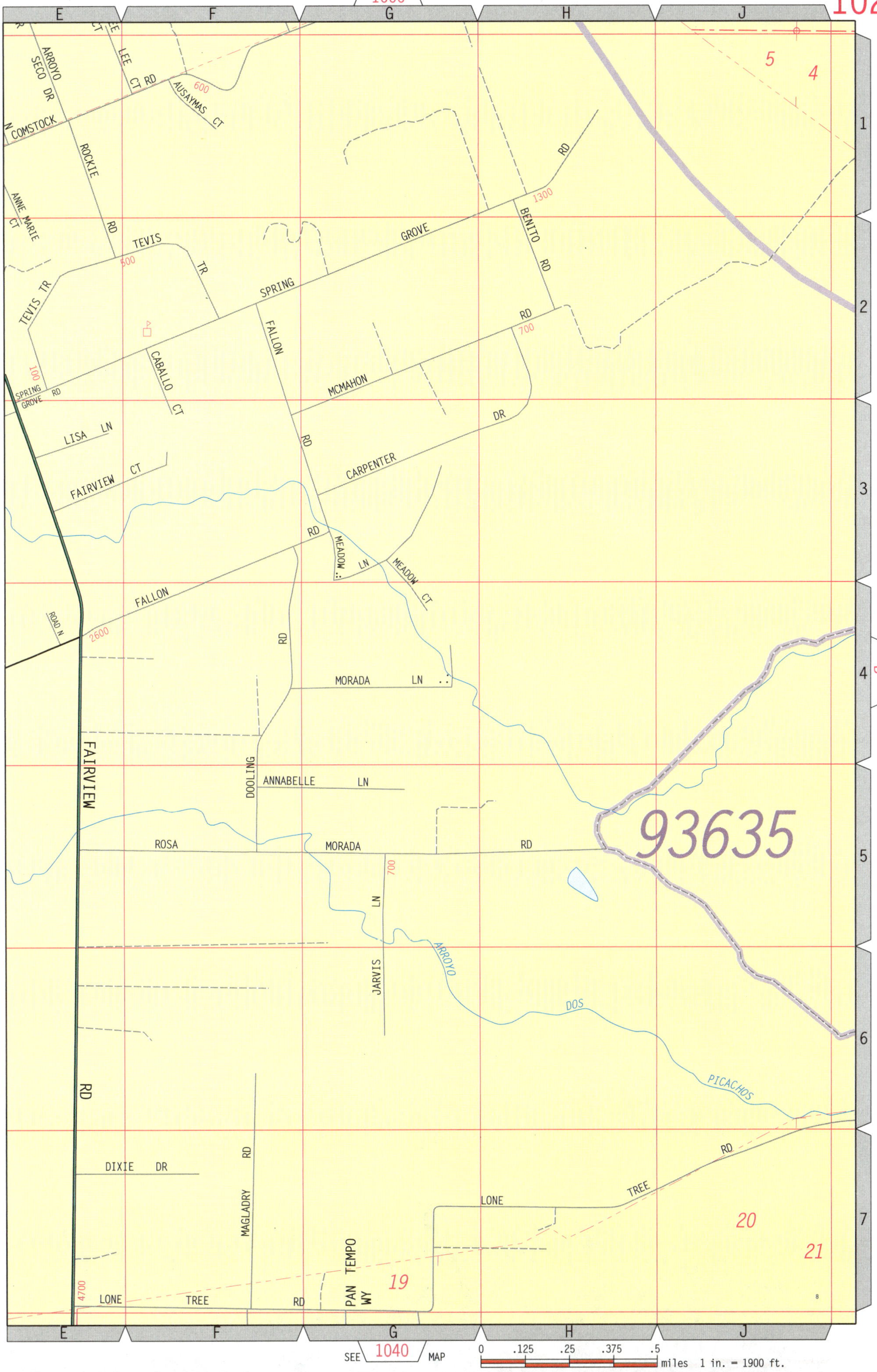
SEE 1000 MAP
SANTA CLARA CO.
SEE B MAP
SEE 1040 MAP
ARROYO SECO DR
LEE CT
RD
AUSAYMAS CT
COMSTOCK
ROCKIE RD
ANNE MARIE CT
TEVIS TR
SPRING GROVE RD
BENITO RD
FALLON RD
CABALLO CT
MCMAHON
LISA LN
FAIRVIEW CT
CARPENTER DR
MEADOW LN
MEADOW CT
ROAD N
MORADA LN
DOOLING RD
ANNABELLE LN
FAIRVIEW RD
ROSA MORADA RD
JARVIS LN
ARROYO DOS PICACHOS
93635
DIXIE DR
MAGLADRY RD
PAN TEMPO WY
LONE TREE RD
miles 1 in. = 1900 ft.

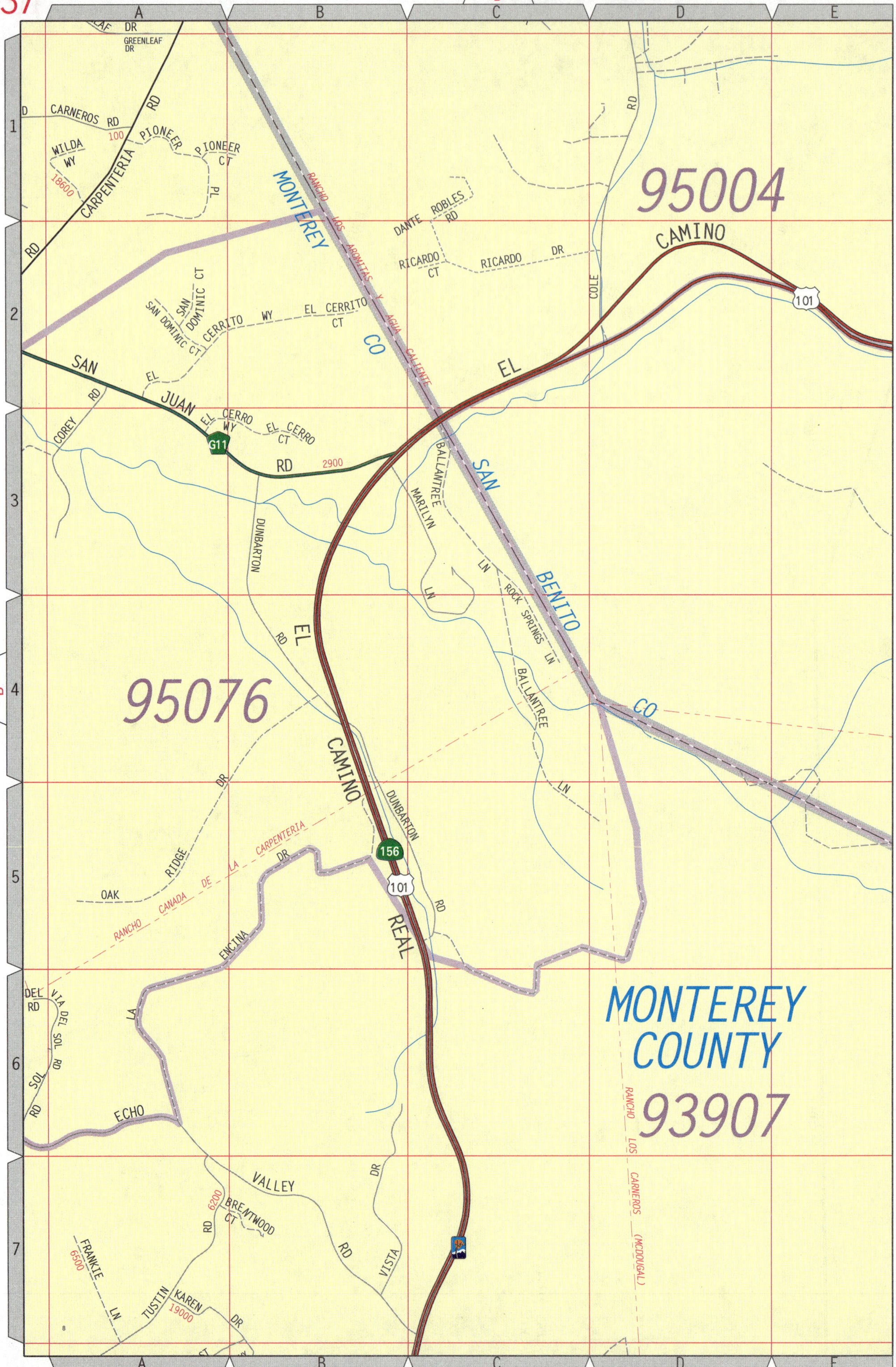

SANTA CLARA CO.
SEE B MAP
95004
95076
MONTEREY COUNTY
93907
CARNEROS RD
CARPENTERIA RD
PIONEER
PIONEER CT
WILDA WY
GREENLEAF DR
MONTEREY
SAN BENITO CO
EL CAMINO REAL
SAN JUAN RD
DANTE ROBLES RD
RICARDO CT
RICARDO DR
COLE RD
EL CERRITO WY
EL CERRITO CT
SAN DOMINIC CT
EL CERRO WY
EL CERRO CT
COREY RD
DUNBARTON RD
BALLANTREE LN
MARILYN LN
ROCK SPRINGS LN
OAK RIDGE DR
ENCINA DR
LA ENCINA DR
VIA DEL SOL RD
DEL SOL RD
ECHO VALLEY RD
BRENTWOOD CT
VISTA DR
FRANKIE LN
TUSTIN
KAREN DR
RANCHO LOS AROMITAS Y AGUA CALIENTE
RANCHO CANADA DE LA CARPENTERIA
RANCHO LOS CARNEROS (MCDOUGAL)
101
156
G11
0 .125 .25 .375 .5 miles 1 in. = 1900 ft.

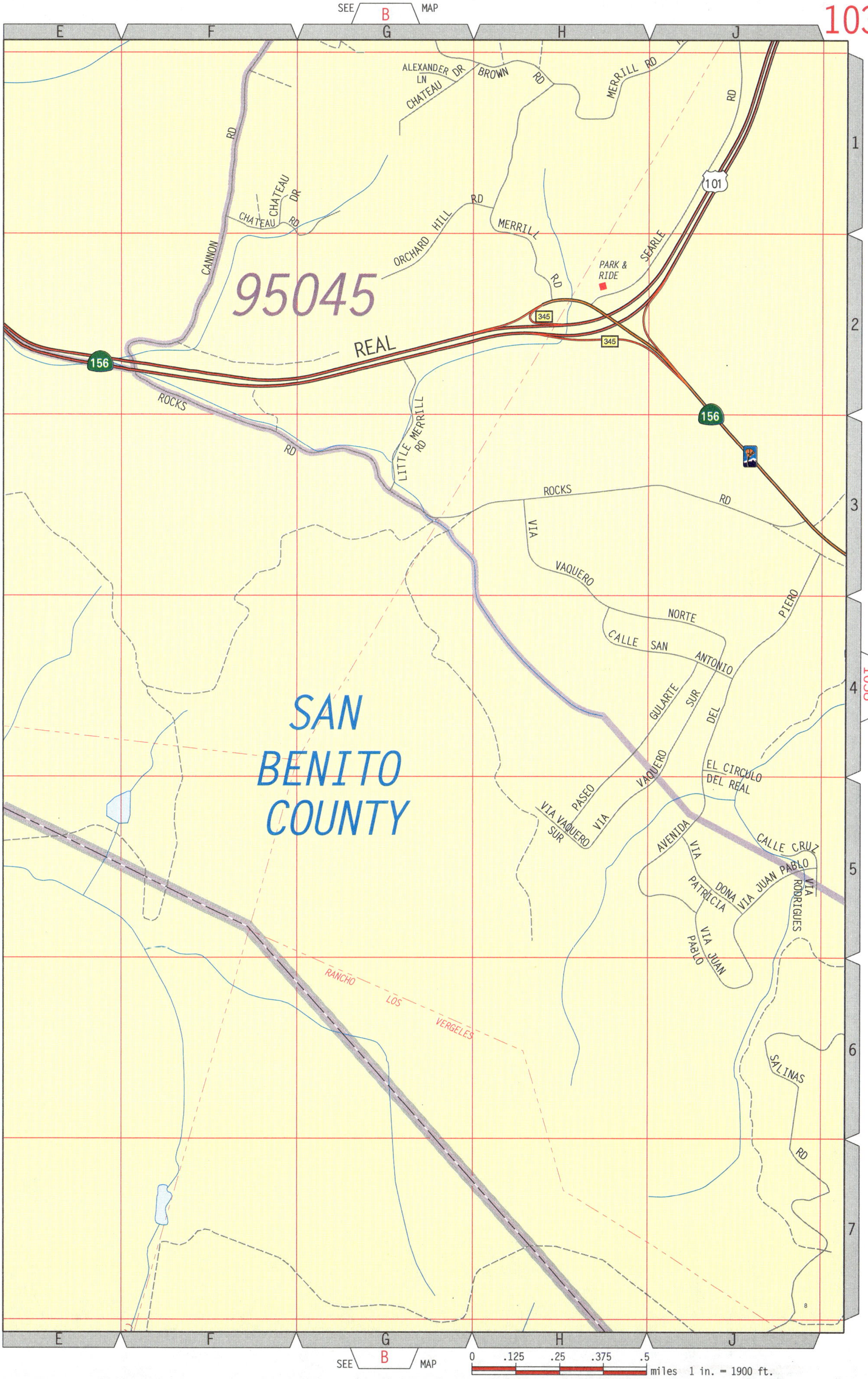

SEE B MAP
E
F
G
H
J
1
2
3
4
5
6
7
SEE 1038 MAP
ALEXANDER LN
CHATEAU DR
BROWN RD
MERRILL RD
RD
101
CHATEAU DR
CHATEAU RD
CANNON RD
ORCHARD HILL RD
MERRILL RD
PARK & RIDE
SEARLE
95045
345
345
REAL
156
156
ROCKS RD
LITTLE MERRILL RD
ROCKS RD
VIA VAQUERO
NORTE
PIERO
CALLE SAN ANTONIO
GULARTE
SUR
DEL
SAN BENITO COUNTY
EL CIRCULO DEL REAL
PASEO
VAQUERO
VIA VAQUERO SUR
VIA
AVENIDA
VIA
CALLE CRUZ
DONA PATRICIA
VIA JUAN PABLO
VIA RODRIGUES
VIA JUAN PABLO
RANCHO LOS VERGELES
SALINAS RD
SEE B MAP
0 .125 .25 .375 .5
miles 1 in. = 1900 ft.

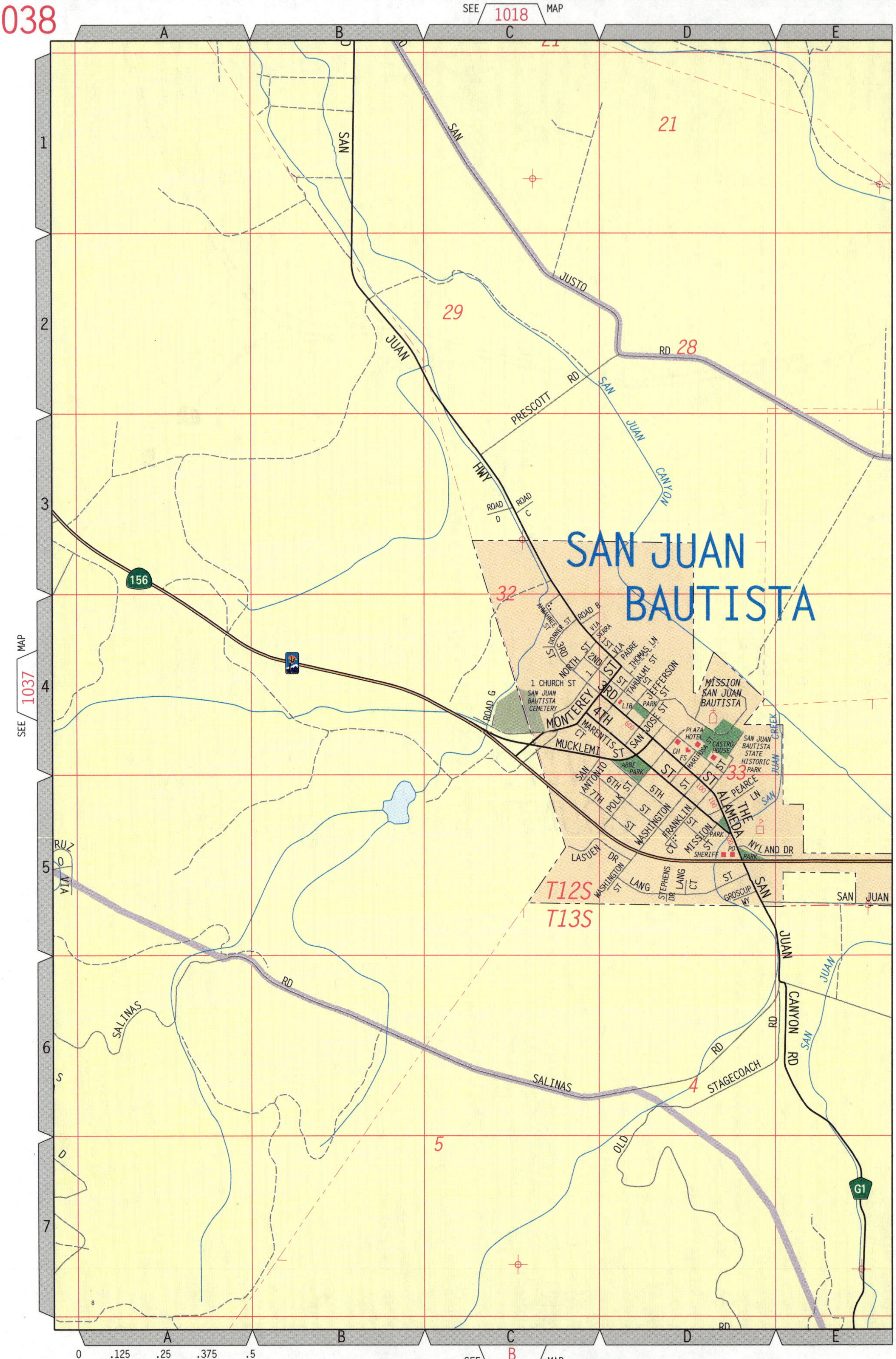
SEE 1018 MAP
SEE 1037 MAP
SEE B MAP
SAN JUAN BAUTISTA
SAN JUAN HWY
SAN JUSTO RD
PRESCOTT RD
SAN JUAN CANYON
ROAD D
ROAD C
ROAD G
ROAD B
156
G1
SALINAS RD
OLD STAGECOACH RD
SAN JUAN CANYON RD
SAN JUAN CREEK
MISSION SAN JUAN BAUTISTA
SAN JUAN BAUTISTA STATE HISTORIC PARK
SAN JUAN BAUTISTA CEMETERY
ABBE PARK
PLAZA HOTEL
CASTRO HOUSE
MONTEREY ST
MUCKLEMI ST
MARENTIS CT
3RD ST
4TH ST
2ND ST
1ST ST
NORTH ST
1 CHURCH ST
SAN JOSE ST
JEFFERSON ST
THOMAS LN
TAHUALMI ST
VIA PADRE
VIA SERRA
DONNER ST
AHWAHNEE ST
SAN ANTONIO
6TH ST
7TH ST
5TH ST
POLK ST
WASHINGTON ST
FRANKLIN ST
MISSION ST
MARIPOSA ST
THE ALAMEDA
PEARCE LN
NYLAND DR
LASUEN DR
WASHINGTON ST
LANG ST
STEPHENS DR
LANG CT
GROSCUP WY
SAN JUAN RD
RUZ O VIA
LIB
PARK
CH
FS
SHERIFF
PO
21
28
29
32
33
4
5
T12S
T13S
0 .125 .25 .375 .5 miles 1 in. = 1900 ft.

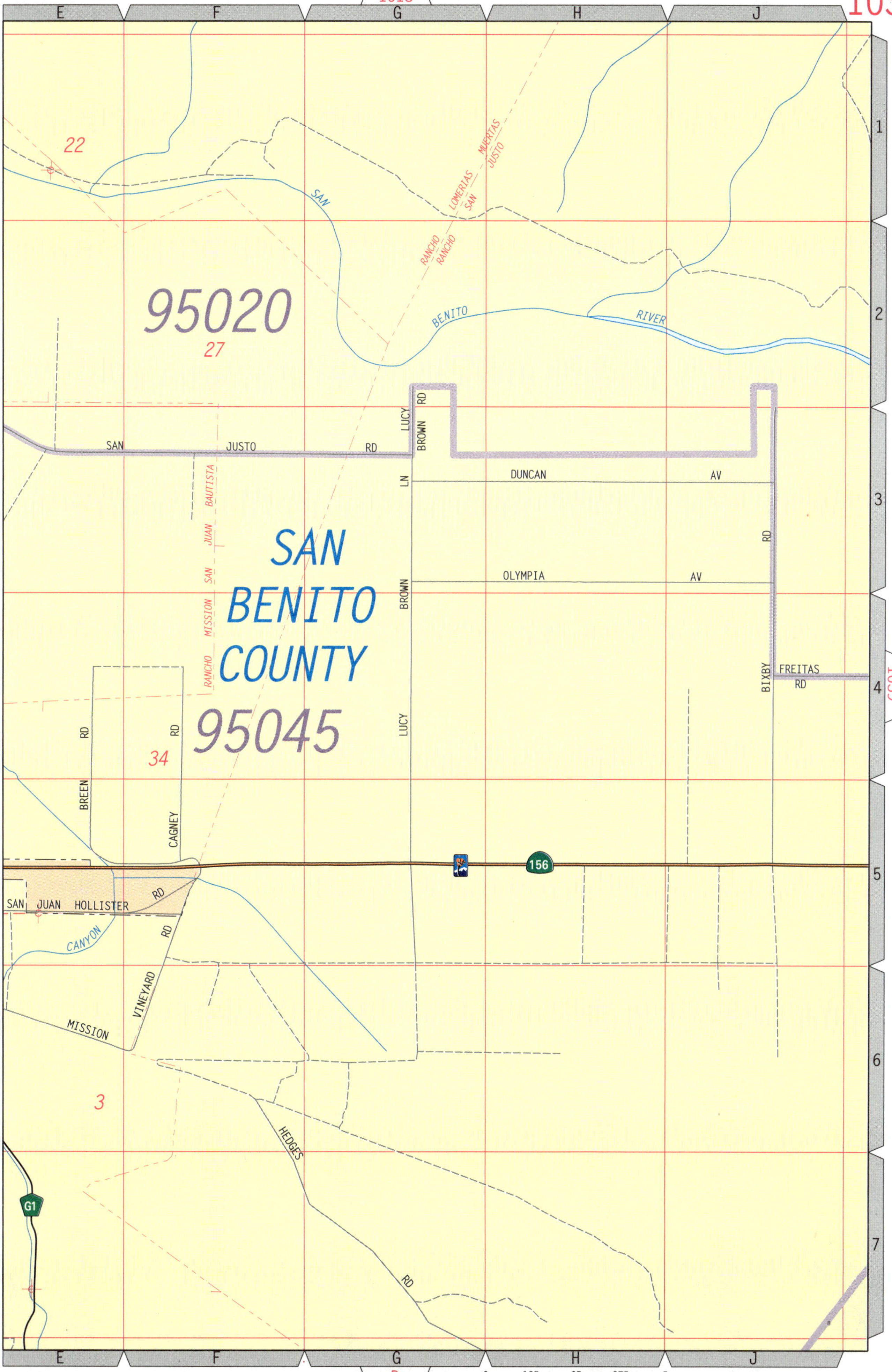
SEE 1018 MAP
E
F
G
H
J
1
2
3
4
5
6
7
22
SAN
RANCHO LOMERIAS MUERTAS
RANCHO SAN JUSTO
95020
27
BENITO
RIVER
SAN JUSTO RD
LUCY RD
BROWN LN
DUNCAN AV
OLYMPIA AV
RANCHO SAN JUAN BAUTISTA
MISSION SAN JUAN BAUTISTA
SAN BENITO COUNTY
95045
34
BREEN RD
CAGNEY RD
BROWN
LUCY
BIXBY RD
FREITAS RD
SEE 1039 MAP
156
SAN JUAN HOLLISTER RD
CANYON
VINEYARD RD
MISSION
3
HEDGES RD
G1
SEE B MAP
0 .125 .25 .375 .5 miles 1 in. = 1900 ft.
SANTA CLARA CO.

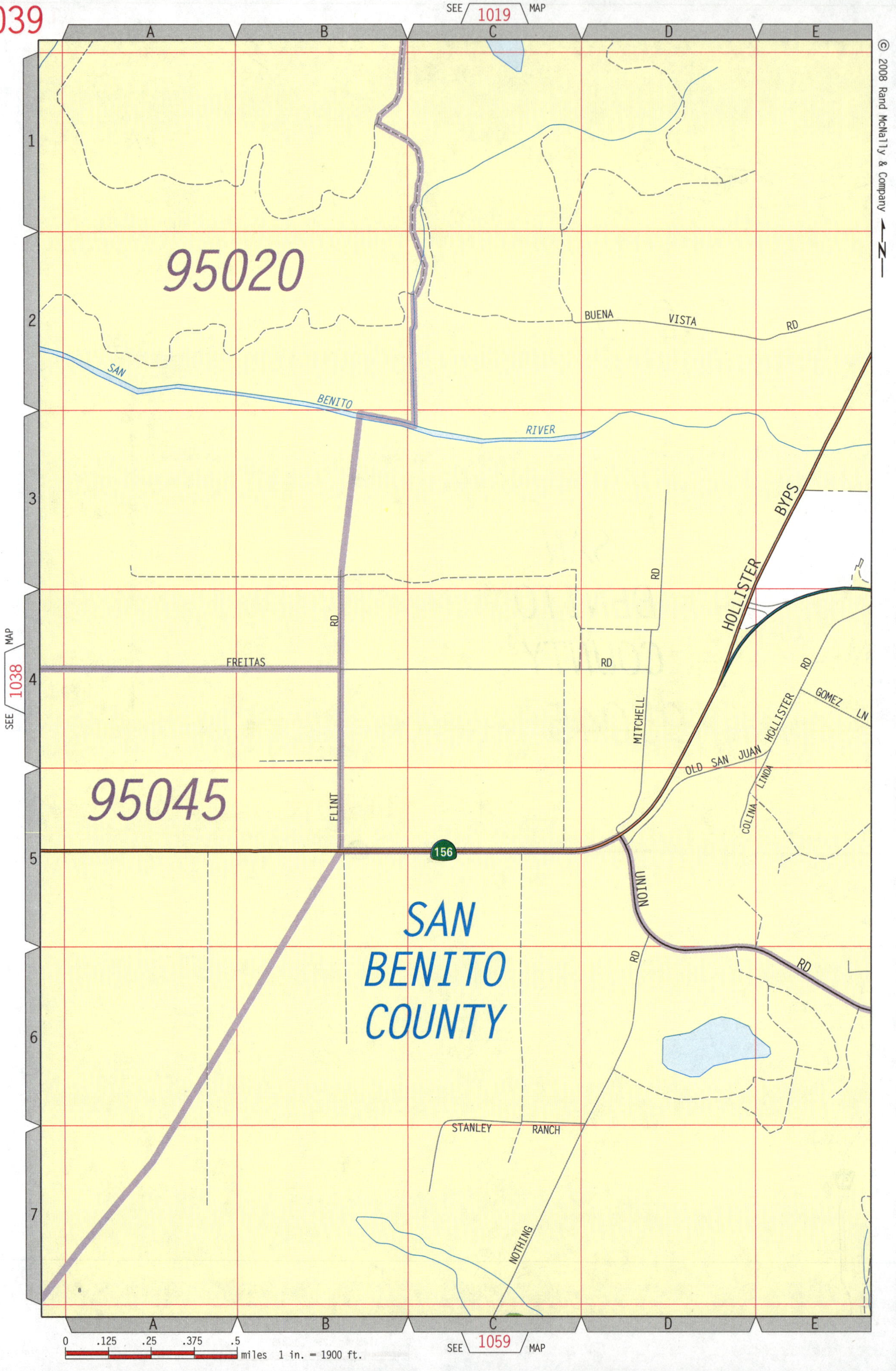
SEE 1019 MAP
SEE 1038 MAP
SEE 1059 MAP
SANTA CLARA CO.
95020
95045
BUENA VISTA RD
SAN BENITO RIVER
FREITAS RD
FLINT RD
MITCHELL RD
HOLLISTER BYPS
GOMEZ LN
RD
OLD SAN JUAN HOLLISTER
COLINA LINDA
156
UNION RD
SAN BENITO COUNTY
STANLEY RANCH
NOTHING
A
B
C
D
E
1
2
3
4
5
6
7
0 .125 .25 .375 .5 miles 1 in. = 1900 ft.

SEE 1019 MAP

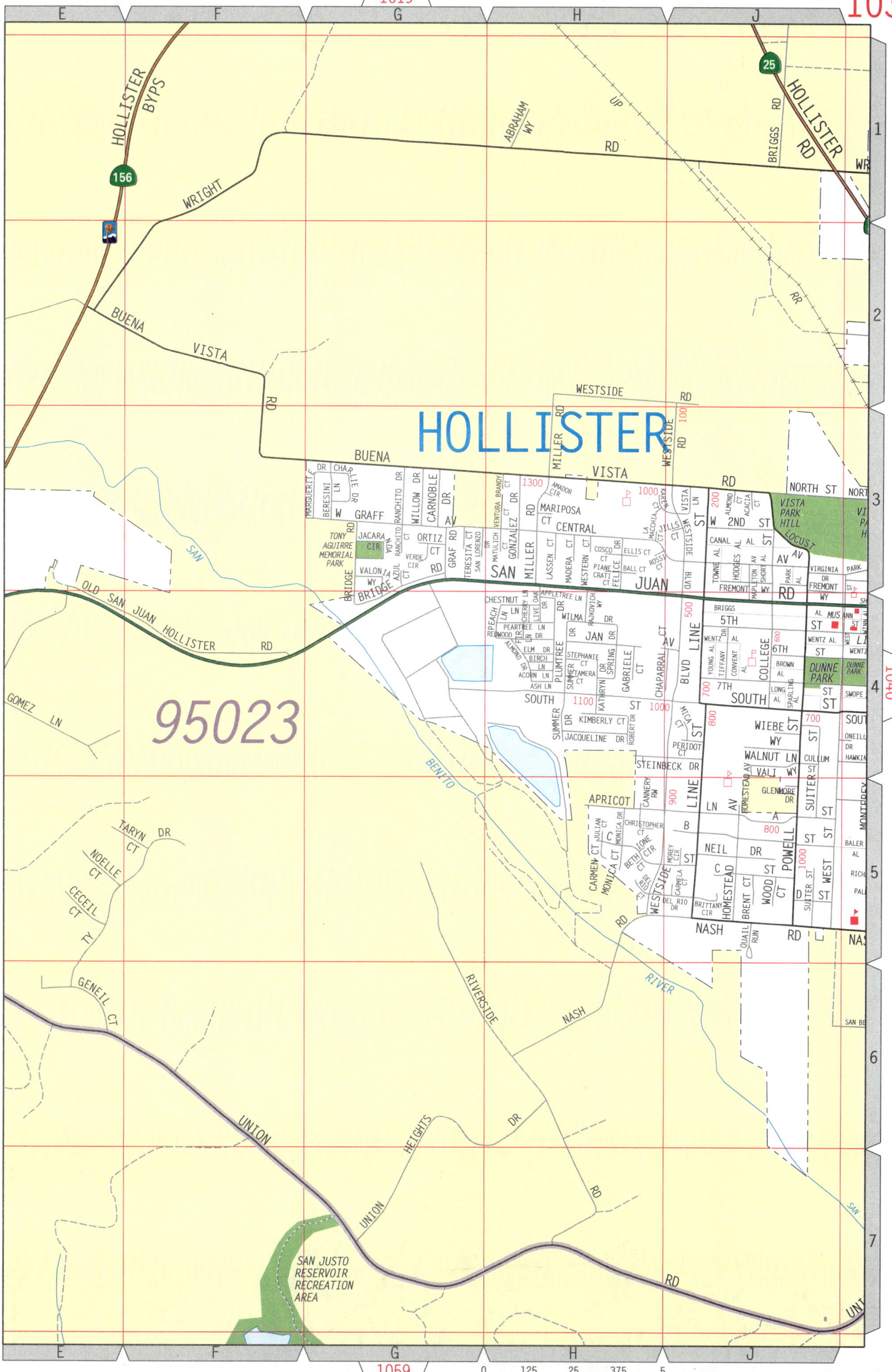

SEE 1040 MAP
SEE 1059 MAP

0 .125 .25 .375 .5 miles 1 in. = 1900 ft.

SEE 1020 MAP

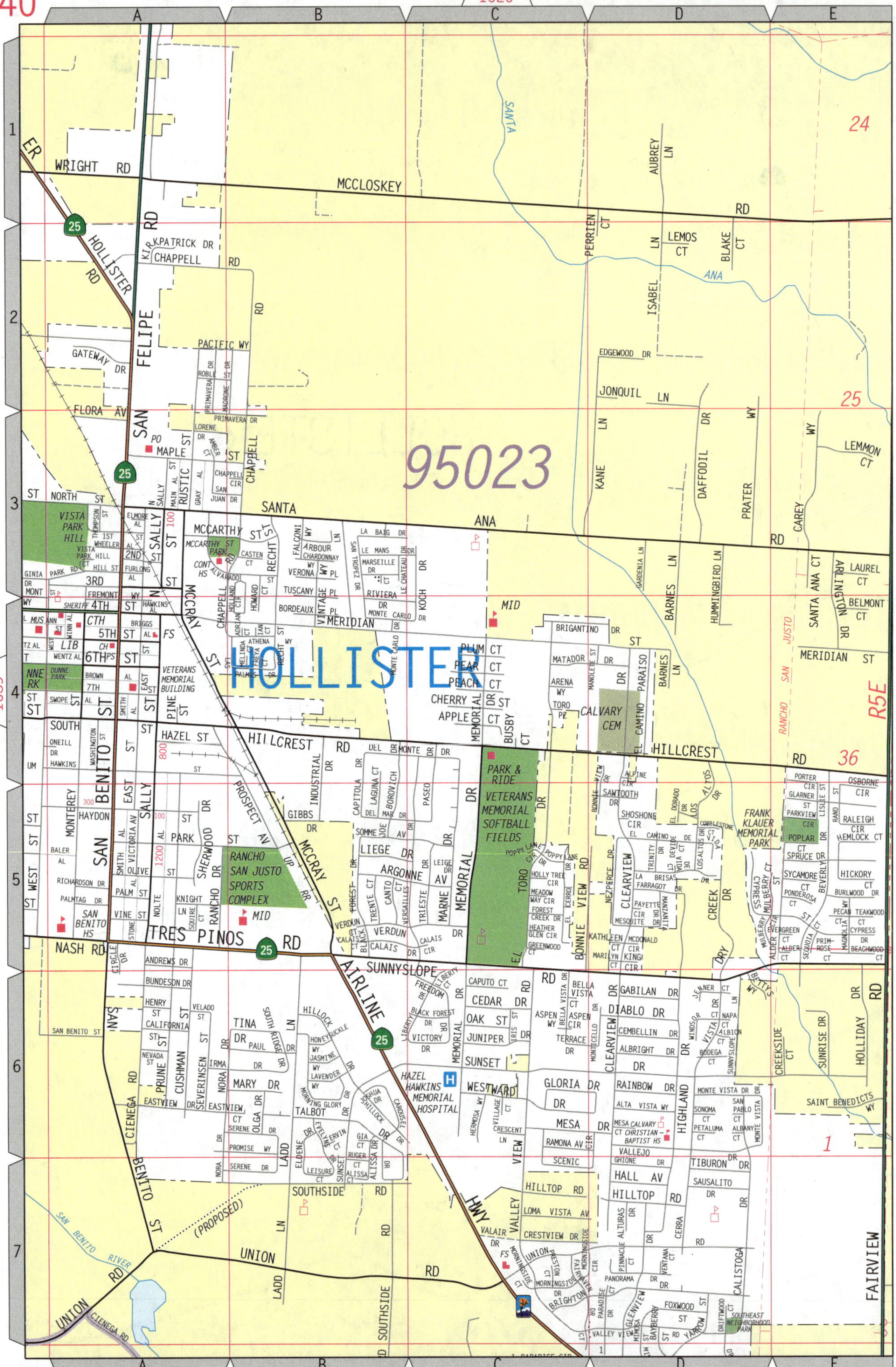

SEE 1039 MAP

SEE 1060 MAP

0 .125 .25 .375 .5 miles 1 in. = 1900 ft.

SANTA CLARA CO.

SEE 1020 MAP

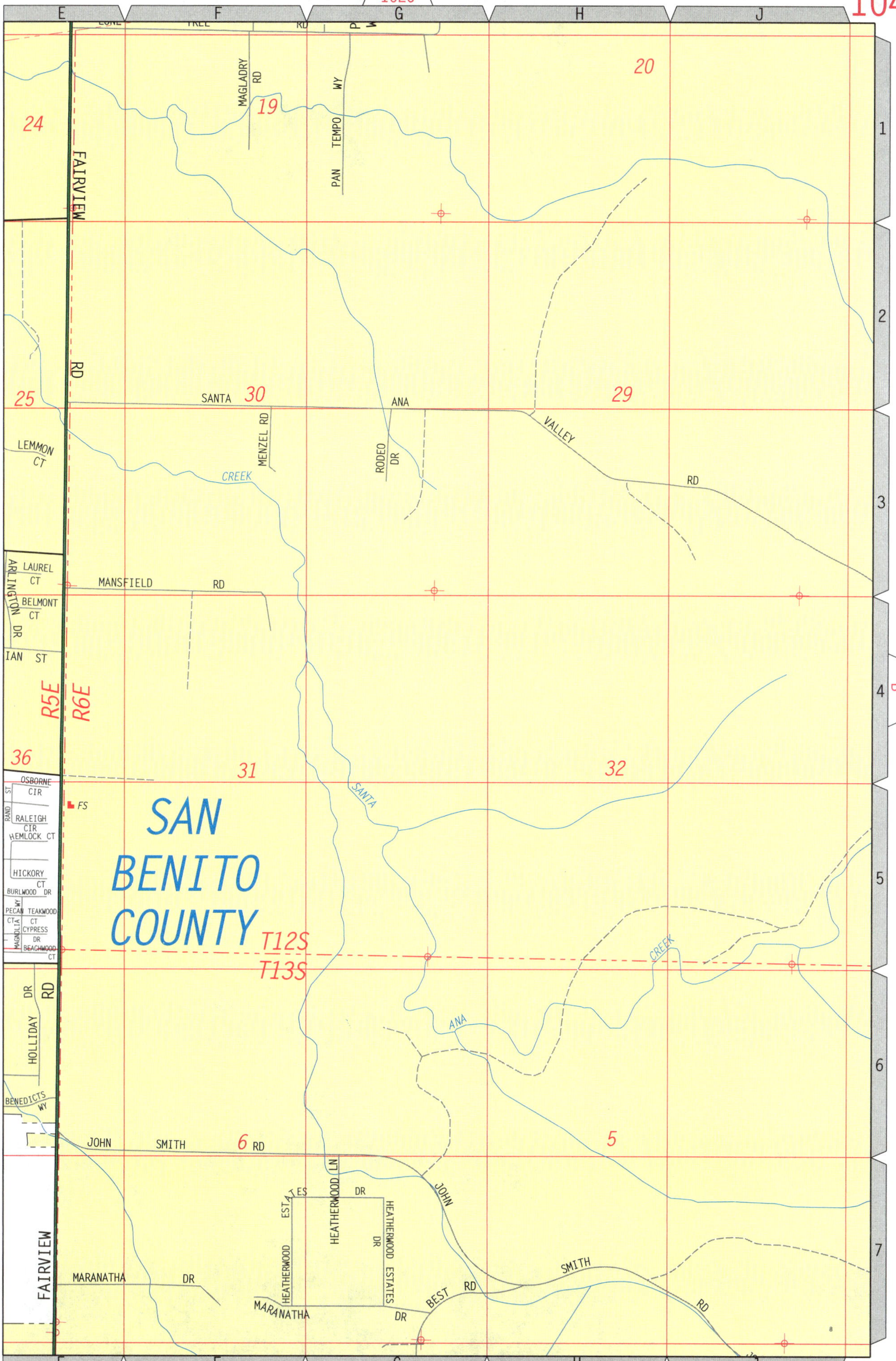

SAN BENITO COUNTY
FAIRVIEW RD
MAGLADRY RD
PAN TEMPO WY
SANTA ANA VALLEY RD
MENZEL RD
RODEO DR
CREEK
LEMMON CT
LAUREL CT
ARLINGTON DR
BELMONT CT
MANSFIELD RD
IAN ST
R5E
R6E
T12S
T13S
OSBORNE CIR
RAND ST
RALEIGH CIR
HEMLOCK CT
HICKORY CT
BURLWOOD DR
PECAN WY
TEAKWOOD CT
MAGNOLIA CT
CYPRESS DR
BEACHWOOD CT
FS
SANTA ANA CREEK
HOLLIDAY DR
BENEDICTS WY
JOHN SMITH RD
HEATHERWOOD LN
HEATHERWOOD ESTATES DR
MARANATHA DR
BEST RD
24
19
20
25
30
29
36
31
32
6
5
E F G H J
1 2 3 4 5 6 7
0 .125 .25 .375 .5 miles 1 in. = 1900 ft.

SEE B MAP

SANTA CLARA CO.

SEE 1060 MAP

SEE 1039 MAP

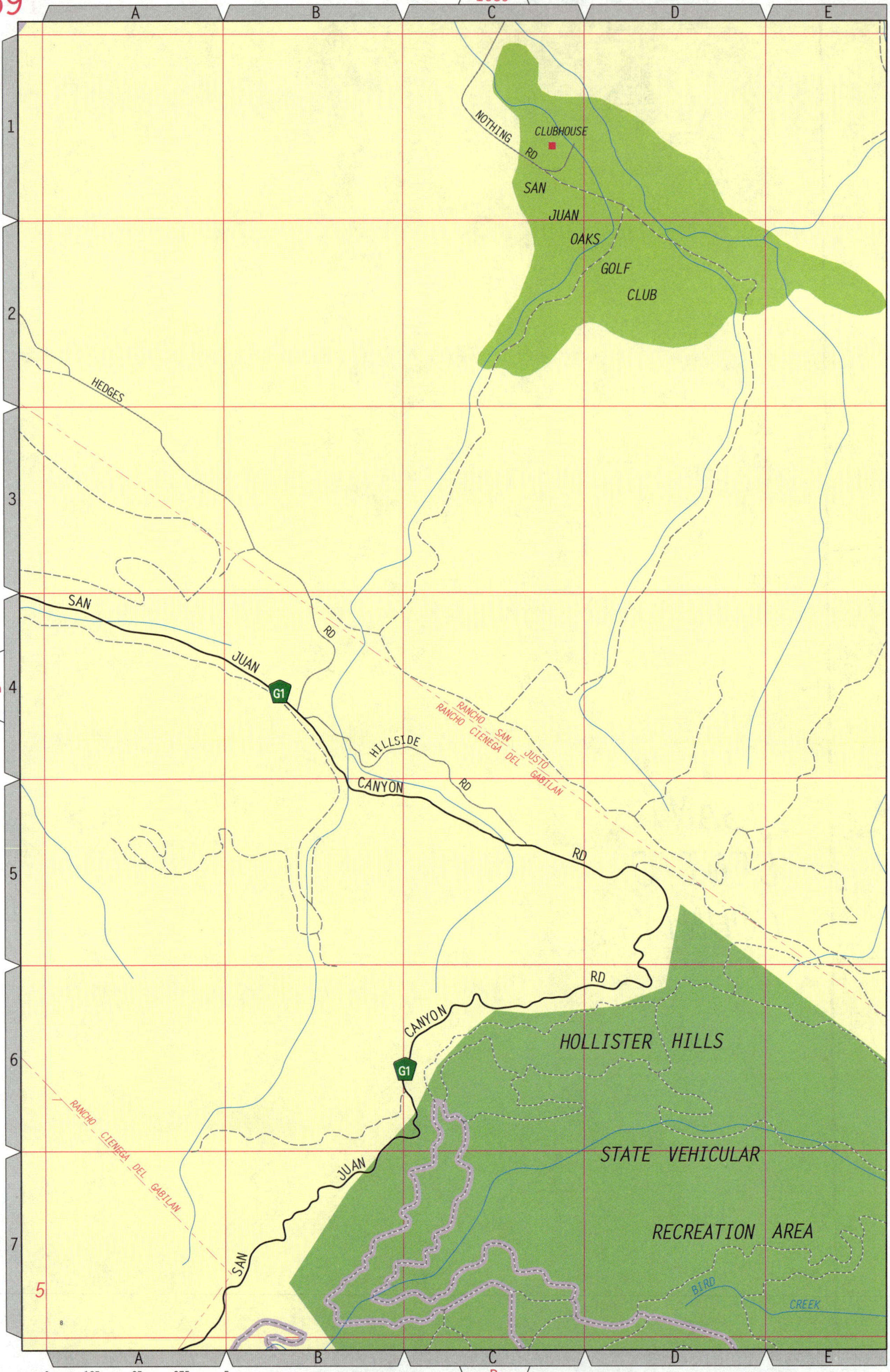

SANTA CLARA CO.

0 .125 .25 .375 .5 miles 1 in. = 1900 ft.

SEE B MAP

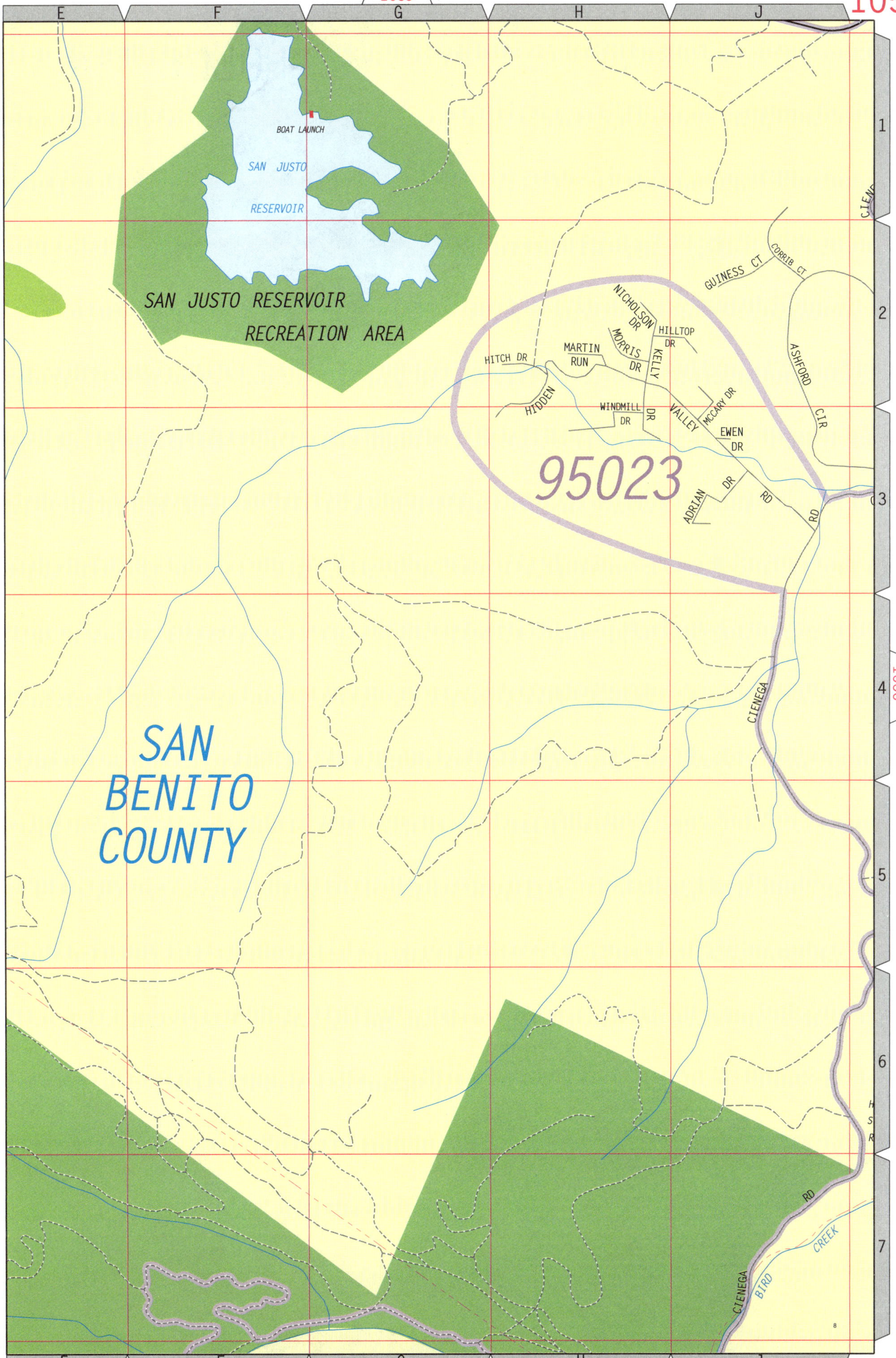
SEE 1039 MAP
E
F
G
H
J
1
2
3
4
5
6
7
BOAT LAUNCH
SAN JUSTO
RESERVOIR
SAN JUSTO RESERVOIR
RECREATION AREA
NICHOLSON DR
HILLTOP DR
MORRIS DR
KELLY DR
MARTIN RUN
HITCH DR
HIDDEN
WINDMILL DR
VALLEY RD
MCCARY DR
EWEN DR
GUINESS CT
CORRIB CT
ASHFORD CIR
ADRIAN DR
95023
SEE 1060 MAP
CIENEGA RD
SAN BENITO COUNTY
BIRD CREEK
SANTA CLARA CO.
SEE B MAP
0 .125 .25 .375 .5
miles 1 in. = 1900 ft.

SEE 1040 MAP

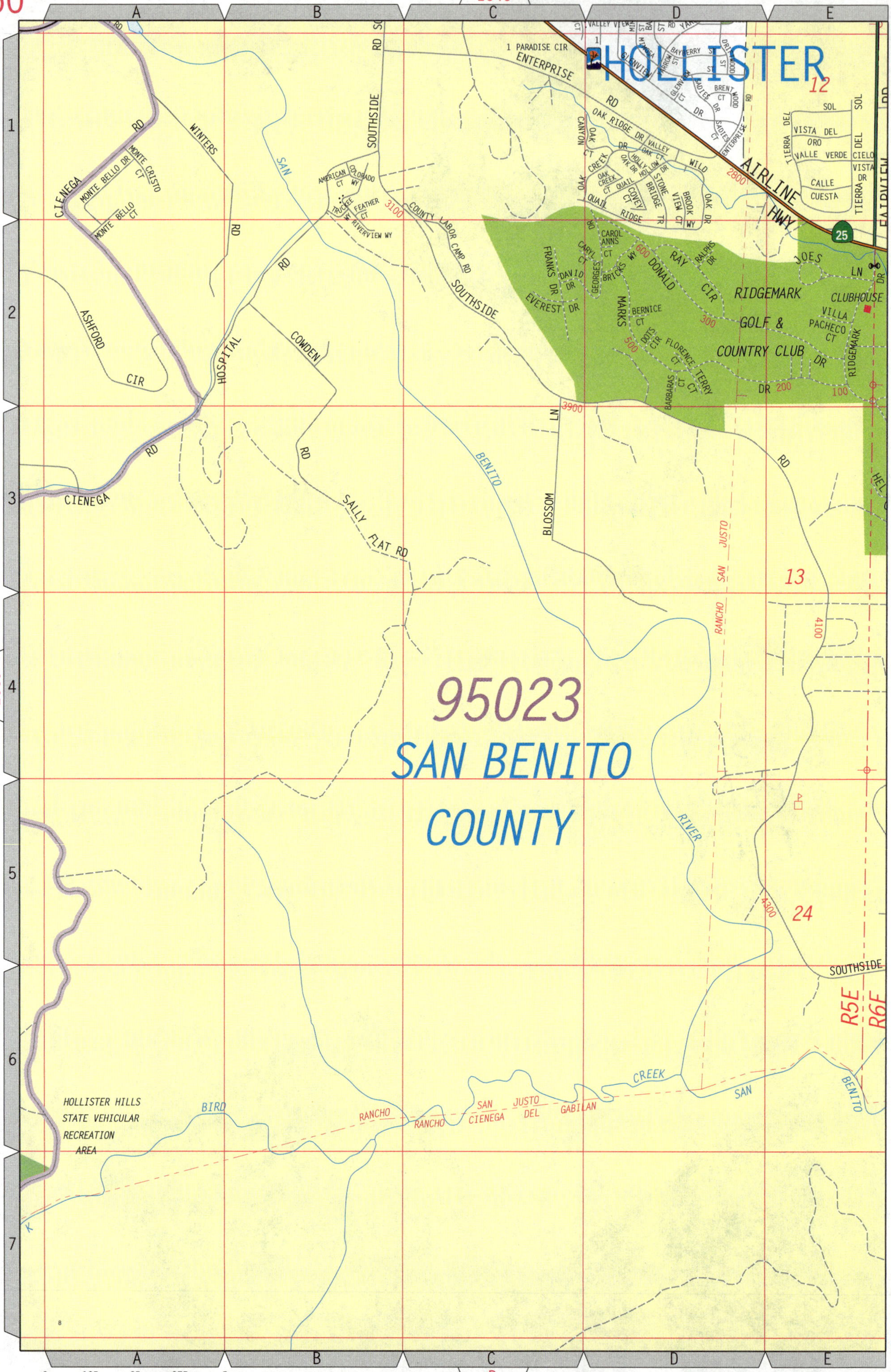

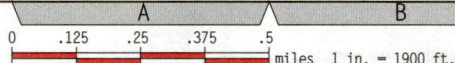

0 .125 .25 .375 .5 miles 1 in. = 1900 ft.

SEE 1059 MAP

SEE B MAP

SEE 1040 MAP

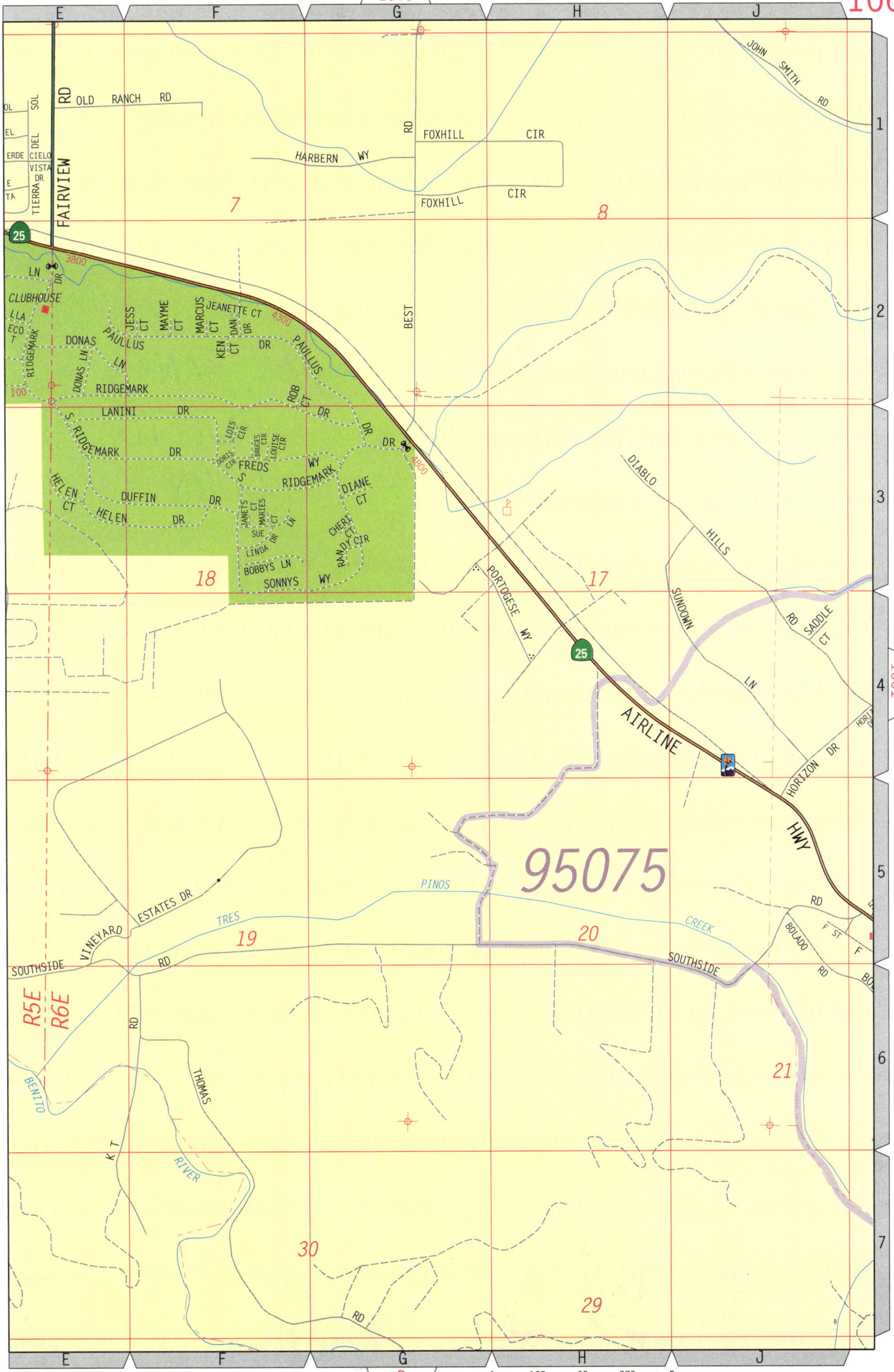

SANTA CLARA CO.

SEE 1061 MAP

SEE B MAP

0 .125 .25 .375 .5 miles 1 in. = 1900 ft.

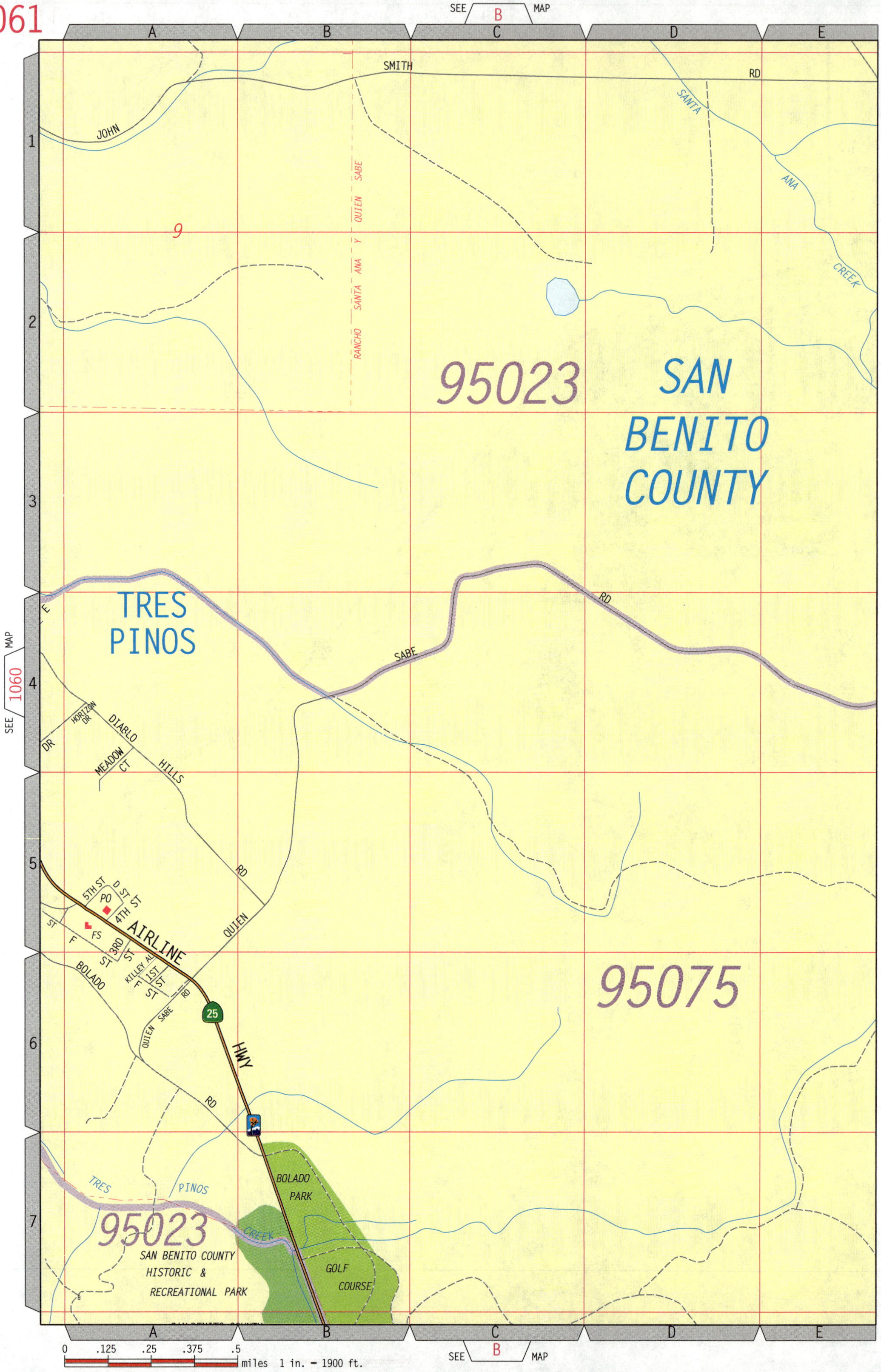
SEE B MAP
A
B
C
D
E
1
2
3
4
5
6
7
SMITH RD
JOHN
SANTA ANA CREEK
RANCHO SANTA ANA Y QUIEN SABE
9
95023
SAN BENITO COUNTY
TRES PINOS
E
SEE 1060 MAP
QUIEN SABE RD
HORIZON DR
DIABLO HILLS RD
DR
MEADOW CT
5TH ST
D ST
PO
4TH ST
ST
FS
F ST
3RD ST
AIRLINE
BOLADO
KILLEY AL
1ST ST
F ST
QUIEN SABE RD
25
HWY
95075
RD
TRES PINOS CREEK
BOLADO PARK
95023
SAN BENITO COUNTY HISTORIC & RECREATIONAL PARK
GOLF COURSE
0 .125 .25 .375 .5
miles 1 in. = 1900 ft.
SEE B MAP

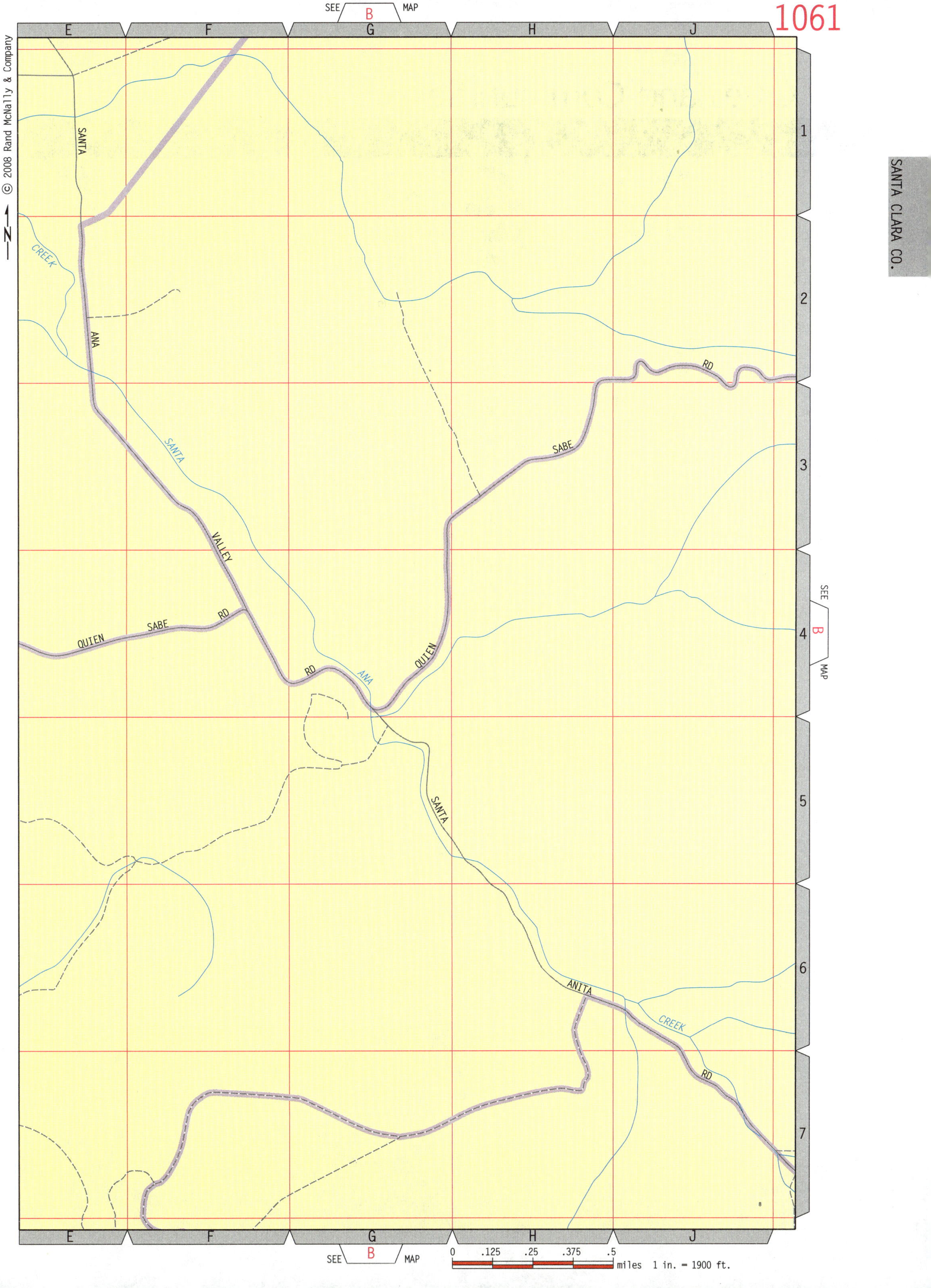
SEE B MAP
E
F
G
H
J
1
2
3
4
5
6
7
SEE B MAP
SANTA
ANA
VALLEY
RD
QUIEN SABE RD
CREEK
SANTA
ANA
SABE
RD
QUIEN
SANTA
ANITA
CREEK
RD
SANTA CLARA CO.
0 .125 .25 .375 .5
miles 1 in. = 1900 ft.

Cities and Communities

Community Name	Abbr.	ZIP Code	Map Page	Community Name	Abbr.	ZIP Code	Map Page
Aldercroft Heights		95030	913	* Milpitas	MPS	95035	794
Alum Rock		95127	834	Monta Vista		95014	852
Alviso		95002	793	* Monte Sereno	MSER	95030	873
Berryessa		95132	814	* Morgan Hill	MGH	95037	937
Burbank		95128	853	* Mountain View	MTVW	94040	811
Cambrian Park		95124	873	New Almaden		95042	894
* Campbell	CMBL	95008	853	* Palo Alto	PA	94301	791
Chemeketa Park		95030	912	Paradise Valley		95037	936
Coyote		95013	896	Rancho Rinconada		95014	852
* Cupertino	CPTO	95014	852	. Redwood Estates		95044	912
East Foothills		95127	814	Rucker		95020	957
Evergreen		95121	855	* San Jose	SJS	95103	834
* Gilroy	GIL	95020	977	San Martin		95046	937
Holy City		95026	913	* Santa Clara	SCL	95050	833
Idylwild		95030	912	-- Santa Clara County	SCIC		
* Los Altos	LALT	94022	811	San Tomas		95008	853
* Los Altos Hills	LAH	94022	811	* Saratoga	SAR	95070	872
* Los Gatos	LGTS	95030	873	Stanford		94305	790
Loyola		94024	831	* Sunnyvale	SUNV	94086	812
Madrone		95037	916				

*Indicates incorporated city

List of Abbreviations

PREFIXES AND SUFFIXES

AL	ALLEY
ARC	ARCADE
AV, AVE	AVENUE
AVCT	AVENUE COURT
AVD	AVENIDA
AVD D LA	AVENIDA DE LA
AVD D LOS	AVENIDA DE LOS
AVD DE	AVENIDA DE
AVD DE LAS	AVENIDA DE LAS
AVD DEL	AVENIDA DEL
AVDR	AVENUE DRIVE
AVEX	AVENUE EXTENSION
AV OF	AVENUE OF
AV OF THE	AVENUE OF THE
AVPL	AVENUE PLACE
BAY	BAY
BEND	BEND
BL, BLVD	BOULEVARD
BLCT	BOULEVARD COURT
BLEX	BOULEVARD EXTENSION
BRCH	BRANCH
BRDG	BRIDGE
BYPS	BYPASS
BYWY	BYWAY
CIDR	CIRCLE DRIVE
CIR	CIRCLE
CL	CALLE
CL DE	CALLE DE
CL DL	CALLE DEL
CL D LA	CALLE DE LA
CL D LAS	CALLE DE LAS
CL D LOS	CALLE DE LOS
CL EL	CALLE EL
CLJ	CALLEJON
CL LA	CALLE LA
CL LAS	CALLE LAS
CL LOS	CALLE LOS
CLTR	CLUSTER
CM	CAMINO
CM DE	CAMINO DE
CM DL	CAMINO DEL
CM D LA	CAMINO DE LA
CM D LAS	CAMINO DE LAS
CM D LOS	CAMINO DE LOS
CMTO	CAMINITO
CMTO DEL	CAMINITO DEL
CMTO D LA	CAMINITO DE LA
CMTO D LAS	CAMINITO DE LAS
CMTO D LOS	CAMINITO DE LOS
CNDR	CENTER DRIVE
COM	COMMON
COMS	COMMONS
CORR	CORRIDOR
CRES	CRESCENT
CRLO	CIRCULO
CRSG	CROSSING
CST	CIRCLE STREET
CSWY	CAUSEWAY
CT	COURT
CTAV	COURT AVENUE
CTE	CORTE
CTE D	CORTE DE
CTE DEL	CORTE DEL
CTE D LAS	CORTE DE LAS
CTO	CUT OFF
CTR	CENTER
CTST	COURT STREET
CUR	CURVE
CV	COVE
DE	DE
DIAG	DIAGONAL
DR	DRIVE
DRAV	DRIVE AVENUE
DRCT	DRIVE COURT
DRLP	DRIVE LOOP
DVDR	DIVISION DR
EXAV	EXTENSION AVENUE
EXBL	EXTENSION BOULEVARD
EXRD	EXTENSION ROAD
EXST	EXTENSION STREET
EXT	EXTENSION
EXWY	EXPRESSWAY
FOREST RT	FOREST ROUTE
FRWY	FREEWAY
FRY	FERRY
GDNS	GARDENS
GN, GLN	GLEN
GRN	GREEN
GRV	GROVE
HTS	HEIGHTS
HWY	HIGHWAY
ISL	ISLE
JCT	JUNCTION
LN	LANE
LNCR	LANE CIRCLE
LNDG	LANDING
LNDR	LAND DRIVE
LNLP	LANE LOOP
LP	LOOP
MNR	MANOR
MT	MOUNT
MTWY	MOTORWAY
MWCR	MEWS COURT
MWLN	MEWS LANE
NFD	NAT'L FOREST DEV
NK	NOOK
OH	OUTER HIGHWAY
OVL	OVAL
OVLK	OVERLOOK
OVPS	OVERPASS
PAS	PASEO
PAS DE	PASEO DE
PAS DE LA	PASEO DE LA
PAS DE LAS	PASEO DE LAS
PAS DE LOS	PASEO DE LOS
PAS DL	PASEO DEL
PASG	PASSAGE
PAS LA	PASEO LA
PAS LOS	PASEO LOS
PASS	PASS
PIKE	PIKE
PK	PARK
PKDR	PARK DRIVE
PKWY, PKY	PARKWAY
PL	PLACE
PLWY	PLACE WAY
PLZ, PZ	PLAZA
PT	POINT
PTAV	POINT AVENUE
PTH	PATH
PZ DE	PLAZA DE
PZ DEL	PLAZA DEL
PZ D LA	PLAZA DE LA
PZ D LAS	PLAZA DE LAS
PZWY	PLAZA WAY
RAMP	RAMP
RD	ROAD
RDAV	ROAD AVENUE
RDBP	ROAD BYPASS
RDCT	ROAD COURT
RDEX	ROAD EXTENSION
RDG	RIDGE
RDSP	ROAD SPUR
RDWY	ROAD WAY
RR	RAILROAD
RUE	RUE
RUE D	RUE D
RW	ROW
RY	RAILWAY
SKWY	SKYWAY
SQ	SQUARE
ST	STREET
STAV	STREET AVENUE
STCT	STREET COURT
STDR	STREET DRIVE
STEX	STREET EXTENSION
STLN	STREET LANE
STLP	STREET LOOP
ST OF	STREET OF
ST OF THE	STREET OF THE
STOV	STREET OVERPASS
STPL	STREET PLACE
STPM	STREET PROMENADE
STWY	STREET WAY
STXP	STREET EXPRESSWAY
TER	TERRACE
TFWY	TRAFFICWAY
THWY	THROUGHWAY
TKTR	TRUCK TRAIL
TPKE	TURNPIKE
TRC	TRACE
TRCT	TERRACE COURT
TR, TRL	TRAIL
TRWY	TRAIL WAY
TTSP	TRUCK TRAIL SPUR
TUN	TUNNEL
UNPS	UNDERPASS
VIA D	VIA DE
VIA DL	VIA DEL
VIA D LA	VIA DE LA
VIA D LAS	VIA DE LAS
VIA D LOS	VIA DE LOS
VIA LA	VIA LA
VW	VIEW
VWY	VIEW WAY
VIS	VISTA
VIS D	VISTA DE
VIS D L	VISTA DE LA
VIS D LAS	VISTA DE LAS
VIS DEL	VISTA DEL
WK	WALK
WY	WAY
WYCR	WAY CIRCLE
WYDR	WAY DRIVE
WYLN	WAY LANE
WYPL	WAY PLACE

DIRECTIONS

E	EAST
KPN	KEY PENINSULA NORTH
KPS	KEY PENINSULA SOUTH
N	NORTH
NE	NORTHEAST
NW	NORTHWEST
S	SOUTH
SE	SOUTHEAST
SW	SOUTHWEST
W	WEST

BUILDINGS

CH	CITY HALL
CHP	CALIFORNIA HIGHWAY PATROL
COMM CTR	COMMUNITY CENTER
CON CTR	CONVENTION CENTER
CONT HS	CONTINUATION HIGH SCHOOL
CTH	COURTHOUSE
FAA	FEDERAL AVIATION ADMIN
FS	FIRE STATION
HOSP	HOSPITAL
HS	HIGH SCHOOL
INT	INTERMEDIATE SCHOOL
JR HS	JUNIOR HIGH SCHOOL
LIB	LIBRARY
MID	MIDDLE SCHOOL
MUS	MUSEUM
PO	POST OFFICE
PS	POLICE STATION
SR CIT CTR	SENIOR CITIZENS CENTER
STA	STATION
THTR	THEATER
VIS BUR	VISITORS BUREAU

OTHER ABBREVIATIONS

BCH	BEACH
BLDG	BUILDING
CEM	CEMETERY
CK	CREEK
CO	COUNTY
COMM	COMMUNITY
CTR	CENTER
EST	ESTATE
HIST	HISTORIC
HTS	HEIGHTS
LK	LAKE
MDW	MEADOW
MED	MEDICAL
MEM	MEMORIAL
MT	MOUNT
MTN	MOUNTAIN
NATL	NATIONAL
PKG	PARKING
PLGD	PLAYGROUND
RCH	RANCH
RCHO	RANCHO
REC	RECREATION
RES	RESERVOIR
RIV	RIVER
RR	RAILROAD
SPG	SPRING
STA	SANTA
VLG	VILLAGE
VLY	VALLEY
VW	VIEW

A

STREET Block	City	ZIP	Pg-Grid
A RD			
-	SUNV	94089	812-J3
4100	SCIC	95127	815-C6
A ST			
-	CPTO	95014	831-H6
-	SCIC	94024	831-H3
-	LALT	94024	831-H3
100	MLPK	94025	790-H3
500	HOLL	95023	1039-J5
AARON CT			
7400	SJS	95139	895-G1
AARON PL			
7500	SJS	95139	895-G1
AARON PARK DR			
700	MPS	95035	794-A5
ABBEY CT			
3800	SJS	95008	853-C6
ABBEY LN			
2000	SJS	95008	853-C6
2100	CMBL	95008	853-C6
ABBEYFIELD CT			
6200	SJS	95120	874-C7
ABBEYGATE CT			
4500	SJS	95124	873-J3
ABBOTSFORD CT			
-	SJS	95138	855-F7
ABBOTT AV			
-	MPS	95035	793-J6
-	MPS	95035	813-J1
1100	CMBL	95008	873-B1
S ABBOTT AV			
100	MPS	95035	813-J1
ABBY WOOD CT			
100	LGTS	95032	873-B2
ABDON AV			
14000	SJS	95127	814-H7
14000	SCIC	95127	814-H7
ABDULLA WY			
14000	SAR	95070	852-H7
ABED CT			
2500	SJS	95116	834-J4
ABEL AV			
4100	PA	94306	811-C2
N ABEL ST			
-	MPS	95035	793-J6
-	MPS	95035	794-A5
S ABEL ST			
-	MPS	95035	793-J7
200	MPS	95035	813-J1
200	MPS	95035	814-A1
ABELIA CT			
3000	SJS	95121	854-J4
ABELIA WY			
100	EPA	94303	791-D3
ABERDEEN CT			
-	GIL	95020	977-F3
600	MPS	95035	794-B6
1800	SJS	95122	854-G1
12800	SAR	95070	852-F6
ABERDEEN DR			
900	SUNV	94087	832-B4
ABERDEEN ST			
3500	SCL	95054	813-E6
ABERDEEN WY			
500	MPS	95035	794-B6
ABERFELDY WY			
1200	MPS	95035	814-C1
ABERFORD DR			
1200	SJS	95131	814-E6
ABERHAVEN CT			
-	SJS	95111	875-A1
ABIGAIL LN			
-	SJS	95121	855-A3
ABINANTE LN			
1900	SJS	95124	873-G1
ABINGTON CT			
1700	SJS	95131	834-D1
ABORN CT			
2800	SJS	95148	855-D2
ABORN RD			
1500	SJS	95121	855-A3
2400	SJS	95148	855-F2
2900	SJS	95122	855-B3
3200	SJS	95135	855-H1
3800	SCIC	95135	855-H1
ABORN SQUARE LOOP RD			
2900	SJS	95121	855-B3
ABRA CT			
200	SJS	95139	895-G2
ABRAHAM CT			
-	MTVW	94040	811-G6
ABRAHAM WY			
-	SBnC	95023	1039-H1
ABRAMS CT			
-	SCIC	94305	791-A7
ABRYAN WY			
2000	SMCo	94061	790-B4
ACACIA AV			
400	PA	94306	811-B1
800	SUNV	94086	812-F7
1000	LALT	94022	811-E4
ACACIA CT			
-	HOLL	95023	1039-J3
2000	SCL	95050	833-D3
ACACIA DR			
-	ATN	94027	790-G1
ACACIA LN			
900	SJS	95138	875-F6
ACACIA ST			
100	SJS	95110	834-A5
ACACIA WY			
1500	MGH	95037	917-D6
ACADIA AV			
1100	MPS	95035	814-C1
1200	MPS	95035	794-D7
ACADIA CT			
20600	CPTO	95014	832-D6
ACALANES DR			
100	SUNV	94086	812-B7
ACAPULCO DR			
3700	SJS	95008	853-B6
ACCOLTI WY			
400	SCL	95053	833-F5
ACOMA WY			
200	FRMT	94539	793-J1
ACORN			
-	PTLV	94028	830-D2
ACORN CT			
-	SCIC	95037	896-D7
3100	SJS	95117	853-D3
ACORN LN			
-	LALT	94022	811-E5
200	HOLL	95023	1039-H4
ACORN WY			
-	GIL	95020	977-E1
-	ATN	94027	790-G1
3100	SJS	95117	853-D3
ACQUISTAPACE RD			
100	SBnC	95023	1020-D2
ACTON CT			
14500	SCIC	95124	873-G4
ACTON DR			
14800	SCIC	95124	873-G3
ADA AV			
100	MTVW	94043	812-A5
ADAGIO WY			
600	SJS	95111	855-B7
ADAIR CT			
600	MGH	95037	916-H6
ADAIR LN			
-	PTLV	94028	810-D6
ADAIR WY			
5100	SJS	95124	873-E4
ADALINA CT			
5200	SJS	95124	873-F5
ADAM WY			
-	ATN	94027	790-C2
ADAMO CT			
4700	SJS	95136	874-E2
ADAMO DR			
4600	SJS	95136	874-E2
ADAMS AV			
1400	MPS	95035	794-D6
ADAMS CT			
400	GIL	95020	978-A1
1100	SJS	95132	814-G5
1900	MTVW	94040	831-H1
18600	MGH	95037	916-J4
ADAMS DR			
1100	SJS	95132	814-F5
ADAMS WY			
3000	SCL	95051	833-A7
ADAMSWOOD DR			
3100	SJS	95148	835-E7
ADDIEWELL PL			
1200	SJS	95120	874-C7
1200	SJS	95120	894-C1
ADDINGTON CT			
21500	CPTO	95014	852-B3
ADDISON AV			
100	PA	94301	790-J5
300	PA	94301	791-A4
2000	EPA	94303	791-A2
ADDISON PL			
2800	SCL	95051	833-B2
ADEGA CIR			
-	SJS	95148	855-F1
ADELAIDE WY			
1900	SJS	95124	873-G5
ADELE AV			
2300	MTVW	94043	811-F3
ADELE PL			
1900	SJS	95125	853-J6
ADELHEID CT			
10000	CPTO	95014	852-A1
ADELINE AV			
-	SJS	95125	854-E6
-	SJS	95136	854-E6
ADELONG WY			
-	SJS	95139	875-H7
ADENTRO ARENA			
-	SUNV	94089	812-H4
ADLER AV			
100	CMBL	95008	853-D7
ADLER CT			
3600	SJS	95111	854-G6
ADMIRAL PL			
2000	SJS	95133	814-E7
ADMIRALTY PL			
6000	SJS	95123	874-D5
ADMIRE CT			
1300	MPS	95035	794-C5
ADOBE AV			
100	MPS	95035	793-J6
ADOBE CT			
1300	SJS	95118	874-B2
ADOBE DR			
200	SJS	95131	814-A5
ADOBE LN			
25400	LAH	94022	831-C3
ADOBE PL			
400	PA	94306	811-E1
ADOBE CREEK CT			
1000	SJS	95127	834-J4
ADOBE CREEK LODGE RD			
-	LAH	94022	831-A3
ADOBE RIVER CT			
4600	SJS	95136	874-E2
ADOLFO DR			
1500	SJS	95131	814-C6
ADONIS CT			
800	SUNV	94086	832-G1
ADONIS WY			
2400	SJS	95124	873-E4
ADONNA CT			
27100	LAH	94022	811-A7
ADRA AV			
3400	SCIC	95117	853-D1
3400	SJS	95117	853-D1
ADRAGNA CT			
4400	SJS	95136	874-H1
ADRIAN CT			
-	HOLL	95023	1040-B4
ADRIAN DR			
-	SBnC	95023	1059-J3
ADRIAN PL			
100	LGTS	95032	873-E5
ADRIAN WY			
1100	SJS	95122	834-J5
ADRIANA AV			
10100	CPTO	95014	832-B7
ADRIATIC WY			
3700	SCL	95051	832-H4
ADRIEN DR			
1500	CMBL	95008	873-A1
AERONAUT WY			
19400	SCIC	95033	892-F2
AEROSTAR WY			
-	HOLL	95023	1019-J6
AETNA WY			
2800	SJS	95121	854-J3
2900	SJS	95121	855-A3
AFTON AV			
18700	SAR	95070	852-H7
AFTON CT			
6000	SJS	95123	874-E5
AFUERA ARENA			
-	SUNV	94089	812-H4
AGAPE CT			
4900	SJS	95118	873-J4
AGATE CT			
2600	SCL	95051	832-J1
AGATE DR			
2500	SCL	95051	833-A1
3300	SCL	95051	832-J1
AGATHA WY			
3900	SJS	95136	874-E1
AGENA WY			
100	SUNV	94086	812-D7
AGNES WY			
900	PA	94303	791-C5
AGNEW RD			
2000	SCL	95054	813-C5
AGUA BELIZIE ST			
-	SJS	95131	814-B6
AGUACATE CT			
100	SJS	95116	834-D2
AGUA VISTA DR			
2600	SJS	95132	814-D4
AGUILAR CT			
2100	MPS	95035	794-E6
AHWAHNEE ST			
-	SJB	95045	1038-C4
AHWANEE AV			
600	SUNV	94086	812-G5
N AHWANEE TER			
600	SUNV	94086	812-G5
S AHWANEE TER			
600	SUNV	94086	812-G5
AHWANHEE AV			
100	SUNV	94086	812-F4
AIDA AV			
2600	SJS	95122	855-A2
AIELLO DR			
2700	SJS	95111	854-G5
AIKINS WY			
3500	SJS	95148	855-F1
AINSLEY CT			
3800	SJS	95008	853-C6
AINSLEY PARK DR			
-	CMBL	95008	853-E5
AINSWORTH DR			
10200	CPTO	95014	832-A6
10600	SCIC	94024	832-A6
AINTREE DR			
6800	SJS	95119	895-D1
AIRES LN			
400	SJS	95111	854-F6
AIRLINE HWY Rt#-25			
600	HOLL	95023	1040-B6
1000	SBnC	95023	1040-B6
1600	HOLL	95023	1060-D1
1600	SBnC	95023	1060-D1
5200	SBnC	95075	1060-H4
5900	SBnC	95075	1061-A5
7400	SBnC	95023	1061-A5
AIRPORT BLVD			
500	SJS	95110	833-G1
AIRPORT DR			
-	HOLL	95023	1020-A6
AIRPORT PKWY			
-	SJS	95110	833-H1
AIRPORT RD			
17000	SCIC	95033	913-B1
AIRWAY DR			
-	HOLL	95023	1019-J6
-	HOLL	95023	1020-A6
AITKEN AV			
2100	MTVW	94040	811-F5
AJAX DR			
700	SUNV	94086	832-F1
AKINO CT			
2800	SJS	95148	855-C1
AKIO WY			
1000	SJS	95120	894-F1
AKLAN CT			
300	SJS	95119	875-C7
N AKRON RD			
-	SCIC	94035	812-B2
-	SCIC	94043	812-B2
S AKRON RD			
-	SCIC	94035	812-B2
-	SCIC	94043	812-B2
AKRON WY			
3700	SJS	95117	853-C2
ALADDIN DR			
5400	SJS	95123	875-B4
ALAMEDA CT			
2100	SJS	95126	833-G5
ALAMEDA WY			
2000	SJS	95126	833-G5
ALAMEDA DE LAS PULGAS			
-	ATN	94027	790-B4
ALAMEDA DE LAS PULGAS			
-	WDSD	94027	790-B4
1600	RDWC	94061	790-B4
1800	WDSD	94062	790-B4
2000	SMCo	94062	790-B4
2100	SMCo	94061	790-B4
2300	WDSD	94061	790-B4
3000	SMCo	94025	790-B4
3700	MLPK	94025	790-B4
ALAMITOS DR			
100	SUNV	94086	812-B6
ALAMITOS RD			
21900	SCIC	95120	914-J1
23600	SCIC	95033	914-F3
ALAMITOS CREEK RD			
1000	SJS	95120	894-J3
ALAMO CT			
600	MTVW	94043	812-A4
ALAMO DR			
600	SJS	95123	874-G4
600	SJS	95131	814-A5
600	MGH	95037	937-B4
ALAMO WY			
-	CPTO	95014	852-A2
ALAMOS RD			
-	PTLV	94028	810-E5
ALAN AV			
4900	SJS	95124	873-J4
ALANA DR			
400	SJS	95136	854-E4
ALANA WY			
-	SJS	95136	854-E5
ALANNAH CT			
-	PA	94303	791-C4
ALBA CT			
200	LALT	94022	811-D5
900	SCIC	95127	814-H6
ALBANESE CIR			
600	SJS	95111	854-G3
ALBANY CT			
-	HOLL	95023	1040-D6
1500	MPS	95035	794-D6
ALBANY DR			
100	SJS	95129	853-A1
ALBANY PL			
7100	GIL	95020	977-H4
ALBAR CT			
13900	SAR	95070	872-A1
ALBATROSS CT			
-	CMBL	95008	853-D5
ALBATROSS DR			
1500	SUNV	94087	832-E5
ALBEMAR CT			
3100	SJS	95148	855-D2
ALBERNI ST			
900	EPA	94303	791-A1
ALBERT AV			
1700	SJS	95124	873-H4
ALBERT CT			
100	LGTS	95032	873-B6
ALBERT DR			
200	LGTS	95032	873-B6
ALBERT WY			
600	CMBL	95008	853-C7
ALBERTA AV			
500	SUNV	94087	832-D5
1700	SJS	95125	854-B4
ALBERTA CT			
2300	SCL	95050	833-C2
ALBERTO WY			
400	LGTS	95032	873-B7
ALBERTSTONE DR			
4000	SJS	95130	853-B5
ALBERTSWORTH LN			
10400	LAH	94024	831-E5
ALBION CT			
500	SJS	95136	874-F1
1200	SUNV	94024	832-A4
1600	HOLL	95023	1040-D6
ALBION DR			
500	SJS	95136	874-E1
ALBION LN			
1200	SUNV	94024	832-A4
ALBRIGHT CT			
100	LGTS	95032	873-C3
ALBRIGHT DR			
1400	HOLL	95023	1040-D6
ALBRIGHT WY			
-	LGTS	95032	873-C3
ALBY CT			
1600	SJS	95124	873-J3
ALCALA CT			
-	MGH	95037	917-B3
ALCALDE RD			
17600	CPTO	95014	851-J1
22500	CPTO	95014	852-A1
ALCALDE ST			
2100	SCL	95054	813-C4
ALCANTE DR			
6000	SJS	95129	852-G3
ALCAZAR AV			
21700	CPTO	95014	852-B1
ALCAZAR DR			
5800	SJS	95123	874-G5
ALCOSTA DR			
800	MPS	95035	794-B6
ALCOTT WY			
18400	SAR	95070	872-H1
ALDEAN AV			
300	MTVW	94043	811-F2
ALDEN WY			
3500	SJS	95117	853-C1
ALDER CT			
-	HOLL	95023	1040-E5
13400	SAR	95070	852-E7
13400	SAR	95070	872-E1
ALDER DR			
500	MPS	95035	813-H2
ALDER PL			
-	MLPK	94025	790-H2
ALDER ST			
-	HOLL	95023	1040-E5
700	GIL	95020	977-J6
ALDERBROOK LN			
700	CPTO	95014	852-F2
1000	SJS	95129	852-F3
ALDERBROOK WY			
19700	CPTO	95014	852-F2
ALDER CREEK CT			
1600	SJS	95148	835-D4
ALDERCROFT HEIGHTS RD			
20600	SCIC	95033	912-J1
20600	SCIC	95033	913-A1
ALDER LAKE CT			
1300	SJS	95131	814-B5
ALDERMONT CT			
-	MGH	95037	937-A1
ALDERNEY CT			
22100	SCIC	94024	832-A6
ALDER SPRING WY			
7100	SJS	95139	895-F1
ALDERWOOD AV			
1200	SUNV	94089	812-J3
ALDERWOOD DR			
2500	SJS	95132	814-C3
ALDO AV			
400	SCL	95054	813-E6
ALDO CT			
14000	SJS	95127	835-A4
ALDRICH WY			
1500	SJS	95121	854-J3
1500	SJS	95121	855-A2
ALDWORTH DR			
2700	SJS	95148	835-E7
ALEGRA TER			
400	MPS	95035	793-G3
ALEGRE AV			
1000	LALT	94024	831-H2
ALEGRE PL			
-	SJS	95126	833-D1
ALEGRIA LP			
-	SJS	95128	853-G4
ALEJANDRA AV			
-	ATN	94027	790-E3
-	MLPK	94027	790-E3
ALEJANDRO DR			
26800	LAH	94022	811-A5
ALELANTO LN			
3100	SJS	95135	855-E3
ALERCHE DR			
100	LGTS	95032	873-H7
ALES PL			
300	SCIC	95046	937-E7
ALESSANDRO DR			
3000	SJS	95135	855-E2
ALESSI CT			
11000	SCIC	95020	958-B1
ALESTER AV			
600	PA	94303	791-C4
ALEX DR			
4400	SJS	95130	853-A7
4500	SJS	95130	852-J7
ALEXANDER AV			
-	SJS	95116	834-H2
100	SMCo	94061	790-B2
200	LGTS	95030	872-J7
3000	SCL	95051	833-A6
16300	MSER	95030	872-J7
ALEXANDER CT			
-	SJS	95116	834-H2
1600	LALT	94024	832-A4
ALEXANDER LN			
200	SBnC	95045	1037-G1
ALEXANDER PL			
26300	LAH	94022	811-B6
ALEXANDER ST			
6900	GIL	95020	978-A3
ALEXANDER WY			
400	MPS	95035	794-D5
1600	LALT	94024	832-A4
ALEXANDRA CT			
-	SJS	95125	854-D6
ALEXANDRIA LN			
4800	SJS	95129	853-B2
ALEXIAN DR			
2100	SJS	95116	834-G3
ALEXIS CT			
-	MLPK	94025	790-C7
900	SJS	95116	834-H5
ALEXIS DR			
900	PA	94304	830-F1
3000	PA	94304	810-F7
3200	LAH	94022	810-G7
ALEXIS MANOR PL			
-	SJS	95120	894-J4
ALFORD AV			
1800	LALT	94024	832-A4
1900	LALT	94024	831-J5
ALFRED ST			
3000	SCL	95054	813-D7
ALFRED WY			
2300	SJS	95122	834-J6
2400	SJS	95122	835-A5
ALGEN LN			
100	ScrC	95076	976-A7
ALGER DR			
400	PA	94306	791-D7
400	PA	94306	811-D1
ALGIERS AV			
1000	SJS	95122	834-G7
ALGONQUIN WY			
5600	SJS	95138	875-F1
ALHAMBRA AV			
10000	CPTO	95014	832-C7
ALHAMBRA CT			
-	PTLV	94028	810-D6
ALHAMBRA DR			
2500	SCL	95051	833-B1
ALICANTE DR			
-	MGH	95037	917-C2
-	SJS	95134	813-F3
ALICANTE LN			
25900	LAH	94022	811-C6
ALICANTE PL			
-	MGH	95037	917-C2
ALICANTE CIRCULA			
-	MGH	95037	917-B2
ALICE AV			
-	CMBL	95008	853-E6
400	MTVW	94041	812-A7
ALICE DR			
1100	SCL	95050	833-D4
ALICE LN			
900	MLPK	94025	790-F4
ALICE WY			
900	SUNV	94087	832-G4
ALICIA CT			
10400	CPTO	95014	851-J1
ALICIA WY			
300	LALT	94022	811-F5
ALISA CT			
17400	MGH	95037	917-D5
ALISAL AV			
1500	SJS	95125	854-A7
1500	SJS	95125	874-A1
ALISAL CT			
800	MPS	95035	794-B5
ALISO WY			
-	SMCo	94028	810-E3
ALISON AV			
1500	MTVW	94040	811-H7
ALISSA CT			
-	HOLL	95023	1040-B7
ALISSA DR			
-	HOLL	95023	1040-B7
ALISTER CT			
-	GIL	95020	977-D3
ALKAE CT			
1200	SJS	95121	855-A4
ALKIRE AV			
400	MGH	95037	936-H1
ALL AMERICA WY			
700	SUNV	94086	832-D1
ALLARDICE WY			
800	SCIC	94305	810-J2
ALLEGADO AL			
-	SJS	95128	853-G4
ALLEGAN CIR			
400	SJS	95123	875-A6
ALLEGHANY CT			
6500	SJS	95120	894-C6
ALLEGHENY DR			
600	SUNV	94087	832-D1
ALLEGRO LN			
4700	SJS	95111	875-A1
ALLEN AV			
5600	SJS	95123	874-F5
ALLEN CT			
-	MPS	95035	794-C7
700	PA	94303	791-D6
3300	SCL	95051	832-J7
ALLEN RD			
-	MTVW	94043	812-A1
ALLEN WY			
1000	CMBL	95008	853-B7
3100	SCL	95051	833-A7
3200	SCL	95051	832-J7
ALLENDALE AV			
18400	SAR	95070	872-G1
ALLENTOWN CT			
2300	SJS	95125	854-D3
ALLENWOOD CT			
2900	SJS	95148	855-D1
ALLENWOOD DR			
3000	SJS	95148	855-D1
3100	SJS	95148	835-D7
ALLEY WY			
-	MTVW	94040	811-F3
ALLISON WY			
700	SUNV	94087	832-C4
1800	SJS	95132	814-C4
ALLSTON CT			
1100	SJS	95120	894-F2
ALLSTON WY			
1100	SJS	95120	894-F2
W ALMA AV			
-	SJS	95110	854-C2
200	SJS	95125	854-C2
ALMA CT			
-	LALT	94022	811-E5
1200	SJS	95112	854-D2
21500	SCIC	95033	912-J3
ALMA LN			
-	MLPK	94025	790-G3
ALMA LP			
1400	SJS	95125	854-C3
ALMA ST			
-	MLPK	94025	790-G3
-	PA	94301	790-H4
1200	PA	94301	791-B7
1500	PA	94306	791-B7
2900	PA	94306	811-D1
3900	MTVW	94040	811-E2
E ALMA ST			
100	SJS	95112	854-D2
ALMA TER			
1500	SJS	95125	854-C3
ALMA BRIDGE RD			
17000	SCIC	95033	892-J3
17200	SCIC	95033	893-A4
19200	SCIC	95033	913-A1
ALMA COLLEGE RD			
19000	SCIC	95033	892-H6
ALMADEN AV			
100	MPS	95035	793-J6
100	SJS	95110	834-C1
100	MPS	95035	794-A6
400	SJS	95110	834-B7
800	SUNV	94086	812-H5
21800	CPTO	95014	852-B1
N ALMADEN AV			
-	SJS	95113	834-A6
-	SJS	95110	834-A6
S ALMADEN AV			
-	SJS	95113	834-B6
N ALMADEN BLVD			
-	SJS	95110	834-B6
100	SJS	95113	834-B6
S ALMADEN BLVD			
-	SJS	95113	834-B6
-	SJS	95110	834-B6
ALMADEN CT			
26800	LAH	94022	830-J2
26800	LAH	94022	831-A2
ALMADEN EXWY			
3700	SJS	95118	874-C1
3800	SJS	95136	874-C1
ALMADEN EXWY Rt#-G8			
700	SJS	95125	854-C6
3300	SJS	95118	854-C6
3300	SJS	95136	854-C6
3400	SJS	95136	874-D2
3500	SJS	95118	874-D2
9000	SJS	95123	874-D2
11900	SJS	95120	874-D2
15700	SJS	95120	894-F2
ALMADEN RD			
1300	SJS	95110	854-C5
1600	SJS	95125	854-C5
3600	SJS	95118	874-C1
5900	SJS	95120	874-D6
6300	SJS	95120	894-E1
19400	SCIC	95120	894-J5
20200	SCIC	95120	895-A6
21700	SCIC	95120	914-J1
ALMADEN RD Rt#-G8			
3100	SJS	95125	854-D3
ALMADEN WY			
21700	SCIC	95120	894-J7
21700	SCIC	95120	914-J1
ALMADEN LAKE DR			
900	SJS	95123	874-D6
ALMADEN VALLEY DR			
1400	SJS	95120	874-A6
ALMADEN VILLAGE RD			
1000	SJS	95120	894-G3
ALMA JO CT			
15100	MSER	95030	872-J4
ALMANOR AV			
600	SUNV	94086	812-E4
1000	MLPK	94025	790-H1
ALMANOR CT			
1400	SJS	95132	814-F5
ALMANSA CT			
3200	SJS	95127	814-H6
ALMARIDA DR			
600	CMBL	95008	853-E5
1000	CMBL	95128	853-E3
1000	SJS	95128	853-E3
ALMENDRA AV			
200	LGTS	95030	873-A7
ALMENDRA LN			
-	LALT	94022	811-E6
ALMENDRAL AV			
-	ATN	94027	790-C3
ALMERIA DR			
700	SJS	95123	874-F5
ALMOND AV			
-	LALT	94022	811-E6
500	LALT	94024	811-E6
ALMOND CT			
-	EPA	94303	791-C2
-	HOLL	95023	1039-J3
ALMOND DR			
-	HOLL	95023	1039-H4
2900	SJS	95148	835-C7
ALMOND WY			
1500	MGH	95037	917-D6
ALMOND BLOSSOM CT			
100	LGTS	95032	873-J6
ALMOND BLOSSOM LN			
1600	SJS	95124	873-H6
1700	LGTS	95032	873-H6
ALMOND HILL CT			
100	LGTS	95032	873-C3
ALMOND ORCHARD DR			
1200	MGH	95037	916-G7
ALMONDWOOD WY			
700	SJS	95120	894-H3
ALOHA AV			
14600	SAR	95070	872-D3
ALOHA DR			
200	SJS	95136	854-G7
ALONDRA LN			
15100	SAR	95070	872-F4
ALONSO DR			
1100	SJS	95126	853-G3
ALPET DR			
1900	SCIC	95037	917-D4
ALPHA CT			
600	CMBL	95008	873-C1
ALPINE AV			
-	LGTS	95030	893-B1
200	SJS	95127	834-H1
1300	SCL	95051	833-A4
ALPINE CIR			
1300	HOLL	95023	1040-D4
1300	SBnC	95023	1040-D4
ALPINE DR			
10100	CPTO	95014	832-A7
22600	CPTO	95014	831-J7
ALPINE RD			
-	PTLV	94028	810-D7
-	PTLV	94028	830-C1
-	SMCo	94028	830-D5
2400	SMCo	94025	790-E7
2400	MLPK	94025	790-E7
2400	MLPK	94025	810-E3
2500	SMCo	94025	810-E3
2900	SMCo	94028	810-E3
ALPINE TER			
900	SUNV	94086	812-D6
ALRIC CT			
300	SJS	95123	875-B7
ALRIC DR			
300	SJS	95123	875-B7
ALRIDGE DR			
1300	SUNV	94087	832-D4
ALSACE CT			
-	SJS	95135	855-F3

STREET Block City ZIP Pg-Grid

ALTA AV
1000 MTVW 94043 811-H1
ALTA CT
2200 SJS 95131 814-A5
N ALTA LN
13000 LAH 94022 831-C1
S ALTA LN
13000 LAH 94022 831-C1
ALTA RD
- SClC 94304 810-F1
ALTADENA DR
26100 LAH 94022 811-B6
ALTADENA LN
3900 SClC 95127 815-A7
3900 SClC 95127 835-A1
ALTA GLEN CT
1500 SJS 95125 853-J4
ALTA GLEN DR
1500 SJS 95125 853-J5
ALTA HEIGHTS CT
100 LGTS 95030 893-B1
ALTAIR WY
300 SUNV 94086 812-E7
ALTA MAR TER
- SJS 95126 833-D1
ALTAMARA AV
- SJS 95135 855-F2
- SJS 95148 855-F2
ALTAMEAD DR
1100 LALT 94024 831-H2
ALTA MESA AV
4100 PA 94306 811-D2
ALTA MIRA DR
1000 SCL 95051 832-J4
ALTA MIRA PL
1800 SJS 95124 873-H1
ALTAMONT AV
1500 SJS 95125 874-A1
ALTAMONT CIR
27700 SClC 94022 830-G1
ALTAMONT CT
800 SUNV 94086 812-G5
12100 LAH 94022 831-B3
ALTAMONT DR
400 MPS 95035 794-A5
ALTAMONT LN
27300 LAH 94022 831-A2
ALTAMONT RD
25300 LAH 94022 831-A2
26600 LAH 94022 830-H1
ALTA OAK WY
- GIL 95020 977-J5
ALTA PASEO CT
6500 SJS 95120 894-B2
ALTA TIERRA CT
100 LGTS 95032 893-G1
ALTA TIERRA RD
12800 LAH 94022 831-B1
ALTA VISTA AV
100 LALT 94022 811-D6
13900 SAR 95070 872-E2
ALTA VISTA DR
100 ATN 94027 790-B5
ALTA VISTA LN
100 SCrC 95033 913-A7
ALTA VISTA TER
- FRMT 94539 793-J1
ALTA VISTA WY
1400 HOLL 95023 1040-D6
15700 SClC 95127 815-B6
E ALTA VISTA WY
15700 SClC 95127 815-B6
15700 SJS 95127 815-B6
ALTHAM CT
1500 SJS 95132 814-F4
ALTHOFF WY
700 SJS 95116 834-F6
ALTIA AV
- SJS 95135 855-G3
ALTIMIRA CIR
- MGH 95037 917-B3
ALTINO BLVD
- SJS 95136 854-E5
ALTIPLANO WY
6700 SJS 95119 875-D7
ALTISSIMO PL
- SJS 95131 814-B6
ALTO CT
2500 SJS 95148 835-D6
ALTO LN
- MLPK 94025 790-G4
ALTON ST
- MPS 95035 793-J7
ALTOS OAKS DR
700 LALT 94024 831-G2
ALTO VERDE LN
12800 LAH 94022 811-B6
ALTREE CT
- ATN 94027 790-H1
ALTSCHUL AV
900 MLPK 94025 790-D6
1000 SMCo 94025 790-D6
ALTURAS AV
200 SUNV 94086 812-F4
ALTURAS DR
1400 HOLL 95023 1040-D7
ALTURA VISTA
100 LGTS 95032 872-J2
ALUM ROCK AV
1100 SJS 95116 834-E4
12900 SClC 95127 815-B6
14600 SJS 95127 815-B6
ALUM ROCK AV Rt#-130
700 SJS 95116 834-H3
2700 SClC 95127 834-H3
2700 SJS 95127 834-H3
4600 SClC 95127 835-A1
4600 SJS 95127 835-A1
5100 SClC 95127 815-A7
ALUM ROCK RD
16100 SJS 95127 815-B5

STREET Block City ZIP Pg-Grid

ALUM ROCK FALLS RD
18200 SJS 95127 815-B5
18200 SJS 95132 815-C5
20000 SClC 95127 815-F5
20000 SClC 95140 815-F5
20000 SClC 95132 815-F5
ALVARADO AV
- LALT 94022 811-E5
700 SUNV 94086 812-G5
ALVARADO CT
700 SClC 94305 810-J1
5900 SJS 95120 874-A7
13400 SAR 95070 852-H7
13400 SAR 95070 872-H1
ALVARADO DR
2400 SCL 95051 833-C2
ALVARADO RW
500 SClC 94305 790-H7
500 SClC 94305 810-H1
ALVARADO ST
- HOLL 95023 1040-A3
ALVAREZ COM
- MPS 95035 813-J1
- MPS 95035 814-A1
ALVAREZ CT
- MPS 95035 814-A1
ALVERNAZ DR
1100 SJS 95121 855-A5
ALVES CT
1400 SJS 95131 814-A4
ALVES DR
20500 CPTO 95014 832-D7
ALVESWOOD CIR
2500 SJS 95131 814-C4
ALVIENA DR
2900 SClC 95133 834-H1
ALVIN AV
2400 SJS 95121 854-J2
2600 SJS 95121 855-A2
ALVIN ST
2400 MTVW 94043 811-F2
ALVINA CT
700 LALT 94024 831-G2
ALVISO ST
- SCL 95050 833-E3
500 SCL 95053 833-F5
1100 SJS 95050 833-F5
1100 SJS 95126 833-F5
ALVISO ADOBE CT
- MPS 95035 794-D6
ALVISO-MILPITAS RD
- MPS 95035 813-G1
1500 SJS 95134 813-F1
ALWOOD CT
2800 SJS 95148 835-D7
ALYSHEBA AV
200 SJS 95111 875-B3
ALYSSA CT
700 SJS 95138 875-F4
ALYSSA DR
6600 SJS 95138 875-F4
ALYSSUM LN
- SJS 95128 853-E1
AMADOR AV
- ATN 94027 790-C3
400 LALT 94024 811-F7
800 SUNV 94086 812-H5
AMADOR CIR
1200 HOLL 95023 1039-H3
AMADOR CT
2300 SJS 95122 834-J5
AMADOR DR
2200 SJS 95122 834-J5
AMADOR OAK CT
10000 CPTO 95014 831-C7
AMALFI WY
1900 MTVW 94040 831-H1
AMANDA AV
8500 GIL 95020 977-H1
AMANDA DR
700 SJS 95136 874-E1
AMANDA LN
100 LGTS 95032 873-D6
AMANDA LYNE CT
- SJS 95120 894-H4
AMAPOLA DR
5800 SJS 95129 852-G3
AMAPOLO CT
23800 CPTO 95014 831-G5
AMARANTA AV
4000 PA 94306 811-C2
AMARANTA CT
4100 PA 94306 811-C3
AMARGOSA CT
400 SJS 95111 854-G7
AMARILLO AV
900 PA 94303 791-D5
AMARILLO CT
48700 FRMT 94539 793-J2
AMARO LN
- SJS 95135 855-F2
AMARYL CT
2500 SJS 95132 814-E6
AMARYL DR
2400 SJS 95132 814-E5
AMATO AV
- CMBL 95008 853-C5
AMBAR WY
300 MLPK 94025 790-F6
AMBASSADOR CT
200 LGTS 95030 893-A1
AMBER CT
- HOLL 95023 1040-A3
1400 GIL 95020 977-F3
AMBER DR
3400 SJS 95117 853-C3
AMBER LN
800 LALT 94024 831-E1
AMBERGROVE DR
1400 SJS 95131 814-C7
AMBERLY LN
- SJS 95121 855-A3

STREET Block City ZIP Pg-Grid

AMBER OAK CT
100 LGTS 95032 873-B2
AMBERWOOD CT
2000 SJS 95132 814-D3
AMBERWOOD LN
2000 SJS 95132 814-D2
14700 SClC 95037 937-C4
AMBLER CT
3900 SJS 95111 855-A6
AMBLER WY
3900 SJS 95111 855-A6
AMBLESIDE LN
18600 SAR 95070 872-H3
AMBOY DR
500 SJS 95136 874-F2
AMBRA WY
3400 SJS 95132 814-G2
AMBRIC KNOLLS RD
21000 SAR 95070 872-C3
AMBROSE CT
4000 SJS 95121 855-A5
AMBROSE RD
17000 SClC 95070 872-B7
AMBUM AV
3400 SJS 95148 835-E7
AMBY DR
5400 SJS 95124 873-J6
AMD PL
1000 SUNV 94086 812-H6
AMELIA CT
10100 CPTO 95014 832-A7
AMELIA DR
5100 SJS 95118 874-A4
AMELIA WY
1800 SCL 95050 833-C3
AMERICA AV
300 SUNV 94086 812-F6
AMERICAN CT
- SBnC 95023 1060-B1
6500 SJS 95120 894-C6
AMERICAN WY
1300 SMCo 94025 790-D5
AMERICAN OAK DR
8600 SJS 95135 855-J6
AMERICUS DR
3300 SJS 95148 835-E7
AMES AV
700 PA 94303 791-D7
1100 MPS 95035 814-C1
AMES CT
800 PA 94303 791-E7
AMESBURY WY
1400 SJS 95127 835-A4
AMETHYST CT
5000 SJS 95136 874-E3
AMETHYST DR
2100 SCL 95051 833-A1
AMHERST AV
- SMCo 94025 790-D1
AMHERST CT
3500 MTVW 94040 831-J2
14100 LAH 94022 810-H5
AMHERST DR
19600 CPTO 95014 832-F7
AMHERST LN
3200 SJS 95117 853-D3
AMHERST ST
2000 PA 94306 810-J1
2100 PA 94306 811-A1
AMHERST TR
- SUNV 94087 832-D1
AMIDY GARDEN WY
- SJS 95136 854-E3
AMIGOS CT
24400 LAH 94024 831-E2
AMISTAD CT
10300 CPTO 95014 851-J1
AMISTAD LN
12000 SClC 95046 937-H7
12000 SClC 95046 957-H1
AMONDO DR
5000 SJS 95129 852-J3
AMOS WY
4000 SJS 95135 855-F3
AMPHITHEATRE PKWY
- MTVW 94043 811-H1
AMSTEL CT
2100 SJS 95116 834-G3
AMSTUTZ DR
900 SJS 95129 853-A3
AMULET DR
21200 CPTO 95014 832-C6
AMULET PL
21300 CPTO 95014 832-C6
AMUR CT
2000 MPS 95035 793-J3
AMUR CREEK CT
7100 SJS 95120 894-G4
AMUR OAK LN
100 SJS 95116 834-G4
ANACAPA CT
400 SUNV 94086 812-F5
700 MPS 95035 794-B6
12900 LAH 94022 811-A6
ANACAPA DR
26300 LAH 94022 811-A6
ANACONDA WY
900 SUNV 94087 832-B4
ANAHEIM TER
- SUNV 94086 812-E7
ANAMOR ST
1600 RDWC 94061 790-A2
ANA PRIVADA
1100 MTVW 94040 832-H6
ANCHOR WY
1800 SJS 95132 814-C4
ANCHOR BAY TER
100 SUNV 94086 812-E7
ANCIL WY
3500 SJS 95117 853-C2
ANCORA CT
2200 LALT 94024 831-H6
ANCRUM CT
3000 SJS 95148 855-C2

STREET Block City ZIP Pg-Grid

ANDALUSIA WY
1600 SJS 95125 853-J7
1600 SJS 95125 854-A7
ANDARE CT
2800 SJS 95135 855-G5
ANDERSON CT
- MTVW 94043 811-J4
ANDERSON DR
700 LALT 94024 831-F1
ANDERSON RD
10200 SClC 95127 815-B7
10200 SClC 95127 835-B1
ANDERSON WY
- MLPK 94025 790-E7
- MLPK 94025 810-E1
ANDETTA WY
100 SMCo 94028 810-D3
ANDORA DR
3100 SJS 95148 835-B5
ANDORA TER
- SJS 95135 855-G2
ANDOVER DR
1100 SUNV 94087 832-B1
ANDOVER LN
1600 SJS 95124 873-J3
ANDOVER PL
900 GIL 95020 977-H4
ANDOVER WY
900 LALT 94024 831-H5
ANDRE AV
1100 MTVW 94040 832-A2
ANDRE CT
100 LGTS 95032 873-B7
ANDREA CT
3500 SJS 95117 853-C3
ANDREA DR
1000 SJS 95117 853-C3
ANDREA PL
1700 SCL 95051 833-A3
ANDREW CT
14800 SAR 95070 872-F3
ANDREWS AV
1800 SJS 95124 873-H2
ANDREWS CT
16100 MSER 95030 873-A6
ANDREWS DR
- HOLL 95023 1040-A5
ANDREWS ST
100 LGTS 95030 873-A6
300 MSER 95030 873-A6
ANDSBURY AV
200 MTVW 94043 811-J5
ANFIELD CT
4000 SJS 95136 874-D1
ANGEL AV
300 SUNV 94086 812-E7
ANGEL CT
100 LGTS 95032 873-D6
ANGELA CT
300 LALT 94022 811-F6
2200 SJS 95008 873-E1
6600 GIL 95020 977-J5
ANGELA DR
1400 LALT 94022 811-E6
ANGELA ST
1600 SJS 95125 854-C3
ANGELICA WY
- MGH 95037 916-H4
ANGELICO CT
- SJS 95135 855-J3
ANGELICO DR
- SJS 95135 855-G2
ANGELICO PL
- SJS 95135 855-J3
ANGELICO WY
- SJS 95135 855-J3
ANGELINA DR
3400 SCL 95051 832-J4
ANGELINA RD
26100 SCrC 95033 912-H7
ANGELL CT
- SClC 94305 790-J7
- SClC 94305 791-A7
ANGELO LN
6900 SClC 95020 978-H1
ANGELO WY
- SJS 95110 833-H2
ANGELONI PL
- SClC 95111 854-G5
- SJS 95111 854-G5
ANGIE AV
2100 SJS 95116 834-H5
ANGMAR CT
1100 SJS 95121 855-A5
ANGUS CT
19900 SAR 95070 852-F7
ANGUS DR
400 MPS 95035 794-B6
ANITA AV
300 SClC 94024 831-F2
ANJOU CREEK CIR
7000 SJS 95120 894-G3
ANJOU CREEK CT
7100 SJS 95120 894-G3
ANN PL
600 MPS 95035 794-B4
ANN RD
- PTLV 94028 810-A6
ANN ST
- HOLL 95023 1040-A4
ANNA AV
300 MTVW 94043 811-F3
ANNA DR
1900 SCL 95050 833-C4
4800 SJS 95124 873-G4
ANNABELLE LN
200 SBnC 95023 1020-F5
ANNANDALE PL
3400 SJS 95121 855-D5
ANNAPOLIS ST
2500 EPA 94303 791-B1
ANNAPOLIS WY
1300 SJS 95118 874-B4

STREET Block City ZIP Pg-Grid

ANN ARBOR AV
10300 CPTO 95014 832-C7
ANN ARBOR CT
100 LGTS 95032 873-D7
10200 CPTO 95014 832-C7
ANN ARBOR DR
100 LGTS 95032 873-D7
ANN DARLING DR
300 SJS 95133 834-E3
ANNE CT
1800 SJS 95124 873-H5
ANNE LN
700 MGH 95037 917-D7
19100 CPTO 95014 852-G1
ANNE WY
100 LGTS 95032 873-G5
1800 SJS 95124 873-G5
ANNE MARIE CT
- SBnC 95023 1020-E1
1800 SJS 95132 814-D3
ANNERLY CT
2000 SJS 95121 855-C5
ANNETTE LN
1900 LALT 94024 831-J5
1900 LALT 94024 832-A4
ANNETTE WY
1000 CPTO 95014 852-D3
ANNIE LN
18500 SClC 95120 894-G1
ANNIE LAURIE AV
- MTVW 94043 812-B3
ANNIE LAURIE WY
1600 SJS 95121 855-B3
ANN MARIE CT
13400 SClC 95046 937-D7
ANNONA AV
2200 SJS 95122 834-J7
2200 SJS 95122 835-A7
ANO NUEVO AV
300 SUNV 94086 812-C5
ANSDELL WY
6100 SJS 95123 875-B6
ANSEL LN
- SMCo 94025 810-E2
ANSHEN CT
800 SUNV 94086 832-F2
ANSLEY PL
18800 SAR 95070 852-H6
ANSON AV
10300 CPTO 95014 832-C7
ANSON CT
1600 GIL 95020 977-F1
ANT CT
- MGH 95037 937-C2
ANTELOPE DR
2300 SJS 95133 834-F1
ANTERO WY
800 SJS 95133 814-F7
ANTHONY CT
1800 MTVW 94040 811-F5
ANTHONY DR
2000 SJS 95008 853-B6
ANTHONY PL
10200 CPTO 95014 831-J7
ANTIGUA CT
5800 SJS 95120 874-C5
ANTIGUA DR
5800 SJS 95120 874-C5
ANTIGUA RD
2700 SJS 95111 854-H4
ANTIGUA WY
5700 SJS 95120 874-C5
ANTIQUE CT
- SJS 95125 854-C6
ANTOINETTE DR
10500 CPTO 95014 852-E2
ANTON CT
400 PA 94301 791-B6
ANTON WY
10000 CPTO 95014 832-C7
10000 CPTO 95014 852-C1
ANTONACCI CT
3400 SJS 95148 835-D6
ANTONIO CT
- PTLV 94028 810-C7
600 GIL 95020 977-J5
600 GIL 95020 978-A5
ANTONIO LN
1300 SJS 95117 853-D4
ANTWERP LN
1200 SJS 95118 874-B5
ANVIL CT
600 SJS 95133 834-F1
ANVILWOOD AV
1200 SUNV 94089 812-J3
ANVILWOOD CT
1000 SUNV 94089 812-J3
ANZA DR
13000 SAR 95070 852-G7
ANZA RD
- SJS 95134 813-G3
ANZA ST
400 MTVW 94041 811-J6
ANZAR RD
900 SBnC 95045 1018-A7
APACHE CT
600 SJS 95123 874-G5
1500 GIL 95020 957-F7
APACHE TR
- SClC 95033 913-A2
17900 SClC 95033 912-J2
APENNINES CIR
5100 SJS 95138 855-F6
APOLLO CT
- HOLL 95023 1020-B5
2600 SJS 95121 854-H3
APOLLO DR
2600 SJS 95121 854-H3
APOLLO WY
- HOLL 95023 1020-A6
1200 SUNV 94086 812-J7
13000 SAR 95070 852-D7
APOLLO HEIGHTS CT
15600 SClC 95070 872-C5

STREET Block City ZIP Pg-Grid

APPALOOSA DR
13700 SClC 95046 937-E6
APPALOOSA WY
27000 LAH 94022 830-J2
APPERSON PL
- SCL 95050 833-D2
APPERSON RIDGE CT
3100 SJS 95148 855-E2
APPERSON RIDGE DR
3100 SJS 95148 855-E2
APPIAN LN
1000 SJS 95116 834-E6
APPIAN WY
1000 MGH 95037 937-A4
APPLAUSE PL
600 SJS 95134 813-F2
APPLE CT
900 HOLL 95023 1040-C4
APPLE TER
700 SJS 95111 855-B7
APPLE BLOSSOM DR
5300 SJS 95123 875-A3
APPLE BLOSSOM LN
- CMBL 95008 853-D5
APPLEBLOSSOM LN
16400 SClC 95032 873-C5
APPLEGATE CT
6400 SJS 95119 875-C7
APPLEGATE DR
6400 SJS 95119 875-C7
APPLE GROVE CT
7000 SJS 95135 876-A1
APPLETON DR
3500 SJS 95117 853-C2
APPLE TREE DR
20000 CPTO 95014 832-E7
APPLETREE LN
- HOLL 95023 1039-H4
1800 MTVW 94040 831-G1
APPLE VALLEY DR
800 SJS 95125 854-D5
APPLEWOOD DR
4600 SJS 95129 852-J2
4600 SJS 95129 853-A2
APPLEWOOD LN
- PTLV 94028 810-C7
APPLEY WY
2400 SJS 95124 873-E5
APRICOT AV
900 CMBL 95008 853-F6
APRICOT LN
100 LGTS 95030 872-J7
200 MTVW 94040 831-J2
300 HOLL 95023 1039-H5
300 SBnC 95023 1039-H5
2500 SJS 95121 855-E4
APRICOT HILL CT
14000 SAR 95070 872-H2
APRIL DR
100 SJS 95138 875-D4
APRIL WY
400 CMBL 95008 853-G5
APRILSONG CT
1700 SJS 95131 814-D7
APSIS AV
2400 SJS 95124 873-D3
APSIS CT
2300 SJS 95124 873-E3
APTOS AV
4500 SJS 95111 875-A1
APTOS BEACH CT
7100 SJS 95139 895-F1
AQUARIUS DR
500 SJS 95111 854-F6
AQUILA AV
4000 SJS 95124 873-E3
AQUINO WY
18500 SAR 95070 872-H3
ARABELLE WY
- SJS 95132 814-G5
ARABIAN CT
2300 MGH 95037 917-F6
5900 SJS 95123 874-J5
ARABIAN ST
400 SJS 95123 874-J5
ARABICA TER
- SJS 95126 833-D1
ARAGLIN CT
4000 SJS 95136 854-E5
ARAGON CT
2500 SJS 95125 853-J7
ARAGON WY
2400 SJS 95125 853-J7
2600 SJS 95125 873-J1
ARAKI RD
- SCrC 95033 892-A7
ARAM AV
600 CMBL 95128 853-F4
600 SJS 95128 853-F4
ARAMIS DR
3200 SJS 95127 835-B3
ARANA CT
1700 MPS 95035 794-D5
ARAPAHO DR
900 GIL 95020 957-F7
5700 SJS 95123 874-H5
ARAPAHOE CT
- PTLV 94028 810-B6
ARAPAHOE TR
17700 SClC 95033 913-C2
ARASTRADERO RD
500 PA 94306 811-A5
800 PA 94304 811-A5
900 LAH 94022 811-A5
1500 PA 94304 810-F6
1700 SClC 94304 810-H5
1700 PTLV 94028 810-F6
27100 SClC 94304 811-A5
27500 LAH 94022 810-H5
ARATA CT
1500 SJS 95125 854-C3
ARATA WY
18800 CPTO 95014 852-H1

STREET Block City ZIP Pg-Grid

ARAUJO ST
1300 SJS 95131 814-C7
ARBELECHE LN
20400 SAR 95070 872-D2
ARBOL DR
4000 PA 94306 811-C2
ARBOLADO WY
18500 SAR 95070 872-H3
ARBOLEDA DR
300 LALT 94024 811-F7
300 LALT 94024 831-F1
ARBOL GRANDE CT
- SMCo 94025 790-D5
ARBOR AV
1200 SClC 94024 831-G3
E ARBOR AV
100 SUNV 94086 812-F6
W ARBOR AV
100 SUNV 94086 812-E5
ARBOR CT
1200 MTVW 94040 832-A2
ARBOR DR
1600 SJS 95125 854-C4
ARBOR RD
- MLPK 94025 790-E4
ARBOR ST
8700 GIL 95020 977-H1
ARBOR WY
700 MPS 95035 793-J4
ARBOR DELL WY
5600 SJS 95124 873-J6
ARBORETA CT
- SJS 95116 834-F7
ARBORETUM DR
5200 LALT 94024 831-J6
ARBORETUM RD
300 SClC 94305 790-H5
300 PA 94304 790-H5
ARBOR PARK CT
1300 SJS 95126 853-H3
ARBOR PARK DR
1300 SJS 95126 853-H3
ARBOR REAL WY
- PA 94306 811-D2
ARBOR VALLEY DR
200 SJS 95119 875-E7
ARBOR VALLEY PL
200 SJS 95119 875-E7
ARBOR VISTA WY
1100 SJS 95126 853-H3
ARBOUR LN
500 HOLL 95023 1040-B3
ARBUCKLE AV
3700 SJS 95124 873-H2
ARBUCKLE CT
1500 SCL 95054 813-D7
ARBUELO WY
- LALT 94022 811-E5
ARBUTUS AV
600 SUNV 94086 832-F1
3500 PA 94303 791-E7
ARBUTUS DR
1500 SJS 95118 874-A5
ARC RD
200 CMBL 95008 853-F5
ARCADE AV
- SJS 95148 855-F1
ARCADIA AV
- SCL 95051 832-J7
ARCADIA DR
3300 SJS 95117 853-D1
3300 SClC 95117 853-D1
ARCADIA PL
1400 PA 94303 791-B4
ARCADIA TER
600 SUNV 94086 812-G5
ARCADIAN ST
48200 FRMT 94539 793-J1
ARCADIA PALMS DR
14000 SAR 95070 872-H2
ARCHANGEL DR
- SJS 95002 813-C1
ARCHBOW CT
4700 SJS 95136 874-H3
ARCHBURY CT
3200 SJS 95148 855-F1
ARCHCOVE CT
400 SJS 95111 875-C1
ARCHER CT
1500 CMBL 95008 873-A1
ARCHER ST
- SJS 95112 833-J2
1300 SJS 95002 793-B7
ARCHER WY
1100 CMBL 95008 873-A1
ARCHFIELD CT
1500 MGH 95037 917-D6
ARCHGLEN WY
400 SJS 95111 875-C1
ARCHIBALD DR
15400 SClC 95070 872-C4
ARCHSHIRE CT
3200 SJS 95148 835-F7
ARCHWOOD CIR
2900 SJS 95148 855-D1
ARCO CT
300 SJS 95123 874-J4
ARCOLA CT
3100 SJS 95148 855-D2
ARCTIC AV
2500 SJS 95111 854-G4
ARDEN CT
- RDWC 94061 790-A1
19500 SAR 95070 852-F5
ARDEN RD
200 MLPK 94025 790-F2
ARDEN WY
2300 SJS 95122 834-J5
ARDEN FARMS PL
3900 SJS 95111 854-J7
ARDENWOOD DR
1500 SJS 95129 852-F5
ARDILLA CT
2500 SJS 95128 853-F4

STREET
Block City ZIP Pg-Grid

ARDIS AV
300 SJS 95117 853-D2
300 SCIC 95117 853-D1
ARDIS DR
2000 SJS 95125 854-C5
ARDMORE CT
19500 SAR 95070 852-F5
ARDMORE WY
5300 SJS 95118 874-A5
ARDSLEY CT
1100 SJS 95120 874-C6
ARENA WY
900 HOLL 95023 1040-C4
AREQUIPA CT
200 SJS 95119 875-D7
AREZZO DR
5200 SJS 95138 855-E7
5200 SJS 95138 875-F1
AREZZO WY
5200 SJS 95138 855-E7
5200 SJS 95138 875-E1
ARGONAUT CT
20200 SAR 95070 852-E7
ARGONAUT DR
10100 SAR 95070 852-E7
ARGONNE AV
600 HOLL 95023 1040-B5
ARGONNE DR
13300 SAR 95070 852-D7
ARGUELLO AV
- MGH 95037 917-B3
ARGUELLO CT
- MGH 95037 917-B3
ARGUELLO PL
2300 SCL 95050 833-C3
ARGUELLO ST
600 SCIC 94305 790-H7
ARGUS WY
600 SCL 95054 813-E5
ARGYLE CT
1500 SJS 95132 814-F3
ARIC LN
26400 LAH 94022 811-B5
ARIEL CT
400 SJS 95123 874-J5
ARIEL DR
400 SJS 95123 874-J5
ARIEL-JOSHUA DR
- SJS 95135 855-G2
ARIES WY
100 SUNV 94086 812-E7
ARIZONA AV
1100 MPS 95035 794-A3
1800 MPS 95035 793-J3
ARIZONA WY
1900 RDWC 94061 790-A3
ARKANSAS CT
48400 FRMT 94539 793-J1
ARLEE DR
18000 MSER 95030 872-J6
ARLEEN AV
1300 SUNV 94087 832-F4
ARLEEN WY
2100 SJS 95130 852-J6
ARLEN CT
3700 SJS 95132 814-F2
ARLENE DR
2300 SCL 95050 833-C5
ARLETA AV
300 SCIC 95128 853-G1
ARLIA DR
1300 SCIC 95046 937-J7
ARLINE LN
2000 SCIC 95037 917-D4
ARLINGTON CT
900 SUNV 94087 832-C1
1400 SCIC 95046 937-G4
ARLINGTON DR
2500 SBnC 95023 1040-E3
ARLINGTON LN
1000 SJS 95129 852-E3
ARLINGTON WY
- SMCo 94025 790-H2
- MLPK 94025 790-H2
ARMAND AV
- MTVW 94043 811-J2
ARMAND CT
1000 GIL 95020 977-H4
ARMAND DR
1700 MPS 95035 794-D6
ARMANINI AV
600 SCL 95050 833-C5
ARMDALE CT
3000 SJS 95148 855-C2
ARMED CT
300 SJS 95111 875-B2
ARMONK CT
5300 SJS 95123 875-B3
ARMORY DR
- HOLL 95023 1020-A5
ARMOUR DR
4600 SCL 95054 813-D4
ARMSBY LN
15300 SCIC 95037 936-G6
ARMSTEAD CT
2800 SJS 95121 855-A2
ARMSTRONG PL
2400 SCL 95050 833-C5
ARNERICH RD
14200 LGTS 95032 893-H2
14200 SCIC 95032 893-H2
ARNERICH HILL RD
14500 LGTS 95032 893-G1
14500 SCIC 95032 893-G1
ARNICA CT
4900 SJS 95111 875-A2
ARNO CT
- SJS 95138 855-E7
- SJS 95138 875-E1
ARNOLD AV
- SCIC 94043 812-A2
1200 SJS 95110 833-J2
ARNOLD DR
300 GIL 95020 977-H1
ARNOLD WY
700 MLPK 94025 790-J2
800 SJS 95128 853-F4
ARNOTT WY
1000 CMBL 95008 853-G6
ARPEGGIO AV
4100 SJS 95136 874-G1
ARQUEADO DR
3200 SJS 95148 835-D7
ARQUES AV
1200 SUNV 94086 812-J7
1200 SUNV 94086 813-A7
E ARQUES AV
100 SUNV 94086 812-F6
W ARQUES AV
100 SUNV 94086 812-E6
ARRAN CT
500 SUNV 94087 832-E4
ARREZO POINTE CT
- SJS 95148 855-G2
ARREZO POINTE LN
- SJS 95148 855-G2
ARRIBA CT
1500 SCIC 94024 831-G3
ARRIBA DR
200 SUNV 94086 812-B7
ARROBA WY
3000 SJS 95118 874-A1
ARROW LN
1100 SJS 95126 853-H4
ARROWHEAD DR
600 SJS 95123 874-H6
5400 SJS 95123 875-B4
ARROWHEAD LN
- SMCo 94025 790-D1
- SMCo 94063 790-D1
21400 SAR 95070 852-B5
ARROWHEAD WY
1000 PA 94303 791-D5
ARROWOOD CT
600 LALT 94024 831-F2
ARROWOOD LN
2000 SJS 95130 853-A6
ARROW ROCK PL
900 SUNV 94087 832-B4
ARROYO CIR
7500 GIL 95020 978-B1
ARROYO CT
4200 PA 94306 811-C4
ARROYO DR
100 SJS 95131 814-A5
2400 SCL 95051 833-B4
ARROYO LN
17900 SAR 95070 852-D5
ARROYO RD
700 LALT 94024 811-G6
ARROYO WY
100 SJS 95112 834-D5
ARROYO DE ARGUELLO
12000 SAR 95070 852-D6
ARROYO DEL RANCHO
500 LGTS 95032 893-G1
ARROYO DE ORO
1700 SJS 95116 834-F3
ARROYO DE PLATINA
1800 SJS 95116 834-F3
ARROYO GRANDE WY
100 LGTS 95032 873-C4
ARROYO OAKS
11500 LAH 94024 831-F4
ARROYO SECO DR
- SBnC 95023 1000-E7
- SBnC 95023 1020-E1
1100 CMBL 95008 853-G6
1500 SCIC 95125 853-G6
ARTHUR AV
3200 SJS 95127 835-B3
ARTHUR CT
1200 LALT 94024 831-H4
3000 SCL 95051 833-A7
ARTHUR LN
- ATN 94027 790-C2
ARTHUR PL
1100 SJS 95127 835-A3
ARTISAN WY
- SJS 95125 853-J4
ARUNDEL CT
4900 SJS 95136 874-F2
ASBURY PL
700 SCL 95051 833-B5
ASBURY ST
- SJS 95110 834-A4
300 SJS 95110 833-J5
700 SJS 95126 833-H6
ASBURY WY
1000 MTVW 94043 811-H4
ASCENSION DR
19600 SAR 95070 852-F5
26400 LAH 94022 811-B6
ASCENTE COMS
- SJS 95125 854-E5
ASCHAUER CT
1100 SJS 95131 834-D1
ASCOT CT
17000 MGH 95037 917-E6
ASCOT LN
3000 SJS 95111 854-H5
ASH CT
100 LGTS 95032 873-A3
600 CMBL 95008 853-F5
1500 MGH 95037 917-D6
ASH LN
- HOLL 95023 1039-H4
100 PTLV 94028 810-E4
ASH ST
400 RDWC 94061 790-B1
1800 PA 94306 791-A7
1800 SCL 95054 813-D5
3200 PA 94306 811-B1
ASHBOURNE CT
10700 CPTO 95014 852-C6
ASHBOURNE DR
600 SUNV 94087 832-E4
ASHBROOK CIR
4100 SJS 95124 873-E3
ASHBURTON DR
6000 SJS 95123 875-A6
ASHBURY CT
6000 GIL 95020 977-J6
ASHBY AV
4500 SJS 95124 873-F3
ASHBY DR
700 PA 94301 791-B3
ASHBY LN
100 LALT 94022 811-D5
ASHCROFT CT
1700 SCIC 95020 958-A2
ASHCROFT LN
1200 SJS 95118 874-C5
ASHCROFT WY
1100 SUNV 94087 832-A5
ASHDALE DR
10200 SCIC 95127 835-B2
ASHEBORO CT
1400 SJS 95131 814-C6
ASHER CT
3900 SJS 95124 873-E3
ASHFIELD CT
6500 SJS 95120 894-C1
ASHFIELD RD
- ATN 94027 790-E2
ASHFORD CIR
- SBnC - 1059-J2
- SBnC - 1060-A2
ASHFORD CT
1200 SJS 95131 834-C1
ASHGLEN WY
2300 SJS 95133 834-F1
ASH GROVE CT
100 SJS 95123 875-A3
ASHLAND DR
1400 MPS 95035 794-D7
ASHLAND WY
1900 SJS 95130 852-J6
ASHLER AV
- LGTS 95030 873-A6
ASHLEY CT
2800 SJS 95135 855-G5
12800 SAR 95070 852-D6
ASHLEY PL
1000 MTVW 94040 811-F5
ASHLEY WY
2800 SJS 95135 855-G5
20500 SAR 95070 852-D6
ASHLEY RIDGE CT
4700 SJS 95138 855-E5
ASHLING CT
- SJS 95136 854-E5
ASHLOCK CT
1100 CMBL 95008 873-A1
ASHMEADE CT
1800 SJS 95125 853-G4
ASHMONT DR
4800 SJS 95111 875-B1
ASHRIDGE LN
3700 SJS 95121 855-C4
ASHTON AV
500 PA 94306 791-D7
2000 SMCo 94025 790-D6
ASHTON CT
- SJS 95111 854-J6
3400 PA 94306 791-D7
19600 SAR 95070 852-F5
ASHTON LN
- SJS 95111 854-J6
ASHTON OAKS WY
700 SJS 95138 875-F5
ASHWOOD CT
- SJS 95131 814-A4
ASHWOOD LN
2000 SJS 95132 814-E2
ASHWORTH WY
3000 SJS 95148 835-E7
ASILOMAR TER
900 SUNV 94086 812-C6
ASKAM LN
1700 LALT 94024 832-A5
ASKHAM PLACE CT
1700 SJS 95121 855-C4
ASPEN CIR
1200 HOLL 95023 1040-C6
ASPEN CT
4800 SJS 95124 873-H4
ASPEN DR
2900 SCL 95051 833-A7
22800 LALT 94024 831-J5
ASPEN WY
- GIL 95020 977-G1
400 LALT 94024 831-J5
800 PA 94303 791-E7
1200 HOLL 95023 1040-C6
17000 MGH 95037 917-D6
ASPEN LAKE CT
1300 SJS 95131 814-B5
ASPENRIDGE DR
200 MPS 95035 793-J4
ASPESI CT
18600 SAR 95070 872-H1
ASPESI DR
18500 SAR 95070 872-H1
ASSINIBOINE TR
20800 SCIC 95033 913-C2
ASSISI CT
5800 SJS 95138 875-G1
ASSUNTA WY
1900 SJS 95124 873-G1
ASTER AV
900 SUNV 94086 832-G1
ASTER CT
900 SUNV 94086 832-G1
1400 CPTO 95014 852-D4
ASTER DR
- SJS 95123 875-B6
ASTER LN
1200 CPTO 95014 852-D4
ASTER TER
- FRMT 94539 793-J3
ASTER WY
100 EPA 94303 791-D3
ASTIN CANYON CT
- SJS 95138 855-C5
ASTON CT
- MGH 95037 917-A6
ASTOR CT
- MTVW 94043 811-G2
ASTORIA DR
900 SUNV 94087 832-B4
ASTRAHAN LN
2200 SJS 95148 835-D5
ASTRO CT
1900 SJS 95131 814-D6
ASTRO DR
- HOLL 95023 1020-A5
ATHENA WY
- HOLL 95023 1040-B4
ATHENE DR
10200 SCIC 95127 835-A3
ATHENOUR CT
1400 SJS 95120 874-A7
ATHERTON AV
- ATN 94027 790-C4
4700 SJS 95130 852-J5
4700 SJS 95130 853-A5
4800 SJS 95129 852-J5
ATHERTON CIR
14500 MGH 95037 937-C5
ATHERTON CT
100 SMCo 94061 790-B4
12900 LAH 94022 831-C1
ATHERTON DR
3000 SCL 95051 833-A7
ATHERTON WY
200 MGH 95037 937-C5
200 MGH 95046 937-C5
ATHERTON OAKS LN
- ATN 94027 790-D5
ATHERWOOD AV
- RDWC 94061 790-B2
6300 CPTO 95014 852-F2
ATHERWOOD PL
- RDWC 94061 790-B2
ATHOS PL
19300 SAR 95070 872-G1
ATKINSON LN
1000 MLPK 94025 790-E5
ATLANTA AV
300 SJS 95125 854-A2
ATLANTIC CT
4200 SCL 95054 813-C5
ATLAS AV
- SJS 95126 833-J7
ATMEL WY
2100 SJS 95131 813-G7
ATRIUM CIR
12200 SAR 95070 852-E5
ATRIUM DR
12000 SAR 95070 852-E5
ATTEBERRY LN
1400 SJS 95131 814-A4
ATWOOD CT
- SJS 95131 814-A4
100 LGTS 95032 873-D6
ATWOOD DR
2900 SJS 95121 855-B3
2900 SJS 95122 855-B3
AUBREY LN
1300 SBnC 95023 1040-D1
AUBURN CT
19600 CPTO 95014 832-F7
AUBURN DR
19600 CPTO 95014 832-F7
AUBURN WY
400 SJS 95129 853-A1
600 MGH 95037 937-B4
AUDREY AV
900 CMBL 95008 873-B2
AUDREY DR
16700 MGH 95037 917-C7
AUDREY LN
20000 MonC 93907 1037-D7
AUDREY SMITH LN
600 SUNV 94089 812-H4
AUDUBON DR
1000 SJS 95122 834-G7
1000 SJS 95122 854-G1
AUGUST CIR
300 MLPK 94025 790-F6
AUGUST DR
5600 SJS 95138 875-D4
AUGUST LN
7900 CPTO 95014 852-C2
AUGUSTA CT
- LGTS 95030 873-A6
2800 SCL 95051 833-B2
AUGUSTA CT E
1500 MPS 95035 794-D3
AUGUSTA PL
2100 SCL 95051 833-B2
AUGUSTA WY
4900 SJS 95129 852-J4
AUGUSTINE AV
15700 LGTS 95032 873-C5
AUGUSTINE DR
2400 SCL 95054 813-B6
AULIN DR
2900 SJS 95125 854-B7
AURA CT
900 LALT 94024 831-G3
AURA WY
900 LALT 94024 831-G3
AURELIAN LN
1400 SJS 95126 853-H4
AURORA AV
700 SJS 95129 853-A2
AURORA LN
100 LGTS 95032 873-E5
AUSAYMAS CT
100 SBnC 95023 1020-F1
AUSTIN AV
- ATN 94027 790-C2
1600 LALT 94024 831-J4
AUSTIN CT
100 SJS 95110 854-D2
AUSTIN DR
100 SJS 95119 875-D5
AUSTIN PL
2400 SCL 95050 833-C6
AUSTIN WY
18400 SCIC 95030 872-G5
18400 MSER 95030 872-H5
19000 SAR 95070 872-G5
AUSTWICK CT
6900 SJS 95119 895-D1
AUTINORI CT
- SJS 95148 855-G1
AUTOETCH LN
- SJS 95119 875-C5
AUTOMATION PKWY
1600 SJS 95131 814-C5
AUTREY ST
100 MPS 95035 793-J3
100 MPS 95035 794-A3
AUTUMN CT
400 SJS 95110 834-A6
AUTUMN LN
- SJS 95138 875-D4
200 MGH 95037 937-B5
1000 LALT 94024 831-H3
N AUTUMN ST
- SJS 95110 834-A6
- SJS 95113 834-A6
S AUTUMN ST
Rt#-82
- SJS 95113 834-A7
- SJS 95110 834-A7
AUTUMN ESTATES
2800 SJS 95135 855-G5
AUTUMN GOLD DR
1900 SJS 95131 814-C6
AUTUMN RIDGE LN
1300 SJS 95132 814-G4
AUTUMNSONG WY
1100 SJS 95131 834-D1
1100 SJS 95131 814-D7
AUTUMNTREE CT
2000 SJS 95131 814-C6
AUTUMNVALE DR
2400 SJS 95131 814-C4
2500 SJS 95132 814-C3
AUTUMN WIND
- MPS 95035 814-J1
AUTUMNWOOD CT
3000 SJS 95148 855-E1
AUZERAIS AV
300 SJS 95110 834-B7
400 SJS 95126 834-B7
400 SJS 95126 854-A1
800 SJS 95126 853-J1
AUZERIAS CT
100 LGTS 95032 873-H7
100 LGTS 95032 893-H1
AVALANI AV
400 SJS 95133 834-E2
AVALON CT
3100 PA 94306 791-D7
AVALON DR
- LALT 94022 811-F6
1100 SJS 95125 854-B7
AVALON HEIGHTS TER
47400 FRMT 94539 794-A1
AVANTE PL
700 MGH 95037 917-B6
AVATI CT
1700 SJS 95131 814-D7
AVELAR ST
- EPA 94303 791-B1
AVENIDA LN
10300 CPTO 95014 851-J1
AVENIDA ABETOS
300 SJS 95123 874-H3
AVENIDA ALMENDROS
5300 SJS 95123 874-H3
AVENIDA ALONDRA
600 SUNV 94089 812-H4
AVENIDA ARBOLES
300 SJS 95123 874-H3
AVENIDA BENITO
- SJS 95131 814-B6
AVENIDA CARLOS
- SUNV 94089 812-H4
AVENIDA CRESTA
16200 LGTS 95032 873-F7
AVENIDA DE ANGELINA
4900 SCL 95054 813-D3
AVENIDA DE CARMEN
4900 SCL 95054 813-D3
AVENIDA DE COBRE
1800 SJS 95116 834-F3
AVENIDA DE GUADALUPE
2300 SCL 95054 813-C3
AVENIDA DE LAGO
4900 SCL 95054 813-D3
AVENIDA DE LAS FLORES
2000 SCL 95054 813-D4
AVENIDA DE LAS ROSAS
1900 SCL 95054 813-D3
AVENIDA DE LOS ALUMNOS
2200 SCL 95054 813-C3
AVENIDA DE LOS ARBOLES
4800 SCL 95054 813-D3
AVENIDA DE LOS PADRES
- MGH 95037 917-B3
AVENIDA DEL PIERO
- SBnC - 1037-J4
- SBnC 95045 1037-J4
AVENIDA DEL PRADO
- SCL 95054 813-C4
AVENIDA DEL ROBLE
300 SJS 95123 874-H3
AVENIDA DEL SOL
100 LGTS 95032 872-J2
AVENIDA ELISA
- SJS 95131 814-B6
AVENIDA ESPANA
- SJS 95139 875-G7
100 SJS 95139 895-F1
AVENIDA FELIPE
- SUNV 94089 812-J4
AVENIDA FERNANDO
- SUNV 94089 812-H4
AVENIDA GRANDE
- SUNV 94089 812-H4
- SJS 95139 875-F7
AVENIDA JOSE
- SUNV 94089 812-H4
AVENIDA LAGO
16100 LGTS 95032 873-F7
16300 SCIC 95032 873-F7
AVENIDA LA JUNTA
- SUNV 94089 812-H4
AVENIDA LAS BRISAS
- SJS 95131 814-B6
AVENIDA LEON
- SUNV 94089 812-H4
AVENIDA MANZANOS
300 SJS 95123 874-H3
AVENIDA MARCOS
- SUNV 94089 812-H4
AVENIDA MONTEZ
- SUNV 94089 812-H4
AVENIDA NOGALES
300 SJS 95123 874-H3
AVENIDA PALMAS
300 SJS 95123 874-H3
AVENIDA PINOS
300 SJS 95123 874-H3
AVENIDA PRIVADO
16100 LGTS 95032 873-F6
AVENIDA RICARDO
600 SUNV 94089 812-H4
AVENIDA ROTELLA
6800 SJS 95139 875-G6
AVENUE A
2700 SJS 95127 834-H2
2700 SCIC 95127 834-H2
AVENUE B
100 SCIC 95127 834-H2
100 SJS 95127 834-H2
AVENUE C
2700 SCIC 95127 834-H2
AVERNUS CT
3400 SJS 95135 855-G6
AVERY CT
4900 SJS 95136 874-F2
AVERY LN
500 LGTS 95032 873-A6
AVEZAN WY
- GIL 95020 957-G7
AVIARA CT
- SJS 95135 855-H3
AVIATION AV
- SCL 95050 833-G3
- SJS 95050 833-G3
1200 SJS 95110 833-G3
1200 SCL 95110 833-G3
AVIGNON LN
- SJS 95135 855-F2
AVIGON CT
5800 SJS 95138 875-H1
AVILA AV
2200 SCL 95050 833-E2
AVILA CT
13100 LAH 94022 810-J7
AVIS DR
1100 SJS 95126 853-J3
AVOCA DR
4000 SJS 95136 854-E5
AVOCADO PL
10100 CPTO 95014 852-F1
AVON CT
4200 SJS 95136 874-G1
AVON LN
18500 MSER 95030 872-H4
18500 SAR 95070 872-H4
AVON WY
500 LALT 94024 831-F1
AVONDALE ST
1000 SJS 95129 852-E3
AVOSET TER
100 SUNV 94087 832-E4
AVY AV
1800 MLPK 94025 790-D6
1800 SMCo 94025 790-D6
AWALT CT
1500 LALT 94024 832-A3
AWALT DR
1100 MTVW 94040 832-A2
AYALA CT
100 LGTS 95032 873-G6
AYALA DR
1100 SUNV 94086 812-B6
AYER AV
- SJS 95110 834-A5
AYER DR
1000 GIL 95020 977-G3
AYER LN
1100 MPS 95035 794-C6
AYER ST
1200 MPS 95035 794-C6
AYRES LN
- MLPK 94025 790-E7
AYRSHIRE DR
5300 SJS 95118 874-C4
AYRSHIRE FARM LN
- SCIC 94305 790-J7
AZA DR
2100 SCL 95050 833-C3
AZALEA DR
800 SUNV 94086 832-G1
6900 SJS 95120 894-G3
AZALEA LN
600 SJS 95136 854-E7
AZALEA WY
500 LALT 94022 811-F6
16100 SCIC 95032 873-D5
AZALIA DR
100 EPA 94303 791-C2
AZARA PL
600 SUNV 94086 832-F1
AZARA ST
- GIL 95020 977-D1
AZEVEDO CIR
- SJS 95125 854-E4
AZEVEDO CT
- SJS 95125 854-E5
600 SCL 95051 833-B6
AZEVEDO PKWY
- SJS 95125 854-E5
AZORES ST
- SJS 95136 854-E6
AZTEC AV
100 SJS 95136 854-G7
AZTEC WY
2400 PA 94303 791-D5
AZTEC RIDGE DR
16200 LGTS 95030 893-C3
16200 SCIC 95030 893-C3
16200 SCIC 95033 893-C3
AZUCAR AV
- SJS 95111 875-B3
AZUL CT
- HOLL 95023 1039-G3
AZULE AV
600 SJS 95123 874-G5
AZURE ST
800 SUNV 94087 832-E2
AZZARELLO CT
4400 SJS 95121 855-F4

B

B CT
- GIL 95020 977-E1
B RD
- SUNV 94089 812-J3
15000 SCIC 95127 815-C6
B ST
500 HOLL 95023 1039-J5
900 LALT 94024 831-H3
7600 CPTO 95014 831-G5
BABB CT
- SJS 95125 854-D5
BABBS CREEK DR
700 GIL 95020 977-J6
BABERO AV
1600 SJS 95118 874-A1
1600 SJS 95118 873-J1
BABE RUTH CT
1800 SJS 95132 814-D4
BABE RUTH DR
2700 SJS 95132 814-D4
BACCHUS DR
1200 SJS 95122 834-G7
1200 SJS 95122 854-G1
BACH CT
12700 SAR 95070 852-G6
BACHMAN AV
100 LGTS 95030 873-A7
300 LGTS 95030 872-J6
300 MSER 95030 872-J6
BACHMAN CT
300 LGTS 95030 872-J6
300 LGTS 95030 873-A7
BACHMANN CT
2400 SJS 95124 853-H7
BACIGALUPI DR
100 LGTS 95032 873-H6
BADEN CT
1600 SJS 95132 814-E4
BADGER PASS RD
14600 MGH 95037 937-C5
BADGERWOOD LN
1900 MPS 95035 793-J3
BAERWALDT CT
900 SCIC 95046 937-E3
BAGDAD WY
- SJS 95123 875-B4
BAGDHAD PL
800 SJS 95116 834-J4
BAGELY WY
1300 SJS 95122 854-H1
BAGGINS CT
3300 SJS 95121 855-A4
BAGPIPE WY
1600 SJS 95121 855-B3
BAGSHAW CT
300 SJS 95123 875-A5
BAGUIO CT
6400 SJS 95119 875-C7
BAGWORTH CT
3100 SJS 95148 855-C2
BAHAMA WY
1400 SJS 95122 834-H6
BAHIA AV
100 SJS 95136 854-G7
BAHIA CT
200 SJS 95119 875-E7
BAHL ST
22300 CPTO 95014 832-A7
BAHRE LN
- SJS 95131 814-B6
BAILEY AV
300 MTVW 94043 811-H5
300 MTVW 94041 811-H5
400 SJS 95141 896-A4
400 SJS 95141 895-H6
2200 SCIC 95128 833-F7
2200 SJS 95128 833-F7
BAILEY PL
- SCL 95050 833-C2
BAILEY RD
- SCIC 94035 812-B3
- SCIC 94043 812-B3
500 SJS 95141 895-G6

SANTA CLARA CO.

STREET Block City ZIP Pg-Grid

BAILEY RD
500 SJS 95139 895-G6
BAILY AV
- SCIC 95137 896-B3
- SJS 95137 896-B3
- SJS 95139 896-B3
- SJS 95141 896-B3
BAINBRIDGE CT
900 SUNV 94087 832-B4
BAINS ST
- EPA 94303 791-C3
BAINTER AV
19100 SAR 95030 872-G5
19100 SAR 95070 872-G5
19100 SCIC 95030 872-G5
BAINTER WY
19400 SCIC 95030 872-F5
BAINTREE PL
100 LGTS 95032 873-B3
BAIRD AV
700 SCL 95054 813-E6
BAKER AV
4100 PA 94306 811-C2
BAKER CT
1000 SUNV 94087 832-B4
BAKER LN
27800 LAH 94022 811-A6
BAKER PL
1900 SJS 95131 814-D6
BALANCE DR
500 SJS 95111 854-F6
BALARDO WY
3000 SJS 95148 835-E7
3000 SJS 95148 855-E1
BALBACH ST
100 SJS 95110 834-C7
BALBOA AV
- SJS 95116 834-F3
BALBOA CT
1200 SUNV 94086 812-B6
BALBOA DR
100 MPS 95035 793-J5
BALBOA RD
22500 CPTO 95014 851-J2
BALBOA ST
- SJS 95134 813-G3
BALCOM RD
3800 SCIC 95148 835-F6
BALD EAGLE WY
4300 SJS 95118 874-C2
BALDERSTONE DR
6200 SJS 95120 874-C7
6200 SJS 95120 894-C1
BALDWIN DR
3800 SCL 95051 832-H7
21800 SCIC 95033 913-A3
BALER AL
- HOLL 95023 1039-J5
- HOLL 95023 1040-A5
BALERI RANCH RD
14100 LAH 94022 810-H6
BALFOUR DR
600 SJS 95111 854-H4
BALGRAY CT
3000 SJS 95148 855-C2
BAL HARBOR WY
1100 SJS 95122 834-H6
BALI CT
1300 SJS 95122 854-H1
BALL CT
1100 HOLL 95023 1039-H3
BALLANTREE LN
3800 MonC 95076 1037-C3
BALLANTREE WY
1500 SJS 95118 874-A4
BALLARD CT
1200 SJS 95131 814-D7
BALLATORE DR
100 SJS 95134 813-D2
BALLYBUNION CT
- GIL 95020 977-F5
BALLYBUNION DR
- GIL 95020 977-G5
BALLYMORE CIR
- SJS 95136 854-E4
BALME DR
2300 SJS 95122 854-H2
BALMORAL DR
3000 SJS 95132 814-E3
BALSA AV
1700 SJS 95124 873-H1
BALSAM AV
300 SUNV 94086 812-F5
N BALSAMINA WY
100 SMCo 94028 810-E3
S BALSAMINA WY
200 SMCo 94028 810-E4
BALSAMO DR
6200 SJS 95129 852-F3
BALTIC WY
400 SJS 95111 854-G4
600 SUNV 94089 812-G2
BALTUSROL DR
- GIL 95020 977-H6
BALUSTROL CT
22300 CPTO 95014 852-A2
BAMBI LN
2100 SJS 95116 834-H4
BAMBOO CT
500 SJS 95111 854-G6
BAMBOO DR
700 SUNV 94086 832-F1
BAMBOO PALM CT
- SJS 95133 814-J4
BAN CT
3500 SJS 95117 853-C3
BANANA GROVE LN
100 SJS 95123 874-J3
BANBERRY WY
4800 SJS 95124 873-H4
BANCROFT AV
18100 MSER 95030 872-J6
BANCROFT ST
400 SCL 95051 833-A7
BANCROFT WY
6200 SJS 95129 852-F3
BANDERA DR
3100 PA 94304 830-G1
BANDLEY DR
10000 CPTO 95014 832-D7
10000 CPTO 95014 852-D1
BANES LN
100 GIL 95020 978-B4
BANFF DR
1700 SUNV 94087 832-B6
BANFF ST
600 SJS 95116 834-F6
BANFF SPRINGS CT
100 SJS 95139 875-E7
BANFF SPRINGS WY
100 SJS 95139 875-E7
200 SJS 95139 895-E1
BANGOR AV
- SJS 95123 875-A4
300 SJS 95123 874-J4
BANKHEAD WY
2500 SJS 95121 855-C3
BANK MILL RD
21000 SAR 95070 872-C3
BANNER CT
6100 SJS 95123 874-J6
BANNER DR
6100 SJS 95123 874-J6
BANNING AV
400 SUNV 94086 812-F6
BANNISTER AV
2800 SCIC 95020 958-C3
BANNOCK CIR
4700 SJS 95130 852-J7
4700 SJS 95130 853-A7
BANTA CT
600 SJS 95136 874-F2
BANTRY CT
700 SUNV 94087 832-F4
BANYAN CT
- GIL 95020 957-D7
- GIL 95020 977-D1
- SJS 95131 814-A5
BANYAN LN
15400 MSER 95030 872-J4
BANYAN ST
- GIL 95020 957-D7
BARALAY PL
5100 SJS 95136 874-J3
BARANGA LN
14800 SAR 95070 872-F4
BARBANO AV
- CMBL 95008 853-F6
BARBARA AV
200 MTVW 94040 811-G7
BARBARA DR
200 LGTS 95032 873-G5
1400 SCL 95050 833-C4
1900 PA 94303 791-C5
BARBARA LN
- MLPK 94025 790-E5
10100 CPTO 95014 852-D1
BARBARA WY
2600 SJS 95125 854-C6
BARBARAS CT
- SBnC 95023 1060-D2
BARBEE CT
15100 SCIC 95127 814-J5
BARBER CT
600 MPS 95035 813-H1
BARBER LN
700 MPS 95035 813-H1
BARBERRY CT
1500 SJS 95121 855-A3
BARBERRY LN
1500 SJS 95121 855-A3
1700 SJS 95122 855-A2
BARB WERNER LN
6100 SJS 95119 875-D5
BARCELLS AV
2600 SCL 95051 833-B6
BARCELONA AV
1700 SJS 95124 873-H3
BARCELONA CT
400 MTVW 94040 811-J7
15400 MGH 95037 937-A4
BARCLAY CT
300 PA 94306 811-D2
6100 SJS 95123 875-A6
BARD ST
900 SCIC 95127 814-H6
900 SJS 95127 814-H6
BARDEN WY
1600 SJS 95128 853-G3
BARDOLINO LN
- SJS 95135 855-F2
BAREOAK CT
3300 SJS 95148 835-E7
BARK LN
7000 SJS 95129 852-E3
BARKER DR
3800 SJS 95117 853-B3
BARKER ST
100 MPS 95035 793-J7
BARKLEY AV
2600 SCL 95051 833-A3
BARKSDALE CT
14200 SAR 95070 872-E2
BARKWOOD WY
2900 SJS 95128 853-E4
BARLETTA LN
3100 SJS 95127 834-J1
3100 SCIC 95127 834-J1
BARLEY CT
3500 SJS 95127 835-C2
BARLEY HILL RD
12200 LAH 94024 831-D2
BARLOW AV
2200 SJS 95122 834-J5
BARMETTA WY
- ATN 94027 790-D2
BARNARD AV
- SJS 95125 854-D3
BARNARD RD
17900 SCIC 95037 917-D3
BARNELL AV
16700 MGH 95037 937-A1
BARNES CT
- SJS 95120 894-H4
- SCIC 94305 791-A7
BARNES LN
100 SBnC 95023 1040-D4
1100 SJS 95120 894-H4
BARNEY AV
- ATN 94027 790-C5
- SMCo 94025 790-C5
BARNEY CT
- SMCo 94025 790-D5
BARNHART AV
- SCIC 95037 896-F7
18600 CPTO 95014 852-G2
BARNHART CT
10500 CPTO 95014 852-G2
BARNHART PL
7400 CPTO 95014 852-D4
BARNHEISEL RD
- SBnC 95023 1000-C3
100 SCIC 95020 1000-C3
BARNSDALE CT
6600 SJS 95120 894-C1
BARNSLEY WY
600 SUNV 94087 832-E4
BARNSWELL WY
5800 SJS 95138 875-D4
BARON DR
5300 SJS 95124 873-F5
BARON PL
600 MPS 95035 794-B3
BARONET CT
3900 SJS 95121 855-D5
BARONI AV
100 SJS 95136 854-H7
100 SJS 95136 874-G1
BARONI CT
19900 SAR 95070 872-F1
BARONI GREEN DR
300 SJS 95136 874-J7
BARONSCOURT WY
3000 SJS 95132 814-E3
BAROQUE PL
- SJS 95135 855-J3
BARRANCA DR
10800 CPTO 95014 832-A6
BARRETT AV
- MGH 95037 937-B1
1500 SCIC 95037 917-D7
1500 SCIC 95037 937-D1
2100 SJS 95124 873-F3
2500 MGH 95037 917-F7
BARRINGTON CT
1100 SJS 95121 855-B5
BARRINGTON BRIDGE CT
10800 CPTO 95014 852-C6
BARRINGTON BRIDGE LN
10800 CPTO 95014 852-C6
BARRON AV
500 PA 94306 811-B2
BARRON PL
6400 GIL 95020 978-A5
BARRON ST
500 MLPK 94025 790-G3
BARRON PARK CT
400 SJS 95136 874-F2
BARRON PARK DR
900 SJS 95136 874-G3
BARROW CT
2800 SJS 95121 855-A3
BARRY LN
- ATN 94027 790-D4
15900 MSER 95030 873-A5
BARRYMORE DR
4100 SJS 95117 853-A3
4100 SJS 95129 853-A3
BARSON TER
300 SUNV 94086 812-D7
BARSTOW CT
900 SUNV 94086 812-H5
BARTLETT AV
200 SUNV 94086 812-F7
BARTLETT CT
14800 SCIC 95046 937-G2
BARTLETT CREEK CT
1100 SJS 95120 894-G3
BARTO ST
400 SCL 95051 833-A6
BARTON CT
13800 LAH 94022 811-D7
BARTON DR
1400 SUNV 94087 832-A5
BARTON PL
100 MLPK 94025 790-J2
BARTON ST
1800 SMCo 94061 790-B4
BARTON WY
300 MLPK 94025 790-J3
BASALT CT
2300 SJS 95133 814-H3
BASCH AV
- SJS 95116 834-F3
BASCOM AV
- SCL 95050 833-F6
- SCL 95128 833-F6
- SCIC 95128 833-F7
- SJS 95128 853-G5
- SJS 95128 833-F6
500 SCIC 95128 853-G5
1300 SJS 95050 853-F6
1400 CMBL 95125 853-G5
1400 SJS 95125 853-G5
1400 CMBL 95008 853-G5
1800 CMBL 95128 853-G5
1800 SJS 95126 853-G5
2200 SJS 95008 853-G5
2600 SCIC 95008 853-G5
2600 SCIC 95008 873-E1
2600 SJS 95008 873-E1
2600 SJS 95124 853-G5
2600 SJS 95124 873-E1
S BASCOM AV
300 SJS 95128 853-G1
300 SCIC 95128 853-G1
3100 SJS 95124 873-E3
3100 SJS 95008 873-E3
3500 CMBL 95008 873-E3
14500 CMBL 95032 873-E3
14700 LGTS 95032 873-E3
BASCOM CT
1900 CMBL 95008 873-E2
BASIL AV
- MGH 95037 916-G4
BASIL CT
- MGH 95037 916-G4
BASILE AV
1800 SCIC 95128 853-G1
1800 SJS 95128 853-G1
BASIN CT
500 SJS 95111 854-G4
BASKING LN
- SJS 95138 875-G5
BASKING RIDGE AV
6600 SJS 95138 875-F4
BASS CT
4800 SJS 95130 852-J6
BASSETT LN
- ATN 94027 790-F2
25700 LAH 94022 831-B3
BASSETT ST
- SJS 95112 834-A6
- SJS 95113 834-A6
- SJS 95110 834-A6
2000 SCL 95054 813-D6
BASSWOOD CT
4800 SJS 95124 873-H4
BASTIA LN
- SJS 95127 834-C1
BASTILLE CT
- SJS 95135 855-G2
BASUNI WY
- SCIC 95037 917-D5
BATAAN CT
400 SJS 95133 834-G2
BATEMAN WY
3500 SJS 95148 855-F1
BATES CT
3000 SJS 95148 855-E1
BATHGATE LN
3400 SJS 95121 855-C3
BATISTA DR
- SJS 95136 854-E6
BATON ROUGE CT
2800 SJS 95133 814-G7
BATON ROUGE DR
2400 SJS 95133 834-G1
2600 SJS 95133 814-G7
BATTAGLIA CIR
2400 SJS 95132 814-E6
BATTEN WY
- SJS 95135 855-F3
BATTERSEA CT
1700 SJS 95132 814-J3
BATTLE DANCE DR
300 SJS 95111 875-B2
BAUMANN CT
500 MGH 95037 916-H3
500 SCIC 95037 916-H3
BAUTISTA CT
900 PA 94303 791-E6
BAUTISTA PL
- SJS 95126 854-A1
BAVA CT
6100 SJS 95123 875-A6
BAXLEY CT
22000 CPTO 95014 852-A2
BAXTER AV
10700 SCIC 94024 832-A6
BAY RD
300 ATN 94027 790-H1
300 MLPK 94025 790-H1
500 SMCo 94025 790-H1
900 EPA 94303 791-A1
BAY ST
300 SJS 95123 874-J5
800 MTVW 94041 811-J6
900 MTVW 94040 811-J6
BAY TER
500 SUNV 94089 812-G3
BAYARD DR
1100 SJS 95122 854-H2
BAYBERRY
- PTLV 94028 830-D1
BAYBERRY COM
200 FRMT 94539 793-H1
BAYBERRY CT
3000 SJS 95148 855-D2
BAYBERRY LN
3000 SJS 95148 855-C2
BAYBERRY ST
- HOLL 95023 1040-D7
- HOLL 95023 1060-D1
BAYBERRY WY
- MPS 95035 794-A6
BAYFRONT PZ
5400 SCL 95054 813-A3
BAYHAVEN DR
2000 SJS 95122 835-A7
BAY LAUREL DR
1100 MLPK 94025 790-F5
BAY LAUREL LN
1100 SJS 95132 814-H5
BAYLEAF CT
800 SJS 95128 853-F4
BAYLISS CT
7500 SJS 95139 895-G1
BAYLISS DR
200 SJS 95139 895-F2
BAYLISS PL
7400 SJS 95139 895-G1
BAYLOR AV
18200 SJS 95130 852-J7
18200 SAR 95070 852-J7
BAYLOR DR
700 SCL 95051 832-J6
BAYLOR ST
2500 EPA 94303 791-B1
BAYNE PL
4300 SJS 95130 853-A4
BAYO CLAROS CIR
1800 MGH 95037 917-D6
BAYOU DR
3400 SJS 95111 854-J5
BAYO VISTA
3500 SJS 95132 814-H5
BAYPOINTE DR
100 SJS 95134 813-F3
BAYPOINTE PKWY
100 SJS 95134 813-F2
BAY RIDGE CT
1300 SJS 95120 894-C2
N BAYSHORE W
700 SJS 95112 834-C3
BAYSHORE FRWY U.S.-101
- EPA - 790-J1
- EPA - 791-E5
- MLPK - 790-J1
- MLPK - 791-E5
- MTVW - 791-E5
- MTVW - 811-G1
- MTVW - 812-C4
- PA - 791-E5
- SCL - 813-B6
- SCIC - 812-C4
- SCIC - 855-B5
- SJS - 813-B6
- SJS - 833-G1
- SJS - 834-C2
- SJS - 854-H1
- SJS - 855-B5
- SJS - 875-C1
- SUNV - 812-C4
- SUNV - 813-B6
BAYSHORE PKWY
2400 MTVW 94043 791-F7
2600 MTVW 94043 811-G1
E BAYSHORE RD
700 EPA 94303 791-A1
1900 PA 94303 791-D4
W BAYSHORE RD
1200 EPA 94303 791-B2
1900 PA 94303 791-D4
BAYSIDE CT
2300 SJS 95133 834-F2
BAYSIDE PKWY
47000 FRMT 94538 793-F1
BAYSLAND CT
1300 SJS 95131 814-D7
BAYSMILL CT
2800 SJS 95121 854-J3
BAY SPRINGS RD
18500 SCIC 95070 872-D7
BAYTECH DR
100 SJS 95134 813-D1
BAYTON DR
- SJS 95193 875-C4
BAY TREE DR
1100 GIL 95020 977-F1
BAY TREE LN
- SCIC 95127 815-A6
- LALT 94022 831-D1
BAYVIEW AV
- LGTS 95030 872-J7
200 SCIC 95127 815-A7
200 SUNV 94086 812-E7
200 SUNV 94086 832-E1
N BAYVIEW AV
200 SUNV 94086 812-F6
S BAYVIEW AV
100 SUNV 94086 812-E7
BAYVIEW CT
- LGTS 95030 872-J7
BAYVIEW DR
- FRMT 94538 793-G1
18100 SCIC 95033 912-H3
BAYVIEW PARK DR
400 MPS 95035 794-D5
BAYWOOD AV
100 MLPK 94025 790-J3
600 SJS 95128 833-E7
S BAYWOOD AV
300 SJS 95128 853-E1
1100 CMBL 95128 853-E3
BAYWOOD CT
400 MTVW 94040 811-F4
10500 CPTO 95014 832-F7
BAYWOOD DR
10400 CPTO 95014 832-F7
BAYWOOD SQ
1800 SJS 95132 814-E3
BAZOS ST
- GIL 95020 957-H7
BEACHWOOD CT
- HOLL 95023 1040-E5
BEACON DR
- MPS 95035 794-D6
BEACON LN
3300 SJS 95118 874-A1
BEACON ST
- MTVW 94040 811-F3
600 MLPK 94025 790-J2
BEACONSFIELD RD
1100 SJS 95121 855-A5
BEAD GRASS TER
- FRMT 94539 793-J3
BEAL CT
6400 SJS 95123 875-B7
BEAN AV
200 LGTS 95030 873-A7
200 LGTS 95030 872-J7
BEAR CANYON RD
100 SCrC 95033 912-C1
BEARCAT CT
6700 GIL 95020 978-B4
BEAR CLAW WY
- SJS 95136 874-H2
BEAR CREEK RD
17200 SCIC 95033 892-G6
18500 SCrC 95033 892-A7
20300 SCrC 95033 912-C1
21400 SCIC 95033 912-F1
BEAR CREEK RD Rt#-35
20000 SCIC 95033 912-F1
22000 SCIC 95033 912-E1
BEAR CREEK WY
21800 SCrC 95033 892-A7
BEARDEN DR
1600 CMBL 95032 872-J2
BEARDON DR
10100 CPTO 95014 832-D7
BEARDSLEY RD
19100 SCIC 95033 892-F4
BEAR GULCH DR
- PTLV 94028 810-D6
BEAR MOUNTAIN RD
1000 SCrC 95033 912-E1
BEAR PAW
- PTLV 94028 830-C1
BEAR VALLEY LN
2300 SJS 95133 814-H3
2300 SJS 95133 834-F1
BEATRICE CIR
21400 SCIC 95033 912-J3
BEATRICE CT
2000 SJS 95128 853-G3
BEATRICE LN
26900 LAH 94022 811-C7
BEATRICE ST
100 MTVW 94043 811-H4
BEATTIE CT
1300 SJS 95120 874-B6
BEAUCHAMP CT
20800 SAR 95070 852-D5
BEAUCHAMPS LN
11900 SAR 95070 852-D5
BEAUJOLAIS CT
8400 SJS 95135 855-H7
BEAULIEU CT
1200 SJS 95125 853-G4
BEAUME CT
400 MTVW 94043 811-G2
BEAUMERE WY
100 MPS 95035 794-A4
BEAUMONT AV
13200 SAR 95070 852-E7
13400 SAR 95070 872-E1
BEAUMONT DR
1000 SJS 95129 852-J3
BEAUMONT SQ
3300 MTVW 94040 831-J2
BEAUMONT CANYON DR
- SJS 95138 855-E6
BEAVEN DR
21700 CPTO 95014 832-B7
BEAVER LN
26900 LAH 94022 811-A5
BEAVER CREEK WY
700 SJS 95133 814-H3
700 SJS 95133 834-F1
BEAVERTON CT
800 SUNV 94087 832-C4
BECK AV
18400 MSER 95030 872-H6
BECK DR
1600 SJS 95130 853-B5
BECKER LN
400 LALT 94022 811-D5
BECKET DR
1200 SJS 95121 854-J3
BECKHAM DR
300 SJS 95123 875-B7
BECKLEY DR
300 SJS 95135 855-F3
BECKWITH RD
19200 SCIC 95030 872-G7
BECKY LN
15000 MSER 95030 872-J4
25400 LAH 94022 831-C2
BEDAL LN
300 CMBL 95008 873-D1
BEDAL PARK CT
300 CMBL 95008 873-D1
BEDFORD AV
1300 SUNV 94024 832-A5
1400 SUNV 94087 832-A5
BEDFORD CT
1200 SUNV 94024 832-A4
BEDFORD DR
- MTVW 94043 812-B6
BEDFORD LP
- MTVW 94043 812-B5
BEDFORD ST
10000 SCIC 95127 835-A3
BEDIVERE DR
600 SJS 95127 814-H7
BEE CT
1000 MPS 95035 814-D2
BEEBE CIR
4000 SJS 95135 855-F3
BEECH ST
900 EPA 94303 791-C2
1700 SCL 95054 813-D5
BEECHER CT
2800 SJS 95121 855-A2
BEECH GROVE CT
5300 SJS 95123 874-J3
BEECHMONT AV
4200 SJS 95136 874-D1
BEECHNUT AV
300 SUNV 94086 812-E5
BEECHVALE CT
300 SJS 95119 895-D1
BEECHWOOD AV
2400 SJS 95128 833-E7
BEECHWOOD DR
5300 LALT 94024 831-J6
BEEGUM WY
200 SJS 95123 875-A4
BEEKMAN PL
19800 CPTO 95014 832-F6
BEEMAN DR
10300 SJS 95127 835-B4
BEEMER AV
100 SUNV 94086 812-E7
BEETHOVEN LN
- LGTS 95032 873-D3
BEGEN AV
1500 MTVW 94040 811-H7
1600 MTVW 94040 831-H1
BEGGS RD
20000 SCIC 95033 892-D3
BEGONIA DR
5400 SJS 95124 873-J6
BEGONIA LN
600 SJS 95136 854-E7
BEGONIA WY
600 SUNV 94086 832-F1
BEHLER DR
3500 SJS 95132 814-F2
BEIGNET WY
- SJS 95133 834-G1
BELA DR
4800 SJS 95129 852-J4
4800 SJS 95129 853-A4
BEL AIR AV
1600 SJS 95126 833-F7
1700 SJS 95128 833-F7
BEL AIR CT
- MTVW 94043 812-B5
BELAIR CT
23400 SCrC 95033 913-D7
BEL AIR PL
17300 MGH 95037 917-B6
BEL AIR WY
500 MGH 95037 917-B6
BEL AIRE CT
11000 CPTO 95014 852-B3
BEL AIRE DR
100 SJS 95131 814-A4
BEL AIRE HILLS RD
- SJS 95138 855-F6
BEL AYRE DR
100 SCL 95117 833-C7
100 SCL 95117 853-C1
BELBLOSSOM DR
200 LGTS 95032 873-G6
BELBLOSSOM WY
200 LGTS 95032 873-H6
BELBROOK CT
6500 SJS 95120 894-C1
BELBROOK PL
1200 MPS 95035 793-J4
BELBROOK WY
- ATN 94027 790-B6
1100 MPS 95035 793-J4
1100 MPS 95035 794-A4
BEL CANTO DR
4900 SJS 95124 873-F4
BELCREST DR
100 LGTS 95032 873-H7
BELDEN CT
600 LALT 94022 811-E5
BELDEN DR
- LALT 94022 811-E5
200 SJS 95123 875-A4
BELDER DR
1000 SJS 95120 894-H4
BEL ESCOU DR
4900 SJS 95124 873-F4
15000 SCIC 95124 873-F4
BEL ESTOS DR
4900 SJS 95124 873-F4
15000 SCIC 95124 873-F4
BELFAIR CT
700 SUNV 94087 832-C4
BELFAST CT
500 SUNV 94087 832-E4
BELFAST DR
2700 SJS 95127 835-A5
BELFORD DR
1000 SJS 95132 814-F6
BELFRY WY
500 SUNV 94087 832-D4
BELGATOS LN
200 LGTS 95032 873-H7
BELGATOS RD
100 LGTS 95032 873-H6
BELGLEN LN
100 LGTS 95032 873-H6
BELGLEN WY
100 LGTS 95032 873-H6
BELGRAVIAN CT
2700 SJS 95121 855-D3
BELGROVE CIR
3200 SJS 95148 855-F1
BELGROVE CT
3300 SJS 95148 855-F1
BELHAVEN DR
100 LGTS 95032 873-H6
BELICK ST
3100 SCL 95054 813-F7
BELKNAP CT
1200 CPTO 95014 852-C3
BELKNAP DR
7800 CPTO 95014 852-C3
BELL AV
2900 SCIC 95133 834-H1
BELL CT
- EPA 94303 791-B2
BELL RD
13000 SCrC 95033 912-F6
BELL ST
300 EPA 94303 791-B2
BELLA CALAIS WY
- SJS 95138 875-G5
BELLA CORTE
400 MTVW 94043 811-G2

STREET
Block City ZIP Pg-Grid

BELLADONNA CT
600 SUNV 94086 832-F1
BELLAGIO DR
5600 SJS 95118 874-B5
BELLAIR WY
1100 MLPK 94025 790-D6
1100 SMCo 94025 790-D6
BELLA LADERA DR
24500 LAH 94024 831-E2
BELLA MADEIRA LN
- SCIC 95127 835-F4
BELLA MONTE WY
- SJS 95148 855-G2
BELLARMINE CT
3200 SCL 95051 833-A2
BELLA TERRA CT
- SJS 95132 814-G5
BELLA VINA
18800 SAR 95070 852-D7
BELLA VISTA
19900 SAR 95070 872-E3
BELLA VISTA AV
100 LGTS 95030 873-B7
200 LGTS 95032 873-B7
3400 SCL 95051 832-J3
BELLA VISTA CT
100 LGTS 95032 873-B7
1500 HOLL 95023 1040-C6
3400 SCL 95051 832-J3
BELLA VISTA DR
1500 HOLL 95023 1040-C6
BELLA VISTA LN
- SCIC 95020 976-C5
- SCrC 95076 976-C5
BELLE CT
15100 SAR 95070 872-F4
BELLEAU AV
- ATN 94027 790-D2
BELLEMEADE ST
1200 SJS 95131 834-C1
BELLEROSE DR
100 SJS 95128 833-F7
100 SCIC 95128 833-F7
200 SCIC 95128 853-F1
200 SJS 95128 853-F1
BELLE TERRE CT
- CMBL 95008 853-A1
BELLETTO DR
17400 MGH 95037 917-B6
BELLEVILLE WY
1200 SUNV 94024 832-A5
1400 SUNV 94087 832-A5
BELLEVUE AV
- SJS 95110 854-D2
22300 CPTO 95014 852-A1
BELLEVUE CT
300 LALT 94024 831-F1
BELLEW DR
700 MPS 95035 813-H1
BELLFLOWER AV
600 SUNV 94086 832-F2
BELLFLOWER CT
15000 SCIC 95127 814-J5
BELLGROVE CIR
11800 SAR 95070 852-G7
BELLHURST AV
900 SJS 95122 834-F7
BELLINGHAM CT
1100 SJS 95121 854-J3
BELLINGHAM DR
1000 SJS 95121 854-J3
BELLINGHAM WY
1300 SUNV 94024 832-B4
1300 SUNV 94087 832-B4
BELLINGTON CT
- SJS 95138 855-D5
BELLINI CT
2800 SJS 95132 814-F5
BELLINI WY
- MGH 95037 937-A4
BELLIS CT
700 SJS 95123 874-G6
BELLO AV
2100 SJS 95125 853-J6
2100 SJS 95125 854-A6
BELLOMO AV
900 SUNV 94086 832-F3
BELLOMY ST
700 SCL 95053 833-E5
700 SCL 95050 833-E5
1600 SCL 95128 833-E5
BELLVIEW CT
2100 PA 94303 791-C5
BELLWOOD CT
1300 LALT 94024 831-J4
BELLWOOD DR
400 SCL 95054 813-E5
19100 SAR 95070 852-G6
BELLWORTH CT
- SJS 95135 855-F4
BEL MIRA WY
- SJS 95135 855-H3
BELMONT AV
100 SMCo 94061 790-B3
200 LGTS 95030 872-J7
16300 MSER 95030 872-J7
BELMONT CT
- SBnC 95023 1040-E4
BELMONT DR
400 SJS 95125 854-C3
BELMONT TER
900 SUNV 94086 812-D6
BELNAP WY
15400 SAR 95070 872-C4
15400 SCIC 95070 872-C4
BELRIDGE DR
100 LGTS 95032 873-H7
BELSHAW DR
1300 MTVW 94040 832-A2
BELTANE DR
7700 SJS 95135 856-A6
BELTHORN CT
2200 SJS 95131 814-E6
BELTIERA CT
- SJS 95135 855-H1
BELTIERA PL
- SJS 95135 855-H1
BELTRAMI DR
1100 SJS 95127 835-B3
BELVALE DR
100 LGTS 95032 873-H6
BELVEDERE DR
4200 SJS 95129 853-A2
BELVEDERE LN
1000 SJS 95129 852-F3
BELVOIR DR
1600 SCIC 94024 831-G4
BELVUE DR
100 LGTS 95032 873-H6
BELWOOD CT
100 LGTS 95032 873-H6
BELWOOD LN
100 LGTS 95032 873-H6
BELWOOD GATEWAY
- LGTS 95032 873-H6
BENASSI DR
7600 GIL 95020 977-G3
BENBOW AV
100 SJS 95123 875-B5
BENBOW DR
9300 GIL 95020 957-G7
BEND AV
700 SJS 95136 874-E1
BEND DR
600 SUNV 94087 832-D4
BENDER CIR
100 MGH 95037 916-J5
BENDIGO DR
1700 LALT 94024 831-H4
BENDMILL WY
1000 SJS 95121 854-J4
BENDORF DR
100 SJS 95111 875-B3
BENEDICT LN
15500 LGTS 95032 873-C5
BENEFIT CT
400 SJS 95133 834-G2
BENETTI CT
21800 CPTO 95014 832-B7
BENGAL CT
5100 SJS 95111 875-A2
BENGAL DR
5000 SJS 95111 875-A2
BEN HUR CT
2300 SJS 95124 853-G7
BENICIA AV
900 SUNV 94086 812-D5
BENITO RD
300 SBnC 95023 1020-H1
BENJAMIN AV
2800 SJS 95124 873-F1
BENJAMIN CT
2900 SJS 95124 873-F1
BENJAMIN DR
2400 MTVW 94043 811-F2
BEN LOMOND DR
4000 PA 94306 811-E2
BEN LOMOND WY
3300 SJS 95121 855-B3
BENNETT AV
3400 SCL 95051 832-J7
BENNETT CT
100 GIL 95020 957-H7
BENNETT ST
100 GIL 95020 957-H7
BENNETT WY
1000 SJS 95125 854-B5
16300 LGTS 95032 873-D4
BENNETTA LN
11700 SCIC 95020 957-J1
BENNIGHOF CT
2100 SJS 95121 855-C3
BENNINGTON DR
1100 SUNV 94087 832-B1
BENNY CT
1100 SJS 95131 834-C1
BEN ROE DR
1400 LALT 94024 831-J4
1500 LALT 94024 832-A4
BENSON LN
2500 SJS 95125 854-A7
2600 SJS 95125 874-A1
BENT DR
1000 CMBL 95008 853-G6
BENT GRASS TER
- FRMT 94539 793-J3
BENTLEY AV
- LGTS 95030 873-A7
BENTLEY CT
26000 LAH 94022 811-D7
BENTLEY DR
1800 SJS 95132 814-E4
17600 MGH 95037 917-B6
BENTLEY SQ
100 MTVW 94040 811-J7
BENTLEY RIDGE DR
- SJS 95138 855-E5
BENTOAK CT
1100 SJS 95129 852-H3
BENT OAK LN
2900 MGH 95037 917-G6
BENTOAK LN
1000 SJS 95129 852-H3
BENTON CT
1500 SUNV 94087 832-H5
BENTON ST
500 SCL 95050 833-C4
1600 SCL 95051 832-H5
1600 SUNV 94087 832-H5
2400 SCL 95051 833-A5
BENVENUE AV
300 LALT 94024 811-F7
BENZO DR
6300 SJS 95123 875-A7
BERCAW LN
14300 SCIC 95124 873-G3
14300 SJS 95124 873-G3
BERENDA WY
- SMCo 94028 810-E3
BERESFORD AV
100 SMCo 94061 790-B3
100 RDWC 94061 790-B3
BERESFORD CT
- SMCo 94061 790-B3
100 MPS 95035 794-A7
BERESFORD PL
- SMCo 94061 790-B3
BERESINI LN
- HOLL 95023 1039-G3
BERG CT
1100 MPS 95035 794-B4
BERGAMO CT
5600 SJS 95118 874-B5
BERGER DR
1400 SJS 95112 834-B1
BERGERAC DR
1400 SJS 95118 874-A6
BERGESEN CT
- ATN 94027 790-B4
BERGIN PL
1400 SCL 95051 833-A4
BERGMAN CT
2500 SJS 95121 855-E4
BERING DR
1800 SJS 95112 833-J1
2100 SJS 95131 813-H7
2100 SJS 95131 833-J1
BERINGER CT
1400 SJS 95125 853-G4
BERKELAND CT
4900 SJS 95111 875-C1
BERKELEY AV
500 SMCo 94025 790-H1
1000 MLPK 94025 790-H1
BERKELEY CT
22100 SCIC 94024 832-A7
BERKELEY TER
100 SUNV 94086 812-E7
BERKELEY WY
2200 SJS 95116 834-H4
BERKSFORD WY
600 CMBL 95008 853-C7
BERKSHIRE AV
- SMCo 94063 790-C1
900 SUNV 94087 832-C1
BERKSHIRE CT
10100 CPTO 95014 831-C7
18300 MGH 95037 916-H5
BERKSHIRE DR
100 MGH 95037 916-H5
1100 SJS 95125 854-C7
10400 LAH 94024 831-E5
10400 SCIC 94024 831-E5
BERKSHIRE PL
600 MPS 95035 794-B3
BERLAND CT
7600 CPTO 95014 852-D3
BERLIN DR
- SCIC 95046 937-G5
BERMUDA CT
900 SUNV 94086 832-G1
BERMUDA WY
1500 SJS 95122 834-H6
BERN CT
900 SJS 95112 834-B1
BERNA ST
1600 SCL 95050 833-C3
BERNAL AV
600 SUNV 94086 812-G6
BERNAL RD
- SJS 95119 875-F6
- SJS 95138 875-F6
100 SJS 95139 875-F6
100 SJS 95139 895-E1
100 SJS 95119 895-E1
100 SCIC 95119 895-D1
500 SJS 95120 895-C2
BERNAL WY
- SJS 95139 875-F7
- SJS 95119 875-F7
BERNARDO AV
600 SUNV 94087 812-B7
600 SUNV 94087 832-B2
1500 CPTO 95014 832-B5
N BERNARDO AV
400 MTVW 94043 812-C6
400 MTVW 94086 812-C6
S BERNARDO AV
100 MTVW 94041 812-B7
100 SUNV 94086 812-B7
BERNICE CT
- SBnC 95023 1060-D2
BERNICE WY
1800 SJS 95124 873-G2
BERONA WY
1400 SJS 95122 834-J5
1500 SJS 95122 835-A6
BERRENDO DR
- MPS 95035 794-A5
BERRY AV
600 LALT 94024 831-G2
BERRY CT
200 MGH 95037 916-J7
600 SCIC 94043 812-A3
BERRY DR
600 SCIC 94043 812-B2
BERRY WY
3500 SCL 95051 832-J2
14500 SJS 95124 873-G3
14500 SCIC 95124 873-G3
BERRYBUSH CT
- GIL 95020 977-J5
BERRYESSA RD
700 SJS 95112 834-B3
900 SJS 95133 834-C2
1100 SJS 95131 814-E7
1100 SJS 95133 814-E7
1200 SJS 95131 834-C2
2400 SJS 95132 814-G6
BERRYESSA ST
600 MPS 95035 793-J6
600 MPS 95035 794-A6
BERRY HILL CT
14100 LAH 94022 810-H6
BERRY HILL LN
14200 LAH 94022 810-J6
BERRYWOOD DR
1600 SJS 95133 834-E3
BERT DR
- HOLL 95023 1020-B5
BERTINI CT
3700 SJS 95117 853-C2
BERTLAND CT
1300 SJS 95131 814-D7
BERTRAM RD
21100 SCIC 95120 895-A7
21200 SCIC 95120 894-J7
21200 SCIC 95120 914-J1
BERWICK LN
- GIL 95020 977-D3
BERWICK ST
13200 SAR 95070 852-H7
BERWICK WY
100 SUNV 94087 832-E4
BERWICKSHIRE WY
6400 SJS 95120 894-C1
BERYLWOOD LN
- MPS 95035 793-J3
BESS CT
1300 SJS 95128 853-F4
BEST CT
2100 SJS 95131 814-E7
BEST RD
- SBnC 95023 1060-G2
700 SBnC 95023 1040-G7
BESTOR ST
200 SJS 95112 854-D1
400 SJS 95112 834-E7
BESTVIEW CT
15300 SAR 95070 872-F4
BESWICK DR
5600 SJS 95123 875-B4
BETA CT
600 CMBL 95008 853-C7
BETABEL RD
- SBnC 95020 1018-B4
9500 SBnC 95045 1018-B4
BETH CT
1300 HOLL 95023 1039-H5
3600 SCL 95054 813-E6
BETH DR
400 SJS 95111 854-H5
BETH WY
1500 CMBL 95008 873-A1
BETHANY AV
1700 SJS 95132 814-D4
BETHANY CT
1800 SJS 95132 814-D4
BETHEL AV
10000 SCIC 95127 835-A3
BETLIN AV
800 CPTO 95014 852-F2
BETLO AV
2400 MTVW 94043 811-F2
2500 PA 94306 811-F2
BETLO CT
5000 SJS 95130 852-J6
BETSY WY
2800 SJS 95133 814-H7
2800 SJS 95133 834-G1
BETSY ROSS DR
5200 SCL 95054 813-A3
BETTE AV
800 CPTO 95014 852-F2
BETTEN CT
1000 SJS 95127 834-J4
BETTENCOURT WY
- MPS 95035 814-A4
BETTIO RD
- SCIC 94035 812-B3
BETTY CT
700 SUNV 94086 832-F2
1600 SCL 95051 833-A3
BETTY LN
- ATN 94027 790-C4
BETTY ANN CT
21500 SCIC 95033 913-A3
BETTYS WY
- HOLL 95023 1040-D6
- SBnC 95023 1040-D6
BEVANS DR
400 SJS 95129 852-J1
BEVERLY BLVD
- SJS 95116 834-F4
BEVERLY CT
200 CMBL 95008 853-C6
BEVERLY DR
- SBnC 95023 1040-E5
1200 HOLL 95023 1040-E5
BEVERLY LN
100 LALT 94022 811-E6
BEVERLY ST
- MTVW 94043 812-B5
BEVIL CT
6400 SJS 95123 875-B7
BEVIN BROOK DR
1700 SJS 95112 854-F1
BEWCASTLE CT
2900 SJS 95132 814-D3
BEXLEY LNDG
1800 SJS 95132 814-C4
BIANCA WY
- GIL 95020 977-F2
BIANCHI WY
10000 CPTO 95014 852-D1
BIANCO WY
3400 SJS 95135 855-E3
BIARRITZ CIR
1200 LALT 94022 811-E6
BIARRITZ CT
18800 SAR 95070 852-H6
BIARRITZ LN
18800 SAR 95070 852-H6
BIARRITZ PL
5500 SJS 95138 875-F1
BIBBITS DR
3900 PA 94303 791-F7
3900 PA 94303 811-F1
BIBEL AV
6400 SJS 95129 852-F4
BICKLEY CT
5100 SJS 95136 874-E3
BICKNELL RD
600 LGTS 95030 873-A4
600 LGTS 95032 873-A4
800 MSER 95030 872-H4
800 MSER 95032 872-H4
800 LGTS 95030 872-H4
800 LGTS 95032 872-H4
18000 MSER 95030 873-A4
BIDDLEFORD CT
100 SJS 95139 875-G7
BIDWELL AV
900 SUNV 94086 812-C6
BIEBER DR
200 SJS 95123 875-A4
BIELAWSKI RD
- SCIC 95070 871-F7
- SCrC 95033 871-F7
BIEN CT
3300 SJS 95148 835-D7
BIEN WY
3300 SJS 95148 835-D7
BIENNA CT
- SJS 95131 814-B6
BIG BASIN DR
1400 MPS 95035 814-D2
BIG BASIN WY
Rt#-9
14400 SAR 95070 872-D3
22900 SCrC 95006 871-A4
22900 SCrC 95033 871-A4
26500 SCIC 95030 871-A4
BIG BEAR CT
900 MPS 95035 814-C1
BIG BEND DR
1500 MPS 95035 794-D7
BIGELOW CT
6000 SJS 95123 875-B6
BIGGS CT
600 SJS 95136 874-F2
BIGHORN CT
48700 FRMT 94539 793-J2
BIGOAK CT
1000 SJS 95129 852-H3
BIGOAK DR
5500 SJS 95129 852-H3
BIG OAK LN
- MPS 95035 793-J3
BIG SUR DR
1000 SJS 95120 894-H4
BIG TALK CT
1200 SJS 95120 874-C7
BIG WOOD DR
2900 SJS 95127 834-H2
BIKINI AV
1900 SJS 95122 854-H1
BILBO CT
1300 SJS 95121 855-A4
BILBO DR
3000 SJS 95121 855-A4
BILICH PL
10100 CPTO 95014 832-F7
BILL GRAHAM PKWY
- MTVW 94043 791-J7
- MTVW 94043 811-J1
BILLINGS CIR
- SCL 95054 813-E4
BILLINGS PL
- SCL 95050 833-D3
BILL RAY CT
- SJS 95125 854-F5
BILTMORE LN
- MLPK 94025 790-C6
BIMBER CT
3100 SJS 95148 835-D7
BIMMERLE PL
900 SJS 95123 874-E5
BING DR
800 SCL 95051 832-J5
1300 SJS 95129 852-G4
BINGHAM CT
5300 SJS 95123 874-J3
BIRCH AV
800 SUNV 94086 812-F7
1600 SCIC 95125 853-H5
1600 SJS 95125 853-H5
BIRCH DR
600 CMBL 95008 853-F5
BIRCH LN
- SCIC 95127 834-H2
4200 SJS 95129 853-A2
100 HOLL 95023 1039-H4
BIRCH PL
- GIL 95020 977-G1
BIRCH ST
1800 PA 94306 791-A6
3300 PA 94306 811-C1
BIRCH WY
400 SCL 95051 833-A7
6200 SJS 95138 875-F6
17100 MGH 95037 917-D6
BIRCH GROVE DR
5300 SJS 95123 875-A3
BIRCH HILL WY
26600 LAH 94022 811-B7
BIRCH LAKE CT
1700 SJS 95131 814-B5
BIRCHMEADOW CT
1300 SJS 95131 814-B6
BIRCHMEADOW LN
1300 SJS 95131 814-B6
BIRCH RIDGE CIR
100 SJS 95123 874-G7
BIRCH SPRING CT
11600 CPTO 95014 852-C4
BIRCHTREE LN
2600 SCL 95051 833-B6
BIRCH WOOD CT
100 LGTS 95032 873-B2
BIRCHWOOD CT
600 LALT 94024 831-F1
BIRCHWOOD DR
1200 SUNV 94089 812-J4
BIRCHWOOD LN
3200 SJS 95132 814-E2
BIRD AV
300 SJS 95126 854-A2
400 LGTS 95032 873-A7
400 SJS 95125 854-A2
BIRDSONG ST
500 GIL 95020 977-H1
BIRDVALE WY
- MGH 95037 916-H3
BIRKDALE CT
5200 GIL 95020 977-E4
BIRKDALE WY
5000 SJS 95138 855-E7
BIRKENSHAW PL
4500 SJS 95136 874-F2
BIRKHAVEN PL
- SJS 95138 875-G5
BIRMINGHAM CT
4800 SJS 95136 874-G2
BIRMINGHAM DR
4800 SJS 95136 874-G2
BISCAY CT
- CMBL 95008 853-A1
BISCAYNE CT
500 MGH 95037 917-A6
BISCAYNE WY
1700 SJS 95122 834-H6
BISCEGLIA AV
- MGH 95037 937-A1
BISCOTTI PL
4000 SJS 95134 813-D2
BISHOP AV
300 SUNV 94086 832-E1
BISHOP CT
8700 SCIC 95020 958-E5
BISHOP LN
- SMCo 94025 810-F1
BISMARCK DR
1000 CMBL 95008 853-B5
1000 SJS 95130 853-B5
1000 SJS 95008 853-B5
BISON CT
6500 SJS 95119 875-D7
BITTERN DR
1300 SUNV 94087 832-E5
BITTERNUT CT
1100 SJS 95131 814-D7
BITTER OAK ST
22200 CPTO 95014 832-A6
22200 LALT 95014 832-A6
BITTERROOT PL
6700 SJS 95120 894-G2
BIXBY DR
100 MPS 95035 794-D7
19700 CPTO 95014 852-F1
BIXBY RD
100 SBnC 95045 1038-J4
500 SBnC 95020 1038-J4
BLACHARD RD
600 SJS 95139 895-J2
600 SCIC 95139 895-J2
BLACK RD
18200 SCIC 95033 892-C3
20300 SCrC 95033 892-C3
BLACK ARROW RD
20000 SCIC 95033 892-E4
BLACKBERRY CT
- GIL 95020 977-J5
BLACKBERRY TER
1100 SUNV 94087 832-B3
BLACKBERRY HILL RD
15200 LGTS 95030 893-C2
15200 SCIC 95030 893-D2
BLACKBIRD CT
6000 SJS 95120 874-B7
BLACKBURN AV
100 MLPK 94025 790-J3
BLACKFEET TR
17600 SCIC 95033 913-C2
BLACKFIELD CT
1000 SCL 95051 833-B5
BLACKFIELD DR
1100 SCL 95051 833-C4
BLACKFIELD WY
1000 MTVW 94040 811-F5
BLACKFOOT CT
700 SJS 95123 874-H6
BLACKFORD AV
3700 SJS 95117 853-B2
4200 SJS 95129 853-A2
BLACKFORD CIR
4100 SJS 95117 853-B2
BLACKFORD CT
600 SJS 95117 853-C2
BLACKFORD LN
1600 SCIC 95125 853-H4
1900 SJS 95125 853-H4
BLACK FOREST DR
1100 HOLL 95023 1040-B5
BLACKHAWK CT
1400 SUNV 94087 832-E5
5600 SJS 95123 874-H4
BLACKHAWK DR
1500 SUNV 94087 832-E5
BLACKHAWK CANYON RD
4900 SCIC 95020 976-F3
BLACKLOCK CT
6000 SJS 95123 875-A6
BLACKMORE CT
1800 SJS 95132 814-D4
BLACK MOUNTAIN CT
900 LALT 94024 831-H2
BLACK MOUNTAIN RD
27200 LAH 94022 830-J1
27600 LAH 94022 831-A1
BLACK MOUNTAIN GRADE
- SCIC 95138 876-F6
BLACK OAK CT
17600 MGH 95037 936-F1
BLACK OAK LN
6100 SJS 95120 874-D7
BLACK OAK WY
- CPTO 95014 831-G5
BLACKOAK WY
5400 SJS 95129 852-H3
BLACKPOOL CT
5500 SJS 95138 875-H1
BLACK PRINCE CT
600 MGH 95037 937-B5
BLACK RIVER CT
4600 SJS 95136 874-G2
BLACKSMITH DR
1200 GIL 95020 957-F7
BLACKSTONE AV
1400 SJS 95118 874-B1
BLACK WALNUT CT
800 MGH 95037 917-B6
14400 SAR 95070 872-F2
BLACK WALNUT WY
800 MGH 95037 917-B6
BLACKWELDER CT
100 SCIC 94305 790-J7
BLACKWELL DR
300 LGTS 95032 873-D4
BLACKWING WY
1400 GIL 95020 957-E7
BLACKWOOD DR
6300 CPTO 95014 852-F2
BLACKWOOD TER
- SUNV 94086 832-F1
BLAINE CT
- SJS 95125 854-D6
BLAIR AV
600 SUNV 94087 832-B1
BLAIR CT
700 SUNV 94087 832-C1
900 PA 94303 791-C5
BLAIRBETH DR
300 SJS 95119 895-D1
BLAIRBURRY WY
500 SJS 95123 874-G4
BLAIRGOWRY CT
- GIL 95020 977-E4
BLAIRMORE CT
4000 SJS 95121 855-B5
BLAIRWOOD CT
700 SJS 95120 894-H3
BLAISDELL CT
700 SJS 95117 853-D2
BLAKE AV
- SCL 95051 833-A7
BLAKE CT
- SBnC 95023 1040-D2
900 GIL 95020 977-H3
BLAKE ST
400 MLPK 94025 790-F4
BLAKE WILBUR DR
900 PA 94304 790-G6
900 PA 94305 790-G6
BLALOCK ST
1000 MPS 95035 794-B5
BLANCHARD DR
17600 MSER 95030 873-A5
BLANCHARD WY
700 SUNV 94087 832-C4
BLANCO DR
4600 SJS 95129 852-J3
4600 SJS 95129 853-A3
BLAND AV
100 CMBL 95008 853-D5
BLANDING AV
2100 SJS 95121 855-C3
BLANDOR WY
10500 LAH 94024 831-D5
BLANEY AV
1000 SJS 95129 852-E4
N BLANEY AV
10000 CPTO 95014 832-F6
10000 CPTO 95014 852-F1
S BLANEY AV
10100 CPTO 95014 852-F2
BLANEY CT
10300 CPTO 95014 852-E1
BLANGE WY
- SJS 95134 813-D2
BLAUER CT
6200 SJS 95135 855-H6
BLAUER DR
20200 SAR 95070 852-E7
BLAUER LN
6200 SJS 95135 855-H6
BLAZINGWOOD AV
700 CPTO 95014 852-F2
BLAZINGWOOD DR
900 SUNV 94089 812-J5
BLEDSOE CT
- LAH 94022 831-B3
BLENHEIM AV
2700 SMCo 94063 790-C1
BLENHEIM LN
3400 SJS 95121 855-D3
BLEWETT AV
1100 SJS 95125 854-A3
BLINN CT
600 LALT 94024 811-G6
BLISS AV
2100 MPS 95035 794-E7
BLISS CT
500 SJS 95136 874-F1
BLOCK DR
1100 SCL 95050 833-C4
BLOM DR
500 SJS 95111 875-B1
BLOOMFIELD AV
Rt#-G7
1200 SCIC 95020 978-H7
1300 SCIC 95020 998-E1

STREET Block	City	ZIP	Pg-Grid
BLOOMFIELD AV Rt#-25			
100	SCIC	95020	998-C2
BLOOMFIELD DR			
4200	SJS	95124	873-J3
BLOOMSBURY WY			
3600	SJS	95132	814-F2
BLOSSOM AV			
5600	SJS	95123	874-H5
BLOSSOM CT			
300	SCIC	95037	916-E3
BLOSSOM DR			
800	SCL	95050	833-C5
BLOSSOM LN			
-	SBnC	95023	1060-C3
100	MTVW	94041	811-H5
20500	CPTO	95014	852-D2
BLOSSOM WY			
5400	SJS	95123	875-B4
BLOSSOM ACRES DR			
5400	SJS	95124	873-F6
BLOSSOM CREST WY			
2100	SJS	95124	873-F6
BLOSSOM DALE DR			
5400	SJS	95124	873-F6
BLOSSOM GARDENS CIR			
5400	SJS	95123	875-A3
BLOSSOM GLEN CT			
600	GIL	95020	977-J4
BLOSSOM GLEN WY			
100	LGTS	95032	873-E5
200	LGTS	95124	873-E5
200	SJS	95124	873-E5
BLOSSOM HILL RD Rt#-G10			
-	LGTS	95030	873-C6
-	SJS	95111	875-A4
-	SJS	95138	875-A4
-	SJS	95193	875-A4
-	LGTS	95032	873-E5
-	SJS	95123	875-A4
300	SJS	95123	874-E4
600	SCIC	95123	874-E4
1100	SJS	95118	874-A6
1500	SJS	95124	874-A6
1500	SJS	95124	873-G6
15500	SCIC	95032	873-C6
BLOSSOM PARK LN			
5600	SJS	95118	874-A6
5600	SJS	95124	874-A6
BLOSSOM RIVER DR			
1000	SJS	95123	874-D4
BLOSSOM RIVER WY			
1000	SJS	95123	874-D4
BLOSSOM TERRACE CT			
5400	SJS	95124	873-F6
BLOSSOM TREE LN			
5400	SJS	95124	873-F6
BLOSSOM VALLEY DR			
200	SJS	95124	873-E5
300	LGTS	95032	873-E5
2200	LGTS	95124	873-E5
BLOSSOMVIEW DR			
3500	SJS	95118	874-B1
BLOSSOM VILLA WY			
200	LGTS	95032	873-F6
200	SJS	95124	873-F6
BLOSSOM VISTA AV			
5400	SJS	95124	873-F6
BLOSSOM WOOD DR			
5400	SJS	95124	873-E6
BLUEBELL AV			
2200	SJS	95122	854-J1
BLUEBELL DR			
8400	GIL	95020	977-C1
BLUEBELL WY			
900	SUNV	94086	832-G1
BLUEBERRY TER			
500	SJS	95129	853-B2
BLUEBERRY HILL			
100	LGTS	95032	873-D7
BLUEBIRD AV			
1000	SCL	95051	832-H5
BLUEBIRD CT			
1300	SUNV	94087	832-E4
BLUEBIRD DR			
3100	SJS	95117	853-D4
BLUEBONNET CT			
1800	MGH	95037	917-D6
BLUEBONNET DR			
900	SUNV	94086	832-G2
BLUEBONNET WY			
1400	MGH	95037	917-D6
BLUE CREEK CT			
3200	SJS	95135	855-E2
BLUE DOLPHIN DR			
3600	SJS	95136	854-G7
BLUEFIELD CT			
500	SJS	95136	874-F1
BLUEFIELD DR			
200	SJS	95136	874-G1
BLUE GRASS CT			
3400	MGH	95037	917-G4
BLUEGRASS LN			
5600	SJS	95118	874-B5
BLUE GUM CT			
15000	SAR	95070	872-G4
BLUE GUM DR			
3900	SCIC	95127	835-B1
3900	SJS	95127	835-B1
BLUE HERON CT			
9600	GIL	95020	957-E7
BLUE HILL DR			
6900	SJS	95129	852-E3
BLUE HILLS DR			
21200	SAR	95070	852-C5
BLUEJACKET WY			
2000	SJS	95133	814-E7
2000	SJS	95133	834-E1
BLUE JAY CT			
17400	MGH	95037	917-F4
BLUEJAY CT			
700	EPA	94303	791-B1
BLUE JAY DR			
900	SJS	95125	854-C6
17400	MGH	95037	917-F4
BLUEJAY DR			
1600	SUNV	94087	832-E6
10900	CPTO	95014	832-E6
BLUE LAGOON DR			
2300	SCL	95054	813-C5
BLUE LAKE SQ			
1100	MTVW	94040	832-A2
BLUE LYNX CT			
-	MGH	95037	917-A2
BLUE MEADOWS CT			
12400	SAR	95070	852-D5
BLUE MIST PL			
1000	SJS	95120	894-F2
BLUE MOUNTAIN DR			
3200	SJS	95127	835-B4
BLUE OAK CT			
3400	SJS	95148	835-E6
BLUE OAK LN			
300	LALT	94306	811-D5
BLUE OAKS CT			
-	PTLV	94028	830-D3
BLUE OAKS PL			
-	LAH	94022	831-A3
BLUE OAKS RD			
3900	SCIC	95020	958-F2
BLUE PARROT CT			
1200	GIL	95020	977-F3
BLUERIDGE AV			
2300	MLPK	94025	790-D7
BLUE RIDGE DR			
4600	SJS	95129	853-A4
4700	SJS	95129	852-J4
BLUERIDGE DR			
2000	MPS	95035	814-E1
BLUERING CT			
6000	SJS	95120	874-B7
BLUE ROCK CT			
2500	SJS	95133	834-F1
BLUE SAGE DR			
700	SUNV	94086	832-F1
BLUE SPRUCE CT			
1800	MPS	95035	814-A4
BLUE SPRUCE WY			
1600	MPS	95035	813-J3
1700	MPS	95035	814-A3
BLUESTONE CT			
2500	SJS	95122	835-A5
BLUEWATER CT			
3000	SJS	95148	835-B5
BLUEWOOD CIR			
1900	SJS	95132	814-F3
BLUFF CT			
-	SJS	95135	875-J1
BLUFFWOOD CT			
6800	SJS	95120	894-H2
BLYTHE AV			
600	SUNV	94086	812-G5
BLYTHE CT			
600	SUNV	94086	812-G5
19900	SAR	95070	852-F6
BLYTHSWOOD DR			
18500	MSER	95030	872-H5
18500	SCIC	95030	872-H5
BOA VISTA DR			
1200	SJS	95122	854-H1
BOBBIE AV			
5000	SJS	95130	852-J6
BOBBYS LN			
-	SBnC	95023	1060-F3
BOBBYWOOD AV			
5400	SJS	95124	873-H5
BOBOLINK CIR			
500	SUNV	94087	832-E4
BOBOLINK DR			
2500	SJS	95125	854-D6
BOBWHITE AV			
1300	SUNV	94087	832-E4
BOB WHITE PL			
1400	SJS	95131	814-D7
BODEGA CT			
1600	HOLL	95023	1040-D6
BODEGA DR			
1100	SUNV	94086	812-C6
BODEGA WY			
300	SJS	95119	875-C7
BODIE CT			
5600	SJS	95123	875-A4
BOEGER LN			
3500	SJS	95148	835-D5
BOGALUSA CT			
600	FRMT	94539	793-J1
BOHANNON DR			
1900	SCL	95050	833-D6
BOHLMAN RD			
14900	SAR	95070	872-C4
15400	SCIC	95070	872-C5
18700	SCIC	95070	892-D1
BOISE CT			
600	SUNV	94087	832-D4
BOISE DR			
1000	CMBL	95008	853-B5
3900	SJS	95130	853-B5
BOLADO DR			
6900	SJS	95119	875-E7
6900	SJS	95119	895-E1
BOLADO RD			
300	SBnC	95075	1060-J5
300	SBnC	95075	1061-A6
BOLD CT			
600	SJS	95111	875-B1
BOLD DR			
600	SJS	95111	875-B1
700	SJS	95111	855-B7
BOLERO DR			
4500	SJS	95111	855-A7
4500	SJS	95111	875-A1
BOLIVAR DR			
600	SJS	95123	874-G5
BOLIVAR LN			
100	PTLV	94028	810-D5
BOLLA CT			
-	SJS	95124	873-G1
BOLLINGER RD			
5400	CPTO	95014	852-D2
5400	SJS	95129	852-G2
5800	SJS	95014	852-D2
BOLSA RD			
-	SBnC	95023	1019-G2
400	SCIC	95020	998-C1
1200	GIL	95020	978-B7
1200	GIL	95020	998-C1
1200	SCIC	95020	978-B7
1300	SBnC	95023	1020-A1
BOLSENA ST			
3300	SJS	95135	855-G6
BOLTON CT			
600	SJS	95129	853-A2
BOLTON DR			
800	MPS	95035	794-A2
8400	GIL	95020	977-J1
BOLTON PL			
-	MLPK	94025	790-F5
BONACCORSO PL			
600	SJS	95133	814-G7
BONAIR			
200	SCIC	94305	790-J7
BONAIR CT			
1000	SJS	95117	853-D3
BONANZA CT			
600	SUNV	94087	832-D4
BONAVENTURA DR			
-	SJS	95134	813-G6
BONBON DR			
2600	SJS	95148	835-C7
BONCHEFF DR			
2700	SJS	95133	814-G7
BOND CT			
100	LGTS	95030	893-C1
BOND ST			
800	SCL	95051	832-J6
BOND WY			
700	MTVW	94040	831-H1
BONESO CIR			
4100	SJS	95134	813-D3
BONGATE CT			
1400	SJS	95130	853-A4
BONGIOVANNI PL			
-	SCL	95054	813-D5
BONITA			
-	MTVW	94043	811-J2
BONITA AV			
-	RDWC	94061	790-B1
200	SJS	95116	834-F5
900	MTVW	94040	811-H7
3400	SCL	95051	832-J2
BONITA CT			
-	MTVW	94040	811-H6
3400	SCL	95051	832-J2
BONITA DR			
18700	MGH	95037	916-H5
BONITA RD			
100	SMCo	94028	830-D4
BONNER CT			
14900	SCIC	95037	937-C4
BONNET CT			
1300	SJS	95132	814-F5
BONNET WY			
18800	SAR	95070	852-G7
18800	SAR	95070	872-H1
BONNEVILLE WY			
900	SUNV	94087	832-B4
BONNIE CT			
1400	RDWC	94061	790-A2
BONNIE DR			
2500	SCL	95051	833-B2
BONNIE LN			
16300	LGTS	95032	873-D7
BONNIE BRAE LN			
20100	SAR	95070	872-E4
BONNIE BRAE WY			
20100	SAR	95070	872-E3
BONNIE JOY AV			
1500	SJS	95129	852-F4
BONNIE RIDGE WY			
19700	SAR	95070	852-F7
19900	SAR	95070	872-E1
BONNIE VIEW CT			
500	MGH	95037	916-H7
BONNIE VIEW DR			
800	HOLL	95023	1040-D5
BONNIE VIEW RD			
800	HOLL	95023	1040-C5
800	SBnC	95023	1040-C5
BONNY DR			
10200	CPTO	95014	852-D1
BONNY ST			
100	MTVW	94043	811-G4
BONSEN CT			
100	SMCo	94062	790-A4
BON VISTA CT			
10000	SCIC	95127	815-C7
10000	SCIC	95127	835-D1
BOOK LN			
2100	SCL	95054	813-C4
BOOKER AV			
300	SUNV	94086	812-D7
BOOKER CREEK RD			
24000	SCIC	95070	871-G3
BOOKSIN AV			
1800	SJS	95125	853-J6
2200	SJS	95125	854-A6
2900	SJS	95125	874-A1
BOONE DR			
1500	SJS	95118	874-A6
BOONEWOOD CT			
700	SJS	95120	894-H2
BORANDA AV			
900	MTVW	94040	811-H6
BORANDA CT			
-	MTVW	94040	811-H7
BORAX DR			
2400	SCL	95051	833-A1
BORCHERS DR			
1900	SJS	95124	873-G1
BORDEAUX DR			
1100	SUNV	94089	812-F3
BORDEAUX LN			
-	SJS	95127	834-C2
BORDEAUX PL			
400	HOLL	95023	1040-B4
BORDELAIS DR			
1400	SJS	95118	874-A6
BORDEN DR			
3700	SCIC	95148	835-G7
BORDENRAE CT			
700	SJS	95117	853-D2
BORDER RD			
1000	SCIC	94024	831-F2
BORDER HILL DR			
12600	SCIC	94024	831-F2
BORDWELL CT			
4700	SJS	95118	874-B3
BORDWELL DR			
4700	SJS	95118	874-B3
BORELLO DR			
2400	SJS	95128	853-F4
BORELLO WY			
700	MTVW	94041	812-A7
BOREN DR			
2400	SJS	95121	854-H2
BORGE CT			
3400	SJS	95132	814-G4
BORGES CT			
10600	SCIC	95020	958-A3
BORGWOOD CT			
800	SJS	95120	894-H4
BORINA DR			
4200	SJS	95129	853-A2
4600	SJS	95129	852-J2
BORNEO CIR			
5200	SJS	95123	874-J3
BORREGAS AV			
500	SUNV	94086	812-E5
900	SUNV	94089	812-F3
BOSCO LN			
900	GIL	95020	977-G2
BOSE CT			
6500	SJS	95120	894-D1
BOSE LN			
6300	SJS	95120	874-D7
6300	SJS	95120	894-D1
BOSQUE ST			
-	GIL	95020	957-H7
BOSTON AV			
-	SCIC	95128	833-G7
-	SCIC	95128	853-G1
-	SJS	95128	853-G1
BOSTON POST CT			
6500	SJS	95120	894-E1
BOSWALL CT			
3200	SJS	95121	855-C3
BOTHELL CIR			
6200	SJS	95123	875-A7
BOTHELO AV			
-	MPS	95035	794-A7
-	MPS	95035	814-A1
BOTTICELLI DR			
-	SJS	95135	855-G2
BOTTLE BRUSH LN			
1300	SJS	95118	874-B5
BOUCHARD DR			
1400	SJS	95118	874-A6
BOUDIN CT			
-	SJS	95131	814-C4
BOUGAINVILLEA CT			
14600	SAR	95070	872-C3
BOUGAINVILLEA DR			
5000	SJS	95111	875-A2
BOUGAINVILLEA TER			
-	SUNV	94086	832-H1
BOULAY CT			
200	SCIC	95037	896-C7
BOULDER BLVD			
-	SJS	95193	875-C4
BOULDER DR			
800	SJS	95132	815-A4
BOULDER ST			
200	MPS	95035	794-A3
BOULDER MOUNTAIN WY			
6500	SJS	95120	874-F7
6500	SJS	95120	894-F1
BOUNTIFUL ACRES WY			
19200	SAR	95070	872-G5
BOUQUET PARK LN			
-	SJS	95135	855-G2
BOURBON CT			
800	MTVW	94041	812-A7
BOURET DR			
1200	SJS	95118	874-B3
BOURGEOIS WY			
3100	SJS	95111	854-H5
BOURGOGNE CT			
-	SJS	95135	855-F3
BOURNEMOUTH CT			
3500	SJS	95136	874-D1
BOURNEMOUTH DR			
3500	SJS	95136	874-D1
BOUVERON CT			
2800	SJS	95148	855-D2
BOW WY			
-	PTLV	94028	810-B6
BOWDEN AV			
14900	SCIC	95037	936-J5
BOWDEN CT			
17000	SCIC	95037	936-J6
17000	SCIC	95037	937-A6
BOWDOIN ST			
700	SCIC	94305	810-J1
900	SCIC	94305	790-J7
2000	PA	94306	810-J1
2100	PA	94306	811-A1
BOWE AV			
1400	SCL	95051	833-B4
BOWEN AV			
800	SJS	95123	874-E5
BOWEN CT			
5900	SJS	95123	874-E5
BOWERS AV			
1700	SCL	95051	833-B2
2900	SCL	95051	813-B7
3000	SCL	95054	813-B7
BOWERY LN			
-	SJS	95135	855-F4
BOWHILL CT			
20900	SAR	95070	852-C5
BOWLING LN			
1600	SJS	95118	873-J4
BOWLING GREEN DR			
1600	SJS	95121	854-J2
1600	SJS	95121	855-A2
BOX CANYON RD			
1300	SJS	95120	894-D3
BOXLEAF CT			
400	SJS	95117	853-C1
BOXWOOD DR			
2200	SCL	95128	833-E6
2400	SCL	95128	833-E6
BOYCE AV			
800	PA	94301	791-A4
BOYCE LN			
20700	SAR	95070	872-D1
BOYD CT			
6000	SJS	95123	875-A6
BOYD RD			
-	SCIC	94035	812-B1
-	SCIC	94043	812-B1
BOYD ST			
200	MPS	95035	794-A3
BOYER LN			
-	LGTS	95030	873-A7
BOYER WY			
6400	MonC	93907	1037-B7
BOYNTON AV			
300	SJS	95117	853-C1
BOYSEA DR			
1300	SJS	95118	874-B2
BOYSOL CT			
3500	SJS	95132	814-F2
BRACCIANO CT			
3200	SJS	95135	855-C7
BRACE AV			
1100	SJS	95125	854-A4
BRACEBRIDGE CT			
1200	CMBL	95008	873-B2
BRACH WY			
3600	SCL	95051	832-H4
BRACKETT AV			
2800	SJS	95148	835-D7
BRACKETT WY			
-	SCL	95054	813-E4
BRADBURY DR			
2900	SJS	95122	855-B3
BRADBURY LN			
200	RDWC	94061	790-B2
BRADDALE AV			
1400	LALT	94024	831-J3
BRADDOCK CT			
1700	SJS	95125	853-G5
BRADEN CT			
3300	SJS	95148	835-E7
BRADFORD DR			
100	SUNV	94089	812-F4
BRADFORD WY			
1600	MGH	95037	917-D6
1700	SJS	95124	873-H2
BRADLEY AV			
300	SCIC	95128	853-F1
300	SJS	95128	853-F1
BRADLEY CT			
-	SMCo	94061	790-B4
BRADLEY WY			
1000	EPA	94303	791-A1
BRADSHAW DR			
3000	SJS	95148	855-D1
BRADWELL CT			
100	SJS	95138	875-E4
BRADY CT			
2600	SCL	95051	833-B3
BRADY PL			
-	MLPK	94025	790-H2
BRAEBRIDGE RD			
1300	SJS	95131	814-D7
BRAEBURN CT			
3900	SJS	95130	853-B4
BRAEMAR CT			
19500	SAR	95070	852-F7
BRAEMAR DR			
19500	SAR	95070	852-F7
19600	SAR	95070	872-F1
BRAEMER CT			
1100	SJS	95132	814-F6
BRAHMS AV			
2500	SJS	95122	855-A1
BRAHMS CT			
1900	SJS	95122	855-A1
BRAHMS WY			
100	SUNV	94087	832-E2
BRAID CT			
-	GIL	95020	977-D3
BRALY AV			
1500	MPS	95035	794-D6
BRAMBLE TR			
18100	SCIC	95033	912-J4
BRAMBLE WOOD LN			
-	SJS	95131	814-A6
BRANBURY DR			
200	CMBL	95008	853-C5
BRANBURY WY			
900	SJS	95133	834-E1
1000	SJS	95133	814-E7
BRANDEIS CT			
2900	SJS	95148	855-C7
BRANDERMILL CT			
700	SJS	95138	875-G5
BRANDON WY			
300	MLPK	94025	790-F6
BRANDT CT			
-	MPS	95035	794-C7
BRANDY CT			
-	SBnC	95023	1039-H3
BRANDY LN			
3200	SJS	95132	814-G5
BRANDYBUCK WY			
1100	SJS	95121	855-A4
BRANDYWINE CT			
12900	SAR	95070	852-D6
BRANDYWINE DR			
3000	SJS	95121	855-A3
12800	SAR	95070	852-D7
BRANHAM LN			
100	SJS	95136	874-G2
100	SCIC	95136	874-G2
900	SJS	95136	875-A2
1100	SJS	95118	874-B3
1500	SJS	95124	874-B3
1600	SJS	95118	873-H4
1600	SJS	95124	873-H4
1800	SCIC	95124	873-H4
BRANHAM LN E			
-	SJS	95138	875-C2
100	SJS	95111	875-A2
BRANHAM PARK PL			
1600	SJS	95118	873-H7
BRANNAN PL			
2400	SCL	95050	833-C5
BRANNER DR			
2300	MLPK	94025	810-E1
2300	SMCo	94025	790-E7
2300	SMCo	94025	810-E1
2300	MLPK	94025	790-E7
BRANSTON CT			
14800	SCIC	95037	937-A5
BRANTLEY DR			
1900	SJS	95131	814-D7
BRAQUET LN			
9200	SCIC	95020	957-B7
BRASILIA WY			
5800	SJS	95120	874-D5
BRASSWOOD CT			
400	SCL	95054	813-F6
BRATER CT			
1900	SJS	95131	814-D7
BRAVO CT			
12700	SCIC	95046	937-H6
BRAXTON DR			
600	SJS	95111	875-B1
BRAY AV			
2000	SCL	95050	833-C4
BREA LN			
-	SJS	95138	875-G5
BREA TER			
-	SUNV	94086	812-G5
BREECH AV			
100	SCL	95051	833-C7
100	SCL	95051	853-C1
BREEN CT			
3000	SJS	95121	855-A4
BREEN RD			
300	SBnC	95045	1038-E5
BREEZEWOOD CT			
1100	SUNV	94089	812-J4
BREEZYGLEN CT			
500	SJS	95133	834-F1
BREGA CT			
2200	MGH	95037	917-E6
BREGA LN			
2200	MGH	95037	917-E6
BREM LN			
6600	GIL	95020	978-B4
BREMERTON DR			
800	SUNV	94087	832-C4
BRENDA AV			
5300	SJS	95124	873-J5
BRENDA CT			
19900	CPTO	95014	852-F1
BRENDA LEE DR			
600	SJS	95123	874-H7
BRENDEL DR			
12900	LAH	94022	831-C1
BRENFORD DR			
2500	SJS	95122	834-J5
BRENNAN ST			
500	SJS	95131	813-H6
BRENNER WY			
1500	SJS	95118	874-A5
BRENNING DR			
2400	SJS	95111	854-G3
BRENT CT			
-	MLPK	94025	790-C7
1000	HOLL	95023	1039-J5
BRENT DR			
800	CPTO	95014	852-F2
BRENTON AV			
1200	SJS	95129	852-J4
BRENTON CT			
100	MTVW	94043	812-A5
BRENTWOOD CT			
-	HOLL	95023	1060-D1
700	LALT	94024	831-G2
2200	EPA	94303	791-C2
19600	MonC	93907	1037-B7
BRENTWOOD DR			
-	SJS	95131	814-A5
600	SJS	95129	853-A2
700	SJS	95129	852-J2
BRENTWOOD LN			
1600	GIL	95020	977-F1
BRENTWOOD PL			
700	LALT	94024	831-G2
BRENTWOOD ST			
1200	LALT	94024	831-G2
BRESANO LN			
-	LGTS	95030	873-B4
BRET AV			
10000	CPTO	95014	852-H1
BRET COVE CT			
100	SJS	95120	894-G2
BRET HARTE CT			
100	SCL	95050	833-D7
BRET HARTE DR			
6600	SJS	95120	894-F2
BRET HARTE ST			
800	PA	94303	791-B5
BRET HILL CT			
100	SJS	95120	894-G2
BRET KNOLL CT			
100	SJS	95120	894-G2
BRETMOOR WY			
1100	SJS	95129	852-F4
BREVINS LP			
-	SJS	95125	854-D7
BREWER AV			
10400	CPTO	95014	832-C7
BREWSTER AV			
4900	SJS	95124	873-F4
15000	SCIC	95124	873-F4
BREWSTER LN			
1500	SCIC	95037	936-H4
BRIAN CT			
300	SJS	95123	875-B6
1400	MPS	95035	794-C5
BRIAN LN			
100	SCL	95051	833-A7
BRIANA CT			
900	SJS	95120	894-H2
BRIAR CT			
13400	SAR	95070	852-E7
13400	SAR	95070	872-E1
BRIARBERRY CT			
1200	SJS	95131	814-D7
BRIARBERRY LN			
1400	GIL	95020	957-E7
BRIARBROOK CT			
3500	SJS	95132	814-F2
BRIARBUSH CT			
1700	SJS	95131	814-D7
BRIARCLIFF CT			
600	SCL	95051	832-J6
BRIARCLIFF DR			
600	SJS	95123	874-G5
BRIARCREEK CT			
1200	SJS	95131	814-C7
BRIARCREST CT			
1600	SJS	95131	834-C1
BRIARCREST DR			
1100	SJS	95131	834-C1
1200	SJS	95131	814-C7
BRIARGLEN DR			
3900	SJS	95118	874-C1
BRIAR HILLS CT			
-	SJS	95138	855-E5
BRIARLEAF CIR			
1200	SJS	95131	834-C1
BRIARPOINT DR			
1600	SJS	95131	834-C1
BRIAR RANCH LN			
600	SJS	95120	894-G4
BRIAR RIDGE DR			
5600	SJS	95123	874-G7
BRIARTREE DR			
1500	SJS	95131	834-C1
BRIARWOOD CT			
1100	LALT	94024	831-G2
BRIARWOOD DR			
200	SJS	95131	814-A4
1800	SCL	95051	832-J3
2100	SJS	95125	853-J6
2600	SJS	95125	854-A7
2600	SJS	95125	874-A1
2800	SJS	95118	874-A1
BRIARWOOD WY			
100	LGTS	95032	873-G6
700	SCIC	95008	853-F7
4100	PA	94306	811-E2
BRICE CT			
100	SJS	95111	875-A2
BRICKS WY			
-	SBnC	95023	1060-D2
BRICKWAY CT			
-	LGTS	95032	873-A6
BRIDAL PTH			
-	SJS	95111	854-G4
BRIDAL PLACE CT			
3600	SJS	95121	855-B4
BRIDGE CT			
7100	SJS	95120	894-G4
BRIDGE RD			
100	SBnC	95023	1039-G4
100	HOLL	95023	1039-G4
BRIDGECASTLE CT			
2000	SJS	95121	855-C5
BRIDGE PARK CT			
11500	CPTO	95014	852-C4
BRIDGEPORT CT			
3600	SJS	95117	853-C3
BRIDGEPORT TER			
-	SUNV	94087	832-D1
BRIDGEPORT LAKE DR			
5800	SJS	95123	874-G7
BRIDGET DR			
700	SJS	95136	874-E1
BRIDGETON CT			
100	LALT	94022	811-D6
BRIDGEVIEW CT			
-	SJS	95138	855-D5
BRIDGEVIEW LN			
-	SJS	95138	855-D5
BRIDGEVIEW TER			
-	SJS	95138	855-D6
BRIDGEWOOD WY			
900	SUNV	94089	812-J5
BRIDLE LN			
2100	SCIC	95046	938-A7
BRIDLE WY			
5800	SJS	95123	874-J5
BRIDLE PATH CT			
2400	SCIC	95020	958-C2
BRIDLE PATH DR			
2400	SCIC	95020	958-C1
BRIDLE RIDGE CT			
5000	SJS	95138	855-E5

STREET
Block City ZIP Pg-Grid

BRIGADOON WY
3200 SJS 95121 855-C3
BRIGANTINE DR
1000 SJS 95129 852-G3
BRIGANTINO DR
- HOLL 95023 1040-C4
BRIGGS AL
- HOLL 95023 1039-J4
- HOLL 95023 1040-A4
BRIGGS CT
200 SJS 95139 895-F1
BRIGGS RD
100 SBnC 95023 1039-J1
400 HOLL 95023 1019-J7
400 SBnC 95023 1019-J7
BRIGHAM RD
16200 SCIC 95030 872-G7
BRIGHTEN AV
1700 SJS 95124 873-H2
BRIGHT OAK PL
1000 SJS 95120 894-F2
BRIGHT OAKS CT
1300 LALT 94024 831-J3
BRIGHTON DR
- HOLL 95023 1040-C7
BRIGHTON LN
200 RDWC 94061 790-B2
BRIGHTON PL
1000 MTVW 94040 811-F5
BRIGHTSIDE CT
1100 SJS 95127 835-A4
BRIGHT WILLOW CIR
- SJS 95131 814-A5
BRIGHTWOOD CT
3100 SJS 95148 835-D7
BRIGHTWOOD DR
2800 SJS 95148 835-D7
BRILL CT
100 SJS 95116 834-G2
BRINDOS CT
- SJS 95123 874-F7
BRIONA CT
- SJS 95124 873-G1
BRIONES CT
27600 LAH 94022 830-H1
BRIONES WY
12400 LAH 94022 830-H1
BRIONNE DR
5600 SJS 95118 874-A6
BRISA PURA DR
- SJS 95116 834-E5
BRISAS DR
- SJS 95134 813-F3
BRISA SUAVE COM
- MPS 95035 813-J1
BRISBANE CT
7100 SJS 95129 852-E4
BRISBANE TER
100 SUNV 94086 812-E7
BRISBANE WY
7100 SJS 95129 852-E4
BRISTLECONE CT
1400 GIL 95020 977-G3
BRISTLE GRASS TER
FRMT 94539 793-J3
BRISTOL DR
2700 SJS 95127 835-A5
BRISTOL WY
2700 RDWC 94061 790-A3
BRISTOLWOOD LN
2100 SJS 95132 814-E2
BRITT WY
2400 SJS 95148 855-B1
2500 SJS 95148 835-C7
BRITTANY CIR
800 HOLL 95023 1039-J5
BRITTANY CT
3200 SJS 95135 855-F3
9000 GIL 95020 977-H1
10200 CPTO 95014 852-E1
BRITTANY MEADOWS
- ATN 94027 790-E3
BRITTON AV
100 ATN 94027 790-E3
300 SUNV 94086 832-F1
1100 SJS 95125 853-J3
1100 SJS 95125 854-A3
N BRITTON AV
500 SUNV 94086 812-G6
S BRITTON AV
300 SUNV 94086 812-G6
BRITWELL CT
4400 SJS 95136 874-F2
BRIX WY
- MGH 95037 917-E6
BRIXTON CT
1800 SJS 95132 814-E3
BROADACRES DR
- SCIC 95120 894-C2
- SJS 95120 894-C2
BROAD ACRES RD
- ATN 94027 790-C5
BROADLEAF LN
800 SJS 95128 833-F7
BROADMOOR DR
700 SJS 95129 853-A2
BROADVIEW DR
- SCIC 95033 913-A1
10200 SCIC 95127 835-B2
BROADWAY
- LGTS 95030 872-J7
- LGTS 95030 892-J1
- LGTS 95030 893-A1
1000 SJS 95125 854-A2
BROADWAY CT
1000 SJS 95125 854-A2
BROADWAY RD
21400 SCIC 95033 912-J2
BROADWAY ST
400 GIL 95020 977-H2
BROCASTLE WY
100 SJS 95032 873-B4
BROCK WY
3900 SCIC 95111 855-A6

BROCK WY
3900 SJS 95111 855-A6
BROCKENHURST DR
300 SJS 95119 895-D1
BROCKHAMPTON CT
1000 SJS 95136 874-C2
BROCKTON LN
19100 SAR 95070 852-G6
BRODERICK DR
400 SJS 95111 875-C2
BRODERICK WY
2700 MTVW 94043 791-G6
BRODIE DR
3300 SJS 95111 854-J5
3400 SJS 95111 855-A5
BROKAW RD
- SJS 95131 833-H1
- SJS 95110 833-H1
- SJS 95112 833-H1
200 SCL 95050 833-F3
E BROKAW RD
100 SJS 95131 833-H1
100 SJS 95112 833-H1
200 SJS 95131 813-J7
200 SJS 95112 813-J7
700 SJS 95131 814-A7
700 SJS 95112 814-A7
BROKEN ARROW DR
5000 SJS 95136 874-H2
5000 SJS 95136 875-A2
BROKEN LANCE CT
5200 SJS 95136 875-B3
BROKEN OAK CT
2800 SJS 95148 835-E7
BROMLEY CROSS DR
200 SJS 95119 895-D1
BRONSON AV
14500 SCIC 95124 873-G3
BROOK LN
19000 SAR 95070 852-G5
BROOK PL
1300 MTVW 94040 832-A2
BROOK WY
- GIL 95020 977-J5
BROOKDALE AV
1200 MTVW 94040 811-G7
BROOKDALE DR
1400 SJS 95125 853-J4
3200 SCL 95051 833-A5
3300 SCL 95051 832-J5
BROOKE ACRES CT
16200 LGTS 95032 893-D1
BROOKE ACRES DR
100 LGTS 95032 873-D7
100 LGTS 95032 893-D1
BROOK ESTATES CT
3000 SJS 95135 855-G5
BROOKFIELD AV
1200 SUNV 94087 832-B1
BROOK GLEN DR
- SJS 95129 852-G6
11800 SAR 95070 852-G6
BROOKGLEN DR
1300 SAR 95070 852-G5
1300 SJS 95129 852-G5
BROOKGROVE LN
900 CPTO 95014 852-G2
BROOKHAVEN DR
19000 SAR 95070 852-G4
BROOKHOLLOW DR
- SJS 95132 814-E5
BROOKHOLLOW LN
- SBnC 95023 1019-D4
BROOKHOLLOW RD
900 SBnC 95023 1019-C4
BROOKHURST CT
5600 SJS 95129 852-H4
BROOKINGS LN
1200 SUNV 94024 832-B4
BROOK LEAF CT
3300 SJS 95132 814-G4
BROOKLINE DR
800 SUNV 94087 832-C1
BROOKLYN AV
- LGTS 95030 893-A1
- SJS 95119 875-D5
- SJS 95126 833-G7
- SCIC 95128 833-G7
- SCIC 95128 853-G1
200 SJS 95128 833-G7
BROOKMERE DR
300 SJS 95123 875-B7
BROOKMILL RD
1400 LALT 94024 832-A3
BROOKMONT CT
- MGH 95037 937-A1
BROOKNOLL CT
19100 SAR 95070 852-G4
BROOKRIDGE DR
11800 SAR 95070 852-G5
BROOKS AV
200 LGTS 95030 872-J7
500 SJS 95125 854-A2
BROOKSIDE AV
- SCL 95117 833-C7
- SCL 95117 853-C1
BROOKSIDE DR
100 PTLV 94028 810-B7
BROOKS RANGE LNDG
- SJS 95131 814-A6
BROOKSTONE CT
- MPS 95035 794-C2
BROOKTREE CT
7100 SJS 95120 894-H3
BROOKTREE WY
7000 SJS 95120 894-H2
BROOKVALE DR
1500 SJS 95129 852-E4
BROOK VIEW CT
- SBnC 95023 1060-D1
BROOKVIEW CT
1000 MGH 95037 937-B5
BROOKVIEW DR
19000 SAR 95070 852-G5

BROOKWELL DR
10700 CPTO 95014 852-F2
BROOKWOOD AV
300 SJS 95116 834-E6
BROOKWOOD LN
20500 SAR 95070 872-D2
BROWER AV
3300 MTVW 94040 832-A2
BROWN AL
- HOLL 95023 1039-J4
- HOLL 95023 1040-A4
BROWN AV
2000 SCL 95051 833-A2
12900 SCIC 95111 854-H6
BROWN CT
2000 SCL 95051 833-B3
BROWN RD
300 SBnC 95045 1037-H1
BROWN ST
300 SJS 95125 854-B1
BROWNHILL CT
3200 SJS 95135 855-E2
BROWNING AV
200 CMBL 95008 873-D3
3000 SJS 95124 873-G2
BROWNS LN
14300 LGTS 95032 873-B2
BROWNSTONE CT
2500 SJS 95122 835-A5
BROWNWOOD WY
3600 SCL 95054 813-F6
BRUCE AV
17500 LGTS 95030 873-A5
17700 MSER 95030 873-A5
BRUCE CT
2800 SCL 95051 833-B2
15800 MSER 95030 873-A5
BRUCE DR
800 PA 94303 791-D6
BRUCE WY
1100 SCIC 95120 894-H5
BRUCES CIR
- SBnC 95023 1060-F3
BRUCITO AV
1100 LALT 94024 831-H4
BRUCKNER CIR
3400 MTVW 94040 832-A2
BRULE CT
14900 SCIC 95127 835-B1
BRUNDAGE WY
10900 SCIC 95127 815-B6
BRUNNHILDE WY
1500 SJS 95121 854-J4
1500 SJS 95121 855-A3
BRUNO CT
- SJS 95136 854-F7
BRUNO DR
- SJS 95136 854-F7
BRUNSWICK AV
4500 SJS 95124 873-F3
BRUSH RD
20800 SCIC 95033 912-H1
BRUSHCREEK CT
1600 SJS 95121 855-D7
BRUSHCREEK WY
3400 SJS 95121 855-D7
BRUSHGLEN WY
2300 SJS 95133 834-F2
BRUT WY
4200 SJS 95135 855-G3
BRYAN AV
400 SUNV 94086 832-E1
1000 SJS 95118 874-B2
BRYANT AV
100 MTVW 94040 831-J2
700 MTVW 94040 832-A2
BRYANT CT
300 PA 94301 790-H4
BRYANT ST
100 MTVW 94041 811-H5
100 PA 94301 790-H4
1000 PA 94301 791-B6
2500 PA 94306 791-C7
3200 PA 94306 811-D1
BRYANT WY
900 SUNV 94087 832-G4
BRYCE CT
500 MPS 95035 794-D7
500 MPS 95035 814-D1
BRYCE DR
300 MGH 95037 937-A2
800 SJS 95123 874-F4
BRYN MAWR CT
- MTVW 94043 811-G2
BRYSON AV
500 PA 94306 791-C6
BRYSON CT
15200 SCIC 95037 937-A5
BUBB RD
1100 CPTO 95014 852-C1
BUBBLINGWELL PL
6600 SJS 95120 894-F1
BUCHANAN CT
- EPA 94303 791-C1
1000 SCL 95051 833-B5
BUCHANAN DR
1100 SCL 95051 833-B4
BUCHER AV
500 SCL 95051 833-B6
BUCHER DR
15900 SCIC 95037 936-J3
BUCHSER WY
800 SJS 95125 854-B3
BUCK CT
- WDSD 94062 790-A5
BUCKEYE
- PTLV 94028 830-C1
BUCKEYE CT
800 MPS 95035 813-J3
900 SUNV 94086 832-G2
BUCKEYE DR
500 SJS 95111 854-J6
1500 MPS 95035 813-J3

BUCKHAVEN DR
7600 SJS 95135 856-A6
7600 SJS 95135 855-J6
BUCKHAVEN LN
19900 SAR 95070 852-F7
BUCK HILL CT
- MGH 95037 936-J2
BUCKHILL CT
2500 SJS 95148 835-C6
BUCKINGHAM AV
- SMCo 94063 790-C1
BUCKINGHAM CT
19100 SAR 95070 872-G1
BUCKINGHAM DR
100 SCL 95051 833-B7
100 SCL 95051 853-B1
1000 LALT 94024 831-H2
3300 SJS 95118 874-C1
BUCKINGHAM PARK CT
400 SJS 95136 874-F1
BUCKLEY ST
3600 SCL 95051 832-H3
BUCK MEADOW DR
- PTLV 94028 830-D3
BUCKNALL RD
600 CMBL 95008 853-A6
800 SJS 95008 853-B6
4300 SJS 95130 853-A6
4800 SJS 95130 852-J6
18500 SAR 95070 852-H6
BUCKNAM AV
800 CMBL 95008 873-B1
BUCKNAM CT
1100 CMBL 95008 873-B1
BUCKNER DR
3400 SJS 95127 835-A3
14100 SCIC 95127 835-A3
BUCKSKIN CT
16600 MGH 95037 917-F6
BUCKTHORN WY
- ATN 94025 790-E2
- MLPK 94025 790-E2
BUCKTHORNE WY
1300 SJS 95129 852-E4
BUCKWOOD CT
800 SJS 95120 894-H3
BUDD AV
- CMBL 95008 853-C7
BUDD CT
600 CMBL 95008 853-C7
BUDDLAWN WY
600 CMBL 95008 853-C7
BUENA CREST CT
2800 SJS 95121 855-F4
BUENA KNOLL CT
2800 SJS 95121 855-F4
BUENA LUNA
1400 SJS 95128 853-F4
BUENA MONTE DR
900 SJS 95111 855-A6
BUENA PARK CT
4300 SJS 95121 855-F4
BUENA POINT CT
2700 SJS 95121 855-F4
BUENA VIEW CT
2700 SJS 95121 855-F4
BUENA VISTA AV
- GIL 95020 957-H5
- SCIC 95020 957-H5
- SJS 95126 853-H1
100 SJS 95126 833-H7
200 SUNV 94086 812-C6
300 SCIC 95126 853-H1
400 SMCo 94061 790-B3
800 SCIC 95020 958-A5
17100 LGTS 95030 873-B4
BUENA VISTA DR
100 SJS 95131 814-A5
11600 LAH 94022 830-H2
BUENA VISTA RD
800 HOLL 95023 1039-G3
800 SBnC 95023 1039-D2
BUFFETT PL
6000 SJS 95123 874-D5
BUFKIN CT
5800 SJS 95123 875-A5
BUFKIN DR
5900 SJS 95123 875-A6
BUGATTI CT
400 SJS 95123 874-H3
BUGATTI PL
700 MGH 95037 917-B6
BUGGYWHIP CT
6600 SJS 95120 894-C5
BULLDOG BLVD
1000 SJS 95116 834-D4
BULLION CIR
1300 SJS 95120 874-B6
BULLION CT
1400 SJS 95120 874-B6
BULLION PL
1400 SJS 95120 874-B6
BUNCE CT
1100 SJS 95132 814-G5
BUNDESON DR
- HOLL 95023 1040-A6
BUNDY AV
300 SJS 95117 853-D2
300 SCIC 95117 853-D1
BUNDY ESTATES PL
- SJS 95117 853-D1
BUNGALOW CT
- SJS 95125 854-C6
BUNKER CT
2800 SJS 95121 855-A2
BUNKER HILL CT
6600 SJS 95120 894-C5
BUNKER HILL LN
2800 SCL 95054 813-A3
BUNTING CT
- GIL 95020 957-E6
BURBANK DR
800 SCL 95051 832-J5

BURBANK ST
- SCIC 95046 937-E6
BURCHELL AV
5800 SJS 95120 874-B6
BURCHELL CT
5900 SJS 95120 874-B7
BURCHELL RD
8300 SCIC 95020 977-B1
8300 GIL 95020 977-B1
8700 SCIC 95020 957-A7
10000 SCIC 95020 956-J7
BURDETT WY
1100 MPS 95035 794-C5
BURDETTE DR
1600 SJS 95121 854-J1
BURDICK LN
- SCL 95054 813-E4
BURDICK WY
2800 SJS 95148 855-C1
BURGESS DR
300 MLPK 94025 790-G4
BURGOYNE ST
300 MTVW 94043 811-H3
BURGUNDY CT
1200 SJS 95132 814-H5
BURGUNDY DR
3300 SJS 95132 814-G5
BURGUNDY WY
19400 SAR 95070 872-F3
BURKE DR
400 GIL 95020 978-A1
4500 SCL 95054 813-D4
BURKE LN
25600 LAH 94022 811-D7
BURKE RD
13200 LAH 94022 831-C1
13300 LAH 94022 811-D7
16700 LGTS 95032 873-J7
16700 SJS 95120 873-J7
16700 SJS 95124 873-J7
BURKE ST
400 SJS 95112 854-F3
BURKETTE DR
1200 SJS 95129 853-A4
BURL CT
2800 SJS 95121 855-E3
22800 SCrC 95033 912-J5
BURL WY
2700 SJS 95121 855-E3
BURLEY DR
1600 MPS 95035 794-D6
BURLINGAME WY
2600 SJS 95121 855-D3
BURLINGTON ST
- SJS 95193 875-C4
BURLWOOD DR
- HOLL 95023 1040-E5
900 SJS 95120 894-G2
BURMAN DR
900 SJS 95111 855-A6
BURNBANK PL
6000 SJS 95120 874-C7
BURNETT AV
100 MGH 95037 916-H3
100 SCIC 95037 916-J2
300 SCL 95051 833-A7
800 SCIC 95037 917-A1
BURNETT DR
20900 SAR 95070 852-C5
BURNHAM CT
100 CMBL 95008 853-B5
BURNHAM DR
1100 SJS 95132 814-F5
BURNHAM WY
2400 PA 94303 791-D5
BURNING TREE CT
6900 SJS 95119 875-E7
BURNING TREE DR
100 SJS 95119 875-E7
200 SJS 95119 895-E1
BURNLEY WY
1100 SCL 95051 832-H4
1100 SUNV 94087 832-H4
BURNS AV
100 ATN 94027 790-E2
BURNS WY
14200 SAR 95070 872-D2
BURNSIDE DR
6800 SJS 95120 894-G3
BURNTWOOD AV
1000 SUNV 94089 812-J5
BURNTWOOD CT
1100 SUNV 94089 812-J5
BURREL CT
1500 SJS 95126 833-G6
BURROWS RD
1200 CMBL 95008 873-B1
BURTON AV
- SJS 95112 834-A3
BURTON DR
3900 SCL 95054 813-D5
BURTON RD
16100 LGTS 95032 873-D3
BUSBY CT
700 HOLL 95023 1040-C4
BUSH CIR
- SCIC 94043 812-A2
BUSH ST
- SJS 95126 834-A7
100 MTVW 94041 811-J6
BUSHNELL RD
10000 SCrC 95018 912-E5
BUSHNELL ST
- SCIC 94035 812-B2
- SCIC 94043 812-B2
BUSINESS CIR
2200 SJS 95128 853-F1
BUSKIRK ST
100 MPS 95035 793-J3
100 MPS 95035 794-A3
BUTANO AV
100 SUNV 94086 812-B6
BUTANO CT
6100 SJS 95123 874-G6

BUTANO DR
1600 MPS 95035 814-E2
BUTANO TER
14700 SAR 95070 872-D3
BUTCH DR
2500 SCIC 95020 958-D1
BUTCHER DR
3400 SCL 95051 832-J5
BUTLER ST
- MPS 95035 793-J7
BUTTE CT
1000 SUNV 94087 832-B4
BUTTE ST
2800 SCL 95051 833-A4
BUTTERCUP LN
1000 GIL 95020 977-G2
BUTTERFIELD BLVD
- MGH 95037 937-B1
18500 MGH 95037 916-J4
18500 MGH 95037 917-A6
BUTTERFLY DR
1200 SJS 95120 874-C7
BUTTERFLY LN
3200 SCIC 95037 917-F4
BUTTITTA LN
1400 SCL 95051 833-A4
BUTTONWOOD CT
2700 SJS 95148 835-E6
BYERLEY AV
700 SJS 95125 854-B5
BYERLY CT
10100 CPTO 95014 831-C7
BYERS DR
1900 MLPK 94025 791-A2
BYERS ST
1000 GIL 95020 977-H3
BYINGTON DR
4800 SJS 95121 855-F5
4800 SJS 95138 855-F5
BYRD LN
13100 LAH 94022 810-J7
BYRNE AV
10000 CPTO 95014 852-B1
BYRNE CT
21800 CPTO 95014 852-B1
BYRNE PARK LN
27200 LAH 94022 830-J2
27200 LAH 94022 831-A2
BYRON DR
1900 SJS 95124 873-G2
BYRON ST
100 PA 94301 790-J3
1100 PA 94301 791-A4
2700 PA 94306 791-C6
4100 PA 94306 811-F2

C

C CT
- GIL 95020 977-E1
S C RD
- SUNV 94089 812-J3
C ST
- CPTO 95014 831-H5
100 MLPK 94025 790-G3
600 HOLL 95023 1039-H5
1100 SUNV 94089 812-E2
CABALLO CT
- SBnC 95023 1020-F2
1100 SJS 95132 814-G5
CABALLO LN
- SCIC 94304 810-F6
CABANA DR
1700 SCIC 95125 853-H6
CABERNET CIR
- MGH 95037 917-E6
CABERNET CT
- MGH 95037 917-D6
8200 SJS 95135 855-J6
CABERNET DR
18800 SAR 95070 852-H5
CABERNET WY
48800 FRMT 94539 794-A2
CABERNET VINEYARDS CIR
3600 SJS 95117 853-C3
CABERNET VINEYARDS CT
900 SJS 95117 853-C2
CABOT AV
- SCL 95051 832-J7
- SCL 95051 852-J1
CABOT PL
1100 SJS 95129 852-F3
CABRAL AV
5800 SJS 95123 874-F5
CABRILLO AV
600 SCIC 94305 810-H1
1200 SCL 95050 833-D3
1200 SJS 95132 814-E5
1900 SCL 95051 832-J3
2400 SCL 95051 833-B2
CABRILLO CT
- GIL 95020 977-G1
2000 SCL 95051 833-B3
CABRILLO DR
800 SJS 95131 814-A5
CABRILLO RD
2000 SJS 95134 813-G3
CACTUS DR
5500 SJS 95123 875-B4
CADBURRY CT
500 SJS 95123 874-G4
CADET PL
900 SJS 95133 814-E7
CADILLAC CT
1100 MPS 95035 793-H5
CADILLAC DR
3100 SJS 95117 853-D4
CADIZ DR
5800 SJS 95123 874-F5
CADMILL CT
2800 SJS 95121 854-J4

CADWALLADER AV
3500 SJS 95121 855-D3
CADWELL CT
100 SJS 95138 875-D4
CAGGIANO CT
1000 SJS 95120 894-G3
CAGGIANO DR
1000 SJS 95120 894-G3
CAGNEY RD
200 SBnC 95045 1038-F5
CAHALAN AV
5600 SJS 95123 874-G4
CAHALAN CT
700 SJS 95123 874-G4
CAHEN DR
7100 SJS 95120 894-H4
CAHILL ST
- SJS 95110 834-A7
- SJS 95113 834-A7
CAHILL PARK DR
- SJS 95126 834-A7
CAIRO CT
10000 SCIC 95127 835-A3
CAITLIN WY
- FRMT 94539 793-H2
CAJON WY
- GIL 95020 977-J7
CALABAZAS BLVD
1300 SCL 95051 833-A2
2300 SCL 95051 832-J2
CALABAZAS CT
1300 SCL 95051 833-A4
CALABAZAS CREEK CIR
6900 SJS 95129 852-E4
CALABRESE WY
1500 GIL 95020 977-F2
CALADO AV
100 CMBL 95008 853-A5
300 SJS 95130 853-A5
CALADO CT
1600 CMBL 95008 853-A5
CALAIS CIR
800 HOLL 95023 1040-C5
CALAIS CT
600 HOLL 95023 1040-B5
4700 SJS 95124 874-A3
CALAIS DR
700 HOLL 95023 1040-B5
CALARO CT
2300 MGH 95037 917-E6
CALAVERAS AV
1400 SJS 95126 833-H7
CALAVERAS BLVD
1400 MPS 95035 794-D6
CALAVERAS BLVD Rt#-237
300 MPS 95035 793-J7
300 MPS 95035 813-J1
500 MPS 95035 794-A7
CALAVERAS CT
- MPS 95035 794-C6
CALAVERAS RD
2000 MPS 95035 794-E6
3100 SCIC 95035 794-H5
4000 SCIC 95140 794-J2
CALAVERAS RIDGE DR
800 MPS 95035 794-C4
CALBOONYA CT
1600 SJS 95125 854-D3
CALBORO DR
1000 SJS 95117 853-D3
CALCATERRA CT
1100 SJS 95120 894-G3
CALCATERRA DR
7000 SJS 95120 894-F3
CALCATERRA PL
300 PA 94306 811-E2
CALCO CREEK DR
- SJS 95127 835-C3
CALDERON AV
100 MTVW 94041 811-J6
CALDERWOOD LN
5200 SJS 95118 874-B4
CALDWELL AV
200 LGTS 95032 873-B7
CALDWELL CT
200 SCIC 95037 896-C7
1200 SUNV 94024 832-A4
CALDWELL PL
700 SCL 95051 833-B5
CALEB CT
2100 SJS 95121 855-C4
CALEDONIA DR
7700 SJS 95135 856-A6
7900 SJS 95135 855-J5
CALEDONIA WY
- GIL 95020 977-D3
CALENDULA CT
- SJS 95136 874-G2
CALERA CREEK HEIGHTS DR
1600 MPS 95035 794-C3
CALERO AV
200 SJS 95123 875-A5
300 SJS 95123 874-F5
CALERO ST
800 MPS 95035 793-J6
CALERO HILLS CT
7100 SJS 95139 895-H2
CALFHILL CT
- LGTS 95032 873-B6
CALGARY CT
10100 SCIC 95127 835-B3
CALGARY DR
1700 SUNV 94087 832-B6
CALHOUN ST
800 SJS 95116 834-D5
CALI AV
20400 CPTO 95014 852-E1
CALICO AV
3300 SJS 95124 873-F2
3600 SCIC 95124 873-F2

SANTA CLARA CO.

STREET
Block City ZIP Pg-Grid

CALICO CT
700 SUNV 94086 832-F1
2600 MGH 95037 917-F6
CALICO TRAIL RDG
- MGH 95037 917-G4
- SCIC 95037 917-G4
CALICOWOOD PL
5100 SJS 95111 875-C2
CALIDA DR
4900 SJS 95136 874-F2
CALIENTE DR
600 SUNV 94086 812-G5
CALIENTE WY
- GIL 95020 977-J7
1400 SJS 95132 814-E4
CALIFORNIA AV
- SCIC 95046 937-D6
400 SCL 95050 833-D5
900 SJS 95125 854-B4
900 SUNV 94086 812-G7
E CALIFORNIA AV
100 SUNV 94086 812-F7
N CALIFORNIA AV
- PA 94301 791-B6
700 PA 94303 791-C5
S CALIFORNIA AV
100 PA 94306 791-A7
500 PA 94304 791-A7
700 PA 94304 811-A1
700 PA 94306 811-A1
1600 PA 94305 811-A1
1600 SCIC 94305 811-A1
W CALIFORNIA AV
100 SUNV 94086 812-D6
CALIFORNIA CIR
1200 MPS 95035 793-H4
CALIFORNIA ST
- HOLL 95023 1040-A6
200 CMBL 95008 853-D7
500 MTVW 94041 811-G4
1700 MTVW 94040 811-F3
CALIFORNIA OAK WY
10000 CPTO 95014 831-J7
CALINOMA DR
1500 SJS 95118 874-A5
CALIRI CT
8600 SCIC 95020 958-E5
CALISTOGA DR
1800 SJS 95124 873-H1
1900 HOLL 95023 1040-D7
CALISTOGA WY
- MTVW 94043 812-A5
CALLA CT
- SJS 95133 814-F7
CALLA DR
700 SUNV 94086 832-F2
CALLADO WY
- ATN 94027 790-C5
CALLAN ST
100 MPS 95035 793-J3
100 MPS 95035 794-A3
CALLE ALEGRE
1400 SJS 95120 874-B7
CALLE ALFREDO
- SUNV 94089 812-G4
CALLE ALICIA
- SUNV 94089 812-J4
CALLE ALMADEN
1100 SJS 95120 874-D6
CALLE ALOUDRA
5400 SJS 95111 875-C3
CALLE ANITA
- SUNV 94089 812-H4
CALLE ARTIS
700 SJS 95131 814-A5
CALLE ASTA
400 MGH 95037 917-A6
CALLE ATAVIO
400 MGH 95037 917-A7
CALLE BONITA
6200 SJS 95120 874-B7
6200 SJS 95120 894-B1
CALLE BUENA VISTA
- MGH 95037 917-A6
CALLE CABALLERIA
400 MGH 95037 917-A7
CALLE CABALLERIA CT
500 MGH 95037 917-A6
CALLE CABEZAL
300 MGH 95037 917-A7
CALLE CARLOTTA
- SUNV 94089 812-J4
CALLE CELESTINA
12300 SCIC 95020 956-J3
CALLE CENTRAL
17700 MGH 95037 917-A5
CALLE CERRO
300 MGH 95037 917-A6
CALLE CIELO
11800 SCIC 95020 956-J4
CALLECITA
100 LGTS 95032 872-J2
CALLECITA ST
1400 SJS 95125 853-J6
1400 SJS 95125 854-A6
CALLE CONCHITA
- SUNV 94089 812-H4
CALLE CONSUELO
- SUNV 94089 812-H4
CALLE CORTA
- LGTS 95032 872-J2
CALLE CRUZ
- SBnC 95045 1037-J5
CALLE CUERVO
200 SJS 95111 875-C3
CALLE CUESTA
100 SBnC 95023 1060-E1
CALLE DE AIDA
1500 SJS 95118 874-A3
CALLE DE AMOR
6000 SJS 95124 873-J7
CALLE DE ARROYO
4400 SJS 95118 874-A2
CALLE DE BARCELONA
19300 CPTO 95014 852-G1
CALLE DE CUESTANDA
1200 MPS 95035 814-E1
CALLE DE ESCUELA
4900 SCL 95054 813-C3
CALLE DE FARRAR
4300 SJS 95118 874-B3
CALLE DE FELICE
6000 SJS 95124 873-J7
CALLE DE GILDA
1400 SJS 95118 874-B3
CALLE DE GUADALUPE
- SJS 95116 834-G3
CALLE DE LA PAZ
1400 SJS 95120 874-B7
CALLE DE LAS ESTRELLA
2900 SJS 95148 855-B2
CALLE DE LAS FLORES
2900 SJS 95148 855-B2
CALLE DEL CONEJO
6100 SJS 95120 874-B7
CALLE DEL MUNDO
2200 SCL 95054 813-C3
CALLE DEL PRADO
600 MPS 95035 794-B5
CALLE DEL REY
8700 GIL 95020 977-F1
9200 GIL 95020 957-F7
CALLE DEL SOL
1400 MPS 95035 793-H3
5100 SCL 95054 813-C3
17300 MGH 95037 917-A7
26300 LAH 94022 831-B1
CALLE DE LUCIA
4700 SJS 95124 874-A3
CALLE DE LUNA
2200 SCL 95054 813-C3
CALLE DE PLATA
1700 SJS 95116 834-F3
CALLE DE PRIMAVERA
2000 SCL 95054 813-C4
CALLE DE PROSPERO
1600 SJS 95124 873-J7
CALLE DE RICO
6000 SJS 95124 873-J7
CALLE DE STUARDA
1500 SJS 95118 874-A2
CALLE DE SUERTE
6000 SJS 95124 873-J7
CALLE DE TOSCA
4500 SJS 95118 874-A3
CALLE DE VERDE
800 SJS 95136 874-E2
CALLE DOLORES
- SUNV 94089 812-H4
CALLE DORITA
- SUNV 94089 812-J4
CALLE EL KOWALIK
1600 SJS 95124 874-A3
CALLE EL PADRE
100 LGTS 95032 873-A2
CALLE ENRIQUE
15300 MGH 95037 937-B4
CALLE ESPERANZA
6100 SJS 95120 874-B7
CALLE ESTORIA
100 LGTS 95032 873-A2
CALLE ESTRELLA
- SUNV 94089 812-H4
CALLE EULALIA
- SUNV 94089 812-H4
CALLE FLORENCIA
- MGH 95037 917-A6
CALLE GALONDRINA
- SJS 95111 875-B3
CALLE GAVIOTA
300 SJS 95111 875-C3
CALLE GLORIA
- SUNV 94089 812-H4
CALLE GRANADA PK
- MTVW 94043 811-H4
CALLE HERMOSA
17700 MGH 95037 917-A6
CALLE ISABELLA
- SUNV 94089 812-H4
CALLE JUANITA
- SUNV 94089 812-H4
CALLE LARGA
- LGTS 95032 872-J2
- LGTS 95032 873-A2
CALLE LOLITA
200 LGTS 95032 873-A2
CALLE LUCIA
- SUNV 94089 812-H4
CALLE LUPE
1000 SUNV 94089 812-J4
CALLE MARGUERITA
100 LGTS 95032 873-A2
CALLE MARIA
- SUNV 94089 812-J4
CALLE MAZATAN
17200 MGH 95037 917-B7
CALLE MESA ALTA
2000 MPS 95035 814-E1
CALLE MONIZ
19100 SCIC 95037 916-J3
CALLE MONTALVO
20200 SAR 95070 872-E3
CALLE NIVEL
100 LGTS 95032 872-J2
CALLE ORIENTE
1100 MPS 95035 794-C5
CALLE PINTADA
5400 SJS 95111 875-C3
CALLE ROSITA
- SUNV 94089 812-H4
CALLE SAN ANTONIO
- SBnC 95045 1037-J4
CALLE SERRA
- MGH 95037 917-B3
CALLE SIENA
- MGH 95037 917-A6
CALLE SUENO
- MGH 95037 937-B3
CALLE TACUBA
13600 SAR 95070 872-E1
CALLE TERESA
- SUNV 94089 812-H4
CALLE TIERRA
- MGH 95037 917-A6
CALLE UVAS
12200 SCIC 95020 956-J3
CALLE VENTURA
1100 SJS 95120 894-E2
CALLE VERDE
400 MGH 95037 917-A6
CALLE VICTORIA
- SUNV 94089 812-H4
CALLE VIENTO
- MGH 95037 917-A6
CALLE VIENTO CT
- MGH 95037 917-A6
CALLE VISTA VERDE
2100 MPS 95035 814-E1
CALL OF THE WILD RD
21900 SCIC 95033 913-A3
CALMA CT
2500 SJS 95128 853-F4
CALMOR AV
5600 SJS 95123 874-F4
CALMOR CT
5600 SJS 95123 874-F5
CALOOSA CT
1700 SJS 95131 814-D7
CALPELLA DR
500 SJS 95136 874-F2
CALPINE DR
5600 SJS 95123 875-B4
CALUMET CT
1000 SJS 95112 834-D3
CALVARY WY
- SJS 95118 854-C7
CALVELLI CT
3500 SJS 95124 873-E2
CALVERT CT
200 SCL 95051 832-J7
CALVERT DR
200 CPTO 95014 852-H1
200 SJS 95014 852-H1
200 SCL 95051 832-J7
CALVIEW AV
2000 SJS 95122 834-J6
CALVIEW LN
1400 SJS 95122 834-J6
CALVIN AV
3200 SJS 95124 873-F2
3300 SCIC 95124 873-F2
CALWA CT
5000 SJS 95111 875-A2
CALYPSO CT
1100 SJS 95127 835-A4
CALZAR DR
3000 SJS 95118 874-A1
CAMACHO WY
1800 SJS 95132 814-D3
CAMANO CT
1100 SJS 95122 854-H2
CAMARDA CT
20100 CPTO 95014 832-E7
CAMARENA PL
- SJS 95121 855-A3
CAMARGO CT
2900 SJS 95132 814-D3
CAMARGO DR
1700 SJS 95132 814-D3
CAMARILLO CT
1000 MPS 95035 794-C4
3200 SJS 95135 855-G4
CAMAS AV
400 SJS 95116 834-J3
CAMBERLEY LN
10100 CPTO 95014 851-J1
CAMBERLY WY
400 RDWC 94061 790-B2
CAMBER TREE CT
1100 SJS 95120 874-D7
CAMBRIA CT
- SJS 95124 873-J3
CAMBRIAN DR
500 SCIC 95008 853-F7
500 SJS 95008 853-F7
CAMBRIANNA DR
1900 SJS 95124 873-G2
CAMBRIAN VIEW WY
100 LGTS 95032 873-G6
CAMBRIDGE AV
200 PA 94306 791-A7
600 MLPK 94025 790-G5
900 SUNV 94087 832-C1
CAMBRIDGE DR
500 SCL 95051 832-J6
2800 SJS 95125 854-C7
12500 SAR 95070 852-G6
CAMBRIDGE LN
3500 MTVW 94040 831-J2
CAMDEN AV
700 CMBL 95008 873-E1
700 CMBL 95008 853-E7
1300 SCIC 95008 873-E1
1300 SJS 95120 894-C1
1400 SJS 95008 873-E1
1500 SJS 95124 873-E2
2100 SCIC 95124 873-E2
4400 SJS 95118 873-H3
6000 SJS 95120 873-J7
6000 SJS 95120 874-A7
CAMDEN OAKS CT
1500 SJS 95124 873-J6
1500 SJS 95124 874-A6
CAMDEN VILLAGE CIR
5700 SJS 95124 873-J6
5700 SJS 95124 874-A6
CAMDEN VILLAGE CT
5700 SJS 95124 874-A6
CAMELFORD WY
2900 SJS 95127 834-H1
CAMELIA DR
6400 SJS 95120 894-D1
CAMELLIA AV
100 RDWC 94061 790-B2
CAMELLIA CT
- EPA 94303 791-C3
600 LALT 94024 811-G6
CAMELLIA DR
1100 EPA 94303 791-D2
CAMELLIA TER
100 LGTS 95032 873-C6
16100 SCIC 95032 873-C6
CAMELLIA WY
500 LALT 94024 811-F6
900 SJS 95117 853-B3
CAMELOT DR
15100 SCIC 95132 814-H4
CAMEO CT
300 CMBL 95008 853-G6
CAMEO DR
1000 CMBL 95008 853-G6
1400 SJS 95129 852-J4
CAMERON BLVD
- GIL 95020 978-C4
CAMERON CIR
- MPS 95035 794-B7
CAMERON CT
- MPS 95035 794-B7
CAMERON DR
- MTVW 94043 812-B6
CAMERON PL
- MPS 95035 794-C7
1100 SJS 95129 852-F3
CAMERON WY
3000 SCL 95051 833-A7
CAMILLE CIR
400 SJS 95134 813-H4
CAMILLE CT
300 MTVW 94040 811-H6
1500 SCIC 95037 937-E1
CAMILLE LN
- MTVW 94040 811-J6
CAMINA ESCUELA
600 SJS 95129 853-A2
CAMINO DR
600 SCL 95050 833-F5
CAMINO AL LAGO
200 ATN 94027 790-C5
200 SMCo 94025 790-C5
CAMINO A LOS CERROS
- ATN 94027 790-C5
- SMCo 94027 790-C5
1800 SMCo 94025 790-C5
CAMINO ARROYO
- SCIC 95020 978-D5
8000 GIL 95020 978-B1
CAMINO BARCO
13900 SAR 95070 872-H1
CAMINO CERRADO
1400 SJS 95128 853-F5
CAMINO DE LAS ROBLES
- PA 94301 790-H5
CAMINO DEL CERRO
100 LGTS 95032 873-E5
16000 SCIC 95032 873-E6
CAMINO DE LOS ROBLES
- ATN 94027 790-D5
1800 SMCo 94025 790-D5
CAMINO DEL REY
2600 SJS 95132 814-E5
CAMINO DEL SOL
16100 LGTS 95032 873-D4
CAMINO ECCO
2600 SJS 95121 854-J2
2600 SJS 95121 855-A2
CAMINO HERMOSA
23300 LAH 94024 831-E4
CAMINO LEONOR
- SJS 95131 814-B6
CAMINO MEDIO LN
12700 LAH 94022 811-B6
CAMINO MONDE
1500 SJS 95125 853-J4
CAMINO NOLA CT
- SJS 95132 814-E5
CAMINO PABLO
1100 SJS 95125 853-J3
CAMINO POR LOS ARBOLES
- ATN 94027 790-D5
CAMINO RAMON
1000 SJS 95125 853-J4
CAMINO RICARDO
1000 SJS 95125 853-J3
CAMINO RICO
13600 SAR 95070 872-E1
CAMINO ROBLES CT
1400 SJS 95120 874-B7
1400 SJS 95120 894-B1
CAMINO ROBLES WY
1300 SJS 95120 874-B7
1300 SJS 95120 894-B1
CAMINO VERDE DR
6000 SJS 95119 875-C7
CAMINO VISTA DR
10100 CPTO 95014 851-J1
CAMINO VISTA WY
15900 SCIC 95127 815-B6
CAMLOOP DR
2600 SJS 95130 852-J7
CAMP AV
700 MTVW 94043 811-H2
CAMPANA DR
4000 PA 94306 811-C2
CAMPANULA PL
4800 LGTS 95124 873-E4
CAMPBELL AV
- SJS 95193 875-C4
500 LALT 94024 811-F7
500 LALT 94024 831-F1
900 SCL 95050 833-G4
1100 SJS 95126 833-G4
1200 SCL 95126 833-G4
4700 SJS 95130 852-J5
4700 SJS 95130 853-A6
5000 SJS 95129 852-J5
E CAMPBELL AV
- CMBL 95008 853-E6
1600 SCIC 95125 853-G6
W CAMPBELL AV
- CMBL 95008 853-B6
700 SJS 95008 853-B6
1700 SJS 95130 853-B6
CAMPBELL DR
- MTVW 94043 812-B5
CAMPBELL LN
- MLPK 94025 810-E1
- MLPK 94025 790-E7
CAMPBELL ST
900 MPS 95035 794-B5
CAMPBELL TECHNOLOGY PKWY
- CMBL 95008 853-E7
CAMPERDOWN WY
1900 SJS 95121 855-C3
CAMPESINO AV
200 PA 94306 791-C7
200 PA 94306 811-C1
CAMPHOR AV
100 FRMT 94539 793-H1
CAMPHOR CT
1800 MPS 95035 813-J4
CAMPHOR WY
700 EPA 94303 791-B2
CAMPISI CT
4500 SCIC 95020 976-J1
6800 SJS 95120 894-F2
CAMPISI WY
900 CMBL 95008 853-F5
CAMPO RD
100 PTLV 94028 810-C7
CAMPO BELLO
- MLPK 94025 790-E7
CAMPO BELLO CT
- MLPK 94025 790-E7
CAMPOBELLO CT
700 MGH 95037 937-B5
CAMPO CALLE WY
14400 SAR 95070 872-G3
CAMPOLI DR
100 MGH 95037 916-H5
CAMPOS VERDES
100 LGTS 95032 873-G6
CAMPO VISTA LN
13900 LAH 94022 811-C7
CAMPUS DR
100 SCIC 94305 790-G6
800 SCIC 94305 810-H1
CAMPUS DR E
300 SCIC 94305 810-G1
700 SCIC 94305 790-H7
CAMPUS DR W
300 SCIC 94305 790-F7
900 SCIC 94305 810-F1
CAMROSE AV
2200 SJS 95130 852-J7
12700 SJS 95070 852-J7
CAMROSE CT
- GIL 95020 977-G1
CANADA DR
700 MPS 95035 794-B6
CANADA RD
3000 SCIC 95020 978-J2
CANAL AL
600 HOLL 95023 1039-J3
CANAL WY
1800 SJS 95132 814-C4
CANARIO WY
12700 LAH 94022 811-A6
CANARY DR
1600 SUNV 94087 832-E5
CANARY LN
1200 SJS 95117 853-D4
CANARY ISLAND CT
2000 SCL 95050 833-C3
CANARY PALM CT
- SJS 95133 814-J4
CANBERRA CT
4700 SJS 95124 873-J3
CANBERRA DR
1600 SJS 95124 873-J3
CANDACE WY
1600 LALT 94024 832-A4
CANDIA DR
1100 SJS 95121 854-H2
CANDLELIGHT WY
1100 CPTO 95014 852-D3
CANDLER AV
14000 SJS 95127 835-B4
CANDLESTICK WY
500 SJS 95127 835-B2
CANDLEWOOD AV
1000 SUNV 94089 812-J5
CANDLEWOOD CT
1100 SUNV 94089 812-J4
6300 CPTO 95014 852-F2
CANDLEWOOD DR
800 CPTO 95014 852-G2
CANDY CT
12200 SAR 95070 852-F5
CANDY LN
12100 SAR 95070 852-F5
CANDY LYNN CT
6100 SJS 95120 874-D7
CANELA WY
- SJS 95136 874-G2
CANFIELD CT
800 SJS 95136 874-D2
CANMORE CT
200 SJS 95136 874-J3
CANNA CT
1500 MTVW 94043 811-H4
CANNA LN
1600 SJS 95124 873-J6
CANNERY CIR
- CMBL 95008 853-E6
CANNERY RW
- HOLL 95023 1039-H5
CANNERY WY
- GIL 95020 978-A2
CANNES PL
- SJS 95138 875-H1
CANNETO DR
- SJS 95129 852-J5
CANNIKIN CT
200 SJS 95116 834-G4
CANNIKIN DR
200 SJS 95116 834-G4
CANNON RD
200 SBnC 95045 1037-F2
200 SBnC 95004 1037-F2
CANOAS CREEK CIR
- SJS 95136 854-D6
CANOAS CREEK CT
- SJS 95136 854-D7
CANOAS GARDEN AV
2100 SJS 95125 854-D5
2300 SCIC 95125 854-D5
CANOAS VILLA CT
- SJS 95136 854-D6
CANON DR
15500 SCIC 95030 872-F5
CANONGATE CT
3300 SJS 95121 855-C5
CANON VISTA
11000 SCIC 95127 815-A5
11000 SJS 95127 815-A5
CANOPY CT
- GIL 95020 977-H5
CANTADA CT
3200 SJS 95135 855-G3
CANTAMAR CT
- SJS 95135 855-H3
CANTARA CT
- SJS 95127 835-B3
CANTATA WY
25200 LAH 94022 831-D2
CANTERBURY CT
6300 SJS 95129 852-F4
CANTERBURY PL
- GIL 95020 957-J7
600 MPS 95035 794-B3
CANTERBURY WY
1500 LALT 94024 831-J3
CANTO CT
- HOLL 95023 1040-B5
CANTO DR
4900 SJS 95124 873-J4
4900 SJS 95118 873-J4
CANTON DR
500 SJS 95123 874-H4
1200 MPS 95035 794-C7
CANTOR CT
16500 MGH 95037 917-G6
CANTOR DR
2700 MGH 95037 917-F6
CANYON CT
- GIL 95020 957-F7
CANYON DR
- SBnC 95023 1000-G7
100 PTLV 94028 810-C7
200 PTLV 94028 830-C1
11000 SCIC 95127 815-A6
CANYON RD
27500 PA 94304 830-H2
27500 SCIC 95014 830-H2
CANYON CLIFF CT
- SJS 95138 855-F6
CANYON CREEK DR
3400 SJS 95132 814-G2
CANYON HILLS LN
- SJS 95138 855-E6
CANYON OAK WY
- CPTO 95014 831-H6
CANYON RIDGE DR
3800 SJS 95148 835-G7
CANYON RIVER CT
4700 SJS 95136 874-E2
CANYON TRAIL WY
4800 SJS 95136 874-H2
CANYON VIEW CT
3400 SJS 95132 814-G3
CANYON VIEW DR
1500 SJS 95132 814-G2
11300 CPTO 95014 852-A3
20500 SAR 95070 872-C2
CANYON VISTA CT
11000 CPTO 95014 852-A2
CAPAY CT
4600 SJS 95118 874-B3
CAPAY DR
4600 SJS 95118 874-B3
CAPE ANITA PL
900 SJS 95133 814-E7
CAPE ANN PL
1900 SJS 95133 834-E1
CAPE ASTON CT
1700 SJS 95133 834-D1
CAPE BLANCO CT
500 SUNV 94087 832-D4
CAPE BRETON PL
800 SJS 95133 834-E1
CAPE BUFFALO DR
900 SJS 95133 834-D1
CAPE CANAVERAL PL
900 SJS 95133 834-D1
CAPE COD CT
3600 SJS 95117 853-C3
CAPE COLONY DR
800 SJS 95133 834-E1
CAPE CORAL DR
1700 SJS 95133 834-E1
CAPE DIAMOND DR
800 SJS 95133 834-E1
CAPE FLATTERY PL
800 SJS 95133 834-E1
CAPE GEORGE PL
900 SJS 95133 834-E1
CAPE HATTERAS WY
1700 SJS 95133 834-E1
CAPE HILDA PL
1900 SJS 95133 834-E1
CAPE HORN CT
1700 SJS 95133 834-E1
CAPE HORN DR
1800 SJS 95133 834-E1
CAPE HORN PL
1700 SJS 95133 834-E1
CAPE JASMINE PL
1700 SJS 95133 834-E1
CAPE JESSUP DR
900 SJS 95133 834-E1
900 SJS 95133 814-E7
CAPE KENNEDY DR
800 SJS 95133 834-E1
CAPELAW CT
3100 SJS 95135 855-F3
CAPELLA WY
- MPS 95035 813-J2
200 SUNV 94086 812-E7
CAPE MARY PL
900 SJS 95133 814-E7
CAPE MAY PL
800 SJS 95133 834-E1
CAPE MISTY DR
1700 SJS 95133 834-D1
CAPE MORRIS PL
900 SJS 95133 834-E1
CAPE POINT PL
900 SJS 95133 834-E1
CAPE TOWN PL
800 SJS 95133 834-E1
CAPE TRINITY PL
800 SJS 95133 834-E1
CAPE VERDE PL
800 SJS 95133 834-E1
CAPE VINCENT PL
800 SJS 95133 834-E1
CAPEWOOD CT
2900 SJS 95132 814-D3
CAPEWOOD LN
2800 SJS 95132 814-D3
CAPE YORK PL
800 SJS 95133 834-E1
CAPILANO DR
5700 SJS 95138 855-H7
CAPISTRANO AV
4800 SJS 95129 852-J1
4800 SJS 95129 853-A1
CAPISTRANO DR
2200 SCL 95051 832-J2
CAPISTRANO PL
100 LGTS 95032 873-A3
CAPISTRANO WY
- MGH 95037 917-B3
23000 LALT 94024 831-H4
CAPITANCILLOS DR
1500 SJS 95120 874-A7
CAPITANCILLOS PL
1600 SJS 95120 874-A7
CAPITOL AV
- SJS 95116 834-J4
- SJS 95127 834-J4
- SCIC 95127 834-G2
300 SJS 95133 834-G2
600 SJS 95133 814-G7
1300 SJS 95127 835-A5
1700 SJS 95148 835-A5
1900 EPA 94303 791-B2
E CAPITOL AV
500 MPS 95035 814-B3
2100 SJS 95132 814-B3
N CAPITOL AV
700 SJS 95133 814-F7
900 SJS 95132 814-C4
1700 SJS 95131 814-C4
W CAPITOL AV
100 MPS 95035 814-A2
200 MPS 95035 813-J2
CAPITOL CT
1200 SJS 95127 834-J5
CAPITOL EXWY
100 SJS 95136 854-D7
400 SJS 95136 874-F1
700 SJS 95127 834-J4
700 SJS 95116 834-J4
900 SJS 95111 854-G7
1000 SJS 95122 834-J4
1000 SCIC 95111 854-G7
1300 SJS 95127 835-A6
1300 SJS 95122 835-A6
1700 SJS 95121 854-G7
1800 SJS 95148 835-A6
1800 SJS 95121 855-B3
2300 SJS 95122 855-B3
2300 SJS 95148 855-B3
CAPITOLA AV
4500 SJS 95111 875-A1
CAPITOLA DR
800 HOLL 95023 1040-B5
CAPITOLA TER
- FRMT 94539 794-A1
CAPITOLA WY
900 SCL 95051 832-J5
CAPITOL PARK CT
- SJS 95132 814-C4
CAPITOL REEF CT
4500 SJS 95136 874-G2
CAPITOL VILLAGE CIR
200 SJS 95136 874-G1
CAPPANELLE TER
- SJS 95129 852-J5

SANTA CLARA COUNTY STREET INDEX
CENTERHART CT

© 2008 Rand McNally & Company

SANTA CLARA CO.

STREET
Block City ZIP Pg-Grid

CAPPELLETTI CT
- MTVW 94043 811-G3
CAPPER CT
- SMCo 94061 790-B4
CAPPY CT
- SJS 95111 875-A2
CAPRI DR
900 CMBL 95008 873-C2
14100 LGTS 95032 873-C2
CAPRI WY
6500 SJS 95129 852-F3
CAPRIANA CIR
3200 SJS 95135 855-G3
CAPRIC DR
400 SJS 95123 875-B3
CAPRICE CT
500 MGH 95037 917-B7
CAPRICORN CT
400 SJS 95111 854-F6
CAPRISTA CT
19600 SCIC 95037 916-F4
CAPURSO WY
1400 SJS 95125 854-B3
CAPUTO CT
1000 HOLL 95023 1040-C6
CAPUTO DR
16600 MGH 95037 937-C1
CARACAS CT
2100 SJS 95122 834-J7
CARADO CT
25700 LAH 94022 811-C5
CARASCO WY
- SJS 95135 855-G3
CARASTON WY
2700 SJS 95148 835-C7
2700 SJS 95148 855-C1
CARAVAN WY
- SJS 95123 875-B3
CARAVELLA DR
3700 SJS 95117 853-B4
CARAWAY CT
4500 SJS 95129 853-B2
CARBONERA AV
100 SUNV 94086 812-B7
CARDEL WY
1700 SJS 95124 873-H5
CARDIFF CT
1100 SJS 95117 853-D3
CARDIFF LN
1000 RDWC 94061 790-B2
CARDIFF PL
600 MPS 95035 794-B3
CARDIGAN DR
700 SUNV 94087 832-F4
CARDIN AV
3300 SJS 95118 874-A1
E CARDINAL DR
900 SUNV 94087 832-A2
W CARDINAL DR
800 SUNV 94087 832-B2
CARDINAL LN
100 LGTS 95032 873-C7
2700 SJS 95125 854-B7
CARDINAL WY
1000 PA 94303 791-D5
CARDINGTON DR
2000 SJS 95132 814-D3
CARDONA WY
1200 SJS 95131 814-E7
CARDOZA CT
3400 SJS 95132 814-G3
CARERA CT
- SJS 95123 874-F6
CAREY AV
2900 MGH 95037 917-G6
2900 SCIC 95037 917-G6
15400 SCIC 95037 937-H1
CAREY WY
- SBnC 95023 1040-E3
E CARIBBEAN DR
200 SUNV 94089 812-G2
CARIBE WY
300 SJS 95133 834-G2
CARIBOU CT
700 SUNV 94087 832-C4
CARICK PLACE WY
3500 SJS 95121 855-B4
CARIGNAN WY
- SJS 95135 855-G6
CARIGNANE DR
700 GIL 95020 977-J7
700 GIL 95020 978-A7
CARILLO LN
13400 LAH 94022 811-A5
CARINO TR
- MPS 95035 813-J1
CARIS CT
11400 SCIC 95046 957-G3
CARL AV
1600 MPS 95035 794-D6
CARL RD
- SUNV 94089 812-F1
CARL ST
300 SCL 95050 833-F3
CARLA CT
500 MTVW 94040 811-H7
1100 SJS 95120 874-D7
CARLA DR
1100 SJS 95120 874-D7
CARLA WY
700 GIL 95020 977-H1
CARLESTER DR
200 LGTS 95032 873-D4
CARLETON CT
1600 RDWC 94061 790-A2
CARLETON PL
3000 SCL 95051 833-A6
CARLING CT
100 SJS 95111 875-A2
CARLISLE WY
100 SUNV 94087 832-E4
CARLITOS CT
3700 PA 94306 811-B2
E CARLO ST
- MPS 95035 793-J7
- MPS 95035 794-A7
CARLOS AV
100 RDWC 94061 790-B1
CARLO SCIMECA CT
2600 SJS 95132 814-F5
CARLO SCIMECA DR
2600 SJS 95132 814-F5
CARLOS PRIVADA
1100 MTVW 94040 832-H6
CARLOTTA CT
700 SJS 95136 874-E1
CARLOW CT
100 SUNV 94087 832-E4
CARLS CT
11400 SJS 95123 875-B3
CARLSBAD CT
600 MPS 95035 794-E7
CARLSBAD DR
1100 SJS 95118 874-C4
CARLSBAD RD
48500 FRMT 94539 793-J2
CARLSBAD ST
500 MPS 95035 794-E7
CARLSEN WY
1300 SJS 95118 874-B1
CARLSON CIR
3700 PA 94306 811-E1
CARLSON CT
3800 PA 94306 811-E1
CARLSON DR
16300 SCIC 95037 936-G3
CARLTON AV
100 LGTS 95032 873-D5
1100 MLPK 94025 790-J1
2000 SJS 95124 873-E4
2000 SCIC 95124 873-E4
15900 LGTS 95124 873-E4
CARLTON CT
200 LGTS 95032 873-D4
CARLTON WY
200 LGTS 95032 873-D4
CARLYLE CT
- SCL 95054 813-D4
200 GIL 95020 977-H1
CARLYN AV
- CMBL 95008 853-D5
CARLYN CT
500 SUNV 94086 832-E1
CARLYSLE AV
3600 SCL 95051 832-H6
CARLYSLE ST
100 SJS 95113 834-B6
200 SJS 95110 834-B6
CARM AV
5000 SJS 95124 873-H5
CARMEL AV
- SUNV 94086 812-G5
800 LALT 94022 811-D4
CARMEL CT
900 LALT 94022 811-D4
CARMEL DR
1400 SJS 95125 854-B3
2300 PA 94303 791-D4
CARMEL ST
7200 GIL 95020 977-H1
CARMEL TER
1200 LALT 94024 831-H2
CARMEL WY
100 SMCo 94028 830-E3
1100 SCL 95050 833-D4
CARMELA CT
1300 HOLL 95023 1039-J5
CARMELITA DR
100 MTVW 94040 811-J7
CARMELLA COMS
- SJS 95148 855-J2
CARMELLA CT
- SJS 95148 855-J1
CARMELLA PL
- SJS 95148 855-J2
CARMELO CT
- MGH 95037 917-B3
CARMEN CT
1200 HOLL 95023 1039-H5
1400 SJS 95121 854-J2
CARMEN RD
10000 CPTO 95014 832-A7
10000 CPTO 95014 852-A1
CARMINE WY
1400 SJS 95131 814-C6
CARMONA CT
10000 CPTO 95014 852-B1
CARNABY CT
4500 SJS 95136 874-E2
CARNADERO RD
800 GIL 95020 998-C1
800 SCIC 95020 978-C7
800 SCIC 95020 998-C1
800 GIL 95020 978-C7
CARNATION CT
800 LALT 94024 831-E1
CARNATION LN
900 GIL 95020 977-G1
CARNAVON WY
1400 SJS 95131 814-C7
CARNEGIE DR
- MPS 95035 794-C7
CARNEGIE SQ
- SJS 95116 834-D5
CARNELIAN CIR
14500 SAR 95070 872-E2
CARNELIAN DR
1100 SJS 95122 834-G7
CARNELIAN GLEN CT
14500 SAR 95070 872-E3
CARNEROS AV
400 SUNV 94086 812-B7
CARNEROS RD
100 MonC 95004 1037-A1
CARNFORTH CT
1100 SJS 95120 894-G4
CARNIEL AV
12700 SAR 95070 852-D6
CARNIEL CT
12800 SAR 95070 852-D6
CARNIVAL WY
- SJS 95112 834-B3
7200 SJS 95120 894-H4
CARNOBLE DR
200 HOLL 95023 1039-G3
CARNOT DR
1500 SJS 95126 853-H4
CARNOUSTE CT
- GIL 95020 977-F3
CARNOUSTIE CT
22300 CPTO 95014 852-A2
CAROB CT
- GIL 95020 957-E7
CAROB LN
1500 LALT 94024 831-H3
CAROBWOOD CT
3400 SJS 95132 814-E2
CAROBWOOD LN
2100 SJS 95132 814-E2
CAROL AV
2200 MTVW 94040 831-J1
CAROL DR
2400 SCIC 95125 854-E5
2400 SJS 95125 854-E5
2400 SCIC 95136 854-E5
CAROL LN
12000 SAR 95070 852-E5
CAROLA AV
900 SJS 95130 853-B4
CAROLA CT
4100 SJS 95130 853-B4
CAROL ANNS CT
- SBnC 95023 1060-D2
CAROLE CT
700 EPA 94303 791-B1
CAROLE WY
1500 RDWC 94061 790-A1
CAROLINA AV
600 SUNV 94086 812-F5
2400 RDWC 94061 790-A3
CAROLINA LN
- ATN 94027 790-C2
200 PA 94306 811-D2
CAROLINE DR
22000 CPTO 95014 832-A6
CAROLINE LN
- GIL 95020 978-A2
CAROLINE WY
4800 SJS 95124 873-H4
CAROL LEAF CT
3200 SJS 95148 855-E1
CAROL LEE DR
10100 CPTO 95014 832-E7
CAROLYN AV
1000 SJS 95125 853-J3
1000 SJS 95125 854-A3
CAROLYN CT
10600 SCIC 95020 957-J3
CAROLYN DR
1100 SCL 95050 833-C4
CARON CT
2700 SJS 95121 854-H3
CAROUSEL DR
- HOLL 95023 1040-B6
- SBnC 95023 1040-B6
- SJS 95111 854-G4
CARPENTER DR
- SBnC 95023 1020-G3
CARPENTER PL
2000 SCL 95051 833-D1
CARPENTERIA RD
500 MonC 95004 1037-A1
CARPENTIER WY
400 SJS 95111 854-F6
CARR PL
7200 GIL 95020 977-H4
CARRABELLE WY
900 SJS 95120 894-H2
CARRACCI LN
- SJS 95135 855-G2
CARRAGATA DR
- SJS 95134 813-D3
CARRERA CT
- SJS 95148 855-G1
CARRIAGE CIR
7700 CPTO 95014 852-C2
CARRIAGE CT
- MLPK 94025 790-C7
- LALT 94022 811-E5
CARRIAGE DR
300 SCL 95050 833-D6
1700 GIL 95020 977-E1
18200 MGH 95037 916-H6
CARRIAGE COVE CT
3300 SJS 95111 854-J5
CARRIAGE HILL DR
18700 SCIC 95120 894-G1
CARRIAGE LAMP WY
17300 MGH 95037 917-B6
CARRICK AV
13100 SAR 95070 852-H7
CARRICK CT
500 SUNV 94087 832-E4
CARRIE ST
100 SJS 95112 834-C7
CARRIE LEE WY
1100 SJS 95118 874-B1
CARRIL CT
15500 MSER 95030 873-A5
CARRINGTON CIR
- SJS 95125 854-A7
- SJS 95125 874-B1
27200 LAH 94022 830-J1
CARRINGTON CT
- SJS 95125 854-A7
- SJS 95125 874-B1
CARROLL ST
100 SUNV 94086 812-E7
100 SUNV 94086 832-E1
CARROLL OAKS WY
7700 SCIC 95120 895-D5
CARRYBACK AV
5200 SJS 95111 875-C2
CARRYDUFF WY
3700 SJS 95121 855-C4
CARRYWOOD WY
700 SJS 95120 894-J3
CARSON CT
100 SUNV 94086 812-C7
CARSON DR
800 SUNV 94086 812-C6
CARSON WY
1000 MPS 95035 794-B4
2700 SJS 95124 873-G1
CARTA BLANCA ST
22300 CPTO 95014 832-A7
CARTAGO CT
200 SJS 95116 834-D2
CARTER AV
4900 SJS 95118 873-J4
5100 SJS 95118 874-A5
CARTER WY
- MLPK 94025 790-C7
300 SCL 95051 832-J7
CARTERWOOD PL
1300 SJS 95121 854-J2
CARTWRIGHT WY
20200 CPTO 95014 832-E7
CARVER DR
10500 CPTO 95014 852-H2
CARVER PL
1100 MTVW 94040 811-F5
CARVER ST
11900 SCIC 95127 814-H7
11900 SJS 95127 814-H7
CARVO CT
1300 LALT 94024 831-H3
CARYL CT
- SBnC 95023 1060-C2
CAS DR
3500 SJS 95111 854-H6
CASA CT
1300 SCL 95051 832-H4
CASA LN
17700 MGH 95037 917-B5
17700 SCIC 95037 917-B5
CASABA CREEK CT
1100 SJS 95120 894-G3
CASABELLA AV
- SJS 95148 855-F1
CASABELLA CT
- SJS 95148 855-F1
CASA BLANCA AV
400 SJS 95129 852-J1
CASABLANCA CIR
1400 GIL 95020 977-F3
CASA BLANCA LN
18600 SAR 95070 872-H1
CASA BONITA CT
700 LALT 94024 831-F1
CASA DE PINO WY
- SCIC 95014 851-E4
CASA DE PONSELLE
1500 SJS 95118 874-A3
CASA GRANDE
100 LGTS 95032 872-J2
CASA GRANDE AV
- MTVW 94043 812-A2
CASA GRANDE CT
2700 MGH 95037 917-F6
4100 SJS 95118 874-C2
CASA GRANDE WY
3900 SJS 95118 874-B2
CASALEGNO CT
- SJS 95148 855-F2
CASALINO CT
3400 SJS 95148 835-D6
CASA LOMA CT
400 SJS 95129 852-B7
CASA LOMA RD
300 SCIC 95037 915-G4
300 SCIC 95037 935-B2
300 SJS 95141 915-E5
CASALS CT
2800 SJS 95148 855-C6
CASA MADEIRA LN
4300 SCIC 95127 835-F4
CASA MIA DR
2000 SJS 95124 873-F2
CASA MIA WY
12400 LAH 94024 831-E2
CASA NUEVA CT
- SJS 95124 873-G1
CASANUEVA PL
900 SCIC 94305 810-J2
CASA VERDE AV
4900 SJS 95129 852-B7
CASA VIEW DR
- SJS 95129 852-J1
CASCADE CT
1000 MLPK 94025 790-D6
CASCADE DR
500 SUNV 94087 832-C4
700 SJS 95129 853-A2
1000 MLPK 94025 790-C6
CASCADE ST
2200 MPS 95035 814-E1
CASCADE TER
1300 SUNV 94087 832-D4
CASCADES CT
300 MGH 95037 937-A2
CASCADITA TER
400 MPS 95035 793-G3
CASCIANO CIR
- GIL 95020 977-G1
CASCO CT
2600 SJS 95121 854-H3
CASEY AV
2500 MTVW 94043 791-F6
CASEY ST
- GIL 95020 977-J1
CASEY WY
2600 SJS 95121 855-D3
CASHDAN CT
3300 SCL 95051 833-A1
CASHEW BLOSSOM DR
- SJS 95123 875-A3
CASHMERE CT
500 SUNV 94087 832-D4
CASHMERE TER
1300 SUNV 94087 832-D4
CASINO REAL
15700 MGH 95037 937-A4
CASITA CT
400 LALT 94022 811-F5
400 SJS 95129 852-B7
CASITA WY
- GIL 95020 977-J7
400 LALT 94022 811-F5
CASITAS BULEVAR
100 LGTS 95032 872-J2
CASPAR LN
- SJS 95124 873-G7
CASPER ST
- MPS 95035 793-J7
CASPIAN CT
100 SUNV 94089 812-F2
CASPIAN DR
200 SUNV 94089 812-G2
CASPIAN SEA DR
1200 SJS 95126 853-G3
CASS PL
10100 CPTO 95014 852-A1
CASS WY
3700 PA 94306 811-C2
CASSADAY CT
600 SJS 95136 874-E1
CASSANDRA WY
- MTVW 94043 812-A4
CASSATT WY
500 SJS 95125 854-C4
CASSELINO DR
- SJS 95136 854-F6
CASSIA WY
1000 SUNV 94086 832-G2
CASSIAR DR
1600 SJS 95130 853-B5
CASSIS CT
- SJS 95148 855-G2
CASSLAND CT
1300 SJS 95131 814-D7
CASSWELL CT
100 SJS 95138 875-D4
CASSWOOD CT
700 SJS 95120 894-J3
CASTANO DR
5800 SJS 95129 852-G3
CASTANO CORTE
500 LALT 94022 811-E5
N CASTANYA WY
100 SMCo 94028 810-E3
S CASTANYA WY
200 SMCo 94028 810-E4
CASTELLO DR
6000 SJS 95120 874-C7
CASTELLO WY
2500 SCL 95051 832-J1
CASTEN CT
100 HOLL 95023 1040-B3
CASTERWOOD CT
700 SJS 95120 894-H2
CASTILE CT
2300 SJS 95125 853-J7
CASTILLEJA AV
1500 PA 94306 791-A6
CASTILLEJA CT
900 LALT 94024 831-H2
CASTILLON WY
100 SJS 95119 875-C6
CASTINE AV
10300 CPTO 95014 832-C7
CASTLE DR
2800 SJS 95125 854-C7
CASTLE LN
600 LALT 94024 811-G6
600 LALT 94022 811-G6
CASTLE WY
1100 MLPK 94025 790-F4
CASTLEBRIDGE DR
- SJS 95116 834-F3
CASTLEBROOK CT
1700 SJS 95133 834-E3
CASTLEBURY DR
2000 SJS 95116 834-G3
CASTLE CANYON WY
3100 SJS 95135 876-A2
CASTLECREST DR
- SJS 95116 834-G3
CASTLEGATE DR
1700 SJS 95132 814-E3
CASTLE GLEN AV
5400 SJS 95129 852-H3
CASTLE HILL DR
18300 MGH 95037 916-F6
CASTLE HILL WY
20500 SCIC 95033 912-J1
CASTLEKNOLL DR
6100 SJS 95129 852-C7
CASTLE LAKE CIR
1100 MGH 95037 916-G6
CASTLE LAKE DR
18600 MGH 95037 916-G6
CASTLEMAINE CT
- SJS 95136 854-E5
CASTLE MANOR DR
5400 SJS 95129 852-H4
CASTLEMONT AV
1200 SJS 95128 853-E4
CASTLE RIDGE DR
18300 MGH 95037 916-F6
CASTLEROCK CT
500 SUNV 94087 832-D4
CASTLEROCK DR
6800 SJS 95120 894-E3
CASTLEROCK TER
500 SUNV 94087 832-D4
CASTLETON CT
2500 SJS 95148 855-C1
CASTLETON DR
2500 SJS 95148 855-C1
CASTLETON ST
21500 CPTO 95014 852-B3
CASTLETON TER
1300 SUNV 94087 832-H4
CASTLETON WY
1000 SUNV 94087 832-H4
CASTLETREE CT
1700 SJS 95131 814-C5
CASTLEWOOD CT
4900 SJS 95129 852-J3
CASTLEWOOD DR
300 LGTS 95032 873-B2
4600 SJS 95129 852-J3
4600 SJS 95129 853-A3
CASTRO CT
300 CMBL 95008 853-A5
CASTRO DR
1600 CMBL 95008 853-A6
1600 SJS 95130 853-A6
CASTRO PL
2300 SCL 95050 833-C3
CASTRO ST
100 MTVW 94041 811-H5
900 MTVW 94040 811-H5
CASTRO VALLEY RD
1000 SCIC 95020 998-A2
1200 SCIC 95020 997-G2
CASUAL CT
6800 SJS 95120 894-F2
CASUAL WY
1100 SJS 95120 894-F2
CATALA CT
600 SCL 95050 833-D5
CATALANO CT
- CPTO 95014 852-C3
CATALDI DR
2900 SJS 95132 814-E4
CATALINA AV
3100 SCL 95051 833-A5
CATALINA CT
- LALT 94022 811-E5
8100 GIL 95020 977-F2
11200 CPTO 95014 852-B3
CATALINA DR
4500 SJS 95129 853-A3
CATALINA WY
700 LALT 94022 811-E5
CATALONIA WY
1600 SJS 95125 853-J7
CATALPA DR
- ATN 94027 790-F1
CATALPA LN
- CMBL 95008 853-D6
CATAMARAN ST
6500 SJS 95119 875-D7
CATERPILLAR CT
- SJS 95135 855-D3
CATHARINE CT
26200 LAH 94022 811-B6
CATHAY DR
1100 SJS 95122 834-H5
CATHCART WY
1000 SCIC 94305 810-J2
1000 SCIC 94305 811-A2
CATHEDRAL DR
700 SUNV 94087 832-C4
CATHERINE CT
- PTLV 94028 810-A5
600 GIL 95020 977-J5
CATHERINE ST
900 SJS 95002 793-B7
1600 SCL 95050 833-D4
CATHY PL
- MLPK 94025 790-F5
CATKIN CT
600 SJS 95128 853-F2
CATRINA CT
1900 SJS 95124 873-G5
CATRON DR
23200 SCIC 95033 913-C6
CAUDILLO TER
400 MPS 95035 793-H3
CAUSEY LN
200 LGTS 95030 873-C7
200 LGTS 95030 893-C1
CAVALIER CT
400 LALT 94022 811-D4
1800 SJS 95124 853-G7
CAVENDISH DR
3300 SJS 95132 814-F3
CAXTON CT
3900 SJS 95130 853-B4
CAYENNE DR
- MGH 95037 916-G4
CAYMAN PL
3100 SJS 95127 814-G6
CAYMAN WY
900 SJS 95127 814-G6
CAYMUS CT
100 SUNV 94086 812-C6
CAYUGA CT
600 SJS 95123 874-H7
CAYUGA DR
600 SJS 95123 874-H7
CEANOTHUS LN
6200 SJS 95119 875-D5
CEBALO LN
- ATN 94027 790-C1
CEBU CT
6400 SJS 95119 875-C7
CECALA DR
6000 SJS 95120 874-C7
CECEIL CT
- SBnC 95023 1039-E5
CECELIA CT
500 LALT 94022 811-F5
CECELIA WY
300 LALT 94022 811-F5
300 MTVW 94040 811-F5
CECIL AV
2200 SCIC 95128 853-F1
2200 SJS 95128 853-F1
3200 SCL 95117 833-D7
3200 SCL 95117 853-C1
CEDAR AV
800 SUNV 94086 812-F7
2000 SMCo 94025 790-D6
CEDAR CT
- MPS 95035 814-A3
- SMCo 94025 790-D6
1300 GIL 95020 977-G3
CEDAR DR
1000 HOLL 95023 1040-C6
CEDAR LN
- PA 94306 811-D2
- SCIC 95127 834-H2
6200 SJS 95138 875-F6
CEDAR PL
1400 LALT 94024 831-J6
CEDAR ST
1100 PA 94301 791-B4
CEDAR WY
- MPS 95035 814-A3
400 SCL 95051 833-B7
CEDAR BROOK
100 MTVW 94041 811-J6
CEDAR BROOK TER
20500 CPTO 95014 832-D6
CEDARCREEK CT
1600 SJS 95121 855-D7
CEDARCREEK DR
1600 SJS 95121 855-D7
CEDARCREST LN
3100 SJS 95132 814-E3
CEDARCREST PL
100 LGTS 95032 873-B3
CEDARDALE CT
2800 SJS 95148 835-E7
CEDARDALE DR
3400 SJS 95148 835-E6
CEDAR FLAT CT
3500 SJS 95127 835-C3
CEDAR GABLES DR
1000 SJS 95118 874-C2
CEDAR GARDENS CT
- SJS 95123 874-H4
CEDARGATE LN
200 SJS 95136 874-J3
CEDAR GROVE CIR
5300 SJS 95123 874-J3
5300 SJS 95123 875-A3
CEDARHURST LN
- SJS 95136 874-D2
CEDAR KNOLL CT
- SJS 95121 855-B4
CEDAR LAKE CT
1700 SJS 95131 814-B6
CEDARMEADOW CT
1300 SJS 95131 814-B6
CEDARMEADOW LN
1700 SJS 95131 814-B6
CEDAR RIDGE CT
3000 SJS 95148 835-G7
3000 SJS 95148 855-G1
CEDARSIDE CT
- SJS 95116 834-F7
CEDAR SPRING CT
11500 CPTO 95014 852-C4
CEDAR TREE CT
10500 CPTO 95014 832-E7
CEDAR TREE LN
20000 CPTO 95014 832-E6
CEDARVILLE LN
700 SJS 95133 834-F1
700 SJS 95133 814-F7
CEDARWOOD DR
- SJS 95131 814-A4
CEDARWOOD LN
2100 SJS 95125 853-J6
CEDARWOOD WY
1100 RDWC 94061 790-B2
CEDRO ST
300 SJS 95111 854-H6
CEDRO WY
700 SCIC 94305 810-J2
CEFALU DR
3600 SJS 95124 873-J2
CELEBRATION CT
600 SJS 95134 813-F2
CELEBRATION DR
- MPS 95035 814-J2
CELEO LN
10600 SCIC 95127 815-B7
CELESTE CIR
20600 CPTO 95014 832-D6
CELESTE CT
- SJS 95133 814-E7
CELESTINE AV
900 SJS 95125 854-C5
CELIA WY
900 PA 94303 791-D5
CELILO DR
1000 SUNV 94087 832-B4
CEMBELLIN DR
1400 HOLL 95023 1040-D6
CENTENNIAL BLVD
4900 SCL 95054 813-C4
CENTENNIAL CT
1300 SJS 95129 852-G4
CENTER AV
10500 SCIC 95020 958-A3
11400 SCIC 95020 957-J1
11900 SCIC 95046 937-G3
11900 SCIC 95046 957-J1
CENTER DR
500 PA 94301 791-B3
CENTER RD
2200 SJS 95134 813-F3
CENTER ST
100 RDWC 94061 790-B1
CENTERHART CT
5200 SJS 95123 874-F7

STREET Block	City	ZIP	Pg-Grid
CENTER RIDGE DR			
1600	SJS	95121	854-J2
1600	SJS	95121	855-A2
CENTERWOOD CT			
2800	SJS	95148	835-D7
CENTERWOOD WY			
3000	SJS	95148	835-D7
CENTRAL AV			
-	SJS	95125	854-E4
-	LGTS	95030	893-A2
-	MGH	95037	916-J7
-	MGH	95037	917-A6
-	RDWC	94061	790-B1
100	MTVW	94043	811-J4
100	MTVW	94043	812-A4
200	SUNV	94086	812-A4
200	SUNV	94086	832-E1
300	MLPK	94025	791-A3
600	HOLL	95023	1039-H3
1400	SBnC	95023	1039-H3
E CENTRAL AV			
-	MGH	95037	917-A6
300	SCIC	95037	917-A6
N CENTRAL AV			
-	CMBL	95008	853-E5
1000	CMBL	95128	853-E3
1200	SJS	95128	853-E3
W CENTRAL AV			
-	LGTS	95030	893-A2
CENTRAL CT			
-	LGTS	95030	893-A1
CENTRAL DR			
-	MLPK	94025	790-J1
26900	LAH	94022	830-H2
CENTRAL EXWY			
Rt#-G6			
-	MTVW	94086	812-A5
-	PA	94306	811-G3
-	SCL	94086	812-H7
500	MTVW	94043	812-A5
500	MTVW	94041	812-A5
700	SCL	95050	833-D1
700	SJS	95054	833-D1
700	MTVW	94041	811-G3
700	MTVW	94043	811-G3
800	SCL	95054	833-D1
1600	MTVW	94040	811-G3
2200	SCL	95051	833-D1
2700	SCL	95051	813-A7
2700	SCL	95054	813-A7
3000	SUNV	95054	813-A7
3200	SUNV	94086	813-A7
3400	SUNV	94086	812-H7
3400	SCL	95051	812-H7
CENTRAL WY			
600	SCIC	95128	853-F2
2200	SJS	95128	853-F2
CENTRALIA CT			
500	SUNV	94087	832-D4
CENTRAL PARK DR			
2100	SJS	95008	853-E7
2100	CMBL	95008	853-E7
CENTRE ST			
-	MTVW	94041	811-J6
-	MTVW	94041	812-A6
CENTRE POINTE DR			
1400	MPS	95035	814-B3
CENTURY CT			
800	CMBL	95008	853-C7
CENTURY DR			
300	CMBL	95008	853-C7
2200	SJS	95008	853-C7
6400	SJS	95129	852-F3
CENTURY CENTER CT			
100	SJS	95110	833-H2
CENTURY CROSS CT			
400	SJS	95111	875-C3
CENTURY HILL CT			
5400	SJS	95111	875-C3
CENTURY MANOR CT			
5500	SJS	95111	875-D3
CENTURY MEADOW CT			
5400	SJS	95111	875-C3
CENTURY OAKS CT			
400	SJS	95111	875-C3
CENTURY OAKS WY			
400	SJS	95111	875-C3
CENTURY PARK WY			
5400	SJS	95111	875-C3
CENTURY PLAZA WY			
5400	SJS	95111	875-C3
CERA DR			
900	SJS	95129	853-A3
CEREUS CT			
48400	FRMT	94539	793-J1
CEREZA CT			
-	SJS	95112	834-B4
CEREZA DR			
700	PA	94306	811-C2
CERRA VISTA DR			
1500	HOLL	95023	1040-D7
CERRITO AV			
100	RDWC	94061	790-A4
100	SMCo	94061	790-A4
CERRITO CT			
3300	SJS	95148	835-D7
CERRITO PL			
-	SMCo	94061	790-A4
CERRITO WY			
1000	PA	94306	811-C3
3200	SJS	95148	835-D7
CERRO CHICO			
200	LGTS	95030	873-C7
CERRO CREST DR			
-	SJS	95138	875-H6
CERRO KAMUK CT			
2100	SJS	95116	834-F3
CERROS MNR			
-	SMCo	94025	790-D5
CERRO TERBI CT			
2100	SJS	95116	834-G3
CERRO VERDE			
1300	SJS	95120	894-B1
CERRO VISTA CT			
2700	MGH	95037	917-F6
15900	LGTS	95032	873-D7
CERRO VISTA DR			
2700	MGH	95037	917-F6
15900	LGTS	95032	873-D7
15900	LGTS	95032	893-E1
CERVANTES RD			
100	PTLV	94028	810-C5
CERVANTES WY			
2200	SJS	95008	853-C7
CERVANTEZ CT			
1000	MPS	95035	794-C4
CESANO CT			
400	PA	94306	811-D3
CESSNA CT			
6300	SJS	95123	874-J7
CESTARIC DR			
500	MPS	95035	794-C5
CEYLON AV			
1900	SJS	95122	834-J7
CEYLON CT			
2100	SJS	95122	834-J7
CEYNOWA LN			
-	SCIC	95121	855-C3
-	SJS	95121	855-C3
CEZANNE DR			
600	SUNV	94086	832-E2
800	SUNV	94087	832-E2
CHABLIS CIR			
3500	SJS	95132	814-H4
CHABLIS CT			
19300	SAR	95070	872-G3
CHABOT TER			
2400	PA	94303	791-D4
CHABOT WY			
1400	SJS	95122	834-J5
CHABOYA CT			
4200	SCIC	95148	835-H7
CHABOYA RD			
4000	SCIC	95148	855-G1
4000	SJS	95148	855-G1
4000	SCIC	95148	835-H7
CHABOYA HILLS CT			
4200	SCIC	95148	835-G7
CHABRANT WY			
900	SJS	95125	854-A3
CHACE DR			
10400	CPTO	95014	832-A7
10500	SCIC	94024	832-A7
CHAD DR			
300	MPS	95035	794-A5
CHADBOURNE LN			
18300	MSER	95030	872-J4
CHADWICK CT			
21100	SAR	95070	852-C7
CHADWICK PL			
11100	CPTO	95014	852-B3
CHADWICK ST			
7200	GIL	95020	977-H4
CHAGALL CT			
-	SJS	95138	875-G5
CHAGALL LN			
-	SJS	95138	875-G5
CHAGALL RD			
-	SJS	95138	875-G5
CHAGALL WY			
-	SJS	95138	875-G5
CHALET AV			
100	SJS	95127	834-H1
CHALET LN			
20300	SAR	95070	872-E1
CHALET PL			
100	CMBL	95008	853-F7
CHALET CLOTILDE DR			
13400	SAR	95070	852-C7
CHALET WOODS CIR			
100	CMBL	95008	853-F6
CHALLENGER AV			
200	SJS	95127	834-H1
CHAMBERER DR			
-	SJS	95135	855-F2
CHAMBERLAIN DR			
3500	SJS	95121	855-C3
CHAMBERLIN CT			
-	CMBL	95008	873-B1
CHAMBERS DR			
1500	SJS	95118	874-A2
CHAMBERTIN DR			
5600	SJS	95118	874-A5
CHAMBERY DR			
-	SJS	95127	834-J1
CHAMBORD CT			
-	SJS	95127	834-C2
CHAMISAL AV			
300	LALT	94022	811-D6
CHAMPAGNE LN			
1100	SJS	95132	814-G5
CHAMPION CT			
100	SJS	95134	813-E3
CHANCELLOR WY			
3300	SJS	95111	854-F6
CHANDLER CT			
5700	SJS	95123	874-J4
CHANDON CT			
1300	SJS	95125	853-G4
CHANNEL DR			
6300	SJS	95123	874-J7
CHANNEL DR E			
-	SJS	95002	813-C1
CHANNEL DR W			
-	SJS	95002	813-B1
CHANNING AV			
100	PA	94301	790-J5
400	PA	94301	791-A4
1200	PA	94303	791-C4
2500	SJS	95131	813-F7
CHANT CT			
2500	SJS	95122	834-J5
CHANTAL WY			
-	RDWC	94061	790-A1
CHANTEL CT			
6800	SJS	95129	852-E4
CHANTILLEY CT			
7100	SJS	95139	895-F1
CHANTILLEY LN			
100	SJS	95139	875-F7
100	SJS	95139	895-F1
CHANTILLEY PL			
200	SJS	95139	875-F7
CHANTRELLE CT			
-	GIL	95020	977-E2
CHAPALA DR			
3400	SJS	95148	835-D6
CHAPARRAL AV			
12700	SJS	95070	852-J6
12700	SJS	95130	852-J6
CHAPARRAL CT			
600	HOLL	95023	1039-H4
CHAPARRAL RD			
13100	SCIC	95037	956-H1
CHAPARRAL WY			
27300	LAH	94022	831-A3
CHAPEL DR			
1100	SCL	95050	833-D4
CHAPEL LN			
-	MLPK	94025	790-J2
CHAPELHAVEN CT			
-	SJS	95111	874-J1
CHAPEL HILL WY			
900	SJS	95122	854-G1
CHAPIN RD			
25600	LAH	94022	811-C7
25600	LAH	94022	831-C1
CHAPMAN CT			
500	SCL	95050	833-F5
CHAPMAN DR			
400	CMBL	95008	873-C1
CHAPMAN ST			
500	SJS	95126	833-G5
CHAPPELL CIR			
-	HOLL	95023	1040-A3
CHAPPELL CT			
200	GIL	95020	957-H7
CHAPPELL RD			
-	SBnC	95023	1040-B3
-	HOLL	95023	1040-A2
CHARA CT			
4900	SJS	95118	873-J5
CHARBONO CT			
8300	SJS	95135	855-H6
CHARCOAL RD			
-	SCIC	95014	851-C6
-	SCIC	95030	851-C6
CHARCOT AV			
100	SJS	95131	813-J6
700	SJS	95131	814-A6
CHARD DR			
4000	SJS	95136	854-D7
4000	SJS	95136	874-C1
CHARDONAY CT			
8000	SJS	95135	855-H6
CHARDONNAY CT			
19500	SAR	95070	852-F7
48800	FRMT	94539	793-J2
CHARDONNAY DR			
400	FRMT	94539	793-J2
400	FRMT	94539	794-A2
CHARDONNAY LN			
10500	SCIC	94024	831-F5
CHARDONNAY WY			
400	HOLL	95023	1040-B3
CHARGER DR			
2000	SJS	95131	814-E7
CHARGIN DR			
300	MGH	95037	936-J1
CHARING CROSS LN			
3400	SJS	95132	814-J2
CHARISE CT			
1200	SJS	95120	894-G5
CHARISMA WY			
1200	SJS	95131	814-B6
CHARLEMAGNE DR			
-	SJS	95135	855-H1
CHARLEMAGNE WY			
-	SJS	95135	855-H1
CHARLENE CT			
6700	SJS	95129	852-E3
CHARLES AV			
100	SUNV	94086	812-D7
300	SUNV	94086	832-D1
28000	LAH	94022	810-J7
28000	LAH	94022	830-J1
CHARLES ST			
-	LGTS	95030	873-B7
-	LGTS	95032	873-B7
400	SUNV	94086	832-D1
500	SJS	95112	834-B2
CHARLES CALI DR			
500	SJS	95117	853-D1
CHARLES MARX WY			
-	PA	94304	790-G5
CHARLESTON CT			
700	PA	94303	811-E1
CHARLESTON DR			
1600	CMBL	95008	853-B5
1600	SJS	95130	853-B5
CHARLESTON RD			
1200	MTVW	94043	811-H1
2000	MTVW	94043	812-A1
E CHARLESTON RD			
100	PA	94306	811-E1
500	PA	94303	811-F1
900	PA	94043	811-F1
900	MTVW	94043	811-G1
W CHARLESTON RD			
200	PA	94306	811-D2
CHARLIE DR			
-	HOLL	95023	1039-G3
CHARLOTTE AV			
15000	SCIC	95124	873-F4
CHARMAIN CIR			
600	MTVW	94041	812-B7
CHARMAIN DR			
600	CMBL	95008	853-C5
CHARMAT CT			
3200	SJS	95135	855-G3
CHARMERAN AV			
1800	SJS	95124	873-F3
14500	SCIC	95124	873-F3
CHARMES CT			
3200	SJS	95135	855-G3
CHARMGLOW CT			
2100	SJS	95121	855-C4
CHARMWOOD CT			
1100	SUNV	94089	812-J4
CHARMWOOD SQ			
1300	SJS	95117	853-C4
CHARNWOOD CT			
1800	SJS	95132	814-E3
CHARSAN LN			
11400	CPTO	95014	852-C4
CHARTER HALL CT			
3600	SJS	95136	874-D1
CHARTER OAK PL			
6600	SJS	95120	894-G1
CHARTER OAKS CIR			
100	LGTS	95032	873-C3
CHARTER OAKS DR			
200	LGTS	95032	873-C3
CHARTER PARK CT			
3600	SJS	95136	854-F7
CHARTER PARK DR			
3700	SJS	95136	854-F7
CHARTERS AV			
19600	SAR	95070	852-F7
CHARTERS CT			
19900	SAR	95070	852-E7
CHASE RD			
-	SCIC	95033	913-B5
19300	SCIC	95033	892-G5
CHASEWOOD DR			
23200	SCIC	95033	913-C6
CHATEAU CT			
6800	SJS	95120	894-E2
20000	SAR	95070	852-E7
CHATEAU DR			
-	MLPK	94025	790-F3
200	LALT	94022	811-E6
200	SBnC	95045	1037-F1
1100	SJS	95120	894-D2
20000	SAR	95070	852-E6
CHATEAU RD			
-	SBnC	95045	1037-F1
CHATEAU BOUSSY RD			
23500	SCIC	95033	913-B5
CHATEAU DU LAC			
-	SJS	95148	855-F1
CHATEAU LA SALLE DR			
100	SJS	95111	854-F5
CHATEAUVIEUX PL			
-	SJS	95135	855-G2
CHATHAM CT			
-	SJS	95139	875-G7
300	MTVW	94040	831-J1
CHATHAM WY			
100	MTVW	94040	831-J1
CHATSWORTH LN			
400	RDWC	94061	790-B2
CHATSWORTH PL			
600	SJS	95128	853-H2
CHAUCER DR			
1700	SJS	95116	834-G5
CHAUCER ST			
300	MLPK	94025	791-A3
300	PA	94301	791-A3
CHAUMONT DR			
1500	SJS	95118	874-A6
CHAUNCEY CT			
600	SJS	95128	853-H2
CHAUNCEY WY			
600	SJS	95128	853-H2
CHAVEZ CT			
1400	SJS	95131	814-C7
CHAVEZ WY			
1300	SJS	95131	814-C7
CHAVOYA DR			
20100	CPTO	95014	832-E7
CHECKERS DR			
-	SJS	95116	834-F3
300	SJS	95133	834-F3
CHEENEY ST			
4000	SCL	95054	813-C4
CHEHALIS DR			
900	SUNV	94087	832-B4
CHELAN DR			
900	SUNV	94087	832-B4
CHELMSFORD DR			
18200	CPTO	95014	852-H2
CHELSEA CRSG			
-	SJS	95138	875-G5
CHELSEA CT			
1300	LALT	94024	831-J3
CHELSEA DR			
1300	LALT	94024	831-J3
15000	SCIC	95124	873-F3
CHELSEA WY			
100	RDWC	94061	790-B2
CHELTENHAM CT			
100	SJS	95139	895-G1
CHELTENHAM PL			
100	SJS	95139	895-G1
CHELTENHAM WY			
-	SJS	95139	875-G7
100	SJS	95139	895-G1
CHEMEKETA CT			
700	SJS	95123	874-G4
CHEMEKETA DR			
600	SJS	95123	874-G4
CHEMIN DE RIVIERE			
3500	SJS	95148	855-F1
CHEMISE DR			
900	SJS	95136	874-D1
CHEMOWA CT			
700	SUNV	94087	832-C4
CHEN ST			
1100	SJS	95131	834-D1
CHENEY CT			
1600	SJS	95128	853-G3
CHENEY DR			
1700	SJS	95128	853-G3
CHENIN BLANC DR			
48800	FRMT	94539	793-J2
48800	FRMT	94539	794-A2
CHENIN BLANC LN			
8400	SJS	95135	855-H7
CHENLAN CT			
2000	SJS	95121	855-C4
CHERI CT			
-	SBnC	95023	1060-G3
CHERIS CT			
5300	SJS	95123	874-J3
CHERIS DR			
100	SJS	95123	874-J3
CHEROKEE CT			
-	PTLV	94028	810-C6
CHEROKEE LN			
-	SCIC	95127	815-A7
CHEROKEE TR			
17600	SCIC	95033	913-A2
CHEROKEE WY			
100	PTLV	94028	810-C6
CHERRY AV			
200	LALT	94022	811-D5
300	MLPK	94025	790-G3
900	SJS	95126	853-J3
1000	SJS	95125	853-J3
1200	SJS	95125	854-A4
3000	SJS	95118	854-A6
3000	SJS	95118	874-B1
10000	SCIC	95020	958-A4
CHERRY CT			
200	MGH	95037	937-B6
900	SJS	95126	853-J3
1300	SJS	95118	874-C2
CHERRY LN			
-	CMBL	95008	853-D6
-	HOLL	95023	1039-H4
900	SCL	95051	832-J5
20100	SAR	95070	852-E6
CHERRY ST			
900	HOLL	95023	1040-C4
CHERRY BLOSSOM DR			
-	SJS	95123	875-A3
CHERRY BLOSSOM LN			
-	CMBL	95008	853-C5
-	LGTS	95032	873-C6
15600	SCIC	95032	873-D6
CHERRY BROOK LN			
5200	SJS	95136	875-D1
CHERRY CREEK CIR			
800	SJS	95126	853-J2
CHERRY CREST LN			
-	SJS	95136	875-D1
CHERRYDALE DR			
1400	SJS	95125	853-J5
CHERRY GARDEN LN			
1400	SJS	95125	854-A7
CHERRY GATE LN			
5200	SJS	95136	875-D1
CHERRY GLEN WY			
1500	SJS	95125	853-J4
CHERRY GROVE DR			
1700	SCIC	95125	853-H5
1700	SJS	95125	853-H5
CHERRY HILL CT			
100	LGTS	95032	873-C3
CHERRYHILLS LN			
1700	SJS	95125	853-J5
CHERRY OAKS PL			
4100	PA	94306	811-C3
CHERRY RIDGE CT			
-	SJS	95136	875-A3
CHERRY RIDGE LN			
-	SJS	95136	875-D1
CHERRYSTONE CT			
100	LGTS	95032	873-D6
CHERRYSTONE DR			
800	LGTS	95032	873-C6
2000	SJS	95128	833-E6
CHERRYTHORNE LN			
4800	SJS	95129	852-B7
CHERRYTON LN			
-	SJS	95136	875-A3
CHERRYTREE LN			
1700	MTVW	94040	811-G7
1700	MTVW	94040	831-G1
10300	CPTO	95014	832-E7
CHERRY VALLEY DR			
1400	SJS	95125	853-J4
CHERRYVIEW LN			
1100	SJS	95118	874-C3
CHERRY WOOD CT			
100	LGTS	95032	873-B2
CHERRYWOOD CT			
-	GIL	95020	957-F7
900	SJS	95129	853-A2
CHERRYWOOD DR			
500	SUNV	94087	832-D2
4600	SJS	95129	853-A2
4700	SJS	95129	852-J2
CHERRYWOOD SQ			
1400	SJS	95117	853-C4
CHERTSEY CT			
1300	SJS	95131	814-E6
CHERYL DR			
20600	CPTO	95014	852-D1
CHERYL PL			
-	MLPK	94025	790-F5
CHERYL WY			
2100	SJS	95125	854-A6
CHERYL ANN CT			
2700	SJS	95124	873-J1
CHERYL BECK CT			
-	SJS	95119	875-C6
CHERYL BECK DR			
100	SJS	95119	875-C6
CHERYL KEN WY			
-	SJS	95119	875-D5
CHESAPEAKE CIR			
2600	SJS	95148	855-C7
CHESAPEAKE PL			
800	GIL	95020	977-H4
CHESAPEAKE TER			
1300	SUNV	94089	812-H3
CHESBRO AV			
5400	SJS	95123	874-G5
CHESBRO WY			
1200	GIL	95020	977-G1
CHESBRO LAKE DR			
17200	SCIC	95037	936-D1
CHESHIRE DR			
3400	SJS	95118	874-C1
CHESHIRE WY			
600	SUNV	94087	832-E4
CHESLEY AV			
300	MTVW	94040	831-J1
500	MTVW	94040	832-A1
CHESLEY CT			
500	MTVW	94040	831-J1
CHESLEY DR			
2100	SJS	95130	853-A7
CHESSINGTON DR			
1200	SJS	95131	834-C1
CHESTER AV			
13900	SAR	95070	872-G2
CHESTER CIR			
-	LALT	94022	811-E4
CHESTER ST			
-	SCIC	95046	937-E6
-	LGTS	95030	873-A6
-	LGTS	95032	873-A6
100	MLPK	94025	791-A2
300	MLPK	94025	790-J2
CHESTERFIELD CT			
5800	SJS	95138	875-H1
CHESTERTON CIR			
1600	SJS	95133	834-D1
CHESTNUT AV			
-	LGTS	95030	872-H7
100	SUNV	94086	812-E6
200	PA	94306	791-C7
200	PA	94306	811-C1
400	MPS	95035	793-H6
CHESTNUT CT			
-	MGH	95037	937-C5
2200	MGH	95037	917-F6
CHESTNUT LN			
-	HOLL	95023	1039-H4
CHESTNUT ST			
700	SJS	95110	833-H4
1000	MLPK	94025	790-F3
1700	SCL	95054	813-D5
6600	GIL	95020	978-A2
S CHESTNUT ST			
6300	GIL	95020	978-B5
CHESTNUT PARK CT			
400	SJS	95136	874-G2
CHESWICK DR			
900	SJS	95121	854-H3
CHET CT			
-	SJS	95148	855-F2
CHETAMON CT			
1700	SUNV	94087	832-B6
CHETWOOD DR			
-	MTVW	94043	812-B5
CHEVALIER DR			
1700	SJS	95124	873-H5
CHEVERY CT			
12600	SAR	95070	852-E6
CHEWPON AV			
1200	MPS	95035	814-C2
CHEYENNE CT			
19000	MGH	95037	917-A2
CHEYENNE DR			
-	GIL	95020	957-F7
500	SUNV	94087	832-D4
CHEYENNE LN			
400	SJS	95123	874-H5
CHEYENNE PT			
-	PTLV	94028	810-C6
CHIALA LN			
6800	SJS	95129	852-E3
CHIANTI CT			
8300	SJS	95135	855-J6
CHIAPAS TER			
-	SJS	95126	833-D1
CHICAGO AV			
-	LGTS	95030	893-A1
CHICKADEE CT			
1400	SUNV	94087	832-E5
CHICKASAW CT			
500	SJS	95123	874-H6
CHICO CT			
1000	SUNV	94086	812-J5
CHICORY CT			
1100	SJS	95120	894-C5
CHIECHI AV			
500	SJS	95126	853-H1
CHIERI CT			
-	SJS	95148	855-F2
CHIERI PL			
-	SJS	95148	855-F2
CHIESA DR			
8100	GIL	95020	977-H2
CHIHONG DR			
1400	SJS	95131	814-B7
CHILANIAN LN			
1200	SJS	95120	894-G4
CHILBERG CT			
400	SJS	95133	834-G2
CHILES CT			
5000	SJS	95136	874-F2
CHILES DR			
4900	SJS	95136	874-F2
CHILLUM CT			
3100	SJS	95148	855-E2
CHILOQUIN CT			
500	SUNV	94087	832-D4
CHILTERN WY			
2900	SJS	95127	835-A4
CHILTON CT			
-	SJS	95111	854-J6
CHIMALUS AV			
500	PA	94306	811-B2
CHIMAY WY			
4200	SJS	95135	855-G4
CHINABERRY CT			
400	SJS	95129	853-B2
CHINOOK CT			
-	MGH	95037	917-A2
CHINOOK LN			
400	SJS	95123	874-H5
CHIPLAY DR			
1300	SJS	95122	834-H6
CHIPMAN DR			
900	MPS	95035	814-E1
CHIPPENDALE CT			
100	LGTS	95032	873-A3
CHIPPENHAM DR			
3000	SJS	95132	814-F4
CHIQUITA AV			
200	MTVW	94041	811-G5
CHIQUITA CT			
12800	SAR	95070	852-C6
CHIQUITA WY			
21000	SAR	95070	852-C7
CHIRCO CT			
16700	LGTS	95032	873-C5
CHIRCO DR			
16600	LGTS	95032	873-C5
CHIRI CT			
1500	SCIC	95046	937-J7
CHISHOLM AV			
10400	CPTO	95014	832-C7
CHISIN ST			
-	SJS	95121	855-D5
CHITAMOOK CT			
1700	SUNV	94087	832-B6
CHIVAS CT			
3100	SJS	95117	853-D4
CHIVAS PL			
3100	SJS	95117	853-D4
CHOCTAW CT			
600	SJS	95123	874-H6
CHOCTAW DR			
600	SJS	95123	874-G6
CHONA CT			
21400	SCIC	95120	895-B4
CHOPIN AV			
2600	SJS	95122	855-A2
CHOPIN DR			
700	SUNV	94087	832-F3
CHRIS DR			
5800	SJS	95123	875-A5
CHRIS LN			
1600	SCIC	95046	937-H5
CHRISANDRA LN			
7400	SCIC	95020	978-H3
CHRISLAND AV			
10200	SCIC	95127	835-A3
CHRISLAND CT			
10200	SCIC	95127	835-A2
CHRISMARA CT			
1200	SJS	95120	874-C7
CHRISTENSEN DR			
10200	CPTO	95014	832-C7
CHRISTEPH DR			
18100	MGH	95037	916-H6
CHRISTIAN DR			
4200	SJS	95135	855-F3
CHRISTIE DR			
13300	SAR	95070	852-G7
CHRISTINA CT			
17400	MGH	95037	917-D5
CHRISTINA DR			
1600	LALT	94024	832-A4
CHRISTINE CT			
5500	GIL	95020	977-J7
CHRISTINE DR			
700	PA	94303	791-E7
CHRISTINE LYNN DR			
100	MGH	95037	916-J6
CHRISTOBAL PRIVADA			
1200	MTVW	94040	832-A1
CHRISTOPHER AV			
-	CMBL	95008	853-C6
CHRISTOPHER CT			
300	PA	94306	811-F2
800	SCL	95051	833-A5
1100	HOLL	95023	1039-H5
CHRISTOPHER ST			
1500	SJS	95122	834-G6
CHRISTOPHERS LN			
28300	LAH	94022	810-H5
CHROMA TER			
-	SJS	95112	834-B3
CHROMITE DR			
2400	SCL	95051	833-A2
CHUCKWOOD DR			
1300	SJS	95131	814-C7
CHUKAR CT			
1400	SUNV	94087	832-E5
CHULA VISTA			
11000	SCIC	95127	815-A6
CHULA VISTA CT			
11300	SCIC	95127	815-A5
CHULA VISTA DR			
11000	SCIC	95127	815-A5
CHULA VISTA TER			
1000	SUNV	94086	812-C6
CHULETA CT			
2100	LALT	94024	831-H5
CHURCH AV			
-	SCIC	95046	957-H1
-	SCIC	95020	957-H1
1400	SCIC	95046	937-J7
1400	SCIC	95046	938-A7
1400	SCIC	95020	937-J7
1400	SCIC	95020	938-A7
CHURCH DR			
1400	SJS	95118	874-B2
CHURCH ST			
-	SBnC	95045	1038-C4
-	SJB	95045	1038-C4
100	MTVW	94041	811-H5
100	MTVW	94041	812-A6
100	LGTS	95030	893-A1
6400	GIL	95020	978-A3
7400	GIL	95020	977-J1

STREET Block City ZIP Pg-Grid

CHURCH ST
8800 GIL 95020 957-H6
16000 MGH 95037 937-A1
CHURCHILL AV
- SMCo 94062 790-A4
- PA 94301 790-A4
- PA 94301 791-A6
- WDSD 94062 790-A4
- PA 94306 790-A4
- PA 94306 791-A6
CHURCHILL DR
2000 MPS 95035 794-B2
CHURCHILL PL
100 GIL 95020 978-A5
CHURCHILL RD
300 SBnC 95023 1020-C1
CHURCHILL PARK DR
400 SJS 95136 874-F3
CHURCHWOOD CT
3100 SJS 95148 855-D1
CHURIN DR
3400 MTVW 94040 831-J2
CHURTON AV
1900 LALT 94024 832-A5
2000 LALT 94024 831-J5
CHYNOWETH AV
100 SJS 95136 874-D3
100 SJS 95123 874-G3
500 SCIC 95136 874-G3
700 SJS 95123 875-A3
700 SJS 95136 875-A3
CHYNOWETH CT
- SJS 95136 874-F3
CHYNOWETH PARK CT
5200 SJS 95136 875-A3
CICERO WY
2800 SJS 95148 855-C1
CICERONE LN
13800 LAH 94022 811-C6
CIELITO DR
- LALT 94022 811-E6
CIELITO WY
6600 SJS 95119 875-D7
CIELO LINDO COM
- MPS 95035 813-J1
- MPS 95035 814-A1
CIELO LINDO DR
- SJS 95116 834-F5
CIELO VISTA CT
- GIL 95020 957-E6
CIELO VISTA DR
- SBnC 95023 1060-E1
CIELO VISTA LN
- GIL 95020 957-E6
CIELO VISTA WY
4700 SJS 95129 853-A1
CIENEGA RD
1500 HOLL 95023 1040-A6
1600 SBnC 95023 1040-A6
2600 SBnC 95023 1060-A3
2600 SBnC - 1060-A1
2900 SBnC - 1040-A7
3900 SBnC 95023 1059-J4
4000 SBnC - 1059-J4
CIERVOS RD
- SMCo 94028 830-D4
CILKER CT
- LGTS 95032 873-B6
CIMA WY
- PTLV 94028 810-C7
- PTLV 94028 830-C1
CIMARRON DR
2000 MGH 95037 917-E6
2300 SCL 95051 833-C2
CIMARRON ST
1900 SCIC 95037 917-D4
CIMARRON RIVER CT
- SJS 95136 874-E2
CIMINO AV
200 SJS 95125 854-D4
CIMITY CT
700 SJS 95138 875-F4
CINDERELLA LN
1800 SJS 95116 834-H5
CINERARIA CT
5000 SJS 95111 875-A2
CINNABAR ST
500 SJS 95110 834-A6
700 SJS 95126 833-J6
CINNABAR HILLS RD
10000 SCIC 95120 895-A7
10000 SJS 95120 895-A7
10000 SCIC 95120 915-A1
10000 SJS 95120 915-A1
10100 SCIC 95120 914-J1
10100 SJS 95120 914-J1
CINNAMON DR
500 SJS 95111 854-G7
CINNAMON FERN COM
- FRMT 94539 793-J3
CIOLINO AV
100 MGH 95037 937-A1
CIOPPINO CT
7700 SCIC 95020 958-G6
CIRCLE DR
- SUNV 94089 812-H3
- HOLL 95023 1040-A5
600 EPA 94303 791-B3
700 SCL 95050 833-F5
CIRCLE LN
- MLPK 94025 790-J2
16400 MGH 95037 917-G6
CIRCLE HILL DR
6500 SJS 95120 894-B1
CIRO AV
100 SCIC 95128 833-F7
100 SJS 95128 833-F7
CIROLERO ST
1300 MPS 95035 794-B4
CIRONE WY
2000 SJS 95124 873-F1
CIRRUS WY
100 SUNV 94087 832-E2

CISCO WY
- SJS 95134 813-G4
CITATION CT
14900 MGH 95037 937-B5
22400 SCrC 95033 912-H5
CITATION DR
- LALT 94024 831-J5
22300 SCrC 95033 912-H4
CITATION WY
- HOLL 95023 1020-A7
CITRON AV
700 SUNV 94087 832-B1
CITRUS CT
500 SJS 95117 853-D1
CITRUS LN
19200 SAR 95070 872-G5
CITRUS GROVE CT
1500 SJS 95121 855-A3
CITY LIGHTS PL
- SJS 95136 854-E5
CITYSCAPE PL
- SJS 95136 854-E5
CITY VIEW PL
1200 SJS 95127 835-C3
CIVIC CENTER DR
- CMBL 95008 853-E6
800 SCL 95050 833-D3
CIVIC PARK LN
- CPTO 95014 852-E1
CLAIR CT
3300 SCL 95051 833-A3
CLAIRE CT
2500 MTVW 94043 811-F2
CLAIRE PL
300 MLPK 94025 790-F5
CLAITOR WY
3900 SJS 95132 815-A5
CLAMPETT CT
1500 SJS 95131 814-D5
CLAMPETT LN
1500 SJS 95131 814-D5
CLAMPETT PL
1500 SJS 95131 814-D5
CLAMPETT WY
1500 SJS 95131 814-D5
CLARA DR
700 PA 94303 791-D6
CLARA ST
14800 SCIC 95032 873-B4
14800 MSER 95030 873-B4
CLARA WY
- GIL 95020 978-A2
CLARA FELICE WY
500 SJS 95125 854-C5
CLARA SMITH PL
- SJS 95135 855-F5
CLARA VISTA AV
600 SCL 95050 833-C5
CLARDY PL
500 SJS 95117 853-C1
CLARE CT
1800 SJS 95124 873-H1
CLAREBANK WY
2500 SJS 95121 855-D3
CLAREMONT AV
- SCL 95051 832-J7
- SCL 95051 852-J1
N CLAREMONT AV
- SCIC 95127 834-J1
- SCIC 95127 835-A1
200 SCIC 95127 814-J7
S CLAREMONT AV
- SCIC 95127 835-A1
100 SJS 95127 835-A1
CLAREMONT CT
700 MGH 95037 936-H1
CLAREMONT DR
500 MGH 95037 916-H7
600 MGH 95037 936-H1
CLAREMONT PL
- MLPK 94025 790-H4
CLAREMONT WY
300 MLPK 94025 790-H4
CLARENCE AV
200 SUNV 94086 812-C7
CLARENCE CT
1700 SJS 95124 853-H6
CLARENDON DR
4600 SJS 95129 853-A4
4800 SJS 95129 852-J4
CLARENDON ST
7000 SJS 95129 852-E3
CLARET CT
8200 SJS 95135 855-J6
CLARET DR
- MGH 95037 917-E6
CLAREVIEW AV
- SCIC 95127 835-A1
100 SJS 95127 835-A1
CLAREVIEW CT
200 SJS 95127 835-A1
CLARICE DR
1700 SJS 95122 854-J1
1900 SJS 95122 855-A1
2000 SJS 95122 835-A7
CLARIDAD LP
- MPS 95035 813-J1
CLARIDGE CT
20300 SAR 95070 852-E6
CLARINDA WY
1900 SJS 95124 873-G5
CLARION CT
2700 SJS 95148 835-E6
CLARITA AV
1400 SJS 95130 853-B4
1500 SJS 95008 853-B4
CLARK AV
100 LALT 94024 811-F7
900 MTVW 94040 811-F5
2000 SCL 95051 833-B2
N CLARK AV
200 LALT 94022 811-F6
1100 MTVW 94040 811-F6

CLARK CT
500 LALT 94024 811-F7
CLARK RD
- MTVW 94043 812-B2
- SCIC 94043 812-B2
CLARK ST
1100 SJS 95125 854-B2
CLARK WY
- PA 94304 790-F6
1000 GIL 95020 977-H3
1100 SJS 95125 854-A5
CLARKE AV
1800 EPA 94303 791-C1
CLARKE CT
- EPA 94303 791-C2
CLARKE LN
200 SCIC 95037 916-F4
CLARKSPUR LN
1500 SJS 95129 852-F5
CLARKSTON AV
11000 CPTO 95014 852-B3
CLARKSTON DR
700 SJS 95136 874-E1
CLARKWOOD CT
400 SCL 95054 813-F6
CLARMAR WY
2000 SJS 95128 833-F7
CLASSIC CT
21000 CPTO 95014 852-C3
CLASSICO AV
3000 SJS 95135 855-E3
CLAUDIA DR
10200 SCIC 95127 835-A2
CLAUSEN CT
12800 LAH 94022 831-D2
12800 LAH 94024 831-D2
CLAUSER DR
400 MPS 95035 794-A5
CLAVERING HILL RD
4100 SCIC 95127 815-D7
CLAY DR
- ATN 94027 790-C4
1500 LALT 94024 832-A4
CLAY ST
1600 SCL 95050 833-D4
20200 CPTO 95014 852-E2
CLAYBURN LN
1100 SJS 95121 855-B6
CLAYCOMB CT
1100 SJS 95118 874-G3
CLAYTON AV
- SJS 95110 834-A5
19000 MGH 95037 916-H4
CLAYTON DR
2100 MLPK 94025 790-E7
CLAYTON RD
1100 SJS 95127 835-B3
3400 SCIC 95127 835-F1
11200 SJS 95148 835-C4
CLAYWOOD WY
6900 SJS 95120 894-J3
CLEAR BROOK CT
- SJS 95111 854-J5
CLEARCREEK CT
22000 CPTO 95014 832-A7
CLEAR LAKE AV
1500 MPS 95035 814-D2
CLEAR LAKE CT
1100 MPS 95035 814-D1
CLEAR PARK CIR
200 SJS 95136 874-H2
CLEAR PARK PL
4300 SJS 95136 874-H1
CLEAR RIVER CT
4700 SJS 95136 874-E2
CLEAR SPRINGS CT
600 SJS 95133 834-B2
CLEARVIEW DR
400 HOLL 95023 1040-D5
400 LGTS 95032 873-B3
400 SBnC 95023 1040-D5
500 SCIC 95032 873-B3
700 SJS 95133 814-F7
CLEAR VIEW TER
- FRMT 94539 794-B1
CLEAR VISTA CT
- SJS 95138 875-H6
CLEARWATER CT
500 SUNV 94087 832-D4
CLEARWOOD CT
22000 CPTO 95014 832-A7
CLEAVES AV
- SJS 95126 833-J7
200 SCIC 95126 833-J7
200 SCIC 95126 853-J1
CLELAND AV
- LGTS 95030 893-A1
CLELAND PL
- MLPK 94025 790-J3
CLEMATIS DR
1000 SUNV 94086 832-H2
5700 SJS 95124 873-J7
CLEMENCE AV
1200 SJS 95122 834-F7
1500 SJS 95122 854-G1
CLEMENCE CT
1400 SJS 95122 834-F7
CLEMO AV
4100 PA 94306 811-C3
CLEMSON AV
18300 SAR 95070 852-J7
CLEO AV
20600 CPTO 95014 852-D3
CLEO SPRINGS CT
1500 SJS 95131 814-C6
CLEVELAND AV
- SCIC 95128 833-G7
- SCIC 95128 853-G1
1600 SJS 95126 833-G7
1800 SJS 95128 833-G7
CLIFDEN WY
20300 CPTO 95014 852-E2
CLIFF DR
1400 SJS 95132 814-G3

CLIFFORD CT
6600 CPTO 95014 852-F2
CLIFFORD DR
6500 CPTO 95014 852-F2
CLIFFORD LN
600 MPS 95035 794-B5
CLIFFORD ST
1800 SCL 95050 833-D4
CLIFFWOOD DR
1300 SJS 95122 834-H6
CLIFTON AV
- LGTS 95030 872-J7
- LGTS 95030 892-J1
300 SCIC 95128 853-G1
300 SJS 95128 853-G1
400 CMBL 95128 853-E3
CLIFTON CT
3200 PA 94303 791-E6
CLINTON AV
3400 SCL 95051 832-J7
CLINTON PL
700 SJS 95126 833-J6
700 SJS 95126 834-A6
CLINTON RD
800 LALT 94024 831-G2
CLINTONIA AV
800 SJS 95125 854-A2
CLIPPER CT
1100 SJS 95132 814-G5
CLISE CT
400 SJS 95123 875-A6
CLOGSTON CT
400 SJS 95133 834-G2
CLOUD AV
900 MLPK 94025 790-D6
900 SMCo 94025 790-D6
CLOUD DR
4800 SJS 95111 875-B1
CLOUD WK
- MPS 95035 814-J1
CLOVE DR
2200 SCIC 95128 853-F2
CLOVER AV
600 SJS 95128 833-E7
S CLOVER AV
300 SJS 95128 853-E1
CLOVER LN
100 MLPK 94025 790-J3
CLOVER WY
100 LGTS 95032 873-D7
CLOVERBROOK DR
- MGH 95037 937-C4
1000 SJS 95120 874-E7
CLOVERCREST DR
5300 SJS 95118 874-C4
CLOVERDALE CT
1400 SUNV 94087 832-B4
CLOVERDALE LN
1600 SJS 95130 853-B5
CLOVERFIELD CT
- SJS 95138 855-C5
CLOVERHILL DR
6100 SJS 95120 874-E7
CLOVERLY CT
22100 SCIC 94024 832-A7
CLOVER MEADOW CT
- SJS 95135 855-H7
CLOVER OAK DR
3400 SJS 95148 835-E6
CLOVEWOOD LN
3200 SJS 95132 814-E2
CLOVIS AV
1600 SJS 95124 873-J5
CLUB DR
- GIL 95020 977-D3
5400 SCIC 95127 815-A7
5400 SJS 95131 814-A5
CLUBHOUSE CT
4000 SJS 95135 855-H6
CLUBHOUSE LN
10600 CPTO 95014 852-A2
CLUB VIEW TER
11900 SCIC 94024 831-G3
CLYDA DR
2400 SJS 95116 834-H4
CLYDE AV
400 MTVW 94043 812-C4
700 SCL 95054 813-E6
CLYDE CT
400 MTVW 94043 812-C4
500 MPS 95035 794-B6
CLYDE BANK CT
1100 SUNV 94087 832-H4
CLYDELLE AV
4700 SJS 95124 873-E4
15100 SCIC 95124 873-E4
CLYDESDALE AV
5900 SJS 95123 874-J5
COACH CT
1100 SJS 95120 894-E1
COACHELLA AV
800 SUNV 94086 812-H5
COACHLIGHT DR
3300 SJS 95111 854-J5
COAKLEY DR
400 SJS 95117 853-C1
COALBROOK DR
1600 SJS 95126 853-H4
COALMINE VW
- PTLV 94028 830-C1
COAST AV
2600 MTVW 94043 791-G7
COASTLAND AV
1700 SJS 95125 854-C4
COASTLAND CT
- SJS 95125 854-C5
COASTLAND DR
700 PA 94303 791-C6
COBALT WY
300 SUNV 94086 812-J7
COBBERT DR
3600 SJS 95148 835-F7

COBBLESTONE CT
- HOLL 95023 1040-D5
6500 SJS 95120 894-C6
COBBLESTONE DR
1200 CMBL 95008 853-B7
COBURN CT
- SJS 95139 875-G7
- SJS 95139 895-G1
COCHISE CT
600 FRMT 94539 793-J2
COCHRANE CIR
100 MGH 95037 916-H4
COCHRANE RD
200 MGH 95037 916-J5
800 MGH 95037 917-B2
1800 SJS 95037 917-B2
1800 SCIC 95037 917-B2
COCONUT DR
2500 SJS 95148 835-C7
CODY CT
3600 SCL 95051 832-H7
CODY LN
- LALT 94022 811-E6
14700 SAR 95070 872-E3
CODY RD
- SCIC 94035 812-C2
CODY WY
1800 SJS 95124 853-G7
COE AV
400 SJS 95125 854-A2
COELHO CT
400 MPS 95035 794-A3
COELHO ST
100 MPS 95035 794-A4
COEUR D ALENE WY
900 SUNV 94087 832-B4
COFFEEBERRY DR
- SJS 95123 875-B6
COFFEEWOOD CT
700 SJS 95120 894-H3
COFFEY CT
700 SJS 95123 874-F5
COGHLAN LN
- ATN 94027 790-C4
COHANSEY AV
- GIL 95020 957-J6
- SCIC 95020 957-J6
500 GIL 95020 958-A6
800 SCIC 95020 958-A6
COHANSEY DR
2900 SJS 95132 814-D3
COHASSET WY
5700 SJS 95123 875-B4
COIT DR
2500 SJS 95124 853-G7
2600 SJS 95124 873-G1
COLBY AV
900 SMCo 94025 790-H1
10100 CPTO 95014 832-F7
COLBY CT
19700 SAR 95070 852-F5
COLD HARBOR AV
10100 CPTO 95014 852-F1
COLDWATER DR
3100 SJS 95148 835-B5
COLE DR
14500 SCIC 95124 873-G3
14900 SJS 95124 873-G3
COLE PL
- SCL 95054 813-E5
COLE RD
600 SBnC 95004 1037-D2
COLEMAN AV
400 SJS 95110 834-A5
500 SJS 95110 833-G3
600 MLPK 94025 790-H2
800 SMCo 94025 790-H2
1100 SCL 95050 833-G3
1100 SCL 95110 833-G3
COLEMAN PL
- MLPK 94025 790-J2
COLEMAN RD
- SJS 95123 874-A6
1000 SJS 95120 874-A6
1500 SJS 95120 873-J7
COLERAINE CT
600 SUNV 94087 832-E4
COLERIDGE AV
100 PA 94301 791-A6
COLFAX CT
3100 SCL 95051 833-A3
COLFAX DR
400 SJS 95123 874-J4
COLGATE AV
3200 SCL 95051 833-A6
COLIBRI CT
200 SJS 95119 875-D7
COLIMA CT
- SJS 95131 814-B6
COLINA DR
12200 LAH 94024 831-E2
COLINA LINDA
3500 SBnC 95023 1039-D5
COLINTON WY
1300 SUNV 94087 832-B4
COLLEEN CT
300 MGH 95037 916-J7
600 SJS 95123 874-H7
COLLEEN DR
600 SJS 95123 874-F6
1800 LALT 94024 831-J4
COLLEEN WY
- CMBL 95008 853-B5
COLLEGE AV
- SMCo 94025 790-H2
- LGTS 95030 893-A1
200 PA 94306 791-A7
600 MLPK 94025 790-G5
700 SCL 95050 833-F5
900 PA 94306 811-A1
1500 PA 94306 810-J1
COLLEGE CT
700 LALT 94024 831-E1

COLLEGE DR
600 SJS 95128 853-H2
COLLEGE ST
100 HOLL 95023 1039-J4
100 MTVW 94040 811-F4
COLLEGE PARK DR
- SJS 95110 834-B5
COLLEGE PARK WY
- SJS 95110 834-A5
COLLEGE TERRACE CT
100 LGTS 95030 893-A1
COLLETTE DR
1000 SJS 95132 814-H5
COLLINGSWORTH ST
21700 CPTO 95014 852-B3
COLLINGWOOD AV
1600 SJS 95125 854-A5
COLLINS CT
4300 MTVW 94040 811-E3
COLLINS LN
1200 SJS 95129 852-J4
COLLINWOOD CT
400 SCL 95054 813-F5
COLLOMIA CT
4900 SJS 95111 875-A1
COLMERY CT
4000 SJS 95118 874-A2
COLMERY LN
1500 SJS 95118 874-A2
COLOMBARD CT
8300 SJS 95135 855-J7
COLOMBO DR
4200 SJS 95130 853-A4
4300 SJS 95070 853-A4
4300 SJS 95129 853-A4
COLONADE SQ
100 SJS 95127 834-J3
COLONIAL LN
900 PA 94303 791-D5
1100 SJS 95132 814-H5
COLONIAL PL
- SMCo 94061 790-B3
COLONIAL WY
3000 SJS 95128 853-E4
COLONIAL OAKS DR
1200 LALT 94024 831-J3
COLONNA AV
- SJS 95148 855-F1
COLONY AV
13000 SCIC 95046 937-E5
COLONY CT
1700 GIL 95020 977-E1
COLONY DR
200 SJS 95131 814-A4
COLONY ST
1900 MTVW 94043 811-G2
COLONY WY
1700 GIL 95020 977-E1
COLONY COVE DR
400 SJS 95123 874-G3
COLONY CREST DR
400 SJS 95123 874-G3
COLONY FIELD DR
5300 SJS 95123 874-G3
COLONY GREEN DR
5300 SJS 95123 874-G3
COLONY HILLS LN
1000 CPTO 95014 852-D3
COLONY KNOLL DR
400 SJS 95123 874-G3
COLONY PARK CIR
5300 SJS 95123 874-G3
COLORADO AV
100 PA 94301 791-B7
100 PA 94306 791-D6
700 PA 94303 791-D6
COLORADO CT
100 LGTS 95032 873-H7
100 LGTS 95032 893-H1
COLORADO PL
1000 PA 94303 791-E5
COLORADO WY
- SBnC 95023 1060-B1
COLORVIEW CT
5900 SJS 95120 874-B7
COLT WY
1300 SJS 95121 855-B4
COLTER PL
6000 SJS 95123 874-G6
COLTON AV
1000 SUNV 94089 812-F4
COLTON PL
500 SJS 95110 834-C7
COLTWOOD CT
3400 SJS 95148 835-D6
COLTWOOD DR
2700 SJS 95148 835-D6
COLUMBET AV
11100 SCIC 95020 957-J1
11900 SCIC 95046 937-F2
11900 SCIC 95046 957-J1
COLUMBIA AV
- SMCo 94063 790-D1
500 SJS 95126 854-A1
500 SUNV 94086 812-F6
COLUMBIA DR
1600 MTVW 94040 811-G7
COLUMBIA ST
2100 PA 94306 810-J1
2200 PA 94306 811-A1
COLUMBIA RIVER CT
4600 SJS 95136 874-G2
COLUMBINE AV
1100 SUNV 94086 832-H2
COLUMBINE CT
8700 GIL 95020 977-D1
19200 SAR 95070 852-G6
COLUMBINE DR
3500 SJS 95127 835-C4
3500 SJS 95148 835-C4
COLUMBUS AV
21200 CPTO 95014 852-B3

COLUMBUS CIR
1300 MPS 95035 794-B4
COLUMBUS DR
1000 MPS 95035 794-B4
COLUMBUS PL
2700 SCL 95051 833-B3
COLUMN CT
3200 SJS 95111 854-F6
COLUSA AV
900 SUNV 94086 812-H6
COLUSA WY
1900 SJS 95130 852-J6
COLVILLE DR
300 SJS 95123 875-A5
300 SJS 95123 874-J5
COMANCHE CT
5600 SJS 95123 874-H4
COMANCHE DR
5600 SJS 95123 874-H5
COMANCHE TR
17800 SCIC 95033 913-A2
COMER DR
20900 SAR 95070 852-C6
COMET DR
100 MPS 95035 814-J2
COMET LN
2900 SJS 95127 834-J2
COMMERCE DR
2100 SJS 95131 814-B5
COMMERCIAL AV
800 PA 94303 791-F7
800 PA 94303 811-F1
COMMERCIAL CT
1000 SJS 95112 834-C1
COMMERCIAL ST
100 SUNV 94086 812-G7
100 SUNV 94086 832-G1
100 SJS 95112 834-B2
800 SJS 95133 834-B2
COMMODORE DR
1600 SJS 95133 834-D1
2000 SJS 95133 814-E7
COMMUNICATIONS HILL BLVD
- SJS 95125 854-D4
- SJS 95136 854-F7
COMMUNITY LN
- PA 94301 791-B4
COMO LN
3300 SJS 95118 874-A1
COMPONENT DR
100 SJS 95131 813-H6
COMPTON CT
3600 SJS 95130 853-C4
COMPTON LN
3600 SJS 95130 853-B4
COMSTOCK CIR
- SCIC 94305 790-J7
COMSTOCK LN
1700 SJS 95124 853-H7
COMSTOCK RD
100 SBnC 95023 1020-E1
600 SBnC 95023 1000-G7
800 SBnC 93635 1000-G7
COMSTOCK ST
800 SCL 95054 833-D1
COMSTOCK WY
1700 SJS 95124 853-J7
COMSTOCK QUEEN CT
- MTVW 94043 811-J3
CONCANNON CT
300 SCL 95050 833-D6
CONCEPCION RD
12300 LAH 94022 831-B1
12300 LAH 94022 811-B7
CONCERTO DR
4400 SJS 95111 855-A7
CONCERTO WY
4400 SJS 95111 855-A7
CONCETTA CT
- SJS 95127 834-H2
CONCORD AV
700 SJS 95128 853-H2
1300 LALT 94024 831-H3
CONCORD CIR
- MTVW 94040 811-F3
15000 MGH 95037 937-C2
CONCORD DR
- SJS 95123 875-B4
- SJS 95193 875-B4
200 MLPK 94025 790-J3
CONCORD LN
600 SCL 95051 833-A6
CONCORD PL
7100 GIL 95020 977-J4
CONCORD RIDGE CT
- SJS 95138 855-F6
CONCOURSE DR
1900 SJS 95131 814-B5
CONDENSA ST
2500 SCL 95051 833-B1
CONDIT RD
1100 MGH 95037 917-C6
16100 SCIC 95037 917-B5
17300 MGH 95037 937-D1
CONDON CT
300 SCL 95050 833-D6
CONDOR CIR
5700 SJS 95118 874-A6
CONDOR CT
5700 SJS 95118 874-A6
CONDOR WY
1500 SUNV 94087 832-E5
CONEJO CT
26500 LAH 94022 811-B6
CONEJO DR
200 SJS 95119 875-C7
CONESTOGA WY
300 SJS 95123 875-A6
300 SJS 95123 874-J6
CONGRESS PL
10000 CPTO 95014 832-C7
CONGRESS HALL LN
21700 SAR 95070 872-B3

STREET Block City ZIP Pg-Grid

CONGRESS JUNCTION CIR
18900 SAR 95070 852-B7
CONGRESS SPRINGS LN
21700 SAR 95070 872-B3
CONGRESS SPRINGS RD Rt#-9
20900 SAR 95070 872-A3
22100 SCIC 95070 872-A3
22100 SCIC 95070 871-G2
22500 SCIC 95030 871-G2
CONIFER CT
1900 SJS 95132 814-E2
CONIFER LN
1900 SJS 95132 814-E2
CONIFER ST
48200 FRMT 94539 793-J1
CONIL WY
300 SMCo 94028 810-D4
CONISTON CT
1300 SJS 95118 874-B4
CONISTON WY
5600 SJS 95118 874-C4
CONLIN CT
400 SJS 95123 874-J5
CONNECTICUT DR
1400 RDWC 94061 790-A2
CONNELL CT
9000 GIL 95020 957-H7
CONNEMARA WY
500 SUNV 94087 832-E4
CONNIE DR
700 CMBL 95008 873-C1
CONNOLLY WY
2300 EPA 94303 791-C1
CONRAD AV
1700 SJS 95124 873-H4
CONRADIA CT
21500 CPTO 95014 852-B3
CONSTANCE DR
500 SJS 95117 853-C2
CONSTANSO CT
1400 SJS 95129 852-J4
CONSTANSO WY
1400 SJS 95129 852-J4
CONSTANZO ST
500 SCIC 94305 810-H1
CONSTITUTION AV
18000 MSER 95030 872-J5
CONSTITUTION CT
1800 SJS 95124 853-H6
CONSTITUTION DR
2100 SJS 95124 853-H6
CONSUELO AV
2200 SCL 95050 833-D6
CONTE WY
1800 MGH 95037 917-D6
CONTEMPLATION PL
- MPS 95035 814-J1
CONTESSA CT
6300 SJS 95123 874-J7
CONTI CT
500 SJS 95111 854-G3
CONTINENTAL CIR
700 MTVW 94040 812-A7
700 MTVW 94040 831-A1
21400 SAR 95070 852-C6
CONTINENTAL DR
500 SJS 95111 855-A7
900 MLPK 94025 790-C6
CONVENT AL
- HOLL 95023 1039-J4
CONWAY AV
14700 SCIC 95124 873-G4
CONWAY CT
14700 SCIC 95124 873-G4
CONWAY RD
600 SUNV 94087 832-D3
CONWAY ST
1600 MPS 95035 794-A3
COOK ST
1100 SJS 95126 833-G5
COOKSEY LN
700 SCIC 94305 810-H1
COOLEY AV
1900 EPA 94303 791-B2
COOLEY DR
1700 SJS 95116 834-G4
COOLIDGE AV
800 SUNV 94086 812-D7
1100 SJS 95125 854-A3
COOLIDGE DR
2000 SCL 95051 833-B3
COONEY CT
- SJS 95123 874-G4
COONEY PL
- SJS 95123 874-G4
COOPER AV
15000 SCIC 95124 873-F4
COOPER CT
100 LGTS 95030 873-B5
100 LGTS 95032 873-B5
COOPER DR
3400 SCL 95051 832-J2
COOPER LP
- SCIC 94035 812-B2
- SCIC 94043 812-B2
COOPER PL
- GIL 95020 957-F7
COOPER RIVER DR
1100 SJS 95126 853-G3
COPAL CT
900 SCIC 95127 814-H6
COPCO LN
200 SJS 95123 875-A4
COPELAND CT
5400 SJS 95124 873-H6
COPELAND LN
5400 SJS 95124 873-H6
COPELAND PL
5500 SJS 95124 873-H6
COPPER RD
2900 SCL 95051 812-J7

COPPER RD
2900 SCL 95051 832-J1
COPPERAGE CT
6500 SJS 95120 894-C6
COPPERFIELD DR
4200 SJS 95136 854-F7
4200 SJS 95136 874-F1
COPPER HILL DR
17000 MGH 95037 917-G5
17000 SCIC 95037 917-G5
COPPER HILL PL
17100 SCIC 95037 917-G4
COPPER LEAF DR
3300 SJS 95132 814-G4
COPPER PEAK LN
1100 SJS 95120 894-G5
COPPER SPRING CT
11500 CPTO 95014 852-A4
COPPERWOOD CIR
6500 SJS 95120 894-E2
COQUITO CT
- SMCo 94028 810-D4
COQUITO WY
100 SMCo 94028 810-D4
CORA CT
1200 CMBL 95008 873-C1
CORAL CT
600 LALT 94024 811-G6
3000 SJS 95121 854-J4
3000 SJS 95121 855-A4
CORAL BELL CT
2200 GIL 95020 977-D1
CORAL CANYON DR
5500 SJS 95123 875-B4
CORALEE DR
1700 SJS 95124 873-H4
CORAL GABLES CIR
7000 SJS 95139 895-E1
CORAL SANDS DR
3600 SJS 95136 854-G7
CORALTREE PL
1600 SJS 95131 814-D5
CORALWOOD WY
5700 SJS 95123 874-F5
CORBAL CT
3100 SJS 95148 855-F2
CORBETTA LN
12500 LAH 94022 831-B2
CORBIN AV
5000 SJS 95118 874-C3
CORBY DR
3100 SJS 95148 855-E2
CORCEL CT
16700 LGTS 95032 873-C5
CORD CT
2900 SJS 95148 855-D1
CORDA DR
2800 SJS 95122 855-B2
CORDELIA AV
1100 SJS 95129 852-H4
CORDETERRA CIR
- SCIC 95111 854-G4
- SJS 95111 854-G3
CORDEVALLE CLUB DR
- SCIC 95046 957-C2
CORDILLERAS AV
1300 SUNV 94087 832-D4
CORDOBA WY
2400 SJS 95125 853-J7
CORDOVA CT
- PTLV 94028 810-D6
700 MGH 95037 937-A4
CORDOVA RD
10500 CPTO 95014 851-J2
CORDOY LN
5100 SJS 95124 873-H5
CORDWOOD CT
14300 SAR 95070 872-H2
COREY RD
- MonC 95076 1037-A3
CORIANDER AV
- MGH 95037 916-G4
CORIE CT
1100 SJS 95112 814-B7
CORINA CT
3800 PA 94303 791-E7
CORINA WY
3700 PA 94303 791-E7
3800 PA 94303 811-E1
CORINE LN
1300 MLPK 94025 790-E4
CORINNE DR
15400 LGTS 95032 873-C5
CORINTHIA DR
400 MPS 95035 794-A5
CORKERHILL WY
3600 SJS 95121 855-C3
CORK OAK WY
3300 PA 94303 791-D7
CORKTREE LN
2100 SJS 95132 814-E2
CORKWOOD CT
100 SJS 95136 874-H1
CORLISS WY
500 CMBL 95008 853-C6
CORLISTA DR
800 SJS 95128 853-H2
CORMORANT CT
1500 SUNV 94087 832-E5
CORNELIA CT
600 MTVW 94040 811-H7
CORNELL DR
600 SCL 95051 833-A6
1600 MTVW 94040 811-G7
5400 SJS 95118 874-A5
CORNELL RD
- MLPK 94025 790-G4
CORNELL ST
2000 PA 94306 791-A7
2200 PA 94306 811-A1
CORNFLOWER CT
1000 SUNV 94086 832-H2

CORNICHE DR
700 MGH 95037 917-B6
CORNING AV
- MPS 95035 814-A1
100 MPS 95035 813-J1
CORNING DR
3300 SJS 95118 874-A1
CORNWALL CT
800 SUNV 94087 832-F4
CORNWALL DR
2700 SJS 95127 835-A5
CORONA DR
4500 SJS 95129 853-A3
CORONA WY
100 SMCo 94028 810-D4
CORONACH AV
1500 SUNV 94087 832-B5
CORONADO AV
- LALT 94022 811-D6
600 SCIC 94305 810-J1
CORONADO DR
1200 SUNV 94086 812-B6
2500 SCL 95054 833-B1
2900 SCL 95054 813-B7
7000 SJS 95129 852-E3
CORONET DR
2100 LGTS 95032 873-E5
2100 LGTS 95124 873-E5
2100 SJS 95124 873-E5
CORPORATE CT
2000 SJS 95131 814-B5
CORPORATE LIMIT
600 CMBL 95008 853-F6
CORPORATION WY
1000 PA 94303 791-F7
CORRAL AV
100 SUNV 94086 812-B6
CORRALES DR
4700 SJS 95136 874-D2
CORRALITOS LN
14800 SCIC 95127 835-A1
CORRIB CT
- SBnC - 1059-J2
CORRIDA CIR
4600 SJS 95129 853-A1
CORSA PL
- MGH 95037 917-B6
CORSICA CT
- SJS 95148 855-G2
CORTE VIA
1600 SCIC 94024 831-G4
CORTE ARQUETA
400 MGH 95037 917-B7
CORTE BELLA CT
- SJS 95148 855-F1
CORTE BELLA DR
- SJS 95148 855-F1
CORTE BONITA
1300 SJS 95120 874-B7
CORTE CABANIL
400 MGH 95037 917-B7
CORTE CABAS
400 MGH 95037 917-B7
CORTE CAMULA
6100 SJS 95120 874-C7
CORTE DE ANNA
1600 SJS 95124 874-A3
CORTE DE ARBOL
3100 SJS 95118 874-A1
CORTE DE ARGUELLO
12800 SAR 95070 852-C6
CORTE DE AVELLANO
4700 SJS 95136 874-E2
CORTE DE BELLEZA
6100 SJS 95120 874-C7
CORTE DE BLANCO
800 SJS 95136 874-E2
CORTE DE BOLEYN
4300 SJS 95118 874-A2
CORTE DE CALLAS
1600 SJS 95124 874-A3
CORTE DE CERVATO
4700 SJS 95136 874-D2
CORTE DE FLORES
2000 SCL 95054 813-D4
3000 SJS 95118 874-A1
CORTE DE LA REINA
6100 SJS 95120 874-B7
CORTE DEL CONEJO
6100 SJS 95120 874-B7
CORTE DE MADRID
10400 CPTO 95014 852-G1
CORTE DE MEDEA
1600 SJS 95124 874-A3
CORTE DE MOFFO
1500 SJS 95118 874-B3
CORTE DE PEARSON
1500 SJS 95124 874-A3
CORTE DE PLATA
800 SJS 95136 874-E2
CORTE DE PONS
1600 SJS 95124 874-A3
CORTE DE PRIMAVERA
2000 SCL 95054 813-C3
CORTE DE ROSA
1400 SJS 95120 894-B1
CORTE DE SEVILLE
10400 CPTO 95014 852-G1
CORTE DE TEBALDI
4200 SJS 95118 874-A3
CORTE DE THAIS
1400 SJS 95118 874-B3
CORTE KORN
10500 SCIC 95020 958-A3
CORTE MADERA AV
900 SUNV 94086 812-D5
CORTE MADERA CT
400 SUNV 94086 812-C5
CORTE MADERA LN
12600 LAH 94022 811-B7
21800 CPTO 95014 832-B7
CORTE MADERA RD
100 PTLV 94028 830-C1

CORTE MADERA RD
100 PTLV 94028 810-C7
CORTESE CIR
3100 SJS 95127 814-J7
CORTESE LN
16900 MGH 95037 917-D6
CORTE VERDE DR
5000 SJS 95111 875-A2
CORTEZ AV
100 SJS 95136 854-G7
1700 SJS 95122 834-H6
CORTEZ DR
1200 SUNV 94086 812-B6
2500 SCL 95051 833-B1
CORTEZ LN
12900 LAH 94022 830-J1
CORTEZ ST
1600 MPS 95035 794-A3
CORTINA DR
2900 SJS 95132 814-F5
CORTO ST
700 MTVW 94043 811-J4
CORTONA CT
- SJS 95135 855-G3
CORTONA DR
3200 SJS 95135 855-F2
CORUMBA CT
5800 SJS 95120 874-C5
CORVALLIS CT
1100 SJS 95120 894-F2
CORVALLIS DR
800 SUNV 94087 832-C4
1100 SJS 95120 894-F2
CORVETTE DR
1000 SJS 95129 852-F3
CORVIN DR
2900 SCL 95051 813-A7
2900 SCL 95051 833-A1
CORWIN CT
5000 SJS 95111 875-C1
CORY AV
2300 SJS 95128 833-E7
CORY CT
21000 CPTO 95014 852-C2
CORY DR
- MGH 95037 917-B7
16700 MGH 95037 937-B1
CORY LN
16600 MGH 95037 937-B1
COSCO CT
1100 HOLL 95023 1039-H3
COSENZA LP
4200 SJS 95134 813-D2
COSMO AV
100 MGH 95037 937-A2
COSMO PL
- SJS 95118 874-C3
COSSAREK DR
- SJS 95135 855-F2
COSTA AV
- SJS 95112 854-E3
COSTA MESA DR
300 SJS 95111 854-J7
COSTA MESA TER
- FRMT 94539 794-B1
400 SUNV 94086 812-C5
COSTELLO CT
300 SCIC 94024 831-E2
COSTELLO DR
300 SCIC 94024 831-E2
COSTIGAN CIR
500 MPS 95035 794-B5
COT CT
500 SJS 95117 853-D1
COTHRAN RD
- SCIC 95033 913-D4
COTO CT
- SJS 95148 855-F1
COTSWALD CT
1100 SUNV 94087 832-H4
COTTAGE CT
- MTVW 94043 811-G2
COTTAGE PL
6000 SJS 95123 874-D5
COTTAGE GROVE AV
- SJS 95110 854-D2
COTTAGE GROVE TER
- SUNV 94087 832-D4
COTTERELL DR
1200 SJS 95121 855-A4
COTTLE AV
1500 SJS 95125 854-A5
COTTLE RD
- SJS 95193 875-B5
200 SJS 95119 875-B5
300 SJS 95123 875-B6
6400 SCIC 95123 895-B1
COTTON CT
6000 SJS 95123 875-B6
COTTON PL
- MLPK 94025 790-F5
COTTON ST
300 MLPK 94025 790-F5
COTTON TAIL AV
700 SJS 95116 834-H4
COTTON WOOD CT
- SJS 95131 814-A5
COTTONWOOD CT
- MTVW 94043 812-B5
2900 SCL 95051 833-A6
6300 CPTO 95014 852-F2
COTTONWOOD DR
500 MPS 95035 813-J4
800 CPTO 95014 852-F2
COTTONWOOD ST
48200 FRMT 94539 793-J1
COTTRELL WY
900 SCIC 94305 810-J2
COTY WY
200 SJS 95136 874-G1
COULOMBE DR
4100 PA 94306 811-C3
COUNTESS CT
1100 SJS 95129 852-G4

COUNTESS DR
5900 SJS 95129 852-G3
COUNT FLEET CT
700 MGH 95037 937-B5
COUNTRY DR
2100 GIL 95020 977-D1
COUNTRY LN
- SMCo 94061 790-B2
4700 SJS 95129 852-J4
4700 SJS 95129 853-A4
14600 SCIC 95037 937-C4
COUNTRY WY
13300 LAH 94022 810-H7
COUNTRYBROOK
2400 SJS 95132 814-C4
COUNTRY CLUB CT
3000 PA 94304 810-H7
COUNTRY CLUB DR
1200 MPS 95035 794-C4
1200 SCIC 94024 831-G3
COUNTRY CLUB PKWY
5300 SJS 95138 855-F7
5300 SJS 95138 875-F1
COUNTRY FIELDS LN
- SJS 95136 875-D1
COUNTRY FORGE LN
5200 SJS 95136 875-A3
COUNTRY LEAF CT
3300 SJS 95132 814-G4
COUNTRY OAK CT
5200 SJS 95136 875-D1
COUNTRY OAK LN
- SJS 95136 875-D1
COUNTRYSIDE CT
- MPS 95035 794-C4
COUNTRYSIDE LN
5200 SJS 95136 875-A3
COUNTRY SPRING CT
11500 CPTO 95014 852-C4
COUNTRY SQUIRE CT
12100 SAR 95070 852-G5
COUNTRY SQUIRE DR
12200 SAR 95070 852-G5
COUNTRY SQUIRE LN
12000 SAR 95070 852-G5
COUNTRY SQUIRE WY
12100 SAR 95070 852-G5
COUNTRY TREE CT
- SCIC 95127 835-B1
COUNTRY VIEW CT
22600 SCIC 95119 895-E4
22600 SCIC 95139 895-E4
22600 SCIC 95120 895-E4
COUNTRY VIEW DR
22500 SCIC 95120 895-D5
22600 SCIC 95139 895-D5
COUNTRY VIEW LN
22500 SCIC 95120 895-E5
COUNTRY VISTA CT
3900 SJS 95121 855-D4
COUNTRYWALK CIR
2700 SJS 95132 814-E3
COUNTRYWOOD CT
3600 SJS 95130 853-C4
COUNTY DOWN WY
- GIL 95020 977-F4
COUNTY LABOR CAMP RD
- SBnC 95023 1060-C1
COUR DE CHARLES
- SJS 95148 855-F1
COUR DE JEUNE
- SJS 95148 855-G1
COUR DU VIN
3500 SJS 95148 855-G1
COURTLAND AV
1000 MPS 95035 814-D1
COURTLAND CT
900 MPS 95035 814-D1
COURTNEY AV
1700 SJS 95122 854-G1
COURTSIDE DR
5200 SJS 95138 855-G7
COURTYARD DR
1300 SJS 95118 874-B2
COVE CT
2000 SJS 95148 835-B6
COVE LANE RD
- SCrC 95033 913-C7
COVENTRY CIR
800 MPS 95035 794-A5
COVENTRY CT
800 SUNV 94087 832-F4
COVENTRY DR
100 CMBL 95008 853-C5
2700 SJS 95127 835-A5
COVENTRY WY
800 MPS 95035 794-A5
COVEWOOD CT
2900 SJS 95148 855-D1
COVEY CT
- SBnC 95023 1060-D1
COVINA AV
- SJS 95123 874-J5
COVINA CT
12000 SAR 95070 852-E5
COVINGTON CT
100 SJS 95136 874-H1
900 LALT 94024 831-G2
COVINGTON RD
100 LALT 94024 831-E1
COWDEN PL
13100 LAH 94022 831-A1
COWDEN RD
500 SBnC 95023 1060-B2
COWELL LN
- ATN 94027 790-D5
400 SCIC 94305 810-H1
COWELL RD
16000 SCIC 95030 893-C2
16000 LGTS 95030 893-C2
COWLES COMS
- SJS 95125 854-C4

COWPER CT
1500 SJS 95120 874-A7
3400 PA 94306 791-D7
3400 PA 94306 811-D1
COWPER ST
100 PA 94301 790-J4
800 PA 94301 791-A5
2500 PA 94306 791-C7
3500 PA 94306 811-E1
COX AV
100 SCIC 95046 937-E7
18500 SAR 95070 852-E6
COY DR
100 SJS 95123 874-J3
100 SJS 95123 875-A3
COYNE CT
2100 SJS 95122 834-J7
COYOTE RD
400 SJS 95111 854-J7
400 SJS 95111 855-A7
700 SJS 95111 875-C1
700 SCIC 95111 875-C1
700 SCIC 95111 855-B7
17700 SCIC 95037 917-C3
18100 MGH 95037 917-C3
COYOTE ST
700 MPS 95035 793-J6
COYOTE CREEK CIR
400 SJS 95116 834-D4
COYOTE CREEK CT
1200 SJS 95116 834-D4
COYOTE CREEK PL
1200 SJS 95116 834-D4
COYOTE CREEK GOLF DR
- SCIC 95037 896-C6
- SJS 95037 896-D5
COYOTE HILL
- PTLV 94028 830-C1
COYOTE HILL RD
3100 PA 94304 811-A3
3100 SCIC 94304 810-J3
3100 SCIC 94304 811-A3
COYOTE LAKE RD
13300 SCIC 95046 938-C1
13300 SCIC 95020 938-C1
COYOTE MOON LN
- GIL 95020 957-E6
COYOTE RANCH RD
5800 SCIC 95137 875-H7
5800 SCIC 95137 895-J1
5900 SCIC 95137 896-A1
5900 SJS 95137 896-A2
5900 SJS 95137 895-J2
COYOTE RESERVOIR RD
11000 SCIC 95020 938-E7
11000 SCIC 95046 938-C3
12600 SCIC 95020 958-F1
COZETTE LN
19100 CPTO 95014 852-G1
COZUMEL CIR
2800 SCL 95051 833-A4
COZY CT
500 SJS 95123 874-J7
COZY DR
500 SJS 95123 874-J6
CRABAPPLE WY
500 SJS 95111 854-J6
CRABTREE AV
18600 CPTO 95014 852-H1
CRACOLICE WY
1200 MPS 95035 814-D2
CRAFT DR
10000 CPTO 95014 852-G1
N CRAGMONT AV
- SCIC 95127 834-J1
- SCIC 95127 835-A1
200 SCIC 95127 814-J7
S CRAGMONT AV
- SCIC 95127 835-A1
200 SJS 95127 835-A1
CRAGWOOD LN
1500 SJS 95127 835-A5
CRAIG AV
600 CMBL 95008 853-C7
CRAIG CT
2300 MTVW 94043 811-G3
20600 CPTO 95014 852-D1
CRAIG DR
1000 SJS 95129 852-F3
CRAIG RD
- SCIC 95030 871-E5
- SCrC 95033 871-E5
CRAIG WY
100 LGTS 95032 873-E6
CRAIGEN CIR
20200 SAR 95070 852-E6
CRAILFORD CT
1300 SJS 95121 855-B5
CRAMER CIR
2700 SJS 95111 854-G4
CRANBERRY AV
1100 SUNV 94087 832-B3
CRANBERRY CIR
7900 CPTO 95014 852-C2
CRANBERRY DR
900 CPTO 95014 852-C2
CRANBROOK CT
6400 SJS 95120 894-C1
CRANDALL CIR
- SCL 95054 813-E5
CRANDANO CT
1100 SUNV 94087 832-B3
CRANE AV
1700 MTVW 94040 831-H1
CRANE CT
1600 SJS 95112 833-J1
CRANE ST
900 MLPK 94025 790-F3
CRANE RIDGE CT
- SJS 95138 855-C5
CRANE RIDGE LN
- SJS 95138 855-C5

CRANFORD CIR
4100 SJS 95124 873-E3
CRANWORTH CIR
2000 SJS 95121 855-C4
CRATER LN
2900 SJS 95132 814-F5
CRATER LAKE AV
1500 MPS 95035 794-E7
1500 MPS 95035 814-D1
CRATER LAKE CT
500 SUNV 94087 832-D4
CRAVENS CT
300 SJS 95133 834-G2
CRAWFORD CT
7400 GIL 95020 977-H4
CRAWFORD DR
500 SUNV 94087 832-D2
7300 GIL 95020 977-G3
CRAY CT
3000 SJS 95121 854-J4
CRAYCROFT CT
48400 FRMT 94539 793-J1
CRAYCROFT DR
300 FRMT 94539 793-J1
CRAYSIDE LN
12200 SAR 95070 852-D5
CRAZY PETES RD
- SMCo 94028 830-C6
CREAGER CT
3700 SJS 95130 853-C4
CREE CT
600 SJS 95123 874-H6
CREE DR
600 SJS 95123 874-H6
CREED ST
1000 MPS 95035 794-B4
CREEDEN WY
2100 LALT 94022 811-F5
2100 MTVW 94040 811-F5
CREEK DR
600 MLPK 94025 790-G5
1500 SJS 95125 854-C4
E CREEK DR
100 MLPK 94025 790-H3
E CREEK PL
- MLPK 94025 790-H4
CREEK BANK CT
6500 SJS 95120 894-F1
CREEK BED CT
2200 SCL 95054 813-C5
CREEKBED CT
17100 MGH 95037 917-B7
CREEK ESTATES
5200 SJS 95135 855-G5
CREEK ESTATES CT
3000 SJS 95135 855-G5
CREEKFIELD DR
700 SJS 95136 854-E7
CREEKLAND CIR
700 SJS 95133 834-E2
CREEKLINE DR
7800 CPTO 95014 852-C2
CREEKMORE WY
3100 SJS 95148 835-F7
CREEK PARK DR
- PTLV 94028 810-E7
CREEKPOINT DR
2900 SJS 95133 814-G6
CREEKSIDE CIR
17000 MGH 95037 917-B7
CREEKSIDE CT
- GIL 95020 977-G1
- SBnC 95023 1040-E6
900 MGH 95037 937-B5
17300 MSER 95030 873-A4
22000 CPTO 95014 832-A7
CREEKSIDE DR
- MGH 95037 937-C5
100 PA 94306 811-E2
2700 SJS 95132 814-E3
3100 SJS 95131 814-A4
CREEKSIDE LN
400 MGH 95037 917-B7
CREEKSIDE PL
700 SCL 95051 833-A5
CREEKSIDE WY
700 CMBL 95008 853-F5
CREEKSIDE VILLAGE DR
- LGTS 95032 873-A7
CREEKSTONE CIR
1700 SJS 95133 834-E2
CREEKVIEW CT
6600 SJS 95120 894-G1
12400 SCIC 95046 938-A6
CREEKVIEW DR
300 MGH 95037 917-B7
CREEKVIEW MEADOW CT
- SJS 95135 855-H7
CREEKVIEW MEADOW LN
- SJS 95135 855-G7
CREEKWOOD CT
300 MGH 95037 917-B7
CREEKWOOD DR
1000 SJS 95129 852-J3
CREFFIELD HTS
- LGTS 95030 873-A6
CREIGHTON CT
1200 MPS 95035 814-C1
CREIGHTON PL
3300 SCL 95051 832-J2
CRENSHAW CT
6500 SJS 95120 894-E1
CRESCENDO AV
4200 SJS 95136 874-G1
CRESCENT AV
100 PTLV 94028 810-C7
100 PTLV 94028 830-C1
100 SUNV 94087 832-E3
CRESCENT CT
10100 CPTO 95014 832-A7

SANTA CLARA CO.

STREET
Block City ZIP Pg-Grid

CRESCENT DR
- PA 94301 791-B3
1100 SJS 95125 854-A3
17000 LGTS 95030 893-C1
E CRESCENT DR
500 PA 94301 791-B3
W CRESCENT DR
500 PA 94301 791-B3
CRESCENT LN
1100 HOLL 95023 1040-C6
25400 LAH 94022 831-C2
CRESCENT RD
10000 CPTO 95014 832-A7
CRESCENT TER
600 SUNV 94087 832-E3
CRESENT TER
1000 MPS 95035 814-E1
CRESPI DR
1100 SUNV 94086 812-C6
1400 SJS 95129 852-J5
CREST AV
17600 MGH 95037 916-J7
CREST DR
300 SCIC 95127 815-A6
CREST LN
2300 MLPK 94025 790-D7
CRESTA VISTA LN
500 PTLV 94028 810-D5
CRESTA VISTA WY
200 SJS 95119 875-C6
CRESTBROOK DR
19600 SAR 95070 872-F1
CRESTFIELD DR
1300 SJS 95125 854-B7
CRESTHAVEN LN
1400 SJS 95118 874-B2
CRESTHAVEN ST
2200 MPS 95035 814-E1
CREST HILL CT
9000 GIL 95020 957-E7
9000 GIL 95020 977-E1
CREST HILL WY
- GIL 95020 957-E7
CRESTLINE DR
1100 CPTO 95014 852-D3
CRESTMONT DR
1800 SJS 95124 853-H7
CRESTMOOR CT
700 SJS 95129 852-J2
CRESTMOOR DR
600 SJS 95129 852-J2
CRESTOAK CT
6000 SJS 95120 874-C7
CRESTON DR
10200 CPTO 95014 832-A6
10200 SCIC 94024 832-A6
13100 CPTO 94024 832-A6
CRESTON LN
1100 SJS 95122 834-G7
CRESTPOINT DR
1200 SJS 95131 834-C1
CRESTRIDGE CT
- SJS 95138 875-H6
CRESTRIDGE DR
11500 LAH 94024 831-E4
19400 SCIC 95030 872-F5
CRESTRIDGE LN
- SJS 95138 875-H6
CREST VIEW COM
- FRMT 94539 794-B1
CRESTVIEW CT
8100 SCIC 95020 976-J2
CRESTVIEW DR
200 SCL 95050 833-D7
500 SJS 95117 833-D7
1000 MTVW 94040 812-B7
1000 MTVW 94040 832-B1
1200 HOLL 95023 1040-C7
1200 SBnC 95023 1040-C7
1600 SCIC 94024 831-G4
CRESTWOOD CT
900 SUNV 94089 812-J5
CRESTWOOD DR
1300 SJS 95118 854-B7
CREWE CT
1800 SJS 95132 814-F3
CREWS RD
7300 SCIC 95020 978-F1
7500 SCIC 95020 958-G6
CRIBARI BEND
5400 SJS 95135 855-H5
CRIBARI CIR
5300 SJS 95135 855-H5
CRIBARI CT
5400 SJS 95135 855-H5
CRIBARI GN
5300 SJS 95135 855-H5
CRIBARI HTS
5200 SJS 95135 855-H5
CRIBARI LN
5000 SJS 95135 855-H5
CRIBARI PL
5100 SJS 95135 855-H5
CRIBARI BLUFFS
5000 SJS 95135 855-H5
CRIBARI CORNER
5200 SJS 95135 855-H5
CRIBARI CREST
5300 SJS 95135 855-H5
CRIBARI DALE
5200 SJS 95135 855-H5
CRIBARI DELL
5300 SJS 95135 855-H5
CRIBARI HILLS
5300 SJS 95135 855-H5
CRIBARI KNOLLS
5100 SJS 95135 855-H5
CRIBARI VALE
5000 SJS 95135 855-H5
CRICKET HILL RD
10100 CPTO 95014 851-J1
CRIDER CT
100 LGTS 95032 873-J7

CRIMSON DR
5900 SJS 95120 874-B7
CRIMSONBERRY WY
500 SJS 95129 852-B7
CRINAN DR
1800 SJS 95122 854-G1
CRIOLLO WY
1900 MGH 95037 917-D6
CRISANTO AV
1900 MTVW 94040 811-G4
CRISP AV
19300 SAR 95070 872-G3
CRIST DR
2000 LALT 94024 832-A5
CRISTAL CT
- SJS 95127 835-C3
CRISTICH LN
100 CMBL 95008 853-E7
500 CMBL 95008 873-E1
CRISTINA AV
1300 SJS 95125 854-B3
CRISTO REY DR
2400 LALT 94024 831-H6
2400 CPTO 95014 831-H6
22500 SCIC 94024 831-H6
23700 SCIC 95014 831-H6
25200 LALT 94024 832-A6
CRITTENDEN LN
2100 MTVW 94043 791-J7
2100 MTVW 94043 792-A7
CROCKER CT
- SJS 95111 875-A2
CROCKER DR
- SJS 95111 875-B2
CROCKER LN
7100 GIL 95020 978-B3
CROCKER WY
2200 SCL 95051 832-J2
CROCKETT AV
600 CMBL 95008 853-B7
900 CMBL 95008 873-B1
CROCUS CT
- SMCo 94025 790-E6
1100 SUNV 94086 832-H2
CROCUS DR
4500 SJS 95136 874-F2
CROFT DR
2700 SJS 95148 855-D2
CROMART CT
100 SUNV 94087 832-E4
CRONER AV
1700 MLPK 94025 790-E5
1700 SMCo 94025 790-E5
CRONER PL
- SJS 95131 814-D6
CRONIN DR
- SCL 95051 833-A7
- SCL 95051 853-A1
CRONWELL DR
1300 CMBL 95008 853-G5
1900 CMBL 95125 853-G5
CROOK RD
- SCrC 95033 913-A7
CROOKED CREEK DR
900 LALT 94024 831-G4
CROPLEY AV
2600 SJS 95132 814-F2
CROPLEY CT
3300 SJS 95132 814-F2
CROSBY CT
2700 SCL 95051 833-B3
6700 SJS 95129 852-E3
CROSBY PL
4100 PA 94306 811-C4
CROSLEY CT
1400 SJS 95132 814-G3
CROSS WY
- LGTS 95030 893-B1
1500 SJS 95125 854-C3
CROSSBOW CT
1000 SJS 95120 874-E6
CROSSBROOK CT
6000 SJS 95120 874-E6
CROSSFIELD CT
6000 SJS 95120 874-E6
CROSSGATES LN
1200 SJS 95120 874-C7
1200 SJS 95120 894-D1
CROSSLEES DR
400 SJS 95111 875-C2
CROSSMAN AV
1200 SUNV 94089 812-G3
CROSSMILL CT
2800 SJS 95121 854-J3
CROSSMONT CIR
5900 SJS 95120 874-D6
5900 SCIC 95120 874-D6
CROSSMONT CT
6000 SJS 95120 874-D6
CROSSPOINT CT
1000 SJS 95120 874-D6
CROSS SPRINGS CT
1000 SJS 95120 874-D6
CROSS SPRINGS DR
1000 SJS 95120 874-D6
CROSSVIEW CIR
6000 SJS 95120 874-D6
CROSSVIEW CT
5900 SJS 95120 874-D6
CROSSWIND CT
1000 SJS 95120 874-D6
CROTHERS RD
10200 SCIC 95127 815-B6
10200 SCIC 95127 835-D1
11800 SJS 95127 815-B6
CROTHERS WY
300 SCIC 94305 790-H7
CROW CT
400 SJS 95123 874-H4
1600 SUNV 94087 832-E5
CROW LN
5600 SJS 95123 874-H4
CROW TR
17800 SCIC 95033 912-J2

CROW TR
17800 SCIC 95033 913-C2
CROWDER AV
1800 SJS 95124 873-H3
CROWLEY AV
1100 SCL 95051 833-B4
CROWN BLVD
6500 SJS 95120 894-E2
CROWNER AV
14400 MGH 95046 937-D4
14400 SCIC 95046 937-D4
CROWN RIDGE COM
- FRMT 94539 794-B2
CROY RD
4600 SCIC 95037 936-A3
4900 SCIC 95037 935-C5
CROYDEN CT
500 SUNV 94087 832-E4
CROYDON AV
5600 SJS 95118 874-C4
CRUCERO CT
1400 SJS 95122 834-G7
CRUCERO DR
1300 SJS 95122 834-G7
CRUDEN BAY CT
- SJS 95138 855-E6
CRUDEN BAY WY
- GIL 95020 977-E4
CRUMP CT
5800 SJS 95120 874-B6
CRYSTAL CT
- MPS 95035 793-J7
- MPS 95035 794-A7
CRYSTAL DR
2400 SCL 95051 833-A1
18000 MGH 95037 916-F7
CRYSTALBERRY TER
500 SJS 95129 853-B2
CRYSTAL CREEK DR
2900 SJS 95133 814-G6
CRYSTAL GLEN LN
800 SCL 95050 833-A5
CRYSTAL HILLS CT
- SJS 95138 855-F6
CRYSTAL HOLLOW PL
- SJS 95138 855-C5
CRYSTAL SPRINGS CT
6700 SJS 95120 894-D2
CRYSTAL SPRINGS DR
6400 SJS 95120 894-D2
CRYSTAL SPRINGS WY
- SJS 95123 875-D2
CUCIZ LN
1300 MPS 95035 814-D2
CUEN CT
3600 SJS 95136 874-D1
CUERNAVACA CT
1400 SJS 95120 874-B7
CUERNAVACA CIRCULO
1200 MTVW 94040 832-A1
CUESTA CT
3400 SJS 95148 835-D5
CUESTA DR
- LALT 94022 811-E7
200 MTVW 94040 811-G7
200 LALT 94024 811-E7
2100 MPS 95035 814-E1
3200 SJS 95148 835-D6
CUESTA DE LOS GATOS WY
100 LGTS 95032 873-B7
CULBERTSON DR
10000 CPTO 95014 852-G2
CULLEN CT
- CMBL 95008 853-B7
- CMBL 95008 873-B1
CULLEN LN
3300 SCIC 95020 958-G6
CULLIGAN BLVD
1000 SJS 95120 894-D1
1100 SJS 95120 874-D7
CULLODEN CT
1000 SJS 95121 855-A5
CULLUM ST
500 HOLL 95023 1039-J4
CULP DR
8500 GIL 95020 977-G1
CULPEPPER DR
1200 SJS 95121 854-H2
CULVERT DR
6300 SJS 95123 874-J7
CUMBERLAND AV
800 SUNV 94087 832-C1
CUMBERLAND DR
700 GIL 95020 977-H4
12700 SAR 95070 852-F6
CUMBERLAND PL
1000 SJS 95125 854-D3
CUMBRA VISTA CT
13000 LAH 94022 831-A1
CUMMINS AV
- SCIC 94035 812-B2
- SCIC 94043 812-B2
CUMULUS AV
100 SUNV 94087 832-E2
CUNARD CT
3400 SJS 95132 814-J2
CUNNINGHAM AV
1500 SJS 95122 854-H1
1600 SJS 95122 834-H7
2100 SJS 95148 835-A6
2100 SJS 95122 835-A6
CUNNINGHAM CT
2000 SJS 95148 835-C5
CUNNINGHAM PL
20400 SAR 95070 852-D7
CUNNINGHAM ST
1600 SCL 95050 833-C3
CUPERTINO RD
22200 CPTO 95014 832-A7

CUPERTINO RD
22200 CPTO 95014 852-A1
CUPPLES CT
600 SCL 95051 833-B6
CURCI DR
1400 SJS 95126 853-H3
CURCI PARK CT
- SCIC 95126 853-H3
CURCI PARK LN
- SCIC 95126 853-H3
- SJS 95126 853-H3
CURETON PL
300 SCIC 95127 835-A2
300 SJS 95127 835-A2
CURIE CT
6400 SJS 95123 875-A7
CURIE DR
200 SJS 95119 875-C7
300 SJS 95123 875-A7
500 SJS 95123 874-J7
CURLING CT
3200 SJS 95121 855-B3
CURRAGHMORE CT
4000 SJS 95136 854-E5
CURRENT DR
6200 SJS 95123 874-J7
CURRY AV
- MGH 95037 916-G4
CURRY CT
12400 SAR 95070 852-H6
CURSOR CT
- SJS 95134 813-C1
CURTIS AV
900 SCL 95051 832-J5
E CURTIS AV
- MPS 95035 814-A2
CURTIS ST
800 MLPK 94025 790-F3
CURTIS WY
700 MLPK 94025 790-G4
CURTISS AV
1100 SJS 95125 854-B3
CURTNER AV
- CMBL 95008 873-E1
100 SJS 95125 854-D4
200 PA 94306 811-C1
200 SCIC 95008 873-E1
400 SJS 95008 873-E1
900 SJS 95124 873-G1
1600 SJS 95125 853-J7
1700 SJS 95124 853-G7
CURTNER CT
400 MPS 95035 794-A3
CURTNER DR
400 MPS 95035 794-A4
CURTNER GLEN CT
2600 SJS 95008 873-F1
CUSHMAN ST
1500 HOLL 95023 1040-A6
CUSTER DR
2500 SJS 95124 853-H7
2500 SJS 95124 873-H1
CUTFORTH CT
1300 SJS 95132 814-F5
CUVILLY CT
- SAR 95070 872-D4
CUVILLY WY
- SAR 95070 872-D4
CYCLAMEN CT
- SJS 95111 875-A2
CYNTHIA AV
18600 CPTO 95014 852-H2
CYNTHIA LN
1000 SJS 95129 852-E3
CYNTHIA WY
2000 LALT 94024 832-A5
CYPRESS AV
- SCL 95117 853-D1
- SCL 95117 833-D7
100 SCL 95050 833-E7
300 SUNV 94086 812-F5
S CYPRESS AV
300 SJS 95117 853-C2
400 SCIC 95117 853-D1
CYPRESS CT
- LALT 94022 811-D6
1200 GIL 95020 977-G2
10500 CPTO 95014 832-F6
CYPRESS DR
- HOLL 95023 1040-E5
300 MPS 95035 813-H1
300 LALT 94022 811-D6
10400 CPTO 95014 832-F7
CYPRESS LN
500 CMBL 95008 853-F5
3700 PA 94306 811-C1
6200 SJS 95138 875-F6
CYPRESS RDG
2500 SCIC 95148 835-E6
CYPRESS ST
- HOLL 95023 1040-D5
100 RDWC 94061 790-B1
1100 EPA 94303 791-C2
CYPRESS WY
16200 LGTS 95030 893-C1
CYPRESS PARK CT
400 SJS 95136 874-F1
CYPRESS POINT DR
500 MTVW 94043 811-J4
500 MTVW 94043 812-A4
CYRIL PL
18900 SAR 95070 852-H6
CYRUS AV
3000 SJS 95124 873-H1
CYRUS HEIGHTS LN
17200 LGTS 95032 893-G2
17200 SCIC 95032 893-G2

D

D CT
- GIL 95020 977-E1
D RD
15000 SCIC 95127 815-D6

D ST
- SUNV 94089 812-H3
- SBnC 95075 1061-A5
300 MLPK 94025 790-G3
500 HOLL 95023 1039-J5
S D ST
- SUNV 94089 812-J3
DADE CT
6400 SJS 95123 875-B7
6400 SJS 95123 895-B1
DADIS WY
600 SJS 95111 854-H4
DADO ST
600 SJS 95131 813-J6
DAFFODIL CT
700 SUNV 94086 832-F2
1400 MGH 95037 917-D6
DAFFODIL DR
- SBnC 95023 1040-D3
DAFFODIL PL
- GIL 95020 977-G1
DAFFODIL TER
- FRMT 94539 793-J3
DAFFODIL WY
700 SJS 95117 853-B3
DAGGETT DR
- SJS 95134 813-G5
DAGMAR CT
700 SJS 95136 874-E1
DAGMAR DR
13400 SAR 95070 872-H1
14600 SAR 95070 852-G7
DAHILL CT
3500 SJS 95121 855-C3
DAHLBERG CT
2100 SCIC 95037 936-F2
DAHLBERG DR
2000 SCIC 95037 936-F1
DAHLIA CT
- SJS 95133 814-E7
1100 SUNV 94086 832-H2
DAHLIA DR
1100 SUNV 94086 832-H2
DAHLIA LP
- SJS 95126 833-G4
DAHLIA WY
15900 SCIC 95032 873-D6
15900 LGTS 95032 873-D6
DAILEY AV
700 SJS 95123 874-F4
DAILEY RD
- SCIC 94035 812-B3
- SCIC 94043 812-B3
DAIMLER CT
5300 SJS 95123 874-H3
DAISY CT
1000 SUNV 94086 832-H2
DAISY DR
- SJS 95123 875-B5
DAISY LN
400 EPA 94303 791-D2
8100 GIL 95020 977-G2
DAISYDELL CT
400 SJS 95129 853-B2
DAKAN CT
3100 SJS 95136 854-D7
DAKE AV
4100 PA 94306 811-F2
DAKIN AV
1900 SMCo 94025 790-D6
DAKOTA DR
600 SJS 95111 854-H5
700 MGH 95037 917-B6
DALBON CT
6900 SJS 95119 875-F6
DALE AV
900 MTVW 94040 812-A7
1200 MTVW 94040 832-A1
1300 SJS 95125 854-A5
DALE DR
- SCIC 95127 834-J2
- SCIC 95127 835-A2
DALE HOLLOW CT
- MGH 95037 936-J2
DALEHURST DR
1600 LALT 94024 831-J4
DALEWOOD CT
700 SJS 95120 894-J3
DALLAS CT
1600 LALT 94024 831-J3
3100 SCL 95051 833-A3
DALLAS DR
200 SCIC 95008 873-E1
DALMA DR
- MTVW 94041 811-J6
- MTVW 94041 812-A6
DALMENY CT
6800 SJS 95120 894-H2
DALMUIR CT
2500 SJS 95121 855-D5
DALTON DR
1600 SJS 95124 873-J5
1700 MPS 95035 794-D7
DALTON PL
1800 SJS 95124 873-J5
DALTREY WY
1700 SJS 95132 814-D4
DAMASCUS CT
2300 SJS 95125 853-J6
DAMEY DR
2300 SJS 95116 834-G2
DAMIAN WY
900 LALT 94024 831-J2
DAMICO DR
2800 SJS 95148 855-D2
DAMON LN
13900 SAR 95070 872-A1
13900 SCIC 95070 872-A1
DAMSEN DR
200 SJS 95116 834-G2
DAN DR
- SBnC 95023 1060-F2
DANA AV
- SJS 95128 853-H1

DANA AV
- SJS 95126 853-H1
100 SJS 95128 833-G7
100 SJS 95126 833-G6
1200 PA 94301 791-A3
1300 PA 94303 791-A3
E DANA ST
800 MTVW 94041 812-A6
1200 SUNV 94086 812-B6
W DANA ST
200 MTVW 94041 811-H4
800 MTVW 94041 812-A5
DANBURY DR
1000 SJS 95129 852-F3
DANBURY LN
- RDWC 94061 790-B2
DANBY AV
1300 SJS 95132 814-F4
DANCING WIND WY
- GIL 95020 957-E6
DANDERHALL WY
2000 SJS 95121 855-C3
DANDINI CIR
1800 SJS 95128 853-G3
DANFORTH CT
1200 SJS 95121 854-H2
DANFORTH DR
600 SUNV 94087 832-D2
DANFORTH TER
700 SUNV 94087 832-D1
DANIEL CT
1200 MPS 95035 794-C5
3900 SCIC 95020 978-H1
7000 SCIC 95020 957-A7
7000 SCIC 95020 976-J1
7000 SCIC 95020 977-A1
DANIEL WY
600 SJS 95128 833-F7
3700 SCL 95051 832-H7
S DANIEL WY
300 SJS 95128 853-F1
DANIELLE PL
15000 MSER 95030 872-J4
DANIEL MALONEY DR
1700 SJS 95121 855-B3
DANNA CT
- SJS 95138 875-G6
DANNY BOY CT
900 MGH 95037 937-B5
DANRIDGE DR
6500 SJS 95129 852-E3
DANROMAS WY
1600 SJS 95129 852-F5
DANTE CT
2900 SJS 95135 855-E3
DANTE ROBLES RD
500 SBnC 95004 1037-B2
DANUBE DR
10100 CPTO 95014 852-E1
DANUBE WY
1300 SJS 95116 834-F5
DANVILLE DR
200 LGTS 95032 873-F6
DANWOOD CT
2800 SJS 95148 835-C7
DANZE DR
100 SJS 95111 875-B3
DAPHNE CT
- EPA 94303 791-D3
DAPHNE DR
1200 SJS 95129 852-F4
DAPHNE WY
- EPA 94303 791-D3
DARBYS CT
100 SJS 95110 854-D2
DARCEY LN
1400 SJS 95135 855-F2
DARDANELLI LN
100 LGTS 95032 873-B2
DARIEN WY
12700 SAR 95070 852-G6
DARKNELL CT
3500 SJS 95148 835-E6
DARKNELL WY
2700 SJS 95148 835-E6
DARK STAR CT
14800 MGH 95037 937-B5
DARLENE AV
1400 SJS 95125 854-A7
DARLING LN
13400 LAH 94022 811-D7
DARLINGTON CT
4200 PA 94306 811-D2
DARNELL CT
2300 SJS 95133 834-F1
DARNIS CIR
2100 MGH 95037 917-E6
DARRINGTON CT
1000 SUNV 94087 832-B5
DARRYDOON CT
1200 SJS 95121 855-A5
DARRYL CT
3600 SJS 95130 853-C4
DARRYL DR
- CMBL 95008 853-C5
1300 SJS 95130 853-C4
1500 CMBL 95130 853-C4
DARTMOOR WY
6400 SJS 95129 852-E4
DARTMOUTH DR
5400 SJS 95118 874-A5
DARTMOUTH LN
1000 LALT 94024 831-H2
DARTMOUTH PL
700 GIL 95020 977-J4
DARTMOUTH ST
2000 PA 94306 810-J1
2100 PA 94306 811-A1
DARTSHIRE CT
1400 SUNV 94087 832-G4
DARTSHIRE WY
700 SUNV 94087 832-F4
DARWIN CT
1300 SJS 95122 834-G7

DARWIN WY
1700 SJS 95122 834-H7
DARYA CT
- MTVW 94043 812-B5
DARYLVIEW CT
- SJS 95138 855-E6
DASH CT
5800 SJS 95120 874-B6
DASHWOOD AV
2400 SJS 95121 855-D3
DATE BLOSSOM CT
5400 SJS 95123 875-A3
DATORO DR
2100 SJS 95130 853-A7
DAUPHINE PL
200 LALT 94022 811-E6
DAURINE CT
2900 SCIC 95020 958-F7
DAVENPORT CT
500 SUNV 94087 832-D5
DAVENPORT DR
500 SJS 95127 835-B2
DAVENPORT WY
200 PA 94306 811-D2
DAVES AV
17500 MSER 95030 873-A5
17700 LGTS 95030 873-A5
17900 MSER 95030 872-J5
18200 SCIC 95030 872-J5
DAVID AV
300 CMBL 95008 853-E4
2800 SJS 95128 853-E4
3000 SJS 95008 853-E4
3100 PA 94303 791-D6
DAVID CT
3100 PA 94303 791-D6
8400 GIL 95020 977-J1
DAVID DR
- SBnC 95023 1060-C2
DAVID LN
1300 MPS 95035 814-D2
DAVIDSON AV
4300 SCIC 95020 998-F1
DAVIDWOOD WY
2900 SJS 95148 855-D1
DA VINCI CIR
- MGH 95037 937-A5
DA VINCI CT
- SJS 95148 855-F1
DAVIS CT
22600 SCIC 95120 895-C4
DAVIS ST
1200 SJS 95126 833-F6
4000 SCL 95054 813-D5
DAVISON AV
10400 CPTO 95014 852-F2
DAWES CT
2800 SJS 95148 855-D2
DAWN DR
500 SUNV 94087 832-D2
DAWN LN
12100 LAH 94022 811-A7
DAWN WY
600 GIL 95020 977-J7
DAWNBROOK CT
800 SJS 95111 855-A5
DAWNRIDGE DR
24300 LAH 94024 831-E3
DAWNVIEW CT
900 SJS 95136 874-D3
DAWSON AV
400 SJS 95125 854-C3
DAWSON DR
300 SCL 95051 832-H7
11600 LAH 94024 831-E3
DAY CT
2600 SCL 95051 833-B3
DAY RD
- SCIC 95020 957-G6
400 GIL 95020 957-E5
800 SCIC 95046 957-A4
DAYLIGHT WY
2900 SJS 95111 854-G6
DAYO CT
2800 SJS 95148 855-D2
DAYTON AV
300 SCL 95051 832-J7
DAYTONA DR
1900 SJS 95122 834-J6
DE ALTURA COMS
- SJS 95126 833-G4
DEAN AV
1100 SJS 95125 854-A4
DEAN CT
22000 CPTO 95014 852-A1
DEANNA CT
1100 MGH 95037 916-G7
DEANNA DR
1000 MLPK 94025 790-D6
DEANS PLACE WY
3700 SJS 95121 855-B4
DE ANZA AV
100 SJS 95136 854-G7
N DE ANZA BLVD
10000 CPTO 95014 832-E7
10000 CPTO 95014 852-E1
S DE ANZA BLVD
900 SJS 95129 852-D3
1300 CPTO 95014 852-E2
DE ANZA CIR S
22200 CPTO 95014 852-A2
DE ANZA CT
800 MPS 95035 794-B5
14500 MGH 95037 937-C5
DE ANZA LN
200 LALT 94022 811-E7
DE ANZA WY
1500 SJS 95125 853-J4
DEARBORN PL
800 GIL 95020 977-J4
DEARWELL WY
- SJS 95138 875-D4
DEB CT
1300 SJS 95120 874-C7

STREET Block City ZIP Pg-Grid

DEBBIE CT
3100 SCIC 95020 958-F7
DEBBIE LN
13500 SAR 95070 872-D1
20500 SAR 95070 852-D7
DEBBIE RD
17600 SCrC 95033 912-F6
DEBELL DR
- ATN 94027 790-G2
DE BELL RD
14300 LAH 94022 811-C5
DEBOER LN
700 SJS 95111 855-A6
DEBORAH DR
2200 SCL 95050 833-C2
DEBRA WY
3600 SJS 95117 853-C2
DE BRUIN WY
10800 SCIC 95046 957-F4
DEBUSSY TER
- SUNV 94087 832-E2
DEBUT CT
800 SJS 95134 813-F2
DE CARLI CT
500 CMBL 95008 873-C1
DECATUR DR
1800 SJS 95122 834-H6
DECATUR RD
18500 MSER 95030 872-H6
18500 SCIC 95030 872-H6
DECKER AV
1600 SCIC 95046 937-H5
DECKER WY
- SCIC 95127 835-A1
100 SCIC 95127 834-J1
DECLARATION CT
100 SJS 95116 834-H3
DECLARATION DR
2500 SJS 95116 834-H3
DECLARATION WY
100 SJS 95116 834-H3
DECORAH LN
- CMBL 95008 853-G6
DECOTO CT
900 MPS 95035 794-B5
DEDALERA DR
200 SMCo 94028 810-E4
DEDERICK CT
- SJS 95125 854-D7
DEE ST
800 SUNV 94087 832-D2
DEEDHAM CT
3800 SJS 95148 835-G7
DEEDHAM DR
3500 SJS 95148 835-F7
DEEP CLIFF DR
10600 CPTO 95014 852-A2
DEEP CREEK CT
1800 SJS 95148 835-D4
DEEP HARBOR CT
- SJS 95111 854-J5
DEEP PURPLE WY
5500 SJS 95123 874-F3
DEEPROSE PL
10100 CPTO 95014 852-F1
DEEPWELL CT
21100 SAR 95070 872-C3
DEEPWELL LN
- LALT 94022 831-D1
DEER CT
500 SJS 95123 874-H4
DEER CANYON LN
14400 SAR 95070 872-C2
DEER CREEK CT
1700 SJS 95148 835-D4
DEER CREEK RD
3400 PA 94304 810-J4
3400 SCIC 94304 810-J4
3400 PA 94304 811-A4
DEER CREST CT
- SJS 95138 855-F6
DEERFIELD DR
1500 SJS 95129 852-G5
13600 LAH 94022 811-D7
DEERFIELD RD
- SCIC 95037 936-F3
23300 SCrC 95033 913-C7
DEER HILL RD
- SCIC 95037 917-D3
DEER HOLLOW CT
6500 SJS 95120 874-F7
DEER HOLLOW DR
6400 SJS 95120 874-F7
DEER ISLE DR
2700 SJS 95121 855-E4
DEERLAND CT
5900 SJS 95124 873-J7
DEER MEADOW CT
900 SJS 95122 854-G2
DEER MEADOW LN
100 PTLV 94028 810-C5
DEER PARK CT
14500 LGTS 95032 893-G2
14500 SCIC 95032 893-G2
DEERPARK CT
20500 SAR 95070 872-D1
DEER PARK LN
- PTLV 94028 810-C5
DEER PARK RD
17200 LGTS 95032 893-G1
17200 SCIC 95032 893-G1
DEER PATH DR
- SMCo 94028 830-E4
DEER PATH RD
24000 SCIC 95070 871-G3
DEER RIDGE CIR
100 SJS 95123 874-G7
DEER RUN CIR
- SJS 95136 874-J2
DEER RUN CT
17900 MGH 95037 936-F1
DEER SPRING CT
14500 SAR 95070 872-C2
DEER SPRINGS WY
27200 LAH 94022 830-J2
DEER TRAIL CT
13400 SAR 95070 852-B7
DEER VIEW TER
- FRMT 94539 794-B1
DEERWOOD CT
300 MTVW 94040 811-F4
DEERWOOD DR
2800 SJS 95148 835-C7
DEEVA CT
2800 SCIC 95020 958-F7
DE FALCO WY
1300 SJS 95131 814-C7
1300 SJS 95131 834-C1
DE FOE DR
7400 CPTO 95014 852-D2
DEFRANCE AV
- MTVW 94043 812-B2
- SCIC 94043 812-B2
DEGAS CT
10200 CPTO 95014 851-J1
DEGAS RD
100 PTLV 94028 810-C5
DE GUIGNE DR
300 SUNV 94086 812-H7
DEHAVILLAND CT
19400 SAR 95070 852-G6
DEHAVILLAND DR
19100 SAR 95070 852-G6
DELACROIX CT
- SJS 95135 855-G1
DE LA CRUZ BLVD
500 SJS 95110 813-F6
500 SJS 95131 813-F6
500 SCL 95054 813-E5
600 SJS 95054 813-F6
700 SJS 95054 833-F2
700 SJS 95110 833-F2
2100 SCL 95050 833-F2
2500 SJS 95050 833-F2
DE LA FARGE DR
7400 CPTO 95014 852-D2
DELANCEY CT
- SJS 95135 855-F3
DELAND AV
700 SJS 95128 853-H2
DELANO CT
1300 SJS 95121 855-B2
DELANTE TER
- SJS 95118 874-A4
DE LA PENA AV
1800 SCL 95050 833-D5
DEL AVION LN
- SJS 95138 875-G5
DEL AVION WY
- SJS 95138 875-G5
DELAWARE AV
700 SJS 95123 874-F4
2400 RDWC 94061 790-A3
DELAWARE TR
17600 SCIC 95033 913-A2
DELBARR CT
2000 SJS 95125 854-C4
DELBERT WY
900 SJS 95126 853-J3
DEL CAMBRE DR
1000 SJS 95129 852-J3
DEL CANTO DR
200 SJS 95119 875-C6
DEL CARLO CT
100 LGTS 95032 873-D6
DEL CENTRO WY
700 LALT 94024 831-F1
DEL CERRO CT
15800 LGTS 95032 873-E5
DELFINO WY
1300 MLPK 94025 790-D5
DEL FRANCO CT
2100 SJS 95131 814-A4
DEL FRANCO ST
2100 SJS 95131 814-A4
DELGADO CT
3700 SJS 95008 853-B7
DELIA ST
100 SCIC 95127 814-J7
100 SCIC 95127 834-J1
200 SJS 95127 814-J7
DELL AV
400 MTVW 94043 811-F2
900 CMBL 95008 873-D1
900 CMBL 95008 853-D7
DELL CT
1600 SJS 95118 873-J4
DEL LOMA CT
4700 SJS 95008 873-A1
DEL LOMA DR
2800 SJS 95008 873-A1
2900 CMBL 95008 873-A1
DELLWOOD DR
- SJS 95131 814-A4
DELLWOOD WY
5200 SJS 95118 874-B4
DEL MAR AV
800 SJS 95128 853-G3
DEL MAR DR
600 HOLL 95023 1040-B5
DELMAS AV
- SJS 95110 834-A7
- SJS 95113 834-A7
200 SJS 95126 834-A7
600 SJS 95125 854-B2
DEL MEDIO AV
100 MTVW 94040 811-E3
DEL MEDIO CT
2700 MTVW 94040 811-E2
DEL MONTE AV
- LALT 94022 811-D4
2000 SCL 95051 832-J2
16400 MGH 95037 937-A1
17300 MGH 95037 917-A7
17400 MGH 95037 916-J6
DEL MONTE CIR
200 MGH 95037 916-H6
DEL MONTE DR
600 HOLL 95023 1040-B4
DEL MONTE LN
200 MGH 95037 916-J6
DEL MONTE PL
900 SJS 95117 853-D2
DEL MONTE WY
23000 SCrC 95033 913-D7
DELNA MANOR LN
1100 SJS 95128 853-F3
DELNO ST
1000 SJS 95126 833-G5
DEL NORTE AV
200 SUNV 94086 812-F5
1000 MLPK 94025 790-H1
DEL NORTE DR
3400 SJS 95132 814-G3
DE LOACH CT
1300 SJS 95125 853-G4
DEL ORO CT
600 CMBL 95008 853-C5
5500 SJS 95124 873-G6
DEL ORO DR
5400 SJS 95124 873-H6
DEL ORO PL
5500 SJS 95124 873-G6
DEL ORO WY
1100 GIL 95020 977-F1
DEL PASO AV
1700 SJS 95124 873-H3
DELPHI CIR
200 LALT 94022 811-E5
DELPHI CT
200 LALT 94022 811-E4
DEL PRADO DR
- CMBL 95008 853-C6
DEL REY AV
500 SUNV 94086 812-D5
4400 SJS 95111 875-A1
DEL REY CT
300 SJS 95111 875-A1
8600 GIL 95020 977-F1
DELRIDGE DR
400 SJS 95111 875-C2
DEL RIO CIR
- GIL 95020 957-H7
DEL RIO CT
900 MPS 95035 794-B5
1000 HOLL 95023 1039-H5
DEL RIO DR
900 HOLL 95023 1039-J5
6900 SJS 95119 875-E7
7000 SJS 95119 895-E1
DEL ROBLE PL
18300 SCIC 95120 894-G1
18300 SJS 95120 894-G1
DEL ROBLES CT
6100 SJS 95119 875-C6
DEL ROY CT
600 CMBL 95008 853-C5
DELSEA PL
6000 SJS 95123 874-E5
DELSON CT
13100 LAH 94022 811-A7
DELTA CT
8300 GIL 95020 977-F2
DELTA DR
8100 GIL 95020 977-F2
DELTA RD
2900 SJS 95135 855-F3
DELUCA DR
1500 SJS 95131 814-C6
DEL VAILE CT
800 MPS 95035 794-B5
DELYNN WY
1100 SJS 95125 854-B6
DEMARET DR
4600 SCL 95054 813-D4
DE MARIETTA AV
1600 SJS 95126 853-G4
DE MARIETTA CT
1700 SJS 95126 853-G4
DE MATTEI CT
1000 SJS 95112 834-C3
DEMEREST LN
5400 SJS 95138 875-C3
DEMETER ST
800 SJS 95117 853-B3
DE MILLE DR
4100 SJS 95117 853-A3
4100 SJS 95129 853-A3
DEMOCRACY WY
3000 SCL 95054 813-A4
DEMPSEY RD
- MPS 95035 794-C7
400 MPS 95035 814-C1
DEMPSEY WY
1100 MPS 95035 794-C6
DEMPSTER AV
10300 CPTO 95014 832-B7
DENAIR AV
2200 SJS 95122 854-H1
DENALI DR
- SCIC 95037 937-A2
300 MGH 95037 937-A2
DENALI WY
1500 SJS 95122 854-J1
DENEVI DR
2400 SJS 95130 853-A7
DENEVI LN
16500 SCIC 95030 872-H7
DENIO AV
- GIL 95020 957-H5
- SCIC 95020 957-H5
500 SCIC 95020 958-A4
DENISE DR
2200 SCL 95050 833-C4
DENISE LN
400 SMCo 94061 790-B4
DENISE WY
1100 SJS 95125 854-C6
DENISON AV
10100 CPTO 95014 832-F7
DENNIS AV
300 SUNV 94086 812-C7
1400 MPS 95035 794-D6
DENNIS CT
10000 SCIC 95127 835-A3
DENNIS DR
900 PA 94303 791-D5
DENNIS LN
1500 MTVW 94040 811-G6
DENNYWOOD CT
2800 SJS 95148 835-D7
DENSMORE CT
3300 SJS 95148 835-E7
DENSMORE DR
2900 SJS 95148 835-E7
DENT AV
4900 SJS 95118 874-A3
DENTON WY
3200 SJS 95121 855-C3
DENTWOOD DR
1200 SJS 95118 874-B4
DENVER DR
1000 CMBL 95008 853-B5
DEODAR LN
16200 MSER 95030 872-H6
DEODAR ST
- PA 94306 811-D3
DEODAR WY
200 SUNV 94086 812-F7
200 SUNV 94086 832-F1
DEODARA DR
10400 CPTO 95014 832-F7
DEODARA GROVE CT
5300 SJS 95123 875-A3
DEODORA DR
- ATN 94027 790-G1
500 LALT 94024 831-J5
2100 LALT 94024 832-A5
DE PALMA CT
1400 SJS 95120 894-A1
DE PALMA DR
1400 SJS 95120 894-A1
DE PALMA LN
20000 CPTO 95014 852-E1
DE PAUL CIR
11900 SCIC 95046 938-B7
DE PAUL DR
18500 MGH 95037 917-A4
DE PAUL PL
2200 SCL 95051 832-J2
DEPOT CT
- GIL 95020 978-A3
DEPOT ST
13000 SCIC 95046 937-E6
17000 MGH 95037 917-A7
DERBE DR
800 SJS 95122 854-F1
DERBY CT
600 SUNV 94087 832-E4
DERBYSHIRE DR
1000 CPTO 95014 852-C3
DEREK DR
5100 SJS 95136 874-J3
DERMOTT DR
1100 SJS 95129 853-A3
DEROCHE CT
1300 SUNV 94087 832-B4
DE ROSE WY
1500 SJS 95126 853-G3
DERRY LN
500 MLPK 94025 790-F3
DE SANKA AV
12300 SAR 95070 852-E6
DESCANSA CT
15800 MGH 95037 937-A3
DESCANSO DR
- SJS 95134 813-F3
DESDEMONA CT
1500 SJS 95121 854-J4
1500 SJS 95121 855-A2
DESERT BLOOM PL
- GIL 95020 957-F6
DESERT FLAME DR
6200 SJS 95120 874-C7
6300 SJS 95120 894-C1
DESERT ISLE DR
800 SJS 95117 853-B3
DESERT SANDS WY
- SJS 95123 875-B4
DESERT WILLOW DR
- SJS 95123 875-D5
DESERTWOOD LN
3200 SJS 95132 814-E2
DESIDERIO WY
- GIL 95020 957-H7
DESIN DR
4400 SJS 95118 874-C2
DESMET DR
- SJS 95125 854-C7
DESMET LN
- SJS 95125 854-C7
DESMET WY
- SJS 95125 854-C7
DES MOINES PL
600 SJS 95133 814-G7
DE SOTO AV
3600 SCL 95051 832-H7
DE SOTO DR
300 LGTS 95032 873-D4
700 PA 94303 791-B4
2400 SJS 95124 873-D4
DE SOTO RD
- SJS 95134 813-G3
DESTRY CT
100 SJS 95136 875-A3
DE TRACY ST
1400 SJS 95128 853-E5
DETROIT CT
600 SJS 95133 814-G7
DE VARONA PL
2300 SCL 95050 833-C5
DEVCON CT
100 SJS 95112 833-J1
DEVCON DR
200 SJS 95112 833-J1
DEVERON CT
7500 SJS 95135 855-J6
DE VIDA CT
1400 HOLL 95023 1040-D5
DEVIDE CT
- HOLL 95023 1040-D5
DEVILLE CT
8100 GIL 95020 977-F2
DE VILLE WY
6500 SJS 95129 852-F3
DEVIN DR
2300 SCIC 95148 835-E5
E DEVINE ST
- SJS 95112 834-B6
W DEVINE ST
- SJS 95113 834-B6
100 SJS 95110 834-B6
DEVLIN CT
600 SJS 95133 834-B2
DEVON AV
18500 SAR 95070 852-H7
DEVON PL
2100 MPS 95035 794-A2
DEVON WY
6800 SJS 95129 852-E4
DEVONA TER
1000 SUNV 94087 832-B4
DEVON PARK CT
5100 SJS 95136 874-F3
DEVONSHIRE AV
- MTVW 94043 812-B3
2700 SMCo 94063 790-C1
DEVONSHIRE CT
500 MTVW 94043 812-B3
DEVONSHIRE DR
6300 SJS 95129 852-F3
DEVONSHIRE WY
700 SUNV 94087 832-F4
DEVOS CT
3400 SCL 95051 832-J3
DEVOTO ST
800 MTVW 94041 812-A7
DEVRI CT
2500 MTVW 94043 811-F2
DEVRIES CT
10000 SCIC 95020 957-D6
DEWEY CIR
- MGH 95037 937-C5
DEWEY WY
6200 SJS 95123 874-J7
DEWITT AV
16100 SCIC 95037 936-J3
16700 MGH 95037 936-J1
17600 MGH 95037 916-H7
DEXTER AV
- SMCo 94063 790-D1
DEXTER DR
5300 SJS 95123 874-J3
21300 CPTO 95014 832-C7
DEYON PL
6600 GIL 95020 978-A5
DEZAHARA WY
26900 LAH 94022 831-A2
DIABLO AV
200 MTVW 94043 811-F3
DIABLO CT
300 PA 94306 811-E2
DIABLO DR
1300 HOLL 95023 1040-D6
DIABLO WY
1200 SJS 95120 894-D1
DIABLO HILLS RD
- SBnC 95023 1060-H3
- SBnC 95075 1060-H3
- SBnC 95075 1061-A4
DIADEM DR
700 SJS 95116 834-H4
DIAL WY
5900 SJS 95129 852-F4
DIAMENTE CT
1800 SJS 95116 834-F3
DIAMOND AV
14000 SJS 95127 835-A4
DIAMOND CT
1100 LALT 94024 831-G2
DIAMOND WY
200 MPS 95035 793-H6
DIAMOND HEAD DR
3500 SJS 95136 854-G7
DIAMOND OAKS CT
21200 SAR 95070 852-C6
DIANA AV
300 MGH 95037 917-A7
800 SJS 95116 834-H5
1000 SCIC 95037 917-E4
DIANA LN
700 SJS 95116 834-H4
DIANA PL
100 SJS 95116 834-H3
DIANE CT
- SBnC 95023 1060-G3
8400 GIL 95020 977-H1
DIANE MARIE WY
2400 SCL 95050 833-C5
DIANNE DR
2200 SCL 95050 833-C4
12600 LAH 94022 831-D1
DIAS DR
1400 SCIC 95046 937-F2
3200 SJS 95148 835-D6
DIBBLE CT
3000 SCL 95051 833-A6
DICKENS AV
15000 SCIC 95124 873-F4
DICKENS WY
- GIL 95020 977-H3
DICKINSON DR
4800 SJS 95111 875-B1
DICKINSON WY
600 SJS 95111 875-B1
DIDION CT
6300 SJS 95123 875-A7
DIDION WY
6300 SJS 95123 875-A7
DIDUCA WY
14800 SCIC 95032 873-F7
14800 SCIC 95032 893-G1
DIEL DR
1500 MPS 95035 794-B3
DIERICX CT
22300 MTVW 94040 832-A1
DIERICX DR
2500 MTVW 94040 832-A1
DIESSNER AV
500 SCIC 95046 937-F6
DI FIORE DR
800 SJS 95128 853-G2
DIGITAL DR
- MGH 95037 916-J6
- MGH 95037 917-A6
DI GIULIO AV
900 SCL 95050 833-E3
DI GIULIO CT
- SCL 95050 833-E2
DILLARD CT
1100 SJS 95128 853-F3
DILLION CT
2500 SJS 95133 814-F7
DILLON AV
- CMBL 95008 853-E6
DILLON LN
1700 RDWC 94061 790-A2
DINA CT
1500 SJS 95121 855-A3
DINA LN
2700 SJS 95121 855-A3
DINAHS CT
600 PA 94306 811-D3
DI NAPOLI DR
1000 SJS 95129 852-G3
DINES CT
- EPA 94303 791-C2
DINKEL CT
1100 SJS 95118 874-C3
DINKLESPIEL STATION LN
- ATN 94027 790-E2
DINNY ST
3500 SCL 95054 813-E6
DIONNE WY
900 SJS 95133 834-E1
DIOR TER
- LALT 94022 811-E6
DIPPER CIR
500 SJS 95117 853-D1
DI SALVO AV
100 SCIC 95128 833-F7
100 SJS 95128 833-F7
200 SCIC 95128 853-F1
200 SJS 95128 853-F1
DISCOVERY AV
5000 SJS 95111 875-B3
DISHMAN DR
17600 LGTS 95030 893-B2
DISK CT
- SJS 95134 813-D1
DISK DR
- SJS 95002 793-C7
- SJS 95134 793-C7
- SJS 95134 813-D1
DISNEY LN
6100 CPTO 95014 852-G2
DISTEL CIR
300 LALT 94022 811-F4
DISTEL DR
500 LALT 94022 811-E5
DITTOS LN
- LGTS 95030 893-A1
DIVISION ST
500 CMBL 95008 873-C2
E DIVISION ST
600 LGTS 95032 873-C2
600 CMBL 95008 873-C2
DIX WY
500 SJS 95125 854-C4
DIXIE DR
- SBnC 95023 1020-E7
1600 SJS 95122 854-J1
DIXON DR
2500 SCL 95051 833-B5
DIXON PL
3800 PA 94306 811-E2
DIXON RD
- MPS 95035 793-J3
100 MPS 95035 794-A3
DIXON WY
700 LALT 94022 811-C4
DIXON LANDING RD
- FRMT 94538 793-H4
- SJS 95002 793-H4
- MPS 95035 793-H4
1600 MPS 95002 793-H4
DOANE AV
1700 MTVW 94043 811-H3
DOBBIN DR
1700 SJS 95133 834-E2
DOBERN AV
2200 SJS 95116 834-H4
DOBIE DR
- SJS 95123 875-B4
DODD LN
16100 SCIC 95037 936-J3
DOGAWAY DR
100 SJS 95111 875-B2
DOGWOOD CT
800 SJS 95128 853-F4
DOGWOOD DR
6200 SJS 95138 875-F6
DOGWOOD WY
1300 MGH 95037 917-D6
DOHERTY WY
100 SMCo 94061 790-B4
DOLE WY
21600 SCIC 95033 912-H4
DOLLAR MOUNTAIN DR
200 SJS 95127 834-H1
DOLORES AV
- SCL 95128 833-D6
900 LALT 94024 831-G3
2200 SCL 95050 833-D6
21800 CPTO 95014 852-B1
DOLORES DR
400 MPS 95035 794-E7
1700 SCIC 95125 853-H4
DOLORES ST
400 SCIC 94305 810-H1
DOLPHIN DR
2400 SJS 95124 873-E4
13600 SAR 95070 872-G1
DOMA DR
400 SCIC 95117 853-C1
400 SJS 95117 853-C1
DOMAINE CT
- MGH 95037 917-E6
DOMAINE DR
- MGH 95037 917-E6
5500 SJS 95118 874-A5
DOME AV
1800 SCL 95050 833-E6
1800 SCL 95128 833-E6
DOMINICAN DR
3500 SCL 95051 832-J6
DOMINICK CT
3400 SJS 95127 835-B2
DOMINICK WY
3400 SJS 95127 835-B2
DOMINION AV
1500 SUNV 94087 832-B5
DON AV
1300 SCL 95050 833-D3
1600 SJS 95124 873-J1
DON CT
1600 MTVW 94022 811-G6
1600 MTVW 94040 811-G6
2000 SCL 95050 833-D3
DONA AV
700 SUNV 94087 832-B1
DONAHE DR
300 MPS 95035 794-A6
DONAHE PL
400 MPS 95035 794-A6
DONALD CT
3500 SJS 95127 835-B2
DONALD DR
- SBnC 95023 1060-D2
4100 PA 94306 811-C3
DON ALFONSO CT
5500 SJS 95123 874-E6
DON ALFONSO WY
300 SJS 95123 874-E6
DON ANDRES CT
400 SJS 95123 874-E6
DON ANDRES WY
5400 SJS 95123 874-E6
DONAS LN
- SBnC 95023 1060-E2
DON BASILLO CT
5400 SJS 95123 874-E6
DON BASILLO WY
300 SJS 95123 874-E6
DON CARLOS CT
400 SJS 95123 874-E6
DONCASTER WY
1200 SJS 95127 835-A4
DON CORRELLI CT
400 SJS 95123 874-H2
DON CORRELLI WY
5400 SJS 95123 874-H2
DON DEL MONICO CT
400 SJS 95123 874-E7
DONDERO WY
200 SJS 95119 875-C6
DON DIABLO CT
400 SJS 95123 874-H2
DON DIEGO CT
5400 SJS 95123 874-H2
DON EDGARDO CT
400 SJS 95123 874-H2
DON EDMONDO CT
5400 SJS 95123 874-H2
DONEGAL DR
7500 CPTO 95014 852-D4
DONEGAN WY
- SCL 95054 813-E5
DONELSON PL
14100 LAH 94022 811-B6
DON ENRICO CT
5500 SJS 95123 874-E7
DON FERNANDO WY
400 SJS 95123 874-E6
DON GIOVANNI CT
300 SJS 95123 874-E6
DONINGTON DR
1100 SJS 95129 852-G4
DONIZETTI CT
2800 SJS 95132 814-F5
DON JOSE WY
300 SJS 95123 874-H3
DON JUAN CIR
5400 SJS 95123 874-G4
DON KIRK ST
1300 LALT 94024 831-J4
DON MANRICO CT
5400 SJS 95123 874-E7
DON MARCELLO CT
5400 SJS 95123 874-E7
DON MARCO CT
400 SJS 95123 874-H2
DON MATEO CT
5400 SJS 95123 874-H2
DONNA CT
19200 SCIC 95037 916-J2
DONNA LN
1700 SJS 95124 873-H2
14400 SAR 95070 872-F2
DONNA ADELLE CT
- SCIC 95127 835-A1

STREET Block City ZIP Pg-Grid

DONNER CT
100 SUNV 94086 812-C7
DONNER DR
14800 SCIC 95124 873-G4
DONNER PL
2300 SCL 95050 833-C7
DONNER ST
- SJB 95045 1038-C4
DONNICI ST
- SJS 95136 854-E6
DONNORA CT
1100 SJS 95132 814-G5
DON OCTAVIO CT
5500 SJS 95123 874-E7
DONOHOE ST
100 EPA 94303 791-A2
100 MLPK 94025 791-A2
DONOHUE CT
1900 SJS 95131 814-D6
DONOHUE DR
1200 SJS 95131 814-D6
DONOVAN AV
2600 SCL 95051 833-B3
DONOVAN CT
2000 SJS 95125 853-G4
DON PEDRO CT
5500 SJS 95123 874-E6
DON PIZARRO CT
5400 SJS 95123 874-E7
DON RICARDO CT
5500 SJS 95123 874-E7
DON RODOLFO CT
5400 SJS 95123 874-H2
DON SCALA CT
5500 SJS 95123 874-E7
DON SEVILLE CT
400 SJS 95123 874-E6
DOOLING RD
- SBnC 95023 1020-F5
DOON CT
1100 SUNV 94087 832-H4
DOORN LN
5600 SJS 95118 874-B5
DORADO LN
15500 MSER 95030 873-A5
DORAL CT
1600 SCIC 95020 957-D6
DORALEE WY
1100 SJS 95125 854-B6
DORCEY LN
1500 SJS 95120 874-A7
DORCHESTER DR
- MTVW 94043 812-B4
19400 SAR 95070 852-F6
DORCHESTER LN
1200 SJS 95118 874-C5
DORCICH CT
- SAR 95070 852-J7
DORCICH ST
3100 SCL 95050 833-D7
3100 SCL 95117 833-D7
DOREL DR
800 SCIC 95132 814-J5
800 SJS 95132 814-J5
DORENE CT
14100 SAR 95070 872-B2
DORENE PL
6600 SJS 95120 894-F2
DORI LN
26200 LAH 94022 831-C1
DORIAN CT
900 SCIC 95127 814-H6
DORIS AV
200 SCIC 95127 834-J3
DORIS CIR
- SBnC 95023 1060-F3
DORIS CT
- RDWC 94061 790-A1
8400 GIL 95020 977-H1
10300 SCIC 95127 834-J3
DORIS DR
1800 MLPK 94025 790-E6
DORMAR CT
10600 SCIC 95127 815-B7
DORN CT
6000 SJS 95123 875-B6
DORNOCH AV
1300 SJS 95122 854-H1
DORNOCH CT
- GIL 95020 977-F3
DOROTHY AV
400 SJS 95125 854-B3
DOROTHY WY
21600 SCIC 95033 912-H3
DOROTHY ANN WY
11700 CPTO 95014 852-B4
DORRANCE CT
1900 SJS 95125 853-J6
DORRANCE DR
1700 SJS 95125 853-J6
DORRIE AV
700 SJS 95116 834-E6
DORSET WY
600 SUNV 94087 832-E4
DORSEY WY
21000 SAR 95070 872-C2
DORVAL DR
2300 SJS 95130 853-A6
DOS LOMA VISTA LN
- PTLV 94028 810-D4
DOS PALOS CT
21800 CPTO 95014 832-B7
DOT AV
- CMBL 95008 853-D6
DOT CT
1400 SJS 95120 874-B6
DOTEY CT
600 SJS 95111 875-B1
DOTS CIR
- SBnC 95023 1060-D2
DOTTIELYN AV
3700 SJS 95111 854-J6
DOUD DR
- LALT 94022 811-F6

DOUGHERTY AV
100 SCIC 95037 896-B4
500 MGH 95037 916-G3
500 SCIC 95037 916-E1
500 SCIC 95037 916-E1
DOUGLANE AV
100 SCL 95117 833-D7
100 SCL 95117 853-D1
DOUGLAS CT
- MPS 95035 794-C7
DOUGLAS ST
1400 SCIC 95126 853-H1
1400 SJS 95126 853-H1
DOUGLASS LN
14000 SAR 95070 872-E2
DOUGLASS WY
- ATN 94027 790-F3
DOVE CT
- GIL 95020 957-E7
DOVE LN
1400 SUNV 94087 832-E4
DOVE RD
- SCIC 95111 855-B6
- SJS 95111 855-B6
DOVE HILL RD
3400 SJS 95121 855-B4
DOVELA WY
3000 SJS 95118 874-A1
DOVE OAK CT
10000 CPTO 95014 831-J7
10000 CPTO 95014 851-J1
DOVER CT
100 LGTS 95032 873-E6
800 LALT 94022 831-D1
12400 SAR 95070 852-F5
DOVER ST
100 LGTS 95032 873-E5
DOVER WY
400 CMBL 95008 853-G5
10200 SCIC 95127 834-J3
DOVERTON SQ
2700 MTVW 94040 832-A2
DOVETAIL CT
- SJS 95135 875-J1
DOVETAIL WY
- GIL 95020 957-E6
DOW DR
3000 SJS 95136 854-D7
DOWDY ST
7200 GIL 95020 977-J3
DOWNING AV
400 SCIC 95128 853-F3
400 SJS 95128 853-F3
DOWNING CT
1900 SCL 95051 833-A3
DOWNING LN
700 PA 94301 790-J4
DOWNING RD
800 MPS 95035 794-E4
1000 SCIC 95035 794-E2
DOWNING OAK CT
15000 LGTS 95032 873-F5
DOWNS DR
7200 SJS 95139 895-F1
DOWNSGLEN WY
500 SJS 95133 834-G1
DOWNSWICK DR
1000 SJS 95136 874-D1
DOWNSWOOD CT
800 SJS 95120 894-H3
DOXEY CT
1400 SJS 95131 814-D6
DOXEY DR
1900 SJS 95131 814-D6
DOXEY PL
- SJS 95131 814-D6
DOYLE CIR
- SCL 95054 813-D5
DOYLE CT
4600 SJS 95129 853-A3
DOYLE DR
1400 SJS 95129 852-H4
DOYLE PL
1100 MTVW 94040 811-J7
DOYLE RD
400 SJS 95129 852-J1
4500 SJS 95129 853-A3
DOYLE ST
1000 MLPK 94025 790-F3
DRACENA LN
400 LALT 94022 811-F7
DRACENA WY
1800 SJS 95122 834-H7
DRAGONFLY CT
700 SJS 95133 834-F2
DRAGONFLY WY
700 SJS 95133 834-F1
DRAKE CT
300 SCL 95051 833-A7
19700 CPTO 95014 832-F6
DRAKE DR
19600 CPTO 95014 832-F6
DRAKE ST
400 SJS 95126 854-A1
600 SJS 95125 854-A2
DRAKES CT
100 LGTS 95032 873-D4
DRAKES BAY AV
100 LGTS 95032 873-D4
DREA RD
10900 CPTO 95014 852-A2
DREAM CATCHER WY
- GIL 95020 957-E6
DRESDEN WY
1100 SJS 95129 852-F3
DRESSER CT
- SJS 95008 873-F3
DREW AV
1700 MTVW 94043 811-H3
DREXEL WY
1000 SJS 95121 854-H3
DRIFTER DR
6200 SJS 95123 874-J6

DRIFTWOOD CT
- HOLL 95023 1040-D7
1100 SUNV 94089 812-J4
DRIFTWOOD DR
800 PA 94303 791-E7
2900 SJS 95128 853-E4
DRIFTWOOD ST
- HOLL 95023 1040-D7
- HOLL 95023 1060-D1
DRIFTWOOD TER
1100 GIL 95020 977-G3
DRISCOLL CT
600 PA 94306 811-C3
DRISCOLL PL
4100 PA 94306 811-C2
DRUCILLA DR
500 MTVW 94040 811-H7
DRUMHEAD CT
1900 SJS 95131 814-C6
DRUMM CT
7400 SJS 95139 895-G1
DRUMM PL
7500 SJS 95139 895-G2
DRUMMOND DR
16200 SCIC 95030 872-H5
DRY BED CT
4200 SCL 95054 813-C5
DRY CREEK CT
2200 SJS 95008 853-G7
16700 MGH 95037 936-J1
DRY CREEK DR
- HOLL 95023 1040-D5
- SBnC 95023 1040-D5
DRY CREEK RD
700 CMBL 95008 853-F7
800 SJS 95008 853-G7
1200 SJS 95124 853-J6
1300 SJS 95125 854-A5
1400 SJS 95125 853-J6
1700 SCIC 95125 853-J6
DRY CREEK WY
2000 SJS 95124 853-H6
DRYDEN AV
2300 SCIC 95020 958-E6
10800 CPTO 95014 852-B2
DRYDEN DR
1300 SJS 95131 814-D7
DRY OAK CT
5900 SJS 95120 874-B6
DRY OAK DR
5800 SJS 95120 874-B6
DRY OAK PL
5900 SJS 95120 874-C6
DRYSDALE CT
5700 SJS 95124 873-J6
DRYSDALE DR
100 LGTS 95032 873-E6
1300 SUNV 94087 832-B4
5400 SJS 95124 873-J5
DRYTOWN PL
5900 SJS 95120 874-C6
DRYWOOD LN
3100 SJS 95132 814-D2
DRY YARD DR
500 SJS 95117 853-D1
DUANE AV
600 SUNV 94086 812-G6
800 SCL 95054 813-D7
E DUANE AV
100 SUNV 94086 812-F5
W DUANE AV
300 SUNV 94086 812-E5
DUANE CT
1000 SUNV 94086 812-H6
DUANE ST
- SJS 95110 854-C1
DUARTE CT
200 MPS 95035 794-A4
DUBANSKI DR
700 SJS 95123 874-F6
DUBERT LN
1300 SJS 95122 834-G7
DUBLIN DR
2700 SJS 95127 835-A5
DUBLIN WY
500 SUNV 94087 832-E4
DUBOIS ST
2200 MPS 95035 814-E1
DUBON AV
10100 CPTO 95014 851-J1
DUCHESS CT
3400 SJS 95132 814-J3
DUCKETT WY
1500 SJS 95129 852-E4
DUCK LAKE CT
800 SJS 95123 874-E5
DUDASH CT
1100 SJS 95122 854-H1
DUDLEY AV
500 SJS 95128 853-E2
DUDLEY LN
- SCIC 94305 791-A7
DUENA ST
500 SCIC 94305 790-H7
DUESENBERG DR
5300 SJS 95123 874-G3
DUET CT
6000 SJS 95120 874-C7
DUFF CT
800 SUNV 94086 832-F2
DUFFIN DR
600 SBnC 95023 1060-F3
DUFFY CT
200 SJS 95116 834-F4
DUFFY WY
200 SJS 95116 834-G4
DUGGAN DR
3900 SJS 95118 874-A2
DUKE CT
3300 SCL 95051 832-J6
DUKE DR
10200 SCIC 95020 958-C3
DUKE WY
900 MTVW 94040 811-G7

DUKE WY
1300 SJS 95125 854-A5
DULCEY DR
4100 SJS 95136 874-G1
DULUTH CIR
300 PA 94306 811-D2
DUMAS DR
7500 CPTO 95014 852-D2
DUMBARTON AV
- SMCo 94063 790-C1
2000 EPA 94303 791-A2
2500 SJS 95124 853-H7
2600 SJS 95124 873-H1
DUMONT CIR
2400 SJS 95122 834-J5
DUMONT CT
2500 SJS 95122 834-J5
DUNBAR CT
- GIL 95020 977-F3
DUNBAR DR
20600 CPTO 95014 832-D7
DUNBARTON RD
- MonC 95076 1037-B3
DUNCAN AV
200 SBnC 95045 1038-H3
1000 SUNV 94089 812-F4
DUNCAN PL
3800 PA 94306 811-E1
DUNCAN ST
500 SJS 95127 814-H7
11900 SCIC 95127 814-H7
DUNCANVILLE CT
700 CMBL 95008 853-F6
DUNCARDINE WY
700 SUNV 94087 832-F4
DUNDALE DR
3700 SJS 95121 855-A5
DUNDEE AV
400 MPS 95035 794-A6
18700 SAR 95070 852-H7
DUNDEE CT
1300 SJS 95122 854-H1
DUNDEE DR
2300 SCL 95051 833-B2
DUNDONALD CT
3200 SJS 95121 855-C5
DUNFORD WY
1000 SUNV 94087 832-G5
1000 SCL 95051 832-G5
DUNHOLME WY
500 SUNV 94087 832-E5
DUNIGAN CT
- SJS 95123 874-F7
DUNLAP AV
1700 SCIC 95020 978-D1
2500 SCIC 95020 958-E7
DUNN AV
5900 SJS 95123 874-J5
DUNNE AV
- MGH 95037 917-G6
400 SCIC 95037 917-G2
2400 SCIC 95037 918-A2
E DUNNE AV
- MGH 95037 937-A1
100 MGH 95037 917-D6
2700 SCIC 95037 917-E6
W DUNNE AV
- MGH 95037 937-A1
300 MGH 95037 936-J1
DUNNE ST
- SBnC 95023 999-J3
- SBnC 95023 1000-A4
7100 SCIC 95020 999-H3
DUNNOCK WY
1300 SUNV 94087 832-E4
DUNNVILLE WY
- SBnC 95023 999-J4
DUNRAVEN CT
600 SJS 95136 874-F2
DUNSBURRY CT
5500 SJS 95123 874-F4
DUNSBURRY WY
5500 SJS 95123 874-G4
DUNSMUIR TER
- SUNV 94086 812-E6
DUNSTER DR
200 CMBL 95008 853-D5
DUNWELL CT
100 SJS 95138 875-E4
DUNWICH CT
3100 SJS 95148 855-E2
DUPONT ST
200 SJS 95126 834-A7
200 SJS 95126 854-A1
DURAND RD
- SCIC 94035 812-B2
- SCIC 94043 812-B2
DURAND WY
- PA 94304 790-G5
DURANGO CT
5000 SJS 95118 874-A4
DURANGO LN
9400 GIL 95020 957-F7
DURANGO RIVER CT
4700 SJS 95136 874-G2
DURANT AV
2900 SJS 95111 854-H5
DURAZNO WY
100 SMCo 94028 810-D3
DURBAN CT
5000 SJS 95138 855-F7
DURBAN DR
1900 SJS 95138 855-F7
DURHAM CT
1000 SUNV 94087 832-H5
19900 SAR 95070 872-E2
DURHAM ST
100 MLPK 94025 791-A2
300 MLPK 94025 790-J2
DURLANE CT
900 SUNV 94087 832-G5
DURNESS PL
1000 SJS 95122 854-G1

DURSHIRE WY
600 SUNV 94087 832-F5
DU SAULT DR
6400 SJS 95119 875-C7
DUSTIN CT
- SJS 95123 874-F7
DUTCHESS CT
2400 SCIC 95020 958-C2
DUTTONWOOD LN
- MPS 95035 793-J3
DUVAL CT
3000 SCIC 95020 958-E5
DUVAL WY
26100 LAH 94022 831-B1
DUVALL CT
- SCL 95054 813-C4
500 SUNV 94087 832-D4
DUVALL DR
1500 SJS 95130 853-A5
1700 SJS 95130 852-J5
DWIGHT AV
800 SUNV 94086 812-F7
5500 SJS 95118 874-A5
DWYER AV
1000 SJS 95120 894-D1
DWYER CT
6400 SJS 95120 894-E1
DYMOND CT
400 PA 94306 791-C7

E

E CT
- GIL 95020 977-E1
E ST
1100 SUNV 94089 812-E3
EAGLE DR
1600 SUNV 94087 832-E5
EAGLE CLIFF WY
7200 SJS 95120 894-F4
EAGLE CREST CT
7300 SJS 95120 894-E4
EAGLEHAVEN CT
- SJS 95111 874-J1
EAGLE HILLS CT
- SJS 95138 855-F5
EAGLE HILLS WY
9400 GIL 95020 957-F7
EAGLEHURST DR
1700 SJS 95121 855-C4
EAGLE ISLAND CT
- MGH 95037 936-J2
EAGLE LAKE DR
4600 SJS 95136 874-D2
EAGLE PARK CT
- SJS 95138 855-F5
EAGLE RIDGE CT
- GIL 95020 977-G5
EAGLE RIDGE DR
- GIL 95020 977-F4
EAGLE RIDGE WY
1000 MPS 95035 814-E1
EAGLE ROCK RD
4700 SJS 95136 874-J2
4800 SJS 95136 875-A2
EAGLES LN
5400 SJS 95123 875-A4
EAGLES NEST LN
1400 GIL 95020 957-E7
EAGLE SPRINGS CT
600 MGH 95037 916-H6
EAGLE TREE LN
- SCrC 95018 912-D5
EAGLE VALLEY CT
7100 SJS 95120 894-F4
EAGLE VIEW DR
19000 MGH 95037 917-A2
EAGLE VIEW TER
- FRMT 94539 794-B1
EAGLE VIEW WY
9400 GIL 95020 957-F7
E EAGLEWOOD AV
200 SUNV 94086 812-F5
W EAGLEWOOD AV
100 SUNV 94086 812-E5
EARL DR
3400 SCL 95051 832-J2
EARLANDER ST
10200 SCIC 95127 835-A2
EARLE AV
- SCIC 95126 853-J1
EARLINGTON CT
1000 SUNV 94087 832-B5
EARLS CT
19900 SCIC 95037 916-F3
EARLSWOOD CT
7100 SJS 95120 894-H4
EARLY MORNING LN
- SJS 95135 875-J1
- SJS 95138 875-J1
EASINGTON WY
1500 SJS 95126 853-H4
EAST CT
300 SJS 95116 834-E3
8400 GIL 95020 977-J1
EAST LN
- MPS 95035 814-A1
EAST ST
200 HOLL 95023 1040-A4
7200 GIL 95020 978-B3
EASTBOURNE CT
- SJS 95138 855-E6
EASTBOURNE DR
- SJS 95138 855-E7
EASTBROOK AV
1700 SCIC 94024 831-F4
11000 LAH 94024 831-E3
EASTBROOK CT
23200 SCIC 94024 831-G5
EASTER AV
400 MPS 95035 793-J6
EASTGATE AV
- SJS 95116 834-F4

EAST HILLS CT
10400 SCIC 95127 835-B1
EAST HILLS DR
3000 SCIC 95127 834-J3
3000 SJS 95127 834-J3
3100 SCIC 95127 835-B1
3400 SJS 95127 835-B1
EASTIN PL
- SCL 95051 832-J4
EAST LAKE DR
1500 SJS 95126 853-G3
EASTMAN CANYON RD
13400 SCIC 95037 956-B1
EASTMAN LAKE DR
5900 SJS 95123 874-G7
EASTON CT
2500 SJS 95133 834-G1
EASTON DR
500 SJS 95133 834-F1
12500 SAR 95070 852-H6
EASTON LN
2500 SJS 95133 834-G1
EASTON PL
2500 SJS 95133 834-G1
18900 SAR 95070 852-H6
EASTON TER
600 SJS 95133 834-B2
EASTRIDGE AV
2200 MLPK 94025 790-D7
EASTRIDGE BLVD
2400 SJS 95122 855-B1
EASTRIDGE DR
100 LGTS 95032 873-D6
3500 SJS 95148 835-D4
EASTRIDGE LN
2200 SJS 95122 835-A7
EASTRIDGE LP
- SJS 95122 855-A1
100 SJS 95122 835-A7
EASTRIDGE WY
2200 SJS 95122 835-A7
2200 SJS 95122 855-A1
EASTSIDE DR
200 SJS 95127 834-H1
200 SCIC 95127 834-H1
EAST SUNSET DR
13000 LAH 94022 831-D1
EASTUS DR
4600 SJS 95129 852-J3
4600 SJS 95129 853-A3
EAST VALLEY CT
2200 SCIC 95148 835-E5
EASTVIEW CT
- HOLL 95023 1040-A6
EASTVIEW DR
- HOLL 95023 1040-A6
14500 LGTS 95032 873-B3
14700 SCIC 95032 873-B3
EASTWOOD CIR
3600 SCL 95054 813-F6
EASTWOOD CT
- SJS 95116 834-F4
1000 LALT 94024 831-H2
EASTWOOD DR
1000 LALT 94024 831-H2
EASTWOOD PL
900 LALT 94024 831-H2
EASY ST
100 MTVW 94043 812-A4
600 MGH 95037 937-C5
900 SCIC 95037 937-C5
EATON LN
400 MTVW 94043 812-B5
17100 MSER 95030 873-A4
EATON PL
21700 CPTO 95014 832-B7
EATON TER
- SUNV 94086 812-B7
EBANO CT
1300 SJS 95121 854-J3
EBBESEN AV
2100 SJS 95124 873-F3
EBBETTS DR
700 CMBL 95008 853-A7
700 CMBL 95008 873-A1
EBENER ST
1300 RDWC 94061 790-B1
EBERHARD ST
1600 SCL 95050 833-C3
EBERLY DR
4900 SJS 95111 875-A1
EBERTS DR
1600 SCIC 95046 937-G4
EBONY WY
2800 SJS 95148 835-F7
ECHO AV
100 CMBL 95008 853-D7
ECHO DR
800 LALT 94024 831-F2
22500 SCIC 95033 913-B4
ECHO LN
- PTLV 94028 810-C7
ECHO LP
7100 SJS 95120 894-E3
ECHO CANYON CT
- SJS 95138 855-C5
ECHO HILL CT
- CPTO 95014 852-D3
ECHO KNOLLS RD
- SCIC 95140 815-C7
4100 SCIC 95127 815-C7
ECHO RIDGE CT
1200 SJS 95120 894-E4
ECHO RIDGE DR
7100 SJS 95120 894-E4
ECHO VALLEY DR
1200 SJS 95120 894-D3
ECHO VALLEY RD
500 MonC 95076 1037-A6
500 MonC 93907 1037-A6
ECKBERG CT
- SJS 95127 834-J2
ECKER CT
600 CMBL 95008 853-C7

ECOLA LN
1500 SUNV 94087 832-A5
EDALE DR
700 SUNV 94087 832-C3
EDDINGTON PL
1400 SJS 95129 852-E4
EDE LN
- MPS 95035 814-A3
EDELEN AV
100 LGTS 95030 873-A7
EDELWEISS DR
400 SJS 95136 874-F2
EDEN AV
600 SJS 95117 853-D3
1500 CMBL 95117 853-D4
1500 CMBL 95008 853-D4
N EDEN AV
500 SUNV 94086 812-G5
S EDEN AV
500 SUNV 94086 812-G5
W EDEN AV
600 SUNV 94086 812-F5
EDEN CT
500 SCL 95051 832-J6
EDEN DR
3400 SCL 95051 832-J6
EDEN ST
500 GIL 95020 977-H1
EDENBANK CT
2900 SJS 95148 855-D2
EDENBANK DR
3000 SJS 95148 855-D1
EDENBURY LN
900 SJS 95136 874-D1
EDENHALL DR
1000 SJS 95129 852-G3
EDEN PARK PL
5800 SJS 95138 875-E4
EDENVALE AV
- SJS 95125 854-E4
200 SJS 95136 875-A2
EDEN VIEW DR
4900 SJS 95111 875-B2
EDENWOOD CT
3800 SJS 95121 855-C4
EDENWOOD DR
3800 SJS 95121 855-C5
EDES CT
100 MGH 95037 937-A2
EDGAR CT
4900 SJS 95118 874-C3
EDGE LN
700 LALT 94024 831-G2
EDGE RD
- ATN 94027 790-G1
EDGEBANK DR
1900 SJS 95122 855-A1
EDGEBROOK CT
6500 SJS 95120 894-C1
EDGECLIFF PL
12100 LAH 94022 831-C3
EDGECREST DR
1900 SJS 95122 855-A1
EDGEDALE CT
2500 SJS 95122 855-A1
EDGEFIELD CT
2500 SJS 95122 855-A1
EDGEFIELD DR
3600 SCL 95054 813-F5
EDGEFORT CT
1900 SJS 95122 855-A1
EDGEGATE DR
2000 SJS 95122 855-A1
EDGEHILL DR
400 SCL 95054 813-F5
EDGEHILL WY
1200 MPS 95035 814-F1
EDGEMAN CT
3500 SJS 95148 835-E6
EDGEMONT DR
10900 SCIC 95127 815-B6
EDGEMOOR WY
6300 SJS 95129 852-F3
EDGERTON RD
27600 LAH 94022 830-J1
EDGESTONE CIR
1900 SJS 95122 855-A1
EDGEVIEW CT
2500 SJS 95122 855-A1
EDGEVIEW DR
1900 SJS 95122 855-A1
EDGEWATER DR
- MPS 95035 794-A6
3500 SJS 95136 854-G7
EDGEWOOD DR
- SBnC 95023 1040-D2
1400 PA 94301 791-B3
1500 PA 94303 791-C4
EDGEWOOD LN
700 LALT 94022 831-E1
1800 MLPK 94025 790-E6
EDGEWOOD WY
1500 SJS 95125 854-A6
EDINA LN
19700 SAR 95070 852-F6
EDINBURGH DR
20000 SAR 95070 852-E7
EDINBURGH WY
- GIL 95020 977-E4
EDISON DR
500 SJS 95133 834-H1
2900 SCIC 95133 834-H1
E EDITH AV
100 LALT 94022 811-E6
W EDITH AV
- LALT 94022 811-D6
400 LAH 94022 811-D6
EDITH ST
1100 SJS 95122 834-H5
EDLEE AV
200 PA 94306 811-D2
EDMINTON DR
18300 CPTO 95014 852-H2

STREET
Block City ZIP Pg-Grid

EDMOND CT
1500 SJS 95125 854-A7
EDMONDS CT
1000 SUNV 94087 832-B5
EDMONDS WY
900 SUNV 94087 832-B5
EDMONTON AV
1600 SUNV 94087 832-B5
EDMUND DR
15800 LGTS 95032 873-E5
EDMUNDSON AV
400 SCIC 95037 936-H4
E EDMUNDSON AV
- MGH 95037 937-B2
W EDMUNDSON AV
300 MGH 95037 937-B2
500 SCIC 95037 936-J3
500 SCIC 95037 937-A3
EDMUNDSON CT
1400 SCIC 95037 936-H4
EDMUNDSON DR
1800 SCIC 95037 936-G4
EDNA AV
- SCIC 95127 835-A2
EDNA CT
300 LALT 94022 811-F7
EDNAMARY WY
1700 MTVW 94040 811-F5
EDQUIBA RD
- SCIC 94035 812-B3
EDSEL DR
1100 MPS 95035 794-D7
6300 SJS 95129 852-F3
EDUCATIONAL PARK DR
300 SJS 95133 834-E1
EDWARD AV
3200 SCL 95054 813-F6
EDWARD WY
21500 CPTO 95014 852-B2
EDWARDS AV
- SJS 95110 854-C1
EDWARDS LN
- ATN 94027 790-D3
EDWARDS RD
17600 SCIC 95033 913-C2
17800 SCIC 95033 912-J2
EDWIN JONES CT
16800 MGH 95037 936-J1
EGGO WY
400 SJS 95116 834-D3
N EGRET CT
- GIL 95020 957-E7
S EGRET CT
9100 GIL 95020 957-E7
EGRET DR
1300 SUNV 94087 832-F4
EHRHORN AV
600 MTVW 94041 811-J6
EICHLER CT
1200 MTVW 94040 811-H6
EICHLER DR
900 MTVW 94040 811-G6
EIGLEBERRY ST
7000 GIL 95020 978-A3
7600 GIL 95020 977-J2
EILEEN CT
18100 SCIC 95033 912-H3
EILEEN DR
5100 SJS 95129 852-H4
EISENHOWER DR
500 SJS 95128 853-F3
1400 SCL 95054 813-D4
EL ABRA WY
1100 SJS 95125 854-A3
ELAINE CT
- MSER 95030 873-A5
17800 MGH 95037 916-H7
ELAINE DR
3100 SJS 95124 873-G2
EL ALTILLO
100 LGTS 95032 872-J2
ELAM AV
1200 CMBL 95008 853-B7
ELAN VILLAGE LN
300 SJS 95134 813-G4
EL BOSQUE AV
200 SJS 95134 813-F2
EL BOSQUE DR
100 SJS 95134 813-E3
EL BOSQUE ST
100 SJS 95134 813-F2
ELBRIDGE WY
800 PA 94303 791-D6
EL CAJON DR
200 SJS 95111 854-J6
EL CAJON WY
200 LGTS 95032 873-C4
900 PA 94303 791-C5
EL CAMINITO
9200 GIL 95020 957-F7
9200 GIL 95020 977-F1
EL CAMINITO AV
100 CMBL 95008 853-D6
EL CAMINITO RD
23400 LAH 94024 831-E5
EL CAMINO WY
4000 PA 94306 811-C2
EL CAMINO DE VIDA
1200 HOLL 95023 1040-D5
EL CAMINO GRANDE
15100 SAR 95070 872-G4
EL CAMINO HIGUERA
1100 MPS 95035 794-B4
1300 SCIC 95035 794-B4
EL CAMINO PARAISO
400 HOLL 95023 1040-D4
400 SBnC 95023 1040-D4
EL CAMINO REAL
300 SJS 95139 895-J1
500 SJS 95037 896-D6
500 SCIC 95037 896-D6
1200 SJS 95141 896-D6
5300 SJS 95111 875-H7
5400 SJS 95138 875-H7
5800 SJS 95139 875-H7
5800 SJS 95137 875-H7
5800 SJS 95137 895-J1
5900 SJS 95139 896-D6
5900 SCIC 95137 895-J1
5900 SCIC 95137 896-D6
6000 SJS 95137 896-D6
11200 SJS 95037 916-H4
11200 SCIC 95037 916-H4
13600 MGH 95037 916-H4
EL CAMINO REAL Rt#-82
- MLPK 94025 790-F3
- PA 94301 790-F3
- PA 94304 790-F3
100 ATN 94027 790-C1
100 SMCo 94025 790-C1
200 SCIC 94305 790-F3
200 PA 94305 790-F3
400 SCL 95050 833-F3
400 SCL 95053 833-F3
1000 ATN 94025 790-F3
1400 MLPK 94027 790-F3
1500 PA 94306 790-F3
1500 PA 94306 791-A6
1500 SCIC 94305 791-A6
2300 PA 94304 791-A7
2400 SCL 95051 833-A4
2600 RDWC 94061 790-C1
2600 SMCo 94063 790-C1
2800 PA 94304 811-B1
2900 PA 94306 811-B1
3300 SCL 95051 832-J4
4200 LALT 94022 811-B1
E EL CAMINO REAL Rt#-82
100 SUNV 94086 832-E2
100 SUNV 94087 832-G4
400 MTVW 94040 812-A7
400 MTVW 94041 812-A7
800 SCIC 94087 832-G4
1100 SCL 95051 832-G4
1100 SCL 94086 832-G4
W EL CAMINO REAL Rt#-82
- MTVW 94040 811-F4
- MTVW 94041 811-F4
100 MTVW 94041 812-A7
100 MTVW 94040 812-A7
100 SUNV 94086 832-C1
100 SUNV 94087 832-C1
1000 LALT 94022 811-F4
1100 SUNV 94087 812-B7
1100 SUNV 94086 812-B7
EL CAMINO REAL U.S.-101
- MonC 93907 1037-B4
- MonC 95076 1037-B4
- SBnC - 1037-C2
- SBnC 95004 1037-C2
- SBnC 95020 1018-C1
- SBnC 95045 1018-B3
- SBnC 95045 1037-C2
- SCIC 95020 978-A4
- SCIC 95020 998-B1
- SCIC 95020 1018-C1
5300 GIL 95020 978-A4
7800 GIL 95020 977-J2
8500 GIL 95020 957-G3
10400 SCIC 95020 957-G3
11000 SCIC 95046 957-G3
11800 MGH 95037 916-J6
12600 SCIC 95046 937-F7
13700 MGH 95046 937-F7
14800 MGH 95037 937-A1
17000 MGH 95037 917-A7
EL CAMINO SENDA
15000 SAR 95070 872-G4
EL CAMPO DR
- SCIC 95127 835-A1
100 SCIC 95127 834-J1
EL CAPITAN AV
2000 SCL 95050 833-C3
EL CAPITAN PL
400 PA 94306 811-E1
EL CARMELO AV
100 PA 94306 791-C7
EL CENTRO
- MTVW 94043 811-J2
- MTVW 94043 812-A2
EL CENTRO ST
3700 PA 94306 811-B2
EL CERRITO CT
19200 MonC 95076 1037-B2
EL CERRITO RD
- CPTO 95014 851-J2
3900 PA 94306 811-B3
EL CERRITO WY
300 GIL 95020 977-H2
19100 MonC 95076 1037-A2
EL CERRO CT
19300 MonC 95076 1037-B3
EL CERRO DR
800 HOLL 95023 1040-C5
800 SBnC 95023 1040-C5
EL CERRO WY
19300 MonC 95076 1037-A3
EL CIRCULO DEL REAL
- SBnC 95045 1037-J4
EL CODO WY
1700 SJS 95124 873-H1
EL CORAL CT
4100 SJS 95118 874-C2
EL CORAL WY
3900 SJS 95118 874-C2
ELDAMAR CT
1200 SJS 95121 855-A4
ELDEN DR
600 SJS 95008 853-F7
600 SJS 95124 853-F7
ELDENE DR
- HOLL 95023 1040-B7
ELDER AV
1100 MLPK 94025 790-E5
ELDER CT
- MLPK 94025 790-E5
500 SJS 95123 874-J7
ELDERBERRY DR
1200 SUNV 94087 832-B3
ELDERBERRY WY
1600 SJS 95125 853-J5
ELDERWOOD CT
7600 CPTO 95014 852-D2
ELDIVA CT
- SJS 95148 855-F2
EL DORA DR
- MTVW 94041 811-J6
- MTVW 94041 812-A6
EL DORADO AV
100 PA 94306 791-C7
100 SJS 95136 854-G7
1600 SJS 95126 833-F6
EL DORADO CT
- SJS 95002 813-B1
20500 SAR 95070 872-D1
EL DORADO DR
- SBnC 95023 1040-D5
ELDORADO DR
1500 GIL 95020 977-F2
EL DORADO ST
1300 SJS 95002 793-B7
1500 SJS 95002 813-B1
EL DORI DR
5800 SJS 95123 874-E5
EL DORIC CT
8800 SCIC 95020 976-J1
ELDRIDGE DR
6800 SJS 95120 894-G2
ELEANOR AV
- LALT 94022 811-E7
ELEANOR DR
100 WDSD 94062 790-A5
400 ATN 94027 790-A5
400 WDSD 94027 790-A5
400 ATN 94062 790-A5
ELEANOR WY
900 SUNV 94087 832-G4
ELECTA CT
- GIL 95020 957-J7
ELECTIONEER RD
- SCIC 94305 790-F7
ELECTRA AV
3500 SJS 95118 874-B1
ELENA AV
- ATN 94027 790-D3
ELENA RD
25300 LAH 94022 831-A1
27000 LAH 94022 811-A7
27500 LAH 94022 810-J6
ELENA WY
100 LGTS 95032 873-B3
ELENA PRIVADA
1100 MTVW 94040 832-A1
ELENDA DR
20800 CPTO 95014 832-D7
EL ESCARPADO CT
400 SCIC 94305 810-G1
ELESTER CT
2300 SJS 95124 873-E4
ELESTER DR
4800 SJS 95124 873-E4
EL GATO LN
15500 LGTS 95032 873-D5
15500 SCIC 95032 873-D5
EL GATO WY
- GIL 95020 977-G1
ELGIN LN
3300 SJS 95118 874-A1
EL GRANDE CT
3600 SJS 95132 814-J5
EL GRANDE DR
3500 SJS 95132 814-J5
EL INVIERNO DR
- GIL 95020 957-H7
ELISA AV
19700 SAR 95070 852-F5
ELISE CT
24200 LAH 94024 831-D4
ELIZABETH DR
900 SCL 95050 833-C5
ELIZABETH LN
700 MLPK 94025 790-F3
ELIZABETH ST
400 SJS 95113 834-C6
400 SJS 95112 834-C6
900 SJS 95002 793-B7
ELIZABETH WY
- ATN 94027 790-C2
900 SUNV 94087 832-G4
ELJA WY
5800 SJS 95123 874-F5
ELK LN
2300 SJS 95133 814-F7
ELKA AV
1400 SJS 95129 852-F4
2400 MTVW 94043 811-F2
ELK CREEK PL
200 SJS 95127 834-H1
ELKHORN CT
2200 SJS 95125 854-A6
ELKINS WY
2300 SJS 95121 855-C3
ELKO DR
1100 SUNV 94089 812-J3
1200 SUNV 94089 813-A3
ELK RIDGE CT
3000 SJS 95136 854-E3
ELK RIDGE WY
500 SJS 95136 854-E7
ELKWOOD DR
1100 MPS 95035 793-J5
ELLA CT
5000 SJS 95111 875-B1
ELLA DR
500 SJS 95111 875-B1
ELLEGE RD
18400 SCIC 95033 892-F5
ELLEN AV
1800 SJS 95125 854-B4
ELLEN RD
- SCrC 95018 912-F4
ELLENA DR
2200 SCL 95050 833-C2
ELLENWOOD AV
- LGTS 95030 872-J7
W ELLENWOOD AV
16200 LGTS 95030 872-J6
16200 MSER 95030 872-J6
ELLERBROOK WY
6100 SJS 95123 875-B6
ELLERY ST
11900 SCIC 95127 814-H7
11900 SJS 95127 814-H7
ELLIOT AV
16500 LGTS 95032 873-C5
ELLIOT CT
2500 SCL 95051 833-B2
ELLIOT ST
2400 SCL 95051 833-B2
ELLIOTT DR
100 MLPK 94025 791-A2
ELLIOTT ST
1800 SCIC 95128 853-G1
2100 SJS 95128 853-G1
ELLIS AV
900 SJS 95125 854-B4
1500 MPS 95035 794-D6
15700 SCIC 95037 937-E1
ELLIS CT
1100 HOLL 95023 1039-H3
ELLIS ST
400 MTVW 94043 812-B4
600 MTVW 94035 812-B4
600 SCIC 94035 812-B4
EL LISA DR
900 SJS 95123 874-E4
ELLMAR OAKS CT
200 SJS 95136 874-G1
ELLMAR OAKS DR
3900 SJS 95136 874-G1
ELLMAR OAKS LP
200 SJS 95136 874-G1
ELLSWORTH PL
700 PA 94303 791-D6
ELLWELL DR
1700 MPS 95035 794-D6
ELLYRIDGE CT
200 SJS 95123 874-J3
ELLYRIDGE DR
5400 SJS 95123 874-J3
ELM AV
100 MLPK 94025 791-A2
300 MLPK 94025 790-J2
400 MPS 95035 793-H6
ELM CT
100 SUNV 94086 832-F1
400 MPS 95035 793-J6
21400 CPTO 95014 852-C2
ELM DR
100 HOLL 95023 1039-H4
ELM LN
- PA 94306 811-D2
ELM PK
15000 MSER 95030 873-A4
15000 MSER 95030 872-J4
ELM PL
- ATN 94027 790-G2
ELM RD
17700 MGH 95037 917-C4
17700 SCIC 95037 917-C4
ELM ST
- LGTS 95030 873-A7
100 GIL 95020 978-A2
600 SJS 95126 833-G5
ELMAR WY
1500 SJS 95129 852-F4
EL MARCERO CT
6900 SJS 95119 895-E1
EL MATADOR DR
8000 SCIC 95020 976-J1
9200 SCIC 95020 956-J7
ELMBERD RD
- LAH 94022 831-A1
ELMBRIDGE DR
6000 SJS 95129 852-G3
ELMBROOK WY
500 SJS 95111 855-A7
ELMDALE PL
2600 PA 94303 791-D5
ELMGATE CT
3100 SJS 95148 855-E2
ELMGROVE CT
5000 SJS 95130 852-J6
ELMGROVE LN
2000 SJS 95130 852-J6
ELMHURST AV
3400 SCL 95051 832-J7
ELMHURST CT
100 SCL 95051 832-J7
ELMHURST DR
1500 LALT 94024 832-A3
4500 SJS 95129 853-A2
ELMIRA DR
800 SUNV 94087 832-C2
ELM LAKE CT
- SJS 95131 814-B6
ELM LEAF CT
2000 SCL 95050 833-C3
EL MOLINO WY
300 SJS 95119 875-B7
EL MONTE AV
200 LALT 94022 811-G6
200 LALT 94024 811-G6
900 MTVW 94040 811-G6
1000 MTVW 94022 811-G6
7600 LALT 94024 831-E1
7600 LALT 94022 831-E1
EL MONTE CT
100 LALT 94022 811-F6
EL MONTE RD
- LALT 94024 831-D2
700 LALT 94022 831-D2
700 LAH 94024 831-D2
700 LAH 94022 831-D2
EL MONTE WY
2700 SJS 95127 835-A5
ELMORE AL
- HOLL 95023 1040-A3
EL MORO DR
1200 CMBL 95008 853-G6
ELM PARK CT
15200 MSER 95030 872-J4
ELMSDALE DR
7000 SJS 95120 894-G3
ELMSFORD CT
1100 CPTO 95014 852-C3
ELMSFORD DR
1100 CPTO 95014 852-C3
ELMTREE CT
1800 SJS 95131 814-C5
ELMWOOD CT
100 LGTS 95032 873-A2
ELMWOOD DR
4900 SJS 95130 852-J6
ELMWOOD PL
- MLPK 94025 790-H2
ELMWOOD ST
100 MTVW 94043 811-J4
EL NIDO AV
- LGTS 95030 893-B1
EL NIDO CT
- LGTS 95030 893-C1
- LGTS 95030 873-B7
EL NIDO RD
100 SMCo 94028 830-D4
ELNORA CT
1400 LALT 94024 831-J4
ELODIE WY
100 SJS 95116 834-H2
ELOISE CIR
10600 SCIC 94024 831-F5
EL OLIVAR
100 LGTS 95032 872-J2
EL OSO DR
1400 SJS 95129 852-J5
EL PAJARO CT
15800 MGH 95037 937-A3
EL PASEO DR
6300 SJS 95120 874-D7
6300 SJS 95120 894-D1
EL PASEO DE LOS PASTORES
3600 SCIC 95148 835-F7
EL PATIO CT
100 CMBL 95008 853-F5
EL PATIO DR
500 CMBL 95008 853-F5
EL PINAR
100 LGTS 95032 872-J2
EL PORTAL WY
200 SJS 95119 875-B6
300 SJS 95123 875-B6
EL PORTON
100 LGTS 95032 872-J2
EL PRADO AV
200 SMCo 94061 790-A4
EL PRADO CT
1100 SJS 95120 874-D7
EL PRADO DR
1100 SJS 95120 874-D7
EL PRADO WY
10200 CPTO 95014 851-J1
EL PUENTE WY
14500 SAR 95070 872-F3
EL QUITO WY
15000 SAR 95070 872-H4
EL RANCHITO WY
600 MTVW 94041 811-J6
EL RANCHO AV
17300 MSER 95030 873-B5
EL RANCHO VERDE CT
200 SJS 95116 834-G3
EL RANCHO VERDE DR
100 SJS 95116 834-F3
EL REY RD
- SMCo 94028 830-D4
EL RIO DR
800 SJS 95125 854-C5
EL ROBLE CT
5000 SJS 95118 874-B4
7600 GIL 95020 977-H3
ELROSE AV
5000 SJS 95124 873-H5
EL SERENO AV
- LALT 94024 832-A5
EL SERENO CT
- LALT 94024 832-A5
EL SERENO DR
700 SJS 95123 874-G6
ELSIE AV
1700 MTVW 94043 811-H3
ELSIE WY
- LAH 94022 811-B7
ELSINORE CT
900 PA 94303 791-C5
ELSINORE DR
900 PA 94303 791-C5
ELSMAN CT
1400 SJS 95120 874-A7
EL SOBRANTE ST
2700 SCL 95051 833-A4
EL SOLYO AV
1100 CMBL 95008 853-G6
EL SOMBROSO DR
700 SJS 95123 874-G5
ELSONA CT
1300 SUNV 94087 832-B4
ELSONA DR
1300 SUNV 94087 832-B4
ELTON CT
14900 SCIC 95124 873-G4
ELTON DR
14800 SCIC 95124 873-G4
EL TORO CT
100 MGH 95037 916-J7
6100 SJS 95123 874-F6
EL TORO DR
300 GIL 95020 977-H2
300 HOLL 95023 1040-C5
700 SBnC 95023 1040-C5
EL TORO ST
- MGH 95037 916-J7
EL TORO WY
300 GIL 95020 977-J1
ELVA AV
14300 SAR 95070 872-D2
EL VERANO AV
100 PA 94306 811-C1
300 PA 94306 791-D7
EL VERANO WY
- GIL 95020 957-H7
ELVIRA CT
1200 SJS 95122 834-H5
ELVIRA ST
14000 SAR 95070 872-D2
ELVIS DR
500 SJS 95123 874-J7
EL VISTA WY
2700 SJS 95148 835-D7
ELWELL CT
1000 PA 94303 791-F6
ELWOOD CT
6600 SJS 95120 894-E2
ELWOOD DR
1300 CMBL 95032 872-J1
ELWOOD RD
6600 SJS 95120 894-E3
ELY CT
200 SJS 95123 875-A4
ELY PL
100 PA 94306 811-E1
ELYSIAN PL
- SJS 95125 854-B5
EL ZUPARKO DR
5800 SJS 95123 874-E5
EMADO AV
600 SJS 95139 896-A3
600 SJS 95139 895-J3
EMAMI CT
7200 SJS 95120 894-H4
EMAMI DR
7200 SJS 95120 894-H4
EMANUEL CT
3600 SJS 95121 855-A5
18500 SAR 95070 852-H7
18500 SAR 95070 872-H1
EMBARCADERO RD
- SCIC 94305 790-J6
- PA 94301 790-J6
100 PA 94301 791-C4
600 PA 94303 791-E3
EMBARCADERO WY
2400 PA 94303 791-E3
EMBEE DR
5800 SJS 95123 875-A5
EMERALD WY
900 SJS 95117 853-D3
EMERALD HILL
14400 SAR 95070 872-H2
EMERALD HILLS CIR
2200 SJS 95131 814-D6
EMERALD HILLS LN
12000 LAH 94022 831-D3
EMERALD ISLE LN
- SJS 95135 855-F2
EMERICK AV
300 SCIC 95127 835-A2
300 SJS 95127 835-A2
EMERSON AV
1100 CMBL 95008 873-D3
EMERSON CT
500 SJS 95126 833-H6
8500 GIL 95020 977-G1
EMERSON LN
100 MTVW 94043 812-B5
EMERSON ST
100 PA 94301 790-H4
1100 PA 94301 791-A6
2500 PA 94306 791-B7
3000 PA 94306 811-C1
EMIG CT
1700 SCL 95051 832-J3
EMILIE AV
- ATN 94027 790-E3
EMILIE DR
13200 SJS 95127 834-J3
13500 SCIC 95127 834-J3
EMILINE DR
5000 SJS 95124 873-G5
EMILY DR
600 MTVW 94043 812-A3
EMLYN CT
6000 SJS 95123 875-B6
EMMA CT
900 SJS 95120 894-G4
EMMA LN
100 MLPK 94025 791-A3
EMMETT CT
2200 SCL 95051 832-J2
EMMETT PL
3400 SCL 95051 832-J2
EMMETT WY
2500 EPA 94303 791-B1
EMMONS DR
400 MTVW 94043 811-G2
EMORY AV
600 CMBL 95008 853-D7
700 CMBL 95008 873-D1
EMORY ST
500 SJS 95110 833-H6
600 SJS 95126 833-H6
1700 SJS 95128 833-F7
EMPEROR WY
1500 SUNV 94087 832-F5
EMPEY WY
600 SCIC 95128 853-F2
EMPIRE AL
- SJS 95110 834-A5
EMPIRE AV
10100 CPTO 95014 832-B7
EMPIRE CT
- MTVW 94040 811-F3
E EMPIRE ST
- SJS 95112 834-C4
EMPOLI ST
- SJS 95136 854-F6
EMPRESS CT
6200 SJS 95129 852-F3
ENBORG LN
2200 SCIC 95128 853-F2
ENCANTO WY
- SJS 95135 855-G3
ENCHANTMENT PL
- MPS 95035 814-J1
ENCHANTO VISTA
11200 SCIC 95127 815-A5
ENCINA AV
- PA 94301 790-J5
200 RDWC 94061 790-B1
300 ATN 94027 790-E1
300 SMCo 94025 790-E1
ENCINA CT
15000 SAR 95070 872-G4
ENCINA WY
2500 SCL 95051 833-B4
ENCINA GRANDE DR
600 PA 94306 811-C2
ENCINAL AV
100 ATN 94027 790-F2
100 MLPK 94025 790-F2
100 MLPK 94027 790-F2
ENCINAL CT
23200 LAH 94024 831-E5
ENCINAL DR
6100 SJS 95119 875-C6
ENCINITAS CT
2800 SJS 95132 814-D3
ENCINO CT
100 SUNV 94086 812-C6
ENCINO DR
500 MGH 95037 937-A4
ENCINO RD
- ATN 94027 790-G1
ENCLAVE DR
- SJS 95134 813-C2
ENCORE WY
600 SJS 95134 813-F2
ENDERBY WY
1000 SUNV 94087 832-B4
ENDERS LN
- SCrC 95018 912-B7
ENDERSON CT
18200 SCIC 95037 916-H6
ENDFIELD WY
10000 SCIC 95127 835-A3
ENDICOTT BLVD
1400 SJS 95193 875-C4
ENDICOTT DR
500 SUNV 94087 832-D5
1400 SJS 95122 834-J5
ENDMOOR CT
300 SJS 95119 895-D1
ENDMOOR DR
6700 SJS 95119 895-D1
ENESCO AV
1600 SJS 95121 855-A2
1700 SJS 95122 855-A2
ENGLE WY
6200 GIL 95020 978-B5
ENGLERT CT
300 SJS 95133 834-F2
ENGLEWOOD AV
16300 LGTS 95032 873-C7
16300 SCIC 95032 873-C7
16500 LGTS 95030 873-C7
ENGLEWOOD DR
4600 SJS 95129 852-J4
4600 SJS 95129 853-A4
ENGLISH CT
1600 SJS 95129 852-H5
ENGLISH DR
1400 SJS 95129 852-H4
ENGLISH PL
400 SJS 95138 875-E3
ENGLISH OAK CIR
- GIL 95020 977-G2
ENGLISH OAK WY
10100 CPTO 95014 831-J7
ENGLISH WALNUT CT
800 MGH 95037 917-B6
ENGLISH WALNUT WY
800 MGH 95037 917-B6
ENNING AV
5600 SJS 95123 874-J4
ENOCHS ST
1100 SCL 95051 812-J7
ENOS CT
600 SCL 95051 833-B6
ENRIGHT AV
600 SCL 95050 833-D5
ENRIQUEZ CT
200 MPS 95035 794-A5
ENRIQUITA CT
700 SJS 95123 874-G5
ENSALMO AV
3100 SJS 95118 873-J1
3100 SJS 95118 874-A1
ENSENADA DR
1600 CMBL 95008 853-A6
ENSENADA WY
1300 LALT 94024 831-J4
ENSIGN WY
700 PA 94303 811-E1
1900 SJS 95133 814-E7
1900 SJS 95133 834-E1

SANTA CLARA CO.

STREET Block City ZIP Pg-Grid

ENTERPRISE DR
- SJS 95112 814-A7
ENTERPRISE RD
100 SBnC 95023 1060-C1
900 HOLL 95023 1060-D1
ENTERTAINMENT CT
- SJS 95112 834-A3
ENTRADA PL
11300 LAH 94024 831-F4
11300 SCIC 94024 831-F4
ENTRADA WY
500 SMCo 94025 790-H2
ENTRADA CEDROS
- SJS 95123 874-H3
ENTRADA OLEANDROS
5300 SJS 95123 874-H3
ENTRADA OLMOS
5200 SJS 95123 874-H3
ENZO DR
200 SJS 95138 875-E4
EPERNAY CT
- SJS 95127 834-J1
EPPLING LN
5000 SJS 95111 875-C2
EQUESTRIAN WY
15400 MSER 95030 872-J5
ERIC DR
19300 SAR 95070 852-F5
ERIC LN
1600 SCIC 95020 958-B3
ERICA CT
2900 SJS 95121 854-J3
ERICA DR
900 SUNV 94086 832-G2
ERICA WY
100 SMCo 94028 810-D3
ERIE CIR
700 MPS 95035 794-A6
ERIE CT
700 MPS 95035 794-A5
4200 SCL 95054 813-C5
ERIE DR
300 MPS 95035 794-A5
600 SUNV 94087 832-D2
ERIE PL
700 MPS 95035 794-A5
ERIE WY
200 CMBL 95008 853-B5
ERIN WY
1100 SCIC 95008 873-E1
7500 CPTO 95014 852-D2
ERINBROOK PL
1700 SJS 95131 834-D1
ERINWOOD CT
1200 SJS 95121 855-A4
ERNESTINE LN
1300 MTVW 94040 811-G6
ERSKINE CT
5800 SJS 95123 875-A5
ERSTWILD CT
- PA 94303 791-B4
ERVIN CT
- GIL 95020 978-A5
- HOLL 95023 1040-B6
ERVIN WY
11000 SCIC 95127 835-D4
ESBERG RD
1700 SCIC 94024 831-G4
ESCALON AV
1000 SUNV 94086 812-C5
ESCALON CT
1000 SUNV 94086 812-C5
ESCALONIA CT
2400 SJS 95121 855-D4
ESCANYO WY
100 SMCo 94028 810-E4
ESCAZU CT
100 SJS 95116 834-G3
ESCHENBURG DR
700 GIL 95020 977-H3
ESCOBAR AV
100 LGTS 95032 873-E5
300 SCIC 95032 873-D5
ESCOBAR CT
100 LGTS 95032 873-E5
ESCOBAR RD
100 PTLV 94028 810-C4
ESCOBITA AV
1500 PA 94306 791-A6
ESCONDIDO CT
6100 SJS 95119 875-C6
ESCONDIDO LN
1100 MLPK 94025 790-F3
ESCONDIDO RD
600 SCIC 94305 790-H7
800 SCIC 94305 810-J1
ESCOVER LN
5300 SJS 95118 874-C4
ESCUELA AV
100 MTVW 94041 811-G4
100 MTVW 94040 811-G4
ESCUELA PKWY
400 MPS 95035 794-A4
ESCUELA PL
600 MPS 95035 794-A5
ESFAHAN CT
- SJS 95111 854-F5
ESFAHAN DR
- SJS 95111 854-F5
ESHNER CT
27300 LAH 94022 831-A2
ESMERALDA CT
200 SJS 95116 834-F3
ESPADA CT
13800 SAR 95070 872-J1
ESPANA CT
- MGH 95037 917-B3
ESPANA WY
- MGH 95037 917-B3
ESPARANZA WY
- SJS 95138 875-G5
ESPERANCA AV
2200 SCL 95054 813-C4

ESPERANZA CT
- SJS 95135 855-G3
ESPERANZA DR
26300 LAH 94022 811-B6
ESPINOZA LN
100 MTVW 94043 812-B5
ESPLANADA WY
800 SCIC 94305 810-J1
ESPLANADE LN
- SJS 95138 875-G6
ESPRIT CT
- SJS 95131 814-C4
ESQUIRE PL
10500 CPTO 95014 832-C6
ESSENDON WY
- SJS 95139 875-G7
ESSEX AV
1000 SUNV 94089 812-F4
ESSEX PL
2000 SCL 95051 833-D2
ESSEX ST
1400 SJS 95002 793-C7
ESSEX WY
1300 SJS 95117 853-D4
ESTACADA DR
25800 LAH 94022 811-C5
ESTACADA WY
25800 LAH 94022 811-C5
ESTANCIA CT
- SJS 95131 814-B6
ESTANCIA DR
- SJS 95134 813-F3
ESTATE DR
1200 LALT 94024 831-H3
ESTATES CT
1600 SJS 95127 835-B5
ESTATES DR
900 CPTO 95014 852-F2
9300 SCIC 95020 958-D3
E ESTATES DR
2000 CPTO 95014 852-F1
W ESTATES DR
10800 CPTO 95014 852-F2
ESTATE VIEW CT
3500 SJS 95148 835-D4
ESTATE VIEW WY
2000 SJS 95148 835-D4
ESTEBAN WY
200 SJS 95119 875-C7
ESTEE CT
- SJS 95133 814-E7
ESTELLA DR
2500 SCL 95051 833-B7
ESTELLE AV
1500 SJS 95118 874-A1
ESTERLEE AV
14400 SAR 95070 872-C3
ESTHER AV
200 CMBL 95008 853-E5
ESTHER CT
21400 SCIC 95033 912-J3
ESTHER DR
4400 SJS 95124 873-F3
14200 SCIC 95124 873-F2
ESTONIA CT
600 SJS 95123 874-G4
ESTRADA DR
- MTVW 94043 812-A5
ESTRADA TER
1200 SUNV 94086 812-B7
ESTRADE DR
5200 SJS 95118 874-A4
ESTRALITA PL
13100 LAH 94022 811-A7
13100 LAH 94022 831-A1
ESTRELLITA WY
1000 LALT 94022 811-D4
1300 CMBL 95008 873-B1
ESTUDILLO RD
700 SCIC 94305 810-H2
ETHAN CT
3600 SJS 95136 874-D1
ETHYL CT
100 MPS 95035 813-J1
ETHYL ST
300 MPS 95035 813-J1
ETOILE CT
3300 SJS 95135 855-G3
ETON AV
14100 SCIC 95127 835-A3
ETON WY
900 SUNV 94087 832-G5
ETRUSCAN DR
- SJS 95135 855-E2
ETTERSBERG DR
5800 SJS 95123 875-A5
EUCALYPTUS CT
2000 SCL 95050 833-C3
EUCALYPTUS DR
400 SJS 95134 813-D2
15500 SCIC 95030 872-H5
EUCALYPTUS LN
26000 LAH 94022 811-B6
EUCALYPTUS TER
- SUNV 94086 832-F1
EUCLID AV
- ATN 94027 790-B4
- LGTS 95030 892-J1
- LGTS 95030 893-A1
1900 MLPK 94025 791-B3
2000 EPA 94303 791-B3
EUCLID PL
500 EPA 94303 791-B2
EUGENE AV
1000 SJS 95126 833-J7
EUGENE CT
1000 SUNV 94087 832-B5
EUGENIA LN
- WDSD 94062 790-A5
EUGENIA WY
2000 LALT 94024 832-A5
16400 LGTS 95030 893-C2
16400 SCIC 95030 893-C2

EULALIE DR
2600 SJS 95121 854-J3
EUNICE AV
100 MTVW 94040 831-J1
13100 MTVW 94040 832-A1
EUREKA AV
1100 LALT 94024 831-H3
EUREKA CT
200 SUNV 94086 812-F5
1200 LALT 94024 831-H3
EUROPE CT
3600 SCL 95051 832-H4
EVA AV
1200 LALT 94024 831-H4
EVA CT
2400 SJS 95008 853-B7
EVANDALE AV
- MTVW 94043 812-A3
EVANGELHO CIR
6800 SBnC 95075 1060-J5
6800 SBnC 95075 1061-A5
EVANGELINE CT
6200 SJS 95123 874-G7
EVANGELINE DR
6100 SJS 95123 874-G6
EVANS CT
900 MPS 95035 794-C4
EVANS LN
1800 SJS 95125 854-D5
14300 SAR 95070 872-H2
EVANS RD
- MPS 95035 794-C5
- SCIC 95035 794-C5
EVANSTON PL
6000 SJS 95123 874-E5
EVCO CT
3200 SJS 95127 814-J7
EVELYN AV
2000 SJS 95122 834-J6
E EVELYN AV
- MTVW 94041 812-A5
300 SUNV 94086 812-E7
300 SUNV 94086 832-F1
W EVELYN AV
- MTVW 94041 812-A5
100 MTVW 94041 811-H4
200 SUNV 94086 812-C6
EVELYN ST
900 MLPK 94025 790-F4
EVELYN TER
900 SUNV 94086 832-H1
E EVELYN TER
900 SUNV 94086 832-H1
W EVELYN TER
900 SUNV 94086 832-H1
EVELYNS DR
- HOLL 95023 1040-B6
EVE MARIE AV
1600 LALT 94024 832-A4
EVENING SPRING CT
11500 CPTO 95014 852-A4
EVENING STAR CT
- MGH 95037 917-B3
100 MPS 95035 814-A2
EVENING STAR PL
- MGH 95037 917-A3
EVERDALE CT
2900 SJS 95148 855-C1
EVERDALE DR
2000 SJS 95148 855-C1
EVEREST DR
- SBnC 95023 1060-C2
EVERETT AV
100 PA 94301 790-H4
200 CMBL 95008 853-E6
1600 SJS 95125 854-A4
EVERETT CT
500 PA 94301 790-J4
EVERGLADE AV
1700 SJS 95122 834-H6
EVERGLADES DR
1500 MPS 95035 814-D1
1700 MPS 95035 794-E7
EVERGLOW CT
2900 SJS 95127 835-A4
EVERGREEN CT
- GIL 95020 977-F1
- HOLL 95023 1040-E5
EVERGREEN DR
3500 PA 94303 791-E7
16900 MGH 95037 936-J1
EVERGREEN LN
23000 SCrC 95033 913-C7
EVERGREEN ST
600 MLPK 94025 790-E6
EVERGREEN WY
100 MPS 95035 814-A3
2800 SJS 95121 855-E3
EVERGREEN VILLAGE SQ
- SJS 95135 855-F2
EVERMONT CT
1900 SJS 95127 835-A5
1900 SJS 95148 835-A5
EVERSOLE DR
2700 SJS 95133 814-G7
EVERWOOD CT
1900 SJS 95127 835-A5
1900 SJS 95148 835-A5
EVORA DR
2600 SJS 95124 873-G1
EVULICH CT
15900 SCIC 95127 815-B6
EWEN DR
- SBnC 95023 1059-J3
EWER DR
1700 SJS 95124 873-H3
EWERT RD
- SJS 95050 833-F1
- SJS 95110 813-F7
- SJS 95110 833-F1
EXCALIBER CT
14600 MGH 95037 937-B5
EXCALIBER DR
14700 MGH 95037 937-A5

EXCALIBUR DR
500 SJS 95116 834-J4
EXCELL CT
2000 MTVW 94043 811-G2
EXETER CT
100 SUNV 94087 832-E5
5900 SJS 95138 855-G7
EXMOOR WY
900 SUNV 94087 832-G5
EYE RD
- SUNV 94089 812-H3
EZIE ST
500 SJS 95111 854-J6

F

F ST
- SUNV 94089 812-H3
6800 SBnC 95075 1060-J5
6800 SBnC 95075 1061-A5
FABER PL
2400 PA 94303 791-E4
FABIAN DR
1700 SJS 95124 853-J7
1700 SJS 95124 873-J1
FABIAN WY
3700 PA 94303 791-F7
3800 PA 94303 811-F1
FABLE CT
- MTVW 94043 812-B5
FABLED OAK CT
3300 SJS 95148 835-E7
FAHRNER CT
2900 SJS 95135 855-F3
FAIR AV
900 SJS 95122 854-G1
FAIR LN
- LGTS 95030 873-A7
FAIRBANKS AV
200 CMBL 95008 873-E2
FAIRBANKS CIR
- SJS 95131 814-B6
FAIRBROOK CT
1000 SJS 95132 814-F6
FAIRBROOK DR
1100 MTVW 94040 832-A2
FAIRCHILD DR
- MTVW 94043 812-A3
FAIRCLIFF CT
2900 SJS 95125 854-A7
2900 SJS 95125 874-A1
FAIRCREST DR
2200 SJS 95124 873-E3
FAIRDELL DR
2500 SJS 95125 853-J7
2500 SJS 95125 854-A7
FAIRFAX AV
- ATN 94027 790-D1
2800 SJS 95148 855-C1
FAIRFAX CT
2800 SJS 95148 855-C1
FAIRFIELD AV
900 SCL 95050 833-D4
FAIRFIELD CT
200 PA 94306 811-E2
FAIRFORD CT
1100 SJS 95129 852-G3
FAIRFORD WY
1100 SJS 95129 852-G3
FAIRGLEN DR
2200 SJS 95125 854-A7
FAIRGROVE CT
2300 SJS 95125 853-J7
FAIRHAVEN CT
- HOLL 95023 1040-C7
- HOLL 95023 1060-C1
- MTVW 94041 811-J6
1400 SJS 95118 874-B1
FAIRHAVEN DR
- HOLL 95023 1040-C7
1400 SJS 95118 874-B1
FAIR HILL DR
1700 MPS 95035 794-D5
FAIRHILL LN
2200 SJS 95125 853-J6
FAIRHOPE PL
6000 SJS 95123 874-E5
FAIRLANDS AV
700 CMBL 95008 873-C1
FAIRLANDS CT
1100 CMBL 95008 873-C1
FAIRLANE AV
600 SCL 95051 833-A6
FAIRLAWN AV
1600 SJS 95125 854-A7
1600 SJS 95125 853-J7
FAIRLAWN CT
2200 SJS 95125 854-A7
FAIRMEAD AV
600 PA 94306 811-C3
FAIRMEAD LN
100 LGTS 95032 873-D6
FAIRMEADOW WY
200 MPS 95035 794-C2
FAIRMONT AV
400 MTVW 94041 811-H6
FAIRMONT CT
2100 SJS 95148 835-D5
FAIRMONT DR
2100 SJS 95148 835-D5
FAIROAK CT
2400 SJS 95125 853-J7
FAIR OAKS AV
1000 SUNV 94089 812-G4
N FAIR OAKS AV
- SUNV 94086 812-F7
900 SUNV 94089 812-F7
S FAIR OAKS AV
100 SUNV 94086 812-F7
100 SUNV 94086 832-F2
FAIR OAKS LN
- ATN 94027 790-E2

FAIR OAKS ST
100 MTVW 94040 811-F4
FAIR OAKS WY
500 SUNV 94089 812-G3
FAIRORCHARD AV
1600 SJS 95125 854-A7
1600 SJS 95125 853-J7
FAIRPLACE CT
1700 SJS 95122 854-G1
FAIRVALLEY CT
2200 SJS 95125 853-J6
FAIRVIEW AV
- ATN 94027 790-C5
- LGTS 95030 872-J7
1000 SJS 95125 854-B4
FAIRVIEW CT
- SBnC 95023 1020-E3
FAIRVIEW DR
400 GIL 95020 977-J4
400 GIL 95020 978-A4
FAIRVIEW LN
- SJS 95111 854-G4
2400 SCL 95051 833-C2
FAIRVIEW PZ
- LGTS 95030 872-J7
FAIRVIEW RD
- SBnC 95023 1060-E1
300 HOLL 95023 1040-E7
300 SBnC 95023 1040-E1
3900 SBnC 95023 1020-D1
7800 SBnC 95023 1000-B6
9800 SBnC 95023 999-J5
FAIRVIEW WY
300 MPS 95035 793-H5
FAIRWAY CIR
15000 LGTS 95030 873-A4
15000 MSER 95030 873-A4
FAIRWAY DR
1300 SCIC 94024 831-F3
5300 SCIC 95127 815-A7
FAIRWAY ENTRANCE DR
- SJS 95131 814-C7
FAIRWAY GLEN DR
2000 SCL 95054 813-C4
FAIRWAY GLEN LN
100 SJS 95139 895-E1
FAIRWAY GREEN CIR
1500 SJS 95131 814-C7
FAIRWEATHER LN
1100 SJS 95126 853-H4
FAIRWOOD AV
900 SUNV 94089 812-J5
1600 SJS 95125 854-A6
1600 SJS 95125 853-J7
FAIRWOODS CT
20900 CPTO 95014 852-D1
FAITH CT
3200 SJS 95127 814-J7
FALA TER
- SUNV 94087 832-F6
FALCATO DR
100 MPS 95035 794-E7
FALCON AV
1400 SUNV 94087 832-F4
FALCON CT
1400 GIL 95020 957-E7
1400 SUNV 94087 832-F5
FALCON DR
1200 MPS 95035 814-B3
FALCONI WY
- HOLL 95023 1040-B3
FALCON KNOLL CT
7000 SJS 95120 894-G4
FALCON KNOLL DR
1100 SJS 95120 894-G4
FALCON RIDGE CT
7000 SJS 95120 894-G4
FALERNO WY
3200 SJS 95135 855-G3
FALK CT
- SJS 95116 834-G3
400 MLPK 94025 791-A3
FALKIRK CT
100 SUNV 94087 832-E5
FALKIRK DR
7600 SJS 95135 855-J6
7600 SJS 95135 856-A6
FALL AV
1500 SJS 95127 835-C4
FALL CT
7900 CPTO 95014 852-C2
FALLBROOK AV
1600 SJS 95130 853-A5
1800 SJS 95130 852-J5
FALLCREEK SPRING CT
11500 CPTO 95014 852-A4
FALLEN LEAF DR
1100 MPS 95035 814-A3
1700 MPS 95035 813-J4
FALLEN LEAF LN
1400 LALT 94024 832-A3
FALLENLEAF LN
7300 CPTO 95014 852-D3
7300 SJS 95129 852-D3
FALLEN OAK CT
3200 SJS 95148 855-D2
FALLEN OAK DR
5000 SCIC 95037 935-H3
FALLINGTREE DR
2200 SJS 95131 814-C5
FALLING WATER CT
2300 SCL 95054 813-C5
FALLON AV
600 SCL 95050 833-D5
FALLON RD
- HOLL 95023 1020-B5
300 SBnC 95023 1020-F2
FALL RIVER DR
6500 SJS 95120 894-D1
FALL RIVER TER
500 SUNV 94087 832-D2

FALLS CREEK CT
4200 SJS 95135 855-F4
FALLS CREEK DR
3000 SJS 95135 855-F4
FALLSTONE CT
4500 SJS 95124 873-F3
FALLWOOD LN
2900 SJS 95132 814-D3
FALMOUTH CT
19300 SAR 95070 852-G5
FALMOUTH ST
3200 SJS 95132 814-F3
FALON WY
5800 SJS 95123 875-A5
FAMILLE CT
3300 SJS 95135 855-G3
FAN ST
1700 SJS 95131 834-D1
FAN WY
1700 SJS 95131 834-C1
FANCHER CT
100 LGTS 95030 873-A6
FANELLI CT
- SJS 95136 874-E1
FANITA WY
500 MLPK 94025 790-E6
FAN PALM CT
2000 SCL 95050 833-D3
FANTAIL CT
1500 SUNV 94087 832-F5
FANWOOD CT
1700 SJS 95133 834-D1
FANYON ST
100 MPS 95035 794-C6
FARADAY CT
1600 SJS 95124 873-J3
FARADAY DR
4300 SJS 95124 873-J3
FARADAY PL
4400 SJS 95124 873-J3
FARALLON DR
400 MGH 95037 936-J1
FARALLONE DR
10200 CPTO 95014 852-E2
FARAONE CT
4400 SJS 95136 874-E2
FARAONE DR
600 SJS 95136 874-E2
FARGATE CIR
1100 SJS 95131 834-C1
FARGHER DR
2800 SCL 95051 833-B3
FARGO DR
20600 CPTO 95014 832-D7
FARIS DR
900 SJS 95111 855-A6
FARLEY RD
16400 SCIC 95032 873-C5
16600 LGTS 95032 873-C5
W FARLEY RD
17400 LGTS 95030 873-A5
17400 LGTS 95032 873-A5
FARLEY ST
300 MTVW 94043 811-G4
FARM DR
700 SJS 95136 854-D7
FARM RD
- LALT 94024 831-J5
100 PTLV 94028 810-A5
100 WDSD 94062 810-A5
FARMAN LN
100 SCIC 95020 978-B6
FARMAN FRONTAGE RD
5300 GIL 95020 978-B6
5300 SCIC 95020 978-B6
FARMCREST ST
2200 MPS 95035 814-E1
FARM HILL WY
100 LGTS 95032 873-C4
6300 SJS 95120 874-E7
6300 SJS 95120 894-E1
FARMHOUSE CT
- SJS 95123 874-F4
FARMINGHAM WY
18400 CPTO 95014 852-C6
FARNDON AV
1800 LALT 94024 832-A4
2000 LALT 94024 831-J5
FARNHAM CT
100 SJS 95139 895-G1
FARNSWORTH DR
2300 SJS 95138 855-F6
FARR CT
1300 SJS 95125 854-A4
FARRAGOT DR
- HOLL 95023 1040-D5
- SBnC 95023 1040-D5
FARRAGUT LN
18500 MSER 95030 872-H5
18500 SCIC 95030 872-H5
FARRAGUT WY
1900 SJS 95133 814-E7
1900 SJS 95133 834-E1
FARREL CT
400 MTVW 94043 812-B5
FARRELL AV
- GIL 95020 957-H7
FARRELL PL
- SCL 95054 813-E5
FARRINGDON CT
1500 SJS 95127 835-A5
FARRINGDON DR
1200 SJS 95127 835-A4
FARRINGTON WY
2500 EPA 94303 791-B1
FARR RANCH CT
12300 SAR 95070 852-C6
FARR RANCH RD
12200 SAR 95070 852-C6
FARTHING WY
3200 SJS 95132 814-F3
FAR VUE LN
16500 SCIC 95030 872-G7

FARWELL AV
14600 SAR 95070 872-F3
FARWELL CT
14800 SAR 95070 872-F3
FARWELL LN
- LGTS 95030 892-J1
FASCINATION PL
- MPS 95035 814-J1
FATJO PL
2300 SCL 95050 833-C3
FAULSTICH CT
800 SJS 95112 834-B1
FAUST CT
2600 SJS 95121 854-J2
FAVONIA RD
100 PTLV 94028 810-C4
FAVRE RIDGE RD
18000 SCrC 95033 892-A4
FAWN CT
1600 CMBL 95008 873-A1
FAWN DR
1100 CMBL 95008 873-A1
3000 SJS 95124 873-G2
FAWN LN
- PTLV 94028 810-C5
FAWN TR
18100 SCIC 95033 912-J3
FAWN CREEK CT
27800 LAH 94022 810-H6
FAWNDALE DR
15100 SCIC 95032 893-F1
15100 LGTS 95032 893-F1
FAWNWOOD CT
3100 SJS 95148 855-D1
FAXON RD
- ATN 94027 790-D4
FAXON FOREST
- ATN 94027 790-D4
FAY DR
1600 SJS 95124 873-J2
FAY WY
200 MTVW 94043 811-G3
FAYE PARK DR
600 SJS 95136 874-E1
FAYETTE DR
2600 MTVW 94040 811-E3
FAZELI CT
- SJS 95008 873-F1
FEAFEL CT
4100 SJS 95134 813-D2
FEAFEL DR
4100 SJS 95134 813-D2
FEASEL CT
- SJS 95131 814-A6
FEATHER CT
- SBnC 95023 1060-B1
FEBRUARY DR
100 SJS 95138 875-D4
FEDALIZO CT
- SCIC 95046 937-H6
FEDERATION CT
5300 SJS 95123 875-B3
FEDORA CT
1400 SJS 95121 854-J2
FEHREN DR
13000 SCIC 95111 854-G6
13000 SJS 95111 854-G6
FELDER DR
6300 SJS 95123 875-B7
FELDSPAR DR
400 SJS 95111 854-G4
FELICE CT
100 SJS 95138 875-G7
FELICE DR
200 HOLL 95023 1039-H3
FELIPE AV
900 SJS 95122 834-F6
FELIX WY
500 SJS 95125 854-C4
FELIZ CT
16700 MGH 95037 917-F6
FELL AV
4800 SJS 95136 874-E3
FELL CT
900 SJS 95136 874-E3
FELLER AV
700 SJS 95127 835-B2
FELLOM CT
400 GIL 95020 978-A1
FELTER RD
4600 SCIC 95035 794-J6
4600 SCIC 95140 794-J6
5500 SCIC 95132 815-D1
5500 SCIC 95140 815-E1
FELTON DR
100 MLPK 94025 790-F2
FELTON PL
100 MLPK 94025 790-F2
FELTON WY
10500 CPTO 95014 852-D2
FENIAN DR
2200 SJS 95008 853-B6
FENLEY AV
300 SCIC 95117 853-D1
300 SJS 95117 853-D2
FENNEL CT
- MGH 95037 916-G4
FENNWOOD DR
- ATN 94027 790-F2
FENTON ST
400 SJS 95127 814-J7
500 SCIC 95127 814-J7
FENWAY CT
21000 CPTO 95014 832-C7
FENWICK WY
2900 SJS 95148 855-C2
FERGUSON DR
200 MTVW 94043 812-C5
FERGUSON RD
Rt#-G9
2600 SCIC 95020 958-E7
2600 SCIC 95020 978-F1
FERGUSON WY
1400 SJS 95129 852-J4

STREET
Block City ZIP Pg-Grid

FERN AV
18100 SCIC 95033 912-H3
FERN DR
5400 SJS 95124 873-J6
FERNANDEZ CT
400 SCL 95050 833-C6
FERNANDO AV
200 PA 94306 811-C1
FERNBROOK CT
18900 SAR 95070 852-H5
FERNCREST CT
13600 SAR 95070 872-H1
E FERNDALE AV
200 SUNV 94086 812-F5
W FERNDALE AV
100 SUNV 94086 812-F5
FERNDALE CT
700 SJS 95133 834-F2
FERNDALE DR
1500 SJS 95118 874-A5
FERNDALE WY
2300 SJS 95133 834-F1
FERNE AV
100 PA 94306 811-E2
FERNE CT
100 PA 94306 811-E2
FERNGLEN DR
900 SJS 95123 874-E5
FERNGROVE DR
800 CPTO 95014 852-G2
FERNHILL DR
23700 LAH 94024 831-E4
FERNIE CT
- GIL 95020 977-D3
FERNISH DR
1900 SJS 95148 835-D5
FERNLEAF DR
1000 SUNV 94086 832-G2
FERN PINE CT
1600 SJS 95131 834-D1
FERN RIDGE CT
500 SUNV 94087 832-D5
FERNSIDE SQ
3100 SJS 95132 814-E3
FERNSIDE ST
1900 RDWC 94061 790-A3
1900 WDSD 94062 790-A3
FERNWOOD AV
2400 SCL 95128 833-E7
2400 SJS 95128 833-E7
2500 SJS 95117 833-D7
N FERNWOOD CIR
300 SUNV 94086 812-F5
S FERNWOOD CIR
300 SUNV 94086 812-F5
W FERNWOOD CIR
600 SUNV 94086 812-F5
FERNWOOD LN
1300 GIL 95020 977-G3
FERRAGALLI CT
- GIL 95020 957-G7
FERRANT CT
13100 SCIC 95046 937-J5
FERRARI AV
- SJS 95110 833-J3
FERREIRA CT
400 MPS 95035 794-E7
FERREL CT
1300 SJS 95132 814-F5
FERRIS AV
16400 LGTS 95032 873-C7
16500 LGTS 95030 873-C7
FERRUM CT
2900 SJS 95148 855-D2
FERRY MORSE WY
100 MTVW 94041 812-A6
FESTA AGLIO CT
- GIL 95020 977-G1
FESTA AGLIO DR
- GIL 95020 957-G7
- GIL 95020 977-G1
FESTIVAL CT
7900 CPTO 95014 852-C2
FESTIVAL DR
7700 CPTO 95014 852-C2
FETZER DR
- SJS 95125 853-G4
FEVER DR
- SJS 95123 874-J6
- SJS 95123 875-A6
FEWTRELL DR
1000 CMBL 95008 853-G6
FICUS TER
- SUNV 94086 832-F1
FIDDLERS GRN
1200 SJS 95125 854-E6
FIDDLETOWN PL
5900 SJS 95120 874-C6
FIELDCREST DR
400 SJS 95123 875-B7
2000 MPS 95035 814-E1
FIELDFAIR CT
1300 SUNV 94087 832-F4
FIELDGATE CT
3200 SJS 95148 855-E1
FIELDING DR
800 PA 94303 791-D6
FIELDS DR
1400 SJS 95129 852-J4
FIELDSHIRE WY
1400 MGH 95037 917-D6
FIELDSTONE CT
- SJS 95133 814-E7
FIELDSTONE DR
14600 SAR 95070 872-C3
FIELDWOOD CT
800 SJS 95120 894-H3
FIESTA LN
7800 CPTO 95014 852-C2
FIESTA WY
- LGTS 95030 893-A1
FIFE AV
1000 PA 94301 791-A4

FIFE WY
700 SUNV 94087 832-F5
3400 SJS 95132 814-G3
FIFEWOOD CT
6500 SJS 95120 894-F1
FIG AV
1000 SUNV 94087 832-B2
FIG GROVE CT
5300 SJS 95123 875-A3
FIG TREE CT
19800 CPTO 95014 832-F7
FIGWOOD CT
800 SJS 95120 894-H3
FIJI DR
800 SJS 95127 814-H6
FILAN WY
- SJS 95135 855-E3
FILBERT WY
700 CMBL 95008 853-B7
FILBRO DR
6700 GIL 95020 977-J5
FILICE DR
7400 GIL 95020 977-H3
FILIP RD
700 LALT 94024 831-G2
FILLIPELLI DR
800 GIL 95020 977-G2
FILLMER AV
- LGTS 95030 873-B7
- LGTS 95032 873-B7
FILLMORE ST
1800 SCL 95050 833-D3
4300 SCL 95054 813-C5
FILOMENA AV
100 SJS 95110 834-A5
FILOMENA CT
3300 MTVW 94040 831-J2
FINCH AV
10000 CPTO 95014 832-G7
10000 CPTO 95014 852-G1
FINCH DR
3100 SJS 95117 853-D3
FINCH LN
1400 GIL 95020 957-F7
FINCH WY
1500 SUNV 94087 832-F5
FINCHWELL CT
- SJS 95138 875-D5
FINCHWOOD WY
700 SJS 95120 894-H3
FINDHORN CT
7900 SJS 95135 856-A5
FINDLEY DR
1700 MPS 95035 794-D6
FINE DR
1700 GIL 95020 977-E1
FINEO CT
1400 SJS 95131 814-C7
FINKA PL
- SJS 95126 833-D1
FINLEY PL
- SCL 95050 833-D2
FINLEY RIDGE CT
17700 SCIC 95037 918-A3
FINLEY RIDGE RD
17700 SCIC 95037 917-J2
17700 SCIC 95037 918-A3
FINN LN
12000 LAH 94022 831-C3
FIR AV
500 SUNV 94086 812-F6
FIR LN
- HOLL 95023 1039-H4
400 LALT 94024 831-J5
FIR ST
- MGH 95037 917-B7
- MGH 95037 937-B1
FIRCREST DR
12900 SCIC 95046 937-J5
12900 SCIC 95046 938-A5
FIRE WK
- MPS 95035 814-J1
FIREBIRD WY
1400 SUNV 94087 832-F4
FIREFLY DR
6200 SJS 95120 874-C7
6300 SJS 95120 894-C1
FIRENZE CT
- SJS 95138 855-E7
- SJS 95138 875-E1
FIRESIDE DR
2900 SJS 95128 853-E3
FIRESTONE CT
- SJS 95138 875-H1
FIRESTONE DR
1500 SJS 95116 834-F5
FIRESTONE LP
1500 SJS 95116 834-F5
FIRETHORN CT
2000 MPS 95035 793-J3
FIRETHORN ST
- MPS 95035 793-J3
FIRETHORN TER
- SUNV 94086 832-F2
FIRETHORN WY
- PTLV 94028 810-D7
FIRETHORNE DR
11000 CPTO 95014 832-D6
FIREWOOD CT
700 SJS 95120 894-H3
FIRLOCH AV
400 SUNV 94086 832-F1
E FIRST ST
500 MLPK 94025 790-H3
FIRTH CT
1000 SUNV 94087 832-H5
FIRTH WY
3200 SJS 95121 855-B3
FIR TREE CT
300 MPS 95035 813-J3
FIRWOOD DR
10000 CPTO 95014 851-J1
FISHBURNE AV
5800 SJS 95123 874-F5

FISHER AV
500 MGH 95037 937-E1
500 SCIC 95037 937-E1
1800 SCIC 95037 917-G7
4200 SCIC 95127 835-A2
16100 LGTS 95032 873-B6
FISHER RD
100 SCIC 95037 895-J6
100 SCIC 95037 896-A6
100 SJS 95037 896-A6
100 SJS 95141 895-J6
FISHER HAWK DR
1300 SUNV 94087 832-F4
FISK AV
500 SJS 95125 854-A2
FISK PL
- SCL 95050 833-C2
FITCHVILLE AV
1500 SJS 95126 853-H3
FITZGERALD AV
400 SCIC 95020 957-F3
400 SCIC 95046 957-F3
FITZGERALD CT
10900 SCIC 95046 957-E4
FITZGERALD DR
21500 CPTO 95014 832-B7
FITZGERALD RD
400 SCIC 95020 958-E1
700 SCIC 95020 938-E7
FITZPATRICK WY
- SCL 95054 813-E5
FIVE OAKS CT
- SBnC 95023 1000-E6
FIVE WOUNDS LN
1300 SJS 95116 834-E4
FLAGG AV
400 SCIC 95128 853-F1
FLAGLER ST
500 SJS 95127 814-H7
11900 SCIC 95127 814-H7
FLAGSTAD CT
2700 SJS 95121 855-A3
FLAGSTAFF CT
48700 FRMT 94539 793-J2
FLAGSTAFF PL
48400 FRMT 94539 793-J2
FLAGSTAFF RD
48500 FRMT 94539 793-J2
FLAGSTONE DR
2500 SJS 95132 814-F6
FLAMEWOOD AV
900 SUNV 94089 812-J5
FLAMINGO DR
200 CMBL 95008 853-G7
FLAMINGO WY
1400 SUNV 94087 832-F5
FLAMING OAK LN
16300 MGH 95037 917-G6
FLANDERS DR
3100 SJS 95132 814-G5
FLANIGAN DR
1400 SJS 95121 854-J2
1600 SJS 95121 855-A2
FLANNERY ST
500 SCL 95051 833-A6
FLATER DR
3000 SJS 95148 855-C2
FLAT ROCK CIR
4900 SJS 95136 874-J2
FLAX MOSS CT
1200 SJS 95120 894-C1
FLAXWOOD ST
1100 SJS 95120 874-D6
FLEDERMAUS CT
1500 SJS 95121 854-J4
FLEET ST
5800 SJS 95120 874-B6
FLEETWOOD DR
1000 SJS 95120 874-D7
FLEMING AV
- SCIC 95127 835-A1
- SJS 95127 835-C2
FLEMING CT
100 SJS 95127 835-A1
FLETCHER DR
- ATN 94027 790-B5
FLEUR PL
- ATN 94027 790-C4
FLEUR DE LIS CT
3200 SJS 95132 814-G5
FLICKER WY
1300 SUNV 94087 832-F4
FLICKINGER AV
1100 SJS 95131 814-C5
FLICKINGER CT
1700 SJS 95131 814-C5
FLICKINGER PL
1700 SJS 95131 814-C5
FLICKINGER RD
1800 SJS 95131 814-C4
FLICKINGER WY
1800 SJS 95131 814-C4
FLIN WY
800 SUNV 94087 832-F5
FLINT AV
1800 SJS 95148 835-C5
2000 SCIC 95148 835-C5
FLINT CT
3300 SJS 95148 835-D5
FLINT RD
- SBnC 95023 1039-B5
- SBnC 95045 1039-B5
700 SBnC 95020 1039-B5
FLINTBURY CT
2000 SJS 95148 835-C5
FLINT CREEK CT
1800 SJS 95148 835-D4
FLINT CREEK DR
3500 SJS 95148 835-D4
FLINT CREEK WY
1700 SJS 95148 835-D4
FLINTCREST CT
2000 SJS 95148 835-C5

FLINTCREST DR
2000 SJS 95148 835-C5
FLINTDALE DR
3200 SJS 95148 835-C5
FLINTFIELD DR
2000 SJS 95148 835-D5
FLINTHAVEN DR
3100 SJS 95148 835-B5
FLINTHILL CT
3400 SJS 95148 835-D5
FLINTLOCK RD
15900 SCIC 95014 851-E4
FLINTMONT CT
3200 SJS 95148 835-C5
FLINTMONT DR
3200 SJS 95148 835-C5
FLINTMORE CT
2100 SJS 95148 835-D5
FLINTRIDGE DR
15500 LGTS 95032 873-C5
FLINTSHIRE ST
21500 CPTO 95014 852-B3
FLINTSIDE CT
2100 SJS 95148 835-D5
FLINTVIEW CT
3200 SJS 95148 835-D7
FLINTWELL CT
100 SJS 95138 875-D4
FLINTWELL WY
- SJS 95138 875-D4
FLINTWICK CT
2000 SJS 95148 835-D5
FLINTWOOD CT
2600 SJS 95148 835-D6
FLOOD CIR
- ATN 94027 790-G1
FLOOD DR
1800 SJS 95124 873-H1
FLORA AV
- HOLL 95023 1040-A3
- SBnC 95023 1040-A3
1200 SJS 95117 853-B4
1200 SJS 95130 853-B4
FLORAL ST
- GIL 95020 977-H1
FLORALES DR
600 PA 94306 811-C2
FLORA VISTA AV
300 SUNV 94086 832-E1
3400 SCL 95051 832-J3
10300 CPTO 95014 832-D7
FLORENCE AV
2700 SJS 95127 834-J3
2800 SCIC 95127 834-J3
FLORENCE CT
- SBnC 95023 1060-D2
3100 SJS 95127 834-J2
3100 SJS 95127 835-A2
17600 MGH 95037 916-H7
FLORENCE DR
10400 CPTO 95014 832-B6
FLORENCE LN
900 MLPK 94025 790-F4
FLORENCE ST
100 SUNV 94086 812-D7
300 SUNV 94086 832-D1
400 PA 94301 790-J4
FLORENCE WY
200 SJS 95110 834-A7
1000 CMBL 95008 873-D1
FLORENCE PARK DR
3000 SJS 95135 855-E2
FLORENTINE DR
500 SJS 95123 875-B3
FLORES
- MTVW 94043 811-J2
FLORESTA DR
3200 SJS 95148 835-D6
E FLORESTA WY
100 SMCo 94028 810-E3
W FLORESTA WY
200 SMCo 94028 810-E3
FLORIDA AV
1300 SJS 95122 834-H6
FLORY DR
2400 SJS 95121 854-J2
FLOWER CT
1300 CPTO 95014 852-D4
FLOWER LN
400 MTVW 94043 812-B5
FLOWER GARDEN LN
1600 SJS 95124 873-J6
FLOWERING MEADOW CT
- SJS 95135 855-H7
FLOWERING MEADOW LN
- SJS 95135 855-H7
FLOWERING PEAR DR
11000 CPTO 95014 832-D6
FLOWERING PLUM RD
6200 SJS 95120 874-D7
FLOWERS LN
3100 PA 94306 791-D7
FLOYD AV
1400 SUNV 94087 832-E4
FLOYD ST
- SJS 95110 854-C2
FLUME CT
700 MPS 95035 794-B5
FLYNN AV
300 MTVW 94043 812-A4
FLYNN RD
- HOLL 95023 1019-J6
- SBnC 95023 1019-J6
- HOLL 95023 1020-A7
FOGL CT
- SMCo 94061 790-B4
FOLEY AV
1100 SCL 95051 833-B4
1400 SJS 95122 834-G7
FOLIGNO WY
5700 SJS 95138 875-G1

FOLKESTONE DR
7900 CPTO 95014 852-C3
FOLKLORE CT
6600 SJS 95120 894-C5
FOLLE BLANCHE DR
- SJS 95135 855-G6
FOLSOM CIR
400 MPS 95035 794-A6
FOLSOM CT
400 MPS 95035 794-A6
FOLSOM PL
100 MPS 95035 794-A6
FONICK DR
400 SJS 95111 875-C1
FONT TER
- SJS 95126 854-A1
FONTAINBLEAU TER
300 LALT 94022 811-E5
FONTAINBLEU AV
1200 MPS 95035 794-A4
FONTAINBLEU CT
1200 MPS 95035 794-A4
FONTAINE DR
13300 SAR 95070 852-G7
FONTAINE RD
2400 SJS 95121 854-J2
FONTANA DR
200 SCL 95051 833-B7
FONTANELLE CT
400 SJS 95111 875-C2
FONTANELLE DR
300 SJS 95111 875-C1
FONTANELLE PL
4900 SJS 95111 875-C1
FONTANOSO WY
400 SJS 95138 875-D3
FONTENAY WY
- SJS 95135 855-G3
FONTENBLEU
900 SUNV 94087 832-B4
FONTEVILLE CT
- SJS 95127 834-C2
FOOTE AV
- CMBL 95008 853-F6
FOOTHILL AV
10500 SCIC 95020 958-A1
11800 SCIC 95020 938-A7
12000 SCIC 95046 937-H3
12000 SCIC 95046 938-A7
14600 MGH 95046 937-G1
15600 SCIC 95037 917-G7
15600 SCIC 95037 937-G1
FOOTHILL BLVD
10200 CPTO 95014 852-A1
FOOTHILL BLVD
Rt#-G5
2400 LALT 94024 832-A7
2400 CPTO 95014 832-A7
8400 SCIC 94024 832-A7
8700 CPTO 94024 832-A7
10300 CPTO 95014 852-A1
FOOTHILL CT
100 MGH 95037 937-A1
800 SJS 95123 874-F6
FOOTHILL DR
700 SJS 95123 874-E5
FOOTHILL EXWY
Rt#-G5
100 LALT 94022 811-C5
100 LALT 94022 831-F1
200 LALT 94024 831-F1
400 SCIC 94024 831-F1
2600 PA 94304 811-C5
2600 SCIC 94304 810-J3
2600 SCIC 94304 811-C5
2600 PA 94304 810-J3
4100 PA 94306 811-C5
4400 LALT 94024 832-A6
7100 CPTO 95014 832-A6
14000 LAH 94022 811-C5
14000 LALT 94306 811-C5
FOOTHILL LN
12100 LAH 94022 831-A1
12800 SAR 95070 852-D6
FOOTHILL RD
400 SBnC 95023 1000-E4
FOOTHILL GLEN CT
6000 SJS 95123 874-F6
FOOTHILL GLEN DR
6000 SJS 95123 874-F6
FOOTHILL MEADOWS CT
1400 SJS 95131 814-C7
FOOTPATH WY
- SCrC 95033 871-C4
FORBES AV
2100 SCL 95050 833-B6
2500 SCL 95051 833-A6
3200 SCL 95051 832-J6
FORBES CT
3100 SCL 95051 833-A6
FORBES DR
6200 SJS 95123 874-J7
FORD AV
1400 SJS 95110 854-D2
FORD RD
- SJS 95138 875-D3
FORDHAM CT
1500 MTVW 94040 811-G7
FORDHAM DR
2000 SCL 95051 833-A2
2000 SCL 95051 832-J2
FORDHAM ST
2400 EPA 94303 791-B1
FORDHAM WY
1100 MTVW 94040 811-G7
1700 MTVW 94040 831-G1
FORDWELL CT
- SJS 95138 875-D4
FOREST AV
100 PA 94301 790-J5
600 PA 94301 791-A3
1800 SCIC 95128 833-F7
1800 SJS 95128 833-E7

FOREST AV
2300 SJS 95050 833-E7
2400 SCL 95050 833-E7
2500 SCL 95128 833-E7
2500 SJS 95117 833-C7
3100 SCL 95117 833-C7
20000 CPTO 95014 832-E7
FOREST CT
1000 PA 94301 791-A3
1800 MPS 95035 813-J4
1800 MPS 95035 814-A4
FOREST DR
200 MGH 95037 937-B5
16900 MGH 95037 917-D6
FOREST LN
100 MLPK 94025 790-E2
FOREST ST
7100 GIL 95020 978-A1
8400 GIL 95020 977-J1
8800 GIL 95020 957-J7
FORESTBROOK WY
4000 SJS 95111 854-J6
4000 SJS 95111 855-A7
FOREST CREEK DR
1100 SJS 95129 852-J3
1200 HOLL 95023 1040-C5
FORESTDALE AV
700 SJS 95116 834-E7
FORESTER CT
3800 SJS 95121 855-E3
FOREST GLEN DR
5000 SJS 95129 852-J2
FOREST HILL DR
100 LGTS 95032 873-G5
2600 SJS 95130 852-J7
FOREST HILLS DR
20400 SAR 95070 872-D3
FOREST KNOLL DR
1000 SJS 95129 852-G3
FOREST PARK DR
100 SCL 95051 833-A7
FOREST RIDGE DR
800 SJS 95129 852-J2
FOREST SPRING CT
11500 CPTO 95014 852-C4
FOREST VIEW DR
5000 SJS 95129 852-J2
FORESTWOOD DR
3800 SJS 95121 855-D3
FORGE DR
18900 CPTO 95014 832-H6
FORGE WY
- CPTO 95014 832-D6
- SUNV 94087 832-D6
- SUNV 95014 832-D6
FORGEMILL CT
1000 SJS 95121 854-J4
FORGETREE CT
2000 SJS 95131 814-C5
FORGEWOOD AV
1200 SUNV 94089 812-J3
FORMAN AV
1600 SJS 95124 873-J3
FORMAN DR
500 CMBL 95008 853-F7
FORMBY CT
- SJS 95138 855-E6
FORMOSA DR
1200 SJS 95131 814-B7
FORMOSA RIDGE DR
1100 SJS 95127 835-B3
FORMWAY CT
100 LALT 94022 811-F6
FORREST AV
- LGTS 95032 873-B6
FORRESTAL AV
1200 SJS 95110 833-J2
FORRESTER CT
200 LGTS 95032 893-D1
FORRESTER RD
200 LGTS 95032 893-D1
FORSUM CT
100 SJS 95138 875-G6
FORSUM RD
7200 SJS 95138 875-G6
FORT BAKER DR
900 CPTO 95014 852-B2
FORTINI RD
21100 SCIC 95120 895-B4
FORT LARAMIE DR
500 SUNV 94087 832-D5
FORTRAN CT
4400 SJS 95134 813-D1
FORTRAN DR
4600 SJS 95134 813-D1
FORTROSE CT
- SJS 95139 875-H7
FORT ROYAL PL
4600 SJS 95136 874-F2
FORTUNA CT
13600 SAR 95070 872-H1
FORTUNATA PL
- GIL 95020 978-A2
FORTUNE DR
1900 SJS 95131 814-B4
FOSGATE AV
2300 SCL 95050 833-D7
FOSS AV
- SJS 95116 834-H3
FOSTER CT
1500 SJS 95120 874-A7
FOSTER RD
- LGTS 95030 893-B2
100 SCIC 95030 893-A2
18200 SCIC 95033 893-A2
FOUNDERS LN
800 MPS 95035 794-B4
FOUNDRY CT
500 SJS 95133 834-G1
FOUNTAIN AL
- SJS 95113 834-B6
FOUNTAIN AV
16600 MGH 95037 917-E6

FOUNTAIN CIR
100 SJS 95131 814-A5
FOUNTAIN CT
16600 MGH 95037 917-E6
FOUNTAIN OAKS DR
2100 MGH 95037 917-E6
FOUNTAIN PALM CT
- SJS 95133 814-J4
FOUNTAIN PARK LN
800 MTVW 94043 811-J4
FOUNTAIN VIEW DR
3700 SJS 95136 854-G7
FOUR CORNERS DR
- SBnC 95023 999-J5
FOURIER DR
800 SJS 95127 835-C2
FOUR OAKS CIR
1400 SJS 95131 814-D5
FOUR OAKS CT
2300 SJS 95131 814-D5
FOUR OAKS RD
1300 SJS 95131 814-D5
FOUR SEASONS CT
2300 SJS 95131 814-D5
FOURTH PLAIN CT
2700 SJS 95121 855-D3
FOWLER AV
3100 SCL 95051 833-A3
3300 SCL 95051 832-J3
FOWLER CT
- SJS 95135 855-E3
FOWLER LN
1400 LALT 94024 831-J3
FOWLER RD
2900 SJS 95135 855-G3
3300 SCIC 95135 855-H2
FOWLER ST
7200 GIL 95020 977-H4
FOX AV
- SJS 95110 834-A5
W FOX CT
500 RDWC 94061 790-C1
FOX DR
1700 SJS 95131 814-A6
FOX LN
800 SJS 95131 814-A5
FOX RUN
- SCrC 95033 871-D3
FOXBORO PL
3200 SJS 95135 855-E3
FOXBOROUGH DR
300 MTVW 94041 812-A6
FOXCHASE DR
900 SJS 95123 874-D4
FOXDALE CT
1500 SJS 95122 834-J5
FOXDALE DR
2400 SJS 95122 834-J5
2500 SJS 95122 835-A5
FOXDALE LP
1200 SJS 95122 835-A5
1200 SJS 95122 834-J5
FOXGLOVE CT
- GIL 95020 977-J6
FOXGLOVE DR
900 SUNV 94086 832-G2
FOXHALL LP
1300 SJS 95125 853-G4
FOXHILL CIR
- SBnC 95023 1060-G1
FOX HOLLOW CIR
100 MGH 95037 916-H6
FOXHOLLOW CT
1100 MPS 95035 794-C5
FOXHURST WY
1000 SJS 95120 894-G4
FOX MEADOW CT
1100 SJS 95120 894-G4
FOXRIDGE PL
700 SJS 95133 814-G7
FOXRIDGE WY
700 SJS 95133 814-G6
FOXSWALLOW CT
900 SJS 95120 894-G2
FOXTAIL
- PTLV 94028 830-C1
FOXTAIL CT
- SJS 95138 855-F6
FOXTAIL DR
600 SUNV 94086 832-F2
FOXWELL CT
- SJS 95138 875-D4
FOXWOOD DR
1200 SJS 95118 874-C4
FOXWOOD RD
100 SMCo 94028 830-D4
FOXWOOD ST
- HOLL 95023 1040-D7
FOXWOOD WY
1200 SJS 95118 874-B4
FOXWORTHY AV
1000 SJS 95125 854-B7
1000 SJS 95136 854-C7
1100 SJS 95118 854-B7
1300 SJS 95118 874-A1
1300 SJS 95125 874-A1
1500 SJS 95118 873-G1
1600 SJS 95125 873-G1
1600 SJS 95124 873-F1
FRAGRANT HARBOR CT
200 SJS 95123 874-J3
FRAMPTON CT
25600 LAH 94024 831-E4
FRAN CT
- SJS 95123 874-F7
FRANCEMONT DR
- LAH 94022 831-B3
N FRANCES AV
100 SUNV 94086 812-E7
FRANCES DR
200 LALT 94022 811-E6
S FRANCES ST
100 SUNV 94086 812-E7

STREET Block City ZIP Pg-Grid

S FRANCES ST
400 SUNV 94086 832-E1
FRANCES WY
400 MTVW 94041 811-J6
FRANCESCA CT
- MSER 95030 873-A6
FRANCHERE PL
1300 SUNV 94087 832-B4
FRANCIS AV
1900 SCL 95051 833-A2
FRANCIS CT
17900 SCIC 95033 912-J3
FRANCIS DR
300 SJS 95133 834-H1
300 SCIC 95133 834-H1
1900 SCIC 95133 814-H7
1900 SJS 95133 814-H7
FRANCISCAN CT
2400 SCL 95051 833-B2
6100 SJS 95120 874-A7
FRANCISCAN RDG
- PTLV 94028 830-C1
FRANCISCAN WY
6100 SJS 95120 874-A7
6100 SJS 95120 894-A1
FRANCISCO AV
1100 SJS 95126 853-H4
FRANCIS OAKS WY
15300 LGTS 95032 873-E6
FRANCK AV
1700 SCL 95051 833-C3
FRANCO CT
10800 CPTO 95014 832-D6
FRANCO LN
- SCIC 94024 831-F2
FRANCOLIN TER
- SUNV 94087 832-F5
FRANDON CT
4100 PA 94306 811-C3
FRANELA DR
3000 SJS 95124 873-J1
FRANK AV
16700 LGTS 95032 873-C5
FRANK CT
2000 MPS 95035 794-E6
16900 LGTS 95032 873-C5
FRANKFURT ST
1100 SJS 95126 833-G5
FRANKIE LN
6500 MonC 93907 1037-A7
FRANKLIN AV
13100 MTVW 94040 832-A1
20100 SAR 95070 872-E1
FRANKLIN CT
- SJB 95045 1038-D5
700 SJS 95127 814-H7
22400 MTVW 94040 832-A1
FRANKLIN ST
- SJB 95045 1038-D5
100 MTVW 94041 811-H5
600 SCL 95050 833-E4
700 SCL 95053 833-E4
FRANKS DR
- SBnC 95023 1060-C2
FRANKS LN
1400 SMCo 94025 790-D5
FRANQUETTE AV
800 SJS 95125 854-B5
FRASCHINI CIR
5300 SJS 95123 874-H3
FRASER DR
1400 SUNV 94087 832-B5
FRASER PL
- SCL 95050 833-E3
FRAZER LAKE RD
1900 SCIC 95020 978-F5
6900 SBnC 95023 999-A3
6900 SBnC 95023 1019-F1
6900 SBnC 95020 999-A2
6900 SBnC 95020 1019-F1
7400 SBnC 95020 998-H1
7400 SBnC 95023 998-H1
7800 SCIC 95020 998-H1
FREDA CT
1200 CMBL 95008 873-A1
FREDERICK AV
- ATN 94027 790-H1
700 SCL 95050 833-D5
FREDERICK COMS
- SJS 95126 834-A7
FREDERICK CT
- MTVW 94043 812-B5
- SMCo 94025 790-H1
100 LALT 94022 811-E6
FREDERICKSBURG CT
12200 SAR 95070 852-E6
FREDERICKSBURG DR
12200 SAR 95070 852-E6
FREDS WY
- SBnC 95023 1060-F3
FREED AV
3900 SJS 95117 853-B4
FREEDOM CIR
3900 SCL 95054 813-B6
FREEDOM CT
6700 SJS 95120 894-C5
FREEDOM DR
- HOLL 95023 1040-C6
21000 CPTO 95014 832-C7
FREEDOM LN
- MTVW 94040 811-E3
FREELAND DR
1500 MPS 95035 794-D7
FREEMAN AV
14800 SCIC 95127 814-J6
14800 SJS 95127 814-J6
FREEMAN CT
9000 GIL 95020 957-H7
FREESTONE AV
1000 SUNV 94087 832-B2
FRWY I-280
- SJS - 853-H2
FRWY Rt#-17
- CMBL - 853-F3

FRWY Rt#-17
- CMBL - 853-F4
- CMBL - 873-E1
- LGTS - 873-B7
- LGTS - 873-D3
- LGTS - 892-J1
- LGTS - 893-A1
- SCIC - 892-J2
- SJS - 853-F2
FRWY U.S.-101
- SCIC - 998-C2
FREEWAY VISTA
19200 SCIC 95037 916-J3
FREITAS RD
100 SBnC 95023 1039-A4
600 SBnC 95045 1038-J4
600 SBnC 95045 1039-A4
700 SBnC 95020 1038-J4
700 SBnC 95020 1039-A4
FREMONT AV
100 LALT 94022 831-E1
100 LALT 94024 831-E1
1100 SUNV 94087 832-A3
1200 SUNV 94024 832-A3
14000 LALT 94024 832-A3
E FREMONT AV
500 SUNV 94087 832-E4
600 SCIC 94087 832-E4
W FREMONT AV
500 SUNV 94087 832-B4
1200 SUNV 94024 832-B4
FREMONT BLVD
47000 FRMT 94538 793-F1
FREMONT PL
900 MLPK 94025 790-F4
FREMONT RD
500 SCIC 94305 790-F7
13500 LAH 94022 811-D7
W FREMONT RD
12800 LAH 94022 811-B5
FREMONT ST
500 MLPK 94025 790-F4
600 SCL 95050 833-D4
1100 SJS 95126 833-H6
FREMONT TER W
1200 SUNV 94087 832-C3
FREMONT WY
500 HOLL 95023 1039-J3
500 HOLL 95023 1040-A4
FREMONTIA
- PTLV 94028 830-C1
FREMONT PINES LN
13900 LAH 94022 811-C6
FRENCH CT
100 SJS 95139 895-G1
400 MLPK 94025 791-A3
1200 MPS 95035 814-D2
FRENCH ST
2500 SCL 95051 832-J2
2500 SUNV 94086 832-J2
FRENCHMANS RD
700 SCIC 94305 810-H2
FRENCH OAK DR
8600 SJS 95135 855-J6
FRENI CT
1400 SJS 95121 854-J2
FRESNO ST
2800 SCL 95051 833-A4
FREYA CT
500 HOLL 95023 1040-B4
FREYA DR
2200 SJS 95148 855-D2
FRIAR CT
5900 SJS 95129 852-G3
FRIAR WY
100 CMBL 95008 853-D7
5800 SJS 95129 852-G3
FRIARS CT
2300 LALT 94024 831-J6
FRIARS LN
2300 LALT 94024 831-J6
FRICKA CT
2700 SJS 95121 854-J4
2700 SJS 95121 855-A3
FRINGE TREE TER
- SUNV 94086 832-F1
FRITZEN ST
1100 SJS 95122 834-H5
FROBISHER WY
1700 SJS 95124 853-H7
FROLIC WY
1200 SJS 95129 852-J3
FRONDA DR
3200 SJS 95148 835-D6
FRONT LN
500 MTVW 94041 811-J5
FRONTAGE RD
- SJS 95110 833-J4
- SJS 95110 834-A5
6700 SJS 95120 894-F2
FRONTENAC AV
1300 SUNV 94087 832-B4
FRONTERO AV
1500 SCIC 94024 831-G3
FRONTIER TRAIL DR
- SJS 95136 874-H2
2600 SJS 95136 875-A2
FROST DR
1500 SJS 95131 814-C6
FROST RD
- SCIC 95037 917-F1
FRUIT BARN LN
8700 SJS 95135 856-A6
FRUITDALE AV
1100 SJS 95126 853-H2
1300 SJS 95128 853-E2
2000 SCIC 95128 853-F2
FRUITDALE CT
900 SJS 95126 853-J2
FRUITVALE AV
13600 SAR 95070 872-F3
FRUITWOOD CT
1600 SJS 95125 853-J5

FRYE LN
6100 SBnC 95023 999-G6
FUCHSIA CT
8800 GIL 95020 977-G1
FUCHSIA DR
1500 SJS 95125 854-A7
FUJIKO DR
1500 SJS 95131 814-D5
FUJIKO WY
2100 SJS 95131 814-D5
FUJIYAMA LN
1300 SJS 95132 814-G4
FULBAR CT
1200 SJS 95132 814-G4
FULLER AV
300 SJS 95125 854-A2
FULLER ST
4400 SCL 95054 813-C4
FULLER TER
- SUNV 94086 812-C7
FULLERTON CT
400 SJS 95111 875-C1
FULLERTON DR
400 SJS 95111 875-C1
FULTON AV
1000 SUNV 94089 812-F4
FULTON CT
400 SCL 95051 832-H7
700 MPS 95035 794-A5
FULTON ST
- CMBL 95008 853-A6
100 PA 94301 790-J3
600 PA 94301 791-A4
700 PA 94303 791-B5
FUME BLANC CT
8500 SJS 95135 855-H7
FUMIA CT
- SJS 95131 814-B6
FUMIA DR
- SJS 95131 814-A6
FUMIA PL
- SJS 95131 814-A6
FUNSTON DR
4100 SJS 95136 874-E1
FURLONG AL
- HOLL 95023 1040-A3
FURLONG AV
7200 SCIC 95020 978-E1
FURLONG DR
800 SJS 95123 874-D5
FUSCHIA DR
1000 SUNV 94086 832-H2
FUSTERIA CT
200 FRMT 94539 793-H1
FUTAMASE CT
2400 SJS 95111 854-G3
FYNES CT
1100 SJS 95131 834-C1

G

G CT
- GIL 95020 977-E1
G RD
- SUNV 94089 812-H3
G ST
1100 SUNV 94089 812-E3
GABARDA WY
100 SMCo 94028 810-D4
GABILAN AV
200 SUNV 94086 812-C7
GABILAN DR
1400 HOLL 95023 1040-D6
GABILAN ST
400 LALT 94022 811-E7
500 LALT 94022 831-E1
GABLE DR
100 FRMT 94539 793-H1
GABLE LN
1700 SJS 95124 873-H5
GABRIAL AV
2300 MTVW 94040 811-F3
GABRIELA CT
- SJS 95131 814-B6
GABRIELE CT
- HOLL 95023 1039-H4
N GADSDEN DR
- MPS 95035 794-C6
S GADSDEN DR
- MPS 95035 794-D6
GAFFEY RD
- SCrC 95076 976-A6
GAGE CT
- GIL 95020 977-J6
3900 SJS 95124 873-E3
GAIL AV
500 SUNV 94086 832-F3
GAILEN AV
700 PA 94303 811-F1
800 PA 94303 791-F7
GAILEN CT
700 PA 94303 811-F1
GAILEN LN
700 PA 94303 811-E1
GAILLARDIA WY
1100 EPA 94303 791-C3
GAINSBOROUGH DR
1200 SUNV 94087 832-E3
GAINSVILLE AV
1300 SJS 95122 834-J5
GALA CT
2900 SCL 95051 833-A7
GALAHAD AV
700 SJS 95116 834-J4
1100 SJS 95122 834-J4
GALAHAD CT
2500 SJS 95122 834-J4
GALAXY CT
400 MPS 95035 813-J3
GALE DR
700 CMBL 95008 853-C5
GALEN DR
400 SJS 95123 874-J7

GALENA DR
1500 SJS 95121 855-A2
GALEWOOD CT
1700 SJS 95133 834-E3
GALINDO CT
800 MPS 95035 814-E1
GALLANT FOX AV
5100 SJS 95111 875-B2
GALLANT FOX WY
14600 MGH 95037 937-C5
GALLATIN DR
800 SCL 95051 832-J5
GALLEON CT
600 SJS 95133 814-F7
600 SJS 95133 834-F1
GALLERIA DR
400 SJS 95134 813-H4
GALLI CT
300 LALT 94022 811-F6
7100 SJS 95129 852-E3
GALLI DR
100 LALT 94022 811-E6
7000 SJS 95129 852-E3
GALLOP DR
16700 MGH 95037 917-F6
GALLOWAY CT
1400 SUNV 94087 832-B4
GALLOWAY DR
7600 SJS 95135 855-J6
7600 SJS 95135 856-A6
GALLUP DR
2400 SCL 95051 833-B2
5600 SJS 95118 874-C4
GALOWAY CT
- GIL 95020 977-D3
GALVESTON AV
2100 SJS 95122 854-G2
GALVEZ ST
100 SCIC 94305 790-H6
GALWAY CT
2300 SCL 95050 833-C2
GALWAY DR
1600 CPTO 95014 852-D5
GAMAN LN
- SJS 95112 834-B3
GAMAY CT
400 FRMT 94539 793-J2
3400 SJS 95148 835-D5
GAMAY DR
48800 FRMT 94539 793-J2
48800 FRMT 94539 794-A2
GAMBETTA LN
3700 SJS 95136 854-G7
GAMBIER CT
- PTLV 94028 810-C7
GAMBLIN CIR
1500 SUNV 94087 832-B5
GAMBLIN CT
2600 SCL 95051 833-B7
GAMBLIN DR
200 SCL 95051 833-B7
GAMEL WY
1900 MTVW 94040 811-G4
GAMMA CT
600 CMBL 95008 853-C7
GAMMEL BROWN PL
- SCL 95050 833-D2
GANA CT
2000 SJS 95148 835-B5
GANCI LN
21100 SCIC 95120 895-B5
GANTRY WY
700 MTVW 94040 831-H1
GARBER PL
1100 SJS 95127 835-A3
GARBINI ST
8700 GIL 95020 977-H5
GARBO WY
1200 SJS 95117 853-B3
GARCAL DR
14900 SCIC 95127 835-C1
GARCES AV
5800 SJS 95123 874-F5
GARCIA AV
2300 MTVW 94043 791-G7
2300 MTVW 94043 811-H1
GARCIA CT
300 MPS 95035 794-A4
GARCIA LN
10400 SCIC 95020 957-J3
GARDEN AV
2700 SJS 95111 854-G5
3000 SCIC 95111 854-G5
GARDEN CT
6700 GIL 95020 978-A4
GARDEN DR
700 SJS 95126 833-F6
700 SJS 95128 833-F6
GARDEN LN
200 LGTS 95032 873-C4
1300 MLPK 94025 790-E4
GARDEN ST
100 EPA 94303 791-A1
GARDEN TER
2100 MTVW 94040 831-J1
GARDEN WY
- SCL 95050 833-F5
17800 MGH 95037 916-J6
GARDENA CT
21200 CPTO 95014 832-C6
GARDENA DR
21000 CPTO 95014 832-C6
GARDEN BING CIR
1900 SJS 95131 814-C4
GARDEN BING CT
1900 SJS 95131 814-C4
GARDEN CREST CT
20600 CPTO 95014 852-B7
GARDENDALE DR
2700 SJS 95125 854-C7
3000 SJS 95118 854-C7
3100 SJS 95118 874-C1
GARDEN GATE DR
20600 CPTO 95014 832-D7
GARDENGLEN WY
1500 SJS 95125 854-A7

GARDEN GROVE CIR
- MGH 95037 916-H3
GARDEN HILL DR
100 LGTS 95032 873-C5
GARDEN HILL WY
100 LGTS 95032 873-C4
GARDEN HOUSE WY
8700 SJS 95135 856-A6
GARDENIA CT
- EPA 94303 791-C3
GARDENIA DR
- SJS 95123 875-B5
GARDENIA LN
- SBnC 95023 1040-D3
GARDENIA WY
100 EPA 94303 791-D3
800 LALT 94024 831-E1
1000 SUNV 94086 832-G2
15500 SCIC 95032 873-D5
GARDEN MANOR CT
20600 CPTO 95014 852-B7
GARDENOAK CT
6500 SJS 95120 894-C1
GARDEN PLACE CT
20700 CPTO 95014 852-B7
GARDENSIDE CIR
1100 CPTO 95014 852-D3
GARDENSIDE LN
1100 CPTO 95014 852-D3
GARDENSIDE PL
- SJS 95138 855-D6
GARDEN TERRACE DR
11400 CPTO 95014 852-B7
GARDENVIEW LN
21800 CPTO 95014 832-B7
GARDENWOOD DR
1000 SJS 95129 852-G2
GARDIE PLACE WY
3800 SJS 95121 855-B4
GARFIELD AV
1100 SJS 95125 853-J3
1100 SJS 95125 854-A3
GARFIELD CT
400 GIL 95020 958-A7
400 GIL 95020 978-A1
GARLAND AV
600 SUNV 94086 832-F2
1000 SJS 95126 833-J7
GARLAND DR
100 MLPK 94025 790-F5
700 PA 94303 791-C5
3700 SJS 95136 854-G7
GARLAND PL
- MLPK 94025 790-F5
E GARLAND TER
600 SUNV 94086 832-E2
N GARLAND TER
600 SUNV 94086 832-E2
W GARLAND TER
600 SUNV 94086 832-E2
GARLAND WY
100 LALT 94022 811-E6
GARLIC FARM DR
- GIL 95020 978-B6
GARLIC PASS WY
- GIL 95020 978-B7
GARLOUGH DR
5800 SJS 95123 874-E5
GARLOUGH PL
900 SJS 95123 874-E5
GARNER CT
700 SCL 95050 833-C5
GARNER DR
100 SUNV 94089 812-E4
GARNET DR
3200 SJS 95117 853-D2
GARNETT CT
19900 SAR 95070 852-E6
GARRANS DR
1300 SJS 95130 853-A4
1300 SJS 95129 853-A4
GARRETT CT
1100 SJS 95120 894-F3
GARRETT DR
3500 SCL 95054 813-A7
GARRISON CIR
5300 SJS 95123 875-B3
GARRISON DR
- CMBL 95008 853-D5
GARRITY WY
- SCL 95054 813-E4
GARROD RD
- SAR 95070 852-A7
- SCIC 95070 852-A7
GARTHWICK CT
1300 LALT 94024 831-J3
GARTHWICK DR
1300 LALT 94024 831-J3
GARVEY PL
1500 SJS 95132 814-E4
GARWOOD DR
5200 SJS 95118 874-B4
GARWOOD WY
400 MLPK 94025 790-F3
GARY AV
800 SUNV 94086 832-F3
GARY CT
100 MTVW 94041 811-J6
400 PA 94306 791-C7
GARY ST
700 GIL 95020 977-H1
GARZA LN
1600 SCIC 95020 958-A2
GARZONI PL
- SCL 95054 813-D4
GASCOIGNE DR
10500 CPTO 95014 852-H2
GASCONY CT
- GIL 95020 957-G7
GASPAR CT
2700 PA 94306 791-C6
GASPAR VISTA
- SJS 95126 854-A1

GASSMANN DR
2600 SJS 95121 854-H3
GATELAND CT
3200 SJS 95148 855-E1
GATELIGHT CT
3200 SJS 95148 855-E1
GATES DR
4100 SJS 95124 873-H3
GATES ST
- EPA 94303 791-C2
GATEVIEW CT
800 SJS 95133 814-F7
GATEVIEW DR
700 SJS 95133 814-F7
700 SJS 95133 834-F1
GATEWAY BLVD
3400 FRMT 94538 793-F1
GATEWAY DR
- HOLL 95023 1040-A2
100 LGTS 95032 873-D4
GATEWAY PL
2000 SJS 95110 833-H1
GATEWOOD LN
5200 SJS 95118 874-A4
GATON DR
1600 SJS 95125 853-J5
GATTUCIO DR
4900 SJS 95124 873-J4
GAUCHO CT
1400 SJS 95118 874-B2
GAUNDABERT LN
500 SCIC 95123 874-F3
500 SJS 95136 874-F3
GAUNT AV
8200 GIL 95020 977-G2
GAVELLO AV
700 SUNV 94086 832-F2
GAVILAN CT
400 GIL 95020 958-A7
2800 SJS 95148 855-C1
GAVILAN DR
2700 SJS 95148 855-C1
GAVIN CT
- SJS 95136 874-G2
GAVOTA AV
3200 SJS 95124 873-J2
GAWAIN DR
3100 SJS 95127 814-H7
GAY AV
1200 CMBL 95008 873-C1
2700 SJS 95127 834-H2
2700 SCIC 95127 834-H2
GAYLE DR
4200 SJS 95124 873-H3
GAYLOR LN
3300 SJS 95118 874-A1
GAYWOOD CT
3000 SJS 95148 855-D1
GAZANIA DR
4900 SJS 95111 875-A2
GAZDAR CT
1300 SCL 95051 832-H4
GAZELLE DR
2800 SJS 95008 873-A1
2800 SJS 95008 872-J1
GEBHART AV
- SJS 95116 834-H3
GEHRIG AV
1100 SJS 95132 814-F5
GEIST CT
1600 SJS 95132 814-G2
GELIA WY
- SJS 95118 874-C3
GEM AV
- LGTS 95030 873-C7
GEMINI AV
200 MTVW 94043 811-H4
GEMINI CT
100 LGTS 95032 873-J6
GEMINI LN
3400 SJS 95111 854-F6
GEMMA DR
300 MPS 95035 794-A5
GEMSTONE DR
200 MPS 95035 793-H6
300 MPS 95035 794-A7
GENEIL CT
- SBnC 95023 1039-E6
GENERAL ELECTRIC
- SJS 95125 854-E4
GENEVA AV
500 RDWC 94061 790-B1
GENEVA DR
1200 SUNV 94089 812-G2
3300 SCL 95051 832-J7
GENEVA RD
200 MPS 95035 794-A6
GENEVA ST
1800 SJS 95124 873-G2
GENEVIEVE CT
3100 PA 94303 791-E6
GENEVIEVE LN
600 SJS 95128 833-E7
S GENEVIEVE LN
300 SJS 95128 853-E1
GENG RD
1700 PA 94303 791-D3
GENIE LN
5400 SJS 95123 875-B4
GENINE CT
600 SJS 95127 814-J7
GENINE DR
500 SJS 95127 814-H7
GENNARO WY
- GIL 95020 978-A2
GENOA DR
400 SJS 95133 834-G1
GENTIAN CT
4900 SJS 95111 875-A2
GENTRY CT
2700 SCL 95051 833-B2
GENTRY OAKS PL
6700 SJS 95138 875-G4

GEOMAX CT
4900 SJS 95118 874-C3
GEORGE ST
- SJS 95110 834-A5
900 SCL 95054 813-E7
16100 LGTS 95032 873-C6
GEORGE BLAUER PL
- SJS 95135 855-F5
GEORGE HOOD LN
300 PA 94306 811-D2
GEORGE OAKS DR
4400 SJS 95118 874-C2
GEORGES DR
- SBnC 95023 1060-D2
GEORGE SELLON CIR
- SCL 95054 813-D5
GEORGETOWN CT
- MTVW 94043 812-B5
600 SUNV 94087 832-D2
GEORGETOWN DR
- MTVW 94043 812-B5
GEORGETOWN LN
- SJS 95126 833-J7
GEORGETOWN PL
- SJS 95126 833-J7
- SJS 95126 834-A7
700 GIL 95020 977-J4
3300 SCL 95051 833-A2
3300 SCL 95051 832-J2
GEORGETTA DR
1400 SJS 95125 854-A6
1500 SJS 95125 853-J6
GEORGIA AV
500 PA 94306 811-C2
600 SUNV 94086 812-F5
2000 SJS 95122 834-H5
GEORGIA LN
100 PTLV 94028 810-C7
GEORGIA KATE PL
- SJS 95125 854-B4
GEORGINIA AV
2500 SJS 95116 834-H4
GERALD WY
2400 SJS 95125 854-B6
GERALDINE CT
17800 SCIC 95033 913-A2
GERALD ZAPPELLI CT
20400 SAR 95070 872-D2
GERARD WY
800 SJS 95127 835-B2
GERBER CT
900 SUNV 94087 832-B5
GERDTS DR
6100 SJS 95135 855-H6
GERHARDT AV
1400 SJS 95125 854-A7
GERI LN
200 GIL 95020 957-E6
200 SCIC 95020 957-E6
GERINE BLOSSOM DR
5300 SJS 95123 875-A3
GERLACH DR
1400 SJS 95118 874-B3
GERMAINE CT
1800 SJS 95122 854-G1
GERNEIL CT
14900 SAR 95070 872-E2
GERONA RD
400 SCIC 94305 810-H1
GERONIMO DR
6100 SJS 95123 874-H6
GERTH LN
2200 LAH 94304 810-H4
GEST DR
800 MTVW 94040 831-G1
GETTYSBURG DR
500 SJS 95123 874-H4
GETTYSBURG WY
700 GIL 95020 977-J4
GEYSER DR
1400 SJS 95131 814-C7
GHIONE DR
1400 HOLL 95023 1040-D7
GHIRLANDA CT
7700 GIL 95020 978-A2
GIA CT
- HOLL 95023 1040-B6
GIAMPAOLI DR
1900 SCIC 95046 938-A6
GIANERA ST
2300 SCL 95054 813-C4
GIANNI ST
400 SCL 95054 813-E7
GIANNINI DR
400 SCL 95051 832-H7
GIANNOTTA WY
400 SJS 95133 834-G1
GIANT WY
3400 SJS 95127 835-B2
GIBBONS CT
400 MPS 95035 813-J3
GIBBS DR
- HOLL 95023 1040-B5
- SBnC 95023 1040-B5
GIBERSON RD
- LGTS 95030 893-A1
GIBRALTAR CT
100 SUNV 94089 812-F3
600 MPS 95035 814-B1
GIBRALTAR DR
200 SUNV 94089 812-F3
500 MPS 95035 814-B2
GIBSON AV
3400 SCL 95051 832-J7
GIBSON CT
3500 SCL 95051 832-J7
GIBSON GIRL WY
2300 SJS 95148 835-D5
GIDDINGS CT
100 SJS 95139 895-G1
GIER CT
700 SJS 95111 854-G3

STREET Block	City	ZIP	Pg-Grid
GIFFIN RD			
-	LALT	94022	831-E1
GIFFORD AV			
100	SJS	95110	834-A7
300	SJS	95126	834-A7
300	SJS	95126	854-B1
GIGI CT			
2800	SJS	95111	854-H4
GIGLI CT			
12300	LAH	94022	811-A7
GIGUERE CT			
600	SJS	95133	834-F2
GILA DR			
3400	SJS	95148	835-D5
GILBERT AV			
-	SCL	95051	833-A7
100	MLPK	94025	791-A2
200	MLPK	94025	790-J2
GILCHRIST DR			
800	SJS	95133	814-F7
GILCHRIST WALKWAY			
800	SJS	95133	814-F7
GILDA WY			
1700	SJS	95124	873-H6
GILES WY			
-	SJS	95136	854-E7
GILHAM CT			
-	SJS	95148	855-C1
GILHAM WY			
-	SJS	95148	835-C7
-	SJS	95148	855-C1
GILLETTE DR			
21900	SCIC	95033	913-A3
GILLIAN WY			
1800	SJS	95132	814-D3
GILLICK WY			
20300	CPTO	95014	852-E2
GILLMOR ST			
4700	SCL	95054	813-C4
GILLS DR			
6500	SJS	95120	894-C2
GILMAN AV			
-	CMBL	95008	853-E6
GILMAN RD			
1000	GIL	95020	978-C2
1000	SCIC	95020	978-C2
GILMAN ST			
600	PA	94301	790-J4
GILMORE CT			
400	SJS	95111	854-J6
GILMORE ST			
1400	MTVW	94040	811-G6
GILROY HOT SPRINGS RD			
4200	SCIC	95020	958-G1
5700	SCIC	95020	938-J7
GIMELLI CT			
2500	SJS	95133	834-G1
GIMELLI WY			
2500	SJS	95133	834-G1
GINA CT			
12600	SCIC	95127	814-J5
GINA LN			
-	SBnC	95023	1020-D1
GINASHELL CIR			
6200	SJS	95119	875-C6
GINDEN CT			
1400	CMBL	95008	853-B7
GINDEN DR			
600	CMBL	95008	853-B7
GINGER LN			
900	SCIC	95128	853-F2
1000	SJS	95128	853-F3
GINGER WY			
-	MGH	95037	916-H4
GINGERWOOD DR			
1100	MPS	95035	793-J4
GINKGO CT			
400	SJS	95111	854-G7
GINKO TER			
-	SUNV	94086	832-F1
GINNY LN			
26300	LAH	94022	831-B1
GION AV			
4000	SCIC	95127	834-J1
GIOVANNI CT			
300	SJS	95133	834-H1
GIRALDA DR			
600	LALT	94024	811-F7
GIRARD DR			
1700	MPS	95035	794-D7
GIRARD RD			
-	SCIC	94035	812-B3
GIRAUDO DR			
500	SJS	95111	875-B1
E GISH RD			
-	SJS	95112	834-B1
W GISH RD			
100	SJS	95112	833-J3
200	SJS	95110	833-J3
GIST RD			
19800	SCIC	95033	892-D5
19800	SCrC	95033	892-D5
GITANA CT			
2400	MGH	95037	917-F6
GITTLE CT			
600	SJS	95116	834-H4
GIUFFRIDA AV			
400	SJS	95123	874-H4
GIUFFRIDA CT			
5400	SJS	95123	874-H4
GIUSEPPE CT			
-	SJS	95127	834-J2
GIUSTI DR			
5100	SJS	95111	875-B2
GLACIER DR			
1100	MPS	95035	814-C1
1300	MPS	95035	794-D7
1300	SJS	95118	874-B2
GLADDING CT			
1500	MPS	95035	814-C3
GLADE DR			
2400	SCL	95051	833-A2
GLADIOLA DR			
800	SUNV	94086	832-F2
GLADSTONE AV			
1700	SJS	95124	873-J3
GLADYS AV			
-	MTVW	94043	812-A4
GLADYS CT			
-	MTVW	94043	812-A4
GLADYS WY			
1800	SJS	95124	853-G7
GLAMORGAN CT			
3400	SJS	95127	835-B3
GLARNER ST			
1900	HOLL	95023	1040-E5
GLASGLOW CT			
400	MPS	95035	794-B6
GLASGOW CT			
3500	SJS	95127	835-B2
13200	SAR	95070	852-E7
GLASGOW DR			
19900	SAR	95070	852-E7
GLAUSER DR			
2700	SJS	95133	814-G7
GLEASON AV			
3500	SJS	95130	853-B4
GLEN CT			
600	MPS	95035	794-B5
GLEN PL			
21200	CPTO	95014	832-C7
GLEN WY			
2000	EPA	94303	791-B1
GLENA CT			
1300	SJS	95122	854-H1
GLEN ALDEN CT			
2900	SJS	95148	835-C7
GLEN ALMA WY			
2500	SJS	95148	835-C7
GLEN ALPINE CT			
-	MTVW	94043	812-A4
GLEN ALTO CT			
3100	SJS	95148	855-D1
GLEN ALTO DR			
500	LALT	94024	831-F1
GLEN AMADOR CT			
2700	SJS	95148	835-B7
GLEN ANGUS WY			
2400	SJS	95148	835-C7
GLEN ARBOR CT			
12700	SAR	95070	852-E6
GLEN ASCOT WY			
2800	SJS	95148	835-C7
GLEN AYRE DR			
18400	MGH	95037	916-F6
GLENBAR AV			
900	SUNV	94087	832-G5
GLENBLAIR WY			
1100	CMBL	95008	873-B1
GLENBOROUGH DR			
700	MTVW	94041	812-A6
GLEN BRAE CT			
20300	SAR	95070	852-E7
GLEN BRAE DR			
12800	SAR	95070	852-F6
19600	SAR	95070	872-E1
GLENBRAE LN			
1200	SJS	95118	874-C4
GLENBRIAR DR			
2600	SJS	95130	852-J7
GLENBROOK AV			
1000	SJS	95125	853-J3
GLENBROOK DR			
600	PA	94306	811-D3
GLENBURRY WY			
500	SJS	95123	874-E3
GLEN CANYON CT			
-	MGH	95037	937-A1
GLENCO DR			
10200	CPTO	95014	832-D7
GLENCOE CT			
700	SUNV	94087	832-F4
GLEN COMO WY			
2900	SJS	95148	835-C7
GLEN COTSWOLD CT			
2600	SJS	95148	835-C7
GLEN CRAIG CT			
2900	SJS	95148	835-C7
GLEN CREEK CT			
-	SJS	95138	855-G6
GLENCREST CT			
1500	SJS	95118	874-A2
GLENCREST DR			
1500	SJS	95118	874-A2
GLENCREST WY			
1500	SJS	95118	874-A2
GLEN CROW CT			
2900	SJS	95148	835-C7
GLENDALE AV			
400	SUNV	94086	812-F5
3000	SMCo	94063	790-D1
GLENDALE DR			
-	SJS	95193	875-C4
GLEN DARBY CT			
2900	SJS	95148	835-C7
GLEN DECKER CT			
2800	SJS	95148	835-B7
GLEN DELL DR			
1200	SJS	95125	853-J4
1200	SJS	95125	854-A4
GLENDENNING AV			
2300	SCL	95050	833-C7
GLEN DIXON CT			
2800	SJS	95148	835-B7
GLEN DONEGAL DR			
2800	SJS	95148	835-B7
GLEN DOON CT			
2600	SJS	95148	835-B7
GLENDORA CT			
6200	SJS	95123	874-F6
GLEN DUFF WY			
2400	SJS	95148	835-B7
GLEN DUNDEE CT			
2500	SJS	95148	835-C7
GLEN DUNDEE WY			
2500	SJS	95148	835-B7
GLENEAGLES CIR			
5800	SJS	95138	875-H1
GLENEAGLES DR			
5800	SJS	95138	875-H1
GLEN ECHO AV			
1000	SJS	95125	853-J3
18400	MSER	95030	872-J6
GLENEDEN WY			
3100	SJS	95117	853-D3
GLEN ELK CT			
2600	SJS	95148	835-B7
GLEN ELLEN WY			
1400	SJS	95125	853-J5
1400	SJS	95125	854-A5
GLEN ELM WY			
2400	SJS	95148	835-C7
GLEN EVANS CT			
2700	SJS	95148	835-B7
GLEN EXETER WY			
2400	SJS	95148	835-B7
GLEN EYRIE AV			
100	SJS	95125	853-J3
100	SJS	95125	854-A2
GLEN FALL CT			
2500	SJS	95148	835-C7
GLEN FALLS CT			
-	SBnC	95023	1000-F7
GLEN FARM CT			
2600	SJS	95148	835-C7
GLEN FENTON WY			
2600	SJS	95148	835-B7
GLEN FERGUSON CIR			
2700	SJS	95148	835-C7
GLENFIELD CT			
1600	SJS	95125	854-A7
GLENFIELD DR			
1600	SJS	95125	854-A7
GLENFINNAN CT			
1000	SJS	95122	854-G1
GLENFINNAN DR			
900	SJS	95122	854-G1
GLEN FIRTH DR			
2700	SJS	95133	814-G7
GLENFORD PARK CT			
300	SJS	95136	874-F1
GLEN FOX CT			
2400	SJS	95148	835-C7
GLEN FROST CT			
2800	SJS	95148	835-C7
GLENGARRY DR			
3800	SJS	95121	855-C4
GLENGROVE WY			
3800	SJS	95121	855-C4
GLEN HAIG WY			
2400	SJS	95148	835-C7
GLEN HANCOCK CT			
2600	SJS	95148	835-C7
GLEN HANLEIGH DR			
2400	SJS	95148	835-B7
GLEN HARBOR DR			
6000	SJS	95123	875-A6
GLEN HARDY CT			
2600	SJS	95148	835-B7
GLEN HARWICK CT			
2600	SJS	95148	835-C7
GLEN HASTINGS CT			
2500	SJS	95148	835-C7
GLEN HAVEN CT			
5600	SJS	95129	852-H3
GLEN HAVEN DR			
1200	SJS	95129	852-H4
GLEN HAWKINS CT			
2800	SJS	95148	835-C7
GLEN HEATHER DR			
2700	SJS	95133	814-G7
GLEN HEDGE CT			
2500	SJS	95148	835-C7
GLEN HOLLOW WY			
-	SJS	95132	814-E5
GLENHURST DR			
1600	SJS	95124	873-J2
1600	SJS	95124	874-A2
GLEN IAN CT			
2500	SJS	95148	835-B7
GLEN KEATS CT			
2800	SJS	95148	835-C7
GLEN KELLER CT			
2500	SJS	95148	835-B7
GLEN KEW CT			
2500	SJS	95148	835-B7
GLENKIRK CT			
2200	SJS	95124	853-H6
GLENKIRK DR			
2100	SJS	95124	853-H6
GLEN LAKE CIR			
-	MGH	95037	937-A1
GLEN LOMAN WY			
2600	SJS	95148	835-B7
GLEN MEAD CT			
700	SJS	95133	814-G7
GLENMEAD CT			
-	MTVW	94040	811-F3
GLEN MEADOW CT			
1100	SJS	95125	854-A4
GLENMONT DR			
4100	SJS	95136	874-D1
21200	SAR	95070	872-C2
GLENMOOR CIR			
400	MPS	95035	793-H5
GLENMOOR CT			
500	MPS	95035	793-J5
GLENMOOR WY			
1200	SJS	95129	852-F4
GLENMORE DR			
-	HOLL	95023	1039-J5
GLENN AV			
400	CMBL	95008	873-C1
1100	SJS	95125	853-J3
1100	SJS	95125	854-A3
GLENN WY			
1500	RDWC	94061	790-A2
GLENNAN CT			
5400	SJS	95129	852-H4
GLENOAK CT			
5500	SJS	95129	852-H3
GLENPARK DR			
4300	SJS	95136	874-D2
GLEN PINE DR			
1400	SJS	95125	854-A4
GLENPROSEN CT			
-	SJS	95148	855-F1
GLEN RIDGE AV			
-	LGTS	95030	872-J7
GLENRIDGE DR			
900	SJS	95136	874-D1
GLENRIO DR			
2600	SJS	95121	855-C3
GLENROCK CT			
1600	SJS	95124	873-J7
GLENROY DR			
1600	SJS	95124	873-J2
1600	SJS	95124	874-A2
GLEN SHARON WY			
2800	SJS	95148	835-B7
GLENSIDE DR			
700	SJS	95123	874-G6
GLENSTONE CT			
1700	SJS	95121	855-C4
GLENTREE CT			
5100	SJS	95129	852-J2
GLENTREE DR			
5000	SJS	95129	852-J2
GLEN UNA AV			
1700	SJS	95125	854-B4
GLEN UNA CT			
-	MTVW	94040	811-J7
GLEN UNA DR			
15500	SCIC	95030	872-E5
15500	SAR	95030	872-F5
15900	SAR	95070	872-F5
GLENVIEW AV			
10400	CPTO	95014	852-F1
GLENVIEW CT			
-	HOLL	95023	1060-D1
800	MPS	95035	814-E1
6800	GIL	95020	977-J4
GLENVIEW DR			
-	HOLL	95023	1060-D1
1400	HOLL	95023	1040-D7
2100	MPS	95035	814-E1
6700	SJS	95120	894-F2
6800	GIL	95020	977-J4
GLENVILLE DR			
1600	SJS	95124	873-J2
1600	SJS	95124	874-A2
GLEN WILLOW CT			
-	SJS	95125	854-G5
GLEN WOOD			
800	MTVW	94041	811-J6
GLENWOOD AV			
100	ATN	94027	790-F2
400	MLPK	94025	790-F2
1200	SJS	95125	854-A4
1400	SJS	95125	853-J4
GLENWOOD DR			
8200	GIL	95020	977-J1
20200	SCrC	95033	912-J7
20200	SCrC	95033	913-A7
GLIDER DR			
6100	SJS	95123	874-J7
GLIESSEN TER			
-	SUNV	94089	812-G3
GLIN TER			
-	SUNV	94089	812-G4
GLISTENING CT			
-	MPS	95035	793-H6
GLITHERO CT			
1000	SJS	95112	834-D3
GLORIA AV			
300	SCIC	95127	835-A2
GLORIA CIR			
-	MLPK	94025	790-H2
GLORIA CT			
18100	SCIC	95033	912-J3
GLORIA DR			
1100	HOLL	95023	1040-C6
GLORIA WY			
2400	EPA	94303	791-B1
GLORIETTA CIR			
2700	SCL	95051	833-B7
GLOUCESTER CT			
1000	SUNV	94087	832-G5
GLOUCHESTER CT			
5000	SJS	95136	874-F3
GLOWING CT			
5900	SJS	95120	874-B6
GNARLED OAK LN			
16700	MGH	95037	917-G6
GOBLE LN			
-	SJS	95111	854-F5
GODDESS CT			
6200	SJS	95129	852-F3
GODFREY RD			
2800	SCIC	95020	958-F7
GOEBEL AV			
4100	PA	94306	811-C2
GOEBEL CT			
18100	SCIC	95033	912-J3
GOLD ST			
1300	SJS	95002	793-B7
1500	SJS	95002	813-B1
GOLD CREEK CT			
7200	SJS	95120	894-H4
GOLD CREEK WY			
7200	SJS	95120	894-H4
GOLDEN DR			
5000	SJS	95129	852-J3
GOLDEN WY			
1000	LALT	94024	831-G2
1800	MTVW	94040	831-G2
GOLDEN ACRE CT			
1000	SJS	95136	874-C2
GOLDEN ASPEN WY			
11000	CPTO	95014	832-D6
GOLDEN CREEK TER			
700	SJS	95111	855-B7
GOLDEN CREST COMS			
-	SJS	95125	854-E4
GOLDEN DEW CIR			
2100	SJS	95121	855-C3
GOLDEN GATE AV			
1000	SCIC	95020	957-G5
GOLDEN GATE DR			
7000	SJS	95129	852-E3
GOLDEN HILL CT			
13600	LAH	94022	811-C7
GOLDEN HILLS DR			
100	PTLV	94028	810-C5
1700	MPS	95035	794-D6
GOLDENLAKE RD			
1300	SJS	95131	814-D6
GOLDEN LEAF CT			
-	SJS	95136	874-J7
GOLDEN MEADOW SQ			
1400	SJS	95117	853-C4
GOLDEN OAK CT			
700	SUNV	94086	832-F2
GOLDEN OAK DR			
-	PTLV	94028	810-D5
700	SUNV	94086	832-F2
GOLDEN OAK WY			
1200	SJS	95120	874-C6
GOLDENRAIN AV			
300	FRMT	94539	793-H1
GOLDEN RAIN CT			
200	SJS	95111	875-A1
GOLDEN RAIN DR			
-	SJS	95111	875-A2
GOLDENROD CIR			
-	GIL	95020	977-F1
GOLDENROD CT			
800	SUNV	94086	832-F2
GOLDEN SKY WY			
-	GIL	95020	957-E6
GOLDENSPUR LP			
-	SJS	95138	875-G6
GOLDEN STATE DR			
3400	SCL	95051	832-J5
GOLDENTREE DR			
1600	SJS	95131	814-C5
GOLDFIELD DR			
5600	SJS	95123	874-J4
GOLDFINCH WY			
1500	SUNV	94087	832-F5
GOLD MEADOW CT			
-	SJS	95135	855-H7
GOLDPINE CT			
6800	SJS	95120	894-E3
GOLDPINE WY			
6800	SJS	95120	894-E3
GOLDRIDGE CT			
3200	SJS	95135	855-D2
GOLD RUN WY			
100	SJS	95136	874-G1
GOLDRUSH CT			
1400	SJS	95131	814-D6
GOLDWOOD CT			
2600	SJS	95148	835-D6
GOLETA AV			
12200	SAR	95070	852-E5
GOLETA CT			
12300	SAR	95070	852-E5
GOLF CT			
1000	MTVW	94040	812-A7
GOLF DR			
3100	SJS	95127	814-H7
3200	SCIC	95127	814-J6
3900	SCIC	95127	815-A6
GOLF LN			
-	SMCo	94025	810-E3
-	SCIC	94304	810-E3
GOLF COURSE LN			
7000	SJS	95139	895-E1
7000	SCIC	95119	895-E1
GOLF CREEK DR			
1300	SJS	95120	894-D2
GOLF LINKS CIR			
2200	SCL	95050	833-C6
GOLF LINKS DR			
14700	LGTS	95032	873-B3
14700	SCIC	95032	873-B3
GOLF VIEW DR			
400	SCIC	95127	815-A6
GOLI CT			
-	MTVW	94043	812-B5
GOLZIO CT			
2400	SJS	95133	814-F7
GOMES CT			
200	CMBL	95008	853-E5
GOMES DR			
2600	SJS	95132	814-E5
GOMEZ LN			
-	SBnC	95023	1039-E4
GONDOLA WY			
6300	SJS	95120	874-C7
6300	SJS	95120	894-C1
GONZAGA PL			
3300	SCL	95051	832-J2
GONZAGA ST			
2400	EPA	94303	791-C1
GONZALEZ DR			
-	HOLL	95023	1039-H3
GOODWIN AV			
800	SJS	95128	853-H2
2900	RDWC	94061	790-A2
GOODY LN			
1400	SJS	95131	814-C7
GOODYEAR ST			
-	SJS	95110	854-C2
GOOSEBERRY CT			
1200	SUNV	94087	832-B3
GOOSE LAKE CT			
800	SJS	95123	874-E5
GORDOLA CT			
300	SJS	95111	875-A1
GORDON AV			
300	SCIC	95127	815-A7
600	SCIC	95127	814-J6
2000	SMCo	94025	790-D6
2900	SCL	95051	812-J7
GORDON AV			
2900	SCL	95051	832-J1
GORDON CT			
20500	SAR	95070	852-D6
GORDON ST			
1000	MPS	95035	794-B5
1200	RDWC	94061	790-A1
N GORDON WY			
-	LALT	94022	811-E6
S GORDON WY			
-	LALT	94022	811-E7
GORDY DR			
1400	SJS	95131	814-C7
GORSKY RD			
-	SCIC	94035	812-B3
GOSFORD CT			
-	SJS	95139	875-G7
GOSHAWK CT			
1400	GIL	95020	977-F1
GOSSER ST			
300	MPS	95035	794-A3
GOULARTE WY			
100	SJS	95116	834-G4
GOULD CT			
1700	SCIC	95020	938-A7
1700	SCIC	95020	958-A1
GOULD LN			
18100	SCIC	95037	917-B4
GOURMET AL			
7400	GIL	95020	978-A3
GOVERNORS AV			
500	SCIC	94305	790-G7
GOWER DR			
5300	SJS	95118	874-A5
GOYA DR			
400	SUNV	94087	832-E2
GOYA RD			
100	PTLV	94028	810-C4
GRAACH CT			
4100	SJS	95135	855-G3
GRACE AV			
100	EPA	94303	791-B1
1400	SCIC	95125	853-H4
1700	CMBL	95125	853-H5
GRACE CT			
-	CMBL	95125	853-H5
GRACE DR			
500	MLPK	94025	790-E6
GRACKLE WY			
1500	SUNV	94087	832-F5
GRADELL PL			
3300	SJS	95148	835-D6
GRAF RD			
200	HOLL	95023	1039-G3
W GRAFF AV			
400	SBnC	95023	1039-G3
500	HOLL	95023	1039-G3
GRAFTON WY			
2800	SJS	95148	835-E7
GRAHAM LN			
1600	SCL	95050	833-C3
GRAHAM ST			
100	SJS	95110	854-C1
GRAMERCY PL			
100	SJS	95116	834-G2
GRANADA AV			
1400	SCL	95051	833-A4
3300	SCL	95051	832-J4
21700	CPTO	95014	852-B1
GRANADA CT			
-	PTLV	94028	810-D6
3300	SCL	95051	832-J4
20700	SAR	95070	852-D5
GRANADA DR			
100	MTVW	94043	811-H4
GRANADA WY			
100	LGTS	95032	873-A3
900	SJS	95122	854-G1
GRAND AV			
200	SCIC	95126	833-J7
200	SCIC	95126	853-J1
200	SJS	95126	833-J7
200	SJS	95126	853-J1
21500	CPTO	95014	832-B7
GRAND BLVD			
1200	SJS	95002	793-C7
1200	SJS	95002	813-B1
GRANDBROOK WY			
3800	SJS	95111	855-A5
GRANDBY DR			
2400	SJS	95130	852-J7
GRAND COULEE AV			
600	SUNV	94087	832-D5
GRAND FIR AV			
500	SUNV	94086	832-F2
GRANDIN CT			
300	SJS	95123	874-J4
GRAND MEADOW LN			
6300	SJS	95135	855-J7
GRAND OAK WY			
-	SJS	95135	875-J1
-	SJS	95135	876-A1
GRANDPARK CIR			
300	SJS	95136	874-G1
GRAND PRIX WY			
17200	MGH	95037	917-A6
GRANDSTAND WY			
-	SJS	95111	854-G4
GRAND TETON DR			
1500	MPS	95035	814-D1
GRANDVIEW AV			
15900	MSER	95030	872-J6
GRANDVIEW DR			
2600	SJS	95133	814-G7
15900	MSER	95030	872-J6
GRANDVIEW TER			
-	SJS	95133	814-G7
GRANDWELL WY			
-	SJS	95138	875-D4
GRANDWOOD WY			
6900	SJS	95120	894-J3
GRANGER AV			
1700	LALT	94024	831-H3
1700	SCIC	94024	831-H3
GRANGER TER			
500	SUNV	94087	832-D5
GRANITE CT			
-	MPS	95035	794-A6
14900	SAR	95070	872-G3
GRANITE LN			
2300	SJS	95133	834-F1
GRANITE WY			
800	SJS	95133	834-F2
14600	SAR	95070	872-G3
GRANITE CREEK PL			
2800	SJS	95127	834-J4
2900	SJS	95127	835-A4
GRANITE ROCK WY			
100	SJS	95136	854-G7
GRANT AV			
100	PA	94306	791-B7
GRANT CT			
400	GIL	95020	978-A2
1300	LALT	94024	831-J3
GRANT RD			
800	SBnC	95023	1020-D3
1000	MTVW	94040	811-J7
1100	LALT	94024	831-J4
1100	MTVW	94040	831-J1
1100	SCIC	94040	831-J1
2100	LALT	94024	832-A5
GRANT ST			
100	CMBL	95008	853-E5
200	SJS	95110	854-B1
1500	SCL	95050	833-E3
GRANT PARK LN			
1800	LALT	94024	831-J4
1800	LALT	94024	832-A4
GRANVILLE CT			
200	SJS	95139	895-F1
GRAPE AV			
600	SUNV	94087	832-B2
GRAPELEAF WY			
4100	SJS	95135	855-G3
GRAPEVINE WY			
6500	SJS	95120	894-D1
GRAPE WAGON CIR			
8700	SJS	95135	855-J6
8700	SJS	95135	856-A6
GRAPNEL PL			
10600	CPTO	95014	832-C6
GRASSINA ST			
-	SJS	95136	854-E6
GRASS VALLEY CT			
3400	SJS	95127	835-C4
GRAVES AV			
5000	SJS	95129	852-J5
GRAY AL			
-	HOLL	95023	1040-A3
GRAYS LN			
-	LGTS	95030	873-A7
GRAYSON CT			
300	MLPK	94025	790-J1
300	MLPK	94025	791-A1
GRAYSON TER			
-	SJS	95126	834-A7
GRAYSON WY			
600	MPS	95035	794-B4
GRAYSTONE LN			
6600	SJS	95120	894-F1
6700	SCIC	95120	894-G1
GRAYSTONE MEADOW CIR			
6400	SJS	95120	874-F7
GRAYSTONE MEADOW DR			
6400	SJS	95120	874-F7
GRAYWOOD DR			
1400	SJS	95129	852-G4
GREAT AMERICA PKWY			
-	SJS	95002	813-B3
4100	SCL	95054	813-B3
GREATHOUSE DR			
400	MPS	95035	794-A3
GREAT MALL DR			
-	MPS	95035	814-A2
GREAT MALL PKWY			
400	MPS	95035	814-A2
800	MPS	95035	813-J2
GREAT OAK WY			
5400	SJS	95123	875-B4
GREAT OAKS BLVD			
-	SJS	95119	875-D5
GREAT OAKS DR			
5100	SJS	95111	875-C2
GRECIA CT			
200	SJS	95116	834-F3
GRECO AV			
400	SUNV	94087	832-E3
GREEN CT			
500	PA	94301	791-C6
GREEN ST			
100	EPA	94303	791-B2
100	MLPK	94025	791-A2
GREEN ACRES CT			
2100	SCIC	95037	936-F3
GREEN ACRES LN			
2100	SCIC	95037	936-F3
GREENBANK CT			
5300	SJS	95118	874-C4
GREENBAY CT			
800	SJS	95128	853-F4
GREENBRIAR AV			
1100	SJS	95128	853-E4
GREENBRIAR CT			
3000	SJS	95128	853-E4
GREENBROOK CT			
18900	SAR	95070	852-H5
GREEN CREEK DR			
1800	SJS	95124	853-H7
GREENDALE DR			
100	LGTS	95032	873-D5
GREENDALE WY			
200	SJS	95129	853-A1
GREENE DR			
1400	SJS	95129	852-H4

SANTA CLARA CO.

STREET
Block City ZIP Pg-Grid

GREENFIELD DR
- GIL 95020 977-J6
GREENFIELD PL
100 LGTS 95032 873-B3
GREENFORD CT
3100 SJS 95148 855-E2
GREEN FOREST RD
- SCrC 95033 892-C5
GREENGATE DR
2400 SJS 95132 814-E5
GREEN GLEN CT
1100 SJS 95126 853-H3
GREEN HILL WY
100 LGTS 95032 873-C4
2500 SJS 95121 855-E3
GREEN HILLS CT
12000 LAH 94022 831-B2
GREENLAKE DR
600 SUNV 94089 812-G4
GREENLAND WY
3200 SJS 95135 855-E2
GREENLEAF DR
20600 CPTO 95014 832-C6
GREENLEAF LN
2800 SJS 95121 855-D3
GREENLEE DR
3500 SJS 95117 853-C1
GREENMEADOW LN
12400 SAR 95070 852-D6
GREENMEADOW WY
100 PA 94306 811-E2
500 SJS 95129 853-A2
GREENMOOR DR
1200 SJS 95118 874-C2
GREENOAK DR
5500 SJS 95129 852-H3
GREEN OAK LN
1200 LALT 94024 831-H4
GREENOAKS DR
100 ATN 94027 790-G1
GREENPARK WY
300 SJS 95136 874-G2
GREENRIDGE TER
16000 LGTS 95032 873-F6
GREENROCK RD
2500 MPS 95035 814-F1
GREENSBORO CT
1500 SJS 95131 814-C6
GREENSIDE DR
5300 SClC 95127 815-A6
GREENSTONE CT
2500 SJS 95122 835-A5
GREENTREE CIR
- MPS 95035 814-A3
GREENTREE WY
- MPS 95035 814-A3
3000 SJS 95128 853-E3
3100 SJS 95117 853-D3
GREEN VALLEY DR
100 SClC 95020 957-F4
GREEN VALLEY RD
48700 FRMT 94539 794-A1
48900 MPS 95035 794-A1
GREENVIEW DR
800 MTVW 94040 812-A7
800 MTVW 94040 832-A1
GREENVIEW PL
700 SClC 94024 831-F3
GREENWAYS DR
2100 WDSD 94062 790-A5
GREENWICH AV
900 SUNV 94087 832-C1
GREENWICH CT
1300 SJS 95125 853-G4
GREENWICH DR
800 GIL 95020 977-H4
E GREENWICH DR
700 PA 94303 791-C5
GREENWOOD AV
1000 PA 94301 791-B4
1000 SJS 95126 833-G5
2100 MGH 95037 936-E1
15900 MSER 95030 872-H6
16100 SClC 95030 872-H6
GREENWOOD CIR
- MGH 95037 916-H3
GREENWOOD CT
1200 HOLL 95023 1040-C5
19500 CPTO 95014 852-F1
GREENWOOD DR
400 SCL 95054 813-F6
17500 SClC 95033 913-A3
19300 CPTO 95014 852-G1
GREENWOOD LN
16000 MSER 95030 872-H6
16100 SClC 95030 872-G6
GREENWOOD RD
15900 MSER 95030 872-H6
GREENWOOD WY
1500 MPS 95035 813-J3
1500 MPS 95035 814-A3
GREENYARD CT
- SJS 95138 855-C5
GREENYARD ST
- SJS 95138 855-C5
GREER RD
500 PA 94303 791-C4
GREG CT
800 SClC 95020 957-G2
GREGG CT
200 LGTS 95032 873-G5
GREGG DR
200 LGTS 95032 873-G5
800 LGTS 95124 873-G5
1800 SJS 95124 873-G5
GREGORICH DR
6900 SJS 95138 875-G6
GREGORY LN
200 RDWC 94061 790-B2
GREGORY PL
18200 MSER 95030 872-J4
GREGORY ST
400 SJS 95126 854-A1
500 SJS 95125 854-A2

GREMLIN CT
400 SJS 95111 854-F6
GRENACHE CT
8400 SJS 95135 855-H7
GRENACHE WY
- GIL 95020 977-G4
GRENADINE WY
1800 SJS 95122 854-G1
GRENOLA DR
21100 CPTO 95014 832-C7
GRESHAM AV
500 SUNV 94086 812-F6
GRESHAM CT
7400 SJS 95139 895-G1
GRESHAM LN
- ATN 94027 790-C1
GRETCHEN LN
900 SJS 95117 853-B3
GRETEL LN
1200 MTVW 94040 811-J7
GREY CT
2200 SJS 95124 873-E5
GREY CLIFFS CT
- SJS 95138 855-C5
GREY FEATHER CIR
4900 SJS 95136 874-J3
GREY GHOST AV
200 SJS 95111 875-B2
GREY GHOST CT
500 MGH 95037 937-C5
GREYHAWK CT
- MTVW 94043 812-B5
GREYLANDS DR
1400 SJS 95125 853-G5
GREYMONT DR
3600 SJS 95136 854-F7
GREYSTONE CT
800 GIL 95020 977-G1
GRIDLEY CT
300 SJS 95127 814-J7
GRIDLEY ST
300 SJS 95127 814-H6
300 SClC 95127 814-H6
GRIFFIS WY
15600 SClC 95037 936-F5
GRIFFITH LN
100 CMBL 95008 853-E7
GRIFFITH PL
100 LGTS 95030 873-A6
GRIFFITH ST
10000 SJS 95127 835-A3
GRIGLIO DR
500 SJS 95134 813-D2
GRIMLEY LN
1100 SJS 95120 894-H4
GRIMSBY CT
2300 SJS 95130 852-J7
GRIMSBY DR
4400 SJS 95130 853-A7
4800 SJS 95130 852-J7
GRIMSWOOD CT
700 SJS 95120 894-J3
GRINNELL CT
300 SCL 95051 832-H7
GRISCOM WY
15500 SCrC 95018 912-F4
GRISWOLD LN
15900 SClC 95037 936-H3
GRIZILO DR
1600 SJS 95124 873-J1
GROESBECK HILL RD
3600 SJS 95148 835-E6
GRONWALL CT
1200 SClC 94024 831-F3
GRONWALL LN
1200 SClC 94024 831-F2
GROSBEAK AV
1600 SUNV 94087 832-F5
GROSCUP WY
- SJB 95045 1038-D5
GROSS ST
300 MPS 95035 794-A3
GROSSETO CT
- SJS 95138 855-E7
GROSSMONT DR
3300 SJS 95132 814-H5
GROSVENOR CT
17200 MSER 95030 873-B4
GROSVENOR DR
1900 SJS 95132 814-F3
GROTH CT
3100 SJS 95111 854-F6
GROTH DR
500 SJS 95111 854-F6
GROTH PL
500 SJS 95111 854-F6
GROTON CT
800 SUNV 94087 832-C2
GROUSE WY
500 SJS 95133 834-F1
GROVE AV
3700 PA 94303 791-E7
3800 PA 94303 811-E1
GROVE CT
- SJS 95134 813-C2
- PTLV 94028 810-B7
3800 PA 94303 811-E1
GROVE DR
- PTLV 94028 810-B6
100 MGH 95037 937-B5
GROVE LN
3900 PA 94303 811-E1
GROVE ST
- LGTS 95030 893-A1
GROVELAND DR
10600 SClC 94024 832-A6
GROVELAND ST
- PTLV 94028 830-C1
GROVETREE CT
1500 SJS 95131 814-D5
GROVEWOOD CT
800 SJS 95120 894-H3
GRUBER CT
7100 SJS 95139 875-F7

GRUWELL PL
1000 SJS 95129 853-A3
GUADALAJARA CT
1600 SJS 95120 874-A7
GUADALAJARA DR
1500 SJS 95120 874-A7
GUADALUPE AV
1700 SJS 95125 854-C4
GUADALUPE DR
400 LALT 94022 811-D5
GUADALUPE FRWY Rt#-87
- SClC - 854-D6
- SClC - 874-E1
- SJS - 834-A5
- SJS - 854-C3
- SJS - 854-D6
- SJS - 874-E1
- SJS - 833-H2
GUADALUPE PKWY Rt#-87
800 SJS 95110 833-G1
1500 SJS 95110 834-A4
GUADALUPE MINES CT
6000 SJS 95120 873-J7
GUADALUPE MINES RD
6000 SJS 95120 873-J7
6000 SJS 95120 893-H2
GUANACASTE CT
200 SJS 95116 834-F3
GUAVA CT
20100 SAR 95070 852-E6
GUAVA BLOSSOM CT
- SJS 95123 875-D1
GUAYMAS CT
9000 GIL 95020 977-F1
GUERRA CT
500 SJS 95111 854-G3
GUERRA DR
500 SJS 95111 854-G3
GUERRERO CT
1300 MPS 95035 794-C5
GUIBAL AV
8800 SClC 95020 958-A1
GUILDFORD PL
4000 SJS 95135 855-F3
GUILDHALL DR
2700 SJS 95132 814-C3
GUINDA ST
300 PA 94301 790-J3
500 PA 94301 791-A4
1700 PA 94303 791-B5
GUINESS CT
- SBnC - 1059-J2
GUITI GARDEN CT
- SJS 95136 854-E7
GULLANE WY
- GIL 95020 977-E4
GULLO AV
900 SJS 95129 852-J2
GULUZZO DR
3300 SJS 95148 835-C5
GUMDROP DR
2500 SJS 95148 835-C7
GUM TREE DR
3500 SJS 95111 854-G6
GUM TREE LN
15600 LGTS 95032 873-E6
GUNAR DR
2200 SJS 95124 853-G7
GUNDERSEN DR
2200 SJS 95125 853-J6
GUNNERA CT
- GIL 95020 957-D7
GUNNERA LN
- GIL 95020 957-D7
- GIL 95020 977-D1
GUNSTON WY
1700 SJS 95124 873-H3
1900 SClC 95124 873-H3
GUNTER WY
6200 SJS 95123 874-H6
GUNTHER CT
19200 SAR 95070 852-G6
GURNEY CT
1100 SJS 95132 814-G5
GURRIES DR
200 GIL 95020 977-J2
GUSTAFUS DR
8700 SClC 95020 958-F5
GUTEDEL WY
- SJS 95135 855-G6
GWEN DR
700 CMBL 95008 853-A7
700 CMBL 95008 873-A1
GWINN AV
1700 SClC 95046 937-J6
1700 SClC 95046 938-A6
GWINN CT
400 SJS 95111 875-C2
GYPSY AV
2000 SClC 95046 938-A7
GYPSY HILL RD
14600 SAR 95070 872-G4
GYPSY MOTH PL
6000 SJS 95123 874-E5
GYPSY PLACE CT
1600 SJS 95121 855-B4

H

H CT
- GIL 95020 977-E1
H ST
1100 SUNV 94089 812-D3
HABBITTS CT
- SJS 95111 854-G4
HACIENDA AV
300 CMBL 95008 873-A1
4500 SJS 95008 873-A1
E HACIENDA AV
200 CMBL 95008 873-D1

HACIENDA CT
300 LALT 94022 811-D5
1300 CMBL 95008 873-B1
HACIENDA DR
200 SJS 95131 814-A5
1000 GIL 95020 977-G3
HACIENDA WY
300 LALT 94022 811-D5
HACIENDA VALLEY DR
- MGH 95037 916-H3
HACK AV
1400 CMBL 95008 873-B2
HACKBERRY ST
48200 FRMT 94539 793-J1
HACKETT AV
1600 MTVW 94043 811-G3
HACKETT DR
- GIL 95020 977-D3
HADDON WY
3200 SJS 95135 855-E3
HADEOCK CT
1600 SJS 95132 814-E4
HADLEY AV
500 SJS 95126 833-G7
HADLEY CT
400 GIL 95020 978-A3
HAGA DR
3100 SJS 95111 854-H5
10400 SClC 95111 854-H6
HAGA WY
10300 SClC 95111 854-H6
HAGEMAN CT
- SJS 95125 854-D6
HAGEN CT
7300 GIL 95020 977-H4
HAGER CT
12600 SClC 95046 937-H7
HAIG ST
3500 SCL 95054 813-D6
HAIGHT ST
100 MLPK 94025 791-A1
HAINES AV
4000 SJS 95136 874-E1
HAITI RD
500 SJS 95111 854-G4
HALBREATH CT
3200 SJS 95121 855-C5
HALE AV
17400 MGH 95037 916-H6
HALE PL
10600 CPTO 95014 832-C6
HALE ST
400 PA 94301 790-J3
400 PA 94301 791-A3
HALEY CT
500 SJS 95123 874-J7
HALF RD
1000 MGH 95037 917-A5
1000 SClC 95037 917-B4
HALF CROWN LN
1800 SJS 95132 814-J2
HALF MOON CT
3200 SJS 95111 854-H5
HALFORD AV
1200 SCL 95051 832-H3
HALF PENCE CT
3300 SJS 95132 814-F3
HALF PENCE WY
1800 SJS 95132 814-F3
HALGRIM CT
3000 SJS 95132 814-G5
HALIFAX DR
5100 SJS 95130 852-J7
5100 SJS 95130 872-J1
HALKINS DR
4000 SJS 95124 873-E3
HALL AV
1500 HOLL 95023 1040-D7
HALL CT
19900 CPTO 95014 852-F1
HALL RD
- SClC 94035 812-B2
HALLADALE CT
7600 SJS 95135 855-J6
HALLBROOK DR
1500 SJS 95118 874-A3
1600 SJS 95124 873-J3
1600 SJS 95124 874-A3
HALLCREST DR
1500 SJS 95118 874-A2
HALLECK DR
5700 SJS 95123 874-E5
HALLMARK CIR
- MLPK 94025 790-C6
HALLMARK LN
1700 SJS 95124 873-H2
HALSEY AV
- SClC 95128 853-F1
HAMANN DR
600 SJS 95117 853-C2
HAMIDA CT
1200 SJS 95120 894-E2
HAMILTON AV
100 PA 94301 790-J5
100 MTVW 94043 811-F3
200 MPS 95035 794-A6
700 CMBL 95008 853-J5
700 PA 94301 791-A3
1400 SJS 95125 853-J5
1500 PA 94303 791-B3
1600 SClC 95125 853-J5
1800 CMBL 95125 853-J5
E HAMILTON AV
- CMBL 95008 853-F5
800 SJS 95128 853-F5
800 CMBL 95128 853-F5
900 CMBL 95125 853-F5
900 SJS 95125 853-F5
W HAMILTON AV
- CMBL 95008 853-C5
900 SJS 95130 853-C5
4800 SJS 95130 852-J5
4800 SJS 95129 852-J5

HAMILTON CT
- HOLL 95023 1020-B6
100 LALT 94022 811-D6
100 PA 94301 791-A3
HAMILTON LN
600 SCL 95051 833-A6
HAMILTON PL
1400 SJS 95125 853-G4
HAMILTON WY
1400 SJS 95125 853-J5
HAMILTON PARK DR
3900 SJS 95130 853-B4
HAMLET CT
2300 SJS 95131 814-D5
HAMLIN CT
900 SUNV 94089 812-E4
HAMLINE ST
- SJS 95110 833-J4
900 SJS 95126 833-G5
HAMMERTON CT
5300 SJS 95118 874-C4
HAMMERWOOD AV
1200 SUNV 94089 812-J3
HAMMETT CT
- SJS 95132 814-G3
HAMMOND AV
- FRMT 94539 793-H1
HAMMOND WY
- CPTO 95014 831-H6
600 MPS 95035 814-A1
HAMMONS AV
13300 SAR 95070 852-E7
13400 SAR 95070 872-E1
HAMPSHIRE CT
18300 MGH 95037 916-H5
HAMPSHIRE PL
4300 SJS 95136 874-D2
HAMPSTEAD WY
1700 SJS 95132 814-F3
HAMPSWOOD CT
900 SJS 95120 894-H3
HAMPSWOOD LN
900 SJS 95120 894-H3
HAMPSWOOD WY
800 SJS 95120 894-H3
HAMPTON AV
1600 RDWC 94061 790-A2
HAMPTON CT
- LALT 94022 811-D6
900 MPS 95035 794-B4
1100 SJS 95120 894-E2
HAMPTON DR
1300 SUNV 94087 832-G4
6500 SJS 95120 894-D2
HAMPTON BROOK DR
2600 SCL 95051 833-B4
HAMPTON CREEK DR
2700 SCL 95051 833-B4
HAMPTON FALLS PL
4600 SJS 95136 874-D2
HAMPTON KNOLL DR
1300 SCL 95051 833-B4
HAMPTON LAKE DR
1300 SCL 95051 833-B4
HAMPTON PARK DR
2700 SCL 95051 833-B4
HAMRICK CT
2800 SJS 95121 855-A2
HAMSHIRE CT
1000 SUNV 94087 832-H5
HAMWOOD TER
- MTVW 94043 812-B3
HANALEI PL
4400 SJS 95118 874-B2
HANCHETT AV
1100 SJS 95126 833-H7
1700 SJS 95128 833-H7
1700 SJS 95128 853-H1
HANCOCK AV
6100 SJS 95123 874-G6
HANCOCK CT
14600 LGTS 95032 873-B3
HANCOCK DR
3700 SCL 95051 832-H7
HANCOCK RD
18500 SClC 95033 892-F5
HANFORD DR
20600 CPTO 95014 832-D7
HANI CT
2800 SJS 95111 854-H4
HANK LN
1500 SClC 95046 937-J7
HANNA DR
18600 CPTO 95014 852-H2
HANNA ST
7000 GIL 95020 978-A4
7100 GIL 95020 977-J1
HANNA WY
- MLPK 94025 790-H2
HANNAH CT
- SJS 95126 854-A1
HANNAH ST
400 SJS 95126 854-A1
HANOVER AV
800 SUNV 94087 832-C2
HANOVER DR
6300 SJS 95129 852-F4
HANOVER ST
2000 PA 94306 810-J1
2000 PA 94306 811-A1
2400 PA 94304 811-A1
HANS AV
200 MTVW 94040 811-H7
HANS WY
300 SJS 95133 834-F2
HANSELL DR
5300 SJS 95123 874-J3
HANSEN WY
600 PA 94304 811-A1
HANSON AV
300 SClC 95117 853-D1
300 SJS 95117 853-D1
HANSON CT
900 MPS 95035 793-J5

HAPLAND CT
1300 SJS 95131 814-D7
HAPPY ACRES RD
- LGTS 95032 893-E1
100 LGTS 95032 873-E7
HAPPY HOLLOW LN
- SMCo 94025 810-E1
HAPPY VALLEY AV
1000 SJS 95129 852-J3
HARBERN WY
100 SBnC 95023 1060-F1
HARBOR CT
3400 SJS 95127 835-B2
HARBOR VIEW AV
1800 SJS 95122 834-J7
1800 SJS 95122 835-A7
1800 SJS 95122 854-J1
HARDER ST
5700 SJS 95129 852-H3
HARDING AV
100 LGTS 95030 873-B7
100 LGTS 95032 873-B7
700 SJS 95126 833-J6
3000 SCL 95051 833-A7
12200 SClC 95046 937-D5
12200 SClC 95046 957-E1
HARDY AV
100 CMBL 95008 853-D6
HARDY LN
15500 SClC 95037 936-G5
HAREFIELD CT
1300 SJS 95131 834-C1
HAREFIELD DR
1200 SJS 95131 834-C1
HARGIS WY
- SCL 95054 813-E4
HARGRAVE WY
18900 SAR 95070 852-H6
HARKER AV
1000 PA 94301 791-B4
HARKING DR
700 SUNV 94087 832-C5
HARKINS AV
2100 MLPK 94025 790-D7
2100 SMCo 94025 790-D7
HARLAN CT
1000 SJS 95129 852-G2
HARLAN DR
1000 SJS 95129 852-G3
HARLEIGH CT
13700 SAR 95070 872-G1
HARLEIGH DR
18600 SAR 95070 872-G1
HARLISS AV
800 SJS 95110 854-B1
HARLOW WY
5400 SJS 95124 873-H6
HARMIL WY
1700 SJS 95125 854-B4
HARMON AV
- SJS 95126 853-J1
HARMONY LN
400 SJS 95111 855-A7
HARMONY PL
- MPS 95035 814-J1
HARMONY WY
4900 SJS 95130 852-J6
HARNEY WY
900 SUNV 94087 832-B5
HAROLD AV
- SCL 95117 833-C7
- SCL 95117 853-C1
100 SCL 95050 833-C7
HARPER AV
1000 SUNV 94087 832-B5
HARPER DR
13400 SAR 95070 852-G7
13400 SAR 95070 872-G1
HARPSTER DR
800 MTVW 94040 811-H6
HARRIER CT
1400 SUNV 94087 832-F4
HARRIET AV
- SClC 95127 834-J2
- SClC 95127 835-A2
600 CMBL 95008 853-B7
800 CMBL 95008 873-A1
HARRIET ST
900 PA 94301 791-B4
HARRIETT CT
1300 CMBL 95008 873-A2
HARRIGAN DR
- SCL 95054 813-E5
HARRINGTON AV
500 LALT 94024 831-F1
HARRINGTON CT
400 LALT 94024 831-F1
HARRIS AV
1800 SJS 95124 853-G7
HARRIS CT
2300 SJS 95124 853-H7
HARRIS LN
- SCrC 95033 912-J7
HARRIS WY
2300 SJS 95131 814-A4
HARRISBURG PL
- SJS 95133 814-G7
- SJS 95133 834-G1
HARRISON AV
- CMBL 95008 853-E5
HARRISON CT
1500 SUNV 94087 832-B5
HARRISON ST
500 SJS 95125 854-A1
600 SCL 95050 833-C4
HARRISON WY
- SMCo 94025 790-E6
HARROW WY
600 SUNV 94087 832-E5
HARRY RD
600 SJS 95120 895-A2
600 SJS 95119 895-A2
20200 SJS 95120 894-J3
20300 SClC 95120 894-J3

HARRY RD Rt#-G8
20400 SClC 95120 894-J4
20400 SJS 95120 894-J4
HART AV
2300 SCL 95050 833-C5
HART CT
- MTVW 94043 812-B5
HARTE DR
1700 SJS 95124 853-J7
HARTFORD AV
800 SJS 95125 854-A2
HARTLEY CT
1400 SJS 95130 853-B4
HARTMAN DR
22300 CPTO 95014 832-A6
22300 SClC 94024 832-A6
HARTOG DR
1800 SJS 95131 813-J6
HARVARD AV
300 SCL 95051 832-J6
600 MLPK 94025 790-G4
600 SUNV 94087 832-C2
HARVARD CT
14500 LAH 94022 810-H5
HARVARD DR
5400 SJS 95118 874-A5
HARVARD PL
7100 GIL 95020 977-J4
HARVARD ST
2000 PA 94306 810-J1
2000 PA 94306 811-A1
HARVEST DR
1500 SJS 95127 835-C4
HARVEST LN
- SAR 95070 852-E5
200 MGH 95037 937-B5
HARVEST ESTATES
5100 SJS 95135 855-G5
HARVEST MEADOW CT
1000 SJS 95136 874-C2
HARVEST OAK WY
6000 SJS 95120 874-D6
HARVESTWOOD CT
3000 SJS 95148 835-E7
3000 SJS 95148 855-E1
HARVEY WY
19800 SClC 95033 892-J7
HARWALT DR
1300 LALT 94024 832-A3
HARWELL CT
5700 SJS 95138 875-D4
HARWICK WY
100 SUNV 94087 832-E5
HARWOOD CT
100 LGTS 95032 873-H7
HARWOOD RD
4400 SJS 95124 873-H3
16000 LGTS 95032 873-H7
HASSINGER RD
400 SJS 95111 875-C2
HASSLER PKWY
- SJS 95111 855-C6
- SJS 95138 855-C6
HASTINGS AV
3900 SJS 95118 874-A2
HASTINGS CT
1900 SCL 95051 833-A3
HASTINGS DR
900 MPS 95035 794-B3
HASTINGS PL
6400 GIL 95020 978-A5
HASTINGS PARK CT
3900 SJS 95136 874-F1
HATCHER CT
2200 CMBL 95008 873-E2
HATFIELD WALKWAY
4700 SJS 95124 873-E4
HATHAWAY CT
600 SJS 95136 874-F2
HATTON ST
- SJS 95128 853-E1
HAUCK DR
1400 SJS 95118 874-B1
HAUGHTON DR
2800 SJS 95148 855-D1
HAUN CT
14900 SAR 95070 872-F3
HAVANA DR
1500 SJS 95122 834-H7
HAVEN CT
4100 SJS 95124 873-E3
HAVENHURST DR
1600 LALT 94024 832-A3
HAVENWOOD AV
1100 SUNV 94089 812-J5
1100 SUNV 94089 813-A5
HAVENWOOD DR
1300 SJS 95132 814-E5
HAVERHILL CT
100 SJS 95136 895-G1
HAVERHILL DR
700 SUNV 94087 832-C2
HAVRE CT
1000 SUNV 94087 832-B5
HAWES CT
1500 RDWC 94061 790-A1
HAWES ST
1200 RDWC 94061 790-A1
HAWK CT
1400 SUNV 94087 832-F4
HAWK VW
- PTLV 94028 830-D1
HAWKCREEK PL
6000 SJS 95123 874-E5
HAWKCREST CIR
3100 SJS 95135 876-A1
HAWKHURST PL
1200 SJS 95125 854-E6
HAWKINGTON CT
2500 SCL 95051 833-B2
HAWKINS AL
- HOLL 95023 1040-A4
HAWKINS DR
1700 LALT 94024 832-A3

STREET
Block City ZIP Pg-Grid

HAWKINS LN
2500 SCIC 95037 936-D2
HAWKINS ST
- HOLL 95023 1040-A4
400 HOLL 95023 1039-J4
HAWKSTONE WY
5000 SJS 95138 855-E7
HAWLEY CT
5000 SJS 95118 874-A4
HAWTHORNE AV
- LALT 94022 811-E7
100 PA 94301 790-H4
400 LALT 94024 811-F7
400 SUNV 94086 832-F1
500 CMBL 95008 853-F5
W HAWTHORNE AV
- LALT 94022 811-D7
HAWTHORNE CT
500 LALT 94024 811-F7
HAWTHORNE DR
- ATN 94027 790-F1
HAWTHORNE ST
6000 GIL 95020 977-J6
HAWTHORNE WY
- SJS 95110 834-A5
HAY CT
1000 MPS 95035 814-D2
HAYDEN DR
3700 SJS 95117 853-C3
HAYDON ST
- HOLL 95023 1040-A5
400 HOLL 95023 1039-J5
HAYES AV
- SJS 95123 875-A3
- SJS 95193 875-A3
200 SCL 95051 833-A7
HAYES LN
1900 SCIC 95046 936-J7
1900 SCIC 95046 937-A7
HAYES ST
400 SJS 95112 834-C6
HAYFIELD CT
- SAR 95070 872-E2
HAYFIELD ST
- GIL 95020 977-J6
HAYFORD DR
1600 SJS 95130 853-B5
HAY LOFT CT
2700 MGH 95037 917-F6
HAY LOFT WY
2700 MGH 95037 917-F6
HAYMAN PL
900 LALT 94024 831-H2
HAYMEADOW DR
21000 SAR 95070 872-C3
HAYWARD DR
2500 SCL 95051 833-B5
HAYWORTH DR
1800 SJS 95148 835-C5
HAZEL AV
900 CMBL 95008 853-B7
HAZEL ST
- HOLL 95023 1040-A4
HAZEL WY
18100 SCIC 95033 912-J4
HAZELAAR WY
1600 LALT 94024 831-H3
HAZELBROOK DR
21000 CPTO 95014 832-C7
HAZELDELL WY
500 SJS 95129 853-A2
HAZELNUT CT
800 SUNV 94087 832-B2
HAZELTON AV
200 SUNV 94086 812-E6
HAZELTON CT
200 MGH 95037 916-H6
HAZELWOOD AV
900 CMBL 95008 853-B7
1000 SJS 95125 854-B5
3000 SCL 95051 833-A6
HAZELWOOD WY
2500 EPA 94303 791-B1
HAZEN ST
200 MPS 95035 794-A4
HAZLETT CT
1200 SJS 95131 834-C1
HAZLETT WY
1200 SJS 95131 834-C1
HEACOX RD
19600 SMCo 94028 830-C6
HEADEN WY
- SCL 95054 813-D4
HEADQUARTERS DR
- SJS 95134 813-D2
HEALY AV
2400 SCIC 95111 854-F4
2400 SJS 95111 854-F4
HEARTH CT
1100 SJS 95120 894-C5
HEARTHSTONE DR
1400 SJS 95122 854-F1
HEARTHSTONE WY
800 SJS 95122 854-F1
HEARTLAND WY
6900 SJS 95135 876-A1
7100 SJS 95138 876-A1
HEARTWOOD WY
800 SJS 95133 834-F2
HEATH ST
- MPS 95035 793-H6
13000 SAR 95070 852-H7
HEATH CLIFF PL
400 SJS 95111 875-C1
HEATHCOT CT
3600 SJS 95121 855-C4
HEATHER CT
400 LALT 94022 811-D5
800 MPS 95035 794-B5
2300 MTVW 94043 811-G3
14300 SJS 95124 873-G5
HEATHER DR
- ATN 94027 790-F1
14800 SJS 95124 873-F5

HEATHER LN
100 PA 94303 791-C4
HEATHER WY
900 GIL 95020 977-G2
HEATHERBRAY CT
400 SJS 95136 874-F1
HEATHER BROOK CT
- SJS 95138 855-F6
HEATHERCREEK WY
6100 SJS 95123 874-H6
HEATHERDALE AV
1400 SCL 95050 833-F6
1600 SJS 95050 833-F6
1600 SJS 95126 833-F6
1800 SJS 95128 833-F6
HEATHERFIELD LN
1000 SJS 95132 814-F6
HEATHER GLEN CIR
1200 HOLL 95023 1040-C5
HEATHER GLEN DR
- SJS 95130 853-A6
HEATHER HEIGHTS PL
24600 SCIC 95030 871-D1
HEATHER HEIGHTS RD
24600 SCIC 95030 851-D7
24600 SCIC 95030 871-D2
HEATHERKIRK CT
600 SJS 95123 874-H6
HEATHER RIDGE CT
3200 SJS 95136 854-E3
HEATHER RIDGE DR
3100 SJS 95136 854-E3
HEATHERSTONE WY
800 MTVW 94040 832-A1
900 SUNV 94087 832-B1
HEATHERTREE LN
500 SJS 95129 852-B7
HEATHERWOOD DR
7400 CPTO 95014 852-D2
HEATHERWOOD LN
- SBnC 95023 1040-G7
HEATHERWOOD WY
17000 MGH 95037 917-E6
HEATHERWOOD ESTATES DR
- SBnC 95023 1040-F7
HEATHFIELD CT
6800 SJS 95120 894-G2
HEATHFIELD DR
6600 SJS 95120 894-G2
HEATHVIEW DR
- SJS 95130 853-A6
HEATON MOOR DR
6700 SJS 95119 895-D1
HEAVENLY PL
- MPS 95035 814-J1
HEAVENLY BAMBOO CT
1700 SJS 95131 834-D1
HEAVENLY VALLEY CT
5300 SJS 95136 874-F7
HEBARD RD
20300 SCIC 95033 892-J7
HEBARD WY
20300 SCIC 95033 892-H7
HEBER WY
21700 SAR 95070 872-A2
HEBRIDES WY
700 SUNV 94087 832-F5
HEBRON AV
2400 SJS 95121 855-C3
HEBRON CT
3200 SJS 95121 855-C3
HECATE CT
2400 SJS 95124 873-D3
HECATE PL
2300 SJS 95124 873-D3
HECKER PASS HWY Rt#-152
300 SCrC 95076 976-B7
900 GIL 95020 977-F2
3200 SCIC 95020 977-B2
4400 SCIC 95020 976-F3
HECKMAN WY
1300 SJS 95129 852-G4
HEDDA CT
3200 SJS 95127 814-H6
HEDDING ST
2100 SJS 95128 833-F7
E HEDDING ST
- SJS 95112 834-A3
900 SJS 95133 834-A3
W HEDDING ST
- SJS 95110 834-A4
100 SJS 95110 833-J4
700 SJS 95126 833-G6
1700 SJS 95128 833-E7
2400 SCL 95128 833-E7
HEDEGARD AV
200 CMBL 95008 853-D5
HEDERA CT
1000 SUNV 94086 832-H2
HEDGECROFT PL
1000 SJS 95120 894-F2
HEDGEROW CT
400 MTVW 94041 812-A6
HEDGES RD
- SBnC - 1059-A2
300 SBnC 95045 1038-F6
HEDGESTONE CT
- MPS 95035 794-C2
HEDLUND CT
900 SJS 95123 874-E5
HEFLIN ST
700 MPS 95035 794-B4
HEIDI CT
300 MGH 95037 916-J7
2900 SJS 95132 814-F5
HEIDI DR
300 MGH 95037 916-J7
2900 SJS 95132 814-F5

HEIMGARTNER LN
1900 SJS 95124 873-F4
HEINTZ CT
100 LGTS 95032 873-G6
HEIRLOOM CT
600 SJS 95127 835-B2
HEITMAN CT
3100 SJS 95132 814-G5
HEITZ CT
7200 SJS 95120 894-H4
HELEN AV
- SCL 94086 832-H3
900 SCL 95051 832-H3
900 SUNV 94086 832-H3
HELEN CT
500 SBnC 95023 1060-E3
1900 LALT 94024 831-J4
HELEN DR
- SBnC 95023 1060-E3
HELEN PL
- MLPK 94025 790-F5
HELEN ST
700 SJS 95125 854-A1
HELEN WY
17900 SCIC 95033 912-J3
HELENA DR
700 SUNV 94087 832-B5
HELENA WY
2000 SMCo 94061 790-A4
HELENE CT
16900 MGH 95037 917-G5
HELENE LN
16900 MGH 95037 917-G5
HELLER WY
100 SJS 95116 834-G4
HELLYER AV
- SCIC 95138 855-B7
500 SJS 95111 854-J6
500 SJS 95111 855-A6
700 SCIC 95111 855-A6
3100 SJS 95138 855-B7
5500 SJS 95138 875-D1
HELMOND LN
1400 SJS 95118 874-B5
HELMSDALE CT
7600 SJS 95135 855-J6
HELMSDALE DR
7600 SJS 95135 855-J6
7600 SJS 95135 856-A6
HELMSLEY DR
2600 SJS 95132 814-F6
HELWEH CT
- SJS 95126 833-H6
HELZER RD
- SJS 95136 854-E6
HEMATITE CT
- SJS 95135 856-A7
- SJS 95135 876-A1
HEMLOCK AV
300 RDWC 94061 790-B1
2800 SJS 95128 853-E1
E HEMLOCK AV
100 SUNV 94086 812-F4
W HEMLOCK AV
100 SUNV 94086 812-F4
HEMLOCK CT
- GIL 95020 977-E1
- HOLL 95023 1040-E5
- MPS 95035 794-D6
100 PA 94306 811-E2
400 SCL 95054 813-F5
HEMLOCK LN
- MPS 95035 794-D6
HEMMINGWAY CT
- SJS 95132 814-G3
HEMMINGWAY RD
- SJS 95132 814-G3
HEMPSTEAD PL
1700 RDWC 94061 790-A3
HENARD WY
100 LGTS 95032 873-B7
HENDERSON AV
700 SUNV 94086 832-H4
1000 MLPK 94025 790-J1
1300 SUNV 94087 832-H4
HENDERSON DR
300 SJS 95123 875-A6
HENDON CT
500 SUNV 94087 832-E5
HENDRIX CT
4400 SJS 95124 873-J3
HENDRIX WY
4200 SJS 95124 873-J3
HENDRY DR
17300 SCIC 95037 917-E5
E HENDY AV
100 SUNV 94086 812-E7
W HENDY AV
100 SUNV 94086 812-E7
HENDY LN
- SJS 95124 873-E4
HENESSY DR
2700 SJS 95148 835-D7
HENEY CREEK PL
10400 CPTO 95014 831-J6
HENNESSEY WY
100 GIL 95020 957-H7
HENNESSY PL
- SJS 95118 874-B4
HENNING CT
100 LGTS 95032 873-C3
HENNING PL
- SCL 95050 833-D5
HENRIETTA AV
700 SUNV 94086 832-F2
HENRIETTA CT
- HOLL 95023 1020-B6
HENRIETTE CT
- SJS 95135 855-G3
HENRY AV
100 SCL 95117 833-D7
200 SCL 95117 853-D1
300 SCIC 95117 853-D1
300 SJS 95117 853-D2

HENRY AV
500 SJS 95117 833-D7
N HENRY AV
200 SCL 95117 833-D7
200 SCL 95117 853-D1
HENRY CT
- EPA 94303 791-B2
HENRY ST
- HOLL 95023 1040-A6
HENRY FORD II DR
100 SJS 95134 813-G4
HENSLEY ST
- SJS 95112 834-B5
HENWOOD RD
20400 SCIC 95120 894-J2
20400 SJS 95120 894-J2
HENZI LN
1600 SCIC 95020 958-A2
HEPPLEWHITE CT
100 LGTS 95032 872-J3
HEPPNER LN
3700 SJS 95136 874-E1
HERALD AV
1100 SJS 95116 834-F6
HERBAL LP
- GIL 95020 978-B7
HERBERT DR
5200 SJS 95124 873-G5
5300 LGTS 95032 873-G5
HERBERT LN
- CMBL 95008 853-G6
HERCHELL DR
10800 SCIC 95127 835-A1
HERCUS CT
6500 SJS 95119 875-C7
HEREDIA CT
300 SJS 95116 834-F3
HERITAGE CT
- CMBL 95008 853-H7
- ATN 94027 790-E1
1200 LALT 94024 831-H3
2300 SJS 95124 853-H7
18500 MGH 95037 916-H5
HERITAGE DR
2200 SJS 95124 853-H7
HERITAGE PL
- CMBL 95008 853-E6
HERITAGE WY
- GIL 95020 977-F3
1300 SCIC 95020 956-H4
HERITAGE BAY CT
- SJS 95138 855-C5
HERITAGE BAY DR
- SJS 95138 855-C6
HERITAGE BAY PL
- SJS 95138 855-C6
HERITAGE CREEK CT
- SAR 95070 872-F1
HERITAGE ESTATES CT
3100 SJS 95148 855-E2
HERITAGE ESTATES DR
3300 SJS 95148 855-E2
HERITAGE MANOR DR
2400 SCIC 95020 958-B1
HERITAGE MANOR PL
11400 SCIC 95020 958-B1
HERITAGE OAK
- SAR 95070 872-E2
HERITAGE OAKS CT
3200 SJS 95148 855-F2
HERITAGE OAKS DR
3400 SJS 95148 855-F2
HERITAGE PARK CIR
2600 SJS 95132 814-E5
HERITAGE POINT CT
3200 SJS 95148 855-F2
HERITAGE SPRINGS CT
3100 SJS 95148 855-E2
HERITAGE VALLEY CT
3400 SJS 95148 855-F2
HERITAGE VALLEY DR
3100 SJS 95148 855-E2
HERITAGE VILLAGE LN
- CMBL 95008 853-E5
HERITAGE VILLAGE WY
- CMBL 95008 853-E5
HERLONG AV
100 SJS 95123 875-A5
HERMA ST
5600 SJS 95123 874-J5
5800 SJS 95123 875-A5
HERMES CT
600 SJS 95111 854-G3
HERMINA ST
1000 MPS 95035 793-J5
HERMISTON DR
800 SJS 95136 874-D1
HERMITAGE AV
500 SJS 95134 813-E2
HERMITAGE CT
500 SJS 95134 813-F2
HERMITAGE DR
500 SJS 95134 813-F2
HERMITAGE LN
600 SJS 95134 813-E2
HERMITAGE PL
500 SJS 95134 813-E2
HERMITAGE ST
500 SJS 95134 813-E2
HERMITAGE WY
500 SJS 95134 813-F2
HERMOCILLA WY
- SJS 95116 834-F5
HERMOSA
- MTVW 94043 812-A2
HERMOSA AV
21800 CPTO 95014 852-B1

HERMOSA CT
900 SUNV 94086 812-D6
2200 MGH 95037 917-E6
HERMOSA DR
800 SUNV 94086 812-D6
HERMOSA PL
- MLPK 94025 790-F5
HERMOSA WY
300 MLPK 94025 790-E4
1200 SJS 95125 854-B5
1900 HOLL 95023 1040-C6
HERNANDEZ AV
- LGTS 95030 872-H7
- MSER 95030 872-H7
HERNANDEZ LN
18400 MSER 95030 872-H7
HERON AV
1500 SUNV 94087 832-F5
HERON CT
- SJS 95133 814-F7
HERRICK AV
300 SJS 95123 874-J4
HERRIMAN AV
19900 SAR 95070 872-E1
HERRING AV
15000 SCIC 95124 873-F3
HERSHNER CT
200 LGTS 95032 873-G5
HERSHNER DR
300 LGTS 95032 873-G5
400 SJS 95124 873-G5
HERSHNER WY
400 LGTS 95032 873-G5
HERSMAN AV
1300 SCIC 95046 937-J4
HERSMAN DR
1200 GIL 95020 977-G3
HERTEL LN
1600 SCIC 95046 937-J6
HERVEY LN
1400 SJS 95125 854-B3
HESKET CT
6400 SJS 95123 875-B7
HESKETH CT
- MLPK 94025 790-E5
HESKETH DR
- MLPK 94025 790-E5
HESS RD
1400 RDWC 94061 790-B1
HESSELBEIN WY
2600 SJS 95148 835-C7
2600 SJS 95148 855-C1
HESTER AV
1100 SJS 95126 833-H7
1600 SJS 95128 833-H7
1700 SJS 95128 853-G1
HESTIN CT
- SJS 95123 874-F7
HEWES CT
- SJS 95138 875-G5
HEWLETT ST
- SJS 95112 834-C6
HIAWATHA CT
1000 SUNV 94087 832-B2
4300 SJS 95111 855-A7
HIAWATHA DR
700 SJS 95111 855-A7
HIBERNIA WY
700 SUNV 94087 832-F5
HIBISCUS CT
400 EPA 94303 791-D2
22000 CPTO 95014 832-A6
HIBISCUS DR
22000 CPTO 95014 832-A6
HIBISCUS LN
700 SJS 95117 853-B3
HICHBORN DR
- SCL 95054 813-B6
HICKERSON CT
1200 SJS 95127 835-B3
HICKERSON DR
3200 SJS 95127 835-B3
HICKORY CT
- HOLL 95023 1040-E5
500 SCL 95051 833-A6
HICKORY PL
400 SCL 95051 833-A6
HICKORY WY
- GIL 95020 977-H1
700 SJS 95129 853-A2
HICKORY HILL WY
20200 SAR 95070 852-E7
HICKORYNUT CT
1000 SUNV 94087 832-B2
HICKS AV
1400 SJS 95125 853-J4
1700 SJS 95125 854-A5
HICKS RD
16700 LGTS 95032 873-J7
16700 LGTS 95032 893-H2
17400 SCIC 95032 893-H2
18400 SCIC 95032 894-B3
19400 SCIC 95120 894-B3
19600 SCIC 95033 894-B3
22700 SCIC 95033 914-E1
22700 SCIC 95120 914-E1
HIDALGO CT
700 MGH 95037 936-J1
2900 SJS 95125 873-J1
HIDDEN DR
15900 SCIC 95030 872-F5
HIDDEN CREEK CT
6400 SJS 95120 894-E1
HIDDEN CREEK DR
6400 SJS 95120 894-E1
HIDDEN HILL PL
15700 SAR 95030 872-G5
HIDDEN HILL RD
15700 SAR 95030 872-G5
HIDDENLAKE DR
300 SUNV 94089 812-G4
HIDDEN MEADOW CT
6200 SJS 95135 855-H7

HIDDEN MINE RD
1300 SJS 95120 894-C2
HIDDEN OAKS DR
1100 MLPK 94025 790-E5
HIDDEN SPRING LN
14100 SCIC 95037 936-G7
14100 SCIC 95037 956-G1
HIDDEN SPRINGS CT
14100 LAH 94022 831-B3
HIDDEN SPRINGS LN
- SCrC 95033 912-A1
19200 SCrC 95033 892-A7
HIDDEN VALLEY LN
- PTLV 94028 810-A5
- WDSD 94062 810-A5
4000 SCIC 95127 815-A7
4000 SCIC 95127 835-A1
HIDDEN VALLEY RD
- SBnC 95023 1059-H3
HIDDEN VIEW LN
- SAR 95070 872-C3
HIERRA CT
11500 SCIC 94024 831-G4
HIGATE DR
1500 SJS 95122 834-J5
HIGDON AV
100 MTVW 94041 811-G4
HIGGINS AV
- LALT 94022 811-F6
1700 SCL 95051 833-B3
HIGGINS PL
3000 PA 94303 791-E5
HIGH RD
1000 WDSD 94062 790-A5
HIGH ST
200 PA 94301 790-H4
2100 PA 94301 791-B7
17300 LGTS 95030 893-B2
HIGH GLEN DR
600 SJS 95133 814-G7
HIGHGROVE CT
14400 SCIC 95127 835-B3
HIGHLAND AV
- LGTS 95030 893-B2
200 SCIC 95046 957-E1
1000 SCL 95050 833-F5
HIGHLAND CT
1000 SCL 95050 833-F5
1300 MPS 95035 814-E2
HIGHLAND DR
1300 SBnC 95023 1040-D6
1500 HOLL 95023 1040-D6
15700 SCIC 95127 815-A6
HIGHLAND TER
200 LGTS 95030 893-B2
HIGHLAND WY
24300 SCIC 95033 913-B4
HIGHLAND ESTATES LN
200 SCIC 95046 957-F1
HIGHLAND OAKS DR
100 LGTS 95032 873-C4
HIGHLAND OAKS WY
100 LGTS 95032 873-C4
HIGHLAND PARK LN
2200 SJS 95008 853-E7
HIGHLANDS CIR
800 LALT 94024 831-G5
HIGHLAND VIEW CT
1400 LALT 94024 831-H4
HIGH MEADOW CT
6200 SJS 95135 855-J7
HIGH MEADOW LN
3000 SJS 95135 855-H7
HIGH SCHOOL CT
- LGTS 95030 893-A1
HIGH SCHOOL WY
900 MTVW 94041 811-H5
HIGHWAY Rt#-17
- SCIC 95033 892-J2
- SCIC 95033 912-J1
- SCIC 95033 913-A2
22200 SCrC 95033 912-J4
22200 SCrC 95033 913-A6
HIGHWAY Rt#-129
2100 SBnC 95045 1018-A5
HIGHWAY Rt#-156
- SBnC - 1039-D5
- SBnC 95023 1000-C3
- SBnC 95023 1020-B1
- SBnC 95023 1039-D4
- SBnC 95045 1037-H2
- SBnC 95045 1039-A5
- SCIC 95020 1000-C2
- SJB 95045 1038-C5
1600 SBnC 95045 1038-A3
HIGHWOOD DR
2600 SJS 95116 834-J4
13500 SCIC 95127 834-J3
13700 SCIC 95127 835-A3
HIGUERA PL
1300 MPS 95035 794-A4
HIGUERA RD
3800 SCIC 95148 835-F5
HIGUERA HIGHLAND LN
3900 SCIC 95148 835-G5
HIKIDO DR
1900 SJS 95131 814-D7
HILARY AV
- MTVW 94040 811-F3
HILARY DR
3000 SJS 95124 873-G2
HILBAR LN
500 PA 94303 791-C4
HILFORD CT
1100 SJS 95132 814-G5
HILL AV
900 SJS 95125 854-B4
20100 SAR 95070 872-E4
HILL LN
18300 SCIC 95120 874-G7
18300 SJS 95120 874-G7

HILL RD
15500 SCIC 95037 917-D5
15500 SCIC 95037 937-F1
15700 MGH 95037 917-E6
HILL ST
300 HOLL 95023 1040-A3
HILL WY
13500 LAH 94022 811-D7
HILLARY LN
- SMCo 94061 790-B4
HILLBRIGHT CIR
5700 SJS 95123 874-J5
HILLBRIGHT CT
5700 SJS 95123 874-J5
HILLBRIGHT PL
500 SJS 95123 874-J5
HILLBROOK DR
- PTLV 94028 810-D6
100 LGTS 95032 873-D6
HILLCAP AV
3400 SCIC 95136 854-G7
3400 SJS 95136 854-G7
HILLCREST CT
1300 SJS 95120 894-D3
HILLCREST DR
1200 SJS 95120 894-D3
HILLCREST RD
100 HOLL 95023 1040-B4
400 SBnC 95023 1040-D4
10000 CPTO 95014 832-A7
HILLMAN CT
- MGH 95037 917-A6
HILLMONT AV
1500 SJS 95127 835-A5
1700 SJS 95148 835-A5
HILLMOOR DR
20800 SAR 95070 852-D6
HILLOCK DR
- HOLL 95023 1040-B6
HILL PARK DR
2500 SJS 95124 853-H7
2500 SJS 95124 873-H1
HILLPARK LN
11500 LAH 94024 831-E4
HILLROSE DR
5900 SJS 95123 874-E5
HILLSBORO AV
900 SUNV 94087 832-C2
HILLSBOROUGH WY
3400 SJS 95121 855-D3
HILLSDALE AV
100 SCIC 95136 854-F7
200 SCL 95051 832-H7
200 SJS 95136 854-C7
900 SJS 95125 854-C7
1100 SJS 95118 854-C7
1200 SJS 95118 874-A1
1500 SJS 95118 873-H2
1500 SJS 95124 873-H2
HILLSDALE CT
3700 SCL 95051 832-H6
HILL SIDE
20500 SCIC 95033 912-J1
HILLSIDE AV
- LGTS 95030 893-B1
100 SMCo 94025 790-C6
HILLSIDE CT
100 WDSD 94062 790-A5
3300 SJS 95132 814-G4
HILLSIDE RD
400 SBnC - 1059-B4
HILLSLOPE PL
1100 SCIC 94024 831-F2
HILLSTONE DR
2100 SJS 95138 855-E5
HILL TOP CT
16800 MGH 95037 917-G5
HILLTOP CT
1500 MPS 95035 794-C3
HILL TOP DR
100 LGTS 95032 873-E7
100 LGTS 95032 893-E1
HILLTOP DR
100 SBnC 95023 1059-H2
11900 LAH 94024 831-E3
HILLTOP RD
1200 SBnC 95023 1040-C7
1200 HOLL 95023 1040-D7
HILLTOP WY
14200 SAR 95070 872-H2
HILL TOP VIEW CT
- SJS 95138 855-C6
HILL TOP VIEW LN
- SJS 95138 855-C6
HILL TOP VIEW PL
- SJS 95138 855-D6
HILL TOP VIEW TER
- SJS 95138 855-C6
HILLVALE AV
16100 MSER 95030 872-H6
HILLVIEW AV
- LALT 94022 811-E7
3200 PA 94304 811-A3
5800 SJS 95123 874-E5
HILLVIEW CT
900 MPS 95035 794-B6
E HILLVIEW CT
1400 GIL 95020 977-F2
W HILLVIEW CT
1500 GIL 95020 977-F2
HILLVIEW DR
1100 MLPK 94025 790-E5
1500 SCIC 94024 831-F3
18400 SCIC 95030 872-H5
18400 MSER 95030 872-H5
24100 LAH 94024 831-E3
N HILLVIEW DR
100 MPS 95035 794-B4
S HILLVIEW DR
100 MPS 95035 794-B7
200 MPS 95035 814-B1
HILLVIEW LN
17500 SCIC 95037 917-D4

SANTA CLARA CO.

STREET Block City ZIP Pg-Grid

HILLVIEW PL
1300 MLPK 94025 790-E5
5900 SJS 95123 874-E5
HILL VISTA CT
- SJS 95148 835-E6
HILLWOOD CT
300 MTVW 94040 811-F4
HILLWOOD DR
800 SJS 95129 852-J2
HILLWOOD LN
18000 MGH 95037 916-H6
HILMAR ST
500 SCL 95050 833-F5
HILO CT
2300 MTVW 94040 831-J1
HILOW CT
100 LGTS 95032 873-D6
HILOW RD
100 LGTS 95032 873-C7
16300 SCIC 95032 873-C7
HILTIBRAND DR
1600 SJS 95131 834-C1
HILTON AV
4300 SJS 95130 853-A5
HILTON CT
1500 SJS 95130 853-A5
HIMMEL AV
1100 SMCo 94061 790-B3
HINDIYEH LN
200 SCIC 95046 937-F7
HINES CT
300 SJS 95111 875-A1
HINES TER
- SUNV 94087 832-D5
HIRABAYASHI DR
6400 SJS 95120 894-C1
HIRASAKI AV
- GIL 95020 957-G7
8700 GIL 95020 977-G1
HIRASAKI CT
8700 GIL 95020 977-G1
HITCH DR
300 SBnC 95023 1059-H2
HOBART AV
3100 SCIC 95127 834-J2
3100 SCIC 95127 835-A2
3100 SJS 95127 834-J2
HOBART CT
600 FRMT 94539 793-J1
HOBART ST
500 MLPK 94025 790-E5
HOBART TER
500 SCL 95051 833-A6
HOBBS CT
- MPS 95035 794-C7
HOBIE LN
400 SJS 95127 835-B2
HOBSON ST
- SJS 95110 834-A5
400 SJS 95110 833-J5
HOCKING WY
2600 SJS 95124 853-F7
2600 SJS 95124 873-F1
HODGES AL
- HOLL 95023 1039-J3
HODGES AV
2500 SCIC 95128 853-F1
HOEFLER DR
23200 SCIC 95033 913-C6
HOESCH WY
900 GIL 95020 977-G1
HOFFMAN CT
5600 SJS 95118 874-C4
HOFFMAN LN
1200 CMBL 95008 873-E2
HOFFMAN TER
800 SCIC 94024 831-G4
HOFFMAN RANCH RD
21800 SCrC 95033 892-A7
HOGAN DR
1700 SCL 95054 813-C4
HOGAN WY
1200 GIL 95020 957-F7
HOGAR DR
1700 SJS 95124 873-J1
HOGARTH TER
- SUNV 94087 832-E3
HOGUE CT
1100 SCIC 95046 937-H7
20100 CPTO 95014 832-E7
HOITING DR
3300 SJS 95148 835-E6
HOKETT WY
6200 SJS 95123 874-G7
HOLBROOK LN
- ATN 94027 790-E1
HOLBROOK PL
700 SUNV 94087 832-C2
HOLDEN CT
- PTLV 94028 810-D6
14300 SCIC 95124 873-H4
HOLDEN WY
14800 SCIC 95124 873-H4
HOLDERMAN DR
3300 SJS 95148 835-D6
3400 SCIC 95148 835-D6
HOLGATE AV
5900 SJS 95123 875-A5
HOLGER WY
- SJS 95134 813-D2
HOLIDAY CT
2800 MGH 95037 917-E3
13400 SAR 95070 852-G7
13400 SAR 95070 872-H1
HOLIDAY DR
13400 SAR 95070 872-G1
17000 MGH 95037 917-E3
17000 SCIC 95037 917-G4
HOLIN WY
1700 SJS 95131 834-D1
HOLLAND CIR
200 HOLL 95023 1040-B4
HOLLAND CT
100 MTVW 94040 831-J1
1300 SJS 95118 874-B5
HOLLAND LN
5600 SJS 95118 874-B5
HOLLAND ST
100 EPA 94303 791-A1
HOLLANDERRY PL
7500 CPTO 95014 852-D3
HOLLENBECK AV
600 SUNV 94087 832-D2
HOLLERAN CT
1500 SJS 95132 814-F3
HOLLIDALE CT
1400 LALT 94024 831-J4
HOLLIDAY DR
- SBnC 95023 1040-E6
HOLLINGSWORTH DR
600 LALT 94022 811-F5
1500 MTVW 94022 811-F5
HOLLIS AV
100 CMBL 95008 853-D7
HOLLISTER BYPS
Rt#-156
- HOLL 95023 1019-G4
- HOLL 95023 1039-D4
- SBnC 95023 1019-G4
- SBnC 95023 1020-A3
- SBnC 95023 1039-E1
HOLLISTER RD
Rt#-25
700 HOLL 95023 1039-J1
700 HOLL 95023 1040-A2
700 SBnC 95023 1039-J1
1400 HOLL 95023 1019-H6
1400 SBnC 95023 1019-E2
1800 SCIC 95020 998-F4
2200 SBnC 95020 998-F4
2800 SBnC 95020 999-A6
2800 SBnC 95020 1019-D1
HOLLOWAY RD
900 GIL 95020 978-B4
HOLLOWCREEK CT
1600 SJS 95121 855-D7
HOLLOWCREEK PL
1600 SJS 95121 855-D7
HOLLOWGATE LN
4400 SJS 95124 873-J3
HOLLOW LAKE WY
7000 SJS 95120 894-F4
HOLLOW PARK CT
1100 SJS 95120 894-F3
HOLLOW TREE WY
7000 SJS 95120 894-F4
HOLLY AV
1300 LALT 94024 831-H3
1700 MLPK 94025 790-E6
HOLLY CT
- MTVW 94043 812-B5
1400 GIL 95020 977-G3
HOLLY DR
3300 SCIC 95127 814-H6
3300 SJS 95127 814-J6
4100 SCIC 95127 815-A6
HOLLY LN
600 SJS 95136 854-E7
HOLLY TER
- SUNV 94086 832-F1
HOLLY WY
400 MPS 95035 794-D7
HOLLY ANN PL
1100 SJS 95120 894-E2
HOLLY BERRY CT
400 SJS 95129 853-B2
HOLLY BRANCH CT
2000 SCL 95050 833-C3
HOLLYBURNE AV
1000 MLPK 94025 790-J1
HOLLYCREST DR
100 LGTS 95032 873-D5
HOLLY GILLINGHAM LN
6300 SJS 95119 875-D5
HOLLYHEAD LN
1100 CPTO 95014 852-D3
HOLLY HILL DR
1000 SJS 95122 854-G1
1300 SJS 95122 834-H7
HOLLY HILL WY
100 LGTS 95032 873-C4
HOLLY HOCK CT
400 SJS 95117 853-C1
HOLLYHOCK CT
- GIL 95020 977-D2
HOLLYHOCK LN
2000 GIL 95020 977-E2
HOLLY LEAF LN
5600 SJS 95118 874-B5
HOLLY OAK CIR
1100 SJS 95120 874-D7
HOLLY OAK DR
- SBnC 95023 1060-D1
700 PA 94303 791-D7
HOLLYOAK DR
21400 CPTO 95014 852-C2
HOLLY TREE CIR
1200 HOLL 95023 1040-C5
HOLLYWOOD AV
- LGTS 95030 873-B7
- SJS 95112 854-D2
100 LGTS 95030 893-B1
HOLMES AV
1000 CMBL 95008 873-D3
HOLMES DR
- SCIC 95127 815-A7
HOLMES LN
- SCIC 95127 815-A7
HOLMES PL
- SCL 95051 833-B3
HOLSCLAW RD
6600 GIL 95020 978-D2
6600 SCIC 95020 978-D1
8300 SCIC 95020 958-C7
HOLSCLAW ST
1800 SCIC 95020 958-D7
1800 SCIC 95020 978-D1
HOLSTON RIVER CT
4700 SJS 95136 874-E2
HOLT AV
1300 LALT 94024 831-J4
1500 LALT 94024 832-A5
HOLY CITY RD
19200 SCIC 95033 913-A2
HOLYCON CIR
4600 SJS 95136 874-H2
HOLYOKE CT
12600 SAR 95070 852-F6
W HOME ST
800 SJS 95126 853-J1
800 SJS 95126 854-A1
HOME CREST DR
2500 SJS 95148 835-A6
HOME GATE DR
1700 SJS 95148 835-A6
HOMEPARK CT
3900 SJS 95121 855-D5
HOMER AV
100 PA 94301 790-J5
500 PA 94301 791-A4
HOMER LN
- SMCo 94025 810-E1
HOMERITE DR
3900 SJS 95124 873-G3
14500 SCIC 95124 873-G3
HOMES DR
12700 SAR 95070 852-G6
HOMESTEAD AV
1000 HOLL 95023 1039-J5
HOMESTEAD CT
2200 CPTO 94024 832-A6
2200 LALT 94024 832-A6
HOMESTEAD RD
- SJS 95193 875-C5
1100 SUNV 94087 832-A5
1600 CPTO 95014 832-A5
2200 CPTO 94024 832-A5
2200 LALT 94024 832-A5
E HOMESTEAD RD
100 SCL 95051 832-G6
100 CPTO 95014 832-G6
100 SUNV 94087 832-G6
700 SUNV 95014 832-G6
900 SCL 95050 833-D5
2400 SCL 95051 833-A6
W HOMESTEAD RD
200 CPTO 95014 832-C5
600 SUNV 94087 832-C5
700 SUNV 95014 832-C5
HOMEWARD PL
- SJS 95123 874-F4
HOMEWOOD DR
2200 SJS 95128 833-E7
E HOMEWOOD PL
- MLPK 94025 790-H3
HOMME WY
- MPS 95035 793-J4
HONEY CT
- GIL 95020 977-H5
HONEYBEE CT
8100 SCIC 95020 977-A2
HONEYCOMB LN
8100 SCIC 95020 977-A2
HONEYDALE CT
4000 SJS 95121 855-A5
HONEY LOCUST TER
- SUNV 94086 832-F1
HONEYSUCKLE DR
1600 SJS 95122 854-J1
HONEY SUCKLE LN
3900 SJS 95136 854-E7
HONEYSUCKLE PL
1500 LALT 94024 831-J6
1500 LALT 94024 832-A6
HONEYSUCKLE TER
- FRMT 94539 793-J3
- MPS 95035 793-J3
HONEYSUCKLE WY
- HOLL 95023 1040-B6
HONEYWOOD CT
700 SJS 95120 894-J3
HONFLEUR CT
900 SUNV 94087 832-B5
HONFLEUR DR
1600 SUNV 94087 832-B5
HONG KONG DR
1200 SJS 95131 814-B7
HONOLULU CT
3900 SJS 95111 854-J6
HONOLULU DR
3700 SJS 95111 854-J6
HOOD CT
1600 SCL 95051 833-A3
HOO HOO CT
22300 CPTO 95014 852-A1
HOOKE LN
100 LGTS 95032 873-B3
HOOPER LN
11200 LAH 94024 831-D4
HOOSHANG CT
800 CPTO 95014 852-C2
HOOT OWL WY
17400 SCIC 95037 917-F3
17400 MGH 95037 917-F3
HOOVER AV
500 SJS 95126 833-J6
HOOVER CT
500 GIL 95020 978-A3
2100 SCL 95051 833-C2
HOOVER DR
2000 SCL 95051 833-B3
HOOVER ST
1200 MLPK 94025 790-F3
HOPE DR
1400 SCL 95054 813-D4
HOPE ST
100 MTVW 94041 811-H5
1200 SJS 95002 793-B7
3000 SCIC 95111 854-G6
3000 SJS 95111 854-G6
HOPE TER
500 SUNV 94087 832-D5
HOPETON AV
2300 SJS 95122 854-H2
HOPETON CT
2300 SJS 95122 854-H2
HOPI CIR
6200 SJS 95123 874-H7
HOPI CT
6200 SJS 95123 874-H7
HOPI LN
- GIL 95020 957-F6
HOPKINS AV
1100 PA 94301 791-B5
HOPKINS DR
1100 SJS 95122 834-H6
HOPKINS ST
500 MLPK 94025 790-G3
HOPPE ST
1000 SJS 95002 813-B1
HORACE AV
2500 SJS 95124 853-G7
HORCAJO CIR
900 MPS 95035 794-B4
HORCAJO ST
800 MPS 95035 794-B5
HORGAN AV
- RDWC 94061 790-B2
HORIZON AV
100 MTVW 94043 811-J4
HORIZON CIR
200 SJS 95002 813-B1
HORIZON CT
- SJS 95148 855-G2
HORIZON DR
- SBnC 95075 1060-J5
- SBnC 95075 1061-A4
700 MPS 95035 794-B7
HORIZON LN
- SJS 95148 855-G2
HORNBEAM WY
500 SJS 95111 854-J6
HORNBLOWER CT
500 SJS 95136 874-F2
HORNING ST
400 SJS 95112 834-B3
HORNLEIN CT
- GIL 95020 978-A3
HORSESHOE BEND
- PTLV 94028 830-C1
HORSESHOE CT
1700 SCIC 95046 937-G3
14500 SAR 95070 872-E3
28000 LAH 94022 811-A5
HORSESHOE DR
14500 SAR 95070 872-E3
HORSESHOE LN
27000 LAH 94022 811-A5
HORSETAIL FERN COM
- FRMT 94539 793-J3
HORTON CT
6000 SJS 95123 875-A6
HORWEDEL DR
2800 SJS 95148 855-D2
HOSKINS CT
- SCIC 94305 790-J7
HOSPITAL DR
2400 MTVW 94040 831-H1
HOSPITAL PKWY
200 SJS 95119 875-B6
HOSPITAL PZ
- MLPK 94025 790-J2
HOSPITAL RD
- SBnC 95023 1060-B2
HOSTA LN
5900 SJS 95124 873-J7
HOSTETTER RD
1600 SJS 95131 814-C6
2300 SJS 95132 814-G3
HOTSPUR CT
1400 SJS 95125 854-A4
HOUGE CT
- SJS 95124 873-E3
HOUGHTON CT
1000 SJS 95112 834-D3
HOUGHTON ST
200 MTVW 94041 811-J5
HOULTON CT
100 SJS 95139 875-G7
100 SJS 95139 895-G1
HOUNDSBROOK WY
4100 SJS 95111 855-A7
HOUNDS ESTATES
5300 SJS 95135 855-G5
HOUNDS ESTATES CT
3000 SJS 95135 855-G5
HOUNDSHAVEN WY
4400 SJS 95111 874-J1
4600 SJS 95111 875-A1
HOUNSLOW DR
2100 SJS 95131 814-D6
HOURET CT
1700 MPS 95035 814-B3
HOURET DR
200 MPS 95035 814-B3
HOUSTON CT
13000 SAR 95070 852-D7
HOWARD AV
900 GIL 95020 977-G1
HOWARD CT
- CPTO 95014 852-F2
200 HOLL 95023 1040-B4
900 GIL 95020 977-G1
HOWARD DR
300 SCL 95051 832-H7
HOWARD ST
400 SJS 95110 834-A6
HOWARD WY
- ATN 94027 790-E3
HOWDEN CT
6900 SJS 95119 875-F6
HOWELL AV
700 SCL 95051 833-A6
HOWELL LN
2400 SCIC 95020 938-D7
2400 SCIC 95020 958-C1
HOWEN DR
13500 SAR 95070 872-E1
HOWES CT
200 LGTS 95032 873-G5
HOWES DR
100 LGTS 95032 873-G5
HOWES LN
4900 SJS 95118 873-J4
5100 SJS 95118 874-A4
HOWSON ST
100 GIL 95020 977-J2
HOXETT ST
900 GIL 95020 977-H4
HOYA LN
- GIL 95020 957-D7
HOYET DR
5200 SJS 95129 852-J4
HOYLAKE CT
- GIL 95020 977-D4
HUBBARD AV
500 SCL 95051 832-H6
HUBBARD WY
10700 SCIC 95127 815-B7
10700 SCIC 95127 835-B1
HUBBARTT DR
4100 PA 94306 811-C3
HUBBELL WY
500 LGTS 95030 873-A6
500 LGTS 95032 873-A6
HUCKLEBERRY CT
1000 SUNV 94087 832-B3
HUCKLEBERRY DR
- SJS 95123 875-B6
HUDDERSFIELD CT
1500 SJS 95126 853-H3
HUDNER LN
400 SBnC 95023 1019-E3
HUDSON DR
600 SCL 95051 832-H6
1700 SJS 95124 853-H7
HUDSON PL
700 GIL 95020 977-J4
HUDSON ST
1200 RDWC 94061 790-B1
HUDSON WY
1000 SUNV 94087 832-B2
HUERTO CT
2500 SJS 95128 853-F4
HUERTO DR
2400 SJS 95128 853-F4
HUFF AV
900 MTVW 94043 811-H1
2800 SJS 95128 853-E2
HUGO LN
1400 SJS 95118 874-B2
HULA DR
3500 SJS 95136 854-F7
HULET ST
600 SJS 95125 854-A1
HULL AV
300 SJS 95125 854-A2
1700 SMCo 94061 790-A3
HULME CT
- SCIC 94305 790-J7
HUMBER CT
500 SUNV 94087 832-E5
HUMBERSIDE CT
3100 SJS 95148 855-E2
HUMBOLDT AV
2800 SCL 95051 833-A4
HUMBOLDT CT
200 SUNV 94089 812-F3
HUMBOLDT ST
- SJS 95110 854-C2
- SJS 95112 854-D1
E HUMBOLDT ST
200 SJS 95112 854-D1
HUME DR
15100 SAR 95070 872-E4
HUMEWICK WY
800 SUNV 94087 832-F5
HUMMEL CT
2400 SJS 95148 855-B1
HUMMINGBIRD DR
800 SJS 95125 854-C6
HUMMINGBIRD LN
- SBnC 95023 1040-D4
- SCIC 95046 956-J1
- SCIC 95046 957-B1
1600 SUNV 94087 832-F5
HUNKEN DR
2900 SJS 95111 854-H5
HUNSAKER RD
- MTVW 94043 812-A1
- SCIC 94035 812-A1
- SCIC 94043 812-A1
HUNT WY
- CMBL 95008 853-C6
HUNTER PL
- SCL 95054 813-C5
HUNTER WY
18800 CPTO 95014 852-H2
HUNTERS HILL RD
20400 SCIC 95120 895-A4
HUNTERSTON PL
1000 CPTO 95014 852-C3
HUNTINGDON AV
1000 SJS 95129 852-H3
HUNTINGDON DR
1000 SJS 95129 852-H4
HUNTINGTON CT
- MTVW 94043 812-B5
HUNTINGTON LN
2000 LALT 94024 831-H4
HUNTRIDGE LN
7700 CPTO 95014 852-C2
HUNTSFIELD CT
7000 SJS 95120 894-G4
HUNTSWOOD CT
700 SJS 95120 894-J3
HURAN CT
2500 SJS 95122 855-A1
HURAN DR
2100 SJS 95122 834-J7
2200 SJS 95122 854-J1
2400 SJS 95122 855-A1
HURLINGHAM WY
1400 SJS 95127 835-A4
HURLSTONE LN
900 SJS 95120 894-G2
HURST AV
1600 CMBL 95125 853-H6
1600 SCIC 95125 853-H6
1600 SJS 95125 853-H6
HURSTGLEN WY
3800 SJS 95121 855-C4
HURSTWOOD CT
1700 SJS 95121 855-C4
HUSTED AV
1100 SJS 95125 854-A7
1600 SJS 95125 853-J7
1700 SJS 95124 873-J1
HUSTON CT
2400 MGH 95037 917-F6
HUTCHINGS DR
- SJS 95111 854-G4
HUTCHINSON AV
900 PA 94301 791-B4
HUTCHINSON RD
22000 SCrC 95033 912-H5
24700 SCrC 95066 912-F7
HUTTON CT
100 SUNV 94087 832-E5
6100 SJS 95123 875-A6
HUXLEY CT
1800 SJS 95125 853-G4
HYACINTH LN
1600 SJS 95124 873-J7
HYANNIS DR
500 SUNV 94087 832-D2
HYANNISPORT DR
8000 CPTO 95014 852-B2
HYDE AV
800 CPTO 95014 852-G2
1000 SJS 95129 852-G3
HYDE CT
1600 CMBL 95032 872-J2
HYDE DR
1500 CMBL 95032 872-J2
HYDE PARK DR
400 SJS 95136 874-F3
600 SUNV 94087 832-D2
6300 GIL 95020 978-A5
HYDRANGEA CT
800 SUNV 94086 832-F2
HYDRANGEA LN
1600 SJS 95124 873-J6
HYLAND AV
4300 SCIC 95127 834-J2
4600 SCIC 95127 834-J2
4800 SCIC 95127 835-A1

I

I RD
- SUNV 94089 812-H3
IAN CT
- HOLL 95023 1040-B4
IBERIS CT
1000 SUNV 94086 832-H2
ICEFIELD CT
3100 SCL 95051 833-A1
ICON TER
- SJS 95112 834-B3
IDA DR
17900 SCIC 95033 913-A3
20400 SCIC 95033 912-J2
IDA WY
2000 SJS 95124 873-E2
IDAHO CT
900 MPS 95035 794-A5
2000 RDWC 94061 790-A3
IDAHO ST
1100 SJS 95126 833-G5
1300 SCL 95050 833-G5
IDALYN DR
18000 SCIC 95033 912-J2
IDLEBROOK CT
6500 SJS 95120 894-C1
IDLEWILD CT
6500 SJS 95120 894-C1
IDLEWOOD CT
900 SJS 95121 854-H3
IDLEWOOD DR
900 SJS 95121 854-H3
IDLEWOOD LN
12700 SAR 95070 852-E6
IDYLLWILD AV
1800 SMCo 94061 790-B3
IDYLLWILD CT
300 SMCo 94061 790-B4
IDYLWILD DR
18100 SCIC 95033 892-J7
20400 SCIC 95033 912-J1
IDYLWILD RD
18200 SCIC 95033 912-J1
20600 SCIC 95033 913-A1
IGNEOUS CT
2300 SJS 95133 814-H3
ILIKAI AV
1400 SJS 95118 874-A3
ILIMA CT
800 PA 94306 811-B2
ILIMA WY
900 PA 94306 811-B3
ILLIAD CT
1100 SJS 95118 874-G3
ILLINOIS AV
400 SJS 95126 854-A1
500 SJS 95125 854-A1
ILLINOIS ST
2400 EPA 94303 791-C1
ILLSLEY CT
4400 SJS 95136 874-H1
ILLUMINATION PL
- MPS 95035 814-J1
IMAGES CIR
- MPS 95035 794-A6
- MPS 95035 793-J6
IMAGINATION PL
- MPS 95035 814-J2
IMPALA CT
500 MGH 95037 917-B6
IMPALA DR
3100 SJS 95117 853-D4
IMPATIENS DR
5000 SJS 95111 875-A2
IMPERIAL AV
10100 CPTO 95014 852-B1
IMPERIAL DR
6600 GIL 95020 977-J5
IMPERIAL WY
6400 SJS 95129 852-F3
IMPRESARIO WY
3500 SJS 95127 835-C2
IMPRESSION WY
- SJS 95125 853-J4
IMWALLE CT
2000 SJS 95131 814-E7
INCA CT
16200 SCIC 95030 893-C2
INCLINE CT
2100 MPS 95035 814-E1
INCLINE WY
200 SJS 95139 895-E1
E INDEPENDENCE AV
700 MTVW 94043 811-G1
INDEPENDENCE DR
400 SJS 95111 854-H5
INDIAN AV
5600 SJS 95123 874-G6
INDIAN CRSG
- PTLV 94028 830-C1
INDIAN DR
2400 PA 94303 791-D5
INDIAN BROOM DR
300 SJS 95111 875-B2
INDIAN CREEK CT
1800 SJS 95148 835-D4
INDIAN RIVER CT
4800 SJS 95136 874-H3
INDIAN RIVER DR
4800 SJS 95136 874-H2
INDIAN ROCK WY
- SCrC 95033 871-C3
INDIAN SPRINGS CT
6600 SJS 95120 894-D2
INDIAN SPRINGS DR
5400 SJS 95123 875-D2
INDIAN SUMMER CT
1000 SJS 95122 854-F2
INDIAN TRAIL RD
12300 SCIC 95030 871-C3
12300 SCrC 95033 871-C3
INDIAN VALLEY CT
7100 SJS 95139 895-H2
INDIAN WELLS CT
7000 SJS 95139 895-E1
INDIGO DR
4200 SJS 95136 874-F2
INDIGO OAK CT
- SJS 95138 855-C5
INDIGO OAK LN
- SJS 95138 855-C5
INDIO CT
12600 SAR 95070 852-E6
INDIO WY
300 SUNV 94086 812-E6
INDUS CT
3200 SJS 95127 814-H6
INDUSTRIAL AV
800 PA 94303 791-G7
800 PA 94303 811-G1
1400 SJS 95112 834-A1
INDUSTRIAL DR
800 HOLL 95023 1040-B5
INDUSTRIAL ST
300 CMBL 95008 853-E7
INDUSTRIAL WY
100 MPS 95035 794-A7
400 LGTS 95030 873-A6
INEZ WY
500 SCIC 95117 853-D2
INFINITE LP
20300 CPTO 95014 832-E6
INGALLS CT
2700 SJS 95111 854-G4
INGERSOLL CT
3200 SJS 95148 855-F1
INGERSOLL DR
3200 SJS 95148 855-E1
INGLESIDE CT
6500 SJS 95120 894-B2
INGLEWOOD DR
3700 SCL 95054 813-E5
INGLEWOOD LN
- ATN 94027 790-D3
INGLIS LN
1600 SJS 95118 873-J5
INGRAM CT
200 SJS 95139 895-G2
1000 SUNV 94087 832-B2
INGRID CT
12000 SAR 95070 852-G5
INMAN WY
2000 SJS 95122 834-J7
INNERWICK LN
3300 SJS 95121 855-C3
INNOVATION DR
100 SJS 95134 813-F4
INNSBRUCK DR
1200 SUNV 94089 812-G3
INSKIP DR
1400 CMBL 95008 853-B7
INSPIRATION CT
3300 SJS 95132 814-G4

© 2008 Rand McNally & Company

STREET Block City ZIP Pg-Grid

INSPIRATION DR
3200 SJS 95132 814-G4
INSPIRATION PL
- MPS 95035 814-J1
INTERBAY DR
2000 SJS 95122 834-J7
2000 SJS 95122 835-A7
INTERDALE WY
4100 PA 94306 811-D2
INTERNATIONAL CIR
200 SJS 95119 875-C5
INVERNESS AV
1100 SCL 95050 833-D4
INVERNESS CIR
1500 SJS 95124 874-A3
INVERNESS DR
700 MPS 95035 794-B2
INVERNESS WY
200 SUNV 94087 832-E5
INVICTA WY
3200 SJS 95118 874-B1
INWOOD CT
1400 CMBL 95008 853-B7
INWOOD DR
500 CMBL 95008 853-B7
INYO PL
- SMCo 94061 790-B4
ION CT
100 CMBL 95008 853-D7
IONE CIR
1200 HOLL 95023 1039-H5
IONE CT
12700 SAR 95070 852-E6
IONE DR
2700 SJS 95132 814-F5
IOOF AV
- GIL 95020 978-A2
IOWA AV
100 SUNV 94086 832-D1
W IOWA AV
400 SUNV 94086 832-D1
700 SUNV 94086 812-B7
IOWA DR
6100 SJS 95123 874-H6
IRAZU CT
200 SJS 95116 834-G3
IRENE CT
- MTVW 94043 812-B5
IRENE ST
700 SJS 95110 833-J5
IRIS AV
600 SUNV 94086 832-F2
IRIS CT
1300 SJS 95125 854-A3
IRIS ST
1600 HOLL 95023 1040-C6
IRIS WY
100 PA 94303 791-C4
IRIS BLOSSOM CT
100 SJS 95123 875-A4
IRIS GARDENS CT
- SJS 95125 854-A2
IRISH CT
900 GIL 95020 977-G2
IRLANDA PL
- SJS 95126 833-D1
IRLANDA WY
3000 SJS 95124 873-J1
IRMA DR
200 HOLL 95023 1040-A6
IRMA LYLE DR
21600 SCIC 95033 912-H3
IRONBARK ST
- GIL 95020 977-D1
IRONBRIDGE WY
1200 SJS 95118 874-C4
IRONSHOE DR
- SJS 95138 855-E7
IRONSIDE CT
3000 SJS 95132 814-E3
IRON SPRINGS RD
20300 SCIC 95033 892-H7
20300 SCIC 95033 912-H1
IRONSTONE CT
1100 SJS 95132 814-F6
IRONWOOD DR
800 SJS 95125 854-C6
IRONWOOD TER
500 SUNV 94086 832-F2
IROQUOIS CT
600 SJS 95123 874-G4
IROQUOIS TR
- PTLV 94028 810-B6
IRVEN CT
500 PA 94306 811-D2
IRVING AV
- ATN 94027 790-F1
300 SCIC 95128 853-G1
300 SJS 95128 853-G1
IRWINDALE DR
2900 SJS 95122 855-B3
ISABEL DR
1600 SCIC 95125 853-H4
ISABEL LN
- SBnC 95023 1040-D2
ISABELLA AV
- ATN 94027 790-E2
ISABELLA ST
500 SCL 95050 833-D4
ISABELLA WY
- GIL 95020 977-F3
ISABELLE AV
1300 MTVW 94040 811-G7
ISABELLE CT
- LGTS 95030 873-C7
ISADORA DR
3100 SJS 95132 814-F3
ISDLIO CT
- SJS 95123 874-F6
ISENGARD DR
1200 SJS 95121 855-A4
ISHIMATSU PL
5100 SJS 95124 873-G5
ISIS WY
- MTVW 94043 812-B6
ISLAND DR
100 PA 94301 791-B3
ISLAND PALM CT
- SJS 95133 814-J4
ISLAND PINE WY
6200 SJS 95119 875-D5
ISLA VISTA TER
600 SUNV 94086 812-F5
ISLAY CT
700 SUNV 94087 832-F5
ISSAC CT
- SJS 95136 854-E7
ITHACA AV
800 SUNV 94087 832-C2
IVALYNN CIR
3500 SJS 95132 814-G4
IVALYNN CT
3500 SJS 95132 814-G4
IVALYNN PL
3500 SJS 95132 814-G4
IVAN PL
1500 SJS 95120 874-A7
IVAN WY
3300 MTVW 94040 832-A2
6900 SCIC 95020 978-H2
IVANHOE CT
400 SJS 95136 874-G3
IVEGILL CT
6800 SJS 95119 895-D1
IVERSEN CT
2600 SCL 95051 833-B7
IVES TER
400 SUNV 94087 832-E2
IVORY CREEK DR
900 SJS 95120 894-J4
IVY LN
1900 PA 94303 791-C4
6300 SJS 95129 852-F4
IVY ST
100 GIL 95020 978-A1
IVY CANYON CT
- SJS 95121 855-B4
IVYCREEK CIR
1500 SJS 95121 855-D7
IVY ESTATES CT
2800 SJS 95135 855-G5
IVYGATE LN
3000 SJS 95136 874-J3
IVY GLEN DR
- SJS 95133 814-E7
IVY HILL WY
100 LGTS 95032 873-C4
IVY MILLS LN
1700 SJS 95122 854-G1
IVYWOOD CT
2800 SJS 95121 855-E4
IXIAS CT
1600 SJS 95124 873-J7
IXIAS LN
5800 SJS 95124 873-J7
IZORAH WY
15700 LGTS 95032 873-C5

J

J RD
- SUNV 94089 812-H3
JABIL LN
23900 LAH 94024 831-D4
JACANA CT
5200 SJS 95123 874-F7
JACANA LN
5200 SJS 95123 874-F7
JACARANDA CIR
- HOLL 95023 1039-G3
JACARANDA DR
- MTVW 94043 812-B5
JACARANDA LN
- PA 94306 791-B7
JACARANDA WY
400 SUNV 94086 832-F1
9100 GIL 95020 957-G7
16100 SCIC 95032 873-D6
JACCARANDA CT
13000 SAR 95070 852-F7
JACINTO WY
100 SUNV 94086 812-C6
JACKDOW CT
- GIL 95020 957-E7
JACKIE DR
400 SJS 95111 854-H5
JACKLIN CIR
- MPS 95035 794-A5
JACKLIN CT
- MPS 95035 794-A5
JACKLIN PL
- MPS 95035 794-A5
JACKLIN RD
- MPS 95035 794-A5
JACKPINE CT
700 SUNV 94086 832-F2
JACKS RD
20800 SAR 95070 872-D3
JACKSOL DR
3700 SJS 95124 873-E3
JACKSON AV
200 SUNV 94086 812-E7
N JACKSON AV
- SJS 95116 834-G3
300 SJS 95133 834-F1
900 SJS 95133 814-E7
S JACKSON AV
- SJS 95116 834-H4
JACKSON CT
2000 SCL 95050 833-D3
JACKSON DR
500 PA 94303 791-C4
JACKSON ST
- LGTS 95030 893-A1
- SJS 95112 834-A4
500 SCL 95050 833-D3
900 MTVW 94043 811-H4
JACKSON WY
- SJS 95002 793-C7
JACKSON OAKS CT
3600 MGH 95037 917-H5
JACKSON OAKS DR
15800 MGH 95037 917-G5
JACOB AV
1500 SJS 95118 874-A2
1600 SJS 95124 873-J2
1600 SJS 95124 874-A2
JACOBS CT
400 PA 94306 811-C2
JACOBS WY
- SCIC 95020 957-G3
JACQUELINE CT
16100 MGH 95037 937-C1
JACQUELINE DR
- HOLL 95023 1039-H4
JACQUELINE WY
1000 SJS 95129 852-E3
JACQUES DR
5900 SJS 95123 874-G6
JADE AV
3200 SJS 95117 853-D3
JADELAKE CT
800 SUNV 94089 812-H5
JAFFE LN
1500 SCIC 95046 937-J6
JAGGERS DR
200 SJS 95119 875-C7
JAI DR
300 SJS 95119 875-C7
JALAND CT
1100 SJS 95120 894-H4
JAMAICA RD
2700 SJS 95111 854-G4
JAMAICA WY
2000 SJS 95122 834-J7
JAMES AV
- ATN 94027 790-F1
JAMES CT
1300 SCIC 95037 917-C6
3100 SCL 95051 833-A3
JAMES DR
200 MTVW 94043 812-A4
JAMES PL
1900 SJS 95125 853-J6
JAMES RD
400 PA 94306 811-D2
JAMES LEX LN
17200 MGH 95037 917-B6
JAMES TOWN CT
12000 SAR 95070 852-D5
JAMES TOWN DR
1600 CPTO 95014 852-D4
JAMESTOWN DR
1100 SUNV 94087 832-B2
JAMIE CT
100 LGTS 95032 873-H6
JAMIE LN
800 EPA 94303 791-C1
JAMIESON WY
6300 GIL 95020 978-B5
JAMISON PL
2000 SCL 95051 833-A3
JAN AV
1100 HOLL 95023 1039-H4
JAN DR
8700 GIL 95020 977-F1
JAN WY
4000 SJS 95124 873-H3
JANA LN
800 SJS 95111 855-A6
JANARY WY
6300 SJS 95129 852-F4
JANE LN
2300 MTVW 94043 811-G3
JANE ANN WY
- CMBL 95008 853-C6
JANELLE DR
3200 SJS 95148 855-E2
JANET AV
1900 SJS 95124 873-G2
JANETS CT
- SBnC 95023 1060-F3
JANICE AV
22200 CPTO 95014 852-A1
JANICE DR
1100 SCL 95050 833-C4
JANICE WY
3400 PA 94303 791-E6
JANIS WY
1100 SJS 95125 854-B6
JANKU CT
3200 SJS 95127 814-H6
JANMARIE CT
1100 SJS 95121 855-A5
JANOR CT
15200 MSER 95030 872-J4
JANSEN AV
800 SJS 95125 854-B4
JANUARY DR
100 SJS 95138 875-C4
JAPAUL LN
1400 SJS 95132 814-F3
JAPONICA WY
4600 SJS 95129 853-A1
JARDIN DR
100 LALT 94022 811-E5
300 MTVW 94040 811-E5
JARDINE CT
- SJS 95126 833-D1
JARED LN
- LGTS 95030 893-C1
JARVIS AV
3000 SJS 95118 874-A1
JARVIS CT
300 SUNV 94086 832-E1
1500 SJS 95118 874-B2
JARVIS DR
400 MGH 95037 916-J5
400 MGH 95037 917-A4
JARVIS LN
700 SBnC 95023 1020-G6
JARVIS PL
1500 SJS 95118 874-B2
JARVIS WY
2000 LAH 94304 810-H4
JASMINE CIR
- SJS 95135 855-H3
JASMINE CT
- MTVW 94043 812-B5
100 MPS 95035 794-D6
JASMINE DR
800 SUNV 94086 832-F2
JASMINE WY
- HOLL 95023 1040-B6
100 EPA 94303 791-D3
1200 MGH 95037 917-D6
16100 SCIC 95032 873-D6
JASON CT
6100 SJS 95123 875-A6
JASON DR
- MPS 95035 793-J4
JASON WY
200 MTVW 94043 811-J5
JASPER CT
1100 MGH 95037 936-H1
JASPER DR
1500 SUNV 94087 832-B5
JASPER ST
600 SJS 95116 834-F5
JASPER HIGHLANDS DR
1800 MGH 95037 916-F7
JASPER HILL WY
- SJS 95135 855-F6
E JAVA DR
200 SUNV 94089 812-G3
W JAVA DR
100 SUNV 94089 812-F2
JAY ST
500 LALT 94022 811-F6
3200 SCL 95054 813-C7
JAYBEE PL
100 SJS 95123 875-A3
JAZZ CT
800 SJS 95134 813-F2
JEAN CT
1700 MGH 95037 917-D5
JEAN ELLEN DR
10100 SCIC 95020 957-C6
JEANETTE CT
- SBnC 95023 1060-F2
7800 CPTO 95014 852-C2
JEANETTE LN
14800 SCIC 95127 835-B1
JEANIE LN
2100 SCIC 95020 958-A1
JEANNE AV
800 SJS 95116 834-E7
JEFFERS WY
- CMBL 95008 853-D6
JEFFERSON CT
600 SJS 95133 814-G7
JEFFERSON DR
500 PA 94303 791-C4
800 MTVW 94040 811-G7
2000 SCIC 95020 957-C6
JEFFERSON ST
- SJB 95045 1038-D4
200 SCL 95050 833-D4
JEFFERY AV
1400 SJS 95118 874-B1
JEFFERY CT
1700 SCL 95051 833-A3
JEFFREY AV
600 CMBL 95008 853-C7
JEFFRY LN
10200 SCIC 95020 958-C3
JENA TER
- SUNV 94089 812-G4
JENEANE MARIE CIR
- SJS 95122 854-G2
JENECE CT
17400 MGH 95037 917-D5
JENKINS AV
3000 SJS 95118 854-B7
3000 SJS 95118 874-B1
JENKINS CT
100 SCIC 94305 790-J7
JENKINS LN
100 MTVW 94043 812-B5
JENKINS PL
- SCL 95051 833-A7
JENNER CT
1400 HOLL 95023 1040-D6
JENNIFER CT
300 MTVW 94040 811-F4
JENNIFER LN
1500 SCIC 95020 958-A1
JENNIFER WY
700 MPS 95035 794-A5
3000 SJS 95124 873-G2
JENNINGS DR
600 SJS 95111 854-J5
JENNINGS LN
- ATN 94027 790-D1
JENNY CT
700 SJS 95138 875-F4
JENNY ST
700 SJS 95138 875-F4
JENNY LIND CT
5900 SJS 95120 874-C6
JENSON SPRINGS RD
- SCrC 95033 912-G3
JENVEY AV
1500 SJS 95125 854-A6
JEPSEN CT
12800 SAR 95070 852-D6
JERABEK CT
3900 SJS 95136 874-F1
JERALD AV
2900 SCL 95051 833-A3
JEREMIE CT
6500 SJS 95120 894-E1
JEREMIE DR
6500 SJS 95120 894-E1
JERICHO LN
3300 SJS 95117 853-D3
JERILYN CT
10200 SCIC 95127 835-A2
JERILYN DR
400 SJS 95127 835-A2
14000 SCIC 95127 835-A2
JEROME ST
300 SJS 95125 854-B1
JERRIES DR
14000 SAR 95070 872-E2
JERVIS AV
1100 EPA 94303 791-A1
JESS CT
- SBnC 95023 1060-F2
JESSE JAMES DR
500 SJS 95123 874-J7
JESSICA LN
11600 LAH 94024 831-E4
JESSICA WY
1600 SJS 95121 855-A2
JESSIE CT
2900 SJS 95124 873-F1
JESSIE LN
300 MTVW 94041 811-J6
JESSIE WY
21500 SCIC 95033 912-J3
JEWELL DR
2100 SJS 95124 873-F1
JEWELL PL
2000 MTVW 94043 811-G3
JILINDA CT
10800 SCIC 95127 835-A1
JILL AV
500 SJS 95117 833-D7
700 SCL 95050 833-D7
JILLS CT
100 HOLL 95023 1039-H3
JIM DR
500 SJS 95133 814-H7
JIM ELDER DR
- CMBL 95008 853-C6
JIMS WY
13600 SAR 95070 872-E1
JISHIN TER
- SJS 95112 834-B3
JO DR
100 LGTS 95032 873-D4
JOAN WY
1800 SCL 95050 833-D3
JOANDRA CT
500 SCIC 94024 831-F3
JOANNE AV
3300 SCIC 95127 814-H6
3400 SJS 95127 814-J6
JOAQUIN RD
- SMCo 94028 830-D4
900 MTVW 94043 811-J1
JOE BOROVICH DR
800 HOLL 95023 1040-B5
JOE DIMAGGIO CT
1400 SJS 95122 834-G7
JOEL WY
1700 LALT 94024 832-A2
JOES LN
- SBnC 95023 1060-E2
JOHANNA AV
600 SUNV 94086 812-G6
JOHANSEN DR
10600 CPTO 95014 852-G2
JOHN DR
6600 CPTO 95014 852-E2
JOHN WY
800 CPTO 95014 852-D2
JOHN KIRK CT
100 CMBL 95008 853-A6
JOHN MISE CT
400 SJS 95129 852-J2
JOHN MONTGOMERY DR
2500 SJS 95148 835-A6
JOHN SMITH RD
200 SBnC 95023 1040-E6
1300 SBnC 95023 1060-J1
1300 SBnC 95023 1061-A1
JOHNSON AV
100 LGTS 95030 893-B1
1000 SJS 95129 852-G3
1400 SAR 95070 852-G3
10200 CPTO 95014 852-H2
JOHNSON PL
2400 SCL 95050 833-C6
JOHNSON ST
1000 RDWC 94061 790-A1
1100 MLPK 94025 790-E4
JOHNSON WY
600 GIL 95020 977-J5
JOHNSON HOLLOW
100 LGTS 95030 893-B1
JOHNSTON AV
1700 SJS 95125 854-C4
JOHN TELFER DR
16900 MGH 95037 916-H7
16900 MGH 95037 936-H1
JOHN WILSON WY
100 MGH 95037 937-C4
100 SCIC 95037 937-C4
JOLEEN WY
16800 MGH 95037 917-B7
JOLENE CT
12400 SAR 95070 852-H6
JOLLY CT
1600 LALT 94024 831-H4
JOLLYMAN DR
1000 CPTO 95014 852-D2
JOLLYMAN LN
10700 CPTO 95014 852-D2
JONATHAN AV
1700 SJS 95125 854-B4
JONATHAN CT
900 CMBL 95008 873-B1
JONATHAN ST
1300 SCL 95050 833-E5
JONES AV
1700 SCL 95051 833-A3
JONES LN
1600 LALT 94024 832-A5
JONES RD
200 LGTS 95030 893-A1
200 LGTS 95030 892-J1
JONES WY
800 CMBL 95008 853-C7
JONESBORO CT
1500 SJS 95131 814-C6
JONESPORT AV
2000 SJS 95131 814-E7
JONESPORT CT
1100 SJS 95131 814-E7
JONQUIL DR
4300 SJS 95136 874-F1
JONQUIL LN
- SBnC 95023 1040-D2
JOPLIN DR
1300 SJS 95118 874-B3
JORDAN AV
- LALT 94022 811-E4
JORDAN CT
- MTVW 94043 812-B6
JORDAN PL
- PA 94303 791-B4
JORDAN WY
200 PA 94304 790-G6
JORDAN HEIGHTS DR
100 LGTS 95032 873-E7
100 LGTS 95032 893-E1
JORN CT
700 SJS 95123 874-G6
JOSEFA LN
25700 LAH 94022 831-B2
JOSEFA ST
200 SJS 95110 834-A7
300 SJS 95126 834-A7
300 SJS 95126 854-A1
JOSE FIGUERES AV
- SJS 95116 834-G3
JOSEPH AV
2700 SJS 95008 873-F1
JOSEPH CIR
20100 CPTO 95014 832-E7
JOSEPH LN
700 MGH 95037 917-D7
5000 SJS 95118 873-J4
5000 SJS 95118 874-A4
JOSEPHINE AV
1900 SJS 95124 873-G1
JOSEPH SORCI PL
- SJS 95148 855-G2
JOSEPH SPECIALE DR
4500 SJS 95136 874-G3
JOSHUA DR
- HOLL 95023 1040-B6
JOSHUA WY
400 SUNV 94086 832-G1
JOSINA AV
600 PA 94306 811-B2
JOSSLYN DR
7100 SJS 95120 894-H4
JOY BELL LN
12600 SCIC 95046 937-H7
JOYCE CT
10200 SCIC 95127 835-A3
JOYERIN CT
1400 SJS 95131 814-D7
JOYNER CT
1300 SJS 95131 814-D6
JUAN HERNANDEZ DR
- MGH 95037 917-C7
16300 MGH 95037 937-C1
JUAN HERNANDEZ RD
16100 MGH 95037 937-C1
JUANITA AV
1600 SJS 95125 854-B4
JUANITA DR
400 SCL 95050 833-D6
JUANITA WY
300 LALT 94022 811-C5
1200 CMBL 95008 873-B1
JUARCEYS CT
1500 SJS 95120 874-A7
JUAREZ AV
1600 LALT 94024 831-J4
JUAREZ CT
1900 SJS 95132 814-D3
JUBILEE CT
- SMCo 94061 790-A3
JUBILEE LN
2400 SJS 95131 814-C4
JUDI ANN CT
- SJS 95148 855-F1
JUDITH CT
21400 SCIC 95033 912-J3
JUDITH ST
5400 SJS 95123 874-J4
JUDKINS CT
2700 SJS 95148 855-C1
JUDRO WY
3500 SJS 95117 853-C1
JUDSON DR
1000 MTVW 94040 811-F5
JUDY AV
10000 CPTO 95014 852-G1
JUERGEN DR
3500 SJS 95121 855-C3
JULIAN CT
1200 HOLL 95023 1039-H5
E JULIAN ST
- SJS 95112 834-C5
300 SJS 95116 834-E4
W JULIAN ST
- SJS 95113 834-A6
100 SJS 95110 834-A6
700 SJS 95126 833-J6
700 SJS 95126 834-A6
JULIANA CT
2000 SCL 95050 833-D6
JULIE CT
1000 SCL 95051 832-J5
3500 PA 94306 811-B2
JULIE LN
1500 LALT 94024 831-J3
12300 SAR 95070 852-D5
JULIET AV
800 SJS 95127 835-C2
JULIET PARK DR
3700 SJS 95127 835-C1
JULIETTA LN
27100 LAH 94022 831-A2
JULIETTE LN
3600 SCL 95054 813-C6
JULI LYNN DR
1200 SJS 95120 874-C7
JULIO AV
2700 SJS 95124 873-J1
JULY DR
100 SJS 95138 875-D4
JUNA CT
19500 SAR 95070 872-F4
JUNCTION AV
1700 SJS 95112 833-J1
1700 SJS 95112 834-A1
1700 SJS 95112 813-H6
1700 SJS 95112 814-A7
1800 SJS 95131 813-H6
2100 MTVW 94043 811-G2
2400 SJS 95134 813-G4
JUNCTION CT
1700 SJS 95112 834-A1
JUNE AV
1400 SJS 95122 834-H7
JUNE CT
18100 SCIC 95033 912-J3
JUNE DR
100 SJS 95138 875-D4
JUNE WY
14000 SAR 95070 872-E2
JUNEAU WY
- SJS 95131 814-B6
JUNEBERRY CT
100 SJS 95136 874-H1
JUNESONG WY
900 SJS 95133 834-E1
1000 SJS 95131 834-E1
1100 SJS 95131 814-D7
JUNEWOOD AV
1800 SJS 95132 814-D3
JUNGFRAU CT
800 MPS 95035 814-D1
JUNIPER CT
- CPTO 95014 831-G6
400 SUNV 94086 832-G1
JUNIPER DR
- ATN 94027 790-G1
1000 HOLL 95023 1040-C6
1200 GIL 95020 977-G2
JUNIPER LN
14100 SAR 95070 872-E2
JUNIPERO AV
1100 RDWC 94061 790-A1
JUNIPERO DR
200 MPS 95035 813-J1
200 MPS 95035 814-A1
JUNIPERO WY
19600 SAR 95070 852-F6
JUNIPERO SERRA BLVD Rt#-G5
- MLPK 94025 790-F7
100 SCIC 94305 790-F7
100 SCIC 94304 790-F7
100 SCIC 94305 810-G1
100 SCIC 94304 810-G1
JUNIPERO SERRA FRWY I-280
- CPTO - 832-F6
- LAH - 810-F3
- LAH - 811-A7
- LAH - 831-B1
- LALT - 831-G5
- LALT - 832-F6
- MLPK - 810-C1
- PA - 810-F3
- SCL - 832-F6
- SCL - 852-H1
- SCIC - 810-F3
- SCIC - 831-G5
- SCIC - 832-F6
- SJS - 852-H1
- SJS - 852-J1
- SJS - 853-A1
- SMCo - 790-A6
- SMCo - 810-C1
- SUNV - 832-F6
- WDSD - 790-A6
JUNIPERO SERRA LN
4300 SJS 95129 853-A1
JUPITER CT
600 FRMT 94539 793-J1
1400 MPS 95035 794-D6
JUPITER DR
1500 MPS 95035 794-D6
JUPITER WY
1500 MPS 95035 794-D6
JURA WY
700 SUNV 94087 832-F5
JURGENS DR
200 MPS 95035 793-J4
JURY CT
800 SJS 95112 834-B1
JUSTINE DR
3700 SJS 95124 873-H2
JUSTIN MORGAN DR
2300 SCIC 95020 958-D5
JUSTINO DR
1700 MGH 95037 917-D5
JUSTO CT
100 CMBL 95008 853-D7

STREET Block City ZIP Pg-Grid

K

K RD
- SUNV 94089 812-H3
KAHALA CT
13300 SAR 95070 852-E7
KAISER DR
3000 SCL 95051 833-A5
KAISER RD
- SCIC 94035 812-B3
KALANA AV
- SCIC 95037 896-D7
- SJS 95037 896-D7
100 SCIC 95037 916-C1
KALISPELL CT
1600 SUNV 94087 832-B5
KALLIAM DR
2800 SCL 95051 833-B7
KAMIAH WY
900 SUNV 94087 832-B5
KAMMERER AV
1700 SJS 95116 834-G5
KAMSACK CT
- SUNV 94087 832-B5
KAMSACK DR
1600 SUNV 94087 832-B5
KAMSON WY
100 CMBL 95008 853-D5
KANDICE CT
- SJS 95123 874-F7
KANDLE WY
1100 RDWC 94061 790-B1
KANE CT
1300 SJS 95121 854-J3
19800 SAR 95070 852-F6
KANE DR
100 SBnC 95023 1040-D3
12600 SAR 95070 852-F6
KANEKO DR
6500 SJS 95119 875-D6
KANNELY LN
11600 SCIC 95020 957-H1
KANSAS ST
1600 RDWC 94061 790-A2
KANSAS WY
100 FRMT 94539 793-J2
KARA WY
900 CMBL 95008 853-B7
900 CMBL 95008 873-B1
KARAMEOS CT
1700 SUNV 94087 832-B6
KARAMEOS DR
1700 SUNV 94087 832-B6
KAREN CT
- HOLL 95023 1039-H3
200 LGTS 95032 873-D7
1700 SJS 95124 873-H1
5500 GIL 95020 977-J7
KAREN DR
2300 SCL 95050 833-C5
19000 MonC 93907 1037-A7
KAREN WY
100 ATN 94027 790-B5
1000 MTVW 94040 811-F5
KARIE ANN WY
1200 SJS 95118 874-C1
KARINA CT
- SJS 95131 833-H1
KARINA WY
1300 SCL 95051 832-H4
KARL AV
14800 LGTS 95030 873-A4
14800 MSER 95030 873-A4
KARL ST
1100 SJS 95122 834-J5
KARLSTAD DR
1100 SUNV 94089 812-G4
KARMEN CT
1100 SCL 95051 832-H4
KARN CIR
19900 SAR 95070 852-E6
KARO CT
800 SUNV 94086 832-F2
KASKI CT
6100 SJS 95123 874-G6
KASRA DR
- MTVW 94043 812-B6
KASSEL TER
- SUNV 94089 812-G4
KASSON CT
1300 SJS 95121 854-J2
KATE DR
- LAH 94022 831-C4
- LAH 94024 831-C4
KATHERINE CT
900 SJS 95126 833-G6
KATHLEEN CT
- HOLL 95023 1040-C5
KATHLEEN ST
3400 SJS 95124 873-G2
KATHRYN DR
- HOLL 95023 1039-H4
KATHY CT
100 LGTS 95032 872-J3
KATHY LN
1500 LALT 94024 831-J3
17200 LGTS 95032 893-E2
KATHY WY
1100 MTVW 94022 811-G6
1100 MTVW 94040 811-G6
KATIE CT
1100 MTVW 94040 811-J7
KATO RD
47600 FRMT 94538 793-G1
48700 FRMT 94539 793-H3
KATO TER
48800 FRMT 94539 793-H2
KATON CT
700 SUNV 94086 832-F2
KATRINA WY
2500 MTVW 94040 832-A2
KATRINE CT
1000 SUNV 94087 832-G5
KATYBETH WY
1900 MGH 95037 917-E6
KAUAI DR
3700 SJS 95111 855-A6
KAUFMANN CT
700 SJS 95116 834-E6
KAVENY DR
5400 SJS 95129 852-H4
KAVIN LN
15400 MSER 95030 873-A5
15700 LGTS 95030 873-A5
KAWALKER LN
3100 SJS 95127 814-H6
KAY DR
1800 SJS 95124 873-G6
1900 LALT 94024 831-J5
2300 SCL 95050 833-C4
KAYAK DR
100 SJS 95111 875-B2
KAYBE CT
200 SJS 95139 895-F1
KAYELLEN CT
1100 SJS 95125 854-G5
KAYLA CT
2300 SJS 95124 853-G7
KAYLENE CT
1200 SJS 95127 835-B3
KAYLENE DR
3400 SJS 95127 835-B3
KAY SPRINGS CT
600 MGH 95037 916-H6
KEARNEY AV
2800 SCL 95051 833-A2
KEARNEY ST
200 SJS 95110 834-A7
KEARNY TER
800 SUNV 94086 812-D7
KEATON LP
3300 SJS 95121 855-D2
KEATS CT
600 PA 94306 811-F2
3600 SCIC 95127 834-J1
KEEBLE AV
- SJS 95126 833-J7
KEEBLE CT
- SJS 95126 833-J7
KEELER CT
200 SJS 95139 895-F1
KEENAN WY
1300 SJS 95125 853-G4
KEENE DR
5200 SJS 95124 873-F5
KEESLING AV
1500 SJS 95125 853-J5
1800 SCIC 95125 853-H5
KEEVER CT
- SJS 95127 834-J3
KEEWAYDIN CT
700 SJS 95111 855-A7
KEHOE CT
100 SJS 95136 874-J2
KEITH DR
1500 SJS 95008 853-B7
1500 CMBL 95008 853-A7
KEITH LN
800 SCL 95054 813-E6
KEITH WY
16100 MGH 95037 937-B2
KELDON CT
1000 SJS 95121 854-H2
KELDON DR
1000 SJS 95121 854-H3
KELEZ CT
6200 SJS 95120 874-D7
KELEZ DR
1100 SJS 95120 874-D7
KELL CT
13600 SCIC 95037 956-F2
KELL WY
- SJS 95136 854-C7
KELLER CT
3300 SCL 95054 813-E7
KELLER DR
500 MTVW 94043 812-A3
KELLER ST
3200 SCL 95054 813-E7
KELLEY WY
- SCL 95054 813-D4
KELLEY PARK CIR
1200 MGH 95037 917-C6
KELLOGG AV
100 PA 94301 791-A5
KELLOGG WY
- SCL 95051 833-A7
KELLY CT
1400 SJS 95116 834-F5
KELLY DR
100 SBnC 95023 1059-H2
1000 SJS 95129 852-J3
KELLY LN
10200 SCIC 95020 958-A4
KELLY WY
500 PA 94306 811-D3
KELOWNA CT
1400 SUNV 94087 832-B4
KELSEY DR
1100 SUNV 94087 832-B3
KELSO CT
3600 SCIC 95127 834-J1
KELTNER AV
900 SJS 95117 853-C3
KELTON CT
3600 SCIC 95127 834-J1
KELTON DR
8200 GIL 95020 977-G2
KELVINGTON CT
4000 SJS 95121 855-A5
KEN CIR
200 CMBL 95008 853-D5
KEN CT
- SBnC 95023 1060-F2
KENBAR RD
10300 SCIC 94024 831-F5
KENBRIDGE CT
1000 SUNV 94087 832-B2
KENBROOK CIR
300 SJS 95111 854-G6
KENDALL AV
500 PA 94306 811-B2
KENDALL CT
1100 SJS 95120 894-G4
KENDLE ST
22200 CPTO 95014 832-A7
KENDRA WY
3600 SJS 95130 853-C4
KENDRICK CIR
2600 SJS 95121 854-H3
KENESTA WY
2300 SJS 95122 855-A1
KENHILL DR
3100 SJS 95111 854-G6
KENILWORTH CT
500 SUNV 94087 832-E5
KENILWORTH WY
10100 SCIC 95127 835-A3
KENISTON AV
300 MPS 95035 793-J7
KENLAND DR
3100 SJS 95111 854-G6
KENLAR DR
4900 SJS 95124 873-G4
KENLEY WY
700 SUNV 94087 832-F5
KENMAR CT
1100 SJS 95132 814-F5
KENMORE AV
300 SUNV 94086 832-F1
KENMORE CT
1000 CPTO 95014 852-C2
KENNARD WY
900 SUNV 94087 832-G5
KENNEBEC CT
1500 MGH 95037 917-A3
KENNEBEC PL
- MGH 95037 917-A3
KENNEDY AV
- CMBL 95008 853-E6
2000 SJS 95122 834-H5
KENNEDY CT
200 LGTS 95030 893-D1
200 LGTS 95032 893-D1
400 GIL 95020 957-J7
400 GIL 95020 958-A7
KENNEDY DR
1300 MPS 95035 794-C5
KENNEDY RD
200 LGTS 95030 873-C7
200 SCIC 95030 873-C7
15200 LGTS 95032 893-D1
15200 SCIC 95032 893-G1
16100 LGTS 95030 893-D1
16200 LGTS 95032 873-D7
S KENNEDY RD
16000 LGTS 95030 893-C1
16300 LGTS 95030 873-C7
16300 LGTS 95032 873-C7
KENNEDY KNOLLS LN
100 LGTS 95030 873-D7
100 LGTS 95032 873-D7
KENNETH AV
500 CMBL 95008 853-C7
800 CMBL 95008 873-C1
KENNETH DR
3300 PA 94303 791-E6
KENNETH ST
400 CMBL 95008 853-C7
2900 SCL 95054 813-D7
2900 SCL 95054 833-D1
KENNEWICK CT
1500 SUNV 94087 832-C5
KENNEWICK DR
1500 SUNV 94087 832-C5
KENNEY CT
400 SUNV 94086 832-E1
KENNY LN
10100 SCIC 95127 835-C1
KENOGA DR
2400 SJS 95121 854-H2
KENOSHA AV
19500 SAR 95070 872-F2
KENPARK CT
1800 SJS 95124 853-H7
KENSINGTON AV
1100 SUNV 94087 832-H5
1100 SCL 95051 832-H5
1600 LALT 94024 831-H4
KENSINGTON CIR
1500 LALT 94024 831-H3
KENSINGTON PL
6400 GIL 95020 978-A5
KENSINGTON RD
2700 RDWC 94061 790-A3
KENSINGTON WY
100 LGTS 95032 873-G6
200 SJS 95124 873-G6
KENSINGTON PARK CT
400 SJS 95136 874-F1
KENSON DR
4900 SJS 95124 873-G4
KENT AV
1100 SUNV 94087 832-H5
KENT CT
- SJS 95139 875-G7
KENT DR
- MTVW 94043 812-B5
1900 LALT 94024 831-H5
KENT PL
- MLPK 94025 790-H3
- PA 94301 791-B4
KENT WY
20300 SCIC 95033 892-H7
KENTDALE PL
- SJS 95126 834-A7
KENTFIELD AV
1300 RDWC 94061 790-A2
KENTFIELD DR
5200 SJS 95124 873-G5
5300 LGTS 95032 873-G5
KENTMERE CT
400 MTVW 94040 811-J7
400 MTVW 94040 812-A7
KENTON CT
3700 SJS 95136 874-D1
KENTON LN
3700 SJS 95136 874-D1
KENTRIDGE DR
2900 SCIC 95133 834-H1
KENTUCKY PL
- SJS 95116 834-F4
KENTUCKY ST
1600 RDWC 94061 790-A2
KENTWOOD AV
1000 CPTO 95014 852-D3
1200 SJS 95129 852-D3
KENTWOOD CT
7500 GIL 95020 977-G3
KENTWORTH WY
2600 SCL 95051 833-B1
KENWOOD AV
2200 SJS 95128 833-E6
2400 SCL 95128 833-E6
KENWOOD DR
500 MLPK 94025 790-G4
KENYON CT
3600 SCIC 95127 834-J1
18000 SAR 95070 852-D5
KENYON DR
3300 SCL 95051 832-J6
KENZO CT
3300 MTVW 94040 831-J2
KEONCREST AV
1200 SJS 95110 833-J2
KEPPLER CT
2700 SJS 95148 855-B1
KEPPLER DR
2600 SJS 95148 855-B1
KERLEY DR
1400 SJS 95112 833-J2
KERMATH DR
3100 SJS 95132 814-E3
KERN AV
1100 SUNV 94086 812-H6
2700 SJS 95121 854-J3
8100 GIL 95020 977-G2
9000 GIL 95020 957-G7
9000 SCIC 95020 957-G7
9000 SCIC 95020 977-G2
KERN CT
1200 MTVW 94040 832-A2
KERN LP
1800 FRMT 94539 794-A2
KERRI CT
100 SMCo 94061 790-A4
KERRY AV
1000 SUNV 94087 832-H5
KERRY DR
200 SCL 95050 833-D7
KERRYSHIRE LN
2600 SCL 95051 833-C1
KERSTEN DR
3400 SJS 95124 873-H2
KERWIN RANCH CT
19200 SAR 95070 872-G1
KERWOOD CT
3600 SCIC 95127 834-J1
KESEY LN
2700 SJS 95132 814-D4
KESTER CT
14400 SCIC 95046 937-G3
KESTER DR
10800 CPTO 95014 852-A2
KESTRAL WY
- SJS 95133 814-F7
KESTREL CT
- GIL 95020 957-E7
KESWICK CT
3600 SCIC 95127 834-J1
KETCH PL
900 SJS 95133 814-E7
KETCHUM DR
200 SJS 95127 834-H2
KETTLE CT
6600 SJS 95120 894-E1
KETTMANN RD
3300 SJS 95121 855-D3
3500 SCIC 95121 855-D3
KETZAL CT
- SJS 95116 834-G3
KETZAL WY
- SJS 95116 834-G3
KEVIN DR
1600 SJS 95124 873-J6
KEVIN ST
13100 SAR 95070 852-H7
KEVIN WY
3700 SCL 95054 813-E6
KEVINAIRE DR
500 MPS 95035 794-B5
KEW GARDENS CT
1400 SJS 95120 874-B6
KEYES ST
- SJS 95112 854-D1
1000 SJS 95122 834-E7
1200 SJS 95112 834-E7
KEYMAR DR
5600 SJS 95123 874-J4
KEYSTONE AV
- MGH 95037 916-J7
- MGH 95037 917-A7
2600 SCL 95051 833-B7
KEYSTONE CT
1100 SJS 95132 814-F6
KICKAPOO CT
- MGH 95037 917-B2
KIEL CT
- SUNV 94089 812-G4
KIELY BLVD
- SCL 95051 833-B5
- SCL 95051 853-B1
300 SJS 95129 853-B1
S KIELY BLVD
300 SJS 95129 853-B1
400 SJS 95117 853-B1
KIFER CT
100 SUNV 94086 812-G7
KIFER RD
600 SUNV 94086 812-F7
800 SUNV 94086 832-G1
900 SCL 94086 832-G1
1100 SCL 95051 832-G1
2800 SCL 95051 833-A1
3100 SUNV 94086 833-A1
KIHOLO TER
- SUNV 94089 812-G4
KILBIRNIE CT
800 SUNV 94087 832-F5
KILBRIDE CT
20300 SAR 95070 852-E7
KILBRIDE DR
20000 SAR 95070 852-E7
KILCHOAN CT
1300 SJS 95122 854-H1
KILCHOAN WY
1800 SJS 95122 854-H1
KILDARE AV
1000 SUNV 94087 832-H5
KILKENNY CT
700 SUNV 94087 832-F5
KILKENNY RD
17600 LGTS 95030 893-B2
17600 SCIC 95030 893-B2
KILLARNEY CIR
- SJS 95138 855-G7
- SJS 95138 875-G1
KILLARNEY CT
- GIL 95020 977-F4
800 SUNV 94087 832-F5
KILLARNEY WY
- SJS 95138 855-G7
KILLDEER CT
1700 SUNV 94087 832-F6
KILLEAN CT
100 SUNV 94087 832-E5
KILLEY AL
- SBnC 95075 1061-A6
KILMARNOK DR
7700 SJS 95135 856-A6
KILMER AV
100 CMBL 95008 873-D3
100 LGTS 95008 873-D3
KILO AV
2800 SJS 95124 873-H1
KILROY WY
- ATN 94027 790-B4
KILT CT
19600 SAR 95070 852-F7
19600 SAR 95070 872-F1
KIM CT
1400 CMBL 95008 853-B6
KIM ST
800 CPTO 95014 852-D2
KIMBALL DR
2600 SJS 95121 854-H3
KIMBER CT
3100 SJS 95124 873-H2
KIMBERLIN PL
2000 SCL 95051 833-D2
KIMBERLY CT
- HOLL 95023 1039-H4
1400 SJS 95118 874-B2
2200 SCIC 95037 936-F2
KIMBERLY DR
1100 SJS 95118 874-B1
1700 SUNV 94087 832-B6
KIMBERLY ST
5500 SJS 95129 852-H2
KIMBLE AV
- LGTS 95030 893-A1
KIMLEE DR
3100 SJS 95132 814-F4
KIM LOUISE DR
- CMBL 95008 853-B6
- SJS 95008 853-B6
KIMPTON CT
2400 SJS 95133 834-G1
KINCORA CT
4000 SJS 95136 854-E5
KINDRA HILL DR
7000 SJS 95120 894-H3
KINER AV
1400 SJS 95125 854-A7
KING CIR
- HOLL 95023 1040-D5
KING CT
- MPS 95035 794-C7
1700 SJS 95122 855-A3
2100 SCL 95051 832-J2
18000 SAR 95070 852-D5
KING RD
- SCIC 94035 812-A2
- SCIC 94043 812-A2
N KING RD
- SJS 95133 834-D2
- SJS 95116 834-F3
S KING RD
- SJS 95116 834-G5
1100 SJS 95122 834-H6
2100 SJS 95122 854-J1
2300 SJS 95121 854-J1
2400 SJS 95122 855-A2
2400 SJS 95121 855-A2
KING ST
1100 RDWC 94061 790-A1
KING ARTHURS CT
4100 PA 94306 811-C3
KINGBROOK DR
4800 SJS 95124 873-E4
KINGDALE DR
4800 SJS 95124 873-E4
KING ESTATES
3000 SJS 95135 855-H5
KING ESTATES CT
5300 SJS 95135 855-H5
KINGFIELD WY
2400 SJS 95124 873-D4
KINGFISHER DR
800 SJS 95125 854-C6
KINGFISHER TER
800 SCIC 94087 832-F4
800 SUNV 94087 832-F4
KINGFISHER WY
1300 SUNV 94087 832-F4
KING GEORGE CT
1200 SCIC 95046 937-H7
KINGHURST WY
4800 SJS 95124 873-E4
KINGLET CT
1700 SUNV 94087 832-F6
KINGMAN AV
700 SJS 95128 853-G2
KING PALM CT
- SJS 95133 814-J4
KINGRIDGE DR
4800 SJS 95124 873-D4
KINGS CT
400 CMBL 95008 853-D5
KINGS LN
1400 PA 94303 791-B4
KINGS PL
6400 GIL 95020 978-A5
KINGS RW
700 SJS 95112 834-A1
KINGSBURY CIR
- SCL 95054 813-D5
KINGSBURY CT
7500 CPTO 95014 852-D3
KINGSBURY PL
7400 CPTO 95014 852-D3
KINGS CANYON CT
16400 MGH 95037 937-A1
KINGS CROSS WY
500 SJS 95136 874-F3
KINGSFORD LN
200 RDWC 94061 790-B2
KINGSGATE CT
2800 SJS 95132 814-D3
KINGS GATE DR
1400 SUNV 94087 832-C5
KINGSLAND CT
6500 SJS 95120 894-B1
KINGSLEY AV
100 PA 94301 790-J5
200 PA 94301 791-A5
KINGSLEY WY
14400 LAH 94022 811-B6
KINGSPARK DR
4100 SJS 95136 874-G1
KINGS RIVER CT
4700 SJS 95136 874-E2
KINGSTON CT
1600 LALT 94024 832-A3
KINGSTON RD
2700 SJS 95111 854-G4
KINGSTON WY
- SJS 95193 875-C5
4800 SJS 95130 852-J7
4800 SJS 95130 853-A7
4800 SJS 95130 872-J1
4800 SJS 95130 873-A1
KINGSTON HILL WY
200 LGTS 95032 873-C4
KINGSWOOD WY
600 LALT 94022 811-D5
KINGTON PL
2000 SCL 95051 833-A3
KINGWOOD DR
2500 SCL 95051 833-B2
KINGWOOD WY
4800 SJS 95124 873-E4
KINMAN CT
12600 SAR 95070 852-E6
KINNEY DR
200 SJS 95112 834-A3
KINROSS CT
500 SUNV 94087 832-E5
KINROSS WY
1800 SJS 95122 854-G1
KINSEY CT
- SJS 95131 814-A5
KINSPORT LN
1300 SJS 95120 874-B7
KINST CT
22500 CPTO 95014 851-J2
22500 CPTO 95014 852-A2
KINSULE CT
1300 SJS 95121 855-B5
KINTYRE WY
900 SUNV 94087 832-G5
1300 SJS 95129 852-E4
KIOWA CIR
600 SJS 95123 874-H6
KIOWA CT
- PTLV 94028 810-C6
KIOWA TR
17700 SCIC 95033 913-A2
KIPERASH CT
800 SJS 95133 814-G6
KIPERASH DR
2900 SJS 95133 814-G6
KIPLING CT
1300 SJS 95118 874-C2
KIPLING ST
- GIL 95020 977-H2
200 PA 94301 790-J4
2600 PA 94306 791-C6
KIRBY AV
300 SCIC 95037 916-G2
KIRBY PL
- PA 94301 791-B4
KIRBY WY
1900 SJS 95124 853-G7
1900 SJS 95124 873-F1
KIRBYHILL WY
100 SUNV 94087 832-E5
KIRCHER CT
1700 LALT 94024 832-A4
KIRK AV
- SCIC 95127 835-A1
- SJS 95127 835-A1
100 SCIC 95127 834-J1
100 SJS 95127 834-J1
200 SCIC 95127 814-J7
200 SJS 95127 814-J7
500 SUNV 94086 812-F5
KIRK CT
1600 SJS 95124 873-J3
KIRK RD
3000 SJS 95124 873-J1
4400 SJS 95124 874-A3
KIRKALDY CT
800 SUNV 94087 832-F5
KIRKBROOK DR
12000 SAR 95070 852-E5
KIRKDALE DR
12200 SAR 95070 852-E5
KIRK GLEN CT
600 SJS 95133 814-G7
KIRKHAVEN CT
- SJS 95111 874-J1
KIRKLAND AV
1700 SJS 95125 854-C4
KIRKLAND DR
600 SUNV 94087 832-D5
KIRKLYN DR
1800 SJS 95124 853-H7
KIRKMONT DR
1700 SJS 95124 853-H6
20200 SAR 95070 852-E5
KIRKORIAN WY
15500 MSER 95030 873-A5
KIRKPATRICK DR
- HOLL 95023 1040-A2
KIRKSIDE CT
1100 SJS 95126 853-H3
KIRKWALL PL
600 MPS 95035 794-A3
KIRKWOOD DR
3300 SCIC 95117 853-C1
3500 SJS 95117 853-C1
KIRWIN LN
7400 CPTO 95014 852-D2
KISER DR
900 SJS 95120 894-J4
KISHIMURA DR
300 GIL 95020 957-J7
KISSELL CT
3100 SJS 95111 854-H5
KIT CARSON CT
100 SCL 95050 833-C7
KITCHENER CIR
1000 SJS 95121 855-A5
KITCHENER DR
1600 SUNV 94087 832-C5
KITE DR
- GIL 95020 957-E6
KITIMAT PL
1300 SUNV 94087 832-C4
KITSAP CT
2600 SCL 95051 832-J1
KITTERY CT
- SJS 95139 875-G7
KITTOE DR
100 MTVW 94043 812-A4
KITTRIDGE RD
15300 SAR 95070 872-D4
KITTYHAWK WY
100 MTVW 94041 812-A6
KIZER ST
800 MPS 95035 794-B4
KLAMATH AV
800 SCL 95051 832-J3
KLAMATH DR
1000 MLPK 94025 790-C7
1300 SJS 95130 853-A4
1500 SUNV 94087 832-C5
KLAMATH RD
200 MPS 95035 794-A6
KLAUS DR
3500 SJS 95121 855-C3
KLEE CT
700 SJS 95123 874-G6
1200 SUNV 94087 832-E3
KLEIN CT
3600 SJS 95148 835-E6
KLEIN RD
2400 SCIC 95148 835-E5
2500 SJS 95148 835-E6
KLIPSPRINGER DR
1600 SJS 95124 873-J3
1600 SJS 95124 874-A3
KLOETZEL LN
- SJS 95148 855-F1
KLUNE CT
2300 SCL 95054 813-C4
KNICKERBOCKER DR
600 SUNV 94087 812-B7
600 SUNV 94087 832-A1
KNICKERSON DR
3000 SJS 95148 835-F7
3000 SJS 95148 855-F1
KNIGHT LN
- HOLL 95023 1040-A5
KNIGHTS BRIDGE CT
3000 SJS 95132 814-E4
KNIGHTSBRIDGE LN
- RDWC 94061 790-B2
2500 SCL 95051 833-B2
KNIGHTS BRIDGE RD
2900 SJS 95132 814-E4
KNIGHTS ESTATES
5200 SJS 95135 855-G5
KNIGHTSHAVEN WY
100 SJS 95111 875-A1
KNIGHTSWOOD WY
3100 SJS 95148 835-E1
3100 SJS 95148 855-E1
KNOLL CT
- SJS 95130 853-A6

STREET
Block City ZIP Pg-Grid

KNOLL DR
12500 SCIC 94024 831-F2
KNOLL LN
- SJS 95130 853-A6
KNOLLCREST AV
- SJS 95138 875-G5
KNOLLFIELD WY
800 SJS 95136 874-D2
KNOLLGLEN WY
4000 SJS 95118 874-C2
KNOLL PARK CT
6000 SJS 95120 874-C7
KNOLLS LN
16000 LGTS 95030 893-D1
KNOLL VIEW DR
1200 MPS 95035 794-A4
KNOLL VISTA
- ATN 94027 790-B6
KNOLLWELL WY
5700 SJS 95138 875-D4
KNOLLWOOD AV
1600 SJS 95125 854-A7
KNOLLWOOD DR
19900 SAR 95070 852-E5
KNOLLWOOD LN
1900 LALT 94024 831-H5
KNOPF CT
14600 SCIC 95037 937-A6
KNOWLES AV
400 SCL 95050 833-D6
400 SCL 95128 833-D6
KNOWLES DR
100 LGTS 95032 873-C2
100 CMBL 95008 873-C2
KNOWLTON DR
1400 SUNV 94087 832-C4
KNOX AV
1000 SJS 95116 834-G6
1100 SJS 95122 834-G6
KNUTH RD
18100 SCrC 95033 892-A2
KOA CT
700 SUNV 94086 832-F2
KOBARA LN
1900 SJS 95124 873-G1
KOCH DR
- HOLL 95023 1040-C4
KOCH LN
1100 SJS 95125 854-B7
1500 SJS 95125 874-A1
1600 SJS 95125 873-J1
KOCH TER
1500 SJS 95125 854-A7
KOCHER DR
1800 SCIC 95125 853-H6
KODIAC PL
13400 SAR 95070 852-H7
13400 SAR 95070 872-H1
KODIAK CT
600 SUNV 94087 832-D5
7100 SJS 95139 895-F1
KOHLER RD
3300 SJS 95148 835-D5
KOHNER CT
300 SCL 95050 833-D6
KOLB PL
800 SCL 95050 833-C5
KOLL CIR
100 SJS 95112 833-J2
100 SJS 95112 834-A2
KOLLMAR DR
2700 SJS 95127 834-J4
KOLNES CT
2500 SJS 95121 855-E4
KOMINA AV
20500 SAR 95070 872-D3
KONA CT
6500 SJS 95119 875-D6
KONA PL
100 SJS 95119 875-D6
KONSTANZ TER
- SUNV 94089 812-G4
KOOSER RD
1300 SJS 95118 874-A5
1500 SJS 95124 873-J5
1500 SJS 95124 874-A5
KOREMATSU CT
6400 SJS 95120 894-C1
KORHUMMEL WY
6500 SJS 95119 875-D7
KOSICH CT
12200 SAR 95070 852-H5
KOSICH DR
18600 SAR 95070 852-H5
KOSICH PL
12300 SAR 95070 852-H5
KOTAKE CT
600 SJS 95127 814-H7
KOTENBERG AV
1100 SJS 95125 854-A3
KOVANDA WY
1100 MPS 95035 794-A5
KOZERA DR
800 SJS 95136 874-E2
KOZO CT
5100 SJS 95124 873-G5
KOZO PL
5100 SJS 95124 873-G5
KRAMER LN
- SMCo 94063 790-D1
KREBS CT
1100 SJS 95131 834-D1
KREISLER CT
20700 SAR 95070 852-D5
KRING DR
2700 SJS 95125 854-B7
KRING PL
2400 LALT 94024 831-J6
KRING WY
1400 LALT 94024 831-J6
KRISMER ST
300 MPS 95035 793-J7
KRISTA CT
10300 CPTO 95014 851-J1
KRISTE LN
26000 LAH 94022 831-B1
KRISTEN CT
1000 SJS 95120 894-G3
KRISTIN RIDGE WY
800 MPS 95035 814-E1
KRISTY LN
12000 SAR 95070 852-G5
KROHN LN
13300 SCIC 95046 937-H5
KRUSE DR
2100 SJS 95131 813-J5
KRZICH PL
21300 CPTO 95014 852-C3
K T RD
300 SBnC 95023 1060-E7
KUEHNIS DR
300 CMBL 95008 853-G5
KULLEN CT
- CMBL 95008 853-A6
KUMQUAT DR
500 SJS 95117 853-D2
KUNKEL DR
5200 SJS 95124 873-F5
KURTZ LN
5900 SJS 95123 874-E5
KUYKENDALL PL
3300 SJS 95148 835-E7
KYBURZ PL
5900 SJS 95120 874-C6
KYLE CT
1400 SUNV 94087 832-C4
KYLE ST
700 SJS 95127 814-G6
700 SJS 95133 814-G6
KYLEMORE CT
4000 SJS 95136 854-E5
KYLE PARK CT
- SJS 95125 854-D3
KYRA CIR
1700 SJS 95122 855-A2

L

L RD
- SUNV 94089 812-H3
LA AVD
1000 MTVW 94043 811-J2
1000 MTVW 94043 812-A2
LA AGUA CT
200 MGH 95037 937-B3
LA ALAMEDA DR
15200 MGH 95037 937-A4
LA ALONDRA WY
700 GIL 95020 977-H2
LA ARBOLEDA WY
15300 MGH 95037 937-B3
LA BAIG DR
- HOLL 95023 1040-B3
LA BARBERA DR
800 SJS 95126 853-H3
LA BAREE DR
300 MPS 95035 794-E7
400 MGH 95037 937-B3
LA BARRANCA CT
26800 LAH 94022 831-B1
LA BARRANCA RD
12800 LAH 94022 811-B7
12800 LAH 94022 831-A1
LA BELLA AV
1300 SUNV 94087 832-D4
LA BELLA CT
15600 MGH 95037 937-A3
LA BOHEME WY
1400 SJS 95121 854-J2
LA BRISAS DR
1400 HOLL 95023 1040-D5
LABURNUM DR
800 SUNV 94086 832-F2
LABURNUM RD
- ATN 94027 790-F1
LA CALLE CT
3600 PA 94306 811-B2
LA CANADA CT
100 LGTS 95032 873-C4
400 MGH 95037 937-B4
LA CASTELLET CT
- SJS 95148 855-G2
LAC BLEU CT
- SJS 95148 855-F2
LAC DAZUR CT
- SJS 95148 855-F2
LAC DU VAL CT
- SJS 95148 855-F2
LACEY AV
13900 SAR 95070 872-D2
LACEY DR
2100 MPS 95035 794-E7
LACHINE DR
1600 SUNV 94087 832-C5
E LA CHIQUITA AV
16300 SCIC 95032 873-C7
16300 LGTS 95032 873-C7
W LA CHIQUITA AV
16300 SCIC 95032 873-C7
LA CIENEGA CT
100 LGTS 95032 873-C4
LACKAWANNA CT
1000 SUNV 94087 832-B2
LA COCHE WY
8300 GIL 95020 977-J1
LA CON CT
2000 SJS 95008 853-F7
LACONIA CT
- SJS 95139 875-G7
LA CONNER DR
500 SUNV 94087 832-D5
LA CORONA CT
1900 CMBL 95032 873-A2
LA CORONA DR
1900 CMBL 95032 873-A1
LA CORTE LN
10600 SCIC 95020 957-J3
LA COSTA WY
- SJS 95135 855-H3
LACOUR WY
300 SMCo 94061 790-B3
LA CRESCENT LP
4600 SJS 95136 874-D2
LA CRESCENT PL
200 SJS 95136 874-D2
LA CRESTA CT
12600 LAH 94022 811-B7
LA CRESTA DR
12500 LAH 94022 811-A5
LA CRESTA WY
4700 SJS 95129 852-B7
LA CROIX CT
16500 LGTS 95032 873-D7
LA CROSSE CT
800 SUNV 94087 832-C4
LA CROSSE DR
- MPS 95035 794-D6
100 MGH 95037 937-A3
1400 SUNV 94087 832-C4
LACSA CT
2100 SJS 95116 834-G3
LA CUESTA DR
200 SCIC 94024 831-E2
200 SMCo 94028 810-E3
LADD LN
100 SBnC 95023 1040-B7
1900 HOLL 95023 1040-B7
LADDIE CT
2100 SJS 95121 855-C3
LADDIE WY
1900 SJS 95121 855-C3
LADERA CT
19600 SAR 95070 852-F5
LADERA DR
300 SJS 95134 813-D2
LADIS CT
800 SUNV 94086 832-G2
LADNER DR
5600 SJS 95123 874-J4
LA DONNA ST
3600 PA 94306 811-C2
LADYMUIR CT
2200 SJS 95131 814-D5
LADY PALM CT
- SJS 95133 814-J4
LADYWOOD CT
1300 SJS 95130 853-C4
LA ENCINA DR
- MonC 93907 1037-A6
- MonC 95076 1037-A6
LA ESCUELA CT
15800 MGH 95037 937-A3
LAFAYETTE DR
1100 SUNV 94087 832-B2
LAFAYETTE ST
300 SCL 95050 833-E1
500 SCL 95053 833-E4
2900 SCL 95054 813-B2
2900 SCL 95054 833-E1
LAFAYETTE WY
400 SCL 95050 833-F5
LAFERN CT
6500 SJS 95120 894-C2
LA FIESTA PL
4800 SJS 95129 853-A1
LAGE DR
4600 SJS 95130 853-A7
LA GIRALDA CT
800 MGH 95037 936-H1
LAGO CT
1100 SJS 95121 854-J3
LAGO DE BRACCIANO LN
- SJS 95148 855-J2
LAGO DE BRACCIANO PL
- SJS 95148 855-G2
LAGO DE BRACCIANO ST
- SJS 95148 855-G1
LAGO DE BRACCIANO TER
- SJS 95148 855-J2
LAGO DI COMO PL
- SJS 95136 854-E7
LAGOON WY
2400 SJS 95132 814-C4
LAGO VISTA CIR
4600 SJS 95129 853-A1
4800 SJS 95129 852-B7
LAGO VISTA CT
4600 SCIC 95120 895-E4
LA GRANDE DR
600 SUNV 94087 832-D5
15600 MGH 95037 937-A4
LAGUNA AV
100 SCIC 95037 895-J6
100 SCIC 95037 896-A6
100 SJS 95037 896-A6
100 SJS 95141 895-J6
3500 PA 94306 811-B2
LAGUNA CT
800 HOLL 95023 1040-B5
3400 SCL 95051 832-J3
3500 PA 94306 811-B2
LAGUNA DR
200 SJS 95131 814-A5
300 MPS 95035 793-J5
LAGUNA OAKS PL
3700 PA 94306 811-B2
LAGUNA SECA CT
700 SJS 95123 874-G5
LAGUNA SECA WY
5800 SJS 95123 874-G5
LAGUNITA DR
500 SCIC 94305 790-G7
LA HACIENDA CT
- SJS 95116 834-H3
LAHAINA WY
4400 SJS 95118 874-B3
LA HERNAN DR
200 SCL 95051 832-H7
LAHINCH CT
- GIL 95020 977-F4
LAHINCH DR
- GIL 95020 977-F4
LA HONDA AV
5000 SJS 95129 852-J1
LA HONDA CT
15600 MGH 95037 937-B3
LA HONDA DR
200 MPS 95035 793-J5
LA HONDA SUR
15500 MGH 95037 937-B3
LAINE AV
1700 SCL 95051 833-C3
LAIRD CIR
- SCL 95054 813-E4
LAIRD CT
- SCL 95054 813-E4
LA JENNIFER WY
800 PA 94306 811-B2
LA JOLLA AV
2700 SJS 95124 873-H1
LA JOLLA CT
11200 CPTO 95014 852-B3
15600 MGH 95037 937-B3
LA JOLLA DR
15400 MGH 95037 937-B3
LAKE RD
- SMCo 94028 830-D4
700 SBnC 95023 999-C1
LAKE ALBANO CIR
3100 SJS 95135 855-G6
LAKE ALMANOR DR
5800 SJS 95123 874-G7
LAKEBIRD CT
4800 SJS 95124 873-G4
LAKEBIRD DR
600 SUNV 94089 812-H4
1800 SJS 95124 873-G4
LAKEBIRD PL
4800 SJS 95124 873-G4
LAKEBROOK CT
- SJS 95148 855-G1
LAKECHIME DR
300 SUNV 94089 812-H4
LAKECREST CT
- SJS 95148 855-F2
LAKE CROWLEY PL
5800 SJS 95123 874-G7
LAKEDALE WY
900 SUNV 94089 812-H4
LAKE ESTATES CT
3000 SJS 95135 855-G5
LAKEFAIR DR
600 SUNV 94089 812-G4
LAKEFRONT DR
- SCIC 95046 957-D2
LAKE GARDA DR
3100 SJS 95135 855-G6
LAKEHAVEN DR
600 SUNV 94089 812-H5
LAKEHAVEN TER
600 SUNV 94089 812-G5
LAKE HENNESSY CT
5900 SJS 95123 874-E5
LAKEHOUSE AV
400 SJS 95110 834-A7
LAKE ISABELLA WY
900 SJS 95123 874-G7
LAKEKNOLL DR
800 SUNV 94089 812-H5
LAKE LESINA DR
3200 SJS 95135 855-G6
LAKE MANOR DR
5800 SJS 95123 874-G7
LAKE MCCLURE DR
800 SJS 95123 874-E5
LAKEMONT CT
- SJS 95148 855-F2
LAKEMORE CT
- SJS 95148 855-G1
LAKEMUIR DR
200 SUNV 94089 812-H5
LAKEPARK DR
1600 SJS 95131 814-B6
LAKEPORT CT
- SJS 95148 855-G1
LAKE RANCH RD
- SCIC 95033 892-C1
- SCIC 95070 872-B7
- SCIC 95070 892-C1
LAKE RIDGE LN
- SJS 95148 855-F1
LAKE SANTA CLARA DR
4200 SCL 95054 813-C5
LAKE SHASTA CT
5900 SJS 95123 874-G7
LAKESHIRE CT
900 SJS 95126 853-H3
LAKESHORE CIR
1300 SJS 95131 814-B6
LAKESHORE DR
1200 SMCo 94025 810-A3
4300 SCL 95054 813-C5
LAKESIDE DR
- SJS 95148 855-F1
400 SUNV 94086 812-J7
1300 SUNV 94086 813-A6
2800 SCL 95054 813-A6
LAKE SPRING CT
11500 CPTO 95014 852-C4
LAKE TAHOE CT
900 SJS 95123 874-G7
LAKE TRASINENO DR
3100 SJS 95135 855-C7
LAKETREE CT
1500 SJS 95131 814-D5
LAKEVIEW BLVD
47400 FRMT 94538 793-G1
LAKEVIEW CT
- FRMT 94538 793-G2
- SCIC 95046 957-D2
- SJS 95148 855-F2
18200 SCIC 95033 892-H5
LAKEVIEW DR
100 WDSD 94062 790-A5
17200 MGH 95037 917-F4
LAKEWAY
3000 SUNV 94086 813-A6
LAKEWOOD CT
2100 SJS 95132 814-C3
LAKEWOOD DR
200 SUNV 94089 812-G5
1900 SJS 95132 814-C3
LAKME CT
2600 SJS 95121 854-H4
LAKME WY
1400 SJS 95121 854-H4
LA LANNE CT
25600 LAH 94022 811-C6
LA LOMA CT
24900 LAH 94022 831-C3
LA LOMA DR
- SMCo 94025 790-C6
- MLPK 94025 790-C6
24900 LAH 94022 831-C3
25100 SCIC 94022 831-C3
LALOR DR
5700 SJS 95123 874-G5
LAMA WY
1600 SJS 95118 873-J1
LA MACCHIA CT
- HOLL 95023 1039-H3
LA MAISON DR
600 SJS 95128 853-E2
LA MAR CT
15700 MGH 95037 937-B3
19600 CPTO 95014 852-F1
LA MAR DR
15200 MGH 95037 937-B3
19600 CPTO 95014 852-F1
LA MATA WY
3500 PA 94306 811-B2
LAMBARE WY
- SJS 95135 855-G3
LAMBECK LN
6100 SJS 95119 875-D5
LAMBERT AV
200 PA 94306 791-C7
200 PA 94306 811-B1
LAMBERT LN
2500 SJS 95125 854-B6
LAMBERT WY
500 MTVW 94043 812-B3
LAMBETH CT
600 SUNV 94087 832-E5
2900 SJS 95132 814-E3
LA MESA CT
400 SMCo 94028 810-E3
15600 MGH 95037 937-A3
LA MESA DR
100 SMCo 94028 810-D3
LA MESA LN
3900 SJS 95124 873-J3
LA MESA TER
900 SUNV 94086 812-D6
LA MIEL CT
2000 SJS 95008 853-B6
LA MIEL WY
2100 SJS 95008 853-B6
LA MIRADA CT
15800 MGH 95037 937-B3
LA MIRADA DR
2300 SJS 95125 853-J7
LA MIRADO WY
- SCIC 95030 872-H7
LAMMERHAVEN CT
- SJS 95111 874-J1
LAMMY PL
1100 LALT 94024 831-H2
LAMOND CT
3200 SJS 95148 855-D2
LAMONT CT
600 CMBL 95008 853-B7
1700 SUNV 94087 832-B6
LA MONTAGNE CT
100 LGTS 95032 873-B3
LAMORE DR
1400 SJS 95130 853-A4
LAMPLIGHTER SQ
10000 CPTO 95014 851-J1
LAMPLIGHTER WY
- SJS 95134 813-D2
LANA CT
800 CMBL 95008 853-C7
LANA WY
- HOLL 95023 1020-B6
LANAI AV
1800 SJS 95122 834-H7
2000 SJS 95122 854-H1
LANARK CT
1000 SUNV 94087 832-G5
LANARK LN
19700 SAR 95070 852-F7
19700 SAR 95070 872-F1
LANCASTER CT
2500 SCL 95051 833-C1
LANCASTER DR
1700 SJS 95124 873-H2
LANCASTER RD
15700 SAR 95070 872-G6
15700 SCIC 95030 872-G6
15700 MSER 95030 872-G6
LANCELOT LN
1100 SJS 95127 835-B3
LANCER DR
900 CPTO 95014 852-F3
1000 SJS 95129 852-F3
LANCEWOOD PL
100 LGTS 95032 873-B3
LANCIA DR
17600 MGH 95037 917-A5
LANDA LN
- SMCo 94061 790-A4
LANDAU CT
500 MGH 95037 917-B7
5300 SJS 95123 875-B3
LANDELL CT
1500 LALT 94024 831-J4
1500 LALT 94024 832-A4
LANDEROS DR
200 SCL 95051 833-C7
LANDERWOOD LN
6600 SJS 95120 894-E2
LANDESS AV
1500 MPS 95035 814-D2
1500 SJS 95132 814-D2
LANDINGS DR
1800 MTVW 94043 811-G1
LANDMARK PKWY
1000 MTVW 94043 811-H1
LANDSFORD PL
800 SCL 95050 833-A5
LANDSLIDE CT
2600 SCL 95051 833-A1
LANE AV
900 MTVW 94040 811-H6
LANE PL
- ATN 94027 790-F1
LANE 8 W
- PA 94301 790-J5
LANE A
- SCIC 94305 790-H7
1500 SJS 95112 834-A1
LANE B
500 SCIC 94305 810-H1
1200 SCIC 95020 957-E6
1500 SJS 95112 834-A1
LANE C
500 SCIC 94305 790-H7
500 SCIC 94305 810-H1
600 SJS 95112 834-A1
LANE D
600 SJS 95112 834-A1
LANE E
600 SJS 95112 834-A1
LANE F
600 SJS 95112 834-A1
LANES END CT
- SJS 95121 855-F4
LANES END PL
- SJS 95121 855-F4
LANEVIEW DR
3100 SJS 95132 814-D2
LANE W
500 SCIC 94305 790-H7
LANEWOOD CT
900 SJS 95125 854-C6
LANEWOOD DR
900 SJS 95125 854-C6
LANFAIR CIR
400 SJS 95136 874-F1
LANFAIR CT
600 SJS 95136 874-F1
LANFAIR DR
500 SJS 95136 874-F1
LANG CT
- SJB 95045 1038-D5
LANG ST
- SJB 95045 1038-D5
LANGDON CT
4000 SJS 95121 855-A5
LANGLEY HILL RD
- SMCo 94020 830-A6
LANGPORT DR
1600 SUNV 94087 832-E5
LANGPORT WY
1600 SUNV 94087 832-E6
LANGTON AV
300 LALT 94022 811-D3
LANHAM CT
2300 SJS 95148 855-B1
LANIER LN
2600 SJS 95121 854-J3
LANINI DR
500 SBnC 95023 1060-E3
LANITOS AV
200 SUNV 94086 812-C7
LANNING CT
500 SJS 95133 834-G1
LANNING WY
2300 SJS 95133 834-F2
LANNOY CT
19900 SAR 95070 872-E1
LANO ST
400 SJS 95125 854-C3
LANSBERRY CT
100 LGTS 95032 873-D6
LANSDALE AV
10300 CPTO 95014 852-F1
LANSDALE CT
1100 SJS 95120 894-F2
LANSDOWN CT
800 SUNV 94087 832-C2
LANSFORD AV
2200 SJS 95125 854-A6
LANSING AV
1200 SJS 95118 874-B4
LANTANA AV
12800 SJS 95070 852-J6
12800 SJS 95130 852-J6
LANTANA DR
900 SUNV 94086 832-G2
LANTERN CT
3200 SJS 95111 854-J5
LANTERN WY
3200 SJS 95111 854-J5
LANTIS LN
1700 LALT 94024 832-A4
LANTZ AV
2700 SJS 95124 873-F1
LANTZ DR
100 SCIC 95037 896-C6
LAPA DR
5000 SJS 95129 852-J1
LA PALA CT
3300 SJS 95127 814-J7
15400 MGH 95037 937-B3
LA PALA DR
200 SJS 95127 814-J7
200 SJS 95127 834-J1
LA PALA PL
3300 SJS 95127 814-J7
LA PALMA PL
800 MPS 95035 794-B5
LA PALOMA
- CMBL 95008 853-F7
LA PALOMA AV
20100 SAR 95070 872-E2
LA PALOMA DR
11000 CPTO 95014 852-B3
LA PALOMA RD
13000 LAH 94022 811-C7
13000 LAH 94022 831-B1
LA PALOMA WY
700 GIL 95020 977-H2
LA PARA AV
700 PA 94306 811-C2
LA PAZ
- MTVW 94043 812-A2
- CMBL 95008 853-F7
LA PAZ CT
400 MGH 95037 937-B4
1400 SJS 95118 874-B3
LA PAZ WY
13500 SAR 95070 872-H1
LA PETITE WY
- SJS 95133 814-H7
LA PINTA WY
4700 SJS 95129 852-B7
LA PLATA PZ
800 CMBL 95008 873-C1
LA PLAYA CT
21500 CPTO 95014 852-B3
LA PORTE AV
1700 SJS 95122 834-H6
LA PORTE CT
15800 MGH 95037 937-A3
LA PRADERA DR
1500 CMBL 95008 853-A6
LA PRENDA CT
15800 MGH 95037 937-A3
LA PRENDA RD
400 LALT 94024 831-F1
LAPRIDGE LN
3400 SJS 95124 873-E2
LA PRIMAVERA WY
500 GIL 95020 957-H7
LA QUEBRADA WY
100 SJS 95127 815-C6
LA QUINTA DR
- SJS 95127 815-B6
LARABEE CT
5900 SJS 95120 874-B7
LA RAGIONE AV
2400 SJS 95111 854-G3
LARCH CT
2600 SJS 95121 854-H3
LARCH DR
- ATN 94027 790-G1
LARCH ST
500 MPS 95035 793-H6
LARCH GROVE PL
5300 SJS 95123 875-A3
LARCHMONT AV
12200 SAR 95070 852-F5
LARCHMONT CT
6000 SJS 95123 875-B6
LARCHMONT DR
6000 SJS 95123 875-B6
LARCHWOOD DR
5200 SJS 95118 874-B4
LARCIANO ST
- SJS 95136 854-E6
LAREDO WY
- GIL 95020 957-F6
LA RENA CT
15900 MGH 95037 937-A3
LA RENA DR
25200 LAH 94022 831-C1
LARGA VISTA DR
14900 LGTS 95032 873-F6
LARGO DR
2800 SJS 95132 814-D3
LARGUITA LN
- PTLV 94028 810-B5
LA RHEE DR
2800 SJS 95124 873-J1
LARIAT DR
9300 GIL 95020 957-F7
LARIAT LN
600 SJS 95132 815-A5
LA RINCONADA DR
100 MSER 95030 873-B4
100 MSER 95032 873-B4
100 LGTS 95030 873-B4
100 LGTS 95032 873-B2
14500 SCIC 95032 873-B3
17100 SCIC 95030 873-B4
LARIOS CT
6000 SJS 95123 874-G6
LARIOS WY
6100 SJS 95123 874-G6
LARISA OAKS PL
- SJS 95138 875-E6
LARISSA CT
900 SJS 95136 874-E3
LARK AV
1600 RDWC 94061 790-A2
16500 LGTS 95032 873-C4
17100 LGTS 95030 873-C4
LARK LN
800 SUNV 94087 832-F6
LARK WY
19800 SAR 95070 872-F4
LARKELLEN LN
700 LALT 94024 832-A3
LARK HILLS CT
- SJS 95138 855-F5
LARKIN AV
1400 SJS 95129 852-F4

STREET
Block City ZIP Pg-Grid

LARKMEAD CT
600 SJS 95117 853-C2
LARKMEAD RD
600 SJS 95117 853-C2
LARKSPUR AV
900 SUNV 94086 832-G2
LARKSPUR CT
13400 SCIC 95046 937-E5
LARKSPUR DR
300 EPA 94303 791-D2
1500 SJS 95125 854-A7
LARKSPUR LN
8500 GIL 95020 977-E1
LARKSPUR TER
- FRMT 94539 793-J3
LARKSPUR CANYON DR
- SJS 95138 855-F6
LARKWOOD CT
1500 MPS 95035 793-J4
LARNEL PL
11700 LALT 94024 831-H4
LA ROCCA CT
15200 MGH 95037 937-B4
LA ROCCA DR
15200 MGH 95037 937-A5
LA ROCCA LN
- RDWC 94061 790-A1
LA ROCCA PL
- MGH 95037 937-A4
LA ROCHELLE TER
1100 SUNV 94089 812-G3
LA RODA CT
15900 MGH 95037 937-A3
20000 CPTO 95014 852-E2
LA RODA DR
10500 CPTO 95014 852-E2
LA ROSSA CIR
1500 SJS 95125 854-D3
LA ROSSA CT
200 SJS 95125 854-C3
LARRY CT
3600 SJS 95121 855-A5
LARRY WY
10600 CPTO 95014 832-E6
LARSEN CT
2000 SCL 95051 833-B3
LARSEN PL
1900 SCL 95051 833-B3
LARSENS LNDG
100 LALT 94022 811-D3
LARSON WY
1000 SJS 95117 853-B3
LA SALLE AV
200 SCL 95051 832-J7
LA SALLE DR
1000 SUNV 94087 832-B5
2600 MTVW 94040 831-J1
21500 SCIC 95033 912-J3
LA SALLE WY
2600 SJS 95130 852-J7
LA SANDRA WY
- PTLV 94028 810-B4
LAS ANIMAS AV
- GIL 95020 957-H7
600 GIL 95020 958-A6
600 SCIC 95020 958-A6
LAS ANIMAS CT
8100 GIL 95020 977-H2
LAS ANIMAS RD
- SCIC 95037 896-J1
8500 SCIC 95037 876-G4
LAS ASTAS DR
100 LGTS 95032 873-C4
LAS CAMPANAS CT
2200 LALT 94024 831-H5
LASCAR CT
2300 SJS 95124 873-E3
LASCAR PL
2400 SJS 95124 873-E3
LAS CASAS DE LOS PINOS
2300 SJS 95133 834-F1
LAS CASITAS
- SJS 95126 833-D1
LAS COCHES CT
400 MGH 95037 937-B4
LAS COLINAS LN
- SJS 95119 875-E6
LAS CRUCES CT
5000 SJS 95118 874-B4
LA SELVA DR
3700 PA 94306 811-C1
16900 MGH 95037 936-J1
LAS ENCANTOS CT
1800 CMBL 95032 872-J2
1800 CMBL 95032 873-A2
LA SEYNE PL
5600 SJS 95138 875-F1
LAS FLORES CT
1100 LALT 94022 811-D3
LAS FLORES LN
14800 LGTS 95032 873-G6
LA SIERRA CT
15600 MGH 95037 937-A3
LA SIERRA WY
500 GIL 95020 977-H2
LAS JOYAS CT
1700 CMBL 95032 873-A2
LAS LOMAS DR
700 MPS 95035 794-B6
LAS MIRADAS DR
200 LGTS 95032 873-C4
LAS ONDAS CT
20000 CPTO 95014 852-E1
LAS ONDAS WY
10400 CPTO 95014 852-E1
LAS PALMAS DR
500 HOLL 95023 1040-A4
800 SCL 95051 833-B5
LAS PALMAS WY
- SJS 95133 814-J4
LA SPEZIA PL
- SJS 95138 875-J1

LAS PIEDRAS
- SMCo 94028 830-D5
LAS PIEDRAS CT
1600 CMBL 95032 873-A2
LAS PLUMAS AV
500 SJS 95133 834-E3
LASS DR
2300 SCL 95054 813-C4
LASSEN AV
200 MTVW 94043 811-F3
1100 MPS 95035 814-C1
5000 SJS 95129 852-J4
LASSEN CT
- MLPK 94025 790-C7
200 HOLL 95023 1039-H3
LASSEN DR
900 MLPK 94025 790-C6
LASSEN LN
- SJS 95124 873-G7
LASSEN ST
400 LALT 94022 811-E7
500 LALT 94022 831-E1
LASSEN TER
- SUNV 94086 812-C7
LASSEN WY
15000 MGH 95037 937-B4
LASSENPARK CIR
300 SJS 95136 874-G2
LASSIE CT
2900 SCIC 95020 958-D4
LAS TERRAZAS
- SJS 95131 814-B6
LA STRADA DR
- SJS 95123 875-A5
LASTRETO AV
300 SUNV 94086 812-F6
LASUEN CT
100 LGTS 95032 873-F6
LASUEN DR
- SJB 95045 1038-C5
LASUEN MALL
200 SCIC 94305 790-H6
LASUEN ST
500 SCIC 94305 790-H7
LAS UVAS CT
100 LGTS 95032 873-A2
LAS VIBORAS RD
200 SBnC 95023 1000-D7
200 SBnC 95023 1020-D1
1600 SBnC 93635 1000-D7
LASWELL AV
300 SCIC 95128 853-G1
300 SJS 95128 853-G2
LA TERRACE CIR
1600 SJS 95123 874-D5
LATHAM ST
1200 MTVW 94041 811-F4
1800 MTVW 94040 811-F4
LATHROP CT
5600 SJS 95123 875-A4
LATHROP DR
800 SCIC 94305 810-H2
5600 SJS 95123 875-A4
LATHROP PL
900 SCIC 94305 810-H2
LA TIERRA CT
15600 MGH 95037 937-A4
LA TIERRA DR
15600 MGH 95037 937-A4
LATIMER AV
700 CMBL 95008 853-B5
1100 SJS 95130 853-A4
4500 SJS 95070 853-A4
4500 SJS 95129 853-A4
E LATIMER AV
- CMBL 95008 853-E5
W LATIMER AV
- CMBL 95008 853-D5
LATIMER CIR
500 CMBL 95008 853-D5
LATONA CT
400 SJS 95111 875-C2
LA TORRE AV
4200 SJS 95111 855-A7
LAUELLA CT
200 MTVW 94041 811-G4
LAUFALL LN
- SJS 95111 854-F6
LAUMER AV
- SCIC 95127 835-A1
100 SJS 95127 835-A1
LAURA CT
800 CMBL 95008 853-C7
11000 LAH 94022 831-C4
LAURA DR
600 CMBL 95008 853-C7
5400 SJS 95124 873-G6
LAURA LN
100 PA 94303 791-D4
2300 MTVW 94043 811-F3
6900 SCIC 95020 978-J2
LAURAL AV
6200 SJS 95138 875-F6
LAURANT WY
3500 SJS 95132 814-F2
LAURA VILLE LN
- SJS 95125 854-B4
LAUREDO WY
14500 SCIC 95046 937-G3
LAUREL AV
- SCrC 95033 871-A4
100 LGTS 95030 872-H7
100 MLPK 94025 790-J3
400 MLPK 94025 791-A2
1000 EPA 94303 791-A1
LAUREL CT
- SBnC 95023 1040-E3
LAUREL DR
2200 SCL 95050 833-C4
7500 GIL 95020 977-G3
18300 SCIC 95030 872-J5
18300 SCIC 95033 892-G4
20800 SCIC 95033 913-A1
21300 SCIC 95033 912-J2

LAUREL LN
26600 LAH 94022 811-B7
LAUREL PL
- MLPK 94025 790-F2
LAUREL RD
700 MGH 95037 937-C2
17000 MGH 95037 917-C7
17600 SCIC 95037 917-B5
LAUREL ST
- ATN 94027 790-F2
- MLPK 94025 790-G3
700 SJS 95126 833-H5
LAUREL WY
- MTVW 94040 811-E3
LAUREL CANYON DR
- SJS 95138 855-E6
LAURELDALE LN
900 SJS 95136 874-D2
LAURELEI AV
2000 SJS 95128 833-F7
LAURELES DR
1000 LALT 94022 811-D3
LAURELGLEN CT
4000 SJS 95118 874-C2
LAUREL GLEN DR
900 PA 94304 810-G7
900 PA 94304 830-G1
LAUREL GROVE LN
- SJS 95126 834-A7
LAURELVIEW CT
- FRMT 94538 793-F1
LAURELWOOD DR
1600 SJS 95125 853-J6
LAUREL WOOD LN
17900 MGH 95037 916-G7
LAURELWOOD RD
300 SCL 95054 813-C6
LAURELWOOD CROSSING PL
- SJS 95138 855-C5
LAURELWOOD CROSSING TER
- SJS 95138 855-C6
LAUREN DR
5400 SJS 95124 873-J6
LAURENTIAN WY
1700 SUNV 94087 832-B6
LAURETTA DR
10200 CPTO 95014 832-C7
LAURIE AV
600 SCL 95054 813-E6
1000 SJS 95125 854-B4
LAURIE JO LN
500 SCL 95050 833-C6
LAURINDA DR
1800 SJS 95124 873-G4
LAURYN RIDGE CT
800 MPS 95035 814-E1
LAUSANNE CT
2800 SJS 95132 814-F5
LAUSETT AV
2100 SJS 95116 834-G4
LAUTREC CT
- SJS 95135 855-G2
LAUTREC DR
- SJS 95135 855-G2
LAUTREC TER
- SJS 95135 855-G2
- SUNV 94087 832-E3
LAUTREC WY
- SJS 95135 855-G2
LAVA DR
2300 SJS 95133 834-F1
LAVA WY
600 SJS 95133 834-F1
LAVA ROCK CT
3400 MGH 95037 917-F4
LAVEILLE CT
1200 SJS 95131 814-C7
LA VELA CT
300 MGH 95037 937-B3
LAVENDER DR
- SJS 95123 875-C5
800 SUNV 94086 832-F3
LAVENDER LN
16300 SCIC 95032 873-D5
LAVENDER TER
- SJS 95111 854-G5
LAVENDER WY
- GIL 95020 977-E1
- HOLL 95023 1040-B6
LAVENDULA WY
6100 SJS 95119 875-D5
LAVER CT
1900 LALT 94024 831-H5
LA VERNE DR
18000 SCIC 95033 912-H3
LA VERNE WY
800 LALT 94022 811-D4
LA VIA AZUL
200 MGH 95037 937-B3
LA VIA AZUL CT
200 MGH 95037 937-B3
LA VIDA REAL
12800 LAH 94022 831-A1
LAVINA CT
21000 CPTO 95014 832-C6
LA VISTA CT
900 MGH 95037 936-J3
13000 SAR 95070 852-F7
LA VISTA DR
13000 SAR 95070 852-F7
LAVONA DR
- SJS 95118 874-C4
LA VONNE AV
1700 SJS 95116 834-G5
LA VONNE DR
- CMBL 95008 853-B6
LAWLER RANCH RD
- SMCo 94025 790-A7
- SMCo 94025 810-B1
- WDSD 94062 790-A7
LAWNDALE AV
300 CMBL 95008 853-D5

LAWRENCE CT
1900 SCL 95051 832-J3
LAWRENCE DR
700 GIL 95020 977-H1
LAWRENCE EXWY
2900 SCL 95051 812-J7
2900 SCL 95051 832-J1
LAWRENCE EXWY Rt#-G2
- SAR 95070 852-H3
- SCL 95051 832-J6
- SCL 95051 852-H3
100 SCL 95051 812-J7
200 SUNV 94086 812-J7
300 SJS 95014 852-H3
300 SJS 95129 852-H3
300 CPTO 95014 852-H3
700 SUNV 94089 812-J3
800 SUNV 94087 832-J6
1800 SAR 95129 852-H3
1900 SUNV 94086 832-J6
LAWRENCE LN
900 PA 94303 791-D5
LAWRENCE PL
- SCL 95051 832-J3
LAWRENCE RD
1700 SCL 95051 832-J3
LAWRENCE STATION RD
100 SUNV 94086 832-J1
1200 SUNV 94089 812-J3
LAWSON CT
4800 SJS 95118 873-J4
LAWSON LN
2200 SCL 95054 813-C7
2200 SCL 95054 833-C1
LAWTHER CT
4000 SJS 95135 855-F3
LAWTON AV
900 SJS 95128 853-H3
LAWTON DR
- MPS 95035 794-D6
LAYLA CT
- MTVW 94041 811-H4
LAYNE CT
700 PA 94303 791-D7
LAYTON CT
700 SCL 95051 833-B6
LAYTON ST
700 SCL 95051 833-B5
LAYTON WY
10400 SCIC 95127 834-J3
LAZANEO DR
20100 CPTO 95014 832-D7
LAZO GRANDE DR
- SCIC 95037 936-G7
LAZY LN
3800 SCIC 95135 855-H1
LAZY OAK CT
22500 CPTO 95014 831-C7
LAZY RIVER WY
6700 SJS 95120 894-E2
LEAF CT
600 LALT 94022 811-C5
LEAFTREE CIR
1400 SJS 95131 814-C7
LEAFTREE CT
1400 SJS 95131 814-C7
LEAFWOOD LN
3200 SJS 95111 854-F6
LEAFY CT
1500 MGH 95037 917-D6
LEAHY ST
500 RDWC 94061 790-C1
LEAN AV
5300 SJS 95123 875-A3
LEAN WY
5900 SJS 95123 875-A5
LEANDER DR
12700 LAH 94022 811-B7
LEANN CT
15300 SCIC 95037 937-E2
LEARNARD WY
8700 GIL 95020 977-F1
LEATHERWOOD CT
6700 SJS 95120 894-C5
LEAVESLEY PL
10800 CPTO 95014 852-B2
LEAVESLEY RD
3800 SCIC 95020 958-G4
LEAVESLEY RD Rt#-G9
400 GIL 95020 978-B1
600 GIL 95020 958-C7
1100 SCIC 95020 958-C7
LEAVESLEY RD Rt#-152
- GIL 95020 977-J1
200 GIL 95020 978-A1
LE BAIN DR
2300 SJS 95130 853-A7
LEBANON AV
10200 CPTO 95014 851-J1
LEBANON DR
10100 CPTO 95014 851-J1
LE CHATEAU DR
- HOLL 95023 1040-B3
LE COMPTE PL
800 SJS 95122 834-F7
800 SJS 95122 854-F1
LEDERER CIR
1600 SJS 95131 814-C7
LEDGEWOOD DR
1700 SJS 95124 873-H2
LEDOUX CT
- SJS 95135 855-G1
LEE CT
- SBnC 95023 1000-E7
- SBnC 95023 1020-E1
LEE DR
900 MLPK 94025 790-F3
1600 MTVW 94040 811-G7
21300 SCIC 95033 912-J2

LEE RD
- SBnC 95023 1000-G7
LEE ST
600 LALT 94022 831-E1
LEE TRCT
- SJS 95127 835-C3
LEEDS AV
7500 CPTO 95014 852-D4
LEESA ANN CT
5200 SJS 95124 873-J5
LEEWARD CT
1100 SJS 95122 834-J5
LEEWARD DR
1100 SJS 95122 834-J5
1500 SJS 95122 835-A5
LEEWOOD CT
- LGTS 95032 873-F6
LE FEVRE DR
5500 SJS 95118 874-A5
LEFONT DR
1200 SJS 95131 814-B6
LE FRANC DR
5700 SJS 95118 874-B5
LEGACY WY
- SJS 95125 853-J4
LEGEND CT
- MGH 95037 917-A2
- SJS 95131 834-C1
LEGEND LN
- SJS 95131 834-C1
LEGHORN ST
2000 MTVW 94043 811-F1
2400 PA 94043 811-F1
LEHIGH DR
3500 SCL 95051 832-J6
LEIGE DR
1100 HOLL 95023 1040-C5
LEIGH AV
400 SCIC 95125 853-G7
400 SJS 95125 853-H4
400 CMBL 95008 853-G7
500 SJS 95128 853-G1
900 SJS 95126 853-H4
2200 SJS 95124 853-G7
2600 SJS 95124 873-G2
3000 SCIC 95128 853-G1
3600 SCIC 95124 873-G2
5200 LGTS 95032 873-G6
N LEIGH AV
200 CMBL 95008 853-H5
200 SCIC 95125 853-H5
200 CMBL 95008 853-H5
1500 SJS 95125 853-H5
S LEIGH AV
- SCIC 95125 853-H6
- CMBL 95008 853-H6
LEIGH CT
14400 SCIC 95124 873-G3
LEIGH ST
47900 FRMT 94539 793-J1
LEIGH-ANN PL
1900 SCIC 95125 853-H6
LEIGHTON WY
900 SUNV 94087 832-G5
LEILA CT
15400 LGTS 95032 873-D5
LEISURE CT
- HOLL 95023 1040-B7
3100 SJS 95132 814-G5
LEISURE DR
100 MGH 95037 937-B5
LEITH AV
800 SCL 95054 813-E6
LEKSICH AV
600 MTVW 94041 811-G5
LELAND AV
100 SMCo 94025 790-E6
200 PA 94306 791-A7
300 SCIC 95128 853-G1
300 SJS 95128 853-G1
2100 MTVW 94040 811-F3
LELAND CIR
14400 SAR 95070 872-G3
LELAND PARK CT
6500 SJS 95120 894-C1
LELONG ST
1100 SJS 95110 854-B2
LE MANS DR
- HOLL 95023 1040-B3
LEMANS TER
- SUNV 94089 812-G4
LE MICCINE TER
- SJS 95129 852-J5
LEMMON CT
- SBnC 95023 1040-E3
N LEMON AV
1100 MLPK 94025 790-E5
LEMON ST
400 MLPK 94025 790-E6
LEMON BLOSSOM CT
- SJS 95123 875-B3
LEMONTREE CT
1700 MTVW 94040 831-G1
LEMON TREE RD
1100 SJS 95120 874-D7
LEMONWOOD CT
700 SJS 95120 894-H2
LEMOS CT
500 SBnC 95023 1040-D2
LEMOYNE WY
2200 SJS 95008 853-B7
LENA AV
- SCIC 95020 957-H2
LENA DR
2700 SJS 95124 873-J1
LENARK CT
1100 SJS 95132 814-G5
LENARK DR
3100 SJS 95132 814-G5
LENCAR WY
1700 SJS 95124 873-H3
LENDRUM AV
2300 SJS 95116 834-H3

LENELLE CT
5000 SJS 95118 873-J4
LENFEST RD
600 SJS 95133 834-D2
LENN DR
1800 SJS 95125 853-J5
LENNON WY
1100 SJS 95125 854-A5
LENNOX AV
200 MLPK 94025 790-F2
LENNOX CT
800 SUNV 94087 832-C4
LENNOX WY
1300 SUNV 94087 832-C4
LENOR WY
1000 CMBL 95128 853-E4
LENORA AV
5300 SJS 95124 873-J5
LENORE CT
18200 SCIC 95033 912-H3
LENOX PL
- SCL 95054 813-C4
LENOX WY
13300 LAH 94022 811-D7
LENRAY LN
14300 SCIC 95124 873-G3
LENWOOD WY
6800 SJS 95120 894-F2
LENZEN AV
300 SJS 95110 834-A5
500 SJS 95110 833-J6
600 SJS 95126 833-J6
LENZEN CT
400 SJS 95126 833-J6
LEO AV
200 SJS 95112 854-E3
LEO DR
900 SJS 95129 853-A3
LEOLA CT
10300 CPTO 95014 852-G1
LEOMINSTER CT
- SJS 95139 875-G7
LEON DR
2000 SJS 95128 853-G3
LEON ST
6600 MonC 93907 1037-B7
LEON WY
- ATN 94027 790-F3
LEONA CT
- SJS 95125 854-A2
14200 SCIC 95046 937-F3
LEONA LN
500 MTVW 94040 811-H7
LEONARD CT
3500 SCL 95054 813-D6
LEONARD RD
20500 SAR 95070 852-D7
LEONARD STOCKING DR
- SCL 95054 813-D5
LEONELLO AV
900 LALT 94024 831-G2
LEONG CT
7800 CPTO 95014 852-C2
LEONG DR
600 MTVW 94043 812-A3
LEONTINE CT
48000 FRMT 94539 793-J1
LEOTA AV
100 SUNV 94086 812-C7
LEOTAR CT
100 LGTS 95032 893-D1
LEPA CT
700 SCIC 95020 957-J5
LEPTIS CIR
2300 MGH 95037 917-F6
LERIDA AV
300 LALT 94024 811-F7
LERIDA CT
- SMCo 94028 810-D4
LERMA LN
1100 GIL 95020 977-F1
LERMA WY
1100 GIL 95020 977-F1
LEROY AV
16700 LGTS 95032 873-C5
LERWICK CT
1100 SUNV 94087 832-H5
LE SABRE CT
500 MGH 95037 917-B7
LESHER CT
1400 SJS 95125 854-A5
LESLEY LN
- SBnC 95023 1020-E1
14100 SCIC 95046 937-H3
LESLIE CT
200 MTVW 94043 812-A4
16900 MGH 95037 917-G5
LESLIE DR
1000 SJS 95117 853-B3
LESTER AV
- SJS 95125 853-J3
- SJS 95125 854-A3
LESTER CT
300 SCL 95051 833-B7
LESTER LN
100 LGTS 95032 873-D4
LETITIA CT
1200 SJS 95122 854-H2
LETITIA ST
1200 SJS 95122 854-H2
LEUTAR CT
12300 SAR 95070 852-E5
LEVEE RD
- SJS 95035 813-G1
- SJS 95134 813-G1
LEVEN PLACE WY
3900 SJS 95121 855-C4
LEVIN AV
400 MTVW 94040 831-J2
800 MTVW 94040 832-A2
LEVIN CT
2700 MTVW 94040 831-J2

LEVIN ST
300 MPS 95035 794-A3
LEWIS AV
800 SUNV 94086 812-D7
LEWIS RD
100 SJS 95111 854-H4
200 SCIC 95111 854-G5
LEWIS ST
- GIL 95020 978-A3
1300 SCL 95050 833-E4
LEWISTON CT
700 SUNV 94087 832-C4
LEWISTON DR
700 SJS 95136 874-D1
1300 SUNV 94087 832-C5
LEXANN AV
1500 SJS 95121 855-A3
LEXFORD AV
2700 SJS 95124 873-H1
LEXINGTON AV
- SJS 95119 875-C5
- SJS 95193 875-C5
LEXINGTON CT
13600 SAR 95070 872-E1
18200 MSER 95030 872-E1
LEXINGTON DR
200 MLPK 94025 790-J3
1100 SUNV 94087 832-B2
1300 SJS 95117 853-D4
18200 MSER 95030 872-J5
LEXINGTON PL
700 GIL 95020 977-J4
LEXINGTON ST
700 MPS 95035 793-J6
900 SCL 95050 833-E5
LEXINGTON SCHOOL RD
19800 SCIC 95033 892-J6
LEYLAND PARK DR
6300 SJS 95120 894-C1
LEYTE CT
800 SJS 95111 855-A6
LEYTE TER
- SUNV 94089 812-G4
LIBERATA DR
17700 SCIC 95037 917-D4
LIBERIA CIR
1900 SJS 95116 834-G3
LIBERTY CT
- HOLL 95023 1040-C6
- SJS 95002 793-B7
900 CPTO 95014 852-B2
LIBERTY DR
- HOLL 95023 1040-B6
LIBERTY ST
1400 SJS 95002 813-B1
1600 SJS 95002 793-B7
1900 SCL 95050 833-D5
LIBERTY OAK LN
10000 CPTO 95014 831-C7
LIBERTY PARK AV
2000 SMCo 94025 790-D6
LIBRA LN
3300 SJS 95111 854-F6
LIBRARY LN
- SJS 95116 834-E5
LIBRETTO CT
1800 SJS 95131 814-C4
LICK AV
1000 SJS 95110 854-C2
LICK MILL BLVD
3800 SCL 95054 813-D3
LIDA DR
2300 MTVW 94043 811-F3
LIDDICOAT CIR
14300 LAH 94022 810-H5
LIDDICOAT DR
14400 LAH 94022 810-H5
LIDO WY
1700 SJS 95116 834-G5
12600 SAR 95070 852-E6
LIEB CT
14000 SJS 95127 835-A4
LIEB LN
1500 SJS 95131 814-A5
LIEBELT CT
1000 SJS 95126 853-H3
LIEBRE CT
200 SUNV 94086 812-C7
LIEGE DR
700 HOLL 95023 1040-B5
LIETZ AV
1500 SJS 95118 873-J5
1500 SJS 95118 874-A5
LIGHTFARE CT
3600 SJS 95121 855-A4
LIGHTLAND RD
1100 SJS 95121 855-A5
LIGHTPOST WY
- MGH 95037 916-J4
LIGHTSON ST
- SJS 95113 834-B6
LIGURIAN CT
5200 SJS 95138 855-F6
LIGURIAN DR
5100 SJS 95138 855-G7
LIKA CT
12700 SAR 95070 852-E6
LILAC CT
7800 CPTO 95014 852-C2
LILAC LN
300 EPA 94303 791-B1
600 SJS 95136 854-E7
800 LALT 94024 831-E1
1500 MTVW 94043 811-H3
1800 SCIC 95037 936-G4
16100 SCIC 95032 873-D6
16200 LGTS 95032 873-D6
LILAC WY
700 LGTS 95032 873-C6
800 SCIC 95032 873-C6
7700 CPTO 95014 852-C2
LILAC BLOSSOM LN
5600 SJS 95124 873-J6

STREET Block City ZIP Pg-Grid

LILLIAN AV
1300 SUNV 94087 832-F4
LILLIAN WY
6200 SJS 95120 874-E7
6300 SJS 95120 894-E1
LILLICK DR
1100 SUNV 94087 832-H4
1100 SCL 95051 832-H4
LILLIPUT LN
2500 SJS 95116 834-J4
LILLY AV
100 GIL 95020 977-J1
8600 GIL 95020 957-J7
LILLY LN
700 MGH 95037 917-D7
LILY AV
800 CPTO 95014 852-C2
1000 SUNV 94086 832-H2
LILY CT
7800 CPTO 95014 852-C2
LILY ANN WY
400 SJS 95123 875-B3
LILY BLOSSOM CT
100 SJS 95123 875-A4
LIMA CT
1500 SJS 95126 853-H3
LIMAN AV
- GIL 95020 957-H7
LIME DR
1100 SUNV 94087 832-B3
LIME BLOSSOM CT
100 SJS 95123 875-A3
LIMEKILN LN
- SJS 95124 873-G7
LIMEKILN CANYON RD
16000 SCIC 95033 893-A3
LIMERICK CT
700 SUNV 94087 832-F5
LIMETREE LN
1900 MTVW 94040 831-G1
LIMEWELL CT
- SJS 95138 875-D4
LIMEWOOD DR
1900 SJS 95132 814-E2
LIMON CT
- SJS 95112 834-B4
LINA ST
- SJS 95136 854-F6
LINARIA ST
- GIL 95020 957-D7
LINARIA WY
- SMCo 94028 810-D4
LINBURN CT
2900 SJS 95148 855-B2
LINCOLN AV
100 PA 94301 790-J5
200 SCIC 95126 833-J7
200 SCIC 95126 853-J1
200 PA 94301 791-A4
300 SJS 95126 853-J1
400 SUNV 94086 812-E7
400 SUNV 94086 832-F1
400 LALT 94022 811-D7
500 LALT 94022 831-E1
900 SJS 95126 854-A3
900 SJS 95125 854-A3
13000 SCIC 95046 937-F6
LINCOLN CT
400 GIL 95020 957-J7
400 GIL 95020 958-A7
800 SJS 95125 854-B5
LINCOLN DR
1100 MTVW 94040 831-G1
LINCOLN ST
400 SCL 95128 833-D4
400 SCL 95050 833-D4
2000 EPA 94303 791-A2
LINCOLNSHIRE WY
1100 SJS 95125 854-E6
LINCOLN VILLAGE DR
2400 SJS 95125 854-D3
LINDA AV
15500 SCIC 95032 873-D5
15900 LGTS 95032 873-D6
LINDA DR
- SBnC 95023 1060-F3
900 CMBL 95008 853-C7
900 CMBL 95008 873-B1
LINDA ANN CT
22400 CPTO 95014 832-A6
LINDA ANN PL
10100 CPTO 95014 852-F1
LINDA FLORA ST
600 SCIC 95127 814-J6
LINDAHL CT
1300 SJS 95120 874-C7
LINDAIRE AV
2200 SCIC 95128 853-F3
2200 SJS 95128 853-F3
LINDA MESA DR
17000 MGH 95037 917-E6
LINDA VISTA AV
- ATN 94027 790-C4
800 MTVW 94043 811-J3
18800 SCIC 95030 872-F6
LINDA VISTA DR
10700 CPTO 95014 852-A2
LINDA VISTA LN
9200 SCIC 95020 957-B7
LINDA VISTA PL
22000 CPTO 95014 852-B2
LINDA VISTA ST
600 SCIC 95127 814-H6
LINDA VISTA WY
900 LALT 94024 831-G2
LINDBERGH AV
- MTVW 94043 812-B1
- SCIC 94035 812-B1
2200 SJS 95128 853-F3
LINDBERGH DR
21600 SCIC 95033 912-J3

LINDEN AV
- ATN 94027 790-G1
600 LALT 94022 811-D5
800 SUNV 94086 832-F3
LINDEN DR
- SCL 95050 833-F5
1100 SJS 95126 833-F5
LINDEN LN
1900 MPS 95035 793-J3
LINDENBROOK LN
19800 CPTO 95014 852-F2
LINDENOAKS DR
3200 SJS 95117 853-D2
LINDENTREE LN
2600 SCL 95051 833-B6
LINDENWOOD DR
3600 SJS 95117 853-C2
LINDER HILL CT
1200 SJS 95120 894-G4
LINDER HILL LN
1200 SJS 95120 894-G5
LINDERO DR
3700 PA 94306 811-D1
LINDMUIR DR
3300 SJS 95121 855-A4
LINDO CT
200 MGH 95037 916-J7
LINDO LN
100 MGH 95037 916-J7
LINDSAY AV
10300 CPTO 95014 852-F1
LINDSAY WY
1300 SJS 95118 874-B1
LINDSAY ANN TER
1400 SJS 95131 814-C6
LINDSAY CREEK LN
7100 SJS 95120 894-G4
LINDSTROM CT
500 SJS 95111 875-C2
LINDY LN
21600 CPTO 95014 852-A3
LINDY PL
11400 CPTO 95014 852-B3
LINE ST
- HOLL 95023 1039-J4
LINETTA CT
- SJS 95148 855-G1
LINETTA WY
- SJS 95148 855-G1
LINFIELD DR
400 MLPK 94025 790-G4
E LINFIELD DR
100 MLPK 94025 790-H3
LINFIELD PL
300 MLPK 94025 790-H3
LINKFIELD WY
3000 SJS 95135 855-G3
LINKHORNE CT
300 SJS 95133 834-F2
LINKS RD
900 SCIC 94304 810-F1
LINKSHEAD CT
3100 SJS 95148 855-D1
LINNET CT
- GIL 95020 957-E6
LINNET LN
1700 SUNV 94087 832-F6
10600 CPTO 95014 832-F6
LINTON CT
3800 SJS 95121 855-C4
LINWELL CT
- SJS 95138 875-D5
LINWOOD DR
4100 SJS 95124 873-H3
LINZ TER
- SUNV 94089 812-F4
LIO CT
- SJS 95120 894-H4
LIONS CREEK DR
8700 GIL 95020 977-F1
LIONS PEAK LN
- SCIC 95046 957-D2
LIONWOOD PL
400 SJS 95111 875-C2
LIPPERT PL
- SCL 95050 833-C5
LIQUIDAMBAR WY
400 SUNV 94086 832-G1
LIQUIDAMBER CT
400 SJS 95111 854-G7
LISA CT
700 GIL 95020 977-J7
1200 LALT 94024 831-H3
2100 SCIC 95037 917-E5
LISA LN
- SBnC 95023 1020-E3
500 SJS 95134 813-C2
1100 LALT 94024 831-H3
LISA WY
600 CMBL 95008 853-C4
600 SJS 95130 853-C4
LISBON CT
3600 SJS 95132 814-F1
LISBON DR
3400 SJS 95132 814-E2
LISBON TER
400 MPS 95035 793-G3
LISKA LN
5900 SJS 95119 875-C6
LISLIE ST
800 HOLL 95023 1040-E5
LISMORE CT
3000 SJS 95135 855-F3
LISSOW DR
- SJS 95119 875-C6
LITA LN
- EPA 94303 791-C2
LITCHFIELD PL
2000 SCL 95051 833-D2
LITCHI GROVE CT
100 SJS 95123 874-J3
LITE CT
5900 SJS 95138 875-E5

LITTLE AV
- SJS 95119 875-D5
LITTLE BEAR WY
- SJS 95136 874-H2
LITTLE BOY LN
2600 SJS 95148 835-F7
LITTLE BRANHAM LN
1700 SJS 95124 873-H4
LITTLEBROOK DR
19600 SCIC 95030 872-F6
LITTLE FALLS DR
6400 SJS 95120 894-D1
LITTLEFIELD LN
200 LGTS 95032 873-C7
200 SCIC 95032 873-C7
LITTLEJOHN WY
1100 SJS 95129 852-G3
LITTLE LLAGAS AV
17200 SCIC 95037 936-E2
LITTLEMEADOW CT
4400 SJS 95129 853-A2
LITTLE MERRILL RD
- SBnC 95045 1037-G3
LITTLEOAK CIR
1100 SJS 95129 852-H3
LITTLEOAK DR
1000 SJS 95129 852-H3
LITTLE ORCHARD ST
1400 SJS 95110 854-D2
1400 SJS 95125 854-D3
LITTLE RIVER CT
4700 SJS 95136 874-E2
LITTLE RIVER DR
- SBnC 95023 1000-F7
LITTLE ROCK CT
2800 SJS 95133 814-G7
LITTLE ROCK DR
2800 SJS 95133 814-G7
LITTLETON DR
1200 SJS 95131 834-C1
LITTLETON PL
1600 CMBL 95008 873-A1
LITTLE UVAS RD
4600 SCIC 95037 935-G2
4600 SCIC 95037 936-A3
LITTLE WOOD LN
3000 SJS 95127 834-H1
LITTLEWORTH WY
4100 SJS 95135 855-F3
LITTMAN DR
1200 SJS 95120 894-C1
LITTON CT
600 SUNV 94087 832-E5
LIVE OAK AV
- SCIC 95037 916-E2
- SJS 95037 916-E2
600 MLPK 94025 790-F4
LIVE OAK CT
300 MPS 95035 813-J3
3800 MGH 95037 917-H5
LIVE OAK DR
- HOLL 95023 1039-H4
900 SCL 95051 833-A5
LIVE OAK LN
200 LALT 94022 811-D6
3700 MGH 95037 917-H5
14600 SAR 95070 872-F3
LIVE OAK TER
- SUNV 94086 832-F3
LIVE OAK WY
700 SJS 95129 853-A2
LIVERPOOL AV
1600 SJS 95124 873-J3
LIVERPOOL WY
700 SUNV 94087 832-F5
LIVERY LN
7000 SJS 95135 876-A1
LIVINGSTON AV
1400 SJS 95125 854-A6
LIVONIA PL
- SJS 95111 854-G5
LIVORNO CT
5400 SJS 95138 875-F1
LIZZIE LN
4400 SJS 95118 874-C2
LJEPAVA DR
20000 SAR 95070 852-E7
LLAGAS AV
12000 SCIC 95046 937-E3
12000 SCIC 95046 957-G1
LLAGAS CT
18300 MGH 95037 916-H6
LLAGAS RD
200 MGH 95037 916-H6
800 SCIC 95037 916-H6
1700 MGH 95037 936-F2
1700 SCIC 95037 936-F2
LLAGAS CREEK DR
18200 MGH 95037 916-G6
LLAGAS VISTA DR
600 MGH 95037 916-G6
LLAMA LN
8700 SCIC 95020 958-F5
LLANO LN
- SCIC 95046 957-A1
13900 SCIC 95046 937-A7
LLEWELLYN AV
- CMBL 95008 853-D5
LLOYD WY
1300 MTVW 94040 811-G6
LLOYDEN DR
- ATN 94027 790-D2
LLOYDEN PARK LN
300 ATN 94027 790-D2
LOBELIA LN
1600 SJS 95124 873-J6
LOBOS AV
4500 SJS 95111 875-A1
LO BUE WY
4100 SJS 95111 855-A7
LOCHBURRY CT
500 SJS 95123 874-G3
LOCHINVAR AV
1100 SUNV 94087 832-J5

LOCHINVAR AV
3400 SCL 95051 832-J5
3400 SCL 95051 833-A5
LOCHINVAR WY
15100 SCIC 95132 814-H4
LOCH LOMOND CT
400 MPS 95035 794-A6
500 SUNV 94087 832-E5
LOCH LOMOND LN
1500 SJS 95129 852-E4
LOCH LOMOND ST
3700 SCL 95054 813-E6
LOCHNER DR
1500 SJS 95127 835-A4
LOCHNESS CT
1000 SUNV 94087 832-G5
LOCH NESS WY
1700 SJS 95121 855-B3
LOCHRIDGE DR
300 SJS 95133 834-E3
LOCKE DR
3100 SJS 95111 854-J5
LOCKFORD CT
7500 CPTO 95014 852-D3
LOCKHART LN
100 LALT 94022 811-D6
LOCKHAVEN CT
800 LALT 94024 831-H5
LOCKHAVEN DR
800 LALT 94024 831-H5
LOCKHAVEN WY
1100 SJS 95129 852-G4
LOCKHEED MARTIN WY
1100 SUNV 94089 812-E4
LOCKSLEY PARK DR
1600 SJS 95132 814-F3
LOCKSUNART WY
100 SUNV 94087 832-E5
LOCKWOOD DR
2000 SJS 95132 814-F2
10100 CPTO 95014 851-J1
LOCUST AV
- HOLL 95023 1039-J3
LOCUST DR
17300 SCIC 95033 913-A1
21500 SCIC 95033 912-J3
LOCUST RD
24200 SCIC 95033 913-F7
LOCUST ST
100 RDWC 94061 790-B1
700 SCL 95050 833-F5
700 SJS 95110 854-C1
LODESTONE DR
1200 SJS 95132 814-E5
LODGE CT
1300 SJS 95121 854-J3
LODGEPOLE CT
1400 GIL 95020 977-G3
LODGEWOOD CT
700 SJS 95120 894-H3
LODI LN
2500 SJS 95124 853-J7
LOES WY
3400 SJS 95127 835-B2
LOGAN CT
800 SUNV 94087 832-C5
LOGAN LN
- ATN 94027 790-C2
LOGANBERRY DR
3900 SJS 95121 855-E4
9000 GIL 95020 977-F1
9100 GIL 95020 957-F7
LOGGING RD
17200 SCrC 95033 912-F5
LOGIC DR
2000 SJS 95124 873-F3
LOGSDEN WY
2500 SJS 95122 834-J4
LOGUE AV
300 MTVW 94043 812-C5
LOIRE CT
- SJS 95135 855-F3
LOIS AV
700 SUNV 94087 832-B1
LOIS CIR
- SBnC 95023 1060-F3
LOIS LN
100 PA 94303 791-B4
LOIS ST
2400 MTVW 94043 811-F3
LOIS WY
1400 SCIC 95008 873-E1
LOLA LN
600 MTVW 94040 811-H7
LOLLIE CT
1600 SJS 95124 873-J2
LOLLY CT
12400 SAR 95070 852-H6
LOLLY DR
12300 SAR 95070 852-H5
LOMA CT
- SJS 95131 814-A5
LOMA ST
16700 LGTS 95032 873-C7
LOMA ALMADEN RD
20000 SCIC 95033 913-F1
21600 SCIC 95033 914-A5
LOMA ALTA AV
- LGTS 95030 893-B1
LOMA ALTA CT
16100 SCIC 95037 936-J3
LOMA ALTA DR
3200 SCL 95051 833-A5
LOMA CHIQUITA RD
32900 SCIC 95037 935-A3
LOMA LINDA DR
- SJS 95129 852-J1
LOMA PARK CT
2300 SJS 95124 853-H7
LOMA PARK DR
2200 SJS 95124 853-H7
LOMA PRIETA AV
24100 SCIC 95033 913-F7

LOMA PRIETA AV
24100 SCrC 95033 913-F7
LOMA PRIETA CT
1000 LALT 94024 831-H2
LOMA PRIETA DR
5900 SJS 95123 874-G6
LOMA PRIETA LN
2300 MLPK 94025 790-D7
LOMA PRIETA RD
22500 SCIC 95033 913-H6
23200 SCIC 95033 914-A5
LOMA PRIETA WY
21900 SCIC 95033 913-B3
LOMA RIO DR
14000 SAR 95070 872-E2
LOMAS LN
15600 SCIC 95030 872-G6
LOMAS AZULES CT
8600 SJS 95135 855-J7
LOMAS AZULES PL
8600 SJS 95135 855-J6
LOMA VERDE AV
200 PA 94306 791-C7
700 PA 94303 791-E6
1000 PA 94306 811-C1
LOMA VERDE DR
3100 SJS 95117 853-D4
LOMA VERDE PL
3100 PA 94303 791-D6
LOMA VISTA AV
1200 SBnC 95023 1040-C7
15500 SCIC 95032 873-D5
LOMA VISTA CT
100 LGTS 95032 873-D5
LOMA VISTA LN
2400 SCL 95051 833-C1
LOMAX LN
- MTVW 94043 812-A1
LOMBARD AV
2500 SJS 95116 834-H3
LOMENT CT
2300 SJS 95124 873-E3
LOMENT PL
2400 SJS 95124 873-E3
LOMER WY
400 MPS 95035 794-D7
LOMETA AV
- SUNV 94086 812-C7
LOMITA AV
20500 SAR 95070 872-D3
21600 CPTO 95014 852-B1
LOMITA CT
600 SCIC 94305 810-G1
LOMITA DR
500 SCIC 94305 790-H6
500 SCIC 94305 810-G1
LOMITA LINDA DR
25700 LAH 94024 831-E4
LOMITAS CT
- MLPK 94025 790-F6
LOMOND CT
13500 SAR 95070 872-F1
LOMPICO DR
600 SJS 95123 874-G4
LOMPICO RD
11300 SCrC 95018 912-B7
LON RD
17000 SCrC 95066 912-G7
LONARDO AV
4300 SJS 95118 874-B2
LONDON AV
1100 SUNV 94087 832-H6
LONDON DR
- GIL 95020 978-A5
600 MPS 95035 794-B3
4700 SJS 95008 873-A1
LONDONDERRY DR
700 SUNV 94087 832-F6
3300 SCL 95050 833-C7
LONDONDERRY PL
3300 SCL 95050 833-D7
LONDON PARK CT
400 SJS 95136 874-F1
LONE BLUFF WY
2600 SJS 95111 854-H4
LONE DEER WY
9300 GIL 95020 957-F7
LONE HILL DR
16600 MGH 95037 936-J1
16600 MGH 95037 937-A1
LONE HILL RD
15300 SJS 95124 873-H5
LONE OAK CIR
21800 SCIC 95120 895-C4
LONE OAK CT
2700 GIL 95020 977-D2
LONE OAK DR
2400 SJS 95121 855-E4
LONE OAK LN
10400 LAH 94024 831-E5
LONE PINE LN
1100 SJS 95120 894-E2
LONETREE CT
- MPS 95035 814-A3
LONE TREE RD
- SBnC 95023 1020-E7
LONG AL
- HOLL 95023 1039-J4
LONG CT
6100 SJS 95123 875-A6
LONG ST
1600 SCL 95050 833-D3
LONGACRE CT
2800 SJS 95121 855-A2
LONGBRANCH CT
1100 SJS 95126 853-G4
LONGDALE DR
3100 SJS 95124 873-H2
LONGDEN CIR
2000 LALT 94024 831-G5
LONGDOWN RD
22800 CPTO 95014 851-J1
LONGFELLOW AV
1000 CMBL 95008 873-D3

LONGFELLOW AV
1100 LGTS 95008 873-D3
LONGFELLOW CT
6900 SJS 95129 852-E4
LONGFELLOW WY
1300 SJS 95129 852-E4
LONGFORD DR
2700 SJS 95132 814-E5
LONGHILL CT
- SJS 95138 875-H6
LONGHILL WY
- SJS 95138 875-H6
LONGLEY AV
900 SJS 95125 854-A3
LONGMEADOW DR
100 LGTS 95032 873-D7
1100 GIL 95020 957-E7
LONG OAK LN
10000 CPTO 95014 831-C7
LONG RIDGE RD
- SCIC 95030 871-A1
- SCrC 95033 871-A1
LONGRIDGE RD
200 LGTS 95032 873-D4
LONGSHORE DR
1000 SCIC 95128 853-F3
1000 SJS 95128 853-F3
LONGSPUR
- PTLV 94028 830-C1
LONGSPUR AV
1500 SUNV 94087 832-F5
LONG VALLEY TER
- SJS 95138 875-H6
LONGVIEW DR
200 MGH 95037 916-H7
LONGVIEW ST
1600 SJS 95122 834-G6
LONGWOOD DR
15500 LGTS 95032 873-D5
15500 SCIC 95032 873-D5
LONGWOOD LN
900 SJS 95129 852-J3
LONNA LN
10500 CPTO 95014 852-D2
LONUS ST
800 SJS 95126 853-J2
800 SJS 95126 854-A2
LOO LN
1500 SJS 95131 814-C6
LOOKOUT BEND
6700 SJS 95120 894-D2
LOOMIS CT
2500 SJS 95121 854-J2
LOOMIS DR
2400 SJS 95121 854-H2
LOOP RD
400 SJS 95120 895-B3
LOPEZ CT
15000 SCIC 95046 937-E3
LOPINA DR
- SJS 95129 853-A1
LOQUAT CT
13900 SAR 95070 872-J1
LORA DR
14200 LGTS 95032 873-A2
LORABELLE CT
4200 PA 94306 811-D3
LORAIN PL
100 LGTS 95032 873-B3
LORAINE AV
900 LALT 94024 831-G3
LOREE AV
18600 CPTO 95014 852-G1
LORELEI CT
1200 CMBL 95008 853-B6
LORENE CT
13000 MTVW 94040 832-A1
LORENE DR
100 SBnC 95023 1040-A3
100 HOLL 95023 1040-A3
LORENZEN DR
1700 SJS 95124 853-H7
LORENZO LN
- SJS 95135 855-G2
LORETO ST
200 MTVW 94041 811-J5
LORETTA LN
16100 CMBL 95032 873-D3
LORI AV
800 SUNV 94086 812-D6
LORI DR
- MGH 95037 917-G5
LORIENT TER
- SJS 95133 834-D2
LORNE WY
900 SUNV 94087 832-G5
LORRAINE AV
500 SJS 95110 834-A7
LORWICK WY
1800 SJS 95121 855-C4
LOS ALAMOS DR
17800 SJS 95070 853-A4
LOS ALTOS AV
200 LALT 94022 811-D6
LOS ALTOS CT
200 LALT 94022 811-D6
3800 SJS 95121 855-D3
LOS ALTOS DR
- SBnC 95023 1040-D5
900 HOLL 95023 1040-D5
2700 SJS 95121 855-D3
LOS ALTOS SQ
- LALT 94022 811-E4
LOS ALTURAS
100 LGTS 95032 872-J3
LOS ARBOLES AV
300 SJS 95111 854-J6
500 SCIC 94305 790-F7
1300 SUNV 94087 832-D4
LOS ARBOLES LN
- GIL 95020 977-J7
LOS BUELLIS WY
1400 MPS 95035 793-H3

LOS CERRITOS DR
17000 LGTS 95030 893-C1
LOS CHARROS LN
- PTLV 94028 810-C6
LOS COCHES AV
2200 SCIC 95128 853-F1
2600 SJS 95128 853-F1
LOS COCHES ST
300 MPS 95035 794-B7
LOS COYOTES CT
2500 SCIC 95020 958-D5
LOS ENCINAS CT
1900 CMBL 95032 872-J1
1900 CMBL 95032 873-A2
LOS ENCINOS AV
300 SJS 95134 813-E2
LOS ENCINOS CT
300 SJS 95134 813-E2
LOS ENCINOS DR
300 SJS 95134 813-E2
LOS ENCINOS ST
300 SJS 95134 813-E2
LOS ESTEROS RD
700 SJS 95002 793-D7
700 SJS 95134 793-E6
LOS FELICE DR
17900 SAR 95070 853-A4
17900 SJS 95129 853-A4
LOS GATOS BLVD
200 LGTS 95030 873-B7
2500 SJS 95124 873-B7
2500 LGTS 95032 873-B7
15700 SCIC 95032 873-B7
LOS GATOS ALMADEN RD
200 LGTS 95032 873-D5
200 SJS 95032 873-E5
200 SJS 95124 873-E5
16000 SCIC 95032 873-D5
LOS GATOS SARATOGA RD Rt#-9
- LGTS 95030 873-A6
- LGTS 95032 873-A6
LOS HUECOS DR
600 SJS 95123 874-G6
LOS NINOS WY
400 LALT 94022 811-E5
LOS OLIVOS DR
500 SCL 95050 833-C5
17900 SAR 95070 853-A4
LOS PADRES BLVD
300 SCL 95050 833-C2
LOS PADRES CT
7600 GIL 95020 977-H3
LOS PAJAROS CT
400 LALT 94024 831-F1
LOS PALMOS WY
200 SJS 95119 875-C6
LOS PALOS AV
4200 PA 94306 811-D3
LOS PALOS CIR
4200 PA 94306 811-D3
LOS PALOS CT
4100 SJS 95118 874-C2
LOS PALOS PL
4200 PA 94306 811-D3
LOS PALOS WY
1300 SJS 95118 874-B2
LOS PATIOS
100 LGTS 95032 872-J2
100 LGTS 95032 873-A2
LOS PINOS AV
500 MPS 95035 794-B5
LOS PINOS WY
300 SJS 95119 875-A7
300 SJS 95123 875-A7
LOS POSITOS DR
800 MPS 95035 794-B6
LOS RIOS CT
1500 SJS 95120 874-A7
LOS RIOS DR
1400 SJS 95120 874-A7
1500 SJS 95120 894-A1
LOS ROBLES AV
500 PA 94306 811-C2
LOS ROBLES CT
- SMCo 94025 790-D5
LOS ROBLES WY
17000 LGTS 95030 873-B7
LOSSE ST
500 SJS 95110 834-A5
LOS SERENOS ROBLES
16200 SCIC 95030 872-G6
LOS SUENOS AV
1600 SJS 95116 834-G5
LOSTCREEK CT
3200 SJS 95121 855-D7
LOST LAKE LN
- CMBL 95008 873-D1
LOST OAKS DR
2300 SJS 95124 873-D4
LOST RANCH RD
20700 SCIC 95120 894-J2
LOS TRANCOS CIR
100 SMCo 94028 830-D4
LOS TRANCOS RD
- PA 94304 830-D2
- PTLV 94028 810-D7
100 PA 94304 810-D7
900 PTLV 94028 830-D2
900 SMCo 94028 830-D4
LOST TRAIL CT
- SJS 95136 874-H3
LOST VALLEY RD
- SCrC 95033 892-A6
LOST VIEW RD
7700 SCIC 95120 895-D5
LOTISLAKE CT
700 SUNV 94089 812-H4
LOTUS LN
400 MTVW 94043 811-H4
LOTUS ST
600 SJS 95116 834-F6

STREET
Block City ZIP Pg-Grid

LOTUS WY
100 EPA 94303 791-D3
17300 MGH 95037 917-B6
LOUCKS AV
- LALT 94022 811-D4
LOUIS CT
3500 SJS 95127 835-B2
LOUIS RD
1900 PA 94303 791-C5
3800 PA 94303 811-F1
LOUISA CT
1500 PA 94303 791-B4
LOUISE AV
900 SJS 95125 854-B4
LOUISE CIR
100 SBnC 95023 1060-F3
LOUISE CT
100 LGTS 95032 872-J3
300 MPS 95035 794-E7
600 CMBL 95008 853-C7
LOUISE DR
800 SUNV 94087 832-C5
LOUISE LN
2000 LALT 94024 832-A5
LOUISE ST
1000 MLPK 94025 790-E6
LOUIS HOLSTROM DR
2100 SCIC 95037 936-F3
LOUIS PAUL WY
- SJS 95148 855-F1
LOUMENA LN
400 SJS 95111 854-H5
LOUPE AV
1000 SJS 95121 854-J4
1200 SJS 95121 855-A4
LOUPE CT
200 GIL 95020 977-J1
LOUVRE AV
- SJS 95135 855-F2
LOVE HARRIS RD
20000 SCIC 95033 893-E7
20100 SCIC 95033 913-E1
LOVELAND CT
14200 SAR 95070 872-E2
LOVELEAND CT
900 SCL 95050 833-E3
LOVELL AV
900 CMBL 95008 873-B1
LOVELL PL
2000 SCL 95051 833-A3
LOVERS LN
6500 SBnC 95023 999-G2
8900 SCIC 95020 999-G2
LOVEWOOD WY
2900 SJS 95148 855-D1
LOVOI WY
1000 SJS 95125 854-B5
LOWELL AV
100 PA 94301 791-A6
LOWELL CT
700 SUNV 94087 832-C5
LOWELL DR
300 SCL 95051 832-H7
LOWELL LN
- SJS 95125 854-B7
LOWELL WY
- CMBL 95008 853-E6
LOWENA CT
20700 SAR 95070 852-D5
LOWER ELLEN RD
- SCrC 95018 912-F6
LOWERY DR
- ATN 94027 790-H1
LOWLAND CT
1300 MPS 95035 814-E2
LOWNEY WY
1900 SJS 95131 814-D6
LOWRY DR
3000 SJS 95118 874-B1
LOYALTON DR
800 CMBL 95008 853-A7
800 CMBL 95008 873-A1
LOYE WY
2900 SJS 95148 835-E7
LOYOLA AV
- SMCo 94025 790-D1
2900 SMCo 94063 790-D1
LOYOLA CT
1000 SCL 95051 833-B5
LOYOLA DR
500 SCIC 94024 831-F4
1100 SCL 95051 833-B4
1700 SJS 95122 834-H6
W LOYOLA DR
10100 LAH 94024 831-F5
10100 SCIC 94024 831-F5
LU ANNE DR
100 CMBL 95008 853-B5
LUBEC ST
21400 CPTO 95014 832-C7
LUBICH DR
1200 MTVW 94040 832-A2
LUBY DR
1800 SJS 95133 834-E2
LUCAS CT
3000 SJS 95148 835-F7
LUCAS DR
3600 SJS 95148 835-F7
LUCCA PL
- SJS 95138 855-E7
LUCE CT
700 MTVW 94041 812-A7
LUCENA CT
1400 SJS 95132 814-E4
LUCENA DR
2600 SJS 95132 814-E5
LUCERNE AV
500 RDWC 94061 790-B1
LUCERNE DR
200 SUNV 94086 812-G7
LUCERNE WY
2400 SJS 95122 834-J5
2400 SJS 95122 835-A5
LUCERO LN
12800 LAH 94022 831-A1
LUCERO WY
100 SMCo 94028 810-D3
LUCHESSA AV
- GIL 95020 978-A5
100 SCIC 95020 978-A5
200 SCIC 95020 977-J5
300 GIL 95020 977-J5
LUCHESSA WY
- GIL 95020 978-C5
- SCIC 95020 978-C5
LUCHESSI CT
1100 SJS 95118 874-C2
LUCHESSI DR
1100 SJS 95118 874-C3
LUCIAN AV
3300 SJS 95127 814-J7
14000 SCIC 95127 814-J7
LUCILLE AV
20000 CPTO 95014 832-E6
LUCKY AV
900 SMCo 94025 790-D6
LUCKY CT
10200 SCIC 95046 957-D5
LUCKY RD
16200 MSER 95030 872-G7
16200 SCIC 95030 872-G7
LUCKY OAK ST
10900 CPTO 94024 832-A6
10900 CPTO 95014 832-A6
LUCOT WY
1000 CMBL 95008 873-B2
LUCRETIA AV
1100 SJS 95122 834-F7
1300 SJS 95122 854-G1
2000 SCIC 95122 854-G1
LUCRETIA CIR
900 SJS 95122 854-H2
LUCRETIA CT
1600 SJS 95122 854-F1
LUCY BROWN LN
- SBnC 95045 1038-G4
LUCY BROWN RD
1100 SBnC 95020 1038-G3
1100 SBnC 95045 1038-G3
LUCY MAY TR
18100 SCIC 95033 912-J4
LUDIS LN
- SBnC 95023 1000-B6
LUDLOW CT
3100 SJS 95148 855-C2
LUDLOW WY
300 SJS 95133 834-F2
LUEDKE PL
- SCIC 95111 854-G5
- SJS 95111 854-G5
LUFKIN CT
3600 SJS 95148 835-F7
LUGANO WY
2900 SJS 95132 814-F5
LUIKA PL
1600 CMBL 95008 873-A1
LUJOSO CT
1400 SJS 95128 853-F4
LUKE CT
1800 SJS 95116 834-G5
LULLABY LN
4400 SJS 95111 855-A7
LUMBERTOWN LN
21200 SAR 95070 872-C3
LUNADA CT
- LALT 94022 811-D3
LUNADA DR
300 LALT 94022 811-D3
LUNA PARK DR
- SJS 95112 834-A3
LUNAR CT
7800 CPTO 95014 852-C3
LUND TER
- SUNV 94089 812-G4
LUNDER CT
1900 SJS 95131 814-E7
LUNDY AV
900 SJS 95133 834-D1
1000 SJS 95131 834-D1
1200 SJS 95131 814-B4
LUNDY LN
- LGTS 95030 893-A1
100 PA 94306 811-E2
800 SCIC 94024 831-H4
LUNDY PL
500 MPS 95035 814-B4
500 SJS 95131 814-B4
LUNETA CT
3900 SJS 95136 874-F1
LUNETA DR
4000 SJS 95136 874-F1
LUNING DR
1300 SJS 95118 874-A3
LUPIN LN
- ATN 94027 790-G1
LUPINE AV
3500 PA 94303 791-E7
LUPINE CT
1400 GIL 95020 977-F1
1400 SCIC 95046 937-E5
1500 SJS 95118 874-B1
LUPINE DR
1000 SUNV 94086 832-G2
LUPINE RD
27700 LAH 94022 810-J6
LUPTON AV
1400 SJS 95125 854-A4
LU-RAY DR
100 LGTS 95032 873-E5
LUSARDI DR
2200 SJS 95148 855-D2
LUSTERLEAF DR
700 SUNV 94086 832-G2
LUTHER AV
1000 SJS 95126 833-J7
LUTHER DR
400 SCL 95051 833-B7
LUTHERIA WY
14300 SAR 95070 872-E2
LUX CT
3900 SJS 95136 874-F1
LUXOR CT
- SJS 95126 833-G6
LUZ AV
2200 SJS 95116 834-G3
LUZ CLARA DR
- SJS 95116 834-F5
LUZ DEL SOL LP
- MPS 95035 813-J1
LUZ DEL SOL TR
- MPS 95035 813-J1
LYELL ST
- LALT 94022 811-E7
LYLE CT
2700 SCL 95051 833-B3
LYLE DR
1500 SJS 95125 854-A3
1500 SJS 95129 852-H5
LYLE LN
700 SJS 95008 873-F1
LYLEWOOD CT
- SJS 95138 855-C5
LYMEHAVEN CT
- SJS 95111 874-J1
LYNBROOK CT
18900 SAR 95070 852-H5
LYNBROOK WY
1100 SJS 95129 852-G4
LYNDALE AV
100 SCIC 95127 834-J2
100 SJS 95127 834-J2
10000 SCIC 95127 835-A3
10000 SJS 95127 835-A3
LYNDE AV
13800 SAR 95070 872-D1
LYNDE CT
13800 SAR 95070 872-D2
LYNDON AV
- LGTS 95030 872-J7
LYNETTE WY
200 SJS 95116 834-G4
LYNFIELD LN
4200 SJS 95136 874-D2
LYNG DR
4900 SJS 95111 875-B1
LYNHURST CT
1100 SJS 95118 874-C2
LYNHURST WY
1100 SJS 95118 874-C2
LYNN AV
- MPS 95035 794-D5
1100 SJS 95122 834-G6
2000 SJS 95124 873-F5
15000 LGTS 95032 873-F5
15000 SJS 95032 873-F5
LYNN WY
1000 SUNV 94087 832-B1
LYNNDALE WY
25900 LAH 94022 811-C6
LYNNHAVEN DR
2000 SJS 95128 853-G3
LYNN OAKS DR
3200 SJS 95117 853-D2
LYNTON CT
20100 CPTO 95014 852-E2
LYNVIEW DR
3000 SJS 95148 855-D1
LYNWOOD AV
600 MTVW 94043 812-A3
LYNWOOD TER
2000 SJS 95128 833-F6
2200 MPS 95035 814-E1
LYNX CT
3700 SJS 95136 874-D1
LYNX DR
3500 SJS 95136 874-D1
LYNXWOOD CT
500 SUNV 94086 832-F1
LYON TER
- SUNV 94089 812-G4
LYONBURRY PL
500 SJS 95123 874-G4
LYONCROSS WY
400 SJS 95123 874-J4
LYON ESTATES CT
2900 SJS 95135 855-G5
LYONS CT
2200 SJS 95116 834-H4
18500 SAR 95070 872-H1
LYONS DR
2000 SJS 95116 834-H5
LYONS ST
1100 RDWC 94061 790-A1
LYONSVILLE LN
1300 SJS 95118 874-B5
LYRA ST
48800 FRMT 94539 793-H1
LYRELAKE CT
700 SUNV 94089 812-H4
LYRIC LN
4700 SJS 95111 855-A7
4700 SJS 95111 875-A1
LYTER WY
3200 SJS 95135 855-D2
LYTTON AV
100 PA 94301 790-H4

M

M RD
- SUNV 94089 812-H4
MABEL AV
2000 SJS 95122 834-H5
MABEL CT
12200 SAR 95070 852-G5
MABIE CT
5900 SJS 95123 874-F5
MABURY CT
2800 SJS 95133 814-G7
MABURY RD
600 SJS 95133 834-E1
1100 SJS 95112 834-D2
2400 SJS 95133 814-G7
3100 SJS 95127 814-H6
3200 SCIC 95127 814-H6
12200 SCIC 95133 834-E1
MACADAM CT
5800 SJS 95123 875-A5
MACADAM LN
10100 CPTO 95014 852-E1
MACARA AV
600 SUNV 94086 812-D5
MACARTHUR AV
300 SCIC 95128 853-F1
300 SJS 95128 853-F1
MACAW LN
200 SJS 95123 874-F7
MACAW PL
200 SJS 95123 874-F7
MACAW WY
5200 SJS 95123 874-F7
MACBAIN AV
- ATN 94027 790-E3
MACBETH DR
3700 SJS 95127 835-C2
MACDONALD AV
200 SJS 95116 834-E3
MACDONALD ST
1400 RDWC 94061 790-A2
MACDOWELL TER
- SUNV 94087 832-E2
MACDUEE CT
1800 SJS 95121 855-B3
MACDUEE WY
1800 SJS 95121 855-B3
MACDUFF CT
900 SJS 95127 835-C2
MACE CT
3600 SJS 95127 835-C3
MACE DR
1200 SJS 95127 835-C2
MACEDO PL
- SCL 95054 813-D5
MACGREGOR LN
3500 SCL 95054 813-E6
MACHADO AV
- MPS 95035 813-J1
- MPS 95035 814-A1
1900 SCL 95051 832-J2
1900 SUNV 94086 832-J2
3000 SCL 95051 833-A2
MACHADO LN
1100 SJS 95127 835-C2
MACIAS CT
- SJS 95120 894-H4
MACIAS LN
- SJS 95120 894-H4
MACINTOSH ST
3500 SCL 95054 813-E6
MACINTYRE DR
- SJS 95136 854-E6
MACKALL WY
3100 PA 94306 791-D7
MACKAY DR
4000 PA 94306 811-F2
MACKENZIE CT
- SJS 95127 835-B2
MACKENZIE DR
300 SCL 95051 832-H7
900 SUNV 94087 832-B6
MACKENZIE WY
- GIL 95020 977-D3
MACKEY AV
1600 SJS 95125 854-C3
MACKIN WOODS LN
3200 SJS 95135 855-G3
MACKLIN CT
700 SJS 95133 814-G7
MACLANE ST
200 PA 94306 811-C1
MACLAY CT
6000 SJS 95123 874-E5
14300 SAR 95070 872-G2
MACLAY DR
900 SJS 95123 874-E5
MACON AV
1000 MTVW 94043 811-J2
1000 MTVW 94043 812-A2
1000 SJS 95117 853-D3
MACON RD
- SCIC 94035 812-C1
MACREDES CT
600 SJS 95116 834-E6
MADALEN DR
1200 MPS 95035 794-B4
MADAN LN
- SCL 95051 833-C3
MADDEN AV
2300 SJS 95116 834-G3
MADDEN TER
- SJS 95116 834-G3
MADDUX DR
900 PA 94303 791-D6
1400 RDWC 94061 790-A3
MADELAINE CT
2000 LALT 94024 831-G5
MADELINE DR
3300 SCIC 95127 834-J1
3300 SJS 95127 834-J1
MADELINE LN
900 SCL 95050 833-C5
MADERA
- MTVW 94043 811-J2
MADERA AV
400 SUNV 94086 812-C7
400 SJS 95112 834-B3
1000 MLPK 94025 790-J1
MADERA CT
100 LGTS 95032 873-H7
100 LGTS 95032 893-H1
200 HOLL 95023 1039-H3
MADERA DR
2400 SCL 95051 833-C4
10300 CPTO 95014 832-B7
MADERA RD
22800 CPTO 95014 851-J2
MADIDI PL
- SJS 95128 853-E2
MADISON CT
400 GIL 95020 958-A7
400 SJS 95123 875-A6
MADISON DR
300 SJS 95123 875-A6
800 MTVW 94040 831-G1
MADISON ST
200 SCL 95050 833-E4
MADISON WY
- SMCo 94025 790-H2
500 PA 94303 791-C4
MADOC WY
4400 SJS 95130 853-A6
MADONNA DR
3300 SJS 95117 853-D3
MADONNA WY
800 LALT 94024 831-E2
MADRID CT
3600 SJS 95132 814-F1
MADRID DR
2900 SCIC 95020 957-D6
3400 SJS 95132 814-E2
MADRID RD
10600 CPTO 95014 852-B2
MADRONA AV
1200 SJS 95125 854-B5
MADRONA WY
20300 SCIC 95033 892-H7
20400 SCIC 95033 912-J1
MADRONE AV
- SCrC 95033 871-A4
- SCIC 95037 916-F3
- SJS 95037 916-F3
200 SCL 95051 833-B7
500 SUNV 94086 812-E5
16500 LGTS 95030 872-H7
16600 SCIC 95030 872-H7
MADRONE CT
- CPTO 95014 831-J6
19400 SCIC 95033 892-F4
MADRONE DR
- HOLL 95023 1040-B2
- SBnC 95023 1040-B2
17900 SCIC 95033 912-J2
17900 SCIC 95033 913-A3
MADRONE PKWY
- MGH 95037 916-H4
- MGH 95037 917-A4
MADRONE PL
13900 SCrC 95033 871-C4
MADRONE RD
- ATN 94027 790-G1
MADRONE ST
200 RDWC 94061 790-B1
MADRONE HILL RD
15200 SAR 95070 872-E4
MADRONO AV
1500 PA 94306 791-A6
MADRUGA WY
1200 MPS 95035 814-D2
MAESTRO CT
500 SJS 95134 813-F2
MAESUMI CT
- SJS 95124 873-J7
MAEVE CT
- SJS 95136 854-E5
MAGDALENA AV
500 SCIC 94024 831-F3
600 LALT 94024 831-F3
1200 LAH 94024 831-D4
MAGDALENA CIR
1900 SCL 95051 832-H3
MAGDALENA CT
1200 SCIC 94024 831-F2
MAGELLAN AV
- SJS 95116 834-F3
3600 SCL 95051 832-H7
MAGGI CT
- LGTS 95032 873-B7
MAGGIO CT
1200 CMBL 95008 873-B1
MAGGIORE CT
3100 SJS 95135 855-C7
MAGIC SANDS WY
- SJS 95123 875-D2
MAGLADRY RD
100 SBnC 95023 1020-F7
500 SBnC 95023 1040-F1
MAGLIOCCO DR
2900 SJS 95117 853-D2
2900 SJS 95128 853-E2
MAGNESON LP
100 LGTS 95032 873-C6
MAGNESON TER
100 LGTS 95032 873-C6
MAGNOLIA AV
1300 SJS 95126 833-H7
N MAGNOLIA AV
- SJS 95136 854-E7
S MAGNOLIA AV
700 SJS 95136 854-E7
W MAGNOLIA AV
3900 SJS 95136 854-E7
MAGNOLIA CT
- SAR 95070 872-C1
1600 MLPK 94025 790-F5
2300 MGH 95037 917-E6
MAGNOLIA DR
- ATN 94027 790-F1
3800 PA 94306 811-C2
MAGNOLIA LN
- MTVW 94043 812-B5
- PA 94306 811-D2
400 SCL 95051 833-B7
MAGNOLIA ST
600 MLPK 94025 790-E5
MAGNOLIA WY
- GIL 95020 977-G1
- HOLL 95023 1040-E5
2400 MGH 95037 917-F5
MAGNOLIA BLOSSOM LN
1600 SJS 95124 873-J6
MAGNOLIA LAKE CT
1700 SJS 95131 814-B5
MAGNOLIA TREE CT
1700 SJS 95122 854-G1
MAGNUM DR
2900 SJS 95135 855-E3
MAGPIE LN
1500 SUNV 94087 832-F5
MAHAN DR
400 SJS 95123 875-A6
MAHOGANY CT
- GIL 95020 957-D7
MAHOGANY DR
700 SUNV 94086 832-G2
MAHONEY AV
200 SCIC 95127 835-B1
200 SJS 95127 835-B1
MAIDEN LN
6900 SJS 95120 894-G3
MAIDEN SPRING WY
- MGH 95037 916-H6
MAIN AL
- HOLL 95023 1040-A3
E MAIN AV
- MGH 95037 916-J7
- MGH 95037 917-B6
700 SCIC 95037 917-D4
W MAIN AV
700 MGH 95037 936-H1
900 MGH 95037 916-J7
MAIN ST
- LALT 94022 811-E7
600 SCL 95050 833-D2
E MAIN ST
- LGTS 95030 893-A1
100 LGTS 95030 873-B7
N MAIN ST
- MPS 95035 794-A7
S MAIN ST
- MPS 95035 794-A7
200 MPS 95035 814-A1
W MAIN ST
- LGTS 95030 893-A1
- LGTS 95030 873-A7
100 LGTS 95030 872-J7
MAIN ENTRANCE DR
1400 SJS 95131 814-C7
MAIRWOOD CT
700 SJS 95120 894-J3
MAITLAND DR
5000 SJS 95124 873-H4
MAJESTIC CT
1900 SJS 95132 814-F2
MAJESTIC DR
22400 SCrC 95033 912-H5
MAJESTIC WY
1800 SJS 95132 814-F3
MAJESTIC OAK WY
22700 CPTO 95014 831-J7
MAJORCA CT
6000 SJS 95120 874-B7
MAJORCA DR
1400 MGH 95037 917-D6
MAKATI CIR
5200 SJS 95123 875-B4
MAKATI CT
- SJS 95123 875-B4
MALABAR AV
2800 SCL 95051 833-B7
MALABAR DR
400 SJS 95127 834-J3
400 SJS 95127 835-A3
MALAGA CT
1400 MGH 95037 917-D7
MALAGA DR
2400 SJS 95125 853-J7
16900 MGH 95037 917-D6
MALAGUERRA AV
1800 MGH 95037 917-A2
19000 SCIC 95037 917-A2
19200 SCIC 95037 916-J2
MALARIN AV
600 SCL 95050 833-D5
MALBEC DR
- MGH 95037 917-E6
MALCOM AV
13800 SAR 95070 872-D1
MALDEN AV
1900 SJS 95122 854-H1
MALECH RD
100 SJS 95138 875-J7
100 SCIC 95137 875-J7
100 SCIC 95137 895-J1
100 SCIC 95137 896-A1
MALERO PL
4700 SJS 95129 852-J1
MALIBU DR
1100 SJS 95129 853-A3
MALIBU TER
- FRMT 94539 794-B1
MALLARD WY
1400 SUNV 94087 832-G4
MALLARD RIDGE CIR
1400 SJS 95120 894-F3
MALLARD RIDGE CT
7100 SJS 95120 894-F3
MALLARD RIDGE DR
1400 SJS 95120 894-F3
MALLARD RIDGE LP
7200 SJS 95120 894-F3
MALLET CT
1000 MLPK 94025 790-F4
MALLORY CT
19900 SAR 95070 852-E6
MALO CT
1000 SCIC 95020 958-A4
MALONE PL
2400 SCL 95050 833-C5
MALONE RD
700 SJS 95125 854-B5
MALONEY LN
600 MLPK 94025 790-F3
MALORY CT
- SMCo 94061 790-B3
MALORY DR
6200 SJS 95123 875-B7
MALOTT DR
900 SJS 95121 854-H3
MALPAS LN
5700 SJS 95124 873-J6
MALTON CT
3100 SJS 95148 855-E2
MALVERN CT
10300 CPTO 95014 852-F1
MALVINI DR
3900 SJS 95118 874-B2
MAMMINI CT
13600 SCIC 95046 937-G5
MAMMOTH DR
2300 SJS 95116 834-G2
MANASSAS AV
6400 SJS 95119 875-D5
MANASSAS CT
2000 SJS 95116 834-H5
MANCHESTER AV
200 CMBL 95008 853-G5
MANCHESTER CT
3100 PA 94303 791-D6
MANCHESTER DR
1000 SCL 95050 833-E5
MANCUSO ST
6100 SJS 95120 874-C7
MANDA DR
2800 SJS 95124 873-H1
MANDARIN DR
1200 SUNV 94087 832-B3
MANDARIN WY
- ATN 94027 790-B5
1800 SJS 95122 834-H6
13500 SAR 95070 872-D1
MANDEL CT
1800 SJS 95131 814-D7
MANDELA CT
1000 EPA 94303 791-C1
MANDELAY PL
- SJS 95138 855-E5
MANDERSTON DR
- SJS 95138 855-F7
MANDOLI DR
13400 LAH 94022 811-A5
MANDOLIN DR
300 SJS 95134 813-D2
MANDRILL CT
4700 SJS 95124 873-J3
MANET DR
1000 SUNV 94087 832-E3
MANFRE RD
10300 SCIC 95037 916-C1
MANFRED ST
100 MPS 95035 793-J3
100 MPS 95035 794-A3
MANFROY RANCH RD
3600 SCIC 95020 958-G3
MANGIN WY
2100 SCIC 95148 835-E5
MANGO AV
800 SUNV 94087 832-B2
MANGO BLOSSOM CT
5300 SJS 95123 875-A3
MANGROVE AV
800 SUNV 94086 832-G3
MANGRUM DR
4600 SCL 95054 813-D4
MANHATTAN AV
1900 EPA 94303 791-B3
MANHATTAN CT
1000 SUNV 94087 832-B2
MANHATTAN PL
- SJS 95136 854-E5
2200 SCL 95051 833-A2
MANICHETTI CT
5800 SJS 95123 875-A5
MANILA DR
- MTVW 94035 812-C3
- SCIC 94035 812-C3
- SUNV 94089 812-C3
300 SJS 95119 875-C7
MANILA WY
6400 SJS 95119 875-C7
MANITA CT
21000 CPTO 95014 852-C3
MANITOBA DR
1600 SUNV 94087 832-C5
4700 SJS 95130 853-A7
4800 SJS 95130 852-J7
MANITOU CT
1700 SJS 95120 874-B6
MANLEY CT
100 SJS 95139 895-G1
MANLY CT
300 SCL 95051 833-A7
MANN DR
10000 CPTO 95014 832-B7
MANNA WY
11000 SCIC 95020 957-G3
MANNING AV
- SCIC 95127 834-J2
- SJS 95127 834-J2
MANNING CT
1100 SCIC 95046 937-G4
MANN OAK CT
20000 SCIC 95120 894-J5
MANOA CT
20300 SAR 95070 852-E7
MANOLETE ST
- HOLL 95023 1040-D4
MANOR CT
100 MGH 95037 937-A1
12500 SAR 95070 852-D5
MANOR DR
1100 SJS 95125 854-B6
20500 SAR 95070 852-D5
MANOR PL
- MLPK 94025 790-H3

STREET
Block City ZIP Pg-Grid

MANOR WY
700 LALT 94024 831-G3
MANORWOOD CT
5900 SJS 95129 852-G3
MANRESA CT
200 LALT 94022 831-D1
7500 SJS 95139 895-G2
MANRESA LN
500 LALT 94022 831-D1
500 LAH 94022 831-D1
MANRESA WY
200 LALT 94022 831-D1
MANSFIELD DR
500 MTVW 94040 831-J2
700 SJS 95128 853-G2
MANSFIELD RD
100 SBnC 95023 1040-E3
MANSION CT
- MLPK 94025 790-C7
500 SCL 95054 813-E4
1300 SJS 95120 894-C2
MANSION PARK DR
400 SCL 95054 813-E4
MANTECA CT
6100 SJS 95123 874-G6
MANTECA WY
13600 SAR 95070 872-H1
MANTELLI DR
- GIL 95020 957-D7
500 GIL 95020 977-D1
MANTIS DR
2800 SJS 95148 835-E7
MANTON CT
1600 CMBL 95008 873-A1
MANTON DR
100 SJS 95123 875-B4
MANUEL ST
- SJS 95136 854-F6
MANUELA AV
4100 PA 94306 811-C4
MANUELA CT
4200 PA 94306 811-B4
MANUELA WY
4200 PA 94306 811-B5
MANUELLA RD
4200 LAH 94022 811-C6
4200 PA 94306 811-C5
MANX AV
700 CMBL 95008 853-D7
MANXWOOD PL
5100 SJS 95111 875-C2
MANZANA CT
- SJS 95112 834-B4
MANZANA LN
4000 PA 94306 811-C3
MANZANA PL
- SJS 95112 834-B4
MANZANITA AV
- LGTS 95030 872-H7
- SCIC 95030 872-H7
200 PA 94306 791-A6
200 SCL 95051 833-B7
500 SUNV 94086 812-E5
2000 SMCo 94025 790-C6
MANZANITA CT
- CPTO 95014 831-J7
300 MPS 95035 813-J4
MANZANITA DR
1200 HOLL 95023 1040-D5
3900 SJS 95117 853-B2
4100 SJS 95129 853-A2
17700 SCIC 95037 917-F3
17700 MGH 95037 917-F3
19400 SCIC 95033 892-F4
MANZANITA RD
- ATN 94027 790-G1
MANZANITA WY
- LGTS 95030 872-J7
MANZANO CT
600 MPS 95035 794-B4
MANZANO ST
500 MPS 95035 794-A4
MANZANO WY
1100 SUNV 94089 813-A5
MAPACHE CT
- PTLV 94028 810-A4
MAPACHE DR
100 PTLV 94028 810-A4
MAPLE AV
- ATN 94027 790-E2
400 MPS 95035 793-H6
500 SUNV 94086 812-F6
500 CMBL 95008 853-F6
500 SCIC 95037 937-G1
500 SCIC 95046 937-G1
2300 MGH 95037 937-G1
2300 MGH 95046 937-G1
MAPLE LN
- EPA 94303 791-C1
1500 LALT 94024 831-G3
16700 LGTS 95030 893-A1
MAPLE ST
100 HOLL 95023 1040-A3
200 SBnC 95023 1040-A3
400 MGH 95037 937-B1
400 PA 94301 791-A3
7300 GIL 95020 978-B3
MAPLECREST CT
5500 SJS 95123 874-G4
MAPLE GROVE CT
100 SJS 95123 874-F7
100 SJS 95123 875-A3
MAPLE LAKE CT
1700 SJS 95131 814-B6
MAPLE LEAF CT
- LAH 94022 810-J7
3200 SJS 95121 855-B3
MAPLE LEAF WY
- ATN 94027 790-G2
MAPLETON AV
300 HOLL 95023 1039-J4
MAPLETON CT
- SJS 95131 814-A5
MAPLETREE PL
20500 CPTO 95014 832-D6
MAPLEWOOD AV
300 SCIC 95117 853-D1
300 SJS 95117 853-D1
700 PA 94303 811-F1
MAPLEWOOD LN
2600 SCL 95051 833-B7
MAPLEWOOD PL
700 PA 94303 811-F1
MAPLEWOOD ST
10600 CPTO 95014 832-F6
MARACAIBO DR
5800 SJS 95120 874-C6
MARANATHA DR
- SBnC 95023 1040-E7
MARANTA AV
800 SUNV 94087 832-C2
MARASCHINO DR
1000 SJS 95129 853-A3
1100 SUNV 94087 832-C3
MARATHON DR
300 CMBL 95008 853-C5
MARBELLA CT
4500 SJS 95124 873-F3
16900 MGH 95037 917-D6
MARBELLA DR
2200 SJS 95124 873-F3
MARBLE CT
900 SJS 95120 894-G1
MARBLE ARCH AV
- SJS 95136 854-F7
MARBLE ARCH WY
- SJS 95136 854-F7
MARBRISA CT
- SJS 95135 855-G3
MARBRISA TER
- SJS 95135 855-G2
MARBURG WY
300 SJS 95133 834-E3
N MARBURG WY
300 SJS 95133 834-E3
MARCEL CT
3300 SJS 95135 855-G3
MARCELLA AV
8600 SCIC 95020 958-B4
MARCELLO DR
- SJS 95131 814-B6
MARCELYN AV
2400 MTVW 94043 811-F2
MARCH DR
100 SJS 95138 875-D4
MARCHANT CT
3700 SJS 95127 835-C2
MARCHANT DR
3700 SJS 95127 835-C2
MARCHESE CT
3300 SCL 95051 833-A1
MARCHESE WY
2500 SCL 95051 833-A2
MARCHMONT CT
200 LGTS 95032 873-D7
MARCHMONT DR
200 LGTS 95032 873-C7
16500 SCIC 95032 873-C7
MARCIA AV
1400 SJS 95125 854-A7
MARCIA CT
100 MTVW 94041 811-J6
MARCIA DR
400 MGH 95037 916-H7
MARCO DR
1600 SJS 95131 814-C7
MARCO WY
1600 SJS 95131 814-C7
MARCONI WY
1600 SJS 95125 853-J5
MARCROSS DR
1900 SJS 95131 814-D6
MARCUS CT
- SBnC 95023 1060-F2
MARCUSSEN DR
1000 MLPK 94025 790-G2
MARCY CT
21000 CPTO 95014 832-C7
MARCY LYNN CT
1700 SJS 95124 873-H5
MARDAN DR
1400 SJS 95132 814-F3
MARDEL LN
2000 SJS 95128 853-G3
MARDELL WY
2500 MTVW 94043 811-F2
MARDENE CT
1300 SJS 95121 855-B5
MAREE CT
6100 SJS 95123 874-G6
MARENGO LN
1100 SJS 95132 814-H5
MARENTIS CT
800 SJB 95045 1038-C4
MARE PLACE CT
3800 SJS 95121 855-B5
MARFRANCE DR
3800 SJS 95121 855-A5
MARGARET CT
900 SUNV 94087 832-B2
MARGARET LN
600 CMBL 95008 853-B7
MARGARET ST
- SJS 95112 834-C7
- SJS 95112 854-C1
1700 SJS 95116 834-G5
MARGARET WY
100 SJS 95112 834-C7
MARGARITA AV
200 PA 94306 811-C1
MARGARITA CT
200 LALT 94022 811-D4
MARGATE AV
3500 SJS 95117 853-C2
MARGE WY
500 SCIC 95117 853-D2
MARGO DR
100 MTVW 94041 812-A6
MARGOT PL
1900 SJS 95125 853-J6
MARGUERITE DR
- HOLL 95023 1039-G3
MARIA CT
400 SCL 95050 833-D5
MARIA LN
800 SUNV 94086 832-F3
21100 SAR 95070 852-C5
MARIA ST
200 SCL 95050 833-D5
MARIA WY
700 GIL 95020 977-H1
1300 SJS 95117 853-D4
MARIAN LN
- SCIC 95127 834-J1
- SCIC 95127 835-A2
MARIANELLI CT
1000 SJS 95112 834-C3
MARIANI AV
20300 CPTO 95014 832-D7
MARIANI DR
1600 SUNV 94087 832-F5
MARIANI WY
- SJS 95112 834-B4
MARIANNA LN
- ATN 94027 790-E2
1500 SJS 95128 853-H2
MARIANNA WY
100 CMBL 95008 853-C5
MARIANNE CT
100 MTVW 94040 811-J7
MARIA PRIVADA
1100 MTVW 94040 832-H6
MARIA ROSA WY
10900 CPTO 95014 852-B2
MARIA TERESA CT
100 LGTS 95032 873-E5
MARICH WY
200 LALT 94022 811-F4
400 MTVW 94040 811-F4
MARICOPA DR
100 LGTS 95032 873-D5
MARIE CT
14800 SCIC 95046 937-G2
MARIE LN
700 MGH 95037 917-D7
MARIES CT
- SBnC 95023 1060-F3
MARIETTA CT
800 SCL 95051 833-A5
MARIETTA DR
1500 SJS 95118 874-A4
2900 SCL 95051 833-A5
MARIGOLD CT
1000 SUNV 94086 832-H2
1700 SJS 95133 834-E3
MARIGOLD LN
900 GIL 95020 977-G1
MARILLA AV
1000 SJS 95129 853-A3
MARILLA CT
20100 SAR 95070 852-E5
MARILLA DR
12000 SAR 95070 852-E5
MARILYN CT
- HOLL 95023 1040-D5
1200 MTVW 94040 811-G7
MARILYN DR
700 CMBL 95008 853-C7
800 CMBL 95008 873-C1
900 MTVW 94040 811-G6
MARILYN LN
1100 MonC 95076 1037-C3
14000 SAR 95070 872-H2
MARILYN PL
1300 MTVW 94040 811-G7
MARINA WY
1700 SCIC 95125 853-H5
MARINE WY
2600 MTVW 94043 791-G7
MARINER DR
900 SCIC 94043 811-J3
900 SCIC 94043 812-A3
MARINOVICH WY
1300 LALT 94024 831-J3
MARION AV
400 PA 94301 791-C6
500 PA 94306 791-C6
600 PA 94303 791-C6
MARION DR
- SMCo 94062 790-A4
- WDSD 94062 790-A4
MARION PL
600 PA 94301 791-C6
MARION RD
20500 SAR 95070 872-D2
MARION WY
900 SUNV 94087 832-G4
MARIPOSA AV
- LGTS 95030 873-A6
200 MTVW 94041 811-G5
300 LALT 94022 811-D6
1100 SJS 95126 833-J7
1500 PA 94306 791-A6
MARIPOSA CT
- LGTS 95030 873-A5
1200 HOLL 95023 1039-H3
MARIPOSA ST
- SJB 95045 1038-D4
MARIPOSA WY
1100 GIL 95020 957-F7
MARIST CT
2900 SJS 95148 855-C6
MARITZA CT
- SJS 95121 855-C3
MARJOHN BLVD
4900 SJS 95136 875-A2
MARJORAM DR
- MGH 95037 916-G4
MARJORIE CT
2400 MTVW 94043 811-F2
MARJORIE DR
1000 CMBL 95008 873-B1
MARK AV
- SCIC 94035 812-B2
- SCIC 94043 812-B2
1600 SJS 95124 873-J2
2800 SCL 95051 833-A3
MARKET RW
- SJS 95128 853-E1
MARKET ST
300 SCIC 95020 957-H3
700 SCL 95053 833-D5
800 SCL 95050 833-D5
N MARKET ST
- SJS 95113 834-B6
- SJS 95110 834-B6
S MARKET ST
- SJS 95113 834-B6
200 SJS 95110 834-B7
S MARKET ST Rt#-82
200 SJS 95110 834-B7
MARKHAM AV
- SMCo 94063 790-C1
2300 SJS 95125 854-B6
MARKHAM TER
800 SUNV 94086 812-D7
MARKINGDON AV
2900 SJS 95127 835-A4
MARKROSS CT
17200 MGH 95037 917-A7
MARKS AV
3500 SJS 95118 874-B2
MARKS DR
- SBnC 95023 1060-D2
MARK TWAIN CT
100 SCL 95050 833-D7
MARK TWAIN ST
1800 PA 94303 791-B5
MARKWOOD CT
3100 SJS 95148 835-E7
3100 SJS 95148 855-E1
MARLA CT
6100 SJS 95124 873-J7
MARLBAROUGH AV
1400 LALT 94024 831-J3
MARLBAROUGH CT
1400 LALT 94024 831-J3
MARLBORO CT
2000 SJS 95128 853-G3
MARLBOROUGH AV
2700 SMCo 94063 790-C1
MARLENE CT
1500 SJS 95118 874-G3
MARLETTE DR
3800 SJS 95121 855-A5
MARLINA TER
400 MPS 95035 793-G3
MARLINTON CT
900 SJS 95120 894-G2
MARLOWE DR
4300 SJS 95124 873-J3
MARLOWE ST
400 PA 94301 791-A3
MARLYN WY
1700 SJS 95125 854-A5
MARMON CT
2400 SCL 95051 833-C2
MARMONA CT
200 MLPK 94025 790-J3
MARMONA DR
200 MLPK 94025 790-J2
MARMONT WY
13600 SCIC 95127 834-J3
MARNE DR
1100 HOLL 95023 1040-C5
MARO DR
- SCIC 95127 834-J1
- SCIC 95127 835-A1
MAROEL DR
2100 SJS 95130 853-A7
MAROUN WY
- SJS 95148 855-F1
MARQUES AV
1900 SJS 95125 853-J5
1900 SJS 95125 854-A6
MARQUETTE DR
5400 SJS 95118 874-B5
MARQUETTE ST
3500 SCL 95051 832-J2
MARR LN
2300 SJS 95124 873-E5
MARRIAGE RD
- SCIC 94035 792-D7
- SCIC 94035 812-D1
MARS CT
400 MPS 95035 794-D7
3700 SJS 95121 855-D4
MARS DR
- HOLL 95023 1020-A5
MARSAN CT
1400 CMBL 95008 873-B2
MARSEILLE CT
- HOLL 95023 1040-B3
MARSEILLE DR
- HOLL 95023 1040-B3
MARSEILLES CT
1600 SJS 95138 875-F1
MARSH RD
1000 SMCo 94025 790-F1
1000 ATN 94027 790-F1
MARSH ST
1500 SJS 95122 834-G6
MARSHA WY
2400 SJS 95125 854-B6
MARSHALL AV
400 SJS 95125 854-B2
400 SUNV 94086 812-F7
MARSHALL CT
600 SCL 95051 833-B6
1700 LALT 94024 832-A5
MARSHALL DR
400 SCIC 95020 957-J4
800 PA 94303 791-C5
MARSHALL LN
18500 SAR 95070 872-H2
MARSHGLEN CT
2300 SJS 95133 834-F2
MARSH MANOR WY
3500 SJS 95121 855-D7
MARSHWELL WY
5800 SJS 95138 875-D5
MARSTON LN
- SCL 95054 813-E4
MARSTON WY
3000 SJS 95148 835-F7
3000 SJS 95148 855-F1
MARTELLO DR
1800 SJS 95122 854-G1
MARTEN AV
3100 SJS 95127 835-B5
3100 SJS 95148 835-D4
MARTENS AV
100 MTVW 94040 811-J7
300 MTVW 94040 812-A7
MARTHA AV
18500 SAR 95070 852-H7
MARTHA ST
- SJS 95112 854-C1
300 SJS 95112 834-D7
MARTI WY
200 SJS 95136 874-G1
MARTIGUES CT
- SJS 95148 855-G2
MARTIL WY
300 MPS 95035 794-A5
MARTIN AV
300 SJS 95050 833-F2
300 SJS 95110 833-F2
300 SCL 95050 833-C2
1100 SJS 95126 833-H7
1200 PA 94301 791-A4
1600 SUNV 94087 832-F5
1600 SJS 95128 833-H7
1600 SJS 95128 853-H1
MARTIN RUN
300 SBnC 95023 1059-H2
MARTIN ST
- GIL 95020 978-A3
MARTINIQUE CT
600 SJS 95123 874-G4
MARTIN JUE ST
1700 SJS 95131 834-D1
MARTINSEN CT
400 PA 94306 791-C7
MARTINVALE LN
100 SJS 95119 875-E7
200 SJS 95119 895-E1
MARTINWOOD WY
10600 CPTO 95014 852-E2
MARTIRI CT
- GIL 95020 957-G7
MARTIRI DR
- GIL 95020 957-G7
MARTWOOD WY
7000 SJS 95120 894-H4
MARTY RD
200 SCrC 95033 912-G3
MARVIN AV
- LALT 94022 811-E7
MARY AV
500 SUNV 94086 812-D5
10000 CPTO 95014 832-C7
10000 CPTO 95014 852-C1
N MARY AV
100 SUNV 94086 812-D5
S MARY AV
100 SUNV 94086 812-C7
400 SUNV 94086 832-C2
600 SUNV 94087 832-C2
10800 CPTO 95014 832-C6
MARY CT
800 CMBL 95008 853-C7
1200 SCIC 95020 957-J1
MARY DR
- HOLL 95023 1040-B6
MARY WY
100 LGTS 95032 873-D6
MARY ALICE DR
100 LGTS 95032 873-D4
MARY ALICE WY
21400 SCIC 95033 912-J3
MARYANN DR
800 SCL 95050 833-C5
MARY CAROLINE CT
2900 SJS 95133 814-G6
MARY CAROLINE DR
700 SJS 95133 814-G6
MARY EVELYN DR
600 SJS 95123 874-H7
MARY HELEN LN
- SJS 95136 854-E6
MARY JANE WY
4800 SJS 95124 873-H4
MARY JO CT
5400 SJS 95124 873-H5
MARY JO LN
1400 SCIC 95046 937-H4
MARY JO WY
5300 SJS 95124 873-H6
MARYLAND ST
1700 RDWC 94061 790-A3
MARY LEE WY
1200 SJS 95118 874-B1
MARYLINN DR
- MPS 95035 793-H6
- MPS 95035 794-A6
MARYMEADE LN
1600 LALT 94024 831-J4
MARYMONT AV
- ATN 94027 790-B4
MARYMONTE CT
6500 SJS 95120 894-C1
MARY-VIN LN
800 SCL 95051 832-J6
MASON WY
6700 SJS 95129 852-E3
MASONI PL
- GIL 95020 977-J6
MASONIC AV
- SJS 95125 854-E4
MASONIC DR
2500 SJS 95125 854-D5
MASONWOOD ST
2700 SJS 95148 835-C7
2700 SJS 95148 855-C1
MASSACHUSETTS AV
2800 RDWC 94061 790-A3
MASSACHUSETTS DR
4900 SJS 95136 874-F3
MASSAR AV
400 SJS 95116 834-H4
MASSIDDA CT
1600 SJS 95118 873-J4
MASSIH CT
1300 SJS 95008 873-A1
MASSOL AV
- LGTS 95030 872-J7
100 LGTS 95030 873-A7
MASSOL CT
- LGTS 95030 872-J7
MASSON CT
14700 SAR 95070 872-B2
MASSON TERRACE CIR
18800 SAR 95070 852-B7
MAST ST
100 MGH 95037 937-B1
MASTEN AV
- SCIC 95020 957-G3
700 SCIC 95020 958-A2
MASTERS CT
3700 SJS 95111 854-J6
47800 FRMT 94539 793-H1
MASTIC ST
1000 SJS 95110 854-C2
MASUDA LNDG
1800 SJS 95132 814-C4
MAT AV
300 SJS 95123 874-J5
MATADERO AV
200 PA 94306 811-C1
MATADERO CT
800 PA 94306 811-B2
MATADERO DR
100 SUNV 94086 812-C7
MATADERO CREEK CT
28600 LAH 94022 810-H7
28600 LAH 94022 830-H1
MATADERO CREEK LN
28500 LAH 94022 810-H7
MATADOR DR
900 HOLL 95023 1040-C4
MATARO WY
- SJS 95135 855-G6
MATHER DR
2300 SJS 95116 834-G2
MATHEW ST
300 SCL 95050 833-E2
N MATHILDA AV
100 SUNV 94086 812-E6
800 SUNV 94089 812-E2
S MATHILDA AV
100 SUNV 94086 812-D7
300 SUNV 94086 832-D2
600 SUNV 94087 832-D2
MATHILDA CT
100 MGH 95037 937-A1
MATILIJA DR
15800 SCIC 95030 872-G6
15800 MSER 95030 872-G6
MATISEE PL
- SJS 95148 855-G2
MATISEE TER
- SJS 95148 855-G2
MATISEE WY
- SJS 95148 855-G2
MATISSE CT
1200 SUNV 94087 832-E3
MATOS CT
1800 SCL 95050 833-D5
MATSON DR
1600 SJS 95124 873-J2
MATTERHORN CT
900 MPS 95035 814-D1
MATTERHORN DR
1100 SJS 95132 814-F5
MATTHEW CT
6400 SJS 95123 875-C7
MATTHEWS CT
400 MPS 95035 794-A3
MATTHIAS CT
2700 SJS 95121 854-H3
MATTHIAS DR
2700 SJS 95121 854-H3
MATTIQUE DR
3000 SJS 95135 855-E2
MATTOS AV
3000 SJS 95132 814-F4
MATTOS DR
2300 MPS 95035 794-E7
MATTS CT
900 LALT 94024 831-E1
MATTSON AV
200 LGTS 95032 873-A2
MATULICH CT
200 HOLL 95023 1039-H3
MATZLEY CT
3100 SJS 95124 873-H2
MATZLEY DR
1700 SJS 95124 873-H2
MAUDE AV
18600 SAR 95070 872-H4
E MAUDE AV
100 SUNV 94086 812-F6
W MAUDE AV
100 SUNV 94086 812-D5
800 MTVW 94043 812-C4
MAUDE CT
500 SUNV 94086 812-D5
MAUI CT
3900 SJS 95111 855-A6
MAUI DR
3800 SJS 95111 855-A6
MAUNA KEA LN
1300 SJS 95132 814-F4
MAUNA LOA CT
3000 SJS 95132 814-F5
MAUNEY CT
3700 SJS 95130 853-C4
MAUREEN AV
400 PA 94306 791-D7
MAUREEN WY
20700 SAR 95070 852-D5
MAURER LN
26100 LAH 94022 811-B6
MAURICE LN
1500 SJS 95129 852-H5
MAURICIA AV
2700 SCL 95051 833-A7
3200 SCL 95051 832-J7
MAVERICK CT
1300 SCIC 95046 937-H7
MAXEY DR
1000 SJS 95132 814-G5
MAXIMILIAN DR
2200 SJS 95008 853-C7
MAXINE AV
1400 SJS 95125 854-A6
MAXINE DR
400 SUNV 94086 832-E1
10700 CPTO 95014 832-B6
MAXWELL WY
1300 SJS 95131 814-C7
1300 SJS 95131 834-C1
MAY CT
3800 PA 94303 811-E1
MAY DR
100 SJS 95138 875-D4
MAY LN
- LALT 94022 811-E5
3400 SJS 95124 873-F2
MAYA WY
16100 SCIC 95030 893-C2
MAYALL CT
1700 SJS 95132 814-D4
MAYAN LN
1700 SCIC 95046 938-A7
4200 SCIC 95046 937-J7
MAYBELL AV
500 PA 94306 811-C3
MAYBELL WY
4100 PA 94306 811-C3
MAYBERRY LN
- SJS 95131 834-C1
MAY BROWN AV
1100 MLPK 94025 790-E4
MAYBURY SQ
800 SJS 95133 814-G7
MAYELLEN AV
300 SJS 95126 853-H1
MAYER CT
- LALT 94022 811-F6
MAYETTE AV
1100 SJS 95125 854-B6
MAYFAIR PL
1800 SJS 95116 834-G4
MAYFIELD AV
200 MTVW 94043 811-F3
500 SCIC 94305 790-G7
500 SCIC 94305 810-H1
1900 SJS 95130 852-J6
MAYFIELD CT
4900 SJS 95130 852-J6
MAYFLOWER CT
1700 MTVW 94040 811-F5
5900 SJS 95129 852-G4
MAYGLEN CT
2800 SJS 95133 814-G7
MAYGLEN WY
2800 SJS 95133 814-G7
MAYHEW CT
1300 SJS 95121 854-J2
MAYHEW DR
1200 SJS 95121 854-J2
MAYKIRK CT
1700 SJS 95124 853-H6
MAYKIRK RD
2000 SJS 95124 853-H6
MAYLAND AV
5400 SJS 95138 875-C3
MAYLAND CT
100 SJS 95138 875-C3
MAYME AV
5400 SJS 95129 852-H5
MAYME CT
- SBnC 95023 1060-F2
MAYNARD CT
- LALT 94022 811-E5
MAYNARD WY
- LALT 94022 811-E5
MAYO DR
6200 SJS 95123 875-B7
MAYO WY
300 SJS 95123 875-B7
MAYOCK RD
300 GIL 95020 978-B6
MAYS AV
16000 LGTS 95030 873-A6
16000 MSER 95030 873-A6
MAYSONG CT
1700 SJS 95131 814-D7
MAYSUN CT
1400 CMBL 95008 873-A1
MAYTEN WY
100 FRMT 94539 793-J1
MAYTEN GROVE CT
5300 SJS 95123 874-J3
MAYTEN TREE CT
700 SUNV 94086 832-G2
MAYVIEW AV
700 PA 94303 811-E1
700 PA 94303 791-E7

STREET
Block City ZIP Pg-Grid

MAYWOOD AV
2200 SCIC 95128 853-F3
2200 SJS 95128 853-F3
MAYWOOD CT
900 LALT 94024 831-F1
MAYWOOD LN
- MLPK 94025 790-F5
MAZEY ST
100 MPS 95035 793-J3
100 MPS 95035 794-A3
MAZZAGLIA AV
2300 SJS 95125 854-B6
MAZZONE DR
900 SJS 95120 874-D6
MCABEE RD
5900 SJS 95120 874-C7
6400 SJS 95120 894-C1
17500 SCIC 95120 894-B2
MCABEE ESTATES PL
1200 SJS 95120 874-C7
MCALISTER DR
700 SJS 95128 833-F7
MCANDREW CT
2800 SJS 95121 855-D3
MCANN CT
2800 SJS 95121 855-D3
MCAULEY CT
1000 PA 94301 791-A3
MCBAIN AV
1000 CMBL 95008 853-G5
1700 SCIC 95125 853-G5
MCBAIN CT
1000 CMBL 95008 853-G6
MCBRIDE LP
- SJS 95125 854-C7
MCCALL DR
6900 SJS 95120 894-F3
MCCAMISH AV
400 SJS 95123 875-A6
MCCANDLESS DR
1800 MPS 95035 814-A3
MCCARTHY BLVD
500 MPS 95035 813-H1
N MCCARTHY BLVD
500 MPS 95035 793-H5
500 MPS 95035 813-H1
1700 MPS 95002 793-H5
1900 SJS 95002 793-H5
1900 FRMT 94538 793-H5
MCCARTHY LN
- SJS 95134 793-F7
MCCARTHY ST
100 HOLL 95023 1040-A3
MCCARTY AV
500 MTVW 94041 812-A6
600 MTVW 94041 811-J6
MCCARTY RANCH DR
8700 SJS 95135 855-J6
8700 SJS 95135 856-A6
MCCARTYSVILLE PL
12600 SAR 95070 852-D6
MCCARY DR
- SBnC 95023 1059-J3
MCCLELLAN PL
10500 CPTO 95014 852-D2
MCCLELLAN RD
7800 CPTO 95014 852-A2
MCCLOSKEY RD
100 HOLL 95023 1040-B1
100 SBnC 95023 1040-B1
MCCLUHAN WY
1700 SJS 95132 814-D4
MCCLURE LN
1300 LALT 94024 831-J3
MCCOLLAM DR
500 SJS 95127 814-J7
MCCONNELL DR
12200 SCIC 95046 957-G1
MCCONNELL RD
400 SBnC 95023 1019-F5
MCCOPPIN PARK CT
3500 SJS 95124 873-E2
MCCORD AV
- SCIC 94035 812-B2
- SCIC 94043 812-B2
MCCORMICK DR
1500 SCL 95050 833-C4
MCCORMICK LN
- ATN 94027 790-E1
MCCOVEY LN
400 SJS 95127 835-B2
MCCOY AV
1500 CMBL 95008 853-A7
1500 CMBL 95130 853-A7
4400 SJS 95130 853-A7
4700 SJS 95130 852-J7
18200 SAR 95070 852-H7
MCCRAY ST
- HOLL 95023 1040-A3
300 SBnC 95023 1040-B5
MCCREERY AV
- SJS 95116 834-F4
MCCREERY CT
1800 SJS 95116 834-G5
MCCULLOCH WY
13200 SAR 95070 852-H7
MCDANIEL AV
1400 SJS 95126 833-G6
1700 SJS 95128 833-F7
MCDOLE ST
13100 SAR 95070 852-H7
MCDONALD CIR
- HOLL 95023 1040-D5
MCDONALD LN
2200 SCIC 95037 917-D4
MC DUFF AV
200 FRMT 94539 793-H1
MCDUFF AV
200 FRMT 94539 793-H1
MCEVOY ST
200 RDWC 94061 790-B1
200 SJS 95126 834-A7
200 SJS 95126 854-A1
200 SCIC 95126 854-A1

MCFARLAND AV
18500 SAR 95070 852-H7
MCFARLAND CT
100 SCIC 94305 790-J7
MCGILL RD
16900 SCIC 95070 872-C7
16900 SCIC 95070 892-C1
MCGILVRA CT
5800 SJS 95123 875-A5
MCGINNESS AV
1000 SJS 95127 834-J4
1000 SJS 95127 835-A5
E MCGLINCEY LN
200 CMBL 95008 853-E7
MCGRAW AV
16700 MGH 95037 937-A1
MCGREGOR WY
1000 PA 94306 811-B3
1500 SJS 95129 852-E5
MCINTOSH AV
1200 SUNV 94087 832-C3
MCINTOSH CT
1200 SUNV 94087 832-C3
MCINTOSH CREEK DR
1100 SJS 95120 894-G3
MCKAY DR
1000 SJS 95131 814-B6
MCKEAN CT
7100 SJS 95120 894-J4
MCKEAN RD
19500 SJS 95120 894-H4
MCKEAN RD Rt#-G8
19600 SJS 95120 894-J4
19600 SCIC 95120 894-J4
20000 SCIC 95120 895-A4
22400 SJS 95120 895-F6
22400 SJS 95141 895-F6
23500 SJS 95141 915-G1
23500 SCIC 95141 915-G1
23900 SCIC 95037 915-G1
MCKEE RD
300 SCIC 95127 834-H1
300 SCIC 95127 815-A7
1200 SJS 95116 834-H1
1500 SJS 95133 834-H1
2700 SJS 95127 834-H1
2900 SCIC 95133 834-H1
3600 SCIC 95127 814-J7
3600 SJS 95127 814-J7
5100 SJS 95127 815-A7
MCKELLAR DR
5600 SJS 95129 852-G4
MCKELLAR LN
4200 PA 94306 811-D2
MCKELVY LN
15900 MGH 95037 937-A3
15900 SCIC 95037 937-A3
MCKENDRIE ST
300 SJS 95110 833-J4
800 SJS 95126 833-G6
MCKENDRY DR
100 MLPK 94025 790-J2
MCKENDRY PL
300 MLPK 94025 790-J3
MCKENZIE AV
1300 LALT 94024 831-H2
MCKENZIE PL
- SJS 95131 814-D6
MCKILLOP CT
- SCL 95050 833-G5
MCKINLEY AV
200 SUNV 94086 832-E1
1400 SCIC 95126 853-H3
1400 SJS 95126 853-H3
E MCKINLEY AV
400 SUNV 94086 832-E1
W MCKINLEY AV
400 SUNV 94086 812-B7
MCKINLEY DR
2900 SCL 95051 833-A7
3300 SCL 95051 832-J7
MCKINLEY ST
1100 RDWC 94061 790-A1
MCKINNON CT
1500 SJS 95130 853-A5
MCKINNON DR
4200 SJS 95130 853-A4
17700 SJS 95070 853-A4
MCKLINTOCK LN
10200 CPTO 95014 851-J1
MCLAREN PL
10100 CPTO 95014 832-F7
MCLAUGHLIN AV
500 SJS 95116 834-E5
700 SJS 95122 834-E5
1600 SJS 95122 854-G1
2400 SJS 95121 854-G1
3000 SJS 95121 855-A4
17700 MGH 95037 917-A7
MCLAUGHLIN CT
- MGH 95037 916-J6
- MGH 95037 917-A6
MCLELLAN AV
300 SJS 95110 854-B1
MCMAHON RD
600 SBnC 95023 1020-G2
MCMURDIE DR
1200 CMBL 95008 873-D1
MCNAIR ST
- EPA 94303 791-C3
MCNIFF PL
- SJS 95124 853-H7
MCPHEE RD
- SCIC 95037 935-F7
MC PHERSON ST
1300 SCL 95051 832-J4
MCQUESTEN DR
1300 SJS 95122 834-G7
MCVAY AV
10400 SCIC 95127 835-B1
MCVAY CT
14800 SCIC 95127 835-B1
MEAD AV
2800 SCL 95051 833-A1

MEADOW AV
500 SCL 95051 832-H6
E MEADOW CIR
1000 PA 94303 791-E7
MEADOW CT
- SBnC 95023 1020-G3
- SBnC 95075 1061-A5
1200 MGH 95037 917-C6
E MEADOW DR
100 PA 94306 811-D1
500 PA 94306 791-E7
500 PA 94303 791-E7
W MEADOW DR
200 PA 94306 811-D2
MEADOW LN
- ATN 94027 790-B6
300 SCIC 95127 835-A2
300 SJS 95127 835-A2
600 LALT 94022 811-C4
1400 MTVW 94040 811-G7
1500 SBnC 95023 1020-G3
MEADOW PL
10300 CPTO 95014 851-J1
MEADOWBROOK DR
100 LGTS 95032 873-G6
2400 SCL 95051 833-A2
MEADOW CREEK CT
- PTLV 94028 810-D7
MEADOW CREEK DR
600 SJS 95136 874-E1
MEADOW DALE CT
400 SJS 95136 874-F1
MEADOWFAIRE COM
- FRMT 94539 793-J3
MEADOWFAIRE DR
- SJS 95111 854-G4
MEADOWFAIRE PL
- SJS 95111 854-G4
MEADOWFAIRE WY
- SJS 95111 854-G4
MEADOWFIELD LN
2600 SJS 95135 875-J1
MEADOWGATE WY
2100 SJS 95132 814-D2
MEADOW GLEN CT
1500 SJS 95121 855-B4
MEADOW GLEN WY
1400 SJS 95121 855-B4
MEADOWGREEN WY
- MGH 95037 916-H3
MEADOWHAVEN WY
200 MPS 95035 794-A6
MEADOWHURST CT
4500 SJS 95136 874-E2
MEADOWLAKE DR
200 SUNV 94089 812-H4
MEADOWLAND DR
- MPS 95035 794-A6
MEADOWLANDS LN
2900 SJS 95135 855-H7
3100 SJS 95135 856-A7
MEADOWLARK AV
1200 SJS 95128 833-E6
MEADOWLARK LN
1500 SUNV 94087 832-G5
2400 SCIC 95020 958-C3
MEADOWLEAF CT
2600 SJS 95135 875-J1
MEADOWMONT DR
2300 SJS 95133 814-H3
2300 SJS 95133 834-E1
MEADOW OAK RD
20700 SAR 95070 852-D5
MEADOWOOD DR
100 PTLV 94028 810-B5
900 SJS 95120 894-E1
MEADOW PINE PL
- SJS 95125 854-D5
MEADOW RIDGE CIR
1300 SJS 95131 814-C7
MEADOWSIDE CT
- SJS 95136 874-J7
MEADOWVIEW LN
21800 CPTO 95014 832-B7
MEADOWVILLE CT
4400 SJS 95129 853-A2
MEADOW VISTA CT
6700 SJS 95135 855-J7
6700 SJS 95135 875-J1
MEADOW WAY CIR
1200 HOLL 95023 1040-C5
MEADWELL CT
- SJS 95138 875-D4
MEANDER DR
5800 SJS 95120 874-B6
MEARS CT
900 SCIC 94305 810-J1
MEDALLION DR
1300 SJS 95120 874-B7
MEDEIRAS TER
300 MPS 95035 793-H3
MEDFORD DR
1500 LALT 94024 832-A3
MEDIA WY
2600 SJS 95125 853-J7
MEDICUS CT
18600 CPTO 95014 852-H1
MEDINA CT
22600 CPTO 95014 851-J1
MEDINA LN
22700 CPTO 95014 851-J1
MEDITATION DR
- SJS 95125 854-E4
MEDITATION PL
- MPS 95035 814-J1
MEDLEY CT
1200 SJS 95121 855-A4
MEDLEY DR
- SJS 95121 855-A4
MEDOC CT
400 MTVW 94043 811-G2
MEDWIN CT
3000 SJS 95148 855-C2

MEG CT
9500 SCIC 95020 958-E4
MEG DR
4200 SJS 95136 874-F1
MEI DR
700 MGH 95037 917-D7
MEIGGS LN
19000 CPTO 95014 852-G2
MEKLER CT
500 SJS 95111 854-G3
MELANIE LN
- ATN 94027 790-A5
- WDSD 94027 790-A5
MELANNIE CT
700 SJS 95116 834-F6
MELBA CT
1200 SJS 95120 894-E2
1500 MTVW 94022 811-G5
1500 MTVW 94040 811-G5
MELBOURNE BLVD
900 SJS 95116 834-E6
MELCHESTER DR
3000 SJS 95132 814-E3
MELCHOIR CT
900 SCIC 95046 957-F5
MELINDA CIR
19300 SAR 95070 852-G5
MELINDA CT
500 HOLL 95023 1040-B4
MELISSA CT
2500 SJS 95121 854-J2
10300 CPTO 95014 851-J1
MELLO DR
600 SJS 95134 813-H5
MELLO PL
10100 CPTO 95014 852-F1
MELLO ST
1100 EPA 94303 791-A1
MELLON DR
18900 SAR 95070 852-H6
MELLOWOOD DR
12200 SAR 95070 852-G5
MELNIKOFF DR
3000 SJS 95121 855-C5
MELODY LN
- MGH 95037 937-B5
1600 SJS 95133 834-E3
3800 SCL 95051 832-H6
12400 LAH 94022 830-J1
17000 SCIC 95033 913-A4
MELON CT
700 SUNV 94087 832-C1
MELROSE AV
- SJS 95116 834-F3
MELVILLE AV
100 PA 94301 791-A5
MELVILLE WY
2400 SJS 95130 852-J7
MELVIN DR
6800 SJS 95129 852-E3
MELVIN HENRY CT
- SMCo 94061 790-A4
MELWOOD DR
1300 SJS 95118 874-B4
MEMBRILLO CORTE
3100 SCL 95051 833-A5
MEMOREX DR
900 SCL 95050 833-D2
MEMORIAL DR
400 HOLL 95023 1040-C4
MEMORIAL WY
100 SCIC 94305 790-H6
MEMORY LN
100 CMBL 95008 853-G6
MEMPHIS DR
300 CMBL 95008 853-C5
MENALTO AV
1900 MLPK 94025 791-A2
2100 EPA 94303 791-A1
MENALTO DR
12200 LAH 94022 830-H1
MENARD DR
100 SJS 95138 875-G6
MENAUL CT
7100 SJS 95139 875-F7
MENDELSOHN LN
20000 SAR 95070 872-E3
MENDENHALL DR
1500 SJS 95130 853-B5
MENDOCINO LN
- SJS 95124 873-F4
MENDOCINO WY
700 MGH 95037 937-B5
MENDOTA WY
2000 SJS 95122 834-J7
2100 SJS 95122 835-A7
MENDOZA AV
4700 SJS 95111 875-A1
MENHART DR
10200 CPTO 95014 852-H1
MENKER AV
400 SJS 95128 853-H2
400 SJS 95126 853-H2
MENLO AV
600 MLPK 94025 790-F4
MENLO DR
6300 SJS 95120 874-E7
6300 SJS 95120 894-E1
MENLO OAKS AV
200 SMCo 94025 790-H2
1000 MLPK 94025 790-H2
MENORCA CT
1400 SJS 95120 874-B7
MENTE LINDA LP
- MPS 95035 813-J1
- MPS 95035 814-A1
MENZEL PL
2100 SCL 95050 833-C3
MENZEL RD
- SBnC 95023 1040-F3
MERANO DR
100 SJS 95134 813-D2
MERCADO CT
600 MPS 95035 794-B5

MERCED CT
3100 SCL 95051 833-A3
MERCEDES AV
800 LALT 94022 811-D4
MERCEDES DR
- MGH 95037 917-A6
MERCEDES LN
- ATN 94027 790-D2
MERCEDES RD
22700 CPTO 95014 851-J2
MERCER AV
1400 SJS 95125 853-J5
MERCURY CT
1400 MPS 95035 794-D7
MERCURY DR
- HOLL 95023 1020-A6
400 SUNV 94086 812-J6
MERCURY ST
48000 FRMT 94539 793-J1
MERCY ST
- MTVW 94041 812-A6
- MTVW 94041 811-H5
MEREDITH AV
1100 SJS 95125 854-A3
MERIDA DR
20200 SAR 95070 852-E5
MERIDAN AV
200 SCIC 95126 833-J7
200 SCIC 95126 853-J1
200 SJS 95126 853-J1
200 SJS 95126 833-J7
MERIDIAN AV
500 SJS 95128 853-J6
800 SJS 95126 853-J6
1000 SJS 95125 853-J6
1300 SCIC 95125 853-J6
1900 SJS 95124 853-J6
2600 SJS 95125 873-J1
2600 SJS 95124 873-J1
2900 SJS 95118 873-J1
3000 SCIC 95126 853-J3
3300 SJS 95118 874-A2
3300 SJS 95124 874-A2
5800 SJS 95120 874-B7
6200 SJS 95120 894-C1
MERIDIAN ST
900 HOLL 95023 1040-B4
1100 SBnC 95023 1040-E4
MERIDIAN WY
700 SJS 95126 853-J2
1800 MTVW 94043 811-H4
MERION CT
- GIL 95020 977-H7
MERION DR
200 SJS 95116 834-F5
MERITAGE CT
- SCIC 95020 976-J2
- SCIC 95020 977-A2
MERKELEY ROW ST
10200 SCIC 95127 815-D7
MERLE AV
1000 SJS 95125 854-A3
MERLIN LN
500 SJS 95111 854-F6
MERLONE CT
- SJS 95008 873-F3
MERLOT CT
4200 SJS 95135 855-G4
MERLOT DR
- MGH 95037 917-E6
400 FRMT 94539 793-J2
600 FRMT 94539 794-A2
MERLOT LN
- GIL 95020 977-G4
MERRIBROOK CT
19800 SAR 95070 872-F1
MERRIBROOK DR
19700 SAR 95070 872-F1
MERRICK DR
20200 SAR 95070 872-E1
MERRILL DR
1600 SJS 95124 873-J5
MERRILL LP
1600 SJS 95124 873-J5
1600 SJS 95118 873-J5
MERRILL PL
- SCL 95051 832-J4
MERRILL RD
100 SBnC 95045 1037-H1
MERRILL ST
1000 MLPK 94025 790-F3
MERRIMAC DR
500 CMBL 95008 853-D4
1000 SUNV 94087 832-B2
3300 SJS 95117 853-D4
MERRIMAN LN
12400 SCIC 95020 956-H3
MERRIMAN RD
10300 CPTO 95014 851-J2
MERRITON CT
1600 SJS 95124 873-J4
MERRITT DR
19600 CPTO 95014 832-E7
MERRITT RD
100 LALT 94022 811-E6
MERRITT TER
- SUNV 94086 812-C7
MERRIVALE WEST SQ
1300 SJS 95117 853-C4
MERRIWEATHER LN
400 SJS 95134 813-C2
MERRY LN
1400 SJS 95128 853-E5
MERRYWOOD DR
1300 SJS 95118 874-B4
MERVYNS WY
2700 SJS 95127 834-J4
MERZ CT
200 MPS 95035 794-A5
MESA AV
800 PA 94306 811-B4
MESA CT
- ATN 94027 790-B5
800 PA 94306 811-C4

MESA CT
1400 HOLL 95023 1040-D6
MESA DR
1100 SJS 95118 874-C4
1100 SJS 95131 814-A5
1200 HOLL 95023 1040-C6
MESA RD
200 SCIC 95020 978-A7
200 SCIC 95020 998-A1
5200 GIL 95020 978-A7
5500 GIL 95020 977-J6
MESA OAK CT
900 SUNV 94086 832-G2
MESA VERDE DR
2000 MPS 95035 794-E7
MESCALERO DR
5900 SJS 95123 874-H5
MESITA WY
1800 SJS 95124 873-H1
MESQUITE DR
1400 HOLL 95023 1040-D5
2800 SCL 95051 833-B7
MESQUITE PL
800 SUNV 94086 832-G2
MESSINA DR
1600 SJS 95132 814-F3
META DR
2500 SJS 95130 853-A7
METCALF RD
- SCIC 95037 896-J3
- SCIC 95137 896-J3
- SJS 95037 896-J3
100 SJS 95138 875-J7
200 SJS 95138 876-C6
300 SCIC 95137 876-F5
600 SCIC 95138 876-F5
1100 SCIC 95037 876-F5
METEOR DR
21300 CPTO 95014 832-C6
METEOR PL
10500 CPTO 95014 832-C6
METHILHAVEN CT
3300 SJS 95121 855-C5
METHILHAVEN LN
3300 SJS 95121 855-C5
METHVEN LN
1200 MPS 95035 814-C1
METLER CT
18700 SAR 95070 872-H1
METRO CIR
1000 PA 94303 791-D5
METRO DR
100 SJS 95110 833-H2
METROPOLITAN DR
- MPS 95035 814-J1
METROPOLITAN WY
- SJS 95135 855-F3
METRO WALK DR
- MPS 95035 814-J2
MEYER CIR
3000 SJS 95121 855-B3
3000 SJS 95148 855-B3
MEYERHOLZ CT
21700 CPTO 95014 832-B7
MEZZAMONTE PL
- SJS 95148 855-G1
MIA CIR
4600 SJS 95136 874-H2
MIAMI DR
1600 SJS 95122 834-H7
MICA CT
- HOLL 95023 1039-J4
MICHAEL CT
1400 MPS 95035 794-C5
20300 CPTO 95014 852-E2
MICHAEL DR
200 CMBL 95008 853-F6
MICHAEL LN
15600 MSER 95030 873-A5
MICHAEL ST
600 MPS 95035 794-C5
MICHAEL WY
- SCL 95051 832-J7
MICHAELS DR
20800 SAR 95070 872-C2
MICHAELS WY
- ATN 94027 790-E3
MICH BLUFF DR
1300 SJS 95131 814-D6
MICHELANGELO DR
- SJS 95135 855-F2
900 SUNV 94087 832-E3
MICHELE CT
17400 MGH 95037 917-D5
MICHELE WY
6700 SJS 95129 852-E3
MICHELE JEAN WY
2400 SCL 95050 833-C6
MICHELLE DR
200 CMBL 95008 853-B5
MICHIGAN AV
900 SJS 95125 854-A4
1200 SJS 95002 793-C7
1200 SJS 95002 813-B1
1600 EPA 94303 791-B1
MICHIGAN RD
200 MPS 95035 794-A5
MICHON CT
1700 SJS 95124 873-H4
MICHON DR
1700 SJS 95124 873-J4
MICRO CT
1000 SJS 95120 894-H4
MICRO PL
1000 SJS 95120 894-H4
MIDAS WY
1200 SUNV 94086 812-J6
MIDDLE AV
600 MLPK 94025 790-F5
E MIDDLE AV
- MGH 95046 937-E4
100 SCIC 95046 937-G3
W MIDDLE AV
- MGH 95037 937-C4

W MIDDLE AV
- SCIC 95037 937-C4
MIDDLE CT
400 MLPK 94025 790-F6
MIDDLEBOROUGH CIR
2600 SJS 95132 814-D4
MIDDLEBURY DR
500 SUNV 94087 832-D2
MIDDLEBURY LN
- LALT 94022 811-D6
MIDDLEBURY WY
7200 SJS 95139 875-G7
MIDDLE ELLEN RD
15000 ScrC 95018 912-E5
MIDDLEFIELD AV
- MTVW 94043 811-G2
MIDDLEFIELD RD
- ATN 94027 790-E1
- PA 94301 790-E1
500 MLPK 94025 790-E1
600 PA 94301 791-A4
1600 PA 94303 791-A4
2600 PA 94306 791-A4
3100 SMCo 94063 790-D1
3200 SMCo 94025 790-D1
3600 PA 94303 811-E1
3600 PA 94306 811-E1
E MIDDLEFIELD RD
- MTVW 94043 812-B4
600 MTVW 94086 812-B4
700 SUNV 94086 812-B4
W MIDDLEFIELD RD
500 MTVW 94043 811-H3
500 MTVW 94043 812-A4
700 SCIC 94043 811-H3
MIDDLE FORK LN
13400 LAH 94022 810-J7
MIDDLE GATE ST
- ATN 94027 790-D2
MIDDLE PARK DR
4000 SJS 95135 855-F3
MIDDLETON AV
1600 LALT 94024 831-J4
MIDDLETON CT
1300 LALT 94024 831-J4
MIDDLETOWN DR
2200 SJS 95008 853-B7
MIDFIELD AV
1300 SJS 95122 834-G7
MIDHURST CT
3100 SJS 95135 855-F3
MIDHURST WY
2900 SJS 95135 855-E3
MIDPINE AV
1100 SJS 95122 854-H2
MIDPINE CT
22700 ScrC 95033 912-J5
MIDROCK CORNERS
- MTVW 94043 811-G2
MIDTOWN CT
2700 PA 94303 791-C6
MIDTOWN PL
- SJS 95136 854-E5
MIDVALE LN
800 SJS 95136 874-E1
N MIDWAY ST
- CMBL 95008 853-G6
S MIDWAY ST
200 CMBL 95008 853-G6
MIDWICK DR
- MPS 95035 794-A5
MIELKE DR
400 MLPK 94025 790-G3
MIETTE WY
1300 SUNV 94087 832-C4
MIGNON DR
2600 SJS 95132 814-D4
MIGNOT LN
400 SJS 95111 854-J6
MIGUEL AV
1100 LALT 94024 831-H4
MIGUELITO RD
10200 SCIC 95127 815-B6
10200 SCIC 95127 835-C1
MILAN DR
400 SJS 95134 813-H4
MILANI CT
- ATN 94027 790-E3
MILANO TER
100 LGTS 95030 873-B4
300 MPS 95035 793-H3
MILANO WY
1900 MTVW 94040 831-H1
MILAS CT
7400 GIL 95020 977-H3
MILBRAE LN
200 LGTS 95032 873-B6
MILBURN ST
3500 SJS 95148 835-E6
MILDRED AV
1200 SJS 95125 854-A4
1400 SJS 95125 853-J5
MILES AV
- LGTS 95030 873-A7
MILES CT
800 SCL 95051 833-A5
MILES DR
2900 SCL 95051 833-A5
MILFORD DR
21300 CPTO 95014 832-C7
MILFORD WY
13900 SCIC 95127 835-A3
13900 SJS 95127 835-A3
MILHON CT
2600 SJS 95148 855-B1
MILITARY WY
500 PA 94306 811-C2
MILJEVICH DR
20000 SAR 95070 852-E7
MILKY WY
- SJS 95121 855-D4
1000 CPTO 95014 852-C3
MILL CT
- LGTS 95032 873-C3
18000 SAR 95070 852-D5

SANTA CLARA CO.

STREET	Block	City	ZIP	Pg-Grid
MILL RD				
	-	LGTS	95032	873-C4
	-	SJS	95002	793-B7
MILL ST				
	100	LGTS	95030	893-A1
MILLAR AV				
	-	SCIC	95127	834-J2
	-	SCIC	95127	835-A2
	-	SJS	95127	834-J2
	2800	SCL	95051	833-A3
MILLARD LN				
	21400	CPTO	95014	832-C6
MILLBRAE WY				
	2700	SJS	95121	855-D3
MILLBROOK CT				
	500	CMBL	95008	853-C6
MILLBROOK DR				
	3000	SJS	95148	855-D1
MILL CREEK LN				
	500	SCL	95054	813-E4
	5200	SJS	95136	875-A3
MILL CREEK WY				
	-	MGH	95037	916-H4
MILLER AV				
	-	SJS	95112	854-E3
	800	CMBL	95008	873-B1
	800	CPTO	95014	852-F4
	1000	GIL	95020	977-H4
	1000	SJS	95129	852-F4
	1600	SCIC	94024	831-F4
	2600	MTVW	94040	811-E3
	4200	PA	94306	811-E3
	12000	SAR	95070	852-G6
MILLER CT				
	-	SMCo	94061	790-B3
	4300	PA	94306	811-E3
	19300	SAR	95070	852-F5
MILLER RD				
	-	SBnC	95023	1039-H3
	-	HOLL	95023	1039-H3
MILLER ST				
	600	SJS	95110	834-A4
MILLER RIDGE RD				
	21000	SCrC	95033	892-A3
MILLET CT				
	3500	SJS	95127	835-C2
MILLHAVEN PL				
	100	SJS	95111	874-J1
MILLICENT CT				
	3500	SJS	95148	835-C4
MILLICH DR				
	500	CMBL	95008	853-C4
MILLICH LN				
	500	CMBL	95008	853-C4
	1200	SJS	95117	853-C4
MILLIE AV				
	900	MLPK	94025	790-F4
MILLIGAN DR				
	5400	SJS	95124	873-J6
MILLION CT				
	2600	SJS	95148	835-E6
MILL POND DR				
	300	SJS	95125	854-D5
	400	SCIC	95125	854-D5
MILLRICH DR				
	100	LGTS	95030	873-B4
MILL RISE WY				
	17100	LGTS	95030	893-D1
MILL RIVER LN				
	400	SJS	95134	813-H4
MILL RIVER PL				
	400	SJS	95134	813-F2
MILLS AV				
	600	LALT	94022	811-F6
	2000	SMCo	94025	790-C6
MILLS CT				
	900	SJS	95125	854-B2
	1400	MLPK	94025	790-F3
MILLS ST				
	1200	MLPK	94025	790-F3
MILLS CORNER LN				
	900	SJS	95122	854-G1
MILLSGATE LN				
	1700	SJS	95122	854-G1
MILL STONE LN				
	-	SJS	95136	875-A3
MILL STREAM DR				
	700	SJS	95125	854-D5
MILLSWOOD CT				
	700	SJS	95120	894-J3
MILLWATER CT				
	100	MPS	95035	794-C2
MILMAR WY				
	100	LGTS	95032	873-E5
MILMONT DR				
	-	FRMT	94538	793-H3
	1700	MPS	95035	793-J5
MILMONT ST				
	-	FRMT	94538	793-H2
MILO CT				
	800	SJS	95133	814-G6
N MILPITAS BLVD				
	100	MPS	95035	794-A5
	1100	MPS	95035	793-J3
S MILPITAS BLVD				
	-	MPS	95035	794-B7
	100	MPS	95035	814-B1
MILROY PL				
	1600	SJS	95124	873-J3
N MILTON AV				
	-	CMBL	95008	853-D5
S MILTON AV				
	-	CMBL	95008	853-D6
MILTON CT				
	3300	MTVW	94040	831-J2
MILTON ST				
	1600	SMCo	94061	790-B3
MILTON WY				
	1200	SJS	95125	854-B3
MILVERTON RD				
	600	LALT	94022	831-D1
MIMOSA CT				
	-	GIL	95020	977-E1
	500	LALT	94024	831-J6
MIMOSA ST				
	-	HOLL	95023	1040-D7
	-	HOLL	95023	1060-D1
MIMOSA WY				
	100	SMCo	94028	810-D4
	6200	SJS	95138	875-F6
MINA WY				
	-	SAR	95070	872-C1
MINAKER CT				
	10000	CPTO	95014	852-B1
MINARDI AV				
	1500	SJS	95125	854-A6
MINARET AV				
	200	MTVW	94043	812-A5
MINAS DR				
	4700	SJS	95136	874-D2
MINAS DE ORO				
	1700	SJS	95116	834-F3
MINDEN CT				
	5600	SJS	95123	875-A4
MINDY WY				
	600	SJS	95123	874-J7
MINE HILL RD				
	20500	SCIC	95120	894-H6
MINER PL				
	10100	CPTO	95014	832-E7
MINERAL SPRING WY				
	-	SCIC	95033	913-B3
MINETTE DR				
	10600	CPTO	95014	852-H2
MINETTE PL				
	10600	CPTO	95014	852-H2
MINIDOKA AV				
	100	SJS	95127	834-H1
MINNA WY				
	1900	SJS	95124	873-G1
MINNESOTA AV				
	300	SJS	95125	854-B2
	1200	SJS	95125	853-J4
MINNIS CIR				
	-	MPS	95035	793-J4
MINOCA RD				
	-	PTLV	94028	810-D5
MINOCQUA CT				
	19700	SAR	95070	872-F2
MINOR AV				
	400	SJS	95126	854-B1
	500	SJS	95125	854-B1
MINORCA CT				
	12500	LAH	94022	811-A7
MINORU DR				
	1000	SJS	95120	894-H4
MINTO CT				
	3500	SJS	95132	814-F2
MINTO DR				
	1900	SJS	95132	814-F2
MINTON LN				
	500	MTVW	94041	811-J5
MINTWOOD CT				
	4800	SJS	95129	852-B7
MINUET DR				
	1800	SJS	95131	814-D4
MINUTEMAN WY				
	1500	SJS	95132	814-E4
MIRA WY				
	-	SMCo	94028	810-D4
MIRABEAU CT				
	-	SJS	95132	814-G5
MIRABEAU LN				
	-	SJS	95132	814-G5
MIRA BELLA CIR				
	2700	MGH	95037	917-F7
MIRABELLA CT				
	1600	MPS	95035	794-D6
MIRA BELLA PL				
	16500	MGH	95037	917-F6
MIRABELLI CIR				
	-	SJS	95134	813-D2
MIRACLE MOUNTAIN DR				
	5900	SJS	95123	874-E5
MIRADA AV				
	600	SCIC	94305	810-H1
MIRADA DR				
	-	SJS	95134	813-F3
MIRADERO AV				
	15000	SCIC	95127	815-B6
	15800	SJS	95127	815-B6
MIRADOR CT				
	-	SJS	95116	834-F5
MIRADOR TER				
	-	SJS	95116	834-F5
MIRA FLORES CT				
	16500	MGH	95037	917-G6
MIRAFLORES WY				
	1200	LALT	94024	831-G2
MIRAGE WY				
	3200	SJS	95135	855-G3
MIRA LAGOS DR				
	16500	MGH	95037	917-G7
MIRA LOMA WY				
	3900	SJS	95111	854-J7
MIRALOMA WY				
	200	SUNV	94086	812-J7
	12500	LAH	94024	831-E2
MIRAMAR AV				
	4800	SJS	95129	852-J1
	4800	SJS	95129	853-A1
MIRAMAR WY				
	1100	SUNV	94086	832-H3
	3700	SCL	95051	832-H3
MIRAMESA CT				
	3700	SCL	95051	832-H3
MIRAMONTE AV				
	100	PA	94306	791-A6
	100	SCIC	95037	916-D2
	800	MTVW	94040	811-H7
	900	LALT	94024	831-H2
	900	MTVW	94040	831-H2
MIRAMONTE RD				
	10900	CPTO	95014	851-J2
	10900	CPTO	95014	852-A2
MIRANDA AV				
	3200	PA	94304	811-B4
	3700	PA	94306	811-C4
MIRANDA CT				
	14400	LAH	94022	811-C5
MIRANDA GRN				
	800	PA	94306	811-C5
MIRANDA RD				
	14000	LAH	94022	811-C6
MIRANDA WY				
	14300	LAH	94022	811-C6
MIRA PLAZA CT				
	1900	SCL	95051	832-H3
MIRASOL CT				
	6100	SJS	95123	874-F6
MIRASSOU DR				
	1600	SJS	95124	873-J5
MIRASSOU PL				
	1700	SJS	95124	873-J5
MIRASSOU ESTATE PL				
	-	SJS	95135	855-E2
MIRAVALLE AV				
	1300	LALT	94024	831-J3
MIRAVERDE CT				
	3700	SCL	95051	832-H3
MIRA VISTA CIR				
	3300	SJS	95132	814-H5
MIRA VISTA CT				
	3300	SJS	95132	814-H5
MIRA VISTA RD				
	10200	CPTO	95014	852-A1
MIREILLE DR				
	5600	SJS	95118	874-A6
MIREVAL RD				
	16200	LGTS	95030	893-D2
	16200	SCIC	95030	893-D2
MIRIAM CT				
	1700	SJS	95124	853-H6
MIRMIROU DR				
	13900	LAH	94022	810-H6
MISE AV				
	4900	SJS	95124	873-G4
MISSION AVD				
	-	MGH	95037	917-B3
MISSION DR				
	100	EPA	94303	791-C3
MISSION ST				
	-	SJB	95045	1038-D5
	500	SCL	95050	833-F5
E MISSION ST				
	-	SJS	95112	834-B3
W MISSION ST				
	-	SJS	95110	834-A4
	100	SJS	95110	833-J4
MISSION WY				
	-	CMBL	95008	853-D6
	21500	CPTO	95014	832-B7
MISSION COLLEGE BLVD				
	2000	SCL	95054	813-B5
	3000	SUNV	94089	813-A6
MISSION GLEN DR				
	2300	SCL	95051	833-B2
MISSION GREENS DR				
	2600	SJS	95148	835-C7
	2600	SJS	95148	855-C1
MISSION HILL PL				
	2500	SJS	95148	855-C1
MISSION SPRINGS CIR				
	1500	SJS	95131	814-C6
MISSION SPRINGS CT				
	1500	SJS	95131	814-C6
MISSION VIEW DR				
	18500	MGH	95037	917-A3
	18500	SCIC	95037	917-A3
MISSION VINEYARD RD				
	-	SBnC	95045	1038-E6
	-	SJB	95045	1038-E6
MISTAYA CT				
	1400	SUNV	94087	832-C4
MISTFLOWER DR				
	800	SJS	95122	834-F7
	800	SJS	95122	854-F1
MISTLETOE RD				
	200	LGTS	95032	872-J3
MISTY GLEN CT				
	-	SJS	95111	854-J5
MISTY WILLOW CT				
	6700	SJS	95120	894-E2
MITCHELL AV				
	16800	LGTS	95032	873-C6
MITCHELL CT				
	1000	CMBL	95128	853-E4
MITCHELL LN				
	400	PA	94301	790-H5
	5200	SJS	95111	875-B3
MITCHELL RD				
	-	SBnC	95023	1039-D4
MITTON CT				
	3500	SJS	95148	835-F7
MITTON DR				
	2900	SJS	95148	835-E7
MITTY WY				
	4900	SJS	95129	852-J2
MITZI DR				
	4100	SJS	95117	853-A3
	4200	SJS	95129	853-A3
MIWOK CT				
	-	MGH	95037	917-A2
MIWOK DR				
	6000	SJS	95123	874-H6
MIWOK PL				
	-	MGH	95037	917-A2
MIYUKI DR				
	1600	SJS	95193	875-C5
	2700	SJS	95119	875-C5
MOANA CT				
	800	PA	94306	811-C5
MOCHO CT				
	1300	SJS	95121	854-J2
MOCKINGBIRD CT				
	1100	SJS	95120	894-H4
MOCKINGBIRD LN				
	800	PA	94306	811-B4
	800	SUNV	94087	832-A2
	9200	GIL	95020	957-F7
MOCKINGBIRD HILL LN				
	1100	SJS	95120	894-H5
	10600	SCIC	95120	894-H5
MOCKING PLACE WY				
	1600	SJS	95121	855-B4
MODERN ICE DR				
	-	SJS	95112	834-B3
MODOC CT				
	500	SJS	95123	874-H6
MODOC TR				
	20900	SCIC	95033	913-A2
MODRED DR				
	3100	SJS	95127	814-H7
MOEN CT				
	7300	SJS	95139	895-F1
MOFFAT ST				
	1000	SJS	95002	813-B1
MOFFETT BLVD				
	100	MTVW	94043	811-J4
	400	SCIC	94043	811-J4
	500	MTVW	94043	812-A3
	500	SCIC	94043	812-A3
MOFFETT CIR				
	1000	PA	94303	791-D5
MOFFETT PARK CT				
	900	SUNV	94089	812-H3
MOFFETT PARK DR				
	100	SUNV	94089	812-J2
	1300	SUNV	94089	813-A2
W MOFFETT PARK DR				
	100	SUNV	94089	812-E4
MOFFO CT				
	1400	SJS	95121	854-J3
MOHAWK DR				
	5900	SJS	95123	874-H6
MOHICAN DR				
	600	SJS	95123	874-H5
MOIRA GLEN CT				
	1700	SJS	95112	854-F1
MOJAVE DR				
	6200	SJS	95120	874-D7
	6300	SJS	95120	894-D1
MOJONERA CT				
	100	LGTS	95032	873-C3
MOKELUMNE PL				
	1200	SJS	95120	874-C6
MOLINARO ST				
	3100	SCL	95054	813-E7
MOLINO AV				
	400	SUNV	94086	812-C7
	400	SUNV	94086	832-C1
MOLTZEN DR				
	7400	CPTO	95014	852-D3
MOLUCCA TER				
	-	SUNV	94089	812-G4
MONA WY				
	-	CMBL	95008	853-C4
	3500	SJS	95008	853-C4
	3500	SJS	95130	853-C4
MONACO DR				
	2300	SJS	95124	873-E3
MONARCH CIR				
	-	SJS	95138	875-G5
MONARCH LN				
	-	SJS	95138	875-G5
MONASTERY WY				
	800	SCL	95050	833-D5
MONCONTOUR CT				
	-	SJS	95135	855-G1
MONCUCCO CT				
	-	SJS	95148	855-F1
MONCUCCO WY				
	-	SJS	95148	855-F1
MONDIGO AV				
	2000	SJS	95122	834-J7
	2100	SJS	95122	835-A7
MONET CIR				
	4100	SJS	95136	874-H1
MONET PL				
	4300	SJS	95136	874-H1
MONETA WY				
	200	CMBL	95008	853-G6
MONFERINO DR				
	600	SJS	95112	834-C3
MONICA CT				
	1200	HOLL	95023	1039-H5
MONICA DR				
	-	SCIC	95037	916-G3
	1100	HOLL	95023	1039-H5
MONICA LN				
	600	CMBL	95008	853-E4
	600	SJS	95008	853-E4
	1000	CMBL	95128	853-E4
MONITOR CT				
	2200	SJS	95125	854-D3
MONKTON CT				
	3000	SJS	95148	855-C2
MONMOUTH DR				
	300	MPS	95035	794-D7
MONO WY				
	100	SCL	95051	832-H7
MONO LAKE CT				
	5900	SJS	95123	874-G7
MONROE CT				
	-	LGTS	95032	873-B6
MONROE DR				
	100	MTVW	94040	811-D3
	100	PA	94306	811-D3
MONROE ST				
	-	SCL	95128	833-E5
	-	SCL	95050	833-D2
	500	SJS	95050	833-E7
	500	SJS	95050	853-F1
	500	SJS	95128	833-E7
	500	SJS	95128	853-F1
	1900	SCL	95051	832-J2
	1900	SUNV	94086	832-J2
	2300	SCL	95051	833-A2
S MONROE ST				
	300	SJS	95128	853-E1
MONROVIA DR				
	1700	SJS	95122	855-A2
	1800	SJS	95121	855-A2
MONROVIA ST				
	21500	CPTO	95014	852-B3
MONTAGE CT				
	1800	SJS	95131	814-C4
MONTAGUE CT				
	-	MPS	95035	814-C2
MONTAGUE EXWY				
	3200	SJS	95135	855-E2
	300	MPS	95035	814-B3
	1300	SJS	95131	813-H5
	1300	SJS	95131	814-A4
	1300	MPS	95035	813-H5
	3000	SJS	95132	814-B3
MONTAGUE EXWY Rt#-G4				
	-	SJS	95134	813-F4
	400	SCL	95054	813-D6
	600	MPS	95035	813-F4
	600	SJS	95131	813-F4
MONTALBAN DR				
	1400	SJS	95120	874-A7
	1400	SJS	95120	894-A1
MONTALTO DR				
	1500	MTVW	94040	811-H7
MONTALVO DR				
	5900	SJS	95123	874-G6
MONTALVO LN				
	20400	SAR	95070	872-D4
MONTALVO RD				
	14700	SAR	95070	872-E4
MONTALVO HEIGHTS CT				
	15200	SAR	95070	872-D4
MONTALVO HEIGHTS DR				
	20400	SAR	95070	872-D4
MONTALVO OAKS				
	20400	SAR	95070	872-D3
MONTANA CT				
	6400	SJS	95120	894-E1
MONTANA LN				
	-	SMCo	94025	790-D5
MONTARA CT				
	-	PTLV	94028	810-D6
MONTARA DR				
	-	MPS	95035	814-E1
	19000	SCIC	95033	892-H4
MONTARA TER				
	-	SUNV	94086	812-F6
MONTAUK CT				
	19600	SAR	95070	872-F2
MONTAUK DR				
	19500	SAR	95070	872-F2
MONTAVO PL				
	-	SJS	95008	873-F1
MONTCLAIR AV				
	200	SJS	95116	834-G2
MONTCLAIR CT				
	100	LGTS	95032	872-J3
MONTCLAIR DR				
	300	SCL	95051	832-H7
MONTCLAIR RD				
	100	LGTS	95032	872-J3
	300	LGTS	95032	873-A3
	14600	SAR	95070	872-J3
MONTCLAIRE CT				
	23200	LALT	94024	831-H4
MONTCLAIRE PL				
	1400	LALT	94024	831-H4
MONTCLAIRE WY				
	1300	LALT	94024	831-H4
MONTE CT				
	2000	MPS	95035	814-E1
	21800	CPTO	95014	832-B7
MONTE DR				
	1100	MPS	95035	814-E1
MONTEAGLE DR				
	1200	SJS	95127	835-A4
MONTEBELLO AV				
	200	MTVW	94043	811-G3
MONTE BELLO CT				
	-	SBnC	95023	1060-A2
MONTE BELLO DR				
	-	SBnC	95023	1060-A1
	7700	GIL	95020	977-G2
MONTEBELLO RD				
	-	PA	94304	830-G6
	-	PA	94304	851-A1
	13000	SCIC	95014	851-C3
MONTEBELLO WY				
	-	LGTS	95030	893-A1
MONTEBELLO OAKS CT				
	1500	LALT	94024	831-J3
MONTE CARLO DR				
	-	HOLL	95023	1040-B4
MONTE CARLO WY				
	1800	SCIC	95125	853-H6
MONTECITO AV				
	1400	MTVW	94043	811-G3
MONTECITO CT				
	-	SJS	95135	855-G3
MONTECITO DR				
	3200	SJS	95135	855-G3
MONTECITO WY				
	300	MPS	95035	793-H4
MONTECITO VISTA DR				
	-	SJS	95111	854-F5
MONTECITO VISTA WY				
	-	SJS	95111	854-F5
MONTE CRESTA WY				
	2800	SJS	95132	814-E4
MONTE CRISTO CT				
	-	SBnC	95023	1060-A1
MONTEGO CT				
	6400	SJS	95120	894-B1
MONTEGO DR				
	1400	SJS	95120	894-B1
	1400	SCIC	95120	894-B1
MONTEGO LN				
	-	SMCo	94061	790-B4
	-	WDSD	94061	790-B4
MONTEGO TER				
	-	SUNV	94089	812-G4
MONTELEGRE DR				
	1400	SJS	95120	874-A7
MONTELENA CT				
	300	MTVW	94040	811-E2
MONTELENA DR				
	3200	SJS	95135	855-E2
MONTE LINDO CT				
	2500	SJS	95121	855-D3
MONTELLANO CT				
	1600	SJS	95120	874-A7
	1600	SJS	95120	894-A1
MONTELLANO DR				
	1400	SJS	95120	874-A7
MONTEMAR WY				
	1600	SCIC	95125	853-H5
MONTEREY				
	-	MTVW	94043	811-J2
	-	MTVW	94043	812-A2
MONTEREY AV				
	400	LGTS	95030	873-A6
	2000	SMCo	94025	790-C6
	2100	SCL	95051	833-A2
MONTEREY CIR				
	900	SJS	95138	875-F6
MONTEREY CT				
	1900	SCL	95051	833-A3
	11200	CPTO	95014	852-B3
MONTEREY HWY Rt#-82				
	1400	SJS	95112	854-D2
	1400	SJS	95110	854-D2
	1600	SJS	95125	854-D2
	2400	SCIC	95111	854-F5
	2400	SJS	95111	854-F5
	3100	SJS	95136	854-F5
	4100	SJS	95111	874-H1
	4100	SJS	95136	874-H1
	4600	SJS	95136	875-A2
	4600	SJS	95111	875-A2
	5200	SJS	95123	875-A2
	5200	SJS	95193	875-A2
MONTEREY PL				
	400	LALT	94022	811-D6
MONTEREY RD				
	300	SJS	95139	895-H1
	500	SJS	95037	896-B3
	500	SCIC	95037	896-B3
	1200	SJS	95141	896-B3
	5300	SJS	95111	875-C3
	5400	SJS	95138	875-C3
	5800	SJS	95139	875-C3
	5800	SJS	95137	875-C3
	5800	SJS	95137	895-H1
	5900	SJS	95139	896-B3
	5900	SCIC	95137	895-H1
	5900	SCIC	95137	896-B3
	6000	SJS	95137	896-B3
	11200	SJS	95037	916-F1
	11200	SCIC	95037	916-F1
	13600	MGH	95037	916-F1
MONTEREY RD U.S.-101				
	5300	GIL	95020	978-A4
	8800	GIL	95020	957-H5
	10400	SCIC	95020	957-F1
	11000	SCIC	95046	957-F1
	11600	MGH	95037	916-J6
	12600	SCIC	95046	937-E6
	13700	MGH	95046	937-E6
	14800	MGH	95037	937-A1
	17000	MGH	95037	917-A7
MONTEREY ST				
	-	SBnC	95045	1038-C4
	-	HOLL	95023	1040-A5
	-	SJB	95045	1038-C4
MONTEREY ST U.S.-101				
	7000	GIL	95020	978-A3
	7800	GIL	95020	977-J1
	8500	GIL	95020	957-J7
MONTEREY TER				
	-	SUNV	94089	812-G4
MONTE ROSA DR				
	600	MLPK	94025	790-D7
	600	MLPK	94025	810-D1
MONTE SERENO TER				
	-	FRMT	94539	794-B1
MONTE SOL TER				
	400	MPS	95035	793-G3
MONTE SUNSET DR				
	20700	SCIC	95120	894-H1
MONTEVAL CT				
	1600	SJS	95120	873-J7
	1600	SJS	95120	874-A7
MONTEVAL LN				
	1500	SJS	95120	874-A7
MONTEVAL PL				
	1500	SJS	95120	874-A7
MONTEVARCHI ST				
	-	SJS	95136	854-F7
MONTE VERANO CT				
	-	SJS	95116	834-H3
MONTE VERDE CT				
	1200	LALT	94024	831-H4
MONTEVERDE DR				
	5900	SJS	95120	874-A7
	6100	SJS	95120	894-A1
MONTE VERDE LN				
	3200	SJS	95135	855-G3
MONTEVIDEO LN				
	1600	SJS	95127	835-A5
MONTE VILLA CT				
	100	CMBL	95008	873-E2
MONTEVINA RD				
	18200	SCIC	95033	892-E1
	20200	SCIC	95070	892-E1
MONTEVINO DR				
	5800	SJS	95123	874-G5
MONTE VISTA				
	-	MTVW	94043	812-A2
MONTE VISTA AV				
	-	ATN	94027	790-C4
MONTE VISTA DR				
	-	SJS	95125	854-E5
	1600	HOLL	95023	1040-D6
	15400	SAR	95070	872-G4
MONTE VISTA WY				
	-	GIL	95020	977-H3
MONTEVOIT CT				
	-	SJS	95138	855-F7
MONTEWOOD CT				
	18400	SAR	95070	872-G5
MONTEWOOD DR				
	18400	SAR	95070	872-H5
MONTEZUMA DR				
	2200	SJS	95008	853-B7
MONTFORD CT				
	1800	SJS	95132	814-E3
MONTGOMERY AV				
	1200	SMCo	94061	790-B3
MONTGOMERY BEND				
	6000	SJS	95135	855-H6
MONTGOMERY CT				
	6000	SJS	95135	855-H6
MONTGOMERY DR				
	3200	SCL	95054	813-B7
MONTGOMERY LN				
	-	SBnC	95023	1020-D3
	5400	SJS	95135	855-H6
MONTGOMERY PL				
	6100	SJS	95135	855-H6
MONTGOMERY PL E				
	6000	SJS	95135	855-H6
MONTGOMERY PL S				
	6000	SJS	95135	855-H6
MONTGOMERY PL W				
	6000	SJS	95135	855-H6
MONTGOMERY ST				
	-	LGTS	95030	873-A6
	800	MTVW	94041	811-J6
MONTGOMERY ST Rt#-82				
	-	SJS	95110	834-A7
	200	SJS	95110	854-A1
N MONTGOMERY ST				
	100	SJS	95110	834-A6
S MONTGOMERY ST Rt#-82				
	-	SJS	95110	834-A7
	-	SJS	95113	834-A7
MONTGOMERY CORNER				
	6000	SJS	95135	855-H6
MONTICELLI CT				
	-	GIL	95020	957-G7
MONTICELLI DR				
	-	GIL	95020	957-G7
MONTICELLO AV				
	200	SJS	95125	854-D4
MONTICELLO DR				
	1500	HOLL	95023	1040-D6
MONTICELLO WY				
	2400	SCL	95051	832-J2
	15100	MGH	95037	937-A4
MONTIERRA PL				
	3200	SJS	95135	855-G3
MONTMORENCY CT				
	4300	SJS	95118	874-C2
MONTMORENCY DR				
	1100	SJS	95118	874-B2
MONTORO CT				
	6100	SJS	95120	874-B7
MONTORO DR				
	6000	SJS	95120	874-B7
MONTOYA CIR				
	17400	MGH	95037	917-B6
MONTPELIER DR				
	2300	SJS	95116	834-G2
MONTPERE WY				
	18200	SAR	95070	872-H1
MONTREAL CT				
	4700	SJS	95130	853-A7
MONTREAL DR				
	4700	SJS	95130	853-A7
	4800	SJS	95130	852-J7
MONTROSE AV				
	700	PA	94303	811-F1
MONTROSE CT				
	22700	SCrC	95033	912-J5
MONTROSE ST				
	13000	SAR	95070	852-H7
MONTROSE WY				
	1600	SJS	95124	874-A3
MONTWOOD CIR				
	300	SMCo	94061	790-B4
MONTY CIR				
	800	SCL	95050	833-D5
MONUMENT CT				
	500	FRMT	94539	794-A2
MOODY CT				
	26800	LAH	94022	830-J2
MOODY RD				
	12200	SCIC	95014	830-H2
	12200	LAH	94022	830-H3
	25500	LAH	94022	831-A3
	26600	SCIC	95014	831-A3
MOODY SPRINGS CT				
	12000	LAH	94022	831-B3
MOON CT				
	1100	MPS	95035	814-A2
MOON LN				
	14000	LAH	94022	810-H6
MOON BEAM DR				
	-	MTVW	94043	811-J3
MOONBEAM WY				
	1100	MPS	95035	814-A2
MOON DANCE				
	-	MPS	95035	814-J1
MOONFLOWER CT				
	4100	SJS	95135	855-F3

SANTA CLARA CO.

STREET
Block City ZIP Pg-Grid

MOON GATE PL
1000 SJS 95120 894-G2
MOON GLOW CT
700 SJS 95123 874-F3
MOONLIGHT CIR
1200 MPS 95035 813-J3
MOONLIGHT WY
1200 MPS 95035 813-J2
MOONLITE PL
2600 SCL 95051 833-B4
MOON SHADOW DR
- MPS 95035 814-J1
MOONSTAR CT
3000 SJS 95148 835-B5
MOONSTONE CT
5000 SJS 95136 874-D3
MOORBROOK DR
2600 SJS 95132 814-F6
MOORE DR
- SJS 95116 834-G4
MOORE RD
300 WDSD 94062 790-A6
MOORGLEN CT
2300 SJS 95133 834-F2
MOORPARK AV
1500 SJS 95128 853-E2
2200 SCIC 95128 853-F2
3100 SJS 95117 853-B2
4200 SJS 95129 853-B2
4800 SJS 95129 852-J2
MOORPARK WY
- MTVW 94041 812-A6
MORA CT
1700 SCIC 94024 831-G4
MORA DR
700 SCIC 94024 831-G4
2200 MTVW 94040 811-F3
11200 SCIC 95014 831-F5
MORADA LN
300 SBnC 95023 1020-G4
MORAES CT
1100 SJS 95127 835-B3
MORAGA AV
5800 SJS 95123 874-F5
MORAGA CT
900 PA 94303 791-E6
MORAGA DR
800 MTVW 94041 812-A7
MORAGA ST
1100 SCL 95051 833-A4
MORAGA WY
200 SJS 95119 875-C7
MORA GLEN DR
23100 SCIC 94024 831-G5
MORA HEIGHTS WY
23200 SCIC 94024 831-G5
MORAINE DR
2200 SCL 95051 833-A1
MORAN DR
4300 SJS 95129 853-A3
MORAN LN
19900 SAR 95070 872-F1
MORAQUITA CT
- SCIC 94024 831-F5
MORAY CT
19500 SAR 95070 852-F7
19500 SAR 95070 872-F1
MORDEN DR
4800 SJS 95130 852-J7
4800 SJS 95130 853-A7
MORE AV
200 LGTS 95032 873-A2
200 CMBL 95032 872-J1
200 SJS 95032 872-J1
500 LGTS 95032 872-J4
700 CMBL 95032 873-A2
MORECAMBE DR
7000 SJS 95120 894-G3
MORELAND WY
- SCL 95054 813-E5
4000 SJS 95130 853-B4
MORELY CT
1100 SJS 95122 854-H1
MORENGO DR
10600 CPTO 95014 852-H2
MORENO AV
700 PA 94303 791-D5
3200 SJS 95127 835-B3
MORENO CT
12900 SCIC 95046 937-G6
MORENO LN
600 SCL 95050 833-D5
2100 SCIC 95020 958-C4
MORETTI DR
10300 CPTO 95014 852-H2
MORETTI LN
300 MPS 95035 794-C6
MOREVERN CIR
7500 SJS 95135 855-J6
MOREY CIR
1200 HOLL 95023 1039-J5
MOREY DR
500 MLPK 94025 790-G4
MOREY WY
- GIL 95020 977-G1
MORGAN AV
1800 MGH 95037 917-D6
MORGAN CT
1600 MTVW 94043 811-H2
1900 MGH 95037 917-D5
MORGAN PL
700 LALT 94024 831-G1
3400 SJS 95132 814-G3
MORGAN ST
1600 MTVW 94043 811-H2
MORGRIDGE WY
- SJS 95134 813-G2
MORISET WY
- SJS 95131 814-C4
MORNING GLORY DR
- HOLL 95023 1040-B6
MORNING GLORY LN
1600 SJS 95124 873-J6

MORNINGSIDE
600 LALT 94022 831-D1
MORNINGSIDE CIR
- HOLL 95023 1040-C7
800 GIL 95020 957-G7
MORNINGSIDE CT
- HOLL 95023 1040-C7
9300 GIL 95020 957-G7
MORNINGSIDE DR
- HOLL 95023 1040-C7
1000 SUNV 94087 832-A1
5500 SJS 95138 875-F1
MORNING SPRING CT
11500 CPTO 95014 852-A4
MORNING STAR DR
- SJS 95131 814-C5
1500 MGH 95037 917-A3
MORNING SUN CT
- MTVW 94043 811-J3
MORNING VIEW TER
- FRMT 94539 794-B1
MORO CT
- GIL 95020 957-G7
MORO DR
- GIL 95020 957-G7
MOROCCO DR
1600 SJS 95125 853-J7
MORRELL RD
23500 SCrC 95033 913-D7
MORRENE DR
200 CMBL 95008 853-B5
MORRIE DR
3600 SJS 95127 835-C3
MORRILL AV
1100 SJS 95132 814-D2
MORRILL CT
1100 SJS 95132 814-F5
MORRILL RD
23300 SCrC 95033 913-E6
24100 SCrC 95033 913-E6
MORRIS AV
1000 SJS 95126 853-J1
MORRIS CT
2100 SJS 95126 833-G5
MORRIS DR
200 SBnC 95023 1059-H2
3100 PA 94303 791-E6
MORRIS LN
100 CMBL 95008 853-E7
MORRISON AV
- SJS 95126 833-J7
200 SCIC 95126 833-J7
200 SCIC 95126 853-J1
2000 SCL 95051 833-B3
N MORRISON AV
300 SJS 95126 833-J6
MORRISON LN
300 CMBL 95008 873-C1
MORRO VISTA LN
100 SMCo 94028 810-C3
MORROW CT
100 SJS 95139 875-F7
MORSE AV
200 SUNV 94086 812-F5
900 SUNV 94089 812-G4
MORSE CT
400 SUNV 94086 812-F5
MORSE LN
1600 SCL 95051 833-B4
MORSE ST
500 SJS 95126 833-G5
1100 SCL 95050 833-G5
MORTON AV
1100 SCL 95051 833-B4
1300 LALT 94024 831-J4
1500 LALT 94024 832-A4
MORTON CT
100 MTVW 94040 811-F5
MORTON ST
- PA 94303 791-C5
MORTON WY
- PA 94303 791-C5
5600 SJS 95123 874-F4
MOSEGARD LN
14700 SCIC 95037 937-A5
MOSELLE CT
200 SJS 95119 875-D7
MOSELLE DR
6700 SJS 95119 875-D7
MOSHER DR
- SJS 95135 855-G2
- SJS 95148 855-G1
MOSHER WY
- PA 94304 790-F5
MOSS DR
800 SJS 95116 834-G5
MOSSBROOK AV
1600 SJS 95130 853-A5
MOSSBROOK CIR
4500 SJS 95130 853-A5
MOSSCREEK LN
3300 SJS 95121 855-D7
MOSSDALE WY
2300 SJS 95133 814-F7
2300 SJS 95133 834-E1
MOSSHALL WY
3100 SJS 95135 855-F3
MOSS HOLLOW DR
2800 SJS 95121 855-B2
2800 SJS 95122 855-B2
MOSSLAND DR
1300 SJS 95131 814-D7
MOSSMILL CT
2800 SJS 95121 854-J3
MOSS OAK WY
6100 SJS 95120 874-D7
MOSS POINT DR
2800 SJS 95127 835-A5
MOSSROSE WY
- GIL 95020 977-F1
MOSSWELL CT
100 SJS 95138 875-D4
MOSSWOOD DR
2600 SJS 95132 814-E5

MOSSWOOD LN
2400 SCL 95051 833-C1
MOSSY OAK CT
10000 CPTO 95014 831-J7
10000 CPTO 95014 851-J1
MOULIN LN
- SJS 95135 855-F3
MOULIN PL
- SCL 95054 813-D5
MOULTON DR
- ATN 94027 790-F2
1100 MPS 95035 814-E1
MOUNDHAVEN CT
100 SJS 95111 874-J1
MOUNTAIN DR
20300 SCIC 95120 895-A6
MOUNTAIN WY
15700 SCIC 95030 872-G6
MOUNTAIN CHARLIE RD
17500 SCIC 95033 913-A4
20700 SCIC 95033 912-J4
23800 SCrC 95033 912-J4
MOUNTAIN CREEK CT
1800 SJS 95148 835-D4
MOUNTAINGATE WY
2400 SJS 95133 814-H3
MOUNTAIN HAWK CT
- SJS 95120 894-F4
MOUNTAIN HOME DR
500 SJS 95136 854-E7
MOUNTAIN LAUREL CT
- MTVW 94043 811-H4
MOUNTAIN LAUREL LN
- LGTS 95032 893-H1
MOUNTAIN MEADOW CT
5900 SJS 95135 856-A7
MOUNTAIN QUAIL CIR
1100 SJS 95120 894-F3
MOUNTAIN SHADOWS DR
1200 MTVW 94043 811-H3
MOUNTAIN SHADOWS RD
1000 SJS 95120 894-H4
MOUNTAIN SPRINGS DR
100 SJS 95136 854-E6
MOUNTAIN SWALLOW CT
7100 SJS 95120 894-F3
MOUNTAIN VIEW AV
- LALT 94024 811-G6
- SCIC 95127 815-A7
100 MTVW 94041 811-H5
100 SCIC 95127 814-J7
100 SJS 95127 814-J7
800 MTVW 94040 811-H5
MOUNTAIN VIEW CIR
- MGH 95037 916-H3
MOUNTAIN VIEW CT
18000 SCIC 95033 912-J3
MOUNTN VW-ALVISO RD Rt#-237
- MTVW 94041 812-A6
- MTVW 94043 812-A6
600 MTVW 94041 811-J7
MOUNTAIRE CT
- SJS 95138 855-D6
MOUNTAIRE LN
- SJS 95138 855-D6
MOUNTAIRE PL
- SJS 95138 855-D6
MOUNT BLANC WY
1600 SJS 95127 835-B4
MOUNT CARMEL DR
900 SJS 95120 894-F1
MOUNTCASTLE WY
4100 SJS 95136 874-D2
MOUNT CLARE DR
2900 SJS 95148 835-C7
MOUNTCLIFFE CT
3800 SJS 95136 874-D1
MOUNTCOURSE LN
1200 SJS 95131 814-B7
MOUNT CREST DR
11200 CPTO 95014 852-B3
MOUNT DARWIN DR
1000 SJS 95120 894-F2
MOUNT DAVIDSON CT
3500 SJS 95124 873-E2
MOUNT DAVIDSON DR
2200 SJS 95124 873-E2
MOUNT DIABLO AV
1400 MPS 95035 814-D1
MOUNT DIABLO DR
1400 SJS 95127 835-B4
MOUNT DIABLO LN
- SBnC 95023 1000-D7
MOUNT EDEN CT
21400 SAR 95070 872-B2
MOUNT EDEN RD
21800 SAR 95070 872-B1
21800 SCIC 95070 872-B1
22000 SCIC 95070 852-A7
22600 SCIC 95014 851-J7
22600 SCIC 95070 851-J7
MOUNT EVEREST CT
1500 SJS 95127 835-B4
MOUNT EVEREST DR
3200 SJS 95127 835-B4
MOUNTFORD DR
6200 SJS 95123 875-A7
MOUNT FOREST DR
6500 SJS 95120 894-F1
MOUNT FRAZIER DR
1500 SJS 95127 835-C4
MOUNT HAMILTON AV
- LALT 94022 811-D6

MOUNT HAMILTON RD Rt#-130
11000 SCIC 95127 815-B7
11400 SCIC 95127 835-D1
12400 SCIC 95140 835-G2
12600 SCIC 95140 815-F7
18000 SCIC 95135 856-H1
18000 SCIC 95140 856-H1
MOUNT HAMILTON VIEW DR
1400 SJS 95116 834-E4
MOUNT HERMAN DR
1400 SJS 95127 835-B4
MOUNT HOLLY DR
6600 SJS 95120 894-F1
MOUNT HOOD WY
3100 SJS 95127 835-B4
MOUNT HOPE DR
6600 SJS 95120 894-F1
MOUNT ISABEL CT
3100 SJS 95148 855-E1
MOUNT ISABEL DR
3100 SJS 95148 855-E1
MOUNT KENYA DR
1700 SJS 95127 835-C4
MOUNT LASSEN DR
1400 SJS 95127 835-B4
MOUNT LENEVE DR
6700 SJS 95120 894-F2
MOUNT LOGAN DR
3200 SJS 95127 835-B4
MOUNT MADONNA DR
3300 SJS 95127 835-C4
MOUNT MADONNA RD
400 SCrC 95076 976-C1
400 SCIC 95020 976-C1
1500 SCIC 95020 956-C7
1500 SCIC 95037 956-C7
1500 SCIC 95037 976-C1
MOUNT MCKINLEY CT
3400 SJS 95127 835-C4
MOUNT MCKINLEY DR
3100 SJS 95127 835-C4
MOUNT OLIVEIRA DR
1600 SJS 95127 835-C4
MOUNT OSO DR
3100 SJS 95148 855-E2
MOUNT PAKRON CT
6700 SJS 95120 894-F2
MOUNT PAKRON DR
6600 SJS 95120 894-F2
MOUNT PALOMAR DR
1400 SJS 95127 835-B4
MOUNT PLEASANT CT
3500 SJS 95148 835-C4
MOUNT PLEASANT DR
1500 SJS 95127 835-C4
1500 SJS 95148 835-C4
MOUNT PLEASANT RD
1600 SJS 95148 835-D4
1600 SJS 95127 835-D4
2000 SCIC 95148 835-E5
MOUNT PRIETA DR
3400 SJS 95127 835-C4
MOUNT RAINIER AV
1500 MPS 95035 814-D1
MOUNT RAINIER DR
3100 SJS 95127 835-B4
MOUNT ROYAL DR
6500 SJS 95120 894-F1
MOUNT RUSHMORE DR
1700 SJS 95127 835-C4
MOUNT SAINT HELENA DR
3400 SJS 95127 835-C4
MOUNT SHASTA AV
1300 MPS 95035 814-D1
MOUNT SHASTA DR
1400 SJS 95127 835-B4
MOUNT STANLEY DR
1400 SJS 95127 835-C4
MOUNT UMUNHUM RD
11000 SCIC 95033 914-D1
13600 SCIC 95033 913-J2
MOUNT VERNON CT
1900 MTVW 94040 811-G4
MOUNT VERNON DR
1600 SCIC 95125 853-H5
MOUNT VERNON LN
- ATN 94027 790-E1
MOUNT VERNON WY
7000 GIL 95020 977-J4
MOUNT VISTA DR
3100 SJS 95127 835-B4
MOUNT WELLINGTON DR
6500 SJS 95120 894-F1
MOUNT WHITNEY DR
1400 SJS 95127 835-B4
MOUNT WILSON DR
3200 SJS 95127 835-B4
MOUTON CIR
- EPA 94303 791-C3
MOUVERDE PL
- SJS 95135 855-H2
MOZART AV
2600 SJS 95122 855-A1
16100 CMBL 95032 873-D3
16100 LGTS 95032 873-D3
MOZART CT
500 SUNV 94087 832-E3
MOZART WY
16400 LGTS 95032 873-D3
MOZELLE CT
17800 SCIC 95033 913-A2
MUCKLEMI ST
- SBnC 95045 1038-C4
- SJB 95045 1038-C4
MUELLER AV
2400 SJS 95116 834-G2
MUENCH CT
1300 SJS 95131 814-C7
MUENDER AV
800 SUNV 94086 812-D7

MUIR AV
- SCL 95051 832-J7
MUIR DR
700 MTVW 94041 812-B7
5400 SJS 95124 873-J6
8600 GIL 95020 977-F1
MUIR WY
1000 LALT 94024 831-H2
MUIRDRUM PL
3000 SJS 95148 835-D7
MUIRFIELD CT
- SJS 95116 834-H3
MUIRFIELD DR
- SJS 95116 834-H3
MUIRHOUSE PL
5200 SJS 95136 874-F3
MUIR PLACE CT
3800 SJS 95121 855-B4
MUIRWOOD CT
2100 SJS 95132 814-C3
MUIRWOOD WY
2000 SJS 95132 814-C3
MULBERRY CIR
- HOLL 95023 1040-D5
2100 SJS 95125 853-J6
MULBERRY CT
- HOLL 95023 1040-D5
- MGH 95037 937-B5
MULBERRY DR
14200 LGTS 95032 873-B2
MULBERRY LN
- ATN 94027 790-C5
800 SUNV 94087 832-C1
1600 SJS 95125 853-J6
26000 LAH 94022 811-B6
MULCASTER CT
800 SJS 95136 874-D1
MULLEN AV
- LGTS 95030 873-A7
MULLER PL
- SJS 95126 833-H7
- SJS 95126 853-H1
MULLINIX WY
- SJS 95136 854-F7
MUMFORD PL
3800 PA 94306 811-E1
MUNDELL CT
1000 LALT 94022 811-D4
MUNDELL WY
300 LALT 94022 811-D4
MUNICH TER
- SUNV 94089 812-G4
MUNRO AV
1200 CMBL 95008 873-B1
MUNROE WY
17100 MGH 95037 936-J1
MURAOKA DR
- GIL 95020 957-J7
- GIL 95020 977-J1
MURDOCH CT
3400 PA 94306 791-D7
MURDOCH DR
3400 PA 94306 791-D7
MURFIELD WY
- GIL 95020 977-E4
MURGUIA AV
1900 SCL 95050 833-D5
MURIEL CT
400 SCL 95051 833-B7
1100 SJS 95121 855-A5
MURIEL LN
19100 CPTO 95014 852-G1
MURIETTA LN
3700 SJS 95127 835-D2
11900 LAH 94022 831-A3
MURILLO AV
3500 SCIC 95148 835-E6
3500 SJS 95148 835-E6
3500 SJS 95148 855-G1
MURLAGAN AV
- MTVW 94043 812-A3
MURMAN CT
2900 SJS 95148 855-D2
MURPHY AV
1100 SJS 95131 814-B7
11500 SCIC 95020 957-G1
12200 SCIC 95046 937-E3
12200 SCIC 95046 957-G1
15200 SCIC 95037 937-D1
15300 SCIC 95037 917-C6
15400 MGH 95037 917-C6
15800 MGH 95037 937-D1
N MURPHY AV
100 SUNV 94086 812-E6
S MURPHY AV
100 SUNV 94086 812-E7
400 SUNV 94086 832-E1
MURPHY CT
18400 MGH 95037 916-H5
MURPHY LN
- MGH 95037 917-A3
MURPHY RANCH RD
500 MPS 95035 813-G2
MURPHY SPRINGS CT
18500 MGH 95037 916-H5
MURPHY SPRINGS DR
18300 MGH 95037 916-H6
MURRAY AV
7700 GIL 95020 978-A1
8500 GIL 95020 958-A7
8600 GIL 95020 957-J6
9100 SCIC 95020 957-J6
MURRAY CT
- RDWC 94061 790-B1
MURRAY ST
300 MPS 95035 794-A3
MURRAY WY
3200 PA 94303 791-E6
MURRE LN
1500 SUNV 94087 832-G5
MURTHA DR
2700 SJS 95127 834-J5
2700 SJS 95127 835-A4

MUSCAT CT
1200 SUNV 94087 832-B3
MUSCAT DR
6700 SJS 95119 875-E7
MUSETTA CT
1500 SJS 95121 855-A2
MUSEUM WY
100 SCIC 94305 790-H6
MUSSELBURGH WY
- GIL 95020 977-F3
MUSTANG DR
1400 MPS 95035 814-B3
MUSTANG ST
300 SJS 95123 874-J5
300 SJS 95123 875-A5
MUSTO AV
- SJS 95123 875-B4
MYER PL
10100 CPTO 95014 832-E7
MYERSLY CT
3400 SJS 95148 835-E7
MYLES CT
3200 SJS 95117 853-D2
MYLINDA DR
3900 SJS 95132 815-A4
MYNA CT
5200 SJS 95123 874-F7
MYRA DR
1700 SJS 95124 873-J6
MYREN CT
19000 SAR 95070 872-G1
MYREN DR
13400 SAR 95070 872-G1
MYRNA CT
- SJS 95148 855-F1
MYRTLE AV
- MGH 95037 937-A1
1400 SJS 95118 874-B1
MYRTLE CT
100 EPA 94303 791-C2
MYRTLE DR
1100 SUNV 94086 832-H2
MYRTLE PL
- EPA 94303 791-C2
MYRTLE ST
600 SJS 95126 833-G5
900 EPA 94303 791-C2
MYRTLEWOOD DR
6300 CPTO 95014 852-F2
MYSTIC CT
4100 SJS 95124 873-E3
MYSTIC DR
- SJS 95124 873-E3

N

N RD
- SUNV 94089 812-H4
NADINE CT
15000 SCIC 95124 873-F4
NADINE DR
1100 CMBL 95008 853-B5
NAGAREDA DR
- GIL 95020 977-J1
NAGEL WY
- SJS 95136 854-E6
NAGLEE AV
1100 SJS 95126 833-G7
1800 SJS 95128 833-F7
NAGLEE PL
- SJS 95126 833-G6
NAIDA AV
2000 SJS 95122 834-H6
NAIRN WY
- GIL 95020 977-E3
NAKOOCHE TR
- SCIC 95033 913-C2
NALOR CT
17200 LGTS 95032 873-B3
NAMPEYO ST
48900 FRMT 94539 793-J2
NANCARROW CT
1300 SJS 95120 874-C7
NANCARROW WY
1200 SJS 95120 874-C7
NANCY CT
100 MTVW 94041 811-J6
20600 CPTO 95014 852-D1
NANCY LN
100 SJS 95127 834-J3
200 SCIC 95127 834-J3
800 LALT 94024 831-G3
NANCY WY
- MLPK 94025 790-E6
NANDELL LN
600 SCIC 94024 831-F3
NANDINA WY
1000 SUNV 94086 832-G2
NANTES CT
- SJS 95148 855-G2
NANTUCKET CIR
- SCL 95054 813-D4
NANTUCKET CT
800 SUNV 94087 832-C2
900 SJS 95126 853-J3
12600 SAR 95070 852-F6
NANTUCKET PL
7300 GIL 95020 977-J4
NAOMI CT
1600 RDWC 94061 790-A1
4000 SJS 95136 874-E1
21500 SCIC 95033 912-J3
NAPA CT
1500 HOLL 95023 1040-D6
3200 SJS 95148 835-D6
NAPA DR
3100 SJS 95148 835-D6
NAPA RIVER CT
4500 SJS 95136 874-E2
NAPLES DR
1800 SJS 95122 834-H5
NAPOLI LP
- SJS 95135 855-G2

NAPOLI PL
- SJS 95135 855-G2
NAPOLI TER
- SJS 95135 855-G2
NAPOLI WY
- SJS 95135 855-G2
NARAMORE LN
- LGTS 95032 873-A2
NARANJA WY
- PTLV 94028 810-A5
NARCISO CT
1000 SJS 95129 852-G2
NARCISSO RD
4700 SCIC 95020 998-D4
NARVAEZ AV
3000 SJS 95125 854-D6
3000 SJS 95136 854-E7
3800 SJS 95136 874-E1
NASH AV
600 MLPK 94025 790-H2
NASH CT
3700 SJS 95111 854-J6
NASH RD
300 HOLL 95023 1040-A5
300 SBnC 95023 1040-A5
300 SBnC 95023 1039-H6
500 HOLL 95023 1039-J5
800 LALT 94024 831-E1
NASHUA CT
100 SJS 95139 895-G1
600 SUNV 94087 832-D2
NASHVILLE DR
2900 SJS 95133 814-H7
NASSAU DR
2000 SJS 95122 834-J7
2000 SMCo 94061 790-B4
NATALIE AV
1600 SCL 95051 833-A3
NATALIE CT
1600 SJS 95118 873-J4
NATALIE DR
700 MGH 95037 917-D7
700 MGH 95037 937-C1
NATALYE RD
14900 MSER 95030 873-B4
14900 MSER 95032 873-B4
NATHAN CT
3700 PA 94303 791-F7
NATHAN WY
3700 PA 94303 791-F7
NATHAN ABBOTT WY
- SCIC 94305 790-H7
NATHANSON AV
10500 CPTO 95014 832-C6
NATHHORST AV
100 PTLV 94028 810-C7
NATIONAL AV
400 MTVW 94043 812-B4
4800 SJS 95124 873-D3
4800 LGTS 95032 873-D3
NATIVE DANCER DR
14700 MGH 95037 937-B5
NATOMA CT
12100 SAR 95070 852-E5
NATOMA DR
700 SJS 95123 874-G5
NATOMA RD
13100 LAH 94022 810-J7
27200 LAH 94022 830-J1
27300 LAH 94022 831-A1
28200 LAH 94022 811-A7
NATURE CT
300 SJS 95123 875-B6
NATURE DR
300 SJS 95123 875-B6
NAUTILUS CT
2400 SJS 95128 853-F3
NAVAJO CT
- GIL 95020 957-F7
600 SJS 95123 874-G4
NAVAJO LN
- LALT 94022 811-E6
NAVAJO PL
- PTLV 94028 810-B5
NAVAJO TR
17700 SCIC 95033 913-A2
NAVARO PL
400 SJS 95134 813-H4
NAVARO WY
400 SJS 95134 813-H4
NAVARRO DR
1300 SUNV 94087 832-G4
NAVLET CT
1200 SUNV 94087 832-C3
NAVY PL
1900 SJS 95133 834-E1
NAZARENE WY
900 SJS 95117 853-D3
NAZARETH CT
600 SCL 95051 832-J6
NEAL AV
2700 SJS 95128 853-E2
3100 SJS 95117 853-D2
NECTAR CT
- GIL 95020 977-H5
NECTARINE AV
800 SUNV 94087 832-C2
NEDSON CT
2500 MTVW 94043 811-F2
NEEDHAM LN
19600 SAR 95070 852-F6
NEEDLES DR
400 SJS 95112 854-E2
NEET AV
2900 SJS 95128 853-E3
NEIL DR
600 HOLL 95023 1039-J5
NEILSON CT
300 SJS 95111 875-A1
NELA LN
700 LALT 94022 811-E4
NELIS CT
1200 SUNV 94087 832-C3

© 2008 Rand McNally & Company

STREET
Block City ZIP Pg-Grid

NELLO DR
500 CMBL 95008 853-D7
NELO ST
400 SCL 95054 813-F6
NELSON CT
1400 SCL 95054 813-D4
3900 PA 94306 811-E1
14600 SCIC 95124 873-G3
NELSON DR
1600 SCL 95054 813-D4
3800 PA 94306 811-E1
NELSON RD
- SCIC 94305 790-J6
NELSON WY
1300 SUNV 94087 832-C4
1700 SJS 95124 873-H3
14500 SCIC 95124 873-G3
NEPO CT
6400 SJS 95119 875-C7
NEPO DR
6300 SJS 95119 875-C7
NEPTUNE CT
900 SCIC 94043 811-J4
6600 SJS 95120 894-C1
NERDY AV
300 SJS 95111 854-J6
NERISSA WY
5000 SJS 95124 873-G5
NERO CT
2000 SJS 95008 853-B6
NESBIT CT
1400 SJS 95120 874-B6
NESTA DR
3300 SJS 95118 874-A1
NESTON WY
1500 LALT 94024 831-J5
1500 LALT 94024 832-A5
NESTORITA WY
1800 SJS 95124 873-H1
NETTLE PL
1000 SUNV 94086 832-G2
NETWORK CIR
- SCL 95054 813-D5
NEVA LN
14700 SCIC 95046 957-G3
NEVADA AV
100 PA 94301 791-B6
700 SJS 95125 854-A4
NEVADA PL
1000 SJS 95125 854-B4
NEVADA ST
- HOLL 95023 1040-A6
NEVES CT
2600 SCL 95051 833-C7
NEVES WY
3400 SJS 95127 835-A1
NEVILLE AV
2400 SJS 95130 853-A7
NEVIN WY
700 SJS 95128 853-H2
NEW AV
8500 SCIC 95020 958-C3
11500 SCIC 95020 938-A6
11500 SCIC 95046 938-A6
12900 SCIC 95046 937-J5
NEW CT
5600 SJS 95123 874-H4
NEWARK WY
2800 SJS 95124 873-G1
NEW AUTUMN ST
- SJS 95110 834-A5
NEW BEDFORD CT
1500 SJS 95131 814-C7
NEWBERRY CT
4200 PA 94306 811-D2
NEWBERRY DR
1100 SJS 95118 874-C1
NEWBRIDGE DR
26000 LAH 94022 811-C7
NEWBRIDGE ST
600 MLPK 94025 790-J1
800 MLPK 94025 791-A1
900 EPA 94303 791-A1
NEW BRUNSWICK AV
1500 SUNV 94087 832-C5
NEWCASTLE CT
200 RDWC 94061 790-B2
NEWCASTLE DR
300 RDWC 94061 790-B2
1600 LALT 94024 832-A4
1700 LALT 94024 831-J5
7500 CPTO 95014 852-D4
NEW COMPTON CT
4900 SJS 95136 874-F2
NEW COMPTON DR
600 SJS 95136 874-F2
NEW DORSET CT
600 SJS 95136 874-F2
NEWELL AV
100 LGTS 95032 873-B3
100 LGTS 95030 873-B3
NEWELL CT
100 LGTS 95032 873-B3
NEWELL PL
800 PA 94303 791-B4
NEWELL RD
- EPA 94303 791-B3
400 PA 94303 791-B5
400 PA 94301 791-B4
NEW ENGLAND CT
5000 SJS 95136 874-F3
NEWFOUNDLAND DR
1400 SUNV 94087 832-D4
NEWGATE CT
- SJS 95138 875-H1
NEWHALL DR
- SJS 95110 833-G4
NEWHALL ST
600 SJS 95110 833-H4
800 SJS 95126 833-G5
1400 SCL 95050 833-F5
1900 SCL 95128 833-F5
2100 SJS 95128 833-E6

NEW HAMPTON WY
1300 SCL 95051 833-B4
NEW HAVEN CT
900 CPTO 95014 852-B2
NEWHOUSE CT
19200 SAR 95070 852-G6
NEW IRELAND CT
600 SJS 95136 874-F2
NEW JERSEY AV
2300 SJS 95124 853-G7
2500 SJS 95124 873-G3
14200 SCIC 95124 873-G3
NEWMAN PL
- MTVW 94043 811-H2
NEW MAPLE ST
- SCL 95050 833-G5
NEW MAYFIELD LN
200 PA 94306 791-A7
NEW PENCE CT
1700 SJS 95132 814-J3
NEWPORT AV
1300 SJS 95125 854-A4
NEWPORT CT
12400 SAR 95070 852-F5
NEW RAMSEY CT
4900 SJS 95136 874-F2
NEW RIVER DR
100 SJS 95119 875-E7
100 SJS 95119 895-E1
NEWSOM AV
18700 CPTO 95014 852-H2
NEWTON AV
1900 SJS 95122 834-H6
NEWTON DR
3300 MTVW 94040 831-J2
NEW TRIER AV
5000 SJS 95136 874-E2
NEWVILLE DR
500 LGTS 95032 873-A2
500 LGTS 95032 872-J2
NEW WORLD DR
4900 SJS 95136 874-F3
NEW YORK AV
- LGTS 95030 873-A7
NEZPERCE DR
1000 HOLL 95023 1040-D5
NEZ PERCE TR
20800 SCIC 95033 913-A2
NIAGARA DR
1300 SJS 95130 853-B4
NIBLICK AV
11700 SCIC 94024 831-F4
NICASIO CT
- SJS 95127 834-J2
NICE CT
- SJS 95138 855-E7
NICHOLAS DR
- MTVW 94043 812-B5
2700 SJS 95124 873-F1
NICHOLS AV
- SCIC 95037 916-G2
NICHOLSON AV
200 LGTS 95030 873-A7
200 LGTS 95030 872-J7
300 MSER 95030 872-J7
500 SCL 95051 833-B6
NICHOLSON DR
- SBnC 95023 1059-H2
NICHOLSON LN
100 SJS 95134 813-E3
NICKEL AV
1500 SJS 95121 855-A2
NICKLAUS AV
1000 MPS 95035 794-B4
NICOLE CT
700 GIL 95020 977-J7
700 GIL 95020 978-A7
4800 SJS 95111 875-C1
NICOLE LN
24700 LAH 94024 831-E2
NICOLE WY
5400 GIL 95020 978-A7
5400 GIL 95020 977-J7
NICORA AV
1400 SJS 95133 834-D2
NIDO DR
300 CMBL 95008 853-D7
NIEMAN BLVD
2100 SJS 95121 855-D4
2900 SJS 95148 855-B2
NIEMAN CT
2300 SJS 95121 855-C3
NIEMEYER CT
- SJS 95132 814-E6
NIEVES CT
1200 MPS 95035 794-B4
NIEVES ST
800 MPS 95035 794-B4
NIGHTFALL CT
1000 SJS 95120 894-F2
NIGHTHAWK TER
1600 SUNV 94087 832-G6
NIGHTINGALE AV
1600 SUNV 94087 832-G5
NIGHTINGALE CT
1200 LALT 94024 831-H4
NIGHTINGALE DR
2400 SJS 95125 854-D6
NIGUEL LN
- SJS 95138 875-G5
NIKETTE WY
1100 SJS 95120 894-E3
NIKKIE LN
23200 SCIC 95033 913-D6
NIKULINA CT
1100 SJS 95120 894-F3
NILDA AV
1000 MTVW 94040 811-J7
NILE DR
10100 CPTO 95014 852-E1
NILES RD
15900 SCrC 95033 912-F4
NIMITZ AV
- RDWC 94061 790-B3

NIMITZ AV
- SMCo 94061 790-B3
NIMITZ FRWY I-880
- FRMT - 793-G2
- MPS - 793-H4
- MPS - 813-J1
- SJS - 813-J1
- SJS - 814-A6
- SJS - 833-H5
- SJS - 834-A1
- SJS - 853-F1
NIMRICH LN
2100 SJS 95124 873-F6
NINA CT
100 LGTS 95030 873-C7
NINA LN
16600 MGH 95037 917-C7
16600 MGH 95037 937-C1
NINA PL
26800 LAH 94022 811-A5
NINO AV
400 LGTS 95032 873-B6
NINO WY
200 LGTS 95032 873-B6
NIPOMA CT
- SJS 95135 855-G3
NIPPER AV
500 SJS 95133 834-E3
NISICH CT
1200 SJS 95122 854-H2
NISICH DR
1300 SJS 95122 854-H1
NISQUALLY DR
700 SUNV 94087 832-C5
NITA AV
300 MTVW 94043 811-F2
NOB HILL CT
- SJS 95127 835-B2
NOB HILL DR
3600 SJS 95127 835-B2
15100 SCIC 95127 835-B2
NOB HILL TER
100 MGH 95037 916-J7
100 MGH 95037 917-A7
NOB HILL WY
200 LGTS 95032 873-C4
NOBILI AV
1600 SCL 95051 832-J2
NOBLE AV
3200 SJS 95132 814-H5
11000 SCIC 95132 814-H5
NOBLE CT
100 LGTS 95032 873-D6
NOBLE LN
1000 SJS 95132 814-H5
NOBLE FIR CT
21100 CPTO 95014 852-C2
NOBU DR
1500 SJS 95131 814-C6
NOEL AV
10300 CPTO 95014 832-B7
NOEL DR
1000 MLPK 94025 790-G3
1900 LALT 94024 831-J5
NOELLA WY
5000 SJS 95124 873-H5
NOELLE CT
- SBnC 95023 1039-E5
NOKOMIS DR
500 SJS 95111 854-J7
500 SJS 95111 855-A7
NOLA DR
2100 SJS 95125 854-A6
NOLDEN AV
400 SCIC 95117 853-C1
400 SJS 95117 853-C1
NOLTE AL
900 HOLL 95023 1040-A5
NOMARK CT
1700 SJS 95125 854-A5
NOME CT
1400 SUNV 94087 832-D4
NOME DR
- SJS 95131 814-B6
NONAME UNO
- GIL 95020 958-A6
9400 GIL 95020 957-J6
9700 SCIC 95020 957-H2
NOONAN CT
21600 CPTO 95014 852-B1
NOONWOOD CT
7000 SJS 95120 894-J3
NORA DR
1800 HOLL 95023 1040-A6
NORA WY
- ATN 94027 790-D2
1600 SJS 95124 873-J5
NORADA CT
20700 SAR 95070 852-D5
NORANDA DR
700 CPTO 95014 832-C6
700 SUNV 95014 832-C6
NORBERT CT
2700 SJS 95148 835-F6
NORCLIFFE CT
3700 SJS 95136 874-D1
NORCOTT CT
6700 SJS 95120 894-F2
NORCREST CT
2800 SJS 95148 835-F6
NORCREST DR
2800 SJS 95148 835-F7
NORCROSS CT
3600 SJS 95148 835-F7
NORCROSS DR
2600 SJS 95148 835-F6
NORD LN
1600 SJS 95125 853-J7
1600 SJS 95125 854-A7
1600 SJS 95125 873-J1
NORDALE AV
600 SJS 95112 854-F2
NORDICA CT
3900 SJS 95124 873-E3

NORDYKE DR
400 SJS 95127 835-A3
NOREEN DR
1600 SJS 95124 874-A2
1600 SJS 95124 873-J2
NORELIUS CT
1300 SJS 95120 874-B6
NORFOLK DR
1000 SJS 95129 852-G3
NORFOLK PINE AV
800 SUNV 94087 832-C2
NORIEGA AV
1000 SUNV 94086 812-C7
NORIN CT
900 SCIC 95008 873-E1
NORITA CT
2700 SJS 95127 834-H2
NORLAND DR
1500 SUNV 94087 832-D5
NORMA JEAN WY
1500 SJS 95118 874-G3
NORMAN AV
1400 SCIC 95125 853-H5
1500 SCL 95054 813-D6
NORMAN DR
1200 SUNV 94087 832-G4
21500 SCIC 95033 913-A3
NORMAN ST
1300 RDWC 94061 790-A1
NORMANDALE DR
3900 SJS 95118 874-B2
NORMANDY CT
10300 CPTO 95014 852-E1
NORMANDY DR
1000 SCIC 95008 873-E1
NORMANDY LN
100 ATN 94027 790-D2
12700 LAH 94022 831-D2
NORMANDY WY
1200 SCL 95050 833-E6
1200 SCL 95128 833-E6
7500 CPTO 95014 852-D4
NORMINGTON WY
800 SJS 95136 874-D1
NORRED CT
300 SJS 95119 895-D1
NORSEMAN DR
1800 SJS 95133 834-E2
NORSTAD ST
1000 SJS 95128 853-F3
NORTECH PKWY
100 SJS 95134 813-D1
NORTH DR
100 MTVW 94040 831-H1
NORTH PZ
- MLPK 94025 790-J1
NORTH ST
- SBnC 95023 1040-A3
- SJB 95045 1038-C4
- SCIC 95046 937-E6
400 HOLL 95023 1039-J3
400 HOLL 95023 1040-A3
NORTHAMPTON CT
12500 SAR 95070 852-G6
NORTHAMPTON DR
700 PA 94303 791-B5
2100 SJS 95124 853-H6
19200 SAR 95070 852-F5
NORTHBROOK SQ
20100 CPTO 95014 832-G6
NORTHCOVE SQ
20100 CPTO 95014 832-G6
NORTH CREEK DR
200 SJS 95139 895-F1
NORTHCREST LN
10900 SCIC 94024 831-D4
NORTHCREST SQ
20000 CPTO 95014 832-G6
NORTHDALE CT
6300 SJS 95123 874-J7
NORTHERN RD
400 SJS 95125 854-C3
NORTHFIELD SQ
10800 CPTO 95014 832-G6
NORTHFORDE DR
10700 CPTO 95014 832-F6
NORTH FORK LN
13400 LAH 94022 810-J7
NORTHFRONT WY
- SJS 95131 814-B7
NORTHGATE DR
100 WDSD 94062 790-A5
400 SJS 95111 875-C2
NORTHGATE ST
100 ATN 94027 790-D2
NORTHGLEN SQ
20200 CPTO 95014 832-G6
NORTHGROVE LN
2300 SJS 95133 814-H3
NORTHGROVE WY
2300 SJS 95133 814-H3
NORTHHURST DR
10800 CPTO 95014 832-E6
NORTHLAKE DR
300 SJS 95117 853-C1
NORTHLAWN CT
4900 SJS 95130 852-J6
NORTHLAWN DR
4800 SJS 95130 852-J6
NORTH LOOP DR
1300 SJS 95126 853-H3
NORTHOAK SQ
10800 CPTO 95014 832-G6
NORTHPOINT WY
10800 CPTO 95014 832-G6
NORTHRIDGE DR
6500 SJS 95120 894-E2
NORTHRIDGE SQ
10800 CPTO 95014 832-G6
NORTHRUP AV
700 SJS 95126 853-J2
NORTHRUP ST
700 SJS 95126 853-J2

NORTHSEAL SQ
10900 CPTO 95014 832-G6
NORTHSHORE SQ
10800 CPTO 95014 832-G6
NORTHSIDE PL
- SJS 95112 834-B3
NORTHSKY SQ
10800 CPTO 95014 832-G6
NORTH STAR CIR
1900 SJS 95131 814-C4
NORTH STAR CT
2400 SJS 95131 814-C4
NORTHUMBERLAND AV
300 RDWC 94061 790-B1
NORTHUMBERLAND DR
1100 SUNV 94087 832-B2
NORTHVIEW SQ
10800 CPTO 95014 832-G6
NORTHWEST CIR
1800 SJS 95131 814-B6
NORTHWEST SQ
20100 CPTO 95014 832-G6
NORTHWESTERN PKWY
2500 SCL 95051 833-B1
NORTHWIND SQ
20000 CPTO 95014 832-G6
NORTHWOOD DR
2500 SJS 95132 814-C3
20000 CPTO 95014 832-E6
NORTON AV
- SJS 95126 833-H7
- SJS 95126 853-H1
NORTON RD
15100 SAR 95070 872-D4
NORTREE ST
3600 SJS 95148 835-F7
NORVAL WY
1100 SJS 95125 854-A5
NORVELLA ST
1300 SJS 95122 834-J5
NORWALK DR
4200 SJS 95129 853-B1
NORWICH AV
200 MPS 95035 793-J7
10200 CPTO 95014 832-F7
NORWICH WY
4500 SJS 95008 853-A6
4500 SJS 95130 853-A6
NORWOOD AV
3000 SJS 95148 835-D7
NOTHING RD
- SBnC - 1039-C7
- SBnC - 1059-C1
NOTRE DAME DR
1600 MTVW 94040 811-G7
3400 SCL 95051 832-J2
NOTRE DAME ST
- SJS 95110 834-B6
- SJS 95113 834-B6
NOTTINGHAM AV
- SMCo 94063 790-C1
NOTTINGHAM PL
1000 SJS 95117 853-B3
NOTTINGHAM WY
400 CMBL 95008 853-G5
1000 LALT 94024 831-H4
NOTTOWAY AV
2000 SJS 95116 834-H5
NOVA CT
- MPS 95035 814-A2
NOVA LN
300 MLPK 94025 790-J3
NOVAK DR
600 SJS 95127 814-H7
NOVA SCOTIA AV
3400 SJS 95124 873-E2
3500 SCIC 95124 873-E2
NOVATO AV
400 SUNV 94086 812-C7
400 SUNV 94086 832-C1
NOVEMBER DR
900 CPTO 95014 852-C2
NOYO DR
100 SJS 95123 875-B5
NOYO RIVER CT
4600 SJS 95136 874-G2
NUBE CT
2500 SJS 95148 835-D6
NUESTRA AV
400 SUNV 94086 812-C7
400 SUNV 94086 832-C1
NUESTRA CASTILLO CT
- SJS 95116 834-H3
NUEVA DR
6300 SJS 95119 875-C7
NUEVA ST
- RDWC 94061 790-B1
NUGGET CT
1600 SJS 95127 835-B5
NUNES DR
2000 SJS 95131 814-D6
NUNZIO CT
- SJS 95120 894-H4
NURIA CT
- SCIC 95111 854-G5
- SJS 95111 854-G5
NURIA PL
- SCIC 95111 854-G5
- SJS 95111 854-G5
NUTHATCH LN
1500 SUNV 94087 832-G5
NUTMEG AV
700 SUNV 94087 832-C1
NUTMEG CT
1900 SJS 95131 814-D6
NUTTAL OAK CT
700 SUNV 94086 832-G2
NUTTMAN ST
500 SCL 95054 813-E7
NUT TREE LN
100 MGH 95037 937-B5
NUT TREE PL
1300 SJS 95122 834-F7

NUTWOOD LN
14400 SAR 95070 872-F3
NYLAND DR
- SJB 95045 1038-D5

O

OAHU DR
700 SJS 95111 855-A6
OAHU LN
19100 SAR 95070 872-G1
OAK AV
- SCIC 95046 937-E6
300 RDWC 94061 790-A1
1300 LALT 94024 831-J3
1400 LALT 94040 831-J3
1400 LALT 94040 832-A3
1400 LALT 94024 832-A3
1600 MLPK 94025 790-J2
1600 MTVW 94040 832-A3
1600 MLPK 94025 790-F6
1900 SMCo 94025 790-F6
OAK CT
- SUNV 94086 812-E7
100 MLPK 94025 791-A3
8100 GIL 95020 977-J2
19000 SCIC 95033 892-G4
21500 SCIC 95033 913-B2
OAK DR
900 SJS 95138 875-F6
3500 SMCo 94025 790-E1
3600 ATN 94027 790-E1
11300 SCrC 95018 912-B7
17900 SCIC 95033 912-J2
17900 SCIC 95033 913-A2
18300 MSER 95030 872-H5
18300 SCIC 95030 872-H5
OAK LN
- MTVW 94040 811-J6
900 MLPK 94025 790-F4
3400 SCIC 95037 917-G4
3400 SCIC 95037 936-J7
OAK PL
14400 SAR 95070 872-E3
OAK RD
- SCIC 94305 790-F6
OAK ST
- SJS 95110 854-C1
- LALT 94022 811-D6
100 MTVW 94041 811-H5
1000 HOLL 95023 1040-C6
3400 MGH 95037 917-B7
3400 MGH 95037 937-B1
14400 SAR 95070 872-D3
OAKBERRY WY
300 SJS 95123 875-B6
OAKBLUFF CT
1100 SJS 95131 814-E7
OAKBRIDGE DR
3000 SJS 95121 855-A3
OAK BROOK CIR
100 SJS 95139 895-H2
OAK BROOK WY
- GIL 95020 977-J6
OAK CANYON CT
- SBnC 95023 1060-D1
1400 SJS 95120 874-A6
OAK CANYON DR
1400 SJS 95120 874-A7
16200 MGH 95037 917-H6
OAK CANYON LN
3700 MGH 95037 917-H6
3700 SCIC 95037 917-H6
OAK CANYON PL
1400 SJS 95120 874-A6
OAK CREEK CT
- SBnC 95023 1060-D1
OAK CREEK DR
- SBnC 95023 1060-C1
1300 PA 94304 790-F6
OAK CREEK LN
20500 SAR 95070 852-D5
OAK CREEK WY
1200 SUNV 94089 813-A5
OAKCREST CT
22600 CPTO 95014 831-J7
OAKCREST DR
6400 SJS 95120 894-D1
OAKDALE AV
400 EPA 94303 791-B1
OAKDALE DR
200 LGTS 95032 873-C4
OAKDALE WY
200 MGH 95037 916-H3
OAKDELL DR
1600 MLPK 94025 790-E6
OAKDELL PL
900 SJS 95117 853-D3
21900 CPTO 95014 832-B7
OAKES ST
- EPA 94303 791-C3
OAK ESTATES CT
2800 SJS 95135 855-F5
OAKFIELD AV
100 RDWC 94061 790-B2
OAKFIELD LN
500 MLPK 94025 790-E6
OAK FLAT RD
2300 SJS 95131 814-D5
22800 SCrC 95033 912-G6
OAK FOREST CT
- PTLV 94028 830-D2
OAK FOREST WY
6000 SJS 95120 874-D7
OAKGATE WY
3100 SJS 95148 855-E1
OAK GLEN AV
15200 SCIC 95037 936-C1
17500 SCIC 95037 916-B7
OAKGLEN WY
1200 SJS 95120 874-B6
OAK GLENN DR
18600 SCIC 95030 872-H5

OAK GROVE AV
- ATN 94027 790-G2
- LGTS 95030 892-J1
100 MLPK 94025 790-F3
OAK GROVE CT
200 MGH 95037 916-H6
OAK GROVE DR
400 SCL 95054 813-E5
700 SJS 95129 853-A2
17900 MGH 95037 916-J6
OAK GROVE PZ
700 MLPK 94025 790-F4
OAKHAVEN DR
19700 SAR 95070 852-F5
OAK HAVEN PL
- MTVW 94041 811-G4
OAK HILL AV
- SJS 95125 854-E4
4100 PA 94306 811-B4
OAK HILL CT
3400 MGH 95037 917-H5
OAK HILL WY
- LGTS 95030 893-A1
OAK HOLLOW LN
14000 SAR 95070 872-E1
OAK HOLLOW WY
- MLPK 94025 790-E7
OAKHURST AV
1300 LALT 94024 831-H3
OAKHURST CT
5500 SJS 95129 852-H4
OAKHURST DR
16200 MSER 95030 872-J6
OAKHURST WY
- MPS 95035 794-A6
OAK KNOLL CIR
24000 LAH 94024 831-D3
OAK KNOLL CT
15700 LGTS 95030 872-J5
15700 LGTS 95030 873-A5
OAK KNOLL DR
1200 SJS 95129 852-H4
15600 LGTS 95030 873-A5
15600 MSER 95030 873-A5
OAK KNOLL LN
500 MLPK 94025 790-E6
OAK KNOLL RD
- LGTS 95030 872-J7
- SCIC 95030 872-J7
OAK LAKE CT
1200 SJS 95131 814-B5
OAKLAND AV
400 SJS 95116 834-G4
1000 MLPK 94025 790-H1
OAKLAND PL
100 LGTS 95032 873-B2
OAKLAND RD
900 SJS 95112 834-B1
1000 SJS 95133 834-B1
1500 SJS 95131 814-A5
1500 SJS 95112 814-A5
OAK LEAF CT
3100 MGH 95037 917-G5
OAKLEAF CT
21900 CPTO 95014 832-B7
OAK LEAF DR
16800 MGH 95037 917-F4
OAKLEAF DR
3500 SJS 95127 835-C4
OAK LEAF LN
3000 MGH 95037 917-G5
OAKLEAF PL
10000 CPTO 95014 832-B7
OAKLEY AV
2000 SMCo 94025 790-D6
OAKLEY DR
1400 LALT 94024 831-J4
OAKMEAD PKWY
300 SUNV 94086 813-A7
1200 SUNV 94086 812-J6
OAK MEADOW CT
7700 CPTO 95014 852-C4
OAK MEADOW DR
200 LGTS 95032 873-B6
OAKMEAD VILLAGE CT
3000 SCL 95051 813-A7
OAKMEAD VILLAGE DR
2800 SCL 95054 813-A7
2900 SCL 95051 813-A7
2900 SCL 95051 833-A1
OAKMILL CT
2800 SJS 95121 854-J3
OAKMONT DR
1100 SJS 95117 853-B3
19700 SCIC 95033 892-J7
OAKMONT PL
1000 SJS 95117 853-B3
OAKMONT WY
100 LGTS 95032 873-C4
OAKMORE DR
- SCIC 95127 815-A7
OAKNOLL CT
21900 CPTO 95014 832-B7
OAK PARK CT
12100 LAH 94024 831-D3
OAK PARK DR
100 LGTS 95032 873-C4
700 MGH 95037 936-J1
5400 SJS 95129 852-H4
OAK PARK LN
2500 SJS 95008 853-F7
OAK POINT TER
1500 SUNV 94087 832-D5
OAKRIDGE CT
15600 MGH 95037 917-H4
OAK RIDGE DR
- SBnC 95023 1060-D1
19300 MonC 95076 1037-A5
OAKRIDGE DR
600 SCIC 94024 831-F4
OAKRIDGE LN
16900 MGH 95037 917-H5

STREET Block City ZIP Pg-Grid

OAKRIDGE LN
16900 SCIC 95037 917-H5
OAK RIDGE RD
17900 SCrC 95033 892-B3
OAKRIDGE RD
200 SCIC 95030 872-G6
15800 MGH 95037 917-H5
OAK RIDGE WY
15200 LGTS 95030 873-B4
OAK RIM CT
100 LGTS 95032 873-C5
OAK RIM WY
100 LGTS 95032 873-C6
OAK SPRING CT
11500 CPTO 95014 852-C4
OAK SPRINGS CIR
7700 SCIC 95020 958-G6
OAKTON CT
1800 SJS 95148 835-A5
OAKTREE DR
300 MTVW 94040 811-F4
1000 SJS 95129 852-H3
OAK VALLEY DR
13000 SCIC 95037 956-G1
OAK VALLEY RD
- CPTO 95014 831-G6
- SCIC 95014 831-G6
OAK VIEW CIR
16400 MGH 95037 917-G6
OAK VIEW CT
16400 MGH 95037 917-G6
OAK VIEW LN
3200 MGH 95037 917-G6
OAKVIEW LN
21800 CPTO 95014 832-B7
OAKVIEW RD
1100 SJS 95121 855-A5
OAKVILLE AV
10400 CPTO 95014 852-F2
OAKWOOD AV
1700 SJS 95124 873-H3
OAKWOOD BLVD
- RDWC 94061 790-C1
- ATN 94027 790-C1
E OAKWOOD BLVD
200 RDWC 94061 790-C1
W OAKWOOD BLVD
200 RDWC 94061 790-C1
OAKWOOD CT
600 LALT 94024 831-G2
3300 MGH 95037 917-H6
20500 SAR 95070 852-D7
OAKWOOD DR
- RDWC 94061 790-C1
400 SCL 95054 813-E5
2000 EPA 94303 791-A2
OAKWOOD LN
16300 MGH 95037 917-H6
OAKWOOD PL
300 MLPK 94025 790-H1
OAK WOOD WY
200 LGTS 95032 873-C4
OASIS CT
10200 CPTO 95014 832-A7
OASIS DR
5500 SJS 95123 875-B4
OBATA CT
- GIL 95020 978-C6
OBATA WY
5700 GIL 95020 978-C6
OBERG CT
- MTVW 94043 812-B5
OBERLIN ST
1900 SCIC 94305 791-A7
1900 SCIC 94305 811-A1
2000 PA 94306 811-A1
OBERLIN WY
6400 SJS 95123 875-B7
6400 SJS 95123 895-B1
OBERT DR
100 SJS 95136 874-J2
OBRAD DR
12300 SAR 95070 852-H6
OBRIEN CT
1000 SJS 95126 833-G5
O BRINE LN
- PA 94303 791-D4
OBSERVATORY AV
- SJS 95125 854-F4
OBSERVATORY DR
10400 SCIC 95127 815-B7
10400 SCIC 95127 835-C1
OBSIDIAN CT
7700 CPTO 95014 852-C3
OBURN CT
1500 CMBL 95008 873-B2
OCALA AV
1700 SJS 95122 834-J7
2200 SJS 95148 834-J7
2400 SJS 95122 835-A5
2400 SJS 95148 835-A5
OCALA CT
2900 SJS 95148 835-B5
OCCIDENTAL CT
- SJS 95123 874-F7
OCEAN VIEW DR
18000 SCIC 95033 912-J4
OCHO RIOS DR
6100 SJS 95123 874-G6
OCONNOR DR
100 SCIC 95128 853-F1
100 SJS 95128 833-F7
100 SJS 95128 853-F1
OCONNOR ST
900 EPA 94303 791-C2
100 MLPK 94025 791-A2
500 EPA 94303 791-A2
W OCONNOR ST
100 MLPK 94025 791-A2
300 MLPK 94025 790-J2
OCTAVIUS DR
3200 SCL 95054 813-C7
OCTOBER DR
5500 SJS 95138 875-C4

OCTOBER WY
7900 CPTO 95014 852-C2
ODELL PL
- ATN 94027 790-E2
ODELL WY
900 LALT 94024 831-H1
ODYSSEY CT
100 SJS 95118 874-G3
OELLA CT
4000 SJS 95124 874-A2
OFFENBACH PL
400 SUNV 94087 832-E3
OGALLALA PTH
17600 SCIC 95033 913-A2
OGALLALA WARPATH
17700 SCIC 95033 913-C2
17800 SCIC 95033 912-J2
OGDEN CT
- MPS 95035 793-J7
OGIER AV
100 SCIC 95037 896-E7
O GRADY DR
7000 SJS 95120 894-G3
OHARA CT
2300 SJS 95133 834-F1
OHIGGINS DR
1400 SJS 95126 853-G4
OHIO AV
2400 RDWC 94061 790-A3
OHIO CT
100 MPS 95035 793-J7
OHLONE
- PTLV 94028 830-C2
OHLONE CT
100 LGTS 95032 873-B6
OHLONE DR
2500 SJS 95132 814-E6
10000 SCIC 95020 957-E5
OHLONE LN
26400 LAH 94022 811-B5
OHLONE WY
- GIL 95020 957-F7
OJAI DR
16200 MSER 95030 872-G6
18900 SCIC 95030 872-G6
OJO DE AGUA CT
2000 SJS 95116 834-D2
OKA LN
15000 LGTS 95032 873-D3
OKA RD
14400 LGTS 95032 873-C3
OKANOGAN CT
14100 SAR 95070 872-F2
OKANOGAN DR
14000 SAR 95070 872-F2
OKEEFE CT
- GIL 95020 957-F6
OKEEFE LN
- GIL 95020 957-F6
24900 LALT 94022 831-C1
24900 LAH 94022 831-C1
OKEEFE ST
100 MLPK 94025 791-A2
100 MLPK 94025 790-J2
E OKEEFE ST
100 EPA 94303 791-A2
100 MLPK 94025 791-A2
OKINO CT
5300 SJS 95123 874-J3
OLCOTT ST
3000 SCL 95054 813-C7
OLD ABBEY PL
1300 SJS 95132 814-E6
OLD ADOBE RD
100 LGTS 95032 872-J3
100 SAR 95070 872-J3
200 LGTS 95030 872-J3
4100 PA 94306 811-B4
OLD ADOBE WY
1900 SJS 95132 872-J3
OLD ALMADEN RD
2800 SJS 95125 854-C7
3300 SJS 95136 854-C7
OLD ALTOS RD
200 LALT 94022 811-D7
13600 LAH 94022 811-D7
OLD BAYSHORE HWY
- SJS 95110 833-H1
200 SJS 95112 833-H1
1100 SJS 95112 834-A2
OLD BEAR CREEK RD
- SCrC 95033 892-A7
- SCrC 95033 912-A1
OLD BLOSSOM HILL RD
200 SCIC 95032 873-D6
200 LGTS 95032 873-D6
OLDBRIDGE RD
1800 SJS 95131 814-D7
OLDBROOK CT
500 SJS 95111 855-A7
OLD CALAVERAS RD
1900 MPS 95035 794-E4
1900 SCIC 95035 794-D5
OLD COACH RD
11900 SCIC 95020 956-J4
OLD CREEK DR
900 SJS 95120 894-G2
OLD CREEK RD
3300 SCIC 95020 956-J4
OLD CRESCI RD
- SCrC 95033 912-G7
OLD CREST PL
2400 SJS 95132 814-E6
OLDE DR
100 LGTS 95032 873-D7
14300 LGTS 95030 873-D7
OLD ELM CT
2400 SJS 95132 814-E6
OLD ESTATES CT
2800 SJS 95135 855-G5
OLD EVANS RD
400 MPS 95035 794-D5

OLDFIELD WY
2900 SJS 95135 855-F3
OLD FORGE LN
1200 SJS 95132 814-E6
OLD GATE CT
2400 SJS 95132 814-E6
OLD GILROY ST
100 GIL 95020 978-A3
OLD GLORY LN
2800 SCL 95054 813-B4
OLD GOLD MINE RD
21500 SCIC 95033 913-B2
OLDHAM WY
600 SJS 95111 854-H4
OLD IRONSIDES DR
4700 SCL 95054 813-B4
OLD JAPANESE RD
16000 SCrC 95033 912-G7
W OLD JULIAN ST
100 SJS 95110 834-A6
OLD LOGGING RD
22000 SCrC 95033 912-G5
OLD MANOR PL
1100 SJS 95132 814-E6
OLD MEADOW CT
6500 SJS 95135 855-J7
OLD MIDDLEFIELD WY
1700 MTVW 94043 811-F2
4200 PA 94306 811-F2
4200 PA 94043 811-F2
OLD MILL CT
6600 SJS 95120 894-E1
OLD MILL RD
300 SCrC 95066 912-G7
OLDMINE RD
21400 SCIC 95033 913-B2
OLD MONTEREY RD
4200 SCIC 95020 998-B5
18100 MGH 95037 916-H5
OLD MOUNT RD
100 SCrC 95018 912-E6
OLD MOUNTAIN VIEW-ALVISO RD
900 SUNV 94089 812-J3
1200 SUNV 94089 813-A3
3100 SCL 95054 813-A3
OLD OAK CT
400 LALT 94022 811-D6
OLD OAK DR
1100 SJS 95120 894-E2
OLD OAK LN
2800 MGH 95037 917-F6
OLD OAK WY
13400 SAR 95070 852-C7
13400 SAR 95070 872-C1
OLD OAKLAND RD
1500 SJS 95131 814-B7
OLD ORCHARD CT
100 LGTS 95032 873-G6
OLD ORCHARD DR
100 LGTS 95032 873-G6
OLD ORCHARD RD
700 CMBL 95008 853-D7
800 CMBL 95008 873-D1
OLD PACHECO PASS RD
2100 SCIC 95020 978-F4
OLD PAGE MILL LN
28000 LAH 94304 810-H4
OLD PAGE MILL RD
2000 LAH 94304 810-J4
2000 SCIC 94304 810-J4
2200 PA 94304 810-J4
2300 LAH 94022 810-J4
OLD PARK PL
1300 SJS 95132 814-E5
OLD PIEDMONT RD
1400 SJS 95132 814-G3
1800 SCIC 95132 814-F1
2100 MPS 95035 814-F1
OLD POST WY
2300 SJS 95132 814-E6
OLD QUARRY RD
- SCIC 95120 874-D6
- SJS 95120 874-D6
OLD RANCH LN
11500 LAH 94024 831-E4
OLD RANCH RD
- SBnC 95023 1060-E1
11400 LAH 94024 831-E4
16000 SCrC 95033 912-G4
OLD RIDGE CT
2400 SJS 95132 814-E6
OLD RIDGE RD
15100 SCrC 95033 912-H4
OLD ROSE PL
1300 SJS 95132 814-E5
OLD SAN FRANCISCO RD
300 SUNV 94086 832-E1
OLD SAN JUAN HOLLISTER RD
- HOLL 95023 1039-E3
2800 SBnC 95023 1039-E3
OLD SANTA CRUZ HWY
19800 SCIC 95033 892-H6
20500 SCIC 95033 912-J2
21500 SCIC 95033 913-A1
23400 SCIC 95033 913-A5
OLD SNAKEY RD
12100 LAH 94022 831-B3
OLD SPANISH TR
- SMCo 94028 830-D4
100 PTLV 94028 830-D4
OLD STAGECOACH RD
- SBnC - 1038-D7
- SBnC 95045 1038-D7
OLD STONE PL
1300 SJS 95132 814-E6
OLD STONE WY
1300 SJS 95132 814-D5

OLD SUMMIT RD
17500 SCIC 95070 892-A2
17500 SCIC 95033 892-A2
23500 SCIC 95033 913-C6
OLD SUMMIT RD S
- SCrC 95033 912-J4
- SCrC 95033 913-A5
21000 SCIC 95033 912-J4
OLD TOMS CT
- GIL 95020 977-E4
OLD TOWN CT
900 CPTO 95014 852-B2
OLD TRACE CT
4100 PA 94306 811-B4
OLD TRACE LN
27000 LAH 94022 811-B5
27000 PA 94306 811-B5
OLD TRACE RD
1000 PA 94306 811-B4
OLDTREE CT
1700 SJS 95131 814-D4
OLD TREE WY
13500 SAR 95070 872-E1
OLD TULLY RD
- SJS 95112 854-F4
- SJS 95111 854-F4
200 SCIC 95111 854-F4
OLD VINEYARD RD
- SCrC 95033 892-A3
OLDWELL CT
- SJS 95138 875-D4
OLD WELL RD
21000 SCIC 95033 912-H1
OLD WILLOW PL
1200 SJS 95125 854-E6
OLDWOOD CT
3000 SJS 95148 855-E1
OLD WOOD RD
14200 SAR 95070 872-H2
OLD YERBA BUENA RD
3200 SJS 95135 855-H4
3300 SCIC 95135 855-H4
3300 SCIC 95135 856-A4
OLEA CT
- GIL 95020 957-D7
OLEANDER AV
16100 SCIC 95032 873-C5
16300 LGTS 95032 873-C5
OLEANDER CT
1000 SUNV 94086 832-H2
OLEANDER DR
- SJS 95123 875-C5
OLENA CT
- SJS 95127 834-J2
OLGA DR
- HOLL 95023 1040-B6
3900 SJS 95117 853-B2
4100 SJS 95129 853-B2
OLIN AV
- SJS 95128 853-D1
3100 SJS 95117 853-D1
3100 SCIC 95117 853-D1
OLINDER CT
900 SJS 95122 834-F6
OLIVAS CIR
8700 SJS 95135 855-J6
8700 SJS 95135 856-A6
OLIVE AV
300 PA 94306 791-B7
400 PA 94306 811-B1
14500 SCIC 95037 937-B4
14500 MGH 95037 937-B4
21600 CPTO 95014 852-B1
E OLIVE AV
100 SUNV 94086 832-E1
W OLIVE AV
100 SUNV 94086 832-C1
1000 SUNV 94086 812-B7
OLIVE CT
- MTVW 94041 811-J6
OLIVE DR
10500 SCIC 95127 835-B1
10600 SCIC 95127 815-B7
OLIVE PL
10600 SCIC 95127 815-B7
10600 SCIC 95127 835-B1
OLIVE ST
- HOLL 95023 1040-A5
100 LGTS 95030 873-A6
300 MLPK 94025 790-E5
1800 SJS 95128 833-G7
1800 SCIC 95128 833-G7
OLIVE BRANCH CT
6700 SJS 95120 894-E3
OLIVE BRANCH LN
1100 SJS 95120 894-E2
18000 MGH 95037 916-G7
OLIVEGATE LN
2100 SJS 95136 874-J3
OLIVE GROVE WY
8700 SJS 95135 856-A6
OLIVE HILL DR
- SJS 95125 854-D5
OLIVER CT
- MLPK 94025 790-C6
OLIVER DR
- SJS 95135 855-F4
OLIVER PL
- SCL 95051 832-J4
OLIVER ST
300 MPS 95035 794-A3
1100 RDWC 94061 790-A1
OLIVERA TER
- SUNV 94087 832-E3
OLIVE SPRING CT
11600 CPTO 95014 852-A4
OLIVESTONE WY
2600 SJS 95132 814-E5
OLIVE TREE CT
24700 LAH 94024 831-D5
OLIVETREE DR
1700 SJS 95131 814-C5

OLIVE TREE LN
24600 LAH 94024 831-D4
24700 SCIC 94024 831-D4
OLIVETTI CT
3600 SJS 95148 835-F7
OLIVEWOOD PL
3000 SJS 95148 855-E1
OLIVE WOOD ST
19900 CPTO 95014 832-F6
OLIVIA CT
11400 SCIC 95020 957-G2
OLIVIAN DR
500 SJS 95123 875-B3
OLMO CT
1000 SJS 95129 852-H2
OLMSTED RD
- SCIC 94305 791-A7
- SCIC 94305 810-J1
- SCIC 94305 811-A1
- SCIC 94305 790-J7
OLSEN DR
- SJS 95128 853-E1
3200 SCIC 95117 853-D1
3200 SJS 95117 853-D1
OLSTAD CT
5300 SJS 95111 875-C2
OLYMPIA AV
100 SBnC 95045 1038-H3
1200 SCIC 95008 873-E1
1300 SJS 95008 873-E1
OLYMPIC AV
2300 MLPK 94025 790-D7
OLYMPIC CT
- GIL 95020 977-H7
OLYMPIC DR
1100 MPS 95035 814-D1
16000 MGH 95037 937-A2
OLYMPUS CT
900 SUNV 94087 832-B6
OLYMPUS DR
1300 SJS 95129 853-A4
1300 SJS 95129 852-J4
OMAHA CT
6200 SJS 95123 874-H6
OMAR DR
- SJS 95123 875-B4
OMAR ST
1400 SCIC 95020 958-B4
OMEGA CT
700 SJS 95127 814-H6
OMEGA LN
14400 SAR 95070 872-H3
OMIRA DR
200 SJS 95123 875-A4
ONDINE CT
1000 SJS 95132 814-H5
ONEDA CT
21400 SCIC 95033 913-A2
ONEIDA DR
600 SUNV 94087 832-D2
6100 SJS 95123 874-H6
ONEILL DR
800 HOLL 95023 1039-J4
800 HOLL 95023 1040-A4
ONEL DR
2100 SJS 95131 833-H1
2100 SJS 95131 813-H7
ONE OAK LN
15400 MSER 95030 873-A5
ONEONTA DR
24900 LAH 94022 831-C2
ON ORBIT DR
15500 SCIC 95070 872-C5
ONSLOW WY
3300 SJS 95132 814-G4
ONTARIO CT
600 SUNV 94087 832-D5
ONTARIO DR
1500 SUNV 94087 832-D5
2400 SJS 95124 853-G7
ONTARIO LN
1300 CMBL 95008 853-B5
ONTARIO RD
200 MPS 95035 794-A6
ONYX CT
700 SJS 95117 853-D2
OPAL DR
700 SJS 95117 853-D3
OPENMEADOW CT
4400 SJS 95129 853-A1
OPHELIA AV
2600 SJS 95122 855-A1
OPHELIA CT
2700 SJS 95122 855-A2
OPHIR CT
100 MPS 95035 793-J7
OPTICAL CT
- SJS 95138 875-E3
ORA ST
5400 SJS 95129 852-H3
ORACLE OAK PL
800 SUNV 94086 832-G2
ORANGE AV
300 SCIC 94043 812-A2
400 LALT 94022 811-D7
500 LALT 94022 831-E1
800 SUNV 94087 832-C2
1100 MLPK 94025 790-D5
1100 SMCo 94025 790-D5
10000 CPTO 95014 832-C2
10000 CPTO 95014 852-B1
ORANGE ST
3100 SJS 95127 814-H7
ORANGE BLOSSOM DR
7500 CPTO 95014 852-D4
ORANGE BLOSSOM LN
15700 SCIC 95032 873-D6
ORANGEBRICK WY
1000 SJS 95120 894-F2
ORANGE GROVE DR
1800 SJS 95124 873-G1
ORANGESTONE WY
2600 SJS 95132 814-E5

ORANGETREE LN
1800 MTVW 94040 831-G1
10500 CPTO 95014 832-E7
ORANGEWOOD DR
1500 SJS 95121 855-A3
ORANGEWOOD ST
19800 CPTO 95014 832-F6
ORCHARD AV
- RDWC 94061 790-B1
100 MTVW 94043 812-A4
100 MTVW 94043 811-J5
300 SUNV 94086 812-E6
ORCHARD CT
1600 MGH 95037 917-D6
21100 CPTO 95014 832-A7
ORCHARD DR
3000 SJS 95134 813-F5
7000 GIL 95020 977-J4
ORCHARD GN
200 MTVW 94043 812-A5
ORCHARD PKWY
2100 SJS 95131 813-G7
2700 SJS 95134 813-F5
ORCHARD RD
- SBnC 95023 1000-D5
1200 SCIC 95020 1000-D2
20300 SAR 95070 872-E2
ORCHARD ST
- LGTS 95030 893-A1
ORCHARD CITY DR
- CMBL 95008 853-E6
ORCHARD HILL LN
26900 LAH 94022 811-C7
ORCHARD HILL RD
300 SBnC 95045 1037-G2
ORCHARD HILLS ST
- ATN 94027 790-B4
ORCHARD MEADOW DR
20000 SCIC 95070 852-A7
ORCHARD OAK CIR
100 CMBL 95008 853-F6
ORCHARD PARK DR
5600 SJS 95123 874-J5
ORCHARD SPRING CT
11600 CPTO 95014 852-A4
ORCHARD SPRING LN
11600 CPTO 95014 852-A4
ORCHARD VIEW DR
1600 SJS 95124 873-J6
ORCHID DR
1100 SUNV 94086 832-H2
ORCHID PL
800 LALT 94024 831-E1
ORCHID WY
900 SJS 95117 853-B3
OREGOLD PL
700 SJS 95131 814-B5
OREGON AV
100 PA 94301 791-B6
700 PA 94303 791-B6
2100 RDWC 94061 790-A2
OREGON CT
900 MPS 95035 794-A5
OREGON EXWY
Rt#-G3
- PA 94301 791-C6
- PA 94306 791-C6
2500 PA 94303 791-C6
OREGON WY
1000 MPS 95035 794-A5
ORELLA CT
12600 SAR 95070 852-F6
ORESTES WY
2000 SJS 95008 853-B6
ORI AV
2700 SJS 95128 853-E2
ORICK CT
300 SJS 95123 874-J4
ORILLA CT
1100 LALT 94022 811-D3
ORILLIA CT
1500 SUNV 94087 832-D5
ORIN CT
4100 SJS 95124 873-E3
ORINDA DR
2500 SJS 95121 855-D3
ORINDA ST
3400 PA 94306 811-C1
ORINDA WY
9100 GIL 95020 957-F7
ORIOLE AV
1500 SUNV 94087 832-G5
ORIOLE DR
3100 SJS 95117 853-D3
ORIOLE RD
14000 SAR 95070 872-G4
ORIOLE WY
15100 SAR 95070 872-H4
ORION CT
100 MPS 95035 793-J7
ORION LN
7700 CPTO 95014 852-C3
ORION PL
900 CPTO 95014 852-C3
ORKNEY AV
700 SCL 95054 813-E6
ORLANDO DR
1300 SJS 95122 834-H6
2100 SJS 95122 854-J1
ORLEANS CT
13700 SAR 95070 872-G1
ORLEANS DR
1200 SUNV 94089 812-G3
1600 SJS 95122 854-J1
ORLINE CT
10700 CPTO 95014 852-D2
ORME ST
4100 PA 94306 811-C2
ORMONDE DR
700 MTVW 94043 811-H3
ORMONDE WY
1300 MTVW 94043 811-H3
ORMSBY DR
1400 SUNV 94087 832-D4

ORNELLAS DR
2000 MPS 95035 814-E1
OROGRANDE PL
7700 CPTO 95014 852-C3
OROLETTE PL
1900 SJS 95131 814-D6
ORONSAY CT
200 SJS 95119 875-D7
ORONSAY WY
200 SJS 95119 875-D7
OROPEZA CT
600 SJS 95133 834-G1
OROSI CT
200 SJS 95116 834-F3
OROSI WY
200 SJS 95116 834-F3
OROVILLE RD
400 MPS 95035 794-A6
ORR CT
1600 LALT 94024 831-J4
ORSETTI CT
300 SCIC 95020 957-J5
ORTEGA AV
- MTVW 94040 811-F4
ORTEGA CIR
1000 GIL 95020 977-G3
ORTEGA CT
3700 PA 94303 791-F7
ORTEGA DR
26800 LAH 94022 811-A5
ORTHELLO WY
2800 SCL 95051 833-A4
ORTIZ CT
- HOLL 95023 1039-G3
1200 SUNV 94089 813-A4
ORTO ST
400 SJS 95125 854-D3
ORVIETO CT
5700 SJS 95138 875-G1
ORVIS AV
500 SJS 95112 834-D7
OSAGE AV
- LALT 94022 811-F7
OSAGE CT
600 SJS 95123 874-G4
OSBORN AV
1100 SMCo 94061 790-B3
OSBORNE AV
2300 SCL 95050 833-D7
OSBORNE CIR
2100 HOLL 95023 1040-E5
OSBORNE CT
14900 SCIC 95037 936-J6
OSCAR CT
2000 SCIC 95020 958-C3
OSCAR DR
2000 SCIC 95020 958-B3
OSGOOD CT
400 SJS 95111 875-B2
OSITOS AV
400 SUNV 94086 812-C7
400 SUNV 94086 832-C1
OSLO LN
1300 SJS 95118 874-B5
OSPREY CT
1500 SJS 95127 835-C4
OSTENBERG DR
6000 SJS 95120 874-C7
OSTRICH CT
5200 SJS 95123 874-F7
OSUNA PL
1100 SJS 95129 852-J3
OSWALD PL
1700 SCL 95051 833-B3
OSWEGO DR
800 SJS 95122 854-F1
OTHELLO AV
2600 SJS 95122 855-A2
OTIS WY
- LALT 94022 811-F6
OTONO CT
300 SJS 95111 875-A1
OTOOLE AV
1900 SJS 95131 814-A7
2100 SJS 95131 813-J5
OTOOLE CT
8500 GIL 95020 977-G1
OTOOLE LN
- SJS 95131 814-A6
OTOOLE WY
- SJS 95131 814-A6
OTTAWA CT
1600 SUNV 94087 832-D5
OTTAWA WY
100 FRMT 94539 793-J2
2400 SJS 95130 853-A7
OTTERSON CT
2900 PA 94303 791-D5
OTTERSON ST
500 SJS 95110 834-A7
OTTO CT
900 SJS 95132 814-J5
OUR LN
2400 MTVW 94040 831-J1
OUR LADYS WY
- SCL 95054 813-B5
OUSLEY DR
1400 GIL 95020 977-F1
OUTLOOK CT
3400 SJS 95132 814-G3
OUTLOOK DR
500 SCIC 94024 831-F2
OVATION CT
700 SJS 95134 813-H4
OVERBROOK DR
3200 SJS 95118 874-B1
OVERLAND CT
600 SJS 95111 854-H5
OVERLAND WY
600 SJS 95111 854-H5
OVERLOOK DR
15900 SCIC 95030 872-F6
OVERLOOK RD
16500 SCIC 95030 872-G7

STREET Block City ZIP Pg-Grid

OVERLOOK RD
16600 SCIC 95033 872-G7
18200 LGTS 95030 872-H7
18500 MSER 95030 872-H7
OVERTURE CT
700 SJS 95134 813-H4
OWEN ST
2100 SCL 95054 833-C1
2200 SCL 95054 813-C7
OWENS CT
- MTVW 94043 812-B5
OWENS LAKE DR
800 SJS 95123 874-D5
OWEN SOUND DR
1400 SUNV 94087 832-D4
OWLSWOOD WY
400 SJS 95111 854-F6
OWSLEY AV
900 SJS 95122 834-F7
OXBOW CT
1300 SUNV 94087 832-D4
5100 SJS 95124 873-F5
OXFORD AV
200 PA 94306 791-A7
1200 SUNV 94087 832-B2
OXFORD CT
3500 SCL 95051 832-J6
OXFORD DR
900 LALT 94024 831-H5
3500 SCL 95051 832-J6
OXFORD LN
3200 SJS 95117 853-D3
OXFORD ST
1300 RDWC 94061 790-A1
OXTON DR
1100 SJS 95121 854-J3
OYAMA DR
1400 SJS 95131 814-B7
OYAMA PL
1400 SJS 95131 814-B7
OYSTER BAY DR
4700 SJS 95136 874-D2

P

PACCHETTI WY
100 MTVW 94040 811-E3
PACER LN
2600 SCIC 95111 854-G4
PACHECO CT
2100 SCIC 95020 978-F4
PACHECO DR
800 MPS 95035 794-B6
2300 SJS 95133 834-F1
PACHECO HWY
4300 SBnC 95023 1000-C6
4300 SBnC 95023 1020-B1
PACHECO ST
1300 SCL 95051 833-A4
PACHECO CREEK DR
- SBnC 95023 1000-C5
PACHECO PASS HWY
2800 SCIC 95020 978-F4
PACHECO PASS HWY Rt#-152
600 GIL 95020 978-C3
1400 SCIC 95020 978-G3
4000 SCIC 95020 999-G1
6100 SCIC 95020 1000-A2
PACIFIC AV
800 SCIC 95126 853-J1
1300 SJS 95002 793-C7
PACIFIC DR
400 MTVW 94043 812-B5
2300 SCL 95051 832-J2
PACIFIC WY
200 SBnC 95023 1040-B2
200 HOLL 95023 1040-B2
PACIFICA DR
2000 SJS 95131 814-A5
20000 CPTO 95014 852-E1
PACIFICA WY
200 MPS 95035 793-J4
PACIFIC RIM LN
2400 SJS 95121 855-E4
PACIFIC RIM WY
4400 SJS 95121 855-E4
PACINA DR
2000 SJS 95116 834-H5
PACKING PL
200 SJS 95116 834-G4
PACO DR
400 LALT 94024 811-F7
PADDINGTON WY
1200 SJS 95127 835-A4
PADDON CIR
5800 SJS 95123 875-A5
PADERO AV
13200 SAR 95070 852-C7
PADERO CT
13200 SAR 95070 852-C7
PADILLA WY
3300 SJS 95148 835-D7
PADOVA DR
- GIL 95020 957-G7
- GIL 95020 977-G1
PADRE CT
12100 LAH 94022 831-B2
PADRES CT
1500 SJS 95125 854-C3
PADRES DR
1400 SJS 95125 854-B3
PADUA CT
- MGH 95037 917-B3
PAGANINI AV
2600 SJS 95122 855-A1
PAGE AV
- FRMT 94538 793-G2
PAGE ST
- CMBL 95008 853-F6
300 SCIC 95126 853-H1
300 SJS 95126 853-H1
PAGEANT WY
- LGTS 95030 893-A1

PAGE MILL DR
100 SJS 95111 875-B2
PAGE MILL RD
100 PA 94306 791-B7
600 PA 94304 791-B7
600 PA 94304 811-A2
1000 PA 94304 830-G2
1000 SCIC 95014 830-G2
1400 SCIC 94305 811-A2
1600 PA 94304 811-A2
1800 PA 94304 810-H7
1800 SCIC 94305 810-H7
4100 SCIC 94028 830-F7
11400 LAH 94022 830-G2
11900 SCIC 94022 830-G2
12700 LAH 94022 810-H7
20800 SMCo 94028 830-F7
PAGE MILL RD Rt#-G3
1800 SCIC 94305 810-J4
1800 PA 94304 810-J4
1900 SCIC 94304 810-J4
2100 LAH 94022 810-J4
PAGODA TREE CT
800 SUNV 94086 832-G2
PAGOSA CT
48900 FRMT 94539 793-J2
PAGOSA WY
- FRMT 94539 793-J3
300 FRMT 94539 794-A2
PAINTBRUSH DR
1000 SUNV 94086 832-H3
PAINTED FEATHER CT
- MGH 95037 917-A3
PAINTED FEATHER DR
- MGH 95037 917-A3
PAINTED ROCK DR
2400 SCL 95051 833-A1
PAINTER CT
- GIL 95020 977-G1
PAIUTE LN
400 SJS 95123 874-H5
PAJARO AV
200 SUNV 94086 812-D6
PAJARO CT
100 SUNV 94086 812-D6
6500 SJS 95120 894-D1
PAJARO WY
6500 SJS 95120 894-D1
PALA AV
- SJS 95127 834-H2
- SCIC 95127 834-H2
400 SUNV 94086 812-D7
400 SUNV 94086 832-C1
PALACE DR
- SJS 95129 853-A1
PALACEWOOD CT
4900 SJS 95129 852-J2
PALACIO ESPADA CT
200 SJS 95116 834-F3
PALACIO ROYALE CIR
200 SJS 95116 834-D2
PALACIO VERDE CT
200 SJS 95116 834-D2
PALADIN DR
3900 SJS 95124 873-J3
PALA MESA DR
5800 SJS 95123 875-A5
PALAMOS AV
1100 SUNV 94089 812-J4
1200 SUNV 94089 813-A4
PALANTINO WY
3200 SJS 95135 855-G3
PALA RANCH CIR
- SJS 95133 834-D2
PALEMETTO DUNES CT
- SJS 95138 855-E6
PALERMO CT
13000 SAR 95070 852-F7
PALISADE DR
4200 SJS 95111 855-A7
PALISADES DR
1100 MPS 95035 793-J4
PALM AV
- LGTS 95030 872-J7
- SCIC 95037 896-C7
- SCIC 95037 916-B1
100 SJS 95037 896-C7
500 LALT 94022 811-E7
500 LALT 94022 831-E1
700 RDWC 94061 790-A1
22200 CPTO 95014 852-A1
PALM CT
- MLPK 94025 790-E5
700 SUNV 94086 832-G2
9900 SCIC 95037 916-C1
PALM DR
- SCL 95054 813-D5
100 PA 94305 790-H6
100 SCIC 94305 790-H6
PALM ST
100 HOLL 95023 1040-A5
400 PA 94301 791-A3
600 SJS 95110 854-B1
PALM BEACH WY
2000 SJS 95122 834-J7
2000 SJS 95122 854-J1
PALMDALE CT
2500 SCL 95051 833-B2
PALM DESERT WY
- SJS 95123 875-D1
PALMER AV
100 MTVW 94043 811-G3
PALMER DR
100 LGTS 95032 873-C3
PALMER LN
- PTLV 94028 810-C6
200 SMCo 94025 790-E1
200 ATN 94027 790-E1

PALMER ST
400 MPS 95035 813-J1
PALMETTO DR
400 SUNV 94086 832-G1
500 SJS 95111 854-G6
PALM GROVE CT
5300 SJS 95123 875-A3
PALM HAVEN AV
600 SJS 95125 854-A2
PALMIA DR
- SJS 95123 875-B5
PALMILLA DR
- SJS 95134 813-F3
PALMIRA WY
2200 SJS 95122 854-J1
PALMITA PL
200 MTVW 94041 811-J5
PALMO CT
- SJS 95135 855-G3
PALM RIDGE LN
100 SJS 95123 874-G7
PALM SPRING CT
11600 CPTO 95014 852-A4
PALM SPRINGS CIR
5900 SJS 95123 874-G6
PALMTAG DR
300 HOLL 95023 1040-A5
12300 SAR 95070 852-G6
PALM VALLEY BLVD
- SJS 95123 875-B5
PALM VIEW DR
5400 SJS 95123 875-B4
PALMVIEW WY
1400 SJS 95122 834-H6
PALMWELL WY
- SJS 95138 875-D5
PALMWOOD DR
1400 SJS 95122 834-H6
PALO DR
- PA 94304 790-H5
- SCIC 94305 790-H5
PALO ALTO AV
100 PA 94301 790-J3
200 MTVW 94041 811-G5
1000 PA 94301 791-A3
PALO ALTO WY
1900 SMCo 94025 790-E7
PALO HILLS DR
26700 LAH 94022 811-A5
PALOMA AV
4600 SJS 95111 875-A1
PALOMA CT
23700 CPTO 95014 831-G5
PALOMA DR
100 MGH 95037 916-H5
PALOMA RD
- CPTO 95014 851-J2
- PTLV 94028 810-B5
PALOMAR AV
600 SUNV 94086 812-D5
PALOMAR REAL
- CMBL 95008 853-F7
PALOMAS
- MTVW 94043 811-J2
PALOMINO CT
2400 MGH 95037 917-F6
PALOMINO DR
14600 SCIC 95127 835-B2
14600 SJS 95127 835-B2
PALOMINO LN
300 SCIC 95046 937-E6
PALOMINO WY
14000 SAR 95070 872-B2
PALO OAKS CT
18900 SAR 95070 852-H6
PALO SANTO DR
1600 CMBL 95008 853-A6
PALOS VERDES DR
11100 CPTO 95014 852-B3
15400 MSER 95030 873-A5
PALO VERDE AV
2300 EPA 94303 791-A1
PALO VERDE DR
400 SUNV 94086 832-G2
PALO VERDE WY
400 SUNV 94086 832-G1
PALO VISTA RD
10200 CPTO 95014 852-A1
PAM LN
1500 SJS 95120 874-A7
PAMELA AV
200 SJS 95116 834-G2
PAMELA DR
200 MTVW 94040 811-J6
PAMELA WY
20700 SAR 95070 872-D3
PAMLAR AV
300 CMBL 95008 853-E4
300 SJS 95128 853-F4
PAMPAS CT
20100 SAR 95070 852-E5
PAMPAS DR
1200 SJS 95120 874-D7
PAMPAS LN
300 SCIC 94305 790-J7
1100 GIL 95020 957-F7
PAMPLONA ST
- SJS 95131 814-B6
PANAMA AV
1800 SJS 95122 834-H7
2000 SJS 95122 854-H1
PANAMA ST
100 SCIC 94305 790-G7
PANCHITA WY
400 LALT 94022 811-E5
PANCHO CT
6300 SJS 95123 874-J7
PANDA CT
3800 SJS 95117 853-B3
PANDA DR
900 SJS 95117 853-B3
PANDA LN
3800 SJS 95117 853-B2

PANDA PL
3800 SJS 95117 853-B3
PANDOLFI PL
1100 SJS 95131 814-E7
PANDORA DR
1800 SJS 95124 873-G1
PANELLI PL
800 SCIC 95050 833-F5
PANIGHETTI PL
- LGTS 95030 893-B1
PANMURE CT
3100 SJS 95135 855-F3
PANOCHE AV
1100 SJS 95122 834-F7
PANOCHE CT
- SJS 95122 834-F7
PANORAMA DR
- HOLL 95023 1040-D7
19100 SAR 95070 872-G4
20800 SCIC 95033 913-B2
PANORAMA WY
100 LGTS 95032 873-G6
PANTALIS CT
2500 SJS 95132 814-E6
PANTALIS DR
2500 SJS 95132 814-E6
PAN TEMPO WY
100 SBnC 95023 1020-G7
100 SBnC 95023 1040-G1
PAOLO CT
1900 SJS 95131 814-D6
PAPAC WY
500 SCIC 95117 853-D2
PAPAYA CT
400 SJS 95111 854-G7
PAPPANI DR
1200 GIL 95020 977-G2
PAPPANI WY
- SJS 95148 855-F2
PAPYRUS LN
- SJS 95126 833-G6
PAQUITA ESPANA CT
- SCIC 95037 896-C6
PAR AV
11600 SCIC 94024 831-E3
PARADISE CIR
- HOLL 95023 1040-D7
- HOLL 95023 1060-C1
PARADISE CT
- HOLL 95023 1040-D7
1000 PA 94306 811-B3
PARADISE DR
- HOLL 95023 1040-D7
20600 CPTO 95014 852-D1
PARADISE WY
900 PA 94306 811-B3
PARADISE VIEW RD
1700 SCIC 95037 936-H3
PARAGON CT
- MTVW 94040 811-F3
PARAGON DR
2100 SJS 95131 813-J6
2100 SJS 95131 814-A5
PARAISO CT
200 SJS 95119 875-D7
PARAMOUNT CT
13000 SAR 95070 852-D6
PARAMOUNT DR
13100 SAR 95070 852-D7
PARASOL CT
- SJS 95125 854-C6
PARC LN
- MPS 95035 814-A1
PARC PLACE DR
- MPS 95035 814-A1
PARIA TER
- SUNV 94089 812-G3
PARIS WY
2200 SJS 95132 814-E2
PARISH PL
10200 CPTO 95014 832-E7
PARISH WY
8100 GIL 95020 977-H2
PARK AL
300 HOLL 95023 1039-J3
PARK AV
- LGTS 95030 893-A1
100 PA 94306 791-A7
100 SJS 95113 834-A7
200 SJS 95110 834-A7
400 SJS 95002 793-C7
600 SJS 95126 834-A7
800 SJS 95126 833-G6
800 SCIC 95126 833-J7
2100 SCL 95050 833-F5
2100 SJS 95050 833-F5
2700 SCL 95053 833-F5
PARK BLVD
200 PA 94306 791-A6
3300 PA 94306 811-C1
PARK CIR
10100 CPTO 95014 832-D7
PARK CIR E
10100 CPTO 95014 832-D7
PARK CIR W
10100 CPTO 95014 832-D7
PARK COM
- FRMT 94539 793-J3
PARK CT
500 SCL 95050 833-F5
800 MTVW 94040 811-E6
PARK DR
- ATN 94027 790-D2
- MGH 95037 937-B5
100 GIL 95020 977-H1
800 MTVW 94040 811-G5
1100 MTVW 94022 811-G5
15000 SAR 95070 872-E4
PARK LN
- MLPK 94025 790-J1
- SJS 95123 875-B4
100 ATN 94027 790-D4
2900 SJS 95127 835-B5

PARK PL
20300 SAR 95070 872-E2
PARK RD
- HOLL 95023 1040-A3
PARK ST
- SBnC 95023 1040-A5
- HOLL 95023 1040-A5
100 RDWC 94061 790-B1
PARK TER
- FRMT 94539 793-J3
PARK WY
16100 SCIC 95127 815-B6
16100 SJS 95127 815-B6
17700 MGH 95037 916-J7
PARK ARCADIA DR
4600 SJS 95136 874-J2
PARK BELMONT PL
- SJS 95136 874-J1
PARK BOLTON PL
100 SJS 95136 874-H1
PARK BRISTOL PL
4400 SJS 95136 874-J1
PARK BROOK CT
1100 MPS 95035 794-C6
PARK CHARLES CT
3900 SJS 95111 854-J6
PARK CHERRY PL
4500 SJS 95136 874-J2
PARK CONCORD PL
4600 SJS 95136 874-J2
PARK CREST CT
1500 SJS 95118 874-A6
PARK CREST DR
5600 SJS 95118 874-A6
PARKDALE DR
600 CMBL 95008 853-F7
600 SJS 95008 853-F7
PARKDALE WY
1600 SJS 95127 835-B5
1800 SJS 95148 835-B5
PARK DARTMOUTH PL
100 SJS 95136 874-H1
PARK DOUGLAS PL
4700 SJS 95136 874-J2
PARK ELLEN DR
100 SJS 95136 874-J2
PARK ENTRANCE DR
1300 SJS 95131 814-C7
PARKER AV
- ATN 94027 790-B4
PARKER CT
900 SCL 95050 833-E3
2400 MTVW 94043 811-F3
PARKER ST
700 SCL 95050 833-E3
2400 MTVW 94043 811-F3
PARKER RANCH CT
12400 SAR 95070 852-C6
PARKER RANCH RD
12000 SAR 95070 852-C6
PARK ESSEX PL
- SJS 95136 874-J1
PARK ESTATES WY
2800 SJS 95135 855-F5
PARKFIELD AV
5000 SJS 95129 852-J3
PARK FLETCHER PL
- SJS 95136 874-J1
PARKGATE CT
- SJS 95138 855-C5
PARK GLEN CT
1100 MPS 95035 794-C6
PARK GREEN DR
- CPTO 95014 852-E1
PARK GROTON PL
- SJS 95136 874-J1
PARK GROVE DR
1100 MPS 95035 794-C6
PARKHAVEN CT
3300 SJS 95132 814-F2
PARKHAVEN DR
3200 SJS 95132 814-F3
PARK HEIGHTS DR
1100 MPS 95035 794-C6
PARK HILL DR
- MPS 95035 794-C6
PARKHILLS AV
1600 LALT 94024 831-J4
PARKHURST DR
500 CMBL 95008 853-A7
PARKINGTON AV
1100 SUNV 94087 832-B1
PARKINSON AV
1000 PA 94301 791-A4
PARKINSON CT
1000 SCIC 95126 853-J1
PARK JOHNSON PL
500 SJS 95111 854-J6
500 SJS 95111 855-A6
PARKLAND AV
3400 SJS 95117 853-C3
PARKLAND CT
2500 SCL 95051 833-A1
PARK MANOR DR
5600 SJS 95118 874-A6
PARK MEADOW CT
500 SJS 95129 852-J1
PARK MEADOW DR
500 SJS 95129 852-J2
PARK MILFORD PL
4600 SJS 95136 874-J2
PARKMONT CT
1200 SJS 95131 814-B7
PARKMONT DR
1400 SJS 95131 814-B7
PARKMOOR AV
500 SCIC 95128 853-F1
500 SJS 95128 853-F1
1100 SJS 95126 853-H2
PARK NORTON PL
4600 SJS 95136 874-J2
PARK OAK CT
1100 MPS 95035 794-C6

PARK OXFORD PL
- SJS 95136 874-J2
PARK PAXTON PL
4400 SJS 95136 874-J1
PARK PLEASANT CIR
1300 SJS 95127 835-B3
PARK RIDGE DR
1500 SJS 95118 874-A6
PARKROW LN
2800 SJS 95132 814-E3
PARK ROYAL DR
1900 SJS 95125 853-J6
PARK SHARON DR
- SJS 95136 874-J2
PARKSIDE AV
1600 SJS 95125 854-B4
PARKSIDE CT
17300 MSER 95030 873-B4
PARKSIDE DR
100 PA 94306 811-E2
PARKSIDE LN
10200 CPTO 95014 852-F1
PARKSIDE CENTER DR
- HOLL 95023 1020-A7
- SBnC 95023 1020-A7
PARK SOMMERS WY
4400 SJS 95136 874-J2
PARK SUTTON PL
4600 SJS 95136 874-J2
N PARK VICTORIA DR
- MPS 95035 794-A3
S PARK VICTORIA DR
- MPS 95035 794-C7
500 MPS 95035 814-D1
PARKVIEW AV
1500 SJS 95130 853-A5
PARKVIEW CIR
1900 HOLL 95023 1040-E5
PARKVIEW CT
- CPTO 95014 832-F6
PARK VIEW DR
1100 MPS 95035 794-C6
PARKVIEW DR
17000 MGH 95037 917-G5
17000 SCIC 95037 917-G5
PARKVIEW GREEN CIR
1500 SJS 95131 814-C7
PARK VILLA CIR
8000 CPTO 95014 852-B2
PARK VILLAGE PL
- SJS 95136 874-J1
PARK VISTA CIR
1800 SCL 95050 833-D3
PARK WARREN PL
- SJS 95136 874-J1
PARK WATSON PL
100 SJS 95136 874-J2
PARKWELL CT
100 SJS 95138 875-E4
PARKWEST DR
4500 SJS 95130 853-A5
PARK WILLOW CT
1100 MPS 95035 794-C6
PARK WILSHIRE DR
2500 SJS 95124 853-H7
2600 SJS 95124 873-H1
PARKWOOD DR
- ATN 94027 790-H1
10100 CPTO 95014 832-C7
PARKWOOD WY
1000 RDWC 94061 790-B2
2100 SJS 95125 854-A6
PARLETT PL
10100 CPTO 95014 832-E7
PARLIAMENT CT
3400 SJS 95132 814-J3
PARMA DR
1100 SJS 95120 894-D1
PARMA WY
500 LALT 94024 831-F2
PARMER AV
200 SJS 95116 834-F4
PARNELL DR
2700 SJS 95121 854-J3
PARNELL PL
800 SUNV 94087 832-F6
PARQUET CT
2400 SJS 95124 853-H7
W PARR AV
500 LGTS 95032 873-B2
500 CMBL 95008 873-B2
PARR LN
200 CMBL 95008 853-D6
PARRISH CT
4900 SJS 95111 875-C1
PARRISH VIEW DR
10000 SCIC 95020 957-D6
PARROT AV
1500 SUNV 94087 832-G5
PARROTT ST
500 SJS 95112 854-F3
PARSONS AV
- MTVW 94043 812-A1
- SCIC 94043 812-A1
1300 CMBL 95008 873-E2
PARSONS CT
1300 CMBL 95008 873-E1
PARSONS WY
- LALT 94022 811-E5
PAR THREE DR
10600 CPTO 95014 852-A2
PARTRIDGE AV
600 MLPK 94025 790-G4
1500 SUNV 94087 832-G5
PARTRIDGE CT
4400 SJS 95121 855-E4
PARTRIDGE DR
1300 GIL 95020 977-F1
4100 SJS 95121 855-E4

PARTRIDGE LN
23200 SCIC 94024 831-G4
PARVIN DR
- MTVW 94043 812-B5
700 MPS 95035 794-B5
PASA LN
- SJS 95112 834-B4
PASADENA AV
10100 CPTO 95014 852-B1
PASA ROBLES AV
- LALT 94022 811-D4
PASATIEMPO DR
1700 SJS 95124 873-J3
PASCOE AV
900 SJS 95125 854-B6
PASEO CT
- MTVW 94043 812-B5
PASEO DR
800 HOLL 95023 1040-C5
PASEO LN
- SJS 95124 873-J1
PASEO CARMELO
17400 LGTS 95030 893-D2
PASEO CERRO
12400 SAR 95070 852-H6
PASEO DE ARBOLES
2900 SJS 95135 855-F4
PASEO DEL ORO
2000 SJS 95124 873-F2
PASEO DEL ROBLE
13500 LAH 94022 810-H6
PASEO DEL ROBLE CT
13600 LAH 94022 810-H6
PASEO DEL SOL
2000 SJS 95124 873-F2
PASEO DE PALOMAS
500 CMBL 95008 853-F6
PASEO DE SAN ANTONIO WK
- SJS 95113 834-B6
PASEO ESTERO DR
800 SJS 95122 854-G2
PASEO FLORES
12500 SAR 95070 852-H6
PASEO GULARTE
- SBnC - 1037-J4
- SBnC 95045 1037-J4
PASEO LADO
18500 SAR 95070 852-H7
PASEO LAURA
100 LGTS 95032 873-D3
PASEO OLIVOS
12600 SAR 95070 852-H6
PASEO OLIVOS CT
2000 SJS 95130 852-J6
PASEO OLIVOS WY
4900 SJS 95130 852-J6
PASEO PICO
- SAR 95070 852-H6
PASEO PRESADA
12700 SAR 95070 852-H6
PASEO PUEBLO
18500 SAR 95070 852-H6
PASEO PUEBLO CT
6100 SJS 95120 874-C7
PASEO PUEBLO DR
6000 SJS 95120 874-D7
PASEO REFUGIO
400 MPS 95035 794-B6
PASEO ROBLES AV
2600 SCIC 95046 937-J2
PASEO TIERRA
18500 SAR 95070 852-H6
PASEO TRANQUILLO
14900 SJS 95118 873-H7
PASEO TRANQUILO
9100 SCIC 95020 976-J1
PASEO VISTA AV
2900 SCIC 95046 937-J1
2900 SCIC 95046 938-A1
PASETTA DR
2100 SCL 95050 833-C2
PASHOTE CT
1400 MPS 95035 794-A4
PASITO TER
100 SUNV 94086 812-D6
PASO DEL ARROYO
- PTLV 94028 810-D7
PASO LOS CERRITOS
6000 SJS 95120 874-B7
6300 SJS 95120 894-B1
PASQUALE CT
- SJS 95133 834-H1
PASTEL LN
13300 MTVW 94040 832-A1
PASTEUR DR
100 PA 94304 790-G6
100 SCIC 94305 790-G6
200 PA 94305 790-G6
PASTORIA AV
300 SUNV 94086 812-D7
300 SUNV 94086 832-D1
N PASTORIA AV
200 SUNV 94086 812-D6
S PASTORIA AV
100 SUNV 94086 812-D7
PATCH AV
300 SCIC 95128 853-F1
PATH WY
100 SJS 95136 874-H2
PATINA CT
- SJS 95135 855-H3
PATIO CT
1200 CMBL 95008 853-G6
PATIO DR
1200 CMBL 95008 853-G6
1600 SCIC 95125 853-H6
PATLEN DR
1200 LALT 94024 831-H3
PATRIC CT
20200 CPTO 95014 852-E2
PATRICIA CT
- MTVW 94041 811-J6

STREET Block City ZIP Pg-Grid

PATRICIA CT
400 MPS 95035 794-E7
900 CMBL 95008 873-B1
18100 SCIC 95033 912-H3
PATRICIA DR
- ATN 94027 790-C2
2300 SCL 95050 833-C5
2500 SCL 95051 833-B5
PATRICIA LN
500 PA 94303 791-C4
PATRICIA PL
- MLPK 94025 790-F5
PATRICIA WY
900 SJS 95125 854-A3
PATRICK WY
400 LALT 94022 811-D5
PATRICK HENRY DR
2900 SCL 95054 813-A4
PATRIOT WY
21100 CPTO 95014 832-C7
PATT AV
2800 SJS 95133 814-H7
2800 SJS 95133 834-G1
2800 SCIC 95133 814-H7
PATTERSON AV
- SMCo 94025 790-D5
PATTERSON ST
100 SJS 95112 834-C7
PATTON AV
300 SCIC 95128 853-F1
PAUL AV
- MTVW 94041 811-J6
- MTVW 94041 812-A6
700 PA 94306 811-C2
14300 SAR 95070 872-D2
PAUL DR
300 HOLL 95023 1040-B6
PAULA CT
- SJS 95126 853-J2
400 SCL 95050 833-D6
1200 LALT 94024 831-J2
PAULA DR
1100 CMBL 95008 853-B5
PAULA ST
800 SJS 95126 853-J2
PAULINE DR
1300 SUNV 94087 832-F4
2300 SJS 95124 853-G7
PAULLUS DR
- SBnC 95023 1060-E2
PAUL ROBESON CT
800 EPA 94303 791-B1
PAULSEN LN
200 PA 94301 790-J4
PAVAN CT
2800 SJS 95148 855-D2
PAVAN DR
3000 SJS 95148 855-D2
PAVILION LP
- SJS 95112 834-A3
PAVISO DR
20400 CPTO 95014 832-E7
PAWNEE TR
20700 SCIC 95033 913-C2
PAWTUCKET WY
7300 SJS 95139 895-G1
PAXTON CT
6000 SJS 95123 874-F6
PAYETTE AV
1000 SUNV 94087 832-B6
PAYETTE CIR
1200 HOLL 95023 1040-D5
PAYETTE CT
1300 SJS 95129 852-G4
PAYNE AV
200 CMBL 95128 853-E4
200 SJS 95128 853-E4
200 CMBL 95008 853-E4
200 SJS 95008 853-E4
1300 SJS 95117 853-B4
3100 SJS 95130 853-B4
4200 SJS 95129 853-B4
PAYNE CT
800 SUNV 94087 832-C2
PAYNE DR
1100 LALT 94024 831-H3
PAYTON AV
14900 SCIC 95124 873-G3
PEACEFUL GLEN CT
1400 SJS 95121 855-D7
PEACH AV
700 SUNV 94087 832-C2
PEACH CT
900 HOLL 95023 1040-C4
1100 SJS 95116 834-E5
PEACH LN
- HOLL 95023 1039-H4
PEACH TER
4900 SJS 95008 872-J1
PEACH BLOSSOM DR
7500 CPTO 95014 852-D4
PEACHBLOSSOM LN
15600 SCIC 95032 873-C5
15600 LGTS 95032 873-C5
PEACH GROVE CT
5200 SJS 95123 874-F7
PEACH HILL RD
15300 SAR 95070 872-E5
15300 SCIC 95030 872-E5
15400 SAR 95030 872-E5
PEACHTREE CT
700 CMBL 95008 873-A2
1700 MTVW 94040 831-G1
PEACHTREE LN
2100 SJS 95128 833-E6
20000 CPTO 95014 832-E7
PEACH WILLOW CT
100 LGTS 95032 873-B2
PEACHWOOD CT
2700 SJS 95132 814-E5
PEACHWOOD DR
1600 SJS 95132 814-D4
PEACHWOOD PL
1600 SJS 95132 814-D5

PEACOCK AV
1500 SUNV 94087 832-G5
1700 MTVW 94043 811-H3
PEACOCK CT
- GIL 95020 977-F1
- SCIC 95014 851-G4
3600 SCL 95051 832-H4
PEACOCK LN
16300 SCIC 95032 873-D7
PEACOCK GAP DR
4400 SCIC 95127 815-C5
4400 SJS 95127 815-C5
PEAK AV
17000 MGH 95037 936-J1
17200 MGH 95037 916-J7
PEAK DR
3500 SJS 95127 835-C3
PEAK LN
- PTLV 94028 810-D5
PEAK VIEW DR
48900 FRMT 94539 793-J2
PEANUT BRITTLE DR
3100 SJS 95148 835-D7
PEAR AV
800 SUNV 94087 832-C2
1200 MTVW 94043 811-J2
PEAR CT
900 HOLL 95023 1040-C4
PEAR DR
1900 MGH 95037 917-D5
PEAR LN
- SJS 95112 834-B4
PEAR BLOSSOM CT
- SJS 95123 875-D1
PEARCE LN
100 SJB 95045 1038-D5
PEARCE MITCHELL PL
- SCIC 94305 810-H1
PEARL AV
3000 SJS 95136 854-D7
3200 SJS 95136 874-D1
PEARLROTH DR
6300 SJS 95123 875-A7
PEARLTONE DR
3200 SJS 95117 853-D3
PEARLWOOD WY
700 SJS 95123 874-F5
PEARSON CT
1600 SJS 95122 834-G7
PEARTREE CT
15000 SCIC 95046 937-G2
19800 CPTO 95014 832-F7
PEARTREE LN
100 HOLL 95023 1039-H4
1700 MTVW 94040 811-G7
1700 MTVW 94040 831-G1
2600 SJS 95121 855-E4
19800 CPTO 95014 832-F7
PEBBLE CT
- SJS 95131 814-C7
PEBBLE PL
10600 CPTO 95014 832-C6
PEBBLE BEACH CT
1700 MPS 95035 794-D3
2400 SJS 95125 854-C6
PEBBLE BEACH DR
2400 SJS 95125 854-C6
2500 SCL 95051 833-B1
PEBBLE CREEK CT
200 MGH 95037 917-B7
1000 SJS 95127 834-J4
PEBBLE GLEN DR
4800 SJS 95129 852-J3
4800 SJS 95129 853-A3
PEBBLELAKE CT
800 SUNV 94089 812-H5
PEBBLETREE CT
5100 SJS 95111 875-C2
PEBBLETREE WY
5200 SJS 95111 875-C2
PEBBLEWOOD CT
6600 SJS 95120 894-F1
PECAN CT
- HOLL 95023 1040-E5
800 SUNV 94087 832-C3
1200 SJS 95131 814-D7
1600 RDWC 94061 790-A2
PECAN WY
700 CMBL 95008 853-B7
PECAN BLOSSOM DR
5300 SJS 95123 875-B3
PECAN GROVE CT
100 SJS 95123 874-J3
PECHIN CIR
2400 SJS 95130 853-A7
PECK LN
12000 LAH 94022 831-B3
PECORA WY
100 SMCo 94028 810-D4
PECOS PT
3800 SJS 95132 814-J5
PECOS WY
1100 SUNV 94089 812-J4
PECOS RIVER CT
600 SJS 95111 854-H4
PECTEN CT
1000 MPS 95035 814-C3
PEDRICK CT
1100 SJS 95120 894-D1
PEDRO AV
200 MPS 95035 794-E7
PEDRO ST
1200 SJS 95126 853-J2
1200 SJS 95126 854-A2
PEDRO VIEW RD
- SCIC 95127 835-C1
PEEBLES AV
- MGH 95037 916-H4
500 SCIC 95037 916-J3
900 SCIC 95037 917-A3
PEEBLES PL
- SCL 95051 832-H3

PEEKSKILL DR
700 SUNV 94087 832-C2
PEET RD
18100 SCIC 95037 917-B3
18100 MGH 95037 917-A2
PEGASUS CT
2700 SJS 95148 835-E6
7400 SJS 95139 875-H7
PEGASUS WY
7300 SJS 95139 875-G7
PEGGY AV
1000 CMBL 95008 873-B1
PEGGY CT
1300 CMBL 95008 873-B1
PEIKING DR
1200 SJS 95131 814-B7
PELHAM CT
6400 SJS 95123 875-A7
PELICAN CT
5200 SJS 95123 874-F7
PELICAN RIDGE DR
7200 SJS 95120 894-F3
PELIO LN
- SAR 95070 872-E4
PELLEAS LN
700 SJS 95127 814-H6
PELLIER CT
1300 SJS 95121 854-J2
PELLIER DR
1200 SJS 95121 854-J3
PEMBA CT
200 SJS 95119 875-D6
PEMBA DR
6400 SJS 95119 875-D6
PEMBRIDGE CT
1100 SJS 95118 874-C1
PEMBRIDGE DR
1100 SJS 95118 874-C1
PEMBROKE DR
1100 SJS 95131 814-E7
PEMBROKE PL
- MLPK 94025 790-F6
PENA CT
500 PA 94306 811-C2
PENDERGAST AV
18700 CPTO 95014 852-H2
PENDLETON AV
900 SUNV 94087 832-B6
PENDLETON DR
2800 SJS 95148 855-D1
PENDRAGON LN
2500 SJS 95116 834-J4
PENHURST PL
4000 SJS 95135 855-F3
PENINSULA AV
10000 CPTO 95014 832-B7
10000 CPTO 95014 852-B1
PENINSULA WY
900 SMCo 94025 790-H1
PENINSULAR AV
1000 LALT 94024 831-H4
10700 CPTO 95014 832-A6
PENINSULAR CT
1000 LALT 94024 831-H3
PENITENCIA CT
500 MPS 95035 793-J6
PENITENCIA ST
500 MPS 95035 793-J6
PENITENCIA CREEK RD
2600 SJS 95132 814-F7
2900 SJS 95133 814-F7
3100 SJS 95127 814-F7
3600 SCIC 95127 814-F7
3600 SCIC 95132 814-F7
15100 SJS 95132 815-A5
15100 SJS 95127 815-A5
PENN AV
4900 SCIC 95124 873-E4
4900 SJS 95124 873-E4
PENN WY
200 LGTS 95032 873-D4
PENNINGTON LN
1000 CPTO 95014 852-C3
PENNSYLVANIA AV
- LGTS 95030 872-J7
PENNY LN
2000 MTVW 94043 811-G2
PENNY WY
1700 LALT 94024 832-A4
PENNYHILL DR
200 SJS 95127 834-H1
PENNYROYAL TER
1200 SUNV 94087 832-E3
PENROD PL
600 SJS 95116 834-J4
PENSACOLA DR
1500 SJS 95122 854-H1
1600 SJS 95122 834-J7
PENTLAND CT
3000 SJS 95148 855-C2
PENTLAND WY
2200 SJS 95148 855-C2
PENTZ WY
5800 SJS 95123 875-B5
PENWITH AV
3900 SJS 95130 853-B4
PENWOOD ST
1700 SJS 95133 834-E1
PEONY LN
1600 SJS 95124 873-J6
PEPITA CT
3100 SJS 95132 814-G5
PEPITONE AV
1000 SJS 95110 854-C2
PEPPER AV
400 PA 94304 811-B1
400 PA 94306 791-B7
400 PA 94306 811-B1
1000 SUNV 94087 832-C2
PEPPER CT
100 LALT 94022 811-E7
PEPPER DR
- LALT 94022 811-E7

PEPPER LN
15000 SAR 95070 872-F4
PEPPER GRASS CT
- GIL 95020 977-E1
PEPPERIDGE CT
2700 SJS 95148 835-E6
PEPPERIDGE DR
3400 SJS 95148 835-E6
PEPPERMINT DR
3000 SJS 95148 835-C7
PEPPER TREE CT
800 SCL 95051 833-A5
PEPPERTREE CT
1500 MGH 95037 917-D6
PEPPERTREE DR
16900 MGH 95037 917-D6
PEPPER TREE LN
- LGTS 95032 873-B5
800 SCL 95051 833-A5
3300 SCIC 95127 814-H6
3900 SJS 95127 814-J6
20800 CPTO 95014 852-C1
PEPPERWOOD CT
- MLPK 94025 790-H2
- MTVW 94043 812-B3
PEPPERWOOD DR
4800 SJS 95124 873-H4
PEPPERWOOD LN
2600 SCL 95051 833-B6
PERA CT
- SJS 95112 834-B4
PERALTA AV
- LGTS 95030 872-J7
400 SUNV 94086 832-D1
PERALTA CT
- CPTO 95014 831-J7
1300 SJS 95120 874-C7
14100 SAR 95070 872-C2
PERALTA DR
1200 SJS 95120 874-D7
PERCHERON CT
17100 MGH 95037 917-D6
PERCIVALE DR
3100 SJS 95127 814-H7
PEREGO WY
18500 SAR 95070 872-H1
PEREGRINE CT
900 SCL 95051 832-H5
PEREGRINE DR
1200 GIL 95020 957-E7
PEREGRINO WY
1500 SJS 95125 853-J5
PERICH CT
2300 MTVW 94040 831-J1
PERIDOT CT
- HOLL 95023 1039-J4
PERIDOT DR
2600 SJS 95132 814-F6
PERIDOT PL
2600 SJS 95132 814-F5
PERIE LN
3700 SJS 95132 814-J4
3800 SJS 95132 815-A4
PERIMETER RD
- LAH 94022 831-C2
6300 SJS 95119 875-C5
N PERIMETER RD
- MLPK 94025 790-J1
S PERIMETER RD
600 MLPK 94025 790-J2
W PERIMETER RD
600 MLPK 94025 790-J1
600 SMCo 94025 790-J1
PERINO LN
1500 SCIC 95046 937-J7
PERIVALE CT
3100 SJS 95148 855-E2
PERIWINKLE DR
8600 GIL 95020 977-D1
PERIWINKLE LN
4700 SJS 95129 853-B2
4700 SJS 95129 852-B7
PERIWINKLE TER
- FRMT 94539 793-J3
800 SUNV 94086 832-F3
PERKINS CT
100 LGTS 95032 873-B3
600 SJS 95127 814-J6
PERMANENTE RD
- SCIC 95014 851-G1
PERMANENTE WY
100 MTVW 94041 811-G4
PERNICH CT
1300 SJS 95120 874-C7
PERREIRA DR
900 SCL 95051 832-J5
900 SCL 95051 833-A5
PERRELLI ST
800 GIL 95020 977-H3
PERRIEN CT
- SBnC 95023 1040-D2
PERRIN CT
1500 SJS 95131 814-D6
PERRONE CIR
1800 SJS 95116 834-F3
PERRY AV
1900 SMCo 94025 790-E7
PERRY CT
400 SCL 95054 813-E6
1600 SJS 95116 834-F4
PERRY LN
15200 SCIC 95037 936-J5
PERRY ST
100 MPS 95035 794-C7
PERRYMONT AV
200 SJS 95125 854-D4
PERSHING AV
700 SJS 95126 833-J6
PERSIAN DR
100 SUNV 94089 812-F3
PERSIANWOOD PL
5100 SJS 95111 875-C2
PERSIMMON AV
800 SUNV 94087 832-C2

PERSIMMON PL
4600 SJS 95129 853-A2
PERSIMMON GROVE CT
5300 SJS 95123 874-F7
PERTH CT
600 MPS 95035 794-A6
PERUGIA CIR
2500 SJS 95138 855-G7
PERUKA PL
300 SJS 95116 834-D4
PESCADERO CT
200 MPS 95035 793-J5
PESCADERO DR
700 SJS 95123 874-F5
PESCADERO ST
200 MPS 95035 793-J5
PESCADERO TER
300 SUNV 94086 812-D7
PESCARA CT
2600 SJS 95008 873-F1
PETAL WY
1200 SJS 95129 852-G4
PETALUMA CT
1600 HOLL 95023 1040-D6
1800 MPS 95035 794-D6
S PETER CT
- CMBL 95008 853-G6
N PETER DR
- CMBL 95008 853-G6
S PETER DR
- CMBL 95008 853-G6
PETER COUTTS CIR
- SCIC 94305 811-A2
PETER COUTTS RD
- SCIC 94305 810-J1
100 SCIC 94305 811-A2
PETER PAN AV
700 SJS 95116 834-H4
PETER PAN TR
18100 SCIC 95033 912-J4
PETERS CT
- SCIC 95037 936-D2
PETERSBURG DR
2100 MPS 95035 794-E7
PETERSEN AV
1500 SJS 95129 852-H5
PETERSEN DR
1100 GIL 95020 977-G1
PETERSON CT
1200 LALT 94024 831-J3
PETERSON WY
3600 SCL 95054 813-A6
PETIE CT
1000 MTVW 94040 811-J6
PETRACH TER
- SJS 95135 855-G2
PETRARCH CT
3200 SJS 95135 855-H2
PETRI PL
1600 SJS 95124 873-J5
1600 SJS 95118 873-J5
PETRONI WY
1000 SJS 95120 894-F2
PETTIGREW CT
2900 SJS 95148 855-C2
PETTIGREW DR
2100 SJS 95148 855-C2
PETTIS AV
200 MTVW 94041 811-G5
PETULLA CT
4000 SJS 95124 873-J2
PETUNIA CT
- SAR 95070 872-C1
PFEFFER LN
2400 SCIC 95128 853-F2
2400 SJS 95128 853-F2
PFEIFFER RANCH CT
- SJS 95120 874-E7
PFEIFFER RANCH RD
- SCIC 95120 874-F7
6300 SJS 95120 874-E7
6400 SJS 95120 894-F1
PFEIFLE AV
12900 SCIC 95111 854-H6
PHANTOM AV
1400 SCIC 95125 853-H5
1600 CMBL 95125 853-H5
PHARLAP AV
5000 SJS 95111 875-B2
PHARLAP DR
10000 CPTO 95014 832-B7
PHARMER RD
8400 SCIC 95020 976-J1
8400 SCIC 95020 977-A1
PHEASANT DR
1200 GIL 95020 957-F7
PHEASANT RD
18100 SCIC 95032 893-H3
18100 SCIC 95033 893-H3
PHEASANT HILL CT
1400 SJS 95120 894-G4
PHEASANT HILL DR
1200 SJS 95120 894-F4
PHEASANT HILL WY
1300 SJS 95120 894-F4
PHEASANT RIDGE WY
- SJS 95136 854-E3
PHELAN AV
- SJS 95112 854-E2
800 SJS 95122 854-F1
PHELAN CT
1800 SJS 95122 854-G1
PHELAN WY
1100 SJS 95122 854-G1
PHELAND CT
800 MPS 95035 814-D1
PHELPS AV
1000 SJS 95117 853-C4
PHIL CT
600 CPTO 95014 852-G2
PHIL LN
19100 CPTO 95014 852-G2

PHIL PL
19300 CPTO 95014 852-G2
PHILEO CT
4900 SJS 95118 873-J4
PHILIP CT
2900 SJS 95121 855-A3
PHILLIPS AV
2600 SCL 95051 833-B4
17100 LGTS 95030 893-C1
PHILLIPS CT
1100 SCL 95051 833-B4
PHILLIPS RD
- PA 94303 791-B3
PHINNEY PL
7500 SJS 95139 895-G1
PHINNEY WY
7300 SJS 95139 895-G1
PHOENIX CT
- MPS 95035 813-J2
3800 SJS 95130 853-B4
PHOENIX DR
400 CMBL 95008 853-B5
1400 SJS 95130 853-B5
PHOTINIA LN
300 SCIC 95127 835-B1
PHUNGLAU CT
- SJS 95117 853-C1
PHYLLIS AV
900 MTVW 94040 811-J7
7000 SJS 95129 852-E3
PHYLLIS CT
1100 MTVW 94040 811-J7
PIANE CRATI CT
1100 HOLL 95023 1039-H3
PIAZZA CT
- SCIC 95127 815-A7
PIAZZA DR
500 MTVW 94043 812-B3
PIAZZA LN
11000 SCIC 95020 957-J2
PIAZZA WY
- MGH 95037 937-B2
- SCIC 95127 815-A7
100 SCIC 95127 835-A1
PIAZZA DE VALENCIA
- SJS 95128 853-E1
PICADILLY DR
3100 SJS 95118 874-C1
PICADILLY PL
1400 CMBL 95008 853-G5
PICARDY PLACE CT
3900 SJS 95121 855-B4
PICASSO DR
1200 SUNV 94087 832-F4
PICASSO TER
600 SUNV 94087 832-E3
PICEA CT
12700 SAR 95070 852-B6
PICKEMAN CT
- GIL 95020 977-D3
PICKFORD AV
- SCIC 95127 834-J1
PICNIC GROVE PL
- SJS 95112 834-A3
PICO LN
800 LALT 94022 811-E4
PIEDMONT CT
100 LGTS 95032 873-G6
17000 MGH 95037 936-J1
PIEDMONT RD
- MPS 95035 794-E6
200 SCIC 95035 794-E6
700 MPS 95035 814-F1
1000 SJS 95127 814-F2
1000 SJS 95132 814-F2
1100 SCIC 95035 814-F1
15000 SAR 95070 872-E4
PIEDRA DR
100 SUNV 94086 812-C7
PIEMONTE CT
- SJS 95148 855-F2
PIENZANNA CT
- SJS 95148 855-G1
PIERCE AV
- SJS 95110 834-C7
PIERCE CT
20000 SAR 95070 852-E6
PIERCE RD
- SCrC 95033 912-H6
400 MLPK 94025 790-J1
12700 SAR 95070 852-E6
13400 SAR 95070 872-B1
PIERCE ST
100 GIL 95020 977-J1
1100 SCL 95050 833-D4
PIERCE RANCH RD
1300 SJS 95120 894-C2
PIERCY RD
300 SJS 95138 875-D3
400 SCIC 95138 875-E3
PIERINO AV
700 SUNV 94086 832-F2
PIERS CT
900 PA 94303 791-D6
PIERS LN
- SMCo 94025 810-E2
900 SCIC 94304 810-E2
PIETRO DR
1300 SJS 95131 814-C7
PIETZ CT
6000 SJS 95123 874-F6
PIKE RD
13800 SAR 95070 872-C1
PILAND DR
1300 SJS 95130 853-C4
PILAR CT
5800 SJS 95120 874-C5
PILGRIM AV
1700 MTVW 94040 811-F5
5900 SJS 95129 852-G5
PILINUT CT
1000 SUNV 94087 832-C2

PILOT KNOB DR
2300 SCL 95051 833-B1
PIMA DR
600 SJS 95123 874-H5
PIMENTO AV
1100 SUNV 94087 832-C3
PINA CT
- SJS 95112 834-B4
PINARD ST
2200 MPS 95035 814-E1
PINE
200 CMBL 95008 853-E6
PINE AV
- SCrC 95033 871-A4
500 SUNV 94086 812-E5
600 SJS 95125 854-B4
17000 LGTS 95032 873-B7
PINE LN
- LALT 94022 811-D5
100 MGH 95037 937-B5
PINE ST
100 MGH 95037 937-B1
700 HOLL 95023 1040-A4
1000 MLPK 94025 790-G3
1200 PA 94301 791-B5
PINE TR
17000 SCIC 95033 912-J3
PINE WY
16900 MGH 95037 917-D6
PINEAPPLE AV
800 SUNV 94087 832-C2
PINE BRIDGE PL
- SJS 95008 853-F7
PINE BROOK CT
11700 CPTO 95014 852-C4
PINE BROOK LN
11700 CPTO 95014 852-C4
PINE CONE CT
17500 MSER 95030 873-A5
PINECONE CT
1700 MGH 95037 917-D6
PINE CREEK DR
3300 SJS 95132 814-G3
PINECREST CT
2800 SJS 95121 855-E4
PINECREST DR
500 LALT 94024 831-J5
1700 SCIC 95046 937-J5
1700 SCIC 95046 938-A5
PINEDALE CT
7200 SJS 95139 895-F1
PINEFIELD RD
300 SJS 95134 813-C2
PINE FOREST PL
4800 SJS 95118 873-H7
PINEGATE WY
3200 SJS 95148 855-E1
PINE GROVE WY
1400 SJS 95129 852-G4
PINE HILL CT
4800 SJS 95129 852-J2
PINE HILL RD
800 SCIC 94305 810-J1
PINE HOLLOW CIR
1700 SJS 95133 834-E2
PINEHURST AV
200 LGTS 95032 873-F6
PINEHURST CT W
1700 MPS 95035 794-D3
PINEHURST DR
1400 SJS 95118 874-B2
1600 LALT 94024 832-A3
PINEHURST PL
- GIL 95020 977-D3
PINEHURST SQ
1400 SJS 95117 853-C4
PINE LAKE CT
1300 SJS 95131 814-B5
PINELAND AV
5900 SJS 95123 874-J5
PINE MEADOW CT
- SJS 95135 855-H7
PINEMONT DR
4800 SJS 95008 872-J1
4800 SJS 95008 873-A1
PINE NUT CT
1000 SUNV 94087 832-C2
PINE PASS TER
600 SUNV 94087 832-D5
PINE RIDGE CT
3500 SJS 95127 835-C3
PINE RIDGE WY
- PTLV 94028 810-D5
3500 SJS 95127 835-C3
22000 SCIC 95033 913-B3
PINE SPRING CT
3200 SJS 95121 855-B3
PINETREE CT
- SJS 95131 814-C6
PINETREE TER
5000 SJS 95008 872-J1
PINEVIEW DR
300 SCL 95050 833-D7
500 SJS 95117 833-D7
PINEVIEW LN
100 MLPK 94025 790-D5
PINEVILLE AV
10400 CPTO 95014 852-F2
PINEWELL CT
5600 SJS 95138 875-D4
PINE WOOD CT
500 LGTS 95032 873-B2
PINEWOOD CT
1600 MPS 95035 814-A3
PINEWOOD DR
600 SJS 95129 853-A3
PINE WOOD LN
100 LGTS 95032 873-B2
PINEWOOD PL
1000 SJS 95129 853-A3
3700 SCL 95054 813-E5
PINEWOOD WY
1600 MPS 95035 813-J3
1600 MPS 95035 814-A3

STREET
Block City ZIP Pg-Grid

PINION WY
1700 MGH 95037 917-D6
PINKERTON CT
3300 SJS 95148 835-E7
PINKERTON DR
3200 SJS 95148 835-D7
PINKSTONE CT
1600 SJS 95122 835-A6
PINMORE DR
1500 SJS 95118 874-A4
1700 SJS 95118 873-J4
PINNACLE CT
- HOLL 95023 1040-D7
3500 SJS 95132 814-G3
19300 SAR 95070 872-G3
PINNACLE DR
3300 SJS 95132 814-G4
PINNACLES TER
- SUNV 94086 812-F6
PINNTAGE PKWY
20200 CPTO 95014 852-E1
PIN OAK CT
3400 SJS 95148 835-E7
PIN OAK DR
400 SUNV 94086 832-G1
PINOLE CT
10600 CPTO 95014 852-E2
PINON CT
700 SUNV 94086 832-G2
PINON DR
100 PTLV 94028 810-B4
PINON PL
4400 SJS 95136 874-J1
PINOT CT
200 SJS 95119 875-E7
PINOTAGE CT
8300 SJS 95135 855-J7
PINOT BLANC WY
600 FRMT 94539 794-A2
3200 SJS 95135 855-G3
PINOT GRIGIO PL
- SJS 95135 855-H2
PINOT GRIS WY
4100 SJS 95135 855-G3
PINOTIN CT
- SJS 95148 855-F2
PINOT NOIR CT
8000 SJS 95135 855-H6
PINTA CT
100 LGTS 95030 873-C7
PINTAIL CT
1200 SJS 95118 874-C2
PINTO CT
2400 MGH 95037 917-F6
PINTO DR
600 SJS 95111 854-H5
PINTO PALM TER
- SUNV 94086 832-G4
PINTO RIVER CT
4600 SJS 95136 874-G2
PIONEER AV
- SCIC 94035 812-B1
2400 SCIC 95128 853-F1
PIONEER CT
3000 MonC 95004 1037-A1
PIONEER PL
19200 MonC 95004 1037-A1
PIONEER WY
- MTVW 94041 812-A6
PIPE DREAM CT
1100 SJS 95122 834-F7
PIPER AV
800 SUNV 94087 832-C2
PIPER DR
1200 MPS 95035 814-B2
4100 SJS 95117 853-A3
4100 SJS 95129 853-A3
PIPPIN AV
800 SUNV 94087 832-C2
PIPPIN CREEK CT
1100 SJS 95120 894-G3
PISA CT
- SJS 95138 855-E7
PISCES DR
3400 SJS 95111 854-F6
PISMO CT
6300 SJS 95123 875-A7
PISMO TER
300 SUNV 94086 812-D7
PISTACHIO DR
3400 SJS 95111 854-G6
PISTACHIO GROVE CT
5300 SJS 95123 874-F7
PISTOIA WY
- SJS 95138 855-G7
- SJS 95138 875-G1
PITCAIRN WY
3300 SJS 95111 854-J5
PITCH PINE CT
4300 SJS 95136 874-H1
PITKIN CT
- SJS 95125 854-D6
PITKIN LP
- SJS 95125 854-D6
PITLOCHRY DR
- GIL 95020 977-F4
PITMAN AV
1200 PA 94301 791-A3
1300 PA 94303 791-A3
PITNER CT
3000 SJS 95148 855-D1
PITTSFIELD WY
7200 SJS 95139 875-G7
PIVOTO CT
- SJS 95125 854-B2
PIVOTO PL
- SJS 95125 854-B2
PIXANNE CT
2600 SJS 95148 835-B6
PLACE DE JARDIN
- SJS 95148 855-F2
PLACE DE LOUIS
- SJS 95148 855-G1

PLACER OAKS RD
16800 LGTS 95032 873-B5
PLACER SPRING CT
11800 CPTO 95014 852-C4
PLACID CT
- SJS 95135 875-J1
PLACIDA CT
14600 SAR 95070 872-C3
PLACIDO CT
- SJS 95135 855-H3
PLACITAS AV
- ATN 94027 790-E1
500 SMCo 94025 790-E1
PLAINFIELD DR
4700 SJS 95111 875-B1
PLAINVIEW CT
6500 SJS 95120 894-C1
PLANETREE PL
900 SUNV 94086 832-G2
PLATEAU AV
1500 SCIC 94024 831-F3
PLATEAU DR
- SJS 95125 854-E5
PLATINUM CT
1800 SJS 95116 834-F3
PLATT AV
1100 MPS 95035 814-D1
PLATT CT
800 MPS 95035 814-D1
PLATTE RIVER CT
600 SJS 95111 854-H5
PLAYA DEL REY
5400 SJS 95123 874-F3
PLAZA CT
1700 MTVW 94040 811-G7
1700 MTVW 94040 831-G1
PLAZA DR
100 SUNV 94089 812-F3
800 SJS 95125 854-A2
PLAZA AMERICAS
2600 SJS 95132 814-D4
PLAZA BANDERAS
2600 SJS 95132 814-D4
PLAZA CASITAS
1700 SJS 95132 814-D4
PLAZA CENTRAL
- LALT 94022 811-D7
PLAZA CLAVELES
2600 SJS 95132 814-D4
PLAZA CORONA
5000 SCL 95054 813-C3
PLAZA DE GUADALUPE
2100 SJS 95116 834-G3
PLAZA ESCUELA
4900 SCL 95054 813-C3
PLAZA INVIERNO
600 SJS 95111 875-B1
PLAZA LA POSADA
200 LGTS 95032 872-J3
PLAZA MONTEZ
1900 SJS 95132 814-D3
PLAZA SOL
- SJS 95131 814-B6
PLAZOLETA
100 LGTS 95032 872-J2
PLEASANT AV
- SAR 95070 872-E4
PLEASANT ST
- SJS 95110 834-A6
- LGTS 95030 873-B7
- LGTS 95030 893-B1
PLEASANT WY
800 LALT 94022 811-E4
PLEASANT ACRES DR
2300 SCIC 95148 835-E5
PLEASANT CREST CT
2000 SJS 95148 835-D4
PLEASANT CREST DR
3500 SJS 95148 835-D5
PLEASANT ECHO DR
3500 SJS 95148 835-D4
PLEASANT GROVE CT
- SJS 95112 854-F4
PLEASANT HILLS CT
7000 SJS 95139 895-E1
PLEASANT KNOLL CT
- SCIC 95148 835-D4
- SJS 95148 835-D4
PLEASANT KNOLL DR
3500 SJS 95148 835-D4
PLEASANT RIDGE AV
- SCIC 95127 834-H2
PLEASANT ROW CT
3500 SJS 95148 835-D5
PLEASANT VIEW AV
17300 MSER 95030 873-A5
PLEASANT VISTA DR
3700 SCIC 95148 835-E5
PLENTY TER
- SUNV 94089 812-G4
PLOMOSA CT
600 FRMT 94539 793-J1
PLOMOSA RD
48500 FRMT 94539 793-J2
PLOMOSA WY
- FRMT 94539 793-J1
PLUM AV
1100 SUNV 94087 832-C3
PLUM CT
- MTVW 94043 811-J5
900 HOLL 95023 1040-C4
PLUM ST
1100 SJS 95110 854-C2
PLUMAS DR
2700 SJS 95121 854-J3
2800 SJS 95121 855-A3
12000 SAR 95070 852-E5
PLUM BLOSSOM DR
7400 CPTO 95014 852-D4
PLUM BLOSSOM LN
- CMBL 95008 853-D5
PLUMERIA DR
- SJS 95134 813-F6

PLUM GROVE CT
100 SJS 95123 874-F7
PLUMMER AV
2200 SJS 95125 854-A6
2900 SJS 95125 874-B1
2900 SJS 95118 874-B1
PLUMSTEAD CT
2200 SJS 95148 855-C2
PLUMSTEAD WY
2900 SJS 95148 855-C2
PLUMTREE DR
- HOLL 95023 1039-H4
PLUMTREE LN
900 MTVW 94040 831-G1
10200 CPTO 95014 832-E7
PLYMOUTH AV
6100 SJS 95129 852-G4
PLYMOUTH DR
800 GIL 95020 977-H4
1000 SUNV 94087 832-B2
12500 SAR 95070 852-F6
PLYMOUTH ST
1400 MTVW 94043 811-G1
PLYMPTON CT
100 SJS 95139 875-G7
100 SJS 95139 895-G1
POAS CIR
100 SJS 95116 834-G3
POAS CT
2000 SJS 95116 834-G3
POCATELLO AV
900 SUNV 94087 832-B6
POCATELLO CT
500 SJS 95111 854-H5
POCATELLO DR
400 SJS 95111 854-H5
POCO WY
1900 SJS 95116 834-H5
POE LN
1300 SJS 95130 853-B4
POE ST
300 PA 94301 790-H4
POETRY DR
- SJS 95131 814-D4
POETT LN
2400 SCL 95051 833-B2
POGLIA CT
5600 SJS 95138 875-G1
POINCIANA DR
1100 SCL 95051 832-H3
1100 SUNV 94086 832-H3
POINSETTIA CT
4400 SJS 95136 874-H1
POINT CREEK CT
800 SJS 95133 814-G7
POINT CREEK DR
800 SJS 95133 814-G7
POINTDEXTER CT
2800 SJS 95133 814-G6
POINT DUNES CT
7100 SJS 95139 895-H2
POINTE CLAIRE CT
1400 SUNV 94087 832-D4
POINTE CLAIRE DR
1300 SUNV 94087 832-D4
POKER FLAT PL
1200 SJS 95120 874-C6
POLARIS AV
200 MTVW 94043 811-H4
POLARIS CT
- MPS 95035 814-A3
POLE LINE RD
4800 SCIC 95020 976-C2
POLHEMUS AV
200 ATN 94027 790-C4
POLI RD
9200 SCIC 95020 956-F6
POLITZER DR
- MLPK 94025 790-E5
POLK AV
1000 SUNV 94086 812-B7
2400 SCL 95051 833-C7
POLK CT
400 GIL 95020 978-A2
1900 MTVW 94040 831-G1
POLK LN
1000 SJS 95117 853-C3
POLK ST
- SJB 95045 1038-D5
POLK SPRING CT
1200 SJS 95120 894-G4
POLLACK RD
- SCIC 94035 812-B1
POLLARD AV
100 SCIC 95046 937-D3
POLLARD CT
2300 CMBL 95032 872-J2
POLLARD RD
600 LGTS 95032 873-A2
800 CMBL 95032 873-A2
1400 CMBL 95032 873-A2
1900 LGTS 95032 872-J2
1900 CMBL 95032 872-J2
2000 SAR 95070 872-J2
POLLARD OAKS CT
- LGTS 95032 873-B2
POLLEN CT
2000 SJS 95131 814-D7
POLTONHALL CT
3200 SJS 95121 855-C5
POLTON PLACE WY
3700 SJS 95121 855-B4
POLVADERO DR
6900 SJS 95119 895-E1
POMANDER PL
6600 SJS 95120 894-G1
POME AV
1100 SUNV 94087 832-C3
POMEGRANATE CT
1100 SUNV 94087 832-C3
POMEGRANATE LN
400 SJS 95134 813-C2
POMELO CT
1100 SUNV 94087 832-C3

POMERADO DR
3200 SJS 95135 855-H3
POMERADO WY
3300 SJS 95135 855-G3
POMEROY AV
500 SCL 95051 832-J6
600 SCL 95051 833-A5
3100 SJS 95121 855-C3
POMEROY CT
3200 SJS 95121 855-C3
POMO PL
1000 SCIC 95020 957-F5
POMONA AV
1400 SJS 95110 854-D2
1600 SJS 95125 854-D2
4200 PA 94306 811-C3
POMPANO ST
1200 SJS 95122 834-H6
POMPEY DR
1400 SJS 95128 853-E5
POMPONIO
- PTLV 94028 830-C1
PONCE CT
5700 SJS 95120 874-C5
PONCE DR
4000 PA 94306 811-E2
POND CT
- MPS 95035 794-A7
POND WY
1900 SJS 95132 814-C4
PONDEROSA AV
700 SUNV 94086 832-G3
PONDEROSA CT
- HOLL 95023 1040-E5
16700 MGH 95037 917-E6
PONDEROSA DR
7700 GIL 95020 977-F3
PONDEROSA TER
4900 SJS 95008 872-J1
PONDEROSA WY
2800 SCL 95051 833-A6
PONSELLE CT
2600 SJS 95121 854-J4
PONTIAC AV
20700 SAR 95070 872-D2
PONTIAC DR
5700 SJS 95123 874-H5
PONTIUS CT
5800 SJS 95123 875-A5
PONY PASS CIR
4900 SJS 95136 874-H2
POPE CT
1700 CMBL 95008 873-D2
POPE ST
100 MLPK 94025 791-A3
200 MLPK 94025 790-J2
POPEJOY CT
4800 SJS 95118 873-J4
POPLAR AV
- CMBL 95008 853-F6
100 RDWC 94061 790-B1
800 SUNV 94086 832-G3
1200 SUNV 94087 832-G3
2000 EPA 94303 791-A1
POPLAR CT
- HOLL 95023 1040-E5
900 SUNV 94086 832-G3
POPLAR DR
2200 SJS 95122 834-J5
8700 GIL 95020 977-F1
POPLAR ST
700 SCL 95050 833-F5
POPLAR TER
4900 SJS 95008 872-J1
POPLAR GROVE SQ
22800 CPTO 95014 851-J1
POPLARWOOD WY
2500 SJS 95132 814-C3
POPPY AV
1700 MLPK 94025 790-E6
POPPY CT
100 MPS 95035 794-D6
800 SUNV 94086 832-G3
POPPY DR
22500 CPTO 95014 831-J7
22500 CPTO 95014 832-A7
POPPY LN
- MPS 95035 794-D6
3400 SCIC 95020 957-B7
12400 SCIC 95127 814-J5
15600 MSER 95030 873-A5
POPPY PL
400 MTVW 94043 811-H4
POPPY WY
1200 CPTO 95014 852-D4
POPPY BLOSSOM CT
5300 SJS 95123 875-B3
POPPYFIELD ST
- GIL 95020 977-J5
POPPY HILLS PL
5700 SJS 95138 875-G1
POPPY LANE CIR
1100 HOLL 95023 1040-C5
POPPY LANE DR
1200 HOLL 95023 1040-C5
POPULUS PL
900 SUNV 94086 832-G3
PORGY PL
1300 SJS 95128 853-F4
PORPOISE TER
500 SUNV 94089 812-G3
PORT WY
2100 SJS 95133 814-E7
PORTAGE AV
400 PA 94306 811-B1
PORTAGE MOUNTAIN DR
1500 SJS 95126 853-H4
PORTAL AV
10100 CPTO 95014 852-F1
10600 CPTO 95014 832-F7
PORTAL CT
2200 SJS 95131 814-A5

PORTAL PL
700 PA 94303 791-B5
PORTAL PZ
19800 CPTO 95014 852-F1
E PORTAL RD
- SJS 95125 854-F5
PORTAL WY
2200 SJS 95148 835-D6
PORTER CIR
1900 HOLL 95023 1040-E4
PORTER DR
3100 PA 94304 811-A2
PORTER LN
100 SCIC 95127 815-A7
300 SCIC 95127 835-B1
PORTERFIELD CT
2400 MTVW 94040 831-J1
PORTER PEABODY RD
7600 SCIC 95020 958-G4
PORTIA AV
300 SUNV 94086 812-C7
PORTLAND AV
900 LALT 94024 831-H2
PORTMARNOCH CT
- SJS 95138 855-E6
PORTMARNOCK CT
- GIL 95020 977-F4
PORTMARNOCK WY
- GIL 95020 977-F4
PORTO ALEGRE CT
1100 SJS 95120 874-D5
PORTO ALEGRE DR
5700 SJS 95120 874-C5
PORTO ALEGRE PL
1100 SJS 95120 874-D6
PORTOBELO DR
1400 SJS 95118 874-A3
PORTOFINO PL
- SJS 95125 854-D7
- SJS 95136 854-D7
PORTOFINO TER
400 MPS 95035 793-G3
PORTOGESE WY
- SBnC 95023 1060-H3
PORTOLA AV
1000 SCL 95126 833-G5
1000 SJS 95126 833-G5
1500 PA 94306 791-A6
E PORTOLA AV
- LALT 94022 811-E4
W PORTOLA AV
- LALT 94022 811-D4
PORTOLA CT
200 LALT 94022 811-E4
PORTOLA DR
1500 MPS 95035 814-D1
PORTOLA RD
- CPTO 95014 851-J2
- PTLV 94028 810-A6
PORTOLA GREEN CIR
- PTLV 94028 810-C7
PORTOLA REDWOOD LN
- SJS 95124 873-G7
PORTOS CT
19300 SAR 95070 852-G7
PORTOS DR
19000 SAR 95070 872-G1
19100 SAR 95070 852-G7
PORTOS PL
19100 SAR 95070 872-G1
PORTREE DR
7500 SJS 95135 855-J6
PORT ROWAN DR
6900 SJS 95119 875-F6
PORTRUSH CT
- GIL 95020 977-G6
PORTRUSH LN
- GIL 95020 977-H6
PORTRUSH PL
5600 SJS 95138 875-F1
PORTSMOUTH CT
2000 SJS 95132 814-J2
PORTSWOOD CIR
800 SJS 95120 894-H3
PORTSWOOD DR
700 SJS 95120 894-H3
POSITANO LN
6700 SJS 95138 875-G4
POSSUM LN
- PTLV 94028 810-A6
POST ST
- SJS 95113 834-B6
200 MTVW 94040 811-J7
POSTGATE CT
1900 SJS 95121 855-C3
POST OAK CIR
5900 SJS 95120 874-C6
POSTON DR
4700 SJS 95136 874-J3
POSTWOOD DR
2800 SJS 95132 814-D3
POTOMAC CT
600 SJS 95136 874-F2
POTOMAC DR
100 LGTS 95032 873-D5
POTOMAC PL
7100 GIL 95020 977-H4
POTRERO AV
300 SUNV 94086 812-D6
POTRERO DR
1700 SJS 95124 873-G1
POTTER CT
16700 LGTS 95032 873-C7
POTTERS HATCH CIR
10100 CPTO 95014 851-J1
POTTS DR
10500 SCIC 95111 854-H6
POUGHKEEPSIE RD
- SJS 95119 875-C4
- SJS 95193 875-C4
100 SJS 95123 875-B4
POVERTY FLAT RD
- SCIC 95037 918-J1

POWDERBORN CT N
4600 SJS 95136 874-G2
POWDERBORN CT S
4600 SJS 95136 874-G2
POWDERHORN CT
600 SCIC 95046 957-E1
POWELL CT
1600 SJS 95122 834-G7
POWELL ST
400 HOLL 95023 1039-J5
800 SBnC 95023 1039-J5
POWER CT
- SJS 95133 834-B2
POWERSCOURT WY
- SJS 95136 854-E5
PRADA CT
1300 MPS 95035 794-C5
PRADA DR
400 MPS 95035 794-C5
PRADO CT
- PTLV 94028 810-C7
PRADO LN
3200 SJS 95148 835-D6
PRADO SECOYA
- ATN 94027 790-E4
PRADO VISTA DR
10100 CPTO 95014 851-J1
PRAGUE CT
6500 SJS 95119 875-D7
PRAGUE DR
200 SJS 95119 875-D7
PRAIRIE LN
2900 SJS 95127 834-H1
PRAIRIE OWL CT
- GIL 95020 957-F7
PRAIRIE VIEW CT
200 SJS 95127 834-H1
PRAIRIE WOOD CT
200 SJS 95127 834-H2
PRAMUKHS WY
6600 SJS 95120 894-G1
PRANCER CT
900 MGH 95037 937-B5
PRATER WY
- SBnC 95023 1040-D3
PRATOLA CT
15100 MGH 95037 937-B4
PRATOLINA ST
- SJS 95136 854-F7
PRATT LN
600 SCIC 95037 916-J2
PRELUDE DR
1300 SJS 95131 814-C7
PRENTISS DR
1100 SJS 95120 894-F2
PRESCOTT AV
1100 SUNV 94089 812-J4
1100 SUNV 94089 813-A4
3600 SJS 95124 873-H2
PRESCOTT RD
- SBnC 95045 1038-C3
PRESERVATION CT
18500 MGH 95037 916-H5
PRESERVATION DR
200 SJS 95116 834-G4
PRESERVATION WY
- MGH 95037 916-H5
PRESIDIO DR
8000 CPTO 95014 852-B2
PRESTON CT
- HOLL 95023 1040-C7
2700 MTVW 94040 831-J2
PRESTON DR
100 MTVW 94040 831-J2
5700 SJS 95124 873-J6
PRESTWICK CIR
7700 SJS 95135 856-A5
PRESTWICK CT
- GIL 95020 977-E3
700 SUNV 94087 832-F6
PRETORIA CT
800 SJS 95127 814-H6
PREVITARA CT
- SJS 95110 854-C2
PREVOST CT
1000 SJS 95125 854-G5
PREVOST ST
800 SJS 95125 854-B2
PRICE AV
19800 CPTO 95014 852-F1
PRICE CT
3000 PA 94303 791-D6
16800 MGH 95037 936-H2
PRICE DR
16800 MGH 95037 936-J2
PRICE WY
2300 SJS 95124 853-G7
PRICEWOOD CT
700 SJS 95120 894-H3
PRIDE CT
3200 SJS 95127 814-H6
PRIDE ST
700 SJS 95127 814-H6
PRIETA CT
10900 SCIC 95127 815-B7
PRIMAVERA DR
- HOLL 95023 1040-A2
- SBnC 95023 1040-A3
PRIMERA CT
2600 SJS 95148 835-D6
PRIMERO LN
- SJS 95128 853-G4
PRIMM AV
1400 SJS 95122 834-H6
PRIMO CT
1900 SJS 95131 814-C6
PRIMROSE AV
900 SUNV 94086 832-G3
PRIMROSE CT
- HOLL 95023 1040-E5
PRIMROSE DR
- SJS 95123 875-B5
PRIMROSE LN
1000 GIL 95020 977-G2

PRIMROSE WY
- PA 94303 791-C4
1200 CPTO 95014 852-D4
PRINCE DR
6000 SJS 95129 852-G3
PRINCE ST
200 LGTS 95032 873-A2
PRINCE ALBERT CT
3400 SJS 95132 814-J2
PRINCE CHARLES CT
3400 SJS 95132 814-J2
PRINCE EDWARD WY
1400 SUNV 94087 832-D4
PRINCE ESTATES CT
5300 SJS 95135 855-H5
PRINCE GEORGE DR
1900 SJS 95116 834-F3
PRINCE OF WALES LN
3400 SJS 95132 814-J3
PRINCE PHILIP CT
3400 SJS 95132 814-J2
PRINCE ROYAL PL
4600 SJS 95136 874-F2
PRINCESS PL
600 MPS 95035 794-B4
PRINCESS ANNE DR
900 SJS 95128 853-G3
PRINCESS ELLEENA CT
24000 LAH 94024 831-E3
PRINCESS MARGARET CT
3400 SJS 95132 814-J3
PRINCETON CT
3300 SCL 95051 832-J6
PRINCETON DR
600 SUNV 94087 832-D2
1400 SJS 95118 874-A5
PRINCETON PL
7200 GIL 95020 977-J4
PRINCETON RD
- MLPK 94025 790-G5
PRINCETON ST
2000 PA 94306 791-A7
2000 PA 94306 811-A1
PRINCETON WY
3200 SCL 95051 832-J6
3200 SCL 95051 833-A6
PRINCEVALLE ST
6500 SCIC 95020 978-A5
6500 GIL 95020 978-A5
6600 GIL 95020 977-J3
PRINDIVILLE CT
100 SJS 95138 875-G7
PRINDIVILLE DR
7300 SJS 95138 875-G7
PRING CT
18600 CPTO 95014 852-H1
PRINTEMPO DR
600 SJS 95134 813-H4
PRINTEMPO PL
800 SJS 95134 813-H4
PRINTY AV
500 MPS 95035 794-C5
PRIOR LN
200 ATN 94027 790-F2
PRIROLE DR
- SJS 95117 853-C2
PRISCILLA CT
1700 MTVW 94040 811-G5
PRISCILLA DR
1200 SJS 95129 853-A4
PRISCILLA LN
12300 LAH 94022 831-D3
12300 LAH 94024 831-D3
PRITCHARD CT
700 SCL 95051 833-B6
PRITCHETT CT
1300 LALT 94024 831-J3
PRITCHETT WY
1300 LALT 94024 831-J3
PRIVADA LUISITA
100 LGTS 95030 873-B4
PRIVATE DR
- GIL 95020 957-D7
PRIVET CT
700 SUNV 94086 832-G2
PROM DR
13900 SCIC 95037 936-G7
13900 SCIC 95037 956-G1
PROMENADE CT
800 SJS 95138 875-G5
PROMENADE LN
700 SJS 95138 875-G5
PROMETHEAN WY
100 MTVW 94043 811-J5
100 MTVW 94043 812-A5
PROMISE WY
- HOLL 95023 1040-A6
PROMONTORY WY
3100 SJS 95135 876-A1
PRONTO DR
600 SJS 95123 874-F5
PROSPECT AV
- LGTS 95030 893-A1
- SCIC 95030 893-A1
800 HOLL 95023 1040-B5
24600 LAH 94024 831-C3
24600 LAH 94022 831-C3
PROSPECT CT
100 LGTS 95030 893-A1
PROSPECT RD
1700 SJS 95129 852-F5
5100 SAR 95070 852-B6
7400 CPTO 95014 852-D5
22500 SCIC 95070 852-B6
PROSPECT ST
900 SJS 95110 854-C1
2100 MLPK 94025 790-D7
2100 SMCo 94025 790-D7
PROSPER AV
1100 SJS 95118 874-C2

STREET Block	City	ZIP	Pg-Grid
PROSPERITY CT			
1500	SJS	95131	814-C6
PROUD DR			
1400	SJS	95132	814-G4
PROUTY WY			
1000	SJS	95129	852-H3
PROVANMILL WY			
2100	SJS	95121	855-C4
PROVENCE CT			
-	SJS	95135	855-F3
PROVIDENCE CT			
900	CPTO	95014	852-B2
PROVINCETOWN DR			
1500	SJS	95129	852-G5
PROVO CT			
3100	SJS	95127	814-H6
PRUNE CT			
1000	SUNV	94087	832-C2
PRUNE ST			
900	HOLL	95023	1040-A6
1800	SBnC	95023	1040-A6
PRUNE WY			
600	SJS	95117	853-D1
PRUNE BLOSSOM DR			
5300	SJS	95123	875-D1
13700	SAR	95070	872-D1
PRUNEDALE RD			
4100	SCIC	95020	978-J5
PRUNELLE CT			
1100	SUNV	94087	832-C3
PRUNERIDGE AV			
700	SCL	95051	832-G6
1800	SCL	95050	833-D7
1800	SCL	95128	833-D7
1900	SJS	95117	833-D7
2500	SCL	95051	833-A7
3800	CPTO	95014	832-G6
PRUNETREE CT			
2400	SJS	95121	855-E4
PRUNETREE LN			
4000	SJS	95121	855-E4
10300	CPTO	95014	832-E7
PUCCINI AV			
2600	SJS	95122	855-A1
PUCCINI DR			
500	SUNV	94087	832-E3
PUEBLA CT			
1400	SJS	95118	874-B3
PUEBLO CT			
-	GIL	95020	957-F6
PUEBLO DR			
200	SJS	95131	814-A5
PUEBLO HILL CT			
700	SJS	95127	835-B1
PUEBLO VISTA			
10300	SCIC	95127	835-B2
10300	SJS	95127	835-B2
PUENTE CT			
20000	SAR	95070	852-F6
PUERTO GOLFITO CT			
100	SJS	95116	834-D2
PUERTO LIMON CT			
2000	SJS	95116	834-F3
PUERTO VALLARTA DR			
1500	SJS	95120	874-A7
1600	SJS	95120	893-J1
1600	SJS	95120	894-A1
PUESTA DEL SOL			
100	LGTS	95032	872-J3
PUFFIN CT			
-	CMBL	95008	853-D5
PUGET SOUND WY			
800	SJS	95133	834-E1
PULGAS AV			
1800	EPA	94303	791-C1
PULLMAN WY			
-	SJS	95111	854-F6
PULORA CT			
1100	SUNV	94087	832-C3
PUMPHERSTON CT			
2200	SJS	95148	855-C2
PUMPHERSTON WY			
3200	SJS	95148	855-C2
PUMPKIN CT			
7900	CPTO	95014	852-C2
PUMPKIN DR			
7900	CPTO	95014	852-B2
PURCELL PL			
-	SJS	95131	814-D6
PURDUE CT			
700	SCL	95051	832-J6
PURDUE DR			
18300	SAR	95070	852-J7
PURDUE PL			
5500	SJS	95118	874-A5
PURE CT			
500	SJS	95136	874-G3
PURISSIMA AV			
400	SUNV	94086	832-D1
PURISSIMA RD			
26200	LAH	94022	831-B1
26600	LAH	94022	811-A6
PURISSIMA WY			
-	MGH	95037	917-B3
PURITAN CT			
700	SJS	95123	874-G6
PURITANI CT			
2500	SJS	95121	854-H4
PURITANI WY			
1400	SJS	95121	854-H4
PURPLE CLIFF CT			
6500	SJS	95119	875-D7
PURPLE GLEN DR			
200	SJS	95119	875-D7
PURPLE HILLS DR			
6100	SJS	95119	875-D7
PURPLE KNOLL CT			
6200	SJS	95119	875-D6
PURPLELEAF ST			
48000	FRMT	94539	793-H1
PURPLE SAGE CT			
6100	SJS	95119	875-C6
PURPLE VALE CT			
6500	SJS	95119	875-D7
PUSATERI WY			
1100	SJS	95121	854-J4
PUTNEY CT			
1900	SJS	95132	814-D3
PUTTER AV			
11600	SCIC	94024	831-E4
PUTTER WY			
11700	SCIC	94024	831-F4
PYLE CT			
2200	SCL	95051	833-B2
PYRACANTHA TER			
700	SUNV	94087	832-E3
PYRAMID CT			
1500	SJS	95130	853-B4
PYRUS WY			
800	SUNV	94087	832-C2
Q			
QUADROS LN			
2000	SJS	95131	814-E7
QUAIL			
-	PTLV	94028	830-C1
QUAIL AV			
1500	SUNV	94087	832-H5
QUAIL CT			
-	ATN	94027	790-H1
17200	MGH	95037	917-F4
QUAIL DR			
1500	MPS	95035	794-D5
QUAIL LN			
3100	MGH	95037	917-F4
26000	LAH	94022	811-C7
QUAIL RUN			
1500	HOLL	95023	1039-J5
QUAIL ACRES			
14100	SAR	95070	872-F2
QUAIL BLUFF CT			
-	SJS	95121	855-D4
QUAIL BLUFF LN			
-	SJS	95121	855-D5
QUAIL BLUFF PL			
-	SJS	95121	855-D4
QUAIL BUSH CT			
400	SJS	95117	853-C1
QUAIL CANYON CT			
3800	SCIC	95148	835-F5
QUAIL CANYON RD			
3800	SCIC	95148	835-F5
QUAIL CLIFF WY			
7000	SJS	95120	894-G3
QUAIL COVE CT			
7000	SJS	95120	894-F3
QUAIL COVE WY			
7000	SJS	95120	894-F3
QUAIL CREEK CIR			
1200	SJS	95120	894-F3
QUAIL CREST WY			
7000	SJS	95120	894-F4
QUAIL DUNES WY			
7000	SJS	95120	894-G3
QUAIL HILL RD			
15900	LGTS	95032	873-D6
QUAIL HOLLOW DR			
-	SJS	95128	853-F4
900	SBnC	95023	1060-D1
QUAIL KNOLL CT			
1100	SJS	95120	894-F3
QUAIL MEADOW RD			
1900	SCIC	94024	831-G5
QUAIL RIDGE CT			
1100	SJS	95120	894-F3
QUAIL RIDGE WY			
-	SBnC	95023	1060-D1
QUAIL RUN CT			
1100	SJS	95118	874-C3
15500	SCIC	95070	872-C4
QUAIL VIEW WY			
1000	SJS	95120	894-F3
QUAIL WALK DR			
1400	GIL	95020	957-E7
QUAMME DR			
1100	SJS	95121	854-J3
QUANTICO CT			
2400	SJS	95128	853-F3
QUARRY RD			
100	PA	94304	790-H5
100	SCIC	94305	790-H5
500	PA	94305	790-H5
21300	SAR	95070	872-C1
N QUARRY RD			
16400	LGTS	95030	893-C1
S QUARRY RD			
16400	LGTS	95030	893-C2
QUARRY PARK DR			
4000	SJS	95136	854-E5
QUARRY PARK WY			
4000	SJS	95136	854-E5
QUARTUCCIO WY			
4100	SCIC	95148	835-G7
4100	SCIC	95148	855-G1
QUARTZ WY			
1400	SJS	95118	874-B2
QUEBEC CT			
1500	SUNV	94087	832-D5
QUEBEC WY			
1900	SJS	95124	853-G7
QUEEN ANNE DR			
700	SUNV	94087	832-C3
1000	SJS	95129	852-G3
QUEEN CHARLOTTE DR			
1600	SUNV	94087	832-D5
QUEEN ELIZABETH WY			
1800	SJS	95132	814-J3
QUEEN MARY CT			
1900	SJS	95132	814-J2
QUEENS CT			
-	ATN	94027	790-C4
400	CMBL	95008	853-D5
QUEENS LN			
400	SJS	95112	834-A2
QUEENSBRIDGE CT			
1000	SJS	95120	894-G4
QUEENSBRIDGE WY			
1100	SJS	95120	894-G4
QUEENSBROOK DR			
1000	SJS	95129	852-C7
QUEENSBURRY AV			
1500	LALT	94024	832-A3
QUEENS CROSSING DR			
1400	SJS	95132	814-E4
QUEENS ESTATES CT			
2900	SJS	95135	855-G5
QUEENS OAK CT			
22600	CPTO	95014	831-C7
QUEENSTOWN CT			
1500	SUNV	94087	832-D5
QUEENSTOWN DR			
1700	SJS	95132	814-E3
QUEENSWOOD CT			
7000	SJS	95120	894-H2
QUEENSWOOD WY			
6800	SJS	95120	894-H3
QUEEN VICTORIA WY			
3400	SJS	95132	814-J3
QUERCUS CT			
900	SUNV	94086	832-H3
QUESADA DR			
3200	SJS	95148	835-D7
QUEST LN			
-	SJS	95148	835-C7
QUETTA AV			
700	SUNV	94087	832-D2
QUETTA CT			
800	SUNV	94087	832-D2
QUICKERT RD			
15400	SAR	95070	872-C5
15400	SCIC	95070	872-C5
QUICKSILVER DR			
1000	SJS	95136	874-D2
QUIEN SABE RD			
-	SBnC	-	1061-G4
-	SBnC	95023	1061-E4
-	SBnC	95075	1061-A5
QUIET CIR			
1900	SJS	95132	814-E3
QUIET MEADOW CT			
1400	SJS	95121	855-D7
QUIET POND LN			
-	SJS	95138	855-C6
QUILEN CT			
-	SCIC	94305	790-J7
QUIMBY RD			
1700	SJS	95122	835-G7
1700	SJS	95122	855-B1
2400	SJS	95148	855-E1
3600	SJS	95148	835-G7
3700	SCIC	95148	835-G7
QUINCE AV			
800	SCL	95051	833-A6
1100	SUNV	94087	832-D3
QUINCE LN			
500	MPS	95035	794-D5
QUINCY DR			
400	MTVW	94043	811-F2
1200	SJS	95132	814-G5
QUINLAN LN			
3700	SJS	95118	874-B2
QUINN AV			
500	SJS	95112	854-G3
2100	SCL	95051	833-B2
QUINN CT			
2100	SCL	95051	833-B2
19200	SCIC	95037	916-J2
QUINNHILL AV			
200	SCIC	94024	831-E2
300	LALT	94024	831-E2
QUINTERNO CT			
22200	CPTO	95014	852-A1
QUINTINIA DR			
800	SUNV	94086	832-G3
QUINTO WY			
2700	SJS	95124	873-H1
QUITO RD			
12500	SJS	95130	872-J1
12500	SAR	95070	872-J1
QUITO RD Rt#-G2			
2000	SAR	95070	852-J7
2000	SJS	95130	852-J7
12400	SAR	95130	852-J7
12500	SJS	95130	872-H4
12500	SAR	95070	872-H4
14800	LGTS	95030	872-H4
14800	LGTS	95032	872-H4
14900	MSER	95030	872-H4
15500	SCIC	95030	872-H4
QUITO OAKS WY			
13900	SAR	95070	872-J2
QUME DR			
2200	SJS	95131	814-C5
R			
RABIA DR			
5500	SJS	95123	874-H4
RACE LN			
-	SJS	95126	853-J2
RACE ST			
-	SJS	95126	833-J7
200	SCIC	95126	833-J7
200	SCIC	95126	853-J1
300	SJS	95126	853-J1
RACHEL CT			
5700	SJS	95123	874-J5
RACINE PL			
-	SJS	95111	854-G5
RACOON CT			
17600	MGH	95037	917-E3
RADCLIFF DR			
28100	LAH	94022	810-H5
RADCLIFF WY			
800	SUNV	94087	832-C2
RADCLIFFE DR			
400	SCL	95051	833-A7
900	SJS	95117	853-D3
RADFORD DR			
100	CMBL	95008	853-B5
RADIANT DR			
6200	SJS	95123	874-J7
RADIO AV			
2000	SJS	95125	854-B5
RADKO DR			
6500	SJS	95119	875-D7
RADOYKA DR			
12300	SAR	95070	852-H6
RADTKE AV			
10000	SCIC	95020	957-H5
RAE LN			
22100	CPTO	95014	852-A2
RAEBURN CT			
800	SJS	95136	874-E1
RAFAEL DR			
1000	SJS	95120	874-E7
RAFTER RIDGE DR			
-	SJS	95127	835-C3
RAFTON DR			
4900	SJS	95124	873-J4
RAGGIO AV			
2300	SCL	95050	833-C3
2400	SCL	95051	833-B3
RAHWAY DR			
4700	SJS	95111	875-B1
RAICH DR			
7100	SJS	95120	894-H4
RAILROAD AV			
200	MPS	95035	794-A7
300	MGH	95037	917-A7
400	SCL	95050	833-F3
1800	MGH	95037	937-B1
15400	SCIC	95037	937-C2
N RAILROAD CT			
200	MPS	95035	794-A6
RAILROAD ST			
7300	GIL	95020	978-A3
RAILWAY AV			
-	CMBL	95008	853-E6
RAIMUNDO WY			
700	SCIC	94305	810-J2
1100	SCIC	94305	811-A2
RAIN WK			
-	MPS	95035	814-J1
RAINBOW CT			
21600	CPTO	95014	852-B4
RAINBOW DR			
600	MTVW	94041	812-A7
1400	HOLL	95023	1040-D6
5800	SJS	95129	852-E4
7300	CPTO	95014	852-B4
21500	SCIC	95014	852-B4
RAINBOW PL			
-	MPS	95035	814-J1
21000	CPTO	95014	852-A4
RAIN DANCE			
-	MPS	95035	814-J1
RAINDANCE CT			
-	SJS	95136	874-H2
RAINERI LN			
19200	SCIC	95033	912-J1
RAINFIELD DR			
2700	SJS	95133	834-G1
RAINIER ST			
100	SJS	95126	833-J7
RAINTREE CT			
800	SJS	95129	852-J2
RAINTREE DR			
800	SJS	95129	852-J2
RAINTREE SPRING CT			
11500	CPTO	95014	852-A4
RAINVIEW DR			
2700	SJS	95133	814-G7
2700	SJS	95133	834-G1
RAINWELL CT			
2700	SJS	95133	834-G1
RAINWELL DR			
400	SJS	95133	834-G1
RAINWOOD CT			
2800	SJS	95148	835-D7
RAJKOVICH WY			
400	HOLL	95023	1039-H4
1100	SJS	95120	894-F3
RAKTAD RD			
21100	SCIC	95120	895-B5
RALEIGH CIR			
2100	HOLL	95023	1040-E5
RALEIGH DR			
2400	SJS	95124	853-J7
RALEIGH PL			
18900	SAR	95070	852-G6
RALEIGH RD			
-	SJS	95193	875-C5
200	SJS	95119	875-C5
RALENE CT			
1600	SJS	95131	814-D5
RALENE PL			
1600	SJS	95131	814-D5
RALMAR AV			
2000	EPA	94303	791-A1
RALPH CT			
500	SCIC	95046	937-F4
RALPH LEE CT			
1700	MGH	95037	917-D5
RALPH LEE DR			
1700	MGH	95037	917-D5
RALPHS DR			
-	SBnC	95023	1060-D2
RALSTON CT			
2300	SJS	95148	855-C2
2600	SCL	95051	833-B3
RALSTON DR			
2300	SJS	95148	855-C2
RALSTON RD			
-	ATN	94027	790-C3
RALT CT			
-	SJS	95123	874-F7
RALYA CT			
18500	CPTO	95014	852-H1
RAMA DR			
3100	SJS	95124	873-H2
RAMBLEWOOD DR			
6400	SJS	95120	894-E1
RAMBO CT			
2300	SCL	95054	813-C5
RAMBOW DR			
3400	PA	94306	791-D7
3400	PA	94306	811-D1
RAMEL WY			
100	LGTS	95030	893-B1
RAMIREZ CT			
3800	SJS	95121	855-D3
RAMISH DR			
2100	SJS	95131	814-D6
RAMITA CT			
1400	SJS	95128	853-F5
RAMKE PL			
2400	SCL	95050	833-C6
RAMOHS WY			
100	LGTS	95032	873-G6
RAMON DR			
200	LALT	94024	811-F7
1300	SUNV	94087	832-G4
RAMONA AV			
700	SUNV	94087	832-C1
900	SJS	95125	854-A2
1200	HOLL	95023	1040-C6
RAMONA CIR			
3600	PA	94306	811-D1
RAMONA CT			
2800	SCL	95051	833-B6
22300	CPTO	95014	852-A1
RAMONA RD			
100	SMCo	94028	830-E3
RAMONA ST			
200	PA	94301	790-H4
1100	PA	94301	791-B7
2500	PA	94306	791-B7
3000	PA	94306	811-D1
RAMONA WY			
700	GIL	95020	977-G1
RAMOS CT			
500	MPS	95035	794-D5
2700	MTVW	94040	832-A2
RAMOS WY			
2100	SJS	95128	833-F7
2100	SCIC	95128	833-F7
3100	PA	94304	811-B1
RAMOSO RD			
100	PTLV	94028	810-B4
RAMPART AV			
10400	CPTO	95014	852-F2
RAMSDELL PL			
2600	SJS	95148	835-C7
2600	SJS	95148	855-C1
RAMSGATE WY			
1500	SJS	95127	835-A4
RAMSHALL PL			
-	SCL	95054	813-D5
RAMSTAD DR			
3400	SJS	95127	835-B3
RAMSTREE DR			
1600	SJS	95131	814-C5
RANCH CT			
1400	SJS	95132	814-G3
RANCH DR			
-	MPS	95035	813-H1
100	MPS	95035	793-H7
RANCH PL			
3400	SJS	95132	814-G3
RANCH RD			
3800	SCIC	95135	855-J1
3800	SCIC	95148	855-J1
3800	SCIC	95148	835-J7
RANCHERO DR			
15700	SCIC	95037	937-E1
RANCHERO WY			
1000	SJS	95117	853-B3
RANCH HOUSE WY			
8700	SJS	95135	856-A6
RANCHITA CT			
1400	LALT	94024	831-J3
RANCHITA DR			
1300	LALT	94024	831-J3
RANCHITO CT			
-	HOLL	95023	1039-G3
RANCHITO DR			
200	HOLL	95023	1039-G3
RANCHO DR			
-	SJS	95111	854-H7
100	SCIC	95111	854-H7
1200	HOLL	95023	1040-A5
RANCHO PL			
-	SJS	95126	833-D1
10200	CPTO	95014	852-A1
RANCHO BELLA VISTA			
20100	SAR	95070	872-E3
RANCHO DEEP CLIFF DR			
22300	CPTO	95014	852-A2
22400	CPTO	95014	851-J2
RANCHO HIGUERA RD			
400	MPS	95035	794-A4
RANCHO HILLS CT			
1700	GIL	95020	977-E1
RANCHO HILLS DR			
8700	GIL	95020	977-E1
8900	GIL	95020	957-E6
RANCHO LAS CIMAS WY			
18500	SAR	95070	872-H3
RANCHO MANOR CT			
100	SJS	95111	854-H6
RANCHO MANUELLA LN			
26100	LAH	94022	811-C5
RANCHO MCCORMICK BLVD			
2000	SCL	95050	833-C3
RANCHO MCCORMICK CT			
2100	SCL	95050	833-C3
RANCHO REAL			
8400	GIL	95020	977-F2
RANCHO VENTURA ST			
22300	CPTO	95014	852-A1
RANCHO VIEW CT			
3400	SJS	95132	814-G3
RANCHO VISTA CT			
3300	SCIC	95020	977-C2
RANCHO VISTA DR			
7800	SCIC	95020	977-C3
7900	GIL	95020	977-C3
RAND ST			
800	HOLL	95023	1040-E5
1600	MPS	95035	794-A4
RANDALL CT			
6000	SJS	95123	874-G6
RANDALL PL			
-	MLPK	94025	790-F6
RANDERS CT			
2700	PA	94303	791-C6
RANDLESWOOD CT			
5800	SJS	95129	852-G3
RANDOL AV			
1100	SJS	95126	833-H6
RANDOL CREEK DR			
6900	SJS	95120	894-F3
RANDOLPH AV			
3600	SCL	95051	832-H7
RANDOLPH DR			
1900	SJS	95128	853-G2
2000	SCIC	95128	853-G2
RANDOLPH PKWY			
1600	LALT	94024	831-J4
RANDY CIR			
-	SBnC	95023	1060-G3
RANDY CT			
-	SMCo	94061	790-A3
RANDY LN			
10000	CPTO	95014	832-E6
10000	CPTO	95014	852-E1
RANERE CT			
1000	SUNV	94087	832-C2
RANEY CT			
700	SCL	95050	833-C5
RANFRE LN			
19300	SAR	95070	852-G7
19300	SAR	95070	872-G1
RANGER CT			
16700	MGH	95037	917-F6
RANGEWOOD DR			
-	SJS	95138	855-C6
RANGEWOOD PL			
-	SJS	95138	855-C5
RANGPUR CT			
1000	SUNV	94087	832-D2
RANKIN AV			
-	SJS	95110	834-A5
RANKIN DR			
1000	MPS	95035	794-C4
RANSEN CT			
18200	MGH	95037	916-J6
RANSON DR			
600	SJS	95133	834-F1
RANWICK CT			
4200	SJS	95118	874-C2
RAPHAEL DR			
-	SJS	95135	855-H1
RAPOSA CT			
1100	SJS	95121	855-A4
RAPOSA DR			
1100	SJS	95121	855-A4
RAQUEL CT			
400	LALT	94022	811-C5
1600	SJS	95128	853-G3
14800	SCIC	95046	937-G2
RAQUEL LN			
300	LALT	94022	811-D5
RARITAN PL			
2600	SJS	95148	835-E6
RASMUS CIR			
3000	SJS	95148	855-E1
RASPBERRY CT			
-	GIL	95020	977-J6
RASPBERRY PL			
4700	SJS	95129	853-B2
RATHMANN DR			
2800	SJS	95148	835-E7
RATHMORE LN			
-	MTVW	94043	812-B4
RATTAN CT			
600	FRMT	94539	793-J2
RATTAN TER			
800	SUNV	94086	832-G3
RAVEN CT			
13800	SAR	95070	872-J1
RAVENDALE CT			
3400	SJS	95111	854-G6
RAVENDALE DR			
400	MTVW	94043	812-B6
RAVENNA CT			
5600	SJS	95118	874-B5
RAVENSBURY AV			
22500	SCIC	95014	831-E5
23000	LAH	94024	831-E4
23100	SCIC	94024	831-E5
RAVENSCOURT AV			
900	CMBL	95128	853-F4
900	SJS	95128	853-F4
RAVENS PLACE WY			
1500	SJS	95121	855-B4
RAVENSWOOD AV			
100	ATN	94027	790-G3
100	MLPK	94025	790-G3
RAVENSWOOD CT			
19000	MGH	95037	917-A2
RAVENSWOOD DR			
1400	LALT	94024	832-A3
RAVENSWOOD WY			
3100	SJS	95148	835-E7
3100	SJS	95148	855-E1
RAVENWOOD DR			
13700	SAR	95070	872-H2
RAVINE CT			
2300	SJS	95133	834-F1
RAVINE DR			
2300	SJS	95133	834-F1
RAVINE RD			
15800	SAR	95030	872-G5
15800	SCIC	95030	872-G5
RAVINIA WY			
100	LGTS	95030	893-D2
100	LGTS	95032	893-D2
RAVIZZA AV			
1700	SCL	95051	833-B3
RAWLINGS DR			
900	SJS	95136	874-D2
RAWLS CT			
100	SJS	95139	895-F1
RAWLS WY			
100	SJS	95139	895-F1
RAY AV			
1000	LALT	94022	811-D4
RAY CIR			
-	SBnC	95023	1060-D2
RAYANNA AV			
3300	SCL	95051	832-J3
RAYBAL CT			
6300	SJS	95123	875-A7
RAYMOND AV			
300	SCIC	95128	853-G1
300	SJS	95128	853-G1
RAYMOND ST			
3000	SCL	95054	813-E7
RAYMUNDO AV			
800	LALT	94024	811-G6
RAYOS DE ESTRELLA DR			
-	SJS	95116	834-E5
RAYOS DEL SOL DR			
-	SJS	95116	834-E5
REA ST			
7600	GIL	95020	977-H3
REALM DR			
7000	SJS	95119	875-E7
REAMWOOD AV			
1200	SUNV	94089	813-A3
1200	SCL	95054	813-A3
REBECCA LN			
-	ATN	94027	790-G2
11600	LAH	94024	831-E3
REBECCA WY			
600	SJS	95117	853-B2
REBECCA LYNN WY			
2400	SCL	95050	833-C6
REBECCA PRIVADA			
800	MTVW	94040	832-A1
REBEIRO AV			
2600	SCL	95051	833-B6
REBEL CT			
5000	SJS	95118	874-A4
REBEL WY			
1500	SJS	95118	874-A4
1600	SJS	95118	873-J4
RECHT ST			
-	HOLL	95023	1040-B3
RECIFE WY			
5800	SJS	95120	874-C5
RECREATION AV			
-	MLPK	94025	790-J1
RECREATION DR			
-	SUNV	94089	812-H3
REDBERRY DR			
16300	SCIC	95030	872-F5
16300	SAR	95030	872-F5
REDBERRY RDG			
-	PTLV	94028	830-D2
REDBIRD DR			
800	SJS	95125	854-C6
REDBUD CT			
2400	SJS	95128	853-F4
REDBUSH TER			
2000	SJS	95128	833-F6
REDCLIFF CT			
22500	MTVW	94040	832-A1
REDCLIFF DR			
1200	SJS	95118	854-C7
1200	SJS	95118	874-C1
RED CREEK DR			
4900	SJS	95136	874-J2
4900	SJS	95136	875-A2
REDDING RD			
-	CMBL	95008	873-E2
200	SJS	95008	873-E2
REDEN DR			
4300	SJS	95130	853-A7
REDFIELD CT			
1500	SJS	95121	855-A3
RED FIR CT			
10500	CPTO	95014	852-C2
REDGLEN CT			
3200	SJS	95135	855-E2
RED HAWK DR			
1200	GIL	95020	957-F7
RED HAWK PL			
-	ScrC	95076	976-B7
REDHEAD LN			
-	LGTS	95030	893-B1
RED HILL RD			
20000	SCIC	95030	872-E5
RED HOLLY CT			
7100	SJS	95120	894-D3
RED MAPLE CT			
-	SJS	95138	855-C6
RED MAPLE LN			
-	SJS	95138	855-B6
RED MAPLE WY			
-	SJS	95138	855-B6
REDMOND AV			
900	SJS	95120	894-E1
900	SJS	95120	874-A7
REDMOND CT			
1000	SJS	95120	874-E7
RED OAK DR			
-	SUNV	94086	832-G1

STREET
Block City ZIP Pg-Grid

RED OAK DR E
200 SUNV 94086 832-G1
RED OAK DR W
200 SUNV 94086 832-G1
REDOAKS DR
1100 SJS 95128 853-E3
REDONDO CT
11200 CPTO 95014 852-B3
REDONDO DR
1200 SJS 95125 854-B5
REDONDO TER
300 SUNV 94086 812-D7
RED PEAK LN
- SJS 95135 876-A1
RED PINE CT
1100 SJS 95125 854-A4
RED RIVER WY
100 SJS 95136 875-A3
REDROCK CT
1100 SUNV 94089 812-J4
REDROCK RD
26600 LAH 94022 830-H2
REDSTONE DR
5000 SJS 95124 873-E4
RED TAIL CT
- MGH 95037 917-A2
3700 SCL 95051 832-H5
RED TAIL PL
- MGH 95037 917-A2
REDWING AV
1600 SUNV 94087 832-H5
REDWOOD AV
- MLPK 94025 790-J2
200 SCL 95051 833-A7
200 MPS 95035 793-H6
500 SJS 95050 833-E7
500 SJS 95128 833-E7
900 SUNV 94086 832-H3
2000 RDWC 94061 790-A1
N REDWOOD AV
- SJS 95050 833-E7
1300 SJS 95128 833-E6
S REDWOOD AV
300 SJS 95128 853-E1
REDWOOD CIR
3700 PA 94306 811-D1
REDWOOD CT
700 MTVW 94041 811-G5
REDWOOD DR
100 HOLL 95023 1039-H4
900 SJS 95138 875-F6
1400 LALT 94024 831-J6
17900 SCIC 95033 912-J2
REDWOOD LN
1300 GIL 95020 977-G3
REDWOOD WY
- ATN 94027 790-E2
REDWOOD ESTATES RD
17800 SCIC 95033 913-C2
REDWOOD GULCH RD
13700 SCIC 95070 871-F2
13800 SCIC 95030 871-F2
REDWOOD LAKE CT
1300 SJS 95131 814-B5
REDWOOD RETREAT RD
4100 SCIC 95020 956-E7
5200 SCIC 95037 956-C5
REECE WY
2900 SJS 95133 814-G7
REED AV
900 SUNV 94086 832-G2
REED ST
300 SCL 95050 833-D3
E REED ST
- SJS 95112 834-D7
W REED ST
100 SJS 95110 834-C7
100 SJS 95110 854-C1
REED TER
1000 SUNV 94086 832-H2
REEDHURST AV
3900 SJS 95118 874-A2
REESE ST
1200 RDWC 94061 790-A1
REEVE ST
900 SCL 95050 833-E3
REEVES CT
14600 SCIC 95127 835-B2
REFLECTIONS LN
- MPS 95035 794-A6
- MPS 95035 793-H6
REFREDI CT
21700 CPTO 95014 852-B1
REGABY PLACE CT
3800 SJS 95121 855-B5
REGAL CT
700 MLPK 94025 790-J2
4100 SCIC 95127 814-J6
4100 SCIC 95127 815-A6
REGALO CT
1400 SJS 95128 853-F4
REGAN LN
12700 SAR 95070 852-E6
REGAN ST
10200 SJS 95127 835-B3
REGAS DR
300 CMBL 95008 853-F7
REGATTA LN
1600 SJS 95112 833-J1
REGENCY AV
- SJS 95136 854-F7
REGENCY DR
1200 SJS 95129 852-H4
REGENCY PL
1200 SJS 95129 852-H4
REGENCY KNOLL DR
1000 SJS 95129 852-C7
REGENCY OAKS DR
6100 SJS 95129 852-C7
REGENT CT
100 LGTS 95032 873-G6
900 RDWC 94061 790-B1

REGENT DR
100 LGTS 95032 873-G6
900 LALT 94024 831-H5
REGENT PL
- PA 94301 791-A4
REGENT ST
1300 RDWC 94061 790-A1
REGENT PARK DR
700 SJS 95123 874-F4
REGIA CT
1100 SUNV 94087 832-D3
REGINA CT
2300 SCL 95054 813-C5
REGINA WY
1700 CMBL 95008 873-A1
1800 SJS 95008 873-A1
REGIS CT
3300 SCL 95051 833-A2
REGNART CT
21700 CPTO 95014 852-B3
REGNART RD
21500 CPTO 95014 852-A4
REGNART WY
2800 SCL 95051 833-B7
REGNART CANYON DR
11600 CPTO 95014 852-A4
REID LN
20500 SAR 95070 872-D2
REINCLAUD CT
1100 SUNV 94087 832-C3
REINELL PL
20200 CPTO 95014 832-E7
REINERT CT
2100 MTVW 94043 811-G2
REINERT RD
800 MTVW 94043 811-G2
REINOSO CT
3600 SJS 95136 874-D1
REMBRANDT DR
1000 SUNV 94087 832-F3
REMILLARD CT
900 SJS 95122 834-E7
REMINGTON CT
1100 SUNV 94087 832-A3
2600 MGH 95037 917-F6
3000 SJS 95148 855-D1
E REMINGTON DR
100 SUNV 94087 832-E3
W REMINGTON DR
500 SUNV 94087 832-B2
REMINGTON WY
2900 SJS 95148 855-D1
3100 SJS 95148 835-D7
REMO CT
2300 SCL 95054 813-C5
REMO ST
700 SJS 95116 834-F6
REMSEN CT
1000 SUNV 94087 832-B3
REMUDA LN
1600 SJS 95112 833-J1
RENAISSANCE CT
1700 SCIC 95046 937-J6
RENAISSANCE DR
200 SJS 95134 813-D2
RENATO CT
- RDWC 94061 790-C1
RENEE CT
1000 SJS 95120 894-H4
1200 SCIC 95046 937-H5
RENETTA CT
800 LALT 94024 831-E1
RENFIELD WY
2300 SJS 95148 855-C2
RENFREW CT
2200 SJS 95131 814-D5
N RENGSTORFF AV
- MTVW 94040 811-G3
300 MTVW 94043 811-G1
S RENGSTORFF AV
100 MTVW 94040 811-F4
RENICK CT
2900 SJS 95148 855-C2
RENNIE AV
- SCIC 95127 815-A6
RENO DR
2300 SJS 95148 835-D6
RENOIR CT
1000 SUNV 94087 832-F3
RENOVA DR
500 SCIC 95128 853-F2
RENRAW DR
1200 SJS 95127 835-C3
RENTON CT
800 SJS 95123 874-E5
RENZ LN
700 GIL 95020 978-B3
RENZO CT
4700 SJS 95111 875-B1
REPUBLIC AV
100 SJS 95116 834-H3
REPUBLIC CT
2500 SJS 95116 834-H3
REPUBLIC PL
2500 SJS 95116 834-J3
REQUA CT
2900 SJS 95148 835-E7
RESEARCH PL
3000 SJS 95134 813-G4
RESEDA DR
600 SUNV 94087 832-D1
RESERVE CT
- SJS 95135 855-F2
RESERVOIR RD
- ATN 94027 790-B6
- LGTS 95030 893-A1
RESIDENT LN
- MLPK 94025 790-J2
RESTON TER
- SUNV 94087 832-D5
RESULTS WY
- CPTO 95014 852-B1
RETTUS CT
600 SJS 95111 854-G3

REVA CT
10200 SCIC 95127 835-A3
REVELATION PL
- MPS 95035 814-J1
REVELSTOKE WY
1400 SUNV 94087 832-D5
REVERE AV
1400 SJS 95118 874-B1
REVERE DR
800 SUNV 94087 832-C3
REVERE PL
7100 GIL 95020 977-H4
REVEY AV
100 SJS 95128 833-F7
100 SCIC 95128 833-F7
200 SCIC 95128 853-F1
200 SJS 95128 853-F1
REX CIR
100 CMBL 95008 853-D5
REXFORD WY
2100 SCIC 95128 853-G2
2100 SJS 95128 853-G2
REXWOOD CT
3800 SJS 95121 855-C4
REYNA PL
- MLPK 94025 790-F5
REYNAUD DR
14800 SCIC 95127 835-B1
REYNELLA CT
1100 SUNV 94087 832-D3
REYNOLDS CIR
400 SJS 95112 833-J1
REYNOLDS DR
16300 SCIC 95037 936-G3
REYNOLDS RD
19400 SCIC 95033 894-A4
20300 SCIC 95033 893-J6
RHAPSODY WY
4500 SJS 95111 855-A7
RHINE LN
1400 SJS 95118 874-B5
RHINECASTLE WY
1100 SJS 95120 874-D6
RHINECLIFF WY
1500 SJS 95126 853-H4
RHODA DR
3700 SJS 95117 853-B3
13200 LAH 94022 811-A6
RHODES CT
- SJS 95126 833-J7
400 SCIC 95046 937-F6
RHODES DR
500 PA 94303 791-C4
RHODESIA WY
1500 SJS 95126 853-H4
RHONDA DR
4800 SJS 95129 852-J4
4800 SJS 95129 853-A4
RHONE CT
400 MTVW 94043 811-G3
RHUS RIDGE RD
11800 LAH 94022 831-B3
11900 SCIC 94022 831-B3
RIALTO CT
2000 MTVW 94043 811-G3
RIBBON DR
4000 SJS 95130 853-B4
RIBBONWOOD AV
- SJS 95123 875-C5
RIBCHESTER CT
5700 SJS 95123 874-J4
RIBIER CT
1100 SUNV 94087 832-D3
RIBISI CIR
1000 SJS 95131 814-E7
RIBISI WY
1000 SJS 95131 814-D7
1200 SJS 95131 834-D1
RIC DR
2300 SCIC 95020 958-D6
RICARDO CT
- SBnC 95004 1037-B2
RICARDO DR
400 SBnC 95004 1037-C2
RICARDO RD
22500 CPTO 95014 851-J2
22500 CPTO 95014 852-A2
RICA VISTA WY
15600 SCIC 95127 815-B7
RICE CT
5000 SJS 95111 875-A2
20600 SAR 95070 852-D7
RICE DR
4900 SJS 95111 875-A2
RICE LN
10200 SCIC 95020 957-J4
RICE WY
5000 SJS 95111 875-A2
RICH AV
900 MTVW 94022 811-G5
900 MTVW 94040 811-G5
RICH PL
900 MTVW 94022 811-G5
900 MTVW 94040 811-G5
RICHARD AV
1400 SCL 95050 833-D2
RICHARD CT
2400 MTVW 94043 811-F2
RICHARDS AV
1400 SJS 95125 853-J4
RICHARDSON AV
1100 LALT 94024 831-H4
RICHARDSON CT
800 PA 94303 791-D7
RICHARDSON DR
300 HOLL 95023 1040-A5
3400 SJS 95127 814-J7
RICHDALE AV
400 SJS 95111 854-J6
RICHELIEU CT
300 LALT 94022 811-E5
13700 SAR 95070 872-G1
RICHELIEU PL
1500 SUNV 94087 832-D5

RICHEY DR
15100 SCIC 95124 873-E4
RICHFIELD DR
100 SJS 95129 853-A1
RICHGROVE CT
2800 SJS 95148 835-E7
RICHLAND AV
2800 SJS 95125 854-C7
RICHLAND DR
2200 SJS 95125 854-B6
RICHLEE DR
300 CMBL 95008 853-G5
RICHMOND AV
- SJS 95037 896-A7
- SCIC 95037 896-A7
300 SCIC 95128 853-H2
300 SJS 95128 853-H2
RICHTER CT
1200 MPS 95035 814-C1
RICHWOOD CT
19400 CPTO 95014 852-G1
RICHWOOD DR
10100 CPTO 95014 852-F1
RICKENBACKER ST
1000 SJS 95128 853-F3
RICKY CT
700 CMBL 95008 853-C6
RICKY DR
700 CMBL 95008 853-C6
RIDDER PARK DR
700 SJS 95131 814-A6
700 SJS 95131 834-A1
RIDDLE RD
3100 SJS 95117 853-D2
RIDGE CT
2900 SCL 95051 833-A6
RIDGE RD
700 SCL 95051 833-A6
5000 SCIC 95020 976-C2
20500 SCIC 95033 912-J1
RIDGEBROOK WY
4100 SJS 95111 855-A7
RIDGECLIFF CT
2300 SJS 95131 814-D5
RIDGE CREEK CT
11700 CPTO 95014 852-C4
RIDGECREST AV
16000 MSER 95030 872-H6
RIDGEFARM DR
400 SJS 95123 874-J5
RIDGEGATE DR
2900 SJS 95133 814-G7
RIDGEGLEN WY
2300 SJS 95133 834-G1
RIDGELEY DR
1000 CMBL 95008 853-G5
1800 CMBL 95125 853-G5
RIDGELINE CT
1200 SJS 95127 835-C3
RIDGEMARK DR
200 SBnC 95023 1060-E2
S RIDGEMARK DR
- SBnC 95023 1060-E3
RIDGEMONT DR
1000 MPS 95035 814-E1
2000 SJS 95148 835-B5
2700 SJS 95127 835-B5
3400 MTVW 94040 831-J2
RIDGE OAK CT
1200 SJS 95120 874-C7
RIDGETOP DR
14800 SCIC 95127 814-J6
14800 SJS 95127 814-J6
RIDGETREE WY
1600 SJS 95131 814-D4
RIDGEVIEW AV
10800 SCIC 95127 815-B7
RIDGEVIEW CT
3700 MGH 95037 917-H5
10400 CPTO 95014 832-G7
10700 SCIC 95127 815-B7
RIDGEVIEW DR
- ATN 94027 790-A5
RIDGEVIEW TER
- SCIC 95127 815-B7
RIDGEVIEW WY
10600 SCIC 95127 815-B7
N RIDGE VISTA AV
300 SCIC 95127 814-H7
300 SCIC 95127 834-J1
11900 SJS 95127 814-H7
S RIDGE VISTA AV
300 SCIC 95127 834-J1
300 SJS 95127 834-J1
RIDGEWAY DR
8800 GIL 95020 977-E1
10000 CPTO 95014 851-J1
RIDGEWOOD DR
1300 SJS 95118 874-B4
RIDGEWOOD LN
25800 LAH 94022 831-B2
RIDING CT
6000 SJS 95124 873-J7
RIDLEY WY
1200 SJS 95125 853-J4
RIEDAL PL
10100 CPTO 95014 832-F7
RIEDEL CT
2800 SJS 95135 855-E2
12400 SCIC 95046 938-A6
RIEDEL DR
2800 SJS 95135 855-D3
RIELLY CT
700 SJS 95123 874-F4
RIESLING CT
- FRMT 94539 793-J2
19400 SAR 95070 872-F3
RIESLING ST
- FRMT 94539 793-J2
RIESLING TER
1200 SUNV 94087 832-C3
RIESLING WY
8300 SJS 95135 855-H7

RIGOLETTO DR
1700 SJS 95122 855-A1
RIGOR DR
- SJS 95148 855-F1
RILEY WY
800 RDWC 94061 790-C2
RILMA LN
1000 LALT 94022 811-E4
RIL MARIANNA CT
- MGH 95037 916-H6
RIMROCK DR
1300 SJS 95120 894-D3
RIMWOOD DR
5200 SJS 95118 874-B4
RINCON AV
400 SUNV 94086 832-D1
700 SJS 95008 853-B6
700 CMBL 95008 853-B6
4300 SJS 95130 853-B6
E RINCON AV
- CMBL 95008 853-E6
W RINCON AV
- CMBL 95008 853-D6
RINCON CIR
1000 SJS 95131 813-J4
4100 PA 94306 811-C3
RINCONADA AV
100 PA 94301 791-A6
RINCONADA CT
400 LALT 94022 811-F7
RINCONADA DR
2400 SJS 95125 854-C6
RINCONADA OAKS CT
100 LGTS 95032 872-J3
RINEHART DR
2300 SJS 95133 834-G2
RINGEL CT
1700 MGH 95037 917-D5
RINGEL DR
17300 MGH 95037 917-D5
RINGROSE CT
1300 SJS 95121 855-B1
RINGWOOD AV
- SMCo 94025 790-H2
- ATN 94027 790-H1
800 MLPK 94025 790-H1
1100 SJS 95131 814-B4
RINGWOOD CT
1100 SJS 95131 814-B5
RIO CT
4000 SJS 95134 813-D2
RIO BARRANCA CT
2100 SJS 95116 834-G3
RIO BRAVO DR
3400 SJS 95148 835-D6
RIO CHICO DR
100 SJS 95111 854-J7
RIO DE ESMERALDA
3200 SJS 95121 855-B4
RIO DE JOYAS
3200 SJS 95121 855-A4
RIO DE LATA
3200 SJS 95121 855-A4
RIO DE LOS MOLINOS AV
100 SUNV 94086 812-C6
RIO DE ORO
3200 SJS 95121 855-B4
RIO DE PERLA
3200 SJS 95121 855-B4
RIO DE PLATA
3200 SJS 95121 855-A4
RIO DE PLOMO
1300 SJS 95121 855-B4
RIO GRAND CT
500 MGH 95037 917-A6
RIO GRANDE DR
5200 SJS 95136 874-J3
RIO GRANDE WY
- GIL 95020 957-F6
RIO GUACIMAL CT
2100 SJS 95116 834-G3
RIO HONDO DR
1200 SJS 95120 894-C1
RIO LOBO DR
5200 SJS 95136 874-J3
5200 SJS 95136 875-A3
RIO ORO CT
400 MGH 95037 917-A6
RIORDAN DR
2100 SJS 95130 853-A7
RIORDAN PL
- MLPK 94025 790-H2
RIORDEN TER
- SUNV 94087 832-D5
RIO RITA WY
4700 SJS 95129 853-A1
RIO ROBLES
- SJS 95134 813-E3
RIO ROBLES E
- SJS 95134 813-F3
RIO SERENA AV
- CMBL 95008 853-A5
200 SJS 95130 853-A5
RIO VERDE CT
4900 SJS 95118 874-A3
RIO VERDE DR
4900 SJS 95118 874-A3
RIO VERDE PL
200 MPS 95035 813-J1
RIO VISTA
100 LGTS 95032 872-J2
RIO VISTA AV
4800 SJS 95129 852-J1
4800 SJS 95129 853-A1
RIPARIAN CT
- SJS 95133 814-F7
RIPLEY DR
500 SJS 95133 834-E2
RITA CT
2200 SCL 95050 833-D6
RITA DR
16700 MGH 95037 917-C7

RITANNA CT
20600 SAR 95070 852-D5
RITTENHOUSE AV
- ATN 94027 790-D2
RITZ CT
3600 SJS 95148 835-F7
RIVA RIDGE RD
22300 SCrC 95033 912-H5
E RIVER PKWY
- SCL 95054 813-E4
N RIVER ST
- SJS 95113 834-A6
- SJS 95110 834-A6
RIVERA ST
700 MPS 95035 794-B4
RIVER ASH CT
- SJS 95136 874-H1
RIVERBANK RD
3300 SCIC 95020 956-J4
RIVER BED CT
2200 SCL 95054 813-C5
RIVER BIRCH CT
1600 SJS 95131 834-D1
RIVER BIRCH DR
1600 SJS 95131 834-D1
RIVERBORO PL
- SJS 95123 874-D3
RIVERCREST CT
10300 CPTO 95014 832-A7
RIVERDALE CT
13600 SAR 95070 872-H1
RIVERDALE DR
13600 SAR 95070 872-H1
RIVER FALLS DR
700 SJS 95111 855-A7
RIVERMARK PKWY
- SCL 95054 813-E5
RIVERMONT CT
2600 SJS 95116 834-J4
RIVER OAKS CIR
200 SJS 95134 813-G4
RIVER OAKS PKWY
100 SJS 95134 813-F4
RIVER OAKS PL
- SJS 95134 813-F4
RIVER PARK DR
700 SJS 95111 855-A7
RIVER RANCH CIR
13800 SAR 95070 872-E1
RIVER ROCK CT
400 SJS 95136 854-F7
RIVERRUN DR
2700 SJS 95127 834-H2
RIVERSIDE CT
400 SCL 95054 813-F5
RIVERSIDE DR
600 LALT 94024 831-F1
600 SJS 95125 854-A2
22300 CPTO 95014 852-A2
22400 CPTO 95014 851-J2
RIVERSIDE RD
- SBnC 95023 1039-G6
W RIVERSIDE WY
1000 SJS 95129 852-E2
RIVER TRAIL CT
4800 SJS 95136 874-H3
RIVERVIEW CIR
- GIL 95020 977-J5
RIVER VIEW DR
300 SJS 95111 875-A1
600 SJS 95111 855-B7
RIVERVIEW WY
- SBnC 95023 1060-B2
RIVIERA CT
900 SJS 95129 852-J2
RIVIERA DR
- HOLL 95023 1040-B4
100 LGTS 95032 873-B6
600 LALT 94024 811-G7
RIVIERA RD
10300 CPTO 95014 852-A1
RIVOIR DR
4000 SJS 95118 874-A2
RIXFORD LN
600 LALT 94024 831-F2
RIZAL CT
6400 SJS 95119 875-C7
ROAD A
- SBnC 95023 1000-C7
9500 SJS 95138 875-E2
ROAD B
- SBnC 95023 1000-C7
- SJB 95045 1038-D4
ROAD C
- SBnC 95023 1000-C7
- SBnC 95045 1038-C3
ROAD D
- SBnC 95023 1000-C7
- SBnC 95045 1038-C3
ROAD F
- SBnC 95023 1000-C7
ROAD G
- SBnC 95023 1000-C7
- SBnC 95023 1020-C1
- SBnC 95045 1038-C4
ROAD H
- SBnC 95023 1020-C1
ROAD J
- SBnC 95023 1020-D1
ROAD L
- SBnC 95023 1020-D2
6900 SCIC 95138 876-A2
ROAD N
- SBnC 95023 1020-E4
ROAD O
- SBnC 95023 1020-C5
ROAD P
- SBnC 95023 1020-A4
ROAD Q
- SBnC 95023 1020-B2
ROADING DR
400 SJS 95123 874-J5
ROADRUNNER TER
1300 SUNV 94087 832-H4

ROAN ST
300 SJS 95123 874-J5
ROARING WATER WY
21300 SCIC 95033 913-B2
ROB CT
- SBnC 95023 1060-F2
ROBALO CT
1100 SJS 95132 814-G5
ROBB DR
4500 SJS 95118 874-B2
ROBB RD
26100 LAH 94022 811-B5
26100 PA 94306 811-B5
ROBBIA CT
1200 SUNV 94087 832-F4
ROBBIA DR
1000 SUNV 94087 832-F3
ROBERSON LN
400 SJS 95112 833-J1
ROBERT AV
400 SCL 95050 833-E2
ROBERT DR
- HOLL 95023 1039-H4
ROBERTA CT
2900 SJS 95121 854-J4
ROBERT FOWLER WY
2400 SJS 95148 835-A6
ROBERTS AV
1100 SJS 95122 834-F7
1100 SJS 95122 854-F1
ROBERTS CT
100 SJS 95110 854-D2
ROBERT S DR
- MLPK 94025 790-E4
ROBERTS PL
- SJS 95122 834-F7
ROBERTS RD
- LGTS 95030 873-A6
- LGTS 95032 873-B6
ROBERTSON RD
2400 SCL 95051 833-B2
ROBERTSVILLE CT
500 SJS 95118 874-G3
ROBIE LN
16200 SCIC 95032 873-C6
16200 LGTS 95032 873-C6
ROBIN CT
700 EPA 94303 791-B1
1100 SUNV 94087 832-B3
ROBIN DR
500 SCL 95050 833-C5
1800 SJS 95124 873-H1
ROBIN LN
800 CMBL 95008 853-D7
800 CMBL 95008 873-D1
2000 SCIC 95046 937-H3
ROBIN WY
100 LGTS 95032 873-C7
200 MLPK 94025 790-J3
900 SUNV 94087 832-B2
19800 SAR 95070 872-F4
ROBIN ANN DR
15300 MSER 95030 873-A4
ROBINDELL WY
7700 CPTO 95014 852-C3
ROBIN HOOD CT
1000 LALT 94024 831-H4
ROBIN HOOD DR
2000 LALT 94024 831-H4
ROBIN RIDGE CT
- SJS 95135 875-J1
- SJS 95135 876-A1
ROBINSON AV
2400 SCL 95051 833-B4
ROBLAR LN
2500 SCL 95051 833-B2
ROBLE AV
200 RDWC 94061 790-C1
600 MLPK 94025 790-F4
ROBLE CT
19400 SAR 95070 852-F7
ROBLE DR
500 SCIC 94305 790-G7
600 MGH 95037 937-A4
800 SUNV 94086 832-H3
ROBLE RDG
900 PA 94306 811-B2
ROBLE ST
- HOLL 95023 1040-A2
ROBLE ALTO
27900 LAH 94022 810-H7
ROBLE ALTO CT
13600 LAH 94022 810-H6
ROBLE BLANCO
27900 LAH 94022 810-H7
ROBLEDA CT
26700 LAH 94022 811-C7
ROBLEDA DR
- ATN 94027 790-C2
ROBLEDA RD
12200 LAH 94022 831-B1
13200 LAH 94022 811-C7
ROBLE LADERA RD
12600 LAH 94022 811-A7
ROBLES DEL ORO
15600 SCIC 95030 872-G5
ROBLES RANCH RD
- LALT 94024 831-H4
ROBLE VENENO LN
12600 LAH 94022 811-B7
ROBNICK CT
1300 CMBL 95008 873-A1
ROBSHEAL DR
1300 SJS 95125 854-A5
1400 SJS 95125 853-J5
ROBWAY AV
1100 CMBL 95008 853-G5
ROCHELLE DR
1800 SJS 95124 873-H1
ROCHESTER AV
- SJS 95123 875-B4
- SJS 95193 875-C4
ROCHESTER CT
1000 SUNV 94087 832-B3

STREET
Block City ZIP Pg-Grid

ROCHIN CT
15900 LGTS 95032 873-E5
ROCHIN TER
15900 LGTS 95032 873-D6
15900 SCIC 95032 873-D6
ROCK AV
1000 SJS 95131 814-A5
ROCK ST
1700 MTVW 94043 811-G2
ROCK CANYON CIR
900 SJS 95127 814-J5
ROCKDALE DR
900 SJS 95129 853-A3
ROCKEFELLER DR
900 SUNV 94087 832-B3
ROCKHAVEN DR
1200 SJS 95120 894-E3
ROCKHURST CT
2000 SCL 95051 832-J2
ROCKIE RD
- SBnC 95023 1020-E1
ROCKING HORSE CT
600 SJS 95123 874-J7
ROCKLIN CT
1400 SJS 95131 814-C7
ROCKPOINT LN
- LALT 94024 831-E2
- SCIC 94024 831-E2
ROCKPORT AV
3200 SJS 95132 814-G5
ROCKPORT DR
500 SUNV 94087 832-D3
ROCKRIDGE WY
2400 SCL 95051 833-B2
ROCK RIVER CT
2900 SJS 95111 854-H4
ROCKROSE AV
1000 SUNV 94086 832-G3
ROCKROSE CT
- SJS 95133 814-F7
2000 GIL 95020 977-E1
ROCKS RD
500 SBnC 95045 1037-H3
1100 SBnC - 1037-F2
1500 SBnC 95004 1037-F2
ROCK SPRING CT
11500 CPTO 95014 852-A4
ROCKSPRING DR
1700 SJS 95112 854-F2
ROCK SPRINGS LN
20100 MonC 95076 1037-C3
ROCKTON AV
6800 SJS 95119 875-F6
ROCKTON PL
- SJS 95119 875-F6
ROCKTREE CT
1700 SJS 95131 814-D4
ROCKVIEW CT
6800 SJS 95120 894-C3
ROCKWAY DR
- SCIC 95127 834-J2
- SCIC 95127 835-A2
ROCKWOOD DR
700 SJS 95129 853-A2
ROCKWOOD RANCH RD
- SCIC 95037 936-E3
ROCKY CREEK CT
3600 SJS 95148 835-D4
17000 MGH 95037 917-B7
ROCKY CREEK WY
14500 SAR 95070 872-D3
ROCKY CREST DR
6500 SJS 95120 874-F7
6600 SJS 95120 894-F1
ROCKY GLEN CT
6100 SJS 95123 874-F6
ROCKY MOUNTAIN AV
1600 MPS 95035 814-D2
ROCKY MOUNTAIN DR
3100 SJS 95127 835-B5
ROCKY RIDGE RD
2100 MGH 95037 936-F1
ROCKY WATER LN
3200 SJS 95148 855-B3
RODEO CT
300 SJS 95111 854-H5
RODEO DR
- SBnC 95023 1040-G3
300 SJS 95111 854-H5
9300 GIL 95020 957-F7
RODEO PL
400 SJS 95111 854-H5
RODEO CREEK HOLLOW
13200 SAR 95070 852-D7
RODLING DR
6900 SJS 95138 875-F6
RODLING WY
100 SJS 95138 875-F6
RODNEY DR
1100 SJS 95118 874-C1
RODONI CT
12700 SAR 95070 852-G6
RODONOVAN CT
200 SCL 95051 832-J7
RODONOVAN DR
- SCL 95051 832-J7
- SCL 95051 852-J1
RODRIGUES AV
100 MPS 95035 794-C7
19800 CPTO 95014 852-D1
ROEDER CT
300 SJS 95111 875-B2
ROEDER RD
4900 SJS 95111 875-B2
ROEHAMPTON AV
10000 SCIC 95127 835-A3
ROENOKE WY
2000 SJS 95128 853-G3
ROEWILL DR
1000 SJS 95117 853-B3
ROGER ST
1600 MPS 95035 794-A4

ROGERS AV
1600 SJS 95112 834-A1
1600 SJS 95112 833-J1
1600 SJS 95112 813-J7
ROGERS CT
700 SCL 95051 833-B6
ROGERS LN
7400 GIL 95020 978-B3
ROGERS ST
- LGTS 95030 893-A1
ROGGE RD
100 EPA 94303 791-C1
ROHN WY
5800 SJS 95123 875-A5
ROJO PL
1400 SJS 95128 853-F5
ROLFE CT
14900 SCIC 95127 835-B1
ROLINE CT
15000 SCIC 95124 873-F4
ROLL ST
1600 SCL 95050 833-C3
ROLLINGDELL CT
1100 CPTO 95014 852-D3
ROLLINGDELL DR
7300 CPTO 95014 852-D3
7300 SJS 95129 852-D3
ROLLING GLEN CT
6000 SJS 95123 874-F6
ROLLING HILLS DR
2000 MGH 95037 936-E1
9500 SCIC 95020 958-D3
ROLLING HILLS RD
22000 SAR 95070 852-B5
ROLLING MEADOW CT
6400 SJS 95135 855-J7
ROLLING OAKS CT
6500 SJS 95120 894-C2
ROLLING OAKS DR
6500 SJS 95120 894-C2
ROLLINGSIDE DR
3500 SJS 95148 835-F7
ROLLINGWOOD CT
3000 SJS 95148 835-F7
ROLLY RD
10200 SCIC 94024 831-F5
ROMA CT
2900 SCL 95051 833-A7
ROMAN AV
- GIL 95020 957-H7
- GIL 95020 977-H1
ROMANI CT
- SJS 95125 854-D7
ROMBERG DR
500 SUNV 94087 832-E3
ROME DR
20500 SCIC 95120 895-A6
ROMEO AV
10200 SJS 95127 835-C2
ROMERO ST
2200 SJS 95128 853-F4
ROMFORD DR
5200 SJS 95124 873-H5
ROMITA CT
16000 MSER 95030 872-H6
ROMITTI CT
18000 MSER 95030 872-J6
RONALD AV
400 CMBL 95008 853-C7
RONALD CT
700 LALT 94024 831-G2
1600 SJS 95118 873-J4
1600 SJS 95118 874-A4
RONALD ST
2100 SCL 95050 833-D2
RONALD WY
10900 CPTO 95014 852-B2
RONAN AV
- GIL 95020 957-H7
200 GIL 95020 977-H1
RONCO DR
2700 SJS 95132 814-F5
RONDA DR
14800 SCIC 95124 873-G4
14800 SJS 95124 873-G4
RONDEAU DR
400 SJS 95124 873-J3
RONDEN CT
1600 MTVW 94040 811-G6
RONDO WY
- SMCo 94025 790-D5
RONIE WY
1800 SJS 95124 873-H3
RONNIE WY
13300 SAR 95070 852-G7
13400 SAR 95070 872-G1
ROOP RD
2200 SCIC 95020 958-F2
ROOSEVELT AV
- SCIC 95046 937-E6
200 SUNV 94086 812-F6
1400 RDWC 94061 790-A1
ROOSEVELT CIR
- PA 94306 811-D1
2300 SCL 95051 833-C2
ROOSEVELT CT
2300 SCL 95051 833-C2
ROOSEVELT ST
900 SJS 95112 834-D4
ROOSEVELT WY
- SJS 95002 793-C7
ROOSTER CT
- SJS 95136 874-J2
ROOSTER DR
5200 SJS 95136 874-J3
RORKE WY
800 PA 94303 791-E6
RORTY DR
- SJS 95136 854-E6
ROSA AV
1000 SUNV 94086 832-G3
ROSA CT
- SJS 95126 833-D1
900 SUNV 94086 832-G3

ROSALIA AV
1200 SJS 95117 853-B4
1200 SJS 95130 853-B4
1300 SUNV 94087 832-G4
ROSALIE CT
200 LGTS 95032 873-C7
ROSALIE DR
1300 SCL 95050 833-C4
ROSALIND LN
18500 SCIC 95120 894-G1
ROSALINDA CT
2600 SJS 95121 854-J4
ROSA MORADA RD
600 SBnC 95023 1020-F5
ROSANNA ST
6700 GIL 95020 978-A4
7200 GIL 95020 977-J2
ROSARIO AV
21500 CPTO 95014 852-B2
ROSARIO CT
2800 SJS 95132 814-D3
ROSARIO DR
2800 SJS 95132 814-D3
ROSATO CT
2900 SJS 95135 855-E3
ROSE AV
800 MTVW 94040 831-G1
900 MLPK 94025 790-F4
2800 SJS 95127 834-J3
3000 SCIC 95127 834-J2
4100 SCIC 95127 835-A2
15900 LGTS 95030 873-A6
15900 MSER 95030 873-A6
16000 MSER 95030 872-J6
E ROSE CIR
1000 LALT 94024 831-J2
W ROSE CIR
1100 LALT 94024 831-H2
ROSE CT
100 CMBL 95008 853-D6
900 SCL 95051 833-B5
17900 MSER 95030 872-J6
17900 MSER 95030 873-A6
18000 SCIC 95033 912-J2
ROSE DR
100 MPS 95035 794-A4
ROSE LN
700 LALT 94024 831-F1
15900 LGTS 95030 873-A5
19100 MGH 95037 916-H4
ROSE PL
1200 SJS 95112 854-D1
ROSE TER
- FRMT 94539 793-J3
ROSE WY
2500 SCL 95051 833-B5
ROSE ANNA DR
1500 SJS 95118 874-A5
ROSE ARBOR CT
- SJS 95133 814-E7
ROSEBAY CT
- SJS 95127 834-J2
ROSE BLOSSOM DR
700 CPTO 95014 852-C2
ROSEBRIAR WY
1100 SJS 95131 814-D7
1100 SJS 95131 834-D1
ROSEBUD CT
1900 SJS 95128 853-G3
ROSE CREEK DR
3000 SJS 95148 835-B5
ROSECREST TER
1400 SJS 95126 833-H7
ROSEDALE DR
3200 SJS 95117 853-D2
ROSEFIELD WY
1100 MLPK 94025 790-E5
ROSEGARDEN CT
48900 FRMT 94539 794-A2
ROSEGARDEN LN
1300 CPTO 95014 852-D4
ROSELEAF CT
16300 SCIC 95032 873-D5
ROSELEAF LN
16100 SCIC 95032 873-D5
ROSEMAR AV
3700 SJS 95127 835-B2
ROSEMAR CT
10200 SJS 95127 835-C1
ROSEMARIE PL
19400 CPTO 95014 852-G1
ROSEMARY CIR
17100 MGH 95037 917-B7
ROSEMARY LN
1700 RDWC 94061 790-A2
E ROSEMARY LN
- CMBL 95008 853-E5
- CMBL 95128 853-E5
2900 SJS 95008 853-E5
2900 SJS 95128 853-E5
W ROSEMARY LN
100 CMBL 95008 853-D5
ROSEMARY ST
- SJS 95110 833-J3
- SJS 95112 833-J3
100 SJS 95112 834-A3
ROSEMARY TER
- SUNV 94086 832-G3
ROSEMONT AV
1000 LALT 94024 831-H3
ROSEMONT CT
1000 LALT 94024 831-H3
ROSEMONT DR
300 SCL 95051 832-J7
ROSENBAUM AV
4100 SJS 95136 874-G1
ROSENCRANS WY
7100 SJS 95139 895-F1
ROSENELFE CIR
1900 SJS 95148 835-B5
ROSE ORCHARD CT
18100 MGH 95037 916-G7
ROSE ORCHARD WY
- SJS 95134 813-E2

ROSE RIDGE LN
5900 SJS 95123 874-G7
ROSE TERRASSE CIR
- SJS 95148 855-G1
ROSETTA DR
2200 SCIC 95037 917-E6
ROSETTE CT
900 SUNV 94086 832-G3
ROSETTE TER
800 SUNV 94086 832-G3
ROSETTE WY
- GIL 95020 977-F2
ROSE VIEW DR
10000 SCIC 95127 835-C1
10100 SCIC 95127 815-C7
ROSEWELL CT
- SJS 95138 875-D4
ROSEWELL WY
- SJS 95138 875-D4
ROSEWOOD AV
300 SCIC 95117 853-D1
300 SJS 95117 853-D1
ROSEWOOD CT
600 LALT 94024 831-F1
ROSEWOOD DR
- ATN 94027 790-G1
700 PA 94303 791-C6
ROSEWOOD ST
10600 CPTO 95014 832-F6
ROSITA AV
400 LALT 94024 831-F1
2100 SCL 95050 833-D7
ROSITA CT
2300 SCL 95050 833-D6
ROSLYN CIR
700 MTVW 94043 812-A3
ROSLYN CT
2400 SJS 95121 854-J2
ROSS AV
2800 SJS 95124 873-H2
ROSS CIR
1700 SJS 95124 873-J3
ROSS CT
800 PA 94303 791-D6
ROSS DR
300 SUNV 94089 812-E4
ROSS RD
2300 PA 94303 791-C5
ROSSBURN CT
1600 SJS 95121 855-B6
ROSS CREEK CT
100 LGTS 95032 873-E5
ROSSI CT
- HOLL 95023 1039-H3
500 GIL 95020 978-C6
ROSSI LN
400 GIL 95020 978-C5
400 SCIC 95020 978-C5
ROSSMERE CT
13600 SAR 95070 872-F1
ROSSMORE CT
2900 SJS 95148 855-C1
ROSSMORE LN
2900 SJS 95148 855-C1
ROSSMORE WY
2900 SJS 95148 855-C1
ROSSMOYNE DR
14800 SCIC 95124 873-H4
ROSSOTTO DR
2400 SJS 95130 853-A7
ROSS PARK CT
4000 SJS 95118 874-B2
ROSS PARK DR
4000 SJS 95118 874-B2
ROSSWAY CT
1300 LALT 94024 831-J4
ROSSWOOD DR
1700 SJS 95124 873-G4
ROSWELL CT
300 MPS 95035 794-D7
ROSWELL DR
100 MPS 95035 794-D7
ROTH PL
2000 SCL 95051 833-D1
ROTH WY
100 SCIC 94305 790-G6
ROTHE DR
11300 SCIC 95020 957-G2
ROTHERHAVEN WY
4500 SJS 95111 874-J1
4500 SJS 95111 875-A1
ROTHLAND CT
1300 SJS 95131 814-D7
ROTHROCK DR
100 SJS 95116 834-G2
ROTTERDAM LN
5600 SJS 95118 874-B5
ROUEN CT
- SJS 95127 834-J1
ROUGH AND READY RD
500 SJS 95133 834-G1
500 SJS 95133 814-G7
ROUNDLEAF CT
1900 SJS 95131 814-D6
ROUNDSTONE DR
- GIL 95020 977-D3
ROUNDTABLE DR
- SJS 95111 875-B3
ROUNDTREE CT
4800 SJS 95008 872-J1
ROUNDTREE DR
4700 SJS 95008 873-A1
4800 SJS 95008 872-J1
ROUSE CT
7100 SJS 95139 875-F7
ROUSSEAU DR
1200 SUNV 94087 832-F4
ROWENA CT
3500 SCL 95054 813-E6
ROWLEY DR
3500 SJS 95132 814-F2
ROXANNE DR
5200 SJS 95124 873-H5

ROXBURGHE CT
- SJS 95138 855-F7
ROXBURY CT
1200 SCL 95050 833-F6
ROXBURY LN
500 LGTS 95032 873-A2
ROXBURY ST
- SCL 95050 833-E6
ROX PLACE CT
3600 SJS 95121 855-B4
ROY AV
1000 SJS 95125 854-B6
ROYAL AV
300 SJS 95126 854-A1
ROYAL DR
2000 SCL 95050 833-C3
ROYAL WY
600 GIL 95020 977-J5
ROYAL ACORN PL
6000 SJS 95120 874-D7
ROYAL ACRES CT
1000 SJS 95136 874-C2
ROYAL ANN CT
1100 SUNV 94087 832-D3
1400 SJS 95129 852-G4
ROYAL ANN DR
1100 SUNV 94087 832-D3
5800 SJS 95129 852-G4
ROYALBROOK CT
800 SJS 95111 855-A6
ROYAL CREST DR
1100 SJS 95131 814-C7
1100 SJS 95131 834-D1
ROYALE PARK CT
4500 SJS 95136 874-F2
ROYALE PARK DR
400 SJS 95136 874-F2
ROYAL ESTATES CT
5000 SJS 95135 855-G5
ROYAL FOREST CT
4600 SJS 95136 874-G2
ROYAL GARDEN PL
4600 SJS 95136 874-G2
ROYAL GATE PL
400 SJS 95136 874-G2
ROYAL GLEN CT
600 SJS 95133 814-H7
ROYAL GLEN DR
600 SJS 95133 814-G7
ROYAL GROVE CT
4600 SJS 95136 874-G2
ROYAL MEADOW LN
3000 SJS 95135 855-J7
3200 SJS 95135 856-A7
ROYAL OAK CT
- MTVW 94040 811-F3
6200 SJS 95123 875-A6
ROYAL OAK WY
10000 CPTO 95014 831-C7
ROYAL RIDGE CT
7000 SJS 95120 894-E3
ROYAL RIDGE DR
7000 SJS 95120 894-E3
ROYALRIDGE WY
2500 SCL 95051 833-C1
ROYALTREE CIR
2200 SJS 95131 814-C5
ROYALVALE WY
2700 SJS 95132 814-C4
ROYALWOOD WY
6800 SJS 95120 894-H3
ROYCE DR
300 SJS 95133 834-E3
ROYCE ST
100 LGTS 95030 873-A7
ROYCOTT WY
1100 SJS 95125 854-A5
ROYSTON CT
1100 SJS 95120 894-E2
R T JONES RD
1100 SCIC 94043 812-A2
1100 MTVW 94043 812-A2
RUBIDOUX TER
300 SUNV 94086 812-C7
RUBINO CIR
- SJS 95125 854-D6
RUBINO DR
- SJS 95125 854-D7
RUBION CT
3400 SJS 95148 835-D4
RUBION DR
3400 SJS 95148 835-C5
RUBIS DR
800 SUNV 94087 832-D2
RUBY AV
2100 SJS 95148 835-D5
2300 SJS 95148 855-E1
2300 SCIC 95148 835-D5
4100 SJS 95135 855-F2
RUBY CT
3400 SJS 95148 835-E7
RUBY ST
1200 RDWC 94061 790-A1
RUBY TER
2700 SJS 95148 835-E6
RUBY VW
2700 SJS 95148 835-E6
RUCKER AV
100 SCIC 95020 957-H4
900 SCIC 95020 958-A3
RUCKER DR
1700 SJS 95124 873-H5
21800 CPTO 95014 852-B2
RUDD CT
500 SJS 95111 854-J6
RUDY CT
5700 SJS 95124 873-J6
RUDY DR
5400 SJS 95124 873-J6
RUDY RD
100 SCrC 95033 912-G7
100 SCrC 95066 912-G7
RUDYARD DR
300 MPS 95035 793-J7

RUE AVATI
1300 SJS 95131 814-C6
RUE BORDEAUX
4700 SJS 95136 874-J2
RUE BOULOGNE
100 SJS 95136 874-J2
RUE CALAIS
4800 SJS 95136 874-J2
RUE CANNES
2200 SJS 95136 874-J2
RUE CHENE DOR
4400 SJS 95148 855-F1
RUE FERRARI
5800 SJS 95138 875-E4
RUE LE MANS
4800 SJS 95136 874-J2
RUE LOIRET
4800 SJS 95136 874-J2
RUE LYON CT
4700 SJS 95136 874-J2
RUE MIRASSOU
4400 SJS 95148 855-F1
RUE MONTAGNE
800 CMBL 95008 853-F7
RUE NICE CT
4800 SJS 95136 874-J2
RUE ORLEANS CT
4700 SJS 95136 874-J2
RUE PARIS
100 SJS 95136 874-J2
RUE ROYALE
- SJS 95148 855-G1
RUE TOULON CT
4800 SJS 95136 874-J2
RUE TOURS CT
4800 SJS 95136 874-J2
RUFF DR
900 SJS 95110 833-J4
RUFFINO LN
- SJS 95148 855-F1
RUFFINO TER
- SJS 95129 852-J5
RUGBY CT
1100 SJS 95120 874-C6
RUGE DR
1000 SJS 95132 814-F6
RUGER CT
- HOLL 95023 1040-B7
RUIZ CT
1500 SJS 95129 852-H4
RUMFORD DR
21300 CPTO 95014 832-C7
RUMSEY CT
400 SJS 95111 875-C2
RUNNING BEAR DR
5100 SJS 95136 875-A2
RUNNING FARM LN
- SCIC 94305 790-J7
- SCIC 94305 810-J1
RUNNING SPRINGS RD
- SJS 95135 856-A7
- SJS 95135 875-J1
- SJS 95135 876-A1
RUNNING WATER CT
2300 SCL 95054 813-C5
RUNNINGWOOD CIR
800 MTVW 94040 832-A1
RUNNYMEAD CT
1000 LALT 94024 831-H2
RUNNYMEAD DR
1100 LALT 94024 831-H2
RUNNYMEDE DR
1100 SJS 95117 853-D3
RUNNYMEDE ST
400 EPA 94303 791-C1
RUNO CT
18500 CPTO 95014 852-H1
RUNSHAW PL
1200 SJS 95121 855-A5
RUPERT DR
2300 SJS 95124 873-E3
RUPPELL PL
1100 CPTO 95014 852-D3
RURAL LN
300 MLPK 94025 810-E1
300 SMCo 94025 810-E1
RUSCH PL
- SCIC 95111 854-G5
- SJS 95111 854-G5
RUSHMORE LN
200 LGTS 95032 873-B6
RUSKIN DR
3100 SJS 95132 814-F4
RUSSELIA LN
- SJS 95128 853-E1
RUSSELL AV
900 LALT 94024 831-G2
1600 SCL 95054 813-D6
RUSSELL CT
- MLPK 94025 790-J3
20700 SAR 95070 852-D7
20700 SAR 95070 872-D1
RUSSELL LN
700 MPS 95035 794-B4
20500 SAR 95070 872-D1
RUSSET DR
800 SUNV 94087 832-D2
RUSSET TER
700 SUNV 94087 832-D1
RUSSO COMS
- SJS 95127 834-H1
RUSSO DR
5300 SJS 95118 874-C3
RUSTIC AV
2700 SJS 95124 873-G1
RUSTIC DR
2800 SJS 95124 873-G1
3200 SCL 95051 833-A5
RUSTIC LN
600 MTVW 94040 811-H7
RUSTIC ST
- HOLL 95023 1040-A3
- SBnC 95023 1040-A3

RUSTIC RANCH CT
600 SJS 95120 894-H3
RUSTIC RIDGE CIR
200 SJS 95123 874-G7
RUSTLING OAK CT
16400 MGH 95037 917-G6
RUSTLING OAK LN
16400 MGH 95037 917-G6
RUTH AV
300 MTVW 94043 811-F3
RUTH CT
1000 EPA 94303 791-C1
2800 SCL 95051 833-B6
RUTH DR
1100 SJS 95125 854-C7
RUTH CABRAL WY
2400 SCL 95050 833-C5
RUTHELMA AV
4200 PA 94306 811-D2
RUTHERFORD AV
100 SMCo 94061 790-B2
6800 SJS 95129 852-E4
RUTHERGLEN PL
5200 SJS 95136 874-F3
RUTHER PLACE CT
1600 SJS 95121 855-B4
RUTHER PLACE WY
3600 SJS 95121 855-B4
RUTHLEE CT
- SCIC 94024 831-E2
RUTHVEN AV
400 PA 94301 790-H4
RUTLAND AV
400 SCIC 95128 853-G1
RUTLEDGE PL
2000 SCL 95051 833-D2
RUTTNER CT
4900 SJS 95111 875-C1
RUTTNER PL
4900 SJS 95111 875-C1
RYAN AV
3000 SCL 95051 833-A6
RYAN CT
- SCIC 94305 810-J2
800 GIL 95020 977-H2
RYAN DR
10200 SJS 95127 835-B3
RYANS AL
700 MLPK 94025 790-F4
RYCROFT CT
7000 SJS 95120 894-H3
RYDER ST
100 SCL 95051 812-J7
RYE CT
1000 SJS 95127 835-C2
RYEGATE CT
300 SJS 95133 834-F2
RYLAND ST
100 SJS 95110 834-A5
RYMAR CT
1000 SJS 95133 814-F6
RYMAR DR
2500 SJS 95133 814-F7
RYMAR LN
2500 SJS 95133 814-F7
RYMAR PL
1000 SJS 95133 814-F6
RYMAR TER
1000 SJS 95133 814-F7
RYMAR WY
1000 SJS 95133 814-F7

S

SABAL CT
1100 SJS 95132 814-G5
SABAL DR
1100 SJS 95132 814-F5
SABINA WY
1500 SJS 95118 874-A4
SABINI CT
17800 MGH 95037 916-G7
17800 SCIC 95037 916-G7
SABRINA CT
1200 RDWC 94061 790-A1
SACO TER
- SUNV 94089 812-G4
SACRAMENTO ST
500 EPA 94303 791-B1
SACREMENTO AV
4000 SJS 95111 855-A6
SADDLE CT
- SBnC 95075 1060-J4
27800 LAH 94022 810-J6
SADDLEBACK
- PTLV 94028 830-C1
SADDLEBACK DR
16700 MGH 95037 917-E5
SADDLE BROOK DR
- SJS 95136 874-H2
- SJS 95136 875-A2
SADDLEHORN WY
16800 MGH 95037 917-E6
SADDLE MOUNTAIN DR
14300 LAH 94022 810-J6
SADDLE PARK AV
- SJS 95138 855-D6
SADDLE PARK PL
- SJS 95138 855-D6
SADDLER DR
9300 GIL 95020 957-F7
SADDLE RACK ST
900 SJS 95126 853-J1
SADDLE TREE CT
- SJS 95136 874-H2
SADDLEWOOD DR
1000 SJS 95121 854-H2
SADIE CT
4000 SJS 95008 853-B7
SADIES CT
- HOLL 95023 1060-D1
SADIES DR
- HOLL 95023 1060-D1

STREET
Block City ZIP Pg-Grid

SAFARI DR
400 SJS 95123 874-J6
SAFE HAVEN CT
- SJS 95111 854-J5
SAFFARIAN CT
2000 SJS 95121 855-C3
SAFFLE CT
1400 CMBL 95008 873-B1
SAFFRON CT
- GIL 95020 977-E1
SAFFRON DR
- MGH 95037 916-G4
SAGA LN
- MLPK 94025 790-D7
- MLPK 94025 810-D1
SAGE AV
- MGH 95037 916-G4
SAGE CT
900 CPTO 95014 852-C2
19300 SAR 95070 872-G1
N SAGE CT
1100 SUNV 94087 832-D3
SAGE DR
- SJS 95123 875-B5
SAGE ST
1100 EPA 94303 791-C2
SAGE HEN CT
1200 SJS 95118 874-C2
SAGE HEN WY
1300 SUNV 94087 832-H4
SAGE HILL DR
1400 GIL 95020 957-F7
SAGELAND DR
1700 SJS 95131 814-D7
SAGEMEADOW CT
100 MPS 95035 794-A6
SAGEMILL CT
1200 SJS 95121 854-J3
SAGEMONT AV
4500 SJS 95130 853-A5
SAGE OAK WY
6000 SJS 95120 874-D7
SAGER WY
6200 SJS 95123 874-H7
SAGEWELL WY
5700 SJS 95138 875-D4
SAGEWOOD CT
9200 GIL 95020 957-F7
SAGEWOOD LN
3200 SJS 95132 814-E2
SAGINAW TER
- SUNV 94089 812-G4
SAGITTARIUS LN
3200 SJS 95111 854-F6
SAGUARO CT
- SCIC 95020 977-A2
SAHARA WY
2000 SCL 95050 833-D3
SAICH WY
10000 CPTO 95014 832-D7
10000 CPTO 95014 852-D1
SAIDEL DR
2200 SJS 95124 873-E4
SAINT ANDREWS AV
22300 CPTO 95014 852-A2
SAINT ANDREWS CIR
- GIL 95020 977-F3
SAINT ANDREWS CT
1800 MPS 95035 794-D3
SAINT ANDREWS PL
1800 SJS 95132 814-E3
SAINT ANN CT
19700 SAR 95070 852-F7
SAINT ANNES CT
5100 SJS 95138 855-F7
SAINT ANTHONY CT
1100 LALT 94024 831-J5
SAINT ANTHONY DR
1700 SCIC 95125 853-H5
17100 MGH 95037 917-B7
SAINT ANTHONYS PL
1600 CMBL 95008 873-E2
SAINT BENEDICTS WY
- SBnC 95023 1040-E6
SAINT CATHERINE CT
5400 SCIC 95127 815-A7
SAINT CHARLES CIR
- SJS 95133 834-G1
SAINT CHARLES CT
1100 LALT 94024 831-H5
SAINT CHARLES ST
20700 SAR 95070 872-D3
SAINT CLAIRE CT
2200 SCL 95054 813-C5
SAINT CLAIRE DR
500 PA 94306 791-D7
SAINT CLAR AV
- GIL 95020 957-G7
SAINT CROIX CT
4200 SJS 95118 874-C2
SAINT ELIZABETH CT
- SCIC 95126 853-H3
- SJS 95126 853-H3
SAINT ELIZABETH DR
800 SCIC 95126 853-H3
800 SJS 95126 853-H3
SAINT EMILION CT
400 MTVW 94043 811-G3
SAINT FLORENCE DR
400 SJS 95133 834-G1
SAINT FLORIAN WY
- SJS 95136 854-E6
SAINT FRANCIS CT
500 MLPK 94025 790-F6
7600 GIL 95020 977-G3
SAINT FRANCIS DR
1400 SCIC 95125 853-H5
2100 PA 94303 791-D4
SAINT FRANCIS PL
500 MLPK 94025 790-F6
SAINT FRANCIS RD
26400 LAH 94022 811-A5
SAINT FRANCIS ST
600 RDWC 94061 790-A1
SAINT GABRIEL LN
- SJS 95002 813-C1
SAINT GEORGE LN
7200 SJS 95120 894-G5
SAINT GILES LN
2600 MTVW 94040 831-J2
SAINT IGNATIUS PL
3200 SCL 95051 833-A2
SAINT JAMES DR
700 MGH 95037 937-C1
E SAINT JAMES ST
- SJS 95112 834-C5
1100 SJS 95116 834-E3
W SAINT JAMES ST
- SJS 95113 834-B6
100 SJS 95110 834-B6
SAINT JOAN CT
20700 SAR 95070 852-D5
SAINT JOHN CT
- MGH 95037 937-C1
E SAINT JOHN ST
- SJS 95113 834-C5
- SJS 95112 834-C5
1100 SJS 95116 834-E4
W SAINT JOHN ST
- SJS 95113 834-A6
100 SJS 95110 834-A6
SAINT JOSEPH AV
1800 LALT 94024 831-G5
7500 SCIC 94024 831-G5
7500 CPTO 95014 831-G5
SAINT JOSEPH CT
900 LALT 94024 831-H4
1100 MPS 95035 794-C5
SAINT JOSEPH DR
17100 MGH 95037 917-B7
SAINT JULIE DR
300 SJS 95119 875-C7
SAINT KATHERINE DR
- MGH 95037 917-C3
SAINT KITTS CT
800 SJS 95127 814-G6
SAINT LAURENT CT
5400 SCIC 95127 815-A7
SAINT LAWRENCE DR
1800 SCL 95051 832-J3
2400 SJS 95124 853-G7
16200 MGH 95037 937-C1
SAINT LUCIA CT
800 SJS 95127 814-G6
SAINT MARK CT
1200 LALT 94024 831-J5
SAINT MARKS AV
18700 MGH 95037 917-B2
SAINT MARKS CT
1800 MGH 95037 917-B2
SAINT MARYS PL
3300 SCL 95051 832-J2
SAINT MATTHEW WY
1200 LALT 94024 831-H5
SAINT MICHAEL CT
3300 PA 94306 791-D7
SAINT MICHAEL DR
3300 PA 94306 791-D7
SAINT MICHAEL PL
700 MGH 95037 937-C1
SAINT PALAIS PL
- SCL 95054 813-D4
SAINT PAUL DR
300 CMBL 95008 853-B5
SAINT RAPHAEL LN
- SJS 95002 813-C1
SAINT REGIS DR
1500 SJS 95124 874-A3
1600 SJS 95124 873-J3
SAINT TIMOTHY PL
700 MGH 95037 937-C1
SAJAK AV
1200 SJS 95131 814-C7
SAKURA DR
- SJS 95112 834-B3
SAKURA WY
19300 CPTO 95014 852-G1
SALADO DR
1500 MTVW 94043 791-G7
1500 MTVW 94043 811-G1
SALAMONI CT
- SJS 95133 834-D2
SALAS CT
2100 EPA 94303 791-C2
SALBERG AV
600 SCL 95051 833-B6
SALEM AV
1600 SCIC 95020 957-D6
22300 CPTO 95014 832-A7
22500 CPTO 95014 831-J7
SALEM DR
2900 SCL 95051 833-A6
3100 SJS 95127 814-H6
SALERNO DR
900 SCIC 95008 873-E1
SALERNO TER
- SUNV 94089 812-G4
SALICE WY
- CMBL 95008 853-D6
SALIDA DEL SOL
6000 SJS 95123 874-F6
SALINA DR
4500 SJS 95124 873-F3
SALINAS CT
3300 SJS 95132 814-G3
SALINAS RD
2300 SBnC - 1037-J6
2300 SBnC - 1038-A6
2300 SBnC 95045 1038-C6
SALISBURY DR
1600 SJS 95124 873-J3
SALLY CT
2900 SCL 95051 833-A3
SALLY DR
4400 SJS 95124 873-H4
SALLY ST
400 HOLL 95023 1040-A5
N SALLY ST
- HOLL 95023 1040-A3
SALLY FLAT RD
500 SBnC 95023 1060-B3
SALLY GARDEN CT
- SJS 95136 854-E7
SALMAR AV
400 CMBL 95008 853-F5
SALMON DR
400 SJS 95111 854-G4
SALMON CREEK CT
1500 SJS 95127 835-C3
SALOME CT
2600 SJS 95121 854-H4
SALSBURY DR
200 SCL 95051 833-B7
SALTAMONTES DR
14600 LAH 94022 811-C5
SALT LAKE CT
800 SJS 95133 814-G6
SALT LAKE DR
600 SJS 95133 814-G7
SALUDA CT
1300 SJS 95121 854-J2
SALVATIERRA ST
500 SCIC 94305 810-H1
SALVATORE CT
1200 SJS 95120 874-C6
SALVATORE DR
1200 SJS 95120 874-C6
SAMAR DR
6400 SJS 95119 875-C7
SAMARIA PL
- SCIC 95111 854-G5
- SJS 95111 854-G5
SAMARITAN CT
2500 SJS 95124 873-D4
SAMARITAN DR
2000 SCIC 95124 873-D3
2000 SJS 95124 873-D3
2500 LGTS 95032 873-D3
SAMARITAN PL
2300 SJS 95124 873-E4
SAM CAVA LN
400 CMBL 95008 853-E6
SAMEDRA ST
900 SUNV 94087 832-C5
SAM MCDONALD RD
- SCIC 94305 790-J6
SAMOA WY
2300 SJS 95122 834-J5
SAMSON CT
1700 SJS 95124 873-J3
SAMSON WY
3900 SJS 95124 873-H3
SAMUEL DR
2900 SJS 95121 855-A3
SAMUEL LN
12800 LAH 94022 811-A6
SAN ALESO AV
700 SUNV 94086 812-E5
SAN ANDREAS AV
1500 SJS 95118 874-A1
SAN ANDREAS CT
100 SUNV 94086 812-E7
300 MPS 95035 793-J5
SAN ANDREAS DR
100 MLPK 94025 790-H3
200 MPS 95035 793-J5
SAN ANGELO AV
400 SUNV 94086 812-E6
SAN ANSELMO WY
200 SUNV 94086 812-E6
6300 SJS 95119 875-C7
SAN ANTONIO
- SJB 95045 1038-C5
SAN ANTONIO AV
1400 MLPK 94025 790-F3
SAN ANTONIO CIR
1000 MTVW 94040 811-E3
SAN ANTONIO CT
- MTVW 94040 811-E3
200 SJS 95116 834-F5
SAN ANTONIO DR
- MGH 95037 917-B3
SAN ANTONIO PL
100 MTVW 94040 811-E3
2100 SCL 95051 833-A2
SAN ANTONIO RD
100 PA 94306 811-F2
600 MTVW 94040 811-E3
700 PA 94303 811-F2
700 PA 94043 811-F2
800 PA 94303 791-F6
1000 MTVW 94043 791-F6
1100 MTVW 94303 791-F6
N SAN ANTONIO RD
- LALT 94022 811-E6
S SAN ANTONIO RD
- LALT 94022 811-E7
E SAN ANTONIO ST
100 SJS 95116 834-F4
400 SJS 95112 834-D6
SAN ANTONIO WY
- MGH 95037 917-B3
200 PA 94306 811-F2
SAN ARDO DR
1500 SCIC 95125 853-H4
SAN ARDO WY
800 MTVW 94043 811-J3
SAN BENANCIO WY
- MGH 95037 917-B7
SAN BENITO AV
- ATN 94027 790-E1
400 LGTS 95030 873-A6
500 SMCo 94025 790-E1
15800 MSER 95030 873-A5
SAN BENITO DR
16600 MGH 95037 937-B1
E SAN BENITO DR
1300 FRMT 94539 794-A2
SAN BENITO PL
- MGH 95037 937-B1
SAN BENITO ST
- SBnC 95023 1039-J6
1500 HOLL 95023 1040-A6
1500 SBnC 95023 1040-A6
SAN BENITO ST Rt#-25
400 HOLL 95023 1040-A5
SAN BENITO WY
15800 MSER 95030 873-A5
SAN BERNARDINO WY
300 SUNV 94086 812-E6
3900 SJS 95111 854-J7
SANBORN AV
1400 SJS 95110 854-D2
SANBORN RD
15500 SCIC 95070 871-J5
15500 SCIC 95070 872-B6
SAN BRUNO AV
- SCIC 95037 916-D1
- SJS 95037 896-E7
- SJS 95037 916-D1
SAN BUENA CT
6100 SJS 95119 875-C6
SAN CARLOS AV
100 SMCo 94061 790-B3
700 MTVW 94043 811-J3
700 MTVW 94043 812-A3
SAN CARLOS CT
700 PA 94303 791-C6
SAN CARLOS ST
300 SJS 95126 853-G1
600 SJS 95128 853-G1
800 SCIC 95126 853-G1
1700 SCIC 95128 853-G1
E SAN CARLOS ST
- SJS 95113 834-C7
100 SJS 95112 834-D6
W SAN CARLOS ST
- SJS 95110 834-C7
- SJS 95113 834-C7
600 SJS 95126 854-A1
600 SJS 95110 854-A1
700 SJS 95126 853-J1
700 SCIC 95126 853-J1
700 SCIC 95126 854-A1
W SAN CARLOS ST Rt#-82
100 SJS 95110 834-A7
100 SJS 95113 834-A7
300 SJS 95126 834-A7
500 SJS 95126 854-A1
500 SJS 95110 854-A1
SAN CARLOS WY
- MGH 95037 917-B3
SAN CARRIZO WY
800 MTVW 94043 811-J3
800 MTVW 94043 812-A3
SANCHEZ DR
100 MGH 95037 916-H5
5500 SJS 95123 874-D4
5500 SJS 95136 874-D4
SANCHEZ WY
1100 RDWC 94061 790-A1
SAN CLEMENTE AV
3000 SJS 95118 874-A1
SAN CLEMENTE DR
200 MLPK 94025 790-H3
SAN CLEMENTE WY
700 MTVW 94043 811-H3
SAN CONRADO TER
600 SUNV 94086 812-G5
SAN CRISTOVAL CT
700 MGH 95037 937-C1
SANDALRIDGE CT
900 MPS 95035 794-A5
SANDALWOOD CT
600 MPS 95035 794-A4
1300 SJS 95127 835-A4
2000 PA 94303 791-D4
SANDALWOOD LN
900 MPS 95035 794-A5
1200 LALT 94024 831-H4
SANDALWOOD WY
17200 MGH 95037 917-E6
SAND BLOSSOM ST
100 SJS 95123 875-A3
SAND DUNE WY
5500 SJS 95123 875-B4
SANDEL WY
- SJS 95136 854-E6
SANDERLING CT
- CMBL 95008 853-D5
SANDERS AV
400 SJS 95116 834-G4
SAND HILL CIR
100 MLPK 94025 790-B7
SAND HILL RD
100 MLPK 94025 790-E7
900 PA 94304 790-F6
1100 SMCo 94025 810-A1
1300 SCIC 94305 790-F6
2000 SMCo 94025 790-F6
2400 MLPK 94025 810-C1
SAND HILL WY
2500 SCL 95051 833-C1
SANDHURST DR
- MPS 95035 794-A6
SANDIA AV
1100 SUNV 94089 812-J5
1200 SUNV 94089 813-A5
SAN DIEGO AV
600 SUNV 94086 812-F5
SAN DOMAR DR
1300 MTVW 94043 811-H3
SAN DOMINGO WY
300 LALT 94022 811-C5
SAN DOMINIC CT
3800 MonC 95076 1037-A2
SANDPEBBLE DR
4000 SJS 95136 854-F7
SANDPIPER CT
- CMBL 95008 853-D5
1500 SUNV 94087 832-H5
SAND POINT CT
2700 SJS 95148 855-C1
SAND POINT DR
2600 SJS 95148 855-C1
SANDRA DR
1200 SJS 95125 854-B6
SANDRA PL
2900 PA 94303 791-D6
SANDRINGHAM WY
1400 SJS 95126 833-H7
SANDS DR
500 SJS 95125 854-D6
SANDSTONE
- PTLV 94028 830-C1
SANDSTONE LN
1100 SJS 95132 814-F6
SANDY CT
13000 SCIC 95046 956-J2
SANDY LN
4800 SJS 95124 873-G4
4800 SCIC 95124 873-G4
SANDY CREEK LN
1700 SJS 95125 853-J5
SANDY ROCK CT
1600 SJS 95125 853-J5
SANDY ROCK LN
1600 SJS 95125 853-J5
SAN FELICIA WY
500 LALT 94022 811-E5
SAN FELIPE RD
- SJS 95037 896-J3
500 HOLL 95023 1040-A1
700 SBnC 95023 1040-A1
1500 HOLL 95023 1020-A4
3000 SJS 95135 855-D2
3200 SJS 95148 855-D2
3300 SJS 95121 855-D2
3900 SBnC 95023 1020-A1
4900 SJS 95138 855-F5
5400 SBnC 95023 999-J4
5400 SBnC 95023 1000-A7
6100 SJS 95138 875-J1
6100 SJS 95135 875-J1
6200 SJS 95138 876-A2
6200 SCIC 95138 875-J1
6200 SCIC 95138 876-A2
7000 SCIC 95020 999-H1
7400 SCIC 95037 876-H1
8700 SCIC 95037 856-G7
10500 CPTO 95014 851-J2
SAN FELIPE RD Rt#-25
- HOLL 95023 1040-A3
200 SBnC 95023 1040-A3
SAN FERNANDO AV
10300 CPTO 95014 852-B1
SAN FERNANDO CT
10300 CPTO 95014 852-A1
E SAN FERNANDO ST
- SJS 95113 834-C6
100 SJS 95112 834-C6
100 SJS 95192 834-C6
900 SJS 95116 834-H3
W SAN FERNANDO ST
- SJS 95113 834-A7
200 SJS 95110 834-A7
700 SJS 95126 834-A7
700 SJS 95126 833-J7
SAN FILIPPO CT
1200 SJS 95128 853-E3
SANFORD AV
- CMBL 95008 853-E6
SANFORD DR
6000 SJS 95123 874-F6
SAN FRANCISCO CT
800 SCIC 94305 810-J1
5100 SJS 95138 855-F7
SAN FRANCISCO TER
800 SCIC 94305 810-J1
SAN GABRIEL AV
600 MGH 95037 937-B1
SAN GABRIEL CT
- MGH 95037 937-C1
SAN GABRIEL DR
100 SUNV 94086 812-G7
SAN GABRIEL WY
1500 SCIC 95125 853-H5
SANGER WY
500 SJS 95125 854-C4
SAN GERONIMO WY
200 SUNV 94086 812-G7
SANGIOVESE PL
- SJS 95135 855-H2
SANGO CT
1700 MPS 95035 814-B3
SAN GREGORIO WY
400 SJS 95111 854-J7
SAN IGNACIO AV
6200 SJS 95119 875-D6
SAN JACINTO RD
28800 CPTO 95014 851-J2
SAN JOAQUIN AV
1500 SJS 95118 874-A1
SAN JORGE TER
- SUNV 94089 812-G4
SAN JOSE AV
- SJS 95125 854-D3
- SJS 95110 854-D3
SAN JOSE CT
- MGH 95037 937-B1
SAN JOSE DR
- MGH 95037 937-B1
SAN JOSE ST
- SJB 95045 1038-D4
SAN JUAN AV
- SMCo 94025 790-D5
1200 SJS 95110 833-J3
3000 SCL 95051 833-A2
SAN JUAN CT
100 LALT 94022 811-E4
9000 GIL 95020 977-F1
SAN JUAN DR
100 HOLL 95023 1040-A3
600 SUNV 94086 812-G6
16700 MGH 95037 937-B1
SAN JUAN HWY
800 SBnC 95045 1018-B6
800 SBnC 95045 1038-B1
2100 SBnC 95020 1018-B6
SAN JUAN RD
500 HOLL 95023 1039-H3
500 HOLL 95023 1040-A4
22500 CPTO 95014 851-J2
SAN JUAN RD Rt#-G11
2700 MonC 95076 1037-A2
SAN JUAN ST
500 SCIC 94305 810-H1
SAN JUAN CANYON RD Rt#-G1
- SJB 95045 1038-D5
1700 SBnC - 1059-A4
1700 SBnC 95045 1038-D5
SAN JUAN HOLLISTER RD
100 SBnC 95045 1038-E5
100 SJB 95045 1038-E5
SAN JUDE AV
700 PA 94306 811-B2
SAN JULE CT
700 SUNV 94086 812-G5
SAN JULIAN CT
2000 MTVW 94043 811-G3
SAN JULIAN WY
400 MTVW 94043 811-G2
SAN JUNIPERO DR
800 SUNV 94086 812-G5
SAN JUSTO CT
- GIL 95020 977-J6
700 SUNV 94086 812-G5
SAN JUSTO RD
- GIL 95020 977-J7
1600 SBnC 95045 1038-C1
1600 SBnC 95020 1038-C1
2000 SBnC 95020 1018-B7
2000 SBnC 95045 1018-B7
SAN LAZARO AV
100 SUNV 94086 812-G7
SAN LEANDRO AV
900 MTVW 94043 811-J2
900 MTVW 94043 812-A3
10500 CPTO 95014 852-A2
SAN LORENZO DR
200 HOLL 95023 1039-G3
5600 SJS 95123 874-F4
SAN LUCAR CT
100 SUNV 94086 812-G7
100 SUNV 94086 832-G1
SAN LUCAS AV
700 MTVW 94043 811-J3
700 MTVW 94043 812-A3
SAN LUCAS CT
800 MTVW 94043 811-J3
SAN LUCAS WY
- SJS 95135 855-H3
SAN LUIS AV
300 LALT 94024 811-F7
1400 MTVW 94043 811-G3
SAN LUIS DR
200 MLPK 94025 790-H2
SAN LUIS WY
16700 MGH 95037 937-B1
16700 MGH 95037 917-B7
SAN LUISITO WY
600 SUNV 94086 812-G6
SAN LUIS REY AV
3000 SJS 95118 874-A1
SAN LUPPE DR
800 MTVW 94043 812-A3
SAN MARCOS CIR
900 MTVW 94043 811-H3
SAN MARCOS CT
700 MGH 95037 937-C1
2600 SJS 95132 814-E5
SAN MARCOS DR
1300 SJS 95132 814-E5
SAN MARCOS RD
19200 SAR 95070 872-F3
SAN MARCOS WY
3400 SCL 95051 832-J3
SAN MARDO AV
3300 SCIC 95127 814-H6
SAN MARINO AV
3300 SCIC 95127 814-H6
E SAN MARTIN AV
- SCIC 95046 937-G5
W SAN MARTIN AV
- SCIC 95046 937-A6
SAN MARTIN PL
600 LALT 94024 811-G7
SAN MARTINO CT
- SJS 95126 833-G6
SAN MATEO AV
200 LGTS 95030 873-A6
SAN MATEO CT
800 SUNV 94086 812-G5
SAN MATEO DR
- MLPK 94025 790-E4
100 SJS 95111 854-H7
SAN MICHELE PL
- SJS 95135 855-J3
SAN MIGUEL AV
600 SUNV 94086 812-G6
600 SCL 95050 833-C5
SAN MIGUEL CT
300 MPS 95035 813-J1
SAN MIGUEL ST
1000 GIL 95020 977-G3
SAN MIGUEL WY
4100 SJS 95111 854-J7
SAN MINETE CT
- SJS 95148 855-G1
SAN MORITZ DR
1100 SJS 95132 814-F5
SAN ONOFRE CT
900 SCIC 95127 814-H6
900 SJS 95127 814-H6
SAN PABLO AV
700 SUNV 94086 812-H5
3300 SCIC 95127 814-H6
3400 SJS 95127 814-J6
SAN PABLO CT
- HOLL 95023 1040-D6
500 MGH 95037 937-B1
3700 SCIC 95127 814-J6
SAN PABLO DR
700 MTVW 94043 811-J3
700 MTVW 94043 812-A3
SAN PALO CT
18600 SAR 95070 852-H5
SAN PATRICIO AV
600 SUNV 94086 812-G6
SAN PEDRO AV
- MGH 95037 937-A1
600 SUNV 94086 812-H6
800 MGH 95037 917-C7
1300 SCIC 95037 917-D7
SAN PEDRO LN
600 MGH 95037 917-C7
600 MGH 95037 937-B1
N SAN PEDRO ST
- SJS 95110 834-A4
900 SJS 95110 833-J3
S SAN PEDRO ST
- SJS 95113 834-B6
100 SJS 95110 834-B6
SAN PETRA CT
300 MPS 95035 813-J1
SAN PETRONIO AV
800 SUNV 94086 812-H5
SAN PIER CT
800 SUNV 94086 812-H5
SAN PIERRE WY
500 MTVW 94043 811-H3
SAN RAFAEL AV
800 MTVW 94043 811-J3
2100 SCL 95051 833-A2
SAN RAFAEL CT
2000 SCL 95051 833-A3
SAN RAFAEL PL
700 SCIC 94305 810-H1
SAN RAFAEL ST
- MGH 95037 917-C2
700 SUNV 94086 812-H6
SAN RAMON AV
700 SUNV 94086 812-H5
1200 MTVW 94043 811-G2
SAN RAMON CT
700 MGH 95037 937-C1
900 MTVW 94043 811-H3
SAN RAMON DR
100 SJS 95111 854-H7
16500 MGH 95037 917-C7
16500 MGH 95037 937-C1
SAN RAMON WY
4000 SJS 95111 854-J7
SAN RIVAS DR
3200 SJS 95148 835-D7
SAN SABA CT
900 SUNV 94086 812-H5
SAN SABA DR
3400 SJS 95148 835-D6
E SAN SALVADOR ST
- SJS 95113 834-D6
- SJS 95112 834-D6
100 SJS 95192 834-D6
W SAN SALVADOR ST
- SJS 95110 834-C7
SAN SEBASTIAN PL
700 MGH 95037 937-A4
SAN SIMEON DR
800 MTVW 94043 811-J3
SAN SIMEON ST
600 SUNV 94086 812-H6
SAN SIMEON WY
4000 SJS 95111 854-J7
SANTA ANA AV
400 SJS 95112 834-B3
SANTA ANA CT
1500 SBnC 95023 1040-E4
SANTA ANA RD
- HOLL 95023 1040-B3
200 SBnC 95023 1040-B3
18100 SCIC 95033 912-H3
SANTA ANA ST
2200 PA 94303 791-C4
SANTA ANA VALLEY RD
300 SBnC 95075 1061-E1
300 SBnC 95023 1040-F2
4600 SBnC - 1061-E1
4600 SBnC 95023 1061-E1
SANTA ANITA RD
300 SBnC - 1061-G5
300 SBnC 95075 1061-G5
SANTA ANNA CT
200 SUNV 94086 812-G7
SANTA BARBARA AV
3400 SCL 95051 832-J3
SANTA BARBARA DR
400 LALT 94022 811-F6
1700 SCIC 95125 853-H4
7500 GIL 95020 977-G3
SANTA BARBARA TER
- SUNV 94086 812-F5
SANTA BELLA PL
21700 CPTO 95014 852-B3
SANTA CATALINA ST
2300 PA 94303 791-D4
SANTA CATALINA TER
600 SUNV 94086 812-F5
SANTA CHRISTINA CT
700 SUNV 94086 812-F5
SANTA CLARA AV
100 MTVW 94043 811-J4
100 SCIC 95020 957-H4

STREET Block City ZIP Pg-Grid

SANTA CLARA AV
100 SMCo 94061 790-B3
100 RDWC 94061 790-B3
10000 CPTO 95014 832-B7
SANTA CLARA RD
21500 SCIC 95033 912-J3
SANTA CLARA ST
800 SCL 95053 833-D5
900 SCL 95050 833-D5
E SANTA CLARA ST
- SJS 95113 834-C6
100 SJS 95112 834-C6
800 SJS 95116 834-C6
W SANTA CLARA ST
- SJS 95113 834-A7
- SJS 95110 834-A7
W SANTA CLARA ST Rt#-82
400 SJS 95113 834-A7
600 SJS 95126 834-A7
SANTA COLETA CT
600 SUNV 94086 812-F5
SANTA CROCE CT
- SJS 95148 855-G1
SANTA CRUZ AV
500 MLPK 94025 790-F3
1600 SCL 95051 833-A2
2000 SMCo 94025 790-E6
N SANTA CRUZ AV
- LGTS 95030 873-A6
S SANTA CRUZ AV
- LGTS 95030 873-A7
- LGTS 95030 893-A1
100 LGTS 95030 892-J1
SANTA CRUZ RDG
100 SCrC 95033 913-A6
SANTA CRUZ TER
400 SUNV 94086 812-F5
SANTA ELENA WY
200 SUNV 94086 812-F7
SANTA FE AV
800 SCIC 94305 810-J1
SANTA FE DR
- GIL 95020 957-H7
1300 SJS 95118 874-B3
SANTA FE TER
200 SUNV 94086 812-F7
SANTA INES WY
- MGH 95037 917-B3
SANTA INEZ CT
1900 SCL 95051 832-J3
7600 GIL 95020 977-G3
SANTA INEZ DR
1300 SCIC 95125 853-H4
SANTA LUCIA DR
1700 SCIC 95125 853-H4
3100 SCL 95051 833-A5
SANTA LUCIA RD
10500 CPTO 95014 851-J2
SANTA MARGARITA AV
100 MLPK 94025 790-H3
3000 SJS 95118 874-A1
SANTA MARIA AV
700 SCIC 94305 810-H2
1500 SJS 95125 853-J4
3000 SCL 95051 833-A2
SANTA MARIA CT
7600 GIL 95020 977-G3
SANTA MESA DR
400 SJS 95123 874-J6
SANTA MONICA AV
100 MLPK 94025 790-H3
1500 SJS 95118 874-A1
SANTA MONICA TER
- FRMT 94539 794-B1
SANTANA HTS
- SJS 95128 853-E1
SANTANA RW
- SJS 95128 853-E1
SANTANDER CT
200 LALT 94022 811-D4
SANTA PAULA AV
600 SUNV 94086 812-H6
1200 SJS 95110 833-J2
22300 CPTO 95014 852-A1
SANTA PAULA DR
7500 GIL 95020 977-G3
SANTA RITA AV
100 PA 94301 791-B6
300 MLPK 94025 790-F5
700 LALT 94022 811-D4
SANTA RITA CT
100 LALT 94022 811-D3
SANTA RITA DR
300 MPS 95035 794-B6
SANTA RITA ST
700 SUNV 94086 812-H5
SANTA RITA WY
4100 SJS 95111 854-J7
SANTA ROSA AV
100 MTVW 94043 811-J4
SANTA ROSA CT
1900 SCL 95051 832-J3
SANTA ROSA DR
100 SJS 95111 854-J7
300 LGTS 95032 873-G7
300 LGTS 95032 893-G1
2000 SBnC 95023 1020-B5
SANTA ROSA ST
700 SUNV 94086 812-H5
SANTA SUSANA ST
700 SUNV 94086 812-H5
SANTA SUSANA WY
4100 SJS 95111 854-J7
SANTA TERESA BLVD
5000 SCIC 95020 998-A1
5300 SCIC 95020 978-A7
5400 SJS 95136 874-E5
5500 SJS 95123 874-E5
5600 GIL 95020 978-A7
5700 SCIC 95020 977-J6
5700 GIL 95020 977-F3
6000 SJS 95123 875-A6

SANTA TERESA BLVD
6200 SJS 95119 875-C6
7000 SJS 95139 875-C6
7000 SJS 95139 895-H2
7300 SCIC 95139 895-H2
7300 SCIC 95119 895-H2
7300 SJS 95139 896-A4
7800 SJS 95141 896-A4
9000 GIL 95020 957-G7
9000 SJS 95037 896-A4
10200 SCIC 95046 957-D1
10200 SCIC 95020 957-F4
13000 SCIC 95046 937-D7
14100 SCIC 95037 896-A4
14100 SCIC 95037 936-J2
14100 MGH 95037 937-B6
14100 SCIC 95037 937-B6
14300 MGH 95037 936-J2
14300 SCIC 95037 916-C1
14500 MGH 95037 916-F4
SANTA TERESA DR
10800 CPTO 95014 852-B3
SANTA TERESA ST
100 SCIC 94305 790-G7
300 SJS 95110 834-A5
SANTA THERESA DR
7400 GIL 95020 977-H3
SANTA TRINITA AV
300 SUNV 94086 812-H7
SANTA YNEZ ST
600 SCIC 94305 810-H1
600 SUNV 94086 812-J6
SANTA YSABEL WY
6000 SJS 95123 874-F6
SANTEE DR
1200 SJS 95122 834-G7
SANTEE RIVER CT
600 SJS 95111 854-H4
SANTIAGO AV
- ATN 94027 790-D4
100 SMCo 94061 790-A3
2000 SJS 95122 834-J7
2000 SJS 95122 835-A7
2000 SJS 95122 854-J1
SANTIAGO PL
800 MGH 95037 937-A4
SAN TOMAS CT
1500 SJS 95130 853-B4
SAN TOMAS EXWY
- CMBL 95008 873-D1
SAN TOMAS EXWY Rt#-G4
- CMBL 95008 853-C6
- CMBL 95008 873-D1
- SJS 95008 853-C4
- SCL 95050 833-C6
- SCL 95051 833-C3
- SCL 95051 833-C4
- SCL 95117 833-C4
- SCL 95117 853-C4
100 SJS 95117 853-C4
100 SJS 95130 853-C4
2900 SCL 95054 813-C7
2900 SCL 95054 833-C3
SAN TOMAS LN
16600 MGH 95037 937-B1
SAN TOMAS ST
700 SUNV 94086 812-H5
SAN TOMAS AQUINO PKWY
1300 SJS 95130 853-C4
N SAN TOMAS AQUINO RD
- CMBL 95008 853-B6
- SJS 95008 853-B6
200 SJS 95130 853-B6
1200 SJS 95129 853-B6
1200 SJS 95117 853-B6
S SAN TOMAS AQUINO RD
- SJS 95008 853-A6
200 SJS 95130 853-A6
500 CMBL 95008 853-B7
1000 CMBL 95008 873-B1
SANTORO LN
- SJS 95124 873-G7
SANTOS CT
600 MPS 95035 794-C5
SAN TROPEZ DR
- HOLL 95023 1040-B3
SAN TROPICO CT
- SJS 95135 855-H3
SAN VERON AV
800 MTVW 94043 811-J3
SAN VICENTE AV
22400 SCIC 95120 895-A4
22500 SJS 95120 895-B4
SAN VICENTE CT
- MGH 95037 937-C1
SAN VICENTE DR
600 MGH 95037 937-C1
SAN VICENTE WY
100 SUNV 94086 812-H7
SAN VITO CT
300 SJS 95116 834-F3
SAN YSIDRO AV
8400 GIL 95020 958-A7
8400 GIL 95020 978-A1
SAN YSIDRO WY
2900 SCL 95051 812-J7
2900 SCL 95051 832-J1
4000 SJS 95111 854-J7
SAN ZENO WY
- SUNV 94086 832-J1
SAPA CT
4500 SJS 95136 874-E2
SAPENA CT
400 SCL 95054 813-E7
SAPPHIRE CT
900 SJS 95136 874-E3
SAPWOOD LN
1600 SJS 95133 814-H3
SAPWOOD WY
2300 SJS 95133 814-H3

SARA AV
300 SUNV 94086 812-C7
SARA CT
900 SUNV 94086 812-C7
SARABAND WY
800 SJS 95122 854-F1
SARAFINA WY
- GIL 95020 978-A2
SARAGLEN CT
- SAR 95070 852-F5
SARAGLEN DR
12000 SAR 95070 852-F5
SARAH CT
4000 SJS 95136 874-E1
SARAHILLS CT
21200 SAR 95070 872-C1
SARAHILLS DR
20700 SAR 95070 872-C1
SARA JANE CT
16900 MGH 95037 917-G5
SARA JANE LN
16900 MGH 95037 917-G5
SARALYNN DR
1600 SJS 95121 855-A2
SARANAC DR
700 SUNV 94087 832-C3
SARA PARK CIR
18800 SAR 95070 852-H6
SARASOTA WY
1800 SJS 95122 834-H7
2100 SJS 95122 854-H1
SARATOGA AV
- SCL 95051 833-C7
- SCL 95051 853-B1
100 SCL 95050 833-C7
300 SJS 95129 853-B1
1100 EPA 94303 791-A1
1400 SJS 95129 852-G7
1800 SAR 95070 852-G7
1800 SJS 95130 852-G7
1800 SAR 95129 852-G7
13300 SAR 95070 872-F1
SARATOGA AV Rt#-9
- LGTS 95030 873-B7
- LGTS 95032 873-B7
SARATOGA DR
1400 MPS 95035 814-D1
SARATOGA PL
7100 GIL 95020 977-H4
SARATOGA CREEK DR
12200 SAR 95070 852-G6
SARATOGA GLEN CT
12700 SAR 95070 852-G6
SARATOGA GLEN PL
18900 SAR 95070 852-G6
SARATOGA HEIGHTS CT
14500 SAR 95070 872-B2
SARATOGA HEIGHTS DR
21400 SAR 95070 872-B2
SARATOGA HILLS RD
14000 SAR 95070 872-C1
SARATOGA LOS GATOS RD Rt#-9
300 MSER 95030 872-G5
300 MSER 95030 873-A6
18500 SCIC 95030 872-G5
18800 SAR 95070 872-E3
SARATOGA-SUNNYVALE RD
12000 SAR 95070 852-E7
S SARATOGA-SUNNYVALE RD
12500 SAR 95070 852-E7
13200 SAR 95070 872-E1
SARATOGA TOLL RD
20000 SCrC 95006 871-A5
20000 SCrC 95033 871-A5
SARATOGA VILLA PL
12000 SAR 95070 852-D5
SARATOGA VISTA AV
13500 SAR 95070 872-E1
SARATOGA VISTA CT
20000 SAR 95070 872-E1
SARATOGA WOODS CIR
12700 SAR 95070 852-E6
SARAVIEW CT
20900 SAR 95070 852-D7
20900 SAR 95070 872-C1
SARAVIEW DR
13400 SAR 95070 852-D7
13400 SAR 95070 872-D1
SARGENT DR
1000 SUNV 94087 832-F3
SARGENT RD
- ATN 94027 790-B7
SARGENT ST
8000 GIL 95020 977-J2
SARITA WY
1300 SCL 95051 832-H4
SARK CT
400 MPS 95035 794-A6
SARK WY
3800 SJS 95111 855-A6
SARON DR
- SJS 95116 834-G4
SASKATCHEWAN DR
1400 SUNV 94087 832-D5
SASSAFRAS DR
3400 SJS 95111 854-G6
SASSONE CT
1200 MPS 95035 814-D2
SATINWOOD DR
3600 SJS 95148 835-F7
SATTERLEE LN
8700 SCIC 95020 958-E4
SATURN AV
600 FRMT 94539 793-J1
SATURN CT
1400 MPS 95035 794-D7
SATURN TER
300 SUNV 94086 832-E1

SAUSAL DR
- PTLV 94028 810-C6
SAUSALITO DR
1600 HOLL 95023 1040-D7
SAUTNER DR
400 SJS 95123 875-B7
SAUVIGNON CT
- FRMT 94539 793-J2
8400 SJS 95135 855-J7
SAVAKER AV
800 SJS 95126 853-J2
SAVANNAH CT
19000 MGH 95037 917-A2
SAVANNAH DR
1000 SJS 95117 853-D3
SAVENDISH CT
5200 SJS 95136 874-F3
SAVERIO CT
2100 SJS 95008 853-B6
SAVONA CT
- SJS 95126 833-G6
SAVORY DR
800 SUNV 94087 832-D2
SAVOY DR
4500 SJS 95129 853-A4
SAVSTROM WY
400 SJS 95111 875-B1
SAWGRASS DR
1500 SJS 95116 834-F5
SAWLEAF CT
1500 SJS 95131 814-D6
SAWLEAF ST
48200 FRMT 94539 793-J1
SAW MILL LN
- MTVW 94043 811-J3
SAWTOOTH CT
3600 SJS 95111 854-G6
SAWTOOTH DR
1200 HOLL 95023 1040-D5
1200 SBnC 95023 1040-D5
SAWYER CT
2300 SCL 95054 813-C5
SAXON WY
1100 MLPK 94025 790-F4
SAXONY CT
5600 SJS 95123 874-G4
SAYOKO CIR
4200 SJS 95136 874-H1
SAYRE AV
- SCIC 94035 812-B2
SCAGIA LN
23500 SCIC 95033 913-D6
SCAGLIOTTI RD
500 SBnC 95023 1020-C5
SCALETTA LN
1000 SJS 95120 894-H4
SCANLAN PL
2400 SCL 95050 833-C6
SCARAWAY DR
1400 SJS 95132 814-F4
SCARFF WY
26000 LAH 94022 811-C5
SCARLETT RD
2300 SCIC 95020 958-D5
SCARLETT WY
4900 SJS 95111 875-C1
SCARLETWOOD TER
4800 SJS 95129 852-B7
SCARSBOROUGH WY
100 LGTS 95032 873-A3
SCARSDALE CT
1100 SJS 95120 894-G4
SCARSDALE PL
7100 SJS 95120 894-G4
SCARSDALE WY
7100 SJS 95120 894-G4
SCENERY CT
6500 SJS 95120 894-C1
SCENIC BLVD
10000 CPTO 95014 852-A1
SCENIC CIR
1900 HOLL 95023 1040-C7
10300 CPTO 95014 852-A1
SCENIC CT
10400 CPTO 95014 852-A1
SCENIC SQ
1900 SJS 95132 814-E3
SCENIC HEIGHTS WY
22500 SAR 95070 852-B5
SCENIC MEADOW CT
- SJS 95135 855-H7
SCENIC MEADOW LN
- SJS 95135 855-G7
- SJS 95138 855-G7
SCENIC VISTA CT
- SCIC 95119 895-A1
- SCIC 95120 895-A1
SCENIC VISTA DR
20700 SCIC 95120 894-J2
20800 SCIC 95120 895-A1
20800 SCIC 95119 895-A1
SCEPTER CT
1800 SJS 95132 814-G2
SCHALLENBERGER RD
1500 SJS 95112 814-A7
1500 SJS 95131 814-A7
SCHARFF AV
- SJS 95116 834-G3
SCHELLER AV
- SCIC 95037 896-B7
- SCIC 95037 916-A1
SCHEMBRI LN
700 EPA 94303 791-B1
SCHIELE AV
700 SJS 95126 833-H6
SCHOFIELD CT
11200 SCIC 95020 957-J2
SCHOOLDALE DR
1800 SJS 95124 853-H7
SCHOOLHOUSE RD
700 SJS 95138 875-G5
SCHOONER CT
2800 SJS 95148 855-D1

SCHOTT CT
- SCL 95054 813-C5
SCHOTT ST
100 SJS 95116 834-G2
SCHRADER DR
1900 SJS 95124 853-G7
SCHRAMM WY
- SJS 95127 835-C3
SCHROEDER AV
300 SUNV 94086 812-E6
SCHUBERT AV
2400 SJS 95124 853-G7
SCHUBERT DR
700 SUNV 94087 832-F3
SCHULTE DR
1700 SJS 95133 834-F3
SCHULTIES RD
23400 SCrC 95033 913-A6
SCHWEPPES CT
1800 SJS 95132 814-J3
SCHWIE AL
- MLPK 94025 790-E6
SCOFIELD DR
20500 CPTO 95014 852-D1
SCOFIELD ST
600 EPA 94303 791-B3
SCOLLON CT
1400 SJS 95132 814-F5
SCORPIO DR
1800 SJS 95111 854-G6
SCOSSA AV
1300 SJS 95118 874-B3
SCOSSA CT
- SJS 95118 874-B3
SCOTCH HEATHER CT
3200 SJS 95148 855-E2
SCOTIA TER
- SUNV 94089 812-G4
SCOTLAND DR
1100 CPTO 95014 852-D3
19400 SAR 95070 852-F7
19400 SAR 95070 872-F1
SCOTSGLEN CT
900 SJS 95136 874-D1
SCOTT BLVD
500 SCL 95050 833-D3
1200 SUNV 94086 813-A7
2900 SCL 95054 833-D3
2900 SCL 95054 813-A7
SCOTT CT
800 CMBL 95008 873-C1
SCOTT DR
1700 MGH 95037 916-F7
18400 MSER 95030 872-H6
SCOTT LN
1900 LALT 94024 831-H5
SCOTT ST
300 SJS 95126 853-G1
300 SCIC 95126 853-G1
900 PA 94301 790-J5
1600 SJS 95128 853-E1
1600 SCIC 95128 853-G1
SCOTT CREEK RD
600 FRMT 94539 793-J2
600 FRMT 94539 794-A2
2100 SCIC 95035 794-A2
SCOTT FARM RD
- SCIC 95070 871-G7
- SCrC 95033 871-G7
SCOTTS BLUFF PL
300 MGH 95037 937-A2
SCOTTSDALE CT
2800 SJS 95148 855-C2
SCOTTSDALE DR
2400 SJS 95148 835-B7
2600 SJS 95148 855-B1
SCOTTSFIELD DR
4400 SJS 95136 874-D2
SCOTTSVILLE CT
500 SJS 95133 834-F2
SCOTTY ST
1500 SJS 95122 834-G6
SCOUT CT
4800 SJS 95136 874-J2
SCRIPPS AV
4000 PA 94306 811-E2
SCRIPPS CT
200 PA 94306 811-E2
SCULLY AV
12000 SAR 95070 852-F5
SEABEE PL
1900 SJS 95133 834-E1
SEABISCUIT DR
200 SJS 95111 875-B2
SEABOARD AV
2500 SJS 95131 813-F7
SEABRIDGE DR
- FRMT 94538 793-F1
SEABROOK CT
800 SJS 95111 855-A6
SEABURY DR
800 SJS 95136 874-E2
SEACLIFF DR
2000 MPS 95035 794-E7
2000 MPS 95035 814-E1
SEACLIFF WY
2300 SJS 95122 854-J1
SEACREEK CT
3200 SJS 95121 855-D7
SEACREEK WY
1600 SJS 95121 855-D7
SEAFIELD CT
3000 SJS 95148 855-C2
SEAGRAVES WY
20100 SAR 95070 872-E2
SEA GULL CT
19700 SAR 95070 852-F6
SEA GULL WY
19800 SAR 95070 852-E5
SEALE AV
100 PA 94301 791-A6
600 PA 94303 791-A6
SEAMAN PL
2000 SJS 95133 814-E7

SEAN CIR
5400 SJS 95123 874-J4
SEAN CT
- SJS 95123 874-F7
SEAN LN
5500 SJS 95123 874-J3
SEARCY DR
1300 SJS 95118 874-B2
SEAREEL LN
1400 SJS 95131 814-A4
SEARLE RD
900 SBnC 95045 1037-J2
1200 SBnC 95045 1018-A7
SEARLES AV
1500 SJS 95125 854-A4
SEARS RD
23500 SCIC 95033 913-E6
SEARSVILLE RD
- SCIC 94305 790-F7
SEARVILLE RD
1500 PA 94304 810-G5
1700 SCIC 94304 810-F6
28000 LAH 94022 810-G5
SEASIDE DR
100 MPS 95035 793-J5
SEASIDE WY
1100 MPS 95035 793-J5
SEATON AV
20600 SAR 95070 872-D1
SEAVIEW DR
300 SJS 95002 813-B1
1700 SJS 95122 834-H7
SEAWELL CT
100 SJS 95138 875-E4
SEAWOOD WY
700 SJS 95120 894-J3
SEBASIAN WY
400 SJS 95111 854-J6
SEBASTIAN CT
100 LGTS 95032 873-J6
SEBASTIAN BORELLO DR
2800 SJS 95148 855-D2
SEBREE LN
18200 MSER 95030 872-J5
SECRETARIAT CT
14600 MGH 95037 937-B5
SECRETARIAT WY
- MGH 95037 937-B5
- SCIC 95037 937-B5
SEDLAK CT
2500 SJS 95148 855-B1
SEDONA PL
- SJS 95116 834-F4
SEDONA TER
- SJS 95116 834-F5
SEDONA WY
- GIL 95020 957-F6
SEDUM RD
48600 FRMT 94539 793-J2
SEEBECK CT
2000 SJS 95132 814-F2
SEEBER CT
7700 CPTO 95014 852-C4
SEELY AV
2600 SJS 95134 813-H4
SEENA AV
900 LALT 94024 831-G2
SEGO CT
1600 SJS 95131 834-D1
SEGOVIA CT
3200 SJS 95127 814-H6
SEGURA CT
2800 SJS 95125 873-J1
SEIFERT AV
5600 SJS 95118 874-B4
SEILANS CT
- SJS 95148 855-G2
SEINE CT
- SJS 95127 834-J1
SELBORN PL
1400 SJS 95126 833-H7
SELBY LN
- ATN 94027 790-C2
- SMCo 94063 790-C1
800 SCIC 95127 814-H6
1100 SMCo 94061 790-B3
W SELBY LN
1100 ATN 94027 790-C2
1400 SMCo 94061 790-B3
SELIG LN
1700 LALT 94024 832-A3
SELINDA LN
5000 SJS 95124 873-H4
SELINDA WY
5000 SJS 95124 873-H5
SELKIRK PL
800 SUNV 94087 832-F6
SELMAC AV
- SJS 95136 874-E1
SELO DR
1300 SUNV 94087 832-D4
SELVA DR
3200 SJS 95148 835-D6
SELWYN DR
200 MPS 95035 794-C7
SEMICIRCULAR RD
100 SMCo 94063 790-D1
100 SMCo 94025 790-D1
SEMICONDUCTOR DR
2900 SCL 95051 812-H7
2900 SCL 95051 832-H1
2900 SCL 94086 812-H7
2900 SCL 94086 832-H1
SEMILLON DR
48800 FRMT 94539 793-J2
SEMINARY DR
300 MLPK 94025 790-H2
SEMINOLE WY
700 PA 94303 811-F1
1600 SJS 95122 854-J1
SENATE WY
10000 CPTO 95014 832-C7

SENECA CT
600 SJS 95123 874-G4
SENECA ST
400 PA 94301 790-J3
400 PA 94301 791-A3
SENECA TER
- SUNV 94087 832-D1
SENEGAL CT
1400 GIL 95020 977-F1
SENHORINHA ST
- SJS 95136 854-E6
SENNA CT
400 SUNV 94086 832-G1
SENTER RD
- SJS 95111 854-H5
800 SJS 95112 854-F2
SENTER CREEK CT
2600 SJS 95111 854-G4
SENTINEL ST
5800 SJS 95120 874-B6
SENTRY PALM CT
- SJS 95133 814-J4
SEPTEMBER CT
800 CPTO 95014 852-C2
SEPTEMBER DR
800 CPTO 95014 852-C2
5500 SJS 95138 875-D4
SEPTEMBER SONG CT
1700 SJS 95131 814-D7
SEPULVEDA AV
2000 MPS 95035 794-E6
SEPULVEDA CT
200 MPS 95035 794-E7
SEQUESTER CT
2400 SJS 95133 814-F6
SEQUOIA AV
- SCrC 95033 871-A4
- SJS 95125 854-E4
100 SJS 95126 833-H7
100 SMCo 94061 790-A3
200 PA 94306 791-A6
SEQUOIA CT
- HOLL 95023 1040-E5
- SMCo 94061 790-B3
SEQUOIA DR
400 SUNV 94086 832-G2
500 LALT 94024 831-J5
500 MPS 95035 794-D7
600 MPS 95035 814-E1
1400 GIL 95020 977-G3
SEQUOIA LN
400 SCIC 94305 790-G7
SEQUOIA WY
- SMCo 94061 790-B4
400 LALT 94024 831-J5
SEQUOIA CREEK CT
- SJS 95121 855-D4
SEQUOIA CREEK DR
- SJS 95121 855-D4
SERENA CT
- SCIC 95126 853-H1
100 MTVW 94043 812-A5
SERENA WY
100 SCL 95051 833-B7
100 SCL 95051 853-B1
SERENADE CT
600 SJS 95111 855-A7
SERENADE WY
400 SJS 95111 854-J7
400 SJS 95111 855-A7
SERENA VISTA CT
16200 MSER 95030 872-J6
SERENE CT
800 MGH 95037 917-B6
SERENE DR
- HOLL 95023 1040-A6
17300 MGH 95037 917-A5
17700 SCIC 95037 917-A5
SERENE WY
21000 SCIC 95120 894-J2
SERENE VALLEY CT
1200 SJS 95120 894-E2
SERENITY CT
6800 SJS 95120 894-F2
SERENITY PL
- MPS 95035 814-J2
SERENITY WY
6800 SJS 95120 894-F2
SERENO CT
- CPTO 95014 831-H6
17200 MSER 95030 873-B4
SERENO DR
23300 CPTO 95014 831-H6
SERENO VISTA WY
300 SJS 95116 834-D2
SERGE AV
1900 SJS 95130 852-J6
SERPA DR
1600 MPS 95035 794-D5
3000 SJS 95148 855-C2
SERPENTINE AV
- SJS 95125 854-E4
SERPENTINE CT
600 MGH 95037 916-H6
SERRA AV
2000 SCL 95050 833-C5
SERRA AVD
- MGH 95037 917-B3
SERRA CT
- MGH 95037 917-B3
200 LGTS 95032 873-B6
SERRA ST
- CPTO 95014 831-H6
500 SCIC 94305 790-H7
700 SCIC 94305 791-A7
SERRA WY
100 MPS 95035 793-J7
100 MPS 95035 794-A7
SERRAMONTE DR
18000 SCIC 95030 872-H5
SERRANO AV
300 SCIC 95127 835-A2
SERRANO DR
- ATN 94027 790-C2

STREET Block City ZIP Pg-Grid

SERRAOAKS CT
13700 SAR 95070 872-H1
SERVICE ST
800 SJS 95112 834-B2
SESAME CT
1200 SUNV 94087 832-D3
2500 SJS 95148 835-A6
SESAME DR
1100 SUNV 94087 832-D3
SESSIONS DR
6900 SJS 95119 875-F6
SETAREH CT
1200 SJS 95125 854-A4
SETH CT
1000 SJS 95120 894-G3
SETTLE AV
1100 SJS 95125 854-A3
SEVELY DR
800 MTVW 94041 812-A6
SEVEN ACRES LN
14100 LAH 94022 811-C6
SEVEN SPRINGS DR
11600 CPTO 95014 852-C4
SEVEN SPRINGS LN
11500 CPTO 95014 852-C4
SEVEN SPRINGS PKWY
11700 CPTO 95014 852-C4
SEVEN TREES BLVD
3800 SJS 95111 854-H6
SEVEN TREES VILLAGE WY
3300 SJS 95111 854-G6
SEVERANCE CT
5100 SJS 95136 874-E3
SEVERANCE DR
4900 SJS 95136 874-E3
SEVERANCE ST
9100 GIL 95020 957-H7
SEVERINSEN ST
1700 HOLL 95023 1040-A6
SEVERYNS AV
- SCIC 94035 812-B2
- SCIC 94043 812-B2
SEVIER AV
1000 MLPK 94025 790-J1
SEVILLA DR
- LALT 94022 811-E5
SEVILLA LN
20500 SAR 95070 872-D1
SEVILLE DR
1400 MGH 95037 917-D7
SEVILLE WY
1700 SJS 95131 814-D7
SEVIN TER
- SJS 95133 834-D2
SEVYSON CT
2900 PA 94303 791-D6
SEWARD CT
10100 SCIC 95127 835-A3
SEWELL AV
12200 SCIC 95046 937-E6
SEYFERTH WY
3000 SJS 95118 854-C7
3000 SJS 95118 874-C1
SEYMOUR AV
14700 SCIC 95046 937-D3
SEYMOUR LN
1000 MLPK 94025 790-E5
SEYMOUR ST
300 SJS 95110 833-J5
SHADELANDS DR
6200 SJS 95123 874-H7
SHADE TREE LN
2200 SJS 95131 814-C5
SHADLE AV
1000 CMBL 95008 873-B1
SHADOW CT
500 SJS 95129 853-B2
SHADOW DR
- MPS 95035 814-J1
SHADOW GN
500 SJS 95129 853-A2
SHADOW TR
18100 SCIC 95033 912-J4
SHADOW BROOK DR
900 SJS 95120 894-F2
SHADOW BROOK WY
- MGH 95037 916-H6
SHADOWBROOK WY
18200 MGH 95037 916-H6
SHADOW CREEK DR
600 SJS 95136 854-E7
SHADOW CREEK PL
11600 SCIC 94024 831-G4
SHADOWCREST WY
5400 SJS 95123 874-G4
SHADOW DANCE DR
100 SJS 95125 854-C3
SHADOW ESTATES
5100 SJS 95135 855-G5
SHADOWFAX DR
1200 SJS 95121 855-A4
W SHADOWGRAPH DR
100 SJS 95125 854-D5
SHADOWHILL LN
7400 CPTO 95014 852-D4
SHADOWHURST CT
4500 SJS 95136 874-E2
SHADOWLAKE CT
200 MPS 95035 794-A6
SHADOW LANE CT
14400 MGH 95037 937-C5
SHADOW LEAF DR
3300 SJS 95132 814-G4
SHADOW MIST CT
- SJS 95138 855-F6
SHADOW MOUNTAIN CT
6800 SJS 95120 894-E3
SHADOW MOUNTAIN DR
13000 SAR 95070 852-E7

SHADOW OAKS WY
14000 SAR 95070 872-E2
SHADOW PARK PL
3200 SJS 95121 855-B2
SHADOW RIDGE CT
2100 SJS 95138 855-E5
SHADOW RIDGE WY
2100 SJS 95138 855-E5
SHADOW ROCK CT
700 SJS 95136 854-F7
SHADOW RUN DR
300 SJS 95125 854-C3
SHADOW SPRINGS PL
3000 SJS 95121 855-B1
SHADOWTREE DR
2100 SJS 95131 814-C5
SHADOWVALE WY
2600 SJS 95132 814-C4
SHADOW WOOD CT
- SJS 95136 874-J7
SHADY AV
5000 SJS 95129 852-J4
SHADY LN
2100 SCIC 95037 936-F2
15700 LGTS 95032 873-E6
21300 SCIC 95033 913-B2
SHADY WY
21300 SCIC 95033 912-J4
SHADYBROOK CT
11900 SAR 95070 852-H4
SHADY BROOK LN
1900 SCIC 95037 936-G4
SHADY CREEK CT
1700 SJS 95148 835-D4
SHADY CREEK LN
600 LALT 94024 831-G1
SHADY DALE AV
1100 CMBL 95008 853-G6
SHADY GLEN AV
1500 SCL 95050 833-F6
SHADY GROVE CT
- SJS 95138 855-D6
SHADYGROVE CT
6200 CPTO 95014 852-G2
SHADYGROVE DR
6000 CPTO 95014 852-G2
SHADY GROVE PL
- SJS 95138 855-D7
SHADYHOLLOW CT
3600 SJS 95148 835-G7
SHADY HOLLOW DR
1700 MGH 95037 916-F7
SHADY LANE DR
17000 SCIC 95037 917-G4
SHADY MEADOWS PL
- SJS 95138 855-D6
SHADY OAK CT
19600 SAR 95070 872-F2
SHADY OAK LN
11000 CPTO 95014 832-D6
SHADY OAKS CT
26700 LAH 94022 811-A5
SHADY SPRING LN
3300 MTVW 94040 831-J2
SHADY VIEW LN
16300 LGTS 95032 873-D7
16300 SCIC 95032 873-D7
SHAFER AV
- MGH 95037 917-E6
2200 SCIC 95037 917-E6
SHAFER CT
- SCIC 95037 917-E5
SHAFER DR
3400 SCL 95051 832-J5
SHAFFER DR
1400 SJS 95132 814-F3
SHAKER CT
1100 SJS 95120 894-C5
SHALEN CT
5000 SJS 95130 852-J6
SHAMROCK AV
1700 SCL 95051 833-B3
SHAMROCK DR
300 SCIC 95008 873-E1
2200 SJS 95008 873-E1
SHANDON CT
4000 SJS 95136 854-E5
SHANDWICK CT
1000 SJS 95136 874-D1
SHANG CT
4000 SJS 95127 834-H1
SHANGHAI CIR
1500 SJS 95131 814-B7
SHANGHAI CT
1200 SJS 95131 814-B7
SHANNON CT
2900 SCL 95051 833-A6
21400 CPTO 95014 852-C2
SHANNON RD
14000 LGTS 95032 893-G1
14000 SCIC 95032 893-G1
14900 SCIC 95032 873-C6
14900 LGTS 95032 873-C6
SHANNON HEIGHTS RD
15500 LGTS 95032 873-E7
SHANNON OAKS LN
- LGTS 95032 893-H1
SHANNONS DR
5500 SCIC 95037 935-E2
SHARLENE CT
2100 SCIC 95037 917-D5
SHARMON PALMS LN
700 CMBL 95008 853-C7
800 CMBL 95008 873-C1
SHARON CT
- MLPK 94025 790-D7
100 LGTS 95124 873-E6
100 LGTS 95032 873-E6
800 CMBL 95008 853-C7
800 PA 94303 791-B4
SHARON DR
7000 SJS 95129 852-E4

SHARON LN
5400 SJS 95124 873-G6
SHARON RD
2000 MLPK 94025 790-D7
2000 SMCo 94025 790-D7
SHARON MANOR CT
1400 SJS 95129 852-E4
SHARON OAKS DR
2300 MLPK 94025 790-E7
SHARON PARK DR
100 MLPK 94025 790-C7
SHARP AV
200 CMBL 95008 873-E1
1400 SJS 95008 873-E1
SHARP CT
1300 CMBL 95008 873-E1
SHARY AV
700 MTVW 94041 811-J6
SHASTA AV
1100 SJS 95126 833-H7
1500 SJS 95128 833-H7
1500 SJS 95128 853-G1
SHASTA DR
300 PA 94306 811-E2
3800 SCL 95051 832-H6
SHASTA LN
- MLPK 94025 790-C7
14900 MGH 95037 937-B4
SHASTA ST
- LALT 94022 811-D6
SHASTA FIR DR
700 SUNV 94086 832-G2
SHASTA FIR WY
- SUNV 94086 832-G2
SHASTA SPRING CT
11800 CPTO 95014 852-A5
SHATO PL
100 FRMT 94539 793-H1
SHATTUCK DR
21800 CPTO 95014 852-B2
SHAUNA LN
900 PA 94306 811-B3
SHAW DR
1500 SJS 95118 874-A1
SHAWCROFT DR
5900 SJS 95123 874-J6
SHAWN DR
1300 SJS 95118 874-B3
SHAWNEE LN
400 SJS 95123 874-H5
SHAWNEE PASS
100 PTLV 94028 810-B6
SHAWNEE PL
300 FRMT 94539 793-J1
SHAWNEE WY
300 FRMT 94539 793-J1
SHAYNOR CT
3700 SJS 95130 853-C4
SHEA CT
7200 SJS 95139 895-F1
SHEAN CT
11400 SCIC 95020 957-G2
SHEAR CREEK RD
21000 SCrC 95033 892-A3
SHEARER DR
- ATN 94027 790-C1
SHEARTON DR
600 SJS 95117 853-C2
SHEARWATER DR
6800 SJS 95120 894-H2
SHEEHAN CT
7100 SJS 95120 894-G3
SHEFFIELD AV
1300 CMBL 95008 853-G5
1500 CMBL 95125 853-G5
SHEFFIELD CT
- MTVW 94040 811-F3
300 CMBL 95125 853-H5
SHEFFIELD DR
- SJS 95131 814-A5
SHEFFIELD LN
200 RDWC 94061 790-B2
SHEFFIELD RIDGE CT
2100 SJS 95138 855-F5
SHEILA AV
13800 SCIC 95037 956-G1
13900 SCIC 95037 936-G7
SHEILA CT
- MTVW 94043 811-G2
800 CMBL 95008 873-C1
SHELBURNE WY
17400 LGTS 95030 873-A5
17400 LGTS 95032 873-A5
SHELBY DR
- MTVW 94043 812-B5
SHELBY LN
500 LALT 94024 811-E7
SHELBY CREEK CT
1300 SJS 95120 894-F4
SHELBY CREEK LN
1200 SJS 95120 894-G4
SHELDON AV
4100 SCIC 95020 998-E2
SHELDON RD
16700 SCIC 95030 872-H7
16700 SCIC 95033 872-H7
SHELLBACK PL
2000 SJS 95133 814-E7
2000 SJS 95133 834-E1
SHELLBARK DR
- SJS 95136 874-H1
SHELLEY AV
100 CMBL 95008 873-E2
200 SJS 95008 873-E2
700 SJS 95124 873-E2
SHELLEY CT
500 MPS 95035 794-B6
SHELLY CT
6100 SJS 95123 874-G6
SHELLY DR
20600 CPTO 95014 852-D1
SHELTON DR
- HOLL 95023 1020-B6

SHELTON WY
1000 SJS 95125 853-J3
SHENADO PL
- SJS 95123 875-B3
- SJS 95136 875-B3
SHENANDOAH AV
1500 MPS 95035 794-D7
SHENANDOAH DR
800 SUNV 94087 832-C3
1000 SJS 95125 854-D3
SHEPHERD AV
400 SJS 95125 854-B2
SHERATON DR
600 SUNV 94087 832-C3
2100 SCL 95050 833-C3
SHERBOURNE DR
4300 SJS 95124 874-A3
SHERBROOKE WY
2900 SJS 95127 835-A4
SHEREE CT
12600 SCIC 95127 814-J5
SHEREEN PL
- CMBL 95008 853-C6
SHERI ANN CIR
1800 SJS 95131 814-B6
SHERIDAN AV
100 PA 94306 791-B7
SHERIDAN CIR
12300 SAR 95070 852-E6
SHERIDAN PL
400 SJS 95111 854-G4
SHERIDAN ST
- LALT 94022 831-D1
SHERLAND AV
- MTVW 94043 812-A4
SHERLAND CT
200 MTVW 94043 812-B4
SHERLOCK CT
27300 LAH 94022 830-H2
SHERLOCK DR
2400 SJS 95121 854-H3
SHERLOCK RD
27300 LAH 94022 830-H2
SHERMAN AV
100 PA 94306 791-B7
800 MLPK 94025 790-D6
1100 SMCo 94025 790-D6
SHERMAN CT
- SJS 95193 875-C4
900 MPS 95035 794-B4
SHERMAN ST
400 LALT 94022 811-D7
900 SCL 95050 833-F4
900 SJS 95110 854-C1
SHERMAN OAKS DR
700 SJS 95128 853-G3
SHERRY CT
200 SJS 95119 875-E7
SHERRY LN
1100 SCIC 95046 937-H7
SHERRYS WY
19400 SCIC 95033 892-F3
SHERWIN AV
2100 SCL 95050 833-C5
SHERWOOD AV
1000 SJS 95126 833-G5
1200 SCL 95050 833-G5
1200 SCL 95126 833-G5
SHERWOOD CT
1100 SUNV 94087 832-B3
SHERWOOD DR
300 GIL 95020 977-H1
900 HOLL 95023 1040-A5
900 SUNV 94087 832-B3
SHERWOOD LN
800 LALT 94022 811-E4
SHERWOOD WY
300 MLPK 94025 790-G4
SHETLAND CT
500 MPS 95035 794-B6
700 SJS 95127 814-H6
SHETLAND PL
800 SUNV 94087 832-F6
SHIANGZONE CT
- SJS 95121 855-C4
SHIBLEY AV
2200 SJS 95125 854-A6
SHILLING CT
1800 SJS 95132 814-J2
SHILLINGSBURG AV
21400 SCIC 95120 895-C5
SHILOH AV
2000 MPS 95035 794-E7
SHILOH PL
- SJS 95138 855-D5
SHILSHONE CIR
2400 SJS 95121 854-H3
SHILSHONE WY
2500 SJS 95121 854-H3
SHIMMER CT
- MPS 95035 793-H6
SHINGLE VALLEY RD
- SCIC 95037 876-F7
- SCIC 95037 896-G1
- SCIC 95137 876-F7
- SCIC 95137 896-G1
- SCIC 95138 876-F7
SHIRAZ PL
- SJS 95135 855-H2
SHIRE CT
100 LGTS 95032 873-A3
SHIRECREST CT
600 SJS 95123 874-G4
SHIRLEY AV
800 SUNV 94086 812-D6
1600 SCIC 94024 831-F4
SHIRLEY DR
1100 MPS 95035 794-C7
SHIRLEY WY
400 MLPK 94025 790-J2
SHIRLYNN CT
500 LALT 94022 811-E7
500 LALT 94022 831-E1

SHOFNER PL
3100 SJS 95111 854-F6
SHOLES CT
14200 LAH 94022 811-B6
SHONA CT
4000 SJS 95124 873-J2
4000 SJS 95124 874-A2
SHOOTING STAR CT
- GIL 95020 977-E1
SHOOTING STAR TER
800 SUNV 94086 832-F3
SHOPPE LN
- MLPK 94025 790-J2
SHORE RD
200 SBnC 95023 999-C6
2600 SBnC 95020 999-C6
SHOREBIRD WY
1300 MTVW 94043 811-J1
1300 MTVW 94043 812-A1
SHOREBREEZE CT
- EPA 94303 791-C2
SHOREHAM CT
10200 SCIC 95127 834-J3
SHORELAND DR
1200 SJS 95122 854-H1
N SHORELINE BLVD
200 MTVW 94043 811-J1
1900 MTVW 94043 791-J7
S SHORELINE BLVD
300 MTVW 94043 811-H5
300 MTVW 94041 811-H5
SHORELINE CT
- FRMT 94538 793-G2
SHORESIDE CT
2300 SCL 95054 813-C5
SHOREVIEW CT
1300 SJS 95122 854-H1
SHOREWOOD LN
400 SJS 95134 813-C2
SHORT AL
- HOLL 95023 1039-J3
SHORT RD
- SBnC 95045 1018-A7
15900 LGTS 95032 873-D6
SHORT HILL CT
14000 SAR 95070 872-G2
SHORTRIDGE AV
- SJS 95116 834-F4
SHOSHANA LN
- SJS 95135 855-G2
SHOSHONE CIR
1300 HOLL 95023 1040-D5
SHOSHONE CT
200 SJS 95127 834-H1
SHOSHONE DR
200 SJS 95127 834-H1
SHOSHONE PL
- PTLV 94028 810-B6
SHOWERS CT
- MTVW 94040 811-E3
SHOWERS DR
- MTVW 94040 811-E4
SHREEN CT
1600 SJS 95124 874-A2
SHRIVER CT
1200 SJS 95132 814-G5
SHRIVER DR
3100 SJS 95132 814-G5
SHUBERT CT
19300 SAR 95070 852-G6
SHUBERT DR
19200 SAR 95070 852-G6
SHULMAN AV
1000 SCL 95050 833-E2
1800 SJS 95124 853-G7
SHUMAKER WY
1500 SJS 95131 814-D6
SIBELIUS AV
2600 SJS 95122 855-A1
W SIDE AV
2900 SMCo 94063 790-D1
SIDLAW CT
4600 SJS 95136 874-F2
SIEBER CT
400 SJS 95111 854-F6
SIEBER PL
500 SJS 95111 854-F6
SIEBER WY
3200 SJS 95111 854-F6
SIENA CT
- SJS 95135 855-G1
SIENA DR
- GIL 95020 977-G1
SIENE TER
- SJS 95133 834-D2
SIENNA DR
10300 SJS 95127 835-A4
SIERRA AV
400 MTVW 94041 811-H6
1100 SJS 95126 833-H7
1500 SJS 95126 853-H1
SIERRA CT
100 MGH 95037 916-H5
1200 SJS 95132 814-E5
2300 PA 94303 791-D4
SIERRA DR
1000 MLPK 94025 790-C6
SIERRA LN
- PTLV 94028 810-C5
SIERRA RD
1100 SJS 95131 834-C1
1300 SJS 95131 814-D6
2400 SJS 95132 814-G4
3400 SCIC 95132 814-J3
3500 SCIC 95132 815-A3
3500 SJS 95132 815-A3
5300 SCIC 95140 815-E3
SIERRA ST
1200 RDWC 94061 790-A1
SIERRA AZULE
300 LGTS 95032 873-G7
SIERRA CREEK WY
1400 SJS 95132 814-F3

SIERRA GRANDE CT
- SJS 95116 834-H3
SIERRA GRANDE WY
2500 SJS 95116 834-H3
SIERRA LINDA
100 LGTS 95032 872-J2
SIERRA MADRES TER
- SJS 95126 833-D1
SIERRA MAR DR
1200 SJS 95118 854-C7
1200 SJS 95118 874-B1
SIERRA MEADOW CT
2500 SJS 95116 834-H3
SIERRA MEADOW DR
100 SJS 95116 834-H3
SIERRA MESA DR
100 SJS 95116 834-H3
SIERRA MONTE WY
2500 SJS 95116 834-H3
SIERRA MORENA
100 LGTS 95032 873-E5
SIERRA MORENA CT
15400 MGH 95037 937-A4
SIERRA SERENA
2500 SJS 95116 834-H3
SIERRA SPRING CT
11700 CPTO 95014 852-A5
SIERRA SPRING LN
- CPTO 95014 852-A5
SIERRA VENTURA DR
2100 LALT 94024 831-H5
SIERRA VILLAGE CT
1100 SJS 95132 814-H3
SIERRA VILLAGE PL
1200 SJS 95132 814-H3
SIERRA VILLAGE WY
1200 SJS 95132 814-H3
SIERRAVILLE AV
1400 SJS 95132 814-F4
SIERRA VISTA AV
- MTVW 94043 811-H1
SIERRA VISTA CT
2500 SJS 95116 834-H3
SIERRA VISTA PL
- SJS 95116 834-H3
SIERRA WOOD DR
2000 SJS 95132 814-D3
SIESTA CT
- SMCo 94028 810-D4
SIESTA DR
1500 LALT 94024 831-J3
SIESTA VISTA DR
15800 SCIC 95127 815-C7
SIETA CT
1400 SJS 95118 874-B1
SIGAL DR
20600 SAR 95070 872-D4
SIGRID WY
5300 SJS 95136 874-J3
5300 SJS 95123 874-J3
SILACCI DR
800 CMBL 95008 853-A7
1400 CMBL 95008 873-A1
SILACCI WY
6600 GIL 95020 978-C4
SILBERMAN DR
6100 SJS 95120 874-C7
SILBURY CT
3100 SJS 95148 855-E2
SILCREEK DR
- SJS 95116 834-F3
SILENCE DR
- SJS 95148 835-D4
SILENT HILLS LN
27300 LAH 94022 831-A2
SILER LN
- SJS 95116 834-F5
SILICON DR
900 SJS 95126 833-H5
SILICON VALLEY BLVD
300 SJS 95138 875-F5
SILK CT
3600 SJS 95111 854-G6
SILK OAK WY
700 SUNV 94086 832-G2
SILK WOOD LN
- SJS 95131 814-A6
SILVA AV
300 MTVW 94040 811-E3
4300 SJS 95118 874-B2
4300 PA 94306 811-E3
SILVA CIR
10200 SCIC 95020 958-B4
SILVA CT
4300 PA 94306 811-E3
SILVA PL
- SCL 95054 813-D5
SILVER AV
1600 RDWC 94061 790-A1
SILVERA LN
- SJS 95136 874-D2
SILVERA ST
100 MPS 95035 793-J7
SILVER ACRES CT
5100 SJS 95138 855-F7
SILVERADO AV
20300 CPTO 95014 852-E2
SILVERADO DR
1200 SJS 95120 894-D2
SILVER BELL DR
6900 SJS 95120 894-G6
SILVERBERRY DR
4300 SJS 95136 874-H1
SILVER BLOSSOM CT
2200 SJS 95138 855-E7
SILVER BLUFF WY
2200 SJS 95138 855-G7
SILVER BREEZE CT
2200 SJS 95138 855-G7
SILVER BROOK CT
7000 SJS 95120 894-G5
SILVER CANYON DR
1100 SJS 95120 894-G6

SILVER CLIFF DR
6900 SJS 95120 894-G5
SILVER CLOUD CT
500 MGH 95037 937-C5
SILVER CREEK CT
1700 SJS 95121 855-C4
SILVER CREEK RD
2700 SJS 95121 855-B3
3800 SJS 95138 875-H1
3800 SCIC 95138 875-H1
3900 SJS 95138 855-C4
SILVER CREEK VALLEY RD
400 SJS 95138 875-D3
400 SJS 95111 875-D3
1900 SCIC 95138 875-D3
2400 SJS 95138 855-E6
5000 SJS 95121 855-E6
SILVERCREST DR
1500 SJS 95118 874-A2
SILVERCREST RIDGE CT
- SJS 95135 855-J4
SILVER ESTATES
2800 SJS 95135 855-G5
SILVER FOX DR
6900 SJS 95120 894-G5
SILVER GARDEN WY
5200 SJS 95138 855-E7
SILVERGATE CT
6900 SJS 95120 894-G5
SILVER GLEN CT
1700 SJS 95121 855-C4
SILVER HILL DR
1100 SJS 95120 894-G6
SILVER HOLLOW CT
2100 SJS 95138 855-F7
SILVERIA CT
2300 SCL 95054 813-C4
SILVER KNOLL CT
2200 SJS 95138 855-F7
SILVERLAKE CT
200 MPS 95035 794-A6
SILVERLAKE DR
100 MPS 95035 794-A6
200 SUNV 94089 812-H4
SILVERLAND CT
2900 SJS 95135 855-D3
SILVERLAND DR
2900 SJS 95135 855-E3
SILVER LEAF RD
5600 SJS 95138 875-D4
SILVER LODE LN
7100 SJS 95120 894-H4
SILVER MEADOW CT
1700 SJS 95121 855-B4
SILVER MOON CT
7000 SJS 95120 894-G5
SILVER OAK CT
1100 SJS 95120 874-D7
22600 CPTO 95014 851-J1
SILVER OAK LN
22500 CPTO 95014 831-C7
SILVER OAK WY
22500 CPTO 95014 831-C7
22500 CPTO 95014 832-A7
22600 CPTO 95014 851-J1
SILVER PEAK DR
6900 SJS 95120 894-G5
SILVER PINE CT
700 SUNV 94086 832-G2
SILVER POINT WY
5300 SJS 95138 855-F7
SILVER POND LN
- SJS 95138 855-C6
SILVER RANCH LN
- SJS 95138 855-C6
SILVER RANCH PL
- SJS 95138 855-C6
SILVER RIDGE CT
5200 SJS 95138 855-G6
SILVER RIDGE DR
5100 SJS 95138 855-G6
SILVER SAGE
5500 SJS 95123 875-B4
SILVER SHADOW DR
1100 SJS 95120 894-G5
SILVER SPRING CT
11500 CPTO 95014 852-A4
SILVER SPRINGS WY
- SJS 95123 875-D2
SILVER STAR CT
7000 SJS 95120 894-G5
SILVERSTONE PL
1500 SJS 95122 834-J5
1500 SJS 95122 835-A5
1700 SJS 95148 835-A5
SILVER TERRACE WY
2200 SJS 95138 855-E7
SILVERTIP CT
300 MPS 95035 813-J3
SILVER TIP WY
700 SUNV 94086 832-H2
SILVER TRAIL CT
5200 SJS 95138 855-E7
SILVERTREE DR
1600 SJS 95131 814-C5
SILVER VALE CT
2100 SJS 95138 855-F7
SILVER VIEW CT
- SJS 95138 855-E6
SILVER VISTA WY
5300 SJS 95138 855-G7
SILVERWINGS CT
1800 MGH 95037 917-B2
SILVERWOOD AV
1900 MTVW 94043 811-G4
SILVERWOOD DR
1700 SJS 95124 873-J2
SILVERWOOD CREEK CT
- SJS 95135 855-J4
SILVIA CT
200 LALT 94024 811-F7

1108 SILVIA DR SANTA CLARA COUNTY STREET INDEX STACIA ST

STREET Block City ZIP Pg-Grid

SILVIA DR
300 LALT 94024 811-F7
SILVIA ST
8500 GIL 95020 977-G1
SIMAS DR
500 MPS 95035 794-C5
SIMBERLAN DR
3100 SJS 95148 855-E1
SIMKINS CT
2900 PA 94303 791-D5
SIMON AV
2000 SJS 95122 834-J6
SIMON LN
13300 LAH 94022 810-J7
SIMONI DR
15700 SCIC 95127 815-B7
SIMONS WY
- LGTS 95030 873-B7
SIMONSON CT
1200 SJS 95121 854-J2
SIMONSON WY
1200 SJS 95121 854-J2
SIMPSON WY
1800 SJS 95125 854-A5
SINBAD AV
800 SJS 95116 834-J4
SINCLAIR DR
600 SJS 95116 834-G4
SINCLAIR FRWY I-280
- SCIC - 853-G2
- SJS - 834-C7
- SJS - 834-E7
- SJS - 834-F6
- SJS - 853-G2
- SJS - 854-A2
SINCLAIR FRWY I-680
- FRMT - 793-J1
- FRMT - 794-A2
- MPS - 794-A2
- MPS - 814-E6
- SJS - 814-E6
- SJS - 834-F1
SINCLAIR FRONTAGE RD
200 MPS 95035 794-C7
500 MPS 95035 814-C1
SINGING HILL LN
14400 SAR 95070 872-H3
SINGING RAIN PL
2800 SJS 95127 835-A4
SINGLETARY AV
1100 SJS 95126 833-H7
SINGLETON LN
400 SJS 95111 854-J5
SINGLETON RD
600 SJS 95111 854-J5
10100 SCIC 95111 854-H6
SINGLETREE WY
1500 SJS 95124 873-J6
1500 SJS 95124 874-A6
1500 SJS 95118 874-A6
SINGLEY DR
300 MPS 95035 794-A5
SINNOTT LN
100 MPS 95035 814-A1
SIOUX LN
- LALT 94022 811-E6
400 SJS 95123 874-H5
SIOUX TR
20900 SCIC 95033 913-A2
SIOUX WY
- PTLV 94028 810-C6
SIPPOLA WY
1300 SJS 95121 854-J2
SIRICA CT
700 SJS 95138 875-G4
SIRICA WY
700 SJS 95138 875-F4
SIRINA CT
- SJS 95131 814-C5
SIRTE TER
- SUNV 94089 812-G4
SISKIYOU DR
900 MLPK 94025 790-C7
SISKIYOU PL
- MLPK 94025 790-C7
SITKA TER
1000 SUNV 94086 832-H2
SKALL DR
400 SJS 95111 854-J6
SKIP AWAY CT
- MGH 95037 937-B5
SKIPSTONE CT
400 SJS 95136 854-F7
SKOWHEGAN CT
100 SJS 95139 895-G1
SKUSE CT
- SCIC 95120 894-G1
SKY LN
14700 LGTS 95032 873-F7
14700 SCIC 95032 873-F7
SKYFARM CT
6400 SJS 95120 894-B1
SKYFARM DR
6500 SJS 95120 894-C1
SKYLAKE CT
1100 SUNV 94089 812-J4
SKYLARK DR
2400 SJS 95125 854-C6
SKYLINE BLVD
18000 SCIC 95033 912-H4
SKYLINE BLVD Rt#-35
- SCrC 95033 871-D3
11800 SCIC 95030 851-A7
11800 SCIC 95030 871-B1
12300 SCIC 95070 871-F6
13000 SCIC 95070 892-A2
13500 SCIC 95033 892-D6
13500 SCrC 95033 892-A2
18600 SMCo 94020 830-A4
18600 PTLV 94028 830-A4

SKYLINE BLVD Rt#-35
19000 SCIC 95033 912-E1
19000 SCrC 95033 912-E1
19800 SMCo 94028 830-C7
SKYLINE DR
- HOLL 95023 1020-A5
1900 MPS 95035 814-E1
SKYLINE RDG
- SCIC 95070 892-A2
- SCrC 95033 892-A2
SKY MEADOW LN
6400 SJS 95135 855-J7
SKY OAKS WY
19500 SCIC 95030 872-F5
SKYPORT DR
100 SJS 95110 833-H2
SKYVIEW CT
- MTVW 94043 812-B4
23300 SCrC 95033 913-C7
SKYVIEW DR
15200 SCIC 95132 814-H4
15200 SJS 95132 814-H4
SKYVIEW TER
15300 SCIC 95132 814-J4
23400 SCrC 95033 913-C7
SKYWALKER DR
- SJS 95135 876-A1
SKYWARD PL
- SJS 95136 854-E5
SKYWAY DR
200 SJS 95111 875-A1
200 SJS 95111 874-J1
400 SJS 95136 874-H1
SLADKY AV
800 MTVW 94040 811-G7
SLATER CT
3600 SJS 95132 814-F2
SLEEPER AV
100 MTVW 94040 831-J1
700 MTVW 94040 832-A1
SLEEP VALLEY RD
15600 SCIC 95037 936-F5
SLEEPY CREEK DR
7200 SJS 95120 894-J4
SLEEPY CREEK WY
7200 SJS 95120 894-J3
SLEEPY HOLLOW LN
2300 SJS 95116 834-J5
SLEEPY MEADOW CT
1400 SJS 95121 855-D7
SLIDA DR
6300 SJS 95129 852-F4
SLOAT CT
300 SCL 95051 833-A7
SLOPEVIEW DR
3500 SJS 95148 835-E7
3600 SCIC 95148 835-E7
SLOPING MEADOW CT
6500 SJS 95135 855-J7
SMITH AL
1000 HOLL 95023 1040-A4
SMITH AV
900 CMBL 95008 853-B7
1700 SJS 95112 854-E2
SMITH CREEK DR
100 LGTS 95030 873-A3
SMITHERS DR
2700 SJS 95148 855-C1
SMITH RANCH CT
- LGTS 95030 873-C3
SMITHWOOD ST
- MPS 95035 793-J7
SMITTYS ST
23500 SCIC 95033 913-D6
SMOKE RIVER CT
4600 SJS 95136 874-E2
SMOKE TREE CT
100 SJS 95136 874-H1
SMOKE TREE WY
600 SUNV 94086 832-H2
SMOKEY CT
500 CMBL 95008 853-A7
SMYRNA CT
1100 SUNV 94087 832-D3
SNEAD DR
4600 SCL 95054 813-D4
SNECKNER CT
- SMCo 94025 810-F1
SNELL AV
200 SJS 95123 874-J4
3500 SJS 95136 854-G7
3900 SJS 95136 874-H1
4800 SCIC 95136 874-H1
SNELL CT
200 SJS 95123 874-J3
26600 LAH 94022 811-B5
SNELL LN
26600 LAH 94022 811-B6
SNELL PL
- MPS 95035 814-A3
SNELL RD
16200 SCIC 95030 893-B2
16400 LGTS 95030 893-B2
SNELL WY
5600 SJS 95123 874-J5
SNIVELY AV
3300 SCL 95051 832-J4
3300 SCL 95051 833-A4
SNOW DR
4700 SJS 95111 855-B7
4800 SJS 95111 875-B1
SNOW ST
1200 MTVW 94041 811-G5
SNOW TER
700 SJS 95111 855-B7
SNOWBANK CT
4100 SJS 95135 855-F3
SNOWBERRY CT
- GIL 95020 977-J5
1100 SUNV 94087 832-D3
6100 SJS 95123 875-B6
SNOW CREST RD
- SCIC 95030 871-D3

SNOW CREST RD
- SCrC 95033 871-D3
SNOWDEN AV
- ATN 94027 790-D1
SNOWDON PL
5500 SJS 95138 855-H7
5600 SJS 95138 875-H1
SNYDER AV
400 SJS 95125 854-A2
SNYDER LN
400 MTVW 94043 812-B5
SOARES CT
3300 SCL 95051 832-J5
SOBEY RD
14100 SAR 95070 872-H2
SOBEY MEADOWS CT
14000 SAR 95070 872-H2
SOBEY OAKS CT
14500 SAR 95070 872-G3
SOBRANTE WY
200 SUNV 94086 812-D6
SOBRATO CT
600 CMBL 95008 853-C7
SOBRATO DR
300 CMBL 95008 853-C7
600 CMBL 95008 873-C1
SOBRATO LN
600 CMBL 95008 853-C7
SOBRATO WY
600 CMBL 95008 853-C7
SOCORRO AV
1100 SUNV 94089 812-J5
1200 SUNV 94089 813-A5
SODA SPRINGS RD
15300 SCIC 95033 913-F1
15400 SCIC 95033 893-C6
SOELRO CT
4000 SCIC 95127 815-B7
SOGOL CT
1900 SJS 95122 854-G2
SOGOL DR
- SJS 95122 854-G1
SOLA ST
20800 CPTO 95014 852-D1
SOLACE PL
2500 MTVW 94040 831-J1
SOLANA CT
900 MTVW 94040 811-F5
SOLANA DR
100 LALT 94022 811-F6
1000 MTVW 94040 811-F6
4000 PA 94306 811-C2
9200 GIL 95020 957-F7
19600 SAR 95070 852-F6
SOLANA RD
100 PTLV 94028 810-B5
SOLANO CT
- MGH 95037 917-B3
3300 SCL 95051 832-J5
SOLANO DR
6200 SJS 95119 875-C6
SOLAR CT
- MPS 95035 794-D6
SOLEDAD ST
9000 GIL 95020 977-F1
SOLEIL CT
- SJS 95126 833-D1
SOLERA DR
8600 SJS 95135 855-J6
SOLIS DR
1300 GIL 95020 977-F1
SOLIS RANCHO DR
8000 SCIC 95020 976-H2
SOLITA CT
700 LGTS 95030 873-A4
SOLITO CT
700 SJS 95123 874-G5
SOLOMON CT
6200 SJS 95123 875-B7
SOLOMON TER
- SUNV 94089 812-G4
SOLTERO DR
5800 SJS 95123 874-F5
SOMA WY
- SCIC 95020 956-J4
SOMERSET CT
1900 LALT 94024 831-H5
10300 CPTO 95014 852-E1
SOMERSET DR
- CMBL 95008 853-A1
800 SUNV 94087 832-C3
1100 SJS 95132 814-G5
20000 CPTO 95014 852-E1
SOMERSET LN
- ATN 94027 790-D4
SOMERSET PL
- PA 94301 791-A4
SOMERSET PARK CIR
2600 SJS 95132 814-F5
SOMERSWORTH DR
1900 SJS 95124 853-G7
SOMERVILLE CT
19700 SAR 95070 852-F5
SOMERVILLE DR
19500 SAR 95070 852-F5
SOMME AV
600 HOLL 95023 1040-B5
SONADOR COMS
- SJS 95128 853-G4
SONATA WY
4500 SJS 95111 855-A7
SONDGRATH WY
100 MTVW 94040 811-F3
SONDRA WY
100 CMBL 95008 853-C5
SONG CT
1100 SJS 95131 834-D1
SONI CT
600 SJS 95116 834-H4
SONIA WY
600 MTVW 94040 811-H6
SONNET CT
1800 SJS 95131 814-C4

SONNYS WY
- SBnC 95023 1060-F3
SONOMA AV
- ATN 94027 790-H1
1000 MLPK 94025 790-H1
SONOMA CT
1600 HOLL 95023 1040-D6
SONOMA DR
1500 MPS 95035 814-D1
SONOMA PL
2600 SCL 95051 833-B5
SONOMA ST
100 SJS 95110 834-A7
SONOMA TER
800 SCIC 94305 810-J1
SONORA AV
- SJS 95110 833-H3
SONORA CT
1100 SUNV 94086 832-H1
SONUCA AV
900 CMBL 95008 873-C1
SOPHIA WY
4100 SJS 95134 813-D2
SOPHIST DR
3800 SJS 95132 814-J4
3800 SJS 95132 815-A4
SOQUEL WY
300 SUNV 94086 812-E6
SORCI DR
3600 SJS 95124 873-J2
3600 SJS 95124 874-A2
SORENSON AV
19300 CPTO 95014 852-G1
SORGEPARK PL
200 SJS 95127 834-H1
SORICH RD
- SCIC 95030 851-A7
- SCrC 95033 851-A7
SORREL AV
5900 SJS 95123 874-J5
SORREL DR
16300 MGH 95037 917-F6
SORREL WY
16600 MGH 95037 917-E6
SORRENTO CT
- GIL 95020 977-G1
1900 MTVW 94040 831-H1
SORRENTO DR
- GIL 95020 977-G1
SORRENTO WY
200 SJS 95119 875-C6
SOTERION DR
1600 SJS 95118 873-J5
SOTO CT
1300 SJS 95121 854-J2
SOUSA LN
18600 SAR 95070 872-J1
SOUTH CT
2200 PA 94301 791-C7
2500 PA 94306 791-C7
3100 PA 94306 811-D1
SOUTH DR
100 MTVW 94040 831-H1
2300 SCL 95051 833-C2
SOUTH PZ
- MLPK 94025 790-J2
SOUTH ST
- SCIC 95046 937-F7
- HOLL 95023 1040-A4
300 HOLL 95023 1039-H4
SOUTHAMPTON CT
3600 SJS 95148 835-G7
SOUTHAMPTON DR
700 PA 94303 791-C5
SOUTHBAY DR
300 SJS 95134 813-D2
SOUTHBAY FRWY Rt#-237
- MPS - 813-C1
- SCL - 813-C1
- SJS - 813-C1
- SUNV - 812-D4
- SUNV - 812-F3
- SUNV - 813-C1
SOUTH BREEZE CT
5900 SJS 95138 875-E5
SOUTHBRIDGE CT
5300 SJS 95118 874-C4
SOUTHBRIDGE PL
5200 SJS 95118 874-C4
SOUTHBROOK CT
5900 SJS 95138 875-E5
SOUTHBROOK DR
- SJS 95138 875-E5
SOUTHCREEK CT
- SJS 95138 875-E5
SOUTHCREST WY
5500 SCIC 95123 874-G4
5500 SJS 95123 874-G4
SOUTHERLAND CT
- GIL 95020 977-H6
SOUTHFIELD CT
- SJS 95138 875-E5
SOUTH FORK LN
13400 LAH 94022 810-J7
SOUTH GARDEN CT
5900 SJS 95138 875-F5
SOUTHGATE CT
- SJS 95138 875-E5
100 GIL 95020 978-A4
SOUTHGATE DR
- WDSD 94062 790-A5
SOUTHGATE ST
- ATN 94027 790-D2
SOUTHGROVE DR
700 SJS 95133 834-F1
800 SJS 95133 814-H3
SOUTHGROVE LN
2300 SJS 95133 814-H3
SOUTHLAKE CT
- SJS 95138 875-E5
SOUTHLAKE DR
- SJS 95138 875-E5

SOUTHMAR CT
- SJS 95138 875-E5
SOUTHMONT CT
5900 SJS 95138 875-E5
SOUTHOAKS CT
5900 SJS 95138 875-E5
SOUTH PARK DR
500 SJS 95129 852-J2
SOUTH PARK LN
2400 SCL 95051 833-B2
SOUTHPINE CT
- SJS 95138 875-E5
SOUTHPINE DR
5700 SJS 95138 875-E5
SOUTHPORT CT
- SJS 95138 875-E5
SOUTHRIDGE CT
5900 SJS 95138 875-E5
SOUTH RIDGE DR
1900 HOLL 95023 1040-B6
SOUTHSEA CT
- SJS 95138 875-E5
SOUTHSHORE CT
11600 CPTO 95014 852-C4
SOUTHSIDE DR
- SCIC 95111 854-H5
- SJS 95111 854-H5
500 GIL 95020 978-C6
500 SCIC 95020 978-D6
SOUTHSIDE RD
2200 HOLL 95023 1040-B7
2200 SBnC 95023 1040-B7
2200 SBnC 95023 1060-B1
7400 SBnC 95075 1060-H5
8200 SBnC 95075 1061-A5
SOUTHSUN CT
100 SJS 95138 875-E4
SOUTH SURF CT
5900 SJS 95138 875-E5
SOUTH TERRACE CT
- SJS 95138 875-E5
SOUTH VALLEY FRWY U.S.-101
- GIL - 957-G1
- GIL - 958-A6
- GIL - 978-A1
- MGH - 916-H1
- MGH - 917-A4
- MGH - 937-D1
- SCIC - 875-G6
- SCIC - 895-J1
- SCIC - 896-B3
- SCIC - 916-H1
- SCIC - 917-A4
- SCIC - 937-D1
- SCIC - 937-F4
- SCIC - 957-G1
- SCIC - 978-B5
- SJS - 875-G6
- SJS - 896-B3
- SJS - 916-H1
SOUTHVIEW CT
5900 SJS 95138 875-E4
SOUTHVIEW DR
5700 SJS 95138 875-E5
SOUTHWEST EXWY
1800 SJS 95128 853-G4
1800 SJS 95126 853-G4
SOUTHWICK CT
5100 SJS 95136 874-F3
SOUTHWIND DR
5900 SJS 95138 875-E5
SOUTHWOOD AV
400 SUNV 94086 832-E1
SOUTHWOOD CT
- SJS 95129 853-A4
SOUTHWOOD DR
100 PA 94301 791-B3
1400 SJS 95070 853-A4
1400 SJS 95130 853-A4
1400 SJS 95130 852-J5
11500 SJS 95129 853-A4
SOUTIRAGE LN
- SJS 95135 855-G2
SPACE PARK DR
1400 SCL 95054 813-D7
SPACE PARK WY
1000 MTVW 94043 811-J1
1000 MTVW 94043 812-A1
SPADAFORE AV
900 SJS 95125 854-D3
SPADAFORE CT
900 SJS 95125 854-C6
SPAGNOLI CT
300 LALT 94022 811-D5
SPAICH CT
- SAR 95070 872-E2
SPAICH DR
1100 SJS 95117 853-C4
SPALDING AV
- SUNV 94087 832-E3
23900 SCIC 94024 831-E3
SPANISH CT
- SJS 95121 855-C3
SPANISH BAY CT
1900 SJS 95138 855-F7
SPANISHGATE CT
2100 SJS 95132 814-D3
SPANISH OAK CIR
- GIL 95020 977-G2
SPANISH OAK CT
10000 CPTO 95014 831-C7
SPAR AV
300 SCIC 95117 853-D1
300 SJS 95117 853-D1
SPARGUR DR
500 LALT 94022 811-F6
SPARHAWK DR
600 MGH 95037 916-H6
SPARHAWK WY
18200 MGH 95037 916-H6
SPARKLING WY
1600 SJS 95125 853-J5

SPARLING AL
600 HOLL 95023 1039-J4
SPARROW CT
- EPA 94303 791-C2
1600 SUNV 94087 832-H5
SPARROW GLEN CT
- GIL 95020 957-E6
SPARROW GLEN WY
- GIL 95020 957-E6
SPARTAN CT
500 SJS 95112 854-E1
SPEAK LN
4800 SJS 95118 874-C2
SPECIALE WY
1100 SJS 95125 854-C7
SPENCE AV
100 MPS 95035 793-J7
SPENCER AV
700 SJS 95125 854-B1
16800 LGTS 95032 873-C7
SPENCER CT
700 LALT 94024 831-G1
700 MTVW 94040 831-G1
9000 GIL 95020 977-H1
SPENCER LN
- ATN 94027 790-E3
SPENCER WY
900 LALT 94024 831-G2
SPENO DR
3400 SJS 95117 853-C4
SPERRY LN
15000 SAR 95070 872-H4
SPICE LN
- GIL 95020 978-B6
SPICEWOOD CT
700 SJS 95120 894-H3
SPINDRIFT AV
800 SJS 95134 813-F2
SPINDRIFT DR
700 SJS 95134 813-F2
SPINDRIFT LN
800 SJS 95134 813-F2
SPINDRIFT PL
700 SJS 95134 813-F2
SPINDRIFT ST
700 SJS 95134 813-F2
SPINDRIFT WY
800 SJS 95134 813-F2
SPINNAKER DR
- FRMT 94538 793-F1
5500 SJS 95123 874-J4
SPINNAKER WALKWAY
5400 SJS 95123 874-J4
SPINOSA DR
800 SUNV 94087 832-D3
SPIRO DR
1100 SJS 95116 834-F6
SPIROS WY
- SMCo 94025 790-D5
SPODE WY
300 SJS 95123 875-B6
SPOKANE CT
48400 FRMT 94539 793-J2
SPOKANE DR
1100 SJS 95122 854-H1
SPOKANE PL
48400 FRMT 94539 793-J1
SPOKANE RD
48500 FRMT 94539 793-J2
SPONSON CT
6300 SJS 95123 875-B7
SPONSON LN
6200 SJS 95123 875-B7
SPOONBILL WY
1300 SUNV 94087 832-H4
SPOONWOOD CT
4200 SJS 95136 874-H1
SPOSITO CIR
100 SJS 95136 874-G1
SPRAWLING OAKS CT
20500 SCIC 95120 895-A5
SPRECKELS AV
100 LGTS 95030 893-B1
SPRECKLES AV
1200 SJS 95002 793-C6
SPRIERING DR
1500 CMBL 95008 873-E2
SPRIG CT
1300 SUNV 94087 832-H4
SPRIG WY
- GIL 95020 957-F7
SPRING AV
- SCIC 95046 937-F6
100 MGH 95037 937-A1
100 MGH 95037 936-J2
100 SCIC 95037 936-J2
SPRING DR
100 SJS 95138 875-C4
500 HOLL 95023 1039-H4
SPRING LN
- MGH 95037 937-C5
SPRING ST
- LGTS 95030 893-B1
400 SJS 95110 834-A5
700 SJS 95110 833-J4
1600 MTVW 94043 811-H2
SPRING TR
200 SCIC 95033 912-J4
SPRING BLOSSOM CT
20500 SAR 95070 852-D6
SPRINGBROOK AV
2900 SJS 95148 835-F7
3700 SCIC 95148 835-F7
SPRINGBROOK CT
2900 SJS 95148 835-F7
SPRINGBROOK LN
19000 SAR 95070 872-H3
SPRING CREEK LN
3400 SCIC 95035 794-G5
SPRINGDALE CT
8100 GIL 95020 978-A1
SPRINGDALE DR
4800 SJS 95129 852-J2

SPRINGER AV
14200 SAR 95070 872-D2
SPRINGER CT
14600 SAR 95070 872-D3
SPRINGER RD
100 LALT 94024 811-G7
N SPRINGER RD
- LALT 94024 811-G6
100 MTVW 94040 811-G6
S SPRINGER RD
- MTVW 94040 811-G7
- LALT 94024 811-G7
600 LALT 94024 831-G1
600 MTVW 94040 831-G1
SPRINGER TER
500 LALT 94024 811-F7
SPRINGER WY
6000 SJS 95123 875-B6
SPRINGFIELD DR
700 CMBL 95008 853-B5
3900 SJS 95130 853-B5
SPRINGFIELD TER
800 SUNV 94087 832-C3
SPRINGFIELD WY
3100 SJS 95111 854-H5
SPRING GARDEN DR
2900 SJS 95127 834-H1
SPRING GROVE DR
900 SJS 95126 853-J3
SPRING GROVE RD
300 SBnC 95023 1020-E2
SPRINGHAVEN CT
- SJS 95111 875-A1
SPRING HILL CT
16700 MGH 95037 936-J1
SPRINGHILL CT
13600 SAR 95070 872-H1
SPRING HILL DR
300 MGH 95037 936-J2
SPRINGHILL DR
25800 LAH 94022 811-C5
SPRING HILL WY
900 SJS 95120 894-F4
SPRINGHILL WY
- MGH 95037 916-H3
SPRINGKNOLL CT
3000 SCIC 95127 835-G3
SPRING MEADOW CT
6400 SJS 95135 855-J7
SPRINGPARK CIR
300 SJS 95136 874-G1
SPRINGPATH LN
6500 SJS 95120 894-B1
SPRINGSONG DR
1700 SJS 95131 834-D1
1700 SJS 95131 814-D7
SPRING VALLEY AV
13500 SCIC 95037 936-J7
13500 SCIC 95037 956-J1
SPRING VALLEY LN
200 MPS 95035 794-D5
SPRINGVIEW LN
3100 SCIC 95127 835-G3
SPRINGWOOD DR
600 SJS 95129 852-J2
SPROUL CT
6400 SJS 95120 894-E1
SPRUANCE CT
1400 SJS 95128 853-F4
SPRUANCE ST
1100 SJS 95128 853-F3
SPRUCE
900 SJS 95138 875-F6
SPRUCE AV
- ATN 94025 790-E2
- MLPK 94025 790-E2
SPRUCE CT
1300 GIL 95020 977-G3
SPRUCE DR
- HOLL 95023 1040-E5
600 SUNV 94086 832-H2
SPRUCEGATE CT
3200 SJS 95148 855-E1
SPRUCE HILL CT
100 LGTS 95032 873-C3
SPRUCEMONT PL
100 SJS 95139 895-F1
SPRUCE ROCK ST
3400 SJS 95121 855-D3
SPRUCEWOOD DR
1300 SJS 95118 874-B4
SPUR CT
2400 MGH 95037 917-F6
SPURLING CT
- SJS 95127 835-C3
SPYGLASS HILL RD
100 SJS 95127 815-B6
SQUAREHAVEN CT
- SJS 95111 874-J1
SQUERI DR
3400 SJS 95127 835-C3
SQUIRE CT
100 HOLL 95023 1040-A5
SQUIRECREEK CIR
3500 SJS 95121 855-D7
SQUIRECREEK LN
1500 SJS 95121 855-D7
SQUIREDELL DR
6100 SJS 95129 852-F4
SQUIREHILL CT
7700 CPTO 95014 852-C3
SQUIREWOOD WY
7500 CPTO 95014 852-D3
SQUIRREL HOLLOW LN
14100 SAR 95070 872-E2
STAATS WY
2000 SCL 95050 833-C3
STACEY CT
3400 MTVW 94040 831-J2
STACIA DR
2700 SJS 95124 873-J1
STACIA ST
- LGTS 95030 893-B1

SANTA CLARA CO.
© 2008 Rand McNally & Company

STREET Block City ZIP Pg-Grid

STACIA ST
- LGTS 95030 873-B7
STAFFORD DR
1100 CPTO 95014 852-C3
STAFFORD ST
1900 SCL 95050 833-D4
STAGECOACH RD
21900 SCrC 95033 912-J4
STAGEHAND DR
200 SJS 95111 875-B2
STAGHORN CT
1600 SJS 95121 855-A3
STAGHORN LN
1500 SJS 95121 855-A3
STAGI CT
900 LALT 94024 831-E1
STAGI LN
800 LALT 94024 831-E1
STAGIA LN
23200 SCIC 95033 913-C6
STAHL ST
1300 SJS 95122 834-H5
STALLION WY
2800 SJS 95121 855-A3
STAMM AV
600 MTVW 94040 811-H6
STANDER DR
3200 SJS 95148 855-F1
STANDING OAK CT
22900 CPTO 95014 851-J1
STANDISH DR
14500 SCIC 95124 873-G3
STANDRIDGE CT
6400 SJS 95123 875-B7
STANFIELD DR
600 CMBL 95008 853-F7
600 SJS 95008 853-F7
STANFORD AV
- SCIC 94304 810-J2
100 SMCo 94025 790-E6
200 PA 94306 791-A7
300 MLPK 94025 790-E6
500 SCIC 94305 791-A7
1000 PA 94306 811-F3
1000 SCIC 94305 811-F3
1100 PA 94306 810-J2
1100 SCIC 94305 810-J2
2100 MTVW 94040 811-F3
STANFORD CT
900 MLPK 94025 790-E5
14100 LAH 94022 810-H5
STANFORD PL
2300 SCL 95051 832-J2
2300 SCL 95051 833-A2
7400 CPTO 95014 852-D3
STANHOPE CT
1500 SJS 95121 855-A3
STANHOPE DR
2800 SJS 95121 855-A3
STANISLAUS CT
2300 SJS 95133 834-F1
STANISLAUS DR
700 SJS 95133 834-F1
STANLEY AV
900 LALT 94024 831-G2
1900 SCL 95050 833-D6
STANLEY CT
6000 SJS 95123 875-B6
STANLEY WY
900 PA 94303 791-B4
STANLEY RANCH
- SBnC - 1039-C7
STANTON WY
1300 SJS 95131 814-C7
1300 SJS 95131 834-C1
STANWICH RD
1600 SJS 95131 814-D5
STANWIRTH CT
1200 LALT 94024 831-J3
STANWOOD DR
1300 SJS 95118 874-B4
STAPLES AV
100 SCIC 95127 834-J1
300 SCIC 95127 814-J7
STAPLETON CT
1500 SJS 95118 874-A5
STARBIRD CIR
1100 SJS 95117 853-C3
STARBRIGHT DR
2200 SJS 95124 873-E2
STARBURST CT
- SJS 95127 834-H1
STARBUSH DR
600 SUNV 94086 832-H2
STAR BUSH LN
1300 SJS 95118 874-B5
STARCREST DR
5400 SJS 95123 874-F3
STARDUST CT
1400 SCL 95050 833-D3
STARDUST LN
600 LALT 94024 811-F7
700 SJS 95123 874-F4
STARDUST WY
1100 MPS 95035 813-J2
STARFISH CT
2000 SJS 95148 835-B5
STARFLOWER CT
900 SUNV 94086 832-G3
STARGLO PL
1100 SJS 95131 814-B6
STAR JASMINE CT
1500 SJS 95131 814-C5
STARK WY
1400 SJS 95118 874-B2
STARLIGHT CT
700 SJS 95117 853-D2
STARLING DR
6100 GIL 95020 977-J6
22300 CPTO 95014 832-A6
22300 SCIC 94024 832-A6
22400 CPTO 94024 832-A6
STARLING RIDGE CT
1100 SJS 95120 894-F3

STREET Block City ZIP Pg-Grid

STARLING VALLEY DR
7000 SJS 95120 894-E3
STARLING VIEW DR
1100 SJS 95120 894-E3
STARLITE CT
- MTVW 94043 811-J3
400 MPS 95035 813-J3
48000 FRMT 94539 793-J1
STARLITE DR
1000 MPS 95035 813-J3
1500 MPS 95035 814-A3
STARLITE LN
800 LALT 94024 831-E1
STARLITE WY
100 FRMT 94539 793-J1
STARR CT
600 SCL 95051 833-B6
STARR LN
2100 SCIC 95020 978-F5
STARR WY
- MTVW 94040 811-H7
STARRETT CT
18600 CPTO 95014 852-H2
STAR RIDGE CT
12600 SAR 95070 852-C6
STARR KING CIR
3700 PA 94306 811-D1
STARS & STRIPES DR
5100 SCL 95054 813-B3
STARSWEPT LN
14800 MGH 95046 937-D4
14800 SCIC 95037 937-D4
14800 SCIC 95046 937-D4
STARVIEW DR
3700 SJS 95124 873-E3
STARWOOD CT
1100 SJS 95120 874-C6
STARWOOD DR
5900 SJS 95120 874-C6
STARWOOD PL
1100 SJS 95120 874-C6
STATE ST
- LALT 94022 811-D7
700 SJS 95110 854-C1
1200 SJS 95002 793-B7
STAUFFER BLVD
100 SJS 95125 854-D3
STAUFFER LN
11200 CPTO 95014 852-C4
STAUNTON CT
2100 PA 94306 791-A7
STAYNER RD
1200 SJS 95121 855-B5
STEBBINS AV
2100 SCL 95051 833-B2
STEEPLECHASE LN
1100 CPTO 95014 852-D3
STEFFS CT
12100 SCIC 95046 937-J7
12100 SCIC 95046 957-J1
STEINBAUGH CT
3800 SJS 95132 814-J4
STEINBECK DR
- HOLL 95023 1039-H4
- SBnC 95023 1039-H4
800 SJS 95123 874-E4
STEINHART CT
2800 SCL 95051 833-B6
STEINWAY AV
800 CMBL 95008 873-B1
STEITZ CT
900 SJS 95116 834-H5
STELLA CT
800 SUNV 94087 832-D2
6000 SJS 95123 875-A6
STELLA RD
- CPTO 95014 851-J2
STELLAR WY
1200 MPS 95035 814-A2
STELLING CT
3000 PA 94303 791-D6
STELLING DR
3000 PA 94303 791-D6
STELLING RD
800 CPTO 95014 852-D1
10000 CPTO 95014 832-D7
STEMEL CT
600 MPS 95035 794-D5
STEMEL WY
1300 MPS 95035 794-C5
STEMPLE CT
2800 SJS 95121 855-A2
STENDER WY
2100 SCL 95054 833-C1
2200 SCL 95054 813-B7
STENDHAL LN
600 CPTO 95014 852-G2
STEPHANIE CT
1200 HOLL 95023 1039-H4
3200 SJS 95132 814-F3
STEPHEN CT
6700 GIL 95020 977-J5
6700 GIL 95020 978-A5
STEPHEN PL
6700 GIL 95020 978-A5
STEPHEN WY
1300 SJS 95129 852-G4
STEPHENIE LN
15900 LGTS 95032 873-D6
15900 SCIC 95032 873-D6
STEPHENS DR
- SJB 95045 1038-D5
STERLING AV
2000 SMCo 94025 790-D6
STERLING BLVD
10100 CPTO 95014 852-H2
STERLING GATE CT
7000 SJS 95120 894-G4
STERLING GATE DR
1000 SJS 95120 894-G4
STERLING OAK CT
- SAR 95070 872-H2

STREET Block City ZIP Pg-Grid

STERLING OAKS DR
5900 SJS 95120 874-C6
STERN AV
700 PA 94303 791-D6
10000 CPTO 95014 852-H1
10000 SJS 95014 852-H1
STERN LN
- ATN 94027 790-C4
STEUBEN DR
700 SUNV 94087 832-C3
STEVAL PL
3500 SJS 95136 874-D1
STEVENS CIR
800 SCIC 94043 812-A2
STEVENS CT
1300 CMBL 95008 873-C2
3100 SJS 95148 855-E1
12800 SCIC 95046 957-D1
STEVENS LN
2900 SJS 95148 855-D1
STEVENS PL
1600 LALT 94024 832-A5
STEVENS RD
400 SCIC 94043 812-A2
STEVENS WY
800 SCIC 94043 812-A2
STEVENS CANYON RD
10700 CPTO 95014 852-A2
10700 CPTO 95014 851-J3
10800 SCIC 95014 851-H4
15600 SCIC 95030 851-H6
15600 SCIC 95030 871-F1
15600 SCIC 95070 871-F1
17400 SCIC 95014 871-F1
STEVENS CREEK BLVD
2800 SJS 95128 853-B1
2800 SJS 95050 853-B1
3000 SCL 95050 853-B1
3100 SJS 95117 853-B1
3100 SCL 95117 853-B1
3600 SCL 95051 853-B1
3800 SJS 95129 853-B1
4800 SJS 95129 852-E1
4800 SCL 95051 852-E1
5300 SJS 95014 852-E1
5500 SCL 95014 852-E1
18900 CPTO 95014 852-E1
21600 CPTO 95014 832-A7
22500 CPTO 95014 851-J1
22700 SCIC 95014 831-H7
22700 SCIC 95014 851-J1
STEVENS CREEK FRWY Rt#-85
- CPTO - 832-A1
- LALT - 832-A1
- MTVW - 811-J2
- MTVW - 812-A7
- MTVW - 832-A1
- SUNV - 832-A1
STEVENSON LN
- ATN 94027 790-D3
STEVENSON ST
2800 SCL 95051 833-A6
STEVICK DR
300 ATN 94027 790-B5
STEWART AV
- SCIC 95127 834-J2
- SJS 95127 834-J2
STEWART CT
- SUNV 94086 812-H6
13100 SAR 95070 852-D7
STEWART DR
800 SUNV 94086 812-G6
STEWART LN
- SCL 95054 813-E5
STEWART RD
- SCIC 95033 913-B1
STIERLIN CT
2000 MTVW 94043 811-J1
2000 MTVW 94043 812-A1
STIERLIN RD
700 MTVW 94043 811-J4
STILES WY
10500 SCIC 95127 815-B7
STILLWATER LN
200 SJS 95139 895-F1
STIMSON WY
3100 SJS 95135 855-F3
STIRLING DR
600 MPS 95035 794-A3
STIRRUP WY
27600 LAH 94022 810-J5
STOCKBRIDGE AV
- ATN 94027 790-C3
- SMCo 94061 790-C3
2100 WDSD 94062 790-A5
2100 WDSD 94027 790-C3
STOCKBRIDGE DR
1300 SJS 95130 853-B4
STOCK FARM RD
- SCIC 94305 790-F6
STOCKLMEIR CT
22000 CPTO 95014 852-A1
STOCKTON AV
1000 SJS 95110 833-H4
1000 SJS 95126 833-J5
1000 SJS 95126 834-A6
STOCKTON PL
3100 PA 94303 791-E6
STOCKWELL DR
- MTVW 94043 812-B5
STOESSER CT
7100 SJS 95120 894-G4
STOKES AV
10300 CPTO 95014 832-B6
STOKES ST
600 CMBL 95128 853-F4
600 SJS 95128 853-F4
1000 SJS 95126 853-H4
STONE AL
- HOLL 95023 1040-A5
STONE AV
1700 SJS 95125 854-D3

STREET Block City ZIP Pg-Grid

STONE AV
2100 SCIC 95125 854-D3
STONE CT
400 SJS 95125 854-C3
STONE LN
700 PA 94303 791-E7
STONE TR
18200 SCIC 95033 912-J4
STONEBRIDGE
22700 CPTO 95014 831-H7
22800 CPTO 95014 851-J1
STONEBRIDGE CT
- SJS 95125 854-B3
14600 SCIC 95037 937-A6
STONEBRIDGE DR
14600 SCIC 95037 937-A6
STONE BRIDGE TR
- SBnC 95023 1060-D1
STONEBROOK CT
12300 LAH 94022 831-C2
STONEBROOK DR
10900 LAH 94024 831-D3
10900 SCIC 94024 831-D3
12100 LAH 94022 831-D3
STONE CANYON DR
4300 SJS 95136 874-H1
STONE CREEK DR
1400 SJS 95132 814-F3
STONECRESS ST
- GIL 95020 957-D7
- GIL 95020 977-D1
STONECREST WY
2700 SJS 95133 814-G6
STONEFIELD CT
700 SJS 95136 854-F7
STONEGATE CIR
200 SJS 95125 854-D5
STONE GATE CT
1000 MGH 95037 937-A4
STONEGATE RD
- PTLV 94028 810-B6
STONEGLEN CT
900 SJS 95122 854-G1
STONEHAVEN DR
2000 LALT 94024 831-H5
STONEHEDGE CT
10200 SCIC 95127 835-A3
STONEHEDGE WY
10000 SCIC 95127 835-A3
STONEHILL CT
6500 SJS 95120 874-F7
STONEHILL DR
6500 SJS 95120 874-F7
6500 SJS 95120 894-F1
STONEHURST WY
800 SCIC 95008 853-F7
800 SCIC 95008 873-F3
STONEMAG WY
600 SJS 95127 814-J6
STONE PINE CT
2000 SCL 95050 833-C3
STONE PINE LN
100 MLPK 94025 790-E2
STONERIDGE DR
14600 SAR 95070 872-C3
STONESHIRE CT
7600 SJS 95135 856-A6
STONEWOOD LN
1900 SJS 95132 814-E2
STONEY CT
500 GIL 95020 978-B3
STONEY CREEK PL
- SJS 95138 855-G6
STONEY CREEK WY
- MGH 95037 916-H6
STONEYFORD CT
- SJS 95138 855-E5
STONEYHAVEN WY
4400 SJS 95111 874-J1
STONY BROOK DR
- SBnC 95023 1000-F7
STONYBROOK RD
100 LGTS 95030 873-C7
100 LGTS 95032 873-C7
STONYDALE DR
10200 CPTO 95014 832-A7
STONYLAKE CT
1100 SUNV 94089 812-J4
STORY CT
1300 SJS 95127 835-C3
STORY LN
10600 SJS 95127 835-C3
STORY RD
1100 SJS 95122 834-F7
1400 SJS 95116 834-H5
2700 SJS 95127 834-H5
2700 SJS 95127 835-B2
3000 SCIC 95127 835-B2
STORY BOOK LN
1100 SJS 95116 834-E5
STORY HILL LN
28100 LAH 94022 810-H7
STOWE AV
1800 SJS 95116 834-F4
STOWE CT
- SMCo 94025 810-F1
STOWE LN
- SMCo 94025 810-E1
STOWELL AV
300 SUNV 94086 812-E6
STRADA CIRCOLARE
- SJS 95135 855-G2
STRATA ALMADEN
1100 SJS 95120 874-D6
STRATFORD CT
100 MTVW 94040 831-J1
15000 MSER 95030 872-H4
STRATFORD DR
1800 MPS 95035 794-B2
2200 SJS 95124 873-E3
15000 SCIC 95124 873-F3
STRATFORD PL
- GIL 95020 978-A5
200 LALT 94022 811-D6

STREET Block City ZIP Pg-Grid

STRATFORD PK CT
400 SJS 95136 874-F2
STRATH PL
- GIL 95020 977-D3
STRATHMORE PL
100 LGTS 95032 873-B3
STRATTON PL
2100 SJS 95131 814-D6
STRAUSS WY
1300 SJS 95132 814-F5
STRAWBERRY CT
1100 SUNV 94087 832-D3
STRAWBERRY LN
500 SJS 95129 853-B2
1700 MPS 95035 794-D6
8400 GIL 95020 977-D1
STRAWBERRY PARK DR
4200 SJS 95129 853-A2
4700 SJS 95129 852-J2
STRAWFLOWER LN
5600 SJS 95118 874-C5
STRAYER DR
1100 SJS 95129 852-G3
STREET A
- GIL 95020 977-D3
STREET B
- GIL 95020 977-D3
STRELOW CT
6100 SJS 95120 874-C7
STRICKROTH DR
700 MPS 95035 794-A5
STROHMEYER CT
- SJS 95116 834-G3
STROTMAN CT
9400 SCIC 95020 958-E4
STROUD PL
400 SJS 95111 854-H6
STRUZENBURG CT
13500 SCIC 95037 956-H1
STUART CT
- LALT 94022 811-E5
STUART DR
7500 GIL 95020 977-G3
STUBBINS WY
1400 SJS 95132 814-E4
STUCKEY DR
4900 SJS 95124 873-G4
STUDEBAKER CIR
5300 SJS 95123 874-H3
STUDENT LN
4500 SJS 95130 853-A5
STULMAN DR
300 MPS 95035 794-D7
STURGEON WY
1300 SJS 95129 852-F4
STURLA DR
2400 SJS 95148 855-C1
STUTZ WY
400 GIL 95020 978-B4
2900 SJS 95148 855-D1
SUDBURY CT
100 MPS 95035 794-A5
SUDBURY DR
- MPS 95035 794-A5
SUE AV
2500 SJS 95111 854-G3
SUE LN
- SBnC 95023 1060-F3
SUENO DR
3200 SJS 95148 835-D6
SUEZ TER
- SUNV 94089 812-G4
SUFFOLK CT
1100 LALT 94024 831-H2
SUFFOLK DR
1300 SJS 95127 835-A5
SUFFOLK WY
1000 LALT 94024 831-H2
SUFONET DR
2100 SJS 95124 873-F4
SUGAR BABE DR
9400 SCIC 95020 958-D4
SUGARCREEK CT
3400 SJS 95121 855-D7
SUGARCREEK DR
3400 SJS 95121 855-D7
SUGAR MAPLE DR
100 SJS 95136 874-H1
SUGARPINE AV
800 SUNV 94086 832-H3
SUGAR PINE CT
2800 SJS 95121 855-E3
SUGARPLUM DR
2500 SJS 95148 835-D7
SUISSE DR
400 SJS 95123 874-J6
SUISUN AV
2500 SJS 95121 855-D3
SUISUN DR
20000 CPTO 95014 852-E2
SUITER ST
800 HOLL 95023 1039-J5
SULLIVAN AV
1900 SJS 95122 834-H6
SULLIVAN CT
1800 MGH 95037 917-B3
SULLIVAN DR
500 MTVW 94041 812-A7
3700 SCL 95051 832-H7
SULLIVAN WY
21100 SAR 95070 872-C2
SULPHUR SPRING CT
3000 SJS 95148 855-E1
SULTAN PL
5400 SJS 95123 875-B3
SULTANA DR
1000 SJS 95122 834-G7
1000 SJS 95122 854-G1
SULU CT
6400 SJS 95119 875-C7
SUMAC DR
1000 MPS 95035 813-H2
1000 SUNV 94086 832-G3

STREET Block City ZIP Pg-Grid

SUMATRA AV
1800 SJS 95122 834-H7
SUMBA CT
200 SJS 95123 874-J3
SUMMER CIR
200 MGH 95037 937-B5
SUMMER CT
2300 SJS 95116 834-H4
SUMMER DR
100 SJS 95138 875-D4
500 HOLL 95023 1039-H4
SUMMER PL
5600 SJS 95138 875-D4
SUMMER ST
2300 SJS 95116 834-H4
SUMMERAIN CT
1000 SJS 95122 854-F2
SUMMER BLOSSOM AV
- SJS 95122 834-G7
- SJS 95122 854-G1
SUMMER BLOSSOM CT
- SJS 95122 834-G7
SUMMERBROOK CT
5700 SJS 95123 874-E4
SUMMERBROOK LN
800 SJS 95123 874-E4
SUMMER CREEK DR
3100 SJS 95136 854-E7
SUMMERDALE DR
1000 SJS 95132 814-F6
SUMMERDAYS CT
2800 SJS 95132 814-F6
SUMMER EVE CT
2200 SJS 95122 854-G1
SUMMERFIELD DR
- MPS 95035 813-J2
- MPS 95035 814-A2
900 SJS 95121 854-H4
1500 CMBL 95008 853-A7
SUMMERGARDEN CT
1100 SJS 95132 814-G6
SUMMERHEIGHTS DR
2700 SJS 95132 814-F6
SUMMERHILL AV
24100 SCIC 94024 831-E2
24100 LAH 94024 831-E2
24700 LALT 94024 831-E2
SUMMERHILL CIR
900 GIL 95020 957-G7
SUMMERHILL CT
3000 SJS 95148 835-F7
3000 SJS 95148 855-G1
24500 SCIC 94024 831-E2
SUMMERLAND DR
400 SJS 95134 813-C2
SUMMERLEAF DR
900 SJS 95120 894-G1
SUMMERLEAF PL
900 SJS 95120 894-G1
SUMMERMIST CT
1000 SJS 95122 854-G2
SUMMERPARK CT
1100 SJS 95132 814-F6
SUMMERPLACE DR
1000 SJS 95122 854-G1
SUMMERSHORE CT
1000 SJS 95122 854-F2
SUMMERSIDE DR
900 SCIC 95122 854-G2
900 SJS 95122 854-G2
SUMMERSONG CT
1000 SJS 95132 814-G6
SUMMERTON DR
2100 SJS 95122 854-H2
SUMMERTREE CT
1100 SJS 95132 814-F6
SUMMERVIEW DR
1000 SJS 95132 814-F6
SUMMERWIND CT
1000 SJS 95132 814-F6
SUMMERWIND DR
100 MPS 95035 793-J5
SUMMERWIND WY
1100 MPS 95035 793-J5
SUMMERWINGS CT
1100 SJS 95132 814-F6
SUMMERWOOD CT
1000 SJS 95132 814-F6
SUMMERWOOD DR
100 LGTS 95032 873-B2
SUMMIT AV
5200 SCIC 95127 814-J7
5200 SCIC 95127 815-A7
SUMMIT CT
800 SUNV 94087 832-D2
SUMMIT RD
- SCIC 95037 935-A6
- SCrC 95033 935-A6
1000 SCIC 95037 956-A7
1000 SCrC 95076 956-A7
1100 SCIC 95020 976-A1
1100 SCIC 95037 976-A1
1100 SCrC 95076 976-A1
22300 SCIC 95033 912-J4
22400 SCrC 95033 913-A4
22400 SCIC 95033 913-D7
SUMMIT RD Rt#-35
20700 SCrC 95033 912-F2
21000 SCIC 95033 912-F2
SUMMIT WY
17100 LGTS 95030 873-B4
SUMMIT CANYON RD
300 SCrC 95033 913-C6
SUMMIT RIDGE CT
3600 SJS 95148 835-G7
SUMMIT VIEW TER
- FRMT 94539 794-B1
SUMMIT WOOD CT
11600 LAH 94022 831-C3
SUMMIT WOOD RD
11500 LAH 94022 831-C3
SUMNER DR
12400 SAR 95070 852-E6

STREET Block City ZIP Pg-Grid

SUN CT
1100 MPS 95035 814-A2
SUN LN
1500 SJS 95132 814-F4
SUNBEAM CIR
1300 SJS 95122 834-G6
SUNBERRY DR
200 CMBL 95008 853-D5
SUN BLOSSOM DR
100 SJS 95123 875-A3
SUNBONNET CT
- SJS 95125 854-C6
SUNBONNET LP
- SJS 95125 854-C7
SUNBROOK CT
700 SJS 95111 855-A6
SUNBURST DR
2900 SJS 95111 854-G5
SUNCREST AV
3300 SJS 95132 814-H5
3900 SJS 95132 815-A4
SUND AV
100 LGTS 95030 893-B1
100 SCIC 95030 893-B1
SUN DANCE
- MPS 95035 814-J1
SUNDANCE DR
16800 MGH 95037 917-E6
SUNDERLAND DR
7900 CPTO 95014 852-C3
SUNDOWN LN
- SBnC 95023 1060-J3
- SBnC 95075 1060-J3
1100 SJS 95127 835-A4
SUNDOWN CANYON WY
10400 LAH 94024 831-E5
SUNFLOWER CIR
2400 GIL 95020 977-D1
SUNFLOWER LN
5600 SJS 95118 874-B5
SUN GLORY LN
2200 SJS 95124 873-F1
SUNHILL
- PTLV 94028 830-C2
SUNHILLS DR
10400 SCIC 94024 831-F5
SUNKEN GARDENS TER
900 SUNV 94086 832-G3
SUNKIST CT
300 LALT 94022 811-F5
SUNKIST LN
- LALT 94022 811-F6
SUNLAND CT
1400 SJS 95130 853-A4
SUNLITE DR
700 SCL 95050 833-C5
SUNMOR AV
2000 MTVW 94040 832-A1
SUNNINGDALE WY
- GIL 95020 977-E4
SUNNY CT
400 SJS 95116 834-F5
SUNNYARBOR CT
800 CMBL 95008 873-C1
SUNNYBROOK CT
400 CMBL 95008 853-D7
14500 MGH 95037 937-C5
18900 SAR 95070 852-G5
SUNNYBROOK DR
400 CMBL 95008 853-C7
SUNNY CREEK DR
5100 SJS 95135 855-G5
SUNNY CREEK PL
5100 SJS 95135 855-G5
SUNNYCREST CIR
1300 SJS 95122 854-H1
SUNNYDALE CT
3500 SJS 95117 853-C3
SUNNYDAYS LN
3500 SCL 95051 832-J3
SUNNYGATE CT
3500 SJS 95117 853-C3
SUNNYGLEN DR
2500 SJS 95122 835-A6
SUNNYHAVEN DR
1100 SJS 95117 853-C3
SUNNYHILLS CT
100 MPS 95035 793-J4
SUNNYHILLS DR
1800 MPS 95035 793-J3
1800 MPS 95035 794-A3
SUNNYLAKE CT
3500 SJS 95117 853-C4
SUNNYMEAD CT
3500 SJS 95117 853-C4
SUNNY MEADOW LN
3000 SJS 95135 855-G5
SUNNY MEADOW PL
3000 SJS 95135 855-G5
SUNNYMOUNT AV
500 SUNV 94087 832-D3
E SUNNYOAKS AV
- CMBL 95008 873-D1
W SUNNYOAKS AV
200 CMBL 95008 873-C1
SUNNY OAKS DR
5500 SJS 95123 874-F4
SUNNY ORCHARD LN
5200 SJS 95135 855-G5
SUNNYPARK CT
800 CMBL 95008 873-C1
SUNNYSIDE AV
- CMBL 95008 853-E6
15000 MGH 95037 937-A4
15000 SCIC 95037 937-A4
15900 MGH 95037 936-J3
15900 SCIC 95037 936-J3
SUNNYSIDE DR
19000 SAR 95070 872-G5
SUNNYSIDE RD
21300 SCIC 95033 913-B2
SUNNYSLOPE AV
- SCIC 95127 835-A1

STREET / Block City ZIP Pg-Grid

SUNNYSLOPE AV
100 SJS 95127 835-A1
SUNNYSLOPE LN
- HOLL 95023 1040-D6
- SBnC 95023 1040-D6
SUNNYSLOPE RD
600 HOLL 95023 1040-B6
1300 SBnC 95023 1040-B6
SUNNYVALE AV
- SUNV 94086 812-E6
200 SUNV 94086 832-E1
600 SUNV 94087 832-E1
SUNNYVALE-SARATOGA RD
800 SUNV 94087 832-E5
1600 CPTO 95014 832-E5
SUNNYVIEW LN
2000 MTVW 94040 831-J1
SUNNY VISTA DR
2000 SCL 95128 833-E6
2100 SJS 95128 833-E6
SUNOL ST
- SJS 95126 833-J7
200 SCIC 95126 853-J1
200 SCIC 95126 833-J7
300 SJS 95126 853-J1
500 SJS 95126 854-A2
SUNPARK CT
300 SJS 95136 874-G2
SUNPARK LN
300 SJS 95136 874-G2
SUNPARK PL
300 SJS 95136 874-G2
SUNRAY AV
- SJS 95123 875-C5
SUNRAY DR
16500 LGTS 95032 873-C5
SUN RIDGE LN
100 SJS 95123 874-G7
SUNRISE CT
- MLPK 94025 790-E7
1300 LALT 94024 831-H3
SUN RISE DR
- SJS 95002 813-B1
SUNRISE DR
- SCIC 95033 913-A4
- SBnC 95023 1040-E6
1000 GIL 95020 957-E6
2200 SJS 95124 873-E3
20600 CPTO 95014 852-D1
SUNRISE WY
1200 MPS 95035 813-J2
1200 MPS 95035 814-A3
SUNRISE FARM RD
27400 LAH 94022 830-J1
SUNRISE SPRING CT
11500 CPTO 95014 852-A4
SUNROSE TER
900 SUNV 94086 832-G3
SUNSET AV
100 SUNV 94086 812-D7
500 SJS 95116 834-H5
16100 SCIC 95037 937-A2
16100 MGH 95037 937-A2
N SUNSET AV
- SJS 95116 834-G3
S SUNSET AV
- SJS 95116 834-G4
SUNSET CT
- MLPK 94025 790-D7
2000 SJS 95116 834-G4
SUNSET DR
800 HOLL 95023 1040-C6
800 SCL 95050 833-C5
1000 SBnC 95023 1040-C6
19900 SAR 95070 872-E5
19900 SAR 95030 872-E5
19900 SCIC 95030 872-E5
23400 SCrC 95033 913-C6
SUNSET LN
- MLPK 94025 790-D7
SUNSET GLEN DR
700 SJS 95123 874-F6
SUNSET HILLS CT
- SJS 95138 855-F6
SUNSET RIDGE RD
100 SCrC 95033 892-B6
100 SCrC 95033 912-C1
SUNSET SPRING CT
11500 CPTO 95014 852-A4
SUNSET VIEW CT
2000 SJS 95116 834-G4
SUNSET VIEW RD
- SCrC 95033 913-A7
SUNSHADE LN
1400 SJS 95122 834-G6
SUNSHADOW LN
1300 SJS 95127 835-A4
SUNSHINE CT
700 LALT 94024 811-G7
1400 SJS 95122 834-G7
SUNSHINE DR
700 LALT 94024 811-G7
SUNSHINE LN
17200 SCIC 95033 913-B2
SUNSHINE ST
- MGH 95037 937-C6
- SCIC 95046 937-C6
SUN SONG
- MPS 95035 814-J1
SUNSPRING CIR
5500 SJS 95138 875-C4
SUNTREE CT
900 SUNV 94086 832-H3
SUN VALLEY CT
12600 SAR 95070 852-H6
SUNWOOD DR
2900 SJS 95111 854-H5
SUNWOOD MEADOWS PL
100 SJS 95139 875-F7
SUPERIOR DR
100 CMBL 95008 853-B6
SUPERIOR RD
600 MPS 95035 794-A5
SUPREME DR
1900 SJS 95148 835-A6
SURBER DR
300 SJS 95123 875-A5
SURF CT
3400 SCIC 95127 814-H6
SURIAN CT
1000 SJS 95120 894-G3
SURMONT CT
100 LGTS 95032 873-G6
SURMONT DR
100 LGTS 95032 873-G6
SURREY CIR
10200 CPTO 95014 851-J1
SURREY CT
100 MPS 95035 794-D6
SURREY LN
- ATN 94027 790-F2
13300 SAR 95070 852-D7
SURREY PL
200 LALT 94022 811-D6
2000 SJS 95008 853-F7
SUR VERANO
7200 SJS 95135 855-J5
SUSAN CT
800 GIL 95020 977-J7
800 SCIC 95020 957-G3
6000 SJS 95123 874-F6
16900 MGH 95037 917-G5
SUSAN DR
2300 SCL 95050 833-C4
SUSAN WY
1000 SUNV 94087 832-B1
SUSAN GALE CT
- MLPK 94025 790-C6
SUSIE LN
3400 SCIC 95020 978-H2
SUSQUEHANNA CT
900 SUNV 94087 832-B3
SUSSEX DR
2700 SJS 95127 834-J4
2700 SJS 95127 835-A4
SUSSEX PL
700 MPS 95035 794-A3
1800 MLPK 94025 790-F2
6400 GIL 95020 978-A5
SUSSEX SQ
1100 MTVW 94040 811-J7
SUSSEX WY
2700 RDWC 94061 790-A3
SUSSEX PARK CT
5100 SJS 95136 874-F3
SUTCLIFF AV
4700 SJS 95118 874-B3
SUTHERLAND AV
11100 CPTO 95014 852-B3
SUTHERLAND DR
- ATN 94027 790-B5
3900 PA 94303 811-F1
SUTRO DR
2700 SJS 95124 853-G7
2700 SJS 95124 873-H1
SUTTER AV
700 PA 94303 791-C6
800 SUNV 94086 812-C7
800 SUNV 94086 832-D1
2100 SCL 95050 833-C7
SUTTER BLVD
18500 MGH 95037 916-J4
18500 MGH 95037 917-A4
SUTTER ST
- SJS 95110 854-C1
SUTTER CREEK CIR
5000 SJS 95136 874-J2
5000 SJS 95136 875-A2
SUTTER CREEK LN
- MTVW 94043 811-J3
SUTTERGATE CT
2100 SJS 95132 814-D3
SUTTERGATE WY
2900 SJS 95132 814-D3
SUTTERWIND DR
- MPS 95035 794-A6
SUTTON DR
14800 SCIC 95124 873-H4
SUTTON PARK PL
5900 CPTO 95014 852-G2
SUVIEW DR
15200 LGTS 95032 873-E7
15200 LGTS 95032 893-F1
SUZANNE CT
500 PA 94306 811-D3
1300 SJS 95129 852-H4
SUZANNE DR
4200 PA 94306 811-D3
SUZAY CT
1400 SJS 95122 854-H2
SUZUKI CT
2700 SJS 95121 854-J4
SWAIN WY
- PA 94304 790-G6
1900 SJS 95124 873-G4
SWALLOW DR
600 SJS 95111 854-J5
1600 SUNV 94087 832-H5
SWALLOW LN
1400 GIL 95020 957-F7
SWALLOW WY
3700 SCL 95051 832-H4
3700 CPTO 95014 832-H6
SWANCREEK CT
3300 SJS 95121 855-D7
SWANCREEK WY
1500 SJS 95121 855-D7
SWANER DR
1200 GIL 95020 977-G2
SWANGATE WY
1600 SJS 95124 873-J3
SWAN OAK LN
10000 CPTO 95014 831-C7
SWANSEA CT
2000 SJS 95132 814-J2
SWANSON WY
2600 MTVW 94040 831-J1
SWANSTON LN
200 GIL 95020 978-A2
6000 GIL 95020 977-J1
SWANSTON WY
1700 SJS 95132 814-E4
SWANSWOOD CT
700 SJS 95120 894-J3
SWAPS DR
300 SJS 95111 875-B2
SWARTHMORE DR
18300 SAR 95070 852-J7
SWEET DR
900 SJS 95129 853-A3
SWEETBAY DR
700 SUNV 94086 832-H3
SWEETBERRY CT
100 SJS 95136 874-H1
SWEETBRIAR DR
600 CMBL 95008 853-F7
600 SJS 95008 853-F7
800 SCIC 95008 853-F7
800 SCIC 95008 873-F1
1600 SJS 95125 853-J6
SWEET BROOK CT
- SJS 95111 855-A6
SWEETGUM CT
1900 SJS 95131 814-D7
SWEETLEAF CT
2800 SJS 95148 835-E7
SWEET OAK ST
10800 CPTO 94024 832-A6
10800 CPTO 95014 832-A6
10900 LALT 95014 832-A6
SWEETPEA TER
- FRMT 94539 793-J3
SWEETWATER WY
700 SJS 95133 834-F1
SWEETWOOD TER
- SUNV 94086 832-H1
SWEIGERT RD
3400 SCIC 95132 814-H2
3400 SJS 95132 814-H2
5500 SCIC 95132 815-C1
SWENSEN CT
2000 SJS 95131 814-E7
SWICKARD AV
- SJS 95193 875-D4
- SJS 95119 875-D4
SWIFT AV
2100 SJS 95148 835-A6
SWIFT CT
1600 SUNV 94087 832-H5
SWINDON CT
3100 SJS 95148 855-E2
SWINGING GATE CT
1200 SJS 95120 894-E2
SWISS CREEK LN
- SCIC 95014 851-E4
SWOPE AL
- HOLL 95023 1039-J4
- HOLL 95023 1040-A4
SWORD DANCER CT
14900 MGH 95037 937-B5
SYCAMORE AV
- MGH 95037 917-A1
- SCIC 95037 896-B4
12200 SCIC 95046 937-F2
12200 SCIC 95046 957-H1
SYCAMORE CT
- CPTO 95014 831-G6
- HOLL 95023 1040-E5
- RDWC 94061 790-A2
300 LGTS 95032 873-F5
1200 GIL 95020 977-F1
2200 LALT 94024 831-J6
SYCAMORE DR
- CPTO 95014 831-G5
500 MPS 95035 813-H3
800 PA 94303 791-D6
13500 SCIC 95037 956-H1
13800 SCIC 95037 936-H6
15000 SCIC 95037 937-A5
SYCAMORE GN
1900 SJS 95125 853-J6
SYCAMORE TER
1200 SUNV 94086 832-H4
SYCAMORE WY
2800 SCL 95051 833-A7
SYCAMORE GROVE PL
- SJS 95121 855-D4
SYDENHAM CT
400 SJS 95111 875-C2
SYDNEY CT
- GIL 95020 977-H2
3600 SJS 95132 814-F2
SYDNEY DR
1300 SUNV 94087 832-D4
3500 SJS 95132 814-F2
SYDNOR DR
800 SCIC 95008 853-F7
SYKES CT
2800 SCL 95051 833-B6
SYLVAN AV
300 MTVW 94041 812-A7
2400 SJS 95050 833-E7
2400 SJS 95128 833-E7
SYLVAN CT
17000 SCIC 95033 912-J3
SYLVAN DR
3100 SJS 95148 835-C5
SYLVANDALE AV
600 SJS 95111 854-J6
600 SJS 95111 855-A6
10100 SCIC 95111 854-H6
10100 SCIC 95111 855-A6
SYLVANDALE WY
13200 SCIC 95111 854-H6
SYLVANER WY
600 FRMT 94539 794-A2
6000 SJS 95120 874-D6
SYLVIA AV
100 MPS 95035 813-J1
SYLVIA AV
100 MPS 95035 814-A1
SYLVIA CT
300 MPS 95035 813-J1
SYLVIA DR
1200 SJS 95121 854-J4
1300 SJS 95121 855-A3
SYLVIAN WY
- LALT 94022 811-D6
SYMPHONY LN
4600 SJS 95111 855-A7
SYNTAX CT
- SJS 95002 813-C1
SYRACUSE DR
1000 SUNV 94087 832-B3
SYRAH CT
- GIL 95020 977-G4

T

TAAFFE LN
12900 LAH 94022 831-B1
TAAFFE RD
26200 LAH 94022 831-A1
N TAAFFE ST
100 SUNV 94086 812-E7
S TAAFFE ST
100 SUNV 94086 812-E7
400 SUNV 94086 832-D1
TACONIC CT
5600 SJS 95123 874-H4
TADLEY CT
300 RDWC 94061 790-B1
TAFFY CT
2600 SJS 95148 835-C7
TAFFY DR
2600 SJS 95148 835-C7
TAFT AV
2600 SCL 95051 833-B6
TAFT CT
400 GIL 95020 978-A2
2600 SCL 95051 833-B6
TAFT DR
5200 SJS 95124 873-F5
TAGART DR
2600 SJS 95148 835-C7
2600 SJS 95148 855-C1
TAGLIO CT
6800 SJS 95120 894-H2
TAGUS CT
- PTLV 94028 810-D5
TAHAMA CT
100 SCrC 95033 912-H4
TAHITI CT
2000 SJS 95122 854-H1
TAHOE DR
1600 MPS 95035 814-E1
TAHOE TER
500 MTVW 94041 812-B7
TAHOE WY
2900 SJS 95125 854-B7
3600 SCL 95051 812-H7
14800 MGH 95037 937-B4
TAHUALMI ST
- SJB 95045 1038-D4
TAIDA ST
1100 SJS 95131 834-D1
TAINAN CT
1200 SJS 95131 814-B7
TAINAN DR
1400 SJS 95131 814-B7
TAINAN PL
1200 SJS 95131 814-B7
TAIPEI DR
1500 SJS 95131 814-B7
TAIT AV
- LGTS 95030 872-J7
- LGTS 95030 873-A7
TAJI CT
900 SJS 95122 854-G2
TAJI DR
900 SJS 95122 854-G2
TAKA CT
1300 SJS 95122 854-H1
TALATHY WY
3200 SJS 95135 855-E3
TALBOT CT
- MGH 95037 917-A6
TALBOT DR
800 MGH 95037 917-A6
2000 HOLL 95023 1040-B6
TALESFORE CT
1100 SJS 95131 814-E7
TALIA AV
2100 SCL 95050 833-D7
TALISMAN CT
700 PA 94303 791-E7
TALISMAN DR
800 PA 94303 791-E7
800 SUNV 94087 832-E2
TALLAHASSEE DR
1100 SJS 95122 834-J5
TALLENT AV
700 SCIC 95127 814-J5
TALLMAN CT
800 SJS 95123 874-E4
TALLWOOD CT
- ATN 94027 790-C6
TALMADGE AV
- SCIC 95127 834-J1
TAMALPAIS AV
6300 SJS 95120 874-E7
6300 SJS 95120 894-E1
TAMALPAIS ST
2400 MTVW 94043 811-F3
TAMARACK AV
800 SJS 95128 833-E7
TAMARACK LN
800 SUNV 94086 832-H3
900 SCL 95051 832-H3
TAMARIND CT
21000 CPTO 95014 832-C6
TAMARIND TER
- SJS 95112 834-D7
TAMBOUR WY
1800 SJS 95131 814-C4
TAMERA CT
1200 HOLL 95023 1039-H4
TAMI WY
500 MTVW 94041 812-B7
TAMIE LN
2000 SJS 95130 852-J6
TAMI LEE DR
1300 SJS 95122 834-G7
TAMMEY CT
- SJS 95116 834-G3
TAM O SHANTER DR
6500 SJS 95120 894-D2
TAMPA CT
1600 SJS 95122 854-J1
TAMPA WY
1600 SJS 95122 834-H7
1900 SJS 95122 854-J1
TAMPICO WY
4500 SJS 95118 874-A3
TAMSON CT
15300 MSER 95030 872-J4
TAMWORTH AV
13700 SAR 95070 872-D1
TANAGER CT
900 SUNV 94087 832-A2
TANAKA DR
1400 SJS 95131 814-C7
TANBARK ST
4200 SJS 95129 853-A2
TANDERA AV
5800 SJS 95123 874-F5
TANFIELD LN
400 SJS 95111 854-F6
TANGERINE WY
1100 SUNV 94087 832-D3
TANGLEWOOD DR
2700 SJS 95127 835-A5
TANGLEWOOD LN
26700 LAH 94022 831-A3
TANGO WY
4600 SJS 95111 855-A7
TANKERLAND CT
3500 SJS 95121 855-D3
TANKIT CT
2100 SJS 95008 853-B6
TANKIT DR
2100 SJS 95008 853-B6
TANLAND DR
1000 PA 94303 791-D5
TANNAHILL DR
6600 SJS 95120 894-E1
TANNERY WY
3100 SCL 95054 813-A6
TANNHAUSER CT
1400 SJS 95121 854-H4
TANNHAUSER WY
2600 SJS 95121 854-H4
TAN OAK DR
100 PTLV 94028 830-C1
TANOAK DR
400 SCL 95051 833-B7
TAN OAK TER
- SUNV 94086 832-H1
TANTALLON CT
2900 SJS 95132 814-F4
TANTAU AV
10000 CPTO 95014 852-G1
N TANTAU AV
10100 CPTO 95014 832-G7
10100 CPTO 95014 852-G1
TAO PL
- SJS 95125 854-B2
TAORMINO AV
5900 SJS 95123 874-F5
TAOS DR
14100 SAR 95070 872-F2
TAOS RD
48600 FRMT 94539 793-J2
TAOS WY
- GIL 95020 957-H7
TAPER AV
2800 SCL 95051 833-A3
3000 SJS 95124 873-G2
TAPER CT
1300 SJS 95122 854-H1
TAPER LN
1200 SJS 95122 854-G1
TAPESTRY CT
- CMBL 95008 853-A1
TAPESTRY DR
- GIL 95020 957-F6
- SJS 95135 855-H1
TAPESTRY WY
- SJS 95135 855-H1
TAPROOT CT
2300 SJS 95133 814-H3
TARA ST
100 EPA 94303 791-C1
TARANGA CT
7200 SJS 95139 875-G7
TAROB CT
1800 MPS 95035 814-B3
TARRAGON AV
- MGH 95037 916-H4
TARRYTOWN CT
600 SJS 95136 874-F2
TARTAN DR
2500 SCL 95051 833-B2
TARTARIAN WY
800 SUNV 94087 832-D2
1300 SJS 95129 852-G4
TARTER CT
- SJS 95136 854-E7
TARTER WY
- SJS 95136 854-E7
TARYN CT
- SBnC 95023 1039-E5
TARYN LN
8300 GIL 95020 977-F2
TASMAN CT
- SUNV 94089 812-G4
TASMAN DR
- SJS 95134 813-D3
300 SCL 95054 813-B3
500 SUNV 94089 812-G3
700 MPS 95035 813-H3
1200 SUNV 94089 813-A4
TASSAJARA CIR
17000 MGH 95037 917-E6
TASSASARA DR
800 MPS 95035 794-B5
TASSO ST
100 PA 94301 790-J3
1300 PA 94301 791-A5
TATE ST
- EPA 94303 791-C3
TATRA CT
800 SJS 95136 874-E3
TATRA DR
5000 SJS 95136 874-E2
TATUM AV
500 GIL 95020 957-G7
500 SCIC 95020 957-G7
TATUM LN
- SJS 95128 853-E1
TAUBEH CT
3900 SJS 95136 874-F1
TAWNYGATE WY
1600 SJS 95124 873-J3
1600 SJS 95124 874-A3
TAYLOR AV
19100 MGH 95037 916-H4
E TAYLOR AV
200 SUNV 94086 812-F6
TAYLOR CT
500 MTVW 94043 812-A4
TAYLOR DR
400 MPS 95035 794-A3
TAYLOR ST
900 SJS 95002 793-B7
1200 SJS 95002 813-B1
E TAYLOR ST
- SJS 95112 834-C3
W TAYLOR ST
- SJS 95110 834-A4
300 SJS 95110 833-H6
600 SJS 95126 833-H6
TAYMOUTH WY
- GIL 95020 977-D3
TAYSIDE CT
7500 SJS 95135 855-J5
TEA CT
- EPA 94303 791-C2
TEABERRY CT
6100 SJS 95123 875-B6
TEAK CT
17000 MGH 95037 917-D6
TEAK TER
- SUNV 94086 832-H1
TEAK GROVE CT
100 SJS 95123 874-F7
100 SJS 95123 875-A3
TEAKWOOD AV
800 LGTS 95032 873-B2
TEAKWOOD CT
- HOLL 95023 1040-E5
800 LGTS 95032 873-B2
TEAKWOOD DR
1300 SJS 95128 853-E4
TEAL CT
6100 GIL 95020 977-J6
TEAL DR
900 SCL 95051 832-H5
1100 SUNV 94087 832-H5
TEALE AV
3900 SJS 95117 853-B3
TEAL RIDGE CT
3000 SJS 95136 854-E3
TEA ROSE CIR
1100 SJS 95131 814-B6
TEA ROSE WY
1800 SJS 95131 814-B6
TEA TREE CT
- GIL 95020 957-E7
TEATREE CT
600 SJS 95128 853-F2
TEA TREE TER
- SUNV 94086 832-H1
TEA TREE WY
- GIL 95020 957-E7
- GIL 95020 977-E1
TECHNOLOGY DR
800 MPS 95035 813-G2
1600 SJS 95110 833-H1
18400 MGH 95037 917-A4
TECHNOLOGY PKWY
2300 HOLL 95023 1020-A5
TED AV
12300 SAR 95070 852-E5
TED CT
12300 SAR 95070 852-E5
TEDDINGTON DR
3100 SJS 95148 855-E2
TEERLINK WY
14000 SAR 95070 872-B2
TEHAMA AV
1000 MLPK 94025 790-H1
2100 SJS 95122 834-J6
TEKMAN DR
1000 SJS 95122 854-H2
TELEGRAPH DR
3500 SJS 95132 814-H4
TELFER AV
1100 SJS 95125 854-A4
TELFORD AV
700 MTVW 94043 811-H2
TEMPLE CT
3100 SCL 95051 833-A6
TEMPLE DR
900 SJS 95117 853-B3
N TEMPLE DR
- MPS 95035 794-D6
S TEMPLE DR
- MPS 95035 794-D7
TEMPLEBAR WY
600 LALT 94022 811-D5
TEMPLETON CT
600 SUNV 94087 832-D3
TEMPLETON DR
500 SUNV 94087 832-D3
TEMPLETON PL
13800 LAH 94022 811-D7
TEN CT
- MGH 95037 937-C2
TEN ACRES CT
14100 SAR 95070 872-H2
TEN ACRES RD
18800 SAR 95070 872-G2
TENAKA PL
1500 SUNV 94087 832-D5
TENAYA DR
1300 SJS 95125 854-B7
TENLEY CT
3200 SJS 95148 855-D2
TENLEY DR
3200 SJS 95148 855-D2
TENNANT AV
- MGH 95037 937-B2
- SJS 95138 875-F4
800 SCIC 95037 937-D1
2200 SCIC 95037 917-F7
2200 MGH 95037 917-F7
TENNESSEE LN
200 PA 94306 811-D2
TENNYSON AV
100 PA 94301 791-A6
700 PA 94303 791-A6
TENNYSON DR
- GIL 95020 977-H2
TENNYSON LN
900 SJS 95116 834-G5
TEN OAK CT
13200 SAR 95070 852-F7
TEN OAK WY
12900 SAR 95070 852-F7
TEOLA WY
2000 SJS 95121 855-C3
TEPA WY
11400 LAH 94022 831-B3
TERALBA CT
100 SJS 95139 895-G1
TERESA LN
1100 MGH 95037 916-G7
TERESA WY
- LAH 94022 831-D3
- LAH 94024 831-D3
TERESA MARIE TER
1600 MPS 95035 793-G3
TERESI CT
700 SJS 95117 853-D2
TERESI LN
600 LALT 94024 831-F1
TERESITA CT
200 HOLL 95023 1039-G3
TERESITA DR
1200 SJS 95129 852-J5
TERESITA WY
100 LGTS 95030 893-D1
100 LGTS 95032 893-D1
TERFIDIA LN
- MPS 95035 794-D6
TERILYN AV
1500 SJS 95122 834-G6
2000 SJS 95122 854-H1
TERMAN DR
4200 PA 94306 811-C3
TERMINAL AV
1500 SJS 95112 834-A2
TERMINAL BLVD
2500 MTVW 94043 791-G6
TERMINAL DR
800 SJS 95110 833-G2
TERNER WY
- SJS 95136 874-E3
TERNURA LP
- MPS 95035 813-J1
TERRA CIR
- SJS 95121 855-D4
TERRA PL
- SJS 95121 855-D4
TERRA ALTA CT
2000 MPS 95035 814-E2
TERRA ALTA DR
1200 MPS 95035 814-E2
TERRA BELLA AV
900 SJS 95125 854-B5
900 MTVW 94043 811-H2
900 MTVW 94043 812-A3
TERRA BELLA DR
700 MPS 95035 794-B6
11200 CPTO 95014 852-B3
TERRA BRAVA PL
- SJS 95121 855-D4
TERRA CALIFORNIA WY
1900 MGH 95037 917-E6
TERRACE CT
- SAR 95070 872-D2
- LGTS 95030 893-B1
700 LALT 94024 811-G7
TERRACE DR
400 SJS 95110 834-D4
700 SCIC 94024 831-G4
1200 HOLL 95023 1040-C6
21500 CPTO 95014 852-B3
TERRACE LAKE DR
- SJS 95123 874-E5
TERRACE VIEW DR
- SJS 95123 874-D5
TERRA COTTA CT
3100 SJS 95135 855-E2
TERRA COTTA DR
3100 SJS 95135 855-E2
TERRAINE ST
100 SJS 95113 834-B6
100 SJS 95110 834-B6
TERRA MESA WY
300 MPS 95035 793-H3

STREET
Block City ZIP Pg-Grid

TERRA NOBLE WY
1000 SJS 95132 814-H5
TERRA VILLA AV
2200 EPA 94303 791-C2
TERRA VISTA CT
- MPS 95035 794-C3
TERRAZZO CT
5800 SJS 95123 874-F5
TERRAZZO DR
700 SJS 95123 874-F5
TERRELL ST
900 SJS 95136 874-D1
TERRENA VALLEY DR
3700 SJS 95121 855-D4
TERRENCE AV
12100 SAR 95070 852-F5
TERRENO DE FLORES CIR
- LGTS 95032 873-D4
TERRENO DE FLORES LN
14900 LGTS 95032 873-D4
TERRI CT
9500 GIL 95020 957-J6
9500 GIL 95020 958-A6
9500 SClC 95020 957-J5
TERRI WY
1800 SJS 95124 873-H3
TERRIER CT
6000 SJS 95123 875-A6
TERRI LYNN CT
1400 SClC 95020 958-A2
TERRY CT
- SBnC 95023 1060-D2
TERRY LN
1900 SMCo 94061 790-B4
TERRY WY
10200 CPTO 95014 852-D1
10900 SClC 94024 831-F5
TERRYWOOD CT
3100 SJS 95132 814-D2
TERSINI CT
1800 SJS 95131 814-C7
TERSTINA PL
3700 SCL 95051 832-H3
TESORO CT
5400 SJS 95124 873-G5
TEVIS PL
- PA 94301 791-B4
TEVIS TR
100 SBnC 95023 1020-E2
TEXAS CT
5800 SJS 95120 874-B6
THACKERAY LN
900 SJS 95116 834-G5
THADDEUS DR
2400 MTVW 94043 811-G2
THAIN WY
500 PA 94306 811-C2
THAINWOOD WY
3800 SJS 95121 855-C4
THAMES DR
1100 SJS 95129 852-G3
6600 GIL 95020 978-A5
THAMES LN
100 LALT 94022 811-D4
THAMES PARK CT
400 SJS 95136 874-F1
THATCHER CT
900 LALT 94024 831-H2
THATCHER DR
900 LALT 94024 831-H1
900 MTVW 94040 831-H1
THAYER CT
2200 SJS 95122 854-H1
7300 GIL 95020 977-H4
THE ALAMEDA
- SJB 95045 1038-D5
2600 SCL 95053 833-F4
3100 SCL 95050 833-F4
THE ALAMEDA Rt#-82
600 SJS 95126 834-A7
800 SJS 95126 833-H5
2100 SCL 95126 833-H5
2200 SCL 95050 833-H5
2500 SCL 95053 833-H5
THE AMERICANA
900 MTVW 94040 812-A7
THE BUCKEYE
18600 SClC 95033 912-J1
THE DALLES AV
700 SUNV 94087 832-A4
THELMA AV
20000 SAR 95070 872-E1
THELMA WY
900 SJS 95122 834-F7
900 SJS 95122 854-F1
THENDARA WY
13400 LAH 94022 811-A5
THEO DR
1500 SJS 95131 814-B6
THEODEN CT
1100 SJS 95121 855-A4
THERESA AV
1200 CMBL 95008 873-C2
THERESA LN
2700 SJS 95124 873-F1
THE STRAND AV
1600 SJS 95120 874-B6
THETA CT
400 SJS 95123 875-A7
THE VILLAGES PKWY
2400 SJS 95135 855-G6
THE VILLAGES FAIRWAY DR
2000 SJS 95135 855-H6
2800 SJS 95135 856-A6
THE WOODS DR
3900 SJS 95136 854-H7
3900 SJS 95136 874-H1
THICKET WY
6100 SJS 95119 875-D5
THIMBLEBERRY LN
4600 SJS 95129 853-B2
THIMBLEHALL LN
3400 SJS 95121 855-C3
THISTLE
- PTLV 94028 830-C1
THISTLE CT
1000 SUNV 94086 832-G3
THISTLE DR
4500 SJS 95136 874-F1
THISTLE WY
9200 GIL 95020 957-F7
THISTLEWOOD CT
1300 SJS 95121 855-B1
THOBURN CT
- SClC 94305 790-J7
THOMAS CT
1500 MTVW 94040 811-G6
1500 MTVW 94022 811-G6
THOMAS DR
200 LGTS 95032 873-G5
3300 PA 94303 791-E6
THOMAS LN
- SJB 95045 1038-D4
THOMAS RD
300 GIL 95020 977-J6
300 SClC 95020 977-J6
1600 SCL 95054 813-D6
1900 SBnC 95023 1060-F6
THOMAS GRADE
2700 MGH 95037 917-F5
THOMPSON AV
100 MTVW 94043 811-F3
3300 SJS 95118 874-A1
THOMPSON CT
- MPS 95035 813-J1
2300 MTVW 94043 811-G3
THOMPSON PL
900 SUNV 94086 812-G6
2300 SCL 95050 833-C3
THOMPSON RD
20100 SClC 95033 892-E6
THOMPSON SQ
100 MTVW 94043 811-F3
THOMPSON ST
- MPS 95035 813-J1
- HOLL 95023 1040-A3
THOMPSON CREEK CT
2700 SJS 95121 855-E3
3600 SJS 95135 855-E3
THORNAPPLE DR
600 SUNV 94086 832-H2
THORNBRIAR DR
1500 SJS 95131 834-C1
THORNBURY LN
- SJS 95138 855-B5
THORNCREEK CT
- SJS 95135 855-G5
THORNCREST DR
1500 SJS 95131 814-C7
1500 SJS 95131 834-C1
THORNDALE CT
1000 SJS 95121 855-A5
THORNHAVEN WY
4500 SJS 95111 875-A1
4500 SJS 95111 874-J1
THORNLEAF WY
1500 SJS 95131 834-C1
THORNMILL WY
1200 SJS 95121 854-J3
THORNTON WY
500 SClC 95128 853-F3
500 SJS 95128 853-F2
THORNTREE CT
1100 SJS 95120 874-D6
THORNTREE DR
5900 SJS 95120 874-C6
THORNTREE PL
1100 SJS 95120 874-D6
THORN VALLEY CT
1200 SJS 95131 834-C1
THORNWOOD DR
800 PA 94303 791-E7
5300 SJS 95123 874-E3
THORP PL
- SAR 95030 872-G5
THORPE CT
1200 LALT 94024 831-H3
THORSEN CT
700 SClC 94024 831-G4
THOUSAND OAKS CT
4400 SJS 95136 874-D2
THOUSAND OAKS DR
3600 SJS 95136 874-D1
THOUSAND PINES CT
3200 SJS 95148 855-D2
THRASHER LN
2800 SJS 95125 854-B7
THREADNEEDLE WY
1800 SJS 95121 855-B3
THREE FORKS LN
13400 LAH 94022 810-H7
THREE OAKS CT
14800 SAR 95070 872-F3
THREE OAKS WY
19500 SAR 95070 872-F4
THREE SPRINGS CT
3000 SClC 95127 835-G3
THREE SPRINGS RD
3000 SClC 95127 835-G3
THRESTLEWOOD LN
- SJS 95138 855-B5
THRIFT PL
3300 SJS 95148 835-E6
THRUSH CT
1500 SCL 95051 832-H5
2600 SJS 95125 854-C6
THRUSH DR
2500 SJS 95125 854-C6
THRUSH WY
3700 SCL 95051 832-H5
THUNDERBIRD AV
1300 SUNV 94087 832-H5
1400 SCL 95051 832-H5
THUNDERBIRD WY
1800 SClC 95125 853-H6
THURESON WY
5500 SJS 95124 873-H6
THURLOW ST
300 MLPK 94025 790-G3
THURMAN DR
3000 SJS 95148 855-F1
THURSTON AV
1100 LALT 94024 831-H4
THURSTON ST
200 LGTS 95030 873-A6
THYME AV
- MGH 95037 916-G4
TIA PL
1900 SJS 95131 814-E7
TIANA LN
700 MTVW 94041 812-B7
TIANI CT
1800 SJS 95133 834-E1
TIARA DR
2200 SJS 95116 834-H5
TIARE LN
- LAH 94024 831-E2
TIBER CT
1600 SJS 95138 875-F1
TIBERAN WY
5000 SJS 95130 852-J6
TIBOUCHINA LN
6200 SJS 95119 875-D5
TIBURON DR
1600 HOLL 95023 1040-D7
TICE DR
100 MPS 95035 794-B4
TICONDEROGA DR
800 SUNV 94087 832-B3
TICONDEROGA PL
7200 GIL 95020 977-H4
TIERRA BUENA DR
1400 SJS 95121 854-J2
1500 SJS 95121 855-A2
TIERRA DEL SOL
300 SBnC 95023 1060-E1
TIERRA ENCANTADA CT
- SJS 95116 834-G4
TIERRA ENCANTADA WY
- SJS 95116 834-G4
TIERRA GRANDE CT
21300 SClC 95120 895-C5
TIERRA SOMBRA CT
21600 SClC 95120 895-C5
TIFFANY CT
600 SUNV 94087 832-D3
TIFFANY DR
500 HOLL 95023 1039-J4
TIFFANY WY
1600 SJS 95125 854-A7
TIFFANY CANYON CT
- SJS 95120 894-G5
TIFFANY HILL WY
- SJS 95120 894-G4
TIFFIN DR
100 SJS 95136 874-J2
TIFTON WY
4900 SJS 95118 874-B3
TIGARA CT
3700 SJS 95136 874-D1
TIGER LILY LN
- SJS 95131 814-A5
TIGERWOOD WY
400 SJS 95111 875-C2
TILBURY DR
4400 SJS 95130 853-A6
TILDEN DR
4800 SJS 95124 873-G4
TILLAMOOK DR
6200 SJS 95123 874-H7
TILLMAN AV
- SJS 95126 833-H7
TILSON AV
18700 CPTO 95014 852-G1
TILTON AV
- MGH 95037 916-G4
100 SClC 95037 916-G4
TILTON CT
2600 SJS 95121 854-J3
TILTON DR
1100 SUNV 94087 832-E3
TIMBER CT
6500 SJS 95120 894-E1
TIMBER WY
300 MPS 95035 813-J3
TIMBER COVE DR
- CMBL 95008 853-E7
TIMBER CREEK DR
1500 SJS 95131 814-D5
TIMBERCREST DR
1000 SJS 95120 894-E1
TIMBERLAKE AV
3400 SJS 95148 835-D6
TIMBERLAKE CT
2600 SJS 95148 835-E6
TIMBERLINE
- SCrC 95033 892-C5
TIMBERLINE CT
2800 SJS 95121 855-E3
TIMBERLINE DR
3600 SJS 95121 855-E3
TIMBERLOOP DR
4200 SJS 95136 854-F7
4200 SJS 95136 874-F1
TIMBERPEAK CT
- SJS 95116 834-F7
TIMBERPINE AV
600 SUNV 94086 832-H2
TIMBERPINE CT
1100 SUNV 94086 832-H2
TIMBER SPRING CT
11600 CPTO 95014 852-C4
TIMBERVIEW CT
6500 SJS 95120 894-C1
TIMBERVIEW DR
6500 SJS 95120 894-C2
TIMBERWOOD CT
6800 SJS 95120 894-H2
TIMLOTT CT
3800 PA 94306 811-C2
TIMLOTT LN
800 PA 94306 811-C2
TIMMUS LN
23400 SClC 95033 913-D6
TIMOR CT
700 SJS 95127 814-H6
TIMOR TER
- SUNV 94089 812-G4
TIMOTHY DR
900 SJS 95133 834-C2
TIMOTHY LN
- SClC 95120 895-D5
TIM TAM CT
22400 SCrC 95033 912-H5
TINA DR
- HOLL 95023 1040-B6
TINSLEY ST
- EPA 94303 791-C3
TINTERN LN
- PTLV 94028 810-B6
TINY ST
2000 MPS 95035 793-J3
2000 MPS 95035 794-A3
TIOGA CT
300 PA 94306 811-E2
500 SUNV 94087 832-D3
TIOGA DR
2200 MLPK 94025 790-C6
TIOGA WY
1800 SJS 95124 853-H7
TIPPAWINGO AV
3400 PA 94306 811-B1
TIPTOE LN
1500 LALT 94024 832-A3
7400 CPTO 95014 852-D3
TIROL CT
500 MPS 95035 794-B5
TIROS WY
1200 SUNV 94086 812-J6
TISCH WY
3000 SJS 95128 853-E2
TISDALE WY
5000 SJS 95130 852-J7
TITAN WY
1200 SUNV 94086 812-J6
TITLEIST CT
300 SJS 95127 815-A7
TITUS AV
12000 SAR 95070 852-G6
TITUS CT
19300 SAR 95070 852-G6
TIVERTON DR
3800 SJS 95121 855-B5
TIVOLI WY
1200 SJS 95120 894-E3
TOANO CT
1500 SJS 95131 814-D6
TOBAGO AV
1900 SJS 95122 854-H1
TOBIAS DR
1500 SJS 95118 874-A4
TOBIN CIR
- SCL 95054 813-E5
TOBIN DR
2900 SJS 95132 814-E4
TODD LN
26000 LAH 94022 811-C7
TODD ST
1300 MTVW 94040 811-G6
TODD WY
3000 SJS 95124 873-G2
TOFT ST
400 MTVW 94041 811-G5
TOFTS DR
1100 SJS 95131 814-E6
TOHARA WY
2900 SClC 95037 936-G6
TOIYABE WY
2300 SJS 95133 814-F7
2300 SJS 95133 834-F1
TOKAY CT
3400 SJS 95148 835-C4
TOKAY WY
3400 SJS 95148 835-C4
TOLBERT CT
2300 SJS 95122 854-J1
TOLBERT DR
1500 SJS 95122 854-H1
TOLEDO AV
2600 SCL 95051 833-B6
TOLIN CT
200 SJS 95139 895-F1
TOLL GATE RD
21100 SAR 95070 872-B2
TOLLIVER DR
2900 SJS 95148 855-D2
TOLMAN DR
700 SClC 94305 810-J2
TOLUSA CT
- MGH 95037 917-B4
TOLWORTH DR
1000 SJS 95128 853-F3
2500 CMBL 95128 853-F3
TOMAHAWK DR
5100 SJS 95136 875-A3
TOMAHAWK PL
49000 FRMT 94539 793-J3
TOMASINA CT
2200 SJS 95008 873-E1
TOMI LEA ST
600 LALT 94022 811-E5
TOMKI CT
- CPTO 95014 852-C2
TOMKINS CT
300 GIL 95020 957-J7
TOMLIN WY
2200 SJS 95133 834-F2
TOMLINSON LN
900 SJS 95116 834-G5
TOMMY LN
7400 SClC 95120 894-H5
TOMPKINS DR
5800 SJS 95129 852-G3
TOMRICK AV
4500 SJS 95124 873-F3
TONALEA ST
48900 FRMT 94539 793-J3
TONGA CT
700 SJS 95127 814-H6
TONI CT
10100 CPTO 95014 832-E7
TONI ANN PL
13500 SAR 95070 872-D1
TONINO DR
4600 SJS 95136 874-D2
TONITA WY
10300 CPTO 95014 852-D1
TONOPAH CT
48600 FRMT 94539 793-J2
TONOPAH DR
- FRMT 94539 793-J2
5700 SJS 95123 875-A4
TONY DR
4800 SJS 95124 873-G4
TONY P SANTOS WY
- SJS 95002 793-C7
- SJS 95002 813-C1
TOPAM GLEN CT
7400 SClC 95120 894-J5
TOPAR AV
1400 SClC 94024 831-G3
TOPAZ AV
1000 SJS 95117 853-B4
TOPAZ ST
100 MPS 95035 794-A7
100 MPS 95035 814-B1
TOPEKA AV
- SClC 95128 833-G7
- SClC 95128 853-G1
- SJS 95128 853-G1
100 SJS 95128 833-G7
200 SJS 95126 833-G7
TOPHAM CT
- MPS 95035 794-C5
TOPOCK CT
3500 SJS 95111 854-G7
TOP OF THE HILL CT
15200 LGTS 95032 893-E1
TOP OF THE HILL RD
15200 LGTS 95032 893-F1
15200 SClC 95032 893-F1
TOPPING WY
16400 LGTS 95032 873-C7
16400 SClC 95032 873-C7
TORELLO LN
26000 LAH 94022 811-C6
TORERO PZ
800 CMBL 95008 873-C1
TORLAND CT
500 SUNV 94087 832-D3
TORO CT
- PTLV 94028 810-D6
TORO PZ
900 HOLL 95023 1040-C4
TORONJA CT
- SJS 95112 834-B4
TORO VISTA CT
16700 MGH 95037 917-G6
TORRANCE AV
1200 SUNV 94089 812-J5
10100 SJS 95127 835-A3
TORRE AV
10000 CPTO 95014 852-E1
TORRE CT
1500 SJS 95120 874-A6
TORREGATA LP
- SJS 95134 813-D2
TORRENZIA DR
- SJS 95134 813-D2
TORRES AV
1100 MPS 95035 794-C5
TORREY CT
17200 MGH 95037 936-J1
TORREYA AV
600 SUNV 94086 832-H2
TORREYA CT
700 PA 94303 791-D7
TORREY PINES CIR
- SJS 95124 873-G7
TORRINGTON CT
1400 SJS 95120 874-B6
TORRINGTON DR
600 SUNV 94087 832-D3
TORTOLA WY
400 SJS 95133 834-G2
TORWOOD CT
500 LALT 94022 811-C5
TORWOOD LN
400 LALT 94022 811-D5
TORYGLEN WY
2100 SJS 95121 855-C3
TOSCA CT
1500 SJS 95121 854-J2
TOSCA WY
2500 SJS 95121 854-J2
TOSCANA CT
3000 SJS 95135 855-E3
TOSCANO CT
2100 MPS 95035 794-A2
TOTTENHAM CT
5000 SJS 95136 874-F3
TOULON CT
1600 SJS 95138 875-F1
TOURAINE DR
1400 SJS 95118 874-A6
TOURNEY DR
1200 SJS 95131 814-E6
TOURNEY LP
200 LGTS 95030 893-B2
TOURNEY RD
17500 LGTS 95030 893-B1
17600 SClC 95030 893-B2
TOVAR DR
400 SJS 95123 875-A6
TOWER HILL AV
- SJS 95136 854-F7
TOWERS LN
2900 SJS 95121 855-A3
TOWLE PL
600 PA 94306 791-C7
TOWLE WY
600 PA 94306 791-C7
TOWN AND COUNTRY LN
1900 SCL 95050 833-D6
TOWN CENTER DR
- MPS 95035 794-B6
TOWNCENTER DR
2400 SUNV 94086 812-E7
2400 SUNV 94086 832-E1
TOWN CENTER LN
20300 CPTO 95014 852-E1
TOWN CLUB DR
1600 SJS 95124 873-J2
TOWNE AL
200 HOLL 95023 1039-J3
TOWNE CIR
- MTVW 94040 811-F3
TOWNE PL
- MPS 95035 814-J1
TOWNE TER
100 LGTS 95030 873-A6
100 LGTS 95032 873-A6
TOWNSEND AV
800 SJS 95112 834-B1
1300 SJS 95131 814-C7
1700 SCL 95051 833-A3
TOWNSEND TER
- SUNV 94087 832-B3
TOWNSEND PARK CIR
1200 SJS 95131 814-C7
TOWN SQUARE DR
- MTVW 94043 812-B5
TOWNSQUARE DR
3500 SJS 95127 835-B2
3500 SClC 95127 835-B2
TOY LN
2600 SJS 95121 855-D3
TOYAMA DR
400 SUNV 94089 812-G4
TOYON AV
100 SJS 95127 814-J6
300 LALT 94022 811-D6
600 SUNV 94086 832-H2
TOYON CT
800 SClC 95127 814-J6
800 SJS 95127 814-J6
8700 GIL 95020 977-F1
TOYON DR
2800 SCL 95051 833-A7
15500 SClC 95030 872-J5
TOYON PL
600 PA 94306 791-D7
TOYON RD
- ATN 94027 790-G1
TOYONITA RD
23400 LAH 94024 831-E4
TRABUCO CT
3200 SJS 95135 855-G3
TRACE AV
600 SJS 95126 833-G7
TRACEL DR
6100 SJS 95129 852-F5
TRACY CT
14000 LAH 94022 810-H6
14000 PA 94304 810-H6
TRACY DR
3300 SCL 95051 832-J7
TRACY WY
1600 SClC 95046 937-G4
TRADAN DR
1800 SJS 95132 814-C4
TRADEWINDS CT
5400 SJS 95123 874-J4
TRADEWINDS DR
200 SJS 95123 874-J3
300 SJS 95123 875-A4
TRADEWINDS WALKWAY
5400 SJS 95123 874-J4
TRADE ZONE BLVD
300 MPS 95035 814-B4
300 SJS 95131 814-B4
TRADE ZONE CIR
1900 SJS 95131 814-B4
TRADE ZONE CT
1800 SJS 95131 814-B4
TRADE ZONE PL
2500 SJS 95131 814-B4
TRADE ZONE WY
1800 SJS 95131 814-B4
TRADITION CT
6600 SJS 95120 894-C5
TRAFALGAR PL
3400 SJS 95132 814-J3
TRAIL DR
16600 MGH 95037 917-F6
TRAIL LN
- WDSD 94062 810-A5
TRAILBLAZER WY
9300 GIL 95020 957-F7
TRAIL RUN CT
4800 SJS 95136 874-J2
4800 SJS 95136 875-A2
TRAILS END RD
14200 SCrC 95033 871-D3
TRAILSIDE CT
- SJS 95138 855-B6
TRAILSIDE LN
- SJS 95138 855-B6
TRAILSIDE WY
- SJS 95138 855-C6
TRAILWAY DR
4100 SClC 95127 835-A2
TRAJAN CT
- SJS 95135 855-F2
TRAMIER CT
8300 SJS 95135 855-H7
TRAMWAY DR
200 MPS 95035 794-A5
TRAMWAY PL
400 MPS 95035 794-A5
TRANQUILITY PL
- MPS 95035 814-J1
TRANSILL CIR
- SCL 95054 813-E5
TRANSPORT ST
4000 PA 94303 791-F7
4000 PA 94303 811-G1
TRAPPERS TR
- PA 94304 830-E2
TRAUGHBER ST
1200 MPS 95035 794-C5
TRAVEL PARK CIR
- GIL 95020 978-B6
TRAVERSO AV
300 LALT 94022 811-D4
TRAVERSO CT
400 LALT 94022 811-D4
TRAVIATA PL
- SJS 95117 853-D4
TRAVIS CT
10400 SClC 95020 958-B2
TREADWAY DR
2300 SJS 95133 834-F1
TREATY CT
5000 SJS 95136 875-A2
TREBOL LN
3200 SJS 95148 835-D6
TREE FERN COM
- FRMT 94539 793-J3
TREEHOUSE WY
14300 SCrC 95018 912-E5
TREE TOP CT
5800 SJS 95123 875-A5
TREE VIEW TR
- SCrC 95033 913-D7
TREEWOOD LN
1900 SJS 95132 814-E2
TREGO DR
4700 SJS 95118 874-B3
TRELLIS PL
3200 SJS 95135 855-E3
TRENARY WY
5000 SJS 95118 874-C3
TRENT DR
4800 SJS 95124 873-G4
TRENTE CT
600 HOLL 95023 1040-B5
TRENTON DR
700 SUNV 94087 832-C3
1900 SJS 95124 873-G1
TRENTON PL
7200 GIL 95020 977-J4
TRENTON WY
300 MLPK 94025 790-J3
TRENTS FERRY CT
500 SJS 95133 834-E2
TRESEDER CT
100 LGTS 95032 873-B7
TRES PINOS RD Rt#-25
100 HOLL 95023 1040-A5
TRESSLER CT
- CPTO 95014 852-A2
TRESTLEWOOD DR
- SJS 95138 855-B6
TREVIGNE AV
- SJS 95135 855-F2
TREVINO TER
1000 SJS 95120 894-E1
TREVISO AV
1500 SJS 95118 874-B5
TREVOR DR
1500 SJS 95118 874-A4
TRIANON WY
200 LALT 94022 811-E6
TRIBOROUGH LN
1400 SJS 95126 853-G4
TRICIA WY
20400 SAR 95070 852-E7
TRIESTE CT
1600 SJS 95122 854-F1
TRIESTE DR
1200 HOLL 95023 1040-C5
TRIESTE WY
1500 SJS 95122 854-F1
TRIFONE DR
900 SJS 95117 853-C3
TRIMAR CT
3900 SJS 95111 854-J6
TRIMBLE CT
- GIL 95020 957-H7
2100 SJS 95132 814-C3
TRIMBLE RD
400 SJS 95134 813-F6
500 SJS 95131 813-F6
500 SCL 95054 813-F6
500 SCL 95134 813-F6
2500 SJS 95131 814-C3
2500 SJS 95132 814-C3
2500 MPS 95035 814-C3
TRINA WY
3700 SJS 95117 853-C1
TRINIDAD CT
6500 SJS 95120 894-D1
TRINIDAD DR
6400 SJS 95120 894-E1
TRINIDAD RD
2700 SJS 95111 854-H4
TRINITY AV
13800 SAR 95070 872-D2
TRINITY CT
- MLPK 94025 790-C7
13900 SAR 95070 872-D1

SANTA CLARA CO.

© 2008 Rand McNally & Company

STREET
Block City ZIP Pg-Grid

TRINITY DR
1000 HOLL 95023 1040-D5
1000 MLPK 94025 790-C7
TRINITY PL
3100 SJS 95124 873-F2
TRINITY HILLS CT
- SJS 95138 855-F6
TRINITY PARK DR
- SJS 95002 793-C7
- SJS 95002 813-C1
TRINITY RIVER CT
2900 SJS 95111 854-H4
TRINITY SPRING CT
11700 CPTO 95014 852-A5
TRIPIANO CT
2000 MTVW 94040 831-J1
TRIPOLI AV
1800 SJS 95122 854-G1
TRIPOLI CT
12900 LAH 94022 830-J1
TRIPP AV
1200 SJS 95116 834-D4
TRISTAN AV
3100 SJS 95127 814-H7
TRITON CT
1600 SCL 95050 833-D3
TRIUMPH CT
1400 SJS 95129 852-E4
TROLLEY CT
- SJS 95112 834-B3
TRONA WY
1500 SJS 95125 854-A7
1600 SJS 95125 873-J1
1600 SJS 95125 874-A1
TRONSON CT
3600 SJS 95132 814-F2
TROON CT
- GIL 95020 977-D3
600 MPS 95035 794-B6
TROON DR
1500 SJS 95116 834-F5
TROON WY
- GIL 95020 977-D3
TROPHY DR
900 MTVW 94040 811-G6
TROVARE CT
- SJS 95135 855-G3
TROVATA CT
2800 SJS 95135 855-G5
TROWBRIDGE WY
5600 SJS 95138 855-G7
5800 SJS 95138 875-H1
TROY CT
900 SUNV 94087 832-C3
TROY DR
500 SJS 95117 853-B1
TROY RD
- SCrC 95033 913-C7
TROY PARK PL
1800 SJS 95124 873-G4
TRUCKEE CT
4000 SJS 95136 874-H1
TRUCKEE LN
100 SJS 95136 874-G1
TRUCKEE WY
- SBnC 95023 1060-B1
TRUDEAN WY
1700 SJS 95132 814-D4
TRUDY LN
- SMCo 94025 790-D6
TRUETT CT
2900 SJS 95148 855-C6
TRUFFLE CT
3200 SJS 95148 855-E2
TRUMAN AV
1400 LALT 94024 832-A3
3300 MTVW 94040 832-A3
3500 LALT 94040 832-A3
TRUMAN WY
- SJS 95002 793-C7
- SJS 95002 813-C1
TRUMAR LN
- SCIC 95020 958-A1
TRUMBULL CT
500 SUNV 94087 832-D3
TRUMPETER PL
1200 SJS 95131 814-B6
TRUMPP CT
17700 MGH 95037 916-H7
TRYNA DR
3300 MTVW 94040 832-A2
TUBAC LN
5600 SJS 95118 874-B5
TUBBY ST
400 CMBL 95008 853-E5
TUBMAN CT
500 SJS 95125 854-D5
TUCKER DR
6300 SJS 95129 852-F4
TUCSON AV
1100 SUNV 94089 812-J5
TUCSON DR
5600 SJS 95118 874-D4
TUCSON WY
5500 SJS 95193 875-C4
6600 SJS 95119 875-C4
TUDOR CT
1200 SJS 95127 834-J4
TUDOR DR
1600 MLPK 94025 790-F2
TUERS CT
1000 SJS 95121 854-J4
TUERS RD
2600 SJS 95121 854-H3
3300 SJS 95121 855-A5
TUGGLE AV
18700 CPTO 95014 852-H2
TUGGLE PL
10600 CPTO 95014 852-H2
TULA CT
20800 CPTO 95014 852-D1
TULA LN
10200 CPTO 95014 852-D1

TULANE CT
800 MTVW 94040 811-G7
3400 SCL 95051 832-J6
TULANE DR
600 SCL 95051 832-J6
800 MTVW 94040 811-G7
TULARCITOS DR
1200 MPS 95035 794-D3
TULARE DR
3000 SJS 95132 814-F4
48900 FRMT 94539 794-A2
TULARE HILL DR
7300 SJS 95139 875-G7
TULARE HILL LN
7400 SJS 95139 875-G7
TULARE HILL RD
7300 SJS 95139 875-G7
TULIP CT
900 SUNV 94086 832-G3
TULIP DR
1000 SUNV 94086 832-G3
TULIP LN
- PA 94303 791-C4
TULIP RD
2100 SJS 95128 833-E6
2400 SCL 95128 833-E6
TULIP TER
- FRMT 94539 793-J3
TULIPAN DR
1000 SJS 95129 852-G3
TULIP BLOSSOM CT
100 SJS 95123 875-A4
TULIPTREE DR
- SJS 95123 875-D5
TULIPTREE LN
2600 SCL 95051 833-B7
TULIPWOOD LN
3200 SJS 95132 814-E2
TULITA CT
21000 CPTO 95014 832-C7
TULLY CT
3600 SJS 95148 835-F6
TULLY RD
- SJS 95112 854-F4
200 SJS 95121 854-H2
200 SJS 95122 854-H2
300 SCIC 95111 854-F4
300 SJS 95111 854-H2
1900 SJS 95122 855-A1
2100 SJS 95122 835-B7
2200 SJS 95148 835-E6
2900 SCIC 95148 835-D6
TUMBLE WY
3500 SJS 95132 814-G4
TUMBLE GRASS TER
- FRMT 94539 793-J3
TUNBRIDGE WY
6700 SJS 95120 894-G2
TUNIS AV
3600 SJS 95132 814-F2
TUOLOMNE CT
6100 SJS 95123 874-H6
TUOLUMNE DR
100 FRMT 94539 793-J2
TUPOLO DR
1600 SJS 95124 873-J3
1600 SJS 95124 874-A3
TURANDOT CT
1500 SJS 95121 854-H4
TURLEY CT
1900 SJS 95116 834-H5
TURLEY DR
800 SJS 95116 834-G5
TURLOCK AV
11400 SCIC 95046 957-E3
TURLOCK LN
1400 SJS 95132 814-F4
TURNBERRY PL
5200 SJS 95136 874-F3
TURNBERRY WY
- GIL 95020 977-E4
TURNER CT
100 SJS 95139 895-F1
TURNER DR
400 SCIC 95128 853-F2
TURNER WY
1200 CMBL 95008 873-B1
TURNHOUSE LN
2000 SJS 95121 855-C3
TURNSTONE WY
1300 SUNV 94087 832-H4
TURNWOOD CT
3600 SJS 95130 853-C4
TURQUESA CT
200 SJS 95116 834-F3
TURQUOISE ST
300 MPS 95035 814-B1
48200 FRMT 94539 793-J1
TURRETT DR
1200 SJS 95131 814-D6
TURRIFF WY
1400 SJS 95132 814-E4
TURTLE CREEK CT
300 SJS 95125 854-D4
TURTLEROCK DR
1100 SJS 95122 854-G1
TUSCALOOSA AV
- ATN 94027 790-C3
TUSCAN PARK CT
3200 SJS 95135 855-H2
TUSCANY CIR
- SJS 95135 855-H3
TUSCANY PL
400 HOLL 95023 1040-B3
1000 CPTO 95014 852-D2
TUSCARORA CT
5900 SJS 95123 874-J5
TUSCARORA DR
400 SJS 95123 874-H6
TUSCOLANA WY
- SJS 95125 854-D7
TUSTIN DR
1700 SJS 95122 855-A2

TUSTIN RD
6300 MonC 93907 1037-A7
TWAIN CT
18800 SAR 95070 872-H1
TWEED CT
19500 SAR 95070 852-F7
19500 SAR 95070 872-F1
TWEEDHOLM CT
6200 SJS 95120 894-B1
TWEEDSMUIR CT
2100 SJS 95121 855-C3
TWELVE ACRES DR
600 LALT 94022 811-C5
TWELVE OAKS RD
200 LGTS 95030 893-D1
TWIG LN
19100 CPTO 95014 852-G1
TWILIGHT CT
19900 CPTO 95014 832-F7
TWILIGHT DR
3700 SJS 95124 873-E3
TWINBERRY WY
9200 GIL 95020 957-E7
TWIN BROOK CT
900 SJS 95126 853-J3
TWIN BROOK DR
900 SJS 95126 853-J3
TWIN CREEKS RD
18300 MSER 95030 872-H4
18400 SAR 95070 872-J2
TWIN FALLS CT
3800 SJS 95121 855-D3
TWINKLE CT
- MPS 95035 793-H6
TWINLAKE DR
200 SUNV 94089 812-H5
TWIN OAK CT
- LAH 94022 810-J6
TWIN OAKS DR
100 LGTS 95032 873-D7
TWIN OAKS LN
2700 SJS 95127 835-A5
TWO OAKS LN
7900 GIL 95020 977-D3
TWYLA CT
2400 SJS 95008 853-B7
TWYLA LN
3900 SJS 95008 853-B7
TY DR
- SBnC 95023 1039-E5
TYBALT DR
800 SJS 95127 835-C1
TYHURST CT
5500 SJS 95123 874-J4
TYHURST WALKWAY
5400 SJS 95123 874-J4
TYLER AV
100 SCL 95117 833-D7
100 SCL 95117 853-D1
TYLER CT
100 SCL 95051 833-A7
TYLER PARK WY
1500 MTVW 94040 811-J7
TYMN WY
1900 SJS 95122 834-J6
TYNDALL ST
400 LALT 94022 811-E7
500 LALT 94022 831-E1
TYNE WY
3700 SCL 95054 813-E6
TYR LN
21500 SCIC 95120 895-C5
TYRELLA AV
200 MTVW 94043 812-A4
TYRELLA CT
100 MTVW 94043 812-A4
TYWOOD CT
- SJS 95116 834-F7

U

ULLMAN CT
4400 SJS 95121 855-F4
ULMECA PL
500 FRMT 94539 793-J1
ULMER CT
300 RDWC 94061 790-C1
ULSTER DR
2000 SJS 95131 814-D6
UMATILLA TR
17600 SCIC 95033 913-C2
UMBARGER RD
- SCIC 95111 854-G5
- SJS 95111 854-G5
500 SJS 95121 854-J4
UNDAJON DR
600 SJS 95133 834-E2
UNDERWOOD CT
10000 SCIC 95020 956-J6
UNDERWOOD DR
3700 SJS 95117 853-B2
UNIFIED WY
2200 SJS 95125 854-D4
UNION AV
- CMBL 95008 853-F6
200 LGTS 95032 873-F5
600 SJS 95008 853-F6
800 SCIC 95008 853-F6
1500 RDWC 94061 790-A1
2000 SJS 95124 873-F3
2600 SJS 95124 853-F6
3600 SCIC 95124 873-F3
5200 SJS 95032 873-F5
UNION RD
700 SBnC 95023 1040-A7
900 SBnC 95023 1039-D5
1100 SBnC - 1039-D5
1100 SBnC - 1040-A7
1200 HOLL 95023 1040-C7
UNION ST
- SJS 95110 854-C1
UNION HEIGHTS DR
1800 SBnC 95023 1039-G7

UNITED PL
10000 CPTO 95014 832-D7
UNIVERSITY AV
- PA 94301 790-J4
- LGTS 95030 873-B5
- LALT 94022 811-D6
200 LGTS 95032 873-B5
500 SJS 95110 833-H5
500 LALT 94022 831-E1
600 EPA 94303 791-B2
700 LALT 94024 831-E1
700 PA 94301 791-A3
800 MSER 95030 873-B5
800 MSER 95032 873-B5
900 SJS 95126 833-G6
900 SCIC 94024 831-E1
1700 SJS 95128 833-F7
2100 MTVW 94040 811-F4
UNIVERSITY DR
- MLPK 94025 790-F3
UNIVERSITY ST
700 SCL 95050 833-D5
UNIVERSITY TER
600 LALT 94022 811-D7
600 LALT 94022 831-D1
UNIVERSITY WY
1600 SJS 95126 833-F7
1700 SJS 95128 833-F7
21500 CPTO 95014 832-B7
UPHALL CT
1900 SJS 95121 855-C3
UPLAND CT
11500 CPTO 95014 852-B4
UPLAND WY
11500 CPTO 95014 852-B4
11500 SCIC 95014 852-B4
UPPER ELLEN RD
- SCrC 95018 912-E4
UPPER E ZAYANTE RD
15000 SCrC 95018 912-E4
15000 SCrC 95033 912-F2
UPPER HILL CT
13800 SAR 95070 872-C1
UPPER HILL DR
13800 SAR 95070 872-C1
UPPER HUTCHISON RD
- SCrC 95018 912-D7
UPTON CT
700 SJS 95136 874-E1
UPTON WY
700 SJS 95136 874-E1
URANIUM RD
100 SCL 95051 833-A1
100 SUNV 94086 833-A1
URBAN LN
600 PA 94301 790-H5
URIDIAS RANCH RD
2100 MPS 95035 794-E6
2200 SCIC 95035 794-E6
URLIN CT
6100 SJS 95123 875-B6
URNA AV
1700 SJS 95124 873-H1
URSA DR
48400 FRMT 94539 793-J1
URSHAN CT
100 SJS 95138 875-G6
URSHAN WY
7200 SJS 95138 875-G6
URSULA LN
27200 LAH 94022 830-J1
URSULA WY
1300 EPA 94303 791-B1
URZI CT
2800 SJS 95135 855-E2
URZI DR
3200 SJS 95135 855-E2
USONA DR
1400 SJS 95118 874-B3
UTE CT
6100 SJS 95123 874-H6
UTE DR
6100 SJS 95123 874-H6
UTICA CT
300 SJS 95123 875-B7
500 SUNV 94087 832-D3
UTICA DR
500 SUNV 94087 832-D3
UTICA LN
300 SJS 95123 875-B7
UTICA PL
7100 GIL 95020 977-J4
UTOPIA PL
1100 SJS 95127 835-C2
UVAS AV
200 MPS 95035 793-J6
UVAS CT
700 SJS 95123 874-G5
UVAS RD Rt#-G8
12800 SCIC 95037 956-D1
15500 SCIC 95037 936-A1
17700 SCIC 95037 935-J1
19000 SCIC 95037 916-A5
20400 SCIC 95037 915-J4
UVAS PARK DR
7000 GIL 95020 977-G3
UXBRIDGE CT
- SJS 95139 875-G7

V

VAI AV
21400 CPTO 95014 852-C3
VAL CT
3000 SCIC 95020 958-D3
VALAIR DR
- HOLL 95023 1040-C7
- SBnC 95023 1040-C7
VALBUSA DR
1100 GIL 95020 957-F7
VALCARTIER DR
1400 SUNV 94087 832-D5

VALDEZ PL
900 SCIC 94305 810-J2
VALDOSTA RD
1100 SJS 95121 855-A5
VALE AV
1400 CMBL 95008 873-C2
VALE CT
6100 SJS 95123 875-A6
VALE DR
300 SJS 95123 875-A6
VALELAKE CT
1100 SUNV 94089 812-J4
VALENCIA AV
1000 SUNV 94086 832-C1
VALENCIA CT
- PTLV 94028 810-D6
2300 SJS 95125 853-J6
VALENCIA DR
200 LALT 94022 811-E5
800 MPS 95035 794-B6
VALENCIA PL
- SCL 95050 833-D2
VALERIAN CT
1200 SUNV 94086 832-G3
VALERIAN WY
1000 SUNV 94086 832-G3
VALERIE CT
2200 SJS 95008 853-B7
VALERIE DR
2200 SJS 95008 853-B7
VALERI RUTH CT
500 SCL 95050 833-C6
VALHALLA CT
1700 SJS 95132 814-E4
VALHALLA DR
2900 SJS 95132 814-E4
VALI WY
- HOLL 95023 1039-J4
VALLA DR
1700 SJS 95124 873-H1
VALLCO PKWY
19100 CPTO 95014 832-G7
VALLECITO RD
22000 CPTO 95014 852-A2
VALLECITOS WY
100 LGTS 95032 872-J4
VALLE DEL LAGO
- SJS 95135 855-G4
VALLEJO DR
1300 SJS 95130 853-A4
1500 HOLL 95023 1040-D6
1500 SJS 95070 853-A4
VALLE VERDE
200 SBnC 95023 1060-E1
VALLE VISTA CT
19200 SAR 95070 872-G4
VALLE VISTA DR
19200 SAR 95070 872-F4
VALLEY CT
- ATN 94027 790-A7
- WDSD 94062 790-A7
700 SCL 95051 833-A6
VALLEY RD
- ATN 94027 790-A7
VALLEY ST
200 LALT 94022 811-E7
VALLEY WY
400 MPS 95035 793-J7
600 SCL 95051 833-B6
VALLEYBROOK CT
4100 SJS 95111 855-A7
VALLEY CREST CT
1500 SJS 95131 834-D1
VALLEY CREST DR
1400 SJS 95131 834-C1
VALLEY FORGE DR
1000 SUNV 94087 832-B3
7000 GIL 95020 977-J4
VALLEY FORGE WY
600 CMBL 95008 853-C4
600 SJS 95117 853-C4
VALLEY GLEN CT
6200 SJS 95123 874-G7
VALLEY GLEN DR
6100 SJS 95123 874-G6
VALLEY GREEN DR
20500 CPTO 95014 832-D6
VALLEYHAVEN WY
- SJS 95111 874-J1
VALLEY HEIGHTS DR
2700 SJS 95133 814-G7
VALLEY MEADOW CT
5900 SJS 95135 855-J7
VALLEY OAK
- PTLV 94028 830-C2
VALLEY OAK CT
- SBnC 95023 1060-D1
VALLEY OAK DR
400 SCIC 95037 916-B1
17300 MSER 95030 873-B4
VALLEY OAK TER
- SJS 95112 834-D7
VALLEY OAKS CT
- GIL 95020 957-E7
VALLEY OAKS DR
- GIL 95020 957-E7
- GIL 95020 977-E1
VALLEY PARK CIR
100 SJS 95139 895-H2
VALLEY QUAIL CIR
1100 SJS 95120 894-F3
VALLEY RIDGE LN
3600 SCIC 95148 835-E5
VALLEY SQUARE LN
3300 SJS 95117 853-D4
VALLEY VIEW AV
- SCIC 95127 815-A7
200 SCIC 95127 814-J6
VALLEY VIEW CT
1000 SCIC 94024 831-F2
3200 MGH 95037 917-F4
VALLEY VIEW DR
400 SCIC 94024 831-F2

VALLEY VIEW RD
1500 HOLL 95023 1040-D7
1700 SBnC 95023 1040-C7
VALLEY VISTA CIR
- MGH 95037 916-H4
VALLEY VISTA DR
- SJS 95148 835-E6
VALLEYWOOD CT
3000 SJS 95148 855-E1
VALMAINE CT
3100 SJS 95135 855-F3
VALMY ST
100 MPS 95035 794-A4
VALONIA WY
- HOLL 95023 1039-G3
VALOTA RD
900 RDWC 94061 790-A2
VALPARAISO AV
- ATN 94027 790-E4
- MLPK 94025 790-C6
700 MLPK 94027 790-E4
1800 SMCo 94025 790-D5
VALPARAISO ST
600 SCIC 94305 810-H1
VALPICO DR
1700 SJS 95124 853-J7
1700 SJS 95124 873-J1
VALROY CT
400 SJS 95123 875-A7
VALROY DR
6200 SJS 95123 875-A7
VAN CT
800 SUNV 94087 832-D2
VAN AUKEN CIR
900 PA 94303 791-D5
VAN BUREN CIR
1800 MTVW 94040 831-G1
VAN BUREN RD
400 MLPK 94025 790-J1
VAN BUREN ST
300 LALT 94022 811-C4
VANCE CT
3400 SJS 95132 814-G4
VANCE DR
1300 SJS 95132 814-G4
VANCE LN
- EPA 94303 791-C2
VAN COTT CT
- SJS 95127 834-H3
VANCOUVER CT
14400 SCIC 95127 835-B3
VANDELL WY
400 CMBL 95008 873-D2
VANDER WY
1300 SJS 95112 834-B1
VANDERBILT CT E
1100 SUNV 94087 832-D3
VANDERBILT CT W
1100 SUNV 94087 832-D3
VANDERBILT DR
600 SUNV 94087 832-D3
4300 CMBL 95008 853-A7
4300 SJS 95130 853-A7
4800 SJS 95130 852-J7
18200 SAR 95070 852-J7
VANDERBILT WY
3300 SCL 95051 832-J6
VAN DE WATER WY
500 SJS 95111 854-F6
VAN DUSEN CT
1300 CMBL 95008 873-A1
VAN DUSEN LN
1300 CMBL 95008 873-A2
VAN DYCK CT
800 SUNV 94087 832-F3
VAN DYCK DR
1200 SUNV 94087 832-F3
VANESSA DR
1100 SJS 95126 853-H3
VANGORN CT
3300 SJS 95121 855-A4
VANGORN WY
3300 SJS 95121 855-A4
VANNA CT
1500 SJS 95131 814-B7
VANONI RD
200 SCrC 95076 997-A7
VANPORT CT
1700 SJS 95122 855-B3
VANPORT DR
1700 SJS 95122 855-B3
VAN SANSUL AV
3000 SJS 95128 853-E3
VAN WINKLE LN
2400 SJS 95116 834-J4
VAQUERO CT
13600 SAR 95070 872-C1
VAQUERO DR
700 MTVW 94043 811-J3
VAQUEROS AV
600 SUNV 94086 812-E5
VARDEN AV
2800 SJS 95124 873-G1
VARGAS CT
100 MPS 95035 794-A4
5700 SJS 95120 874-C5
VARGAS DR
1200 SJS 95120 874-C6
VARGAS PL
2300 SCL 95050 833-C3
VARIAN CT
200 SJS 95119 875-D7
VARIAN WY
- PA 94304 790-G5
22200 CPTO 95014 832-A7
VARNER CT
3400 SJS 95132 814-H4
VARSI PL
700 SCL 95053 833-F5
700 SCL 95050 833-F5
VARSITY CT
1000 MTVW 94040 811-G7
VASILAKOS CT
- SMCo 94025 790-C5

VASILAKOS WY
- SMCo 94025 790-D5
VASONA AV
500 LGTS 95032 873-C2
VASONA CT
600 LGTS 95032 873-C2
VASONA ST
600 MPS 95035 793-J6
VASONA TER
500 LGTS 95030 873-B5
VASONA OAKS DR
100 LGTS 95032 873-B5
VASONA PARK RD
- LGTS 95032 873-B6
VASQUEZ AV
1100 SUNV 94086 812-B7
VASQUEZ CT
400 SUNV 94086 812-B7
VASSAR AV
1700 MTVW 94043 811-H3
VASSAR DR
5400 SJS 95118 874-B5
VAUGHN AV
300 SCIC 95128 853-G1
300 SJS 95128 853-G1
VAUXHALL CIR
5300 SJS 95123 874-H3
VEGAS AV
1700 MPS 95035 794-A3
VEGAS DR
6200 SJS 95120 874-E7
6300 SJS 95120 894-E1
VELADO ST
100 HOLL 95023 1040-A6
VELARDE ST
200 MTVW 94041 811-J5
VELASCO DR
300 SJS 95123 874-H4
VELVETLAKE DR
200 SUNV 94089 812-J5
VELVET MEADOW CT
6700 SJS 95120 894-F2
VENADO CT
5600 SJS 95123 875-B4
VENADO WY
100 SJS 95123 875-B4
VENDOME ST
400 SJS 95110 834-A5
VENDURA CT
19300 SAR 95070 852-G6
VENECIA DR
400 SJS 95133 834-G1
VENETIAN WY
15000 MGH 95037 937-B4
VENICE WY
4300 SJS 95129 853-A3
VENN AV
2300 SJS 95124 873-E4
VENNDALE AV
2300 SJS 95124 873-E4
VENNUM DR
1500 SJS 95131 814-C6
VENTANA CT
- HOLL 95023 1040-D7
VENTANA DR
7200 SJS 95129 852-E2
VENTANA PL
7200 SJS 95129 852-E2
VENTURA AV
200 PA 94306 811-C1
4600 SJS 95111 875-A1
VENTURA CT
- MGH 95037 917-B3
100 SBnC 95023 1039-H3
3900 PA 94306 811-C1
VENTURA DR
- MGH 95037 917-B3
48900 FRMT 94539 794-A2
VENTURA PL
2100 SCL 95051 833-A2
VENTURE WY
- GIL 95020 978-C4
VENTURELLA DR
1400 SCIC 95020 957-J2
1400 SCIC 95020 958-A1
VENUS CT
600 FRMT 94539 793-J1
3700 SJS 95121 855-D4
VENUS WY
- MPS 95035 813-J2
VERA LN
5100 SJS 95111 875-B2
VERA CRUZ AV
600 LALT 94022 811-E5
VERA CRUZ DR
5900 SJS 95120 874-A7
VERANDA WY
- SJS 95138 875-G5
VERANO CT
500 SJS 95111 875-B1
VERANO DR
200 LALT 94022 811-F6
VERBENA DR
- GIL 95020 977-E2
100 EPA 94303 791-C3
VERBENA WY
4800 SJS 95129 852-B7
4800 SJS 95129 853-B2
VERDANT WY
3100 SJS 95117 853-D3
VERDE CIR
- HOLL 95023 1039-G3
VERDE CT
100 LGTS 95032 873-E5
20500 SAR 95070 872-C1
VERDE MOOR CT
20800 SAR 95070 852-D6
VERDES ROBLES
17200 LGTS 95030 873-B4
VERDE VISTA CT
13600 SAR 95070 872-D1
VERDE VISTA LN
20500 SAR 95070 872-D1

STREET
Block City ZIP Pg-Grid

VERDI DR
700 SUNV 94087 832-F4
3300 SJS 95111 854-J5
VERDIGRIS CIR
4200 SJS 95134 813-D2
VERDOSA DR
4000 PA 94306 811-C2
VERDUN CT
600 HOLL 95023 1040-B5
VERDUN DR
700 HOLL 95023 1040-B5
VEREDA CT
700 SJS 95123 874-G6
VERMILION CT
3100 SJS 95135 855-E2
VERMONT ST
500 SJS 95110 833-H5
900 SJS 95126 833-H5
VERNA DR
2900 SCIC 95133 814-H7
2900 SCIC 95133 834-H1
VERNAL CT
200 LALT 94022 811-D4
VERNAL DR
1300 SJS 95130 853-B4
VERNAZZA AV
- SJS 95135 855-F2
VERNICE AV
3200 SJS 95127 835-B3
VERNIE CT
900 CPTO 95014 852-D2
VERNIER PL
1000 SCIC 94305 810-J2
VERNON AV
700 SCIC 94043 812-A2
700 MTVW 94043 812-A2
1200 SJS 95125 854-B3
VERNON CIR
800 MTVW 94043 812-A3
VERNON TER
3300 PA 94303 791-E6
VERONA CT
100 LGTS 95030 872-J4
VERONA PL
400 HOLL 95023 1040-B3
VERONA RD
- SJS 95135 855-H3
VERONICA CT
1000 EPA 94303 791-C1
VERONICA DR
19800 SAR 95070 852-F6
VERONICA PL
- PTLV 94028 810-C7
2000 SJS 95124 873-F1
VERSAILLES CT
- SJS 95127 814-J7
- SJS 95127 834-C1
VERSAILLES DR
- MLPK 94025 790-F3
800 HOLL 95023 1040-C5
VERSAILLES WY
19600 SAR 95070 872-F3
VERWOOD DR
2400 SJS 95130 853-A7
VESCA WY
4800 SJS 95129 853-B2
VESPER AV
600 FRMT 94539 793-J1
VESSING CT
18600 SAR 95070 872-H3
VESSING RD
18500 SAR 95070 872-H3
VESTAL ST
400 SJS 95112 834-B3
VESUVIUS LN
3000 SJS 95132 814-F5
VETERAN AV
- SJS 95125 854-E4
VIA ALEGRIA CT
1500 SJS 95121 855-B4
VIA ALMADEN
1100 SJS 95120 874-D6
VIA ALTO CT
13700 SAR 95070 872-H1
VIA AMAROSA
- MGH 95037 916-H3
VIA AMIGOS
6300 SJS 95120 874-D7
6300 SJS 95120 894-D1
VIA AMPARO
7200 SJS 95135 855-J5
VIA ANACAPA
7000 SJS 95139 875-F6
VIA ARLINE
12200 LAH 94022 831-B1
VIA ARRIBA CT
19200 SAR 95070 852-G7
VIA ARRIBA DR
13200 SAR 95070 852-G7
VIA BAHIA
- SUNV 94089 812-H3
VIA BAJA DR
700 MPS 95035 794-B5
VIA BARRANCA
7000 SJS 95139 875-F7
VIA BELLA
7200 SJS 95139 875-F7
VIA BELMONTE
7000 SJS 95135 855-J5
VIA BLANC CT
13100 SAR 95070 852-F7
VIA BLANCA
7000 SJS 95139 875-F7
VIA BONITA
18400 MSER 95030 872-J6
VIA BORGHESE
- SJS 95135 855-F2
VIA BREZZO
7200 SJS 95120 894-G5
VIA CABALLERO
15300 MSER 95030 872-J4
VIA CALZADA
7300 SJS 95135 855-J5
VIA CAMINO CT
22100 CPTO 95014 832-A7
VIA CAMPAGNA
- SJS 95120 893-J1
- SJS 95120 894-A1
VIA CAMPINA
- SJS 95139 875-F6
VIA CAMPO AUREO
- SJS 95120 894-A1
VIA CAMPO VERDE
- SJS 95120 893-J1
- SJS 95120 894-A1
VIA CANCION
1400 SJS 95128 853-F5
VIA CANTARES
7300 SJS 95135 855-J5
VIA CAPRI
- SUNV 94089 812-H3
VIA CARMELA
7100 SJS 95139 875-G7
VIA CARMEN
2800 SJS 95124 873-F1
VIA CARRIZO
7200 SJS 95135 855-J5
VIA CASTANA
15500 MGH 95037 937-A4
VIA CASTANA CT
15700 MGH 95037 937-A4
VIA CERRO GORDO
27600 LAH 94022 830-H1
VIA CIELO
7000 SJS 95135 855-H5
VIA CINCO DE MAYO
1700 SJS 95132 814-D4
VIA CODORNIZ
1400 SJS 95128 853-F4
VIA COLINA
7100 SJS 95139 875-F7
15100 SAR 95070 872-G4
VIA COLLADO
100 LGTS 95032 872-J3
VIA CONTENTA
- MGH 95037 916-H3
1400 SJS 95128 853-F5
VIA CORDURA
7000 SJS 95139 875-F6
VIA CORFINIO
15100 MGH 95037 937-A4
VIA CORITA
27800 LAH 94022 830-J1
27800 LAH 94022 831-A1
VIA CORONA
7100 SJS 95139 875-G7
VIA CORTA
20700 SCIC 95120 894-J2
20700 SCIC 95120 895-A1
VIA CORTINA
- SJS 95120 893-J1
VIA CRESCENTE CT
19200 SAR 95070 852-G7
VIA CRESPI
400 SCIC 94305 790-G7
VIA CRISTOBAL
3900 SJS 95008 853-B6
VIA DE ADRIANNA
6200 SJS 95120 874-B7
6200 SJS 95120 894-B1
VIA DE CABALLE
4800 SJS 95118 874-B3
VIA DE GUADALUPE
- SJS 95116 834-G3
VIA DE LAS ABEJAS
6100 SJS 95120 874-B7
VIA DE LA VISTA
14000 SCIC 95127 835-F3
VIA DEL CASTILLE
600 MGH 95037 937-A4
VIA DEL CIELO
9400 SCIC 95020 958-E3
VIA DEL CORONADO
3000 SJS 95132 814-D3
VIA DEL MAR
3200 SJS 95124 873-F2
VIA DEL ORO
6400 SJS 95119 875-E6
9400 SCIC 95020 958-E3
VIA DE LOS GRANDE
1300 SJS 95120 894-B1
VIA DE LOS REYES
1300 SJS 95120 874-B7
VIA DEL POZO
1000 LALT 94022 811-D4
VIA DEL RIO
7000 SJS 95139 875-F7
VIA DEL SOL
2900 SJS 95132 814-D3
VIA DEL SOL RD
1100 MonC 95076 1037-A6
VIA DEL SUR
15100 MSER 95030 873-A4
VIA DE MARCOS
14500 SAR 95070 872-G3
VIA DE NINOS
15300 MGH 95037 937-B3
VIA DEPAZ
- MGH 95037 916-H3
VIADER CT
600 SCL 95050 833-D5
VIA DESTE
2000 SJS 95008 853-C6
VIA DE TESOROS
100 LGTS 95030 872-J4
100 LGTS 95032 872-J4
VIA DONA PATRICIA
- SBnC - 1037-J5
VIA DONDERA
1300 SCL 95051 833-A4
VIA EDUARDO
15500 MGH 95037 937-A4
VIA EL CAPITAN
1800 SJS 95124 873-H1
VIA ENCANTADA
18100 MSER 95030 872-J4
VIA ENCINITAS
2800 SJS 95132 814-D3
VIA ESCALERA
2100 LALT 94024 831-H5
VIA ESCUELA CT
13000 SAR 95070 852-F7
VIA ESCUELA DR
19500 SAR 95070 852-F7
VIA ESPLENDOR
23000 CPTO 95014 831-H5
VIA FELIZ
27800 LAH 94022 810-J7
VIA FELIZE
- MGH 95037 916-H3
VIA FERRARI
1100 SJS 95122 834-G6
VIA FLORES
1700 SJS 95132 814-D4
VIA FLORES CT
1700 SJS 95132 814-D4
VIA FORTUNA
- SJS 95120 893-J1
- SJS 95120 894-A1
VIA GRANADA
- SUNV 94089 812-H3
VIA GRANDE
700 MGH 95037 936-J1
VIA GRANDE CT
13200 SAR 95070 852-F7
VIA GRANDE DR
13200 SAR 95070 852-F7
VIA GRANJA
7300 SJS 95135 855-J5
VIA HUERTA
1200 LALT 94024 831-H5
VIA JOSE
1100 SJS 95120 874-D7
VIA JUAN PABLO
- SBnC - 1037-J5
- SBnC 95045 1037-J5
VIA LAGO
100 LGTS 95032 872-J2
VIA LAGUNA
7300 SJS 95135 855-J5
VIA LA POSADA
200 LGTS 95032 872-J3
VIA LARGO CT
300 MGH 95037 937-B4
VIA LOMA CT
300 MGH 95037 916-H5
VIA LOMAS
7100 SJS 95139 875-G7
VIA LOMBARDI
20800 CPTO 95014 832-E6
VIA LOMITA
15100 MSER 95030 872-J4
VIA LUGANO
- SJS 95120 893-J1
VIA MADERO DR
5900 SJS 95120 874-A7
VIA MADEROS
2200 LALT 94024 831-J6
VIA MADRONAS CT
19400 SAR 95070 852-F7
VIA MADRONAS DR
13100 SAR 95070 852-F7
VIA MAGGIORE
- SJS 95120 893-J1
VIA MARGUTTA
- SJS 95135 855-F2
VIA MARIA
7100 SJS 95139 875-F7
VIA MATEO
1100 SJS 95120 894-D1
VIA MESA
- SJS 95139 875-F6
VIA MILANO
3800 SJS 95008 853-B6
VIA MIMOSA
7200 SJS 95135 855-J6
VIA MONTALVO
3900 SJS 95008 853-B6
VIA MONTE DR
5600 SJS 95118 874-C4
19400 SAR 95070 852-F7
VIA MONTECITOS
7300 SJS 95135 855-J5
VIA MONTEZ
3000 SJS 95132 814-D3
VIA NAPOLI
2100 SJS 95008 853-B6
20300 CPTO 95014 832-E7
VIA NARETTO
- MGH 95037 937-B3
VIA NAVONA
300 MGH 95037 937-B3
VIA NIDA
- SUNV 94089 812-H3
VIANNA ST
- SJS 95131 814-B6
VIA ORTEGA
400 SCIC 94305 790-G7
VIA PACIFICA
7000 SJS 95139 875-G7
VIA PADRE
- SJB 95045 1038-D4
VIA PALAMOS
20300 CPTO 95014 832-E6
VIA PALOMA
- SJS 95120 893-J1
VIA PALOMINO
15200 MSER 95030 873-A4
15300 MSER 95030 872-J5
VIA PALOU
400 SCIC 94305 790-G7
VIA PASA TIEMPO
- MGH 95037 916-H3
VIA PAVISO
10700 CPTO 95014 832-E7
VIA PIEDRA
7300 SJS 95135 855-J5
VIA PINTO
15200 MSER 95030 873-A4
VIA PISA
1500 SJS 95128 853-H2
VIA PORTADA
7100 SJS 95135 855-J5
VIA PORTOFINO
10800 CPTO 95014 832-E7
VIA PRADERA
7000 SJS 95139 875-F7
VIA PRIMAVERA CT
500 SJS 95111 875-B1
VIA PRIMAVERA DR
300 SJS 95111 875-B1
VIA PUEBLO LN
200 SCIC 94305 790-G6
VIA RAMADA
7000 SJS 95139 875-F7
VIA RANCHERO
900 CMBL 95008 873-C1
VIA RANCHERO CT
13100 SAR 95070 852-G7
VIA RANCHERO DR
13100 SAR 95070 852-G7
VIA REAL DR
19300 SAR 95070 852-G7
VIA REGGIO CT
1900 SJS 95132 814-C4
VIA REGINA
21700 SAR 95070 872-B1
VIA RODRIGUES
- SBnC - 1037-J5
- SBnC 95045 1037-J5
VIA ROMA
2100 SJS 95008 853-B6
VIA ROMERA
7100 SJS 95139 875-F7
VIA RONCOLE
12000 SAR 95070 852-D5
VIA SALICE
3800 SJS 95008 853-B6
VIA SAN MARINO
20300 CPTO 95014 832-E6
VIA SANTA MARIA
100 LGTS 95030 873-C7
100 LGTS 95032 873-C7
VIA SANTA TERESA
20100 SCIC 95120 894-H2
VIA SARONNO
- SJS 95120 893-J1
VIA SENDERO
7200 SJS 95135 855-J5
VIA SERENA
7000 SJS 95139 875-F7
VIA SERENO DR
17500 MSER 95030 873-A5
VIA SERRA
- SJB 95045 1038-D4
VIA SIESTA
- SUNV 94089 812-H3
VIA SOLANA
7100 SJS 95135 855-J5
VIA SORRENTO
400 MGH 95037 937-B4
10800 CPTO 95014 832-E7
VIA TERESA
100 LGTS 95030 872-J4
100 LGTS 95032 872-J4
VIA TESORO CT
19100 SAR 95070 872-G2
VIA VALIENTE
900 SJS 95120 894-G2
VIA VALVERDE
7000 SJS 95135 855-J5
VIA VAQUERO
15400 MSER 95030 872-J5
VIA VAQUERO NORTE
- SBnC 95045 1037-H3
VIA VAQUERO SUR
- SBnC - 1037-H5
- SBnC 95045 1037-H5
VIA VENETO
15500 MGH 95037 937-A4
VIA VENEZIA
- SJS 95125 854-D7
VIA VENTANA
27900 LAH 94022 830-H1
VIA VENTURA
23400 CPTO 95014 831-H6
VIA VICO
7100 SJS 95129 852-E3
VIA VISTA
7200 SJS 95139 875-F7
VIA VIVALDI
- MGH 95037 937-A5
VIA VOLANTE
20300 CPTO 95014 832-E6
VICANNA DR
6300 SJS 95129 852-F4
VICAR LN
900 SJS 95117 853-C3
VICENTE DR
1200 SUNV 94086 812-B7
VICENZA WY
2300 SJS 95138 855-F6
VICEROY CT
10100 CPTO 95014 832-A7
VICEROY WY
800 SJS 95133 814-G6
900 SJS 95132 814-G6
VICKERY AV
400 SCIC 95020 957-G6
14700 SAR 95070 872-D3
VICKERY LN
- GIL 95020 957-H6
- SCIC 95020 957-H6
VICKERY PL
14700 SAR 95070 872-E3
VICKSBURG CT
10200 CPTO 95014 852-F1
VICKSBURG DR
10100 CPTO 95014 852-F1
VICTOR AV
- CMBL 95008 853-C5
VICTOR CT
3200 SJS 95132 814-F3
3300 SCL 95054 813-F6
VICTOR PL
14100 SAR 95070 872-E2
VICTOR ST
3200 SCL 95054 813-F6
VICTOR WY
600 MTVW 94040 811-H6
VICTORIA AV
1000 HOLL 95023 1040-A5
3200 SCL 95051 833-A3
3300 SCL 95051 832-J3
VICTORIA CT
2000 LALT 94024 832-A5
14400 SCIC 95127 835-B3
VICTORIA DR
- ATN 94027 790-F3
- GIL 95020 978-A5
VICTORIA LNDG
1800 SJS 95132 814-C4
VICTORIA PL
300 PA 94306 811-D2
VICTORIA TER
1300 SUNV 94087 832-D4
VICTORIAN PINES PL
- SJS 95117 853-C1
VICTORIA PARK DR
4000 SJS 95136 874-F1
VICTORY AV
400 MTVW 94043 811-F2
VICTORY DR
- HOLL 95023 1040-C6
VICTORY LN
- LGTS 95030 873-A7
VICTORY WY
- SCIC 95037 936-H3
VIDA CT
- MTVW 94043 811-H3
VIDA LARGA LP
- MPS 95035 813-J1
VIDA LEON CT
300 SJS 95116 834-D2
VIENNA DR
- MPS 95035 793-J4
- MPS 95035 794-A4
1200 SUNV 94089 812-H4
VIENTO TER
- MPS 95035 813-J1
VIERRA CT
1300 SJS 95125 854-A5
VIEW DR
1700 MPS 95035 794-D6
VIEW ST
- LALT 94022 811-D6
100 MTVW 94041 811-J5
VIEWCREST CT
20200 SCIC 95120 894-J2
VIEWCREST DR
20200 SCIC 95120 894-H2
VIEWCREST LN
17000 MGH 95037 936-J1
17000 MGH 95037 937-A1
VIEWFIELD RD
15800 MSER 95030 872-J6
VIEWMONT AV
- SCIC 95127 834-J2
- SCIC 95127 835-A2
VIEWMONT CT
3400 SJS 95127 835-A2
3400 SCIC 95127 835-A2
VIEWOAK DR
12100 SAR 95070 852-F5
VIEW OAKS WY
20600 SCIC 95120 894-J2
VIEWPARK CIR
300 SJS 95136 874-G1
VIEWPOINT LN
10000 SJS 95120 894-G4
VIEWRIDGE DR
19700 SAR 95070 852-F5
VIGNOBLE DR
- SCIC 95020 956-J7
VILLA
- MTVW 94043 811-J2
- MTVW 94043 812-A2
VILLA AV
100 LGTS 95030 893-A1
700 SJS 95126 833-H6
VILLA DR
1400 SCIC 94024 831-F3
VILLA PL
2300 SCL 95054 813-C4
VILLA ST
200 MTVW 94041 811-G4
VILLA CENTRE WY
- SJS 95128 853-E1
VILLA CONTESSA CT
- SJS 95135 855-J3
VILLA CONTESSA PL
- SJS 95135 855-J3
VILLA CORTONA WY
- SJS 95125 854-D6
VILLA DE ANZA AV
10600 CPTO 95014 832-E6
VILLA EAST HILLS CT
3100 SJS 95127 835-A3
VILLA FELICE CT
500 LGTS 95030 873-B4
VILLAGE CIR
100 MGH 95037 937-B3
VILLAGE CT
1000 HOLL 95023 1040-C6
1400 MTVW 94040 832-A1
VILLAGE DR
12900 SAR 95070 852-G6
VILLAGE LN
100 MGH 95037 937-B3
300 LGTS 95030 873-A7
VILLAGE PL
- GIL 95020 977-J5
VILLAGE WY
15900 MGH 95037 937-B3
VILLAGE CENTER DR
300 SJS 95134 813-H4
VILLAGEHEART LN
- SJS 95135 855-J3
VILLAGEHEART PL
- SJS 95135 855-J3
VILLAGE HERMOSA LN
8200 SJS 95135 855-J6
VILLAGETREE DR
2000 SJS 95131 814-D6
VILLAGE VIEW DR
7600 SJS 95135 856-A6
VILLAGE VIEW LP
- SJS 95135 856-A6
VILLAGEWOOD WY
6800 SJS 95120 894-H3
VILLAGIO PL
400 SJS 95134 813-H4
VILLA GLEN WY
3800 SJS 95136 874-D1
VILLA MARIA CT
1000 SJS 95125 854-G5
21500 CPTO 95014 852-B3
VILLA MONTEREY
2700 SJS 95111 854-G5
VILLANOVA CT
3300 SCL 95051 833-A2
VILLANOVA RD
2100 SJS 95130 852-J7
2300 SAR 95070 852-J7
VILLA NUEVA CT
100 MTVW 94040 831-J1
VILLA NUEVA WY
2400 MTVW 94040 831-J1
VILLA OAKS LN
21700 SAR 95070 852-B7
21700 SAR 95070 872-B1
21800 SCIC 95070 852-B7
VILLA PACHECO CT
- SBnC 95023 1060-E2
VILLA PARK CT
500 SJS 95118 874-C3
VILLA PARK LN
- SJS 95118 874-G3
VILLA PARK WY
500 SJS 95118 874-C3
VILLA REAL
500 PA 94306 811-C2
VILLA REAL DR
1400 SCIC 95020 958-A2
VILLARITA DR
1500 CMBL 95008 853-A6
1900 SJS 95130 853-A6
VILLA ROBLEDA DR
3300 MTVW 94040 832-A2
VILLA ROSA PL
- SJS 95126 833-H5
VILLA STONE DR
300 SJS 95125 854-D3
VILLA TERESA WY
700 SJS 95123 874-E5
VILLA VERA
4000 PA 94306 811-C2
VILLA VISTA
4000 PA 94306 811-C2
VILLA VISTA RD
100 SJS 95135 855-H4
200 SCIC 95135 855-H4
VILMAR AV
6000 SJS 95120 874-B7
VINA DR
18500 SCIC 95033 892-H4
VINCA CT
700 GIL 95020 977-J6
VINCENT CT
6000 SJS 95123 875-A6
VINCENT DR
200 MTVW 94041 811-J6
2000 SCIC 95046 938-A5
3300 SCL 95051 832-J2
3300 SCL 95051 833-A1
VINCI ST
- SJS 95136 854-F7
VINCI PARK WY
1100 SJS 95131 814-D7
VINE AV
300 SUNV 94086 832-E1
VINE ST
100 HOLL 95023 1040-A5
100 MLPK 94025 790-E6
100 SMCo 94025 790-E6
500 SJS 95110 834-B7
500 SJS 95110 854-C1
1400 SJS 95125 854-C1
14800 SAR 95070 872-E3
VINE TR
18100 SCIC 95033 912-J4
VINEDALE SQ
1900 SJS 95132 814-F3
VINEDO LN
25700 LAH 94022 831-B2
VINEFERA DR
- SJS 95135 855-E2
VINELAND AV
17300 LGTS 95030 873-A5
17300 MSER 95030 873-A5
VINELAND CT
17600 MSER 95030 873-A5
VINEMAPLE AV
600 SUNV 94086 832-J2
VINES CT
- EPA 94303 791-C1
VINEWOOD LN
100 MGH 95037 937-B5
VINEYARD BLVD
15600 MGH 95037 937-B1
VINEYARD CT
100 MGH 95037 937-B2
2200 LALT 94024 831-J5
VINEYARD DR
200 SJS 95119 875-D7
200 SJS 95119 895-D1
1500 LALT 94024 831-J6
1500 LALT 94024 832-A5
VINEYARD LN
- PA 94304 790-G5
19100 SAR 95070 852-G7
VINEYARD CREEK CT
8600 SJS 95135 855-J6
VINEYARD ESTATES DR
6400 SBnC 95023 1060-E5
VINEYARD PARK CT
- SJS 95148 855-C1
VINEYARD PARK DR
- SJS 95148 855-C1
VINEYARD PARK LN
- SJS 95135 855-H2
VINEYARD PARK PL
- SJS 95148 855-C1
VINEYARD PARK WY
- SJS 95135 855-H2
VINEYARD RIDGE CT
8600 SJS 95135 855-J6
VINEYARD RIDGE PL
8600 SJS 95135 855-J6
VINEYARD SPRING CT
11600 CPTO 95014 852-A4
VINFERA PL
- SJS 95135 855-H2
VIN GRANDE CT
3000 SJS 95135 855-E3
VIN SANTO LN
- SJS 95148 855-F1
VINTAGE CT
- SCIC 95046 957-D1
VINTAGE LN
21600 SAR 95070 872-B3
VINTAGE WY
- HOLL 95023 1040-B4
800 SJS 95122 854-F1
VINTAGE ACRES WY
3200 SJS 95148 855-F2
VINTAGE CREST DR
3100 SJS 95148 855-E1
VINTAGE OAKS CT
3200 SJS 95148 855-F2
VINTNER CT
14900 SAR 95070 872-B3
VINTNER WY
1600 SJS 95124 873-H4
VINYARD CT
100 LGTS 95032 872-J3
VIOLA AV
- SJS 95110 834-B7
VIOLA PL
700 LALT 94024 831-E1
VIOLET TER
- FRMT 94539 793-J3
VIOLET WY
- GIL 95020 977-G1
2100 SJS 95008 853-C6
VIOLETA CT
- SJS 95136 874-G2
VIRDELLE DR
21700 SCIC 95033 912-H3
VIREO AV
1500 SCL 95051 832-H5
1500 SUNV 94087 832-H5
VIRGIL PL
1100 SJS 95120 894-H4
VIRGINIA AV
- CMBL 95008 853-C7
900 CMBL 95008 873-C1
1200 RDWC 94061 790-A2
1600 SJS 95116 834-G5
VIRGINIA CT
800 CMBL 95008 873-C1
VIRGINIA DR
400 HOLL 95023 1039-J3
400 HOLL 95023 1040-A3
18000 SCIC 95033 912-J3
VIRGINIA LN
- ATN 94027 790-E1
VIRGINIA PL
1500 SJS 95116 834-F5
E VIRGINIA ST
- SJS 95112 854-C1
200 SJS 95112 834-D7
W VIRGINIA ST
- SJS 95110 854-C1
300 SJS 95125 854-A1
VIRGINIA SWAN PL
10200 CPTO 95014 832-E7
VIRGO LN
3400 SJS 95111 854-F6
VISCAINO AV
1100 SUNV 94086 812-B7
VISCAINO CT
12600 LAH 94022 811-B7
VISCAINO DR
12600 LAH 94022 811-B7
VISCAINO PL
12800 LAH 94022 811-A7
VISCAINO RD
12700 LAH 94022 811-B6
VISCAINO WY
300 SJS 95119 875-C7
VISCONTI PL
- SCL 95050 833-C5
VISO CT
3300 SCL 95054 813-E6
VISTA AV
100 SCIC 95127 814-J7
100 SJS 95127 814-J7
200 SCIC 95127 815-A7
400 PA 94306 811-C2
17700 MSER 95030 873-A5
VISTA CT
900 MGH 95037 936-H1
20200 CPTO 95014 832-E7
VISTA DR
- MonC 93907 1037-B7
10100 CPTO 95014 832-E7
10100 CPTO 95014 852-E1

STREET
Block City ZIP Pg-Grid

VISTA LN
- SCIC 94304 810-F1
- HOLL 95023 1039-J3
15400 LGTS 95032 873-D5
VISTA LP
5900 SJS 95124 873-J7
VISTA WY
400 MPS 95035 794-C7
400 MPS 95035 814-C1
VISTA ARROYO CT
12000 SAR 95070 852-C5
VISTA CLUB CIR
1500 SCL 95054 813-D4
VISTA CREEK DR
2900 SJS 95133 814-G6
VISTA DE ALMADEN
18600 SCIC 95120 874-G7
VISTA DE ALMADEN CT
- SCIC 95120 874-G7
VISTA DE CORDEVALLE
- SCIC 95046 957-E1
VISTA DEL ARBOL
100 LGTS 95030 893-C1
VISTA DEL CAMPO
100 LGTS 95030 873-C7
VISTA DEL LAGO
- LGTS 95032 872-J2
VISTA DEL MAR
100 LGTS 95030 893-C1
1000 SJS 95132 814-J5
VISTA DEL MONTE
100 LGTS 95030 873-C7
100 LGTS 95030 893-C1
VISTA DEL MONTE CT
9100 SCIC 95020 957-B7
VISTA DE LOMAS
19200 SCIC 95037 916-J2
19200 SCIC 95037 917-A3
VISTA DEL ORO
300 SBnC 95023 1060-E1
VISTA DEL PRADO
100 LGTS 95030 893-B1
VISTA DEL ROBLE LN
18400 SCIC 95120 894-G1
VISTA DEL SOL
2500 SJS 95116 834-H3
6900 SCIC 95020 978-J1
VISTA DEL SUR DR
1700 GIL 95020 977-F2
VISTA DEL VALLE
3600 SJS 95132 814-J5
VISTA DEL VALLE CT
16700 MGH 95037 917-F6
VISTA DEL VALLE DR
2700 MGH 95037 917-F6
VISTA DE SIERRA
200 LGTS 95030 893-C1
VISTA DE VALLE CT
13000 LAH 94022 831-A1
VISTAGLEN CT
1700 SJS 95122 835-A6
VISTAGLEN DR
1700 SJS 95122 835-A6
VISTA GRANDE AV
700 LALT 94024 811-G6
700 MTVW 94040 811-G6
VISTA GRANDE WY
18300 SCIC 95033 892-H4
VISTA KNOLL BLVD
10200 CPTO 95014 832-A7
VISTA LOMA
20700 SCIC 95120 894-J2
VISTAMONT DR
3000 SJS 95118 854-B7
3000 SJS 95118 874-C1
VISTA MONTANA
- SJS 95134 813-D2
VISTA NORTE CT
3500 MPS 95035 794-G6
3500 SCIC 95035 794-G6
VISTA OAK
1000 SJS 95132 814-H5
VISTA OAKS CT
20300 CPTO 95014 832-E7
VISTAPARK DR
3900 SJS 95136 874-G1
4000 SJS 95136 854-F7
VISTA PARK HILL CT
- HOLL 95023 1040-A3
VISTA REAL CT
100 LGTS 95032 873-D4
VISTA REGINA
13900 SAR 95070 872-B1
VISTA RIDGE DR
200 MPS 95035 794-G6
500 SCIC 95035 794-G6
VISTA ROMA DR
- SJS 95136 874-G1
VISTA ROMA WY
- SJS 95136 854-G7
- SJS 95136 874-G1
VISTA SERENA
15400 LAH 94022 831-C1
VISTA SPRING CT
500 MPS 95035 794-H6
VISTA VALLE CT
10100 SCIC 95127 815-C7
10100 SCIC 95127 835-C1
VISTA VERDE DR
2200 SJS 95148 835-D5
2200 SCIC 95148 835-C6
VISTA VERDE WY
200 SMCo 94028 830-E5
VISTAVIEW DR
3300 SJS 95132 814-G4
VITERO WY
5800 SJS 95138 875-H1
VITTORIA PL
- SJS 95136 854-F7
VIVIAN DR
16400 LGTS 95030 873-C7
16400 LGTS 95030 893-C1
VIVIAN LN
2800 SJS 95124 873-G1
VIZCAYA CIR
2100 SJS 95008 873-F1
2100 SJS 95008 853-F7
VIZCAYA WY
2100 SJS 95008 873-F1
VOGUE CT
27600 LAH 94022 831-A1
VOLLMER WY
1700 SJS 95116 834-G5
VOLTAIRE ST
- SJS 95135 855-G2
- SJS 95148 855-G2
VOLTERRA CT
5800 SJS 95138 875-G1
VOLTI LN
1100 LALT 94024 831-J2
VONNA CT
700 SJS 95123 874-G5
VOORHEES DR
24500 LAH 94022 831-D2
24500 LAH 94024 831-D2
VOSS AV
22600 CPTO 95014 851-H1
22600 CPTO 95014 852-A1
VOSS PARK LN
2000 SJS 95131 814-E7

W

WABASH AV
- SCIC 95128 833-G7
- SCIC 95128 853-G1
- SJS 95128 853-G1
100 SJS 95128 833-G7
WABASH ST
1200 SJS 95002 793-B7
WABESCO PL
- SJS 95125 854-B2
WACO ST
1000 SJS 95110 833-H4
WADDINGTON AV
400 SUNV 94086 812-F5
WADE AV
1700 SCL 95051 833-B3
WADSWORTH AV
- LGTS 95030 872-J7
WAGMAN DR
400 SJS 95129 852-J1
WAGNER AV
1700 MTVW 94043 811-H3
WAGNER RD
17200 LGTS 95032 893-G3
17200 SCIC 95032 893-G3
WAGON WY
1200 GIL 95020 957-F7
WAIMEA CT
4400 SJS 95118 874-B3
WAINWRIGHT AV
300 SCIC 95128 853-F1
300 SJS 95128 853-F1
WAINWRIGHT DR
800 SJS 95128 853-F4
WAITE AV
500 SUNV 94086 812-F5
WAKEFIELD TER
1500 LALT 94024 832-A3
WAKE FOREST DR
700 MTVW 94043 812-A3
WALBROOK DR
1400 SAR 95070 852-H5
1400 SJS 95129 852-G4
W WALBROOK DR
5800 SJS 95129 852-F4
WALCOTT AV
- SCIC 94035 812-B1
WALDEN CT
12200 SAR 95070 852-F5
WALDEN SQ
2300 SJS 95124 853-H7
WALDHEIM CT
7000 SJS 95120 894-H3
WALDO RD
300 CMBL 95008 853-C7
WALES CT
- SJS 95138 875-H1
WALGLEN CT
900 SJS 95136 874-D1
WALGROVE WY
2900 SJS 95128 853-E3
WALIZER CT
17700 SCIC 95037 917-C4
WALIZER LN
17700 SCIC 95037 917-C3
WALKER CT
1800 SJS 95122 854-G1
WALKER DR
200 MTVW 94043 812-A3
WALKINGSHAW WY
1500 SJS 95132 814-F4
WALL ST
3000 SCIC 95111 854-G5
3000 SJS 95111 854-G5
WALLACE DR
900 SJS 95120 874-E7
900 SJS 95120 894-E1
22100 CPTO 95014 832-A6
WALLACE PL
- SCIC 95037 956-F2
WALLACE ST
2600 SCL 95051 833-B4
WALLA WALLA TR
17700 SCIC 95033 913-A1
WALLEA DR
500 MLPK 94025 790-F4
WALLIN CT
- CPTO 95014 852-C3
WALLIS CT
4100 PA 94306 811-C4
WALLYFORD CT
2500 SJS 95121 855-D5
WALLY PLACE WY
3600 SJS 95121 855-B4
WALNUT AV
- ATN 94027 790-E2
- LGTS 95030 872-J7
100 SUNV 94086 812-E6
20400 SAR 95070 872-D2
WALNUT CIR
10300 CPTO 95014 852-A1
WALNUT DR
- MGH 95037 937-B5
500 MPS 95035 793-J6
1200 CMBL 95008 873-C2
1500 PA 94303 791-B4
1700 MTVW 94040 811-G7
1700 MTVW 94040 831-G1
WALNUT LN
300 GIL 95020 978-A2
600 HOLL 95023 1039-J4
WALNUT ST
- MGH 95037 937-B1
500 SJS 95110 833-J5
WALNUT BLOSSOM DR
5400 SJS 95123 875-A4
WALNUT GROVE AV
1400 SCL 95050 833-F6
1400 SJS 95050 833-F6
1400 SJS 95126 833-F6
2000 SJS 95128 833-E6
2400 SCL 95128 833-E6
WALNUT GROVE DR
17300 MGH 95037 917-B6
WALNUT HILL CT
100 LGTS 95032 873-C3
WALNUT SPRING CT
11600 CPTO 95014 852-A4
WALNUT WOODS CT
1000 SJS 95122 834-F7
WALNUT WOODS DR
900 SJS 95122 834-F7
WALSH AV
600 SCL 95050 833-C1
2300 SCL 95051 833-C1
WALSH CT
- SJS 95123 874-F7
WALSH RD
300 ATN 94027 790-C6
WALTER BRETON DR
2200 SCIC 95037 936-F3
WALTER HAYS DR
100 PA 94303 791-B4
WALTERS AV
1500 CMBL 95008 873-A1
WALTER WELSHER CT
9800 SCIC 95020 958-C4
WALTHAM ST
600 MTVW 94040 831-J2
WALTON AV
21700 SCIC 95120 895-C5
WALTON LN
21700 SCIC 95120 895-C5
WALTON RD
600 LGTS 95032 873-B5
600 LGTS 95030 873-B5
WALTON WY
3200 SJS 95117 853-C3
WALTON HEATH CT
- GIL 95020 977-G6
WALTRIP LN
5600 SJS 95118 874-B5
WALZER WY
- SJS 95136 854-E6
WAR ADMIRAL AV
300 SJS 95111 875-B2
WAR ADMIRAL WY
5000 SJS 95111 875-B1
WARBLER WY
1500 SCL 95051 832-H5
1500 SUNV 94087 832-H5
WARBURTON AV
900 SCL 95050 833-C3
2400 SCL 95051 833-A3
3300 SCL 95051 832-J3
WARD RD
- SCrC 95033 851-A7
WARD WY
2100 SMCo 94062 790-A4
2100 WDSD 94062 790-A4
13400 SAR 95070 852-G7
13400 SAR 95070 872-G1
WARDELL CT
12400 SAR 95070 852-D6
WARDELL RD
12700 SAR 95070 852-D6
WAREC WY
300 LALT 94022 811-D6
WAREHOUSE RD
- MLPK 94025 790-J1
WARFIELD WY
2200 SJS 95122 854-G2
WARM SPRINGS BLVD
47600 FRMT 94539 793-H1
WARM SPRINGS DR
2900 SJS 95127 834-H1
WARMWOOD LN
2000 SJS 95132 814-D2
WARNER AV
1300 SUNV 94087 832-C4
WARNER CT
- MTVW 94043 811-G2
3600 SJS 95127 835-C3
WARNER DR
3500 SJS 95127 835-C3
WARNER RD
- SCIC 94035 812-B2
- SCIC 94043 812-B2
WARNER RANGE AV
2300 MLPK 94025 790-D7
WARREN AV
100 MGH 95037 916-J7
100 MGH 95037 917-A7
1000 SJS 95125 854-B2
WARREN DR
100 SCL 95051 833-B7
WARREN ST
300 SJS 95112 834-B3
WARREN WY
800 PA 94303 791-C5
WARRING DR
700 SJS 95123 874-F4
WARRINGTON AV
2900 SJS 95127 835-A4
WAR WAGON CT
5200 SJS 95136 874-J3
WAR WAGON DR
5100 SJS 95136 874-J3
5100 SJS 95136 875-A3
WARWICK CT
900 SUNV 94087 832-B3
WARWICK DR
100 CMBL 95008 853-C5
WARWICK RD
15300 SJS 95124 873-G5
WASATCH DR
2700 MTVW 94040 832-A2
WASHINGTON AV
100 PA 94301 791-B6
500 SUNV 94086 812-F7
500 SUNV 94086 832-F1
2300 RDWC 94061 790-A2
E WASHINGTON AV
100 SUNV 94086 812-E7
W WASHINGTON AV
400 SUNV 94086 812-B6
WASHINGTON DR
- MPS 95035 793-J4
- MPS 95035 794-A4
WASHINGTON ST
- SJS 95002 813-B1
- SJB 95045 1038-D5
- SCL 95050 833-E4
100 SJS 95112 834-B5
600 LALT 94022 831-E1
800 HOLL 95023 1040-A4
800 MTVW 94043 811-H4
WASHINGTON SQUARE DR
700 MPS 95035 793-J4
WASHOE DR
1100 SJS 95120 894-D1
WASKOW DR
400 SJS 95123 875-A6
WASSON CT
- SJS 95148 855-F1
WATER AV
900 MGH 95037 937-C5
13900 SCIC 95037 937-C5
13900 SCIC 95046 937-C6
WATER ST
3000 SCIC 95111 854-G5
3100 SJS 95111 854-G6
WATER WK
- MPS 95035 814-J1
WATERBIRD WY
1000 SCL 95051 832-H5
WATERBURY CT
3600 SJS 95117 853-C3
WATERFALL CT
5200 SJS 95136 875-B3
WATERFORD CT
- CMBL 95008 853-E5
WATERFORD DR
7500 CPTO 95014 852-D4
WATERFORD MEADOW CT
100 MPS 95035 794-C2
WATERLOO CT
1900 SJS 95132 814-J2
WATERMAN CT
3400 SJS 95127 814-J7
WATERTON CT
300 MGH 95037 937-A2
WATERTON LN
1100 SJS 95131 834-D1
WATERVILLE DR
4500 SJS 95118 874-C3
WATERVILLE PL
- GIL 95020 977-D3
WATER WITCH WY
500 SJS 95117 853-D2
WATKINS AV
- ATN 94027 790-E2
WATKINS WY
4100 SJS 95135 855-F3
WATSON CIR
- SCL 95054 813-E4
WATSON CT
1600 MPS 95035 814-C3
2400 PA 94303 791-D4
WATSON DR
200 CMBL 95008 853-E5
WATSONVILLE CT
14200 SCIC 95037 937-A7
14200 SCIC 95046 937-A7
WATSONVILLE RD
12700 SCIC 95037 956-J2
12700 SCIC 95046 956-J2
13700 SCIC 95037 936-J7
13700 SCIC 95046 936-J7
14000 SCIC 95037 937-A6
14000 SCIC 95046 937-A6
15000 MGH 95037 937-A6
WATSONVILLE RD Rt#-G8
8100 SCIC 95020 977-A1
8200 SCIC 95020 976-J1
9300 SCIC 95020 956-J6
10200 SCIC 95020 957-A4
12300 SCIC 95037 956-J6
12300 SCIC 95046 956-J6
WATTERS CT
- SJS 95127 835-B2
WATTERS DR
14700 SJS 95127 835-B2
14700 SCIC 95127 835-B2
WAUGH DR
18200 SCIC 95037 916-G7
18200 MGH 95037 916-G7
WAVE PL
1900 SJS 95133 834-E1
WAVERLEY CT
- MLPK 94025 790-G3
WAVERLEY ST
100 PA 94301 790-J4
200 MLPK 94025 790-G4
900 PA 94301 791-A5
2600 PA 94306 791-C7
3200 PA 94306 811-D1
WAVERLEY OAKS
100 PA 94301 791-B6
WAVERLY AV
1600 SJS 95122 854-J1
1700 SJS 95122 834-J7
2000 SJS 95122 835-A7
3000 SMCo 94063 790-D1
WAVERLY LN
300 LALT 94022 811-E7
WAVERLY PL
100 MTVW 94040 831-J2
WAVERLY ST
100 SUNV 94086 812-D7
300 SUNV 94086 832-D1
WAWONA DR
1500 SJS 95125 854-A7
1500 SJS 95125 874-A1
WAXWING AV
1500 SUNV 94087 832-H6
WAYCROSS RD
3600 SJS 95121 855-A5
WAYLAND AV
4900 SJS 95118 874-C3
WAYLAND CT
- GIL 95020 977-H1
WAYLAND LN
8000 GIL 95020 977-H1
WAYNE AV
1100 SJS 95131 814-A6
WAYNE CIR
- SJS 95131 814-B6
WAYWORD DR
1500 SJS 95122 834-H7
WEATHERLY DR
500 SJS 95134 813-D2
WEATHERSFIELD WY
1200 SJS 95118 874-B5
WEAVER CT
8900 GIL 95020 957-J7
WEAVER DR
1300 SJS 95125 853-J4
WEAVER RD
16700 SCIC 95033 893-D7
16700 SCIC 95033 913-C1
WEBB RD
100 SCrC 95076 976-A7
WEBB CANYON DR
7000 SCIC 95120 894-E3
7000 SCIC 95120 894-F3
WEBER ST
- SJS 95111 854-G5
WEBSTER CT
2500 PA 94306 791-C6
2500 PA 94301 791-C6
2600 SCL 95051 833-B3
WEBSTER DR
600 SJS 95133 834-F1
WEBSTER ST
100 PA 94301 790-J3
700 PA 94301 791-A4
2500 PA 94306 791-C6
WEDDELL CT
900 SUNV 94089 812-F4
E WEDDELL DR
100 SUNV 94089 812-F4
W WEDDELL DR
100 SUNV 94089 812-E4
WEDGEWOOD AV
100 LGTS 95032 873-A2
WEDGEWOOD CT
5500 SJS 95123 874-F4
WEDGEWOOD DR
700 SJS 95123 874-F4
WEEDIN CT
3600 SJS 95132 814-F2
WEEKES WY
- SJS 95124 873-J5
WEEKS ST
300 EPA 94303 791-B1
WEEPING CREEK WY
3300 SJS 95121 855-D7
WEEPINGGATE LN
1000 SJS 95136 874-J3
WEEPING OAK CT
22600 CPTO 95014 831-C7
WEEPING OAKS CT
1200 SJS 95120 894-E2
WEETH DR
14500 SCIC 95124 873-G2
WEHNER DR
3500 SCL 95051 832-J5
WEHNER WY
6200 SJS 95135 855-H6
WEIBEL WY
1200 SJS 95125 853-G4
WEICHERT DR
800 MGH 95037 917-B6
WEIMAR AV
5900 SJS 95120 874-B6
WEKIVA AV
1000 CMBL 95008 873-B1
WELBURN AV
- GIL 95020 977-F1
WELBY CT
3100 SJS 95111 854-H5
WELCH AV
1000 SJS 95117 853-C3
1800 SJS 95112 854-F2
WELCH RD
700 PA 94304 790-G6
700 PA 94305 790-G6
1000 SCIC 94305 790-G6
WELDON LN
1100 SJS 95131 834-D1
WELDWOOD AV
900 LGTS 95032 873-B2
WELDWOOD CT
900 LGTS 95032 873-B2
WELKER CT
- CMBL 95008 853-B6
WELLCROFT CT
3200 SJS 95148 855-C2
WELLER LN
- MPS 95035 794-A7
- MPS 95035 793-J7
WELLER RD
- SCIC 95035 794-G1
WELLESLEY CT
3500 MTVW 94040 831-J2
WELLESLEY ST
1900 SCIC 94305 791-A7
2100 PA 94306 791-A7
2200 PA 94306 811-A1
WELLFLEET WY
6000 SJS 95129 852-G4
WELLINGTON CT
- MTVW 94040 811-F3
19900 SAR 95070 852-E6
WELLINGTON DR
1800 MPS 95035 794-B2
WELLINGTON PL
800 CMBL 95008 853-B7
WELLINGTON SQ
3800 SJS 95136 874-C1
WELLINGTON PARK DR
4800 SJS 95136 874-F2
4900 SCIC 95136 874-F2
WELLMEADOW CT
6400 SJS 95120 894-C1
WELLS AV
- PA 94301 790-J5
WELLS CT
5600 SJS 95123 874-H4
WELLS ST
800 RDWC 94061 790-B1
WELLSBURY CT
600 PA 94306 791-C7
WELLSBURY WY
600 PA 94306 791-D7
WELL SPRING CT
11500 CPTO 95014 852-A4
WEMA WY
1700 SJS 95124 873-H1
WEMBLEY CT
400 RDWC 94061 790-B2
1800 SJS 95132 814-E3
WENDELL DR
600 CMBL 95008 873-C1
WENDOVER LN
2000 SJS 95121 855-C4
WENDY LN
13500 SAR 95070 872-G1
WENDY WY
1400 SJS 95125 854-A6
1400 SMCo 94025 790-D5
WENLOCK DR
1100 SJS 95122 834-J5
WENRICK CT
1700 LALT 94024 831-J4
WENTE PL
2000 SJS 95125 853-G4
WENTE WY
2000 SJS 95125 853-G4
WENTWORTH ST
1000 MTVW 94043 811-H4
WENTWORTH WY
1200 SJS 95121 855-B5
WENTZ AL
- HOLL 95023 1039-J4
- HOLL 95023 1040-A4
WENTZ DR
900 GIL 95020 977-H4
WERTH AV
1100 MLPK 94025 790-F5
WESCOAT CT
600 SCIC 94035 812-B3
600 SCIC 94043 812-B3
WESCOAT RD
400 SCIC 94035 812-B3
400 SCIC 94043 812-B3
WESLEY CT
1800 SJS 95148 835-A5
WESSEX AV
1400 LALT 94024 831-J3
WESSEX DR
4100 SJS 95136 874-E1
WESSEX PL
800 MPS 95035 794-B3
WEST CT
300 SJS 95116 834-E3
WEST RD
15800 SCIC 95030 872-G6
WEST ST
300 HOLL 95023 1040-A4
500 HOLL 95023 1039-J5
WESTACRES DR
10200 CPTO 95014 852-D1
WESTBERRY DR
2600 SJS 95132 814-E4
WESTBORO CT
- SCIC 95127 834-J3
WESTBORO DR
2900 SCIC 95127 834-J3
2900 SJS 95127 834-J3
2900 SJS 95127 835-A3
2900 SCIC 95127 835-A3
WESTBRANCH DR
2700 SJS 95148 855-C2
WESTBROOK AV
1700 SCIC 94024 831-F4
WESTBURY DR
- SJS 95131 814-A5
WESTCHESTER DR
100 LGTS 95032 873-E5
500 CMBL 95008 853-F7
1000 SUNV 94087 832-B3
2100 SJS 95124 873-E5
2100 LGTS 95124 873-E5
WESTCOTT DR
14500 SAR 95070 872-E3
WEST CREEK DR
1600 SJS 95125 853-J6
WESTDALE DR
4900 SJS 95129 852-J2
WESTERN CT
200 HOLL 95023 1039-H3
WESTERN DR
10100 CPTO 95014 852-D1
WESTFIELD AV
2700 CMBL 95128 853-E3
2700 SJS 95128 853-E3
WESTFIELD DR
1100 MLPK 94025 790-F5
WESTFORD WY
2500 MTVW 94040 832-A2
WEST FORK CT
4800 SJS 95136 874-D2
WESTGATE AV
2200 SJS 95125 854-B6
WESTGROVE LN
2700 SJS 95148 855-C2
WESTHAVEN DR
1600 SJS 95132 814-F3
WEST HILL CT
1000 CPTO 95014 852-D3
WESTHILL DR
100 LGTS 95032 873-G6
WEST HILL LN
7600 CPTO 95014 852-D3
WESTINGHOUSE DR
47500 FRMT 94539 793-H1
WESTLAKE DR
400 SJS 95117 853-C1
WESTLYNN WY
900 CPTO 95014 852-D2
WESTMINISTER CT
1800 SJS 95132 814-E3
WESTMINISTER LN
700 LALT 94022 811-D4
WESTMINSTER AV
1100 EPA 94303 791-A1
WESTMINSTER CT
10100 CPTO 95014 831-C7
WESTMONT AV
1200 CMBL 95008 873-A1
1700 SJS 95008 873-A1
3400 SJS 95008 872-J1
4700 SJS 95130 872-J1
WESTMONT CT
900 SJS 95117 853-C3
WESTMOOR WY
6800 SJS 95129 852-E4
WESTMORELAND AV
2900 SMCo 94063 790-C1
WESTMORELAND CT
2100 SJS 95124 853-H6
WESTMORELAND DR
2100 SJS 95124 853-H6
WESTON DR
500 SJS 95008 853-A6
500 SJS 95130 853-A6
600 CMBL 95008 853-A6
26400 LAH 94022 811-B5
WESTON PL
- SCL 95054 813-C5
WESTOVER DR
13600 SAR 95070 872-G1
WESTPARK DR
2300 SJS 95124 853-H7
WESTRIDGE CT
27800 LAH 94022 830-H1
WESTRIDGE DR
100 PTLV 94028 810-B5
200 SCL 95050 833-D7
200 SCL 95117 833-D7
200 SCL 95117 853-D1
200 SJS 95117 833-D7
900 MPS 95035 814-E1
WESTSHORE CT
11600 CPTO 95014 852-A5
WESTSIDE AV
500 SUNV 94087 832-D3
WESTSIDE BLVD
- HOLL 95023 1039-J3
WESTSIDE RD
- SBnC 95023 1039-H2
WEST SUNSET DR
13200 LAH 94022 831-C1
WEST VALLEY DR
700 CMBL 95008 853-F7
WEST VALLEY FRWY Rt#-85
- CMBL - 873-C2
- CPTO - 832-B7
- CPTO - 852-E5
- LGTS - 873-C2
- SAR - 852-E5
- SAR - 872-H1
- SCIC - 873-C2
- SCIC - 874-C3
- SJS - 852-E5
- SJS - 872-J1
- SJS - 873-C2
- SJS - 874-C3
- SJS - 875-A5
- SUNV - 832-B7
WEST VIEW CT
3700 SCIC 95148 835-E4
WEST VIEW DR
3500 SCIC 95148 835-D5
3500 SJS 95148 835-D5
18600 SAR 95070 852-H5
WESTWARD DR
1000 HOLL 95023 1040-C6

STREET Block City ZIP Pg-Grid

WESTWARD DR
1000 SBnC 95023 1040-C6
WESTWIND WY
25800 LAH 94022 811-B7
WESTWOOD DR
1000 SJS 95125 853-J3
1000 SJS 95131 814-A4
1000 SJS 95131 813-J4
7500 GIL 95020 977-G3
WETMORE DR
3000 SJS 95148 835-F7
3000 SJS 95148 855-F1
WETSAND CT
9300 GIL 95020 957-F7
WEXFORD DR
2700 SJS 95132 814-E4
WEYBRIDGE DR
500 SJS 95123 875-A7
WEYBURN LN
1000 SJS 95129 852-E3
WEYERS CT
2800 SJS 95148 855-D2
WEYMOTH DR
1200 CPTO 95014 852-C4
WHALEY AV
- SJS 95110 833-J4
WHALEY DR
6300 SJS 95135 855-H6
WHARTON CT
- SJS 95132 814-G3
WHARTON RD
- SJS 95132 814-G3
WHEAT CT
1000 SJS 95127 835-C2
WHEATFIELD CT
- GIL 95020 977-J6
WHEATLEY PL
- SJS 95138 855-B5
WHEATON DR
19600 CPTO 95014 832-F7
WHEELER AL
100 HOLL 95023 1040-A3
WHEELER AV
- RDWC 94061 790-B2
100 LGTS 95030 873-B7
WHEELER ST
100 GIL 95020 977-J2
100 GIL 95020 978-A2
WHEELING DR
3300 SCL 95051 832-J6
WHEELSMAN PL
5700 SJS 95123 874-F4
WHELAN CT
100 MTVW 94043 812-B5
WHINNEY PLACE WY
3800 SJS 95121 855-B4
WHIPPLE CT
14700 SCIC 95127 835-B1
WHIPPORWILL DR
2800 MGH 95037 917-E4
WHIRLAWAY DR
100 SJS 95111 875-B2
WHIRLOW PL
1100 SJS 95131 814-D7
WHISKEY HILL LN
10100 SCIC 95020 957-G5
WHISMAN CT
400 MTVW 94043 812-B4
N WHISMAN RD
- MTVW 94043 812-B4
S WHISMAN RD
100 MTVW 94041 812-A6
WHISMAN PARK DR
- MTVW 94043 812-B5
WHISMAN STATION DR
100 MTVW 94043 812-B5
WHISPERING ELM CT
3200 SJS 95148 855-D2
WHISPERING HILLS CIR
2500 SJS 95148 855-B1
WHISPERING HILLS DR
2600 SJS 95148 855-B2
WHISPERING HILLS LN
2700 SJS 95148 855-B2
WHISPERING HILLS LP
2600 SJS 95148 855-B1
WHISPERING HILLS RD
2600 SJS 95148 855-B2
WHISPERING HILLS WY
2600 SJS 95148 855-C2
WHISPERING OAKS DR
20500 SCIC 95120 895-A5
WHISPERING PINES DR
6500 SJS 95120 894-C2
WHISPERING WILLOW WY
- SJS 95125 853-J5
WHITAKER WY
1200 MLPK 94025 790-E5
WHITBOURNE CT
1300 SJS 95120 894-C2
WHITBOURNE DR
6500 SJS 95120 894-C2
WHITBY CT
3100 SJS 95148 855-E2
WHITCLEM CT
200 PA 94306 811-E2
WHITCLEM DR
200 PA 94306 811-D2
WHITCLEM PL
300 PA 94306 811-D2
WHITCLEM WY
200 PA 94306 811-D2
WHITCOMB CT
900 MPS 95035 814-E1

WHITE CT
- MPS 95035 794-C7
3100 SJS 95127 835-A3
WHITE DR
900 SCL 95051 833-B4
N WHITE RD
- SJS 95127 834-J2
- SCIC 95127 834-J2
300 SCIC 95133 834-J2
300 SJS 95133 834-J2
400 SJS 95133 814-H7
400 SCIC 95127 814-H7
400 SCIC 95133 814-H7
500 SJS 95127 814-H7
S WHITE RD
- SCIC 95127 834-J2
- SJS 95127 834-J2
400 SJS 95127 835-C6
1800 SJS 95148 835-C6
2000 SCIC 95148 835-C6
2400 SJS 95148 855-D1
WHITE ST
- SJS 95126 834-A7
WHITE TER
- SJS 95127 834-H1
WHITE ACRES DR
2700 SJS 95148 855-D2
WHITEBICK DR
1000 SJS 95129 852-G3
WHITE CHAPEL AV
- SJS 95136 854-E7
WHITE CHAPEL WY
- SJS 95136 854-F7
WHITE CLIFF DR
1000 SJS 95129 852-F3
WHITE CLOUD CT
14700 MGH 95037 937-B5
WHITE CLOUD DR
900 MGH 95037 937-B5
WHITE CREEK LN
1600 SJS 95125 853-J5
WHITE FIR CT
21000 CPTO 95014 852-C2
WHITE FIR LN
800 SJS 95133 814-H3
800 SJS 95133 834-F1
WHITEGATE AV
1300 SJS 95125 854-B7
WHITEHALL AV
800 CMBL 95128 853-F4
1000 SJS 95128 853-F4
WHITEHALL LN
200 RDWC 94061 790-B2
WHITEHAVEN CT
6000 SJS 95138 875-H1
WHITEHURST CT
1300 SJS 95125 854-B3
WHITEHURST RD
7400 SCIC 95020 976-H4
WHITELEAF CT
3100 SJS 95148 855-E1
WHITELEAF WY
3100 SJS 95148 855-E2
WHITEMARSH CT
1100 SJS 95120 894-E2
WHITE OAK CT
- MLPK 94025 790-E6
3400 MGH 95037 917-G5
WHITE OAK DR
1800 MLPK 94025 790-E6
WHITEOAK DR
1000 SJS 95129 852-H3
WHITE OAK LN
800 SCL 95051 832-J3
800 SUNV 94086 832-J3
WHITE OAK PL
- GIL 95020 977-G2
WHITE OAKS AV
4100 SJS 95124 873-E3
WHITE OAKS CT
1800 CMBL 95008 873-E2
WHITE OAKS RD
1200 CMBL 95008 873-E3
WHITE PINE CT
1100 SJS 95125 854-A4
WHITE RIESLING PL
- SJS 95135 855-H2
WHITEROCK CIR
1500 SJS 95125 853-J5
WHITEROCK CT
1400 SJS 95125 853-J5
WHITE ROCK RD
900 SCrC 95033 912-D3
WHITEROSE CT
3100 SJS 95148 855-E2
WHITEROSE DR
3200 SJS 95148 855-E2
WHITESAND CT
3200 SJS 95148 855-E2
WHITESAND DR
3000 SJS 95148 855-E2
WHITESTONE CT
2500 SJS 95122 835-A5
WHITETAIL LN
- SJS 95138 855-E5
WHITETHORNE DR
600 CMBL 95128 853-F4
600 SJS 95128 853-F4
WHITEWOOD CT
1300 SJS 95131 814-B6
WHITEWOOD DR
1600 SJS 95131 814-B6
WHITE ZINFANDEL PL
- SJS 95135 855-H2
WHITFIELD CT
1200 SJS 95131 814-D7
WHITHAM AV
1700 SCIC 94024 831-F4
WHITMAN CT
300 PA 94301 791-A5
WHITMAN WY
3200 SJS 95132 814-H5

WHITNEY AV
- LGTS 95030 893-B1
100 LGTS 95030 873-B7
WHITNEY CT
- MLPK 94025 790-C7
2400 MTVW 94043 811-F3
WHITNEY DR
1000 MLPK 94025 790-C7
2400 MTVW 94043 811-F3
WHITNEY LN
10000 SCIC 95127 835-C1
WHITNEY PL
- FRMT 94539 793-H2
WHITNEY ST
- LALT 94022 811-E7
WHITNEY WY
300 MGH 95037 937-A2
10500 CPTO 95014 852-E2
WHITS RD
- MTVW 94040 811-F3
WHITSELL ST
3500 PA 94306 811-C1
WHITTIER ST
- MPS 95035 793-J7
WHITTINGTON DR
2800 SJS 95148 855-D1
WHITTON AV
1100 SJS 95116 834-F4
WHITWOOD LN
1600 CMBL 95008 853-A6
4600 SJS 95130 853-A6
WICHITA CT
6200 SJS 95123 874-H6
WICKHAM CT
1700 SJS 95132 814-E4
WICKHAM PL
2500 SCL 95051 833-B2
WICKHAM RD
1600 SJS 95132 814-E4
WIDEN CT
1700 SJS 95132 814-E4
WIDGET DR
800 SJS 95117 853-C2
WIEBE WY
600 HOLL 95023 1039-J4
WIEUCA RD
16200 SCIC 95030 872-G6
WIGAN CT
2200 SJS 95131 814-E7
WIGWAM CT
- SJS 95136 875-B3
WILANETA AV
400 FRMT 94539 793-J2
WILBUR AV
2700 SJS 95127 834-J3
2700 SCIC 95127 834-J3
WILBURN AV
- ATN 94027 790-D1
WILCOX AV
3200 SJS 95118 874-A1
4600 SCL 95054 813-C4
WILCOX WY
1700 SJS 95125 854-A5
WILD WY
17000 LGTS 95030 873-B4
WILDA WY
18400 MonC 95004 1037-A1
WILD BERRY LN
14600 SAR 95070 872-C3
WILDCAT DR
- SAR 95070 872-E4
WILDCAT WY
1500 SJS 95118 874-A6
WILD CREEK DR
7200 SJS 95120 894-J3
WILDCREST DR
13300 LAH 94022 811-C7
13300 LAH 94022 831-C1
WILDER AV
100 LGTS 95030 873-A7
WILDER CT
2000 SCIC 95020 938-A7
WILDERFIELD RD
- SCrC 95018 912-E3
- SCrC 95033 912-E3
WILDERNESS CIR
7000 SJS 95135 876-A2
WILDFLOWER CT
- GIL 95020 977-J7
11600 CPTO 95014 852-D4
WILDFLOWER DR
- SJS 95123 875-A6
WILD FLOWER LN
13700 LAH 94022 811-C7
WILD FLOWER WY
7300 CPTO 95014 852-D4
WILD FLOWER PARK LN
300 MTVW 94043 811-J4
WILDGRASS CT
- GIL 95020 977-J6
WILDHORSE CT
- SJS 95138 875-G6
WILD IRIS DR
8700 GIL 95020 977-E1
WILDMAN DR
1300 SJS 95127 835-C3
WILD MEADOW WY
- SJS 95135 855-J7
- SJS 95135 856-A7
WILD OAK CT
16700 MGH 95037 936-J1
WILD OAK DR
900 SBnC 95023 1060-D1
WILD OAK WY
14500 SAR 95070 872-F3
16700 MGH 95037 936-J1
WILD PLUM LN
14100 LAH 94022 811-C6
WILDROSE CT
2300 GIL 95020 977-D1
WILDROSE WY
1400 MTVW 94043 811-H4

WILD TURKEY LN
3700 SCIC 95020 958-G2
WILDWAY
15000 LGTS 95030 873-B4
15000 LGTS 95032 873-B4
WILDWOOD AV
1200 SUNV 94089 812-J5
1200 SUNV 94089 813-A5
WILDWOOD CT
6600 SJS 95120 894-C5
WILDWOOD LN
- SMCo 94025 810-E1
600 PA 94303 791-C4
WILDWOOD WY
400 SCL 95054 813-E5
14000 SAR 95070 872-D2
WILEY TER
- MTVW 94043 812-B3
WILFORD WY
9800 SCIC 95020 958-B4
WILFRED WY
1900 SJS 95124 873-G4
WILHELMINA WY
1100 SJS 95120 894-F3
WILKEY CT
2700 SJS 95127 834-J4
WILKIE CT
4100 PA 94306 811-D2
WILKIE WY
4000 PA 94306 811-C2
WILKINSON AV
10700 CPTO 95014 852-B3
WILKS ST
- EPA 94303 791-C2
WILL CT
10200 CPTO 95014 832-E7
WILLAMETTE DR
6300 SJS 95123 874-H7
WILLARD AV
400 SCIC 95126 853-H1
400 SJS 95126 853-H1
N WILLARD AV
- SJS 95126 833-H7
- SJS 95126 853-H1
WILLARD CT
800 GIL 95020 977-H1
WILLARD GARDEN CT
1500 SJS 95126 853-H1
WILLESTER AV
2000 SJS 95124 873-F2
WILLETT PL
- SCL 95051 832-J4
WILLIAM AV
3000 SMCo 94063 790-D1
WILLIAM CT
- MLPK 94025 790-E5
E WILLIAM CT
1000 SJS 95116 834-E5
WILLIAM DR
2300 SCL 95050 833-C2
E WILLIAM ST
- SJS 95112 834-D7
- SJS 95113 834-D7
700 SJS 95116 834-G4
W WILLIAM ST
- SJS 95110 834-C7
500 SJS 95125 854-A1
WILLIAM HENRY CT
1700 LALT 94024 831-J4
WILLIAMS AV
20400 SAR 95070 872-D2
WILLIAMS DR
8600 SCIC 95020 958-D6
WILLIAMS RD
2700 SJS 95128 853-E3
3000 SJS 95117 853-C3
4100 SJS 95129 853-A3
4700 SJS 95129 852-J3
WILLIAMS ST
2000 PA 94306 791-A7
WILLIAMS WY
800 MTVW 94040 812-A7
800 MTVW 94040 832-A1
WILLIAMSBURG DR
3100 SJS 95117 853-D4
WILLIAMSBURG LN
20100 SAR 95070 852-E6
WILLIAMSBURG WY
700 GIL 95020 977-J4
WILLIAMSPORT DR
1500 SJS 95131 814-C6
WILLIFORD DR
2500 SJS 95133 814-F7
WILLIS AV
400 SJS 95126 854-B1
600 SJS 95125 854-B1
WILLMAR DR
4100 PA 94306 811-C3
WILLO MAR DR
1200 SJS 95118 854-C7
WILLOW AV
400 MPS 95035 793-J6
1100 SUNV 94086 832-J1
1400 SCIC 95037 936-J7
WILLOW CT
1200 GIL 95020 977-F1
1500 MGH 95037 917-D6
WILLOW DR
200 HOLL 95023 1039-G3
5100 SJS 95124 873-H5
WILLOW PL
- MLPK 94025 790-H3
WILLOW RD
- MLPK 94025 790-J1
1000 MLPK 94025 791-A1
WILLOW RD Rt#-114
- EPA 94303 790-J1
1000 MLPK 94025 790-J1
1100 EPA 94303 791-A1
1100 MLPK 94025 791-A1
WILLOW ST
- SJS 95110 854-C2
400 SJS 95125 854-A3
1100 SJS 95125 853-J3

WILLOW ST
1400 MGH 95037 937-B1
1400 MGH 95037 917-B7
1600 SCIC 95125 853-H4
WILLOW WY
3800 SCL 95054 813-E5
WILLOWBRAE AV
1500 SJS 95125 853-J4
WILLOWBROOK DR
100 PTLV 94028 830-B1
200 PTLV 94028 810-B7
1500 SJS 95118 874-A2
WILLOWBROOK WY
10700 CPTO 95014 852-F2
WILLOW CIRCLE CT
- SJS 95125 854-G5
WILLOW CREEK CT
1700 SJS 95124 873-J1
WILLOW CREEK DR
1600 SJS 95124 873-J1
16700 MGH 95037 936-J1
WILLOWDALE DR
1500 SJS 95118 874-A2
WILLOW ESTATES
5000 SJS 95135 855-G5
WILLOWGATE DR
1500 SJS 95118 874-A2
WILLOWGATE ST
600 MTVW 94043 811-J5
WILLOW GLEN WY
400 SJS 95125 854-A4
WILLOWGROVE LN
6000 CPTO 95014 852-G2
WILLOWHAVEN CT
1100 SJS 95126 853-H3
WILLOWHAVEN DR
1100 SJS 95126 853-H3
WILLOW HILL CT
100 LGTS 95032 873-C3
WILLOWHURST AV
1600 SCIC 95125 853-H5
1600 SJS 95125 853-H5
WILLOW LAKE LN
1600 SJS 95131 814-B6
WILLOWLEAF DR
900 SJS 95128 853-G3
WILLOWMONT AV
1400 SJS 95118 874-A2
1600 SJS 95124 873-J2
1600 SJS 95124 874-A2
WILLOW OAKS DR
1500 SJS 95125 853-J4
WILLOWOOD DR
3500 SJS 95118 874-A2
WILLOWPARK DR
3500 SJS 95118 874-A2
WILLOW POND LN
25500 LAH 94022 831-B3
WILLOWSHIRE WY
- SJS 95125 854-A3
WILLOW SPRINGS RD
600 SCIC 95037 916-F4
WILLOWTREE CT
1400 SJS 95118 874-B1
WILLOWVIEW DR
3500 SJS 95118 874-A2
WILL ROGERS DR
3900 SJS 95117 853-B3
4100 SJS 95129 853-A3
WILL WOOL DR
2200 SJS 95112 854-G2
WILLY CT
400 GIL 95020 978-A1
WILMA DR
1100 HOLL 95023 1039-H4
WILMA WY
4900 SJS 95124 873-E4
WILMINGTON AV
1000 SJS 95129 852-J3
WILSHAM DR
1000 SJS 95132 814-F6
WILSHIRE BLVD
1700 SJS 95116 834-F4
WILSON AV
- SJS 95126 834-A7
300 SUNV 94086 832-F1
WILSON CT
- CMBL 95008 853-C7
600 SCL 95051 833-B6
1900 MTVW 94040 831-G1
21800 CPTO 95014 832-B7
WILSON ST
1200 PA 94301 791-B4
WILSON WY
- SJS 95002 793-C7
- MPS 95035 793-J3
- SJS 95002 813-C1
11700 SCIC 95020 958-A1
WILTON AV
200 PA 94306 811-C1
WILTON DR
100 CMBL 95008 853-D7
WIMBLEDON CT
4000 SJS 95135 855-H5
WIMBLEDON DR
14400 LGTS 95032 873-B3
WIMBLEDON PL
1900 LALT 94024 831-J5
N WINCHESTER BLVD
- SCL 95050 833-E7
- SCL 95050 853-E1
- SCL 95117 853-E1
200 SCL 95128 833-E7
S WINCHESTER BLVD
- CMBL 95008 873-B3
300 SJS 95117 853-E4
300 SJS 95128 853-E4
600 LGTS 95030 873-B3
1500 CMBL 95117 853-E4
1500 CMBL 95128 853-E4
1500 CMBL 95008 853-E4
3300 LGTS 95032 873-B3
15000 MSER 95030 873-B3

WINCHESTER CIR
- LGTS 95032 873-C2
WINCHESTER DR
- ATN 94027 790-E2
WIND WK
- MPS 95035 814-J1
WINDCLIFF LN
- SJS 95138 875-H6
WINDELL CT
700 SJS 95123 874-F4
WINDEMERE CT
2100 SCIC 95037 917-C4
WINDERMERE AV
1000 MLPK 94025 790-J1
WINDHAM LN
100 MTVW 94043 812-A5
WINDIMER DR
1200 LALT 94024 831-H5
WINDING WY
4500 SJS 95129 853-A4
11600 SCIC 94024 831-E4
WINDING CREEK CT
1800 SJS 95148 835-D4
WINDING HILLS CT
- SJS 95138 855-F6
WINDING VISTA COM
- FRMT 94539 794-B1
WINDINGWOOD CT
300 MTVW 94040 811-F4
WINDMILL CT
1100 SJS 95121 854-J4
WINDMILL DR
100 SBnC 95023 1059-H3
WINDMILL ST
500 MGH 95037 937-B1
WINDMILL PARK LN
300 MTVW 94043 811-J4
WIND RIDGE LN
5700 SJS 95123 874-G7
WIND ROSE PL
2100 MTVW 94043 811-G2
WINDROW CT
- SJS 95135 876-A1
WIND SONG
- MPS 95035 814-J1
WINDSONG CT
- MGH 95037 917-A2
WINDSONG PL
- MGH 95037 917-A2
WINDSOR CT
- HOLL 95023 1040-D6
12200 LAH 94022 830-J1
WINDSOR DR
500 MLPK 94025 790-F4
WINDSOR LN
6300 SJS 95129 852-F3
WINDSOR ST
1000 SJS 95129 852-E3
WINDSOR TER
600 SUNV 94087 832-D3
WINDSOR WY
1100 MLPK 94025 790-F4
6800 SJS 95129 852-E4
WINDSOR HILLS CIR
800 SJS 95123 874-E5
WINDSOR HILLS DR
5800 SJS 95123 874-E5
WINDSOR PARK DR
4200 SJS 95136 874-F1
WINDWARD CT
7000 SJS 95135 876-A1
WINE BARREL WY
3400 SJS 95124 873-E2
WINE CASK WY
3400 SJS 95124 873-E2
WINE CORK WY
3400 SJS 95124 873-E2
WINE GARDEN LN
8700 SJS 95135 856-A6
WINE GROWER WY
2500 SJS 95124 873-E2
2200 SJS 95008 873-E2
WINE MAKER WY
2200 SJS 95124 873-E2
WINE MASTER LN
8700 SJS 95135 856-A6
WINERY CT
8000 SJS 95135 855-J6
WINE VALLEY CIR
8800 SJS 95135 855-J6
8800 SJS 95135 856-A6
WINFIELD BLVD
5500 SJS 95136 874-E3
5500 SJS 95123 874-D6
5900 SJS 95120 874-D6
WINFIELD DR
2700 MTVW 94040 831-J2
WING PL
900 SCIC 94305 810-J2
WINGATE DR
600 SUNV 94087 832-D3
WINGED FOOT DR
- GIL 95020 977-H6
WINGHAM PL
4100 SJS 95135 855-F3
WINIFRED DR
- SJS 95122 854-G2
WINN AL
- HOLL 95023 1040-A4
WINN RD
20100 SAR 95070 872-E4
WINNEBAGO CT
6100 SJS 95123 874-H6
WINONA DR
1300 SJS 95125 854-A5
WINSLOW CT
- CMBL 95008 853-A6
WINSLOW DR
1100 SJS 95122 834-G7
WINSOR ST
- MPS 95035 794-A7
WINSTEAD TER
700 SUNV 94087 832-C3

WINSTED CT
100 SJS 95139 875-G7
100 SJS 95139 895-G1
WINSTON CT
1000 SJS 95131 834-C1
WINSTON PL
800 MTVW 94043 812-A3
WINSTON ST
1700 SJS 95131 834-D1
WINSTON WY
- SMCo 94061 790-B3
WINTER LN
5500 SJS 95138 875-C4
19900 SAR 95070 852-E7
WINTERBERRY WY
500 SJS 95129 853-B2
WINTERBROOK DR
6100 SJS 95129 852-C7
WINTERBROOK RD
16000 LGTS 95032 873-D6
WINTERCREEK
- PTLV 94028 830-C2
WINTER CREEK WY
- MGH 95037 916-H6
WINTER GREEN CT
- GIL 95020 977-E1
WINTERGREEN DR
19700 CPTO 95014 852-F1
WINTERGREEN WY
800 PA 94303 791-D6
WINTER PARK WY
1800 SJS 95122 834-J6
WINTERS RD
- SBnC 95023 1060-A1
WINTERSET WY
6500 SJS 95120 894-F1
WINTERSONG CT
1800 SJS 95131 814-D7
1800 SJS 95131 834-D1
WINTON WY
4800 SJS 95124 873-E4
12100 LAH 94024 831-E4
15100 SCIC 95124 873-E4
WINWOOD CT
300 MTVW 94040 811-F4
WINWOOD WY
2900 SJS 95148 835-D7
2900 SJS 95148 855-D1
WISSAHICKON AV
100 LGTS 95030 872-J7
WISTARIA CT
1500 LALT 94024 831-J5
WISTARIA LN
1500 LALT 94024 831-J5
1500 LALT 94024 832-A5
WISTARIA WY
- SCL 95050 833-F5
WISTERIA DR
100 EPA 94303 791-C2
700 GIL 95020 977-J6
WISTERIA TER
1200 SUNV 94086 832-G3
WISTERIA WY
- ATN 94027 790-G1
6300 SJS 95129 852-F4
WITHEY RD
16200 MSER 95030 872-H6
WITHEY HEIGHTS RD
16400 SCIC 95030 872-H6
16500 MSER 95030 872-H6
WITHROW PL
2900 SCL 95051 833-A6
WIVEN PLACE WY
3800 SJS 95121 855-B4
WIZARD CT
2000 SJS 95131 814-D6
WOBURN CT
600 MTVW 94040 831-J2
WODZIENSKI DR
- SJS 95148 855-F1
WOEHL CT
21800 SCIC 95120 895-C4
WOLCOT WY
20300 SAR 95070 852-E6
WOLFBERRY CT
100 SJS 95136 874-H1
WOLFE RD
10000 CPTO 95014 832-G7
10000 CPTO 95014 852-G1
N WOLFE RD
100 SUNV 94086 812-G6
100 SUNV 94086 832-G1
S WOLFE RD
100 SUNV 94086 832-G2
1000 SUNV 94087 832-G5
1000 SCIC 94087 832-G2
WOLLIN WY
100 LGTS 95032 873-D7
WONDERAMA DR
1900 SJS 95148 835-A5
WONG CT
5300 SJS 95123 874-J3
WONG DR
5300 SJS 95123 874-J3
WOOD CT
1000 HOLL 95023 1039-J5
WOOD GRN
800 MTVW 94041 811-J6
WOOD LN
- MLPK 94025 790-E5
WOOD RD
- SCIC 95033 894-B7
- SCIC 95033 914-E1
- SCIC 95120 894-G7
- SCIC 95120 914-E1
100 SCIC 95030 892-J1
WOOD ACRES RD
15700 SCIC 95030 872-G6
WOODALE CT
1300 SJS 95127 835-A4
WOODARD RD
2000 SCIC 95124 873-E2
2000 SJS 95124 873-E2
15900 CMBL 95008 873-D2

STREET
Block City ZIP Pg-Grid

WOODBANK WY
18400 SAR 95070 872-H3
WOODBARK CT
3700 SJS 95117 853-C3
WOODBINE WY
1000 SJS 95117 853-C3
WOODBOROUGH CT
- SJS 95116 834-J7
WOODBOROUGH DR
- SJS 95116 834-E6
WOODBOROUGH PL
- SJS 95116 834-E7
WOODBRAE CT
5000 SJS 95130 852-J7
WOODBRIDGE WY
400 SCL 95054 813-F5
WOODBURN WY
13500 SCIC 95127 834-J3
WOODBURY CT
- SJS 95121 855-E5
WOODBURY DR
21800 CPTO 95014 832-B7
WOODBURY LN
- SJS 95121 855-D5
WOODCLIFF CT
6500 SJS 95120 894-C1
WOODCLIFF DR
6500 SJS 95120 894-C1
WOODCOCK CT
400 MPS 95035 794-A3
WOODCREEK LN
3700 SJS 95117 853-B4
WOODCREEK WY
800 GIL 95020 957-G7
WOODCREST DR
3000 SJS 95118 874-B1
WOOD DELL CT
18700 SAR 95070 852-H6
WOOD DUCK AV
900 SCL 95051 832-H5
WOOD DUCK CT
900 SCL 95051 832-H5
WOODED GLEN DR
2000 LALT 94024 831-G5
WOODED HILLS DR
1200 SJS 95120 894-E3
WOODED LAKE DR
7000 SJS 95120 894-D3
WOODED VIEW DR
100 LGTS 95032 873-E7
200 LGTS 95032 893-E1
WOODELF DR
1300 SJS 95121 855-A3
WOODFALLS CT
1000 SJS 95116 834-E6
WOODFERN
- PTLV 94028 830-C2
WOODFLOWER WY
1100 SJS 95117 853-C4
WOODFORD DR
3500 SJS 95124 873-J2
WOODGATE CT
2900 SJS 95118 873-J1
WOODGLEN DR
2000 SJS 95130 853-A6
WOODGROVE COM
- FRMT 94539 793-J3
WOODGROVE LN
900 SJS 95136 874-D1
WOODGROVE SQ
1400 SJS 95117 853-C4
WOODHAMS RD
- SCL 95051 833-A6
- SCL 95051 853-A1
WOODHAMS OAKS PL
800 SCL 95051 833-A6
WOODHAVEN DR
14000 SCIC 95127 835-A3
14000 SJS 95127 835-A3
WOODHAVEN PL
600 MTVW 94041 811-G5
WOOD HILL CT
11800 CPTO 95014 852-C4
WOOD HOLLOW CT
- SJS 95138 855-F6
WOODHOLLY CT
- SJS 95116 834-J7
WOODHURST LN
5500 SJS 95123 874-F4
WOODING CT
2400 SJS 95128 853-F3
WOODLAND AV
400 LGTS 95032 873-A7
500 MLPK 94025 790-J3
900 MLPK 94025 791-A3
1500 EPA 94303 791-B3
1800 SCL 95050 833-D7
2200 SJS 95128 833-E7
2400 SCL 95128 833-E7
17600 MGH 95037 916-E7
17600 MGH 95037 936-F1
WOODLAND CT
- MPS 95035 814-A3
800 MLPK 94025 790-J3
18100 MGH 95037 936-F1
18100 SCIC 95037 936-F1
WOODLAND LN
300 MTVW 94043 811-J4
WOODLAND RDG
- SCrC 95033 892-C4
WOODLAND TER
- SJS 95112 834-E7
WOODLAND WY
100 MPS 95035 814-A3
WOODLARK WY
7900 CPTO 95014 852-C2
WOODLAWN AV
1200 SJS 95128 853-E4
WOODLEAF CT
3700 SJS 95117 853-C3
WOODLEAF WY
2100 MTVW 94040 831-J1
WOODLEIGH CIR
18800 SAR 95070 852-B7

WOODLEY DR
3500 SJS 95148 835-F7
WOODMAN CT
1300 SJS 95121 855-B2
WOODMEADOW CT
1300 SJS 95131 814-B6
WOODMEADOW LN
1300 SJS 95131 814-B6
WOODMERE DR
4000 SJS 95136 854-F7
WOODMINSTER DR
1000 SJS 95121 854-H2
WOODMONT DR
3000 SJS 95118 874-B1
12700 SAR 95070 852-E6
WOODMOOR DR
2700 SJS 95127 835-A5
WOODPARK CT
- SJS 95116 834-J7
WOODRANCH CT
- SJS 95131 814-E6
WOODRANCH RD
- SJS 95131 814-D6
WOODRIDGE CT
22500 CPTO 95014 851-J1
22500 CPTO 95014 852-A1
WOODRIDGE WY
1600 SJS 95127 835-B5
1600 SJS 95148 835-B5
WOODROE CT
- SJS 95116 834-J7
WOODRUFF DR
1200 SJS 95120 874-C7
WOODRUFF WY
200 MPS 95035 793-J4
WOODS CT
2900 SJS 95148 855-D1
WOODS LN
- LALT 94024 831-J5
WOODS WY
3000 SJS 95148 835-D7
3100 SJS 95148 855-D1
WOODSET CT
- SJS 95116 834-G3
WOODSET LN
- SJS 95116 834-G3
WOODSIDE CT
3300 SJS 95121 855-D3
12400 SAR 95070 852-G5
WOODSIDE DR
12100 SAR 95070 852-G5
WOODSIDE LN
3300 SJS 95121 855-D3
WOODSIDE RD
Rt#-84
400 RDWC 94061 790-B2
1200 SMCo 94061 790-B2
2100 WDSD 94062 790-B2
2100 SMCo 94062 790-B2
WOODSON CT
1500 SJS 95118 874-B2
WOODSTOCK LN
700 LALT 94022 831-E1
3400 MTVW 94040 831-J2
WOODSTOCK WY
500 SCL 95054 813-E5
5200 SJS 95118 874-A4
WOODTHRUSH CT
900 SJS 95120 894-G2
WOODTOWN CT
1000 SJS 95116 834-E6
WOODTREE CT
3400 SJS 95121 855-D3
WOODVALE CT
1000 SJS 95116 834-E6
WOODVIEW AV
300 MGH 95037 916-J4
WOODVIEW DR
- MGH 95037 916-J4
WOODVIEW LN
- WDSD 94062 810-A6
14100 SAR 95070 872-F2
WOODVIEW PL
900 SJS 95120 894-G3
WOODVIEW TER
1200 LALT 94024 831-H5
WOODWARD AV
3200 SCL 95054 813-E6
WOODWARD CT
20700 SAR 95070 872-D1
WOODWARD DR
- MPS 95035 794-A6
WOODWARDIA LN
19400 SCIC 95030 872-F5
WOODWORTH WY
- SCIC 95127 815-D7
- SCIC 95127 835-D1
- GIL 95020 957-H7
WOODY CT
1900 SJS 95132 814-E2
WOODY LN
3200 SJS 95132 814-E3
WOODYEND CT
3400 SJS 95121 855-A4
WOOL AV
12900 SCIC 95111 854-H6
WOOL DR
500 MPS 95035 794-C5
WOOLAROC DR
21600 SCIC 95033 912-H4
WOOL CREEK DR
600 SJS 95112 854-F2
WOOSLEY DR
6200 SJS 95123 875-B6
WOOSTER AV
300 SJS 95116 834-D3
WORCESTER LN
100 LGTS 95030 873-C7
100 LGTS 95030 893-C1
WORCESTER LP
100 LGTS 95030 873-C7
100 LGTS 95030 893-C1
WORDEN WY
14200 SAR 95070 872-E2

WORLEY AV
500 SUNV 94086 812-F6
WORTHAM CT
100 MTVW 94040 831-J2
WORTHING CT
6700 SJS 95120 894-G2
WOZ WY
- SJS 95110 834-B7
WRAIGHT AV
400 LGTS 95032 873-A7
WREN AV
900 SCL 95051 832-J5
900 SUNV 94087 832-J5
7300 GIL 95020 977-H3
8800 GIL 95020 957-H7
8800 SCIC 95020 957-H7
WREN DR
800 SJS 95125 854-C6
WREN WY
200 CMBL 95008 853-C6
2200 SJS 95008 853-C7
WRIGHT AV
- MTVW 94043 812-A1
- SCIC 94043 812-A1
- MGH 95037 916-H7
900 MTVW 94043 811-H4
1200 SUNV 94087 832-B4
WRIGHT CT
1000 SUNV 94087 832-B4
WRIGHT DR
19800 SCIC 95033 892-J7
WRIGHT PL
- SJS 95126 854-A1
3700 PA 94306 811-D1
WRIGHT RD
- SBnC 95023 1039-F1
- SBnC 95023 1040-A1
- HOLL 95023 1040-A1
1300 HOLL 95023 1039-F1
WRIGHT TER
1000 SUNV 94087 832-B4
WRIGHT WY
13200 LAH 94022 811-A7
WRIGHTS STATION RD
22200 SCIC 95033 913-E6
WRIGHT STATION RD
21300 SCIC 95033 913-B2
WRIGLEY WY
800 MPS 95035 794-C7
WUNDERLICH DR
1000 SJS 95129 852-H3
10300 CPTO 95014 852-H1
WYANDOTTE DR
100 SJS 95123 875-B5
WYANDOTTE ST
2100 MTVW 94043 811-F1
WYATT DR
1500 SCL 95054 813-D6
WYCLIFFE CT
2900 SJS 95148 855-C6
WYLIE DR
1700 MPS 95035 794-D7
WYLIE WY
1300 SJS 95130 853-B4
WYMAN WY
800 SJS 95133 814-F7
WYNDHAM DR
- PTLV 94028 810-A6
1600 SJS 95124 874-A3
1600 SJS 95124 873-J3
WYNFAIR RIDGE WY
2100 SJS 95138 855-F5
WYOMA PL
500 MPS 95035 794-B5
WYRICK AV
1700 SJS 95124 873-G2
1800 SCIC 95124 873-H3

X

XAVIER CT
2000 SCL 95051 832-J2
3700 SJS 95008 853-C7

Y

Y RD
- SBnC 95020 1018-B3
2500 SBnC 95045 1018-B3
YAKIMA CIR
3100 SJS 95121 855-A4
YALE CT
14500 LAH 94022 810-H5
YALE DR
1600 MTVW 94040 811-G7
5400 SJS 95118 874-A5
YALE LN
700 SCL 95051 832-J6
YALE RD
- MLPK 94025 790-G4
YALE ST
1900 SCIC 94305 791-A7
2000 PA 94306 791-A7
YAMADA DR
1300 SJS 95131 814-C7
YAMANE DR
200 GIL 95020 957-J7
YAMATO DR
4800 SJS 95111 875-B1
YAMPA CT
48900 FRMT 94539 793-J2
YAMPA RD
- FRMT 94539 793-J2
YAMPA WY
- FRMT 94539 793-J2
400 FRMT 94539 794-A2
YANCY DR
3100 SJS 95148 855-D2
YANKEE POINT CT
1500 SJS 95131 814-D6
YARBOROUGH LN
200 RDWC 94061 790-B2

YARD CT
1100 SJS 95133 834-C2
YARDIS CT
800 MTVW 94040 831-G1
YARMOUNTH TER
1300 SUNV 94087 832-E4
YARMOUTH CT
900 SJS 95120 894-G2
YARMOUTH WY
900 SJS 95120 894-G2
YARROW ST
- HOLL 95023 1040-D7
- HOLL 95023 1060-D1
YARWOOD CT
600 SJS 95128 853-F2
YASOU DEMAS WY
- SJS 95119 875-D5
YASUI CT
100 SJS 95138 875-G7
YATES CT
800 SUNV 94087 832-E2
YEADON WY
6100 SJS 95119 875-C6
YELLOWBIRD CT
6000 SJS 95120 874-B7
YELLOWLEAF CT
3200 SJS 95135 855-E2
YELLOWSTONE AV
1700 MPS 95035 814-D1
YELLOWSTONE DR
300 MGH 95037 937-A2
3900 SJS 95130 853-B4
YELLOWSTONE TER
600 SUNV 94087 832-D3
YERBA BANK CT
2500 SJS 95121 855-E4
YERBA BUENA AV
- LALT 94022 811-D5
300 LALT 94306 811-D5
3500 SJS 95135 855-E3
3600 SJS 95121 855-E3
YERBA BUENA CT
3700 SJS 95121 855-D3
YERBA BUENA PL
200 LALT 94022 811-D5
YERBA BUENA RD
400 SJS 95121 855-A5
800 SJS 95111 855-A5
800 SCIC 95111 855-A5
900 SCIC 95121 855-A5
1500 SJS 95135 855-H3
YERBA BUENA WY
2500 SCL 95054 813-B2
YERBA CLIFF CT
2600 SJS 95121 855-F5
YERBA HILLS CT
2500 SJS 95121 855-E4
YERBA SANTA AV
- LALT 94022 811-D5
YERBA SANTA CT
13800 SAR 95070 872-F1
YERBA VISTA CT
2600 SJS 95121 855-F4
YERMO CT
500 SJS 95111 854-G6
YESLER CT
2300 SJS 95131 814-D4
YEW TREE CT
3600 SJS 95111 854-G6
YNIGO WY
4200 PA 94306 811-C3
YOLANDA CT
1400 SJS 95118 874-B1
YOLO CT
600 SJS 95136 874-E1
YOLO DR
3800 SJS 95136 874-F1
3800 SAR 95070 852-D6
YONA VISTA
11200 SCIC 95127 815-A6
YORK AV
1300 CMBL 95008 873-A1
YORK ST
1600 SJS 95124 873-J2
YORKSHIRE DR
900 LALT 94024 831-H5
1100 CPTO 95014 852-C3
YORKSHIRE WY
2000 MTVW 94040 831-J1
YORKTON DR
2600 MTVW 94040 831-J2
YORKTON WY
5000 SJS 95130 852-J7
YORKTOWN DR
900 SUNV 94087 832-B3
7000 GIL 95020 977-H4
YOSEMITE AV
400 MTVW 94041 811-H6
1100 SJS 95126 833-H7
YOSEMITE DR
400 MPS 95035 814-B1
1300 MPS 95035 794-D7
YOSEMITE WY
- MPS 95035 814-C1
100 LGTS 95032 873-B7
100 LGTS 95030 873-B7
15000 MGH 95037 937-B4
YOSHINO PL
10100 CPTO 95014 852-G1
YOUNG AL
- HOLL 95023 1039-J4
YOUNG CT
24100 SCIC 94024 831-F3
E YOUNGER AV
- SJS 95112 834-A3
W YOUNGER AV
- SJS 95110 833-J3
- SJS 95110 834-A4
YOUNGS CIR
3400 SJS 95127 814-J7
YOUNGS CT
600 SJS 95127 814-J6
YOUNG TOMS CT
- GIL 95020 977-E4

YUBA AV
3200 SJS 95117 853-C3
YUBA CT
19600 SAR 95070 852-F6
YUBA DR
700 MTVW 94041 812-A7
800 MTVW 94041 811-J7
YUBA LN
27800 LAH 94022 810-J7
27800 LAH 94022 811-A7
27800 LAH 94022 830-J1
YUCATAN WY
4900 SJS 95118 874-B3
YUCCA AV
3000 SJS 95124 873-J1
YUKON DR
1400 SUNV 94087 832-D5
YUKON TER
1300 SUNV 94087 832-D4
YUKON WY
2200 SJS 95008 853-B7
YUKON RIVER WY
- SJS 95131 814-B6
YUMA AV
1200 SUNV 94089 812-J5
YUMA DR
3100 SJS 95111 854-H5
YUROK CIR
500 SJS 95123 874-H5
YUROK CT
500 SJS 95123 874-H5
YVETTE CT
1100 SJS 95118 874-C3
YVONNE CT
15100 SCIC 95124 873-F4
YVONNE DR
15100 SCIC 95037 936-H5

Z

ZACHARY CT
- MLPK 94025 790-D7
1200 SJS 95121 854-H2
ZACHARY WY
2400 SJS 95121 854-J2
ZAMORA CT
1000 MPS 95035 794-B4
ZAMZOW CT
200 SCIC 95020 957-J6
ZANKER LN
- SJS 95134 793-E7
ZANKER RD
700 SJS 95134 793-F7
1200 SJS 95134 813-F1
1600 SJS 95112 833-J1
1900 SJS 95112 813-H6
2000 SJS 95131 813-H6
ZAPATA WY
- PTLV 94028 810-A5
ZAPPETTINI CT
12600 LAH 94022 830-H2
ZARICK DR
900 SJS 95129 853-A3
ZATON AV
400 SCIC 95117 853-C1
400 SJS 95117 853-C1
E ZAYANTE RD
13600 SCrC 95018 912-E7
ZEKA DR
1200 SJS 95131 814-C7
ZELLA CT
18100 SCIC 95033 912-H3
ZENA AV
17100 MSER 95030 873-B4
17300 LGTS 95030 873-B4
ZEPHYR CT
1300 SJS 95127 835-A4
ZEPPELIN CT
4900 SJS 95111 875-A2
ZIG ZAG TR
18100 SCIC 95033 912-J3
ZILEMAN CT
5800 SJS 95123 875-A5
ZILEMAN DR
5800 SJS 95123 875-A5
ZINFANDEL CIR
- MGH 95037 917-E6
ZINFANDEL CT
19300 SAR 95070 872-G3
ZINFANDEL ST
- FRMT 94539 793-J2
- FRMT 94539 794-A2
ZINFANDEL WY
- SUNV 94087 832-E2
1100 SJS 95120 874-D6
ZINNIA LN
1600 SJS 95124 873-J6
ZINNIA ST
8700 GIL 95020 977-G1
ZION CT
1300 MPS 95035 794-D7
ZION LN
2900 SJS 95132 814-F5
ZIRCON CT
5000 SJS 95136 874-E3
ZISCH DR
3300 SJS 95118 874-B1
ZOOK RD
- SCIC 94035 792-B7
- SCIC 94035 812-B1
- SUNV 94089 792-B7
ZORIA CIR
2200 SJS 95131 814-D5
ZORIA FARMS LN
- SJS 95127 834-H2
ZORKA AV
20200 SAR 95070 852-E5
ZUNI CT
1500 SJS 95131 814-D6
ZUNI LN
- GIL 95020 957-F6
ZURICH CT
1100 SJS 95132 814-G5
ZURICH TER
1300 SUNV 94087 832-D4

#

1ST AV
- SCIC 94035 812-D1
200 SMCo 94063 790-D1
1000 SUNV 94089 812-D1
1ST ST
- SBnC 95075 1061-A6
100 LALT 94022 811-D7
200 HOLL 95023 1040-A3
600 SUNV 94089 812-H3
700 SJB 95045 1038-D4
900 SBnC 95045 1038-D4
10600 SCIC 95020 957-G3
1ST ST Rt#-152
- GIL 95020 977-H2
N 1ST ST
- SJS 95113 834-A4
100 SJS 95112 834-A4
200 CMBL 95008 853-E6
300 SJS 95110 834-A4
1100 SJS 95110 833-J2
1100 SJS 95112 833-J2
1200 SJS 95002 813-C1
1400 SJS 95131 833-J2
1600 SJS 95131 813-H7
2300 SJS 95134 813-E2
S 1ST ST
- SJS 95113 834-C7
100 CMBL 95008 853-E6
300 SJS 95110 834-C7
500 SJS 95112 834-C7
S 1ST ST Rt#-82
500 SJS 95112 834-C7
500 SJS 95110 834-C7
600 SJS 95112 854-D2
600 SJS 95110 854-D2
W 1ST ST
- MGH 95037 917-A7
- MGH 95037 916-J7
900 MLPK 94025 790-G2
1ST FORK DR
- SCrC 95033 871-C3
2ND AV
200 SMCo 94063 790-D1
1100 SUNV 94089 812-E2
2ND ST
- SUNV 94089 812-H3
- GIL 95020 977-H3
- GIL 95020 978-A2
100 HOLL 95023 1040-A3
100 LALT 94022 811-D6
500 SJB 95045 1038-C4
2000 SCL 95054 813-F3
3900 PA 94306 811-D1
E 2ND ST
100 MLPK 94025 790-G3
N 2ND ST
- SJS 95113 834-A3
- CMBL 95008 853-E6
100 SJS 95112 834-A3
S 2ND ST
- SJS 95113 834-C7
400 SJS 95112 834-C7
900 SJS 95112 854-C1
W 2ND ST
- MGH 95037 917-A7
700 HOLL 95023 1039-J3
3RD AV
200 SMCo 94063 790-D1
1000 SUNV 94089 812-D2
3RD ST
- SBnC 95075 1061-A5
- GIL 95020 978-A2
- MGH 95037 917-A7
- HOLL 95023 1040-A3
- LALT 94022 811-D6
- SCIC 95037 896-D6
- GIL 95020 977-F3
300 SJB 95045 1038-C4
2000 SCL 95054 813-C5
20600 SAR 95070 872-D3
E 3RD ST
400 MLPK 94025 790-H3
N 3RD ST
- CMBL 95008 853-E5
- SJS 95112 834-A3
- SJS 95113 834-B5
S 3RD ST
- SJS 95113 834-C7
100 CMBL 95008 853-E6
300 SJS 95112 834-C7
700 SJS 95112 854-D1
W 3RD ST
600 MLPK 94025 790-G3
4TH AV
- MTVW 94043 812-B5
200 SMCo 94063 790-D1
4TH ST
- SBnC 95075 1061-A5
- SUNV 94089 812-H3
- GIL 95020 978-A3
- MGH 95037 917-A7
- LALT 94022 811-E6
- SJB 95045 1038-C4
100 HOLL 95023 1040-A4
100 GIL 95020 977-H3
10600 SCIC 95020 957-H3
20600 SAR 95070 872-D2
E 4TH ST
600 MLPK 94025 790-G3
N 4TH ST
- SJS 95113 834-B5
- SJS 95112 834-A3
1200 SJS 95112 833-J2
S 4TH ST
- SJS 95113 834-C6
- CMBL 95008 853-E6
- SJS 95112 834-C6
100 SJS 95192 834-C6

W 4TH ST
600 MLPK 94025 790-G3
5TH AV
- SMCo 94063 790-D1
1000 SCIC 94035 812-D2
1000 SUNV 94089 812-D2
5TH ST
- SUNV 94089 812-H3
- GIL 95020 978-A3
- MGH 95037 917-A7
- MGH 95037 937-A1
- SBnC 95075 1061-A5
- SBnC 95075 1060-J5
100 SJB 95045 1038-D5
100 HOLL 95023 1040-A4
100 GIL 95020 977-H3
500 HOLL 95023 1039-J4
10600 SCIC 95020 957-H4
20600 SAR 95070 872-D3
N 5TH ST
- SJS 95113 834-B5
- SJS 95112 834-A3
S 5TH ST
- SJS 95113 834-C7
- SJS 95112 834-C7
700 SJS 95112 854-D1
6TH AV
300 SMCo 94025 790-D1
1000 SUNV 94089 812-E3
6TH ST
- SUNV 94089 812-H3
100 HOLL 95023 1040-A4
300 HOLL 95023 1039-J4
400 SJB 95045 1038-D5
500 GIL 95020 978-B3
10700 SCIC 95020 957-H3
14600 SAR 95070 872-D3
E 6TH ST
- GIL 95020 978-A3
N 6TH ST
- SJS 95113 834-B5
- SJS 95112 834-B4
S 6TH ST
- SJS 95113 834-C7
- SJS 95112 834-C7
800 SJS 95112 854-D1
W 6TH ST
- GIL 95020 978-A3
200 GIL 95020 977-J3
7TH AV
400 SMCo 94025 790-D1
1000 SUNV 94089 812-D3
7TH ST
- SUNV 94089 812-H3
100 HOLL 95023 1040-A4
200 SJB 95045 1038-C5
400 HOLL 95023 1039-J4
E 7TH ST
- GIL 95020 978-A3
N 7TH ST
- SJS 95113 834-B4
- SJS 95112 834-A3
S 7TH ST
- SJS 95113 834-D7
- SJS 95112 834-D7
200 SJS 95112 854-D1
W 7TH ST
- GIL 95020 978-A3
200 GIL 95020 977-J4
8TH AV
300 SMCo 94025 790-D1
1000 SUNV 94089 812-D3
E 8TH ST
200 GIL 95020 978-A3
N 8TH ST
- SJS 95113 834-C5
- SJS 95112 834-B3
S 8TH ST
- SJS 95113 834-D7
- SJS 95112 834-D7
900 SJS 95112 854-D1
W 8TH ST
- GIL 95020 978-A4
300 GIL 95020 977-H4
9TH AV
300 SMCo 94025 790-E1
1000 SUNV 94089 812-E3
9TH ST
- SUNV 94089 812-H3
E 9TH ST
300 GIL 95020 978-A4
N 9TH ST
- SJS 95113 834-B4
- SJS 95112 834-B4
S 9TH ST
- SJS 95113 834-D7
- SJS 95112 834-D7
900 SJS 95112 854-D1
W 9TH ST
- GIL 95020 978-A4
300 GIL 95020 977-J4
10TH ST
- SUNV 94089 812-H3
E 10TH ST
- GIL 95020 978-A4
N 10TH ST
- SJS 95112 834-B2
- SJS 95113 834-B4
S 10TH ST
- SJS 95113 834-D6
- SJS 95112 834-D6
100 SJS 95192 834-D6
900 SJS 95112 854-D1
W 10TH ST
- GIL 95020 978-A4
400 GIL 95020 977-J4
11TH AV
1000 SUNV 94089 812-D3
11TH ST
- GIL 95020 978-A4
N 11TH ST
- SJS 95112 834-B3
S 11TH ST
- SJS 95112 834-D6

STREET Block	City	ZIP	Pg-Grid
S 11TH ST			
1000	SJS	95112	854-E1
N 12TH ST			
-	SJS	95112	834-B3
S 12TH ST			
-	SJS	95112	834-D6
1000	SJS	95112	854-E1
N 13TH ST			
-	SJS	95112	834-B2
S 13TH ST			
-	SJS	95112	834-D6
N 14TH ST			
-	SJS	95112	834-C3
S 14TH ST			
-	SJS	95112	834-D6
N 15TH ST			
-	SJS	95112	834-B2
S 15TH ST			
-	SJS	95112	834-D6
16TH AV			
500	SMCo	94025	790-E1
N 16TH ST			
100	SJS	95112	834-C3
S 16TH ST			
-	SJS	95112	834-D6
17TH AV			
500	SMCo	94025	790-F1
N 17TH ST			
-	SJS	95112	834-C3
S 17TH ST			
-	SJS	95112	834-D5
18TH AV			
600	SMCo	94025	790-F1
N 18TH ST			
100	SJS	95112	834-C3
S 18TH ST			
200	SJS	95116	834-E6
N 19TH ST			
100	SJS	95112	834-C3
S 19TH ST			
-	SJS	95116	834-D5
N 20TH ST			
-	SJS	95116	834-D5
200	SJS	95112	834-D3
S 20TH ST			
-	SJS	95116	834-D5
N 21ST ST			
-	SJS	95116	834-D4
300	SJS	95112	834-C3
S 21ST ST			
-	SJS	95116	834-E5
N 22ND ST			
500	SJS	95112	834-D3
S 22ND ST			
-	SJS	95116	834-E5
N 23RD ST			
700	SJS	95112	834-C3
S 23RD ST			
-	SJS	95116	834-E5
N 24TH ST			
-	SJS	95116	834-E4
S 24TH ST			
-	SJS	95116	834-E5
N 25TH ST			
-	SJS	95116	834-E4
N 26TH ST			
-	SJS	95116	834-E4
S 26TH ST			
-	SJS	95116	834-E5
N 27TH ST			
-	SJS	95116	834-E4
N 28TH ST			
-	SJS	95116	834-E4
S 28TH ST			
-	SJS	95116	834-E5
N 30TH ST			
-	SJS	95116	834-E4
S 30TH ST			
-	SJS	95116	834-E5
N 31ST ST			
-	SJS	95116	834-E4
300	SJS	95133	834-E3
S 31ST ST			
-	SJS	95116	834-F4
N 32ND ST			
-	SJS	95116	834-E4
N 33RD ST			
-	SJS	95116	834-E3
300	SJS	95133	834-E3
S 33RD ST			
-	SJS	95116	834-F4
N 34TH ST			
-	SJS	95116	834-E3
S 34TH ST			
-	SJS	95116	834-F4
I-280 FRWY			
-	SJS	-	853-H2
I-280 JUNIPERO SERRA FRWY			
-	CPTO	-	832-F6
-	LAH	-	810-F3
-	LAH	-	811-A7
-	LAH	-	831-B1
-	LALT	-	831-G5
-	LALT	-	832-F6
-	MLPK	-	810-C1
-	PA	-	810-F3
-	SCL	-	832-F6
-	SCL	-	852-H1
-	SCIC	-	810-F3
-	SCIC	-	831-G5
-	SCIC	-	832-F6
-	SJS	-	852-H1
-	SJS	-	852-J1
-	SJS	-	853-A1
-	SMCo	-	790-A6
-	SMCo	-	810-C1
-	SUNV	-	832-F6
-	WDSD	-	790-A6
I-280 SINCLAIR FRWY			
-	SCIC	-	853-G2
-	SJS	-	834-C7
-	SJS	-	834-E7
I-280 SINCLAIR FRWY			
-	SJS	-	834-F6
-	SJS	-	853-G2
-	SJS	-	854-A2
I-680 SINCLAIR FRWY			
-	FRMT	-	793-J1
-	FRMT	-	794-A2
-	MPS	-	794-A2
-	MPS	-	814-E6
-	SJS	-	814-E6
-	SJS	-	834-F1
I-880 NIMITZ FRWY			
-	FRMT	-	793-G2
-	MPS	-	793-H4
-	MPS	-	813-J1
-	SJS	-	813-J1
-	SJS	-	814-A6
-	SJS	-	833-H5
-	SJS	-	834-A1
-	SJS	-	853-F1
Rt#-G1 SAN JUAN CANYON RD			
-	SJB	95045	1038-D5
1700	SBnC	-	1059-A4
1700	SBnC	95045	1038-D5
Rt#-G2 LAWRENCE EXWY			
-	SAR	95070	852-H3
-	SCL	95051	832-J6
-	SCL	95051	852-H3
100	SCL	95051	812-J7
200	SUNV	94086	812-J7
300	SJS	95014	852-H3
300	SJS	95129	852-H3
300	CPTO	95014	852-H3
700	SUNV	94089	812-J3
800	SUNV	94087	832-J6
1800	SAR	95129	852-H3
1900	SUNV	94086	832-J6
Rt#-G2 QUITO RD			
2000	SAR	95070	852-J7
2000	SJS	95130	852-J7
12400	SAR	95130	852-J7
12500	SJS	95130	872-H4
12500	SAR	95070	872-H4
14800	LGTS	95030	872-H4
14800	LGTS	95032	872-H4
14900	MSER	95030	872-H4
15500	SCIC	95030	872-H4
Rt#-G3 OREGON EXWY			
-	PA	94301	791-C6
-	PA	94306	791-C6
2500	PA	94303	791-C6
Rt#-G3 PAGE MILL RD			
1800	SCIC	94304	810-J4
1800	PA	94304	810-J4
1900	SCIC	94304	810-J4
2100	LAH	94022	810-J4
Rt#-G4 MONTAGUE EXWY			
-	SJS	95134	813-F4
400	SCL	95054	813-D6
600	MPS	95035	813-F4
600	SJS	95131	813-F4
Rt#-G4 SAN TOMAS EXWY			
-	CMBL	95008	853-C6
-	CMBL	95008	873-D1
-	SJS	95008	853-C4
-	SCL	95050	833-C6
-	SCL	95051	833-C3
-	SCL	95051	853-C4
-	SCL	95117	833-C6
-	SCL	95117	853-C4
100	SJS	95117	853-C4
100	SJS	95130	853-C4
2900	SCL	95054	813-C7
2900	SCL	95054	833-C3
Rt#-G5 FOOTHILL BLVD			
2400	LALT	94024	832-A7
2400	CPTO	95014	832-A7
8400	SCIC	94024	832-A7
8700	CPTO	95014	832-A7
10300	CPTO	95014	852-A1
Rt#-G5 FOOTHILL EXWY			
100	LALT	94022	811-C5
100	LALT	94022	831-F1
200	LALT	94024	831-F1
400	SCIC	94024	831-F1
2600	PA	94304	811-C5
2600	SCIC	94304	810-J3
2600	SCIC	94304	811-C5
2600	PA	94304	810-J3
4100	PA	94306	811-C5
4400	LALT	94024	832-A6
7100	CPTO	95014	832-A6
14000	LAH	94022	811-C5
14000	LALT	94306	811-C5
Rt#-G5 JUNIPERO SERRA BLVD			
-	MLPK	94025	790-F7
100	SCIC	94305	790-F7
100	SCIC	94304	790-F7
100	SCIC	94305	810-G1
100	SCIC	94304	810-G1
Rt#-G6 CENTRAL EXWY			
-	MTVW	94086	812-A5
-	PA	94306	811-G3
-	SCL	94086	812-H7
500	MTVW	94043	812-A5
500	MTVW	94041	812-A5
700	SCL	95050	833-D1
700	SJS	95054	833-D1
700	MTVW	94041	811-G3
700	MTVW	94043	811-G3
800	SCL	95054	833-D1
1600	MTVW	94040	811-G3
Rt#-G6 CENTRAL EXWY			
2200	SCL	95051	833-D1
2700	SCL	95051	813-A7
2700	SCL	95054	813-A7
3000	SUNV	95054	813-A7
3200	SUNV	94086	813-A7
3400	SUNV	94086	812-H7
3400	SCL	95051	812-H7
Rt#-G7 BLOOMFIELD AV			
1200	SCIC	95020	978-H7
1300	SCIC	95020	998-E1
Rt#-G8 ALMADEN EXWY			
700	SJS	95125	854-C6
3300	SJS	95118	854-C6
3300	SJS	95136	854-C6
3400	SJS	95136	874-D2
3500	SJS	95118	874-D2
9000	SJS	95123	874-D2
11900	SJS	95120	874-D2
15700	SJS	95120	894-F2
Rt#-G8 ALMADEN RD			
3100	SJS	95125	854-D3
Rt#-G8 HARRY RD			
20400	SCIC	95120	894-J4
20400	SJS	95120	894-J4
Rt#-G8 MCKEAN RD			
19600	SJS	95120	894-J4
19600	SCIC	95120	894-J4
20000	SCIC	95120	895-A4
22400	SJS	95120	895-F6
23400	SJS	95141	895-F6
23500	SJS	95141	915-G1
23500	SCIC	95141	915-G1
23900	SCIC	95037	915-G1
Rt#-G8 UVAS RD			
12800	SCIC	95037	956-D1
15500	SCIC	95037	936-A1
17700	SCIC	95037	935-J1
19000	SCIC	95037	916-A5
20400	SCIC	95037	915-J4
Rt#-G8 WATSONVILLE RD			
8100	SCIC	95020	977-A1
8200	SCIC	95020	976-J1
9300	SCIC	95020	956-J6
10200	SCIC	95020	957-A4
12300	SCIC	95037	956-J6
12300	SCIC	95046	956-J6
Rt#-G9 FERGUSON RD			
2600	SCIC	95020	958-E7
2600	SCIC	95020	978-F1
Rt#-G9 LEAVESLEY RD			
400	GIL	95020	978-B1
600	GIL	95020	958-C7
1100	SCIC	95020	958-C7
Rt#-G10 BLOSSOM HILL RD			
-	LGTS	95030	873-C6
-	SJS	95111	875-A4
-	SJS	95138	875-A4
-	SJS	95193	875-A4
-	LGTS	95032	873-C6
-	SJS	95123	875-A4
300	SJS	95123	874-E4
600	SCIC	95123	874-E4
1100	SJS	95118	874-A6
1500	SJS	95124	874-A6
1500	SJS	95124	873-G6
15500	SCIC	95032	873-C6
Rt#-G11 SAN JUAN RD			
2700	MonC	95076	1037-A2
Rt#-9 BIG BASIN WY			
14400	SAR	95070	872-D3
22900	SCrC	95006	871-A4
22900	SCrC	95033	871-A4
26500	SCIC	95030	871-A4
Rt#-9 CONGRESS SPRINGS RD			
20900	SAR	95070	872-A3
22100	SCIC	95070	872-A3
22100	SCIC	95070	871-G2
22500	SCIC	95030	871-G2
Rt#-9 LOS GATOS SARATOGA RD			
-	LGTS	95030	873-A6
-	LGTS	95032	873-A6
Rt#-9 SARATOGA AV			
-	LGTS	95030	873-B7
-	LGTS	95032	873-B7
Rt#-9 SARATOGA LOS GATOS RD			
300	MSER	95030	872-G5
300	MSER	95030	873-A6
18500	SCIC	95030	872-G5
18800	SAR	95070	872-E3
Rt#-17 FRWY			
-	CMBL	-	853-F3
-	CMBL	-	853-F4
-	CMBL	-	873-E1
-	LGTS	-	873-B7
-	LGTS	-	873-D3
-	LGTS	-	892-J1
-	LGTS	-	893-A1
-	SCIC	-	892-J2
-	SJS	-	853-F2
Rt#-17 HIGHWAY			
-	SCIC	95033	892-J2
-	SCIC	95033	912-J1
-	SCIC	95033	913-A2
22200	SCrC	95033	912-J4
22200	SCrC	95033	913-A6
Rt#-25 AIRLINE HWY			
600	HOLL	95023	1040-B6
1000	SBnC	95023	1040-B6
1600	HOLL	95023	1060-D1
1600	SBnC	95023	1060-D1
Rt#-25 AIRLINE HWY			
5200	SBnC	95075	1060-H4
5900	SBnC	95075	1061-A5
7400	SBnC	95023	1061-A5
Rt#-25 BLOOMFIELD AV			
100	SCIC	95020	998-C2
Rt#-25 HOLLISTER RD			
700	HOLL	95023	1039-J1
700	HOLL	95023	1040-A2
700	SBnC	95023	1039-J1
1400	HOLL	95023	1019-H6
1400	SBnC	95023	1019-E2
1800	SCIC	95020	998-F4
2200	SBnC	95020	998-F4
2800	SBnC	95020	999-A6
2800	SBnC	95020	1019-D1
Rt#-25 SAN BENITO ST			
400	HOLL	95023	1040-A5
Rt#-25 SAN FELIPE RD			
-	HOLL	95023	1040-A3
200	SBnC	95023	1040-A3
Rt#-25 TRES PINOS RD			
100	HOLL	95023	1040-A5
Rt#-35 BEAR CREEK RD			
20000	SCIC	95033	912-F1
22000	SCrC	95033	912-E1
Rt#-35 SKYLINE BLVD			
-	SCrC	95033	871-D3
11800	SCIC	95030	851-A7
11800	SCIC	95030	871-B1
12300	SCIC	95070	871-F6
13000	SCIC	95070	892-A2
13500	SCIC	95033	892-D6
13500	SCrC	95033	892-A2
18600	SMCo	94020	830-A4
18600	PTLV	94028	830-A4
19000	SCIC	95033	912-E1
19000	SCrC	95033	912-E1
19800	SMCo	94028	830-C7
Rt#-35 SUMMIT RD			
20700	SCrC	95033	912-F2
21000	SCIC	95033	912-F2
Rt#-82 S 1ST ST			
500	SJS	95112	834-C7
500	SJS	95110	834-C7
600	SJS	95112	854-D2
600	SJS	95110	854-D2
Rt#-82 S AUTUMN ST			
-	SJS	95113	834-A7
-	SJS	95110	834-A7
Rt#-82 EL CAMINO REAL			
-	MLPK	94025	790-F3
-	PA	94301	790-F3
-	PA	94304	790-F3
100	ATN	94027	790-C1
100	SMCo	94025	790-C1
200	SCIC	94305	790-F3
200	PA	94305	790-F3
400	SCL	95050	833-F3
400	SCL	95053	833-F3
1000	ATN	94025	790-F3
1400	MLPK	94027	790-F3
1500	PA	94306	790-F3
1500	PA	94306	791-A6
1500	SCIC	94305	791-A6
2300	PA	94304	791-A7
2400	SCL	95051	833-A4
2600	RDWC	94061	790-C1
2600	SMCo	94063	790-C1
2800	PA	94304	811-B1
2900	PA	94306	811-B1
3300	SCL	95051	832-J4
4200	LALT	94022	811-B1
Rt#-82 E EL CAMINO REAL			
100	SUNV	94086	832-E2
100	SUNV	94087	832-G4
400	MTVW	94040	812-A7
400	MTVW	94041	812-A7
800	SCIC	94087	832-G4
1100	SCL	95051	832-G4
1100	SCL	94086	832-G4
Rt#-82 W EL CAMINO REAL			
-	MTVW	94040	811-F4
-	MTVW	94041	811-F4
100	MTVW	94041	812-A7
100	MTVW	94040	812-A7
100	SUNV	94086	832-C1
100	SUNV	94087	832-C1
1000	LALT	94022	811-F4
1100	SUNV	94087	812-B7
1100	SUNV	94086	812-B7
Rt#-82 S MARKET ST			
200	SJS	95110	834-B7
Rt#-82 MONTEREY HWY			
1400	SJS	95112	854-D2
1400	SJS	95110	854-D2
1600	SJS	95125	854-D2
2400	SCIC	95111	854-F5
2400	SJS	95111	854-F5
3100	SJS	95136	854-F5
4100	SJS	95111	874-H1
4100	SJS	95136	874-H1
4600	SJS	95136	875-A2
4600	SJS	95111	875-A2
5200	SJS	95123	875-A2
5200	SJS	95193	875-A2
Rt#-82 MONTGOMERY ST			
-	SJS	95110	834-A7
200	SJS	95110	854-A1
Rt#-82 S MONTGOMERY ST			
-	SJS	95110	834-A7
-	SJS	95113	834-A7
Rt#-82 W SAN CARLOS ST			
100	SJS	95110	834-A7
100	SJS	95113	834-A7
300	SJS	95126	834-A7
500	SJS	95126	854-A1
500	SJS	95110	854-A1
Rt#-82 W SANTA CLARA ST			
400	SJS	95113	834-A7
600	SJS	95126	834-A7
Rt#-82 THE ALAMEDA			
600	SJS	95126	834-A7
800	SJS	95126	833-H5
2100	SCL	95126	833-H5
2200	SCL	95050	833-H5
2500	SCL	95053	833-H5
Rt#-84 WOODSIDE RD			
400	RDWC	94061	790-B2
1200	SMCo	94061	790-B2
2100	WDSD	94062	790-B2
2100	SMCo	94062	790-B2
Rt#-85 STEVENS CREEK FRWY			
-	CPTO	-	832-A1
-	LALT	-	832-A1
-	MTVW	-	811-J2
-	MTVW	-	812-A7
-	MTVW	-	832-A1
-	SUNV	-	832-A1
Rt#-85 WEST VALLEY FRWY			
-	CMBL	-	873-C2
-	CPTO	-	832-B7
-	CPTO	-	852-E5
-	LGTS	-	873-C2
-	SAR	-	852-E5
-	SAR	-	872-H1
-	SCIC	-	873-C2
-	SCIC	-	874-C3
-	SJS	-	852-E5
-	SJS	-	872-J1
-	SJS	-	873-C2
-	SJS	-	874-C3
-	SJS	-	875-A5
-	SUNV	-	832-B7
Rt#-87 GUADALUPE FRWY			
-	SCIC	-	854-D6
-	SCIC	-	874-E1
-	SJS	-	834-A5
-	SJS	-	854-C3
-	SJS	-	854-D6
-	SJS	-	874-E1
800	SJS	-	833-H2
Rt#-87 GUADALUPE PKWY			
800	SJS	95110	833-G1
1500	SJS	95110	834-A4
Rt#-114 WILLOW RD			
-	EPA	94303	790-J1
1000	MLPK	94025	790-J1
1100	EPA	94303	791-A1
1100	MLPK	94025	791-A1
Rt#-129 HIGHWAY			
2100	SBnC	95045	1018-A5
Rt#-130 ALUM ROCK AV			
700	SJS	95116	834-H3
2700	SCIC	95127	834-H3
2700	SJS	95127	834-H3
4600	SCIC	95127	835-A1
4600	SJS	95127	835-A1
5100	SCIC	95127	815-A7
Rt#-130 MOUNT HAMILTON RD			
11000	SCIC	95127	815-B7
11400	SCIC	95127	835-D1
12400	SCIC	95140	835-G2
12600	SCIC	95140	815-F7
18000	SCIC	95135	856-H1
18000	SCIC	95140	856-H1
Rt#-152 1ST ST			
-	GIL	95020	977-H2
Rt#-152 HECKER PASS HWY			
300	SCrC	95076	976-B7
900	GIL	95020	977-F2
3200	SCIC	95020	977-B2
4400	SCIC	95020	976-F3
Rt#-152 LEAVESLEY RD			
-	GIL	95020	977-J1
200	GIL	95020	978-A1
Rt#-152 PACHECO PASS HWY			
600	GIL	95020	978-C3
1400	SCIC	95020	978-G3
4000	SCIC	95020	999-G1
6100	SCIC	95020	1000-A2
Rt#-156 HIGHWAY			
-	SBnC	-	1039-D5
-	SBnC	95023	1000-C3
-	SBnC	95023	1020-B1
-	SBnC	95023	1039-D4
-	SBnC	95045	1037-H2
-	SBnC	95045	1039-A5
-	SCIC	95020	1000-C2
-	SJB	95045	1038-C5
1600	SBnC	95045	1038-A3
Rt#-156 HOLLISTER BYPS			
-	HOLL	95023	1019-G4
-	HOLL	95023	1039-D4
-	SBnC	95023	1019-G4
-	SBnC	95023	1020-A3
-	SBnC	95023	1039-E1
Rt#-237 CALAVERAS BLVD			
300	MPS	95035	793-J7
300	MPS	95035	813-J1
500	MPS	95035	794-A7
Rt#-237 MOUNTAIN VW-ALVISO RD			
-	MTVW	94041	812-A6
-	MTVW	94043	812-A6
600	MTVW	94041	811-J7
Rt#-237 SOUTHBAY FRWY			
-	MPS	-	813-C1
-	SCL	-	813-C1
-	SJS	-	813-C1
-	SUNV	-	812-D4
-	SUNV	-	812-F3
-	SUNV	-	813-C1
U.S.-101 BAYSHORE FRWY			
-	EPA	-	790-J1
-	EPA	-	791-E5
-	MLPK	-	790-J1
-	MLPK	-	791-E5
-	MTVW	-	791-E5
-	MTVW	-	811-G1
-	MTVW	-	812-C4
-	PA	-	791-E5
-	SCL	-	813-B6
-	SCIC	-	812-C4
-	SCIC	-	855-B5
-	SJS	-	813-B6
-	SJS	-	833-G1
-	SJS	-	834-C2
-	SJS	-	854-H1
-	SJS	-	855-B5
-	SJS	-	875-C1
-	SUNV	-	812-C4
-	SUNV	-	813-B6
U.S.-101 EL CAMINO REAL			
-	MonC	93907	1037-B4
-	MonC	95076	1037-B4
-	SBnC	-	1037-C2
-	SBnC	95004	1037-C2
-	SBnC	95020	1018-C1
-	SBnC	95045	1018-B3
-	SBnC	95045	1037-C2
-	SCIC	95020	978-A4
-	SCIC	95020	998-B1
-	SCIC	95020	1018-C1
5300	GIL	95020	978-A4
7800	GIL	95020	977-J2
8500	GIL	95020	957-G3
10400	SCIC	95020	957-G3
11000	SCIC	95046	957-G3
11800	MGH	95037	916-J6
12600	SCIC	95046	937-F7
13700	MGH	95046	937-F7
14800	MGH	95037	937-A1
17000	MGH	95037	917-A7
U.S.-101 FRWY			
-	SCIC	-	998-C2
U.S.-101 MONTEREY RD			
5300	GIL	95020	978-A4
8800	GIL	95020	957-H5
10400	SCIC	95020	957-F1
11000	SCIC	95046	957-F1
11600	MGH	95037	916-J6
12600	SCIC	95046	937-E6
13700	MGH	95046	937-E6
14800	MGH	95037	937-A1
17000	MGH	95037	917-A7
U.S.-101 MONTEREY ST			
7000	GIL	95020	978-A3
7800	GIL	95020	977-J1
8500	GIL	95020	957-J7
U.S.-101 SOUTH VALLEY FRWY			
-	GIL	-	957-G1
-	GIL	-	958-A6
-	GIL	-	978-A1
-	MGH	-	916-H1
-	MGH	-	917-A4
-	MGH	-	937-D1
-	SCIC	-	875-G6
-	SCIC	-	895-J1
-	SCIC	-	896-B3
-	SCIC	-	916-H1
-	SCIC	-	917-A4
-	SCIC	-	937-D1
-	SCIC	-	957-G1
-	SCIC	-	978-B5
-	SJS	-	875-G6
-	SJS	-	896-B3
-	SJS	-	916-H1

AIRPORTS

FEATURE NAME Address City, ZIP Code	PAGE-GRID
HOLLISTER MUNICIPAL, HOLL	1019 - J6
MINETA, NORMAN Y SAN JOSE INTL, SJS	833 - G2
PALO ALTO, PA	791 - E2
REID-HILLVIEW, SJS	835 - A6
SOUTH COUNTY, SCIC	937 - G7

BUILDINGS

FEATURE NAME Address City, ZIP Code	PAGE-GRID
FOR DOWNTOWN BUILDINGS SEE PAGE F	-
FLINT CTR 21250 STEVENS CREEK BLVD, CPTO, 95014	852 - C1
IBM RESEARCH LABORATORY LOOP DR, SJS, 95120	895 - B2
IOOF HOME SAN MARCOS RD, SAR, 95070	872 - G3
MAPLES PAVILION CAMPUS DR, SCIC, 94305	790 - J7
STANFORD LINEAR ACCELERATOR CTR 2575 SAND HILL RD, SMCo, 94025	810 - D1

BUILDINGS - GOVERNMENTAL

FEATURE NAME Address City, ZIP Code	PAGE-GRID
ATHERTON CITY HALL 91 ASHFIELD RD, ATN, 94027	790 - E2
CAMPBELL CITY HALL 70 N 1ST ST, CMBL, 95008	853 - E6
CUPERTINO CITY HALL 10300 TORRE AV, CPTO, 95014	852 - E1
EAST PALO ALTO CITY HALL 2415 UNIVERSITY AV, EPA, 94303	791 - B1
ELMWOOD CORRECTIONAL FACILITY 701 ABEL ST, MPS, 95035	814 - A2
GILROY CITY HALL 7351 ROSANNA ST, GIL, 95020	977 - J3
HOLLISTER CITY HALL 375 5TH ST, HOLL, 95023	1040 - A4
LOS ALTOS CITY HALL 1 N SAN ANTONIO RD, LALT, 94022	811 - E6
LOS ALTOS HILLS CITY HALL 26379 W FREMONT RD, LAH, 94022	811 - B6
LOS GATOS CITY HALL 110 E MAIN ST, LGTS, 95030	893 - A1
MENLO PK CITY HALL 701 LAUREL ST, MLPK, 94025	790 - G3
MILPITAS CITY HALL 455 CALAVERAS BLVD, MPS, 95035	794 - B7
MILPITAS CIVIC CTR CALAVERAS BLVD & TOWN CTR DR, MPS, 95035	794 - B7
MONTE SERENO CITY HALL 18041 SARATOGA-LOS GATOS RD, MSER, 95030	872 - J6
MORGAN HILL CITY HALL 17555 PEAK AV, MGH, 95037	936 - J1
MOUNTAIN VIEW CITY HALL 500 CASTRO ST, MTVW, 94041	811 - H5
PALO ALTO CITY HALL 250 HAMILTON AV, PA, 94301	790 - J4
PALO ALTO COURTHOUSE 270 GRANT AV, PA, 94306	791 - B7
PORTOLA VALLEY TOWN HALL 765 PORTOLA RD, PTLV, 94028	810 - A6
SAN BENITO COURTHOUSE 440 5TH ST, HOLL, 95023	1040 - A4
SAN JOSE CITY HALL 200 E SANTA CLARA ST, SJS, 95113	834 - C6
SAN JUAN BAUTISTA CITY HALL 311 2ND ST, SJB, 95045	1038 - D4
SANTA CLARA CITY HALL 1500 WARBURTON AV, SCL, 95050	833 - D3
SANTA CLARA CIVIC CTR 1500 WARBURTON AV, SCL, 95050	833 - D3
SANTA CLARA COUNTY ADMIN BLDG 70 W HEDDING ST, SJS, 95110	834 - A4
SANTA CLARA COUNTY COURTHOUSE 191 N 1ST ST, SJS, 95113	834 - B6
SANTA CLARA COUNTY SERVICE CTR 99 NORTE DAME ST, SJS, 95110	834 - B6
SANTA CLARA COURTHOUSE 1095 HOMESTEAD RD, SCL, 95050	833 - E4
SARATOGA CITY HALL 13777 FRUITVALE AV, SAR, 95070	872 - F1
SOUTH COUNTY COURTHOUSE 12425 MONTEREY RD, SCIC, 95046	957 - F1
SUNNYVALE CITY HALL 456 W OLIVE AV, SUNV, 94086	832 - D1
SUNNYVALE MUNICIPAL COURT 605 W EL CAMINO REAL, SUNV, 94086	832 - D1
U S CUSTOMS AIRPORT BLVD, SJS, 95110	833 - H3
WEST VALLEY COURTHOUSE 14205 CAPRI DR, LGTS, 95032	873 - C2

CEMETERIES

FEATURE NAME Address City, ZIP Code	PAGE-GRID
ALTA MESA MEM PK, PA	811 - C4
CALVARY CATHOLIC CEM, SJS	834 - H2
CALVARY CEM, HOLL	1040 - C4
CEDAR LAWN MEM PK, FRMT	793 - J2
LOS GATOS MEM PK, SJS	873 - E4
MADRONIA CEM, SAR	872 - D3
MISSION CITY MEM PK, SCL	833 - D6
OAK HILL MEM PK, SJS	854 - E4
SAINT MARYS CEM, GIL	977 - H2
SAN JUAN BAUTISTA CEM, SBnC	1038 - C4
SANTA CLARA MISSION CEM, SCL	833 - E5
UNION CEM, RDWC	790 - B1

COLLEGES & UNIVERSITIES

FEATURE NAME Address City, ZIP Code	PAGE-GRID
DE ANZA COLLEGE 21250 STEVENS CREEK BLVD, CPTO, 95014	852 - C1
EVERGREEN VALLEY COMM COLLEGE 3095 YERBA BUENA RD, SJS, 95135	855 - G4
FOOTHILL COLLEGE 12345 S EL MONTE RD, LAH, 94022	831 - C2
GAVILAN COLLEGE 5055 SANTA TERESA BLVD, SCIC, 95020	978 - A7
MARYKNOLL SEMINARY 23000 CRISTO REY DR, SCIC, 94024	831 - H6
MENLO COLLEGE 1000 EL CAMINO REAL, ATN, 94027	790 - E3
MISSION COLLEGE 3000 MISSION COLLEGE BLVD, SCL, 95054	813 - A5
SAINT PATRICKS SEMINARY & UNIV 320 MIDDLEFIELD RD, MLPK, 94025	790 - H2
SAN JOSE CITY COLLEGE 2100 MOORPARK AV, SJS, 95128	853 - G2
SAN JOSE STATE UNIV 125 S 7TH ST, SJS, 95192	834 - C6
SANTA CLARA UNIV 500 EL CAMINO REAL, SCL, 95053	833 - F4
STANFORD UNIV JUNIPERO SERRA BLVD, SCIC, 94305	790 - J6
UNIV OF PHOENIX 3590 N 1ST ST, SJS, 95134	813 - F3
WEST VALLEY COLLEGE 14000 FRUITVALE AV, SAR, 95070	872 - G2

ENTERTAINMENT & SPORTS

FEATURE NAME Address City, ZIP Code	PAGE-GRID
CALIFORNIA THEATRE 345 S 1ST ST, SJS, 95110	834 - C7
GILROY GARDENS THEME PK 3050 HECKER PASS HWY, GIL, 95020	977 - C3
HP PAVILLION AT SAN JOSE 525 W SANTA CLARA ST, SJS, 95110	834 - A6
MILPITAS SPORT CTR N PK VICTRIA DR & CALVRS BLVD, MPS, 95035	794 - C6
MONTGOMERY THEATER 271 S MARKET ST, SJS, 95113	834 - B7
PARAMOUNTS GREAT AMERICA THEME PK GREAT AMERICA PKWY, SCL, 95054	813 - B4
PERFORMING ARTS CTR 255 S ALMADEN BLVD, SJS, 95110	834 - B7
RAGING WATERS 2333 WHITE RD, SJS, 95148	835 - B6
SAN JOSE CIVIC AUDITORIUM 145 W SAN CARLOS ST, SJS, 95113	834 - B7
SAN JOSE MCENERY CONV CTR 150 W SAN CARLOS ST, SJS, 95110	834 - B7
SAN JOSE MUNICIPAL BASEBALL STADIUM E ALMA AV & SENTER RD, SJS, 95112	854 - E1
SANTA CLARA CONV CTR 5001 GREAT AMERICA PKWY, SCL, 95054	813 - B3
SANTA CLARA COUNTY FAIRGROUNDS 344 TULLY RD, SCIC, 95111	854 - F4
SHORELINE AMPHITHEATRE AT MTN VIEW 1 AMPHITHEATRE PKWY, MTVW, 94043	791 - H7
SPARTAN STADIUM S 7TH ST & E ALMA AV, SJS, 95112	854 - E1
STANFORD STADIUM NELSON RD & SAM MCDONALD RD, SCIC, 94305	790 - J6
VILLA MONTALVO 15400 MONTALVO RD, SAR, 95070	872 - D4

GOLF COURSES

FEATURE NAME Address City, ZIP Code	PAGE-GRID
ALMADEN CC, SJS	894 - D2
BLACKBERRY FARM GC, CPTO	852 - A1
BOLADO PK GC, SBnC	1061 - B7
CINNABAR HILLS GC, SJS	915 - H1
CORDEVALLE GC, SCIC	957 - B2
COYOTE CREEK GC, SJS	896 - D5
COYOTE CREEK GC, THE VALLEY COUR, SCIC	896 - C4
CYPRESS GREENS GC, SCIC	835 - C5
DEEP CLIFF GC, CPTO	852 - A2
EAGLE RIDGE GC, GIL	977 - E4
FREMONT HILLS CC, LAH	811 - A7
GAVILAN GC, SCIC	998 - A1
GILROY GC, GIL	977 - D2
GOLF COURSE AT BOULDER RIDGE, SCIC	874 - D6
INSTITUTE GC, MGH	937 - H2
LA RINCONADA CC, LGTS	873 - A3
LOS ALTOS GOLF & CC, SCIC	831 - G4
LOS LAGOS GC, SJS	854 - J4
MENLO CC, WDSD	790 - A4
MOFFETT FIELD GC, SCIC	812 - D1
PALO ALTO HILLS GOLF & CC, PA	830 - G1
PALO ALTO MUNICIPAL GC, PA	791 - D2
PLEASANT HILLS GC, SCIC	835 - C6
PRUNERIDGE GC, SCL	833 - C7
RANCH GC, THE, SJS	855 - D6
RANCHO DEL PUEBLO GC, SJS	834 - F4
RIDGEMARK GOLF & CC, SBnC	1060 - D2
SAN JOSE CC, SCIC	815 - A6
SAN JOSE MUNICIPAL GC, SJS	814 - B7
SAN JUAN OAKS GC, SBnC	1059 - C1
SANTA CLARA GOLF & TENNIS CLUB, SCL	813 - C3
SANTA TERESA GC, SCIC	895 - E1
SARATOGA CC, SAR	852 - B6
SHARON HEIGHTS GOLF & CC, MLPK	790 - B7
SHORELINE GOLF LINKS, MTVW	791 - G7
SILVER CREEK VALLEY CC, SJS	875 - F1
SPRING VALLEY GC, MPS	794 - F5
STANFORD UNIV DRIVING RANGE, SCIC	790 - G7
STANFORD UNIV GC, SCIC	790 - F7
SUMMIT POINTE GC, MPS	794 - D4
SUNKEN GARDENS GC, SUNV	832 - G3
SUNNYVALE GC, SUNV	812 - D4
VILLAGES GOLF & CC, THE, SJS	855 - H6

HISTORIC SITES

FEATURE NAME Address City, ZIP Code	PAGE-GRID
CASTRO HOUSE 2ND ST & WASHINGTON ST, SJB, 95045	1038 - D4
HARRIS-LASS HOUSE 1889 MARKET ST, SCL, 95050	833 - D5
HAYES MANSION HIST LANDMARK EDENVALE AV & RED RIVER WY, SJS, 95136	875 - A2
HIGUERA ADOBE PK N PARK VICTORIA DR & WESSEX PL, MPS, 95035	794 - B3
MISSION SAN JUAN BAUTISTA 2ND ST & FRANKLIN ST, SJB, 95045	1038 - D4
MISSION SANTA CLARA DE ASIS 820 ALVISO ST, SCL, 95053	833 - E4
PERALTA ADOBE 175 W SAINT JOHN ST, SJS, 95110	834 - B6
PLAZA HOTEL 2ND ST & MARIPOSA ST, SJB, 95045	1038 - D4
SAN BENITO CO HIST & REC PK AIRLINE HWY, SBnC, 95023	1061 - A7
SAN JUAN BAUTISTA STATE HIST PK WASHINGTON ST & 2ND ST, SJB, 95045	1038 - D4
WINCHESTER MYSTERY HOUSE 1750 S WINCHESTER BLVD, SJS, 95117	853 - D1

HOSPITALS

FEATURE NAME Address City, ZIP Code	PAGE-GRID
AGNEWS DEVELOPMENTAL CTR 3500 ZANKER RD, SJS, 95134	813 - G3
COMM HOSP OF LOS GATOS 815 POLLARD RD, LGTS, 95032	873 - B2
DE PAUL HEALTH CTR 18550 DE PAUL DR, MGH, 95037	917 - B4
EL CAMINO HOSP 2500 GRANT RD, MTVW, 94040	831 - H1
GOOD SAMARITAN HOSP 2425 SAMARITAN DR, SJS, 95124	873 - E3
HAWKINS, HAZEL MEM HOSP 911 SUNSET DR, HOLL, 95023	1040 - C6
KAISER FOUNDATION HOSP 900 KIELY BLVD, SCL, 95051	833 - A5
KAISER FOUNDATION HOSP - SANTA TERESA 250 HOSPITAL PKWY, SJS, 95119	875 - C6
KAISER PERMANENTE SANTA CLARA 700 LAWRENCE EXWY, SCL, 95051	832 - H6
OCONNOR HOSP 2105 FOREST AV, SJS, 95128	833 - F7
PACKARD, LUCILLE CHILDRENS HOSP-STNFRD 725 WELCH RD, PA, 94305	790 - H6
PALO ALTO MED FOUNDATION 795 EL CAMINO REAL, PA, 94301	790 - J5
REGL MED CTR OF SAN JOSE 225 N JACKSON AV, SJS, 95116	834 - G2
SAINT LOUISE REGL HOSP 9400 NONAME UNO, GIL, 95020	958 - A6
SANTA CLARA VALLEY MED CTR 751 BASCOM AV, SCIC, 95128	853 - F2
STANFORD HOSP & CLINICS 300 PASTEUR DR, PA, 94305	790 - G6
VETERANS ADMIN HOSP PALO ALTO 3801 MIRANDA AV, PA, 94304	811 - B3
VETERANS ADMIN HOSP MENLO PK 795 WILLOW RD, MLPK, 94025	790 - J2

HOTELS

FEATURE NAME Address City, ZIP Code	PAGE-GRID
BEVERLY HERITAGE HOTEL 1820 BARBER LN, MPS, 95035	813 - J4
BILTMORE HOTEL 2151 LAURELWOOD RD, SCL, 95054	813 - C6
COURTYARD BY MARRIOTT 10605 WOLFE RD, CPTO, 95014	832 - G6
COURTYARD BY MARRIOTT 1727 TECHNOLOGY DR, SJS, 95110	833 - H2
COURTYARD BY MARRIOTT - MILPITAS 1480 FALCON DR, MPS, 95035	814 - B3
COURTYARD BY MARRIOTT - PALO ALTO 4320 EL CAMINO REAL, LALT, 94022	811 - D3
CROWNE PLAZA SAN JOSE 282 S ALMADEN BLVD, SJS, 95113	834 - B7
CROWNE PLAZA SAN JOSE-SILICON VALLEY 777 BELLEW DR, MPS, 95035	813 - H1
CROWN PLAZA - PALO ALTO 4290 EL CAMINO REAL, PA, 94306	811 - D3
CYPRESS HOTEL 3 DE ANZA BLVD, CPTO, 95014	852 - D1
DOLCE HAYES MANSION 200 EDENVALE AV, SJS, 95136	875 - A2
DOUBLETREE 2050 GATEWAY PL, SJS, 95110	833 - H1
EMBASSY SUITES 2885 LAKESIDE DR, SCL, 95054	813 - A6
EMBASSY SUITES MILPITAS 901 CALAVERAS BLVD, MPS, 95035	794 - B6
FAIRFIELD INN 1755 N 1ST ST, SJS, 95110	833 - H1
FAIRMONT HOTEL 170 S MARKET ST, SJS, 95113	834 - B7
FOUR POINTS BY SHERATON 1250 LAKESIDE DR, SUNV, 94086	812 - J6
HILTON GARDEN INN 10741 WOLFE RD, CPTO, 95014	832 - F6
HILTON GARDEN INN 30 RANCH DR, MPS, 95035	793 - H7
HILTON GARDEN INN 840 E EL CAMINO REAL, MTVW, 94041	812 - B7
HILTON HOTEL - SANTA CLARA 4949 GREAT AMERICAN PKWY, SCL, 95054	813 - B4
HILTON TOWERS 300 S ALMADEN BLVD, SJS, 95110	834 - B7
HOLIDAY INN SAN JOSE 399 SILICON VALLEY BLVD, SJS, 95138	875 - F4
HOTEL DE ANZA 233 W SANTA CLARA ST, SJS, 95110	834 - B6
HYATT REGENCY SANTA CLARA 5101 GREAT AMERICAN PKWY, SCL, 95054	813 - B3
HYATT SAINTE CLAIRE 302 S MARKET ST, SJS, 95110	834 - C7
HYATT SAN JOSE 1740 N 1ST ST, SJS, 95112	833 - J1
PLAZA SUITES, THE 3100 LAKESIDE DR, SCL, 95054	813 - A6
PRUNEYARD INN, THE 1995 S BASCOM AV, CMBL, 95008	853 - F6
RADISSON INN - SUNNYVALE 1085 E EL CAMINO REAL, SUNV, 94086	832 - H4
RADISSON PLAZA HOTEL 1471 N 4TH ST, SJS, 95112	833 - J2
RESIDENCE INN 1080 STEWART DR, SUNV, 94086	812 - J6
RESIDENCE INN 1501 CALIFORNIA CIR, MPS, 95035	793 - H4
RESIDENCE INN 750 LAKEWAY, SUNV, 94086	813 - A6
RESIDENCE INN HOTEL 1854 W EL CAMINO REAL, MTVW, 94041	811 - G5
SAN JOSE MARRIOTT 301 S MARKET ST, SJS, 95110	834 - B7
SANTA CLARA MARRIOTT 2700 MISSION COLLEGE BLVD, SCL, 95054	813 - B5
SHERATON PALO ALTO 625 EL CAMINO REAL, PA, 94301	790 - H5

FEATURE NAME Address City, ZIP Code	PAGE-GRID
SHERATON SAN JOSE 1801 BARBER LN, MPS, 95035	813 - J4
SHERATON SUNNYVALE 1100 N MATHILDA AV, SUNV, 94089	812 - F3
STANFORD PARK HOTEL 100 EL CAMINO REAL, MLPK, 94025	790 - H4
TOLL HOUSE HOTEL 140 S SANTA CRUZ AV, LGTS, 95030	892 - J1
WESTIN HOTEL - PALO ALTO 675 EL CAMINO REAL, PA, 94301	790 - H5
WILD PALMS HOTEL 910 E FREMONT AV, SUNV, 94087	832 - G4
WYNDHAM HOTEL - SAN JOSE 1350 N 1ST ST, SJS, 95112	833 - J2
WYNDHAM HOTEL - SUNNYVALE 1300 CHESAPEAKE TER, SUNV, 94089	812 - H3

LAW ENFORCEMENT

FEATURE NAME Address City, ZIP Code	PAGE-GRID
ATHERTON POLICE DEPARTMENT 83 ASHFIELD RD, ATN, 94027	790 - E2
CALIFORNIA HIGHWAY PATROL-GILROY 750 RENZ LN, GIL, 95020	978 - B3
CALIFORNIA HIGHWAY PATROL-SAN JOSE 2020 JUNCTION AV, SJS, 95131	813 - J6
CAMPBELL POLICE STA 70 N FIRST ST, CMBL, 95008	853 - E6
EAST PALO ALTO POLICE STA 2415 UNIVERSITY AV, EPA, 94303	791 - B1
GILROY POLICE DEPARTMENT 7301 HANNA ST, GIL, 95020	977 - J3
HOLLISTER POLICE STA 395 APOLLO CT, HOLL, 95023	1020 - B5
LOS ALTOS POLICE DEPARTMENT 1 N SAN ANTONIO RD, LALT, 94022	811 - E6
LOS GATOS POLICE STA 110 E MAIN ST, LGTS, 95030	893 - A1
MENLO PK POLICE DEPARTMENT 801 LAUREL ST, MLPK, 94025	790 - G3
MILPITAS POLICE DEPARTMENT 1275 N MILPITAS BLVD, MPS, 95035	793 - J5
MORGAN HILL POLICE DEPARTMENT 16200 VINEYARD BLVD, MGH, 95037	937 - B2
MOUNTAIN VIEW POLICE DEPARTMENT 1000 VILLA ST, MTVW, 94041	811 - H4
PALO ALTO POLICE DEPARTMENT 275 FOREST AV, PA, 94301	790 - J5
SAN BENITO COUNTY SHERIFFS DEPARTMENT 451 4TH ST, HOLL, 95023	1040 - A4
SAN JOSE POLICE DEPARTMENT 201 W MISSION ST, SJS, 95110	833 - J4
SAN JUAN BAUTISTA SHERIFFS STA 301 THE ALAMEDA, SJB, 95045	1038 - D5
SANTA CLARA POLICE DEPARTMENT 601 EL CAMINO REAL, SCL, 95050	833 - F4
SANTA CLARA COUNTY SHERIFFS OFFICE 55 W YOUNGER AV, SJS, 95110	833 - J3
SUNNYVALE POLICE STA 700 ALL AMERICA WY, SUNV, 94086	832 - D1

LIBRARIES

FEATURE NAME Address City, ZIP Code	PAGE-GRID
ALMADEN BRANCH 6455 CAMDEN AV, SJS, 95120	894 - D1
ALUM ROCK 75 S WHITE RD, SJS, 95127	834 - J2
ALVISO BRANCH 5050 N 1ST ST, SJS, 95002	813 - C1
ATHERTON 2 DINKLESPIEL STATION LN, ATN, 94027	790 - E2
BERRYESSA 3311 NOBLE AV, SJS, 95132	814 - H5
BIBLIOTECA LATINO AMERICANA 690 LOCUST ST, SJS, 95110	854 - B1
CALABAZAS BRANCH 1230 BLANEY AV, SJS, 95129	852 - E3
CAMBRIAN BRANCH 1780 HILLSDALE AV, SJS, 95124	873 - H2
CAMPBELL 77 HARRISON AV, CMBL, 95008	853 - E6
CENTRAL PARK 2635 E HOMESTEAD RD, SCL, 95051	833 - B5
COLLEGE TERRACE BRANCH 2300 WELLESLEY ST, PA, 94306	791 - A7
CUPERTINO 10400 TORRE AV, CPTO, 95014	852 - E1
DOWNTOWN BRANCH 270 FOREST AV, PA, 94301	790 - J5
EAST PALO ALTO BRANCH 2415 UNIVERSITY AV, EPA, 94303	791 - B1
EAST SAN JOSE CARNEGIE 1102 E SANTA CLARA ST, SJS, 95116	834 - E5
EDUCATIONAL PARK 1770 EDUCATIONAL PARK DR, SJS, 95133	834 - F2
EMPIRE BRANCH 491 E EMPIRE ST, SJS, 95112	834 - C4
EVERGREEN BRANCH 2635 ABORN RD, SJS, 95148	855 - D2
GILROY 7387 ROSANNA ST, GIL, 95020	977 - J3
HILLVIEW BRANCH 2255 OCALA AV, SJS, 95122	834 - J6
KING, MARTIN LUTHER JR 150 E SAN FERNANDO ST, SJS, 95112	834 - C6
LOS ALTOS 13 S SAN ANTONIO RD, LALT, 94022	811 - E6
MENLO PARK BRANCH 800 ALMA ST, MLPK, 94025	790 - G3
MILPITAS COMM 40 N MILPITAS BLVD, MPS, 95035	794 - A7
MISSION BRANCH 1098 LEXINGTON ST, SCL, 95050	833 - E4
MITCHELL PK 3700 MIDDLEFIELD RD, PA, 94306	811 - E1
MORGAN HILL 17575 PEAK AV, MGH, 95037	936 - J1
MOUNTAIN VIEW LIBRARIES 585 FRANKLIN ST, MTVW, 94041	811 - H5
PALO ALTO CHILDRENS 1276 HARRIET ST, PA, 94301	791 - B4
PALO ALTO MAIN 1213 NEWELL RD, PA, 94303	791 - B4
PEARL AV BRANCH 4270 PEARL AV, SJS, 95136	874 - E1
PORTOLA VALLEY BRANCH 765 PORTOLA RD, PTLV, 94028	810 - A6
ROSEGARDEN BRANCH 1580 NAGLEE AV, SJS, 95126	833 - G7
SAN BENITO COUNTY 470 5TH ST, HOLL, 95023	1040 - A4
SAN JUAN BAUTISTA 801 2ND ST, SJB, 95045	1038 - D4
SANTA TERESA 290 INTERNATIONAL CIR, SJS, 95119	875 - C6
SARATOGA COMM 13650 SARATOGA AV, SAR, 95070	872 - F1
SEVEN TREES BRANCH 3597 CAS DR, SJS, 95111	854 - H6
SUNNYVALE 665 W OLIVE AV, SUNV, 94086	832 - D1
TULLY COMM 880 TULLY RD, SJS, 95121	854 - H2
VILLAGES 5000 CRIBARI LN, SJS, 95135	855 - H5
WEST VALLEY BRANCH 1243 SAN THOMAS AQUINO RD, SJS, 95117	853 - A4
WILLOW GLEN BRANCH 1157 MINNESOTA AV, SJS, 95125	854 - A4
WOODLAND 1975 GRANT RD, LALT, 94024	831 - J4

MILITARY INSTALLATIONS

FEATURE NAME Address City, ZIP Code	PAGE-GRID
AMES RESEARCH CTR R T JONES RD & CLARK RD, MTVW, 94043	812 - A1
MOFFETT FEDERAL AIRFIELD FAIRCHILD DR & DAILEY RD, SCIC, 94035	812 - D3
MOFFETT FIELD NAVAL AIR STA FAIRCHILD DR & DAILEY DR, SCIC, 94035	812 - C2
NATL GUARD ARMORY 240 N 2ND ST, SJS, 95112	834 - B5
NATL GUARD ARMORY 251 W HEDDING ST, SJS, 95110	833 - J4
U S ARMY RESERVE CTR 155 W HEDDING ST, SJS, 95110	833 - J4

MUSEUMS

FEATURE NAME Address City, ZIP Code	PAGE-GRID
BAYLANDS NATURE INTERPRETIVE CTR 2775 EMBARCADERO RD, PA, 94303	791 - F2
CANTOR ARTS CTR AT STANFORD UNIV 328 LOMITA DR, SCIC, 94305	790 - G6
CHILDRENS DISCOVERY MUS 180 WOZ WY, SJS, 95110	834 - B7
DE SAISSET MUS 500 EL CAMINO REAL, SCL, 95053	833 - F4
FLYING LADY MUS 15060 FOOTHILL AV, SCIC, 95037	917 - G7
GILROY HIST MUS 195 5TH ST, GIL, 95020	977 - J3
LOS ALTOS HIST MUS 51 S SAN ANTONIO RD, LALT, 94022	811 - E6
MOFFETT FIELD MUS SEVERYNS AV, SCIC, 94035	812 - B2
MUS OF AMERICAN HERITAGE 351 HOMER AV, PA, 94301	790 - J5
NASA EXPLORATION CTR MOFFETT BLVD, SCIC, 94043	812 - A3
NEW ALMADEN MUS 21570 ALMADEN RD, SCIC, 95120	894 - J7
PALO ALTO JUNIOR MUS & ZOO 1451 MIDDLEFIELD RD, PA, 94301	791 - B5
ROSICRUCIAN EGYPTAN MUS & PLNTRIUM 1342 NAGLEE AV, SJS, 95126	833 - H6
SAN BENITO COUNTY HIST SOCIETY MUS 498 5TH ST, HOLL, 95023	1039 - J4
SAN JOSE HIST MUS 1650 SENTER RD, SJS, 95112	854 - E2
SAN JOSE MUS OF ART 110 S MARKET ST, SJS, 95113	834 - B6
SANTA CLARA HIST MUS 1509 WARBURTON AV, SCL, 95050	833 - D3
TECH MUS OF INNOVATION, THE 201 S MARKET ST, SJS, 95113	834 - B7
TRITON MUS OF ART 1505 WARBURTON AV, SCL, 95050	833 - D3

OPEN SPACE

FEATURE NAME, City	PAGE-GRID
ARASTRADERO PRESERVE, PA	830 - F1
BAYLANDS NATURE PRESERVE, EPA	791 - D1
BEAR CREEK REDWOODS OPEN SPACE PRES, - SCIC	892 - F6
BYRNE PRESERVE, LAH	830 - J2
COAL CREEK OPEN SPACE, SMCo	830 - C5
EDWARDS, DON SF BAY NATL FOREST, SJS	793 - B3
EL SERENO OPEN SPACE, SCIC	892 - E1
EL SERENO OPEN SPACE PRESERVE, SCIC	892 - G3
FOOTHILLS OPEN SPACE, PA	830 - G3
FREEMONT OLDER OPEN SPACE, SCIC	851 - J5
LONG RIDGE OPEN SPACE, SCrC	871 - A1
LOS TRANCOS OPEN SPACE, PA	830 - F6
MISSION PEAK REGL PRESERVE, FRMT	794 - D1
MONTE BELLO OPEN SPACE, PA	851 - A3
OPEN SPACE, SCIC	815 - F5
PICCHETTI RANCH OPEN SPACE, SCIC	851 - H5
RANCHO CANADA DL ORO OPN SPACE PRES, SJS	935 - E1
RANCHO SAN ANTONIO OPEN SPACE, SCIC	831 - B5
REDWOOD GROVE NATURE PRESERVE, LALT	811 - D7
RUSSIAN RIDGE OPEN SPACE, SMCo	830 - C7
SAINT JOSEPHS HILL OPEN SPACE PRES, LGTS	892 - J2
SARATOGA GAP OPEN SPACE, SCIC	871 - C1
SIERRA AZUL OPEN SPACE PRESERVE, SCIC	913 - F4
UVAS CREEK PRESERVE, GIL	977 - G4
WINDY HILL OPEN SPACE, PTLV	830 - A3

OTHER

FEATURE NAME Address City, ZIP Code	PAGE-GRID
ALLIED ARTS GUILD 75 ARBOR RD, MLPK, 94025	790 - G5
ALPINE HILLS CLUB 4139 ALPINE RD, PTLV, 94028	810 - D7
BAYLANDS ATHLETIC CTR 1900 GENG RD, PA, 94303	791 - D3
CARMELITE MONASTERY HOMESTEAD RD & MONASTERY WY, SCL, 95050	833 - D4
COUNTY OF SANTA CLARA GIRLS RANCH BERNAL RD, SCIC, 95119	895 - D2
DUCK CLUB E CARIBBEAN DR & CROSSMAN AV, SJS, 95002	792 - E3
HAPPY HOLLOW ZOO 1300 SENTER RD, SJS, 95112	854 - E1
HOOVER PAVILION 211 QUARRY RD, PA, 94304	790 - H5
JAMES BOYS RANCH SYCAMORE AV & MALAGUERRA AV, MGH, 95037	917 - B2
JAPANESE FRIENDSHIP TEA GARDEN 1300 SENTER RD, SJS, 95112	854 - E1
MAUSOLEUM LOMITA DR & CAMPUS DR, SCIC, 94305	790 - H6
PALO ALTO ART CTR 1313 NEWELL RD, PA, 94303	791 - B5
PARKSIDE HALL 180 PARK AV, SJS, 95113	834 - B7
RONALD MCDONALD HOUSE 520 SAND HILL RD, PA, 94304	790 - G5
SAN JOSE CLUB PEDRO ST & NORTHROP ST, SJS, 95126	853 - J2
SUNSET MAGAZINE CTR MIDDLEFIELD RD & WILLOW RD, MLPK, 94025	790 - H3
VETERANS MEM BLDG 649 SAN BENITO ST, HOLL, 95023	1040 - A4

PARK & RIDE

FEATURE NAME, City	PAGE-GRID
ALUM ROCK, SJS	834 - J3
BLOCKBUSTER VIDEO, SJS	834 - G1
BLOSSOM HILL CALTRAIN STA, SJS	875 - C4
BLOSSOM HILL STA, SJS	874 - G4
BRANHAM STA, SJS	874 - F2
CAHILL ST & SAN CLARA ST CALTRAIN STA, - SJS	834 - A7
CALIFORNIA AVE CALTRAIN STA, PA	791 - B7
CAMDEN AV, SJS	873 - J4
CAMPBELL SENIOR CTR, CMBL	853 - D6
CAPITOL STA, SJS	874 - E1
CAPITOL STA, SJS	854 - G6
COTTLE STA, SJS	875 - C5
CURTNER STA, SJS	854 - D5
EASTRIDGE MALL, SJS	835 - B7
EL CAMINO REAL & RR AV CALTRAIN STA, SCL	833 - F4
EVELYN AT FRANCIS CALTRAIN STA PK, SUNV	812 - E7
EVELYN LIGHT-RAIL STA, MTVW	811 - J5
GILROY STA, GIL	978 - A4
HOLLISTER, HOLL	1040 - C4
KMART, SCL	832 - H4
KMART, SJS	834 - G2
LAWRENCE CALTRIN STA AT SAN ZENO WY, - SUNV	832 - J1
LOCKHEED MARTIN, SUNV	812 - E4
MAIN AV, MGH	916 - J7
MENLO PK CALTRAIN STA, MLPK	790 - G3
MOORPARK AV, SJS	852 - J3
MORGAN HILL STA, MGH	917 - A7
OHLONE-CHYNOWETH STA, SJS	874 - E3
PAGE MILL & EL CAMINO REAL, PA	791 - B7
PAGE MILL & HWY 280, LAH	810 - H5
PARK & RIDE, MPS	813 - J2
PARK & RIDE, SJS	874 - E3
PARK & RIDE, MPS	814 - A2
PARK & RIDE, SJS	814 - E5
PARK & RIDE, SJS	814 - F7
PARK & RIDE, SBnC	1037 - H2
PARK & RIDE, MPS	794 - A7
RIVER OAKS STA, SJS	813 - F4
SAMTRANS TRANSIT TRANSFER POINT, PA	790 - H5
SAN ANTONIO RD CALTRAIN STA, MTVW	811 - F3
SAN MARTIN STA, SCIC	937 - E6
SANTA TERESA STA SOUTH, SJS	875 - D6
SARATOGA RD, LGTS	873 - A7
SNELL, SJS	874 - J4
SOUTHWEST EXWY & FRUITDALE AV, SJS	853 - H3
TAMIEN STA, SJS	854 - C3
TASMAN DR & LAFAYETTE ST, SCL	813 - C3
UNIVERSITY AVE CALTRAIN STA, PA	790 - H5
VALLCO FASHION PK, CPTO	832 - G7
VTA SANTA TERESA STA NORTH, SJS	875 - D6
VTA SNELL AVENUE STA, SJS	874 - J4
WHISMAN LIGHT-RAIL STA, MTVW	812 - A5
WINFIELD STA, SJS	874 - D5

PARKS & RECREATION

FEATURE NAME, City	PAGE-GRID
ABBE PK, SJB	1038 - D4
ABORN PK, SJS	855 - C2
AGNEW PK, SCL	813 - C5
AGUIRRE, TONY MEM PK, HOLL	1039 - G3
ALBERTSON PARKWAY, SJS	875 - C6
ALMADEN LAKE PK, SJS	874 - D4
ALMADEN MEADOWS PK, SJS	894 - B1
ALMADEN QUICKSILVER COUNTY PK, SCIC	894 - E5
ALMADEN RESERVOIR COUNTY PK, SCIC	914 - G2
ALMADEN WINERY PK, SJS	874 - B6
ALUM ROCK PK, SJS	815 - C5
ALVAREZ PK, SCL	833 - D6
ALVISO MARINA COUNTY PK, SJS	793 - A7
ALVISO PK, SJS	813 - C1
ANDERSON LAKE COUNTY PK, SJS	917 - C1
ARENA GREEN PK, SJS	834 - A6
AUGUSTINE, ALBERT PK, MPS	794 - A3
AVENIDA ESPANA PK, SJS	895 - F1
AZULE PK, SAR	852 - E5
BACHMAN PK, LGTS	872 - J7
BACKESTO PK, SJS	834 - C4
BASKING RIDGE PK, SJS	875 - G5
BEAUCHAMPS PK, SAR	852 - D5
BELGATOS PK, LGTS	873 - H7
BELL STREET PK, EPA	791 - B2
BERNAL PK, SJS	834 - B3
BERRYESSA CREEK PK, SJS	814 - F3
BESTOR ART PK, SJS	854 - D1
BIEBRACH PK, SJS	854 - B1
BLOSSOM HILL PK, LGTS	873 - D6
BOGGINI PK, SJS	855 - D1
BOL PK, PA	811 - B2
BOULWARE PK, PA	811 - B1
BOWDEN PK, PA	791 - B7

FEATURE NAME Address City, ZIP Code	PAGE-GRID
BOWERS PK, SCL	833 - B3
BOWLING GREEN PK, PA	791 - A5
BRACHER PK, SCL	833 - B1
BRALY PK, SUNV	832 - F2
BRANHAM LANE PK, SJS	873 - J3
BRIGADOON PK, SJS	855 - C3
BRIONES PK, PA	811 - C3
BROOKGLEN PK, SAR	852 - G6
BROOKTREE PK, SJS	814 - C5
BUBB PK, MTVW	811 - H7
BURGESS PK, MLPK	790 - G3
BUTCHER PK, GIL	978 - B3
BUTCHER PK, SJS	873 - H2
BYXBEE REC AREA, PA	791 - F3
CADWALLADER PK, SJS	854 - D1
CAHALAN PK, SJS	874 - F5
CAHILL PK, SJS	834 - A7
CALABAZAS PK, SJS	852 - E3
CALERO COUNTY PK, SCIC	915 - C2
CALERO PK, SJS	875 - A5
CALLE ORIENTE PK, MPS	794 - C5
CAMDEN PK, SJS	873 - F2
CAMERON PK, PA	791 - A7
CAMPBELL PK, CMBL	853 - F6
CANNERY PK, SUNV	812 - D6
CANOAS PK, SJS	854 - C6
CAPITOL PK, SJS	834 - J4
CARDOZA PK, MPS	794 - C6
CARLI, STEVE PK, SCL	833 - C5
CARMICHAEL, EARL J PK, SCL	832 - J4
CARRABELLE PK, SJS	894 - H2
CARRIAGE HILLS PK, GIL	957 - E7
CASSELL PK, SJS	834 - J5
CASTLE ROCK STATE PK, SCrC	871 - C6
CASTRO PK, MTVW	811 - G4
CATALDI PK, SJS	814 - E4
CENTRAL PK, SCL	833 - B5
CHESBRO RESERVOIR PK, SCIC	936 - E2
CHETWOOD PK, MTVW	812 - B5
CHILDREN OF THE RAINBOW PK, SJS	834 - G2
CHRISTMAS HILL PK, GIL	977 - H4
CHYNOWETH PK, SJS	875 - A3
CILKER PK, SJS	874 - E3
CIMARRON PK, SJS	814 - H6
CITY PLAZA PK, SCL	833 - E4
CIVIC CTR PK, SCL	833 - D4
CIVIC CTR PK, SUNV	832 - D1
CLARK, ESTHER PK, PA	811 - B5
COE, HENRY W STATE PK, SCIC	918 - G2
COGSWELL PLAZA, PA	790 - H4
COLUMBIA PK, SUNV	812 - F5
COLUMBUS PK, SJS	833 - J5
COMANCHE PK, SJS	874 - H5
COMMUNITY PK, MGH	937 - A2
CONGRESS SPRINGS PK, SAR	852 - F6
CONTE GARDENS PK, MGH	917 - D6
COOPER PK, MTVW	831 - J1
COVINGTON MINI PARK & POOL, LALT	831 - F1
COYOTE CREEK PK, SCIC	895 - J1
COYOTE CREEK PK CHAIN, SCIC	855 - B7
COYOTE LAKE COUNTY PK, SCIC	938 - D3
COY PK, SJS	874 - J3
CREEKSIDE PK, MTVW	812 - A4
CREEKSIDE PK, CPTO	852 - F1
CREIGHTON PK, MPS	814 - D1
CRITTENDEN PK, MTVW	811 - H2
CUESTA PK, MTVW	831 - H1
DANNA ROCK PK, SJS	874 - J1
DE ANZA PK, SUNV	832 - B3
DE ANZA PK, SJS	874 - B5
DEL REY PK, GIL	957 - F7
DEMONSTRATION ORCHARD, SJS	833 - J5
DIANA PK, MGH	917 - B7
DIXON LANDING PK, MPS	793 - J4
DOERR PK, SJS	873 - H1
DOG PK, MTVW	791 - J7
DOVE HILL PK, SJS	855 - B4
DUNNE PK, HOLL	1039 - J4
EAGLE PK, MTVW	811 - H5
EDENVALE GARDEN PK, SJS	875 - A2
EL CAMINO PK, PA	790 - H4
EL PALO ALTO PK, PA	790 - H4
EL QUITO PK, SAR	852 - H6
EL ROBLE PK, GIL	977 - H3
ENCINAL PK, SUNV	812 - D5
ERIKSON PK, SJS	874 - E2
ESCUELA PK, MPS	794 - A4
EVERGREEN PK, SJS	855 - F5
FAIR OAKS PK, SUNV	812 - G6
FAIRWAY GLEN PK, SCL	813 - C3
FAIRWOOD PK, SUNV	813 - A5
FERNISH PK, SJS	835 - C5
FIELD SPORTS COUNTY PK, SCIC	896 - B1
FISCHER, JACK PK, CMBL	873 - B1
FLEISHMAN PK, RDWC	790 - B1
FLICKINGER PK, SJS	814 - D6
FLOOD COUNTY PK, MLPK	790 - H1
FONTANA, JEFFREY PK, SJS	874 - D6
FOOTHILL PK, SJS	874 - F6
FOOTHILL PK, MPS	794 - D7
FOOTHILL PK, SAR	872 - D1
FOREST STREET PK, GIL	978 - A3
FOWLER CREEK PK, SJS	855 - G2
FRANK KLAUER MEM PK, HOLL	1040 - D5
FREMONT, MLPK	790 - F4
FREMONT PK, SCL	833 - D4
FULLER ST PK, SCL	813 - C4
GALVAN PK, MGH	916 - J7
GARDINER PK, SAR	872 - G1
GEMELLO PK, MTVW	811 - F5
GILL, PETER T PK, MPS	794 - B6
GILROY SPORTS PK, SCIC	978 - A6
GLEASON AV PK, SJS	853 - C4
GLENVIEW PK, SJS	894 - F3
GOMEZ, MARY PK, SCL	833 - C6
GRAHAM PK, MTVW	811 - H7
GRANT, JOSEPH D COUNTY PK, SCIC	856 - G2
GRANT PK, LALT	832 - A4
GRAYSTONE PK, SJS	894 - F1
GREAT OAKS PK, SJS	875 - B2
GREENWOOD MANOR PK, SUNV	832 - C1
GREER PK, PA	791 - D5
GREGORY ST PLAZA, SJS	854 - A1

FEATURE NAME Address City, ZIP Code	PAGE-GRID
GROESBECK HILL PK, SJS	835 - E6
GUADALUPE GARDENS, SJS	833 - J5
GUADALUPE OAK GROVE PK, SJS	874 - C6
GUADALUPE RESERVOIR COUNTY PK, SCIC	894 - C4
GUADALUPE RIVER PK, SJS	834 - B7
GULLO PK, SJS	852 - J3
HACIENDA CREEK PK, SJS	834 - D4
HAKONE GARDENS, SAR	872 - C3
HALL MEM PK, MPS	793 - J5
HAMANN PK, SJS	853 - E3
HAMILTON SQUARE PK, MGH	937 - B4
HAPPY HOLLOW PK, SJS	854 - E1
HATHAWAY PK, SJS	853 - A4
HAWES PK, RDWC	790 - A1
HERITAGE OAKS PK, LALT	831 - H2
HERITAGE PK, PA	790 - J5
HERITAGE ROSE GARDEN, SJS	833 - J5
HESTER PK, SJS	833 - G7
HIDDEN LAKE PK, MPS	794 - A6
HILLCREST PK, MPS	814 - E1
HILLSTONE PK, SJS	855 - F6
HILLVIEW COMM CTR, LALT	811 - E6
HILLVIEW PK, SJS	834 - J6
HLSTR HLLS STATE VHCLR REC AREA, SBnC	1059 - E7
HOMERIDGE PK, SCL	833 - A6
HOOVER PK, PA	791 - C7
HOOVER PK, CPTO	852 - D4
HOPKINS CREEKSIDE PK, PA	790 - H4
HOTTS, CHRIS PK, SJS	874 - C5
HOUGE PK, SJS	873 - E3
HUMMINGBIRD PK, SJS	854 - A2
JACKSON PK, MTVW	811 - J4
JACKSON PK, MGH	917 - F6
JOHNSON PK, PA	790 - H4
JOLLYMAN PK, CPTO	852 - D2
KELLEY PK, SJS	834 - E7
KELLOGG PK, PA	791 - A5
KING, MARTIN LUTHER PK, EPA	791 - D2
KIRK PK, SJS	874 - A1
KLEIN PK, MTVW	811 - F4
LA COLINA PK, SJS	875 - A6
LAKE CUNNINGHAM PK, SJS	835 - B6
LAKEWOOD PK, SUNV	812 - H4
LANDELS PK, MTVW	811 - J5
LA RINCONADA PK, LGTS	873 - A3
LAS ANIMAS VETERANS PK, GIL	977 - H1
LAS PALMAS PK, SUNV	832 - D2
LEVIN, ED R COUNTY PK, SCIC	794 - F3
LEXINGTON RESERVOIR COUNTY PK, SCIC	892 - J3
LICK MILL PK, SCL	813 - D4
LINCOLN GLEN PK, SJS	854 - B5
LINCOLN PK, LALT	811 - D6
LINDA VISTA PK, CPTO	852 - A3
LINDEN PK, RDWC	790 - C1
LIVE OAK MANOR PK, LGTS	873 - D4
LIVE OAK PK, SCL	813 - E5
LO BUE PK, SJS	834 - H3
LONE BLUFF MINI PK, SJS	854 - J5
LONE HILL PK, SJS	873 - J4
LONE TREE CREEK PK, FRMT	793 - J1
LOS ARROYOS PK, GIL	957 - G7
LOS GATOS CREEK PK, CMBL	873 - D1
LOS GATOS CREEK TRAIL, CMBL	873 - E1
LOS PASEOS PK, SJS	875 - F7
LYLE, JACK PK, MLPK	790 - F4
MACHADO PK, SCL	832 - J3
MADDUX PK, RDWC	790 - A3
MAGNOLIA PK, MTVW	812 - B5
MANOR, REX PK, MTVW	811 - G3
MARSALLI, LARRY J PK, SCL	833 - E3
MARTIN PK, SJS	834 - E6
MARTIN, T J PK, SJS	874 - B6
MARYMEADE PK, LALT	831 - H3
MAYFAIR PK, SJS	834 - G4
MAYFIELD PK, PA	811 - A1
MAYWOOD PK, SCL	832 - J7
MCCARTHY STREET PK, HOLL	1040 - A3
MCCLELLAN RANCH PK, CPTO	852 - A2
MCENERY PK, SJS	834 - B7
MCKELVEY PK, MTVW	811 - H6
MCKENZIE PK, LALT	831 - G3
MCLAUGHLIN PK, SJS	834 - F7
MEADOWFAIR PK, SJS	855 - B2
MEADOWS PK, SJS	874 - F1
MELODY PK, SJS	855 - A7
MEMORIAL CROSS PK, SJS	833 - F2
MEMORIAL PK, CPTO	832 - C7
MERCY-BUSH PK, MTVW	811 - J5
METCALF PK, SJS	875 - G6
MILL CREEK PK, MGH	937 - B4
MILLER PK, GIL	977 - J2
MILPITAS DOG PK, MPS	794 - E3
MINER PK, SJS	875 - A4
MISE PK, SJS	852 - J1
MITCHELL PK, PA	811 - E1
MOITOZO PK, SJS	813 - F3
MONROE MINI PK, PA	811 - D3
MONTAGUE PK, SCL	813 - E6
MONTA LOMA PK, MTVW	811 - F3
MONTA VISTA PK, CPTO	852 - A1
MONTCLAIRE PK, LALT	831 - H5
MONTGOMERY HILL PK, SJS	855 - G4
MOORE, PAUL PK, SJS	874 - B1
MORAN, KEVIN PK, SAR	852 - F5
MORGAN, JOHN D PK, CMBL	853 - C6
MORTON, RED COMM PK, RDWC	790 - A1
MOTORCYCLE COUNTY PK, SCIC	876 - A7
MOUNT MADONNA COUNTY PK, SCIC	976 - F4
MOUNT PLEASANT PK, SJS	835 - B3
MUNICIPAL ROSE GARDEN, SJS	833 - G7
MURDOCK PK, SJS	852 - H3
MURPHY, MARTIN JR PK, SUNV	812 - E6
MURPHY PK, MPS	814 - D1
NEALON PK, MLPK	790 - G4
NOBLE PK, SJS	814 - H5
NORDSTROM PK, MGH	917 - C6
NORTH COYOTE PK, SJS	834 - B1
NORTHWOOD PK, SJS	814 - C3
OAK CREEK PK, MGH	937 - B5
OAK MEADOW PK, LGTS	873 - B5
OCONNOR PK, SJS	853 - J1
OLINDER, SELMA PK, SJS	834 - E6
ORCHARD GARDENS PK, SUNV	812 - F4

FEATURE NAME Address City, ZIP Code	PAGE-GRID
ORTEGA PK, SUNV	832 - E5
OUR PK, SJS	834 - J4
OVAL PARK, THE, SCIC	790 - H6
OVERFELT GARDENS PK, SJS	834 - F2
PAGE, GEORGE PK, SJS	875 - C6
PALMER, HOLBOOK PK, ATN	790 - E2
PALM HAVEN PK, SJS	854 - A2
PALMIA PK, SJS	875 - B5
PALM PK, RDWC	790 - B1
PALO ALTO FOOTHILLS PK (PRIVATE), PA	830 - F3
P A L SPORTS CTR, SJS	834 - G5
PANAMA PK, SUNV	832 - F4
PARADISE PK, MGH	937 - B3
PARDEE, ELEANOR PK, PA	791 - B4
PARK METROPOLITAN, MPS	814 - B1
PARKVIEW 1 PK, SJS	874 - G1
PARKVIEW 2 PK, SJS	874 - G1
PARKVIEW 3 PK, SJS	874 - H1
PARKWAY PARK, SCL	833 - C7
PARMA PK, SJS	894 - D1
PARQUE DE LA AMISTAD, SJS	834 - G5
PARQUE DE LOS POBLADORES, SJS	834 - C7
PECOT PK, MPS	794 - A3
PEERS PK, PA	791 - A6
PELLIER PK, SJS	834 - B6
PENITENCIA CREEK COUNTY PK, SJS	814 - F7
PFEIFFER PK, SJS	894 - F1
PINEWOOD PK, MPS	814 - A3
PIONEER MEM PK, MTVW	811 - H5
PLATA ARROYO PK, SJS	834 - F3
PLAYA DEL REY PK, SJS	874 - F3
PLAZA DE CESAR CHAVEZ, SJS	834 - B7
PLAZA DEL SOL PK, SUNV	812 - E7
PLOMOSA PK, FRMT	793 - J1
PONDEROSA PK, SUNV	832 - G2
PORTAL PK, CPTO	832 - F7
PRUSCH PK, SJS	834 - G6
RAINBOW PK, GIL	977 - G1
RAINBOW PK, SJS	852 - G4
RAMBLEWOOD PK, SJS	855 - B5
RAMOS PK, PA	791 - E7
RANCHO SAN ANTONIO COUNTY PK, SCIC	831 - G6
RANCHO SAN JUSTO SPORTS COMPLEX, HOLL	1040 - B5
RAVENWOOD PK, SAR	872 - J1
RAYNOR PK, SUNV	832 - G5
RENGSTORFF PK, MTVW	811 - G4
RENZ PK, GIL	977 - J2
REUTHER, WALTER PK, MPS	794 - B5
RINCONADA PK, PA	791 - B5
RIVER GLEN PK, SJS	854 - B4
ROBLES PK, PA	811 - D2
ROGERS, BEN PK, MPS	794 - E7
ROOSEVELT PK, SJS	834 - D5
ROSEMARY GARDEN PK, SJS	833 - H2
ROSICRUCIAN PK, SJS	833 - H6
ROTARY PK, SCL	833 - D3
ROY AVENUE MINI PK, SJS	854 - C5
RUBINO PK, SJS	854 - C7
RYLAND PK, SJS	834 - A5
SAINT JAMES PK, SJS	834 - B6
SAN ANTONIO PK, SUNV	832 - B4
SANBORN-SKYLINE COUNTY PK, SCIC	871 - G6
SANDLEWOOD PK, MPS	794 - B4
SAN JUSTO RESERVOIR REC AREA, SBnC	1059 - F2
SANTANA PK, SJS	853 - E1
SANTA TERESA COUNTY PK, SCIC	875 - C7
SAN TOMAS PK, SJS	853 - B7
SAN VERON PK, MTVW	811 - J3
SAN YSIDRO PK, GIL	978 - A2
SARATOGA CREEK PK, SJS	852 - H4
SCHMIDT, HENRY PK, SCL	833 - C6
SCOTT PK, PA	790 - J5
SCOTTSDALE PK, SJS	874 - A3
SEALE PK, PA	791 - D6
SELWYN PK, MPS	794 - C7
SEMINARY OAKS PK, MLPK	790 - H3
SERRA PK, SUNV	832 - C5
SESQUICENTENNIAL PK, SCL	833 - D4
SHADY OAK PK, SJS	875 - D2
SHARON HILLS PK, MLPK	790 - C6
SHARON PK, MLPK	790 - C7
SHORELINE AT MTN VIEW, MTVW	791 - H7
SHOUP PK, LALT	811 - D7
SILVER CREEK LINEAR PK, SJS	855 - C5
SILVER LEAF PK, SJS	875 - E4
SINNOTT PK, MPS	814 - D1
SLATER PK, MTVW	812 - A5
SOLARI PK, SJS	854 - H6
SOMERSET SQUARE PK, CPTO	852 - B6
SOUTHEAST NEIGHBORHOOD PK, HOLL	1040 - D7
STANFORD HILLS PK, MLPK	790 - E7
STANFORD/PALO ALTO COMM PLAYING FIELDS, PA	791 - A7
STARBIRD PK, SJS	853 - C3
STARLITE PK, MPS	793 - J7
STEVENS CREEK COUNTY PK, SCIC	851 - J3
STEVENSON PK, MTVW	811 - H3
STONE CREEK PK, MGH	917 - B7
STONEGATE PK, SJS	854 - H3
STRAND, JENNY PK, SCL	832 - H7
STRICKROTH PK, MPS	794 - A5
SUNNYVALE BAYLANDS PK, SUNV	812 - J2
SUNRISE PK, GIL	957 - F7
SYLVAN PK, MTVW	812 - A6
TAPESTRY PK, SJS	855 - E2
TERMAN PK, PA	811 - D3
TERRELL PK, SJS	874 - D1
THADDEUS PK, MTVW	811 - G2
THOUSAND OAKS PK, SJS	874 - D1
THREE OAKS PK, CPTO	852 - D3
TINKER PK, MLPK	790 - E5
TOWNSEND PK, SJS	814 - C7
TULLY ROAD BALLFIELDS, SJS	854 - G3
TURTLE ROCK PK, SJS	854 - H1
TWIN CREEKS SPORTS COMPLEX, SUNV	812 - H2
ULISTIC NATURAL AREA, SCL	813 - D3
UNIVERSITY SQUARE, EPA	791 - C3
UPPER STEVENS CREEK COUNTY PK, SCIC	851 - A5
UVAS CANYON COUNTY PK, SCIC	935 - B6
UVAS RESERVOIR PK, SCIC	936 - D7
VARIAN PK, CPTO	832 - A7
VARSITY PK, MTVW	811 - G7
VASONA LAKE COUNTY PK, LGTS	873 - B5

FEATURE NAME Address City, ZIP Code	PAGE-GRID
VETERANS MEM SOFTBALL FIELDS, HOLL	1040 - C5
VICTORY VILLAGE PK, SUNV	812 - F7
VIEW PK, MPS	794 - C4
VILLA MONTALVO ARBORETUM, SCIC	872 - D5
VINCI PK, SJS	814 - D7
VISTA PK, SJS	874 - F2
VISTA PK HILL, HOLL	1039 - J3
WALLENBERG PK, SJS	854 - A6
WALLIS PK, PA	791 - B7
WARBURTON PK, SCL	833 - C3
WASHINGTON CITY PK, SUNV	812 - D7
WASHINGTON PK, SCL	833 - E5
WATERFORD PK, SJS	854 - F7
WATSON PK, SJS	834 - D3
WEISSHAAR PK, PA	811 - A1
WELCH PK, SJS	854 - J1
WERRY PK, PA	810 - J1
WESTWOOD OAKS PK, SCL	832 - H6
WHISMAN PK, MTVW	812 - A4
WIECHERT, HOWARD PK, MGH	937 - A4
WILCOX PK, SJS	854 - A5
WILDWOOD PK, SAR	872 - D2
WILLIAM STREET PK, SJS	834 - E6
WILLOW OAKS PK, MLPK	790 - J2
WILLOW STREET BRAMHALL PK, SJS	853 - J3
WILSON PK, CPTO	852 - F1
WINDMILL SPRINGS PK, SJS	854 - J3
YELLOWSTONE PK, MPS	814 - D1
ZOLEZZI PK, SJS	834 - F5

POST OFFICES

FEATURE NAME Address City, ZIP Code	PAGE-GRID
AGNEW STA 4601 LAFAYETTE ST, SCL, 95054	813 - D4
ALMADEN VALLEY STA 6525 CROWN BLVD, SJS, 95120	894 - E1
ALVISO 1525 GOLD ST, SJS, 95002	813 - B1
BAYSIDE STA 2731 JUNCTION AV, SJS, 95134	813 - H5
BERRYESSA STA 1315 PIEDMONT RD, SJS, 95132	814 - G4
BLOSSOM HILL STA 5706 CAHALAN AV, SJS, 95123	874 - G4
BLOSSOM VALLEY STA 1768 MIRAMONTE AV, MTVW, 94040	831 - H1
CAMBRIAN PK 1769 HILLSDALE AV, SJS, 95124	873 - H2
CAMBRIDGE STA 265 CAMBRIDGE AV, PA, 94306	791 - B7
CAMPBELL 500 W HAMILTON AV, CMBL, 95008	853 - D5
COYOTE 8220 MONTEREY RD, SCIC, 95137	895 - J2
CUPERTINO 21701 STEVENS CREEK BLVD, CPTO, 95014	832 - B7
EAST PALO ALTO 1600 BAY RD, EPA, 94303	791 - B1
ENCINAL STA 526 W FREMONT AV, SUNV, 94087	832 - E4
GARDEN 1165 LINCOLN AV, SJS, 95125	854 - A3
GILROY 100 4TH ST, GIL, 95020	978 - A3
HAMILTON 380 HAMILTON AV, PA, 94301	790 - J4
HILLVIEW STA 2450 ALVIN AV, SJS, 95121	854 - J1
HOLLISTER 100 MAPLE ST, HOLL, 95023	1040 - A3
LOS ALTOS 100 1ST ST, LALT, 94022	811 - D6
LOS GATOS 101 S SANTA CRUZ AV, LGTS, 95030	893 - A1
MILPITAS 450 S ABEL ST, MPS, 95035	814 - A1
MISSION STA 1050 KIELY BLVD, SCL, 95051	833 - B5
MORGAN HILL 16600 MONTEREY RD, MGH, 95037	937 - A1
MOUNTAIN VIEW 211 HOPE ST, MTVW, 94041	811 - J5
NEW ALMADEN 21300 ALMADEN RD, SCIC, 95120	894 - J7
OAK GROVE STA 655 OAK GROVE AV, MLPK, 94025	790 - F3
PALO ALTO 2085 E BAYSHORE RD, PA, 94303	791 - D4
PARKMOOR STA 1545 PARKMOOR AV, SJS, 95126	853 - H2
PLAZA STA 141 S TAAFFE AV, SUNV, 94086	812 - E7
REDWOOD ESTATES MAIN 21432 BROADWAY RD, SCIC, 95033	912 - J2
ROBERTSVILLE STA 1175 BRANHAM LN, SJS, 95118	874 - C2
SAINT JAMES PK 105 N 1ST ST, SJS, 95113	834 - B6
SAN JOSE 1750 LUNDY AV, SJS, 95131	814 - C6
SAN JUAN BAUTISTA 301 THE ALAMEDA, SJB, 95045	1038 - D5
SAN MARTIN 200 E SAN MARTIN AV, SCIC, 95046	937 - F6
SANTA CLARA 1200 FRANKLIN ST, SCL, 95050	833 - E4
SARATOGA MAIN 19630 ALLENDALE AV, SAR, 95070	872 - F1
STANFORD 531 LASUEN MALL, SCIC, 94305	790 - H6
STANFORD UNIV BRANCH LAGUNITA DR & LANE W, SCIC, 94305	790 - H7
STA D 70 S JACKSON AV, SJS, 95116	834 - H3
SUNNYVALE 580 N MARY AV, SUNV, 94086	812 - D5
TRES PINOS 21 4TH ST, SBnC, 95075	1061 - A5
VILLAGE STA 14376 SARATOGA AV, SAR, 95070	872 - E2
WESTGATE STA 4285 PAYNE AV, SJS, 95117	853 - A4
WEST MENLO PK BRANCH 2120 AVY AV, SMCo, 94025	790 - D6
WILLOW GLEN 1750 MERIDIAN AV, SJS, 95125	853 - J5
WOODSIDE PLAZA STA 364 WOODSIDE PZ, RDWC, 94061	790 - A3

SCHOOLS

FEATURE NAME Address City, ZIP Code	PAGE-GRID
ACHIEVER CHRISTIAN ELEM 820 IRONWOOD DR, SJS, 95125	854 - D6
ADDISON ELEM 650 ADDISON AV, PA, 94301	791 - A4
ALLEN ELEM 5845 ALLEN AV, SJS, 95123	874 - F5
ALMADEN COUNTRY ELEM 6835 TRINIDAD DR, SJS, 95120	894 - F1
ALMADEN COUNTRY MID 6835 TRINIDAD DR, SJS, 95120	894 - F1
ALMADEN ELEM 1295 DENTWOOD DR, SJS, 95118	874 - C4
ALMOND ELEM 550 ALMOND AV, LALT, 94022	811 - F6
ALTA VISTA HIGH 1299 BRYANT AV, MTVW, 94040	832 - A2
ALTA VISTA ELEM 200 BLOSSOM VALLEY DR, LGTS, 95032	873 - E5
ANDERSON, ALEX ELEM 5800 CALPINE DR, SJS, 95123	875 - B5
ANDERSON, LEROY ELEM 4000 RHODA DR, SJS, 95117	853 - B3
ANZAR HIGH 2000 SAN JUAN HWY, SBnC, 95045	1018 - B6
APOSTLES LUTHERAN ELEM 5828 SANTA TERESA BLVD, SJS, 95123	874 - G6
APREA, LUIGI ELEM 9225 CL DL REY, GIL, 95020	957 - F7
ARBUCKLE, CLYDE ELEM 1970 CINDERELLA LN, SJS, 95116	834 - H5
ARCHBISHOP MITTY HIGH 5000 MITTY WY, SJS, 95129	852 - J2
ARGONAUT ELEM 13200 SHADOW MOUNTAIN DR, SAR, 95070	852 - E7
ASCENSION SOLORSANO MID 7121 GRENACHE WY, GIL, 95020	977 - G4
ATHENOUR ELEM 5200 DENT AV, SJS, 95118	874 - A4
BACHRODT, WALTER L ELEM 102 SONORA AV, SJS, 95110	833 - J2
BAGBY ELEM 1840 HARRIS AV, SJS, 95124	853 - H7
BAKER, GUSSIE M ELEM 4845 BUCKNALL RD, SJS, 95130	853 - A6
BALDWIN, JULIA ELEM 280 MARTINVALE LN, SJS, 95119	895 - E1
BARRETT ELEM 895 BARRETT AV, MGH, 95037	937 - C1
BARRON PK ELEM 800 BARRON AV, PA, 94306	811 - B2
BELLARMINE COLLEGE PREP 960 W HEDDING ST, SJS, 95126	833 - H5
BERNAL INTERMED 6610 SAN IGNACIO DR, SJS, 95119	875 - D7
BETHEL LUTHERAN ELEM 10181 FINCH AV, CPTO, 95014	852 - G1
BISHOP ELEM 450 N SUNNYVALE AV, SUNV, 94086	812 - F6
BLACH, GEORGINA P INTERMED 1120 COVINGTON RD, LALT, 94024	831 - H2
BLACKFORD ELEM 1970 WILLOW ST, SJS, 95125	853 - H4
BLOSSOM HILL ELEM 16400 BLOSSOM HILL RD, LGTS, 95032	873 - D6
BLOSSOM VALLEY ELEM 420 ALLEGAN CIR, SJS, 95123	875 - A6
BLUE HILLS ELEM 12300 DE SANKA AV, SAR, 95070	852 - E5
BOEGER, AUGUST JR HIGH 1944 FLINT AV, SJS, 95148	835 - C5
BOOKSIN ELEM 1590 DRY CREEK RD, SJS, 95125	853 - J6
BOWERS ELEM 2755 BARKLEY AV, SCL, 95051	833 - B3
BRACHER ELEM 2700 CHROMITE DR, SCL, 95051	833 - B2
BRALY ELEM 675 GAIL AV, SUNV, 94086	832 - F2
BRANHAM HIGH 1570 BRANHAM LN, SJS, 95118	874 - A3
BRIARWOOD ELEM 1930 TOWNSEND AV, SCL, 95051	833 - A3
BRIONES, JUANA ELEM 4100 ORME AV, PA, 94306	811 - C3
BRITTON, LEWIS H MID 80 CENTRAL AV, MGH, 95037	916 - J7
BROADWAY HIGH 4825 SPEAK LN, SJS, 95118	874 - C2
BROOKS, PHILLIPS ELEM 2245 AVY AV, MLPK, 94025	790 - D7
BROOKTREE ELEM 1781 OLIVETREE DR, SJS, 95131	814 - C5
BROWNELL ACADEMY 7800 CARMEL ST, GIL, 95020	977 - J2
BUBB, BENJAMIN ELEM 525 HANS AV, MTVW, 94040	811 - H7
BUCHSER, EMIL MID 1111 BELLOMY ST, SCL, 95050	833 - E5
BULLIS-PURISSIMA ELEM 25890 FREMONT RD, LAH, 94022	811 - C6
BURBANK, LUTHER ELEM 4 WABASH AV, SCIC, 95128	853 - G1
BURNETT ELEM 85 TILTON AV, MGH, 95037	916 - G4
BURNETT, PETER MID 850 N 2ND ST, SJS, 95112	834 - A4
BURNETT, WILLIAM ELEM 400 FANYON ST, MPS, 95035	794 - C5
CABRILLO MID 2550 CABRILLO AV, SCL, 95051	833 - B3
CADWALLADER ELEM 3799 CADWALLADER RD, SJS, 95121	855 - D3
CALAVERAS ELEM 1151 BUENA VISTA RD, HOLL, 95023	1039 - H3
CALAVERAS HILLS HIGH 1331 CALAVERAS BLVD, MPS, 95035	794 - C6
CALLEJON, DON ELEM 4176 LICK MILL BLVD, SCL, 95054	813 - E4
CALVARY CHRISTIAN BAPTIST 1900 HIGHLAND DR, HOLL, 95023	1040 - D6
CAMPBELL CHRISTIAN 1075 W CAMPBELL AV, CMBL, 95008	853 - B6
CAMPBELL MID 295 W CHERRY LN, CMBL, 95008	853 - D6
CANOAS ELEM 880 WREN DR, SJS, 95125	854 - D6
CANTERBURY CHRISTIAN ELEM 101 N EL MONTE AV, LALT, 94022	811 - F6
CAPRI ELEM 850 CHAPMAN AV, CMBL, 95008	873 - C2
CARDEN ELEM, SOUTH VALLEY 1921 CLARINDA WY, SJS, 95124	873 - G4
CARDEN EL ENCANTO 615 HOBART TER, SCL, 95051	833 - B6
CARLTON ELEM 2421 CARLTON AV, SJS, 95124	873 - E4
CARSON, RACHEL ELEM 4245 MEG DR, SJS, 95136	874 - F1
CASSELL, SYLVIA ELEM 1300 TALLAHASSEE DR, SJS, 95122	834 - J5
CASTILLEJA HIGH 1310 BRYANT ST, PA, 94301	791 - A5
CASTILLEJA MID 1310 BRYANT ST, PA, 94301	791 - A5
CASTILLERO MID 6384 LEYLAND PARK DR, SJS, 95120	894 - C1
CASTLEMONT ELEM 3040 E PAYNE AV, SJS, 95008	853 - E4
CASTRO, ELVIRA MID 4600 STUDENT LN, SJS, 95130	853 - A5
CASTRO, MARIANO ELEM 505 ESCUELA AV, MTVW, 94040	811 - G4
CEDAR GROVE ELEM 2702 SUGAR PLUM DR, SJS, 95148	835 - D7
CENTRAL HIGH 17960 MONTEREY RD, MGH, 95037	916 - J6
CERRA VISTA ELEM 2151 CERRA VISTA DR, HOLL, 95023	1040 - D7
CHABOYA MID 3276 CORTONA DR, SJS, 95135	855 - G3
CHALLENGER ALMADEN ELEM 19950 MCKEAN RD, SJS, 95120	894 - J4
CHALLENGER BERRYESSA ELEM 711 GISH RD, SJS, 95112	834 - B1
CHALLENGER MERIDIAN ELEM 2845 MERIDIAN AV, SJS, 95124	873 - J1
CHALLENGER SUNNYVALE ELEM 1185 HOLLENBECK AV, SUNV, 94087	832 - D3
CHARTER OF MORGAN HILL 9530 MONTEREY RD, SJS, 95037	896 - B3
CHAVEZ, CESAR ELEM 2000 KAMMERER AV, SJS, 95116	834 - G4
CHAVEZ, CESAR ELEM 2450 RALMAR AV, EPA, 94303	791 - A1
CHERRY CHASE ELEM 1138 HEATHERSTONE WY, SUNV, 94087	832 - B1
CHERRYWOOD ELEM 2550 GREENGATE DR, SJS, 95132	814 - E5
CHRISTOPHER ELEM 565 COYOTE RD, SJS, 95111	855 - A7
CLARK, CAROLYN ELEM 3701 RUE MIRASSOU, SJS, 95148	855 - F1
COLLINS ELEM 10401 VISTA DR, CPTO, 95014	832 - E7
COLUMBIA MID 739 MORSE AV, SUNV, 94086	812 - F5
CORTE MADERA MID 4575 ALPINE RD, PTLV, 94028	830 - C1
CORY, BENJAMIN ELEM 2280 KENWOOD AV, SJS, 95128	833 - E7
COUNTRY LANE ELEM 5140 COUNTRY LN, SJS, 95129	852 - J4
COVINGTON ELEM 205 COVINGTON RD, LALT, 94024	831 - E1
CRITTENDEN MID 1701 ROCK ST, MTVW, 94043	811 - H2
CUMBERLAND ELEM 824 CUMBERLAND AV, SUNV, 94087	832 - C1
CUPERTINO HIGH 10100 FINCH AV, CPTO, 95014	852 - G1
CUPERTINO MID 1650 BERNARDO AV, SUNV, 94087	832 - B5
CURETON, HORACE ELEM 3720 E HILLS DR, SJS, 95127	835 - B2
CURTNER ELEM 275 REDWOOD AV, MPS, 95035	793 - J6
DAHL, CAPT JASON M ELEM 3200 WATER ST, SJS, 95111	854 - H6
DARLING, ANNE ELEM 333 N 33RD ST, SJS, 95133	834 - E3
DARTMOUTH MID 5575 DARTMOUTH DR, SJS, 95118	874 - A5
DAVES AV ELEM 17770 DAVES AV, MSER, 95030	873 - A5
DAVIS, CAROLINE INTERMED 5035 EDEN VIEW DR, SJS, 95111	875 - B2
DEL BUONO, ANTONIO ELEM 9300 WREN AV, GIL, 95020	957 - H7
DEL MAR HIGH 1224 DEL MAR AV, SJS, 95128	853 - G3
DEL ROBLE ELEM 5345 AVD ALMENDROS, SJS, 95123	874 - H3
DE VARGAS ELEM 5050 MOORPARK AV, SJS, 95129	852 - J2
DILWORTH ELEM 1101 STRAYER DR, SJS, 95129	852 - G3
DORSA, ANTHONY J ELEM 1290 BAL HARBOR WY, SJS, 95122	834 - H6
DOVE HILL ELEM 1460 COLT WY, SJS, 95121	855 - B4
DOWNTOWN COLLEGE PREP HIGH 355 W SAN FERNANDO ST, SJS, 95110	834 - B7
DUVENECK ELEM 705 ALESTER AV, PA, 94303	791 - C4
EASTERBROOK ELEM 4660 EASTUS DR, SJS, 95129	853 - A3

FEATURE NAME Address City, ZIP Code	PAGE-GRID
EAST PALO ALTO CHARTER 1286 RUNNYMEADE ST, EPA, 94303	791 - C1
EAST PALO ALTO CHARTER HIGH 475 POPE ST, MLPK, 94025	790 - J2
EAST VALLEY CHRISTIAN ELEM 2715 S WHITE RD, SJS, 95148	835 - C7
EATON ELEM 20220 SUISUN DR, CPTO, 95014	852 - E2
EDENVALE ELEM 285 AZUCAR AV, SJS, 95111	875 - C2
EDISON-BRENTWOOD ELEM 2086 CLARKE AV, EPA, 94303	791 - C2
EDISON-MCNAIR CHARTER 2033 PULGAS AV, EPA, 94303	791 - C2
EGAN, ARDIS G JR HIGH 100 W PORTOLA AV, LALT, 94022	811 - D4
EISENHOWER ELEM 277 RODONOVAN DR, SCL, 95051	832 - J7
EL CARMELO ELEM 3024 BRYANT ST, PA, 94306	791 - C7
ELIOT ELEM 470 E 7TH ST, GIL, 95020	978 - B3
ELIOT ELEM 7121 GRENACHE WY, GIL, 95020	977 - G4
ELLIS ELEM 550 W OLIVE AV, SUNV, 94086	832 - F1
EL ROBLE ELEM 930 3RD ST, GIL, 95020	977 - H3
EL TORO ELEM 455 E MAIN AV, MGH, 95037	917 - A6
EMPIRE GARDENS ELEM 1060 E EMPIRE ST, SJS, 95112	834 - D4
ENCINAL ELEM 195 ENCINAL AV, ATN, 94027	790 - F2
ENGLISH, C T MID 23800 SUMMIT RD, SCIC, 95033	913 - E7
ERIKSON ELEM 4849 PEARL AV, SJS, 95136	874 - E2
ESCONDIDO ELEM 890 ESCONDIDO RD, SCIC, 94305	810 - J1
EVERGREEN ELEM 3010 FOWLER RD, SJS, 95135	855 - E3
EVERGREEN VALLEY HIGH 3300 QUIMBY RD, SJS, 95148	855 - E1
FAIR, J WILBUR MID 1702 MCLAUGHLIN AV, SJS, 95122	854 - G1
FAIRMEADOW ELEM 500 E MEADOW DR, PA, 94306	811 - E1
FAIRWOOD ELEM 1110 FAIRWOOD AV, SUNV, 94089	812 - J4
FAMMATRE ELEM 2800 NEW JERSEY AV, SJS, 95124	873 - G1
FARIA ELEM 10155 BARBARA LN, CPTO, 95014	852 - D1
FARNHAM ELEM 15711 WOODARD RD, SJS, 95124	873 - E2
FISCHER, CLYDE L MID 1720 HOPKINS DR, SJS, 95122	834 - J6
FISHER, RAYMOND J MID 17000 ROBERTS RD, LGTS, 95032	873 - B6
FIVE WOUNDS ELEM 1390 FIVE WOUNDS LN, SJS, 95116	834 - E4
FOOTHILL HIGH 230 PALA AV, SJS, 95127	834 - H2
FOOTHILL ELEM 13919 LYNDE AV, SAR, 95070	872 - D1
FOOTHILL INTERMED 1966 FLINT AV, SJS, 95148	835 - C5
FOOTHILL SEVENTH-DAY ADVENTIST ELEM 1991 LANDESS AV, MPS, 95035	814 - E2
FORD, HENRY ELEM 2498 MASSACHUSETTS AV, RDWC, 94061	790 - A3
FOREST HILL ELEM 4450 MCCOY AV, CMBL, 95130	853 - A7
FRANKLIN ELEM 420 TULLY RD, SJS, 95111	854 - F3
FREMONT ELEM 335 WEST ST, HOLL, 95023	1040 - A3
FREMONT HIGH 1279 SUNNYVALE-SARATOGA RD, SUNV, 94087	832 - D3
FRENCH AMERICAN OF SILICON VALLE 1522 LEWISTON DR, SUNV, 94087	832 - C5
FROST, EARL ELEM 530 GETTYSBURG DR, SJS, 95123	874 - H4
GABILAN HILLS ELEM 901 SANTA ANA RD, HOLL, 95023	1040 - C3
GALARZA ELEM 1619 BIRD AV, SJS, 95125	854 - C4
GARDEN GATE ELEM 10500 ANN ARBOR AV, CPTO, 95014	832 - C6
GARDNER ELEM 502 ILLINOIS AV, SJS, 95125	854 - B1
GARFIELD CHARTER ELEM 3600 MIDDLEFIELD RD, SMCo, 94025	790 - D1
GEORGE, JOSEPH MID 277 MAHONEY DR, SJS, 95127	835 - B2
GERMAN-AMERICAN OF SAN FRANCISCO 275 ELLIOT DR, MLPK, 94025	791 - A2
GILROY HIGH 750 W 10TH ST, GIL, 95020	977 - J5
GLEN VIEW ELEM 600 W 8TH ST, GIL, 95020	977 - J4
GLIDER ELEM 511 COZY DR, SJS, 95123	874 - J6
GOSS, MILDRED ELEM 2475 VAN WINKLE LN, SJS, 95116	834 - J4
GRAHAM, ISSAC NEWTON MID 1175 CASTRO ST, MTVW, 94040	811 - H6
GRANADA ISLAMIC ELEM 3003 SCOTT BLVD, SCL, 95054	813 - D7
GRANT ELEM 470 E JACKSON ST, SJS, 95112	834 - B4
GRAYSTONE ELEM 6982 SHEARWATER DR, SJS, 95120	894 - H2
GREEN OAKS ELEM 2450 RALMAR AV, EPA, 94303	791 - A1
GUADALUPE ELEM 6044 VERA CRUZ DR, SJS, 95120	874 - A7
GUNDERSON HIGH 622 GAUNDABERT LN, SJS, 95136	874 - F3
GUNN, HENRY M HIGH 780 ARASTRADERO RD, PA, 94306	811 - C4
HACIENDA SCIENCE/ENVIRONMENTAL MAGNET 1290 KIMBERLY DR, SJS, 95118	874 - C1
HAMAN, CW ELEM 865 LOS PADRES BLVD, SCL, 95050	833 - C5
HAMMER MONTESSORI 1325 BOURET DR, SJS, 95118	874 - B3
HARDIN, R O ELEM 881 LINE ST, HOLL, 95023	1039 - J5
HARKER ELEM 4300 BUCKNALL RD, SJS, 95130	853 - A6
HARKER HIGH 500 SARATOGA AV, SJS, 95129	853 - B1
HARTE, BRET MID 7050 BRET HARTE DR, SJS, 95120	894 - G2
HAYES ELEM 5035 POSTON DR, SJS, 95136	874 - J2
HAYS, WALTER ELEM 1525 MIDDLEFIELD RD, PA, 94301	791 - B5
HAZELWOOD ELEM 775 WALDO RD, CMBL, 95008	853 - C7
HELLYER, G W ELEM 725 HELLYER AV, SJS, 95111	855 - A6
HERMAN, LEONARD INTERMED 5955 BLOSSOM AV, SJS, 95123	874 - H5
HESTER ELEM 1460 THE ALAMEDA, SJS, 95126	833 - J6
HILL, ANDREW HIGH 3200 SENTER RD, SJS, 95111	854 - J5
HILLBROOK 300 MARCHMONT DR, LGTS, 95032	873 - D7
HILLVIEW MID 1100 ELDER AV, MLPK, 94025	790 - E5
HOLLY OAK ELEM 2995 ROSSMORE WY, SJS, 95148	855 - C2
HOLY FAMILY ELEM 4850 PEARL AV, SJS, 95136	874 - E2
HOLY SPIRIT 1198 REDMOND AV, SJS, 95120	874 - D7
HOMESTEAD HIGH 21370 HOMESTEAD RD, CPTO, 95014	832 - C6
HOOVER, HERBERT ELEM 445 E CHARLESTON RD, PA, 94306	811 - E1
HOOVER, HERBERT MID 1635 PARK AV, SJS, 95126	833 - H6
HUBBARD, O S ELEM 1745 JUNE AV, SJS, 95122	834 - H7
HUFF, FRANK ELEM 253 MARTENS AV, MTVW, 94040	811 - J7
HUGHES, KATHRYN ELEM 4949 CL DE ESCUELA, SCL, 95054	813 - C3
HYDE MID 19325 BOLLINGER RD, CPTO, 95014	852 - G2
INDEPENDENCE HIGH 1776 EDUCATIONAL PARK DR, SJS, 95133	834 - F2
INTL SCH OF THE PENINSULA COHN CAMPUS 151 LAURA LN, PA, 94303	791 - D3
INTL SCH THE PENINSULA COWPER CAMPUS 3233 COWPER ST, PA, 94306	791 - D7
JACKSON ELEM 2700 FOUNTAIN OAKS DR, MGH, 95037	917 - F6
JORDAN, DAVID STARR MID 750 N CALIFORNIA AV, PA, 94303	791 - C5
KELLEY, ROD ELEM 8755 KERN AV, GIL, 95020	977 - G1
KENNEDY MID 821 BUBB RD, CPTO, 95014	852 - B2
KENNEDY, ROBERT F ELEM 1602 LUCRETIA AV, SJS, 95122	854 - F1
KEYS 2890 MIDDLEFIELD RD, PA, 94306	791 - C6
KINGS ACADEMY HIGH, THE 562 N BRITTON AV, SUNV, 94086	812 - G6
LADD LANE ELEM 161 LADD LN, SBnC, 95023	1040 - B7
LA ENTRADA MID 2200 SHARON RD, MLPK, 94025	790 - D7
LAKESIDE ELEM 19621 BLACK RD, SCIC, 95033	892 - F4
LAKEWOOD ELEM 750 LAKECHIME DR, SUNV, 94089	812 - H4
LANDELS, EDITH ELEM 115 DANA ST, MTVW, 94041	811 - J5
LANEVIEW ELEM 2095 WARMWOOD LN, SJS, 95132	814 - D2
LAS ANIMAS ELEM 8450 WREN AV, GIL, 95020	977 - H1
LAS LOMITAS ELEM 299 ALAMEDA DE LAS PULGAS, ATN, 94027	790 - C5
LATIMER ELEM 4250 LATIMER AV, SJS, 95130	853 - A5
LAUREL ELEM 95 EDGE RD, ATN, 94027	790 - H1
LAURELWOOD ELEM 4280 PARTRIDGE DR, SJS, 95121	855 - E4
LAURELWOOD ELEM 955 TEAL DR, SCL, 95051	832 - H5
LEARNING ACADEMY, THE 5670 CAMDEN AV, SJS, 95124	874 - A6
LEDESMA, RITA ELEM 1001 SCHOOLHOUSE RD, SJS, 95138	875 - G5
LEIGH HIGH 5210 LEIGH AV, SJS, 95124	873 - G5
LELAND HIGH 6677 CAMDEN AV, SJS, 95120	894 - G2
LEXINGTON ELEM 19700 OLD SANTA CRUZ HWY, SCIC, 95033	892 - J6
LEYVA, GEORGE V MID 1865 MONROVIA DR, SJS, 95122	855 - B2
LIBERTY BAPTIST ELEM 2790 S KING RD, SJS, 95122	855 - A2
LIBERTY BAPTIST HIGH 2790 S KING RD, SJS, 95122	855 - A2
LIBERTY HIGH 2177 COTTLE AV, SJS, 95125	854 - B6
LICK, JAMES HIGH 57 N WHITE RD, SJS, 95127	834 - J2
LIETZ ELEM 5300 CARTER AV, SJS, 95118	874 - A5
LINCOLN, ABRAHAM HIGH 555 DANA AV, SJS, 95126	833 - G7
LINCOLN ELEM 21710 MCCLELLAN RD, CPTO, 95014	852 - B2
LINDA VISTA ELEM 100 KIRK AV, SJS, 95127	815 - A7
LIVE OAK HIGH 1505 E MAIN AV, MGH, 95037	917 - C4
LOMA PRIETA ELEM 23800 SUMMIT RD, SCIC, 95033	913 - E7
LONE HILL ELEM 4949 HARWOOD RD, SJS, 95124	873 - H4
LOS ALAMITOS ELEM 6130 SILBERMAN DR, SJS, 95120	874 - C7
LOS ALTOS CHRISTIAN ELEM 625 MAGDALENA AV, LALT, 94024	831 - F2
LOS ALTOS HIGH 201 ALMOND AV, LALT, 94022	811 - E6
LOS ARBOLES ELEM 455 LOS ARBOLES AV, SJS, 95111	854 - J6
LOS GATOS ACADEMY 220 BELGATOS RD, LGTS, 95032	873 - H6
LOS GATOS CHRISTIAN 16845 HICKS RD, LGTS, 95032	873 - J7
LOS GATOS HIGH 20 HIGH SCHOOL CT, LGTS, 95030	893 - A1
LOS PASEOS ELEM 121 AVD GRANDE, SJS, 95139	875 - F7
LOWELL ELEM 625 S 7TH ST, SJS, 95112	834 - D7
LOYOLA ELEM 770 BERRY AV, LALT, 94024	831 - G2
LUTHERAN OF OUR SAVIOR 5825 BOLLINGER RD, CPTO, 95014	852 - G2
LYNBROOK HIGH 1280 JOHNSON AV, SJS, 95129	852 - G4
LYNDALE ELEM 13901 NORDYKE DR, SJS, 95127	834 - J3
LYNHAVEN ELEM 881 S CYPRESS AV, SJS, 95117	853 - C2
MAJESTIC WAY ELEM 1855 MAJESTIC WY, SJS, 95132	814 - F3
MANN, HORACE ELEM 55 N 7TH ST, SJS, 95112	834 - C6
MARSHALL LANE ELEM 14114 MARILYN LN, SAR, 95070	872 - H2
MATHSON, LEE MID 2050 KAMMERER AV, SJS, 95116	834 - H4
MATSUMOTO, TOM ELEM 4121 MACKIN WOODS LN, SJS, 95135	855 - G3
MAYNE, GEORGE ELEM 5030 N 1ST ST, SJS, 95002	813 - C1
MAZE, MARGUERITE MID 900 MERIDIAN ST, SBnC, 95023	1040 - C4
MCAULIFFE, CHRISTA ELEM 12211 TITUS AV, SAR, 95070	852 - G5
MCCOLLAM, MILLARD ELEM 3311 LUCIAN AV, SJS, 95127	814 - J7
MCKINLEY ELEM 651 MACREDES AV, SJS, 95116	834 - E6
MEADOWS, JEANNE R ELEM 1250 TAPER LN, SJS, 95122	854 - H1
MENLO-ATHERTON HIGH 555 MIDDLEFIELD RD, ATN, 94027	790 - G2
MENLO HIGH 50 VALPARAISO AV, ATN, 94027	790 - F3
MENLO MID 50 VALPARAISO AV, ATN, 94027	790 - E3
MEYER, DONALD J ELEM 1824 DAYTONA DR, SJS, 95122	834 - J6
MEYERHOLZ ELEM 6990 MELVIN DR, SJS, 95129	852 - E3
MID-PENINSULA JEWISH COMM 4000 TERMAN DR, PA, 94306	811 - C3
MILLBROOK ELEM 3200 MILLBROOK DR, SJS, 95148	855 - D2
MILLER, GRANDIN ELEM 1250 S KING RD, SJS, 95122	834 - H6
MILLER MID 6151 RAINBOW DR, SJS, 95129	852 - G3
MILLIKIN ELEM 2720 SONOMA PL, SCL, 95051	833 - B5
MILPITAS CHRISTIAN ELEM 3435 BIRCHWOOD LN, SJS, 95132	814 - E2
MILPITAS HIGH 1285 ESCUELA PKWY, MPS, 95035	794 - A4
MINER, GEORGE ELEM 5629 LEAN AV, SJS, 95123	875 - A4
MIRAMONTE ELEM 1175 ALTAMEAD DR, LALT, 94024	831 - H2
MOFFETT HIGH 333 MOFFETT BLVD, MTVW, 94043	811 - J4
MONROE MID 1055 S MONROE ST, SJS, 95128	853 - E3
MONTAGUE ELEM 750 LAURIE AV, SCL, 95054	813 - E6
MONTA LOMA ELEM 460 THOMPSON AV, MTVW, 94043	811 - G3
MONTA VISTA HIGH 21840 MCCLELLAN RD, CPTO, 95014	852 - B2
MONTCLAIRE ELEM 1160 SAINT JOSEPH AV, LALT, 94024	831 - H5
MONTEBELLO ELEM 15101 MONTEBELLO RD, SCIC, 95014	851 - F4
MONTGOMERY, JOHN J ELEM 2010 DANIEL MALONEY DR, SJS, 95121	855 - C3
MORELAND DISCOVERY ELEM 801 HIBISCUS LN, SJS, 95117	853 - B2
MORGAN HILL COUNTRY ELEM 105 JOHN WILSON WY, MGH, 95037	937 - C3
MORRILL MID 1970 MORRILL AV, SJS, 95132	814 - E3
MOST HOLY TRINITY ELEM 1940 CUNNINGHAM AV, SJS, 95122	834 - J7
MOUNTAIN VIEW ACADEMY HIGH 360 S SHORELINE BLVD, MTVW, 94041	811 - H5
MOUNTAIN VIEW HIGH 3535 TRUMAN AV, MTVW, 94040	832 - A2
MOUNT MADONNA HIGH 8750 HIRASAKI CT, GIL, 95020	977 - G1
MOUNT PLEASANT ELEM 14275 CANDLER AV, SJS, 95127	835 - B4
MOUNT PLEASANT HIGH 1750 S WHITE RD, SJS, 95127	835 - B5
MUIR ELEM 6560 HANOVER DR, SJS, 95129	852 - F4

FEATURE NAME	Address City, ZIP Code	PAGE-GRID
MUIR, JOHN MID	1260 BRANHAM LN, SJS, 95118	874 - C3
MULBERRY ELEM	1980 E HAMILTON AV, CMBL, 95125	853 - H5
MURDOCK-PORTAL ELEM	1188 WUNDERLICH DR, SJS, 95129	852 - H3
MURPHY, MARTIN MID	141 AVD ESPANA, SJS, 95139	895 - F1
NATIVITY ELEM	1250 LAUREL ST, MLPK, 94025	790 - F3
NEW VALLEY HIGH	1875 LAWRENCE RD, SCL, 95051	832 - J3
NIMITZ ELEM	545 E CHEYENNE DR, SUNV, 94087	832 - D4
NIXON, LUCILLE M ELEM	1711 STANFORD AV, SCIC, 94305	810 - J2
NOBLE ELEM	3466 GROSSMONT DR, SJS, 95132	814 - H5
NODDIN ELEM	1755 GILDA WY, SJS, 95124	873 - H5
NORDSTROM ELEM	1425 E DUNNE AV, MGH, 95037	917 - D6
NORTH VALLEY BAPTIST	941 CLYDE AV, SCL, 95054	813 - E6
NORTHWOOD ELEM	2760 TRIMBLE RD, SJS, 95132	814 - C3
NORWOOD CREEK ELEM	3241 REMINGTON WY, SJS, 95148	835 - D7
NOTRE DAME HIGH	596 S 2ND ST, SJS, 95112	834 - C7
OAK AVENUE ELEM	1501 OAK AV, LALT, 94024	831 - J3
OAK GROVE HIGH	285 BLOSSOM HILL RD, SJS, 95123	875 - A4
OAK KNOLL ELEM	1895 OAK KNOLL LN, MLPK, 94025	790 - E6
OAK RIDGE ELEM	5920 BUFKIN DR, SJS, 95123	875 - A5
OCALA MID	2800 OCALA AV, SJS, 95148	835 - A6
OHLONE ELEM	950 AMARILLO AV, PA, 94303	791 - D5
OLD ORCHARD ELEM	400 W CAMPBELL AV, CMBL, 95008	853 - C6
OLINDER, SELMA ELEM	890 E WILLIAM ST, SJS, 95116	834 - E6
ORCHARD	921 FOX LN, SJS, 95131	814 - A6
ORMONDALE ELEM	200 SHAWNEE PASS, PTLV, 94028	810 - B6
OSTER ELEM	1855 LENCAR WY, SJS, 95124	873 - H3
OVERFELT, WILLIAM C HIGH	1835 CUNNINGHAM AV, SJS, 95122	834 - J7
PACIFIC WEST CHRISTIAN ACADEMY	1575 MANTELLI DR, GIL, 95020	977 - E1
PAINTER, BEN ELEM	500 ROUGH AND READY RD, SJS, 95133	834 - G1
PALA MID	149 N WHITE RD, SJS, 95127	834 - J2
PALO ALTO HIGH	50 EMBARCADERO RD, PA, 94301	790 - J6
PALO VERDE ELEM	3450 LOUIS RD, PA, 94303	791 - E7
PARADISE VALLEY-MACHADO ELEM	1400 LA CROSSE DR, MGH, 95037	937 - A3
PARKVIEW ELEM	330 BLUEFIELD DR, SJS, 95136	874 - G1
PAYNE, GEORGE C ELEM	3750 GLEASON AV, SJS, 95130	853 - C4
PEGASUS HIGH	1776 EDUCATIONAL PARK DR, SJS, 95133	834 - F2
PENINSULA LTD	920 PENINSULA WY, SMCo, 94025	790 - H1
PETERSON MID	1380 ROSALIA AV, SUNV, 94087	832 - G4
PIEDMONT HILLS HIGH	1377 PIEDMONT RD, SJS, 95132	814 - G4
PIEDMONT MID	955 PIEDMONT RD, SJS, 95132	814 - G5
PINEWOOD HIGH	26800 FREMONT RD, LAH, 94022	811 - B5
PINEWOOD PRIVATE LOWER CAMPUS EL	477 FREMONT AV, LALT, 94024	831 - F2
PINEWOOD PRIVATE OF LOS ALTOS EL	327 FREMONT AV, LALT, 94024	831 - F1
PIONEER HIGH	1290 BLOSSOM HILL RD, SJS, 95118	874 - C4
POMEROY ELEM	1250 POMEROY AV, SCL, 95051	833 - A4
POMEROY, MARSHALL ELEM	1505 ESCUELA PKWY, MPS, 95035	794 - A4
PONDEROSA ELEM	804 PONDEROSA AV, SUNV, 94086	832 - G2
PORTAL, LOUIS ELEM	10300 N BLANEY AV, CPTO, 95014	832 - F7
PRESENTATION HIGH	2281 PLUMMER AV, SJS, 95125	854 - A6
PRICE, IDA MID	2650 NEW JERSEY AV, SJS, 95124	873 - G1
PRIMARY PLUS	3500 AMBER DR, SJS, 95117	853 - D3
PROSPECT HIGH	18900 PROSPECT RD, SAR, 95070	852 - H5
QUEEN OF APOSTLES ELEM	4950 MITTY WY, SJS, 95129	852 - J2
QUIMBY OAK MID	3190 QUIMBY RD, SJS, 95148	855 - E1
RAINBOW BRIDGE CTR	750 N CAPITOL AV, SJS, 95133	814 - G7
RAINBOW BRIDGE CTR ELEM	1500 YOSEMITE DR, MPS, 95035	794 - D7
RAINBOW MONTESSORI ELEM	790 E DUANE AV, SUNV, 94086	812 - G6
RANCHO MILPITAS MID	1915 YELLOWSTONE AV, MPS, 95035	814 - D1
RANCHO SAN JUSTO MID	1201 RANCHO DR, HOLL, 95023	1040 - B5
RANDALL, ROBERT ELEM	1300 EDSEL DR, MPS, 95035	794 - C7
RANDOL, JAMES ELEM	762 SUNSET GLEN DR, SJS, 95123	874 - G6
REDWOOD MID	13925 FRUITVALE AV, SAR, 95070	872 - F1
REED ELEM	1524 JACOB AV, SJS, 95118	874 - B2
REGNART ELEM	1170 YORKSHIRE DR, CPTO, 95014	852 - C3
RESURRECTION ELEM	1395 HOLLENBECK AV, SUNV, 94087	832 - D4
RIVER GLEN ELEM	1088 BROADWAY, SJS, 95125	854 - A3
ROGERS, SAMUEL C MID	4835 DOYLE RD, SJS, 95129	852 - J3
ROGERS, WILLIAM R ELEM	2999 RIDGEMONT DR, SJS, 95127	835 - B5
ROLLING HILLS MID	1585 MORE AV, CMBL, 95032	872 - J2
ROSE, ALEXANDER ELEM	250 ROSWELL DR, MPS, 95035	794 - D7
ROSEMARY ELEM	401 W HAMILTON AV, CMBL, 95008	853 - D5
RUCKER ELEM	325 SANTA CLARA AV, SCIC, 95020	957 - H3
RUSKIN ELEM	1401 TURLOCK LN, SJS, 95132	814 - F4
RUSSELL, THOMAS MID	1500 ESCUELA PKWY, MPS, 95035	794 - A4
RYAN, THOMAS P ELEM	1241 MCGINNESS AV, SJS, 95127	835 - A4
SABRATO, ANN HIGH	401 BURNETT AV, MGH, 95037	916 - H3
SACRED HEART ELEM	13718 SARATOGA AV, SAR, 95070	872 - F1
SACRED HEART ELEM	670 COLLEGE ST, HOLL, 95023	1039 - J4
SACRED HEART PREP HIGH	150 VALPARAISO AV, ATN, 94027	790 - E4
SAINT ANDREWS PRIVATE ELEM	13601 SARATOGA AV, SAR, 95070	872 - F1
SAINT CHRISTOPHER ELEM	2278 BOOKSIN AV, SJS, 95125	854 - A6
SAINT CYPRIAN ELEM	195 LEOTA AV, SUNV, 94086	812 - C7
SAINT ELIZABETH SETON CATHOLIC COMM	1095 CHANNING AV, PA, 94301	791 - B4
SAINT FRANCES CABRINI ELEM	15325 WOODARD RD, SCIC, 95124	873 - F2
SAINT FRANCIS HIGH OF MTN V	1885 MIRAMONTE AV, MTVW, 94040	831 - H1
SAINT JOSEPH OF CUPERTINO ELEM	10120 N DE ANZA BLVD, CPTO, 95014	832 - E7
SAINT JOSEPHS ELEM	1120 MIRAMONTE AV, MTVW, 94040	811 - H6
SAINT JOSEPHS ELEM	50 EMILIE AV, ATN, 94027	790 - E4
SAINT LAWRENCE ACADEMY HIGH	2000 LAWRENCE CT, SCL, 95051	832 - J3
SAINT LAWRENCE ELEM	1977 SAINT LAWRENCE DR, SCL, 95051	832 - J3
SAINT LEO THE GREAT ELEM	1051 W SAN FERNANDO ST, SJS, 95126	833 - J7
SAINT LUCY ELEM	76 E KENNEDY AV, CMBL, 95008	853 - E6
SAINT MARTIN ELEM	597 CENTRAL AV, SUNV, 94086	832 - E1
SAINT MARTIN OF TOURS ELEM	300 OCONNOR DR, SJS, 95128	833 - F7
SAINT MARY	7900 CHURCH ST, GIL, 95020	977 - J2
SAINT MARYS ELEM	30 LYNDON AV, LGTS, 95030	873 - A7
SAINT NICHOLAS ELEM	12816 S EL MONTE RD, LAH, 94022	831 - D2
SAINT PATRICK ELEM	51 N 9TH ST, SJS, 95112	834 - C5
SAINT PIUS ELEM	1100 WOODSIDE RD, RDWC, 94061	790 - B2
SAINT RAYMOND ELEM	1211 ARBOR RD, MLPK, 94025	790 - F4
SAINT SIMON ELEM	1840 GRANT RD, LALT, 94024	831 - J4
SAINT THOMAS MORE	1590 BERRYESSA RD, SJS, 95133	834 - C2
SAKAMOTO ELEM	6280 SHADELANDS DR, SJS, 95123	874 - H7
SAN ANDREAS HIGH	191 ALVARADO ST, HOLL, 95023	1040 - A3
SAN ANSELMO ELEM	6670 SAN ANSELMO WY, SJS, 95119	875 - D7
SAN ANTONIO ELEM	1855 E SAN ANTONIO ST, SJS, 95116	834 - F4
SAN BENITO HIGH	1220 MONTEREY ST, HOLL, 95023	1040 - A5
SANDERS, ROBERT ELEM	3411 ROCKY MOUNTAIN DR, SJS, 95127	835 - C4
SAN JOSE ACADEMY HIGH	275 N 24TH ST, SJS, 95116	834 - D4
SAN JOSE CHRISTIAN	1300 SHEFFIELD AV, CMBL, 95008	853 - G5
SAN JUAN BAUTISTA ELEM	100 NYLAND DR, SJB, 95045	1038 - D5
SAN MARTIN-GWINN ELEM	100 NORTH ST, SCIC, 95046	937 - F6
SAN MIGUEL ELEM	777 SAN MIGUEL AV, SUNV, 94086	812 - G5
SANTA CLARA CHRISTIAN ELEM	3421 MONROE ST, SCL, 95051	832 - J1
SANTA CLARA HIGH	3000 BENTON ST, SCL, 95051	833 - A5
SANTA RITA ELEM	700 LOS ALTOS AV, LALT, 94022	811 - D5
SANTA TERESA ELEM	6200 ENCINAL DR, SJS, 95119	875 - C6
SANTA TERESA HIGH	6150 SNELL RD, SJS, 95123	874 - J6
SANTEE ELEM	1313 AUDUBON DR, SJS, 95122	834 - G7
SAN YSIDRO ELEM	2220 PACHECO PASS HWY, SCIC, 95020	978 - F4
SARATOGA ELEM	14592 OAK ST, SAR, 95070	872 - D3
SARATOGA HIGH	20300 HERRIMAN AV, SAR, 95070	872 - E1
SARTORETTE ELEM	3850 WOODFORD DR, SJS, 95124	873 - J2
SCHALLENBERGER ELEM	1280 KOCH LN, SJS, 95125	854 - B7
SCOTT LANE ELEM	1925 SCOTT BLVD, SCL, 95050	833 - D3
SEDGWICK ELEM	19200 PHIL LN, CPTO, 95014	852 - G2
SELBY LANE ELEM	170 SELBY LN, ATN, 94027	790 - B3
SEVEN TREES ELEM	3975 MIRA LOMA WY, SJS, 95111	854 - J7
SHEPPARD, WILLIAM L MID	480 ROUGH AND READY RD, SJS, 95133	834 - H1
SHERMAN OAKS ELEM	1800 FRUITDALE AV, SJS, 95128	853 - G3
SHIELDS, LESTER W ELEM	2851 GAY AV, SJS, 95127	834 - H2
SHIRAKAWA, GEORGE SR. ELEM	665 WOOL CREEK DR, SJS, 95112	854 - G2
SIERRA ELEM	220 BLAKE AV, SCL, 95051	833 - A7
SIERRAMONT MID	3155 KIMLEE DR, SJS, 95132	814 - F4
SILVER CREEK HIGH	3434 SILVER CREEK RD, SJS, 95121	855 - B4
SILVER OAK ELEM	5000 FARNSWORTH DR, SJS, 95138	855 - G7
SIMONDS ELEM	6515 GRAPEVINE WY, SJS, 95120	894 - D1
SINNOTT, JOHN ELEM	2025 YELLOWSTONE AV, MPS, 95035	814 - E1
SLATER, KENNETH N ELEM	325 GLADYS AV, MTVW, 94043	812 - B5
SLONAKER, HARRY ELEM	1601 CUNNINGHAM AV, SJS, 95122	834 - H7
SMALL WORLD ELEM	1271 ALMA CT, SJS, 95112	854 - D2
SMITH, JAMES FRANKLIN ELEM	2220 WOODBURY LN, SJS, 95121	855 - D5
SMITH, KATHERINE R ELEM	2025 CLARICE DR, SJS, 95122	835 - A7
SOUTHBAY CHRISTIAN ELEM	1134 MIRAMONTE AV, MTVW, 94040	811 - H6
SOUTH PENINSULA HEBREW DAY ELEM	1030 ASTORIA DR, SUNV, 94087	832 - B4
SOUTHSIDE ELEM	4991 SOUTHSIDE RD, SBnC, 95023	1060 - E5
SOUTH VALLEY CHRISTIAN ELEM	145 WRIGHT AV, MGH, 95037	916 - J6
SOUTH VALLEY JR HIGH	385 IOOF AV, GIL, 95020	978 - A2
SPANGLER, ANTHONY ELEM	140 N ABBOTT AV, MPS, 95035	793 - J7
SPRINGER ELEM	1120 ROSE AV, MTVW, 94040	831 - G1
SPRING GROVE ELEM	500 SPRING GROVE RD, SBnC, 95023	1020 - F2
STANFORD, JANE LATHROP MID	480 E MEADOW DR, PA, 94306	811 - D1
ST CATHERINE ELEM	17500 S PEAK AV, MGH, 95037	916 - J7
ST CLARE ELEM	725 WASHINGTON ST, SCL, 95050	833 - E4
STEINBECK MID	820 STEINBECK DR, SJS, 95123	874 - F4
STEVENS CREEK ELEM	10300 AINSWORTH DR, CPTO, 95014	832 - A7
STIPE, SAMUEL ELEM	5000 LYNG DR, SJS, 95111	875 - B1
ST JOHN THE BAPTIST CATHOLIC ELEM	360 S ABEL ST, MPS, 95035	814 - A1
ST JOHN VIANNEY ELEM	4601 HYLAND AV, SJS, 95127	834 - J1
ST JUSTIN ELEM	2655 HOMESTEAD RD, SCL, 95051	833 - B5
STOCKLMEIR, LOUIS V ELEM	592 DUNHOLME WY, SUNV, 94087	832 - E5
STONEGATE ELEM	2605 GASSMANN DR, SJS, 95121	854 - H3
STRATFORD	1196 LIME DR, SUNV, 94087	832 - B3
STRATFORD	220 KENSINGTON WY, LGTS, 95032	873 - G5
ST STEPHENS ELEM	500 SHAWNEE LN, SJS, 95123	874 - H5
ST TIMOTHY ELEM	5100 CAMDEN AV, SJS, 95124	873 - J5
ST VICTOR ELEM	3150 SIERRA RD, SJS, 95132	814 - G5
SUMMERDALE ELEM	1100 SUMMERDALE DR, SJS, 95132	814 - G6
SUNNYSLOPE ELEM	1475 MEMORIAL DR, HOLL, 95023	1040 - C5
SUNNYVALE CHRISTIAN ELEM	445 S MARY AV, SUNV, 94086	812 - C7
SUNNYVALE MID	1080 MANGO AV, SUNV, 94087	832 - B2
SUTTER ELEM	3200 FORBES AV, SCL, 95051	832 - J6
SYLVANDALE MID	653 SYLVANDALE AV, SJS, 95111	854 - J6
TAYLOR, BERTHA ELEM	410 SAUTNER DR, SJS, 95123	875 - B7
TERMAN MID	655 ARASTRADERO RD, PA, 94306	811 - C3
TERRELL ELEM	3925 PEARL AV, SJS, 95136	874 - D1
THEUERKAUF ELEM	1625 SAN LUIS AV, MTVW, 94043	811 - H3
TOYON ELEM	995 BARD ST, SJS, 95127	814 - H6
TRACE, MERITT ELEM	651 DANA AV, SJS, 95126	833 - G7
TRES PINOS ELEM	5635 AIRLINE HWY, SBnC, 95023	1060 - H3
TRINITY EPISCOPAL ELEM	2650 SAND HILL RD, MLPK, 94025	810 - D1
UNION MID	2130 LOS GATOS-ALMADEN RD, SJS, 95124	873 - F5
VALLE VISTA ELEM	2400 FLINT AV, SJS, 95148	835 - D6

FEATURE NAME	Address City, ZIP Code	PAGE-GRID
VALLEY CHRISTIAN HIGH	100 SKYWAY DR, SJS, 95111	874 - J1
VALLEY CHRISTIAN	1450 LEIGH AV, SJS, 95125	853 - H4
VAN METER, LOUISE ELEM	16445 LOS GATOS BLVD, LGTS, 95032	873 - C6
VARGAS ELEM	1054 CARSON DR, SUNV, 94086	812 - C7
VERITAS CHRISTIAN ACADEMY	3800 BLACKFORD AV, SJS, 95117	853 - C2
VINCI PK ELEM	1311 VINCI PARK WY, SJS, 95131	814 - D7
WALDORF OF THE PENINSULA ELEM	11311 MORA DR, LALT, 94024	831 - F1
WALSH, PA ELEM	353 W MAIN AV, MGH, 95037	916 - J7
WASHINGTON ELEM	100 OAK ST, SJS, 95110	854 - C1
WASHINGTON ELEM	270 WASHINGTON ST, SCL, 95050	833 - F5
WELLER, JOSEPH ELEM	345 BOULDER ST, MPS, 95035	794 - A3
WESTMONT HIGH	4805 WESTMONT AV, SJS, 95008	873 - A1
WEST VALLEY ELEM	1635 BELLEVILLE WY, SUNV, 94087	832 - A5
WESTWOOD ELEM	435 SARATOGA AV, SCL, 95050	833 - D6
WHALEY ELEM	2655 ALVIN AV, SJS, 95121	854 - J2
WILCOX, ADRIAN HIGH	3250 MONROE ST, SCL, 95051	833 - A2
WILLIAMS ELEM	1150 RAJKOVICH WY, SJS, 95120	894 - F3
WILLOW GLEN ELEM	1425 LINCOLN AV, SJS, 95125	854 - A4
WILLOW GLEN HIGH	2001 COTTLE AV, SJS, 95125	854 - A5
WILLOW GLEN MID	2105 COTTLE AV, SJS, 95125	854 - A5
WILLOW OAKS ELEM	620 WILLOW RD, MLPK, 94025	790 - J2
WILSON HIGH	1840 BENTON ST, SCL, 95050	833 - D5
WINDMILL SPRINGS ELEM	2880 AETNA WY, SJS, 95121	854 - J3
WOODLAND ELEM	360 LA CUESTA DR, SMCo, 94028	810 - E3
WOODSIDE HIGH	199 CHURCHILL AV, SMCo, 94062	790 - A4
WOODSIDE PRIORY	302 PORTOLA RD, PTLV, 94028	810 - C7
YAVNEH DAY ELEM	14855 OKA RD, LGTS, 95032	873 - C3
YAVNEH DAY	3800 BLACKFORD AV, SJS, 95117	853 - C2
YERBA BUENA HIGH	1855 LUCRETIA AV, SJS, 95122	854 - G1
ZANKER, PEARL ELEM	1585 FALLEN LEAF DR, MPS, 95035	814 - A3

SHOPPING CENTERS

FEATURE NAME	Address City, ZIP Code	PAGE-GRID
ALMADEN PLAZA	5353 ALMADEN EXWY, SJS, 95118	874 - C3
CAPITOL SQUARE MALL	390 N CAPITOL AV, SJS, 95133	834 - G1
EASTRIDGE	1 EASTRIDGE MALL, SJS, 95122	855 - A1
GILROY PREMIUM OUTLETS	681 LEAVESLEY RD, GIL, 95020	978 - B1
GREAT MALL	447 GREAT MALL DR, MPS, 95035	814 - A2
MERVYNS PLAZA	2058 EL CAMINO REAL, SCL, 95050	833 - C4
SAN ANTONIO SHOPPING CTR	2550 W EL CAMINO REAL, MTVW, 94040	811 - E4
SANTANA ROW	355 SANTANA RW, SJS, 95128	853 - E1
SILICON VALLEY WAVE	2502 TOWN CENTER LN, SUNV, 94086	812 - E7
STANFORD SHOPPING CTR	180 EL CAMINO REAL, PA, 94304	790 - G5
VALLCO FASHION PK	10123 N WOLFE RD, CPTO, 95014	832 - G7
WESTFIELD SHOPPINGTOWN OAKRIDGE	925 BLOSSOM HILL RD, SJS, 95123	874 - E3
WESTFIELD SHOPPINGTOWN VALLEY FAIR	2855 STEVENS CREEK BLVD, SCL, 95050	853 - E1
WESTGATE MALL	1600 SARATOGA AV, SJS, 95129	852 - J5

TRANSPORTATION

FEATURE NAME	PAGE-GRID
ACE GREAT AMERICA STA, SCL	813 - C3
ACE SAN JOSE DIRIDON STA, SJS	834 - A7
ALUM ROCK STA, SJS	834 - J3
ALUM ROCK TRANSIT CTR, SJS	834 - J3
AMTRAK SANTA CLARA STA, SCL	813 - C3
BERRYESSA STA, SJS	814 - E6
CALTRAIN ATHERTON STA, ATN	790 - E2
CALTRAIN BLOSSOM HILL STA, SJS	875 - C4
CALTRAIN CALIFORNIA AV STA, PA	791 - B7
CALTRAIN CAPITOL STA, SJS	854 - G6
CALTRAIN COLLEGE PK STA, SJS	833 - H5
CALTRAIN GILROY STA, GIL	978 - A3
CALTRAIN LAWRENCE STA, SUNV	832 - J1
CALTRAIN MENLO PK STA, MLPK	790 - F3
CALTRAIN MORGAN HILL STA, MGH	917 - A7
CALTRAIN MTN VIEW STA, MTVW	811 - J5
CALTRAIN PALO ALTO STA, PA	790 - H5
CALTRAIN SAN ANTONIO STA, MTVW	811 - F3
CALTRAIN SAN JOSE DIRIDON STA, SJS	834 - A7
CALTRAIN SAN MARTIN STA, SCIC	937 - E6
CALTRAIN SANTA CLARA STA, SCL	833 - F4
CALTRAIN STANFORD STA, PA	790 - J5
CALTRAIN SUNNYVALE STA, SUNV	812 - E7
CALTRAIN TAMIEN STA, SJS	854 - C3
CROPLEY STA, SJS	814 - C4
GREAT MALL/MAIN STA, MPS	814 - A2
GREYHOUND BUS STA, SJS	834 - B6
GREYHOUND BUS STA, GIL	978 - A3
HOSTETTER STA, SJS	814 - E5
MCKEE STA, SJS	834 - G1
MONTAGUE STA, MPS	814 - B3
PASEO DE ANTONIO VTA RAIL STA, SJS	834 - C6
PENITENCIA CREEK STA, SJS	814 - F7
REAMWOOD VTA RAIL STA, SUNV	813 - A4
RIVER OAKS VTA RAIL STA, SJS	813 - F4
SAINT JAMES VTA RAIL STA, SJS	834 - B6
SAINT JAMES VTA RAIL STA, SJS	834 - B6
SANTA CLARA VTA RAIL STA, SJS	834 - B6
SANTA CLARA VTA RAIL STA, SJS	834 - B6
SANTA TERESA VTA RAIL STA, SJS	875 - D6
SNELL VTA RAIL STA, SJS	874 - J4
VTA ALMADEN RAIL STA, SJS	874 - D5
VTA BASCOM RAIL STA, SJS	853 - G4
VTA BAYPOINTE RAIL STA, SJS	813 - F3
VTA BAYSHORE NASA RAIL STA, SCIC	812 - C3
VTA BLOSSOM HILL RAIL STA, SJS	874 - G4
VTA BONAVENTURA RAIL STA, SJS	813 - G6
VTA BORREGAS RAIL STA, SUNV	812 - F2
VTA BRANHAM RAIL STA, SJS	874 - E2
VTA CAPITOL RAIL STA, SJS	874 - E1
VTA CHAMPION RAIL STA, SJS	813 - E3
VTA CHILDRENS DISCOVERY MUS STA, SJS	834 - B7
VTA CISCO WY RAIL STA, SJS	813 - G2
VTA CIVIC CTR RAIL STA, SJS	834 - A4
VTA COMPONENT RAIL STA, SJS	813 - G7
VTA CONV CTR RAIL STA, SJS	834 - B7
VTA COTTLE RAIL STA, SJS	875 - C5
VTA CROSSMAN RAIL STA, SUNV	812 - G3
VTA CURTNER RAIL STA, SJS	854 - D5
VTA DOWNTOWN CAMPBELL RAIL STA, CMBL	853 - E6
VTA DOWNTOWN MTN VIEW RAIL STA, MTVW	811 - J5
VTA EVELYN RAIL STA, MTVW	812 - A5
VTA FAIR OAKS RAIL STA, SUNV	812 - G4
VTA FRUITDALE RAIL STA, SJS	853 - H3
VTA GISH RAIL STA, SJS	833 - J2
VTA GREAT AMERICA RAIL STA, SCL	813 - B4
VTA HAMILTON RAIL STA, CMBL	853 - F5
VTA I-880 & MILPITAS RAIL STA, MPS	813 - H2
VTA JAPANTOWN/AYER RAIL STA, SJS	834 - A5
VTA KARINA COURT RAIL STA, SJS	833 - H1
VTA LICK MILL RAIL STA, SCL	813 - C3
VTA LOCKHEED MARTIN RAIL STA, SUNV	812 - E3
VTA METRO/ RAIL STA, SJS	833 - J1
VTA MIDDLEFIELD RAIL STA, MTVW	812 - C4
VTA MOFFETT PK STA, SUNV	812 - E4
VTA OAKRIDGE RAIL STA, SJS	874 - E4
VTA OHLONE-CHYNOWETH RAIL STA, SJS	874 - E3
VTA OLD IRONSIDES RAIL STA, SCL	813 - B4
VTA ORCHARD RAIL STA, SJS	813 - G5
VTA PAS D ANTONIO RAIL STA, SJS	834 - B7
VTA RACE RAIL STA, SJS	853 - J2
VTA SAN FERNANDO RAIL STA, SJS	834 - A7
VTA SAN JOSE DIRIDON RAIL STA, SJS	834 - A7
VTA TAMIEN RAIL STA, SJS	854 - C2
VTA TASMAN RAIL STA, SJS	813 - E3
VTA VIENNA RAIL STA, SUNV	812 - H4
VTA VIRGINIA LIGHT RAIL STA, SJS	854 - B1
VTA WHISMAN RAIL STA, MTVW	812 - B5
VTA WINCHESTER RAIL STA, CMBL	853 - E7

VISITOR INFORMATION

FEATURE NAME	Address City, ZIP Code	PAGE-GRID
GILROY VISITORS BUREAU	MONTEREY ST & IOOF AVE, GIL, 95020	978 - A2
SAN JOSE CONV & VISITORS BUREAU	408 ALMADEN BLVD, SJS, 95110	834 - B7
SANTA CLARA VISITORS BUREAU	2200 LAURELWOOD RD, SCL, 95054	813 - C6
VISITOR CTR	1751 GRAND BLVD, SJS, 95002	793 - D6

CUT ALONG DOTTED LINE

The Thomas Guide®

Thank you for purchasing this Rand McNally Thomas Guide!
We value your comments and suggestions.

Please help us serve you better by completing this postage-paid reply card.
This information is for internal use ONLY and will not be distributed or sold to any external third party.

Missing pages? Maybe not... Please refer to the "Using Your Street Guide" page for further explanation.

Thomas Guide Title: Santa Clara County **ISBN-13# 978-0-5288-6060-7** **MKT: SFB**

Today's Date: ______________ Gender: ☐M ☐F Age Group: ☐18-24 ☐25-31 ☐32-40 ☐41-50 ☐51-64 ☐65+

1. What type of industry do you work in?
   ☐Real Estate ☐Trucking ☐Delivery ☐Construction ☐Utilities ☐Government
   ☐Retail ☐Sales ☐Transportation ☐Landscape ☐Service & Repair
   ☐Courier ☐Automotive ☐Insurance ☐Medical ☐Police/Fire/First Response
   ☐Other, please specify: ______________
2. What type of job do you have in this industry? ______________
3. Where did you purchase this Thomas Guide? (store name & city) ______________
4. Why did you purchase this Thomas Guide? ______________
5. How often do you purchase an updated Thomas Guide? ☐Annually ☐2 yrs. ☐3-5 yrs. ☐Other: ______________
6. Where do you use it? ☐Primarily in the car ☐Primarily in the office ☐Primarily at home ☐Other: ______________
7. How do you use it? ☐Exclusively for business ☐Primarily for business but also for personal or leisure use
   ☐Both work and personal evenly ☐Primarily for personal use ☐Exclusively for personal use
8. What do you use your Thomas Guide for?
   ☐Find Addresses ☐In-route navigation ☐Planning routes ☐Other: ______________
   Find points of interest: ☐Schools ☐Parks ☐Buildings ☐Shopping Centers ☐Other: ______________
9. How often do you use it? ☐Daily ☐Weekly ☐Monthly ☐Other: ______________
10. Do you use the internet for maps and/or directions? ☐Yes ☐No
11. How often do you use the internet for directions? ☐Daily ☐Weekly ☐Monthly ☐Other: ______________
12. Do you use any of the following mapping products in addition to your Thomas Guide?
    ☐Folded paper maps ☐Folded laminated maps ☐Wall maps ☐GPS ☐PDA ☐In-car navigation ☐Phone maps
13. What features, if any, would you like to see added to your Thomas Guide? ______________
14. What features or information do you find most useful in your Rand McNally Thomas Guide? (please specify)
15. Please provide any additional comments or suggestions you have. ______________

We strive to provide you with the most current updated information available if you know of a map correction, please notify us here.

Where is the correction? Map Page #: __________ Grid #: __________ Index Page #: __________

Nature of the correction: ☐Street name missing ☐Street name misspelled ☐Street information incorrect
☐Incorrect location for point of interest ☐Index error ☐Other: ______________

Detail: ______________

CUT ALONG DOTTED LINE

I would like to receive information about updated editions and special offers from Rand McNally
☐via e-mail E-mail address: ______________
☐via postal mail
Your Name: ______________ Company (if used for work): ______________
Address: ______________ City/State/ZIP: ______________

Thank you for your time and help. We are working to serve you better.
This information is for internal use ONLY and will not be distributed or sold to any external third party.

TG-noCD.06

✹ RAND M^cNALLY

The most trusted name on the map.

You'll never need to ask for directions again with these Rand McNally products!

- EasyFinder® Laminated Maps
- Folded Maps
- Street Guides
- Wall Maps
- CustomView Wall Maps
- Road Atlases
- Motor Carriers' Road Atlases

SGTG_07

The Thomas Guide®

San Mateo County
street guide

Contents

Introduction

Maps

Lists and Indexes

RAND McNALLY

Rand McNally Consumer Affairs
P.O. Box 7600
Chicago, IL 60680-9915
randmcnally.com

For comments or suggestions, please call
(800) 777-MAPS (-6277)
or email us at:
consumeraffairs@randmcnally.com

Legend

- Freeway
- Interchange/ramp
- Highway
- Primary road
- Secondary road
- Minor road
- Restricted road
- Alley
- Unpaved road
- Tunnel
- Toll road
- High occupancy vehicle lane
- Stacked multiple roadways
- Proposed road
- Proposed freeway
- Freeway under construction
- One-way road
- Two-way road
- Trail, walkway
- Stairs
- Railroad
- Rapid transit
- Rapid transit, underground

- Ferry
- City boundary
- County boundary
- State boundary
- International boundary
- Military base, Indian reservation
- Township, range, rancho
- River, creek, shoreline
- 98607 ZIP code boundary, ZIP code
- 5 Interstate
- 5 Interstate (Business)
- 3 U.S. highway
- 1 4 8 9 State highways
- Carpool lane
- A Street list marker
- Street name continuation
- Street name change
- Station (train, bus)
- Building (see List of Abbreviations page)
- Building footprint
- Public elementary school
- Public high school

- Private elementary school
- Private high school
- Fire station
- Library
- Mission
- Campground
- H Hospital
- Mountain
- Section corner
- Boat launch
- Gate, locks, barricades
- Lighthouse
- Major shopping center
- Dry lake, beach
- Dam
- Intermittent lake, marsh
- 29 Exit number
- Caltrain Caltrain Station
- samTrans samTrans Transfer/ Park n Ride Centers

we've got you COVERED

Rand McNally's broad selection of products is perfect for your every need. Whether you're looking for the convenience of write-on wipe-off laminated maps, extra maps for every car, or a Road Atlas to plan your next vacation or to use as a reference, Rand McNally has you covered.

Street Guides

Alameda County
Alameda & Contra Costa Counties
Bay Area Metro
Contra Costa County
Marin & Sonoma Counties
Monterey Bay
Napa & Solano Counties
Napa & Sonoma Counties
Sacramento County
Sacramento & Solano Counties
San Francisco & Marin Counties
San Francisco & San Mateo Counties
Santa Clara County
Santa Clara & San Mateo Counties
San Francisco/ Northern Peninsula Cities
San Francisco Bay Area Regional
San Jose/ Silicon Valley
San Mateo/ Redwood City
Santa Cruz/ Watsonville
Santa Rosa/ Sonoma

Folded Maps

EasyFinder® Laminated Maps

California
Concord/ Walnut Creek
Marin County
Monterey/ Carmel
North Bay & the Wine Country
Northern California
Oakland/ Berkeley
Peninsula Cities
San Francisco
San Francisco Bay Area Regional
San Jose/ Santa Clara
Silicon Valley

Paper Maps

California
Citrus Heights/ Carmichael
Concord/ Antioch/ Walnut Creek/ Danville
Fremont/ Hayward
Livermore/ Pleasanton
Marin County
Monterey/ Carmel/ Salinas
Napa/ Fairfield
Oakland/ Berkeley/ Richmond

Wall Maps

Bay Area to Sacramento Regional
California Arterial

Road Atlases

California Road Atlas
Road Atlas
Road Atlas & Travel Guide
Large Scale Road Atlas
Midsize Road Atlas
Deluxe Midsize Road Atlas
Pocket Road Atlas

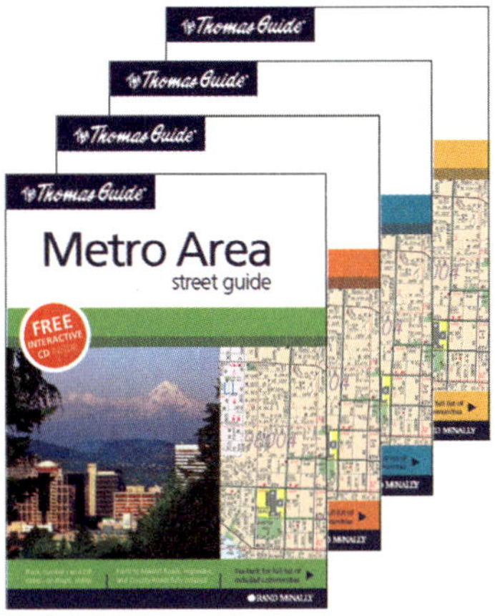

Wherever Rand McNally products are sold or at
www.randmcnally.com

SEE SF 666 MAP

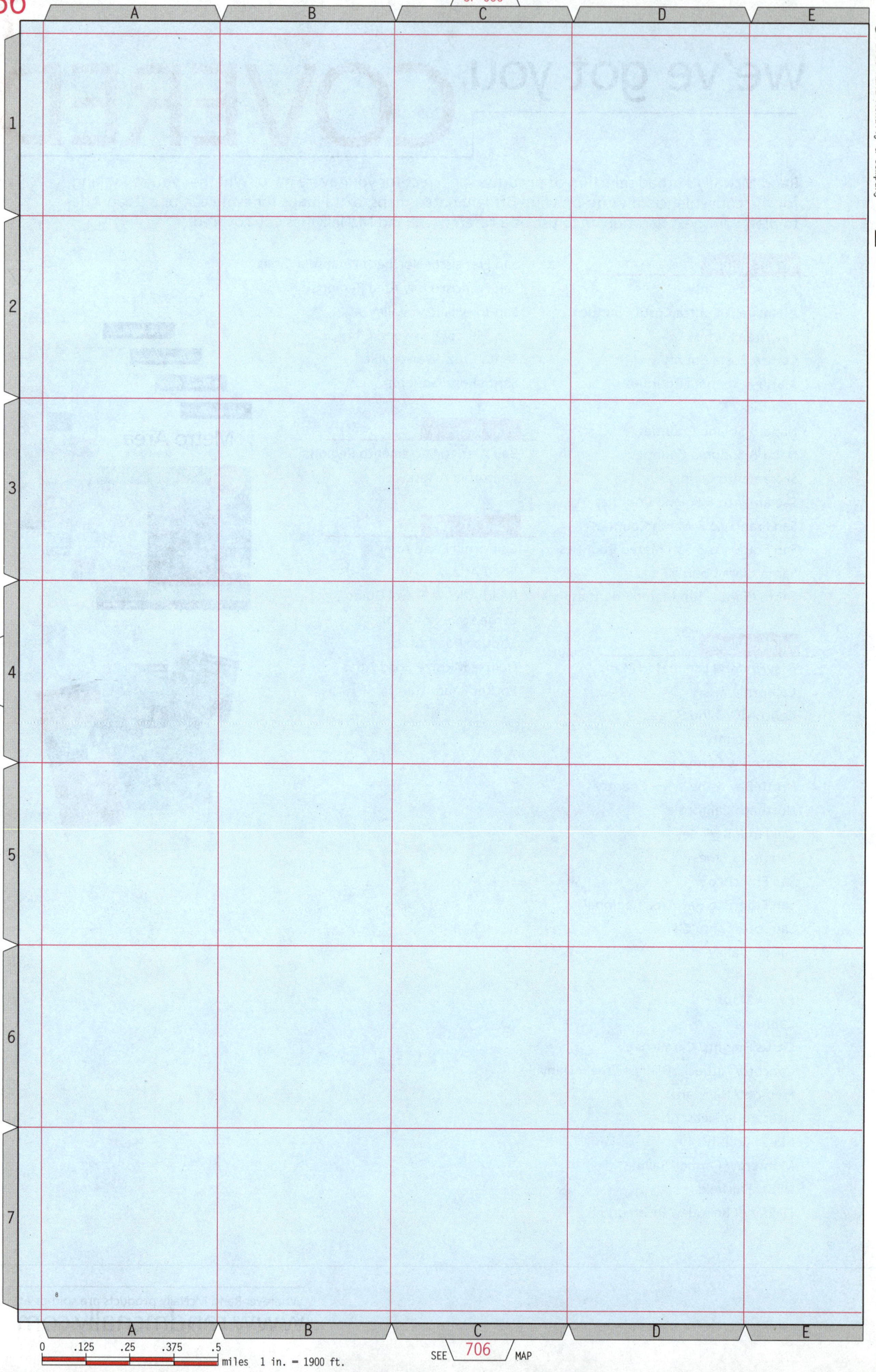

SEE B MAP

SEE 706 MAP

0 .125 .25 .375 .5 miles 1 in. = 1900 ft.

SEE SF 666 MAP
SEE 706 MAP
SEE 687 MAP
SAN MATEO CO.
© 2008 Rand McNally & Company
PACIFIC
OCEAN
GOLDEN GATE
NATIONAL
RECREATION
AREA
HANG GLIDING
HARDING PARK MUNICIPAL GOLF COURSE
LAKE MERCED
JOHN MUIR DR
TRAP & SKEET RANGE
SAN FRANCISCO
94132
THE OLYMPIC COUNTRY CLUB
LAKE SHORE
CLUBHOUSE
SAN FRANCISCO CO
SAN MATEO CO
THE OLYMPIC COUNTRY CLUB
SKYLINE
FLEETWOOD
NORTHGATE AV
WESTMONT
EASTGATE
N MAYFAIR
GLENWOOD DR
GARDEN GROVE
FAIRMONT
WESTON DR
THORNTON STATE BEACH
94015
JOHN DALY BLVD
MAYFAIR
WESTBROOK
ASHLAND
BELFORD
LAKEWOOD
CLIFTON
FAIRLAWN AV
WILDWOOD AV
S MAYFAIR
PARK MANOR DR
OAKMONT DR
SOUTHGATE
CASTLE
GLENROSE
LYNVALE CT
ROSLYN CT
HILLVIEW CT
SKYLINE
T3S
CRESTON AV
87TH ST
BROOKLAWN AV
MONTCLAIR AV
FERNWOOD AV
WESTRIDGE AV
PALISADES DR
PALISADES PARK
SEACLIFF AV
CRESTVIEW AV
MORNINGSIDE DR
WESTMOOR AV
SKYLINE BLVD
11
SEAVIEW DR
UPLAND AV
DR
DALY
CITY
AVALON
SKYLINE DR
NORTHRIDGE PARK
NORTHRIDGE DR
CARMEL AV
HIGHLAND AV
EATON AV
WESTBRAE DR
WAVECREST DR
MENLO AV
HIGATE
OCEANSIDE DR
14
35
E
F
G
H
J
1
2
3
4
5
6
7
0
.125
.25
.375
.5
miles 1 in. = 1900 ft.

SEE SF 667 MAP

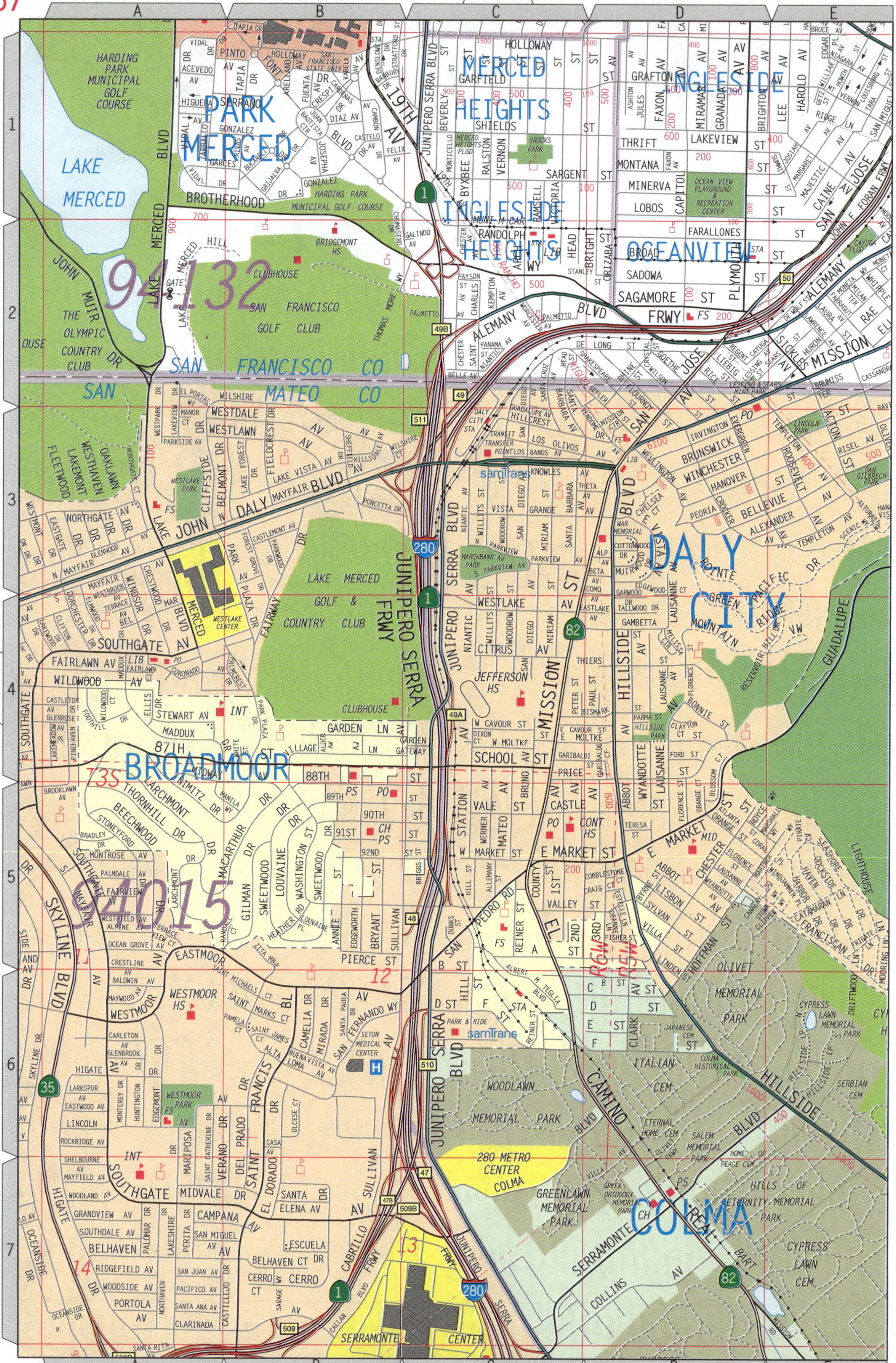
HARDING PARK MUNICIPAL GOLF COURSE
LAKE MERCED
PARK MERCED
MERCED HEIGHTS
INGLESIDE
INGLESIDE HEIGHTS
OCEANVIEW
94132
SAN FRANCISCO GOLF CLUB
THE OLYMPIC COUNTRY CLUB
SAN FRANCISCO CO
SAN MATEO CO
LAKE MERCED GOLF & COUNTRY CLUB
JUNIPERO SERRA FRWY
DALY CITY
BROADMOOR
94015
OLIVET MEMORIAL PARK
CYPRESS LAWN MEMORIAL PARK
WOODLAWN MEMORIAL PARK
280 METRO CENTER COLMA
GREENLAWN MEMORIAL PARK
HILLS OF ETERNITY MEMORIAL PARK
COLMA
SERRAMONTE CENTER
SKYLINE BLVD
JOHN DALY BLVD
MISSION ST
HILLSIDE BLVD
EL CAMINO REAL
SERRAMONTE BLVD
SOUTHGATE AV
WESTLAKE CENTER
JEFFERSON HS
WESTMOOR HS
SETON MEDICAL CENTER
ALEMANY BLVD
SAN JOSE AV
GENEVA AV

0 .125 .25 .375 .5 miles 1 in. = 1900 ft.

SEE 686 MAP

SEE 707 MAP

SEE SF 667 MAP

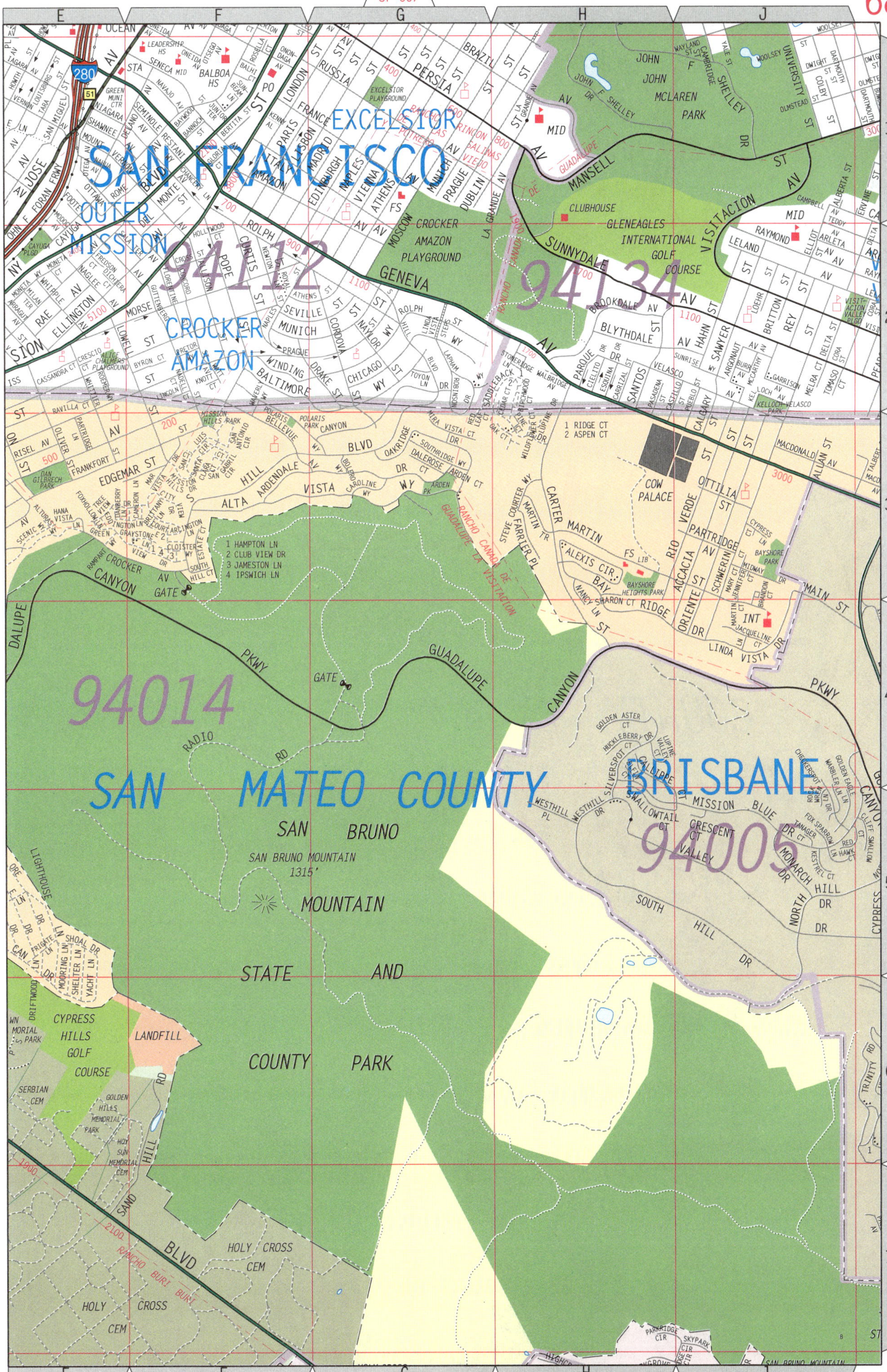

SEE 688 MAP
SEE 707 MAP

0 .125 .25 .375 .5 miles 1 in. = 1900 ft.

SEE SF 668 MAP

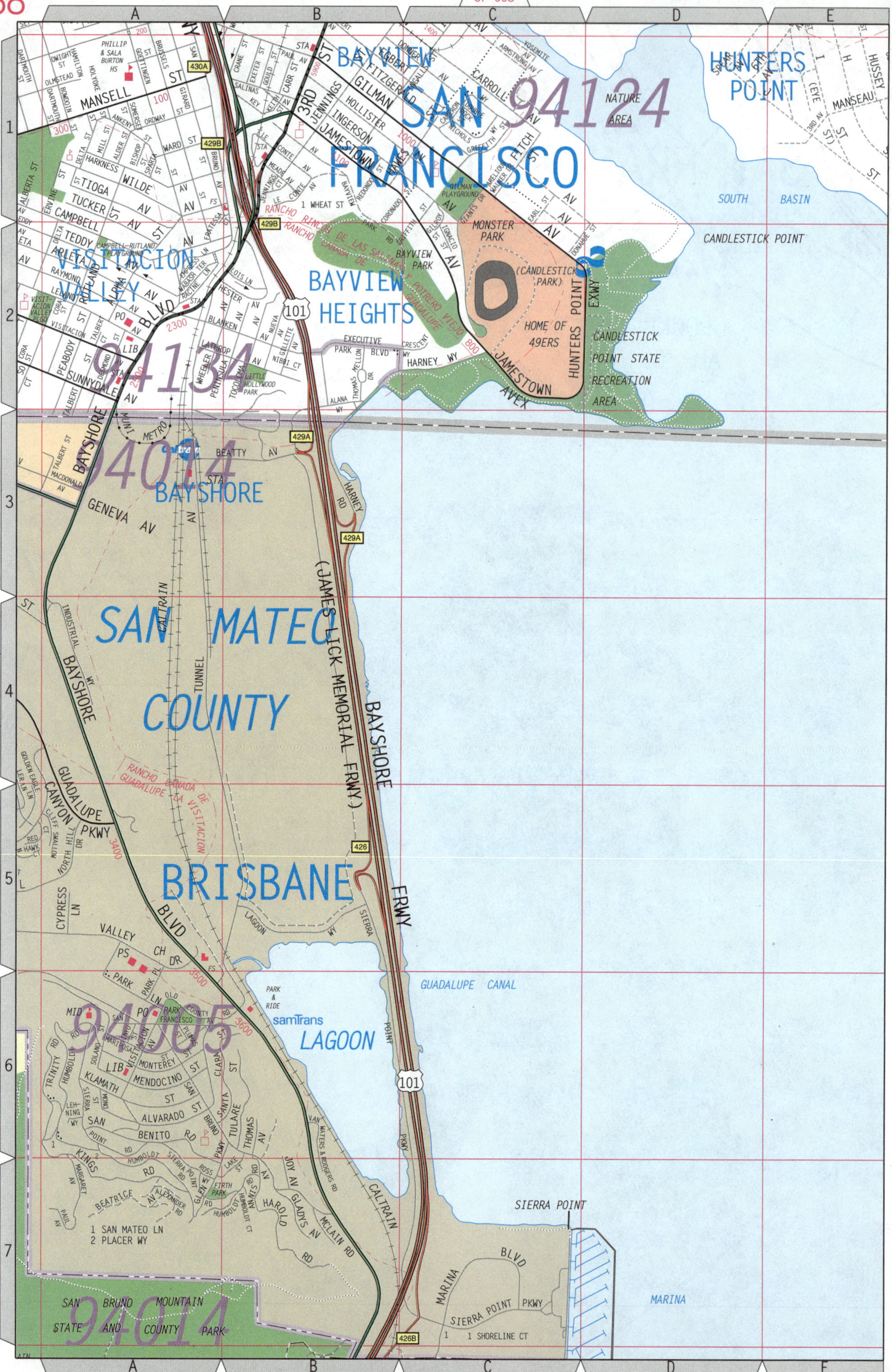
SAN FRANCISCO
94124
HUNTERS POINT
BAYVIEW
VISITACION VALLEY
BAYVIEW HEIGHTS
94134
MONSTER PARK
(CANDLESTICK PARK)
HOME OF 49ERS
CANDLESTICK POINT STATE RECREATION AREA
CANDLESTICK POINT
SOUTH BASIN
NATURE AREA
BAYVIEW PARK
GILMAN PLAYGROUND
94014
BAYSHORE
SAN MATEO COUNTY
BRISBANE
(JAMES LICK MEMORIAL FRWY)
BAYSHORE FRWY
BAYSHORE BLVD
GENEVA AV
GUADALUPE CANYON PKWY
RANCHO GUADALUPE LA VISITACION
LAGOON
GUADALUPE CANAL
SIERRA POINT
SIERRA POINT PKWY
MARINA BLVD
MARINA
94005
SAN BRUNO MOUNTAIN STATE AND COUNTY PARK
1 SAN MATEO LN
2 PLACER WY
1 SHORELINE CT
1 WHEAT ST

SEE 687 MAP
SEE 708 MAP
0 .125 .25 .375 .5 miles 1 in. = 1900 ft.

E
F
G
H
J
1
2
3
4
5
6
7
SEE SF 668 MAP
SEE B MAP
SEE 708 MAP
H
HUSSEY
COCHRANE ST
MORRELL ST
MANSEAU
ST
ST
ST
ST
MAHAN ST
SAN FRANCISCO CO
SAN MATEO CO
SAN FRANCISCO BAY
0 .125 .25 .375 .5
miles 1 in. = 1900 ft.

SEE 686 MAP

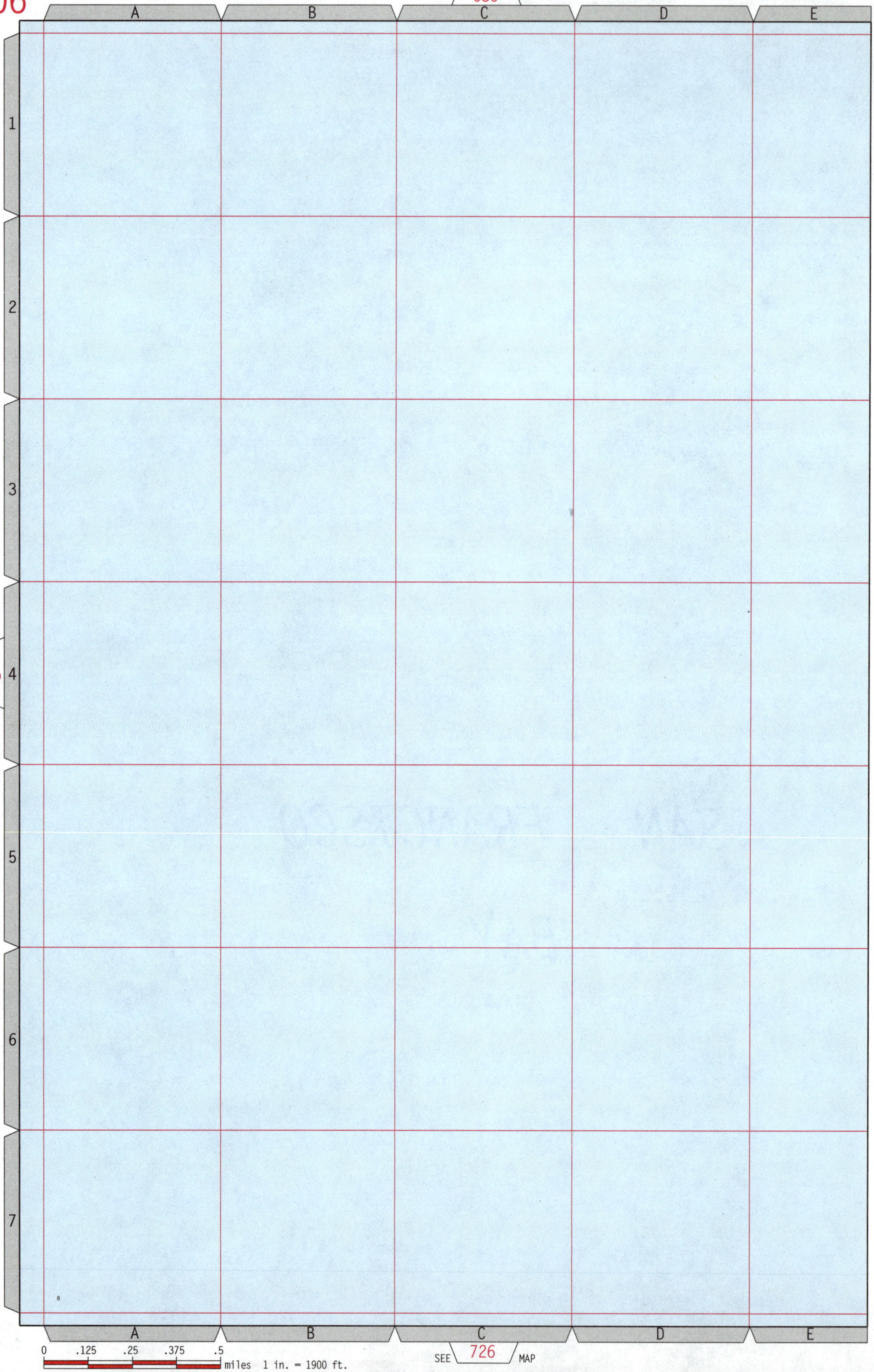

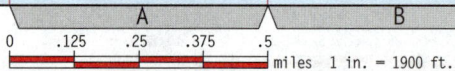

SEE B MAP

0 .125 .25 .375 .5 miles 1 in. = 1900 ft.

SEE 726 MAP

SEE 686 MAP

SEE 726 MAP

0 .125 .25 .375 .5 miles 1 in. = 1900 ft.

SAN MATEO CO.

SEE 687 MAP

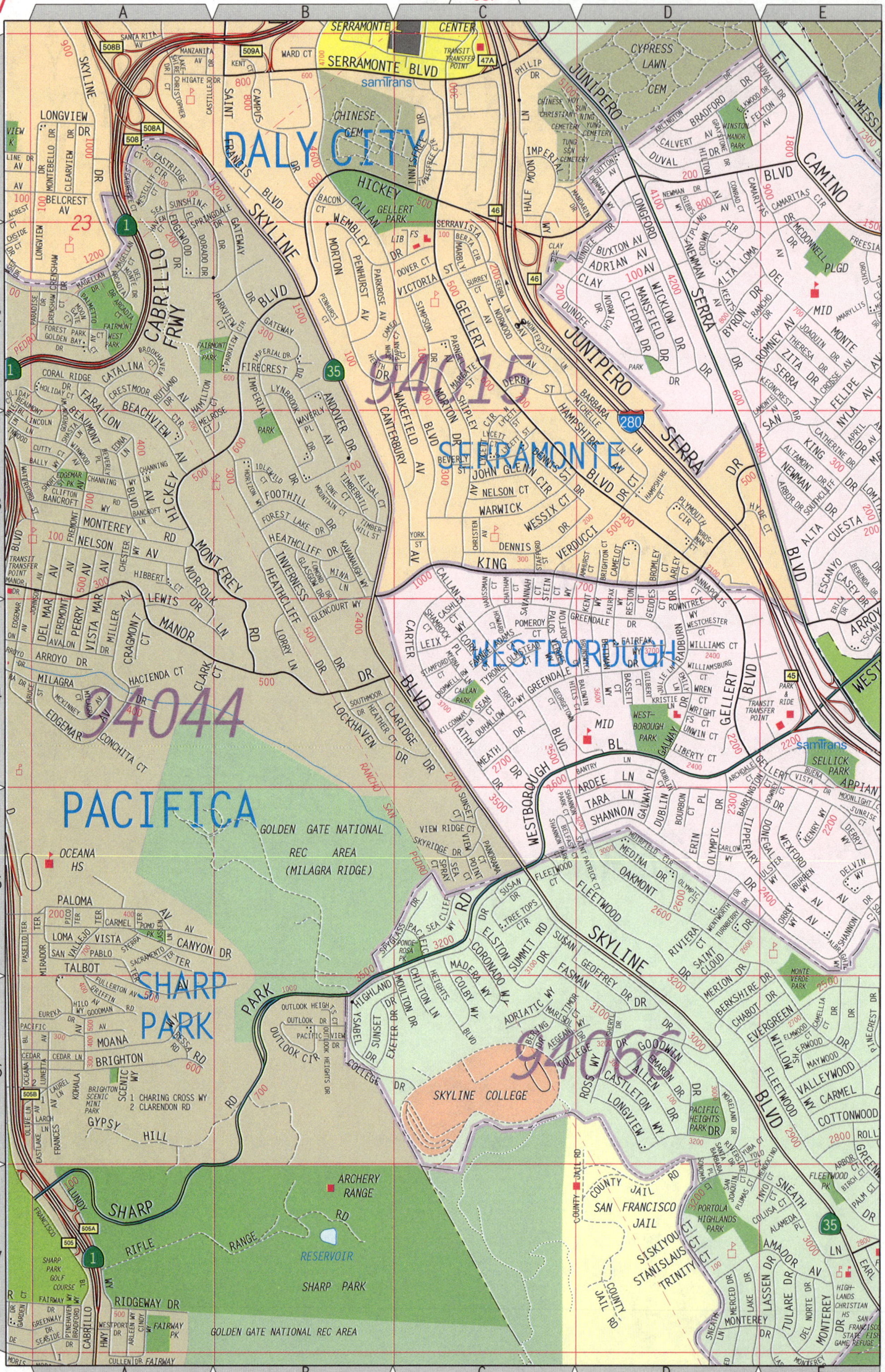

DALY CITY
94015
SERRAMONTE
WESTBOROUGH
94044
PACIFICA
SHARP PARK
94066
SERRAMONTE CENTER
SERRAMONTE BLVD
CHINESE CEM
CYPRESS LAWN CEM
GELLERT PARK
SKYLINE BLVD
JUNIPERO SERRA BLVD
CABRILLO FRWY
HICKEY BLVD
WESTBOROUGH BLVD
GOLDEN GATE NATIONAL REC AREA (MILAGRA RIDGE)
OCEANA HS
SKYLINE COLLEGE
COUNTY JAIL SAN FRANCISCO JAIL
ARCHERY RANGE
RESERVOIR
SHARP PARK
GOLDEN GATE NATIONAL REC AREA
SHARP PARK GOLF COURSE
WEST-BOROUGH PARK
SELLICK PARK
MONTE VERDE PARK
PORTOLA HIGHLANDS PARK
PACIFIC HEIGHTS PARK
FAIRWAY PK
© 2008 Rand McNally & Company
0 .125 .25 .375 .5 miles 1 in. = 1900 ft.

SEE 706 MAP

SEE 727 MAP

SEE 687 MAP

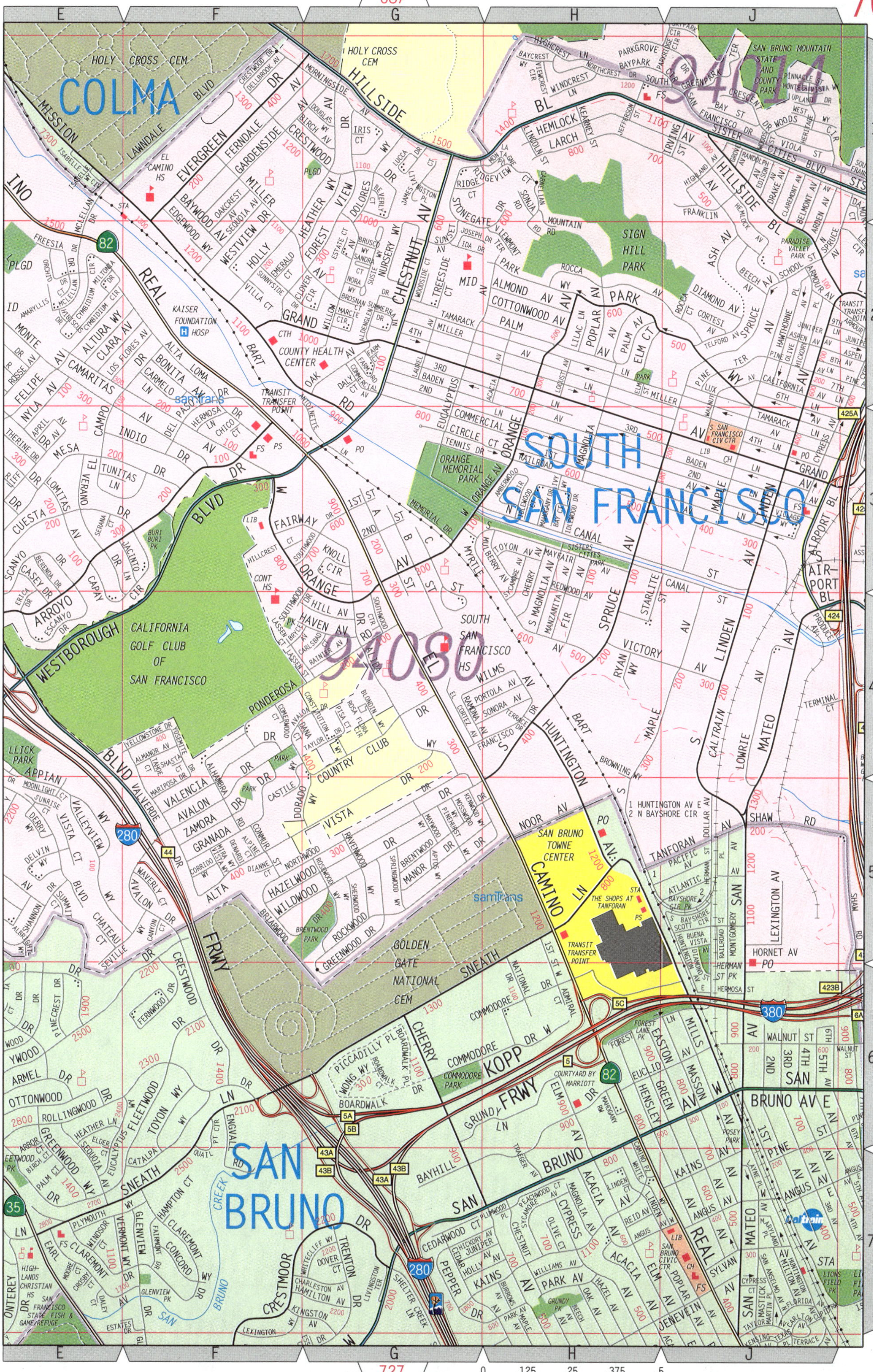

COLMA
SOUTH SAN FRANCISCO
SAN BRUNO
94014
94080
HOLY CROSS CEM
CALIFORNIA GOLF CLUB OF SAN FRANCISCO
GOLDEN GATE NATIONAL CEM
SIGN HILL PARK
ORANGE MEMORIAL PARK
SAN BRUNO MOUNTAIN STATE AND COUNTY PARK
KAISER FOUNDATION HOSP
COUNTY HEALTH CENTER
SOUTH SAN FRANCISCO HS
SAN BRUNO TOWNE CENTER
THE SHOPS AT TANFORAN
TRANSIT TRANSFER POINT
CAMINO REAL
EL CAMINO REAL
MISSION
JUNIPERO SERRA BLVD
HILLSIDE BLVD
WESTBOROUGH BLVD
GRAND AV
AIRPORT BL
HUNTINGTON AV
SNEATH LN
SAN BRUNO AV
SAN MATEO AV
KOPP FRWY
FRWY
SKYLINE BLVD
SAN FRANCISCO STATE FISH & GAME REFUGE
E F G H J
1 2 3 4 5 6 7

SEE 708 MAP

SEE 727 MAP

0 .125 .25 .375 .5 miles 1 in. = 1900 ft.

SEE 688 MAP

SAN BRUNO MOUNTAIN STATE AND COUNTY PARK
94014
SOUTH SAN FRANCISCO
94080
94128
OYSTER COVE MARINA
OYSTER POINT
OYSTER POINT MARINA
OYSTER POINT PARK
POINT SAN BRUNO PARK
POINT SAN BRUNO
SAN BRUNO CANAL
SEAPLANE HARBOR
SAN FRANCISCO INTERNATIONAL AIRPORT
CITY COLLEGE OF SAN FRANCISCO AIRPORT CAMPUS
USCG AIR STATION
UNITED MAINTENANCE
FLYING TIGERS
DELTA CARGO
BUTLER AVIATION
AMERICAN HANGAR
RENTAL CAR FACILITY
LONG TERM PARKING LOT D
LIONS FIELD PARK
7TH AV PARK
7TH & WALNUT PARK
BAYSHORE FRWY
AIRPORT BLVD
OYSTER POINT BLVD
GATEWAY BLVD
GRAND AV
SISTER CITIES BLVD
LINDEN AV
HARBOR WY
LITTLEFIELD AV
FORBES BLVD
GRANDVIEW DR
ALLERTON AV
CABOT RD
MITCHELL AV
SWIFT AV
N ACCESS RD
EMBASSY SUITES SOUTH SAN FRANCISCO
RAMADA INN SAN FRANCISCO NORTH
HOLIDAY INN SAN FRANCISCO INTERNATIONAL AIRPORT NORTH
BEST WESTERN GROSVENOR HOTEL
THE GATEWAY
samTrans
TRANSIT TRANSFER POINT
0 .125 .25 .375 .5 miles 1 in. = 1900 ft.

SEE 707 MAP

SEE 728 MAP

SEE 688 MAP
E
F
G
H
J
1
2
3
4
5
6
7
SAN
FRANCISCO
BAY
SEE B MAP
SEE 728 MAP
0 .125 .25 .375 .5 miles 1 in. = 1900 ft.

SEE 706 MAP
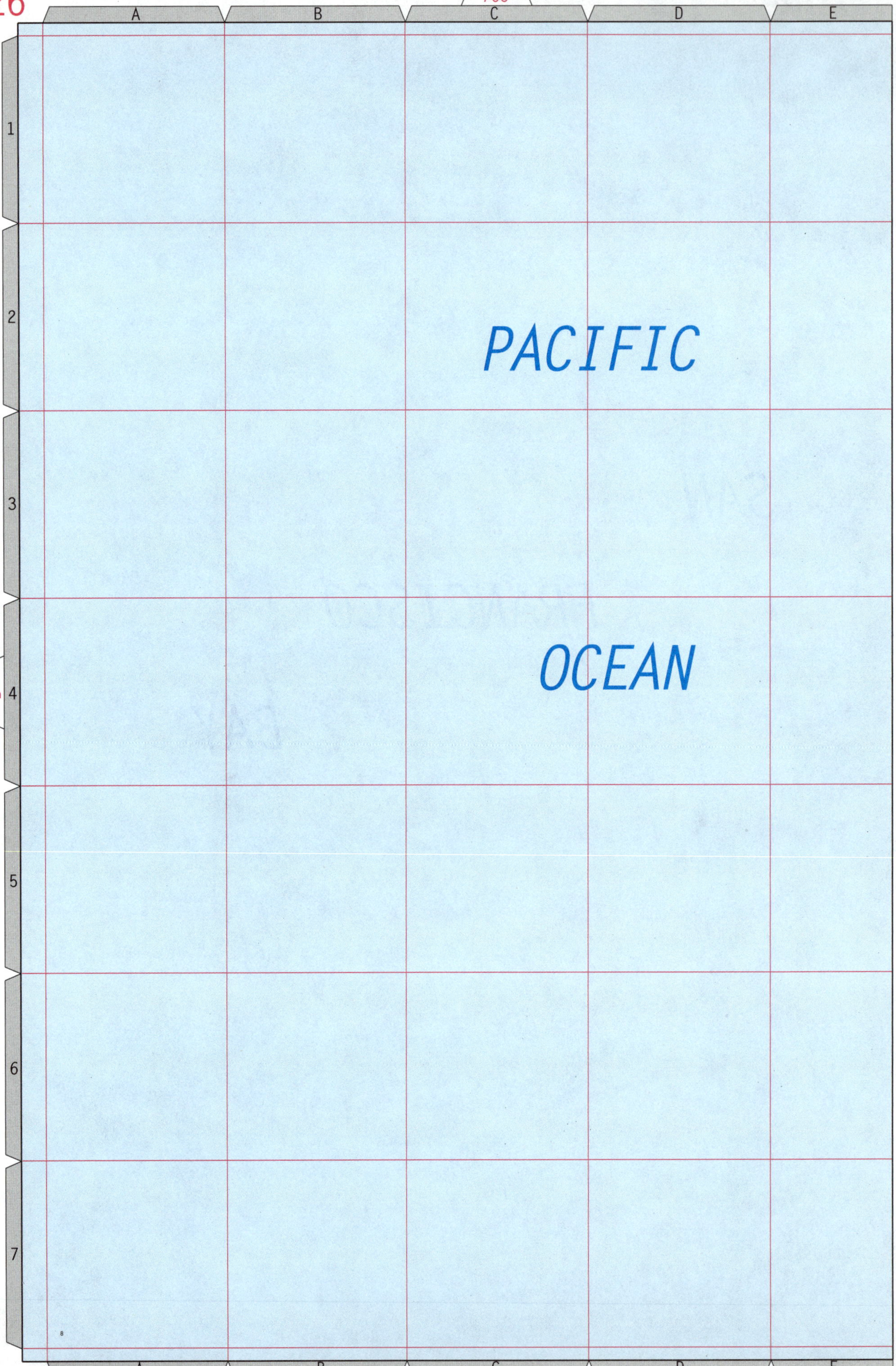

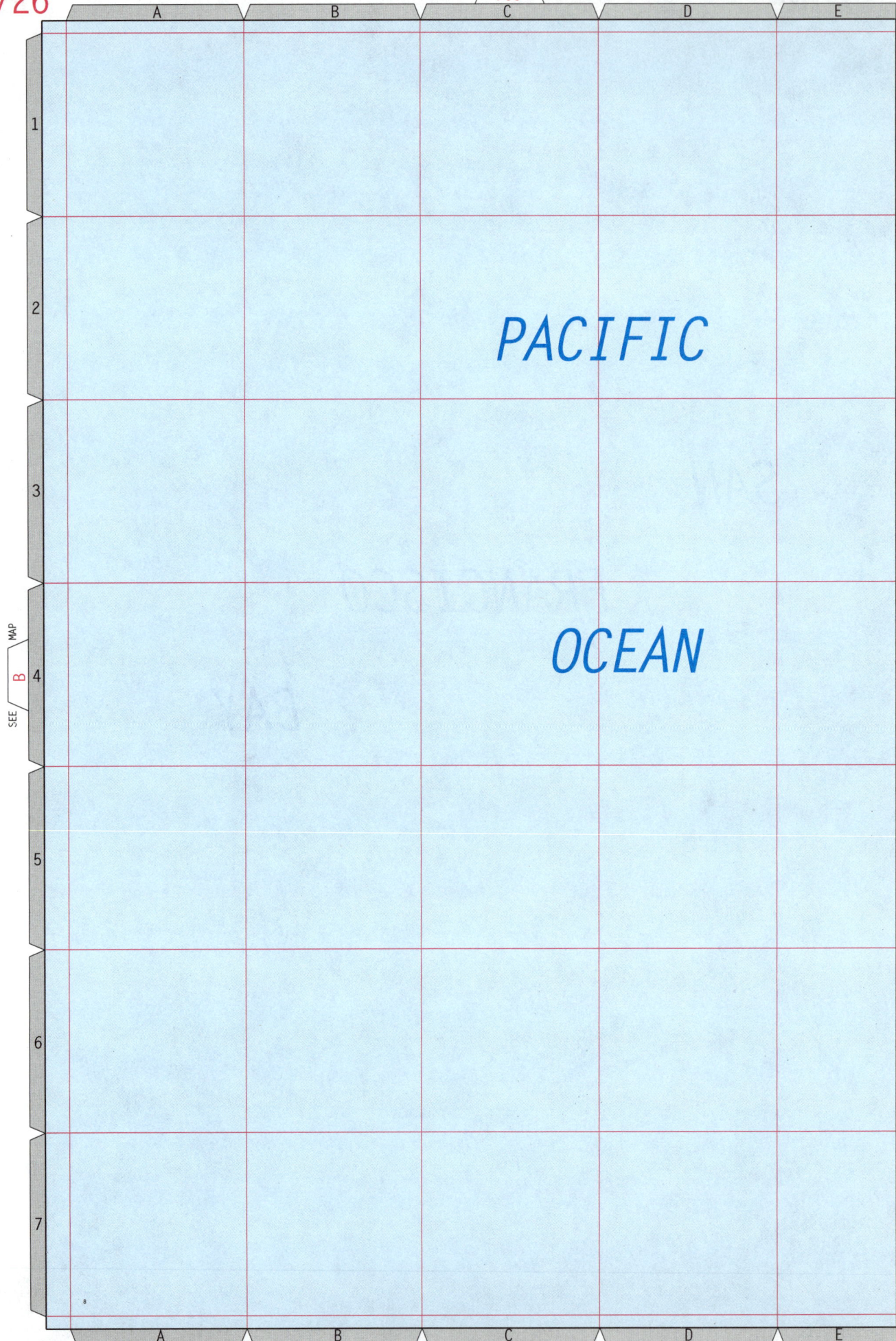

SEE B MAP
SEE 746 MAP
0 .125 .25 .375 .5 miles 1 in. = 1900 ft.

SEE 706 MAP

SEE 727 MAP

SEE 746 MAP

0 .125 .25 .375 .5 miles 1 in. = 1900 ft.

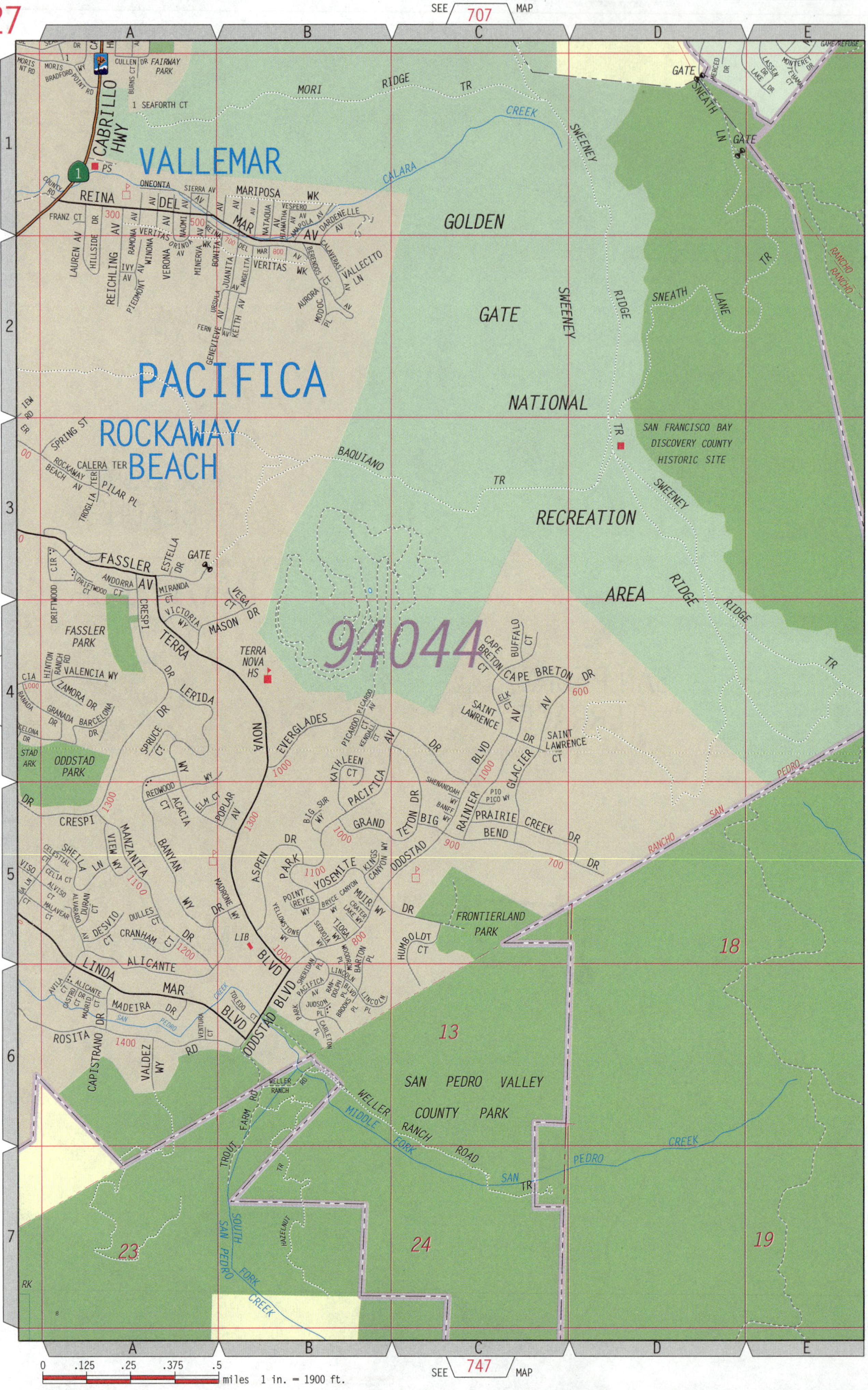
SEE 707 MAP
SEE 726 MAP
SEE 747 MAP
VALLEMAR
PACIFICA
ROCKAWAY BEACH
GOLDEN GATE NATIONAL RECREATION AREA
94044
SAN FRANCISCO BAY DISCOVERY COUNTY HISTORIC SITE
SAN PEDRO VALLEY COUNTY PARK
FAIRWAY PARK
FASSLER PARK
ODDSTAD PARK
FRONTIERLAND PARK
TERRA NOVA HS
CABRILLO HWY
REINA DEL MAR AV
MORI RIDGE TR
SWEENEY RIDGE TR
SNEATH LANE
BAQUIANO TR
CALERA CREEK
FASSLER AV
TERRA NOVA BLVD
CRESPI DR
LINDA MAR BLVD
ODDSTAD BLVD
CAPE BRETON DR
SAINT LAWRENCE BLVD
PRAIRIE CREEK DR
WELLER RANCH ROAD
SAN PEDRO CREEK
MIDDLE FORK
SOUTH FORK
RANCHO SAN PEDRO
13
18
19
23
24
A B C D E
1 2 3 4 5 6 7
0 .125 .25 .375 .5 miles 1 in. = 1900 ft.

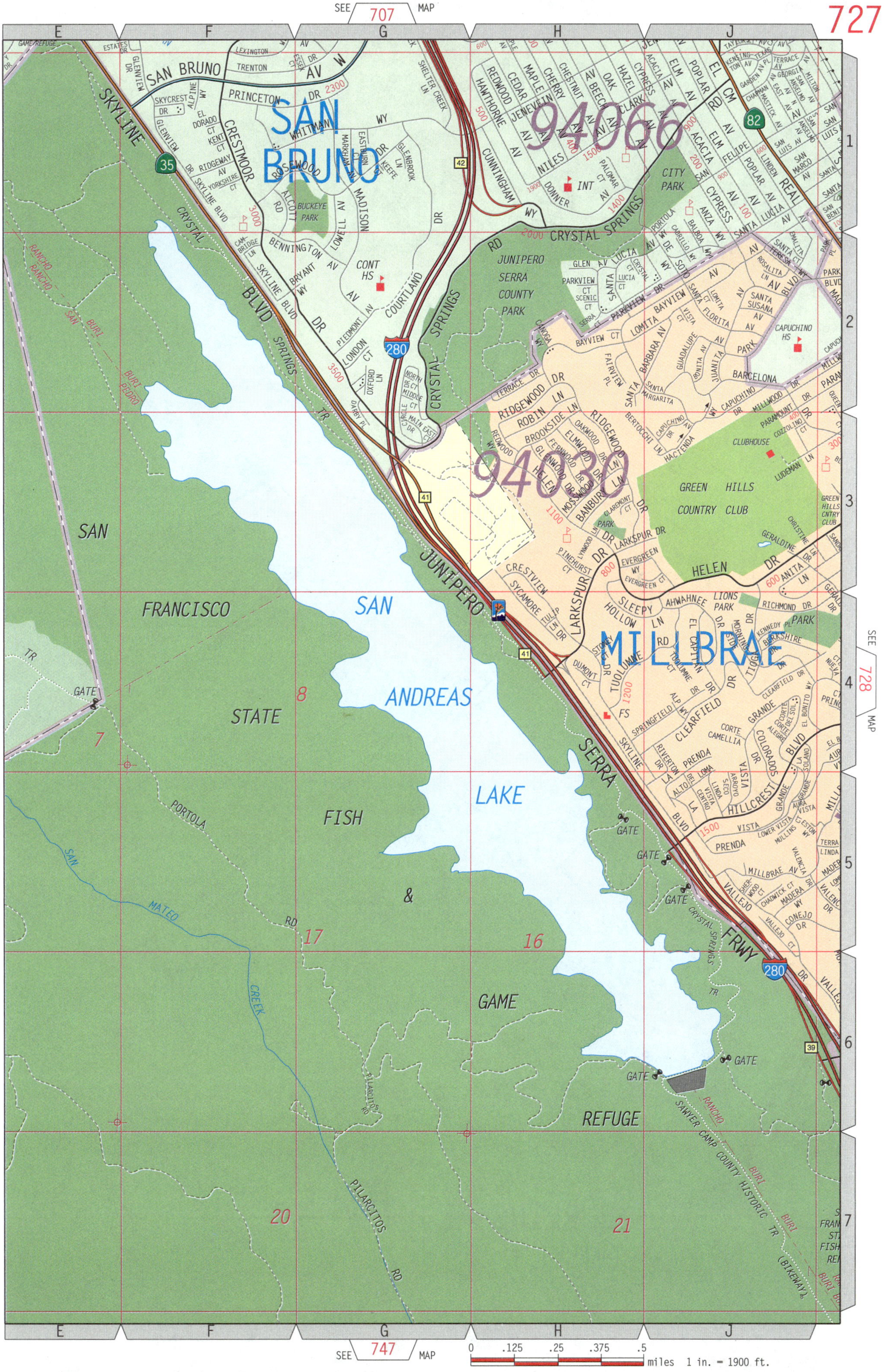
SEE 707 MAP
SEE 728 MAP
SEE 747 MAP
SAN BRUNO
MILLBRAE
94066
94030
SAN ANDREAS LAKE
SAN FRANCISCO STATE FISH & GAME REFUGE
JUNIPERO SERRA COUNTY PARK
GREEN HILLS COUNTRY CLUB
CITY PARK
BUCKEYE PARK
LIONS PARK
SKYLINE BLVD
CRYSTAL SPRINGS RD
JUNIPERO SERRA FRWY
SAN BRUNO AV W
MILLBRAE AV
SAWYER CAMP COUNTY HISTORIC TR (BIKEWAY)
SAN MATEO CREEK
PILARCITOS RD
PORTOLA RD
CAPUCHINO HS
CONT HS
E F G H J
0 .125 .25 .375 .5 miles 1 in. = 1900 ft.

SEE 708 MAP

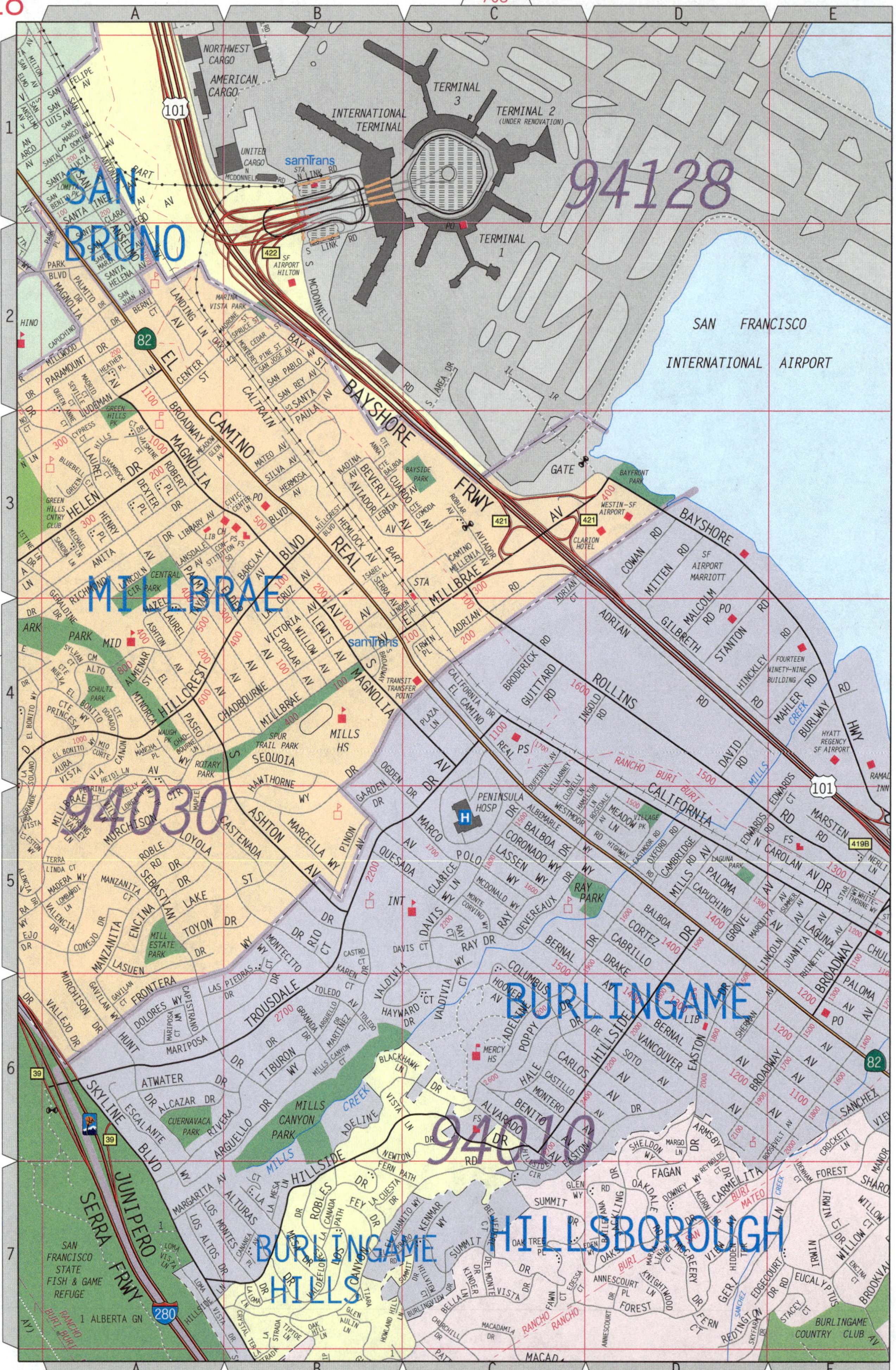

SEE 727 MAP

SEE 748 MAP

0 .125 .25 .375 .5 miles 1 in. = 1900 ft.

© 2008 Rand McNally & Company

N

94128

SAN BRUNO

INTERNATIONAL TERMINAL

TERMINAL 3

TERMINAL 2
(UNDER RENOVATION)

TERMINAL 1

NORTHWEST CARGO

AMERICAN CARGO

UNITED CARGO

samTrans STA LINK RD

BART

SF AIRPORT HILTON

SAN FRANCISCO INTERNATIONAL AIRPORT

BAYSHORE FRWY

BAYSHORE

WESTIN SF AIRPORT

CLARION HOTEL

BAYFRONT PARK

BAYSIDE PARK

GATE

SF AIRPORT MARRIOTT

FOURTEEN NINETY-NINE BUILDING

HYATT REGENCY SF AIRPORT

RAMADA INN

MILLBRAE

EL CAMINO REAL

CALTRAIN

BROADWAY

MAGNOLIA

GREEN HILLS CNTRY CLUB

HILLCREST

MILLS HS

SPUR TRAIL PARK

SEQUOIA

94030

MILLBRAE

MURCHISON

ASHTON

LOYOLA

HAWTHORNE WY

MILL ESTATE PARK

PENINSULA HOSP

RAY PARK

CALIFORNIA

ROLLINS

ADRIAN

BURLWAY HWY

101

419B

BURLINGAME

BROADWAY

TROUSDALE

MILLS CANYON PARK

MERCY HS

HILLSIDE

94010

MILLS CREEK

SERRA FRWY

JUNIPERO

SKYLINE BLVD

SAN FRANCISCO STATE FISH & GAME REFUGE

280

39

BURLINGAME HILLS

HILLSBOROUGH

BURLINGAME COUNTRY CLUB

SEE 708 MAP
SEE 729 MAP
SEE 748 MAP
SAN FRANCISCO BAY
AIRPORT
BAYSIDE PARK
BAYSHORE FRWY
ANZA LAGOON
LAGOON
PENINSULA BEACH
COYOTE POINT COUNTY REC AREA
FIRING RANGE
POPLAR CREEK GOLF COURSE
WASHINGTON PARK
BURLINGAME HS
SAN MATEO
94401
M L KING PARK
PERSHING PARK
EL CAMINO REAL
RAMADA INN
SHERATON GATEWAY
EMBASSY SUITES-SFO BURLINGAME
DOUBLETREE HOTEL
ANZA CORPORATE CENTER
SAN MATEO CONV & VIS BUR
SAN MATEO PERFORMING ARTS CENTER
CITY REC CTR
0 .125 .25 .375 .5 miles 1 in. = 1900 ft.

SEE B MAP
SEE 728 MAP
SEE 749 MAP
SAN FRANCISCO BAY
SAN MATEO POINT
COYOTE POINT MUSEUM
COYOTE POINT MARINA
COYOTE POINT COUNTY REC AREA
COYOTE POINT DR
POPLAR CREEK GOLF COURSE
GATE
SHORELINE PARK (UNDEVELOPED)
POPLAR AV
94401
SAN MATEO
BAYSHORE FWY
101
417A
FOSTER CITY
94404
MARINERS POINT GOLF LINKS
J HART CLINTON DR
SHOREVIEW AV
RYDER COURT PARK
HARBOR VIEW PARK
0 .125 .25 .375 .5 miles 1 in. = 1900 ft.

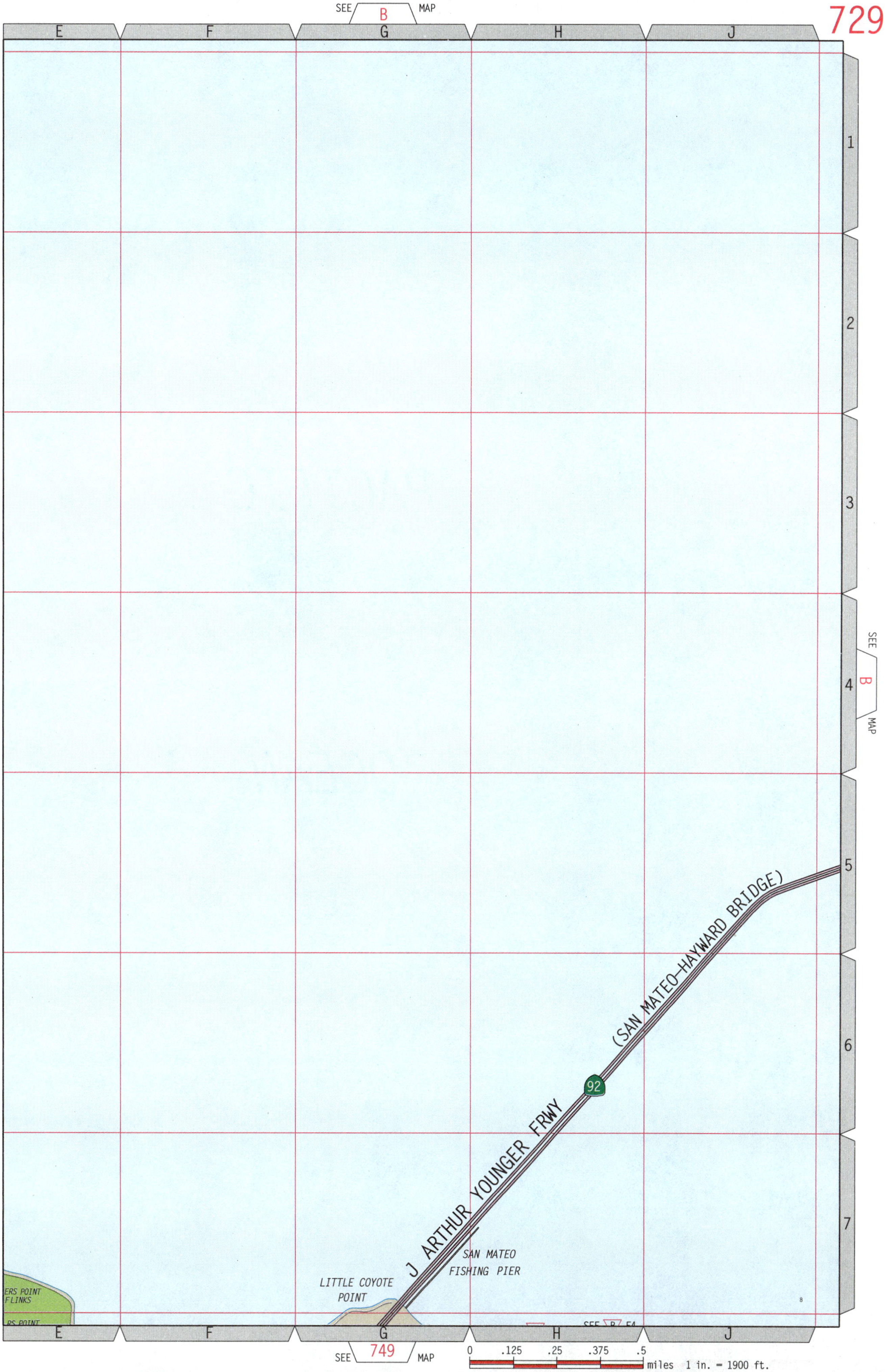
SEE B MAP
E
F
G
H
J
1
2
3
4
5
6
7
SEE B MAP
J ARTHUR YOUNGER FRWY
(SAN MATEO-HAYWARD BRIDGE)
92
SAN MATEO
FISHING PIER
LITTLE COYOTE
POINT
SEE 749 MAP
0 .125 .25 .375 .5 miles 1 in. = 1900 ft.

SEE 726 MAP

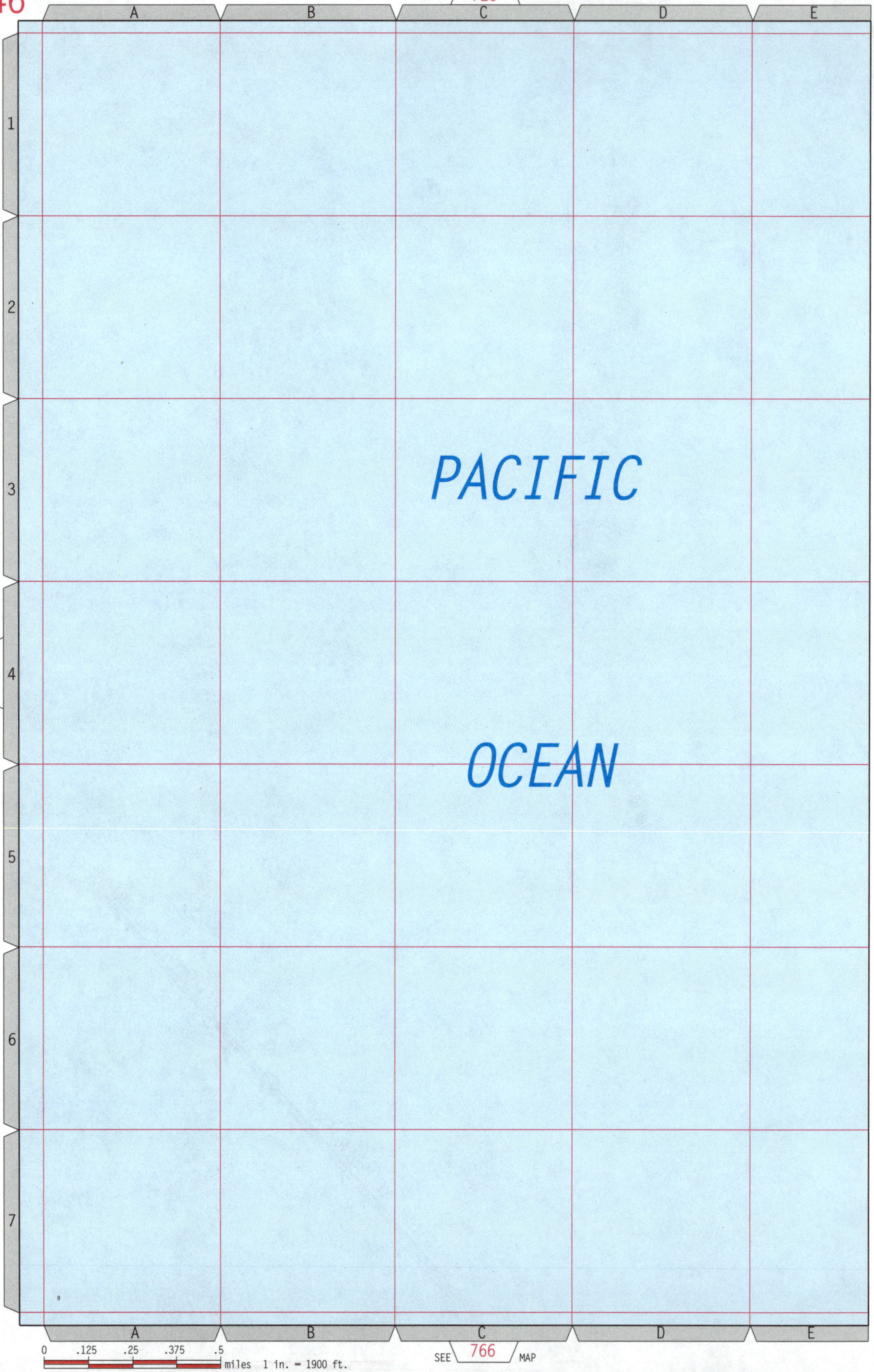

SEE B MAP

0 .125 .25 .375 .5 miles 1 in. = 1900 ft.

SEE 766 MAP

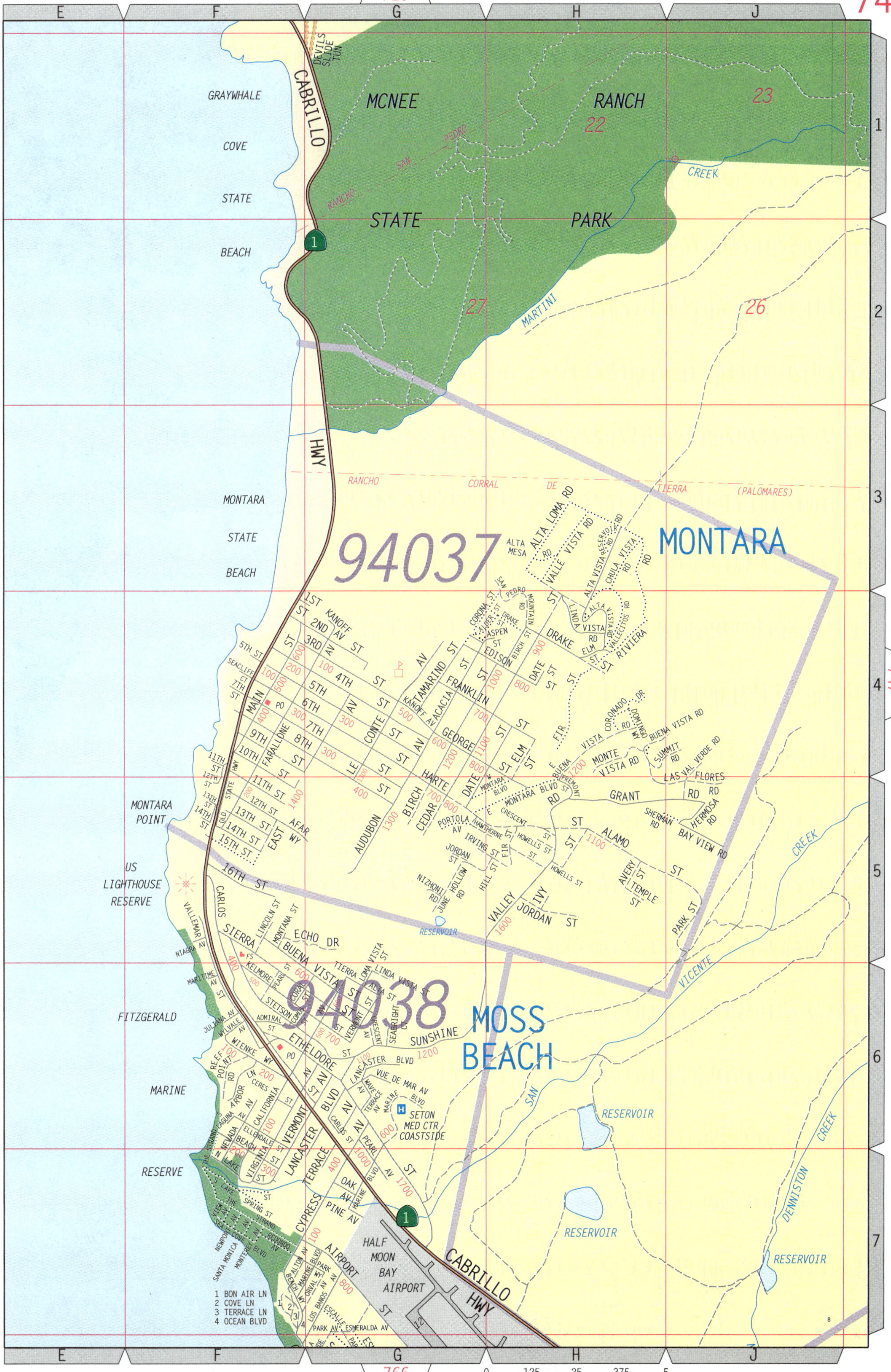
SEE 726 MAP
SAN MATEO CO.
MCNEE RANCH STATE PARK
GRAYWHALE COVE STATE BEACH
CABRILLO HWY
DEVILS SLIDE TUN
MONTARA STATE BEACH
94037
MONTARA
RANCHO CORRAL DE TIERRA (PALOMARES)
RANCHO SAN PEDRO
MARTINI CREEK
MONTARA POINT
US LIGHTHOUSE RESERVE
FITZGERALD MARINE RESERVE
94038
MOSS BEACH
HALF MOON BAY AIRPORT
SETON MED CTR COASTSIDE
RESERVOIR
SAN VICENTE CREEK
DENNISTON CREEK
SEE 747 MAP
1 BON AIR LN
2 COVE LN
3 TERRACE LN
4 OCEAN BLVD
SEE 766 MAP
miles 1 in. = 1900 ft.

SEE 727 MAP

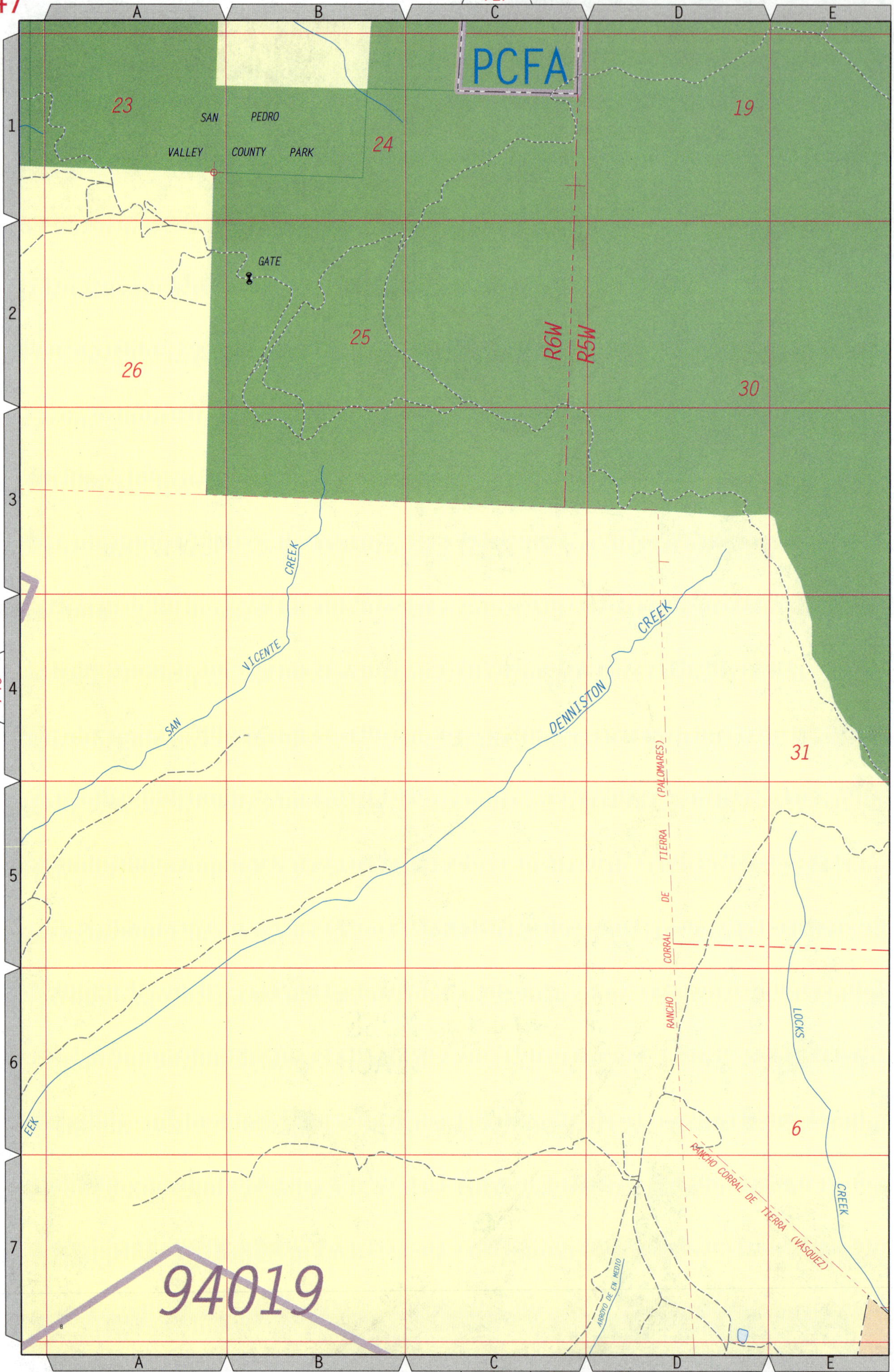

SEE 746 MAP

SEE 767 MAP

0 .125 .25 .375 .5 miles 1 in. = 1900 ft.

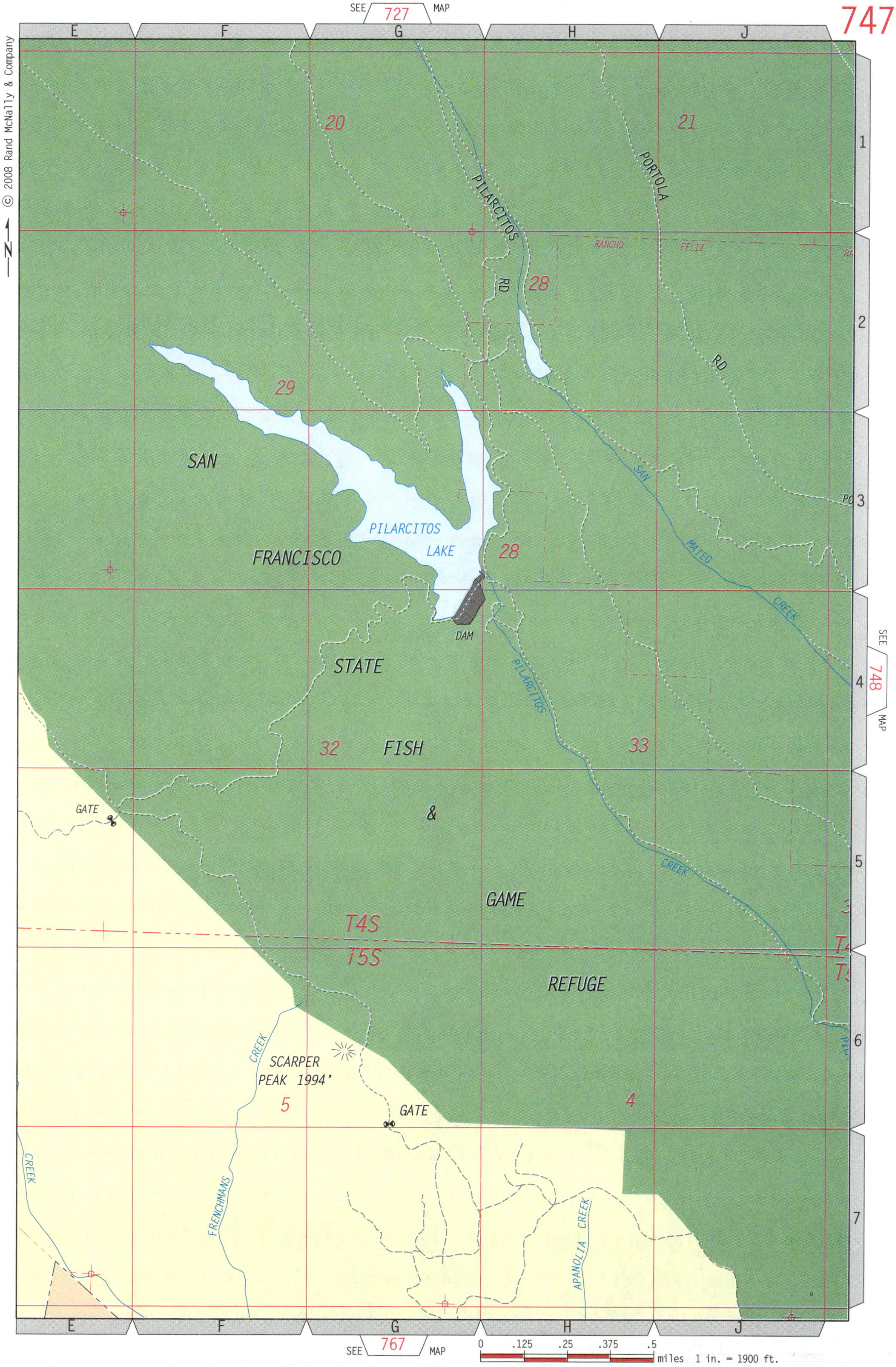
SEE 727 MAP
E
F
G
H
J
1
2
3
4
5
6
7
20
21
PILARCITOS
PORTOLA
RD
RANCHO
FELIZ
28
RD
29
SAN
PILARCITOS
LAKE
FRANCISCO
28
DAM
STATE
PILARCITOS
32
FISH
33
&
GATE
GAME
T4S
T5S
REFUGE
SAN
MATEO
CREEK
CREEK
CREEK
SCARPER
PEAK 1994'
5
GATE
4
CREEK
FRENCHMANS
APANOLIA
CREEK
SEE 748 MAP
SEE 767 MAP
0
.125
.25
.375
.5
miles
1 in. = 1900 ft.

SEE 728 MAP

SEE 747 MAP

0 .125 .25 .375 .5 miles 1 in. = 1900 ft.

SEE 768 MAP

© 2008 Rand McNally & Company

N

A B C D E

BURLINGAME
COUNTRY
CLUB

1

MACADAMIA

SPENCER LAKE

CLUBHOUSE

PLACE

MID

22

RANCHO SAWYER CAMP COUNTY HISTORIC TR (BIKEWAY)

BURI BURI

RANCHO FELIZ

SKYLINE BLVD
SKYLINE BLVD SUMMIT

I-280

1 CHANDLER WY

RANCHO SAN

CHURCHILL
CHURCHILL DR

GLEN AULIN LN
TULIP
TIPOE LN
LIVE OAK
PANORAMA
PRIVET
LEMON CT
BUTTERNUT

PATTON PL
WOODGATE
CHURCHILL DR
PERSIMMON
CINNAMON
EUGENIA DR DR

HOLLY
SANCHEZ CREEK
ORANGE
JACARANDA CT
COTTONWOOD CT
CITRUS CT
PEAR CT
RES
FIR CT

RALSTON
ROBIN
NEW
BARROILHET
FISHHILL
HOMER CT

2

GATE

DAM

GATE
GATE

SAWYER

GOLF FRONTAGE RD
GREVILLEA CT
ROWAN
DARRELL CT
SILKTREE
TEATREE CT
TREE LN
PINE
LAUREL
CORLETT RD
CRAIG
BARBARA WY
PULLMAN
REMILLARD
CASTLE CT
RALSTON
MOSELEY
PULLMAN
WARM CANYON WY
ROBINWOOD
HAYNE
MARLBOROUGH RD

HILLSBOROUGH

CAMP COUNTY

CLUBHOUSE

CRYSTAL
SPRINGS
GOLF
COURSE

GOLF COURSE DR
FS

94010

DARRELL
ALBERTA
ROBERTS WY
DENISE

BLACK MOUNTAIN

3

PORTOLA RD

SAN FRANCISCO

STATE FISH &

GAME REFUGE

HISTORIC TR

PARK & RIDE
36
36

JUNIPERO
SKYLINE
SERRA FRWY

REST AREA
36

TAR PL
HEATHER PL
LAKEY

4

SAN MATEO CREEK

5

34

T4S
T5S

(BIKEWAY)

6

PILARCITOS CREEK

LOWER
CRYSTAL
SPRINGS
RESERVOIR

CRYSTAL SPRINGS RD
SKYLINE

CRYSTAL SPRINGS DAM

7

STONE DAM RESERVOIR
3

PILARCITOS CREEK

RANCHO FELIZ
2

CREEK

SEE A H6
1 GOLDENRIDGE CT
2 GALLOWRIDGE CT
3 NEEDLERIDGE CT
4 CREEKRIDGE CT
5 CRIPPLERIDGE CT
6 TOLLRIDGE CT
7 WEEPINGRIDGE CT
8 HAVENRIDGE CT

SEE 728 MAP

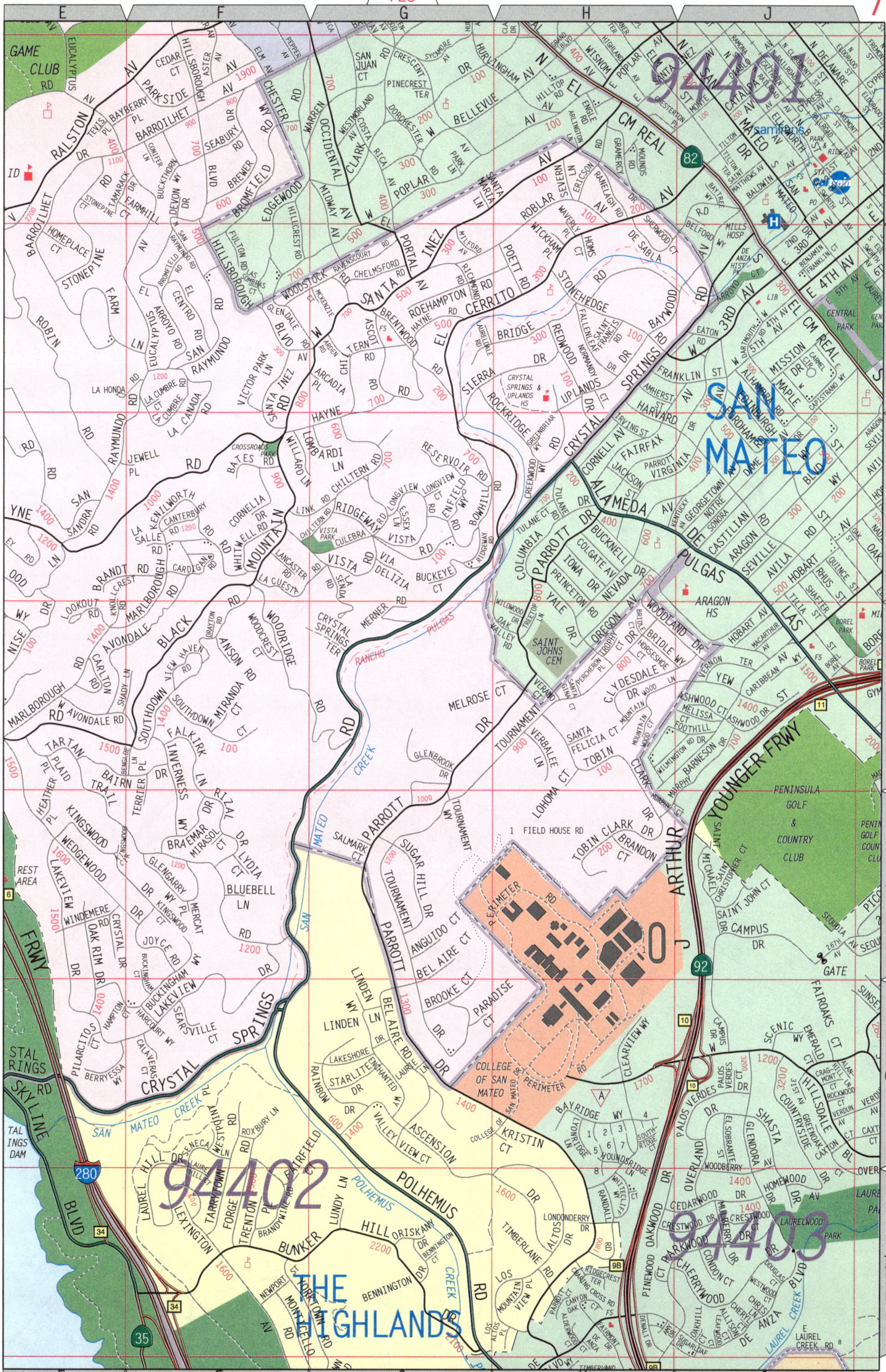

SEE 749 MAP

SEE 768 MAP

0 .125 .25 .375 .5 miles 1 in. = 1900 ft.

SEE 729 MAP

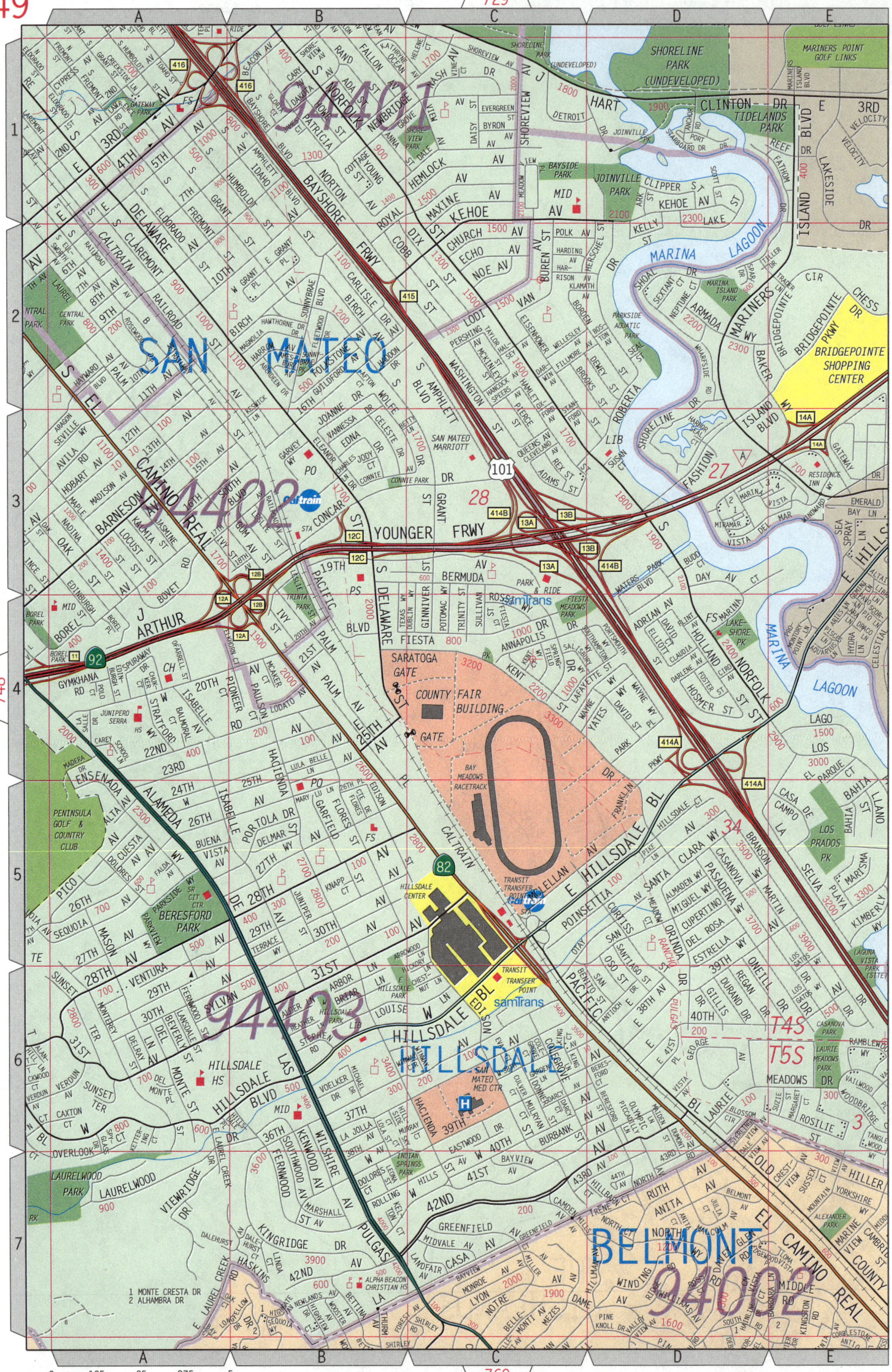
SAN MATEO
HILLSDALE
BELMONT
94401
94402
94403
94002
SHORELINE PARK (UNDEVELOPED)
MARINERS POINT GOLF LINKS
TIDELANDS PARK
BAYSIDE PARK
JOINVILLE PARK
MARINA LAGOON
BRIDGEPOINTE SHOPPING CENTER
CENTRAL PARK
SAN MATEO MARRIOTT
BAYSHORE FRWY
J ARTHUR YOUNGER FRWY
EL CAMINO REAL
CALTRAIN
ALAMEDA DE LAS PULGAS
COUNTY FAIR BUILDING
BAY MEADOWS RACETRACK
SARATOGA GATE
HILLSDALE CENTER
TRANSIT TRANSFER POINT
samTrans
E HILLSDALE BL
HILLSDALE BLVD
PENINSULA GOLF & COUNTRY CLUB
BERESFORD PARK
LAURELWOOD PARK
MATEO MED CTR
LAURIE MEADOWS PARK
LOS PRADOS PK
FIESTA MEADOWS PARK
LAKESHORE PK
RESIDENCE INN
ALPHA BEACON CHRISTIAN HS
1 MONTE CRESTA DR
2 ALHAMBRA DR
T4S
T5S
0 .125 .25 .375 .5 miles 1 in. = 1900 ft.

SEE 748 MAP

SEE 769 MAP

SEE 729 MAP

LITTLE COYOTE POINT
FOSTER CITY
94404
94065
REDWOOD CITY
REDWOOD SHORES
SAN FRANCISCO BAY
BELMONT SLOUGH
STEINBERGER SLOUGH
SALT EVAPORATORS
DON EDWARDS SAN FRANCISCO BAY NATIONAL WILDLIFE REFUGE
J ARTHUR YOUNGER FRWY
BAYSHORE FRWY
HILLSDALE BLVD
EDGEWATER BLVD
FOSTER CITY BLVD
BEACH PARK BL
MARINE PKWY
SHEARWATER PKWY
TWIN DOLPHIN DR
SHORELINE DR
BRIDGEPORT DR
CENTRUM III
HOTEL SOFITEL
BELMONT SPORTS COMPLEX
SEA CLOUD PARK
LEO J RYAN MEMORIAL PARK
BOAT PARK
CATAMARAN PARK
FARRAGUT PARK
BOOTHBAY PARK
PORT ROYAL PARK
RIDGEPOINTE SHOPPING CENTER
R4W R3W
SEE A D3
1 VIA VISTA
2 VISTA CAY
3 VISTA DEL SOL
4 VIA LAGUNA
SEE B F4
1 ANTARES LN
2 CORVUS LN
3 NORMA LN
4 VOLANS LN
5 PHOENIX LN
6 CENTAURUS LN
7 CANIS LN
8 ANDROMEDA LN
9 HERCULES LN
SEE C G6
1 QUADRANT LN
2 MASTHEAD LN
3 STANCHION LN
4 BINNACLE LN
5 CHARTHOUSE LN
6 SKIPJACK LN
SEE D G5
1 SAINT CROIX LN
2 PINRAIL LN
3 WINDLASS LN
4 BOBSTAY LN
5 JIBSTAY LN
6 SAINT VINCENT LN
SEE E H6
1 CAPE HATTERAS CT
2 SEA CLIFF LN
3 STARFISH LN
4 BEACON SHORES DR
5 SEAGATE CT
6 PARK PL
SEE G J4
1 RIVERMIST LN
2 SANDLEWOOD LN
3 KRYSTALLOS LN
4 WINDFIELD LN
5 TREEDUST ST
6 MAKO LN
7 POSEIDON LN
8 ISLEFORD LN
9 WINDLEA LN
10 EYELET LN
SEE F G4
1 LORD IVELSON LN
2 LORD NELSON LN
3 BURKE LN
1 CONSTELLATION CT
1 DEBBIE LN
2 VANNIER DR
1 EXECUTIVE GUILD CIR
2 EXECUTIVE GUILD DR
0 .125 .25 .375 .5 miles 1 in. = 1900 ft.

SEE 750 MAP

SEE 769 MAP

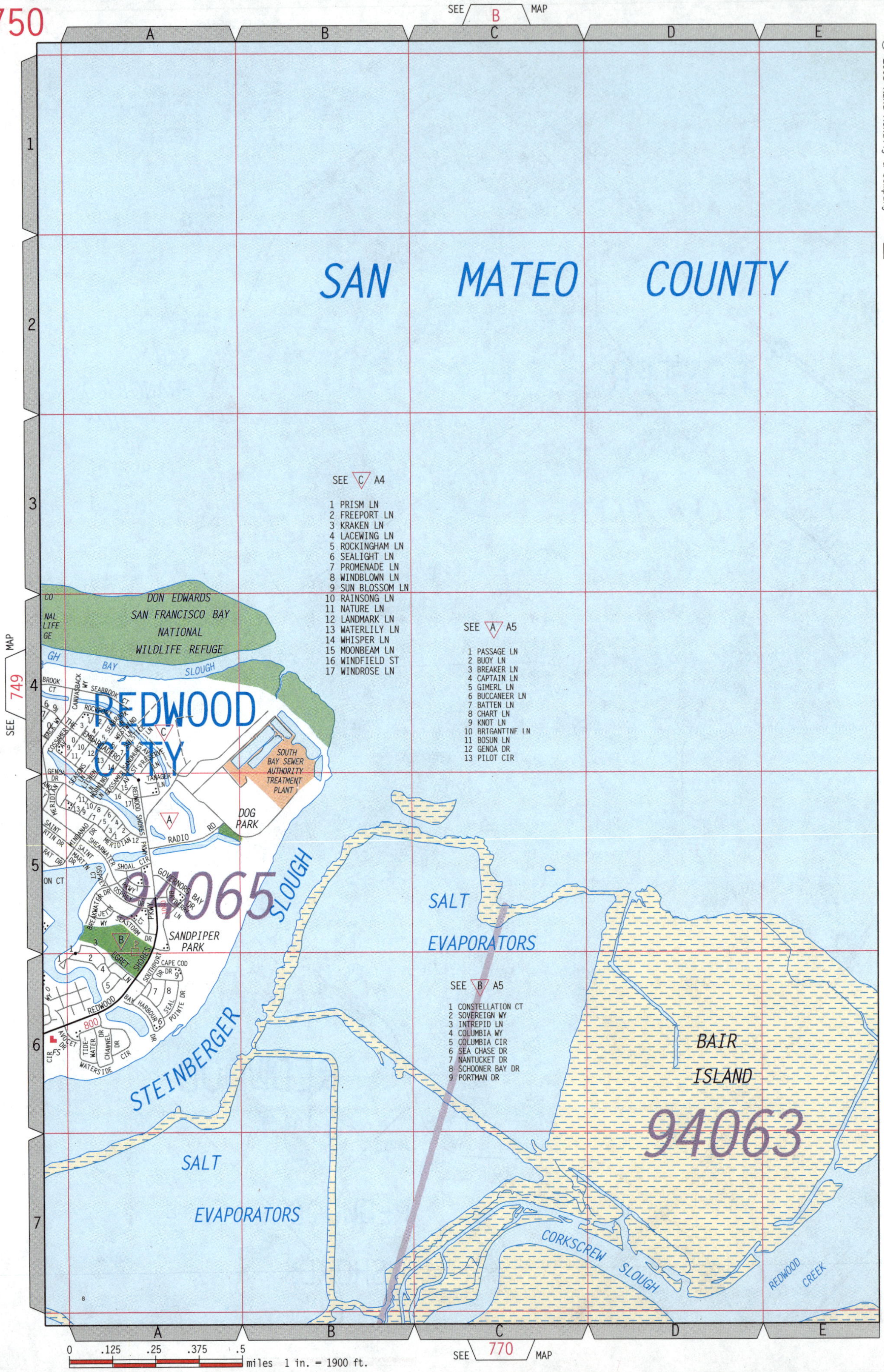
SEE B MAP
A
B
C
D
E
1
2
3
4
5
6
7
SAN MATEO COUNTY
SEE C A4
1 PRISM LN
2 FREEPORT LN
3 KRAKEN LN
4 LACEWING LN
5 ROCKINGHAM LN
6 SEALIGHT LN
7 PROMENADE LN
8 WINDBLOWN LN
9 SUN BLOSSOM LN
10 RAINSONG LN
11 NATURE LN
12 LANDMARK LN
13 WATERLILY LN
14 WHISPER LN
15 MOONBEAM LN
16 WINDFIELD ST
17 WINDROSE LN
SEE A A5
1 PASSAGE LN
2 BUOY LN
3 BREAKER LN
4 CAPTAIN LN
5 GIMERL LN
6 BUCCANEER LN
7 BATTEN LN
8 CHART LN
9 KNOT LN
10 BRIGANTINE LN
11 BOSUN LN
12 GENOA DR
13 PILOT CIR
SEE B A5
1 CONSTELLATION CT
2 SOVEREIGN WY
3 INTREPID LN
4 COLUMBIA WY
5 COLUMBIA CIR
6 SEA CHASE DR
7 NANTUCKET DR
8 SCHOONER BAY DR
9 PORTMAN DR
DON EDWARDS
SAN FRANCISCO BAY
NATIONAL
WILDLIFE REFUGE
BAY
SLOUGH
REDWOOD
CITY
SOUTH
BAY SEWER
AUTHORITY
TREATMENT
PLANT
DOG
PARK
RADIO
RD
94065
SLOUGH
SANDPIPER
PARK
STEINBERGER
SALT
EVAPORATORS
SALT
EVAPORATORS
BAIR
ISLAND
94063
CORKSCREW
SLOUGH
REDWOOD
CREEK
SEE 749 MAP
800
SEE 770 MAP
0 .125 .25 .375 .5
miles 1 in. = 1900 ft.

SEE B MAP

SEE B MAP
SEE 770 MAP

SEE 746 MAP

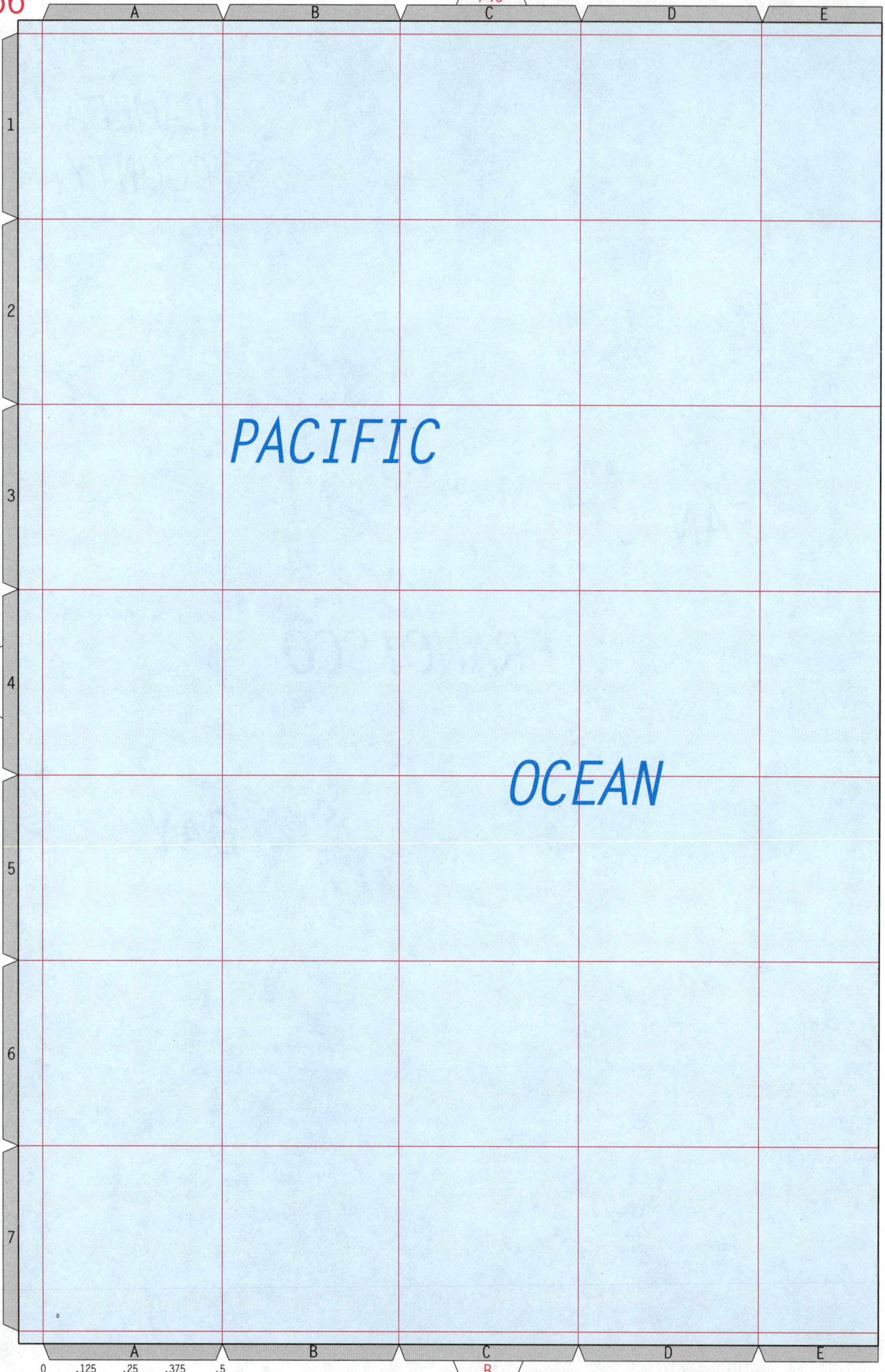

SEE B MAP

SEE B MAP

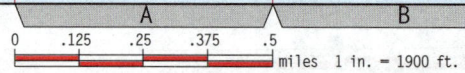

0 .125 .25 .375 .5 miles 1 in. = 1900 ft.

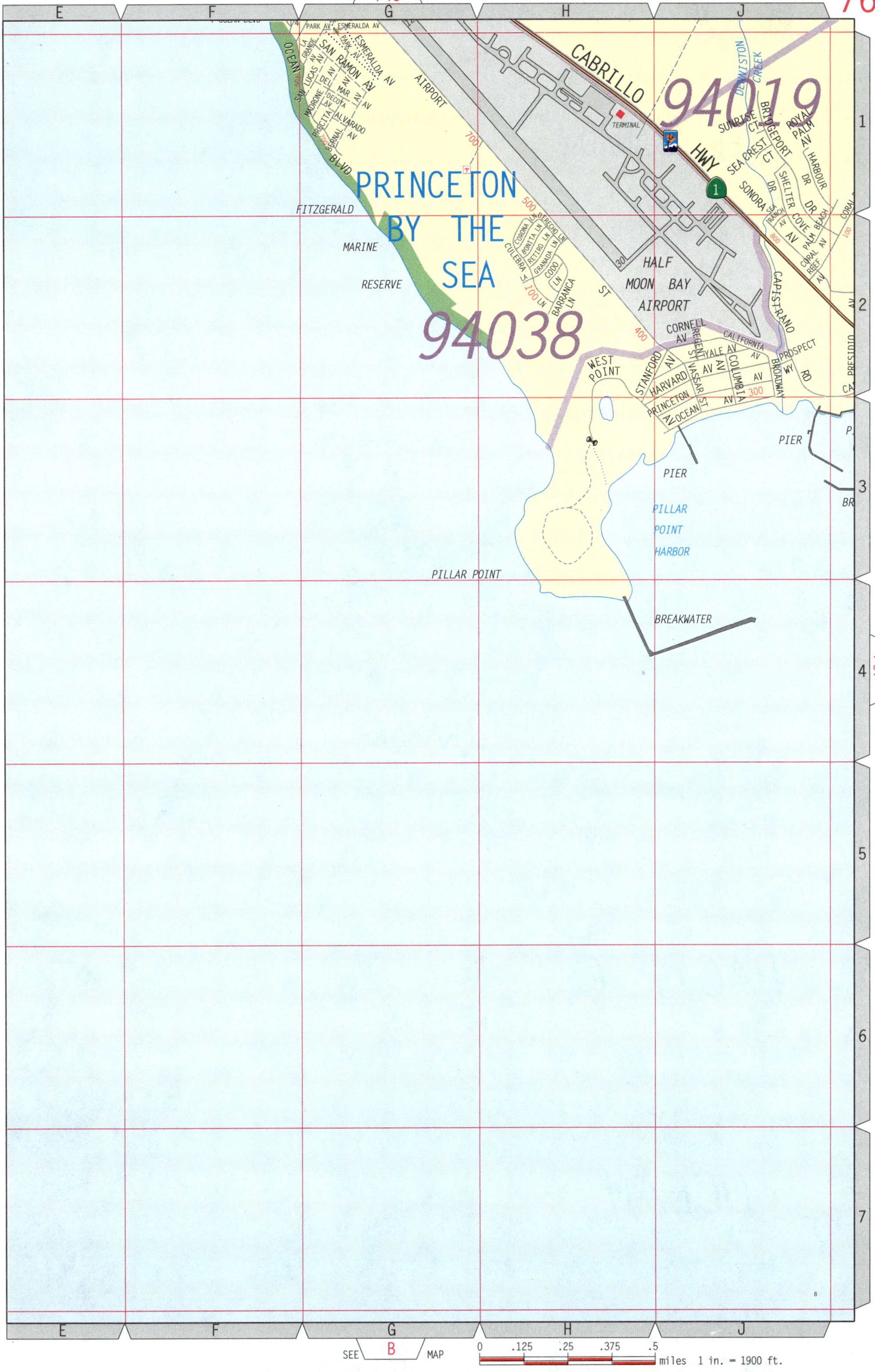
SEE 746 MAP
E
F
G
H
J
PRINCETON BY THE SEA
94038
94019
CABRILLO HWY
HALF MOON BAY AIRPORT
TERMINAL
AIRPORT ST
FITZGERALD MARINE RESERVE
PILLAR POINT
PILLAR POINT HARBOR
BREAKWATER
PIER
PIER
WEST POINT
DENNISTON CREEK
PARK AV
ESMERALDA AV
OCEAN BLVD
SAN RAMON AV
SAN LUCAS AV
ALVARADO AV
CAPISTRANO RD
PROSPECT WY
BROADWAY
CORNELL AV
STANFORD AV
HARVARD AV
PRINCETON AV
OCEAN AV
YALE AV
VASSAR ST
COLUMBIA AV
CALIFORNIA AV
REGENT ST
BARRANCA LN
CODO LN
CULEBRA LN
SUNRISE CT
SEA CREST CT
BRIDGEPORT DR
ROYAL PALM AV
HARBOUR DR
SHELTER COVE DR
SONORA AV
PALM BEACH
CORAL REEF AV
PRESIDIO
1
2
3
4
5
6
7
SEE 767 MAP
SEE B MAP
0 .125 .25 .375 .5 miles 1 in. = 1900 ft.

SEE 747 MAP

SEE 766 MAP

SEE 787 MAP

SEE 747 MAP

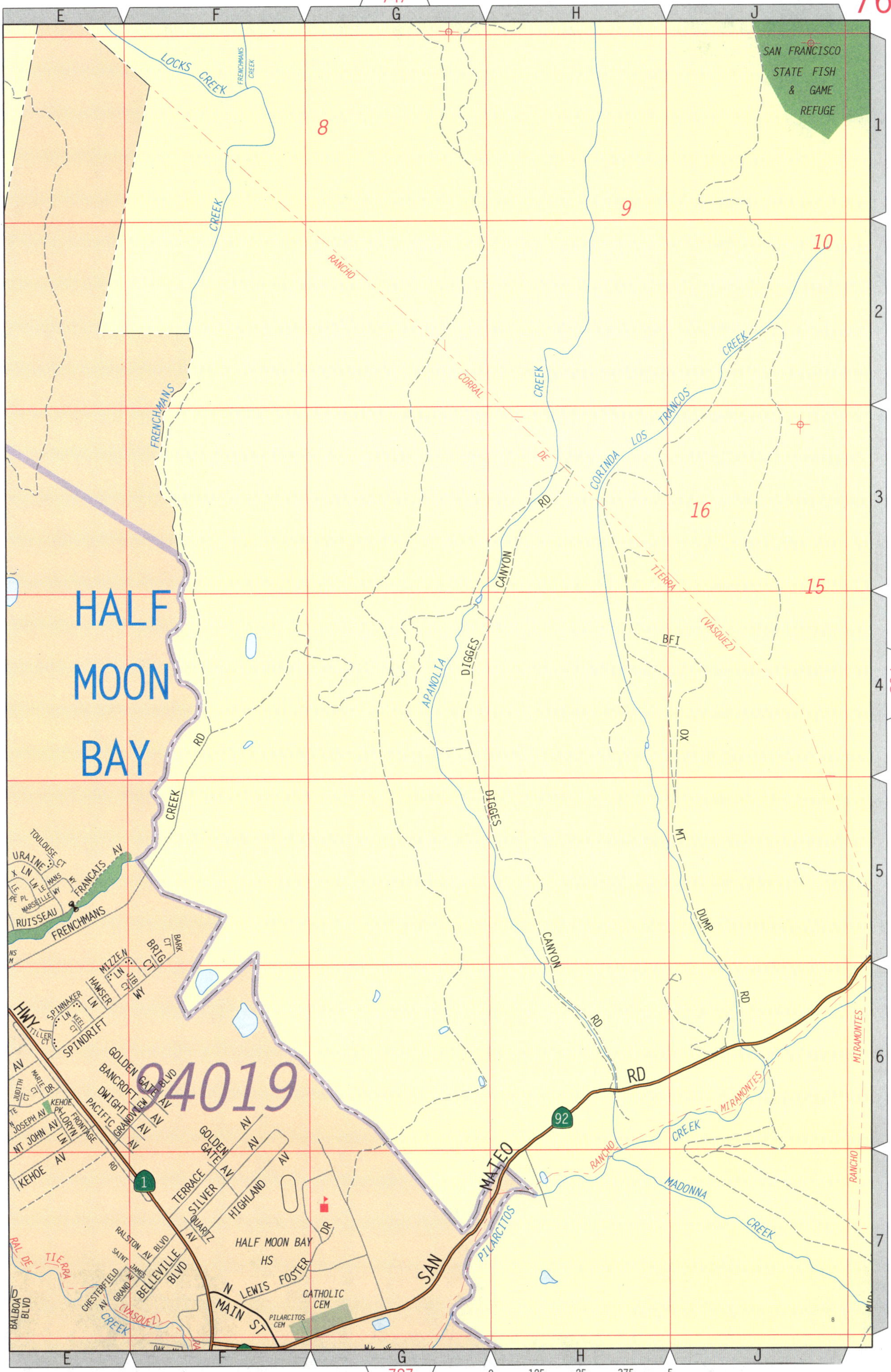

SEE 768 MAP

SEE 787 MAP

0 .125 .25 .375 .5 miles 1 in. = 1900 ft.

SAN MATEO CO.

N

LOCKS CREEK

FRENCHMANS CREEK

CREEK

8

9

10

SAN FRANCISCO
STATE FISH
& GAME
REFUGE

1

RANCHO

CORRAL

CREEK

DE

CORINDA LOS TRANCOS CREEK

2

FRENCHMANS

CREEK RD

HALF

MOON

BAY

RANCHO

TIERRA (VASQUEZ)

16

15

3

APANOLIA

DIGGES

CANYON

RD

BFI

OX

MT

DUMP

4

TOULOUSE CT
URAINE
X LN
LE PL
PE
MARSEILLE WY
LE MANS
FRANCAIS AV
RUISSEAU
FRENCHMANS
NS
M

DIGGES

CREEK

5

BARK
CT
BRIG
CT
MIZZEN
LN
JIB
WY
HAWSER LN
SPINNAKER
LN
TILLER CT
SPINDRIFT

CANYON

CANYON RD

RD

MIRAMONTES

6

HWY

AV
JUDITH
MABLE DR
CT
KEHOE
FLORIN
FRONTAGE
NT JOHN AV
LN
KEHOE AV
JOSEPH AV

SPINDRIFT

GOLDEN GATE BLVD
BANCROFT AV
DWIGHT AV
PACIFIC GRANDVIEW AV
AV

94019

GOLDEN
GATE
AV
AV
TERRACE
SILVER
QUARTZ
HIGHLAND AV
AV
AV

MATEO

RD

RANCHO

MIRAMONTES

CREEK

MADONNA

CREEK

RANCHO

92

6

1

RAL DE TIERRA
BALBOA BLVD

RALSTON AV BLVD
SAINT JAMES
CHESTERFIELD AV
GRAND
BELLEVILLE
BLVD

HALF MOON BAY
HS

N LEWIS FOSTER

DR

CATHOLIC CEM

SAN

PILARCITOS

7

MAIN ST
PILARCITOS
CEM
(VASQUEZ)
CREEK
OAK
M K AVE

8

E F G H J

SEE 748 MAP

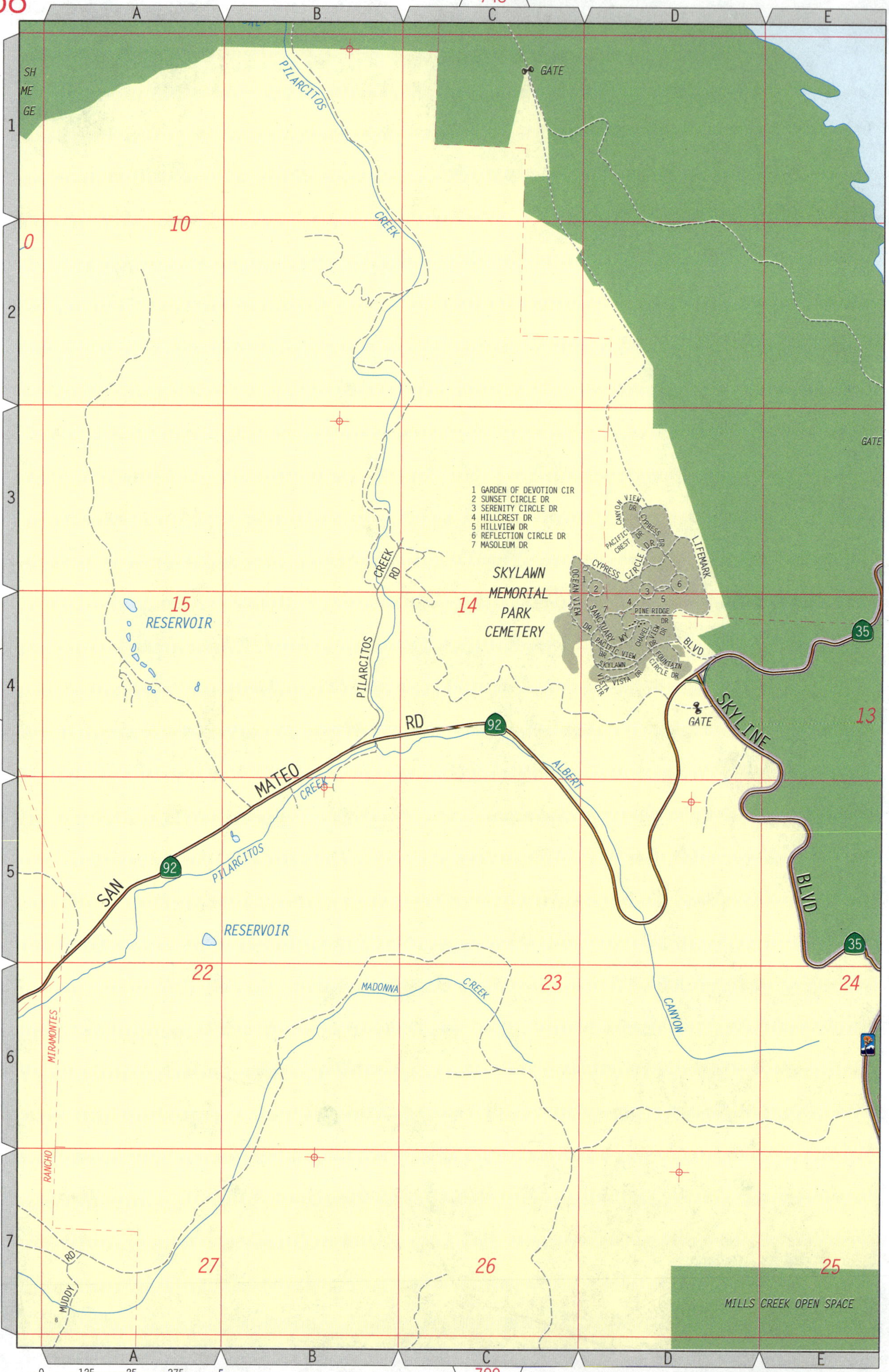
A
B
C
D
E
1
2
3
4
5
6
7
GATE
PILARCITOS
CREEK
10
15
RESERVOIR
14
13
1 GARDEN OF DEVOTION CIR
2 SUNSET CIRCLE DR
3 SERENITY CIRCLE DR
4 HILLCREST DR
5 HILLVIEW DR
6 REFLECTION CIRCLE DR
7 MASOLEUM DR
SKYLAWN MEMORIAL PARK CEMETERY
CANYON VIEW DR
CYPRESS DR
PACIFIC CREST DR
CYPRESS CIRCLE DR
LIFEMARK
OCEAN VIEW DR
SANCTUARY WY
PINE RIDGE DR
CHAPEL VIEW DR
PACIFIC VIEW DR
SKYLAWN
VISTA CIR
VISTA DR
FOUNTAIN CIRCLE DR
BLVD
PILARCITOS CREEK RD
SAN MATEO RD
92
35
SKYLINE BLVD
ALBERT CANYON
PILARCITOS CREEK
RESERVOIR
22
23
24
MADONNA CREEK
MIRAMONTES
RANCHO
MUDDY RD
27
26
25
MILLS CREEK OPEN SPACE

SEE 767 MAP

0 .125 .25 .375 .5 miles 1 in. = 1900 ft.

SEE 788 MAP

SEE 748 MAP

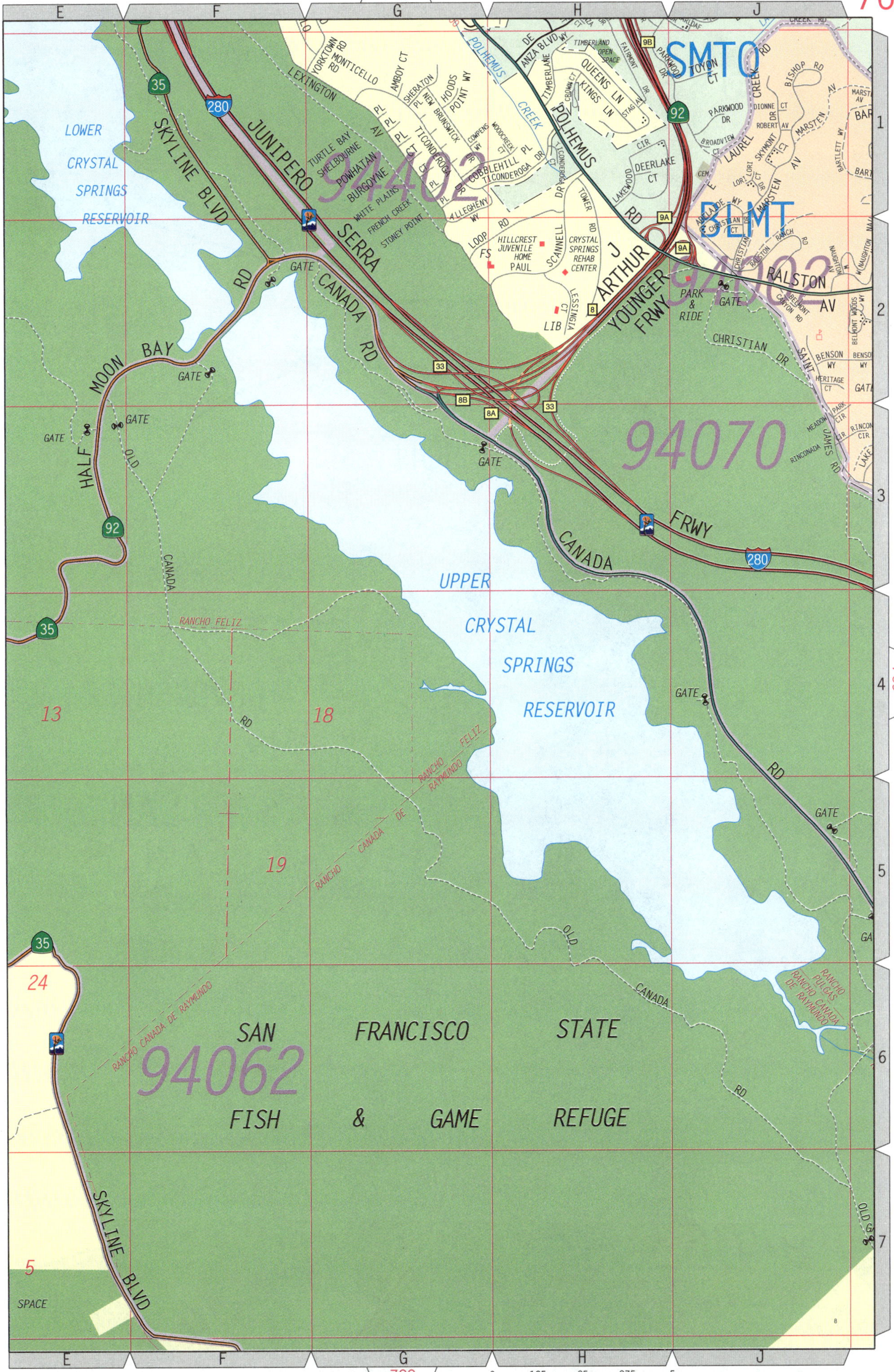

SEE 769 MAP

SEE 788 MAP

SAN MATEO CO.

© 2008 Rand McNally & Company

N

E F G H J

1

SMTO

BLMT

LOWER
CRYSTAL
SPRINGS
RESERVOIR

SKYLINE BLVD

JUNIPERO SERRA

94402

280

35

92

POLHEMUS CREEK

DE ANZA BLVD
TIMBERLAND WY
TIMBERLAKE OPEN SPACE
QUEENS LN
KINGS LN
STAG
POLHEMUS RD
PARKWOOD
TOYON CT
LAUREL
BISHOP RD
MARSTEN
AV

LEXINGTON
YORKTOWN RD
MONTICELLO
AMBOY CT
TURTLE BAY
SHELBOURNE
POWHATAN
BURGOYNE
WHITE PLAINS
SHERATON
PL NEW
BRUNSWICK
TICONDEROGA
COMPENS PL
WOODCREEK
PL
HOODS
POINT WY
FRENCH CREEK
STONEY POINT
ALLEGHENY
COBBLEHILL
TICONDEROGA
DR
LOOP
FS
TOWER RD
LAKEWOOD
RD
CRYSTAL
SPRINGS
REHAB
CENTER
CONCORD
CONDEROGA
CIR
DEERLAKE CT
HILLCREST
JUVENILE
HOME
PAUL
SCANNELL RD
LESSINGIA
CT
LIB
J ARTHUR YOUNGER FRWY

PARKWOOD DR
DIONNE CT
ROBERT AV
BROADVIEW
CEN
SKYMONT
LORI DR
CHRISTIAN
RANCH
BENSON WY
MARSTEN
AV
BARTLETT
BART

92

9B

9A

9A

94002

RALSTON AV

CHRISTIAN DR

BELMONT CANYON RD
PARK & RIDE
GATE

HERITAGE
CT
MEADOW
CIR
PARK
CIR
RINCON
CIR
RINCONADA RD
JAMES RD
LAKE
SAINT
NAUGHTON
W NAUGHTON

2

33

33

8B

8A

GATE

94070

94002

HALF MOON BAY

GATE

OLD

GATE

GATE

GATE

CANADA RD

CANADA

UPPER
CRYSTAL
SPRINGS
RESERVOIR

CANADA RD

FRWY

280

3

RANCHO FELIZ

RANCHO FELIZ RAYMUNDO

RANCHO CANADA DE

GATE

GATE

4

13

18

19

GATE

RANCHO
PULGAS
RANCHO CANADA
DE RAYMUNDO

OLD

CANADA

RD

5

GA

24

35

SAN
94062

FRANCISCO

STATE

FISH

&

GAME

REFUGE

RANCHO CANADA DE RAYMUNDO

OLD

CANADA

6

RD

SKYLINE BLVD

OLD

GA

7

5

SPACE

8

E F G H J

0 .125 .25 .375 .5 miles 1 in. = 1900 ft.

SEE 749 MAP

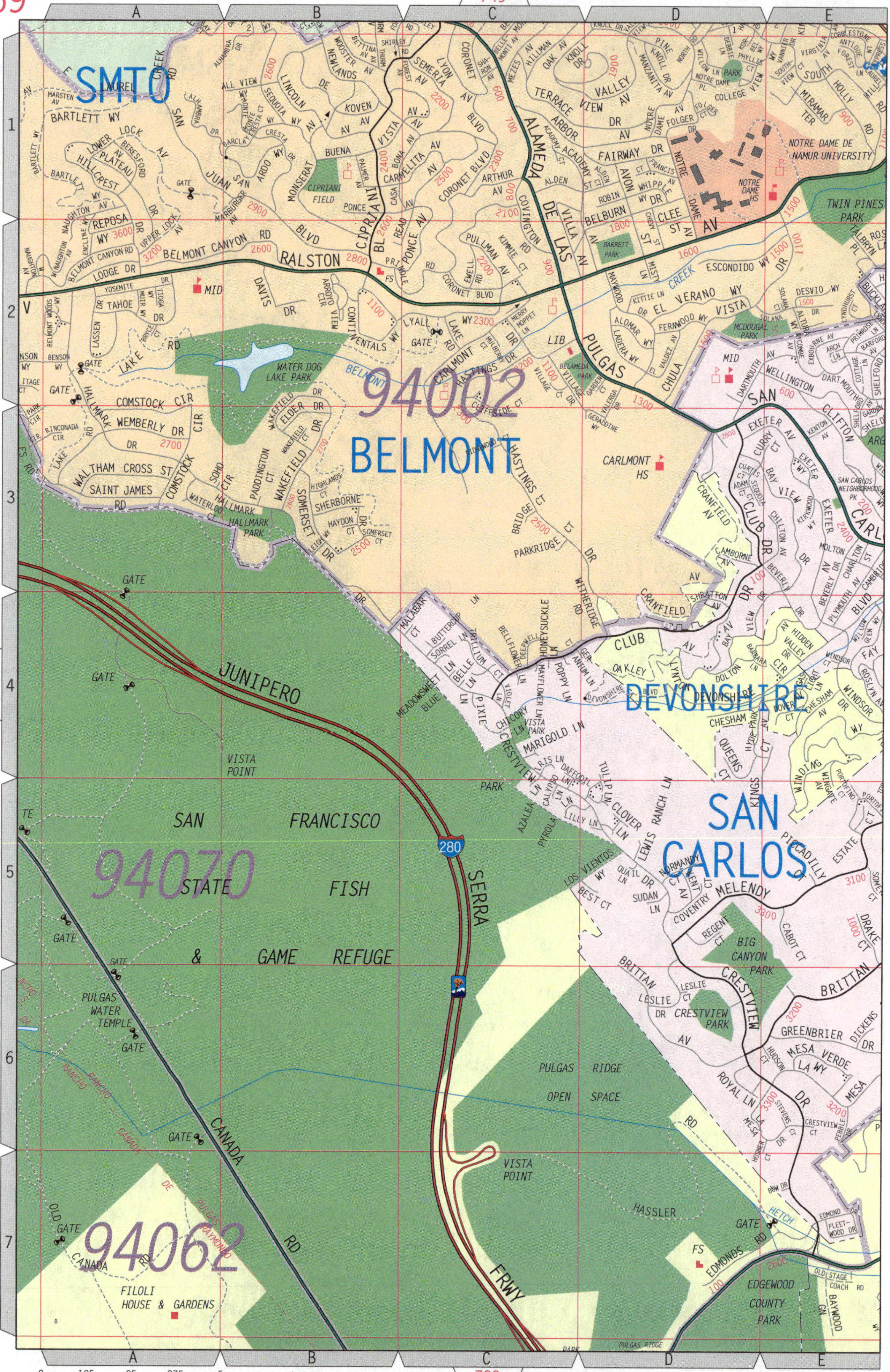

SEE 768 MAP

SEE 789 MAP

0 .125 .25 .375 .5 miles 1 in. = 1900 ft.

SEE 749 MAP

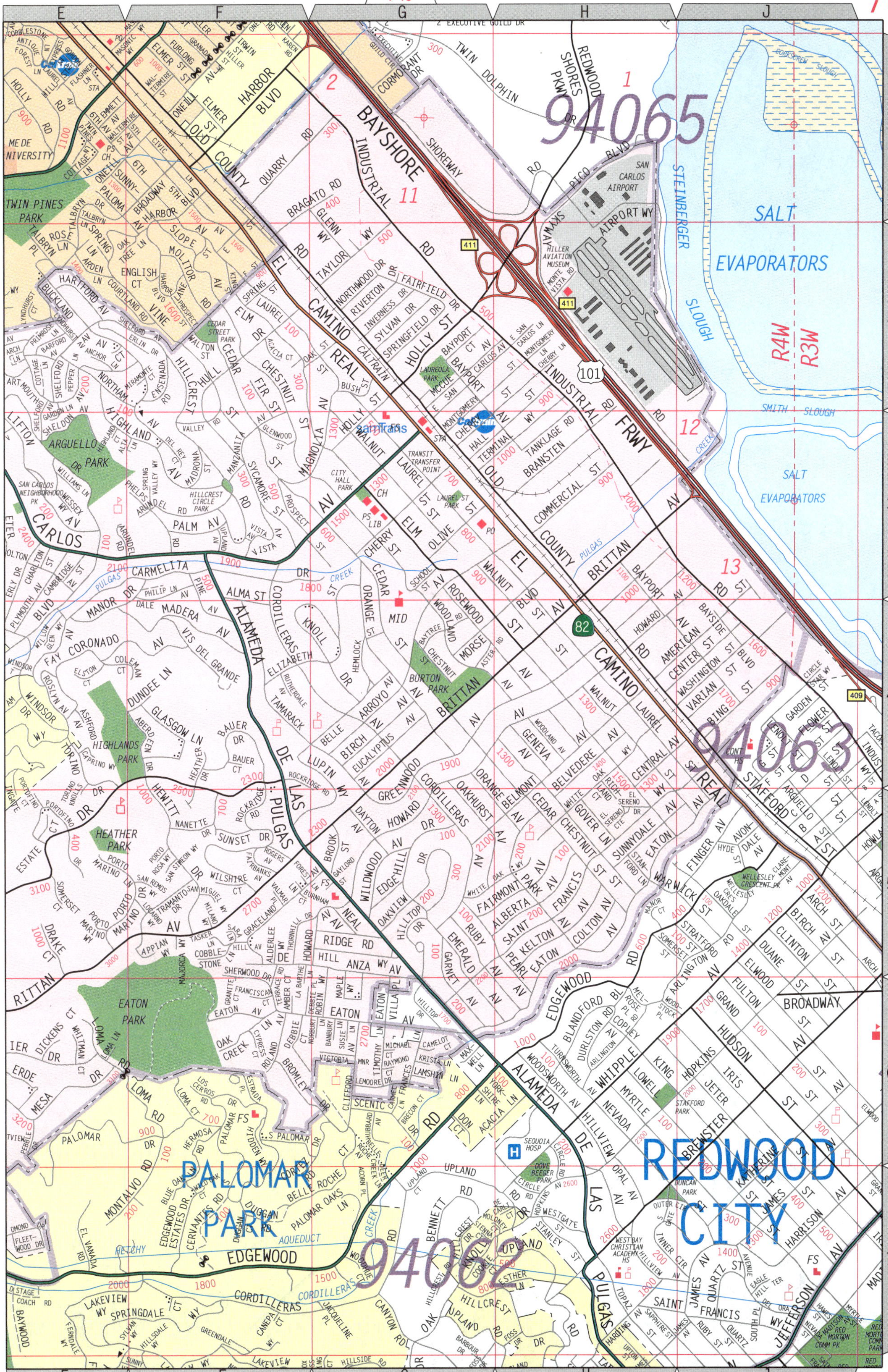

SEE 770 MAP

SEE 789 MAP

0 .125 .25 .375 .5 miles 1 in. = 1900 ft.

SEE 750 MAP

SALT
EVAPORATORS
SALT
EVAPORATORS
SALT
EVAPORATORS
REDWOOD
CREEK
CORKSCREW
SLOUGH
DEEPWATER
SLOUGH
SMITH
SLOUGH
FIRST
SLOUGH
PETES
HARBOR
CEMEX
CEMENT
CEMEX
AGGREGATES
HINMAN
RD
SEAPORT
BLVD
HERKNER RD
BEEGER
RD
MUNICIPAL
MARINA
REDWOOD
MARINA
DOCKTOWN
MARINA
1 LOUIS LN
2 MORESBY LN
3 CHARLOTT LN
4 SYDNEY LN
BAYSHORE RD
BAIR ISLAND
RD
UCCELLI BLVD
CARDINAL
CHESAPEAKE
SAGINAW
GALVESTON DR
PENOBSCOT
DR
BLOMQUIST ST
BAYSHORE
BLVD
MERVYNS
PLAZA
KAISER
FOUNDATION
HOSPITAL
BROADWAY
WOODSIDE
RD
HOOVER
PARK
ANDREW
SPINAS
PARK
SEQUOIA
HS
REDWOOD
CITY
94062
94063
94061
NORTH
FAIR OAKS
EL CAMINO REAL
MIDDLEFIELD
RD
JEFFERSON
AV
VETERANS
BLVD
WHIPPLE
AV
WINSLOW
BREWSTER
AV
MAIN
ST
CHESTNUT
ST
BAY
RD
HUDSON
ST
ROOSEVELT
AV
UNION
CEM
CALTRAIN
HOOVER
ROLISON
LIB
PO
CH
FS
101
84
82
408
409
0 .125 .25 .375 .5
miles 1 in. = 1900 ft.

SEE 769 MAP

SEE 790 MAP

SEE 750 MAP

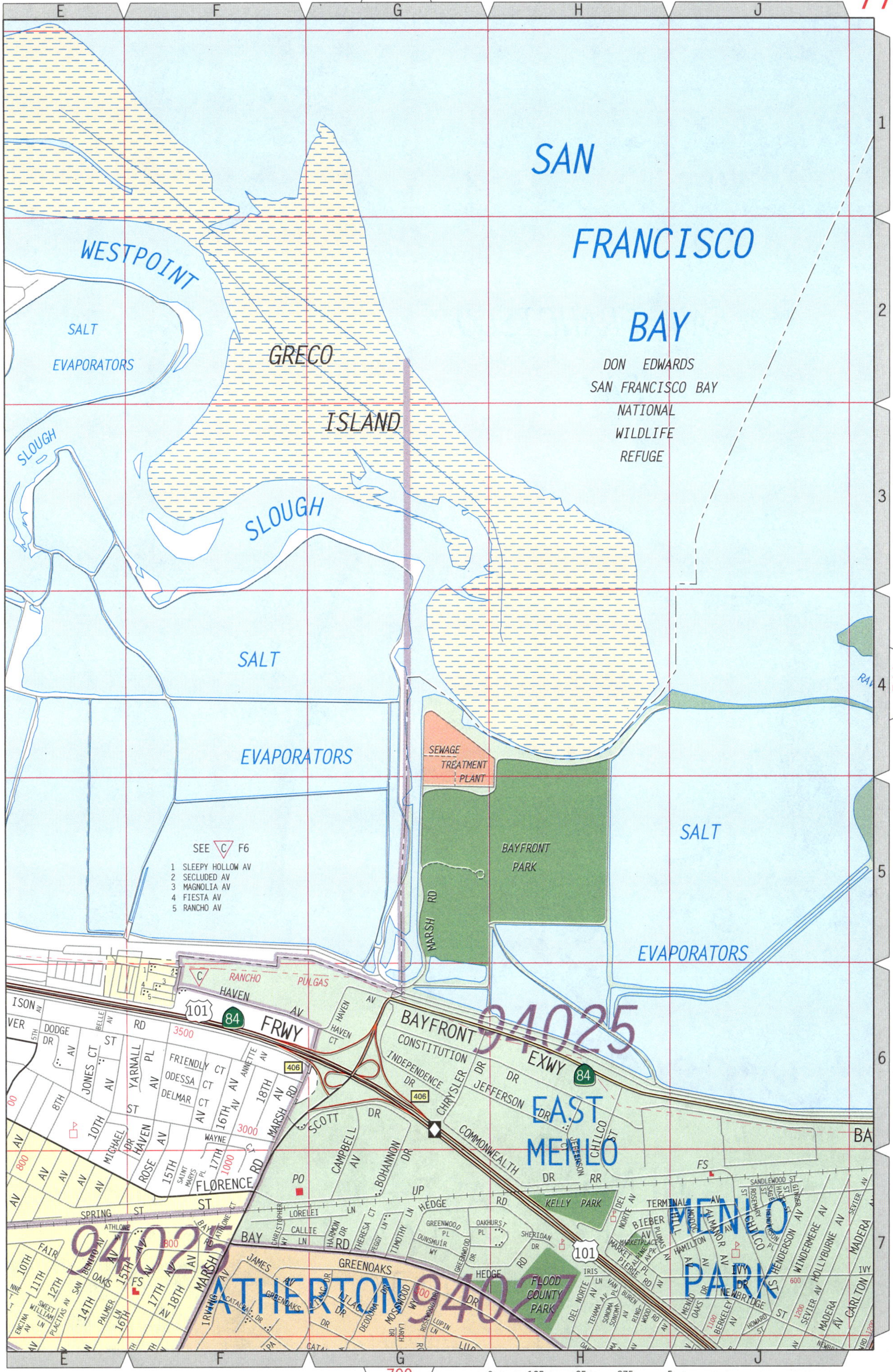
SAN FRANCISCO BAY
DON EDWARDS SAN FRANCISCO BAY NATIONAL WILDLIFE REFUGE
GRECO ISLAND
WESTPOINT SLOUGH
SALT EVAPORATORS
SEWAGE TREATMENT PLANT
BAYFRONT PARK
MARSH RD
SEE C F6
1 SLEEPY HOLLOW AV
2 SECLUDED AV
3 MAGNOLIA AV
4 FIESTA AV
5 RANCHO AV
RANCHO PULGAS
HAVEN AV
BAYFRONT EXWY
FRWY
94025
EAST MENLO
MENLO PARK
ATHERTON
94027
CONSTITUTION DR
INDEPENDENCE DR
CHRYSLER DR
JEFFERSON DR
COMMONWEALTH DR
CHILCO ST
KELLY PARK
FLOOD COUNTY PARK
FLORENCE ST
SPRING ST
BAY RD
GREENOAKS DR
SCOTT DR
CAMPBELL AV
BOHANNON DR
HEDGE RD
TERMINAL AV
IVY DR
NEWBRIDGE ST
HENDERSON AV
WINDERMERE AV
HOLLYBURNE AV
MADERA AV
CARLTON AV
SEVIER AV
MARKET PL
FRIENDLY CT
ODESSA CT
DELMAR CT
YARNALL PL
JONES CT
DODGE DR
WAYNE CT
ROSE AV
MICHAEL DR
MARSH RD
IRVING AV
JAMES AV
LORELEI LN
CALLIE LN
HARMON DR
THERESA CT
TIMOTHY LN
GREENWOOD PL
DUNSMUIR WY
OAKHURST PL
SHERIDAN DR
DEL NORTE AV
BIEBER AV
HAMILTON AV
ALMANOR AV
SANDLEWOOD ST
SEE 771 MAP

SAN MATEO CO.

SEE 790 MAP

0 .125 .25 .375 .5 miles 1 in. = 1900 ft.

SEE B MAP
SEE 770 MAP
SEE 791 MAP
A
B
C
D
E
1
2
3
4
5
6
7
SAN FRANCISCO
BAY
SALT EVAPORATORS
DON EDWARDS
SAN FRANCISCO BAY
NATIONAL WILDLIFF REFUGE
RAVENSWOOD SLOUGH
DUMBARTON BRDG
RAVENSWOOD
OPEN
SPACE
PRESERVE
SALT EVAPORATORS
UP RR
94025
94303
84
109
114
UNIVERSITY AV
BAYFRONT EXWY
WILLOW RD
HAMILTON AV
HAMILTON CT
ADAMS DR
ADAMS CT
MENLO PARK
EAST PALO ALTO
MID-PENINSULA HS
OBRIEN DR
KAVANAUGH DR
CASEY CT
KELLY CT
CARLTON AV
MADERA AV
SEVIER AV
IVY DR
ALBERNI ST
TULANE AV
RUTGERS ST
DREW CT
TEMPLE CT
STEVENS AV
XAVIER ST
HUNTER ST
GEORGETOWN ST
FORDHAM ST
GONZAGA ST
ILLINOIS ST
PURDUE AV
NOTRE DAME AV
ANNAPOLIS ST
BAYLOR ST
FORDHAM ST
JACK FARELL PARK
DEMETER ST
PULGAS AV
TARA ST
BAY RD
BAYLANDS NATURE PRESERVE
COOLEY LANDING
KIRKWOOD CT
CLARENCE CT
GERTRUDE CT
HAZELWOOD WY
GLORIA WY
FARRINGTON WY
EMMETT WY
0 .125 .25 .375 .5 miles 1 in. = 1900 ft.

SEE B MAP

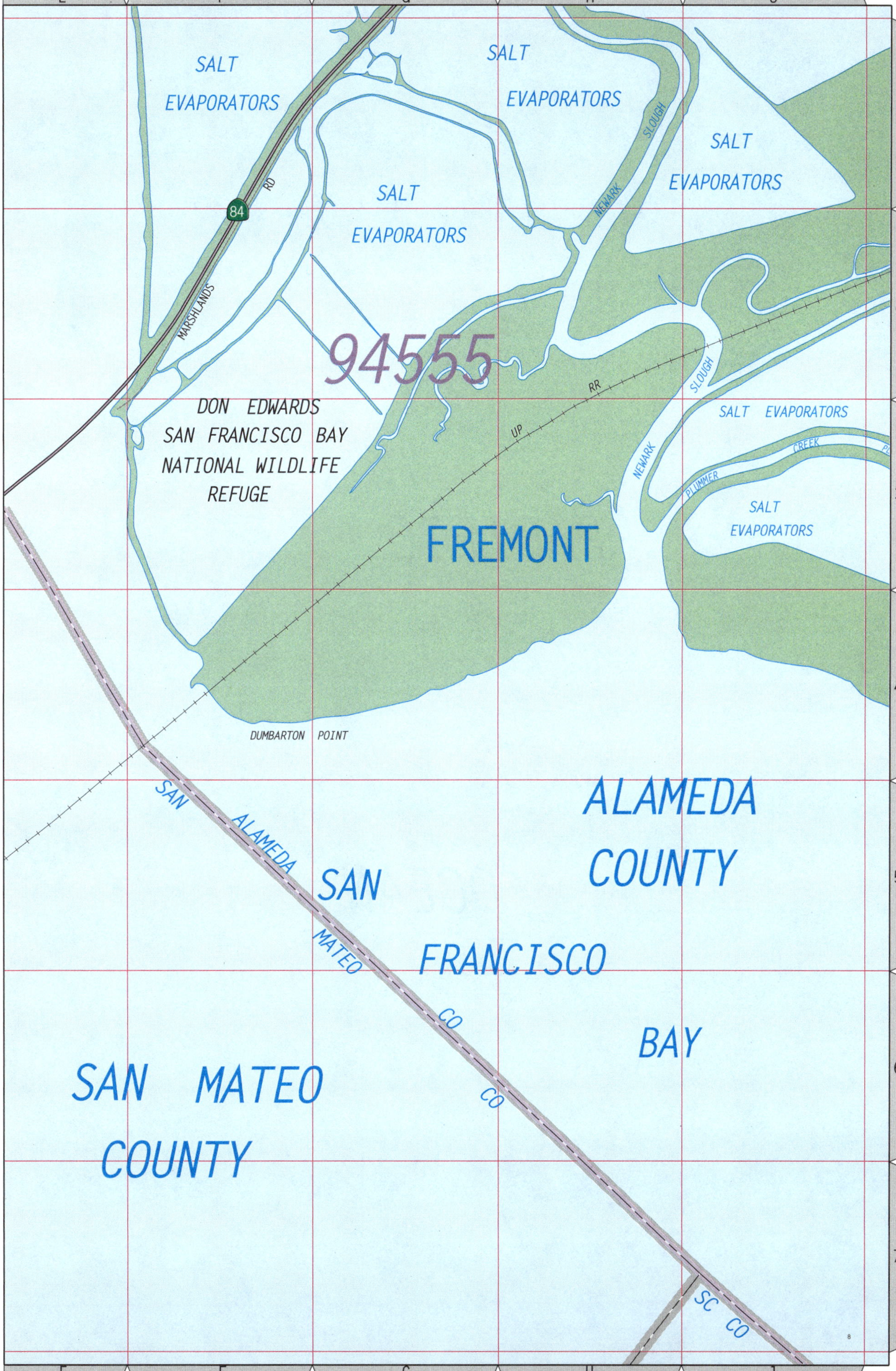
SALT EVAPORATORS
SALT EVAPORATORS
SALT EVAPORATORS
SALT EVAPORATORS
SALT EVAPORATORS
SALT EVAPORATORS
NEWARK SLOUGH
MARSHLANDS RD
84
94555
DON EDWARDS SAN FRANCISCO BAY NATIONAL WILDLIFE REFUGE
UP RR
PLUMMER CREEK
FREMONT
DUMBARTON POINT
ALAMEDA COUNTY
SAN ALAMEDA
SAN MATEO CO
CO
SAN FRANCISCO BAY
SAN MATEO COUNTY
SC CO
E F G H J
1 2 3 4 5 6 7
0 .125 .25 .375 .5 miles 1 in. = 1900 ft.

SEE B MAP
SEE 791 MAP

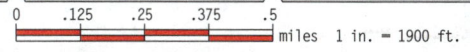

SEE 767 MAP

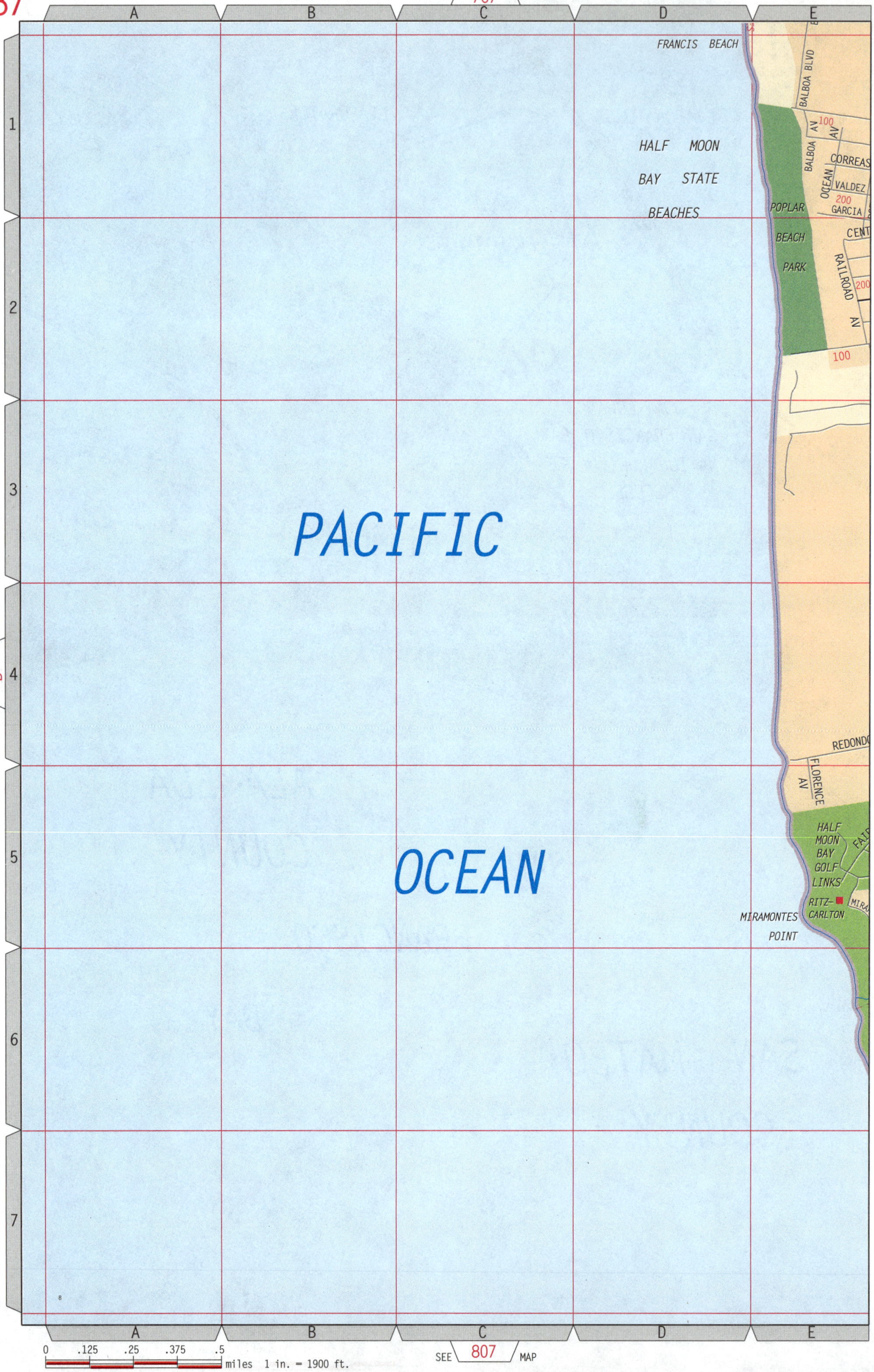

SEE B MAP

0 .125 .25 .375 .5 miles 1 in. = 1900 ft.

SEE 807 MAP

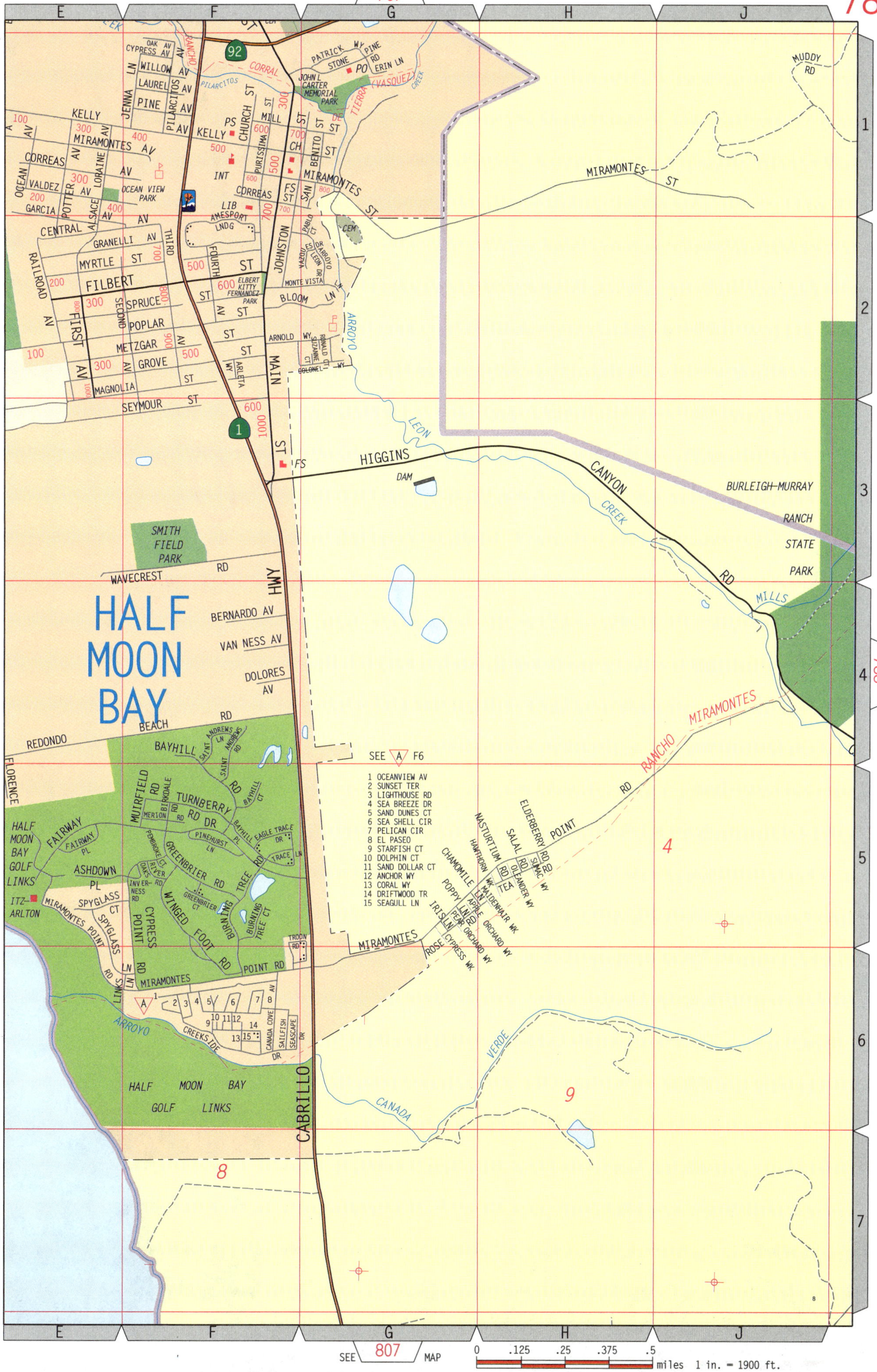
SEE 767 MAP
SAN MATEO CO.
HALF MOON BAY
HIGGINS CANYON RD
BURLEIGH-MURRAY RANCH STATE PARK
SMITH FIELD PARK
HALF MOON BAY GOLF LINKS
CABRILLO HWY
RANCHO MIRAMONTES POINT RD
MIRAMONTES ST
MAIN ST
KELLY AV
FILBERT ST
SEE A F6
1 OCEANVIEW AV
2 SUNSET TER
3 LIGHTHOUSE RD
4 SEA BREEZE DR
5 SAND DUNES CT
6 SEA SHELL CIR
7 PELICAN CIR
8 EL PASEO
9 STARFISH CT
10 DOLPHIN CT
11 SAND DOLLAR CT
12 ANCHOR WY
13 CORAL WY
14 DRIFTWOOD TR
15 SEAGULL LN
SEE 788 MAP
SEE 807 MAP
0 .125 .25 .375 .5 miles 1 in. = 1900 ft.

SEE 768 MAP
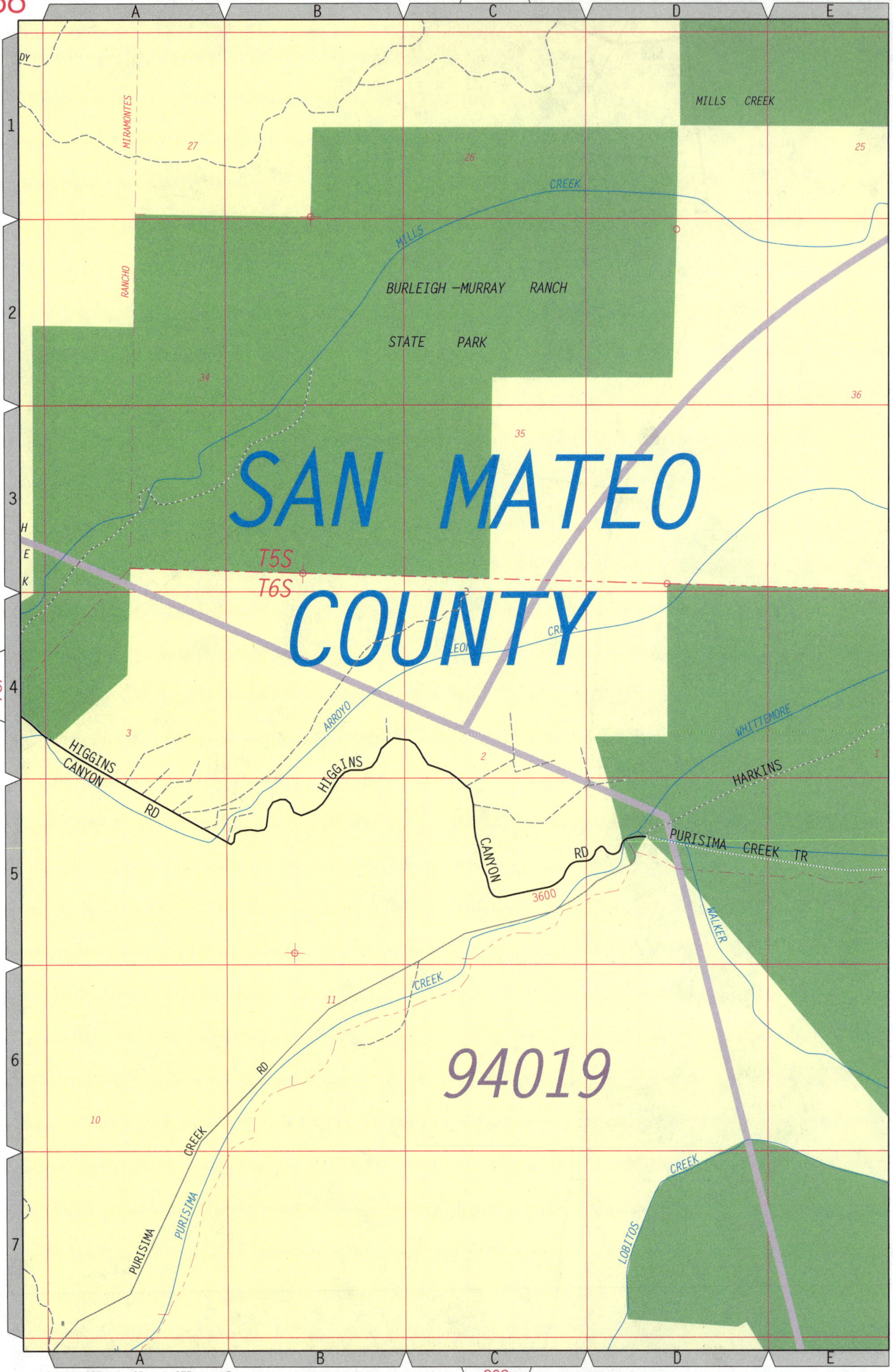

SEE 787 MAP
SEE 808 MAP
0 .125 .25 .375 .5 miles 1 in. = 1900 ft.

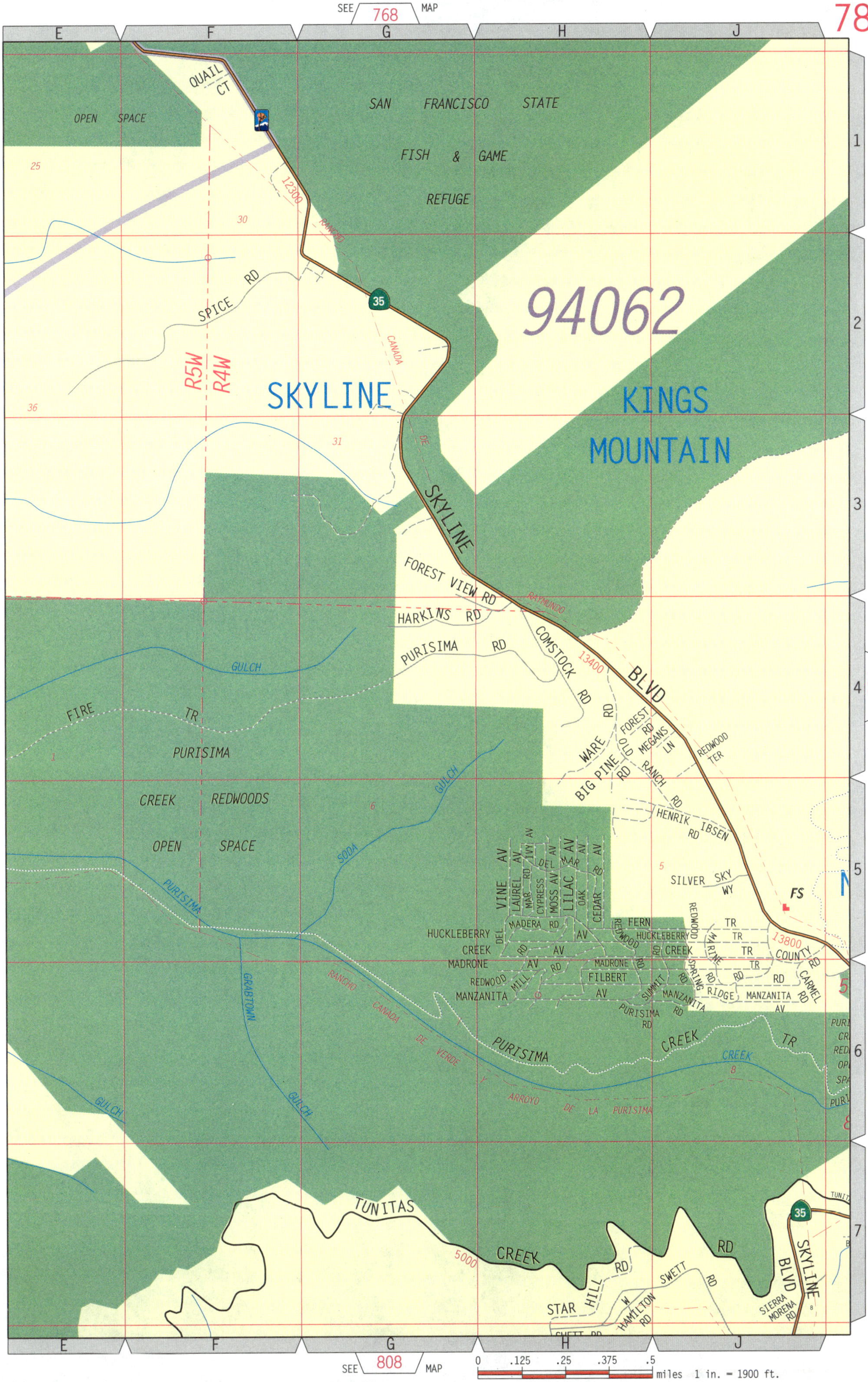
SEE 768 MAP
SEE 789 MAP
SEE 808 MAP
E
F
G
H
J
1
2
3
4
5
6
7
94062
SKYLINE
KINGS MOUNTAIN
SAN FRANCISCO STATE FISH & GAME REFUGE
OPEN SPACE
QUAIL CT
SPICE RD
R5W
R4W
35
CANADA DE RAYMUNDO
RANCHO
SKYLINE BLVD
12300
13400
13800
FOREST VIEW RD
HARKINS RD
PURISIMA RD
COMSTOCK RD
FOREST RD
OLD RANCH RD
MEGANS LN
REDWOOD TER
WARE RD
BIG PINE RD
HENRIK IBSEN RD
SILVER SKY WY
FS
FIRE TR
PURISIMA CREEK REDWOODS OPEN SPACE
GULCH
SODA GULCH
PURISIMA GULCH
GRABTOWN GULCH
VINE AV
LAUREL AV
IVY AV
MAR RD
CYPRESS
DEL MAR AV
MOSS AV
LILAC AV
OAK AV
CEDAR AV
MAR RD
MADERA RD
HUCKLEBERRY
CREEK
MADRONE
REDWOOD
MANZANITA
DEL RD
AV
MILL
FERN
REDWOOD RD
HUCKLEBERRY
CREEK
MADRONE
FILBERT
AV
SUMMIT
SPRING RIDGE
REDWOOD
MARINE
TR
COUNTY RD
CARMEL RD
MANZANITA AV
PURISIMA RD
RANCHO CANADA DE VERDE Y ARROYO DE LA PURISIMA
PURISIMA CREEK TR
CREEK
TUNITAS CREEK RD
5000
STAR HILL RD
W HAMILTON RD
SWETT RD
SWETT RD
SKYLINE BLVD
SIERRA MORENA RD
0 .125 .25 .375 .5 miles 1 in. = 1900 ft.
25
30
36
31
1
6
5
8

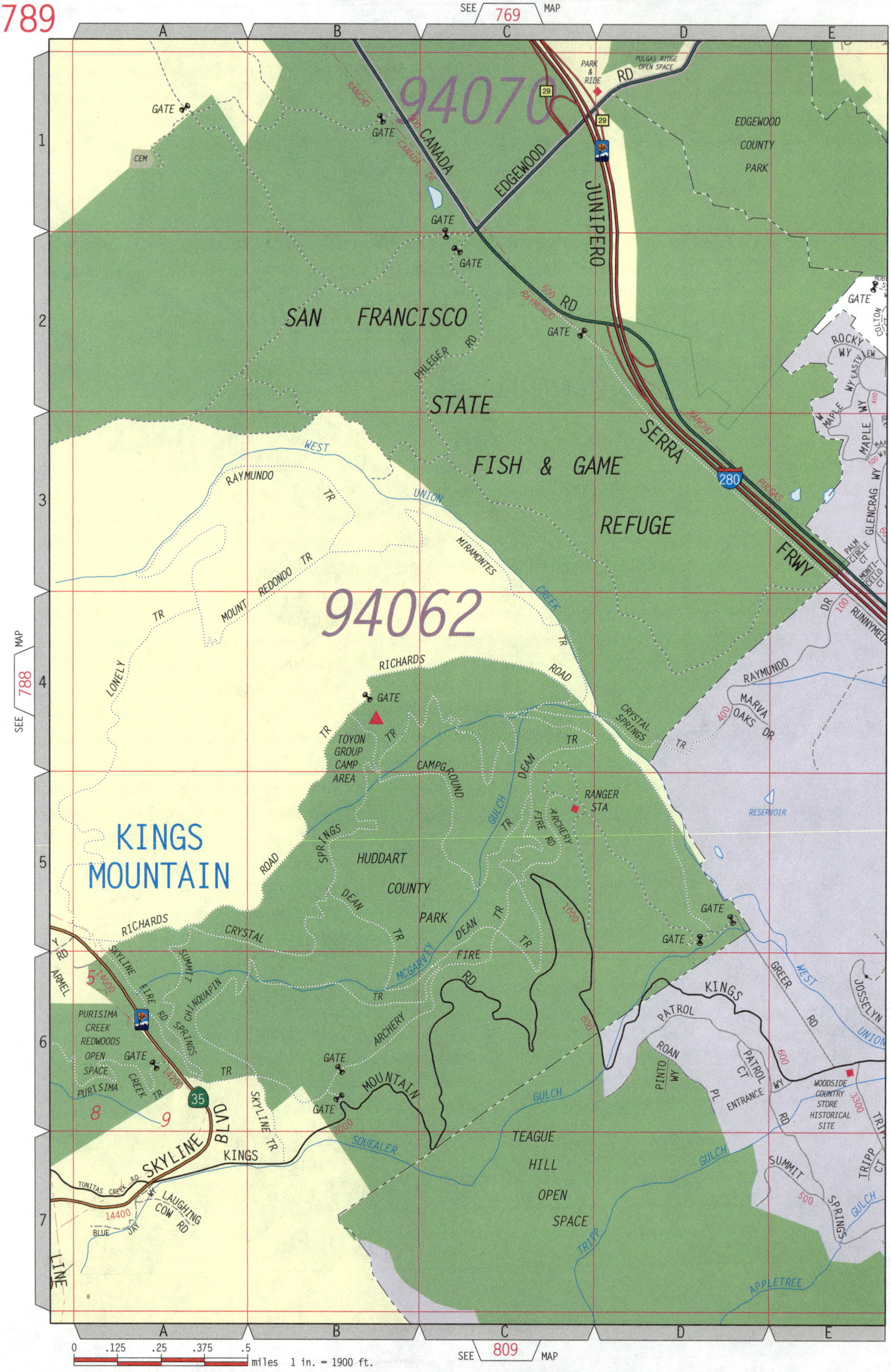
SEE 769 MAP
SEE 788 MAP
SEE 809 MAP
A B C D E
1 2 3 4 5 6 7
94070
94062
SAN FRANCISCO STATE FISH & GAME REFUGE
EDGEWOOD COUNTY PARK
KINGS MOUNTAIN
HUDDART COUNTY PARK
TEAGUE HILL OPEN SPACE
PURISIMA CREEK REDWOODS OPEN SPACE
TOYON GROUP CAMP AREA
RANGER STA
WOODSIDE COUNTRY STORE HISTORICAL SITE
PULGAS RIDGE OPEN SPACE
PARK & RIDE
CEM
GATE
JUNIPERO SERRA FRWY
280
29
35
EDGEWOOD RD
CANADA RD
RAYMUNDO RD
PHLEGER RD
SKYLINE BLVD
KINGS MOUNTAIN RD
TUNITAS CREEK RD
LAUGHING COW RD
BLUE JAY WY
GREER RD
PATROL RD
PATROL CT
ROAN PL
PINTO WY
ENTRANCE WY
SUMMIT SPRINGS RD
TRIPP CT
JOSSELYN LN
RUNNYMEDE
MARVA OAKS DR
ROCKY WY
EASTVIEW WY
MAPLE WY
GLENCRAG WY
PALM CIRCLE CT
MONTICELLO CT
COLTON
ARMEL
WEST UNION CREEK
MCGARVEY GULCH
SQUEALER GULCH
TRIPP GULCH
APPLETREE
RESERVOIR
MIRAMONTES TR
MOUNT REDONDO TR
LONELY TR
RICHARDS ROAD
CRYSTAL SPRINGS TR
CAMPGROUND
DEAN TR
ARCHERY FIRE RD
DEAN FIRE RD
CHINQUAPIN TR
SKYLINE TR
SUMMIT SPRINGS TR
LINE
0 .125 .25 .375 .5 miles 1 in. = 1900 ft.

SEE 769 MAP

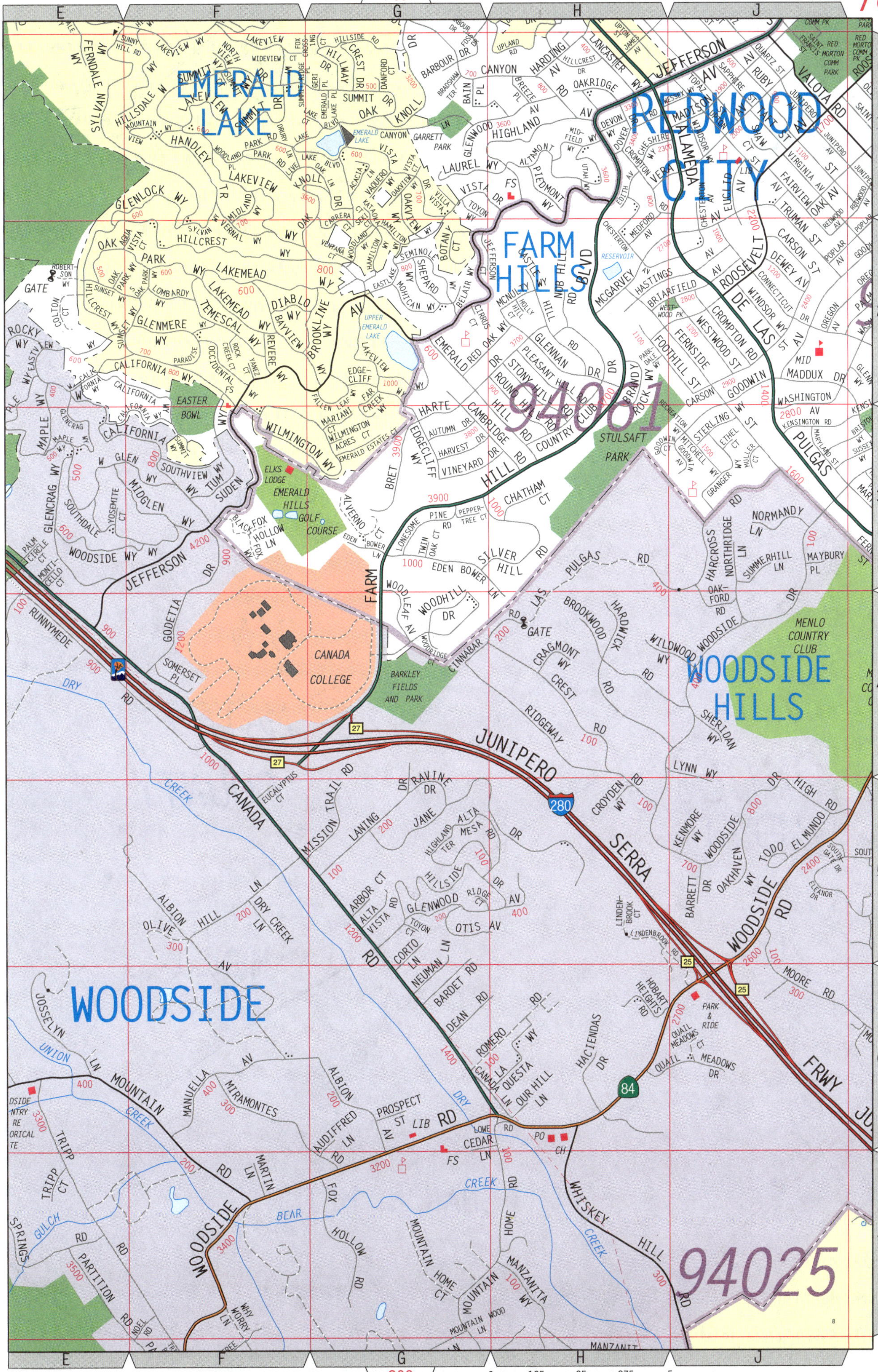

SEE 790 MAP

SEE 809 MAP

0 .125 .25 .375 .5 miles 1 in. = 1900 ft.

SEE 770 MAP

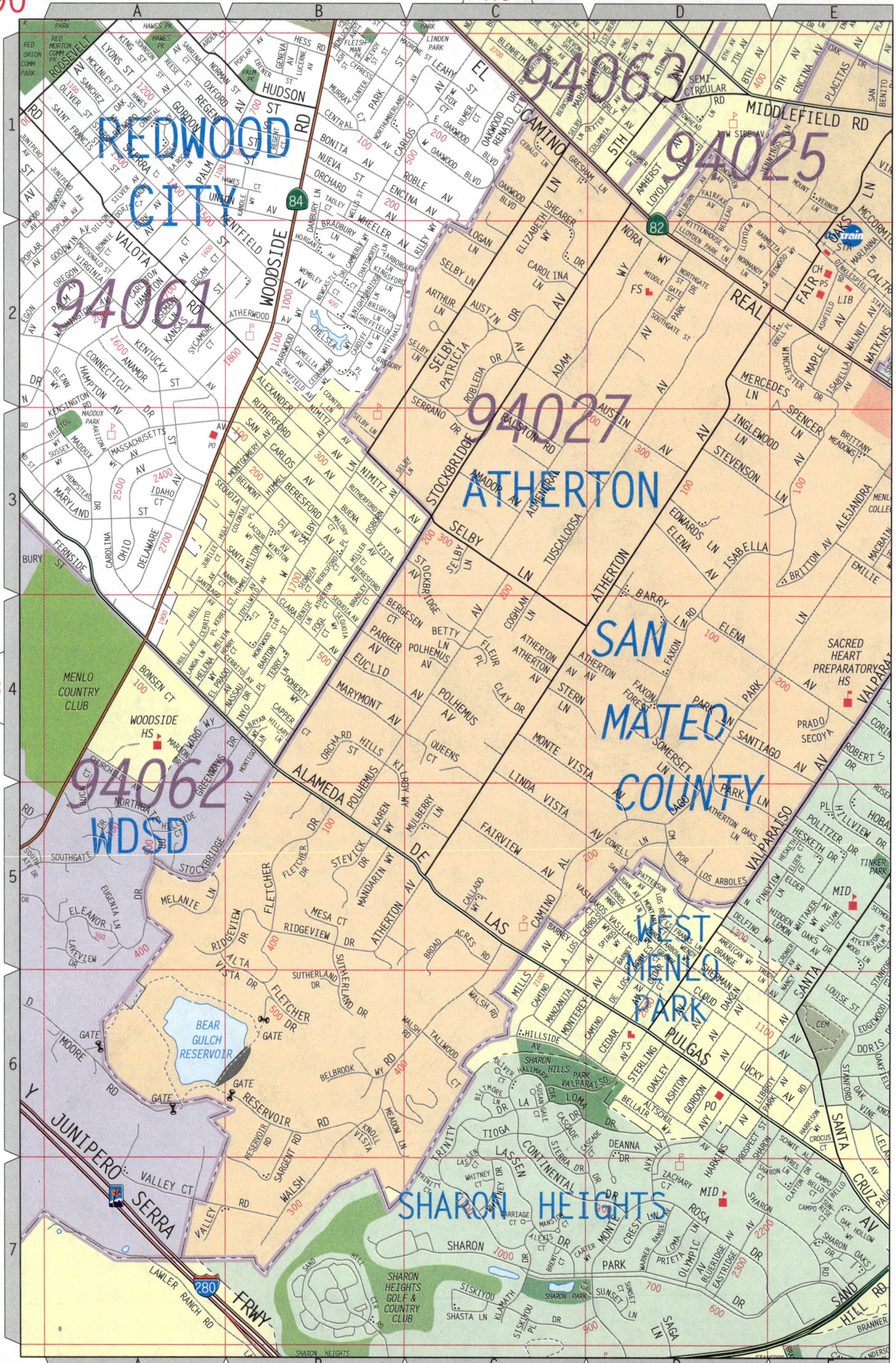

SEE 789 MAP

SEE 810 MAP

0 .125 .25 .375 .5 miles 1 in. = 1900 ft.

SEE 770 MAP

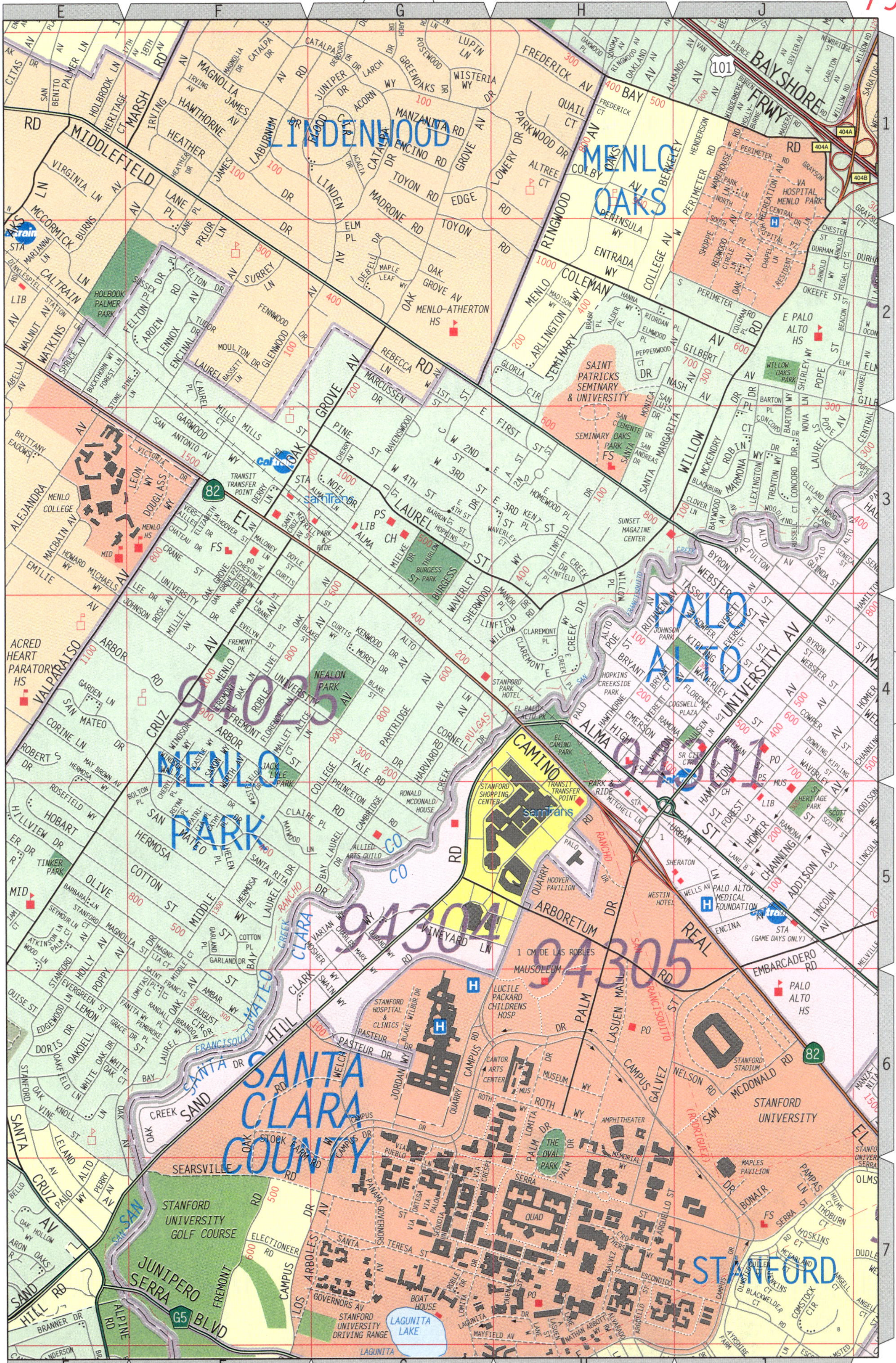
LINDENWOOD
MENLO OAKS
MENLO PARK
PALO ALTO
SANTA CLARA COUNTY
STANFORD
STANFORD UNIVERSITY
STANFORD UNIVERSITY GOLF COURSE
94025
94301
94304
94305
MIDDLEFIELD RD
EL CAMINO REAL
BAYSHORE FRWY
SAND HILL RD
JUNIPERO SERRA BLVD
ALMA ST
UNIVERSITY AV
WILLOW RD
MENLO COLLEGE
HOLBROOK PALMER PARK
MENLO-ATHERTON HS
SAINT PATRICKS SEMINARY & UNIVERSITY
SUNSET MAGAZINE CENTER
STANFORD SHOPPING CENTER
STANFORD HOSPITAL & CLINICS
LUCILE PACKARD CHILDRENS HOSP
PALO ALTO MEDICAL FOUNDATION
PALO ALTO HS
STANFORD STADIUM
MAPLES PAVILION
LAGUNITA LAKE
NEALON PARK
VA HOSPITAL MENLO PARK
E PALO ALTO HS
ACRED HEART PARATORY HS

SEE 791 MAP

SEE 810 MAP

0 .125 .25 .375 .5 miles 1 in. = 1900 ft.

SEE 771 MAP

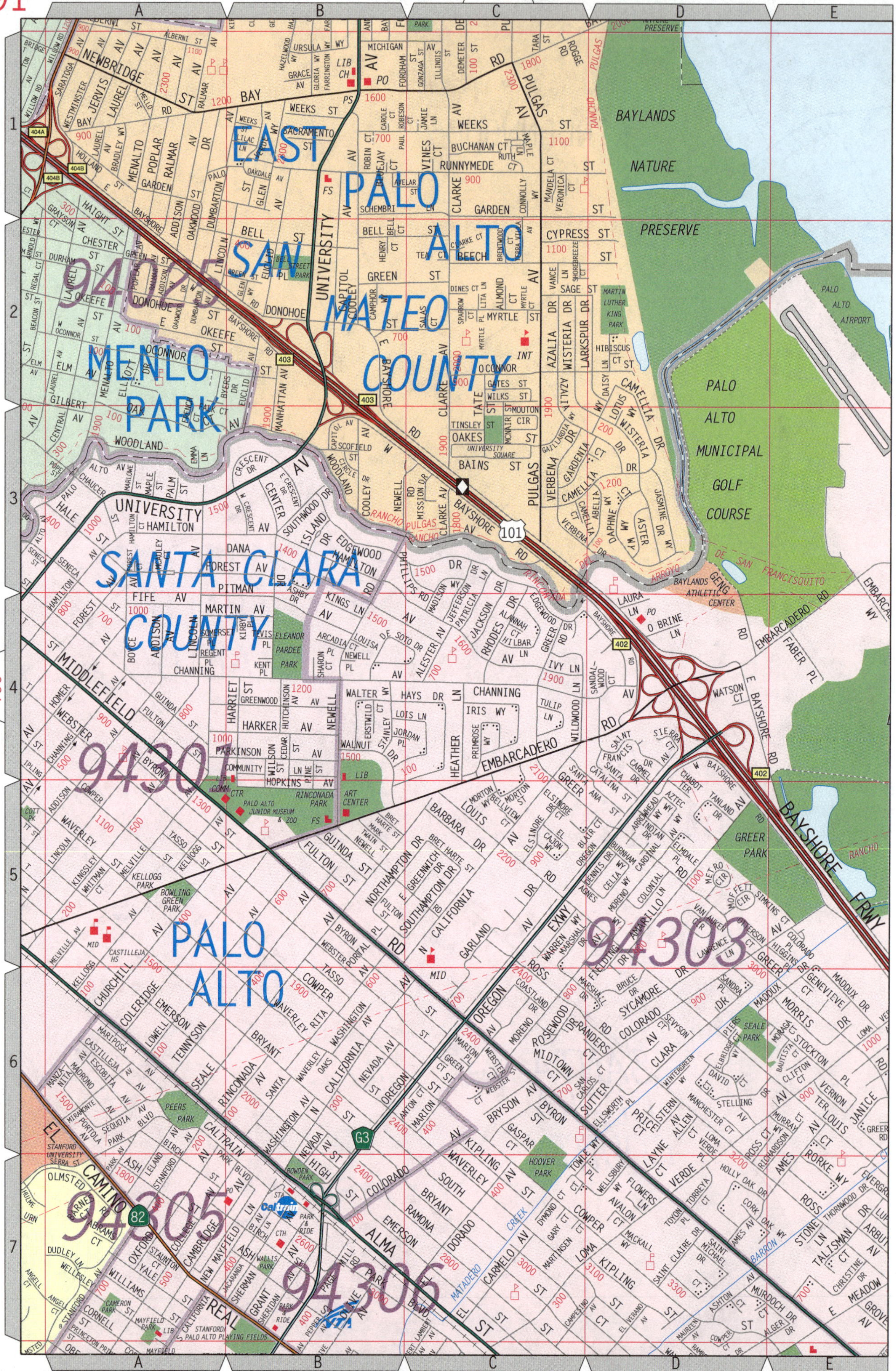

SEE 790 MAP

SEE B MAP

0 .125 .25 .375 .5 miles 1 in. = 1900 ft.

SEE 771 MAP

E
F
G
H
J
1
2
3
4
5
6
7
SAN
FRANCISCO
BAY
SAN MATEO CO
SANTA CLARA CO
SAND POINT
HOOKS POINT
BAYLANDS NATURE PRESERVE
BAYLANDS NATURE INTERPRETIVE CENTER
BOAT LAUNCH
EMBARCADERO RD
EMBARCADERO WY
BYXBEE REC AREA
BAYLANDS
NATURE
PRESERVE
RANCHO RINCON DE SAN FRANCISQUITO
SALT EVAPORATORS
SALT EVAPORATORS
MOUNTAIN VIEW SLOUGH
95002
94043
MOUNTAIN VIEW
SEE B MAP
FRWY
101
SHORELINE AT MOUNTAIN VIEW
PERMANENTE CREEK
SHORELINE GOLF LINKS
CLUBHOUSE
TERMINAL BLVD
SAN ANTONIO RD
BRODERICK WY
CASEY AV
COAST AV
MARINE WY
ELWELL CT
CORPORATION WY
BAYSHORE PKWY
GARCIA AV
SHORELINE
GOLF LINKS
SHORELINE AT MOUNTAIN VIEW
SHORELINE AMPHITHEATRE AT MOUNTAIN VIEW
BILL GRAHAM PKWY
SHORELINE BLVD
DOG PARK
FS
CRITTENDEN LN
SALADO DR
TRANSPORT ST
COMMERCIAL
SAN ANTONIO RD
FABIAN WY
ADOBE CREEK
NATHAN WY
CORINA WY
ORTEGA CT
RD
MEADOW DR
1000
CIR
DR
EVERGREEN DR
ASPEN WY
LUPINE AV
ARBUTUS AV
DRIFTWOOD
RAMOS PARK
MEADOW
GROVE AV
MAYVIEW AV
3600
3800
CHRISTINE DR
CT
MADDUX DR
EVE DR
LOMA VERDE AV
1000
KENNETH DR
THOMAS DR
JANICE WY
GREER RD
CREEK
PL
400C
400B
400C
LO ALTO AIRPORT

0 .125 .25 .375 .5 miles 1 in. = 1900 ft.

SEE B MAP

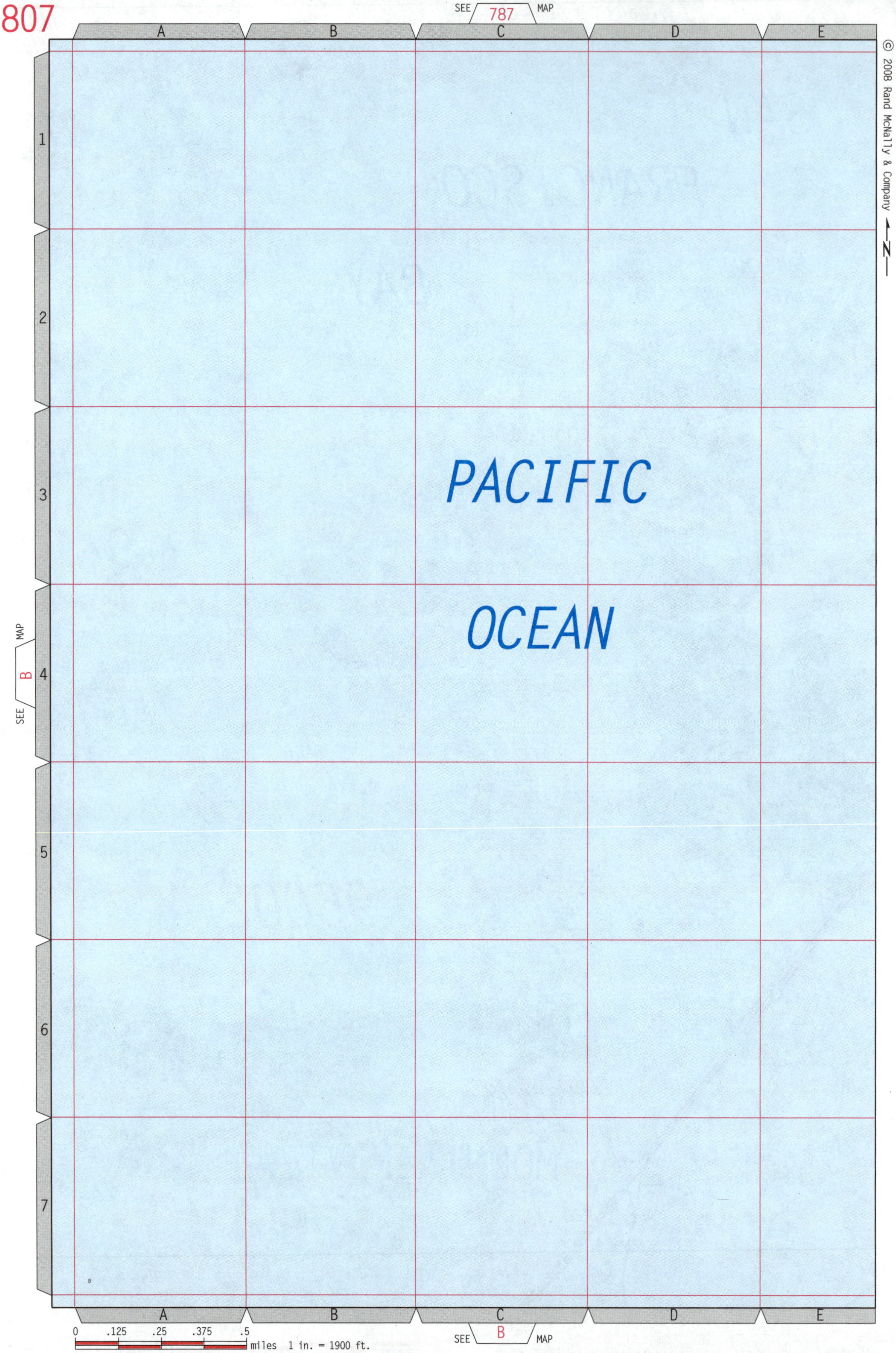
SEE 787 MAP
A
B
C
D
E
1
2
3
4
5
6
7
SEE B MAP
PACIFIC
OCEAN
SEE B MAP
0 .125 .25 .375 .5
miles 1 in. = 1900 ft.

SEE 787 MAP
E
F
G
H
J
1
2
3
4
5
6
7
SAN MATEO COUNTY
94019
CABRILLO HWY
CABRILLO
HWY
1
EEL ROCK
SEAL ROCK
MARTINS BEACH
PURISIMA CREEK RD
PURISIMA
PURISIMA CREEK
VERDE RD
VERDE RD
CEM
RANCHO CANADA DE VERDE Y ARROYO DE LA PURISIMA
RESERVOIR
RESERVOIR
MEYN RD
LOBITOS CREEK RD
LOBITOS CREEK
CREEK
LUCY LN
LOBITOS CREEK CUT
RAILROAD AV
15
16
17
21
SEE 808 MAP
SEE B MAP
0 .125 .25 .375 .5
miles 1 in. = 1900 ft.

SEE 788 MAP

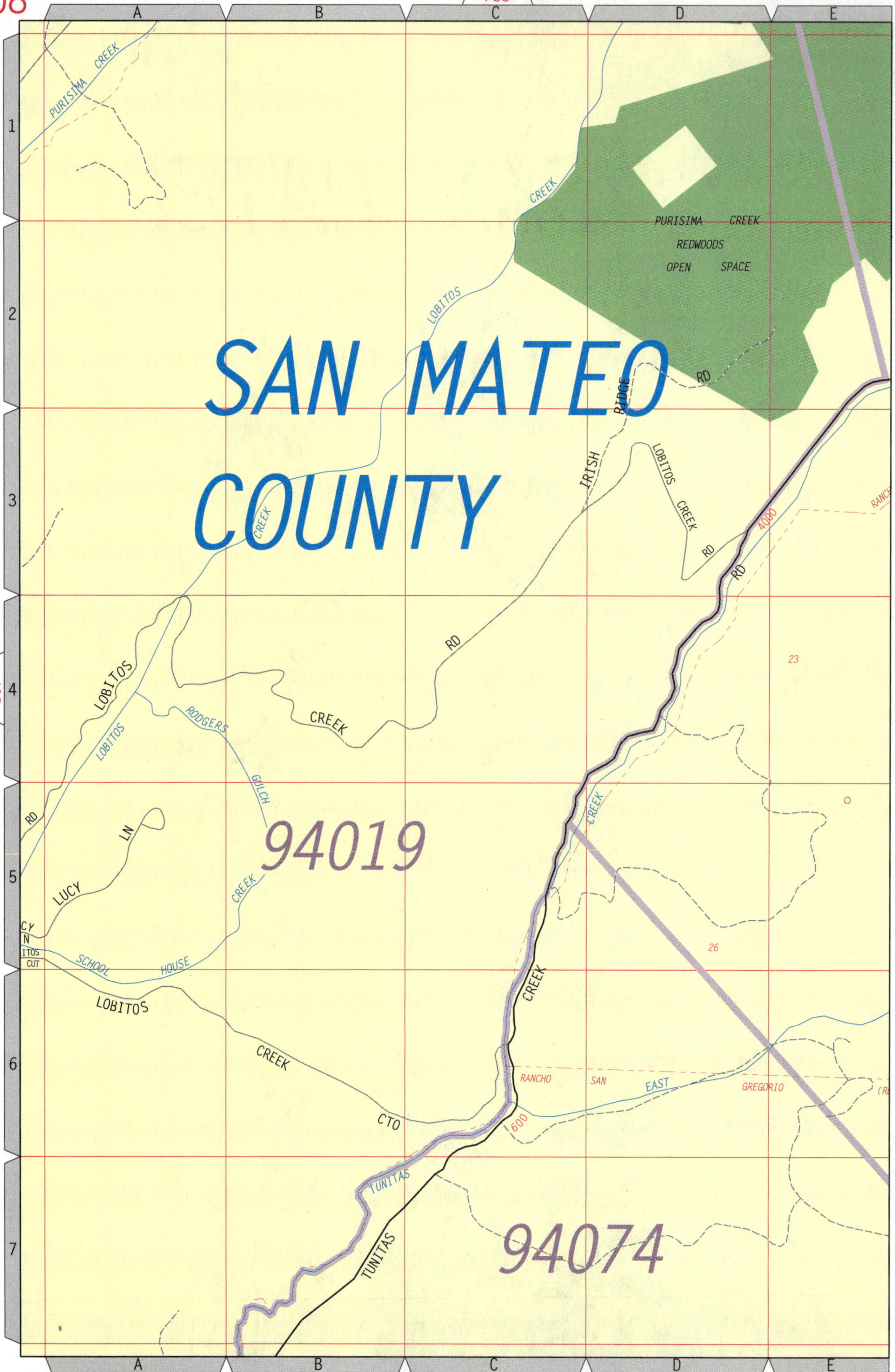

SEE 807 MAP
SEE 828 MAP

0 .125 .25 .375 .5 miles 1 in. = 1900 ft.

SEE 788 MAP
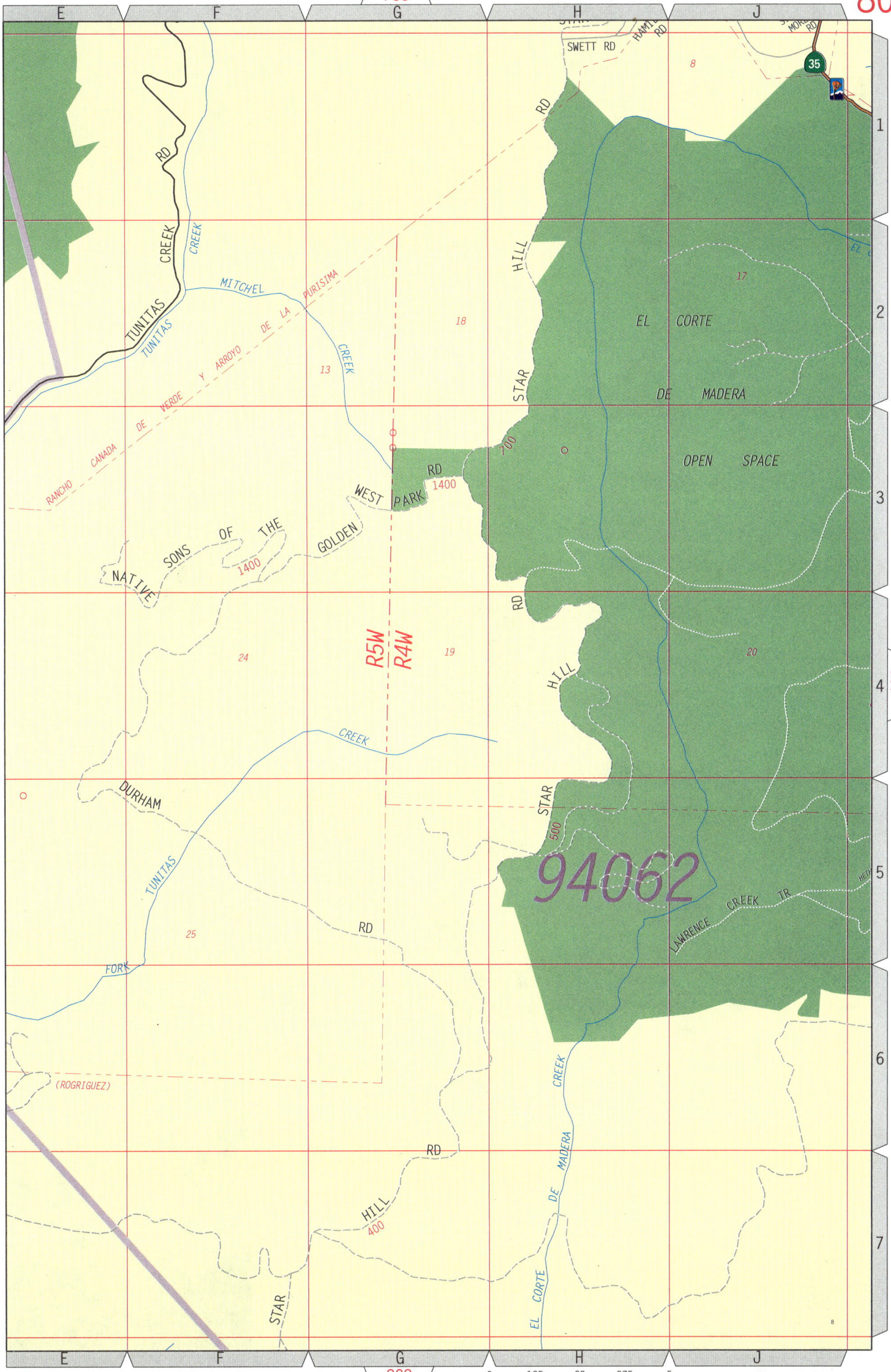

SEE 809 MAP
SEE 828 MAP
0 .125 .25 .375 .5 miles 1 in. = 1900 ft.

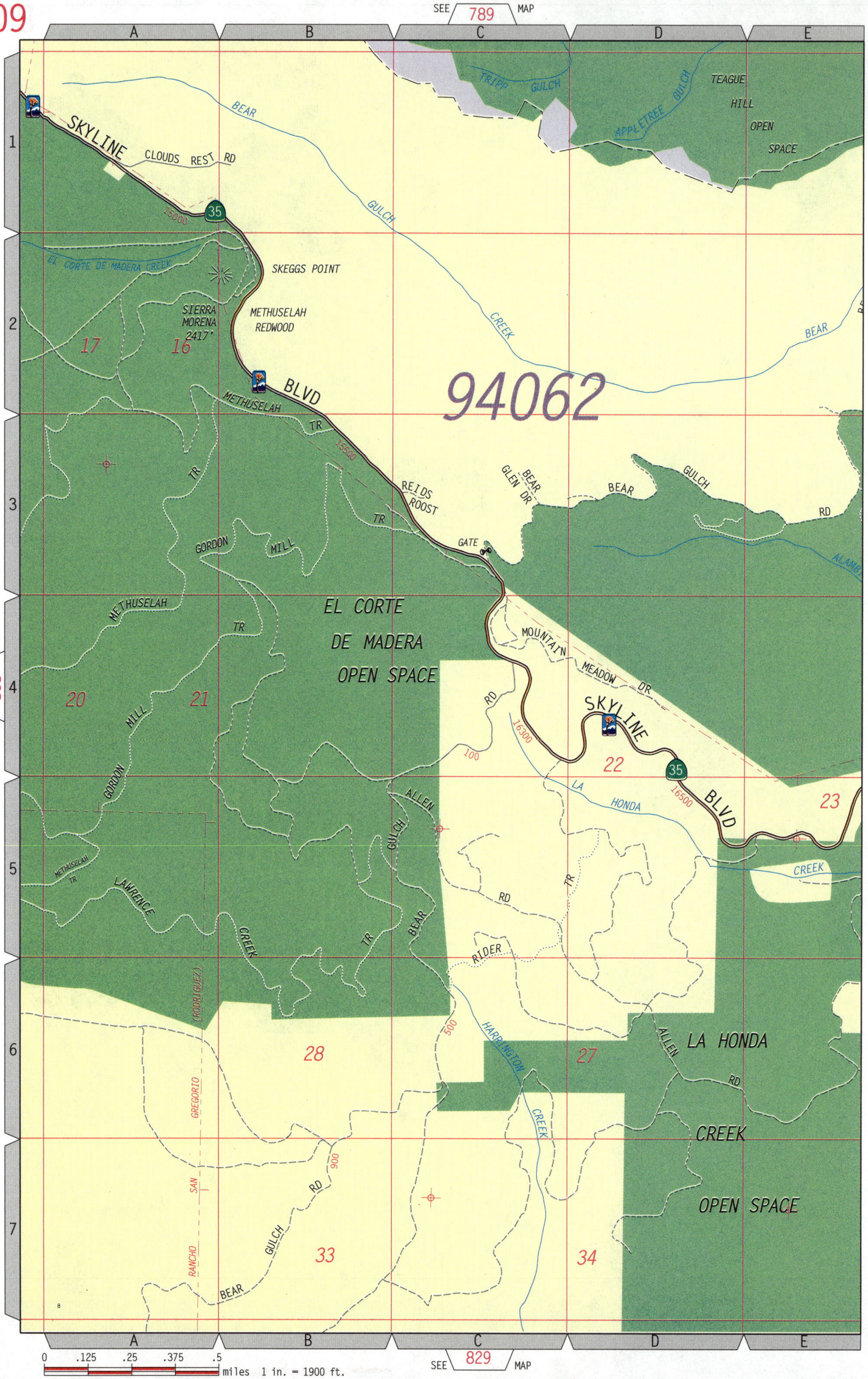
SEE 789 MAP
A
B
C
D
E
1
2
3
4
5
6
7
SKYLINE
CLOUDS REST RD
BEAR
GULCH
CREEK
TRIPP GULCH
APPLETREE GULCH
TEAGUE HILL OPEN SPACE
35
15000
EL CORTE DE MADERA CREEK
SKEGGS POINT
SIERRA MORENA 2417'
METHUSELAH REDWOOD
17
16
BLVD
METHUSELAH TR
15500
94062
BEAR
REIDS ROOST
TR
GLEN DR
BEAR
BEAR GULCH RD
ALAMBA
GATE
GORDON MILL TR
METHUSELAH TR
EL CORTE DE MADERA OPEN SPACE
MOUNTAIN MEADOW DR
SKYLINE BLVD
16300
16500
RD
100
20
21
22
23
MILL
GORDON
ALLEN GULCH
LA HONDA CREEK
METHUSELAH TR
LAWRENCE
CREEK
TR
BEAR
RD
TR
RIDER
(RODRIGUEZ)
500
HARRINGTON CREEK
28
27
ALLEN RD
LA HONDA CREEK OPEN SPACE
GREGORIO
SAN
RANCHO
900
RD
GULCH
BEAR
33
34
SEE 808 MAP
SEE 829 MAP
0 .125 .25 .375 .5 miles 1 in. = 1900 ft.

SEE 789 MAP
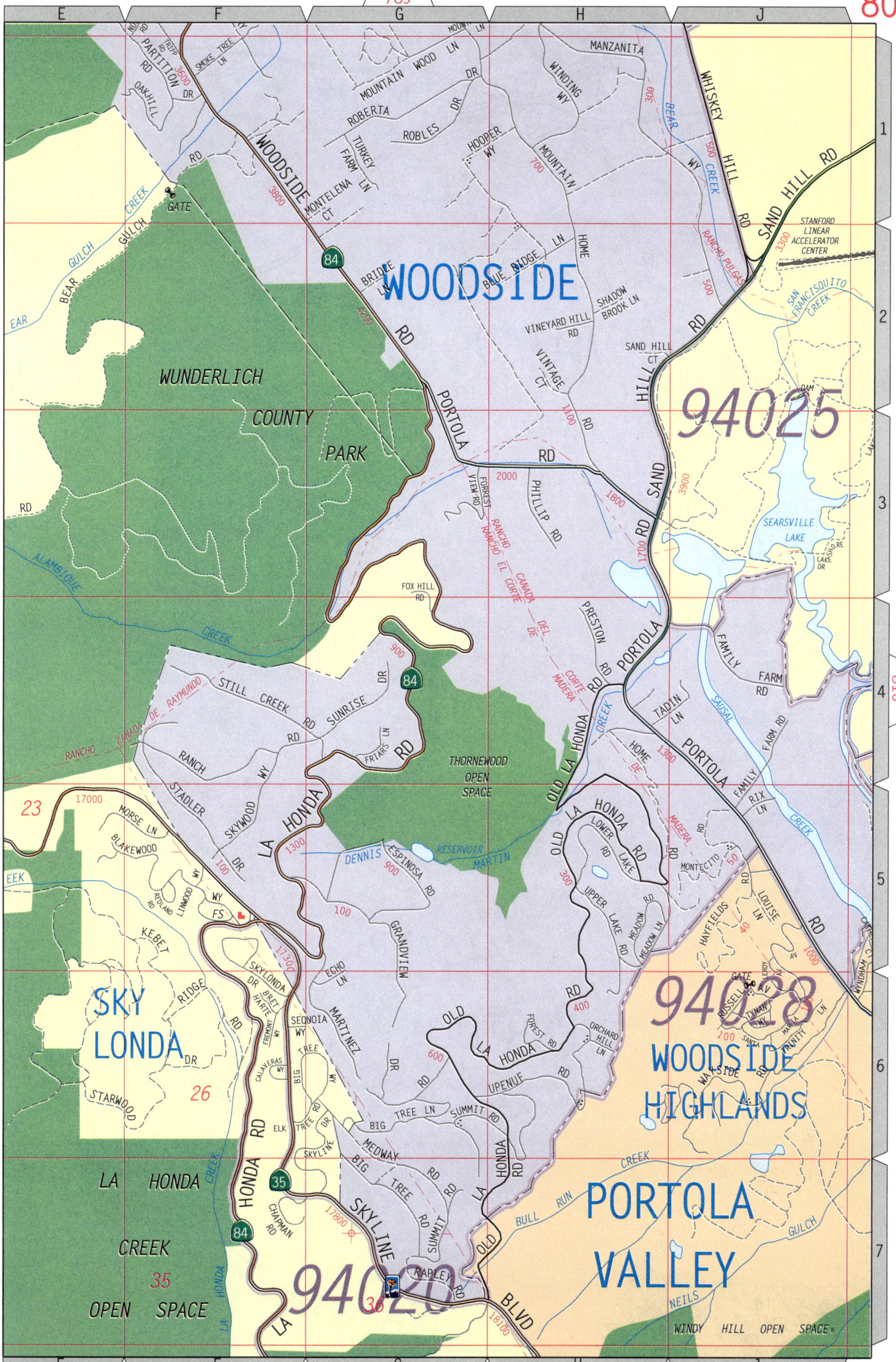

SEE 829 MAP
0 .125 .25 .375 .5 miles 1 in. = 1900 ft.

E F G H J

© 2008 Rand McNally & Company

N

1

WOODSIDE

94025

MANZANITA
WINDING WY
MOUNTAIN WOOD LN
ROBERTA
ROBLES
HOOPER WY
MOUNTAIN
WHISKEY HILL
BEAR CREEK
SAND HILL RD
RANCHO PULGAS
STANFORD LINEAR ACCELERATOR CENTER

WOODSIDE RD
84
BRIDLE LN
MONTELENA CT
TURKEY FARM LN
BLUE RIDGE LN
HOME
SHADOW BROOK LN
VINEYARD HILL RD
VINTAGE CT
SAND HILL CT
SAN FRANCISQUITO CREEK

PARTITION RD
OAKHILL RD
SMOKE TREE LN
GATE
GULCH
BEAR GULCH
CREEK

2

WUNDERLICH
COUNTY
PARK

PORTOLA RD
FOREST VIEW RD
RANCHO
RANCHO EL CORTE
PHILIP RD
CANADA DEL DE
PRESTON RD
CORTE MADERA
FAMILY FARM RD
SEARSVILLE LAKE
LAKE
SHORE
LAKE DR
DAM

3

ALAMBIQUE
CREEK
FOX HILL RD
SAND RD

4

SEE 810 MAP

STILL CREEK RD
SUNRISE DR
FRIARS LN
84
RANCH RD
CANADA DE RAYMUNDO
LA HONDA RD
THORNEWOOD OPEN SPACE
OLD LA HONDA RD
PORTOLA RD
TADIN LN
HOME DE
FAMILY RIX LN
SAUSAL CREEK

23
17000
RANCHO
STADLER
SKYWOOD DR
DENNIS
ESPINOSA RD
RESERVOIR
MARTIN
OLD LA HONDA RD
LOWER LAKE RD
UPPER LAKE RD
MEADOW RD
MONTECITO RD
MADERA
HAYFIELDS
LOUISE AV
WYNDHAM

5

MORSE LN
BLAKEWOOD
REDLAND RD
LINWOOD WY
WY
FS
KEBET
RIDGE
STARWOOD
GRANDVIEW
ECHO LN
MARTINEZ WY
SKYLONDA DR
BRET HARTE WY
FREMONT WY
SEQUOIA WY
CALAVERAS WY
BIG TREE WY
ELK
SKYLINE
CHAPMAN RD
MEDWAY
BIG TREE RD
SUMMIT RD
UPENUF RD
OLD LA HONDA RD
FOREST RD
ORCHARD HILL LN
RUSSELL AV
GATE
DYNANT AV
MARIA
SANTA
TRINITY LN
WATSIDE AV

SKY
LONDA
26

94028
WOODSIDE
HIGHLANDS

6

LA HONDA
CREEK
35
84
CHAPMAN RD
17800
RAPLEY
SKYLINE BLVD
BIG TREE LN
SUMMIT RD
OLD LA HONDA RD
BULL RUN CREEK
NEILS GULCH

94020

PORTOLA
VALLEY

WINDY HILL OPEN SPACE

7

CREEK
35
OPEN SPACE
LA HONDA RD
LA HONDA

SEE 790 MAP

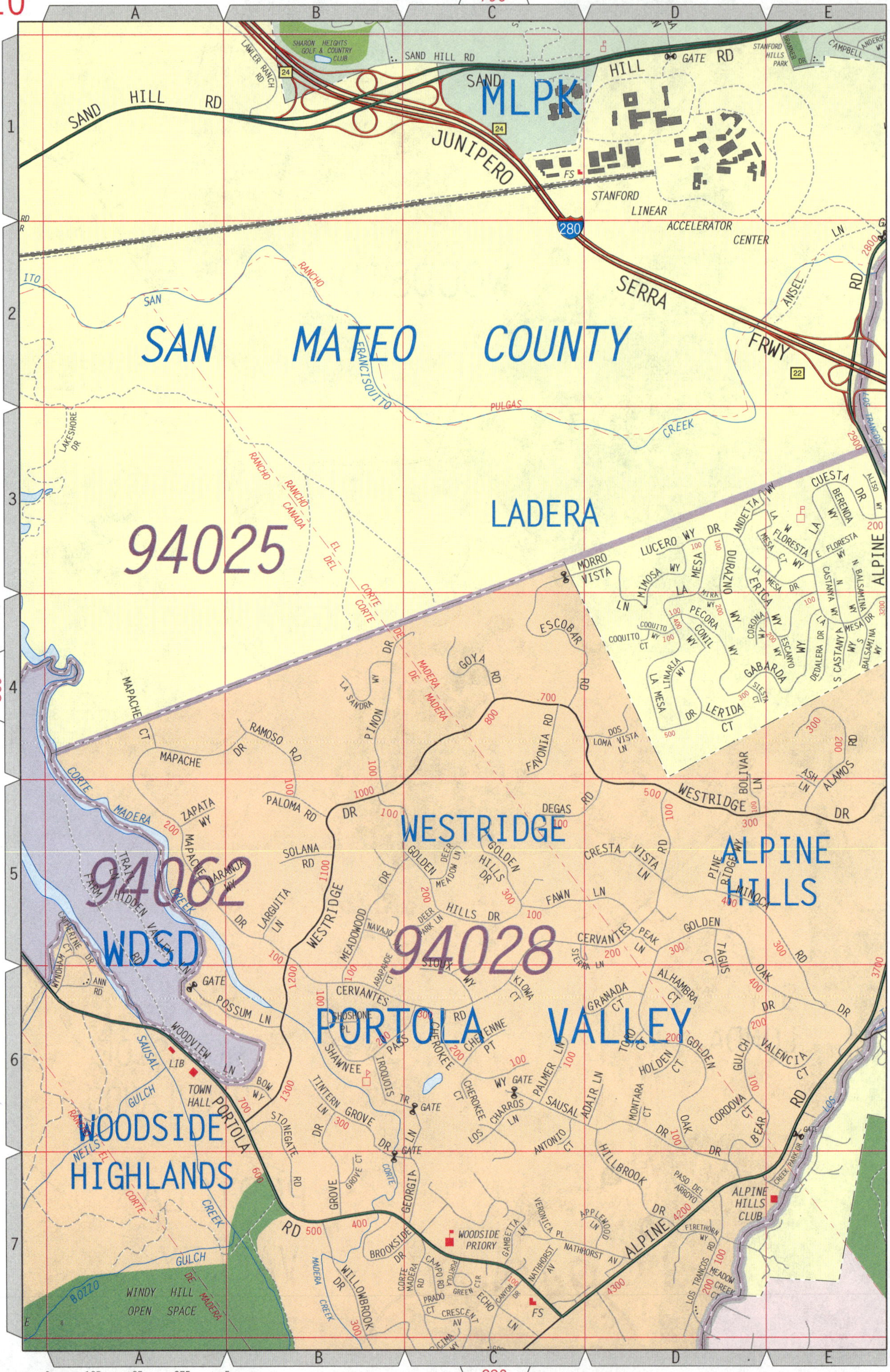

SEE 830 MAP

0 .125 .25 .375 .5 miles 1 in. = 1900 ft.

SEE 790 MAP

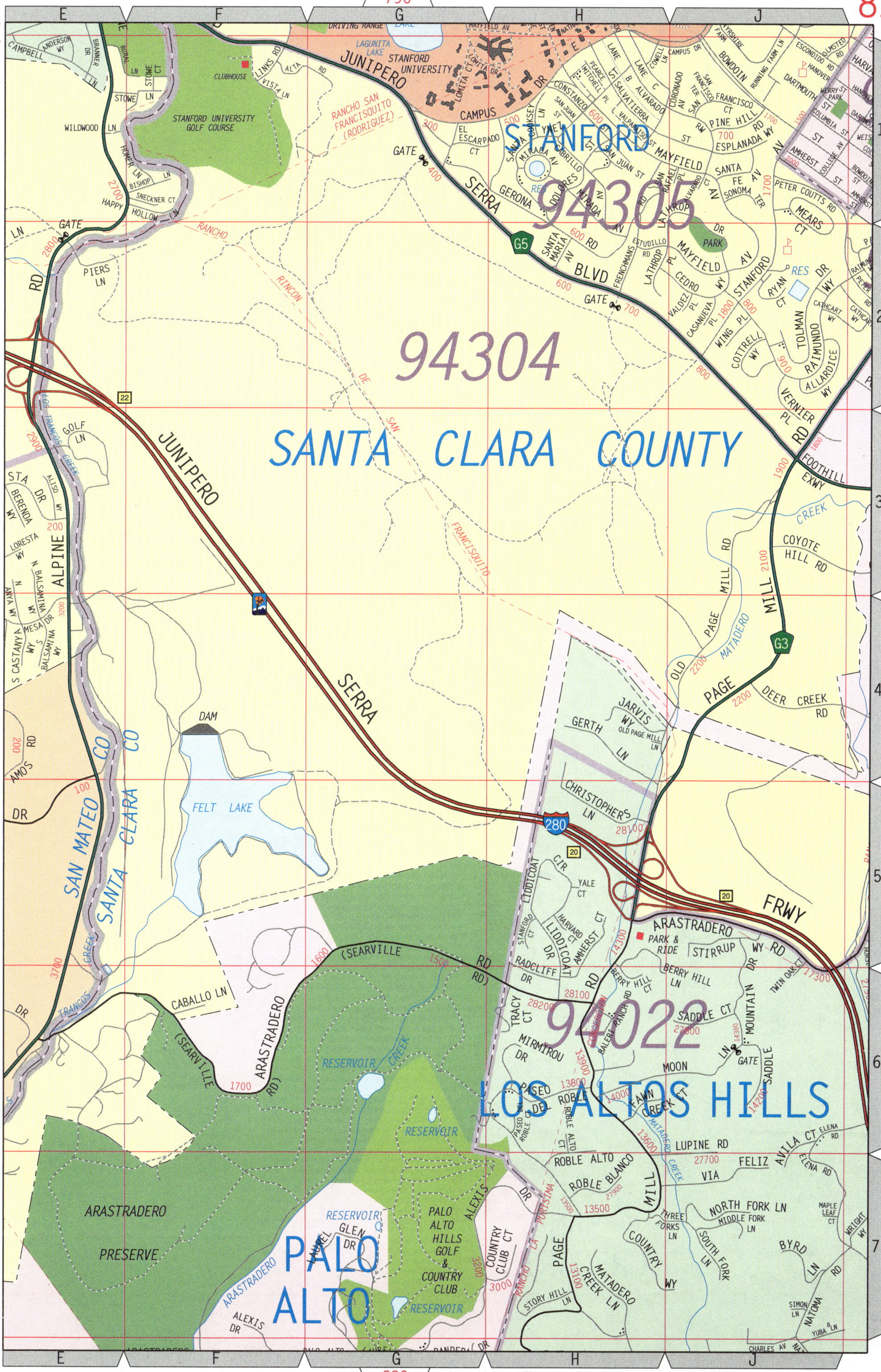

SEE 830 MAP

SEE B MAP

© 2008 Rand McNally & Company

N

STANFORD
94305

94304

SANTA CLARA COUNTY

JUNIPERO

SERRA

BLVD

STANFORD UNIVERSITY GOLF COURSE

STANFORD UNIVERSITY

CAMPUS

LAGUNITA LAKE

DRIVING RANGE

MAYFIELD AV

JUNIPERO

SERRA

ALPINE

SAN MATEO CO

SANTA CLARA CO

FELT LAKE

DAM

FRANCISQUITO

FOOTHILL EXWY

COYOTE HILL RD

PAGE MILL RD

DEER CREEK RD

OLD PAGE MILL LN

JARVIS WY

GERTH LN

CHRISTOPHERS LN

280

20

ARASTRADERO RD

STIRRUP

FRWY

94022

LOS ALTOS HILLS

LIDDICOAT

STANFORD AV

HARVARD CT

RADCLIFF DR

TRACY CT

MIRMIROU DR

PASEO DEL ROBLE

ROBLE ALTO

ROBLE BLANCO

ROBLE ALTO

LUPINE RD

NORTH FORK LN

MIDDLE FORK

SOUTH FORK

MATADERO CREEK LN

COUNTRY WY

MOON

SADDLE CT

GATE

MOUNTAIN LN

SADDLE

FAWN CREEK

VIA FELIZ

ELENA RD

AVILA CT

WRIGHT

BYRD

ARASTRADERO PRESERVE

(SEARVILLE RD)

CABALLO LN

ARASTRADERO RD

RESERVOIR CREEK

RESERVOIR

RESERVOIR

PALO ALTO HILLS GOLF & COUNTRY CLUB

COUNTRY CLUB CT

RESERVOIR

GLEN DR

ALEXIS DR

PALO ALTO

STORY HILL

RANCHO DE LA PURISIMA

PAGE MILL

THREE FORKS LN

0 .125 .25 .375 .5 miles 1 in. = 1900 ft.

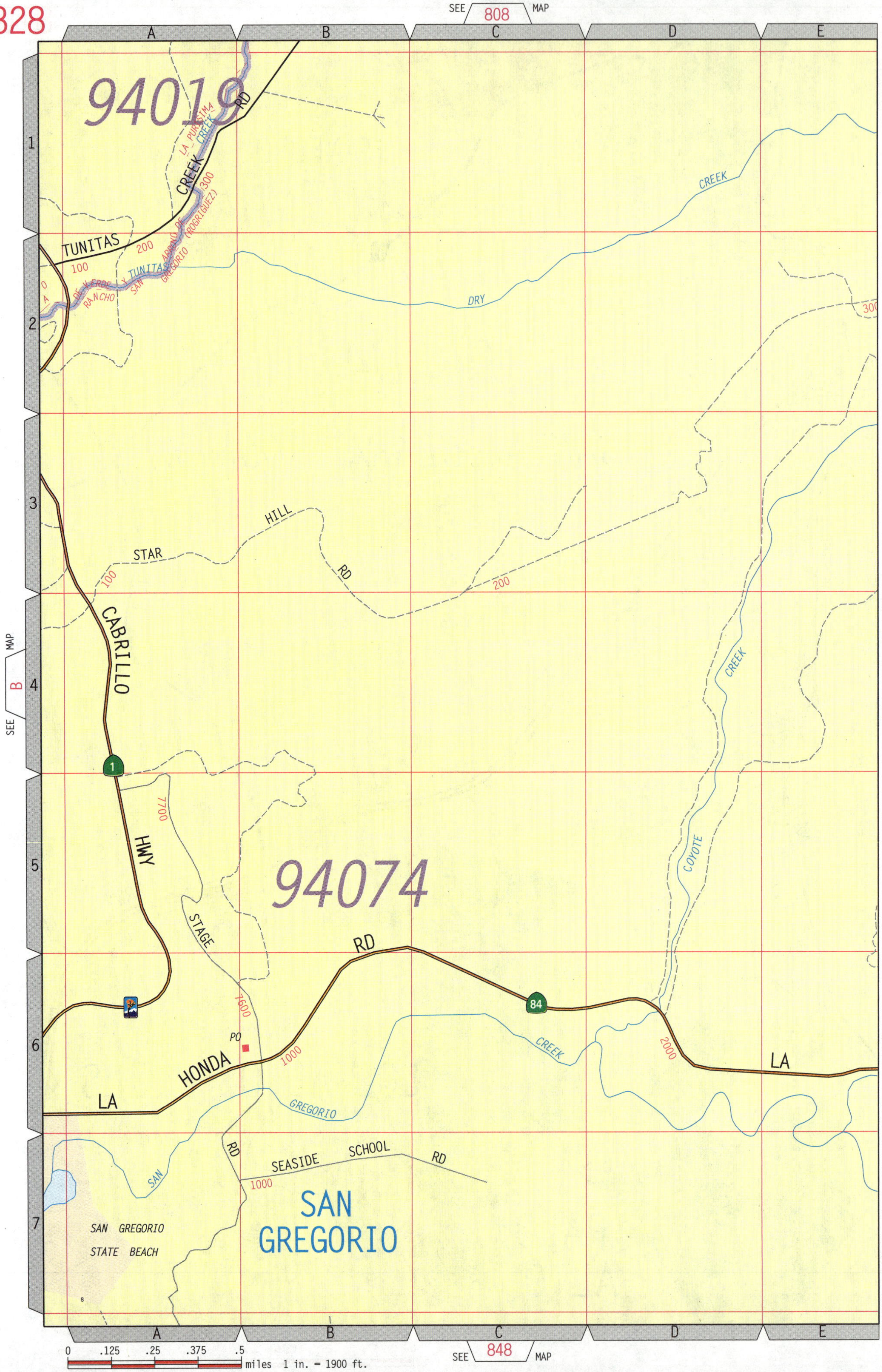
SEE 808 MAP
A
B
C
D
E
1
2
3
4
5
6
7
SEE B MAP
94019
94074
TUNITAS
CREEK
RD
LA PURISIMA CREEK
DRY
CREEK
STAR
HILL
RD
CABRILLO
HWY
1
STAGE
RD
LA
HONDA
RD
84
LA
CREEK
GREGORIO
SAN
COYOTE
CREEK
SEASIDE
SCHOOL
RD
PO
SAN
GREGORIO
SAN GREGORIO
STATE BEACH
100
200
300
1000
2000
7600
7700
SEE 848 MAP
0
.125
.25
.375
.5
miles 1 in. = 1900 ft.

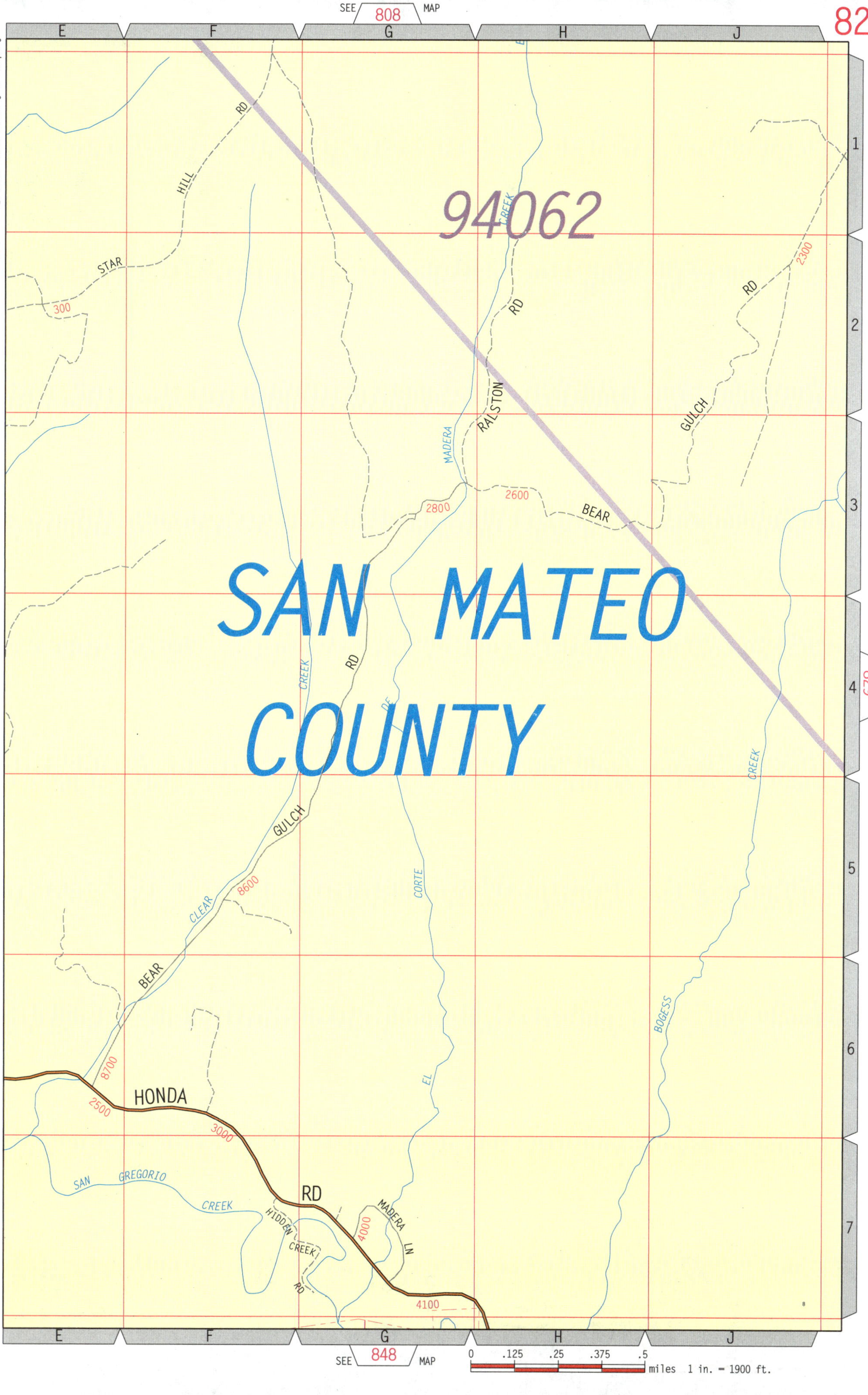
SEE 808 MAP
E
F
G
H
J
1
2
3
4
5
6
7
94062
SAN MATEO
COUNTY
HILL
RD
STAR
300
RALSTON
RD
MADERA
CREEK
GULCH
RD
2300
2800
2600
BEAR
RD
CREEK
GULCH
8600
CLEAR
BEAR
DE
CORTE
EL
BOGESS
CREEK
8700
2500
HONDA
3000
RD
SAN
GREGORIO
CREEK
HIDDEN
CREEK
RD
4000
MADERA
LN
4100
SEE 829 MAP
SEE 848 MAP
0
.125
.25
.375
.5
miles 1 in. = 1900 ft.

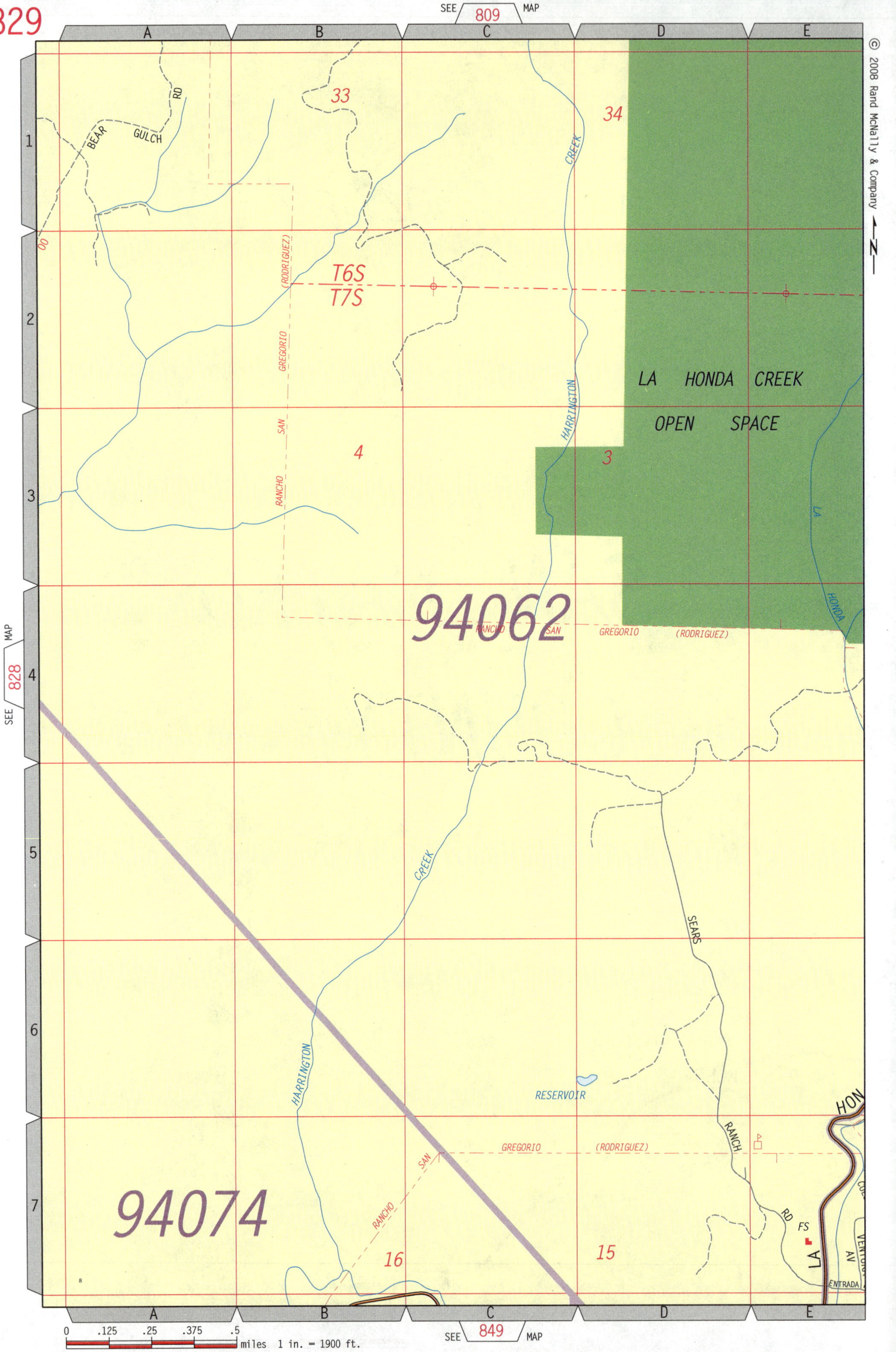
SEE 809 MAP
A
B
C
D
E
1
2
3
4
5
6
7
SEE 828 MAP
SEE 849 MAP
BEAR GULCH RD
33
34
CREEK
T6S
T7S
(RODRIGUEZ)
GREGORIO
SAN
RANCHO
4
3
HARRINGTON
LA HONDA CREEK
OPEN SPACE
LA
HONDA
94062
RANCHO SAN GREGORIO (RODRIGUEZ)
CREEK
HARRINGTON
SEARS
RANCH
RD
RESERVOIR
RANCHO SAN GREGORIO (RODRIGUEZ)
94074
16
15
FS
LA
HON
AV
ENTRADA
0 .125 .25 .375 .5
miles 1 in. = 1900 ft.

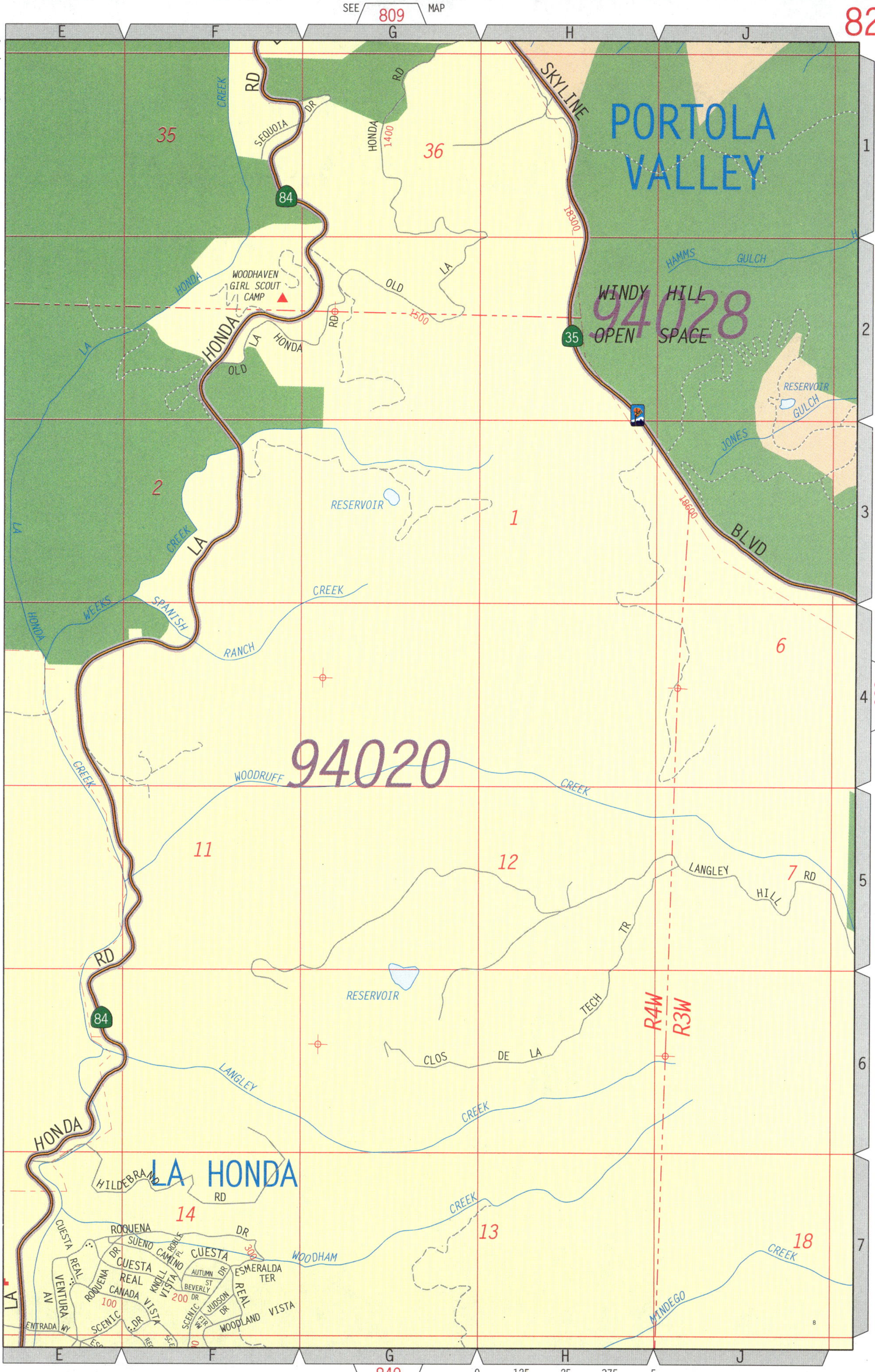

0 .125 .25 .375 .5 miles 1 in. = 1900 ft.

SAN MATEO CO.

E G H J

PORTOLA VALLEY

1

84

WOODHAVEN GIRL SCOUT CAMP

94028

WINDY HILL
OPEN SPACE

35

2

HAMMS GULCH

RESERVOIR

JONES GULCH

BLVD

SKYLINE

2

1

RESERVOIR

3

6

SEE 830 MAP

4

94020

WOODRUFF CREEK

11 12 7 RD

LANGLEY HILL

5

RESERVOIR

TECH

CLOS DE LA

R4W R3W

6

84

LANGLEY

CREEK

LA HONDA

HILDEBRAND
RD

14 13 18

CUESTA
ROQUENA
SUENO CAMINO ROBLE PL
CUESTA CUESTA
KNOLL VISTA ESMERALDA TER
REAL REAL WOODHAM CREEK
ROQUENA AUTUMN ST
VENTURA CANADA VISTA BEVERLY DR JUDSON
AV SCENIC DR WOODLAND VISTA
ENTRADA MINDEGO

7

E F G H J

SEE 810 MAP

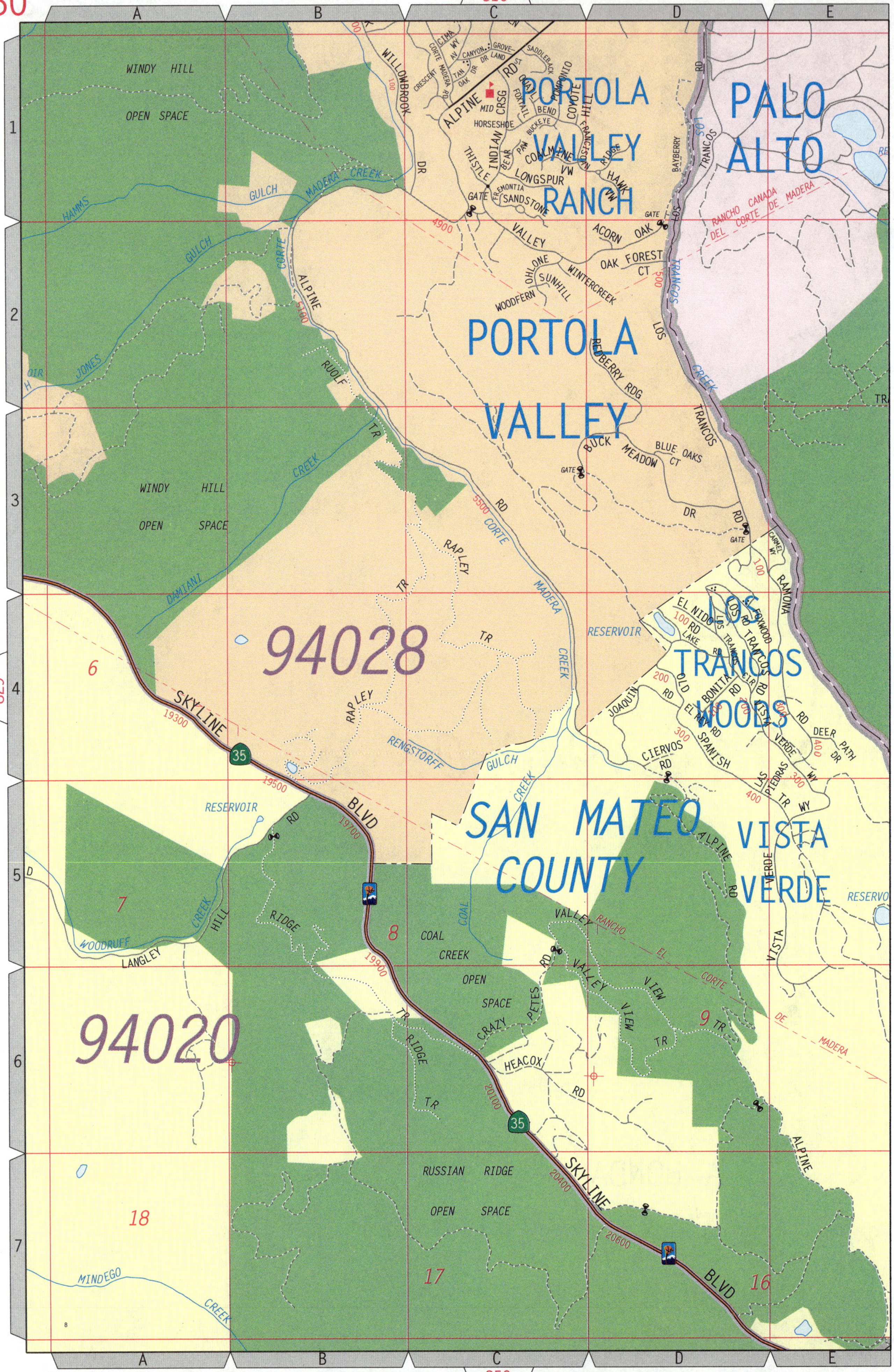
A
B
C
D
E
1
2
3
4
5
6
7
WINDY HILL OPEN SPACE
PORTOLA VALLEY RANCH
PALO ALTO
PORTOLA VALLEY
LOS TRANCOS WOODS
VISTA VERDE
SAN MATEO COUNTY
94028
94020
RUSSIAN RIDGE OPEN SPACE
SKYLINE BLVD
35
ALPINE RD
WILLOWBROOK DR
MADERA CREEK
HAMMS GULCH
CORTE MADERA CREEK
RUOLF TR
RAPLEY TR
RENGSTORFF GULCH
DAMIANI CREEK
JONES
RESERVOIR
LOS TRANCOS RD
LOS TRANCOS CREEK
RANCHO CANADA DEL CORTE DE MADERA
BAYBERRY
ACORN
OAK
OAK FOREST CT
VALLEY
OHLONE
SUNHILL
WINTERCREEK
WOODFERN
REDBERRY RDG
BUCK MEADOW DR
BLUE OAKS CT
GATE
ALPINE
INDIAN
HORSESHOE
THISTLE
LONGSPUR
SANDSTONE
COYOTE HILL
CIMA WY
CRESCENT
GROVE
CANYON
SADDLEBACK
RAMONA
EL NIDO RD
JOAQUIN
CIERVOS RD
SPANISH
DEER PATH DR
VISTA VERDE WY
LAS PIEDRAS TR
COAL CREEK OPEN SPACE
CRAZY PETES RD
VALLEY VIEW TR
HEACOX RD
RIDGE TR
LANGLEY HILL
WOODRUFF CREEK
MINDEGO CREEK
19300
19500
19700
19900
20100
20400
20600
6
7
8
9
16
17
18

SEE 829 MAP

SEE 850 MAP

0 .125 .25 .375 .5 miles 1 in. = 1900 ft.

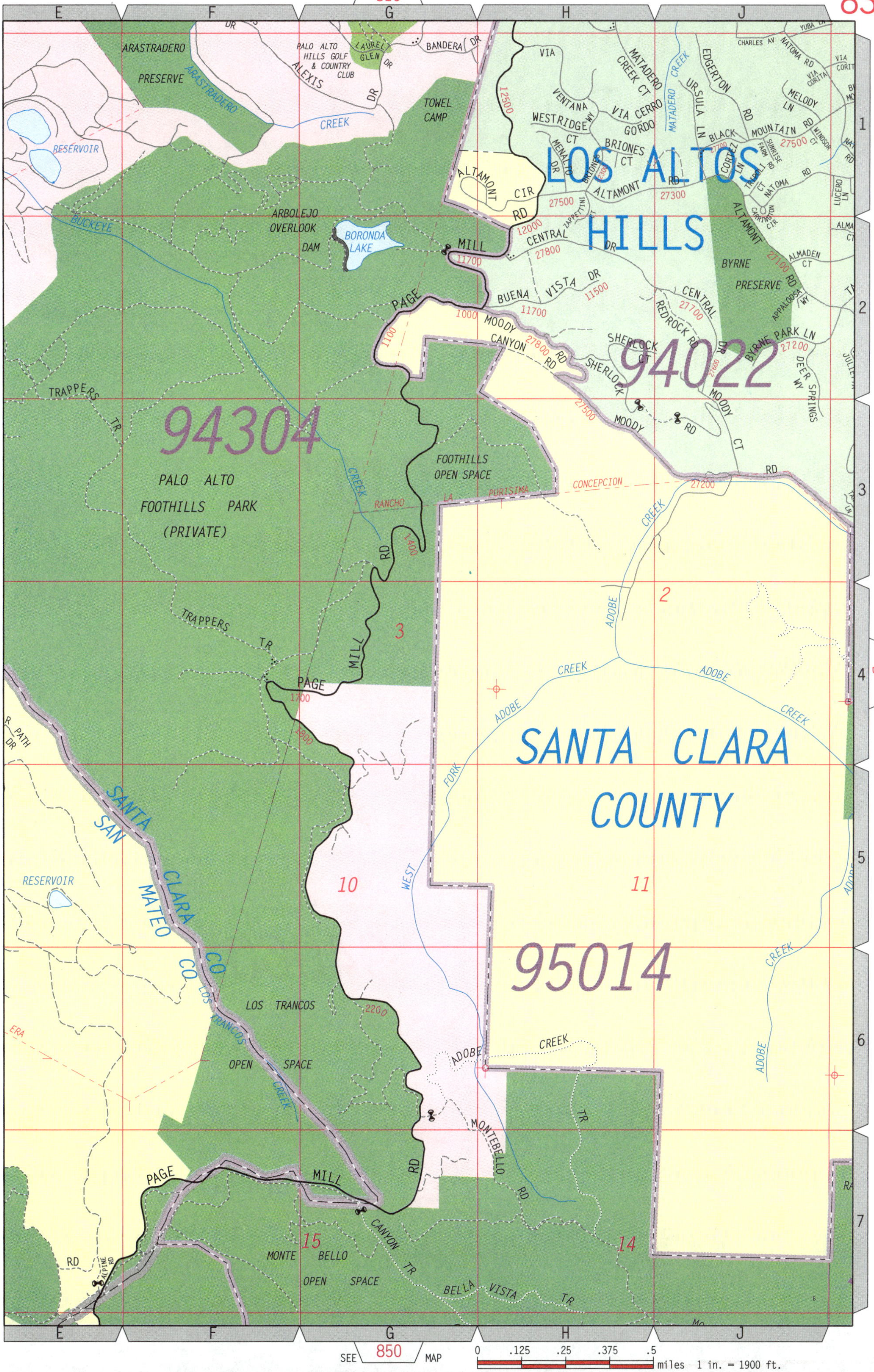
SEE 810 MAP
E
F
G
H
J
1
2
3
4
5
6
7
SEE B MAP
SEE 850 MAP
LOS ALTOS HILLS
SANTA CLARA COUNTY
94304
94022
95014
PALO ALTO FOOTHILLS PARK (PRIVATE)
FOOTHILLS OPEN SPACE
ARASTRADERO PRESERVE
ARASTRADERO CREEK
PALO ALTO HILLS GOLF & COUNTRY CLUB
LAUREL GLEN DR
BANDERA DR
ALEXIS DR
TOWEL CAMP
RESERVOIR
BUCKEYE
ARBOLEJO OVERLOOK
DAM
BORONDA LAKE
PAGE MILL RD
TRAPPERS TR
CREEK
RANCHO LA PURISIMA CONCEPCION
BYRNE PRESERVE
ALTAMONT CIR
ALTAMONT RD
CENTRAL DR
BUENA VISTA DR
MOODY RD
MOODY CANYON RD
SHERLOCK CT
SHERLOCK RD
REDROCK RD
CENTRAL DR
BYRNE PARK LN
DEER SPRINGS WY
APPALOOSA WY
ALMADEN CT
VIA VENTANA
WESTRIDGE CT
VIA CERRO GORDO
BRIONES CT
MENALTO DR
MATADERO CREEK CT
MATADERO CREEK
URSULA LN
EDGERTON RD
BLACK MOUNTAIN RD
MELODY LN
CHARLES AV
NATOMA RD
NATOMA CT
CARRINGTON CIR
LUCERO CT
ADOBE CREEK
WEST FORK ADOBE CREEK
SANTA CLARA CO
SAN MATEO CO
RESERVOIR
LOS TRANCOS OPEN SPACE
LOS TRANCOS CREEK
MONTEBELLO RD
MONTE BELLO OPEN SPACE
CANYON TR
BELLA VISTA TR
ALPINE RD
2
3
10
11
14
15
12500
12000
11700
11500
1000
1100
1400
1700
1900
2200
27500
27300
27800
27700
27600
27200
27100
0 .125 .25 .375 .5 miles 1 in. = 1900 ft.

SEE 828 MAP

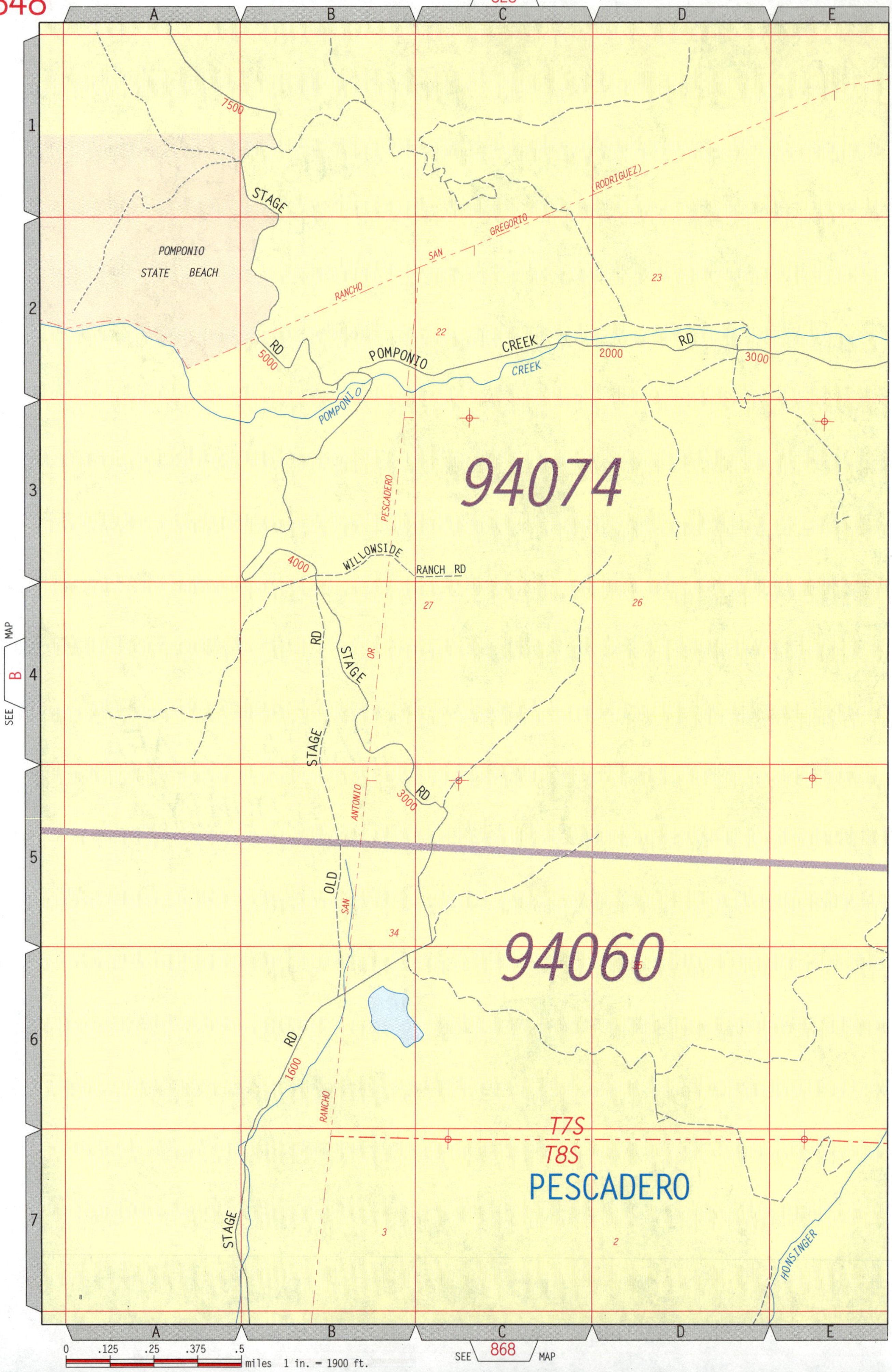

SEE B MAP

SEE 868 MAP

A B C D E

1

7500

STAGE

POMPONIO
STATE BEACH

RODRIGUEZ)

SAN GREGORIO

23

2

RANCHO

RD

5000

POMPONIO CREEK RD

Creek 2000 3000

POMPONIO

PESCADERO

94074

3

4000 WILLOWSIDE RANCH RD

27 26

RD

STAGE OR

STAGE

4

ANTONIO

3000

RD

OLD SAN

34

94060

RD

1600

6

RANCHO

T7S

T8S

PESCADERO

7

STAGE

3

2

HONSINGER

8

A B C D E

0 .125 .25 .375 .5

miles 1 in. = 1900 ft.

SEE 828 MAP

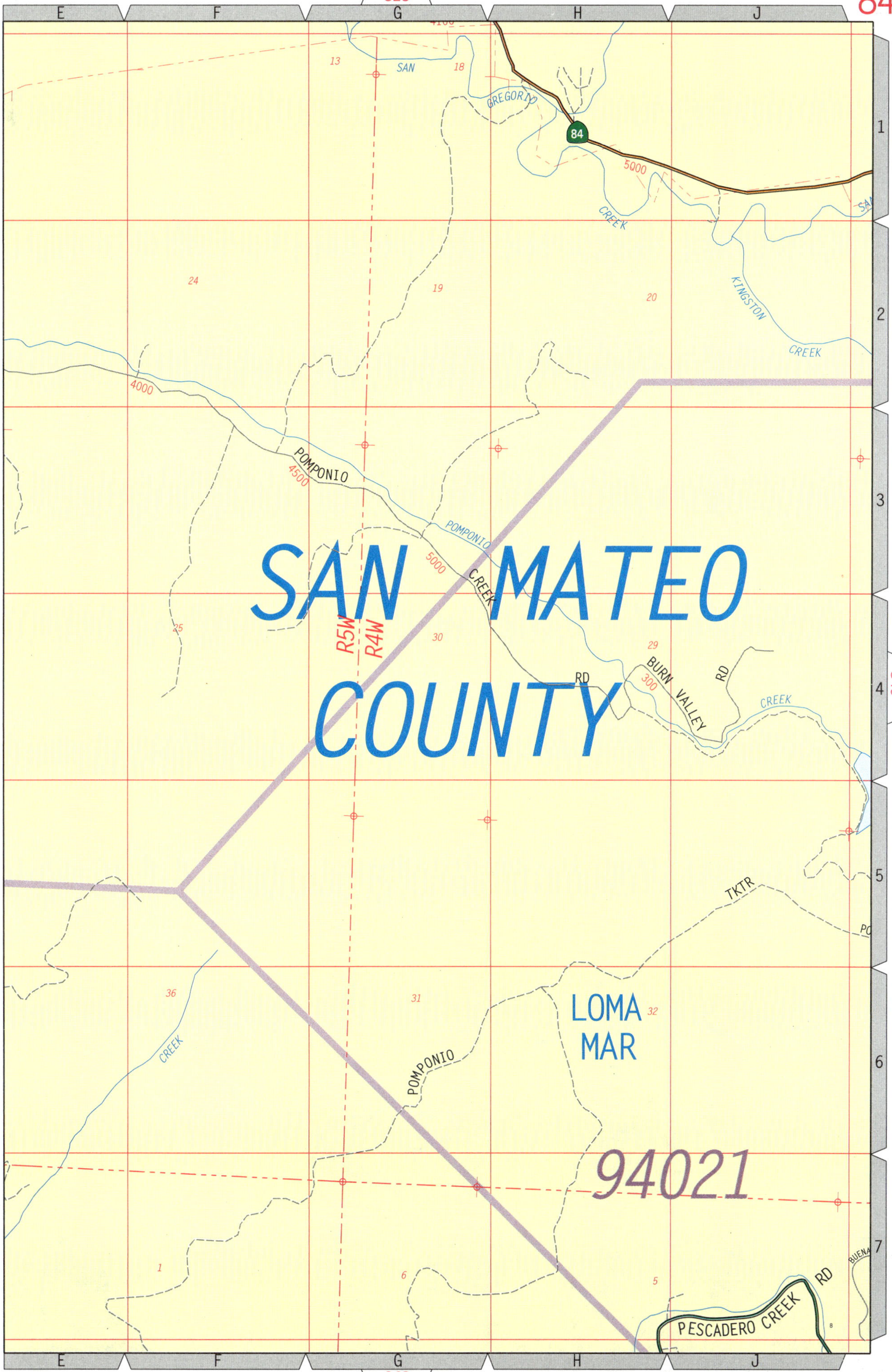

SEE 849 MAP

SEE 868 MAP

0 .125 .25 .375 .5 miles 1 in. = 1900 ft.

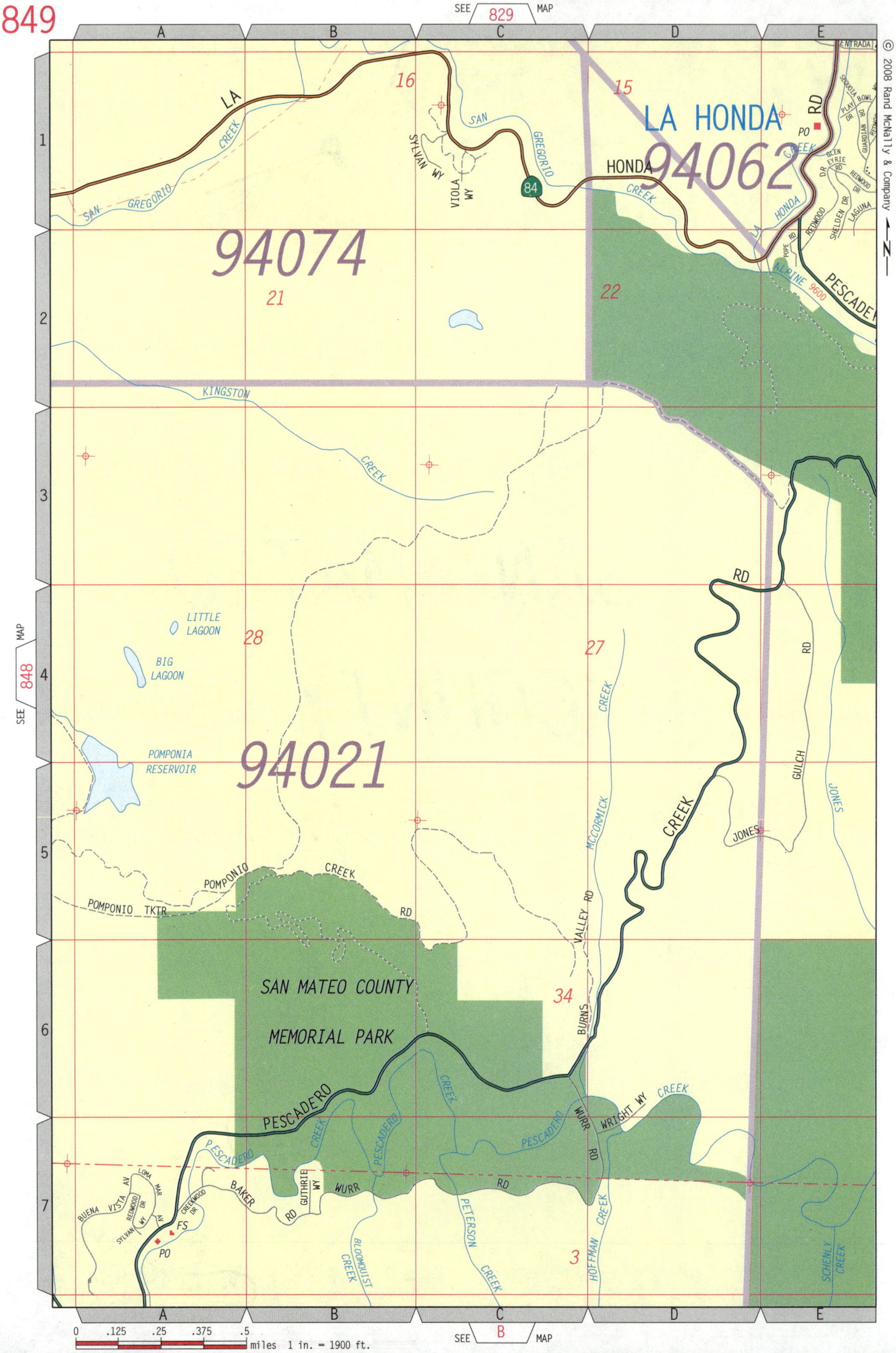
SEE 829 MAP
SEE 848 MAP
SEE B MAP
A
B
C
D
E
1
2
3
4
5
6
7
© 2008 Rand McNally & Company
LA HONDA
94062
94074
94021
LA HONDA RD
84
PO
SAN GREGORIO CREEK
SYLVAN WY
VIOLA WY
LA HONDA CREEK
ENTRADA
SEQUOIA
PLAY BOWL DR
GLEN EYRIE DR
GUARDIAN DR
REDWOOD DR
LAGUNA
SHELDEN DR
POPE RD
ALPINE 9600
PESCADERO
KINGSTON CREEK
LITTLE LAGOON
BIG LAGOON
POMPONIA RESERVOIR
POMPONIO CREEK RD
POMPONIO TKTR
SAN MATEO COUNTY
MEMORIAL PARK
PESCADERO CREEK RD
MCCORMICK CREEK
VALLEY RD
BURNS
GULCH RD
JONES
JONES GULCH
WRIGHT WY
WURR RD
PESCADERO CREEK
BAKER RD
GUTHRIE WY
BUENA VISTA AV
LOMA MAR AV
REDWOOD DR
SYLVAN WY
CREEKWOOD DR
FS
BLOOMQUIST CREEK
PETERSON CREEK
HOFFMAN CREEK
SCHENLY CREEK
15
16
21
22
27
28
34
3
0 .125 .25 .375 .5
miles 1 in. = 1900 ft.

SAN MATEO CO.

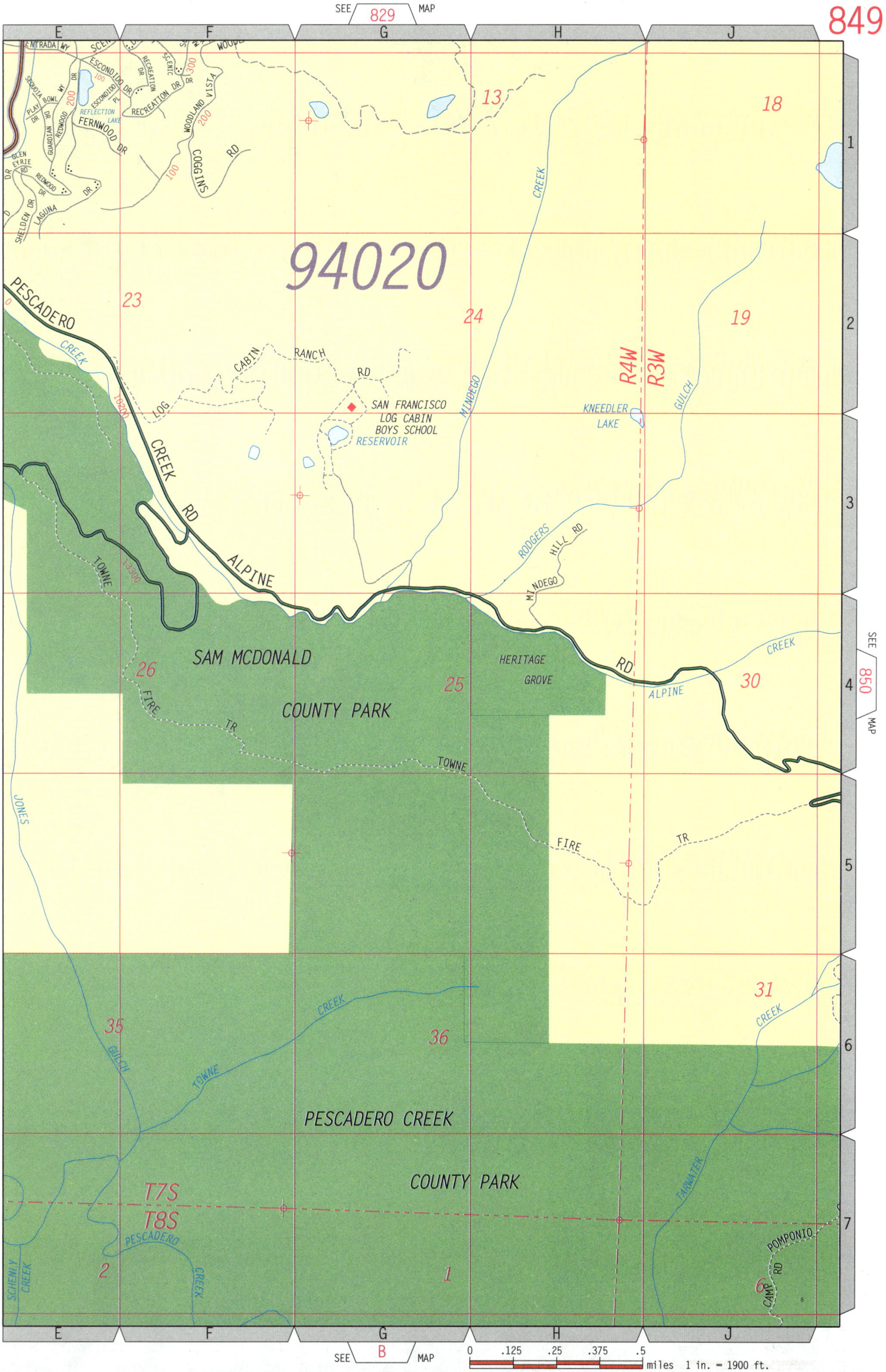
SEE 829 MAP
SEE 850 MAP
SEE B MAP
94020
PESCADERO CREEK RD
ALPINE RD
SAM MCDONALD COUNTY PARK
PESCADERO CREEK COUNTY PARK
HERITAGE GROVE
SAN FRANCISCO LOG CABIN BOYS SCHOOL
RESERVOIR
KNEEDLER LAKE
LOG CABIN RANCH RD
MINDEGO CREEK
RODGERS GULCH
MT MINDEGO HILL RD
TOWNE FIRE TR
TOWNE CREEK
JONES GULCH
SCHENLY CREEK
TARWATER CREEK
POMPONIO RD
CAMP
COGGINS RD
WOODLAND VISTA
FERNWOOD DR
RECREATION DR
ESCONDIDO DR
REFLECTION LAKE
ENTRADA WY
SEQUOIA DR
PLAY BOWL DR
GUARDIAN DR
REDWOOD DR
GLEN EYRIE RD
LAGUNA DR
SHELDEN DR
R4W
R3W
T7S
T8S
0 .125 .25 .375 .5 miles 1 in. = 1900 ft.

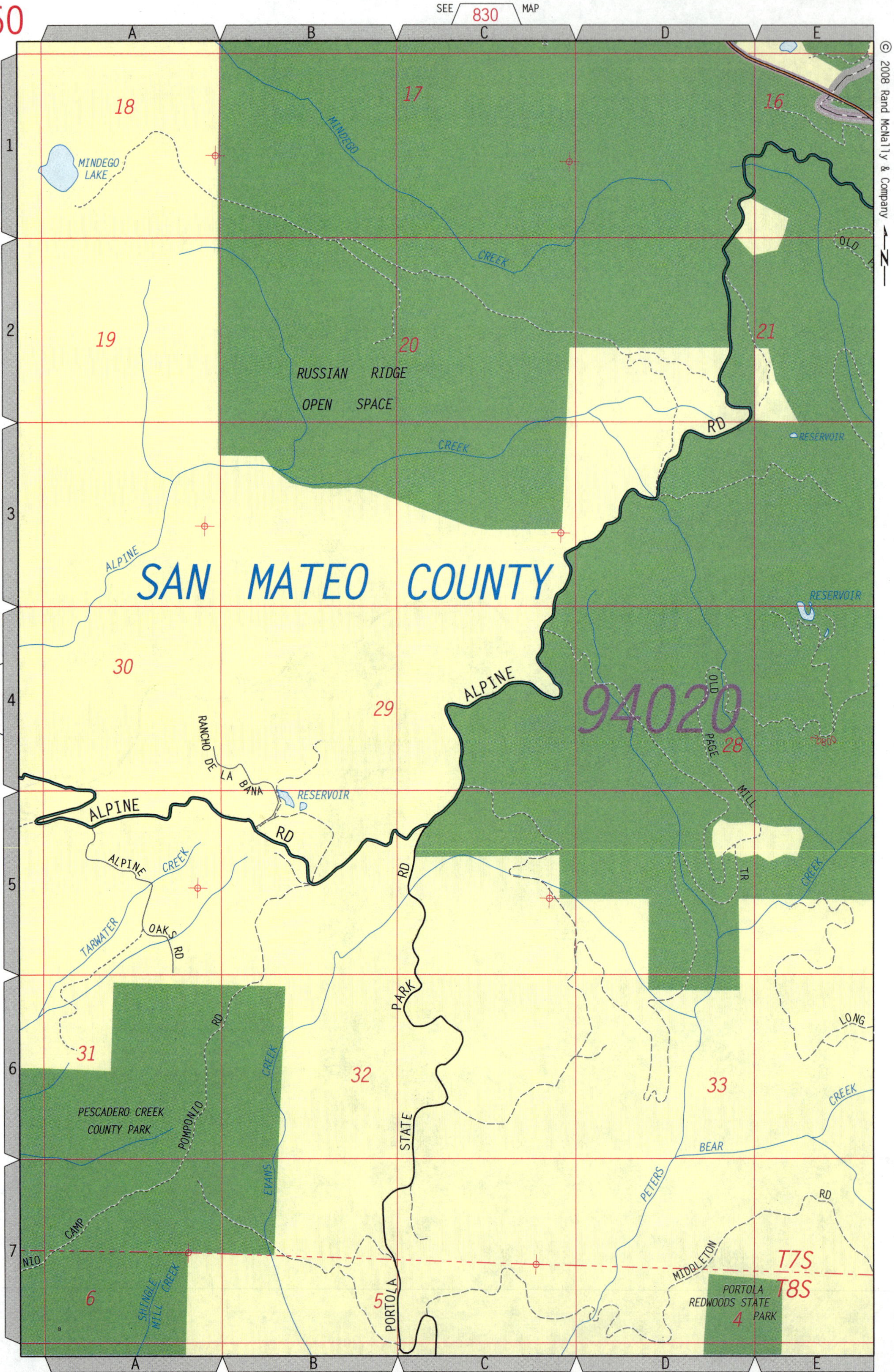
SEE 830 MAP
SAN MATEO COUNTY
94020
RUSSIAN RIDGE
OPEN SPACE
MINDEGO LAKE
MINDEGO
CREEK
ALPINE
ALPINE RD
RANCHO DE LA BANA
RESERVOIR
ALPINE CREEK
TARWATER
OAKS RD
PORTOLA STATE PARK RD
OLD PAGE MILL TR
PESCADERO CREEK
COUNTY PARK
POMPONIO RD
EVANS CREEK
CAMP
SHINGLE MILL CREEK
PETERS
BEAR CREEK
LONG
MIDDLETON RD
PORTOLA REDWOODS STATE PARK
T7S
T8S
SEE 849 MAP
18
17
16
19
20
21
30
29
28
31
32
33
6
5
4

SEE 830 MAP

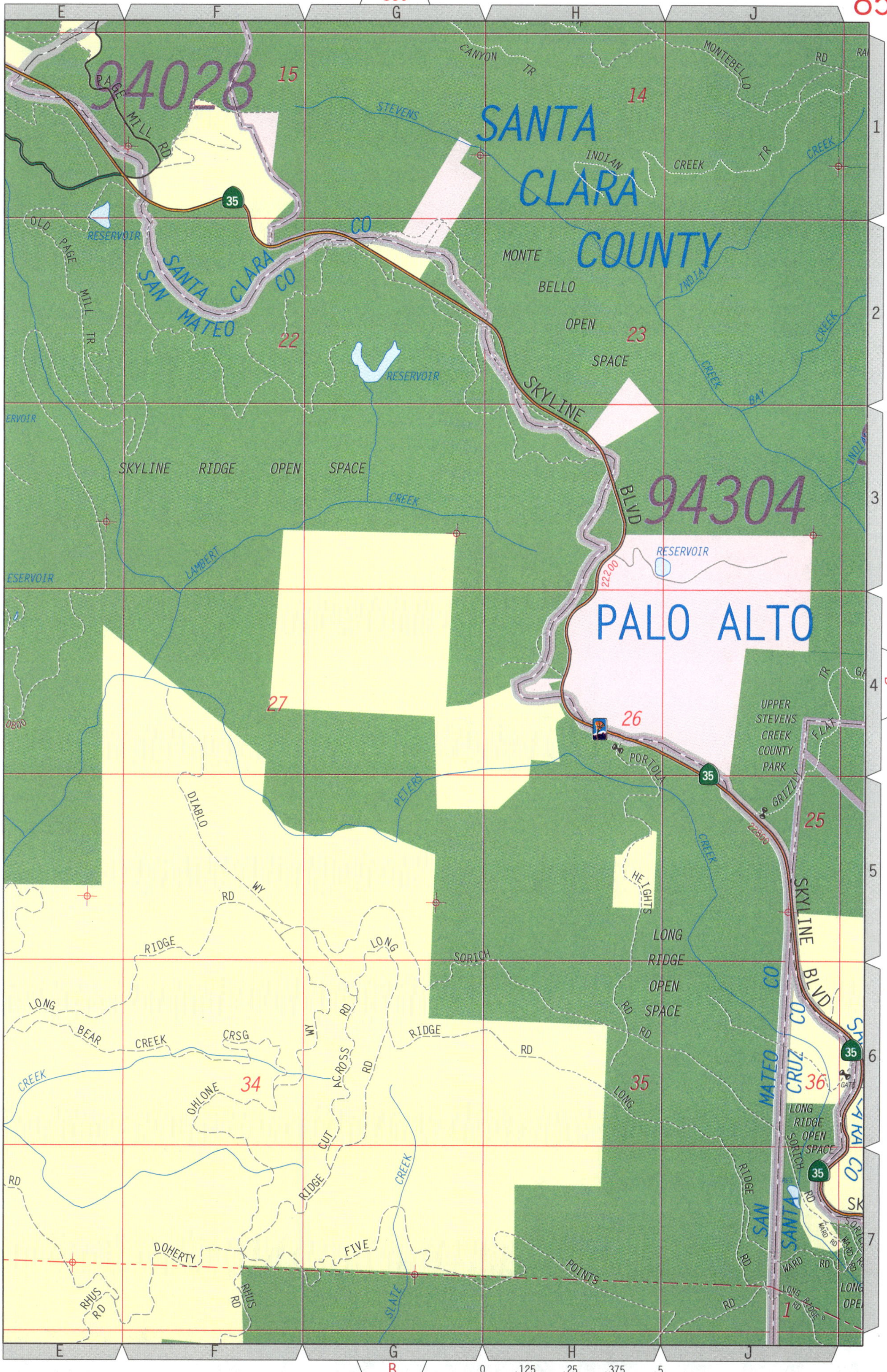

© 2008 Rand McNally & Company

N

E F G H J

94028 15

CANYON TR

STEVENS 14

SANTA

CLARA

COUNTY

1

PAGE MILL RD

35

OLD PAGE MILL TR

RESERVOIR SANTA CLARA CO SAN MATEO CO

MONTEBELLO RD

INDIAN CREEK TR CREEK

MONTE

BELLO

OPEN

SPACE

22 RESERVOIR SKYLINE 23 INDIAN CREEK BAY 2

SKYLINE RIDGE OPEN SPACE

BLVD 94304

CREEK RESERVOIR INDIAN 3

LAMBERT ERVOIR ESERVOIR 0800

212.00

PALO ALTO

26 27 UPPER STEVENS CREEK COUNTY PARK SEE B MAP 4

PORTOLA 35 212.00 GRITZLY TR FLAT GA 25

PETERS CREEK HEIGHTS SKYLINE BLVD 5

DIABLO RD WY LONG SORICH LONG RIDGE OPEN SPACE RD RD SAN MATEO CO SANTA CRUZ CO SK 35 6

RIDGE LONG WY RD RIDGE RD 36 GATE LONG RIDGE OPEN SPACE

LONG BEAR CREEK CRSG ACROSS RD 34 RD 35 LONG RIDGE RD SORICH 35 7

CREEK RD OHLONE CUT RIDGE CREEK SAN SANTA WARD RD WARD RD

DOHERTY FIVE POINTS RD LONG RIDGE B 1 LONG OPE

RHUS RD RHUS RD SLATE CREEK

E F G H J

SEE B MAP
SEE B MAP
0 .125 .25 .375 .5 miles 1 in. = 1900 ft.

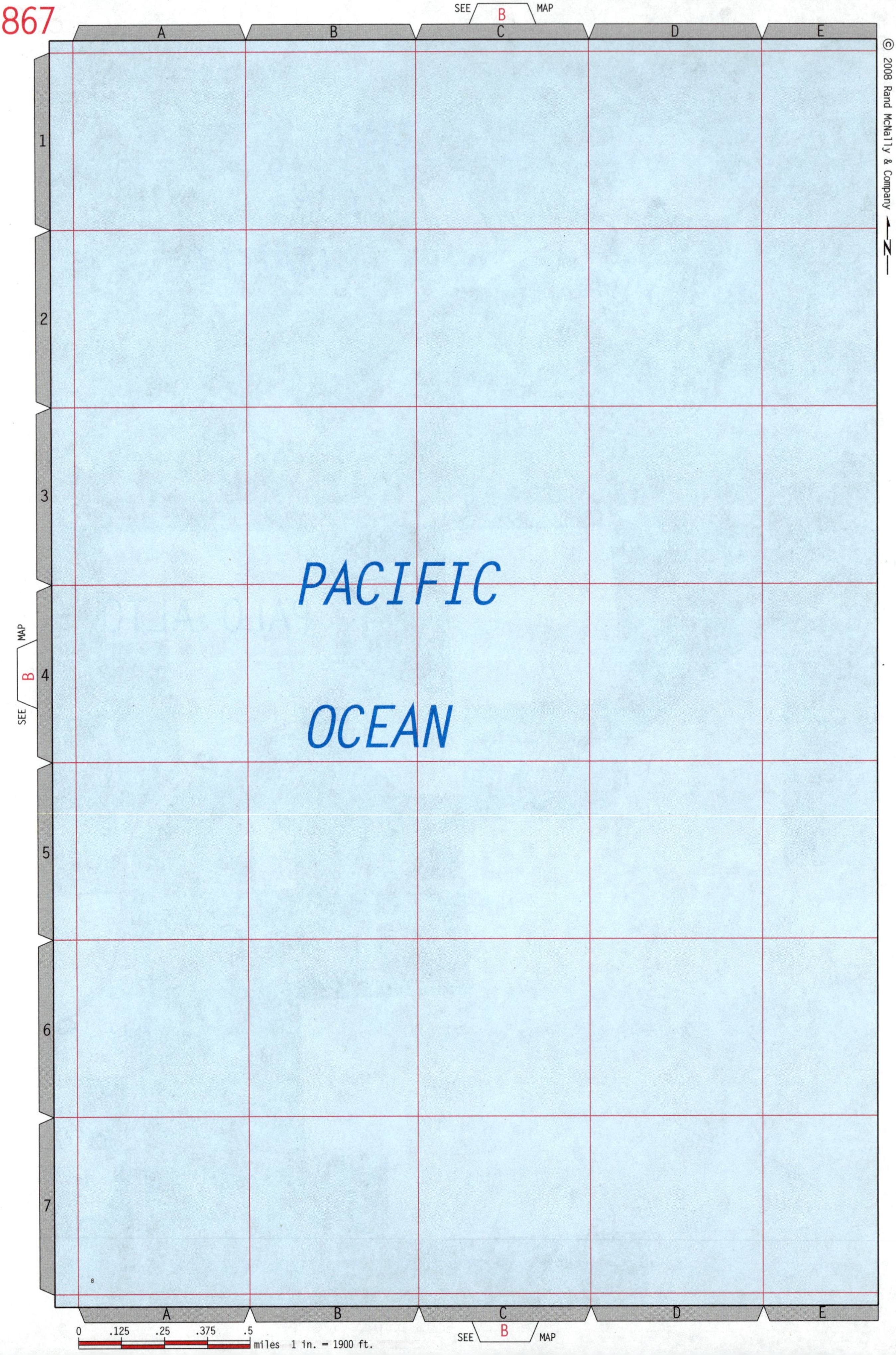
SEE B MAP
A
B
C
D
E
1
2
3
4
5
6
7
PACIFIC
OCEAN
0 .125 .25 .375 .5
miles 1 in. = 1900 ft.

SEE B MAP
E
F
G
H
J
1
2
3
4
5
6
7
PESCADERO STATE BEACH
PESCADERO CREEK
WATER LN
RANCHO BUTANO
BUTANO CREEK
RESERVOIR RD
1000
1100
PESCADERO CREEK RD
LN
FS
HILL RD
RESERVOIR RD
94060
SAN MATEO COUNTY
CABRILLO HWY
1
PEBBLE BEACH
10300
ARTICHOKE RD
500
1000
SEE 868 MAP
PESCADERO POINT
HOLLOW
BEAN
BEAN HOLLOW STATE BEACH
RES
LAKE LUCERNE
ARROYO DE LOS FRIJOLES
10000
BEAN HOLLOW LAKES PARK (PROP PARK)
8
SEE B MAP
0 .125 .25 .375 .5 miles 1 in. = 1900 ft.

SEE 848 MAP

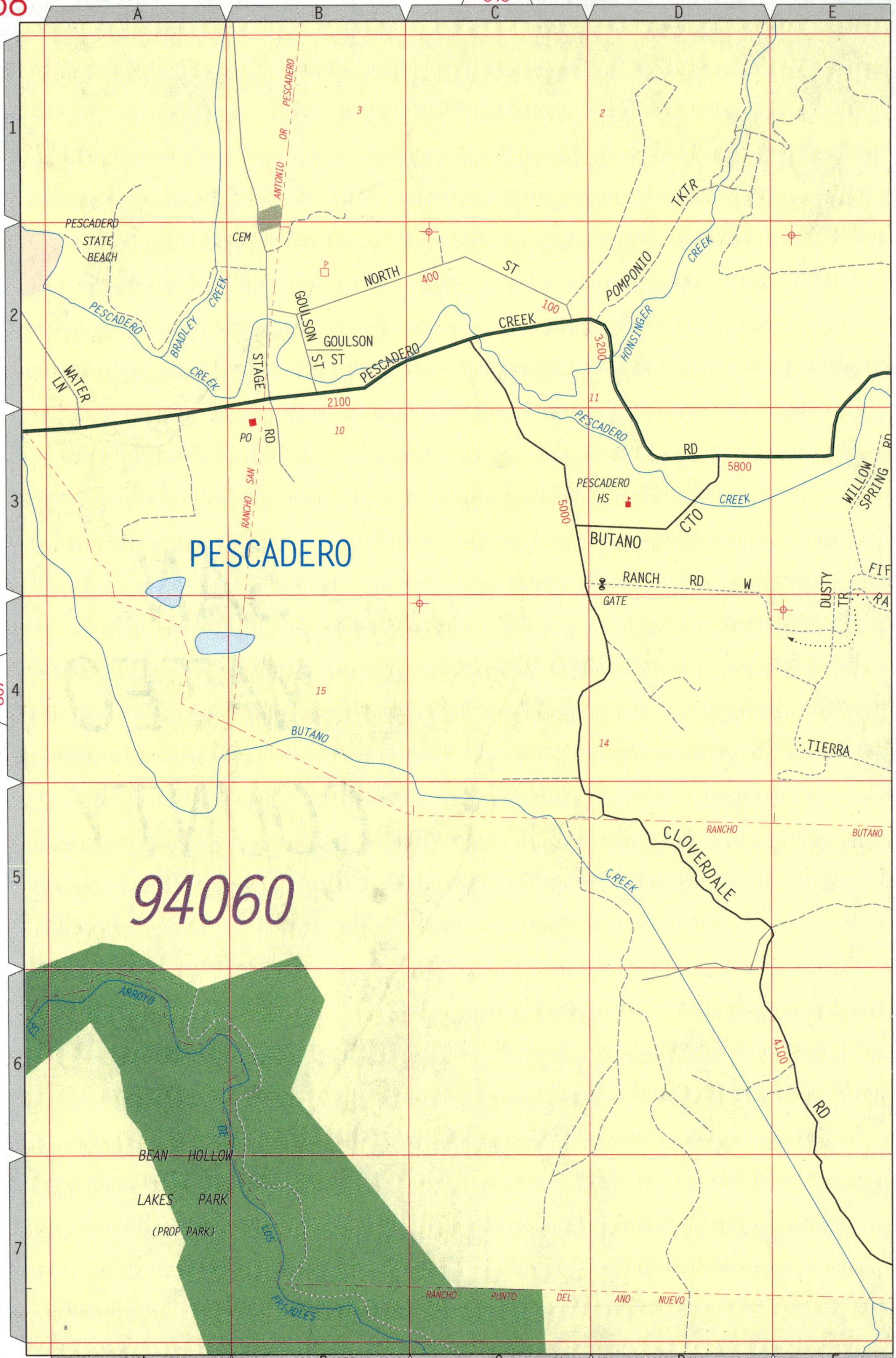

SEE 867 MAP
SEE 888 MAP

0 .125 .25 .375 .5 miles 1 in. = 1900 ft.

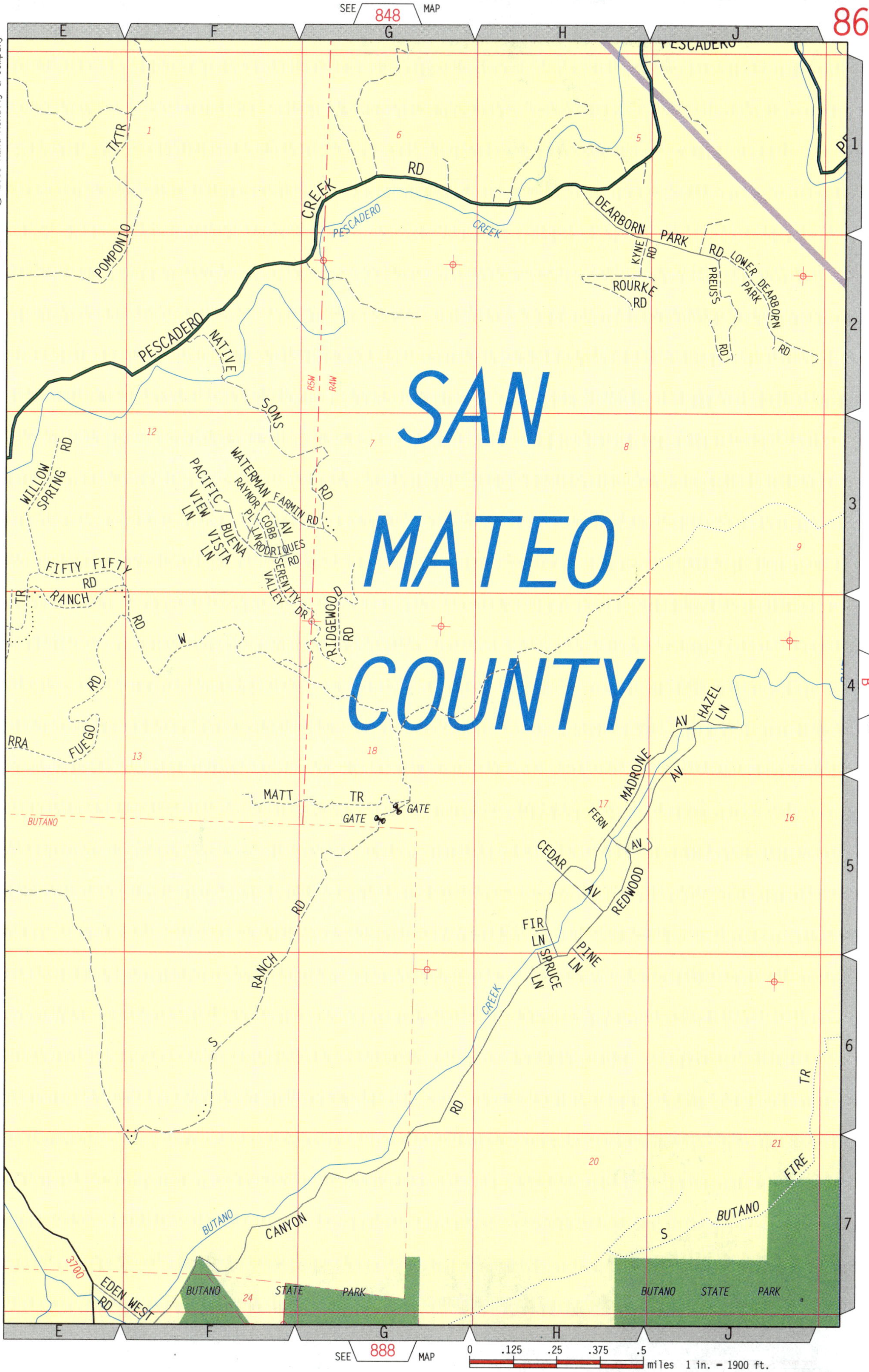
SEE 848 MAP
E
F
G
H
J
SAN MATEO COUNTY
PESCADERO
PESCADERO CREEK RD
PESCADERO CREEK
TKTR
POMPONIO
DEARBORN PARK RD
KYNE RD
ROURKE RD
PREUSS RD
LOWER DEARBORN PARK RD
NATIVE SONS RD
R5W
R4W
WILLOW SPRING RD
WATERMAN AV
RAYNOR PL
PACIFIC VIEW LN
BUENA VISTA LN
COBB LN
FARMIN RD
RODRIQUES RD
SERENITY VALLEY DR
RIDGEWOOD RD
FIFTY FIFTY RD
RANCH TR
W RD
FUEGO
RRA
MATT TR
GATE
GATE
BUTANO
S RANCH RD
HAZEL LN
AV
MADRONE AV
FERN AV
CEDAR AV
REDWOOD
FIR LN
SPRUCE LN
PINE LN
CREEK
RD
BUTANO CANYON
BUTANO
3700
EDEN WEST RD
BUTANO STATE PARK
BUTANO STATE PARK
S BUTANO FIRE TR
1
2
3
4
5
6
7
SEE B MAP
SEE 888 MAP
0 .125 .25 .375 .5 miles 1 in. = 1900 ft.

SAN MATEO CO.

SEE 868 MAP
A
B
C
D
E
1
2
3
4
5
6
7
BEAN HOLLOW LAKES PARK (PROP PARK)
BEAN HOLLOW LAKES
94060
ARROYO DE
PIGEON POINT RD
LIGHTHOUSE VIEW RD
SEE B MAP
SAN MATEO COUNTY
PIGEON POINT RD
RD
6800
CABRILLO HWY
1
COUNTY PARK (PROP)
5500
GAZOS
GAZOS
PACIFIC OCEAN
GAZOS CREEK ANGLING ACCESS
SOUTH COAST BEACHES (PROP PARK)
ANO NUEVO STATE RESERVE
SEE B MAP
0 .125 .25 .375 .5 miles 1 in. = 1900 ft.
N

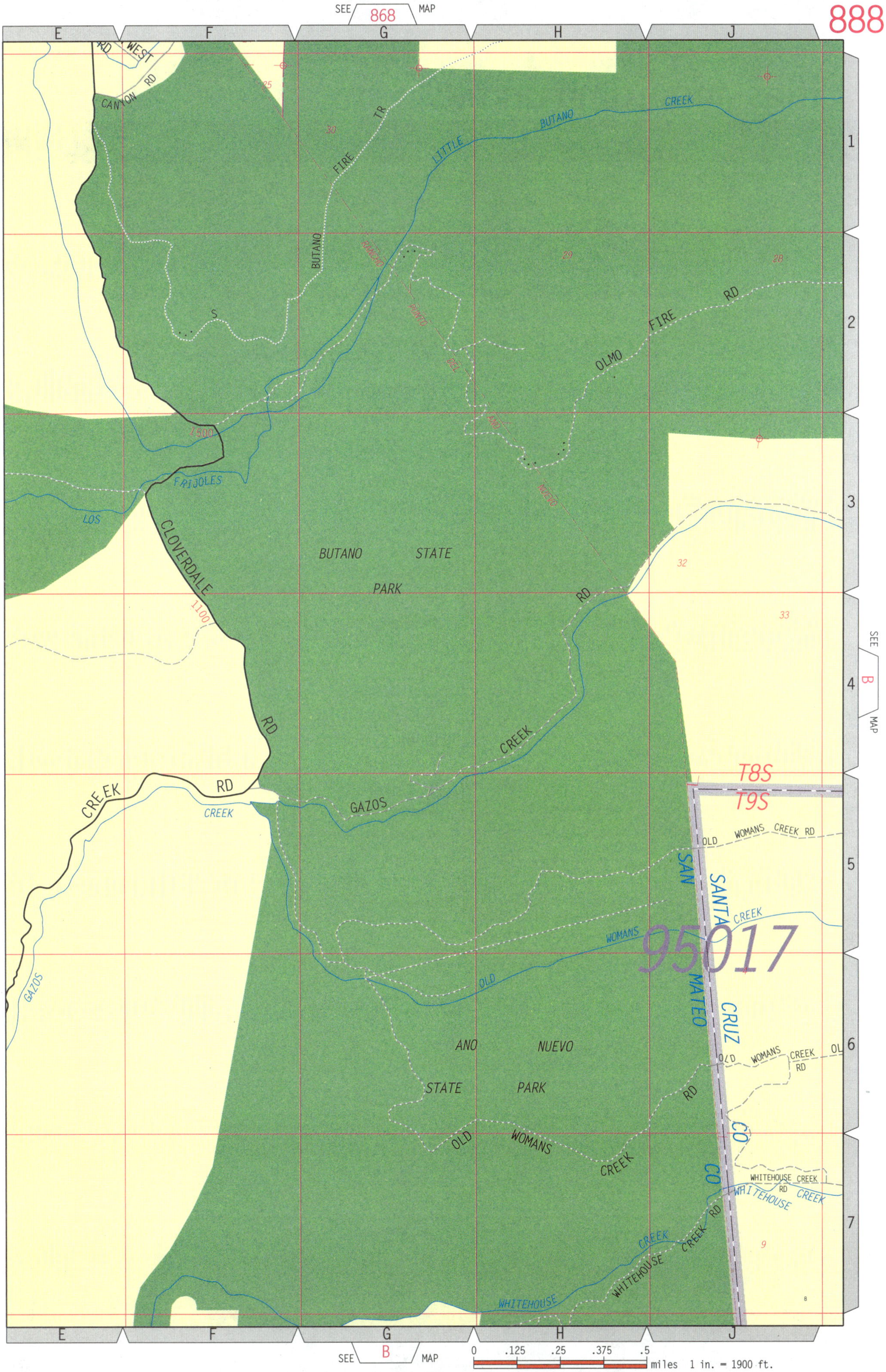
SEE 868 MAP
SEE B MAP
SEE B MAP
E
F
G
H
J
1
2
3
4
5
6
7
WEST
RD
CANYON RD
30
25
FIRE TR
BUTANO
LITTLE BUTANO CREEK
RANCHO
PUNTO
DEL
ANO
NUEVO
29
28
S
OLMO FIRE RD
1500
FRIJOLES
LOS
CLOVERDALE RD
BUTANO STATE PARK
32
33
1100
RD
CREEK
GAZOS
CREEK RD
CREEK
T8S
T9S
OLD WOMANS CREEK RD
SAN MATEO
SANTA CRUZ
CREEK
WOMANS
OLD
95017
GAZOS
ANO NUEVO STATE PARK
OLD WOMANS CREEK RD
OLD WOMANS CREEK RD
CO
CO
WHITEHOUSE CREEK RD
WHITEHOUSE CREEK
WHITEHOUSE CREEK RD
CREEK
WHITEHOUSE
9
8
0 .125 .25 .375 .5
miles 1 in. = 1900 ft.

Cities and Communities

	Community Name	Abbr.	ZIP Code	Map Page
	Alpine Hills		94025	810
*	Atherton	ATN	94027	790
	Bayshore		94005	688
*	Belmont	BLMT	94002	769
*	Brisbane	BSBN	94005	688
	Broadmoor		94015	687
*	Burlingame	BURL	94010	728
	Burlingame Hills		94010	728
*	Colma	CLMA	94014	687
*	Daly City	DALY	94014	687
	Devonshire		94070	769
	East Menlo		94025	770
*	East Palo Alto	EPA	94303	791
	El Granada		94018	767
	Emerald Lake		94062	789
	Farm Hills		94061	789
*	Foster City	FCTY	94404	749
*	Half Moon Bay	HMBY	94019	787
*	Hillsborough	HIL	94010	748
	Hillsdale		94403	749
	Kings Mountain		94062	788
	Ladera		94025	810
	La Honda		94020	849
	Linda Mar		94044	726
	Lindenwood		94025	790
	Loma Mar		94021	848
	Los Trancos Woods		94028	830
	Menlo Oaks		94025	790
*	Menlo Park	MLPK	94025	790
*	Millbrae	MLBR	94030	728
	Miramar		94019	767
	Montara		94037	746
	Moss Beach		94038	746
	North Fair Oaks		94063	770
*	Pacifica	PCFA	94044	727
	Palomar Park		94062	769
	Pescadero		94060	868
*	Portola Valley	PTLV	94028	810
	Portola Valley Ranch		94028	830
	Princeton By The Sea		94018	766
*	Redwood City	RDWC	94061	770
	Redwood Shores		94065	749
	Rockaway Beach		94044	727
*	San Bruno	SBRN	94066	707
*	San Carlos	SCAR	94070	769
	San Gregorio		94074	828
*	San Mateo	SMTO	94401	749
--	San Mateo County	SMCo		
	San Pedro Terrace		94044	726
	Serramonte		94015	707
	Sharon Heights		94025	790
	Sharp Park		94044	707
	Skyline		94062	788
	Sky Londa		94062	809
*	South San Francisco	SSF	94080	707
	The Highlands		94402	748
	Vallemar		94044	727
	Vista Verde		94028	830
	Westborough		94080	707
	West Menlo Park		94025	790
	Westridge		94025	810
*	Woodside	WDSD	94062	789
	Woodside Highlands		94025	809
	Woodside Hills		94062	789

*Indicates incorporated city

List of Abbreviations

PREFIXES AND SUFFIXES

AL	ALLEY
ARC	ARCADE
AV, AVE	AVENUE
AVCT	AVENUE COURT
AVD	AVENIDA
AVD D LA	AVENIDA DE LA
AVD D LOS	AVENIDA DE LOS
AVD DE	AVENIDA DE
AVD DE LAS	AVENIDA DE LAS
AVD DEL	AVENIDA DEL
AVDR	AVENUE DRIVE
AVEX	AVENUE EXTENSION
AV OF	AVENUE OF
AV OF THE	AVENUE OF THE
AVPL	AVENUE PLACE
BAY	BAY
BEND	BEND
BL, BLVD	BOULEVARD
BLCT	BOULEVARD COURT
BLEX	BOULEVARD EXTENSION
BRCH	BRANCH
BRDG	BRIDGE
BYPS	BYPASS
BYWY	BYWAY
CIDR	CIRCLE DRIVE
CIR	CIRCLE
CL	CALLE
CL DE	CALLE DE
CL DL	CALLE DEL
CL D LA	CALLE DE LA
CL D LAS	CALLE DE LAS
CL D LOS	CALLE DE LOS
CL EL	CALLE EL
CLJ	CALLEJON
CL LA	CALLE LA
CL LAS	CALLE LAS
CL LOS	CALLE LOS
CLTR	CLUSTER
CM	CAMINO
CM DE	CAMINO DE
CM DL	CAMINO DEL
CM D LA	CAMINO DE LA
CM D LAS	CAMINO DE LAS
CM D LOS	CAMINO DE LOS
CMTO	CAMINITO
CMTO DEL	CAMINITO DEL
CMTO D LA	CAMINITO DE LA
CMTO D LAS	CAMINITO DE LAS
CMTO D LOS	CAMINITO DE LOS
CNDR	CENTER DRIVE
COM	COMMON
COMS	COMMONS
CORR	CORRIDOR
CRES	CRESCENT
CRLO	CIRCULO
CRSG	CROSSING
CST	CIRCLE STREET
CSWY	CAUSEWAY
CT	COURT
CTAV	COURT AVENUE
CTE	CORTE
CTE D	CORTE DE
CTE DEL	CORTE DEL
CTE D LAS	CORTE DE LAS
CTO	CUT OFF
CTR	CENTER
CTST	COURT STREET
CUR	CURVE
CV	COVE
DE	DE
DIAG	DIAGONAL
DR	DRIVE
DRAV	DRIVE AVENUE
DRCT	DRIVE COURT
DRLP	DRIVE LOOP
DVDR	DIVISION DR
EXAV	EXTENSION AVENUE
EXBL	EXTENSION BOULEVARD
EXRD	EXTENSION ROAD
EXST	EXTENSION STREET
EXT	EXTENSION
EXWY	EXPRESSWAY
FOREST RT	FOREST ROUTE
FRWY	FREEWAY
FRY	FERRY
GDNS	GARDENS
GN, GLN	GLEN
GRN	GREEN
GRV	GROVE
HTS	HEIGHTS
HWY	HIGHWAY
ISL	ISLE
JCT	JUNCTION
LN	LANE
LNCR	LANE CIRCLE
LNDG	LANDING
LNDR	LAND DRIVE
LNLP	LANE LOOP
LP	LOOP
MNR	MANOR
MT	MOUNT
MTWY	MOTORWAY
MWCR	MEWS COURT
MWLN	MEWS LANE
NFD	NAT'L FOREST DEV
NK	NOOK
OH	OUTER HIGHWAY
OVL	OVAL
OVLK	OVERLOOK
OVPS	OVERPASS
PAS	PASEO
PAS DE	PASEO DE
PAS DE LA	PASEO DE LA
PAS DE LAS	PASEO DE LAS
PAS DE LOS	PASEO DE LOS
PAS DL	PASEO DEL
PASG	PASSAGE
PAS LA	PASEO LA
PAS LOS	PASEO LOS
PASS	PASS
PIKE	PIKE
PK	PARK
PKDR	PARK DRIVE
PKWY, PKY	PARKWAY
PL	PLACE
PLWY	PLACE WAY
PLZ, PZ	PLAZA
PT	POINT
PTAV	POINT AVENUE
PTH	PATH
PZ DE	PLAZA DE
PZ DEL	PLAZA DEL
PZ D LA	PLAZA DE LA
PZ D LAS	PLAZA DE LAS
PZWY	PLAZA WAY
RAMP	RAMP
RD	ROAD
RDAV	ROAD AVENUE
RDBP	ROAD BYPASS
RDCT	ROAD COURT
RDEX	ROAD EXTENSION
RDG	RIDGE
RDSP	ROAD SPUR
RDWY	ROAD WAY
RR	RAILROAD
RUE	RUE
RUE D	RUE D
RW	ROW
RY	RAILWAY
SKWY	SKYWAY
SQ	SQUARE
ST	STREET
STAV	STREET AVENUE
STCT	STREET COURT
STDR	STREET DRIVE
STEX	STREET EXTENSION
STLN	STREET LANE
STLP	STREET LOOP
ST OF	STREET OF
ST OF THE	STREET OF THE
STOV	STREET OVERPASS
STPL	STREET PLACE
STPM	STREET PROMENADE
STWY	STREET WAY
STXP	STREET EXPRESSWAY
TER	TERRACE
TFWY	TRAFFICWAY
THWY	THROUGHWAY
TKTR	TRUCK TRAIL
TPKE	TURNPIKE
TRC	TRACE
TRCT	TERRACE COURT
TR, TRL	TRAIL
TRWY	TRAIL WAY
TTSP	TRUCK TRAIL SPUR
TUN	TUNNEL
UNPS	UNDERPASS
VIA D	VIA DE
VIA DL	VIA DEL
VIA D LA	VIA DE LA
VIA D LAS	VIA DE LAS
VIA D LOS	VIA DE LOS
VIA LA	VIA LA
VW	VIEW
VWY	VIEW WAY
VIS	VISTA
VIS D	VISTA DE
VIS D L	VISTA DE LA
VIS D LAS	VISTA DE LAS
VIS DEL	VISTA DEL
WK	WALK
WY	WAY
WYCR	WAY CIRCLE
WYDR	WAY DRIVE
WYLN	WAY LANE
WYPL	WAY PLACE

DIRECTIONS

E	EAST
KPN	KEY PENINSULA NORTH
KPS	KEY PENINSULA SOUTH
N	NORTH
NE	NORTHEAST
NW	NORTHWEST
S	SOUTH
SE	SOUTHEAST
SW	SOUTHWEST
W	WEST

BUILDINGS

CH	CITY HALL
CHP	CALIFORNIA HIGHWAY PATROL
COMM CTR	COMMUNITY CENTER
CON CTR	CONVENTION CENTER
CONT HS	CONTINUATION HIGH SCHOOL
CTH	COURTHOUSE
FAA	FEDERAL AVIATION ADMIN
FS	FIRE STATION
HOSP	HOSPITAL
HS	HIGH SCHOOL
INT	INTERMEDIATE SCHOOL
JR HS	JUNIOR HIGH SCHOOL
LIB	LIBRARY
MID	MIDDLE SCHOOL
MUS	MUSEUM
PO	POST OFFICE
PS	POLICE STATION
SR CIT CTR	SENIOR CITIZENS CENTER
STA	STATION
THTR	THEATER
VIS BUR	VISITORS BUREAU

OTHER ABBREVIATIONS

BCH	BEACH
BLDG	BUILDING
CEM	CEMETERY
CK	CREEK
CO	COUNTY
COMM	COMMUNITY
CTR	CENTER
EST	ESTATE
HIST	HISTORIC
HTS	HEIGHTS
LK	LAKE
MDW	MEADOW
MED	MEDICAL
MEM	MEMORIAL
MT	MOUNT
MTN	MOUNTAIN
NATL	NATIONAL
PKG	PARKING
PLGD	PLAYGROUND
RCH	RANCH
RCHO	RANCHO
REC	RECREATION
RES	RESERVOIR
RIV	RIVER
RR	RAILROAD
SPG	SPRING
STA	SANTA
VLG	VILLAGE
VLY	VALLEY
VW	VIEW

STREET
Block City ZIP Pg-Grid

A

A ST
- SSF 94080 707-G3
100 MLPK 94025 790-H3
100 RDWC 94063 769-J5
100 SMCo 94014 687-C5
100 RDWC 94063 770-A5
400 DALY 94014 687-C5
ABBOT AV
- DALY 94014 687-D5
ABELIA WY
100 EPA 94303 791-D3
ABERDEEN DR
100 SCAR 94070 769-F4
1300 SMTO 94402 749-B2
ABRAMS CT
- SCIC 94305 791-A7
ABRYAN WY
2000 SMCo 94061 790-B4
ACACIA AV
100 SBRN 94066 727-J1
200 SSF 94080 707-H2
400 SBRN 94066 707-H7
ACACIA CT
- PCFA 94044 727-A5
100 SCAR 94070 769-F2
ACACIA DR
- ATN 94027 790-G1
700 BURL 94010 728-F6
ACACIA LN
- SMCo 94062 769-G6
- SMCo 94062 789-G1
ACACIA ST
900 SMCo 94037 746-G4
ACADEMY AV
900 BLMT 94002 769-C1
ACADEMY CT
700 BLMT 94002 769-C1
ACCACIA ST
- DALY 94014 687-J3
- SF 94134 687-J3
N ACCESS RD
100 SSF 94080 708-A5
300 SMCo 94128 708-B6
ACEVEDO AV
- SF 94132 687-A1
ACORN
- PTLV 94028 830-D2
ACORN DR
- HIL 94010 728-D7
ACORN PL
- SMCo 94062 769-G7
ACORN WY
- ATN 94027 790-G1
ACTON ST
- DALY 94014 687-E3
- SF 94112 687-E3
ADA ST
700 SMTO 94401 749-B1
ADAIR LN
- PTLV 94028 810-D6
ADAM CT
- SCAR 94070 769-D3
ADAM WY
- ATN 94027 790-C2
ADAMS CT
1300 MLPK 94025 771-B7
2500 SSF 94080 707-C4
ADAMS DR
1500 MLPK 94025 771-B7
1500 EPA 94303 771-B7
1500 MLPK 94303 771-B7
ADAMS ST
500 RDWC 94062 770-A6
600 RDWC 94061 770-A6
1700 SMTO 94403 749-C3
ADDISON AV
100 PA 94301 790-J5
300 PA 94301 791-A4
2000 EPA 94303 791-A2
ADDISON ST
1300 RDWC 94061 770-B7
ADELAIDE WY
3200 BLMT 94002 768-J2
ADELINE DR
1500 BURL 94010 728-B6
1500 SMCo 94010 728-B6
ADMIRAL CT
1000 SBRN 94066 707-H6
ADMIRAL ST
100 SMCo 94038 746-F6
ADMIRALTY LN
1100 FCTY 94404 749-F2
ADMIRALTY PL
- RDWC 94065 749-H6
ADOBE DR
1300 PCFA 94044 726-H6
ADRIAN AV
100 SSF 94080 707-D2
1300 SMTO 94403 749-D4
ADRIAN CT
- BURL 94010 728-C4
ADRIAN RD
200 MLBR 94030 728-C4
1500 BURL 94010 728-D4
ADRIATIC WY
- SBRN 94066 707-C6
AEGEAN WY
- SBRN 94066 707-C6
AFAR WY
- SMCo 94037 746-F5
AFTON CT
- SMTO 94402 749-B2
AGNES WY
900 PA 94303 791-C5
AGUA VISTA CT
- SMCo 94062 789-E2
AHWAHNEE DR
800 MLBR 94030 727-J4
AIRPORT BLVD
- SSF 94014 708-B1
- BURL 94010 728-F5
- SMTO 94401 728-F5
- SSF 94080 707-J3
400 SSF 94080 708-A2
S AIRPORT BLVD
- SMCo 94128 708-A4
100 SSF 94080 707-J4
100 SSF 94080 708-A4
AIRPORT ST
800 SMCo 94038 746-G7
800 SMCo 94038 766-G1
1000 SMCo 94019 766-G1
AIRPORT WY
400 SCAR 94070 769-H2
500 RDWC 94065 769-H2
ALAMEDA AV
100 SMCo 94019 767-C4
2800 HMBY 94019 767-C4
ALAMEDA PL
- SBRN 94066 707-E7
ALAMEDA DE LAS PULGAS
- ATN 94027 790-B4
- RDWC 94062 769-H6
- WDSD 94027 790-B4
- SMCo 94062 769-H6
100 BLMT 94002 749-A5
200 SMTO 94402 748-H3
300 BLMT 94002 769-C1
400 RDWC 94062 789-J1
400 SCAR 94070 769-F4
400 SMCo 94062 789-J1
600 RDWC 94061 789-J1
1500 SMTO 94403 748-H3
1500 SMTO 94403 749-A5
1600 RDWC 94061 790-B4
1800 WDSD 94062 790-B4
2000 SMCo 94062 790-B4
2100 SMCo 94061 790-B4
2300 WDSD 94061 790-B4
3000 SMCo 94025 790-B4
3700 MLPK 94025 790-B4
ALAMO ST
1100 SMCo 94037 746-H5
ALAMOS RD
- PTLV 94028 810-E5
ALANA WY
- SF 94134 688-B2
100 BSBN 94005 688-B2
ALANHILL LN
3100 SMTO 94403 748-J6
ALANNAH CT
- PA 94303 791-C4
ALBACORE LN
100 FCTY 94404 749-H3
ALBEMARLE WY
1500 BURL 94010 728-C5
ALBERNI ST
900 EPA 94303 771-A7
900 EPA 94303 791-A1
ALBERTA AV
100 SCAR 94070 769-H5
ALBERTA GN
- SMCo 94010 728-A7
ALBERTA ST
- SF 94134 687-J1
ALBERTA WY
300 HIL 94010 748-E3
ALBERT M TEGLIA BLVD
- SMCo 94014 687-C5
ALBION AV
100 WDSD 94062 789-F5
ALBRIGHT WY
2500 SSF 94080 707-E5
ALCALA CT
- PCFA 94044 726-J5
ALCATRAZ AV
- HMBY 94019 767-C4
ALCAZAR DR
3000 BURL 94010 728-A6
ALCOTT RD
200 SBRN 94066 727-F1
ALDEN CT
1200 BLMT 94002 769-D1
ALDEN ST
200 RDWC 94063 770-A5
1800 BLMT 94002 769-C1
ALDENGLEN DR
100 SSF 94080 707-G2
ALDER AV
100 SMCo 94015 687-B4
ALDER LN
400 SMTO 94403 749-B6
ALDER PL
- MLPK 94025 790-H2
ALDER ST
- SMCo 94037 746-G4
- SF 94134 688-A1
ALDERLEE WY
- SCAR 94070 769-F5
ALDERWOOD CT
1800 SMTO 94402 748-H7
ALEJANDRA AV
- ATN 94027 790-E3
- MLPK 94027 790-E3
ALEMANY BLVD
200 SF 94132 687-C2
200 SF 94112 687-E2
ALESTER AV
600 PA 94303 791-C4
ALEXANDER AV
- DALY 94014 687-D3
100 SMCo 94061 790-B2
ALEXANDER RD
- BSBN 94005 688-A7
ALEXIS CIR
500 DALY 94014 687-H3
ALEXIS CT
- MLPK 94025 790-C7
ALEXIS DR
900 PA 94304 830-F1
3000 PA 94304 810-F7
3200 LAH 94022 810-G7
ALGER DR
400 PA 94306 791-D7
ALHAMBRA CT
- PTLV 94028 810-D6
ALHAMBRA DR
2600 BLMT 94002 749-A7
2600 BLMT 94002 769-A1
ALHAMBRA RD
400 SSF 94080 707-F4
500 SMTO 94402 748-J2
ALICANTE DR
1100 PCFA 94044 727-A6
ALICE LN
900 MLPK 94025 790-F4
ALIDA WY
300 SSF 94080 707-G4
300 SMCo 94080 707-G4
ALISAL CT
- PCFA 94044 707-B3
ALISO WY
- SMCo 94028 810-E3
ALLAN ST
500 DALY 94014 687-J3
ALLARDICE WY
800 SCIC 94305 810-J2
ALLEGHENY WY
2200 SMCo 94402 768-G2
ALLEMANY ST
- DALY 94014 687-C5
ALLEN CT
700 PA 94303 791-D6
ALLEN DR
- SBRN 94066 707-D6
ALLEN RD
200 SMCo 94062 809-C5
ALLERTON AV
300 SSF 94080 708-B3
ALLERTON ST
400 RDWC 94063 770-A5
ALLISON CT
3400 SMTO 94403 748-J7
ALLISON ST
- SF 94112 687-F2
ALL VIEW WY
2600 BLMT 94002 769-A1
ALMA LN
- MLPK 94025 790-G3
ALMA ST
- MLPK 94025 790-G3
- PA 94301 790-H4
1200 PA 94301 791-B7
1500 PA 94306 791-B7
2000 SCAR 94070 769-F3
ALMADEN CT
26800 LAH 94022 830-J2
ALMADEN WY
200 SMTO 94403 749-D5
ALMANOR AV
400 SSF 94080 707-F4
1000 MLPK 94025 790-H1
1100 MLPK 94025 770-J7
ALMENAR ST
800 MLBR 94030 728-A4
ALMENDRAL AV
- ATN 94027 790-C3
ALMER RD
500 BURL 94010 728-F6
ALMERIA AV
300 SMCo 94019 767-A2
ALMOND AV
700 SSF 94080 707-H2
ALMOND CT
- EPA 94303 791-C2
ALOMAR WY
1100 BLMT 94002 769-D2
ALP AV
- DALY 94014 687-D3
ALP WY
- MLBR 94030 727-J4
ALPHA ST
- SF 94134 688-A2
ALPINE AV
- DALY 94015 687-A5
800 BURL 94010 728-F6
1100 MLPK 94025 770-H7
ALPINE CT
300 SSF 94080 707-F5
ALPINE RD
- PTLV 94028 810-D7
- PTLV 94028 830-C1
- SMCo 94020 850-C4
- SMCo 94028 830-D5
- SMCo 94020 849-F3
2400 SMCo 94025 790-E7
2400 MLPK 94025 790-E7
2400 MLPK 94025 810-E3
2500 SMCo 94025 810-E3
2900 SMCo 94028 810-E3
ALPINE WY
100 SBRN 94066 727-F1
ALPINE OAKS RD
- SMCo 94020 850-A5
ALSACE LORAINE AV
500 HMBY 94019 787-E2
ALTA AV
500 SMTO 94403 749-A5
ALTA LN
- SCAR 94070 769-E3
ALTA RD
- SCIC 94304 810-F1
ALTAIR AV
600 FCTY 94404 749-E3
ALTA LOMA AV
100 DALY 94015 687-B6
ALTA LOMA DR
100 SSF 94080 707-D2
ALTA LOMA RD
- SMCo 94037 746-H3
ALTA MESA DR
100 SSF 94080 707-E3
ALTA MESA RD
- SMCo 94037 746-H3
100 WDSD 94062 789-G5
ALTAMONT CIR
27700 SCIC 94022 830-G1
ALTAMONT DR
300 SSF 94080 707-E3
ALTAMONT RD
26600 LAH 94022 830-H1
ALTAMONT WY
3500 RDWC 94062 789-H1
ALTA VISTA DR
100 ATN 94027 790-B5
200 SMCo 94080 707-F5
300 SSF 94080 707-F5
600 PCFA 94044 726-J4
ALTA VISTA RD
100 WDSD 94062 789-G5
600 SMCo 94037 746-H4
ALTA VISTA WY
- SMCo 94014 687-F3
- DALY 94014 687-F3
ALTO AV
500 SMCo 94019 767-D4
500 HMBY 94019 767-D4
ALTO LN
- MLPK 94025 790-G4
ALTO LOMA
100 MLBR 94030 727-J5
ALTON AV
100 SMCo 94038 746-F7
ALTREE CT
- ATN 94027 790-H1
ALTSCHUL AV
900 MLPK 94025 790-D6
1000 SMCo 94025 790-D6
ALTURA WY
- SSF 94080 707-E2
900 PCFA 94044 726-J4
1500 BLMT 94002 769-E2
ALTURAS DR
100 SMCo 94010 728-A7
1500 BURL 94010 728-A7
ALTURAS WY
- DALY 94014 687-E3
ALVARADO AV
100 SMCo 94038 766-G1
1200 PCFA 94044 727-A5
1300 BURL 94010 728-C6
1400 SMCo 94010 728-C6
ALVARADO CT
700 SCIC 94305 810-J1
ALVARADO RW
500 SCIC 94305 790-H7
500 SCIC 94305 810-H1
ALVARADO ST
- BSBN 94005 688-A6
ALVERNO CT
- RDWC 94061 789-G3
ALVISO CT
- PCFA 94044 726-J5
- PCFA 94044 727-A5
ALVISO ST
- SF 94127 687-C1
AMADOR AV
- ATN 94027 790-C3
100 SBRN 94066 707-E7
AMALFI WY
400 RDWC 94065 749-J4
AMAPOLA AV
100 PCFA 94044 727-B2
AMARILLO AV
900 PA 94303 791-D5
AMARYLLIS CT
- SSF 94080 707-E2
AMAZON AV
- SF 94112 687-F1
AMBAR WY
300 MLPK 94025 790-F6
AMBER CT
- SCAR 94070 769-F6
AMBERWOOD CIR
- SSF 94080 707-H3
AMBOY CT
- SMCo 94402 768-G1
AMERICAN ST
800 SCAR 94070 769-H4
AMERICAN WY
1300 SMCo 94025 790-D5
AMES AV
700 PA 94303 791-D7
AMES CT
800 PA 94303 791-E7
AMESBURY AV
600 SMTO 94402 749-B2
AMESPORT LNDG
- HMBY 94019 787-F2
AMHERST AV
- SMCo 94025 790-D1
AMHERST CT
14100 LAH 94022 810-H5
AMHERST ST
200 SMTO 94402 748-H2
2000 PA 94306 810-J1
AMHURST CT
- DALY 94015 707-D3
N AMPHLETT BLVD
- SMTO 94401 729-A7
200 SMTO 94401 728-J6
S AMPHLETT BLVD
- SMTO 94401 729-A7
- SMTO 94401 749-B1
800 SMTO 94402 749-B1
AMY DR
- SMTO 94403 748-H7
ANACAPA LN
600 FCTY 94404 749-G5
ANAMOR ST
1600 RDWC 94061 790-A2
ANCHOR CIR
500 RDWC 94065 749-J6
ANCHOR LN
- SCAR 94070 769-E2
ANCHOR RD
400 SMTO 94404 749-D1
ANCHOR WY
- HMBY 94019 787-G5
ANDERSON WY
- MLPK 94025 790-E7
- MLPK 94025 810-E1
ANDETTA WY
100 SMCo 94028 810-D3
ANDORRA CT
- PCFA 94044 727-A3
ANDOVER DR
300 PCFA 94044 707-B2
ANDROMEDA LN
800 FCTY 94404 749-H1
ANGELITA AV
100 PCFA 94044 727-B2
ANGELL CT
- SCIC 94305 790-J7
- SCIC 94305 791-A7
ANGUIDO CT
- HIL 94010 748-G5
ANGUS AV E
200 SBRN 94066 707-J7
500 SBRN 94066 708-A7
ANGUS AV W
- SBRN 94066 707-H7
ANITA AV
800 BLMT 94002 749-D7
ANITA CT
- BLMT 94002 749-D7
ANITA DR
200 MLBR 94030 728-A3
ANITA LN
500 MLBR 94030 727-J3
500 MLBR 94030 728-A3
ANITA RD
- BURL 94010 728-G6
ANKENY ST
- SF 94134 688-A1
ANN RD
- PTLV 94028 810-A6
ANNA ST
900 SMTO 94401 749-B1
ANNAPOLIS CT
3800 SSF 94080 707-D3
ANNAPOLIS DR
1000 SMTO 94403 749-C4
ANNAPOLIS ST
2500 EPA 94303 771-B7
2500 EPA 94303 791-B1
ANNESCOURT DR
- HIL 94010 728-D7
ANNESCOURT PL
- HIL 94010 728-D7
ANNETTE AV
1200 RDWC 94063 770-F6
ANNIE ST
1500 SMCo 94015 687-B5
1500 DALY 94015 687-B5
ANNIS RD
100 BSBN 94005 688-B7
ANSEL AV
600 BURL 94010 728-F6
ANSEL LN
- SMCo 94025 810-E2
ANSON RD
- HIL 94010 748-F4
ANTARES LN
800 FCTY 94404 749-H1
ANTIGUA LN
1400 FCTY 94404 749-G5
ANTIOCH DR
- SMTO 94403 749-D6
ANTIQUE FOREST LN
- BLMT 94002 769-E1
ANTOINETTE LN
400 HMBY 94019 767-E6
800 SSF 94080 707-F2
ANTON CT
400 PA 94301 791-B6
ANTONIO CT
- PTLV 94028 810-C7
ANZA BLVD
100 BURL 94010 728-F5
ANZA DR
900 PCFA 94044 726-H4
ANZA WY
100 SBRN 94066 727-J1
APOLLO RD
700 FCTY 94404 749-F3
APPALOOSA WY
27000 LAH 94022 830-J2
APPIAN WY
- SSF 94080 707-E5
2900 SCAR 94070 769-F5
APPLE ORCHARD WY
- SMCo 94019 787-G5
APPLEWOOD LN
- PTLV 94028 810-C7
APRIL AV
100 SSF 94080 707-E3
APTOS WY
100 SSF 94080 707-G5
AQUARIUS LN
600 FCTY 94404 749-E4
ARA LN
600 FCTY 94404 749-E4
ARAGON BLVD
- SMTO 94401 749-A3
- SMTO 94402 748-J3
- SMTO 94402 749-A3
ARAGON CT
1000 PCFA 94044 726-J5
ARAPAHOE CT
- PTLV 94028 810-B6
ARASTRADERO RD
1500 PA 94304 810-F6
1700 SCIC 94304 810-H5
1700 PTLV 94028 810-F6
27500 LAH 94022 810-H5
ARBALLO DR
300 SF 94132 687-A1
ARBOL GRANDE CT
- SMCo 94025 790-D5
ARBOR AV
1900 BLMT 94002 769-C1
ARBOR CT
100 SBRN 94066 707-E7
100 WDSD 94062 789-G5
ARBOR DR
300 SSF 94080 707-E3
ARBOR LN
100 SMCo 94038 746-F6
100 SMTO 94403 749-B6
ARBOR RD
- MLPK 94025 790-E4
ARBORETUM RD
300 SCIC 94305 790-H5
300 PA 94304 790-H5
ARBUTUS AV
3500 PA 94303 791-E7
ARC WY
1500 BURL 94010 728-E6
ARCADIA CT
100 PCFA 94044 707-A2
ARCADIA DR
- DALY 94015 707-A2
- PCFA 94044 707-A2
ARCADIA PL
- HIL 94010 748-G2
1400 PA 94303 791-B4
ARCH LN
- SCAR 94070 769-E2
ARCH ST
- RDWC 94062 769-J5
- SF 94132 687-C2
100 RDWC 94062 770-A5
ARCHDALE CT
2200 SSF 94080 707-D4
ARCHER CT
- SMTO 94401 729-A6
ARCTURUS CIR
800 FCTY 94404 749-E4
ARDEE LN
2400 SSF 94080 707-D5
ARDEN AV
100 SSF 94080 707-J2
ARDEN CT
- DALY 94014 687-G3
- RDWC 94061 770-A7
- RDWC 94061 790-A1
ARDEN LN
1400 BLMT 94002 769-E2
ARDEN RD
200 MLPK 94025 790-F2
300 HIL 94010 748-G2
ARDENDALE DR
- DALY 94014 687-F3
S AREA DR
- SMCo 94128 728-C2
W AREA DR
- SMCo 94128 708-A7
ARELIOUS WALKER DR
2800 SF 94124 688-C1
ARELLANO AV
- SF 94132 687-B1
ARGONAUT AV
- SF 94134 687-J2
ARGUELLO BLVD
500 PCFA 94044 726-H4
ARGUELLO DR
2700 BURL 94010 728-A6
ARGUELLO ST
300 RDWC 94063 769-J5
600 SCIC 94305 790-H7
800 RDWC 94063 770-A5
ARGUS CT
800 FCTY 94404 749-E4
ARIES LN
700 FCTY 94404 749-E4
ARIZONA WY
1900 RDWC 94061 790-A3
ARK ST
1600 SMTO 94403 749-D1
ARLEEN WY
700 PCFA 94044 707-A7
700 PCFA 94044 727-A1
ARLETA AV
- SF 94134 688-A2
300 SF 94134 687-J2
ARLETA WY
1000 HMBY 94019 787-F2
ARLEY CT
- DALY 94015 707-D3
ARLINGTON DR
- SSF 94080 707-D1
ARLINGTON LN
- DALY 94014 687-F3
300 SMTO 94402 748-H1
ARLINGTON RD
200 RDWC 94062 769-H6
ARLINGTON WY
- SMCo 94025 790-H2
- MLPK 94025 790-H2
ARMADA WY
2200 SMTO 94404 749-D2
ARMOUR AV
200 SSF 94080 708-A2
200 SSF 94080 707-J2
ARMSBY DR
1200 HIL 94010 728-D6
1200 BURL 94010 728-D6
ARMSTRONG AV
1200 SF 94124 688-C1
ARNOLD WY
700 HMBY 94019 787-F2
700 MLPK 94025 790-J2
ARROWHEAD LN
- SMCo 94025 790-D1
- SMCo 94063 790-D1
ARROWHEAD WY
1000 PA 94303 791-D5
ARROWOOD LN
100 SMTO 94403 749-B5
ARROYO AV
1100 SCAR 94070 769-G4
ARROYO CT
- SMTO 94402 748-J2
ARROYO DR
- SSF 94080 707-E4
200 PCFA 94044 706-J4
200 PCFA 94044 707-A4
ARROYO LEON DR
700 HMBY 94019 787-G2
ARROYO SECO
- MLBR 94030 727-J5
ARROYO VIEW CIR
- BLMT 94002 769-B2
ARTHUR AV
2100 BLMT 94002 769-C1
ARTHUR LN
- ATN 94027 790-C2
ARTICHOKE RD
- SMCo 94060 867-H4
ARUBA LN
900 FCTY 94404 749-G4
ARUNDEL RD
- BURL 94010 728-H6
- SCAR 94070 769-E3
ASCENSION DR
1400 SMCo 94402 748-G6
ASCOT RD
300 HIL 94010 748-G2
ASH AV
600 SSF 94080 707-J2
ASH LN
100 PTLV 94028 810-E4
ASH ST
400 RDWC 94061 790-B1
1800 PA 94306 791-A7
ASHBY DR
700 PA 94301 791-B3
ASHDOWN PL
- HMBY 94019 787-E5
ASHFIELD RD
- ATN 94027 790-E2
ASHFORD AV
300 SCAR 94070 769-E4
ASHLAND DR
- DALY 94015 686-J4
ASHTON AV
- MLBR 94030 728-A4
- SF 94112 687-D1
200 SF 94132 687-D1
500 PA 94306 791-D7
2000 SMCo 94025 790-D6
S ASHTON AV
- MLBR 94030 728-B5
1800 BURL 94010 728-B5
ASHTON CT
3400 PA 94306 791-D7
ASHWOOD CT
1300 SMTO 94402 748-J4
ASHWOOD DR
1400 SMTO 94402 748-J4
ASPEN AV
200 SSF 94080 707-J2
200 SSF 94080 708-A2
ASPEN CT
- SF 94134 687-H3
ASPEN DR
1200 PCFA 94044 727-B5
ASPEN ST
900 SMCo 94037 746-H4
ASPEN WY
800 PA 94303 791-E7
ASSOCIATED RD
100 SSF 94080 708-A3
ASTER AV
- HIL 94010 728-F7
- HIL 94010 748-F1
ASTER RD
100 SCAR 94070 769-G4
ASTER WY
100 EPA 94303 791-D3
ATHENIAN WY
400 PCFA 94044 726-G4
ATHENS ST
300 SF 94112 687-G1
ATHERTON AV
- ATN 94027 790-C4
ATHERTON CT
100 SMCo 94061 790-B4
ATHERTON OAKS LN
- ATN 94027 790-D5
ATHERWOOD AV
- RDWC 94061 790-B2
ATHERWOOD PL
- RDWC 94061 790-B2
ATHLONE CT
- SMCo 94025 770-F7
ATHLONE WY
- SMCo 94025 770-E7
ATHY DR
3500 SSF 94080 707-C4
ATKINSON LN
1000 MLPK 94025 790-E5
ATLANTA ST
500 DALY 94014 687-D5
ATLANTIC AV
- SBRN 94066 707-J5
ATWATER DR
2900 BURL 94010 728-A6
AUDIFFRED LN
100 WDSD 94062 789-G7
AUDUBON AV
1200 SMCo 94037 746-G5
AUGUST CIR
300 MLPK 94025 790-F6
AURA VISTA
- MLBR 94030 727-J5
- PCFA 94044 706-J3
- MLBR 94030 728-A4
AURORA CT
- PCFA 94044 727-B2
AUSTIN AV
- ATN 94027 790-C2
AUTUMN DR
3800 RDWC 94061 789-G3
AUTUMN ST
200 SMCo 94020 829-F7
AVALON AV
1000 FCTY 94404 749-F5
AVALON CT
3100 PA 94306 791-D7
AVALON DR
- DALY 94015 686-J6
100 PCFA 94044 706-J4
200 PCFA 94044 707-A4
200 SSF 94080 707-F4
W AVALON DR
100 PCFA 94044 706-J4
AVELAR ST
- EPA 94303 791-B1
AVENUE ALHAMBRA
200 SMCo 94019 767-A3
AVENUE BALBOA
100 SMCo 94019 767-B2
AVENUE CABRILLO
100 SMCo 94019 767-C3
AVENUE DEL ORA
400 RDWC 94062 769-J7
AVENUE DEL ORO
200 SMCo 94019 767-B2
AVENUE GRANADA
100 SMCo 94019 767-A2
AVENUE PORTOLA
- SMCo 94019 767-B2
AVERY ST
- SMCo 94037 746-H5
AVIADOR AV
- MLBR 94030 728-B3
AVIGNON PL
2000 HMBY 94019 767-E5
AVILA CT
1300 PCFA 94044 727-A6
13100 LAH 94022 810-J7
AVILA RD
- SMTO 94402 749-A3
200 SMTO 94402 748-J3
AVOCET CT
200 FCTY 94404 749-H2
AVOCET DR
- RDWC 94065 749-J6
200 RDWC 94065 750-A6
AVON ST
900 BLMT 94002 769-D1
AVONDALE AV
- RDWC 94062 769-J5
AVONDALE RD
1200 HIL 94010 748-E4
W AVONDALE RD
- HIL 94010 748-E4
AVY AV
1800 MLPK 94025 790-D6
1800 SMCo 94025 790-D6
AYRES LN
- MLPK 94025 790-E7
AYRSHIRE FARM LN
- SCIC 94305 790-J7
AZALEA AV
900 BURL 94010 728-F5
AZALEA LN
- SCAR 94070 769-C5
AZALIA DR
100 EPA 94303 791-C2
AZTEC WY
2400 PA 94303 791-D5

B

B ST
100 DALY 94014 687-C5
100 RDWC 94063 769-J5
100 SSF 94080 707-G3
200 SMCo 94014 687-C5
300 CLMA 94014 687-D6
300 RDWC 94063 770-A5
N B ST
- SMTO 94401 748-J1

STREET Block City ZIP Pg-Grid

S B ST
100 SMTO 94401 748-J1
300 SMTO 94401 749-A2
1200 SMTO 94402 749-A2
BACON CT
- DALY 94015 707-B1
BADEN AV
100 SSF 94080 707-G2
BAFFIN CT
- FCTY 94404 749-G6
BAFFIN ST
100 FCTY 94404 749-G5
BAHAMA LN
600 FCTY 94404 749-G5
BAHIA
1800 SMTO 94403 749-E5
BAILEYANA RD
900 HIL 94010 728-D7
BAIN PL
700 RDWC 94062 789-G1
BAINBRIDGE ST
600 FCTY 94404 749-G4
BAINS ST
- EPA 94303 791-C3
BAIR ISLAND RD
500 RDWC 94063 770-B4
BAIRN DR
1400 HIL 94010 748-E4
BAKER RD
- SMCo 94021 849-A7
BAKER ST
100 SSF 94080 708-A3
BAKER WY
900 SMTO 94404 749-D2
BALBOA AV
- HMBY 94019 787-E1
1000 BURL 94010 728-D5
BALBOA BLVD
- HMBY 94019 767-E7
- HMBY 94019 787-E1
BALBOA LN
800 FCTY 94404 749-F3
BALBOA ST
900 FCTY 94404 749-F4
BALBOA WY
100 SBRN 94066 727-J1
1100 PCFA 94044 726-H4
1300 BURL 94010 728-C5
BALCLUTHA DR
1100 FCTY 94404 749-F3
BALDWIN AV
- DALY 94015 687-A6
- SMTO 94401 748-J1
BALDWIN HILLS CT
3600 SSF 94080 707-D4
BALERI RANCH RD
14100 LAH 94022 810-H6
BALHI CT
- SF 94112 687-F1
BALLY WY
400 PCFA 94044 707-A3
400 PCFA 94044 706-J3
BALMORAL CT
2100 SMTO 94403 749-A4
N BALSAMINA WY
100 SMCo 94028 810-E3
S BALSAMINA WY
200 SMCo 94028 810-E4
BALTIC CIR
- RDWC 94065 749-J5
BALTIMORE WY
- SF 94112 687-F2
100 DALY 94014 687-F2
BANBURY DR
- SF 94132 687-B1
BANBURY LN
700 MLBR 94030 727-H3
2700 SCAR 94070 769-G6
BANCROFT AV
900 HMBY 94019 767-E6
BANCROFT LN
400 PCFA 94044 707-A3
BANCROFT RD
- BURL 94010 728-H6
BANCROFT WY
200 PCFA 94044 706-J3
200 PCFA 94044 707-A3
BANDERA DR
3100 PA 94304 830-G1
BANFF WY
- PCFA 94044 727-C5
BANNOCK ST
- SF 94112 687-F1
BANTRY LN
2400 SSF 94080 707-D4
BANYAN WY
1000 PCFA 94044 727-A5
BARBADOS LN
500 FCTY 94404 749-G5
BARBARA DR
1900 PA 94303 791-C5
BARBARA LN
- BLMT 94002 749-E7
- MLPK 94025 790-E5
- SMCo 94070 769-D4
200 DALY 94015 707-D2
BARBARA WY
300 HIL 94010 748-D3
BARBOUR DR
600 RDWC 94062 769-G7
600 RDWC 94062 789-G1
BARCELONA CIR
- RDWC 94065 749-J6
BARCELONA DR
400 MLBR 94030 727-J2
400 MLBR 94030 728-A3
500 SBRN 94066 727-J2
1000 PCFA 94044 726-J4
1000 PCFA 94044 727-A4
BARCLAY AV
200 MLBR 94030 728-B3
BARCLAY WY
2600 BLMT 94002 769-B1
BARDET RD
100 WDSD 94062 789-G6
BARFORD AV
100 SCAR 94070 769-E2
BARK CT
100 HMBY 94019 767-F5
BARK DR
400 RDWC 94065 749-H6
BARKENTINE LN
400 RDWC 94065 749-H7
BARKENTINE ST
100 FCTY 94404 749-G4

BARMETTA WY
- ATN 94027 790-D2
BARNEGAT LN
400 RDWC 94065 749-J6
BARNES CT
- SCIC 94305 791-A7
BARNESON AV
- SMTO 94402 749-A3
200 SMTO 94402 748-J4
BARNEY AV
- ATN 94027 790-C5
- SMCo 94025 790-C5
BARNEY CT
- SMCo 94025 790-D5
BARRANCA LN
100 SMCo 94038 766-H2
BARRETT DR
- WDSD 94062 789-J5
BARRINGTON CT
2200 SSF 94080 707-D5
BARROILHET AV
- SMTO 94402 728-G7
- BURL 94010 728-G7
100 BURL 94010 748-F1
100 SMTO 94402 748-F1
200 HIL 94010 748-F1
BARROILHET DR
1100 HIL 94010 748-E2
BARRON AV
700 SMCo 94063 770-D6
BARRON ST
500 MLPK 94025 790-G3
BARRY LN
- ATN 94027 790-D4
BARTLETT WY
3400 BLMT 94002 768-J1
3400 BLMT 94002 769-A1
BARTON PL
- PCFA 94044 727-B6
100 MLPK 94025 790-J2
BARTON ST
1800 SMCo 94061 790-B4
BARTON WY
300 MLPK 94025 790-J3
E BASIN RD
- SSF 94080 708-D2
W BASIN RD
- SSF 94080 708-C2
BASSETT CT
3600 SSF 94080 707-D4
BASSETT LN
- ATN 94027 790-F2
BATES RD
- HIL 94010 748-F3
BATTEN LN
- RDWC 94065 750-C4
BAUER CT
800 SCAR 94070 769-F4
BAUER DR
800 SCAR 94070 769-F4
BAUTISTA CT
900 PA 94303 791-E6
BAY CT
- SSF 94080 707-H3
3300 BLMT 94002 749-A7
3300 BLMT 94002 769-A1
BAY LNDG
- SMTO 94401 729-B6
BAY RD
- MLPK 94025 770-F7
- ATN 94027 770-F7
300 ATN 94027 790-H1
300 MLPK 94025 790-H1
500 RDWC 94063 770-B6
500 SMCo 94025 790-H1
900 EPA 94303 791-A1
1900 EPA 94303 771-C7
2200 SMCo 94063 770-B6
3700 SMCo 94025 770-F7
BAY ST
- SSF 94014 707-J1
100 MLBR 94030 728-B2
BAYBERRY
- PTLV 94028 830-D1
BAYBERRY LN
900 RDWC 94065 750-A5
BAYBERRY PL
- HIL 94010 748-E1
BAYCREST WY
1300 SSF 94080 707-H1
BAYFRONT EXWY Rt#-84
- MLPK 94025 770-G6
- MLPK 94025 771-A6
BAY HARBOUR DR
800 RDWC 94065 750-A6
BAYHILL CT
2100 HMBY 94019 787-F5
BAYHILL DR
800 SBRN 94066 707-G7
BAYHILL PL
- HMBY 94019 787-F5
BAYHILL RD
300 HMBY 94019 787-F4
BAY LAUREL DR
1100 MLPK 94025 790-F5
BAYLOR ST
2500 EPA 94303 771-B7
2500 EPA 94303 791-B1
BAYPARK CIR
- SSF 94014 707-H1
BAYPORT AV
500 SCAR 94070 769-G2
BAYPORT CT
- SCAR 94070 769-G2
BAY RIDGE DR
500 DALY 94014 687-H3
BAYRIDGE WY
1600 SMTO 94402 748-H6
BAYSHORE BLVD
- SF 94134 688-A3
1500 SF 94124 688-A3
2600 BSBN 94005 688-A4
2600 BSBN 94005 708-B1
2600 BSBN 94080 708-B1
3000 DALY 94014 688-A3
N BAYSHORE BLVD
- SMTO 94401 728-J6
- SMTO 94401 729-A7
S BAYSHORE BLVD
- SMTO 94401 729-A7
500 SMTO 94401 749-B1
N BAYSHORE CIR
- SBRN 94066 707-H5

S BAYSHORE CIR
- SBRN 94066 707-J5
BAYSHORE FRWY U.S.-101
- BLMT - 749-B1
- BLMT - 769-G1
- BSBN - 688-B4
- BSBN - 708-B1
- BURL - 728-F5
- EPA - 790-J1
- EPA - 791-E5
- MLBR - 728-B2
- MLPK - 770-C5
- MLPK - 790-J1
- MLPK - 791-E5
- MTVW - 791-E5
- PA - 791-E5
- RDWC - 769-G1
- RDWC - 770-C5
- SCAR - 769-G1
- SF - 688-B4
- SMCo - 708-A6
- SMCo - 728-B2
- SMTO - 728-F5
- SMTO - 729-A7
- SMTO - 749-B1
- SSF - 708-B1
BAYSHORE HWY
- MLBR 94030 728-D3
1200 BURL 94010 728-D3
BAYSHORE PKWY
2400 MTVW 94043 791-F7
E BAYSHORE RD
500 RDWC 94063 770-A4
700 EPA 94303 791-A1
1900 PA 94303 791-D4
3200 SMCo 94063 770-D5
W BAYSHORE RD
1200 EPA 94303 791-B2
1900 PA 94303 791-D4
BAYSIDE BLVD
1300 SCAR 94070 769-J4
BAYSWATER AV
- BURL 94010 728-H7
1000 SMTO 94401 728-H7
BAYTREE RD
100 SCAR 94070 769-G4
BAYTREE WY
- SMTO 94402 748-J1
BAYVIEW AV
400 MLBR 94030 727-J2
1800 BLMT 94002 749-C7
4000 SMTO 94403 749-C7
BAYVIEW CT
- MLBR 94030 727-H2
BAY VIEW DR
- SCAR 94070 769-E3
200 SMCo 94070 769-D4
BAYVIEW PL
- BURL 94010 728-G5
BAY VIEW RD
- SMCo 94037 746-J5
100 PCFA 94044 726-J3
BAYVIEW WY
700 SMCo 94062 789-F2
BAYVIEW PARK RD
- SF 94124 688-B1
BAYWALK WY
- RDWC 94065 749-H5
BAYWOOD AV
- HIL 94010 748-H2
- SMTO 94402 748-H2
100 MLPK 94025 790-J3
1200 SSF 94080 707-F1
BAYWOOD GN
- SMCo 94062 769-E7
BAYWOOD ST
- SF 94112 687-F1
BEACH AV
400 HMBY 94019 767-E6
BEACH BLVD
1500 PCFA 94044 706-J6
BEACH RD
300 BURL 94010 728-H5
BEACH ST
100 SMCo 94038 746-F6
BEACH WY
100 SMCo 94038 746-F7
BEACH PARK BLVD
- FCTY 94404 749-G1
BEACHSIDE CT
- DALY 94015 706-J2
BEACHVIEW AV
100 PCFA 94044 707-A2
BEACON AV
1200 SMTO 94401 749-B1
BEACON ST
100 SSF 94080 708-A5
600 MLPK 94025 790-J2
BEACON SHORES DR
300 RDWC 94065 749-J2
BEAN HOLLOW RD
200 SMCo 94060 867-H6
BEAR CREEK CRSG
- SMCo 94020 850-E6
BEAR GLEN DR
- SMCo 94062 809-C3
BEAR GULCH DR
- PTLV 94028 810-D6
BEAR GULCH RD
- SMCo 94062 809-E2
- WDSD 94062 809-E2
900 SMCo 94062 829-A1
2000 SMCo 94062 828-H3
2300 SMCo 94074 828-H3
BEAR PAW
- PTLV 94028 830-C1
BEATRICE AV
500 BSBN 94005 688-A7
BEATTY AV
- BSBN 94005 688-A3
BEAUMONT BLVD
100 PCFA 94044 706-J2
200 PCFA 94044 707-A3
BEAU RIVAGE
- PCFA 94044 726-G4
BECKET DR
500 RDWC 94065 749-J7
BEECH AV
400 SBRN 94066 727-H1
400 SSF 94080 707-J2
500 SBRN 94066 707-H7
BEECH ST
100 RDWC 94063 770-B6
900 EPA 94303 791-C2

BEECHWOOD DR
700 DALY 94015 687-A5
800 SMCo 94015 687-A5
BEEGER RD
- RDWC 94063 770-C3
BELAIR WY
- RDWC 94062 789-G2
BEL AIRE CT
- HIL 94010 748-G5
BEL AIRE RD
1300 SMCo 94402 748-G6
1400 HIL 94010 748-G6
BELBROOK WY
- ATN 94027 790-B6
BELBURN DR
1600 BLMT 94002 769-D2
BELCREST AV
- DALY 94015 707-A1
100 DALY 94015 706-J1
BELFAST AV
400 PCFA 94044 726-G4
BELFAST CT
- SSF 94080 707-C5
BELFORD DR
- DALY 94015 686-J4
BELFORD WY
- SMTO 94402 748-J2
BELHAVEN AV
- DALY 94015 687-A7
BELHAVEN CT
- DALY 94015 687-B7
BELL CT
- EPA 94303 791-B2
BELL ST
300 EPA 94303 791-B2
BELLAIR WY
1100 MLPK 94025 790-D6
1100 SMCo 94025 790-D6
BELLA VISTA AV
100 PCFA 94044 706-J5
BELLA VISTA DR
100 HIL 94010 728-C7
BELLE AV
- RDWC 94063 770-E6
- SF 94132 687-C2
1900 SCAR 94070 769-G4
BELLE AIR RD
100 SSF 94080 708-A5
BELLEAU AV
- ATN 94027 790-D2
BELLEMONTI AV
2000 BLMT 94002 749-C7
2000 BLMT 94002 769-C1
BELLE ROCHE AV
- SMCo 94062 769-G6
BELLE ROCHE CT
- SMCo 94062 769-F7
BELLEVILLE BLVD
300 HMBY 94019 767-F7
BELLEVUE AV
- DALY 94014 687-D3
- SF 94112 687-F3
1100 BURL 94010 728-F7
1500 HIL 94010 728-F7
E BELLEVUE AV
- SMTO 94401 748-H1
- SMTO 94401 728-H7
W BELLEVUE AV
- SMTO 94402 748-G1
BELLFLOWER LN
- SCAR 94070 769-C4
BELLVIEW CT
2100 PA 94303 791-C5
BEL MAR AV
- DALY 94015 687-A4
BELMONT AV
100 SMCo 94061 790-B3
100 SSF 94080 707-J2
800 BLMT 94002 749-D7
1100 SCAR 94070 769-H5
BELMONT DR
- DALY 94015 687-A3
BELMONT CANYON RD
2500 BLMT 94002 769-A2
2800 BLMT 94002 768-J2
BELMONT WOODS WY
2900 BLMT 94002 769-A2
BELVEDERE AV
- SCAR 94070 769-H5
BELVEDERE CT
- BURL 94010 728-C7
BENGLOE LN
- HIL 94010 748-E4
BENITO AV
1300 BURL 94010 728-C6
BENJAMIN FRANKLIN CT
- SMTO 94401 748-J2
BENNETT RD
- RDWC 94062 769-G7
BENNINGTON AV
2300 SBRN 94066 727-F2
BENNINGTON CT
- SMCo 94402 748-G7
BENNINGTON DR
- SMCo 94402 748-G7
BENSON WY
2800 BLMT 94002 768-J2
2800 BLMT 94002 769-A2
BEPLER ST
- DALY 94014 687-D2
BERENDA DR
100 SSF 94080 707-E3
BERENDA WY
- SMCo 94028 810-E3
BERENDOS AV
100 PCFA 94044 727-B2
BERESFORD AV
100 SMCo 94061 790-B3
100 RDWC 94061 790-B3
3400 BLMT 94002 769-A1
BERESFORD CT
- SMCo 94061 790-B3
- SMTO 94403 749-D6
BERESFORD PL
- SMCo 94061 790-B3
BERESFORD ST
3800 SMTO 94403 749-D6
BERGESEN CT
- ATN 94027 790-B4
BERING DR
- SBRN 94066 707-C6
BERKELEY AV
500 SMCo 94025 790-H1
1000 MLPK 94025 790-H1

BERKELEY AV
1100 MLPK 94025 770-J7
BERKSHIRE AV
- SMCo 94063 790-C1
200 SMCo 94063 770-D7
BERKSHIRE DR
700 MLBR 94030 727-J4
700 MLBR 94030 728-A4
2600 SBRN 94066 707-D6
BERMUDA DR
400 SMTO 94403 749-C3
BERNAL AV
- SMCo 94038 766-G1
1000 BURL 94010 728-C5
BERNARDO AV
400 HMBY 94019 787-F4
BERNI CT
- MLBR 94030 728-A2
BERRYESSA WY
- HIL 94010 748-E6
BERRY HILL CT
14100 LAH 94022 810-H6
BERRY HILL LN
14200 LAH 94022 810-J6
BERTA CIR
- DALY 94015 707-C2
BERTITA ST
100 SF 94112 687-F1
BERTOCCHI LN
- MLBR 94030 727-H3
BEST CT
700 SCAR 94070 769-D5
BETA AV
- DALY 94014 687-D3
BETTINA AV
2200 BLMT 94002 749-B7
2200 BLMT 94002 769-B1
4200 SMTO 94403 749-B7
BETTMAN WY
3600 SSF 94080 707-D4
BETTY LN
- ATN 94027 790-C4
- SMTO 94402 749-B3
BEVERLY AV
200 MLBR 94030 728-B3
BEVERLY CT
- SSF 94080 707-G1
BEVERLY DR
- SCAR 94070 769-E3
200 SMCo 94020 829-F7
200 SMCo 94070 769-E4
BEVERLY PL
- PCFA 94044 707-A3
BEVERLY ST
- DALY 94015 707-C3
- SF 94132 687-C1
3000 SMTO 94403 749-A6
BFI OX MT DUMP RD
- SMCo - 767-H4
BIARRITZ CT
500 RDWC 94065 749-J5
BIBBITS DR
3900 PA 94303 791-F7
BIDDULPH WY
500 BLMT 94002 749-E7
BIEBER AV
1100 MLPK 94025 770-H7
BIG BEND DR
600 PCFA 94044 727-C5
BIG PINE RD
100 SMCo 94062 788-H5
BIG SUR WY
- PCFA 94044 727-B5
BIG TREE LN
- WDSD 94062 809-G6
- SMCo 94062 809-G6
BIG TREE RD
- SMCo 94062 809-G7
- WDSD 94062 809-G7
BIG TREE WY
- SMCo 94062 809-F6
BILL GRAHAM PKWY
- MTVW 94043 791-J7
BILLINGSGATE LN
200 FCTY 94404 749-F5
BILTMORE LN
- MLPK 94025 790-C6
BING ST
900 SCAR 94070 769-J4
BINNACLE LN
100 FCTY 94404 749-J1
BIRCH AV
400 SMTO 94402 749-B2
1200 SSF 94080 707-F1
1900 SCAR 94070 769-G4
BIRCH CT
100 SBRN 94066 707-E7
BIRCH LN
- PCFA 94044 706-J6
BIRCH ST
- RDWC 94062 769-J5
400 RDWC 94062 770-A6
900 SMCo 94037 746-H4
1800 PA 94306 791-A6
BIRCHWOOD CT
- SF 94134 687-H2
BIRKDALE RD
- HMBY 94019 787-F5
BISCAYNE AV
400 FCTY 94404 749-F6
BISHOP LN
- SMCo 94025 810-F1
BISHOP RD
1900 BLMT 94002 768-J1
BISHOP ST
- SF 94134 688-A1
BISMARK ST
- DALY 94014 687-D4
BLACKBURN AV
100 MLPK 94025 790-J3
BLACKBURN TER
- PCFA 94044 726-G4
BLACK FOX WY
- RDWC 94061 789-F3
- WDSD 94062 789-F3
BLACKHAWK LN
- SMCo 94010 728-B6
BLACK MOUNTAIN RD
800 HIL 94010 748-D4
1600 SMCo 94010 748-D4
27200 LAH 94022 830-J1
BLACKWELDER CT
100 SCIC 94305 790-J7
BLAIR CT
900 PA 94303 791-C5

BLAKE ST
400 MLPK 94025 790-F4
BLAKE WILBUR DR
900 PA 94304 790-G6
900 PA 94305 790-G6
BLAKEWOOD WY
- SMCo 94062 809-E5
BLANDFORD BLVD
800 RDWC 94062 769-H6
BLANKEN AV
- SF 94134 688-A2
600 SF 94124 688-A2
BLENHEIM AV
2700 SMCo 94063 790-C1
BLOMQUIST ST
300 RDWC 94063 770-C5
BLONDIN WY
400 SMCo 94080 707-G4
400 SSF 94080 707-G4
BLOOM LN
700 HMBY 94019 787-F2
BLOOMFIELD RD
- BURL 94010 728-G6
BLOSSOM CIR
100 SMTO 94403 749-D6
BLOSSOM CT
- DALY 94014 687-D5
BLUEBELL CT
- MLBR 94030 728-A3
BLUEBELL LN
- HIL 94010 748-F5
BLUE BELLE LN
- SCAR 94070 769-C4
BLUEFISH CT
300 FCTY 94404 749-H2
BLUEJAY CT
700 EPA 94303 791-B1
BLUE JAY WY
- SMCo 94062 789-A7
BLUE OAK LN
- SMCo 94062 769-F7
BLUE OAKS CT
- PTLV 94028 830-D3
BLUERIDGE AV
2300 MLPK 94025 790-D7
BLUE RIDGE LN
- WDSD 94062 809-G2
BLYTHDALE AV
- SF 94134 687-H2
BLYTHE ST
1100 FCTY 94404 749-G4
BOARDWALK
- PCFA 94044 726-H2
BOARDWALK CT
100 SBRN 94066 707-G6
BOARDWALK DR
100 SBRN 94066 707-G6
BOARDWALK PL
100 SBRN 94066 707-G6
700 RDWC 94065 749-H5
BOARDWALK WY
700 RDWC 94065 749-H6
BOBSTAY LN
600 FCTY 94404 749-J1
BODEGA ST
300 FCTY 94404 749-F5
BOHANNON DR
3800 MLPK 94025 770-G7
BOLERO WY
- DALY 94014 687-G3
BOLIVAR LN
100 PTLV 94028 810-D5
BOLTON PL
- MLPK 94025 790-F5
BONAIR
200 SCIC 94305 790-J7
BON AIR LN
- SMCo 94038 746-F7
BONITA AV
- RDWC 94061 790-B1
100 PCFA 94044 727-B2
200 SSF 94080 707-F2
600 MLBR 94030 727-J2
BONITA LN
100 FCTY 94404 749-H3
100 SMCo 94038 766-H2
BONITA RD
100 SMCo 94028 830-D4
BONNIE CT
1400 RDWC 94061 790-A2
BONNIE LN
- PCFA 94044 706-J3
BONNIE ST
400 DALY 94014 687-D4
BONSEN CT
100 SMCo 94062 790-A4
BOOTHBAY AV
100 FCTY 94404 749-E6
BORDEAUX LN
2000 HMBY 94019 767-E5
BORDEN ST
1600 SMTO 94403 749-C2
BOREL AV
- SMTO 94402 749-A4
400 SMTO 94402 748-J4
BOREL PL
1600 SMTO 94402 749-A4
BORICA ST
- SF 94127 687-C1
BOROUGHWOOD PL
- HIL 94010 748-E3
BOSTON AV
1600 SMTO 94403 749-D2
BOSUN LN
- RDWC 94065 750-C4
BOTANY CT
- RDWC 94062 789-G2
- SMCo 94062 789-G2
500 FCTY 94404 749-F5
BOUNTY DR
500 FCTY 94404 749-G3
BOURBON CT
2300 SSF 94080 707-D5
BOVET RD
- SMTO 94402 749-A4
BOW DR
- SCAR 94070 769-E7
BOW WY
- PTLV 94028 810-B6
BOWDOIN ST
700 SCIC 94305 810-J1
900 SCIC 94305 790-J7
1000 SF 94134 688-A1
2000 PA 94306 810-J1

BOWER RD
800 PCFA 94044 726-H5
BOWFIN ST
300 FCTY 94404 749-H3
BOWHILL RD
700 HIL 94010 748-G3
BOWSPRIT DR
300 RDWC 94065 749-H7
BOWSPRIT LN
100 FCTY 94404 749-G6
BOYCE AV
800 PA 94301 791-A4
BRADBURY LN
200 RDWC 94061 790-B2
BRADFORD DR
- SSF 94080 707-D1
BRADFORD ST
200 RDWC 94063 770-A5
BRADFORD WY
700 PCFA 94044 707-A7
700 PCFA 94044 727-A1
BRADLEY CT
- SMCo 94061 790-B4
1400 SMTO 94401 729-A7
BRADLEY DR
900 DALY 94015 687-A5
900 SMCo 94015 687-A5
BRADLEY WY
1000 EPA 94303 791-A1
BRADSHAW TER
- RDWC 94062 789-G1
BRADY PL
- MLPK 94025 790-H2
BRAEMAR DR
- HIL 94010 748-F5
BRAGATO RD
400 SCAR 94070 769-F1
BRAMBLE CT
300 FCTY 94404 749-H3
BRANDON CT
- DALY 94014 687-J4
- HIL 94010 748-H5
BRANDON WY
300 MLPK 94025 790-F6
BRANDT RD
1300 HIL 94010 748-E3
BRANDY ROCK WY
3600 RDWC 94061 789-H2
BRANDYWINE RD
1500 SMCo 94402 748-F7
BRANNER DR
2300 MLPK 94025 810-E1
2300 SMCo 94025 790-E7
2300 SMCo 94025 810-E1
2300 MLPK 94025 790-E7
BRANSON DR
3400 SMTO 94403 749-D5
BRANSTEN RD
800 SCAR 94070 769-H3
BRAZIL AV
500 SF 94112 687-G1
1100 SF 94134 687-G1
BREAKER LN
- RDWC 94065 750-C4
BREAKWATER DR
- RDWC 94065 750-A5
BRECON CT
100 SMCo 94062 769-G6
BREEZE PL
800 RDWC 94062 789-H1
BRENT CT
- MLPK 94025 790-C7
BRENTWOOD CT
2200 EPA 94303 791-C2
BRENTWOOD DR
- SSF 94080 707-G5
BRENTWOOD RD
200 HIL 94010 748-G2
BRET HARTE
- SMCo 94020 809-F6
BRET HARTE DR
3600 RDWC 94061 789-G3
BRET HARTE ST
800 PA 94303 791-B5
BREWER DR
600 HIL 94010 748-F1
BREWSTER AV
300 RDWC 94063 770-A5
900 RDWC 94062 770-A5
1200 RDWC 94062 769-J6
2700 SMCo 94062 769-J6
BRIAR LN
100 SMTO 94403 749-B6
BRIARFIELD AV
2500 RDWC 94061 789-H2
BRIARFIELD WY
400 BLMT 94002 749-E7
BRIARWOOD DR
400 SSF 94080 707-F5
BRIARWOOD WY
- BLMT 94002 749-E7
BRIDGE CT
- BLMT 94002 769-C3
BRIDGE PKWY
- RDWC 94065 749-G6
BRIDGE RD
- HIL 94010 748-H2
BRIDGEPOINTE CIR
- SMTO 94404 749-E2
BRIDGEPOINTE PKWY
- SMTO 94404 749-E2
BRIDGEPORT DR
100 SMCo 94019 766-J1
100 SMCo 94019 767-A2
BRIDGEPORT LN
600 FCTY 94404 749-F4
BRIDLE CT
- HIL 94010 748-H4
BRIDLE LN
- WDSD 94062 809-G2
BRIDLE WY
1000 HIL 94010 748-H4
BRIG CT
100 HMBY 94019 767-F5
BRIGANTINE LN
- RDWC 94065 750-C4
BRIGGS ST
1500 SMCo 94015 687-C5
1500 DALY 94015 687-C5
BRIGHT ST
- SF 94132 687-D2
BRIGHTON AV
- SF 94112 687-D1
BRIGHTON CT
- DALY 94015 707-D3

STREET
Block City ZIP Pg-Grid

BRIGHTON LN
200 RDWC 94061 790-B2
BRIGHTON RD
100 PCFA 94044 706-J6
200 PCFA 94044 707-A6
BRIONES CT
27600 LAH 94022 830-H1
BRIONES WY
12400 LAH 94022 830-H1
BRISTOL CT
500 FCTY 94404 749-F5
BRISTOL WY
2700 RDWC 94061 789-J3
2700 RDWC 94061 790-A3
BRITTAN AV
800 SCAR 94070 769-H3
BRITTANY LN
- DALY 94014 687-F3
BRITTANY MEADOWS
- ATN 94027 790-E3
BRITTON AV
100 ATN 94027 790-E3
BRITTON ST
- SF 94134 687-J2
BROAD ST
- SF 94112 687-D2
BROAD ACRES RD
- ATN 94027 790-C5
BROADVIEW CT
3500 SMTO 94403 768-J1
BROADWAY
- MLBR 94030 728-A2
- RDWC 94063 770-D6
100 SMCo 94019 766-J2
800 BLMT 94002 769-F1
1000 BURL 94010 728-D6
2700 RDWC 94062 770-B5
2800 RDWC 94062 769-J6
S BROADWAY
- MLBR 94030 728-B4
BRODERICK RD
- BURL 94010 728-C4
BRODERICK WY
2700 MTVW 94043 791-G6
BROMFIELD RD
600 SMTO 94402 748-F1
700 HIL 94010 748-F2
BROMLEY CT
- DALY 94015 707-D3
BROMLEY DR
- SMCo 94062 769-F6
2700 SCAR 94070 769-F6
BROOK ST
100 SCAR 94070 769-G5
BROOKDALE AV
100 SF 94134 687-H2
BROOKE CT
- HIL 94010 748-G6
BROOKHAVEN CT
- PCFA 94044 707-A2
BROOKLAWN AV
- DALY 94015 686-J5
- DALY 94015 687-A5
BROOKLINE WY
3900 SMCo 94062 789-G2
BROOKS PL
- PCFA 94044 727-B6
BROOKS ST
1700 SMTO 94403 749-C2
BROOKSIDE DR
100 PTLV 94028 810 B7
BROOKSIDE LN
800 MLBR 94030 727-H3
BROOKVALE RD
1800 HIL 94010 728-E7
BROOKWOOD RD
100 WDSD 94062 789-H4
BROSNAN CT
100 SSF 94080 707-G2
500 DALY 94015 707-D3
BROTHERHOOD WY
500 SF 94132 687-A1
BROUGHTON LN
500 FCTY 94404 749-G5
BROWNING WY
400 SSF 94080 707-H4
BRUCE AV
- SF 94112 687-E1
BRUCE DR
800 PA 94303 791-D6
BRUCE ST
100 PCFA 94044 707-A4
BRUMISS TER
- DALY 94014 687-E2
BRUNO AV
- DALY 94014 687-C5
BRUNSWICK CT
3700 SSF 94080 707-D4
BRUNSWICK ST
- SF 94112 687-D3
700 DALY 94014 687-D3
BRUSCO WY
900 SSF 94080 707-G2
BRUSSELS ST
700 SF 94134 688-A1
BRYANT CT
300 PA 94301 790-H4
BRYANT ST
100 PA 94301 790-H4
1000 PA 94301 791-B6
1500 DALY 94015 687-B5
2500 PA 94306 791-C7
BRYANT WY
100 SBRN 94066 727-F2
BRYCE AV
200 SSF 94080 707-F4
BRYCE CT
- BLMT 94002 769-A2
BRYCE CANYON WY
- PCFA 94044 727-B5
BRYSON AV
500 PA 94306 791-C6
BUCARELI DR
- SF 94132 687-B1
BUCCANEER LN
- RDWC 94065 750-C4
BUCHANAN CT
- EPA 94303 791-C1
BUCK CT
- WDSD 94062 790-A5
BUCKEYE
- PTLV 94028 830-C1
BUCKEYE CT
- HIL 94010 748-G3

STREET
Block City ZIP Pg-Grid

BUCKEYE ST
- RDWC 94063 770-B6
BUCKINGHAM AV
- SMCo 94063 790-C1
- SMCo 94063 770-C7
BUCKINGHAM CT
- HIL 94010 748-F5
BUCKINGHAM RD
300 PCFA 94044 706-J6
BUCKINGHAM WY
1200 HIL 94010 748-F6
BUCKLAND AV
700 SCAR 94070 769-E2
700 BLMT 94002 769-E2
BUCKLAND CT
- SCAR 94070 769-E2
BUCK MEADOW DR
- PTLV 94028 830-D3
BUCKNELL DR
400 SMTO 94402 748-H3
BUCKTHORN WY
- ATN 94025 790-E2
- HIL 94010 748-F1
- MLPK 94025 790-E2
BUDD CT
1500 SMTO 94403 749-D3
BUEL AV
400 PCFA 94044 726-J2
BUENA VISTA AV
- SMCo 94021 849-A7
- SBRN 94066 707-J5
200 DALY 94015 687-B6
400 SMCo 94061 790-B3
400 SMTO 94403 749-A5
2300 BLMT 94002 769-B1
BUENA VISTA DR
- SSF 94080 707-E4
11600 LAH 94022 830-H2
BUENA VISTA LN
- SMCo 94060 868-F3
BUENA VISTA RD
- SMCo 94037 746-H4
E BUENA VISTA RD
1200 SMCo 94037 746-H4
BUENA VISTA ST
500 SMCo 94038 746-F5
BUFFALO CT
- PCFA 94044 727-C4
BUNKER HILL DR
2000 SMCo 94402 748-F7
2200 SMCo - 748-F7
BUOY LN
- RDWC 94065 750-C4
BURBANK AV
- RDWC 94063 770-C6
- SMTO 94403 749-C6
BURGESS DR
300 MLPK 94025 790-G4
BURGOYNE CT
- SMCo 94402 768-G1
BURKE LN
1100 FCTY 94404 749-J4
BURLINGAME AV
100 BURL 94010 728-G7
BURLINGVIEW DR
2700 BURL 94010 728-C7
BURLWAY RD
700 BURL 94010 728-E4
BURNHAM CT
- SCAR 94070 769-F5
BURNHAM WY
2400 PA 94303 791-D5
BURNING TREE CT
300 HMBY 94019 787-F5
BURNING TREE RD
2200 HMBY 94019 787-F5
BURNS AV
100 ATN 94027 790-E2
BURNS CT
800 PCFA 94044 727-A1
BURNS VALLEY RD
- SMCo 94021 849-C6
BURN VALLEY RD
300 SMCo 94021 848-H4
BURR AV
- SF 94134 687-J2
BURREN WY
2900 SSF 94080 707-E5
BURROWS AV
600 SBRN 94066 707-H7
BURROWS ST
900 FCTY 94404 749-G4
BUSH ST
1100 SCAR 94070 769-G2
BUTANO CTO
300 SMCo 94060 868-C3
BUTLER AV
- SSF 94080 708-A2
BUTTERCUP LN
- SCAR 94070 769-C4
BUTTERNUT DR
2400 HIL 94010 748-C1
BUXTON AV
100 SSF 94080 707-D2
BYERS DR
1900 MLPK 94025 791-A2
BYRD LN
800 FCTY 94404 749-G4
13100 LAH 94022 810-J7
BYRNE ST
100 DALY 94014 687-D5
100 SMCo 94014 687-D5
BYRNE PARK LN
27200 LAH 94022 830-J2
BYRON AV
1800 SMTO 94401 749-C1
BYRON CT
- SF 94112 687-F2
BYRON DR
800 SSF 94080 707-D2
BYRON ST
100 PA 94301 790-J3
1100 PA 94301 791-A4
2700 PA 94306 791-C6
BYXBEE ST
- SF 94132 687-C1

C

C ST
100 MLPK 94025 790-G3
100 RDWC 94063 769-J5
200 SSF 94080 707-J2
300 CLMA 94014 687-D6
300 RDWC 94063 770-A4

STREET
Block City ZIP Pg-Grid

CABALLO LN
- SCIC 94304 810-F6
CABOT CT
400 SSF 94080 708-B3
800 SCAR 94070 769-E5
CABOT LN
800 FCTY 94404 749-F4
CABOT RD
- SSF 94080 708-B3
CABRILLO AV
600 SCIC 94305 810-H1
1000 BURL 94010 728-D5
CABRILLO FRWY Rt#-1
- DALY - 687-B7
- DALY - 707-A2
- PCFA - 707-A2
- PCFA - 706-J5
CABRILLO HWY Rt#-1
- PCFA 94044 707-A7
- HMBY 94019 767-D4
- HMBY 94019 787-G7
- SMCo 94019 767-D4
- SMCo 94038 746-G7
300 PCFA 94044 726-H3
300 PCFA 94044 727-A1
300 SMCo 94037 746-F1
600 SMCo - 746-F1
2000 SMCo - 726-F6
2100 SMCo 94038 766-H1
2100 SMCo - 766-H1
2400 SMCo 94019 787-G7
4000 SMCo 94060 888-B5
9000 SMCo 94060 867-G4
9500 SMCo 94019 766-H1
9600 SMCo 94019 807-G1
9600 SMCo 94019 828-A4
20000 SMCo 94074 828-A4
CABRILLO WY
100 SBRN 94066 727-J1
CADILLAC WY
1000 BURL 94010 728-E5
CADIZ CIR
- RDWC 94065 749-J7
CADIZ CT
- PCFA 94044 726-J4
CAHILL RIDGE RD
- SMCo - 768-D3
CAINE AV
- SF 94112 687-E1
CALAVERAS AV
100 PCFA 94044 727-B2
CALAVERAS CT
- HIL 94010 748-F6
CALAVERAS WY
- SMCo 94020 809-F6
CALERA TER
800 PCFA 94044 727-A3
CALGARY ST
- DALY 94014 687-J3
- SF 94134 687-J3
CALIFORNIA AV
- SMCo 94038 746-F6
100 SMCo 94019 766-J2
100 SSF 94080 708-A3
200 SSF 94080 707-J2
N CALIFORNIA AV
- PA 94301 791-B6
700 PA 94303 791-C5
S CALIFORNIA AV
100 PA 94306 791-A7
500 PA 94304 791-A7
CALIFORNIA DR
- BURL 94010 728-C4
- MLBR 94030 728-C4
CALIFORNIA ST
- RDWC 94063 770-A6
CALIFORNIA WY
500 RDWC 94062 789-E2
600 SMCo 94062 789-E2
700 WDSD 94062 789-E3
W CALIFORNIA WY
500 RDWC 94062 789-E2
500 WDSD 94062 789-E3
CALLADO WY
- ATN 94027 790-C5
CALLAN BLVD
3500 SSF 94080 707-C3
4000 DALY 94015 707-B1
4700 DALY 94015 687-B7
CALLIE LN
- MLPK 94025 770-F7
CALLIPPE CT
- BSBN 94005 687-H4
CALVERT AV
- SSF 94080 707-D1
CALVIN AV
2800 SMCo 94063 770-C7
CALYPSO LN
- SCAR 94070 769-C5
CAMARITAS AV
- SSF 94080 707-D1
CAMARITAS CIR
800 SSF 94080 707-E1
CAMBERLY WY
400 RDWC 94061 790-B2
CAMBON DR
- SF 94132 687-B1
CAMBORNE AV
- SMCo 94070 769-D3
- SCAR 94070 769-D3
CAMBRIDGE AV
200 PA 94306 791-A7
600 MLPK 94025 790-G5
CAMBRIDGE LN
100 SBRN 94066 727-F2
CAMBRIDGE RD
600 RDWC 94061 789-G3
1100 BURL 94010 728-D5
CAMBRIDGE ST
- SCAR 94070 769-E3
500 BLMT 94002 749-E7
700 SF 94134 687-J1
CAMDEN AV
4300 SMTO 94403 749-C7
CAMELIA DR
100 DALY 94015 687-B6
CAMELLIA AV
100 RDWC 94061 790-B2
CAMELLIA CT
- EPA 94303 791-C3
100 SBRN 94066 707-E6
CAMELLIA DR
1100 EPA 94303 791-D2

STREET
Block City ZIP Pg-Grid

CAMELOT CT
- DALY 94015 707-D3
- SCAR 94070 769-G6
CAMEO CT
- DALY 94015 707-B2
CAMERON LN
- DALY 94014 687-F3
CAMERON WY
- SF 94124 688-C1
CAMEROTA WY
400 RDWC 94065 749-J5
CAMINO PZ
700 SBRN 94066 707-H6
CAMINO AL LAGO
200 ATN 94027 790-C5
200 SMCo 94025 790-C5
CAMINO A LOS CERROS
- ATN 94027 790-C5
- SMCo 94027 790-C5
1800 SMCo 94025 790-C5
CAMINO ALTO
- MLBR 94030 728-A4
CAMINO DE LAS ROBLES
- PA 94301 790-H5
CAMINO DE LOS ROBLES
- ATN 94027 790-D5
1800 SMCo 94025 790-D5
CAMINO POR LOS ARBOLES
- ATN 94027 790-D5
CAMINO VISTA CT
- BLMT 94002 749-D7
CAMPANA AV
200 DALY 94015 687-A7
CAMPBELL AV
- SF 94134 688-A1
500 SF 94134 687-J1
4000 MLPK 94025 770-G7
CAMPBELL LN
- MLPK 94025 810-E1
- MLPK 94025 790-E7
CAMPESINO AV
200 PA 94306 791-C7
CAMPHOR CT
- HIL 94010 748-C2
CAMPHOR WY
700 EPA 94303 791-B2
CAMPO RD
100 PTLV 94028 810-C7
CAMPO BELLO
- MLPK 94025 790-E7
CAMPO BELLO CT
- MLPK 94025 790-E7
CAMP POMPONIO RD
- SMCo 94020 849-J7
- SMCo 94020 850-A7
CAMPUS DR
100 SCIC 94305 790-G6
800 DALY 94015 707-B1
800 SCIC 94305 810-H1
2600 SMTO 94403 748-J5
CAMPUS DR E
300 SCIC 94305 810-G1
700 SCIC 94305 790-H7
CAMPUS DR W
300 SCIC 94305 790-F7
900 SCIC 94305 810-F1
CANADA LN
1400 WDSD 94062 789-G6
CANADA RD
- SMCo 94062 768-H3
- SMCo 94070 768-H3
100 SMCo 94062 789-B1
100 SMCo 94402 768-H3
200 SMCo 94062 769-A6
200 SMCo 94070 769-A6
400 SMCo 94070 789-B1
800 WDSD 94062 789-F5
CANADA RD Rt#-92
- SMCo - 768-G2
- SMCo 94062 768-G2
- SMCo 94402 768-G2
CANADA COVE AV
- HMBY 94019 787-F6
CANADA VISTA
- SMCo 94020 829-E7
N CANAL ST
300 SSF 94080 707-H3
S CANAL ST
300 SSF 94080 707-J3
CANANEA AV
3100 BURL 94010 728-B7
CANANEA PL
- BURL 94010 728-B7
CANEPA CT
- SMCo 94062 769-F7
CANIS LN
800 FCTY 94404 749-H1
CANNERY SQ
- DALY 94014 687-D5
CANOE CT
100 RDWC 94065 749-H5
CANOGA WY
- MLBR 94030 727-H2
CANTERBURY AV
- DALY 94015 707-B2
CANTERBURY RD
1200 HIL 94010 748-F3
CANVASBACK WY
1000 RDWC 94065 749-J4
1400 RDWC 94065 750-A4
CANYON CT
- SSF 94080 707-F5
CANYON DR
- SF 94112 687-G3
- DALY 94014 687-G3
100 PTLV 94028 810-C7
200 PTLV 94028 830-C1
500 PCFA 94044 707-A5
CANYON LN
- RDWC 94062 789-G1
- SMCo 94062 789-G1
CANYON RD
- SMCo 94060 868-F7
- SMCo 94060 888-E1
600 RDWC 94062 789-G1
700 RDWC 94062 769-G7
700 SMCo 94062 769-G7
2800 BURL 94010 728-B7
2800 SMCo 94010 728-B7
27500 PA 94304 830-H2
27500 SCIC 95014 830-H2

STREET
Block City ZIP Pg-Grid

CANYON OAK CT
1800 SMTO 94402 748-H7
CANYON VIEW DR
- SMCo - 768-D3
CAPAY CIR
- SSF 94080 707-E3
CAPE BRETON CT
- PCFA 94044 727-C4
CAPE BRETON DR
600 PCFA 94044 727-C4
CAPE COD DR
800 RDWC 94065 750-A6
CAPE HATTERAS CT
- RDWC 94065 749-J2
CAPISTRANO DR
1300 PCFA 94044 727-A6
CAPISTRANO RD
300 SMCo 94019 767-A2
300 SMCo 94019 766-J2
CAPISTRANO WY
600 SMTO 94402 748-J2
1800 BURL 94010 728-A6
E CAPISTRANO WY
500 SMTO 94402 748-J2
W CAPISTRANO WY
700 SMTO 94402 748-J2
CAPITOL AV
- SF 94112 687-D1
1900 EPA 94303 791-B2
CAPPER CT
- SMCo 94061 790-B4
CAPRI LN
500 FCTY 94404 749-G5
CAPRINO WY
300 SCAR 94070 769-E4
CAPSTAN CT
300 RDWC 94065 749-H7
CAPTAIN LN
- RDWC 94065 750-C4
CAPUCHINO AV
900 BURL 94010 728-D5
CAPUCHINO DR
- MLBR 94030 728-A2
500 MLBR 94030 727-J2
CARAVEL LN
700 FCTY 94404 749-G2
CARDENAS AV
- SF 94132 687-B1
CARDIFF LN
1000 RDWC 94061 790-B2
CARDIGAN RD
1200 HIL 94010 748-F3
CARDINAL WY
100 RDWC 94063 770-C3
1000 PA 94303 791-D5
CAREY SCHOOL LN
- SMTO 94403 749-A4
W CARGO RD
- SMCo 94128 708-B7
- SMCo 94128 728-B1
CARIBBEAN WY
600 SMTO 94402 748-J4
CARINA LN
800 FCTY 94404 749-F4
CARLETON AV
- DALY 94015 687-A6
CARLETON CT
1600 RDWC 94061 790-A2
CARLETON PL
- PCFA 94044 727-B6
CARLISLE DR
1100 SMTO 94402 749-B2
CARLMONT DR
2100 BLMT 94002 769-C2
CARLOS AV
100 RDWC 94061 790-B1
1300 BURL 94010 728-C6
CARLOS ST
1300 SMCo 94038 746-F5
CARLOW WY
2900 SSF 94080 707-D5
CARLSBAD CT
- SSF 94080 707-G4
CARLTON AV
200 SBRN 94066 707-J7
200 SBRN 94066 727-J1
800 MLPK 94025 771-A7
1100 MLPK 94025 790-J1
1200 MLPK 94025 770-J7
CARLTON CT
400 SSF 94080 708-B3
CARLTON RD
1400 HIL 94010 748-E4
CARMEL AV
- PCFA 94044 706-J5
- DALY 94015 686-J6
100 SMCo 94019 767-A2
200 PCFA 94044 707-A5
CARMEL CIR
500 SMTO 94402 748-J2
CARMEL DR
2300 PA 94303 791-D4
2500 SBRN 94066 707-E6
CARMEL LN
- SMCo 94062 769-G6
CARMEL RD
100 SMCo 94062 788-J6
CARMEL WY
100 SMCo 94028 830-E3
CARMELITA AV
1100 BURL 94010 728-D7
1900 HIL 94010 728-D7
2500 BLMT 94002 769-B1
CARMELITA DR
1800 SCAR 94070 769-F3
CARMELO LN
200 SSF 94080 707-F2
CARNELIAN RD
100 SSF 94080 707-H1
CAROL AV
1500 BURL 94010 728-G7
E CAROL AV
- BURL 94010 728-G7
CAROLAN AV
200 BURL 94010 728-E5
N CAROLAN AV
1300 BURL 94010 728-E5
CAROLE CT
700 EPA 94303 791-B1
CAROLE WY
1500 RDWC 94061 790-A1
CAROLINA AV
2400 RDWC 94061 790-A3
CAROLINA LN
- ATN 94027 790-C2

STREET
Block City ZIP Pg-Grid

CAROLINE WY
- DALY 94014 687-G3
CARR ST
- SF 94124 688-B1
CARRERA CT
- SMCo 94062 789-G2
CARRIAGE CT
- MLPK 94025 790-C7
CARRINGTON CIR
27200 LAH 94022 830-J1
CARRIZAL ST
- SF 94134 687-H2
CARROLL AV
700 SF 94124 688-C1
CARSON ST
1200 RDWC 94061 789-J2
CARTER DR
3500 SSF 94080 707-C4
CARTER ST
500 DALY 94014 687-H3
500 SF 94134 687-H3
600 SMCo 94014 687-H3
CARTER WY
- MLPK 94025 790-C7
CARTIER LN
900 FCTY 94404 749-G4
CARY AV
1200 SMTO 94401 749-B1
CASA AV
- DALY 94015 687-B6
CASA BONA AV
2300 BLMT 94002 769-B1
CASA DE CAMPO
3100 SMTO 94403 749-E5
CASA DEL MAR DR
400 HMBY 94019 767-E6
CASANOVA DR
3500 SMTO 94403 749-D5
CASANUEVA PL
900 SCIC 94305 810-J2
CASCADE CT
- SMTO 94401 729-A6
1000 MLPK 94025 790-D6
CASCADE DR
1000 MLPK 94025 790-C6
CASEY AV
2500 MTVW 94043 791-F6
CASEY CT
- MLPK 94025 771-A7
CASEY DR
100 SSF 94080 707-E3
CASHLEA CT
2600 SSF 94080 707-C4
CASSANDRA CT
- SF 94112 687-E2
CASSIA ST
400 RDWC 94063 770-B6
N CASTANYA WY
100 SMCo 94028 810-E3
S CASTANYA WY
200 SMCo 94028 810-E4
CASTELO AV
- SF 94132 687-B1
CASTENADA DR
200 MLBR 94030 728-A5
1800 BURL 94010 728-A5
CASTILE WY
300 SSF 94080 707-F5
CASTILIAN WY
100 SMTO 94402 748-J3
CASTILLEJA AV
1500 PA 94306 791-A6
CASTILLEJO DR
- DALY 94015 687-B7
100 DALY 94015 707-A1
CASTILLO AV
1300 BURL 94010 728-C6
CASTILLO ST
- DALY 94014 687-H2
- SF 94134 687-H2
CASTLE CT
- HIL 94010 748-D3
CASTLE ST
- DALY 94014 687-C5
CASTLE WY
1100 MLPK 94025 790-F4
CASTLE HILL RD
600 RDWC 94061 789-H2
CASTLEMONT AV
- DALY 94015 687-B3
CASTLETON AV
- DALY 94015 686-J4
- DALY 94015 687-A4
CASTLETON WY
100 SBRN 94066 707-D6
CASTOR ST
800 FCTY 94404 749-F4
CASTRO CT
- BURL 94010 728-B5
1300 PCFA 94044 727-A6
CATALINA AV
100 PCFA 94044 707-A2
CATALPA AV
200 SMTO 94401 748-J1
CATALPA DR
- ATN 94027 770-F7
- ATN 94027 790-F1
CATALPA WY
2300 SBRN 94066 707-F7
CATAMARAN LN
- DALY 94014 687-E5
CATAMARAN ST
300 FCTY 94404 749-G3
CATHCART WY
1000 SCIC 94305 810-J2
CATHERINE CT
- PTLV 94028 810-A5
CATHERINE DR
300 SSF 94080 707-E3
CATHY PL
- MLPK 94025 790-F5
CAVANAUGH ST
300 SMTO 94401 729-A6
E CAVOUR ST
- DALY 94014 687-C4
W CAVOUR ST
- DALY 94014 687-C4
CAXTON CT
3200 SMTO 94403 748-J6
3200 SMTO 94403 749-A6
CAYMAN LN
600 FCTY 94404 749-G5
CAYUGA AV
- SF 94112 687-D2

STREET
Block City ZIP Pg-Grid

CEBALO LN
- ATN 94027 790-C1
CEDAR AV
- SMCo 94060 868-H5
300 SMCo 94062 788-H5
400 SBRN 94066 727-H1
500 SBRN 94066 707-G7
2000 SMCo 94025 790-D6
CEDAR CT
- DALY 94014 687-H3
- SF 94134 687-H3
- HIL 94010 748-F1
- SMCo 94025 790-D6
CEDAR LN
- WDSD 94062 789-G6
200 PCFA 94044 706-J6
200 PCFA 94044 707-A6
CEDAR PL
800 SSF 94080 708-A2
CEDAR ST
- RDWC 94063 770-B6
- SCAR 94070 769-F2
300 MLBR 94030 728-B2
800 SMCo 94037 746-G5
1100 PA 94301 791-B4
CEDARWOOD CT
1600 SBRN 94066 707-G7
CEDARWOOD DR
1400 SMTO 94403 748-J7
CEDARWOOD WY
1100 RDWC 94061 790-B2
CEDRO WY
700 SCIC 94305 810-J2
CELESTE DR
1600 SMTO 94402 749-B3
CELESTIAL CT
- PCFA 94044 727-A5
CELESTIAL LN
600 FCTY 94404 749-E4
CELIA CT
- PCFA 94044 727-A5
CELIA WY
900 PA 94303 791-D5
CENTAURUS LN
800 FCTY 94404 749-H1
CENTER DR
500 PA 94301 791-B3
CENTER ST
- MLBR 94030 728-A2
- RDWC 94063 770-B7
- RDWC 94061 770-B7
100 RDWC 94061 790-B1
800 SCAR 94070 769-H4
CENTER PARK LN
500 FCTY 94404 749-F3
CENTRAL AV
- RDWC 94061 790-B1
100 BURL 94010 728-G7
200 HMBY 94019 787-E2
300 MLPK 94025 791-A3
1100 SCAR 94070 769-H4
CENTRAL DR
- MLPK 94025 790-J1
26900 LAH 94022 830-H2
CERES ST
- SMCo 94038 746-F6
CERRITO AV
100 RDWC 94061 790-A4
100 SMCo 94061 790-A4
CERRITO PL
- SMCo 94061 790-A4
CERRO CT
300 DALY 94015 687-B7
CERRO DR
- DALY 94015 687-B7
CERROS MNR
- SMCo 94025 790-D5
CERVANTES RD
100 PTLV 94028 810-C5
100 SMCo 94062 769-F7
CERVANTES WY
1100 PCFA 94044 726-H4
CHABOT DR
2600 SBRN 94066 707-D6
CHABOT TER
2400 PA 94303 791-D4
CHADBOURNE AV
- MLBR 94030 728-A4
CHADBOURNE LN
1100 MLBR 94030 728-A4
CHADWICK CT
- MLBR 94030 727-J5
CHALLENGE CT
100 FCTY 94404 749-G2
CHAMOMILE LN
- SMCo 94019 787-G5
CHAMPS ELYSEE BLVD
2900 HMBY 94019 767-D4
CHANCERY LN
- SF 94112 687-F1
CHANDLER WY
- SMCo 94010 728-B7
- SMCo 94010 748-B1
CHANNEL DR
- RDWC 94065 750-A6
CHANNING AV
100 PA 94301 790-J5
400 PA 94301 791-A4
1200 PA 94303 791-C4
CHANNING LN
500 PCFA 94044 707-A3
CHANNING RD
- BURL 94010 728-H6
CHANNING WY
300 PCFA 94044 707-A3
CHANTAL WY
- RDWC 94061 790-A1
CHAPEL LN
- MLPK 94025 790-J2
CHAPEL VIEW DR
- SMCo - 768-D4
CHAPIN AV
1400 BURL 94010 728-F7
CHAPIN LN
100 BURL 94010 728-F7
400 HIL 94010 728-F7
CHAPMAN AV
- SSF 94080 708-A2
300 SBRN 94066 727-J1
CHAPMAN RD
- SMCo 94020 809-F7
CHARING CROSS RD
1800 SMCo 94402 748-H7
1800 SMTO 94402 748-H7

STREET
Block City ZIP Pg-Grid

CHARING CROSS WY
200 PCFA 94044 706-J6
200 PCFA 94044 707-A6
CHARLES AV
28000 LAH 94022 810-J7
28000 LAH 94022 830-J1
CHARLES LN
- SMTO 94402 749-B3
CHARLES MARX WY
- PA 94304 790-G5
CHARLESTON AV
2200 SBRN 94066 707-F7
CHARLOTT LN
- RDWC 94063 770-B4
CHARLTON ST
- SCAR 94070 769-E3
CHART LN
- RDWC 94065 750-C4
CHARTER ST
- RDWC 94063 770-C6
800 SMCo 94063 770-C6
CHARTHOUSE LN
- FCTY 94404 749-J1
CHATEAU CT
- SSF 94080 707-E5
CHATEAU DR
- MLPK 94025 790-F3
400 HIL 94010 748-D2
CHATHAM CT
3800 RDWC 94061 789-H3
3900 SSF 94080 707-C4
CHATHAM RD
400 BURL 94010 728-G6
CHATSWORTH LN
400 RDWC 94061 790-B2
CHAUCER ST
300 MLPK 94025 791-A3
300 PA 94301 791-A3
CHEBEC LN
700 FCTY 94404 749-G2
CHECKERSPOT DR
- BSBN 94005 687-J4
CHELMSFORD RD
500 HIL 94010 748-G2
CHELSEA CT
- DALY 94014 687-D3
CHELSEA WY
100 RDWC 94061 790-B2
CHEMICAL WY
- RDWC 94063 770-C5
CHEROKEE CT
- PTLV 94028 810-C6
CHEROKEE WY
100 PTLV 94028 810-C6
CHERRY AV
- SBRN 94066 707-G6
100 SSF 94080 707-H4
300 MLPK 94025 790-G3
400 SBRN 94066 727-H1
CHERRY LN
800 SCAR 94070 769-H2
CHERRY ST
900 SCAR 94070 769-G3
CHERRYWOOD DR
1400 SMTO 94403 748-J7
CHERYL CT
3400 SMTO 94403 748-J7
CHERYL PL
- MLPK 94025 790-F5
CHESAPEAKE AV
300 FCTY 94404 749-F6
CHESAPEAKE DR
300 RDWC 94063 770-C3
CHESHAM AV
100 SMCo 94070 769-D4
100 SCAR 94070 769-D4
CHESHIRE WY
2300 RDWC 94061 789-H1
CHESS DR
- SMTO 94404 749-E2
1100 FCTY 94404 749-F1
CHESTER AV
- SF 94132 687-C2
CHESTER ST
- SMCo 94014 687-D5
- DALY 94014 687-D5
100 MLPK 94025 791-A2
300 MLPK 94025 790-J2
CHESTER WY
- HIL 94010 748-F1
300 PCFA 94044 707-A3
700 SMTO 94402 748-F1
CHESTERFIELD AV
300 HMBY 94019 767-E7
CHESTERTON AV
300 BLMT 94002 749-E7
800 RDWC 94061 789-H2
CHESTERTON PL
200 SMTO 94401 748-H1
CHESTNUT AV
- SSF 94080 707-G2
200 PA 94306 791-C7
400 SBRN 94066 727-H1
500 SBRN 94066 707-H7
CHESTNUT LN
100 SMTO 94403 749-C6
CHESTNUT ST
- SCAR 94070 769-F2
100 RDWC 94063 770-B6
1000 MLPK 94025 790-F3
CHEVY ST
800 BLMT 94002 769-D1
CHEYENNE PT
- PTLV 94028 810-C6
CHICAGO WY
- SF 94112 687-G2
CHICO CT
- PCFA 94044 726-J4
- SSF 94080 707-F3
CHICORY LN
- SCAR 94070 769-C4
CHILCO ST
1200 MLPK 94025 770-H7
CHILTERN RD
600 HIL 94010 748-G2
CHILTON AV
- SCAR 94070 769-E3
CHILTON LN
3800 SBRN 94066 707-C5
CHRIS LN
3400 SMTO 94403 748-J7
CHRISTEN AV
- DALY 94015 707-C3
CHRISTIAN CT
- BLMT 94002 768-J2
CHRISTIAN DR
3900 BLMT 94002 768-J2
3900 SMCo 94070 768-J2
CHRISTINE DR
700 PA 94303 791-E7
CHRISTINE LN
- MLBR 94030 727-J3
- MLBR 94030 728-A3
CHRISTOPHER CT
- DALY 94015 707-A1
CHRISTOPHER WY
900 MLPK 94025 770-F7
CHRISTOPHERS LN
28300 LAH 94022 810-H5
CHRYSLER DR
1100 MLPK 94025 770-G6
CHRYSOPOLIS DR
800 FCTY 94404 749-G2
CHUKKER CT
100 SMTO 94403 749-A4
CHULA VISTA AV
900 BURL 94010 728-E5
CHULA VISTA DR
1000 BLMT 94002 769-D2
CHULA VISTA RD
- SMCo 94037 746-H3
CHUMASERO DR
- SF 94132 687-B1
CHURCH AV
1500 SMTO 94401 749-C2
CHURCH RD
- SMTO 94401 729-B7
CHURCH ST
300 HMBY 94019 787-F1
CHURCHILL AV
- SMCo 94062 790-A4
- PA 94301 790-A4
- PA 94301 791-A6
- WDSD 94062 790-A4
- PA 94306 790-A4
- PA 94306 791-A6
CHURCHILL DR
2700 HIL 94010 728-C7
2700 HIL 94010 748-B1
CIELITO DR
- SF 94134 687-H2
CIERVOS RD
- SMCo 94028 830-D4
CIMA WY
- PTLV 94028 810-C7
- PTLV 94028 830-C1
CINDY WY
700 PCFA 94044 707-A7
700 PCFA 94044 727-A1
CINNABAR RD
200 WDSD 94062 789-G4
CINNAMON CT
- HIL 94010 748-C1
CIPRIANI BLVD
2100 BLMT 94002 749-C7
2100 BLMT 94002 769-B2
CIRCLE CT
700 SSF 94080 707-G3
CIRCLE DR
- SBRN 94066 727-G3
600 EPA 94303 791-B3
CIRCLE LN
- MLPK 94025 790-J2
CIRCLE RD
- RDWC 94062 769-H6
CIRCLE STAR WY
- SCAR 94063 769-J4
CIRO AV
1400 SMTO 94403 749-D4
CIRRUS CT
- RDWC 94061 789-G2
CITRUS AV
- DALY 94014 687-C4
CITRUS CT
- HIL 94010 748-D2
CITY HALL LN
1300 BURL 94010 728-G7
CITYHOMES LN
- FCTY 94404 749-E3
CITY VIEW DR
- DALY 94014 687-F3
CIVIC LN
1300 BLMT 94002 769-F1
CIVIC CENTER DR
- FCTY 94404 749-F3
CIVIC CENTER LN
- MLBR 94030 728-B3
CLAIRE PL
300 MLPK 94025 790-F5
CLARA AV
- SSF 94080 707-E2
CLARA DR
700 PA 94303 791-D6
CLAREMONT AV
- RDWC 94062 769-J5
100 SSF 94080 707-J1
CLAREMONT CT
- MLBR 94030 727-H3
CLAREMONT DR
1200 SBRN 94066 707-E7
CLAREMONT PL
- MLPK 94025 790-H4
N CLAREMONT ST
- SMTO 94401 728-H7
500 SMTO 94401 748-J1
S CLAREMONT ST
800 SMTO 94401 748-J1
900 SMTO 94401 749-A2
1000 SMTO 94402 749-A2
CLAREMONT WY
300 MLPK 94025 790-H4
CLARENCE CT
- EPA 94303 771-B7
CLARENDON RD
- BURL 94010 728-H6
- PCFA 94044 706-J6
200 PCFA 94044 707-A6
CLARICE LN
2000 BURL 94010 728-C5
CLARIDGE DR
600 PCFA 94044 707-B4
CLARINADA AV
500 DALY 94015 687-A7
CLARK AV
300 DALY 94014 687-D6
300 CLMA 94014 687-D6
300 SMCo 94014 687-D6
900 SBRN 94066 727-H1
CLARK CT
- PCFA 94044 707-A4
CLARK DR
- SMTO 94402 748-G1
- SMTO 94402 728-H7
CLARK WY
- PA 94304 790-F6
CLARKE AV
1800 EPA 94303 791-C1
CLARKE CT
- EPA 94303 791-C2
CLAUDIA AV
1300 SMTO 94403 749-D4
CLAY AV
- SSF 94080 707-D2
CLAY DR
- ATN 94027 790-C4
CLAYTON CT
- DALY 94014 687-D4
CLAYTON DR
2100 MLPK 94025 790-E7
CLEARFIELD DR
600 MLBR 94030 728-A4
600 MLBR 94030 727-J4
CLEARVIEW DR
- DALY 94015 707-A1
CLEARVIEW WY
3000 SMTO 94402 748-H6
CLEARWATER DR
- SSF 94080 708-C5
CLEE ST
1600 BLMT 94002 769-D1
CLELAND PL
- MLPK 94025 790-J3
CLEVELAND AV
1300 SMTO 94403 749-C3
CLEVELAND ST
500 RDWC 94062 770-A7
600 RDWC 94061 770-A7
CLIFDEN DR
200 SSF 94080 707-D2
CLIFFORD AV
- SMCo 94062 769-G6
200 SCAR 94070 769-G6
CLIFFSIDE CT
- BLMT 94002 769-C3
CLIFFSIDE DR
- DALY 94015 687-A3
CLIFF SWALLOW CT
- BSBN 94005 688-A5
CLIFTON AV
200 SCAR 94070 769-E3
CLIFTON CT
3200 PA 94303 791-E6
CLIFTON DR
- DALY 94015 687-A4
CLIFTON RD
200 PCFA 94044 706-J3
200 PCFA 94044 707-A3
CLINTON CT
- RDWC 94061 770-A7
CLINTON ST
- RDWC 94062 769-J5
400 RDWC 94062 770-A6
600 RDWC 94061 770-A6
CLIPPER DR
100 BLMT 94002 749-F6
CLIPPER LN
900 FCTY 94404 749-G3
CLIPPER ST
2300 SMTO 94403 749-D1
CLIPPER WY
- DALY 94014 687-D5
CLOISTER WY
- DALY 94014 687-F3
CLOS DE LA TECH TR
- SMCo 94020 829-G6
CLOUD AV
900 MLPK 94025 790-D6
900 SMCo 94025 790-D6
CLOUDS REST RD
- SMCo 94062 809-A1
CLOVELLY LN
1100 BURL 94010 728-C5
CLOVER CIR
- SSF 94080 707-F2
CLOVER LN
- SCAR 94070 769-D5
100 MLPK 94025 790-J3
CLOVERDALE RD
- SMCo 94060 888-F3
3000 SMCo 94060 868-D5
CLUB DR
- SCAR 94070 769-D3
200 SMCo 94070 769-D4
300 BLMT 94002 769-D4
CLUB VIEW DR
- DALY 94014 687-F3
CLYDESDALE DR
700 HIL 94010 748-H4
COALMINE VW
- PTLV 94028 830-C1
COAST AV
2600 MTVW 94043 791-G7
COAST LN
200 PCFA 94044 726-J2
COASTLAND DR
700 PA 94303 791-C6
COBB LN
- SMCo 94060 868-F3
COBB ST
1100 SMTO 94401 749-B2
COBBLEHILL PL
2100 SMCo 94402 768-G1
COBBLESTONE CT
- DALY 94014 687-C5
COBBLESTONE LN
- BLMT 94002 769-E1
- SCAR 94070 769-F5
COCHRANE ST
- SF 94124 688-E1
COD ST
800 FCTY 94404 749-H3
CODO LN
100 SMCo 94038 766-H2
COGGINS RD
- SMCo 94020 849-F1
COGHLAN LN
- ATN 94027 790-C4
COLBY AV
900 SMCo 94025 790-H1
COLBY ST
600 SF 94134 687-J1
COLBY WY
3800 SBRN 94066 707-C6
COLEGROVE CT
- SMTO 94403 749-C6
COLEGROVE ST
3600 SMTO 94403 749-C6
COLEMAN AV
600 MLPK 94025 790-H2
800 SMCo 94025 790-H2
COLEMAN CT
- SCAR 94070 769-E4
COLEMAN PL
- MLPK 94025 790-J2
COLEPORT LNDG
- RDWC 94065 749-H5
COLERIDGE AV
100 PA 94301 791-A6
COLGATE AV
400 SMTO 94402 748-H3
COLLEGE AV
- SMCo 94025 790-H2
200 PA 94306 791-A7
600 MLPK 94025 790-G5
1000 SMTO 94401 728-J6
1500 PA 94306 810-J1
COLLEGE DR
2800 SBRN 94066 707-C6
COLLEGE OF SAN MATEO DR
100 SMCo 94402 748-G6
3300 SMTO 94402 748-G6
COLLEGE VIEW WY
- BLMT 94002 769-D1
COLLINS AV
800 CLMA 94014 687-D7
1300 CLMA 94014 707-C1
COLMA BLVD
- CLMA 94014 687-C7
COLMA CREEK SERVICE RD
- SSF 94080 708-A4
COLONEL WY
800 HMBY 94019 787-F2
COLONIAL LN
900 PA 94303 791-D5
COLONIAL PL
- SMCo 94061 790-B3
COLORADO AV
100 PA 94301 791-B7
100 PA 94306 791-D6
700 PA 94303 791-D6
COLORADO PL
1000 PA 94303 791-E5
COLORADOS DR
- MLBR 94030 727-J4
COLTON AV
100 SCAR 94070 769-H5
COLTON CT
- RDWC 94062 789-E2
- SMCo 94062 789-E2
COLUMBIA AV
- SMCo 94063 790-D1
100 SMCo 94019 766-J2
COLUMBIA CIR
800 RDWC 94065 750-C6
COLUMBIA DR
600 SMTO 94402 748-H3
COLUMBIA LN
800 FCTY 94404 749-F4
COLUMBIA ST
2100 PA 94306 810-J1
COLUMBIA WY
800 RDWC 94065 750-C6
COLUMBUS AV
1300 BURL 94010 728-C5
COLUMBUS ST
100 SMCo 94019 767-A2
COLUSA CT
100 SBRN 94066 707-D7
COMERWOOD CT
400 SSF 94080 707-F4
COMET DR
600 FCTY 94404 749-G2
COMMANDER LN
300 RDWC 94065 749-H6
COMMERCIAL AV
300 SSF 94080 707-G2
800 PA 94303 791-F7
COMMERCIAL ST
900 SCAR 94070 769-H3
COMMODORE DR W
800 SBRN 94066 707-G6
COMMONS LN
- FCTY 94404 749-E3
COMMONWEALTH DR
100 MLPK 94025 770-G6
COMMUNITY LN
- PA 94301 791-B4
COMO AV
- DALY 94014 687-C3
COMPASS CIR
500 RDWC 94065 749-H7
COMPASS DR
400 RDWC 94065 749-H7
COMPASS LN
900 FCTY 94404 749-H4
COMSTOCK CIR
- SCIC 94305 790-J7
2500 BLMT 94002 769-A3
COMSTOCK RD
100 SMCo 94062 788-H4
COMUS ST
100 SMCo 94038 746-F6
CONCAR DR
- SMTO 94402 749-B3
CONCHITA CT
- PCFA 94044 707-A4
CONCORD DR
200 MLPK 94025 790-J3
CONCORD ST
- SF 94112 687-F2
CONCORD WY
300 BURL 94010 728-G6
2700 SBRN 94066 707-F7
CONCOURSE DR
100 BLMT 94002 749-F6
CONDON CT
- SMTO 94403 748-J7
CONDOR LN
900 FCTY 94404 749-H2
CONEJO DR
- MLBR 94030 728-A5
100 MLBR 94030 727-J5
CONIFER LN
- HIL 94010 748-F1
CONIL WY
300 SMCo 94028 810-D4
CONMUR ST
200 SSF 94080 707-F5
CONNECTICUT DR
1000 RDWC 94061 789-J2
1400 RDWC 94061 790-A2
CONNIE AV
600 SMTO 94402 749-B3
CONNOLLY WY
2300 EPA 94303 791-C1
CONRAD CT
- SSF 94080 707-D1
CONSTANZO ST
500 SCIC 94305 810-H1
CONSTELLATION CT
800 RDWC 94065 750-C6
800 RDWC 94065 749-J5
CONSTITUTION DR
100 MLPK 94025 770-G6
800 FCTY 94404 749-G3
CONSTITUTION SQ
300 MLBR 94030 728-A3
CONSTITUTION WY
400 SMCo 94080 707-G4
400 SSF 94080 707-G4
CONTINENTAL DR
900 MLPK 94025 790-C6
CONTINENTALS WY
1000 BLMT 94002 769-B2
CONVENTION WY
300 RDWC 94063 770-A4
COOKIE CT
100 SMCo 94062 769-G7
COOKSEY LN
700 SCIC 94305 810-H1
COOLEY AV
1900 EPA 94303 791-B2
COOS CT
500 FCTY 94404 749-F5
COPELAND ST
400 PCFA 94044 726-J2
COPLEY AV
- RDWC 94062 769-H6
COQUITO CT
- SMCo 94028 810-D4
COQUITO WY
100 SMCo 94028 810-D4
CORA ST
- SF 94134 688-A2
100 SF 94134 687-J2
CORAL LN
- FCTY 94404 749-E6
CORAL PL
- DALY 94014 687-D5
CORAL ST
800 SMCo 94038 746-F6
CORAL WY
- HMBY 94019 787-G5
CORAL REEF AV
100 SMCo 94019 766-J2
100 SMCo 94019 767-A2
CORAL RIDGE DR
300 PCFA 94044 707-A2
CORBITT DR
500 BURL 94010 728-G6
CORDILLERAS AV
600 SCAR 94070 769-F3
CORDILLERAS CT
- SMCo 94062 769-F7
CORDILLERAS RD
900 SMCo 94062 769-G7
900 RDWC 94062 769-G7
CORDOVA CT
- PTLV 94028 810-D6
800 PCFA 94044 726-J4
CORDOVA ST
- SF 94112 687-G2
500 DALY 94014 687-G2
COREY WY
300 SSF 94080 708-A4
CORINA CT
3800 PA 94303 791-E7
CORINA WY
3700 PA 94303 791-E7
CORINE LN
1300 MLPK 94025 790-E4
CORK PL
3700 SSF 94080 707-C4
CORK HARBOUR CIR
400 RDWC 94065 749-G6
CORK OAK WY
3300 PA 94303 791-D7
CORLETT WY
- HIL 94010 748-C3
CORMORANT DR
- BLMT 94002 769-G1
- RDWC 94065 769-G1
CORNELIA DR
- HIL 94010 748-F3
CORNELL AV
100 SMCo 94019 766-J2
400 SMTO 94402 748-H3
CORNELL RD
- MLPK 94025 790-G4
CORNELL ST
2000 PA 94306 791-A7
CORNISH WY
400 BLMT 94002 749-F7
CORNWALLIS LN
600 FCTY 94404 749-G5
CORONA DR
600 PCFA 94044 726-J4
CORONA LN
100 SMCo 94038 766-H2
CORONA ST
- SF 94127 687-C1
900 SMCo 94037 746-G4
CORONA WY
100 SMCo 94028 810-D4
CORONADO AV
- DALY 94015 687-A4
- SCAR 94070 769-E4
100 SMCo 94019 767-C4
600 SCIC 94305 810-J1
CORONADO DR
- SMCo 94037 746-H4
CORONADO LN
700 FCTY 94404 749-F4
CORONADO ST
- SF 94124 688-B1
CORONADO WY
1600 BURL 94010 728-C5
3700 SBRN 94066 707-C5
CORONET BLVD
2100 BLMT 94002 769-C1
CORPORATE WY
- SSF 94080 708-A3
CORPORATION DR
- SSF 94080 708-A2
CORPORATION WY
1000 PA 94303 791-F7
CORREAS AV
100 HMBY 94019 787-E1
CORREAS ST
500 HMBY 94019 787-F1
CORRIDO WY
400 SSF 94080 707-F5
CORRIENTE POINTE DR
800 RDWC 94065 749-J5
CORSAIR LN
900 FCTY 94404 749-G3
CORSICA LN
1200 FCTY 94404 749-G5
CORTE ALEGRE
- MLBR 94030 727-J4
CORTE ANNA
- MLBR 94030 728-B3
CORTE BALBOA
- MLBR 94030 728-B3
CORTE CAMELLIA
- MLBR 94030 727-J4
CORTE COMODA
- MLBR 94030 728-C3
CORTE DE FLORES
2600 SMTO 94403 749-B5
CORTE DEL SOL
- MLBR 94030 727-J4
CORTE DORADO
- MLBR 94030 728-A4
CORTE MADERA RD
100 PTLV 94028 830-C1
100 PTLV 94028 810-C7
CORTE NUEVA
- MLBR 94030 728-A4
CORTE PRINCESA
- MLBR 94030 728-A4
CORTESI AV
500 SSF 94080 707-J2
CORTEZ AV
100 SMCo 94019 767-C4
1000 BURL 94010 728-D5
CORTEZ LN
800 FCTY 94404 749-G3
12900 LAH 94022 830-J1
CORTEZ RD
- SMCo 94062 769-F7
CORTO LN
- WDSD 94062 789-G6
CORVUS LN
800 FCTY 94404 749-H1
COSSAMER AV
- RDWC 94065 749-J4
- RDWC 94065 750-A4
COSTA RICA AV
100 BURL 94010 728-G7
100 BURL 94010 748-G1
300 SMTO 94402 748-G1
300 HIL 94010 748-G1
COTTAGE LN
- BLMT 94002 769-E1
- SCAR 94070 769-E2
COTTAGE GROVE AV
1400 SMTO 94401 749-B1
COTTON PL
- MLPK 94025 790-F5
COTTON ST
300 MLPK 94025 790-F5
COTTONWOOD AV
700 SSF 94080 707-H2
COTTONWOOD CT
- HIL 94010 748-D1
COTTONWOOD DR
- DALY 94014 687-D3
2400 SBRN 94066 707-E6
COTTRELL WY
900 SCIC 94305 810-J2
COUNTRY LN
- SMCo 94061 790-B2
COUNTRY WY
13300 LAH 94022 810-H7
COUNTRY CLUB CT
3000 PA 94304 810-H7
COUNTRY CLUB DR
- HIL 94010 728-F7
100 SSF 94080 707-G5
200 SMCo 94080 707-G5
3600 RDWC 94061 789-H3
COUNTRYSIDE DR
3200 SMTO 94403 748-J6
COUNTY CIR
200 RDWC 94063 770-A5
COUNTY RD
- SMCo 94062 788-J5
- SMCo 94062 789-A5
100 PCFA 94044 726-J2
100 PCFA 94044 727-A1
COUNTY ST
- DALY 94014 687-C5
COUNTY JAIL RD
- SMCo 94044 707-D7
COURT E
- DALY 94014 687-F3
E COURT LN
100 FCTY 94404 749-F2
COURTLAND DR
200 SBRN 94066 727-G2
COURTLAND RD
1600 BLMT 94002 769-E2
COURT OF SAN MARCO
2900 HMBY 94019 767-D4
COVE LN
- SMCo 94038 746-F7
- RDWC 94065 749-H6
COVENTRY CT
100 SCAR 94070 769-D5
COVINGTON RD
800 BLMT 94002 769-C1
COWAN RD
800 BURL 94010 728-D3
COWELL LN
- ATN 94027 790-D5
400 SCIC 94305 810-H1
COWPENS WY
- SMCo 94402 768-G1
COWPER CT
3400 PA 94306 791-D7
COWPER ST
100 PA 94301 790-J4
800 PA 94301 791-A5
2500 PA 94306 791-C7
COYOTE HILL
- PTLV 94028 830-C1
COYOTE HILL RD
3100 SCIC 94304 810-J3
COYOTE POINT DR
1600 SMTO 94401 728-J6
1700 SMTO 94401 729-A5
COZZOLINO CT
- MLBR 94030 727-J3
CRAGMONT CT
- PCFA 94044 707-A4
- SMTO 94403 748-J6
CRAGMONT WY
- WDSD 94062 789-H4
CRAIG CT
300 DALY 94014 687-C5
CRAIG RD
500 HIL 94010 748-D3
CRANE AV
600 FCTY 94404 749-G1
CRANE ST
- SF 94124 688-B1
900 MLPK 94025 790-F3
CRANFIELD AV
- BLMT 94002 769-D3
- SCAR 94002 769-D3
- SMCo 94002 769-D3
- SMCo 94070 769-D3
- BLMT 94070 769-D3
600 SCAR 94070 769-D3
CRANHAM CT
- PCFA 94044 727-A5
CRATER LAKE WY
- PCFA 94044 727-B5
CRAZY PETES RD
- SMCo 94028 830-C6
CREEK AV
400 SMCo 94062 788-G5
CREEK DR
600 MLPK 94025 790-G5
E CREEK DR
100 MLPK 94025 790-H3
E CREEK PL
- MLPK 94025 790-H4
CREEK TR
- SMCo 94062 788-J5
CREEK PARK DR
- PTLV 94028 810-E7
CREEKRIDGE CT
- SMTO 94402 748-C7
CREEKSIDE DR
- HMBY 94019 787-F6
CREEKSIDE LN
- SMTO 94401 749-A1
CREEKWOOD DR
100 SMCo 94021 849-A7
CREEKWOOD WY
- HIL 94010 748-H3
CRENSHAW CT
- PCFA 94044 707-A2
CRENSHAW DR
- DALY 94015 707-A2
- PCFA 94044 707-A2
CRESCENT AV
100 BURL 94010 728-G7
100 PTLV 94028 810-C7
100 PTLV 94028 830-C1
100 SMCo 94038 746-G6
400 SMTO 94402 728-G7
400 SMTO 94402 748-G1
CRESCENT CT
- BSBN 94005 687-J5
CRESCENT DR
- SSF 94014 707-J1
- PA 94301 791-B3
E CRESCENT DR
500 PA 94301 791-B3
W CRESCENT DR
500 PA 94301 791-B3
CRESCENT ST
- SMCo 94037 746-H5
CRESCENT WY
- SF 94124 688-C2
CRESCIO CT
- SF 94112 687-E2
CRESPI DR
- SF 94132 687-B1
500 PCFA 94044 726-H3
1000 PCFA 94044 727-A4
CREST DR
400 SMCo 94062 789-G1
CREST LN
2300 MLPK 94025 790-D7
CREST RD
100 WDSD 94062 789-H4
CRESTA VISTA LN
500 PTLV 94028 810-D5
CRESTLINE AV
- DALY 94015 687-A5
CRESTMOOR CIR
100 PCFA 94044 707-A2
CRESTMOOR DR
2100 SBRN 94066 707-F7
2600 SBRN 94066 727-F1
CRESTON AV
- DALY 94015 686-J4
CRESTVIEW AV
- DALY 94015 686-J5
500 BLMT 94002 749-E7
CRESTVIEW CT
300 SCAR 94070 769-E6
CRESTVIEW DR
100 SCAR 94070 769-C4
600 SMCo 94070 769-D6
700 MLBR 94030 727-H3
CRESTWOOD CT
1400 SMTO 94403 748-J7
CRESTWOOD DR
- DALY 94015 687-A3
1000 SSF 94080 707-F1
1400 SBRN 94066 707-F5
1500 SMTO 94403 748-H7
CRINGLE DR
500 RDWC 94065 749-H7
CRIPPLERIDGE CT
- SMTO 94402 748-C7
CRITTENDEN LN
2100 MTVW 94043 791-J7
CROCKER AV
- DALY 94014 687-D3
900 SMCo 94014 687-E3
2800 SMCo 94063 770-D7
CROCKETT LN
1700 HIL 94010 728-E6

SAN MATEO CO.

STREET
Block City ZIP Pg-Grid

CROCUS CT
- SMCo 94025 790-E6
CROFTON WY
3800 SSF 94080 707-C4
CROMPTON RD
600 RDWC 94061 789-H1
CROMWELL RW
2600 SSF 94080 707-C4
CRONER AV
1700 MLPK 94025 790-E5
1700 SMCo 94025 790-E5
CROSBY CT
100 SBRN 94066 707-E7
CROSS ST
- SF 94112 687-F2
CROSSWAY RD
700 BURL 94010 728-F6
CROTHERS WY
300 SCIC 94305 790-H7
CROWN CIR
- SSF 94080 707-D2
CROWN CT
- SMCo 94402 768-H1
- SMTO 94402 768-H1
CROYDEN WY
100 WDSD 94062 789-H5
CRYSTAL CT
100 SBRN 94066 727-H2
900 FCTY 94404 749-F5
CRYSTAL DR
1400 HIL 94010 748-E5
CRYSTAL ST
- SF 94112 687-D2
CRYSTAL TER
- SMCo 94010 728-B7
CRYSTAL SPRINGS RD
- HIL 94010 748-H3
- SMTO 94402 748-H3
600 SBRN 94066 727-G2
1100 SMCo 94402 748-E6
1500 SMCo - 748-E6
1500 SMCo 94010 748-E6
2800 SMCo 94030 727-G2
CRYSTAL SPRINGS TER
- HIL 94010 748-G4
CUARDO AV
200 MLBR 94030 728-B3
CUESTA AV
600 SMTO 94403 749-A5
CUESTA DR
100 SSF 94080 707-E3
CUESTA REAL
- SMCo 94020 829-E7
- SMCo 94020 849-E1
CULEBRA LN
100 SMCo 94038 766-H2
CULEBRA RD
800 HIL 94010 748-G3
CULLEN DR
400 PCFA 94044 727-A1
CULVER CT
- SMTO 94403 749-C6
CUMBERLAND CT
900 FCTY 94404 749-E5
CUMBERLAND RD
400 BURL 94010 728-G6
CUNNINGHAM WY
400 SBRN 94066 727-H1
CUPERTINO WY
200 SMTO 94403 749-D5
CUPID RW
100 SBRN 94066 707-J7
CURLEW CT
200 FCTY 94404 749-G1
CURRY CT
- SCAR 94070 769-D3
CURTIS AV
2800 SMCo 94063 770-C7
CURTIS CT
- SCAR 94070 769-D3
CURTIS ST
- SF 94112 687-F2
800 MLPK 94025 790-F3
CURTIS WY
700 MLPK 94025 790-G4
CURTISS ST
3100 SMTO 94403 749-D5
CUT ACROSS RD
- SMCo 94020 850-G7
CUTTER LN
400 FCTY 94404 749-H4
CUTTER ST
300 FCTY 94404 749-H4
CUTTY CT
300 PCFA 94044 707-A3
CUTWATER LN
500 FCTY 94404 749-G6
CYGNUS LN
600 FCTY 94404 749-E4
CYMBIDIUM CIR
1200 SSF 94080 707-E2
CYPRESS AV
100 SBRN 94066 727-H1
100 SMCo 94038 746-F7
200 SSF 94080 707-J3
300 SMCo 94062 788-H5
400 HMBY 94019 787-F1
400 MLBR 94030 727-J1
400 SBRN 94066 707-H7
400 SMTO 94401 748-J1
500 SSF 94080 708-A2
600 SMTO 94401 749-A1
895 BLMT 94002 769-E1
900 SMTO 94401 729-A7
1500 BURL 94010 728-G7
CYPRESS CT
- DALY 94014 687-J3
- MLBR 94030 728-A3
- SBRN 94066 707-J7
- SCAR 94070 769-F6
CYPRESS DR
- SMCo - 768-D3
CYPRESS LN
- BSBN 94005 688-A5
- DALY 94014 687-J3
CYPRESS ST
100 RDWC 94061 790-B1
1100 EPA 94303 791-C2
CYPRESS WK
- SMCo 94019 787-G5
CYPRESS CIRCLE DR
- SMCo - 768-D3
CYPRESS POINT RD
100 HMBY 94019 787-F5

D

D ST
100 DALY 94014 687-C6
100 RDWC 94063 769-J4
300 CLMA 94014 687-D6
300 MLPK 94025 790-G3
DAFFODIL LN
- SCAR 94070 769-C4
DAIRY LN
- BLMT 94002 749-F7
DAISY LN
400 EPA 94303 791-D2
DAISY ST
900 SMTO 94401 749-C1
DAKIN AV
1900 SMCo 94025 790-D6
DAKOTA AV
1200 SMTO 94401 749-B1
DALE AV
100 SCAR 94070 769-F4
1500 SMTO 94401 749-C1
1900 SMTO 94403 749-C1
DALE WY
1200 PCFA 94044 726-G4
DALEHURST AV
700 SMTO 94403 749-A7
DALEHURST CT
3900 SMTO 94403 749-B7
DALEROSE CT
- DALY 94014 687-G3
DALE VIEW AV
500 BLMT 94002 749-D7
DALEY CT
100 SBRN 94066 707-E7
DALHBERG AV
- PCFA 94044 706-J5
DALY CT
- SSF 94080 707-G2
DAMONTE CT
- SSF 94080 708-A1
DANA AV
1200 PA 94301 791-A3
1300 PA 94303 791-A3
DANA CT
- SSF 94080 707-F4
DANA POINTE CT
- RDWC 94065 749-J5
DANBERRY LN
- DALY 94014 687-E3
DANBURY LN
- RDWC 94061 790-B2
DANFORD CT
- SMCo 94062 789-G1
DANMANN AV
1200 PCFA 94044 726-G4
DAPHNE CT
- EPA 94303 791-D3
DAPHNE WY
- EPA 94303 791-D3
DARBY PL
100 SBRN 94066 727-G2
DARCY AV
- SMTO 94403 749-C6
DARCY CT
- SMTO 94403 749-C6
DARDENELLE AV
100 PCFA 94044 727-B1
DARLENE AV
1300 SMTO 94403 749-D4
DARRELL RD
200 HIL 94010 748-C2
DARTMOUTH AV
- SCAR 94070 769-D2
DARTMOUTH RD
100 SMTO 94402 748-J2
DARTMOUTH ST
600 SF 94134 687-J1
800 SF 94134 688-A1
2000 PA 94306 810-J1
DARWIN AV
1500 SMTO 94403 749-C2
DATE ST
900 SMCo 94037 746-H4
DAVEY GLEN RD
- BLMT 94002 749-D7
DAVID AV
3100 PA 94303 791-D6
DAVID CT
2300 SMTO 94403 749-D4
3100 PA 94303 791-D6
DAVID RD
900 BURL 94010 728-D4
DAVID ST
- SMTO 94403 749-D4
DAVIS CT
- BURL 94010 728-B5
DAVIS DR
- BLMT 94002 769-B2
1500 BURL 94010 728-C5
DAVIS ST
1100 RDWC 94061 770-A7
DAVIT LN
600 RDWC 94065 749-J6
DAY AV
1500 SMTO 94403 749-D3
DAYTON AV
1100 SCAR 94070 769-G5
DEAN RD
100 WDSD 94062 789-G6
DEANNA DR
1000 MLPK 94025 790-D6
DEANNE LN
300 DALY 94014 687-D5
DE ANZA AV
100 SCAR 94070 769-F5
100 RDWC 94062 769-F5
DE ANZA BLVD
1400 SMTO 94403 748-J7
1900 SMTO 94402 768-H1
1900 SMTO 94402 748-J7
DE ANZA CT
- SMTO 94402 748-H7
DEARBORN PARK RD
300 SMCo 94060 868-H1
DEBBIE CT
2700 SCAR 94070 769-F6
DEBBIE LN
- BLMT 94002 749-E7
- BLMT 94002 769-D1
DEBBIE PL
2600 SCAR 94070 769-G6
DEBELL DR
- ATN 94027 790-G2

DE CARLI CT
- SMCo 94062 769-H7
DECATUR ST
1100 FCTY 94404 749-G4
DECOTA AV
100 SMCo 94038 766-G1
DEDALERA DR
200 SMCo 94028 810-E4
DEEPWELL CT
- BLMT 94002 769-C4
DEER CREEK LN
- SMCo 94062 769-G6
DEER CREEK RD
3400 PA 94304 810-J4
3400 SCIC 94304 810-J4
DEERLAKE CT
- SMTO 94402 768-H1
DEER MEADOW LN
100 PTLV 94028 810-C5
DEER PARK LN
- PTLV 94028 810-C5
DEER PATH DR
- SMCo 94028 830-E4
DEER SPRINGS WY
27200 LAH 94022 830-J2
DEGAS RD
100 PTLV 94028 810-C5
DE KOVEN AV
2400 BLMT 94002 769-B1
DELANO AV
400 SF 94112 687-F1
DELAWARE AV
2400 RDWC 94061 790-A3
N DELAWARE ST
- SMTO 94401 748-J1
100 SMTO 94401 728-H7
S DELAWARE ST
- SMTO 94401 748-J1
- SMTO 94401 749-A1
400 SMTO 94402 749-A1
1900 SMTO 94403 749-B4
DEL CENTRO
100 MLBR 94030 727-J5
DE LEON LN
900 FCTY 94404 749-F4
DELFINO WY
1300 MLPK 94025 790-D5
DELL RD
800 PCFA 94044 726-H5
DELLBROOK AV
400 SSF 94080 707-F1
DEL MAR AV
100 SMCo 94038 766-G1
400 PCFA 94044 707-A4
DELMAR CT
- RDWC 94063 770-F6
DEL MAR RD
300 SMCo 94062 788-H5
DELMAR WY
200 SMTO 94403 749-B5
DEL MONTE AV
100 SSF 94080 707-E2
DEL MONTE DR
- HIL 94010 728-C7
- PCFA 94044 707-A2
DEL MONTE PL
- SMTO 94403 749-A6
DEL MONTE RD
100 SMCo 94019 767-B2
DEL MONTE ST
- SF 94112 687-F2
3000 SMTO 94403 749-A6
DEL NORTE AV
1000 MLPK 94025 770-H7
1000 MLPK 94025 790-H1
DEL NORTE DR
100 SBRN 94066 707-E7
DE LONG ST
- SF 94112 687-C2
500 DALY 94014 687-C2
DEL PASO DR
- SSF 94080 707-F3
DEL PRADO DR
- DALY 94015 687-B7
DELRAY ST
700 SMTO 94403 749-A6
DEL REY CT
- SCAR 94070 769-F3
DEL ROSA WY
200 SMTO 94403 749-D5
DELTA ST
- SF 94134 688-A1
400 SF 94134 687-J2
DELVIN WY
2200 SSF 94080 707-E5
DEMETER ST
100 EPA 94303 771-C7
100 EPA 94303 791-C1
DENALI DR
- SMTO 94403 748-H7
DENARDI WY
300 SSF 94080 707-F5
DENHAM CT
- HIL 94010 728-E7
DENISE DR
- HIL 94010 748-E4
DENISE LN
400 SMCo 94061 790-B4
DENNIS DR
100 DALY 94015 707-C3
900 PA 94303 791-D5
DENSLOWE DR
100 SF 94132 687-B1
DEODORA DR
- ATN 94027 790-G1
- ATN 94027 770-G7
DERBY ST
- DALY 94015 707-C2
DERECHO LN
100 SMCo 94038 766-H2
DERRY LN
500 MLPK 94025 790-F3
DERRY WY
2200 SSF 94080 707-E5
DE SABLA RD
- SMTO 94402 748-H2
- HIL 94010 748-H2
DESMOND ST
- SF 94134 688-A2
DE SOLO DR
1100 PCFA 94044 726-H4
DE SOTO AV
1300 BURL 94010 728-D6
DE SOTO DR
700 PA 94303 791-B4

DE SOTO LN
900 FCTY 94404 749-F3
DE SOTO ST
- SF 94127 687-C1
DE SOTO WY
100 SBRN 94066 727-J2
600 MLBR 94030 727-J2
DESVIO CT
- PCFA 94044 727-A5
DESVIO WY
1500 BLMT 94002 769-E2
DETROIT DR
1700 SMTO 94404 749-C1
2000 SMTO 94403 749-C1
DEVEREAUX DR
1600 BURL 94010 728-C5
DEVILS SLIDE TUN
- SMCo - 726-G6
- SMCo - 746-G1
DEVON DR
600 HIL 94010 748-F1
DEVON WY
3400 RDWC 94061 789-H1
DEVONSHIRE AV
2700 SMCo 94063 770-C7
2700 SMCo 94063 790-C1
DEVONSHIRE BLVD
- SCAR 94070 769-D4
100 SMCo 94070 769-D4
DEVONSHIRE CIR
- SMCo 94070 769-D4
DEWEY AV
1200 RDWC 94061 789-J2
DEWEY DR
600 FCTY 94404 749-G5
DEWEY ST
1700 SMTO 94403 749-D2
DE WOLF ST
- SF 94112 687-E2
DEXTER AV
- SMCo 94063 790-D1
DEXTER PL
- MLBR 94030 728-A3
DIABLO WY
- SMCo 94020 850-F5
700 SMCo 94062 789-F2
DIAMOND AV
500 SSF 94080 707-J2
DIAMOND ST
100 SBRN 94066 707-J5
DIANNE CT
400 SSF 94080 707-F5
DIAZ AV
- SF 94132 687-B1
DIAZ LN
900 FCTY 94404 749-F3
DICHIERA CT
- SF 94112 687-E2
DICKENS CT
- SCAR 94070 769-E6
DICKEY ST
900 RDWC 94061 770-A7
DIGGES CANYON RD
100 SMCo - 767-G4
DILLER ST
- RDWC 94063 770-A6
DILLON LN
1700 RDWC 94061 790-A2
DINES CT
- EPA 94303 791-C2
DINKLESPIEL STATION LN
- ATN 94027 790-E2
DIONNE CT
- BLMT 94002 768-J1
DIX ST
1100 SMTO 94401 749-C2
DIXON CT
- DALY 94014 687-C4
DNA WY
400 SSF 94080 708-C3
DOCKSIDE CIR
- RDWC 94065 749-J6
DOCKSIDE DR
- DALY 94014 687-E5
DODGE DR
1000 RDWC 94063 770-E6
DOHERTY WY
100 SMCo 94061 790-B4
DOHERTY RIDGE RD
- SMCo 94020 850-F7
DOLAN AV
1500 SMTO 94401 729-B7
DOLLAR AV
100 SSF 94080 707-J5
DOLORES AV
400 HMBY 94019 787-F4
DOLORES CT
400 SMTO 94403 749-B7
DOLORES ST
100 SMCo 94019 767-B2
400 SCIC 94305 810-H1
2300 SMTO 94403 749-A5
DOLORES WY
300 SSF 94080 707-G1
2900 BURL 94010 728-A6
DOLPHIN CT
- HMBY 94019 787-G5
DOLPHIN DR
500 PCFA 94044 706-J4
DOLPHIN ISL
- FCTY 94404 749-H2
DOLPHINE AV
100 SMCo 94019 767-C1
DOLTON AV
100 SMCo 94070 769-D4
100 SMCo 94070 769-D4
DOMINGO WY
- SMCo 94037 746-H4
DOMINICA LN
1400 FCTY 94404 749-G5
DON CT
- SMCo 94062 769-G6
DONAHUE ST
700 SF 94124 688-C2
DONALDSON AV
400 PCFA 94044 726-J2
DONDEE WY
400 PCFA 94044 726-J2
DONEGAL AV
2300 SSF 94080 707-E5
DONNELLY AV
1200 BURL 94010 728-G7
DONNER AV
700 SF 94124 688-B1

DONNER AV
1500 SBRN 94066 727-H1
DONNER ST
3700 SMTO 94403 749-C6
DONOHOE ST
100 EPA 94303 791-A2
100 MLPK 94025 791-A2
DORADO LN
800 FCTY 94404 749-F4
DORADO WY
300 SMCo 94080 707-F5
300 SSF 94080 707-F5
DORCHESTER DR
- DALY 94015 687-A4
DORCHESTER RD
400 SMTO 94402 748-G1
DORE AV
1200 SMTO 94401 729-A7
DORIS CT
- RDWC 94061 790-A1
DORIS DR
1800 MLPK 94025 790-E6
DORY LN
- FCTY 94404 749-F6
500 RDWC 94065 749-J6
DOS LOMA VISTA LN
- PTLV 94028 810-D4
DOUBLE ROCK ST
- SF 94124 688-C1
DOUGLAS AV
400 RDWC 94063 770-D6
400 SMCo 94063 770-D6
1100 BURL 94010 728-G6
DOUGLAS CT
3400 SMTO 94403 748-J7
DOUGLAS WY
1200 SSF 94080 707-G1
DOUGLASS WY
- ATN 94027 790-F3
DOVE LN
1000 FCTY 94404 749-H2
DOVER CT
- DALY 94015 707-C2
- SMCo 94070 769-E4
100 SBRN 94066 707-G7
DOVER LN
1100 FCTY 94404 749-F4
DOVER RD
3300 RDWC 94061 789-H1
DOWNEY CT
2200 SSF 94080 707-E5
DOWNEY WY
- HIL 94010 728-D7
DOWNING LN
700 PA 94301 790-J4
DOYLE ST
1000 MLPK 94025 790-F3
DRACO LN
600 FCTY 94404 749-E4
DRAKE AV
100 SSF 94080 707-J1
1000 BURL 94010 728-D5
DRAKE CT
500 FCTY 94404 749-G5
1000 SCAR 94070 769-E5
DRAKE ST
- SF 94112 687-G2
200 DALY 94014 687-G2
700 SMCo 94037 746-H4
DRAYTON RD
- HIL 94010 748-F4
DREW CT
2800 EPA 94303 771-C6
DRIFTWOOD CIR
- PCFA 94044 727-A4
DRIFTWOOD CT
- PCFA 94044 727-A3
DRIFTWOOD DR
800 PA 94303 791-E7
DRIFTWOOD LN
- DALY 94014 687-E6
DRIFTWOOD TR
- HMBY 94019 787-G5
DRURY LN
500 SMCo 94062 789-F1
DRY CREEK LN
100 WDSD 94062 789-F5
DUANE ST
- RDWC 94062 769-J5
400 RDWC 94062 770-A6
DUBLIN CT
3100 SSF 94080 707-D4
DUBLIN DR
2900 SSF 94080 707-D5
DUBLIN ST
- SF 94112 687-G1
DUBLIN WY
2000 SMTO 94403 749-C4
DUBUQUE AV
500 SSF 94080 708-A3
DUCK CT
200 FCTY 94404 749-H1
DUDLEY LN
- SCIC 94305 791-A7
DUENA ST
500 SCIC 94305 790-H7
DUFFERIN AV
1100 BURL 94010 728-C5
DUGGAN CT
- SMCo 94062 769-F7
DUGGAN RD
100 SMCo 94062 769-F7
DUHALLOW WY
2600 SSF 94080 707-C4
DULLES CT
1100 PCFA 94044 727-A5
DUMBARTON AV
- SMCo 94063 790-C1
100 SMCo 94063 770-C7
2000 EPA 94303 791-A2
DUMBARTON BRDG Rt#-84
- FRMT 94555 771-D4
- MLPK 94303 771-D4
DUMONT CT
- MLBR 94030 727-H4
DUMONT ST
4200 SMTO 94403 749-D6
DUNDEE DR
100 SSF 94080 707-C2
DUNDEE LN
100 SCAR 94070 769-F4
DUNKS ST
- DALY 94014 687-C5

DUNMAN WY
- SSF 94080 707-D1
DUNNE CT
- SMCo 94025 770-E7
DUNSMUIR WY
100 MLPK 94025 770-G7
DURAN CT
- PCFA 94044 727-A5
DURAND DR
3900 SMTO 94403 749-D6
DURAND WY
- PA 94304 790-G5
DURAZNO WY
100 SMCo 94028 810-D3
DURHAM RD
- SMCo 94062 808-E5
DURHAM ST
100 MLPK 94025 791-A2
300 MLPK 94025 790-J2
DURLSTON RD
800 RDWC 94062 769-H6
DUSTY TR
- SMCo 94060 868-E4
DUVAL DR
- SSF 94080 707-D1
DWIGHT AV
900 HMBY 94019 767-E6
DWIGHT RD
- BURL 94010 728-H6
DWIGHT ST
300 SF 94134 688-A1
700 SF 94134 687-J1
DYMOND CT
400 PA 94306 791-C7

E

E ST
100 RDWC 94063 769-J4
300 CLMA 94014 687-D6
300 SF 94124 688-E1
900 BLMT 94002 769-F2
EAGLE LN
1000 FCTY 94404 749-H2
EAGLE HILL TER
- RDWC 94062 769-J7
EAGLE TRACE DR
100 HMBY 94019 787-F5
EARL AV
1700 SBRN 94066 707-E7
EARL ST
500 SF 94124 688-C1
EAST AV
200 SBRN 94066 727-J1
1100 SMCo 94037 746-F5
EAST CT
- SBRN 94066 727-G3
EAST LN
200 BURL 94010 728-G6
EASTBURN CT
100 SBRN 94066 727-G1
EASTGATE DR
- DALY 94015 687-A3
EASTLAKE AV
- DALY 94014 687-C4
- PCFA 94044 707-A6
EASTLAKE WY
3800 RDWC 94062 789-G2
3800 SMCo 94062 789-G2
EASTMOOR AV
- DALY 94015 687-A5
EASTMOOR RD
1100 BURL 94010 728-D5
EASTON AV
500 SBRN 94066 707-H6
EASTON DR
1500 BURL 94010 728-D6
2800 HIL 94010 728-C7
EASTRIDGE AV
2200 MLPK 94025 790-D7
EASTRIDGE CIR
- PCFA 94044 707-A1
EASTRIDGE CT
- PCFA 94044 707-A1
EASTVIEW WY
400 SMCo 94062 789-E2
500 RDWC 94062 789-E2
500 WDSD 94062 789-E2
EASTWOOD AV
- DALY 94015 687-A6
EASTWOOD DR
- SMTO 94403 749-C7
EATON AV
- DALY 94015 686-J6
300 RDWC 94062 769-G6
300 RDWC 94070 769-G6
500 SCAR 94070 769-H5
EATON RD
200 SMTO 94402 748-J2
EATON VILLA PL
- SCAR 94070 769-G6
- RDWC 94062 769-G6
EBENER ST
1100 RDWC 94061 770-A7
1300 RDWC 94061 790-B1
EBKEN ST
300 PCFA 94044 726-J2
ECCLES AV
400 SSF 94080 708-B3
ECHO AV
1500 SMTO 94401 749-C2
ECHO DR
- SMCo 94038 746-F5
ECHO LN
- WDSD 94062 809-G6
- PTLV 94028 810-C7
EDDINGTON LN
- DALY 94014 687-E3
EDDYSTONE CT
- RDWC 94065 749-J6
EDEN WY
- HIL 94010 728-D7
EDEN BOWER LN
900 RDWC 94061 789-G3
EDEN WEST RD
- SMCo 94060 868-E7
- SMCo 94060 888-F1
EDESSA CT
- HIL 94010 728-C7
EDGAR PL
- SF 94112 687-E1
EDGE RD
- ATN 94027 790-G1
EDGECLIFF WY
300 SMCo 94062 789-G2

EDGECLIFF WY
400 RDWC 94061 789-G3
EDGECOURT DR
2100 HIL 94010 728-D7
EDGEHILL DR
100 SCAR 94070 769-G5
800 BURL 94010 728-E6
EDGEMAR AV
500 PCFA 94044 706-J4
600 PCFA 94044 707-A4
EDGEMAR ST
- DALY 94014 687-E3
EDGEMONT DR
- DALY 94015 687-A6
EDGERTON RD
27600 LAH 94022 830-J1
EDGEWATER BLVD
500 FCTY 94404 749-E3
EDGEWOOD CT
- DALY 94014 687-D3
EDGEWOOD DR
100 PCFA 94044 707-A1
1400 PA 94301 791-B3
1500 PA 94303 791-C4
EDGEWOOD LN
1800 MLPK 94025 790-E6
EDGEWOOD PL
- BLMT 94002 749-D7
EDGEWOOD RD
- RDWC 94062 769-H6
300 HIL 94010 748-F1
300 SMTO 94402 748-F1
700 SMCo 94062 769-F7
2400 SMCo 94070 789-C1
2400 RDWC 94062 789-C1
2400 SMCo 94062 789-C1
2400 SMCo 94070 769-F7
EDGEWOOD WY
1200 SSF 94080 707-F1
EDGEWOOD ESTATES DR
- SMCo 94062 769-F7
EDGEWORTH AV
100 SMCo 94015 687-B5
400 DALY 94015 687-B5
EDINBURGH ST
400 SF 94112 687-G1
500 SMTO 94402 748-J2
1200 SMTO 94402 749-A3
1800 SMTO 94403 749-A4
EDISON AV
100 SSF 94080 707-J1
EDISON ST
500 SMCo 94037 746-G4
2600 SMTO 94403 749-B5
EDISON WY
3000 SMCo 94063 770-D7
3200 SMCo 94025 770-D7
EDITH AV
2400 RDWC 94061 789-H1
EDMOND DR
1500 SCAR 94070 769-E7
EDMONDS RD
- SCAR 94070 769-D7
100 SMCo 94070 769-D7
EDNA DR
600 SMTO 94402 749-B3
EDNA LN
300 PCFA 94044 707-A3
EDWARDS CT
- BURL 94010 728-E5
EDWARDS LN
- ATN 94027 790-D3
EDWARDS RD
1000 BURL 94010 728-D5
EGBERT AV
600 SF 94124 688-B1
EGRET LN
800 RDWC 94065 750-A6
EGRET ST
1000 FCTY 94404 749-H1
EISENHOWER ST
1600 SMTO 94403 749-C2
EL ARROYO RD
400 HIL 94010 748-F2
EL BONITO WY
- MLBR 94030 728-A4
200 MLBR 94030 727-J4
ELBRIDGE WY
800 PA 94303 791-D6
EL CAJON WY
900 PA 94303 791-C5
EL CAMINO REAL
- MLBR 94030 728-C4
1700 BURL 94010 728-C4
EL CAMINO REAL Rt#-82
- BURL 94010 728-E6
- CLMA 94014 687-C5
- MLBR 94030 728-A2
- MLPK 94025 790-F3
- PA 94301 790-F3
- SCAR 94070 769-F2
- PA 94304 790-F3
100 ATN 94027 790-C1
100 BLMT 94002 749-D7
100 SBRN 94066 727-J1
100 SSF 94080 707-G4
100 SBRN 94066 707-G4
100 SMCo 94025 790-C1
200 DALY 94014 687-C5
200 SMCo 94014 687-C5
200 SCIC 94305 790-F3
200 PA 94305 790-F3
500 BLMT 94002 769-F2
500 HIL 94010 728-E6
700 CLMA 94014 707-E1
800 SMTO 94402 749-D7
1000 ATN 94025 790-F3
1200 RDWC 94062 769-H3
1200 RDWC 94063 769-H3
1300 SBRN 94066 728-A2
1400 MLPK 94027 790-F3
1400 RDWC 94062 770-A6
1400 RDWC 94063 770-A6
1500 PA 94306 790-F3
1500 PA 94306 791-A6
1500 SCIC 94305 791-A6
1700 MLBR 94030 727-J1
1800 RDWC 94061 770-A6
2300 PA 94304 791-A7
2600 RDWC 94061 790-C1
2600 SMCo 94063 770-A6
2600 SMCo 94063 790-C1

STREET Block City ZIP Pg-Grid

N EL CAMINO REAL Rt#-82
- SMTO 94401 728-G7
- SMTO 94402 728-G7
100 SMTO 94402 748-H1
100 SMTO 94401 748-H1
800 BURL 94010 728-G7
S EL CAMINO REAL Rt#-82
100 SMTO 94403 749-A2
100 BLMT 94002 749-A2
400 SMTO 94402 748-J2
500 SMTO 94402 749-A2
500 SMTO 94401 749-A2
500 SMTO 94401 748-J2
EL CAMPO DR
- SSF 94080 707-E3
EL CAPITAN DR
700 MLBR 94030 727-J4
EL CARMELO AV
100 PA 94306 791-C7
EL CENTRO RD
400 HIL 94010 748-F2
EL CERRITO AV
- SMTO 94402 748-G2
200 HIL 94010 748-G2
EL CORTEZ AV
300 SSF 94080 707-G4
ELDER AV
- MLBR 94030 728-A3
1100 MLPK 94025 790-E5
ELDER CT
- MLPK 94025 790-E5
100 SBRN 94066 707-E6
ELDER DR
- BLMT 94002 769-B3
ELDER LN
- PCFA 94044 706-J6
ELDERBERRY RD
- SMCo 94019 787-H5
EL DORADO AV
100 PA 94306 791-C7
EL DORADO CT
100 SBRN 94066 727-F1
EL DORADO DR
200 PCFA 94044 707-A1
300 DALY 94015 687-B7
N ELDORADO ST
- SMTO 94401 728-J7
- SMTO 94401 748-J1
- SMTO 94401 749-A1
S ELDORADO ST
- SMTO 94401 749-A1
400 SMTO 94402 749-A1
ELEANOR DR
100 WDSD 94062 789-J5
100 WDSD 94062 790-A5
400 ATN 94027 790-A5
400 WDSD 94027 790-A5
400 ATN 94062 790-A5
1600 SMTO 94402 749-B3
ELECTIONEER RD
- SCIC 94305 790-F7
ELENA AV
- ATN 94027 790-D3
ELENA RD
27500 LAH 94022 810-J6
EL ESCARPADO CT
400 SCIC 94305 810-G1
ELFIN CT
- BSBN 94005 687-H4
EL GRANADA BLVD
100 SMCo 94019 767-C2
1600 SMCo - 767-C2
ELIZA CT
100 FCTY 94404 749-G2
ELIZABETH LN
700 MLPK 94025 790-F3
ELIZABETH ST
1700 SCAR 94070 769-F4
ELIZABETH WY
- ATN 94027 790-C2
ELK CT
- PCFA 94044 727-C4
ELKHORN CT
1900 SMTO 94403 749-A4
1900 SMTO 94402 749-A4
ELK TREE RD
- SMCo 94062 809-F6
ELKWOOD DR
- SSF 94080 707-D1
ELLENDALE ST
100 SMCo 94038 746-F6
ELLINGTON AV
- SF 94112 687-E2
ELLIOT ST
300 SF 94134 687-J2
ELLIOTT DR
100 MLPK 94025 791-A2
ELLIOTT ST
2300 SMTO 94403 749-D4
ELLIS DR
800 SMCo 94015 687-A4
N ELLSWORTH AV
- SMTO 94401 728-H7
- SMTO 94401 748-J1
S ELLSWORTH AV
- SMTO 94401 748-J1
400 SMTO 94401 749-A2
ELLSWORTH CT E
400 SMTO 94401 728-H7
ELLSWORTH CT W
400 SMTO 94401 728-H7
ELLSWORTH PL
700 PA 94303 791-D6
ELM AV
100 BURL 94010 748-F1
100 MLPK 94025 791-A2
100 SBRN 94066 727-J1
100 HIL 94010 748-F1
100 BURL 94010 728-F7
100 HIL 94010 728-F7
300 MLPK 94025 790-J2
400 SBRN 94066 707-H6
ELM CT
- PCFA 94044 727-A5
500 SSF 94080 707-H2
ELM PL
- ATN 94027 790-G2
ELM ST
- SCAR 94070 769-F2
100 RDWC 94063 770-B6
100 SMTO 94401 748-H1
400 SSF 94080 707-H2
800 SMCo 94037 746-H4

ELMDALE PL
2600 PA 94303 791-D5
ELMER ST
1000 BLMT 94002 769-F1
1200 SMCo 94002 769-F1
ELMWOOD CT
100 SBRN 94066 707-E6
ELMWOOD DR
- DALY 94015 687-A4
1100 MLBR 94030 727-H3
ELMWOOD PL
- MLPK 94025 790-H2
ELMWOOD RD
1800 HIL 94010 728-E7
EL NIDO RD
100 SMCo 94028 830-D4
EL PARQUE CT
1800 SMTO 94403 749-E4
EL PASEO
- HMBY 94019 787-G5
- MLBR 94030 728-A4
EL PORTAL AV
300 HIL 94010 748-G2
300 SMTO 94402 748-G2
EL PORTAL WY
- DALY 94015 687-A2
EL PRADO AV
200 SMCo 94061 790-A4
EL PRADO RD
2700 BURL 94010 728-B7
EL QUANITO WY
- BURL 94010 728-B7
EL RANCHO DR
- SSF 94080 707-D2
EL REY RD
- SMCo 94028 830-D4
EL SERENO CTE
- SCAR 94070 769-H5
EL SERENO DR
- SCAR 94070 769-H5
ELSINORE CT
900 PA 94303 791-C5
ELSINORE DR
900 PA 94303 791-C5
EL SOBRANTE ST
3300 SMTO 94403 748-J6
ELSTON CT
- SCAR 94070 769-E4
ELSTON DR
3600 SBRN 94066 707-C5
EL VANADA RD
- SMCo 94062 769-E7
EL VERANO AV
300 PA 94306 791-D7
EL VERANO WY
1500 BLMT 94002 769-D2
ELWELL CT
1000 PA 94303 791-F6
ELWOOD ST
- RDWC 94062 769-J5
300 RDWC 94062 770-A6
EMALITA CT
100 SBRN 94066 727-J2
EMARON DR
100 SBRN 94066 707-D6
EMBARCADERO RD
- SCIC 94305 790-J6
- PA 94301 790-J6
100 PA 94301 791-C4
600 PA 94303 791-E3
EMBARCADERO WY
2400 PA 94303 791-E3
EMERALD AV
100 SCAR 94070 769-G5
EMERALD CT
- SMTO 94403 748-J6
- SSF 94080 707-F2
EMERALD BAY LN
100 FCTY 94404 749-E3
EMERALD ESTATES CT
- SMCo 94062 789-G3
EMERALD HILL RD
600 RDWC 94061 789-G2
EMERALD LAKE PL
- SMCo 94062 789-G1
EMERSON ST
100 PA 94301 790-H4
1100 PA 94301 791-A6
2500 PA 94306 791-B7
EMILIE AV
- ATN 94027 790-E3
EMILY LN
2400 SSF 94080 707-D4
EMMA LN
100 MLPK 94025 791-A3
EMMETT AV
800 BLMT 94002 769-E1
EMMETT WY
2500 EPA 94303 771-B7
2500 EPA 94303 791-B1
EMPRESS LN
- SF 94134 688-A2
ENCANTO WY
1100 PCFA 94044 726-H4
ENCHANTED WY
1300 SMCo 94402 748-G6
ENCINA AV
- PA 94301 790-J5
200 RDWC 94061 790-B1
300 ATN 94027 790-E1
300 SMCo 94025 790-E1
500 SMCo 94025 770-E7
ENCINA CT
- HIL 94010 728-E7
ENCINA DR
1200 MLBR 94030 728-A5
ENCINA WY
- SMCo 94019 767-C4
ENCINAL AV
100 ATN 94027 790-F2
100 MLPK 94025 790-F2
100 MLPK 94027 790-F2
ENCINO RD
- ATN 94027 790-G1
ENCLINE WY
3700 BLMT 94002 769-A2
ENFIELD WY
700 HIL 94010 748-G3
ENGLE RD
- SMTO 94402 748-H1
ENGLISH CT
- BLMT 94002 769-F2
ENGVALL RD
2300 SBRN 94066 707-F6

ENSENADA RD
- SCAR 94070 769-F2
ENSENADA WY
2100 SMTO 94403 749-A5
ENSIGN LN
300 RDWC 94065 749-H7
ENTRADA WY
- SMCo 94020 829-E7
- SMCo 94020 849-E1
500 SMCo 94025 790-H2
ENTRANCE WY
- WDSD 94062 789-D6
ERICA DR
300 SSF 94080 707-E4
ERICA WY
100 SMCo 94028 810-D3
ERICKSON LN
800 FCTY 94404 749-F4
ERICSON RD
100 HIL 94010 748-H1
100 SMTO 94402 748-H1
ERIN LN
- HMBY 94019 787-G1
ERIN PL
2300 SSF 94080 707-D5
ERLIN DR
400 SCAR 94070 769-F2
ERRIS CT
3600 SSF 94080 707-C4
ERSTWILD CT
- PA 94303 791-B4
ERVINE ST
- SF 94134 688-A1
ESCALANTE WY
1600 BURL 94010 728-A6
ESCALERO AV
1000 PCFA 94044 726-J4
ESCALLE
- SMCo 94038 746-G7
ESCALONA AV
100 SMCo 94019 767-A1
ESCANYO DR
- SSF 94080 707-E3
ESCANYO WY
100 SMCo 94028 810-E4
ESCOBAR RD
100 PTLV 94028 810-C4
ESCOBITA AV
1500 PA 94306 791-A6
ESCONDIDO DR
100 SMCo 94020 849-E1
ESCONDIDO LN
1100 MLPK 94025 790-F3
ESCONDIDO PL
100 SMCo 94020 849-E1
ESCONDIDO RD
600 SCIC 94305 790-H7
800 SCIC 94305 810-J1
ESCONDIDO WY
1500 BLMT 94002 769-D2
ESCUELA DR
- DALY 94015 687-B7
ESMERALDA AV
800 SMCo 94038 746-G7
800 SMCo 94038 766-G1
ESMERALDA TER
- SMCo 94020 829-F7
ESPINOSA RD
900 WDSD 94062 809-G5
ESPLANADA WY
800 SCIC 94305 810-J1
ESPLANADE
100 PCFA 94044 706-J4
ESQUINA DR
- SF 94134 687-H2
ESSEX CT
100 SBRN 94066 727-G1
ESSEX LN
100 HIL 94010 748-G3
1100 FCTY 94404 749-G5
ESSEX WY
- PCFA 94044 726-G4
ESTATE CT
- SCAR 94070 769-E5
- SSF 94080 707-G2
600 DALY 94014 687-F3
ESTATES DR
100 SBRN 94066 707-E7
ESTELLA DR
- PCFA 94044 727-A3
ESTELLE LN
200 DALY 94014 687-D5
ESTHER LN
700 SMCo 94062 769-H7
ESTON WY
- MLBR 94030 727-J5
- MLBR 94030 728-A5
ESTRADA PL
- SMCo 94062 769-F6
ESTRELLA WY
200 SMTO 94403 749-D5
ESTUDILLO RD
700 SCIC 94305 810-H2
ETHEL CT
- RDWC 94061 789-J3
ETHELDORE ST
700 SMCo 94038 746-F6
EUCALYPTUS AV
- SSF 94080 707-G3
100 HIL 94010 748-E1
600 HIL 94010 728-E7
1900 SCAR 94070 769-G4
EUCALYPTUS CT
- WDSD 94062 789-F5
EUCALYPTUS WY
2400 SBRN 94066 707-E7
EUCLID AV
- ATN 94027 790-B4
100 SBRN 94066 707-H6
1900 MLPK 94025 791-B3
2000 EPA 94303 791-B3
2100 RDWC 94061 789-J1
EUCLID PL
500 EPA 94303 791-B2
EUGENIA DR
- HIL 94010 748-C1
EUGENIA LN
- WDSD 94062 790-A5
EUREKA DR
200 PCFA 94044 706-J6
200 PCFA 94044 707-A6
EVA CT
- SMTO 94403 749-C6
EVELYN ST
900 MLPK 94025 790-F4

EVERETT AV
100 PA 94301 790-H4
EVERETT CT
500 PA 94301 790-J4
EVERGLADES DR
1000 PCFA 94044 727-B4
EVERGREEN AV
- DALY 94014 687-D3
EVERGREEN CT
- MLBR 94030 727-H3
EVERGREEN DR
200 SSF 94080 707-F1
1900 SBRN 94066 707-D6
3500 PA 94303 791-E7
EVERGREEN ST
600 MLPK 94025 790-E6
1800 SMTO 94401 749-C1
EVERGREEN WY
900 MLBR 94030 727-H3
EWELL RD
2200 BLMT 94002 769-C2
EXBOURNE AV
100 SCAR 94070 769-E2
EXCELSIOR AV
900 SF 94112 687-H1
EXECUTIVE DR
- SSF 94080 708-A2
EXECUTIVE GUILD CIR
- BLMT 94002 749-G7
- BLMT 94002 769-G1
- RDWC 94065 749-G7
- RDWC 94065 769-G1
EXECUTIVE GUILD DR
- RDWC 94065 749-G7
EXECUTIVE PARK BLVD
100 SF 94134 688-B2
100 SF 94124 688-B2
EXETER AV
- SCAR 94070 769-D3
EXETER DR
3500 SBRN 94066 707-C6
EXETER ST
- SF 94124 688-B1
EXETER WY
500 SCAR 94070 769-E3
EYE ST
200 SF 94124 688-E1
EYELET LN
100 RDWC 94065 749-J4

F

F ST
100 DALY 94014 687-C6
100 RDWC 94063 769-J4
100 SMCo 94014 687-C6
200 CLMA 94014 687-D6
900 BLMT 94002 769-F2
900 SCAR 94070 769-F2
FABER PL
2400 PA 94303 791-E4
FABIAN WY
3700 PA 94303 791-F7
FAGAN DR
- HIL 94010 728-D7
- BURL 94010 728-D7
FAIRBANKS AV
100 SCAR 94070 769-F5
FAIRFAX AV
- ATN 94027 790-D1
300 SMTO 94402 748-H3
FAIRFAX WY
3700 SSF 94080 707-D4
FAIRFIELD CT
- SMCo 94402 748-F7
FAIRFIELD DR
200 SCAR 94070 769-G2
FAIRFIELD RD
700 BURL 94010 728-E6
FAIRLAWN AV
- DALY 94015 686-J4
- DALY 94015 687-A4
FAIRLAWN CT
- DALY 94015 687-A4
FAIRMONT AV
100 SCAR 94070 769-G5
FAIRMONT DR
- DALY 94015 686-J3
1000 SBRN 94066 707-F7
2000 SMTO 94402 748-H7
2000 SMTO 94402 768-H1
FAIR OAKS AV
2600 SMCo 94063 770-D6
3500 SMCo 94025 770-E7
FAIROAKS CT
- SMTO 94403 748-J6
FAIR OAKS LN
- ATN 94027 790-E2
FAIRVIEW AV
- ATN 94027 790-C5
- DALY 94015 687-A5
1100 RDWC 94061 789-J1
FAIRVIEW PL
- MLBR 94030 727-H2
FAIRWAY CIR
600 HIL 94010 728-F7
FAIRWAY DR
- DALY 94015 687-B4
- SSF 94080 707-F3
100 HMBY 94019 787-E5
200 PCFA 94044 706-J7
300 PCFA 94044 707-A7
1600 BLMT 94002 769-D1
FAIRWAY PL
- HMBY 94019 787-E5
FALDA AV
600 SMTO 94403 749-A5
FALK CT
400 MLPK 94025 791-A3
FALKIRK LN
- HIL 94010 748-F4
FALLENLEAF DR
100 HIL 94010 748-H2
FALLEN LEAF WY
900 SMCo 94062 789-G2
FALLON AV
500 SMTO 94401 729-B7
500 SMTO 94401 749-B1
FAMILY FARM RD
- WDSD 94062 809-J4
300 SMCo 94025 809-J4
FANITA WY
500 MLPK 94025 790-E6

FARALLON AV
200 PCFA 94044 707-A2
FARALLON DR
300 BLMT 94002 749-F6
FARALLONE AV
200 SMCo 94037 746-F4
FARALLONES ST
- SF 94112 687-D2
FAR CREEK WY
900 SMCo 94062 789-G2
FARM CT
- SSF 94080 707-G2
FARM LN
- HIL 94010 748-E2
FARM RD
- SSF 94080 707-G2
100 PTLV 94028 810-A5
100 WDSD 94062 810-A5
FARM HILL BLVD
3500 RDWC 94061 789-G4
4100 WDSD 94062 789-G4
FARMHILL CT
- HIL 94010 748-E1
FARMIN RD
- SMCo 94060 868-F3
FARNEE CT
2600 SSF 94080 707-C4
FARRAGUT AV
- SF 94112 687-E2
FARRAGUT BLVD
900 FCTY 94404 749-F4
FARRIER PL
- DALY 94014 687-H3
FARRINGDON LN
700 BURL 94010 728-F6
FARRINGTON WY
2500 EPA 94303 771-B7
2500 EPA 94303 791-B1
FASHION ISLAND BLVD
- SMTO 94402 749-D3
1300 SMTO 94403 749-D3
1400 SMTO 94404 749-D3
FASMAN DR
3000 SBRN 94066 707-C5
FASSLER AV
800 PCFA 94044 726-J3
800 PCFA 94044 727-A3
FATHOM CT
400 RDWC 94065 749-H7
FATHOM DR
400 SMTO 94404 749-E1
FAVONIA RD
100 PTLV 94028 810-C4
FAWN CT
- HIL 94010 728-C7
FAWN LN
- PTLV 94028 810-C5
FAWN CREEK CT
27800 LAH 94022 810-H6
FAXON AV
- SF 94112 687-D1
FAXON RD
- ATN 94027 790-D4
FAXON FOREST
- ATN 94027 790-D4
FAY AV
- SCAR 94070 769-E4
- SMCo 94070 769-E4
FAY ST
1100 RDWC 94061 770-B7
FELIX AV
- SF 94132 687-B1
FELTON AV
- SSF 94080 707-D1
FELTON DR
100 MLPK 94025 790-F2
FELTON PL
100 MLPK 94025 790-F2
FENNWOOD DR
- ATN 94027 790-F2
FERDINAND AV
100 SMCo 94019 767-B2
FERN AV
- SMCo 94060 868-H5
700 PCFA 94044 727-A2
FERN CT
- HIL 94010 728-D7
FERN PTH
- SMCo 94010 728-B7
FERN TR
- SMCo 94062 788-H5
FERNANDEZ WY
1100 PCFA 94044 726-H4
FERNDALE AV
200 SSF 94080 707-F1
FERNDALE WY
200 SMCo 94062 769-E7
200 SMCo 94062 789-E1
FERNSIDE ST
1000 RDWC 94061 789-J2
1600 WDSD 94062 789-J2
1900 RDWC 94061 790-A3
1900 WDSD 94062 790-A3
FERNWOOD AV
- DALY 94015 686-J5
FERNWOOD DR
- SBRN 94066 707-F6
- SMCo 94020 849-E1
1100 MLBR 94030 727-H3
FERNWOOD ST
2800 SMTO 94403 749-A6
FERNWOOD WY
1700 BLMT 94002 769-D2
FEY DR
100 SMCo 94010 728-B7
N FIELD RD
- SMCo 94128 708-B5
- SSF 94080 708-B5
W FIELD RD
- SMCo 94128 708-A7
FIELDCREST DR
- DALY 94015 687-B3
FIELD HOUSE RD
- SMTO 94402 748-H5
FIELDING DR
800 PA 94303 791-D6
FIESTA AV
- SMCo 94063 770-F5
FIESTA CT
2000 SMTO 94403 749-C4
FIESTA DR
500 SMTO 94403 749-C4
FIFE AV
1000 PA 94301 791-A4

FIFTY FIFTY RD
- SMCo 94060 868-E3
FILBERT RD
- SMCo 94062 788-H6
FILBERT ST
200 HMBY 94019 787-E2
FILLMORE AV
1600 SMTO 94403 749-C2
FINGER AV
- RDWC 94062 769-J5
FIR AV
100 SSF 94080 707-H4
FIR CT
- HIL 94010 748-C2
FIR LN
- SMCo 94060 868-H5
FIR ST
- SMCo 94037 746-H4
100 SCAR 94070 769-F2
FIR VW
- SMCo 94020 829-F7
FIRECREST AV
300 PCFA 94044 707-B2
FIRETHORN WY
- PTLV 94028 810-D7
FIRST AV
600 HMBY 94019 787-E2
E FIRST ST
500 MLPK 94025 790-H3
FISHER ST
400 DALY 94014 687-D5
FITCH ST
2600 SF 94124 688-C1
FITZGERALD AV
500 SF 94124 688-B1
FIVE POINTS RD
- SMCo 94020 850-G7
FLASHNER LN
900 BLMT 94002 769-E1
FLEETWOOD CT
100 SBRN 94066 707-C5
FLEETWOOD DR
- DALY 94015 687-A3
100 SCAR 94070 769-E7
800 SMTO 94402 749-B2
2100 SBRN 94066 707-D5
3900 SSF 94080 707-D5
FLETCHER DR
- ATN 94027 790-B5
FLEUR PL
- ATN 94027 790-C4
FLINT AV
1400 SMTO 94403 749-D4
FLOOD AV
2900 SMCo 94063 770-D7
FLOOD CIR
- ATN 94027 790-G1
FLORENCE AV
600 HMBY 94019 787-E5
FLORENCE LN
900 MLPK 94025 790-F4
FLORENCE ST
- DALY 94014 687-D4
400 PA 94301 790-J4
3600 SMCo 94063 770-F7
3600 RDWC 94063 770-F7
FLORENTINE ST
- SF 94112 687-F2
FLORES DR
1300 PCFA 94044 726-H4
FLORES ST
2200 SMTO 94403 749-B5
E FLORESTA WY
100 SMCo 94028 810-E3
W FLORESTA WY
200 SMCo 94028 810-E3
FLORIBUNDA AV
1200 BURL 94010 728-F7
1600 HIL 94010 728-F7
1800 HIL 94010 748-E1
FLORIDA AV
100 SBRN 94066 707-J7
FLOURNOY ST
- DALY 94014 687-D2
100 SF 94112 687-D2
FLOWER ST
- RDWC 94063 769-J4
FLOWERS LN
3100 PA 94306 791-D7
FLYING CLOUD ISL
100 FCTY 94404 749-G2
FLYING FISH ST
900 FCTY 94404 749-G1
FLYING MIST ISL
100 FCTY 94404 749-G2
FLYNN AV
400 RDWC 94063 770-C6
FOGL CT
- SMCo 94061 790-B4
FOLGER CT
- BLMT 94002 769-D1
FOLGER DR
1500 BLMT 94002 769-D1
FOLKSTONE AV
600 SMTO 94402 749-B2
FONT BLVD
- SF 94132 687-B1
FOOTE AV
- SF 94112 687-E1
FOOTHILL DR
600 PCFA 94044 707-B3
700 SMTO 94402 748-J4
900 SMCo 94015 687-A4
FOOTHILL EXWY Rt#-G5
2600 SCIC 94304 810-J3
2600 PA 94304 810-J3
FOOTHILL ST
1100 RDWC 94061 789-H2
FORBES BLVD
300 SSF 94080 708-B3
FORD ST
400 DALY 94014 687-D4
FORDHAM RD
500 SMTO 94402 748-J3
FORDHAM ST
2400 EPA 94303 791-B1
2500 EPA 94303 771-B7
FORESAIL CT
200 FCTY 94404 749-G4
FOREST AV
100 PA 94301 790-J5
600 PA 94301 791-A3
1900 BLMT 94002 749-B7
2100 BLMT 94002 769-C1

FOREST CT
1000 PA 94301 791-A3
FOREST LN
- SBRN 94066 707-H6
- SCAR 94070 769-F5
100 MLPK 94025 790-E2
FOREST RD
- WDSD 94062 809-H6
- SMCo 94062 788-H4
FOREST GROVE DR
- DALY 94015 687-B3
FOREST LAKE DR
600 PCFA 94044 707-B3
FOREST PARK CT
200 PCFA 94044 707-A2
FOREST VIEW AV
- HIL 94010 728-D7
1500 BURL 94010 728-E7
FOREST VIEW DR
200 SSF 94080 707-G2
FOREST VIEW RD
- SMCo 94062 788-G3
FORGE RD
1400 SMCo 94402 748-F7
FORRESTAL LN
1100 FCTY 94404 749-G4
FORREST VIEW RD
- WDSD 94062 809-G3
FOSS DR
- RDWC 94062 769-H7
- RDWC 94062 789-G1
- SMCo 94062 769-H7
FOSTER ST
2600 SMTO 94403 749-D4
FOSTER CITY BLVD
300 FCTY 94404 749-F1
FOUNTAIN CIRCLE DR
- SMCo - 768-D4
FOURTH AV
300 HMBY 94019 787-F2
W FOX CT
500 RDWC 94061 790-C1
FOX CROSSING CT
100 SMCo 94062 789-F1
FOX HILL RD
- SMCo 94062 809-G3
FOX HOLLOW LN
- RDWC 94061 789-F3
FOXHOLLOW LN
- DALY 94014 687-E3
FOX HOLLOW RD
100 WDSD 94062 789-G7
FOX PLAZA LN
1400 BURL 94010 728-G7
FOX SPARROW LN
- BSBN 94005 687-J5
FOXTAIL
- PTLV 94028 830-C1
FOXWOOD RD
100 SMCo 94028 830-D4
FRANCE AV
- SF 94112 687-F1
FRANCES AV
- PCFA 94044 707-A6
FRANCES LN
200 RDWC 94070 769-G6
200 SCAR 94070 769-G6
200 SMCo 94062 769-G6
FRANCIS AV
1600 BLMT 94002 769-D1
FRANCIS CT
1700 BLMT 94002 769-D1
FRANCISCAN CT
2900 SCAR 94070 769-F6
FRANCISCAN DR
- DALY 94014 687-E5
FRANCISCAN RDG
- PTLV 94028 830-C1
FRANCISCO BLVD
700 PCFA 94044 707-A7
1600 PCFA 94044 706-J6
FRANCISCO DR
100 SSF 94080 707-H4
500 BURL 94010 728-G6
FRANCISCO ST
- SMCo 94019 767-A2
FRANKFORT ST
- DALY 94014 687-E3
FRANKLIN AV
- SSF 94080 707-J1
FRANKLIN PKWY
- SMTO 94403 749-D5
FRANKLIN ST
- RDWC 94063 770-B6
200 SMTO 94402 748-H2
500 SMCo 94037 746-G4
FRANKS LN
1400 SMCo 94025 790-D5
FRANZ CT
100 PCFA 94044 727-A1
FRATESSA CT
- SF 94134 688-A2
FREDERICK AV
- ATN 94027 790-H1
FREDERICK CT
- SMCo 94025 790-H1
FREDSON CT
- SF 94112 687-E2
FREEPORT LN
- RDWC 94065 750-B3
FREESIA DR
- SSF 94080 707-E2
FRWY I-380
- SBRN - 707-G7
FREMONT AV
200 PCFA 94044 707-A3
FREMONT PL
900 MLPK 94025 790-F4
FREMONT RD
500 SCIC 94305 790-F7
FREMONT ST
500 MLPK 94025 790-F4
1100 SMCo 94037 746-H5
N FREMONT ST
- SMTO 94401 728-J7
- SMTO 94401 748-J1
- SMTO 94401 749-A1
S FREMONT ST
- SMTO 94401 749-A1
400 SMTO 94402 749-A1
FREMONT WY
- SMCo 94020 809-F6
FREMONTIA
- PTLV 94028 830-C1

SAN MATEO CO.

STREET
Block City ZIP Pg-Grid

FRENCH CT
400 MLPK 94025 791-A3
FRENCH CREEK PL
- SMCo 94402 768-G2
FRENCHMANS RD
700 SCIC 94305 810-H2
FRENCHMANS CREEK RD
- HMBY 94019 767-E5
- SMCo - 767-E5
FRIARS LN
- WDSD 94062 809-G4
FRIENDLY CT
- RDWC 94063 770-F6
FRIGATE LN
- DALY 94014 687-E5
FROG VALLEY LN
200 BLMT 94002 749-F6
FRONTAGE RD
900 HMBY 94019 767-E6
FRONTERA WY
1200 MLBR 94030 728-A6
1200 BURL 94010 728-A6
FUENTA AV
- SF 94132 687-B1
FULLER ST
300 RDWC 94063 770-A5
FULLERTON AV
400 PCFA 94044 707-A6
FULTON RD
400 SMTO 94402 748-F2
FULTON ST
- RDWC 94062 769-J6
100 PA 94301 790-J3
300 RDWC 94062 770-A7
600 RDWC 94061 770-A7
600 PA 94301 791-A4
700 PA 94303 791-B5
FURLONG ST
1000 BLMT 94002 769-F1
FURTADO LN
400 SMCo 94019 767-D4

G

G ST
100 RDWC 94063 769-J4
GABARDA WY
100 SMCo 94028 810-D4
GAILEN AV
800 PA 94303 791-F7
GAILLARDIA WY
1100 EPA 94303 791-C3
GALINDO AV
- SF 94132 687-C2
GALLEON LN
700 FCTY 94404 749-G2
GALLEY LN
1000 FCTY 94404 749-H4
GALLOWRIDGE CT
- SMTO 94402 748-C7
GALVESTON DR
100 RDWC 94063 770-C4
GALVESTON ST
1000 FCTY 94404 749-F5
GALVEZ DR
1100 PCFA 94044 726-J5
GALVEZ ST
100 SCIC 94305 790-H6
GALWAY DR
2300 SSF 94080 707-D4
GALWAY PL
2400 SSF 94080 707-D5
GAMBETTA LN
- PTLV 94028 810-C7
GAMBETTA ST
- DALY 94014 687-D4
GARCES DR
- SF 94132 687-A1
GARCIA AV
200 HMBY 94019 787-E1
2300 MTVW 94043 791-G7
GARDEN AV
400 SBRN 94066 727-J1
GARDEN CT
- BLMT 94002 769-D2
300 PCFA 94044 706-J7
GARDEN DR
1900 BURL 94010 728-B5
GARDEN LN
- SCAR 94070 769-E3
- SMCo 94015 687-B4
- SMTO 94403 749-C6
1300 MLPK 94025 790-E4
GARDEN ST
- RDWC 94063 769-J4
100 EPA 94303 791-A1
GARDEN GATEWAY
- DALY 94015 687-C4
- SMCo 94015 687-C4
GARDEN GROVE DR
- DALY 94015 686-J3
GARDENIA CT
- EPA 94303 791-C3
GARDENIA WY
100 EPA 94303 791-D3
GARDEN OF DEVOTION CIR
- SMCo - 768-C3
GARDENSIDE AV
200 SSF 94080 707-F1
GARDINER AV
- SSF 94080 708-A2
GARFIELD ST
- SF 94132 687-C1
800 SF 94112 687-C1
2600 SMTO 94403 749-B5
GARIBALDI CT
- DALY 94014 687-D4
GARIBALDI ST
- DALY 94014 687-C4
GARLAND DR
100 MLPK 94025 790-F5
700 PA 94303 791-C5
GARLAND PL
- MLPK 94025 790-F5
GARNET AV
100 SCAR 94070 769-G5
GARRISON AV
- SF 94134 687-J2
GARVEY WY
- SMTO 94402 749-B3
GARWOOD DR
- DALY 94014 687-D3
GARWOOD WY
400 MLPK 94025 790-F3
GARY CT
400 PA 94306 791-C7
GASLIGHT LN
- SMCo 94070 769-E4
GASPAR CT
2700 PA 94306 791-C6
S GATE
- RDWC 94062 769-H7
GATES ST
- EPA 94303 791-C2
GATESHEAD CT
700 FCTY 94404 749-G5
GATEWAY BLVD
200 SSF 94080 708-A3
GATEWAY DR
- DALY 94015 707-B1
- PCFA 94044 707-B1
1800 SMTO 94404 749-E3
1800 FCTY 94404 749-E3
GAVILAN CT
- MLBR 94030 728-A6
GAVILAN WY
1400 MLBR 94030 728-A6
GAYLORD ST
- SCAR 94070 769-G5
GAZOS CREEK RD
- SMCo 94060 888-G5
GEDDES CT
3900 SSF 94080 707-D4
GELLERT BLVD
300 DALY 94015 707-C2
2100 SSF 94080 707-D4
GEMINI LN
700 FCTY 94404 749-E4
GENEVA AV
- SF 94112 687-G2
500 RDWC 94061 790-B1
1300 SCAR 94070 769-H4
1600 SF 94134 687-G2
2100 DALY 94014 687-G2
3100 BSBN 94005 687-G2
3200 BSBN 94005 688-A3
3200 DALY 94014 688-A3
GENEVIEVE AV
300 PCFA 94044 727-A2
GENEVIEVE CT
3100 PA 94303 791-E6
GENEVRA RD
- HIL 94010 728-F7
GENG RD
1700 PA 94303 791-D3
GENOA DR
- RDWC 94065 749-J4
- RDWC 94065 750-C4
GEOFFREY DR
3100 SBRN 94066 707-D5
GEORGE AV
4100 SMTO 94403 749-D6
GEORGE ST
600 SMCo 94037 746-G4
GEORGETOWN AV
300 SMTO 94402 748-J3
GEORGETOWN CT
3600 SSF 94080 707-C4
GEORGETOWN ST
2700 EPA 94303 771-C7
GEORGIA AV
200 SBRN 94066 707-J7
200 SBRN 94066 727-J1
GEORGIA LN
100 PTLV 94028 810-C7
GERALDINE DR
600 MLBR 94030 728-A3
600 MLBR 94030 727-J3
GERALDINE WY
1200 BLMT 94002 769-D3
GERANIUM LN
- SCAR 94070 769-C4
GERI LN
2000 HIL 94010 728-D7
GERI PL
- SMCo 94062 789-G1
GERONA RD
400 SCIC 94305 810-H1
GERTH LN
2200 LAH 94304 810-H4
GERTRUDE CT
- EPA 94303 771-B7
GETZ ST
- SF 94112 687-E1
GIANTS DR
3000 SF 94124 688-C1
GIBBS WY
900 SSF 94080 707-D1
GIBRALTAR LN
500 FCTY 94404 749-F5
GILBERT AV
100 MLPK 94025 791-A2
200 MLPK 94025 790-J2
GILBERT CT
3600 SSF 94080 707-D4
GILBRETH RD
1500 BURL 94010 728-D4
GILLETTE AV
- SF 94134 688-B2
GILLIS DR
3900 SMTO 94403 749-D6
GILMAN AV
500 SF 94124 688-B1
GILMAN DR
1000 SMCo 94015 687-B5
1000 DALY 94015 687-B5
GILMAN ST
600 PA 94301 790-J4
GILROY ST
- SF 94124 688-C2
GIMERL LN
- RDWC 94065 750-C4
GINGER ST
- MLPK 94025 770-J7
GINNIVER ST
1900 SMTO 94403 749-C4
GIRARD ST
700 SF 94134 688-A1
GLACIER AV
1000 PCFA 94044 727-C5
GLADYS AV
- BSBN 94005 688-B7
GLASGOW DR
400 PCFA 94044 707-B3
GLASGOW LN
100 SCAR 94070 769-F4
GLEN AV
1800 SBRN 94066 727-H2
GLEN PKWY
- BSBN 94005 688-A7
GLEN WY
900 HIL 94010 728-C7
2000 EPA 94303 791-B1
W GLEN WY
600 WDSD 94062 789-E3
GLEN AULIN LN
100 SMCo 94010 728-B7
100 SMCo 94010 748-B1
GLENBROOK AV
- DALY 94015 687-A6
GLENBROOK DR
- HIL 94010 748-G4
GLENBROOK LN
100 SBRN 94066 727-G1
GLENCOURT WY
300 PCFA 94044 707-B4
GLENCRAG WY
600 WDSD 94062 789-E3
GLENDALE AV
3000 SMCo 94063 790-D1
GLENDALE RD
300 HIL 94010 748-F2
300 SMTO 94402 748-F2
GLENDORA DR
1400 SMTO 94403 748-J6
GLEN EYRIE RD
- SMCo 94020 849-E1
GLENGARRY WY
- HIL 94010 748-F5
GLENLOCK WY
600 SMCo 94062 789-E1
GLENMERE WY
700 SMCo 94062 789-F2
GLENN WY
- SCAR 94070 769-G1
1500 RDWC 94061 790-A2
GLENNAN DR
500 RDWC 94061 789-H2
GLENROSE AV
- DALY 94015 687-A4
- DALY 94015 686-J4
GLENVIEW DR
700 SBRN 94066 727-F1
900 SBRN 94066 707-F7
GLENWOOD AV
100 ATN 94027 790-F2
100 DALY 94015 687-A3
100 WDSD 94062 789-G5
200 DALY 94015 686-J3
400 MLPK 94025 790-F2
3500 RDWC 94062 789-G1
GLENWOOD DR
1100 MLBR 94030 727-H3
GLENWOOD ST
300 SCAR 94070 769-F3
GLORIA CIR
- MLPK 94025 790-H2
GLORIA CT
- SF 94112 687-F1
600 SMTO 94401 749-B1
GLORIA WY
2400 EPA 94303 791-B1
2500 EPA 94303 771-B7
GLOUCESTER LN
600 FCTY 94404 749-G5
GODETIA DR
900 WDSD 94062 789-F4
GOETHE ST
- DALY 94014 687-D2
100 SF 94112 687-D2
GOETTINGEN ST
700 SF 94134 688-A1
GOLDEN ASTER CT
- BSBN 94005 687-H4
GOLDEN BAY DR
200 PCFA 94044 707-A2
GOLDEN EAGLE LN
- BSBN 94005 687-J4
GOLDEN GATE AV
500 HMBY 94019 767-F6
GOLDEN HILLS DR
100 PTLV 94028 810-C5
GOLDEN OAK DR
- PTLV 94028 810-D5
GOLDENRIDGE CT
- SMTO 94402 748-C7
GOLDHUNTER CT
100 FCTY 94404 749-F2
GOLF LN
- SMCo 94025 810-E3
- SCIC 94304 810-E3
GOLF COURSE DR
- HIL - 748-B2
- SMCo - 748-B2
- SMCo 94010 748-D4
GONZAGA ST
2400 EPA 94303 791-C1
2500 EPA 94303 771-C7
GONZALEZ DR
- SF 94132 687-A1
GOODMAN RD
400 PCFA 94044 707-A6
GOODWIN AV
1900 RDWC 94061 789-J2
2900 RDWC 94061 790-A2
GOODWIN CT
- RDWC 94061 789-H3
GOODWIN DR
100 SBRN 94066 707-D6
GORDON AV
800 BLMT 94002 769-E1
2000 SMCo 94025 790-D6
GORDON ST
1200 RDWC 94061 790-A1
GORDON WY
100 PCFA 94044 707-A3
GOSSAMER AV
- RDWC 94065 750-A5
GOULD ST
- SF 94124 688-B1
GOULSON ST
- SMCo 94060 868-B2
GOVER LN
1500 SCAR 94070 769-H5
GOVERNORS AV
500 SCIC 94305 790-G7
GOVERNORS BAY DR
900 RDWC 94065 750-A5
GOYA RD
100 PTLV 94028 810-C4
GRACE AV
100 EPA 94303 791-B1
GRACE DR
500 MLPK 94025 790-E6
GRACELAND AV
2400 SCAR 94070 769-G5
GRACELAND LN
- SCAR 94070 769-F5
GRAFTON AV
- SF 94112 687-D1
GRAMERCY DR
100 SMTO 94402 748-H1
GRANADA AV
- SF 94112 687-D1
GRANADA CT
- PTLV 94028 810-D6
GRANADA DR
300 SSF 94080 707-F5
1000 PCFA 94044 726-J4
1000 PCFA 94044 727-A4
1500 BURL 94010 728-B6
GRANADA ST
800 BLMT 94002 749-E7
900 BLMT 94002 769-F1
GRAND AV
300 SSF 94080 707-F2
1300 PCFA 94044 726-G4
E GRAND AV
- SSF 94080 707-J3
- SSF 94080 708-A3
GRAND BLVD
- SMTO 94401 748-H1
- SMTO 94401 728-H7
300 HMBY 94019 767-E7
GRAND ST
- RDWC 94062 769-J6
400 RDWC 94062 770-A7
900 RDWC 94061 770-A7
GRAND TETON DR
1000 PCFA 94044 727-B5
GRANDVIEW AV
- DALY 94015 687-A7
GRANDVIEW BLVD
500 HMBY 94019 767-E6
GRANDVIEW DR
- WDSD 94062 809-G5
400 SSF 94080 708-C3
GRANELLI AV
100 HMBY 94019 787-E2
GRANGER WY
1500 RDWC 94061 789-J3
GRANITE CT
- SCAR 94070 769-F6
GRANT AV
100 PA 94306 791-B7
E GRANT PL
800 SMTO 94402 749-B2
W GRANT PL
800 SMTO 94402 749-B2
GRANT RD
1200 SMCo 94037 746-H5
N GRANT ST
- SMTO 94401 729-A7
- SMTO 94401 749-A1
100 SMTO 94401 728-J7
S GRANT ST
- SMTO 94403 749-C3
- SMTO 94401 749-A1
400 SMTO 94402 749-A1
GRAYSON CT
300 MLPK 94025 790-J1
300 MLPK 94025 791-A1
GRAYSTONE DR
- SSF 94080 707-D1
GRAYSTONE LN
- DALY 94014 687-E3
GREBE ST
1000 FCTY 94404 749-H2
GREEN AV
100 SSF 94080 708-A2
500 SBRN 94066 707-H6
GREEN CT
500 PA 94301 791-C6
GREEN RDG
- DALY 94014 687-D4
GREEN ST
100 EPA 94303 791-B2
100 MLPK 94025 791-A2
GREENBRIAR WY
- HIL 94010 748-H3
GREENBRIER CT
- HMBY 94019 787-F5
GREENBRIER DR
1200 SCAR 94070 769-E6
GREENBRIER RD
300 HMBY 94019 787-F5
GREENDALE DR
2100 SSF 94080 707-C4
GREENDALE WY
300 SMCo 94062 769-F7
GREENFIELD AV
200 SMTO 94403 749-C7
GREENFIELD CT
- SMTO 94403 749-C7
- BLMT 94002 749-C7
GREEN HILLS CT
- MLBR 94030 728-A3
GREEN HILLS DR
200 MLBR 94030 728-A3
GREENOAK CT
3000 SMTO 94403 748-J6
3100 SMTO 94403 749-A7
GREENOAKS DR
- ATN 94027 770-F7
100 ATN 94027 790-G1
GREENPARK TER
- SSF 94014 707-J1
GREEN VIEW DR
- DALY 94014 687-E3
GREENVIEW LN
- HIL 94010 728-E7
GREENWAY DR
200 PCFA 94044 706-J7
200 PCFA 94044 707-A7
GREENWAYS DR
2100 WDSD 94062 790-A5
E GREENWICH DR
700 PA 94303 791-C5
GREENWICH LN
600 FCTY 94404 749-F5
GREENWOOD AV
800 SMTO 94402 728-G7
800 SMTO 94402 748-G1
1000 PA 94301 791-B4
1100 SCAR 94070 769-G5
GREENWOOD DR
- SSF 94080 707-G6
1000 MLPK 94025 770-G7
GREENWOOD LN
- RDWC 94063 770-C6
GREENWOOD PL
- MLPK 94025 770-G7
GREENWOOD WY
1400 SBRN 94066 707-E6
GREER RD
100 SMCo 94062 789-E6
100 WDSD 94062 789-E6
500 PA 94303 791-C4
GREGORY LN
200 RDWC 94061 790-B2
GRENADA LN
800 FCTY 94404 749-G4
GRESHAM LN
- ATN 94027 790-C1
GREVILLEA CT
- HIL 94010 748-C2
GRIFFIN AV
400 PCFA 94044 707-A6
GRIFFITH ST
2400 SF 94124 688-C1
GRIJALVA DR
- SF 94132 687-B1
GROVE AV
100 SSF 94080 707-J1
1100 BURL 94010 728-D5
3700 PA 94303 791-E7
GROVE CT
- PTLV 94028 810-B7
GROVE DR
- PTLV 94028 810-B6
GROVE ST
200 HMBY 94019 787-F2
GROVELAND ST
- PTLV 94028 830-C1
GRUNDY LN
900 SBRN 94066 707-G6
GRUNION CT
- FCTY 94404 749-H3
GUADALUPE AV
- DALY 94014 687-C3
600 MLBR 94030 727-J2
GUADALUPE CANYON PKWY
- DALY 94014 687-E4
- BSBN 94005 688-A4
300 SMCo 94014 687-E4
300 BSBN 94005 687-G4
GUARDIAN WY
- SMCo 94020 849-E1
GUERRERO AV
- HMBY 94019 767-D4
GUILDFORD AV
500 SMTO 94402 749-B2
GUINDA ST
300 PA 94301 790-J3
500 PA 94301 791-A4
1700 PA 94303 791-B5
GUITTARD RD
- BURL 94010 728-C4
GULL AV
600 FCTY 94404 749-G1
GULL DR
700 SSF 94080 708-C2
GUM ST
1600 SMTO 94402 749-B3
GUNTER LN
300 RDWC 94065 749-H7
GUTHRIE WY
- SMCo 94021 849-B7
GUTTENBERG ST
- SF 94112 687-F2
300 DALY 94014 687-F2
GYMKHANA RD
400 SMTO 94403 749-A4
GYPSY HILL RD
- PCFA 94044 707-A6

H

H ST
- SF 94124 688-E1
HACIENDA CT
- PCFA 94044 707-A4
HACIENDA ST
2200 SMTO 94403 749-B4
HACIENDA WY
600 MLBR 94030 727-J3
HACIENDAS DR
- WDSD 94062 789-H6
HADDOCK ST
800 FCTY 94404 749-H3
HADDON DR
900 SMTO 94402 749-B2
HAHN ST
- SF 94134 687-J2
HAIGHT ST
100 MLPK 94025 791-A1
HAINLINE DR
400 BLMT 94002 749-D7
HALE DR
2100 BURL 94010 728-C6
HALE ST
400 PA 94301 790-J3
400 PA 94301 791-A3
HALF MOON LN
300 DALY 94015 707-C1
HALF MOON BAY RD
- HMBY 94019 767-F7
- HMBY 94019 787-F1
HALF MOON BAY RD Rt#-92
2900 SMCo - 768-E3
2900 SMCo 94062 768-E3
HALIBUT ST
1300 FCTY 94404 749-H3
HALL ST
900 SCAR 94070 769-G3
HALLING WY
1200 PCFA 94044 726-G4
HALLMARK CIR
- MLPK 94025 790-C6
HALLMARK DR
2400 BLMT 94002 769-A2
HALSEY AV
1400 SMTO 94403 749-C2
2600 SMCo 94063 770-C7
HALSEY BLVD
- FCTY 94404 749-G4
HALYARD LN
300 FCTY 94404 749-G6
HAMILTON AV
100 MLPK 94025 770-J7
100 PA 94301 790-J5
600 MLPK 94025 771-A7
700 PA 94301 791-A3
1500 PA 94303 791-B3
2200 SBRN 94066 707-F7
HAMILTON CT
- PCFA 94044 707-A3
100 PA 94301 791-A3
900 MLPK 94025 771-A7
HAMILTON LN
1100 BURL 94010 728-C5
W HAMILTON RD
200 SMCo 94062 788-H7
200 SMCo 94062 808-H1
HAMILTON ST
500 RDWC 94063 770-A6
600 SF 94134 688-A1
HAMILTON WY
3700 RDWC 94062 789-G2
3700 SMCo 94062 789-G2
HAMLET ST
1700 SMTO 94403 749-C2
HAMPSHIRE AV
- DALY 94015 707-C2
400 SMCo 94063 770-D7
HAMPSHIRE CT
200 DALY 94015 707-D3
HAMPTON AV
1600 RDWC 94061 790-A2
HAMPTON CT
- HIL 94010 748-E6
100 SBRN 94066 707-F7
HAMPTON LN
1700 DALY 94014 687-F3
HANA VISTA LN
- DALY 94014 687-E3
HANCOCK AV
1300 SMTO 94403 749-C2
HANCOCK ST
800 RDWC 94063 770-B7
HANDBURY LN
500 FCTY 94404 749-G5
HANDLEY TR
600 SMCo 94062 789-F1
HANNA WY
- MLPK 94025 790-H2
HANOVER ST
- SF 94112 687-D3
400 DALY 94014 687-D3
2000 PA 94306 810-J1
HANSEN WY
1000 RDWC 94063 770-C5
HAPPY HOLLOW LN
- SMCo 94025 810-E1
HARBOR BLVD
100 SMCo 94002 769-F1
400 RDWC 94063 770-D2
700 BLMT 94002 769-F1
HARBOR DR
- DALY 94014 687-E5
HARBOR WY
100 SSF 94080 708-A3
HARBOR COLONY CT
500 RDWC 94065 749-H6
HARBOR MASTER RD
- SSF 94080 708-D2
HARBOR SEAL CT
100 SMTO 94404 749-D3
HARBOUR DR
100 SMCo 94019 766-J1
100 SMCo 94019 767-A1
HARCOURT WY
1300 HIL 94010 748-F6
HARCROSS RD
100 RDWC 94061 789-J3
100 WDSD 94062 789-J3
HARDING AV
300 SMCo 94062 769-H7
1800 RDWC 94062 769-H7
2000 SMTO 94403 749-C2
2200 RDWC 94062 789-H1
HARDWICK RD
100 WDSD 94062 789-H4
HARKER AV
1000 PA 94301 791-B4
HARKINS AV
2100 MLPK 94025 790-D7
2100 SMCo 94025 790-D7
HARKINS RD
100 SMCo 94062 788-G4
HARKINS FIRE TR
- SMCo 94019 788-D5
- SMCo 94062 788-D5
HARKNESS AV
- SF 94134 688-A1
HARMON DR
900 MLPK 94025 770-G7
HARNEY RD
- SF 94134 688-B3
100 BSBN 94005 688-B3
HARNEY WY
- SF 94134 688-C2
- SF 94124 688-C2
HAROLD AV
- SF 94112 687-E1
HAROLD RD
500 BSBN 94005 688-B7
HARRIET ST
900 PA 94301 791-B4
E HARRIS AV
200 SSF 94080 708-A3
W HARRIS AV
- SSF 94080 708-A4
HARRIS CT
200 SSF 94080 708-A3
HARRISON AV
100 RDWC 94062 770-A6
800 RDWC 94062 769-J7
2000 SMTO 94403 749-C2
HARRISON WY
- SMCo 94025 790-E6
HARROW AV
600 SMTO 94402 749-B2
HARTE ST
600 SMCo 94037 746-G4
HARTFORD AV
- SCAR 94070 769-E2
HARVARD AV
- SMCo 94019 766-H3
600 MLPK 94025 790-G4
HARVARD CT
14500 LAH 94022 810-H5
HARVARD RD
200 SMTO 94402 748-H2
HARVARD ST
2000 PA 94306 810-J1
HARVEST DR
3800 RDWC 94061 789-G3
HARVESTER DR
600 FCTY 94404 749-G2
HARVEY WY
400 PCFA 94044 726-J2
HASKINS DR
3300 BLMT 94002 749-B7
3300 SMTO 94403 749-B7
HASKINS WY
100 SSF 94080 708-C4
HASSLER RD
- SMCo 94070 769-D7
HASTINGS AV
2500 RDWC 94061 789-H2
HASTINGS DR
2200 BLMT 94002 769-C2
HASTINGS SHORE LN
200 RDWC 94065 749-H7
HATCH DR
300 FCTY 94404 749-F1
HATTERAS CT
1000 FCTY 94404 749-F5
HAUSSMAN CT
3900 SSF 94080 707-C4
HAVEN AV
700 SSF 94080 707-G4
800 RDWC 94063 770-F7
3500 MLPK 94025 770-F6
3500 SMCo 94063 770-F6
HAVEN CT
3700 MLPK 94025 770-G6
HAVEN DR
- DALY 94014 687-E5
HAVENRIDGE CT
- SMTO 94402 748-C7
HAWES CT
1500 RDWC 94061 790-A1
HAWES ST
600 RDWC 94061 769-J7
1200 RDWC 94061 790-A1
2300 SF 94124 688-B1
HAWK VW
- PTLV 94028 830-D1
HAWKSBURY LN
400 FCTY 94404 749-F5
HAWSER LN
1500 HMBY 94019 767-E6
HAWTHORN WK
- SMCo 94019 787-G5
HAWTHORNE AV
100 PA 94301 790-H4
400 SBRN 94066 727-H1
HAWTHORNE DR
- ATN 94027 790-F1
1000 SMTO 94402 749-B2
HAWTHORNE PL
600 SSF 94080 707-J2
HAWTHORNE ST
1100 SMCo 94037 746-G5
HAWTHORNE WY
800 MLBR 94030 728-B5
HAYDON CT
- BLMT 94002 769-B3
HAYFIELDS RD
- WDSD 94062 809-J5
- PTLV 94028 809-J5
HAYNE RD
500 HIL 94010 748-G2
HAYWARD AV
- SMTO 94401 749-A2
HAYWARD CT
- BURL 94010 728-B6
HAYWARD DR
2500 BURL 94010 728-C6
HAZEL AV
- MLBR 94030 728-A4
- RDWC 94061 770-B7
300 SBRN 94066 727-H1
500 SBRN 94066 707-H7
HAZEL LN
- SMCo 94060 868-J4
HAZEL ST
- MLPK 94025 770-J7
HAZELWOOD DR
- SSF 94080 707-F5
HAZELWOOD WY
2500 EPA 94303 791-B1
2500 EPA 94303 771-B7
HEACOX RD
19600 SMCo 94028 830-C6
HEAD ST
- SF 94112 687-C2
200 SF 94132 687-C2
800 SF 94127 687-C2
HEATH CT
- DALY 94015 707-B2
HEATHCLIFF DR
300 PCFA 94044 707-B3
HEATHER CT
600 PCFA 94044 707-B4
HEATHER DR
- ATN 94027 790-F1
800 SCAR 94070 769-F4
HEATHER LN
100 PA 94303 791-C4
400 SMTO 94403 749-B6
2500 SBRN 94066 707-E6
HEATHER PL
- HIL 94010 748-E5
- MLBR 94030 728-A2
HEATHER RD
800 SMCo 94015 687-B5
HEATHER WY
300 SSF 94080 707-G2
HEDGE RD
100 MLPK 94025 770-G7
HEIDI LN
- MLBR 94030 728-A4
HELEN DR
200 MLBR 94030 728-A3
500 MLBR 94030 727-H3
HELEN PL
- MLPK 94025 790-F5
HELENA WY
2000 SMCo 94061 790-A4
HELENE CT
1800 SMTO 94401 729-C7
1800 SMTO 94401 749-C1
HELLER ST
200 RDWC 94063 770-B6

STREET Block City ZIP Pg-Grid

HELM LN
1000 FCTY 94404 749-H4
HEMLOCK AV
- RDWC 94061 770-B7
300 RDWC 94061 790-B1
400 SSF 94080 707-H1
500 MLBR 94030 728-B3
1400 SMTO 94401 749-C1
HEMLOCK ST
100 SCAR 94070 769-G4
HEMPSTEAD PL
1700 RDWC 94061 790-A3
HENDERSON AV
1000 MLPK 94025 790-J1
1100 MLPK 94025 770-J7
HENDERSON PL
- MLPK 94025 770-J7
HENRIK IBSEN RD
- SMCo 94062 788-J5
HENRY CT
- EPA 94303 791-B2
HENRY PL
- MLBR 94030 728-A3
HENSLEY AV
600 SBRN 94066 707-H6
HERCULES LN
800 FCTY 94404 749-H1
HERITAGE CT
- ATN 94027 790-E1
- BLMT 94002 768-J2
HERITAGE ST
- SSF 94014 707-J1
HERKNER RD
- RDWC 94063 770-D2
HERMAN ST
1000 SBRN 94066 707-J5
HERMOSA AV
- MLBR 94030 728-B3
400 SMCo 94019 767-D4
1200 PCFA 94044 726-H5
HERMOSA LN
- SSF 94080 707-F3
HERMOSA PL
- MLPK 94025 790-F5
HERMOSA RD
- SMCo 94037 746-J5
- SMCo 94062 769-F6
HERMOSA ST
- SBRN 94066 707-J6
HERMOSA WY
300 MLPK 94025 790-E4
HERSCHEL ST
1700 SMTO 94403 749-D2
HESKETH CT
- MLPK 94025 790-E5
HESKETH DR
- MLPK 94025 790-E5
HESS RD
1400 RDWC 94061 770-B7
1400 RDWC 94061 790-B1
HESTER AV
2000 SF 94134 688-A2
HEWITT DR
1000 SCAR 94070 769-F5
HIAWATHA AV
100 PCFA 94044 727-B2
HIBBERT CT
- PCFA 94044 707-A3
HIBISCUS CT
400 EPA 94303 791-D2
HIBISCUS DR
- SSF 94080 707-E2
HICKEY BLVD
100 PCFA 94044 707-A3
100 SSF 94080 707-B1
300 DALY 94015 707-B1
HICKORY AV
1600 SBRN 94066 707-G7
HICKORY LN
100 SMTO 94403 749-C6
HICKORY PL
700 SSF 94080 707-J2
HIDDEN TER
- HIL 94010 728-D7
HIDDEN WY
- SMCo 94062 769-F6
HIDDEN CREEK RD
- SMCo 94074 828-F7
HIDDEN OAKS DR
1100 MLPK 94025 790-E5
HIDDEN VALLEY DR
- SMCo 94070 769-E4
HIDDEN VALLEY LN
- PTLV 94028 810-A5
- WDSD 94062 810-A5
HIGATE DR
100 DALY 94015 687-A6
100 DALY 94015 707-A1
HIGGINS PL
3000 PA 94303 791-E5
HIGGINS WY
1500 SMCo - 726-H5
1500 PCFA 94044 726-H5
HIGGINS CANYON RD
300 HMBY 94019 787-G3
300 SMCo 94019 787-G3
1700 SMCo 94019 788-A4
HIGH RD
800 WDSD 94062 789-J5
1000 WDSD 94062 790-A5
HIGH ST
200 PA 94301 790-H4
2100 PA 94301 791-B7
HIGHCREST LN
1200 SSF 94080 707-H1
HIGHGATE AV
2800 BLMT 94002 749-B7
HIGH GATE LN
- HIL 94010 728-F7
HIGHLAND AV
- BURL 94010 728-G7
- DALY 94015 686-J6
- SCAR 94070 769-E3
- SMCo 94019 767-C1
- SSF 94080 707-J1
300 SMTO 94401 728-G7
500 HMBY 94019 767-F7
600 SMTO 94401 748-H1
3500 RDWC 94062 789-H1
HIGHLAND CT
1200 SCAR 94070 769-E3
HIGHLAND DR
3100 SBRN 94066 707-B6
HIGHLAND TER
100 WDSD 94062 789-G5

HIGHLANDS CT
- BLMT 94002 769-B3
HIGHVIEW CT
600 SMTO 94403 749-B7
HIGHVIEW DR
4200 SMTO 94403 749-B7
4200 SMTO 94403 769-B1
HIGHWAY Rt#-84
- FRMT 94555 771-G1
- MLPK 94025 771-B5
- MLPK 94303 771-D4
HIGHWAY RD
1400 BURL 94010 728-D5
HIGUERA AV
- SF 94132 687-A1
HILBAR LN
500 PA 94303 791-C4
HILDEBRAND RD
- SMCo 94020 829-E7
HILL AV
- SCAR 94070 769-F5
700 SSF 94080 707-G4
1300 MLPK 94025 770-J7
S HILL BLVD
- SF 94112 687-G2
300 DALY 94014 687-F3
HILL RD
- SMCo 94060 867-G3
HILL ST
- PCFA 94044 726-J2
- DALY 94014 687-C5
- SMCo 94037 746-G5
- SMCo 94014 687-C5
800 BLMT 94002 769-E1
HILL WY
300 SCAR 94070 769-G5
HILLARY LN
- SMCo 94061 790-B4
HILLBARN CT
4200 SMTO 94403 749-D7
HILLBROOK DR
- PTLV 94028 810-D6
HILLCREST BLVD
- SMCo - 727-J5
- MLBR 94030 728-A4
1100 MLBR 94030 727-J5
E HILLCREST BLVD
- MLBR 94030 728-B3
HILLCREST CT
- SSF 94080 707-F3
HILLCREST DR
- SMCo - 768-C3
- DALY 94014 687-C3
400 RDWC 94062 769-G7
400 RDWC 94062 789-H1
400 SMCo 94062 769-G7
3400 BLMT 94002 769-A1
HILLCREST RD
- SCAR 94070 769-F2
400 SMTO 94402 748-F1
500 SMCo 94062 769-G7
500 RDWC 94062 769-G7
HILLCREST WY
400 SMCo 94062 789-E2
HILLER ST
100 BLMT 94002 749-E7
1000 BLMT 94002 769-F1
HILLMAN AV
1700 BLMT 94002 749-D7
1900 BLMT 94002 769-C1
HILLSBOROUGH BLVD
300 HIL 94010 748-F1
300 SMTO 94402 748-F2
800 HIL 94010 728-F7
HILLSDALE AV
- DALY 94015 687-B3
E HILLSDALE BLVD
- SMTO 94403 749-D5
600 FCTY 94404 749-F1
W HILLSDALE BLVD
1700 SMTO 94402 748-J6
1900 SMTO 94403 748-J6
2300 SMTO 94403 749-A6
HILLSDALE CT
- SMTO 94403 749-D5
HILLSDALE PL
- SMTO 94403 749-B6
HILLSDALE WY
200 SMCo 94062 769-F7
200 SMCo 94062 789-E1
HILLSIDE AV
100 SMCo 94025 790-C6
HILLSIDE BLVD
- DALY 94014 687-D4
100 SSF 94080 707-J1
100 SSF 94080 708-A2
1000 SMCo 94014 687-D4
1300 CLMA 94014 687-D6
1400 SMCo 94014 707-G1
1700 CLMA 94014 707-G1
1700 CLMA 94080 687-D6
1700 CLMA 94080 707-G1
HILLSIDE CIR
1300 BURL 94010 728-C6
HILLSIDE CT
100 WDSD 94062 790-A5
3700 SMTO 94403 749-B6
HILLSIDE DR
100 WDSD 94062 789-G5
200 PCFA 94044 727-A2
1500 BURL 94010 728-D6
1500 SMCo 94010 728-D6
HILLSIDE LN
3100 BURL 94010 728-A7
3100 SMCo 94010 728-A7
HILLSIDE LP N
- CLMA 94014 687-E6
HILLSIDE LP S
- CLMA 94014 687-E6
HILLSIDE RD
500 RDWC 94062 789-G1
500 SMCo 94062 789-G1
HILLTOP DR
- RDWC 94062 769-G6
- SCAR 94070 769-G5
HILLTOP RD
- SMTO 94402 748-H1
HILLVIEW AV
- RDWC 94062 769-H6
HILLVIEW CT
- BURL 94010 728-C7
- DALY 94015 686-J4
HILLVIEW DR
- SMCo - 768-C3
1100 MLPK 94025 790-E5

HILLVIEW PL
1300 MLPK 94025 790-E5
HILLWAY DR
300 SMCo 94062 789-G1
HILO WY
300 PCFA 94044 707-A6
HILTON AV
100 SSF 94080 707-D1
HILTON LN
100 PCFA 94044 706-J6
HILTON ST
100 RDWC 94063 770-B6
HILTON WY
100 PCFA 94044 706-J6
HIMMEL AV
1100 SMCo 94061 790-B3
HINCKLEY RD
800 BURL 94010 728-D4
HINMAN RD
- RDWC 94063 770-D2
HINTON RANCH RD
- PCFA 94044 727-A4
HOBART AV
- SMTO 94402 749-A3
200 SMTO 94402 748-J3
HOBART ST
500 MLPK 94025 790-E5
HOBART HEIGHTS RD
100 WDSD 94062 789-H6
HOFFMAN ST
- DALY 94014 687-D6
- CLMA 94014 687-D6
HOLBROOK LN
- ATN 94027 790-E1
HOLDEN CT
- PTLV 94028 810-D6
HOLIDAY CT
- PCFA 94044 706-J2
- PCFA 94044 707-A2
HOLLAND ST
100 EPA 94303 791-A1
2300 SMTO 94403 749-D4
HOLLISTER AV
900 SF 94124 688-B1
HOLLOWAY AV
- SF 94112 687-C1
900 SF 94132 687-B1
1000 SF 94127 687-C1
HOLLY AV
200 SSF 94080 707-F2
1600 SBRN 94066 707-G7
1700 MLPK 94025 790-E6
HOLLY CT
- HIL 94010 748-D1
HOLLY RD
700 BLMT 94002 769-E1
HOLLY ST
600 RDWC 94065 769-G2
600 SCAR 94070 769-G2
HOLLYBURNE AV
1000 MLPK 94025 790-J1
1100 MLPK 94025 770-J7
1400 MLPK 94025 771-A7
HOLLY HILL CT
700 RDWC 94061 789-H2
HOLLY OAK DR
700 PA 94303 791-D7
HOLLYWOOD CT
- SF 94112 687-F2
HOLYOKE ST
- SF 94134 688-A1
HOME RD
- WDSD 94062 809-H4
HOMEPLACE CT
- HIL 94010 748-E2
HOMER AV
100 PA 94301 790-J5
500 PA 94301 791-A4
HOMER LN
- SMCo 94025 810-E1
HOMEWOOD AV
1200 SMTO 94403 748-J7
E HOMEWOOD PL
- MLPK 94025 790-H3
HOMS CT
- HIL 94010 748-H2
HONEYSUCKLE LN
- SCAR 94070 769-C4
HOODS POINT WY
- SMCo 94402 768-G1
HOOPER WY
- WDSD 94062 809-G1
HOOVER AV
1500 BURL 94010 728-C6
HOOVER ST
1200 MLPK 94025 790-F3
3000 RDWC 94063 770-E6
HOPE CT
- RDWC 94061 770-A7
HOPKINS AV
500 RDWC 94063 770-A5
1000 RDWC 94063 769-J6
1000 RDWC 94062 769-J6
1100 PA 94301 791-B5
HOPKINS ST
500 MLPK 94025 790-G3
HORGAN AV
- RDWC 94061 790-B2
HORIZON WY
300 PCFA 94044 707-B3
HORNET AV
200 SSF 94066 707-J5
HORSESHOE BEND
- PTLV 94028 830-C1
HORSESHOE CT
- HIL 94010 748-H4
HOSKINS CT
- SCIC 94305 790-J7
HOSMER CT
300 SCAR 94070 769-D7
HOSMER ST
2600 SMTO 94403 749-D4
HOSPITAL PZ
- MLPK 94025 790-J2
HOUNDSRIDGE LN
- SMTO 94402 748-H6
HOWARD AV
- BURL 94010 728-H6
900 SCAR 94070 769-H6
1000 SMTO 94401 728-H6
HOWARD CT
3800 SSF 94080 707-C4
HOWARD ST
1100 MLPK 94025 770-J7

HOWARD WY
- ATN 94027 790-E3
HOWE ST
700 SMTO 94401 749-B1
HOWELLS ST
1100 SMCo 94037 746-H5
HOWLAND ST
200 RDWC 94063 769-J5
200 RDWC 94063 770-A5
HOWLAND HILL LN
- SMCo 94010 728-B7
HOWTH ST
- SF 94112 687-E1
HUBBARD AV
200 SMCo 94062 769-G6
HUCKLEBERRY AV
300 SMCo 94062 788-G5
HUCKLEBERRY CT
- BSBN 94005 687-H4
HUCKLEBERRY TR
- SMCo 94062 788-H5
HUDSON CT
1100 SCAR 94070 769-E6
HUDSON ST
- RDWC 94062 769-J6
500 RDWC 94062 770-A7
600 RDWC 94061 770-A7
1200 RDWC 94061 790-B1
HUDSON BAY ST
200 FCTY 94404 749-F6
HULL AV
1700 SMCo 94061 790-A3
HULL DR
1200 SCAR 94070 769-F2
HULL LN
1000 FCTY 94404 749-H4
HULME CT
- SCIC 94305 790-J7
HUMBOLDT CT
- BSBN 94005 688-B7
- PCFA 94044 727-C5
HUMBOLDT RD
- BSBN 94005 688-A6
HUMBOLDT ST
- BURL 94010 728-H6
- SMTO 94401 728-H6
N HUMBOLDT ST
- SMTO 94401 728-J6
- SMTO 94401 729-A7
S HUMBOLDT ST
- SMTO 94401 729-A7
- SMTO 94401 749-A1
400 SMTO 94402 749-A1
HUNT DR
1600 BURL 94010 728-A6
HUNTER ST
2700 EPA 94303 771-B7
HUNTERS POINT EXWY
- SF 94124 688-C2
HUNTINGTON AV
200 SBRN 94066 707-J7
200 SBRN 94066 727-J1
200 SBRN 94066 728-A1
1300 SSF 94080 707-H4
2800 SMCo 94063 770-C7
HUNTINGTON AV E
100 SBRN 94066 707-J5
HUNTINGTON DR
- DALY 94015 687-A6
HURLINGAME AV
400 SMCo 94063 770-D6
HURLINGHAM AV
400 SMTO 94402 728-G7
400 SMTO 94402 748-G1
HURON AV
- DALY 94014 687-E2
100 SMTO 94401 729-A7
400 SF 94112 687-E2
HURON CT
- SMTO 94401 729-A7
HUSSEY ST
- SF 94124 688-E1
HUTCHINSON AV
900 PA 94301 791-B4
HYDE CT
- DALY 94015 707-D3
HYDE ST
- RDWC 94062 769-J5
HYDE PARK AV
100 SMCo 94070 769-D4
100 SCAR 94070 769-D4
HYDRA LN
700 FCTY 94404 749-E4

I

I ST
200 SF 94124 688-E1
IDA DR
700 SSF 94080 707-G2
IDAHO CT
2000 RDWC 94061 790-A3
N IDAHO ST
- SMTO 94401 728-J6
500 SMTO 94401 729-A7
S IDAHO ST
400 SMTO 94402 749-B1
800 SMTO 94401 729-A7
800 SMTO 94401 749-A1
IDLEWILD CT
- PCFA 94044 707-B3
IDLEWOOD CT
- SSF 94080 707-H3
IDLEWOOD DR
- SSF 94080 707-H3
IDYLLWILD AV
1800 SMCo 94061 790-B3
IDYLLWILD CT
300 SMCo 94061 790-B4
IGNACIO ST
- SF 94124 688-C2
ILLINOIS ST
2400 EPA 94303 791-C1
2500 EPA 94303 771-C7
IMPERIAL DR
200 PCFA 94044 707-B2
IMPERIAL WY
300 DALY 94015 707-C1
INA CT
- SF 94112 687-H1
INDEPENDENCE DR
100 MLPK 94025 770-G6
INDIAN AV
600 SMTO 94401 728-J7

INDIAN CRSG
- PTLV 94028 830-C1
INDIAN DR
2400 PA 94303 791-D5
INDIO DR
100 SSF 94080 707-E3
INDUSTRIAL AV
800 PA 94303 791-G7
INDUSTRIAL RD
400 SCAR 94070 769-G1
1400 RDWC 94063 769-H2
1400 SCAR 94063 769-H2
1500 SMCo 94002 769-G1
INDUSTRIAL WY
- BSBN 94005 688-A4
100 SSF 94080 708-A3
1300 RDWC 94063 770-A4
1600 RDWC 94063 769-J4
INGALLS ST
2500 SF 94124 688-C1
INGERSON AV
700 SF 94124 688-B1
INGLEWOOD LN
- ATN 94027 790-D3
INGOLD RD
- BURL 94010 728-C4
INNER CIR
- RDWC 94062 769-H7
INNISFREE CIR
300 DALY 94015 707-C1
INNISFREE DR
300 DALY 94015 707-C1
INTREPID LN
800 RDWC 94065 750-C6
INVERNESS DR
300 PCFA 94044 707-B3
900 SCAR 94070 769-G2
INVERNESS RD
- HMBY 94019 787-F5
INVERNESS WY
- HIL 94010 748-F4
INYO CT
100 SBRN 94066 707-E7
INYO PL
- SMCo 94061 790-B4
INYO ST
- BSBN 94005 688-A6
IOWA DR
400 SMTO 94402 748-H3
IPSWICH LN
1800 DALY 94014 687-F3
IRENE CT
100 BLMT 94002 749-D7
IRIS CT
- SMTO 94401 729-A6
- SSF 94080 707-G1
800 PCFA 94044 726-H5
IRIS LN
- SMCo 94019 787-G5
- MLPK 94025 770-H7
- SCAR 94070 769-C4
IRIS ST
- RDWC 94062 769-J6
500 RDWC 94062 770-A7
600 RDWC 94061 770-A7
IRIS WY
100 PA 94303 791-C4
IRISH RIDGE RD
100 SMCo 94019 808-D3
IROQUOIS TR
- PTLV 94028 810-B6
IRVING AV
- ATN 94027 770-F7
- ATN 94027 790-F1
IRVING ST
- SSF 94080 707-J1
200 SMTO 94402 748-H3
1000 SMCo 94037 746-G5
IRVINGTON ST
100 DALY 94014 687-D3
IRWIN CT
700 HIL 94010 728-E7
IRWIN DR
800 HIL 94010 728-E7
IRWIN PL
100 MLBR 94030 728-C4
IRWIN ST
1000 BLMT 94002 749-F7
1000 BLMT 94002 769-F1
ISABEL AL
- MLBR 94030 728-B3
ISABELLA AV
- ATN 94027 790-E2
100 SMCo 94019 767-B3
ISABELLA RD
500 SMCo 94019 767-B2
ISABELLE AV
2000 SMTO 94403 749-A4
ISABELLE CIR
- CLMA 94014 707-E1
ISABELLE WY
- CLMA 94014 707-E1
ISLAND DR
100 PA 94301 791-B3
400 RDWC 94065 749-G6
ISLAND PKWY
- RDWC 94065 749-F6
300 BLMT 94002 749-F6
ISLAND PL
500 RDWC 94065 749-H6
ISLEFORD LN
200 RDWC 94065 749-J3
ITALY AV
- SF 94112 687-F1
IVY AV
- PCFA 94044 727-A2
400 SMCo 94062 788-H5
IVY DR
200 MLPK 94025 770-J7
600 MLPK 94025 771-A7
IVY LN
1900 PA 94303 791-C4
IVY ST
1300 SMCo 94037 746-H5
1700 SMTO 94402 749-A3
IVY WY
- SSF 94080 707-H3

J

J ST
- SF 94124 688-D1
JACARANDA CIR
700 HIL 94010 748-D1

JACARANDA LN
- PA 94306 791-B7
JACINTO LN
- SSF 94080 707-E3
JACKLING DR
900 HIL 94010 728-D7
1200 BURL 94010 728-D7
JACKSON AV
100 RDWC 94061 770-A7
JACKSON DR
500 PA 94303 791-C4
JACKSON ST
300 SMTO 94402 748-H3
JACQUELINE CT
- DALY 94014 687-J4
JACQUELINE LN
- DALY 94014 687-J4
JACQUELINE PL
- SMCo 94062 769-G7
JAMAICA ST
900 FCTY 94404 749-F5
JAMES AV
- ATN 94027 770-F7
- ATN 94027 790-F1
- RDWC 94063 770-A6
- RDWC 94062 770-A6
600 RDWC 94062 769-H7
2000 RDWC 94062 789-H1
2000 SMCo 94062 789-H1
JAMES CT
100 SSF 94080 707-G1
1300 SMTO 94401 749-B1
JAMESTON LN
- DALY 94014 687-F3
JAMESTOWN AV
700 SF 94124 688-B1
JAMESTOWN AVEX
100 SF 94124 688-C2
E JAMIE CT
400 SSF 94080 708-C4
JAMIE LN
800 EPA 94303 791-C1
JANE DR
100 WDSD 94062 789-G5
JANICE WY
3400 PA 94303 791-E6
J ARTHUR YOUNGER FRWY Rt#-92
- BLMT - 768-H2
- FCTY - 729-G7
- FCTY - 749-F2
- HIL - 748-J5
- SMCo - 748-J5
- SMCo - 768-H2
- SMTO - 748-J5
- SMTO - 749-A4
- SMTO - 768-H2
JARVIS WY
2000 LAH 94304 810-H4
JASMINE CT
- MLBR 94030 728-A3
JASMINE ST
1400 SMTO 94402 749-A3
JASMINE WY
100 EPA 94303 791-D3
JEFFERSON AV
400 RDWC 94063 770-B6
1200 RDWC 94062 770-A7
1200 RDWC 94061 770-B6
1900 RDWC 94062 769-J7
1900 RDWC 94061 769-J7
2500 RDWC 94062 789-H1
2500 RDWC 94061 789-H1
3800 SMCo 94062 789-H1
4100 WDSD 94062 789-F3
JEFFERSON CT
- MLPK 94025 770-H6
800 SMTO 94401 728-H7
3700 RDWC 94061 789-G2
JEFFERSON DR
100 MLPK 94025 770-G6
500 PA 94303 791-C4
JEFFERSON ST
- SSF 94080 707-H1
JENEVEIN AV
- SBRN 94066 727-H1
500 SBRN 94066 707-H7
JENKINS CT
100 SCIC 94305 790-J7
JENNA LN
- HMBY 94019 787-F1
JENNIFER CT
- DALY 94014 687-J3
JENNINGS CT
3500 SF 94124 688-B1
JENNINGS LN
- ATN 94027 790-D1
JENNINGS ST
2700 SF 94124 688-B1
JERVIS AV
1100 EPA 94303 791-A1
JETER ST
- RDWC 94062 769-J6
JETTY WY
- RDWC 94065 750-A5
JEWELL PL
- HIL 94010 748-E3
J HART CLINTON DR
1300 SMTO 94401 729-B7
1500 SMTO 94401 749-C1
1700 SMTO 94404 749-C1
JIB CT
100 HMBY 94019 767-F6
JIBSTAY LN
500 FCTY 94404 749-J1
JOANNE DR
600 SMTO 94402 749-B3
JOAQUIN DR
500 SSF 94080 707-E2
JOAQUIN RD
- SMCo 94028 830-D4
JODY CT
- SMTO 94402 749-B3
JOHN DALY BLVD
300 DALY 94014 687-A3
400 DALY 94015 687-A3
800 DALY 94015 686-J4
JOHN F FORAN FRWY I-280
- SF - 687-E2
JOHN F SHELLEY DR
- SF 94134 687-H1
JOHN GLENN CIR
- DALY 94015 707-C3

JOHN MUIR DR
100 SF 94132 687-A2
100 SMCo 94015 687-A2
500 SF 94132 686-J1
JOHN PAPAN CT
- DALY 94015 707-B2
JOHNSON AV
400 PCFA 94044 707-A4
JOHNSON ST
900 RDWC 94061 770-A7
1000 RDWC 94061 790-A1
1100 MLPK 94025 790-E4
JOHNSTON ST
300 HMBY 94019 787-F2
JONES CT
1000 RDWC 94063 770-E6
JONES GULCH RD
- SMCo 94020 849-D5
- SMCo 94021 849-D5
JORDAN PL
- PA 94303 791-B4
JORDAN ST
900 SMCo 94037 746-G5
JORDAN WY
200 PA 94304 790-G6
JOSEPH DR
700 SSF 94080 707-G2
JOSEPHA AV
- SF 94132 687-B1
JOSIAH AV
- SF 94112 687-E1
JOSSELYN LN
100 WDSD 94062 789-E6
JOY AV
- BSBN 94005 688-B7
JOYCE RD
- HIL 94010 748-F5
JUAN BAUTISTA CIR
- SF 94132 687-B1
JUANITA AV
100 PCFA 94044 727-B2
300 MLBR 94030 727-J2
1100 BURL 94010 728-E5
JUBILEE CT
- SMCo 94061 790-A3
JUDITH CT
- HMBY 94019 767-E6
JUDSON DR
400 SMCo 94020 829-F7
JUDSON PL
- PCFA 94044 727-B6
JUDSON ST
1000 BLMT 94002 749-F7
JULES AV
- SF 94112 687-D1
JULIA CT
- BLMT 94002 749-D7
JULIANA AV
- SMCo 94038 746-F6
JULIE LN
2300 SSF 94080 707-D4
JUNE HOLLOW RD
700 SMCo 94037 746-G5
JUNIOR TER
- SF 94112 687-F1
JUNIPER AV
200 SSF 94080 708-A2
200 SSF 94080 707-J2
1600 SBRN 94066 707-G7
JUNIPER DR
- ATN 94027 790-G1
JUNIPER ST
2800 SMTO 94403 749-B5
JUNIPERO AV
1100 RDWC 94061 789-J1
1100 RDWC 94061 790-A1
JUNIPERO SERRA BLVD
400 SSF 94080 707-C1
800 SF 94127 687-C1
900 SF 94132 687-C1
1800 DALY 94014 687-C4
2300 DALY 94015 687-C4
3600 CLMA 94014 687-C6
4200 DALY 94015 707-C1
5000 CLMA 94014 707-C1
JUNIPERO SERRA BLVD Rt#-G5
- MLPK 94025 790-F7
100 SCIC 94305 790-F7
100 SCIC 94304 790-F7
100 SCIC 94305 810-G1
100 SCIC 94304 810-G1
JUNIPERO SERRA BLVD Rt#-1
1100 SF 94132 687-C1
JUNIPERO SERRA FRWY I-280
- DALY - 687-C7
- DALY - 707-C2
- HIL - 748-D4
- LAH - 810-F3
- MLBR - 727-G3
- MLBR - 728-A7
- MLPK - 810-C1
- PA - 810-F3
- SBRN - 707-C2
- SBRN - 727-G3
- SCIC - 810-F3
- SMCo - 727-G3
- SMCo - 728-A7
- SMCo - 748-D4
- SMCo - 768-F1
- SMCo - 769-A4
- SMCo - 789-C1
- SMCo - 790-A6
- SMCo - 810-C1
- SSF - 707-C2
- WDSD - 789-G4
- WDSD - 790-A6
JUNIPERO SERRA FRWY Rt#-1
- DALY - 687-B3
- SF - 687-B3
JUNO LN
800 FCTY 94404 749-F4
JUPITER CT
800 FCTY 94404 749-E3

K

KAINS AV
100 SBRN 94066 707-G7
KALMIA ST
1400 SMTO 94402 749-A3

STREET	Block	City	ZIP	Pg-Grid
KAMMERER CT	-	HIL	94010	728-F7
KANDLE WY	1100	RDWC	94061	790-B1
KANOFF AV	-	SMCo	94037	746-G4
KANSAS ST	1600	RDWC	94061	790-A2
KAREN CT	-	BURL	94010	728-B5
KAREN RD	-	SMCo	94002	749-F7
	-	SMCo	94002	769-F1
KAREN WY	100	ATN	94027	790-B5
KATAOKA CT	-	SMCo	94062	789-G1
KATHERINE AV	500	RDWC	94062	769-J7
KATHLEEN CT	-	PCFA	94044	727-B5
KATHRYN AV	100	SMCo	94019	767-C2
KATHRYNE AV	700	SMTO	94401	749-B1
KAUFFMANN CT	400	SSF	94080	708-C3
KAVANAUGH DR	1300	EPA	94303	771-B7
	1300	MLPK	94025	771-B7
KAVANAUGH WY	200	PCFA	94044	707-B3
KAYNYNE ST	800	RDWC	94063	770-C6
	800	SMCo	94063	770-C6
KEARNEY ST	-	SSF	94080	707-H1
KEATS AV	700	SSF	94080	707-D2
KEBET RIDGE RD	-	SMCo	94062	809-F5
KEDITH ST	1000	BLMT	94002	749-F7
KEEFE CT	100	SBRN	94066	727-G1
KEEL CT	100	HMBY	94019	767-E6
KEEL LN	400	RDWC	94065	749-H6
KEELSON CIR	500	RDWC	94065	749-J6
KEHOE AV	400	HMBY	94019	767-E7
	1200	SMTO	94401	749-C2
	1800	SMTO	94403	749-D1
KEITH AV	300	PCFA	94044	727-B2
KEITH ST	-	SF	94124	688-B1
KELLOCH AV	100	SF	94134	687-J2
KELLOGG AV	100	PA	94301	791-A5
KELLY AV	-	HMBY	94019	787-E1
KELLY CT	-	MLPK	94025	771-A7
KELLY LN	-	MLBR	94030	728-A5
KELLY ST	600	HMBY	94019	787-F1
	1700	SMTO	94403	749-D2
KELMORE ST	500	SMCo	94038	746-F6
KELTON AV	100	SCAR	94070	769-H5
KELTON CT	-	SMTO	94403	749-B7
KEMPTON AV	-	SF	94132	687-C2
KENDALL CT	-	PCFA	94044	727-B4
KENILWORTH RD	1200	HIL	94010	748-F3
KENMAR WY	-	BURL	94010	728-C7
KENMORE WY	100	WDSD	94062	789-J5
KENNEDY PL	-	MLBR	94030	727-J4
KENNETH DR	3300	PA	94303	791-E6
KENNY AL	-	SF	94112	687-F1
KENRY WY	2200	SSF	94080	707-E5
KENSINGTON AV	400	SBRN	94066	727-J1
KENSINGTON RD	2700	RDWC	94061	789-J3
	2700	RDWC	94061	790-A3
KENT AV	700	SCAR	94070	769-D5
KENT CT	-	DALY	94015	707-B1
	-	SMTO	94403	749-C4
	100	SBRN	94066	727-F1
KENT PL	-	MLPK	94025	790-H3
	-	PA	94301	791-B4
KENT RD	-	PCFA	94044	726-G4
KENT ST	2200	SMTO	94403	749-C4
KENT WY	3800	SSF	94080	707-D4
KENTFIELD AV	1300	RDWC	94061	790-A2
KENTON AV	-	SCAR	94070	769-E3
KENTUCKY AV	500	SMTO	94402	748-H3
KENTUCKY ST	1600	RDWC	94061	790-A2
KENWOOD AV	3600	SMTO	94403	749-B6
KENWOOD DR	500	MLPK	94025	790-G4
KENWOOD WY	200	SSF	94080	707-G5
KEONCREST DR	500	SSF	94080	707-D2
KERRI CT	100	SMCo	94061	790-A4
KESTREL CT	-	BSBN	94005	687-J5
KESWICK LN	400	SMTO	94402	749-B3
KETCH CT	100	FCTY	94404	749-G4
KETTERING CT	3400	SMTO	94403	749-A6
KEY AV	900	SF	94124	688-B1
KILCONWAY LN	2700	SSF	94080	707-C4
KILLARNEY LN	1100	BURL	94010	728-C5
KILLDEER CT	200	FCTY	94404	749-G1
KILROY WY	-	ATN	94027	790-B4
KIMBALL WY	100	SSF	94080	708-B4
KIMBERLY WY	3300	SMTO	94403	749-E5
KIMMIE CT	-	BLMT	94002	769-C2
KINDER LN	-	HIL	94010	728-C7
KING CT	-	SMTO	94403	749-C6
KING DR	300	SSF	94080	707-E3
	500	DALY	94015	707-C3
	1100	PCFA	94044	707-C3
KING LN	700	FCTY	94404	749-G4
	3800	SMTO	94403	749-C6
KING ST	-	RDWC	94062	769-H6
	900	RDWC	94061	770-A7
	1100	RDWC	94061	790-A1
	1600	BLMT	94002	769-F2
KINGRIDGE DR	3600	SMTO	94403	749-B7
KINGS CT	100	SCAR	94070	769-D5
KINGS LN	1400	PA	94303	791-B4
	2000	SMCo	94402	768-H1
KINGS RD	-	BSBN	94005	688-A6
KINGS CANYON WY	-	PCFA	94044	727-B5
KINGSFORD LN	200	RDWC	94061	790-B2
KINGSLEY AV	100	PA	94301	790-J5
	200	PA	94301	791-A5
KINGS MOUNTAIN RD	100	WDSD	94062	789-D6
	600	SMCo	94062	789-A7
KINGSTON AV	2200	SBRN	94066	707-F7
	2200	SBRN	94066	727-G1
KINGSTON RD	500	BLMT	94002	749-E7
N KINGSTON ST	-	SMTO	94401	729-A6
S KINGSTON ST	-	SMTO	94401	729-A7
KINGSWOOD CIR	-	HIL	94010	748-E5
KINGSWOOD CT	1400	HIL	94010	748-F5
KINGSWOOD DR	1500	HIL	94010	748-E5
KIOWA CT	-	PTLV	94028	810-C6
KIP LN	3300	BURL	94010	748-B1
KIPLING AV	800	SSF	94080	707-D2
KIPLING ST	200	PA	94301	790-J4
	2600	PA	94306	791-C6
KIRBY PL	-	PA	94301	791-B4
KIRKWOOD CT	-	EPA	94303	771-B7
KIRKWOOD WY	-	SCAR	94070	769-E3
KITTIE LN	-	BLMT	94002	769-D2
KLAMATH AV	2000	SMTO	94403	749-C2
KLAMATH DR	1000	MLPK	94025	790-C7
KLAMATH ST	200	BSBN	94005	688-A6
KNAPP CT	-	SMTO	94403	749-B5
KNIGHTSBRIDGE LN	-	RDWC	94061	790-B2
KNIGHTWOOD LN	-	HIL	94010	728-D7
KNOLL CIR	100	SSF	94080	707-G3
KNOLL DR	600	SCAR	94070	769-F4
KNOLLCREST RD	-	HIL	94010	748-E4
KNOLL VISTA	-	SMCo	94020	829-F7
	-	ATN	94027	790-B6
KNOT LN	-	RDWC	94065	750-C4
KNOTT CT	-	SF	94112	687-F2
KNOWLES AV	-	DALY	94014	687-C3
KOHALA AV	300	PCFA	94044	707-A6
KORBEL WY	-	BLMT	94002	749-D7
	-	BLMT	94002	769-D1
KRAKEN LN	-	RDWC	94065	750-B3
KRAMER LN	-	SMCo	94063	790-D1
KRISTA LN	-	SCAR	94070	769-G6
KRISTIE LN	2300	SSF	94080	707-D4
KRISTIN CT	100	SMCo	94402	748-H6
KRYSTALLOS LN	400	RDWC	94065	749-J3
KYNE RD	-	SMCo	94060	868-H2

L

STREET	Block	City	ZIP	Pg-Grid
LA BARTHE LN	-	SCAR	94070	769-F6
LABURNUM RD	-	ATN	94027	790-F1
LA CANADA PTH	-	SMCo	94010	728-B7
LA CANADA RD	1200	HIL	94010	748-F3
LA CASA AV	200	SMTO	94403	749-B7
LACEWING LN	-	RDWC	94065	750-B3
LACOUR WY	300	SMCo	94061	790-B3
LA CROSSE AV	100	SSF	94080	707-E2
LA CRUZ AV	-	MLBR	94030	728-B4
LA CUESTA DR	100	SMCo	94010	728-B7
	200	SMCo	94028	810-E3
LA CUESTA RD	1000	HIL	94010	748-F3
LA CUMBRE CT	-	HIL	94010	748-F2
LA CUMBRE RD	1200	HIL	94010	748-F3
LADERA WY	600	PCFA	94044	726-J4
	1100	BLMT	94002	769-D2
LAFAYETTE ST	1000	SMTO	94403	749-C4
LAGO	1500	SMTO	94403	749-E4
LAGOON DR	-	RDWC	94065	749-G7
LAGOON WY	100	BSBN	94005	688-B5
LA GRANADA LN	100	SMCo	94038	766-H2
LA GRANDE AV	100	SMCo	94038	766-G1
	100	SMCo	94038	746-G7
	300	SF	94112	687-H1
LAGUNA AV	900	BURL	94010	728-E5
S LAGUNA AV	-	SMCo	94038	746-F6
LAGUNA CIR	900	FCTY	94404	749-F4
LAGUNA DR	-	SMCo	94020	849-E1
LAGUNITA DR	500	SCIC	94305	790-G7
LA HONDA RD	1300	HIL	94010	748-E2
LA HONDA RD Rt#-84	-	SMCo	94074	828-A6
	300	WDSD	94062	809-F5
	400	SMCo	94062	809-F5
	1600	SMCo	94062	829-F3
	1700	SMCo	94020	829-F3
	1700	SMCo	94020	809-F7
	1700	WDSD	94020	809-F5
	4100	SMCo	94074	848-H1
	4300	SMCo	94020	849-A1
	4300	SMCo	94062	849-A1
	4500	SMCo	94074	849-A1
	5200	SMCo	94074	829-E7
LA JOLLA AV	400	SMTO	94403	749-B6
LAKE BLVD	2400	SMCo	94062	789-F1
LAKE CT	-	SMCo	94062	789-G1
LAKE DR	100	SBRN	94066	727-E1
	100	SBRN	94066	707-D7
LAKE RD	-	SMCo	94028	830-D4
	2200	BLMT	94002	769-A2
LAKE ST	100	BSBN	94005	688-B7
	1000	MLBR	94030	728-A5
	1700	SMTO	94403	749-D2
N LAKE ST	200	SMCo	94038	746-F7
S LAKE ST	-	SMCo	94038	746-F7
LAKE FOREST DR	-	DALY	94015	687-B3
LAKEMEAD WY	700	SMCo	94062	789-F2
	3400	RDWC	94062	789-F2
LAKEMEADOW DR	-	DALY	94015	687-A4
LAKE MERCED BLVD	100	SMCo	94015	687-A2
	100	DALY	94015	687-A3
	700	SF	94132	687-A2
LAKE MERCED HILL	-	SF	94132	687-A2
LAKEMONT DR	-	DALY	94015	687-A3
LAKESHIRE DR	200	DALY	94015	687-A7
	500	DALY	94015	707-A1
LAKESHORE DR	100	SMCo	94402	748-G6
	700	RDWC	94065	749-J6
	900	SMCo	94025	809-J3
	1200	SMCo	94025	810-A3
LAKESIDE AV	100	PCFA	94044	706-J6
LAKESIDE DR	300	FCTY	94404	749-E1
LAKEVIEW AV	-	SF	94112	687-D1
	200	PCFA	94044	706-J6
LAKEVIEW DR	-	DALY	94015	687-A3
	100	WDSD	94062	790-A5
	1000	HIL	94010	748-E5
LAKEVIEW LN	200	PCFA	94044	706-J6
LAKEVIEW WY	100	SMCo	94062	769-E7
	300	SMCo	94062	789-F1
	800	RDWC	94062	789-G2
	1000	RDWC	94061	789-G2
LAKE VISTA AV	-	DALY	94015	687-B3
LAKEWOOD CIR	-	SMTO	94402	768-H1
LAKEWOOD DR	-	DALY	94015	686-J4
	-	DALY	94015	687-A4
LA LOMA DR	-	SMCo	94025	790-C6
	-	MLPK	94025	790-C6
LA LOMA LN	100	SMCo	94010	728-B7
LA MANCHA PL	-	MLBR	94030	728-A4
LAMBERT AV	200	PA	94306	791-C7
LA MESA CT	-	BURL	94010	728-B7
	400	SMCo	94028	810-E3
LA MESA DR	100	SMCo	94010	728-B7
	100	SMCo	94028	810-D3
	1500	BURL	94010	728-B7
	3100	SCAR	94070	769-D6
LA MESA LN	-	BURL	94010	728-B7
LA MIRADA DR	900	PCFA	94044	726-J4
LA MONTAGNE PL	-	SSF	94080	707-H1
LAMONTE AV	200	SSF	94080	707-D3
LAMSHIN LN	-	SCAR	94070	769-G6
LANCASTER BLVD	400	SMCo	94038	746-G6
LANCASTER RD	1000	HIL	94010	748-F3
LANCASTER WY	400	RDWC	94062	789-H1
	600	RDWC	94061	789-H1
LANDA LN	-	SMCo	94061	790-A4
LANDFAIR AV	300	SMTO	94403	749-C7
LANDING LN	1100	MLBR	94030	728-A2
LANDMARK LN	-	RDWC	94065	750-B4
LANE PL	-	ATN	94027	790-F1
LANE ST	1000	BLMT	94002	769-F2
LANE 8 W	-	PA	94301	790-J5
LANE A	-	SCIC	94305	790-H7
LANE B	500	SCIC	94305	810-H1
LANE C	500	SCIC	94305	790-H7
	500	SCIC	94305	810-H1
LANE W	500	SCIC	94305	790-H7
LANG RD	300	BURL	94010	728-H5
LANGLEY HILL RD	-	SMCo	94020	829-J5
	-	SMCo	94020	830-A6
LANING DR	100	WDSD	94062	789-G5
LANSDALE AV	300	MLBR	94030	728-A3
LANSDALE ST	3000	SMTO	94403	749-A6
LANYARD DR	400	RDWC	94065	749-H7
LAPHAM WY	-	SF	94112	687-G2
LA PRENDA	-	MLBR	94030	727-J5
LA QUESTA WY	100	WDSD	94062	789-H6
LARCH AV	400	SSF	94080	707-H1
LARCH DR	-	ATN	94027	770-G7
	-	ATN	94027	790-G1
LARCH LN	200	PCFA	94044	706-J6
	200	PCFA	94044	707-A6
LARCHMONT DR	600	SMCo	94015	687-A4
LARGUITA LN	-	PTLV	94028	810-B5
LARK AV	1600	RDWC	94061	790-A2
LARK LN	1000	FCTY	94404	749-H2
LARKSPUR AV	-	DALY	94015	687-A6
LARKSPUR DR	300	EPA	94303	791-D2
	800	MLBR	94030	727-H3
	900	BURL	94010	728-F6
	1000	SMCo	-	727-H4
LA ROCCA LN	-	RDWC	94061	790-A1
LA SALLE DR	2000	SMTO	94403	749-A4
LA SALLE RD	-	HIL	94010	748-F3
LA SANDRA WY	-	PTLV	94028	810-B4
LA SELVA	3000	SMTO	94403	749-E5
LA SENDA RD	-	HIL	94010	748-G3
LAS FLORES RD	-	SMCo	94037	746-H5
LA SOLANO	-	MLBR	94030	727-J4
LAS PIEDRAS	-	SMCo	94028	830-D5
LAS PIEDRAS CT	-	BURL	94010	728-A6
LAS PIEDRAS DR	2800	BURL	94010	728-B6
LAS PULGAS RD	400	WDSD	94062	789-H4
LASSEN CT	-	MLPK	94025	790-C7
	600	SSF	94080	707-F4
LASSEN DR	100	SBRN	94066	707-E7
	100	SBRN	94066	727-E1
	900	MLPK	94025	790-C6
	1000	BLMT	94002	769-A2
LASSEN LN	1000	PCFA	94044	707-A5
LASSEN ST	500	SSF	94080	707-F4
LASSEN WY	1600	BURL	94010	728-C5
LAS SOMBRAS CT	400	SMTO	94402	748-F2
LA STRADA	-	SMCo	94010	728-B7
	-	SMCo	94010	748-B1
LASUEN DR	1200	MLBR	94030	728-A5
LASUEN MALL	200	SCIC	94305	790-H6
LASUEN ST	500	SCIC	94305	790-H7
LATHAM CT	-	HIL	94010	728-F7
LATHROP AV	100	SF	94134	688-A2
LATHROP DR	800	SCIC	94305	810-H2
LATHROP PL	900	SCIC	94305	810-H2
LATHROP ST	-	RDWC	94063	770-B6
LAUGHING COW RD	100	SMCo	94062	789-A7
LAURA LN	100	PA	94303	791-D4
LAURA ST	-	SF	94112	687-E2
LAUREL AV	-	MLBR	94030	728-A3
	100	MLPK	94025	790-J3
	200	SSF	94080	707-G2
	300	SMCo	94062	788-H5
	400	HMBY	94019	787-F1
	400	MLPK	94025	791-A2
	500	SMTO	94401	749-A2
	700	BURL	94010	728-F6
	800	BLMT	94002	769-E1
	1000	EPA	94303	791-A1
LAUREL LN	400	PCFA	94044	707-A6
LAUREL PL	-	MLPK	94025	790-F2
LAUREL ST	-	ATN	94027	790-F2
	-	RDWC	94063	770-C6
	-	SCAR	94070	769-F2
	-	MLPK	94025	790-G3
LAUREL WY	3700	RDWC	94062	789-G1
E LAUREL CREEK DR	3400	SMTO	94403	749-A6
E LAUREL CREEK RD	3000	SMTO	94403	749-A7
	3000	BLMT	94002	749-A7
	3100	SMTO	94403	769-A1
	3100	BLMT	94002	769-A1
	3500	SMTO	94403	768-J1
	3500	BLMT	94002	768-J1
	3500	SMTO	94403	748-J7
	3500	BLMT	94002	748-J7
LAURELDALE RD	-	HIL	94010	748-G2
LAUREL GLEN DR	900	PA	94304	810-G7
	900	PA	94304	830-G1
LAUREL HILL CT	-	SMCo	94402	748-F6
LAUREL HILL DR	1200	SMCo	94402	748-F7
LAURELWOOD DR	700	SMTO	94403	749-A7
LAUREN AV	200	PCFA	94044	727-A2
LAURENT RD	500	HIL	94010	748-D2
LAURIE LN	-	SMCo	94402	748-G6
LAURIE MEADOWS DR	-	SMTO	94403	749-D6
LAUSANNE AV	-	DALY	94014	687-D4
LAWLER RANCH RD	-	SMCo	94025	790-A7
	-	SMCo	94025	810-B1
	-	WDSD	94062	790-A7
LAWNDALE BLVD	-	CLMA	94014	687-F7
	-	CLMA	94014	707-F1
LAWRENCE AV	-	SF	94112	687-E2
	200	SSF	94080	708-B4
LAWRENCE LN	900	PA	94303	791-D5
LAWRENCE RD	800	SMTO	94401	749-A1
LAYNE CT	700	PA	94303	791-D7
LAYNE PL	-	SBRN	94066	707-J7
LEAFWOOD CT	3400	SMTO	94403	748-J7
LEAHY ST	500	RDWC	94061	790-C1
LE BLANC CT	-	HMBY	94019	767-E5
LE CONTE AV	700	SF	94124	688-B1
	1000	SMCo	94037	746-G4
LEE AV	-	SF	94112	687-E1
	400	SMCo	94019	767-D4
LEE DR	900	MLPK	94025	790-F3
LEEWARD LN	1400	FCTY	94404	749-G5
LE HAVRE PL	-	HMBY	94019	767-E5
LEHNING WY	-	BSBN	94005	688-A6
LEIGH WY	2600	BLMT	94002	769-B3
LEIX WY	2600	SSF	94080	707-C4
LELAND AV	-	SF	94134	688-A2
	100	SMCo	94025	790-E6
	200	PA	94306	791-A7
	200	SF	94134	687-J2
LE MANS WY	700	HMBY	94019	767-E5
N LEMON AV	1100	MLPK	94025	790-E5
LEMON CT	-	HIL	94010	748-C1
LEMON ST	400	MLPK	94025	790-E6
LEMOORE DR	-	SCAR	94070	769-G6
LENNOX AV	200	MLPK	94025	790-F2
LENOLT ST	1300	RDWC	94063	770-A5
	1400	RDWC	94063	769-J4
LEO CIR	-	SSF	94080	707-J2
	-	SSF	94080	708-A2
LEO DR	600	FCTY	94404	749-E3
LEON WY	-	ATN	94027	790-F3
LEONA ST	3900	SMTO	94403	749-B7
LERIDA AV	-	MLBR	94030	728-B3
LERIDA CT	-	SMCo	94028	810-D4
LERIDA WY	1200	PCFA	94044	727-A4
LEROY AV	-	PTLV	94028	809-J6
LESLIE CT	900	SCAR	94070	769-D6
LESLIE DR	-	SCAR	94070	769-D6
LESLIE ST	1700	SMTO	94402	749-B3
LESSING ST	-	SF	94112	687-D2
LESSINGIA CT	1900	SMCo	94402	768-H2
LEVEE RD	-	SMTO	94401	729-A6
LEWIS AV	-	MLBR	94030	728-B4
	-	SSF	94080	708-A2
	100	SMCo	94019	767-C1
LEWIS LN	400	PCFA	94044	707-A4
LEWIS FOSTER DR	100	HMBY	94019	767-F7
LEWIS RANCH LN	-	SCAR	94070	769-D5
LEXINGTON AV	100	RDWC	94062	770-A6
	300	SSF	94066	707-J5
	1400	SMCo	94402	748-F7
	1500	SMCo	94402	768-F1
LEXINGTON DR	200	MLPK	94025	790-J3
LEXINGTON WY	300	BURL	94010	728-G6
	2400	SBRN	94066	707-F7
	2400	SBRN	94066	727-F1
LIBERTY CT	2400	SSF	94080	707-D4
LIBERTY LN	700	FCTY	94404	749-G5
LIBERTY PARK AV	2000	SMCo	94025	790-D6
LIBRA LN	600	FCTY	94404	749-E3
LIBRARY AV	200	MLBR	94030	728-A3
LICHEN LN	-	RDWC	94065	750-A5
LIDDICOAT CIR	14300	LAH	94022	810-H5
LIDDICOAT DR	14400	LAH	94022	810-H5
LIDO CIR	-	RDWC	94065	749-J6
LIDO LN	900	FCTY	94404	749-F3
LIDO ST	700	FCTY	94404	749-F3
LIEBIG ST	-	DALY	94014	687-D2
	-	SF	94112	687-D2
LIFEMARK BLVD	-	SMCo	-	768-D3
LIGHT WY	-	SMCo	94025	770-E7
LIGHTHOUSE LN	-	DALY	94014	687-E5
LIGHTHOUSE RD	-	HMBY	94019	787-G5
LIGHTHOUSE VIEW RD	-	SMCo	94060	888-B4
LILAC AV	200	SMCo	94062	788-H5
LILAC DR	-	ATN	94027	770-G7
LILAC LN	-	SSF	94080	707-H2
	300	EPA	94303	791-B1
LILLY LN	-	SCAR	94070	769-C5
LINARIA WY	-	SMCo	94028	810-D4
LINCOLN AV	-	DALY	94015	687-A6
	100	PA	94301	790-J5
	100	RDWC	94061	770-A7
	200	PA	94301	791-A4
	1100	BURL	94010	728-D5
	2400	BLMT	94002	769-B1
LINCOLN BLVD	900	PCFA	94044	727-B6
LINCOLN CIR	400	MLBR	94030	728-A3
LINCOLN CT	-	SF	94112	687-F2
LINCOLN LN	100	PCFA	94044	706-J3
	200	PCFA	94044	707-A3
LINCOLN PL	900	PCFA	94044	727-B6
LINCOLN ST	-	SSF	94080	707-H1
	800	SMCo	94038	746-F5
	2000	EPA	94303	791-A2
LINCOLN CENTRE DR	100	FCTY	94404	749-F1
LINDA CT	700	SMTO	94403	749-B7
LINDA MAR BLVD	500	PCFA	94044	726-H4
	1100	PCFA	94044	727-A6
LINDA VISTA	100	MLBR	94030	727-J5
LINDA VISTA AV	-	ATN	94027	790-C4
LINDA VISTA DR	100	DALY	94014	687-J4
LINDA VISTA RD	800	SMCo	94037	746-H4
LINDA VISTA ST	800	SMCo	94038	746-G6
LINDA VISTA STEPS	-	SF	94112	687-G2
LINDBERGH ST	-	SMTO	94401	729-A7
	200	SMTO	94401	749-B1
LINDEN AV	-	ATN	94027	790-G1
	-	MLBR	94030	727-J1
	-	SSF	94080	707-J3
	-	SBRN	94066	727-J1
	300	SBRN	94066	707-H7
	700	BURL	94010	728-F6
	700	MLBR	94030	728-B4
	900	SSF	94080	708-A2
S LINDEN AV	-	SSF	94080	707-J4
	300	SSF	94066	707-J4
	300	SBRN	94066	707-J4
LINDEN CT	700	SBRN	94066	707-H7
LINDEN LN	100	SMCo	94402	748-G6
LINDEN ST	100	RDWC	94061	770-B7
	600	DALY	94014	687-D5
LINDEN WY	100	SMCo	94402	748-G5
LINDENBROOK CT	300	WDSD	94062	789-H5
LINDENBROOK RD	200	WDSD	94062	789-H5
LINFIELD DR	100	MLPK	94025	790-G4
E LINFIELD DR	100	MLPK	94025	790-H3
LINFIELD PL	300	MLPK	94025	790-H3
LINK RD	900	HIL	94010	748-F3
N LINK RD	-	SMCo	94128	728-B1
S LINK RD	-	SMCo	94128	728-B2
LINKS LN	-	HMBY	94019	787-E6
LINKS RD	900	SCIC	94304	810-F1
LINWOOD WY	-	SMCo	94062	809-F5
LISA CT	800	PCFA	94044	726-H5
LISBON ST	300	SF	94112	687-F1
	500	SMCo	94014	687-D5
	500	DALY	94014	687-D5
LITA LN	-	EPA	94303	791-C2
LITTLEFIELD AV	200	SSF	94080	708-A4
LIVE OAK AV	600	MLPK	94025	790-F4
LIVE OAK LN	-	HIL	94010	748-B1
	500	SMCo	94062	789-F1
LIVINGSTON AV	1300	PCFA	94044	726-G4
LIVINGSTON PL	-	SSF	94080	707-G1
LIVINGSTON TER	2000	SBRN	94066	707-G7
LIVORNO WY	-	RDWC	94065	749-J5
LLANO ST	3200	SMTO	94403	749-E5
LLOYDEN DR	-	ATN	94027	790-D2
LLOYDEN PARK LN	300	ATN	94027	790-D2
LOBITOS CREEK CTO	1200	SMCo	94019	807-J5
	1200	SMCo	94019	808-A6
	1200	SMCo	94074	808-A6
LOBITOS CREEK RD	-	SMCo	94019	807-J5
	-	SMCo	94019	808-D3
LOBOS ST	-	SF	94112	687-D1
LOCARNO WY	1000	SCAR	94070	769-F5
LOCKHAVEN DR	600	PCFA	94044	707-B4
LOCUST AV	300	SSF	94080	707-H2
LOCUST ST	100	RDWC	94061	770-B7
	100	RDWC	94061	790-B1
	1400	SMTO	94402	749-A3
LODATO AV	-	SMTO	94403	749-B4
	-	SMTO	94402	749-B4
LODGE DR	3400	BLMT	94002	769-A2
LODI AV	1300	SMTO	94403	749-C2
	1300	SMTO	94401	749-C2
LOEHR ST	-	SF	94134	687-J2
LOGAN LN	-	ATN	94027	790-C2
LOG CABIN RANCH RD	-	SMCo	94020	849-F3
LOHOMA CT	-	HIL	94010	748-H5
LOIS LN	-	SF	94134	688-B2

STREET
Block City ZIP Pg-Grid

LOIS LN
100 PA 94303 791-B4
LOLA ST
3700 SMTO 94403 749-B6
LOMA CT
700 SMCo 94062 769-F6
LOMA LN
- SCAR 94070 769-E6
LOMA RD
- SCAR 94070 769-E6
- SMCo 94062 769-F6
- SCAR 94062 769-E6
LOMA MAR AV
- SMCo 94021 849-A7
LOMA PRIETA LN
2300 MLPK 94025 790-D7
LOMA VERDE AV
200 PA 94306 791-C7
700 PA 94303 791-E6
LOMA VERDE PL
3100 PA 94303 791-D6
LOMA VISTA
- BLMT 94002 749-E7
LOMA VISTA DR
- BURL 94010 728-A7
- BURL 94010 748-B1
LOMA VISTA LN
100 SMCo 94010 728-A7
LOMA VISTA ST
800 SMCo 94038 746-G6
LOMA VISTA TER
300 PCFA 94044 707-A5
LOMBARDI LN
- MLBR 94030 728-A5
800 HIL 94010 748-F3
LOMBARDY WY
600 SMCo 94062 789-F2
LOMITA AV
300 SBRN 94066 727-H2
300 MLBR 94030 727-H2
LOMITA CT
500 MLBR 94030 727-J2
600 SCIC 94305 810-G1
LOMITA DR
500 SCIC 94305 790-H6
500 SCIC 94305 810-G1
LOMITAS AV
100 SSF 94080 707-E3
LOMITAS CT
- MLPK 94025 790-F6
LOMOND DR
400 PCFA 94044 707-B3
LONDON CT
100 SBRN 94066 727-G2
LONDON LN
200 BLMT 94002 749-F6
LONDON ST
400 SF 94112 687-F1
LONDONDERRY DR
100 SMCo 94402 748-H7
LONE MOUNTAIN CT
- PCFA 94044 707-B3
LONESOME PINE RD
3900 RDWC 94061 789-G3
LONGFELLOW DR
3100 BLMT 94002 749-A7
3100 BLMT 94002 769-A1
LONGFORD DR
- SSF 94080 707-D1
LONG RIDGE RD
- ScrC 95033 850-J7
- SMCo 94020 850-G5
LONGSPUR
- PTLV 94028 830-C1
LONGVIEW CT
- HIL 94010 748-G3
LONGVIEW DR
- DALY 94015 707-A1
2900 SBRN 94066 707-D6
LONGVIEW RD
800 HIL 94010 748-G3
LOOKOUT RD
- HIL 94010 748-E4
LOON CT
200 FCTY 94404 749-H1
LOOP RD
- SMCo 94402 768-G2
LORD IVELSON LN
1100 FCTY 94404 749-J4
LORD NELSON LN
1100 FCTY 94404 749-J4
LOREE LN
- MLBR 94030 728-A5
LORELEI LN
- MLPK 94025 770-F7
LORI CT
3200 BLMT 94002 768-J1
LORI DR
3200 BLMT 94002 768-J1
LORNE LN
- SMCo 94025 770-E7
LORRAINE AV
1500 SMTO 94401 729-A7
LORRY LN
100 PCFA 94044 707-B4
LORTON AV
- BURL 94010 728-G6
LORYN LN
1000 HMBY 94019 767-E6
LOS ALTOS DR
1500 BURL 94010 728-A7
1700 SMCo 94402 748-H7
2100 SMTO 94402 748-H7
LOS ALTOS PL
- SMCo 94402 748-G7
LOS ARBOLES AV
500 SCIC 94305 790-F7
LOS BANOS AV
100 DALY 94014 687-C3
100 SMCo 94038 746-G7
100 SMCo 94038 766-G1
LOS CERROS RD
- SMCo 94062 769-F6
LOS CHARROS LN
- PTLV 94028 810-C6
LOS FLORES AV
- SSF 94080 707-E2
LOS GATOS WY
400 SMTO 94403 749-E5
LOS MONTES DR
100 SMCo 94010 728-A7
1500 BURL 94010 728-A7
LOS OLIVOS AV
- DALY 94014 687-C3
LOS PRADOS
3000 SMTO 94403 749-E4
LOS ROBLES CT
- SMCo 94025 790-D5
LOS ROBLES DR
100 SMCo 94010 728-B7
LOS TRANCOS CIR
100 SMCo 94028 830-D4
LOS TRANCOS RD
- PA 94304 830-D2
- PTLV 94028 810-D7
100 PA 94304 810-D7
900 PTLV 94028 830-D2
900 SMCo 94028 830-D4
LOS VIENTOS WY
100 SMCo 94070 769-C5
100 SCAR 94070 769-C5
LOTUS WY
100 EPA 94303 791-D3
LOUIS LN
- RDWC 94063 770-B4
LOUIS RD
1900 PA 94303 791-C5
LOUISA CT
1500 PA 94303 791-B4
LOUISBURG ST
100 SF 94112 687-E1
LOUISE LN
100 PTLV 94028 809-J5
100 SMTO 94403 749-B6
LOUISE ST
1000 MLPK 94025 790-E6
LOUVAINE DR
1700 SMCo 94015 687-B5
LOUVAINE PL
- SMCo 94015 687-B5
LOWE RD
- WDSD 94062 789-G6
LOWELL AV
100 PA 94301 791-A6
100 SBRN 94066 727-G2
LOWELL ST
- SF 94112 687-E2
- RDWC 94062 769-H6
300 DALY 94014 687-E2
LOWER DEARBORN PARK RD
- SMCo 94060 868-J2
LOWER LAKE RD
100 WDSD 94062 809-H5
LOWER LOCK AV
3300 BLMT 94002 769-A1
LOWER VISTA GRANDE
1200 MLBR 94030 727-J5
LOWERY DR
- ATN 94027 790-H1
LOWRIE AV
1300 SSF 94080 707-J4
LOYOLA AV
- SMCo 94025 790-D1
2900 SMCo 94063 790-D1
LOYOLA DR
200 MLBR 94030 728-A5
1800 BURL 94010 728-A5
LUCCA DR
100 SSF 94080 707-G1
LUCERNE AV
500 RDWC 94061 790-B1
LUCERO WY
100 SMCo 94028 810-D3
LUCIA CT
100 SBRN 94066 727-H2
LUCKY AV
900 SMCo 94025 790-D6
LUCY LN
- SMCo 94019 807-J5
- SMCo 94019 808-A5
LUDEMAN LN
- MLBR 94030 728-A3
300 MLBR 94030 727-J3
LUFF LN
400 RDWC 94065 749-H7
LULA BELLE LN
100 SMTO 94403 749-B4
LUNADO WY
- SF 94127 687-C1
LUNDY LN
- SMCo 94402 748-G7
LUNDY WY
100 PCFA 94044 707-A7
700 PCFA 94044 727-A1
LUNETTA AV
200 PCFA 94044 707-A6
LUPIN LN
- ATN 94027 770-G7
- ATN 94027 790-G1
LUPIN WY
900 SCAR 94070 769-G4
LUPINE AV
3500 PA 94303 791-E7
LUPINE DR
- DALY 94014 687-H3
LUPINE RD
27700 LAH 94022 810-J6
LUPINE WY
- HIL 94010 748-D2
LUPINE VALLEY CT
- BSBN 94005 687-H4
LURLINE DR
700 FCTY 94404 749-G2
LUX AV
100 SSF 94080 707-J2
100 SSF 94080 708-A3
LYALL WY
2300 BLMT 94002 769-C2
LYCETT CIR
- DALY 94015 707-C3
LYCETT CT
- DALY 94015 707-C3
N LYCETT ST
100 DALY 94015 707-C3
S LYCETT ST
100 DALY 94015 707-C3
LYDIA CT
- HIL 94010 748-F5
LYME LN
- FCTY 94404 749-E6
LYNBROOK DR
300 PCFA 94044 707-B2
LYNDHURST AV
100 SCAR 94070 769-E2
200 BLMT 94002 769-E2
LYNDHURST CT
- BLMT 94002 769-E2
LYNGSO LN
- RDWC 94063 770-C5
LYNN WY
100 WDSD 94062 789-J4
LYNTON AV
100 SCAR 94070 769-D4
100 SMCo 94070 769-D4
LYNVALE CT
- DALY 94015 686-J4
LYNWOOD LN
900 MLBR 94030 727-H3
LYNX LN
800 FCTY 94404 749-F4
LYON AV
1900 BLMT 94002 749-C7
2100 BLMT 94002 769-C1
LYONRIDGE LN
- SMTO 94402 748-H6
LYONS ST
1100 RDWC 94061 790-A1
LYTTON AV
100 PA 94301 790-H4

M

MACADAMIA DR
900 HIL 94010 728-C7
900 HIL 94010 748-C1
MACARTHUR AV
400 SMCo 94063 770-C6
600 SMTO 94402 748-J4
MACARTHUR DR
500 SMCo 94015 687-B5
MACBAIN AV
- ATN 94027 790-E3
MACDONALD AV
- DALY 94014 687-J3
- DALY 94014 688-A3
MACDONALD ST
1400 RDWC 94061 790-A2
MACKALL WY
3100 PA 94306 791-D7
MADDUX DR
700 SMCo 94015 687-A4
900 PA 94303 791-D6
900 DALY 94015 687-A4
1400 RDWC 94061 789-J2
1400 RDWC 94061 790-A3
MADEIRA DR
1400 PCFA 94044 727-A6
MADERA AV
- SCAR 94070 769-F4
1000 MLPK 94025 790-J1
1200 MLPK 94025 770-J7
1200 MLPK 94025 771-A7
MADERA DR
500 SMCo 94403 749-A4
500 SMTO 94403 749-A4
MADERA LN
4000 SMCo 94074 828-G7
MADERA RD
400 SMCo 94062 788-H5
MADERA WY
1300 MLBR 94030 728-A5
1300 MLBR 94030 727-J5
3700 SBRN 94066 707-C5
MADISON AV
- SMTO 94402 749-A3
100 RDWC 94061 770-A7
100 SBRN 94066 727-G1
1100 RDWC 94061 769-J7
1500 RDWC 94061 789-J1
MADISON WY
- SMCo 94025 790-H2
500 PA 94303 791-C4
MADRID AV
100 SMCo 94019 767-A2
MADRID CT
- MLBR 94030 728-A2
1300 PCFA 94044 727-A6
MADRID ST
400 SF 94112 687-G1
MADRONA AV
100 SMCo 94019 767-A2
MADRONA ST
- SCAR 94070 769-F3
MADRONE AV
- SMCo 94038 766-G1
- SMCo 94060 868-H5
- SSF 94080 708-A2
500 SMCo 94062 788-G6
MADRONE PL
- HIL 94010 728-E7
MADRONE RD
- ATN 94027 790-G1
MADRONE ST
100 RDWC 94061 770-B7
200 RDWC 94061 790-B1
300 MLBR 94030 728-B2
MADRONE TR
- SMCo 94062 788-H6
MADRONE WY
- PCFA 94044 727-A5
MADRONO AV
1500 PA 94306 791-A6
MAGELLAN AV
100 SMCo 94019 767-C4
MAGELLAN CT
400 PCFA 94044 707-A2
MAGELLAN DR
300 PCFA 94044 707-A2
MAGELLAN LN
800 FCTY 94404 749-G4
MAGNOLIA AV
- SMCo 94063 770-F5
- SSF 94080 707-H3
100 MLBR 94030 728-A2
700 SBRN 94066 707-H7
700 SBRN 94066 727-J2
700 SBRN 94066 728-A2
700 MLBR 94030 727-J2
1200 SCAR 94070 769-F3
S MAGNOLIA AV
- MLBR 94030 728-B4
1800 BURL 94010 728-B4
MAGNOLIA AV S
- SSF 94080 707-H4
MAGNOLIA CT
1600 MLPK 94025 790-F5
MAGNOLIA DR
- ATN 94027 790-F1
600 SMTO 94402 749-B2
MAGNOLIA ST
200 HMBY 94019 787-E2
600 MLPK 94025 790-E5
MAHAN ST
600 SF 94124 688-E1
MAHLER RD
800 BURL 94010 728-E4
MAHOGANY DR
- SSF 94080 707-H3
MAHOGANY RW
700 SBRN 94066 707-H6
MAIDEN LN
4100 SMTO 94403 749-D6
MAIDENHAIR WK
- SMCo 94019 787-H5
MAIN DR
- SBRN 94066 727-G3
MAIN ST
- HMBY 94019 787-F2
100 BSBN 94005 687-J3
100 BSBN 94005 688-A4
200 RDWC 94063 770-B5
300 SMCo 94037 746-F4
N MAIN ST
100 HMBY 94019 767-F7
300 HMBY 94019 787-F1
MAINSAIL CT
200 FCTY 94404 749-G4
MAITLAND RD
400 PCFA 94044 726-J2
MAJESTIC AV
- SF 94112 687-E1
MAJILLA AV
1100 BURL 94010 728-F6
MAJORCA WY
2800 SCAR 94070 769-F6
MAKO LN
200 RDWC 94065 749-J4
MALABAR CT
- SCAR 94070 769-C4
MALAGA ST
900 SMCo 94019 767-C3
MALAVEAR CT
- PCFA 94044 726-J5
- PCFA 94044 727-A5
MALCOLM AV
100 BLMT 94002 749-D7
MALCOLM RD
800 BURL 94010 728-D4
MALLARD ST
800 FCTY 94404 749-G1
MALLET CT
1000 MLPK 94025 790-F4
MALONEY LN
600 MLPK 94025 790-F3
MALORY CT
- SMCo 94061 790-B3
MALTA LN
1200 FCTY 94404 749-F5
MANCHESTER CT
3100 PA 94303 791-D6
MANCHESTER LN
100 BLMT 94002 749-F6
MANDALAY CT
- RDWC 94065 749-J5
MANDALAY PL
- SSF 94014 708-A1
- SSF 94080 708-A1
MANDARIN DR
300 DALY 94015 707-C1
MANDARIN WY
- ATN 94027 790-B5
MANDELA CT
1000 EPA 94303 791-C1
MANGINI WY
- BURL 94010 728-G6
MANHATTAN AV
1900 EPA 94303 791-B3
MANHATTEN CT
- RDWC 94065 749-J5
MANILA WY
600 SMCo 94015 687-A5
MANOR CT
- DALY 94015 687-A3
- RDWC 94062 769-H5
MANOR DR
100 PCFA 94044 706-J3
100 SCAR 94070 769-E4
100 SSF 94080 707-G5
200 PCFA 94044 707-A4
1700 HIL 94010 728-E7
MANOR PL
- MLPK 94025 790-H3
W MANOR PZ
400 PCFA 94044 706-J3
MANSEAU ST
600 SF 94124 688-E1
MANSELL ST
- SF 94134 688-A1
500 SF 94134 687-H1
MANSFIELD DR
200 SSF 94080 707-D2
MANSION CT
- MLPK 94025 790-C7
MANUELLA AV
300 WDSD 94062 789-F6
MANZANITA AV
- DALY 94015 707-A1
- SMCo 94062 788-J6
100 SCAR 94070 769-F3
100 SSF 94080 707-H4
200 PA 94306 791-A6
1600 BLMT 94002 769-D1
2000 SMCo 94025 790-C6
MANZANITA CT
- MLBR 94030 728-A5
MANZANITA DR
1000 PCFA 94044 727-A5
1200 MLBR 94030 728-A5
MANZANITA RD
- ATN 94027 790-G1
200 SMCo 94062 788-J6
MANZANITA ST
- RDWC 94063 770-B7
MANZANITA WY
100 WDSD 94062 789-H7
100 WDSD 94062 809-H1
MAPACHE CT
- PTLV 94028 810-A4
MAPACHE DR
100 PTLV 94028 810-A4
MAPLE AV
- ATN 94027 790-E2
- SSF 94080 707-J3
400 SBRN 94066 727-H1
500 SBRN 94066 707-H7
800 BURL 94010 728-F5
S MAPLE AV
- SSF 94080 707-H4
MAPLE LN
- EPA 94303 791-C1
MAPLE PL
100 MLBR 94030 728-A5
MAPLE ST
- RDWC 94063 770-B5
400 PA 94301 791-A3
500 SMTO 94402 748-J2
900 SMTO 94402 749-A3
MAPLE WY
- SCAR 94070 769-G6
400 WDSD 94062 789-E3
W MAPLE WY
400 WDSD 94062 789-E3
MAPLE LEAF CT
- LAH 94022 810-J7
MAPLE LEAF WY
- ATN 94027 790-G2
MARBLY AV
- DALY 94015 707-C2
MARBURGER AV
3100 BLMT 94002 769-A2
MARCELLA WY
200 MLBR 94030 728-B5
MARCIE CIR
- SSF 94080 707-G2
MARCO WY
100 SSF 94080 708-A5
MARCO POLO WY
1600 BURL 94010 728-C5
MARCUSSEN DR
1000 MLPK 94025 790-G2
MARGARET AV
- BSBN 94005 688-A7
- SF 94112 687-E1
MARGARET CT
4100 SMTO 94403 749-E6
MARGARITA AV
3100 BURL 94010 728-A7
MARGATE ST
- DALY 94015 707-C2
MARGO LN
- HIL 94010 728-D6
MARIALINDA CT
- HIL 94010 728-D7
MARIANI CT
- SMCo 94062 789-G3
MARIANNA LN
- ATN 94027 790-E2
MARIE CT
- HMBY 94019 767-E6
MARIGOLD LN
- SCAR 94070 769-C4
MARIN DR
400 BURL 94010 728-G6
MARINA BLVD
- SSF 94080 708-C2
400 BSBN 94005 688-C7
MARINA CT
1500 SMTO 94403 749-D4
MARINA DR
- RDWC 94065 749-G7
MARINA WY
200 PCFA 94044 706-J7
MARINA VISTA
1500 SMTO 94404 749-D3
MARINE BLVD
100 SMCo 94038 746-G6
MARINE PKWY
100 RDWC 94065 749-G7
MARINE RD
- SMCo 94062 788-J5
MARINE WY
2600 MTVW 94043 791-G7
MARINER WY
- DALY 94014 687-D5
MARINERS ISLAND BLVD
300 FCTY 94404 749-E1
300 SMTO 94404 749-D2
MARINE VIEW AV
300 BLMT 94002 749-E7
300 SMTO 94403 749-E7
MARION AV
400 PA 94301 791-C6
500 PA 94306 791-C6
600 PA 94303 791-C6
MARION DR
- SMCo 94062 790-A4
- WDSD 94062 790-A4
MARION PL
600 PA 94301 791-C6
MARIPOSA AV
100 DALY 94015 687-A7
1500 PA 94306 791-A6
MARIPOSA CT
- BURL 94010 728-A6
MARIPOSA DR
400 SSF 94080 707-F5
2700 BURL 94010 728-A6
MARIPOSA ST
- BSBN 94005 688-A6
MARIPOSA WK
- PCFA 94044 727-B1
MARISMA
3300 SMTO 94403 749-E5
MARISOL DR
- SBRN 94066 707-C6
MARITIME AV
- SMCo 94038 746-F6
MARKET PL
200 MLPK 94025 770-H7
E MARKET ST
- DALY 94014 687-C5
900 SMCo 94014 687-D5
W MARKET ST
- DALY 94014 687-C5
MARKHAM AV
- SMCo 94063 790-C1
400 SBRN 94066 727-G1
MARK TWAIN ST
1800 PA 94303 791-B5
MARLBOROUGH AV
2600 SMCo 94063 770-C7
2700 SMCo 94063 790-C1
MARLBOROUGH RD
1100 HIL 94010 748-E4
MARLIN AV
600 FCTY 94404 749-H2
MARLIN CT
500 RDWC 94065 749-H6
MARLIN DR
500 RDWC 94065 749-J6
MARLOWE ST
400 PA 94301 791-A3
MARMONA CT
200 MLPK 94025 790-J3
MARMONA DR
200 MLPK 94025 790-J2
MARQUETTE LN
900 FCTY 94404 749-G4
MARQUITA AV
1100 BURL 94010 728-D5
MARSEILLE WY
600 HMBY 94019 767-E5
MARSH DR
100 FCTY 94404 749-E1
MARSH RD
800 SMCo 94025 770-F6
800 ATN 94027 770-F6
900 MLPK 94025 770-G5
900 RDWC 94063 770-F6
900 SMCo 94063 770-F6
1000 SMCo 94025 790-F1
1000 ATN 94027 790-F1
1100 RDWC 94025 770-F6
MARSH RD Rt#-84
2300 MLPK 94025 770-F7
MARSHALL AV
900 SMTO 94403 749-B7
MARSHALL CT
600 RDWC 94063 770-B5
MARSHALL DR
800 PA 94303 791-C5
MARSHALL ST
200 RDWC 94063 770-B5
MARSHALL WY
- DALY 94014 687-D5
MARSHLANDS RD
9000 FRMT 94555 771-F2
MARSTEN AV
3500 BLMT 94002 768-J1
3500 BLMT 94002 769-A1
MARSTEN RD
1200 BURL 94010 728-E5
MARTIN AV
1200 PA 94301 791-A4
MARTIN CT
- DALY 94014 687-J4
MARTIN DR
3500 SMTO 94403 749-D5
MARTIN LN
- WDSD 94062 789-F7
MARTIN PL
100 SBRN 94066 707-J7
MARTIN ST
- DALY 94014 687-H3
MARTIN TR
- DALY 94014 687-H3
MARTINEZ DR
2600 BURL 94010 728-B6
MARTINEZ RD
- WDSD 94062 809-G6
MARTINIQUE DR
500 RDWC 94065 749-J7
MARTINIQUE LN
1200 FCTY 94404 749-F5
MARTINSEN CT
400 PA 94306 791-C7
MARVA OAKS DR
100 WDSD 94062 789-D4
MARVILLA CIR
200 PCFA 94044 726-H4
MARVILLA PL
200 PCFA 94044 726-H4
MAR VISTA DR
- DALY 94014 687-F3
MARY CT
- DALY 94014 687-J3
MARYLAND PL
- SBRN 94066 707-J7
MARYLAND ST
1600 RDWC 94061 789-J3
1700 RDWC 94061 790-A3
MARY LU LN
100 SMTO 94403 749-B5
MARYMONT AV
- ATN 94027 790-B4
MASOLEUM DR
- SMCo - 768-C3
MASON DR
1100 PCFA 94044 727-A4
MASON LN
2600 SMTO 94403 749-A5
MASONIC WY
500 BLMT 94002 749-F7
600 BLMT 94002 769-E1
MASSACHUSETTS AV
2800 RDWC 94061 790-A3
2800 RDWC 94061 789-J3
MASSON AV
- SBRN 94066 707-J6
MASTHEAD LN
300 FCTY 94404 749-J1
MASTICK AV
200 SBRN 94066 727-J1
300 SBRN 94066 707-J7
MATADERO CREEK CT
28600 LAH 94022 810-H7
28600 LAH 94022 830-H1
MATADERO CREEK LN
28500 LAH 94022 810-H7
MATEO AV
- DALY 94014 687-C5
- MLBR 94030 728-B3
MATSONIA DR
600 FCTY 94404 749-G2
MATT TR
- SMCo 94060 868-F5
MAUREEN AV
400 PA 94306 791-D7
MAXINE AV
1500 SMTO 94401 749-C1
MAXWELL LN
1200 RDWC 94062 769-G6
MAY BROWN AV
1100 MLPK 94025 790-E4
MAYBURY PL
100 WDSD 94062 789-J3
MAYFAIR AV
500 SSF 94080 707-H3
N MAYFAIR AV
500 DALY 94015 687-A3
500 DALY 94015 686-J3
S MAYFAIR AV
500 DALY 94015 687-A3
700 DALY 94015 686-J4
MAYFIELD AV
- DALY 94015 687-A7
500 SCIC 94305 790-G7
500 SCIC 94305 810-H1
MAYFLOWER LN
- SCAR 94070 769-C4
MAYVIEW AV
700 PA 94303 791-E7
MAYWOOD AV
- DALY 94015 687-A6
MAYWOOD DR
1000 BLMT 94002 769-D2
2300 SBRN 94066 707-E6
MAYWOOD LN
- MLPK 94025 790-F5
MAYWOOD WY
200 SSF 94080 707-G5
MCAKER CT
- SMTO 94402 749-B4
MCAULEY CT
1000 PA 94301 791-A3
MCCARTHY AV
- SF 94134 687-J2
MCCORMICK LN
- ATN 94027 790-E1
MCCREERY DR
- HIL 94010 728-D7
MCCUE AV
900 SCAR 94070 769-G2
MCDONALD WY
1600 BURL 94010 728-C5
MCDONNELL DR
700 SSF 94080 707-E2
N MCDONNELL RD
- SMCo 94128 728-B1
- SMCo 94128 708-A6
S MCDONNELL RD
- MLBR 94030 728-B2
- SMCo 94128 728-B2
MCEVOY ST
200 RDWC 94061 770-B7
200 RDWC 94061 790-B1
MCFARLAND CT
100 SCIC 94305 790-J7
MCGARVEY AV
2100 RDWC 94061 789-H2
MCKENDRY DR
100 MLPK 94025 790-J2
MCKENDRY PL
300 MLPK 94025 790-J3
MCKENZIE CT
- HIL 94010 748-G2
MCKINLEY ST
1100 RDWC 94061 790-A1
1600 SMTO 94403 749-C2
MCKINNEY AV
100 PCFA 94044 707-A4
MCLAIN RD
100 BSBN 94005 688-B7
MCLELLAN AV
- SMTO 94403 749-C5
MCLELLAN DR
- SSF 94080 707-E2
MCNAIR ST
- EPA 94303 791-C3
MCNEILL DR
600 RDWC 94063 770-B4
MCNULTY WY
3600 RDWC 94061 789-H2
MEADE AV
800 SF 94124 688-B1
E MEADOW CIR
1000 PA 94303 791-E7
MEADOW CT
- SMTO 94403 749-D5
E MEADOW DR
500 PA 94306 791-E7
500 PA 94303 791-E7
MEADOW LN
- ATN 94027 790-B6
- RDWC 94063 770-C6
- WDSD 94062 809-H5
- PTLV 94028 809-H5
1500 BURL 94010 728-D5
MEADOW RD
- WDSD 94062 809-H5
MEADOW CREEK CT
- PTLV 94028 810-D7
MEADOW GLEN AV
- MLBR 94030 728-A3
MEADOWOOD DR
100 PTLV 94028 810-B5
MEADOW PARK CIR
- BLMT 94002 768-J3
- BLMT 94002 769-A3
MEADOWSWEET LN
- SCAR 94070 769-C4
MEADOW VIEW PL
2100 SMTO 94403 749-C1
MEARS CT
900 SCIC 94305 810-J1
MEATH DR
2600 SSF 94080 707-C4
MEDFORD AV
2700 RDWC 94061 789-H2
MEDINA DR
2600 SBRN 94066 707-D5
MEDIO AV
100 SMCo 94019 767-C4
MEDITERRANEAN LN
200 RDWC 94065 749-J6
MEDWAY RD
- SMCo 94062 809-G6
- WDSD 94062 809-G6
MEFFERD AV
1400 SMTO 94401 729-A7
MEGANS LN
- SMCo 94062 788-H4
MELANIE LN
- ATN 94027 790-A5
- WDSD 94027 790-A5
MELBOURNE ST
1300 FCTY 94404 749-G5
MELENDY DR
2300 SCAR 94070 769-D5
MELISSA CIR
- DALY 94014 687-D4
MELISSA CT
700 SMTO 94402 748-J4
MELLO ST
1100 EPA 94303 791-A1
MELODY LN
12400 LAH 94022 830-J1
MELRA CT
- SF 94134 687-J2

STREET
Block City ZIP Pg-Grid

MELROSE CT
- HIL 94010 748-G4
- PCFA 94044 707-A3
MELROSE PL
- RDWC 94062 769-H6
MELVILLE AV
100 PA 94301 791-A5
MELVIN HENRY CT
- SMCo 94061 790-A4
MEMORIAL DR
800 SSF 94080 707-G3
MEMORIAL WY
100 SCIC 94305 790-H6
MENALTO AV
1900 MLPK 94025 791-A2
2100 EPA 94303 791-A1
2400 EPA 94303 771-A7
MENALTO DR
12200 LAH 94022 830-H1
MENDOCINO CT
100 SBRN 94066 707-E7
MENDOCINO ST
100 BSBN 94005 688-A6
MENDOCINO WY
600 RDWC 94065 749-J6
MENHADEN CT
300 FCTY 94404 749-H3
MENLO AV
- DALY 94015 686-J7
600 MLPK 94025 790-F4
MENLO OAKS AV
200 SMCo 94025 790-H2
1000 MLPK 94025 770-J7
1000 MLPK 94025 790-H2
MENLO OAKS DR
1100 MLPK 94025 770-J7
MERCAT PL
- HIL 94010 748-F5
MERCED DR
- SBRN 94066 707-D7
- SBRN 94066 727-D1
MERCEDES LN
- ATN 94027 790-D2
MERIDIAN
- RDWC 94065 749-J5
- RDWC 94065 750-A5
MERION DR
2600 SBRN 94066 707-D6
MERION RD
- HMBY 94019 787-F5
MERNER RD
1000 HIL 94010 748-G4
MERRILL ST
1000 MLPK 94025 790-F3
MERRY MOPPET LN
2200 BLMT 94002 769-C2
MESA CT
- ATN 94027 790-B5
MESA VERDE WY
100 SCAR 94070 769-E6
METRO CIR
1000 PA 94303 791-D5
METRO CENTER BLVD
900 FCTY 94404 749-E3
METZGAR ST
200 HMBY 94019 787-E2
MEYN RD
- SMCo 94019 807-H5
MEZES AV
1800 BLMT 94002 749-C7
1900 BLMT 94002 769-C1
MICHAEL CT
- SCAR 94070 769-G6
MICHAEL DR
3400 RDWC 94063 770-E7
3500 SMTO 94403 749-B6
MICHAEL LN
- MLBR 94030 728-A3
- MLBR 94030 727-J3
MICHAELS WY
- ATN 94027 790-E3
MICHELLE CT
200 SSF 94080 708-B4
MICHELLE LN
300 DALY 94015 707-C2
MICHIGAN AV
1600 EPA 94303 791-B1
MIDDLE AV
600 MLPK 94025 790-F5
MIDDLE CT
- SBRN 94066 727-G2
400 MLPK 94025 790-F6
MIDDLE RD
300 BLMT 94002 749-E7
700 BLMT 94002 769-E1
MIDDLEFIELD RD
- ATN 94027 790-E1
- PA 94301 790-E1
400 RDWC 94063 770-A5
500 MLPK 94025 790-E1
600 PA 94301 791-A4
1600 PA 94303 791-A4
2500 SMCo 94063 770-C7
2600 PA 94306 791-A4
3100 SMCo 94063 790-D1
3200 SMCo 94025 790-D1
MIDDLE FORK LN
13400 LAH 94022 810-J7
MIDDLE GATE ST
- ATN 94027 790-D2
MIDDLESEX RD
500 BLMT 94002 749-E7
MIDDLETON RD
- SMCo 94020 850-D7
MIDFIELD WY
3600 RDWC 94062 789-H1
MIDGLEN WY
800 WDSD 94062 789-F3
MIDLAND WY
700 SMCo 94062 789-F1
MIDTOWN CT
2700 PA 94303 791-C6
MIDVALE AV
300 SMTO 94403 749-C7
MIDVALE DR
- DALY 94015 687-A7
MIDWAY AV
400 SMTO 94402 748-G1
500 SMCo 94015 687-A4
MIDWAY CT
- DALY 94014 687-J3
MIDWAY DR
- DALY 94014 687-J3
MIELKE DR
400 MLPK 94025 790-G3

MILAGRA CT
- PCFA 94044 707-A4
MILAGRA DR
100 PCFA 94044 706-J4
200 PCFA 94044 707-A4
MILAN TER
- SF 94112 687-E2
MILANO WY
2700 SCAR 94070 769-F5
MILFORD AV
- HIL 94010 748-G2
MILL RD
400 SMCo 94062 788-H6
MILL ST
- SF 94134 688-A1
600 HMBY 94019 787-F1
MILLBRAE AV
- MLBR 94030 728-B4
1300 MLBR 94030 727-J5
E MILLBRAE AV
- MLBR 94030 728-C4
MILLBRAE CIR
- MLBR 94030 728-A5
MILLER AV
100 SSF 94080 707-F1
500 PCFA 94044 707-A4
1600 BLMT 94002 749-C7
MILLER CT
- SMCo 94061 790-B3
MILLIE AV
900 MLPK 94025 790-F4
MILLS AV
700 SBRN 94066 707-J6
1100 BURL 94010 728-D5
1700 BLMT 94002 749-C7
2000 SMCo 94025 790-C6
MILLS CT
1400 MLPK 94025 790-F3
MILLS ST
1200 MLPK 94025 790-F3
MILLS WY
1000 RDWC 94063 770-D6
MILLS CANYON CT
- BURL 94010 728-B6
MILLWOOD DR
100 MLBR 94030 728-A2
300 MLBR 94030 727-J2
MILTON AV
200 SBRN 94066 727-J1
200 SBRN 94066 728-A1
300 SBRN 94066 707-J7
MILTON ST
1600 SMCo 94061 790-B3
MILTONIA DR
- SSF 94080 707-E2
MIMOSA WY
100 SMCo 94028 810-D4
MINA LN
300 PCFA 94044 707-B3
MINDANAO DR
- RDWC 94065 749-J5
- RDWC 94065 750-A5
MINDEGO HILL RD
- SMCo 94020 849-H4
MINERVA AV
100 PCFA 94044 727-A2
MINERVA ST
- SF 94112 687-D1
MINOCA RD
- PTLV 94028 810-D5
MINORCA WY
- MLBR 94030 728-A4
MIO CTE
- MLBR 94030 728-A4
MIRA ST
100 FCTY 94404 749-E4
MIRA WY
- SMCo 94028 810-D4
MIRADA AV
600 SCIC 94305 810-H1
MIRADA DR
100 DALY 94015 687-B6
MIRADA RD
- SMCo 94019 767-C4
- HMBY 94019 767-C4
MIRADOR TER
900 PCFA 94044 707-A5
MIRAMAR
1400 SMTO 94404 749-D3
MIRAMAR AV
- SF 94112 687-D1
MIRAMAR DR
300 SMCo 94019 767-C4
MIRAMAR TER
700 BLMT 94002 769-E1
MIRAMONTE AV
100 PA 94306 791-A6
MIRAMONTE CT
- SCAR 94070 769-F2
MIRAMONTES AV
100 HMBY 94019 787-E1
MIRAMONTES RD
100 WDSD 94062 789-F6
MIRAMONTES ST
100 HMBY 94019 787-G1
200 SMCo 94019 787-G1
500 SMCo - 787-H1
MIRAMONTES POINT RD
300 SMCo 94019 787-G6
300 HMBY 94019 787-E5
MIRANDA CT
- HIL 94010 748-F4
1500 PCFA 94044 727-A3
MIRASOL CT
- HIL 94010 748-F5
MIRA VISTA CT
- DALY 94014 687-G3
MIRA VISTA WY
300 SSF 94080 707-F5
MIRIAM ST
- DALY 94014 687-C3
MIRMIROU DR
13900 LAH 94022 810-H6
MISSION CIR
- DALY 94014 687-D3
MISSION DR
- SMTO 94402 748-J2
100 EPA 94303 791-C3
MISSION RD
900 SSF 94080 707-E1
1400 CLMA 94014 707-E1
7400 CLMA 94014 687-E7
MISSION ST
4300 SF 94112 687-E2

MISSION ST
5900 DALY 94014 687-E2
MISSION ST Rt#-82
6300 DALY 94014 687-C4
MISSION BLUE DR
- BSBN 94005 687-J5
- BSBN 94005 688-A4
MISSION HILLS DR
- DALY 94014 687-F3
MISSION TRAIL RD
- WDSD 94062 789-F5
MISTY LN
1000 BLMT 94002 769-D2
MITCHELL AV
100 SSF 94080 708-A4
MITCHELL LN
400 PA 94301 790-H5
MITCHELL WY
1400 RDWC 94061 789-J3
MITTEN RD
800 BURL 94010 728-D3
MIZZEN LN
1500 HMBY 94019 767-E6
MOANA WY
200 PCFA 94044 706-J6
200 PCFA 94044 707-A6
MODOC AV
- SF 94112 687-E1
1300 MLPK 94025 770-J7
MODOC PL
200 PCFA 94044 727-B2
MOFFETT CIR
1000 PA 94303 791-D5
MOHICAN WY
800 RDWC 94062 789-G2
MOLITOR RD
1500 BLMT 94002 769-F2
MOLONEY CT
400 SMCo 94062 769-G7
E MOLTKE ST
- DALY 94014 687-C4
W MOLTKE ST
- DALY 94014 687-C4
MOLTON AV
- SCAR 94070 769-E3
MONACO DR
100 RDWC 94065 749-J5
MONARCH DR
- BSBN 94005 687-J5
MONETA CT
- SF 94112 687-E2
MONETA WY
- SF 94112 687-E2
MONO ST
- BSBN 94005 688-A6
MONROE AV
1300 SMTO 94401 729-A7
2000 BLMT 94002 749-C7
MONROE ST
100 RDWC 94063 770-B6
MONSERAT AV
2300 BLMT 94002 769-B1
MONTALVO RD
100 SMCo 94062 769-E7
MONTANA LN
- SMCo 94025 790-D5
MONTANA ST
- SF 94112 687-D1
100 SMCo 94038 746-F5
E MONTARA BLVD
1000 SMCo 94037 746-H5
W MONTARA BLVD
- SMCo 94037 746-G5
MONTARA CT
- PTLV 94028 810-D6
MONTCLAIR AV
- DALY 94015 686-J5
MONTEBELLO DR
- DALY 94015 707-A1
MONTEBELLO RD
- PA 94304 830-G6
- PA 94304 850-J1
MONTECITO AV
100 PCFA 94044 706-J6
400 SMCo 94019 767-A2
MONTECITO RD
- WDSD 94062 809-J5
MONTECITO WY
1800 BURL 94010 728-B5
MONTE CORVINO WY
1600 BURL 94010 728-C5
MONTE CRESTA CT
- BLMT 94002 769-B1
MONTE CRESTA DR
2600 BLMT 94002 769-B1
2600 BLMT 94002 749-A7
MONTE DIABLO AV
- SMTO 94401 748-J1
500 SMTO 94401 728-J7
900 SMTO 94401 729-A7
MONTEGO LN
- FCTY 94404 749-E6
- SMCo 94061 790-B4
- WDSD 94061 790-B4
MONTELENA CT
- WDSD 94062 809-G1
MONTEREY AV
- SMCo 94038 746-F7
1000 FCTY 94404 749-F5
2000 SMCo 94025 790-C6
MONTEREY DR
- DALY 94015 687-A6
1500 SBRN 94066 707-D7
1700 SBRN 94066 727-E1
MONTEREY RD
100 PCFA 94044 706-J3
200 PCFA 94044 707-A3
MONTEREY ST
- MLBR 94030 728-B2
100 BSBN 94005 688-A6
2600 SMTO 94403 749-A6
MONTERO AV
1300 BURL 94010 728-C6
MONTE ROSA DR
600 MLPK 94025 790-D7
600 MLPK 94025 810-D1
MONTE VERDE DR
900 PCFA 94044 726-J5
MONTE VISTA AV
- ATN 94027 790-C4
MONTE VISTA LN
700 HMBY 94019 787-F2
MONTEVISTA LN
100 DALY 94015 707-C2

MONTE VISTA RD
100 SCAR 94070 769-H2
100 SMCo 94037 746-H4
MONTE VISTA WY
- SSF 94014 707-J1
MONTEZUMA DR
600 PCFA 94044 726-H4
MONTGOMERY AV
900 SBRN 94066 707-J5
1200 SMCo 94061 790-B3
MONTGOMERY LN
800 SCAR 94070 769-H2
MONTGOMERY ST
900 SCAR 94070 769-G3
MONTICELLO CT
- WDSD 94062 789-E3
MONTICELLO RD
1700 SMCo 94402 748-F7
1700 SMCo 94402 768-G1
MONTICELLO ST
- SF 94132 687-C1
400 SF 94127 687-C1
MONTROSE AV
- DALY 94015 687-A5
MONTSERRAT DR
- RDWC 94065 749-J5
MONTWOOD CIR
300 SMCo 94061 790-B4
MOODY CT
26800 LAH 94022 830-J2
MOODY RD
12200 SCIC 95014 830-H2
12200 LAH 94022 830-H3
MOON LN
14000 LAH 94022 810-H6
MOONBEAM LN
- RDWC 94065 750-B4
MOON GATE CT
- PCFA 94044 707-A2
MOONLIGHT CT
- SSF 94080 707-E5
MOONSAIL LN
1200 FCTY 94404 749-H3
MOORE CT
100 SBRN 94066 707-E7
MOORE RD
100 WDSD 94062 789-J6
300 WDSD 94062 790-A6
MOORING LN
- DALY 94014 687-E6
MORAGA CT
900 PA 94303 791-E6
MORELAND DR
3200 SBRN 94066 707-D6
3400 SMCo 94044 707-D6
MORENO AV
700 PA 94303 791-D5
MORESBY LN
- RDWC 94063 770-B4
MOREY DR
500 MLPK 94025 790-G4
MORIS POINT RD
100 PCFA 94044 706-J7
100 PCFA 94044 726-J1
100 PCFA 94044 727-A1
MORNING LN
- RDWC 94065 750-A5
MORNINGSIDE AV
1100 SSF 94080 707-G1
MORNINGSIDE DR
- DALY 94015 686-J5
600 MLBR 94030 727-J4
S MORO AV
600 SMCo 94019 767-C3
MORRELL AV
800 BURL 94010 728-F6
MORRELL ST
300 SF 94124 688-E1
MORRIS DR
3100 PA 94303 791-E6
MORRO CT
500 FCTY 94404 749-F5
MORRO VISTA LN
100 SMCo 94028 810-C3
MORSE BLVD
1100 SCAR 94070 769-G4
MORSE LN
- SMCo 94062 809-E5
MORSE ST
- SF 94112 687-F2
MORTON DR
- DALY 94015 707-B2
MORTON ST
- PA 94303 791-C5
MORTON WY
- PA 94303 791-C5
MOSCOW ST
300 SF 94112 687-G2
MOSELEY RD
300 HIL 94010 748-D3
MOSHER WY
- PA 94304 790-F5
MOSS AV
300 SMCo 94062 788-H5
MOSSWOOD LN
800 MLBR 94030 727-H3
MOSSWOOD RD
- HIL 94010 748-D3
MOSSWOOD WY
- ATN 94027 770-G7
200 SSF 94080 707-G5
MOULTON DR
- ATN 94027 790-F2
3800 SBRN 94066 707-C6
MOUNDS RD
- SMTO 94402 748-H1
MOUNTAIN RD
100 SSF 94080 707-H2
MOUNTAIN VW
300 DALY 94014 687-D4
MOUNTAIN HOME CT
300 WDSD 94062 789-G7
MOUNTAIN HOME RD
- WDSD 94062 789-G7
400 WDSD 94062 809-H1
MOUNTAIN MEADOW DR
- SMCo 94062 809-C4
MOUNTAIN VIEW AV
300 BLMT 94002 749-E7
300 SMTO 94403 749-E7
MOUNTAIN VIEW PL
- SMCo 94402 748-H7
MOUNTAIN VIEW WY
500 SMCo 94062 789-F1

MOUNTAIN WOOD CT
- HIL 94010 748-H4
MOUNTAIN WOOD LN
- HIL 94010 748-H4
100 WDSD 94062 789-G7
100 WDSD 94062 809-G1
MOUNT VERNON AV
- SF 94112 687-E1
MOUNT VERNON LN
- ATN 94027 790-E1
MOUTON CIR
- EPA 94303 791-C3
MUDDY RD
- SMCo - 787-J1
- SMCo - 788-A1
- SMCo - 768-A7
MUIR WY
- PCFA 94044 727-B5
1000 BLMT 94002 769-A2
MUIRFIELD CIR
2600 SBRN 94066 707-D5
MUIRFIELD RD
- HMBY 94019 787-F5
MUIRWOOD DR
- DALY 94014 687-D3
MULBERRY AV
100 SSF 94080 707-G3
MULBERRY CT
- BLMT 94002 769-C2
MULBERRY DR
1700 SMTO 94403 748-J7
MULBERRY LN
- ATN 94027 790-C5
MULLER CT
3000 RDWC 94061 789-J3
MULLET CT
300 FCTY 94404 749-H3
MULLINS CT
- MLBR 94030 727-J5
MULRYAN CT
- SMTO 94403 749-C6
MUNICH ST
200 SF 94112 687-G1
MURCHISON DR
500 MLBR 94030 728-A5
1400 BURL 94010 728-A5
MURDOCH CT
3400 PA 94306 791-D7
MURDOCH DR
3400 PA 94306 791-D7
MURPHY CT
- SMTO 94402 748-H5
MURPHY DR
700 SMTO 94402 748-H5
900 HIL 94010 748-H5
MURRAY CT
- RDWC 94061 790-B1
- SMTO 94403 749-B6
MURRAY WY
3200 PA 94303 791-E6
MUSEUM WY
100 SCIC 94305 790-H6
MYRNA LN
3700 SSF 94080 707-C4
MYRTLE AV
500 SSF 94080 707-G3
MYRTLE CT
100 EPA 94303 791-C2
MYRTLE PL
- EPA 94303 791-C2
MYRTLE RD
100 BURL 94010 728-G6
MYRTLE ST
- RDWC 94062 769-H6
200 HMBY 94019 787-E2
600 RDWC 94061 769-J7
900 EPA 94303 791-C2
MYSTIC LN
600 FCTY 94404 749-F4

N

NADELL CT
- SF 94112 687-F2
NADINA AV
400 MLBR 94030 728-B3
NADINA ST
1200 SMTO 94402 749-A3
NAGLEE AV
- SF 94112 687-E2
NAHUA AV
- SF 94112 687-E1
NANCY LN
600 DALY 94014 687-H3
NANCY WY
- MLPK 94025 790-E6
NANETTE DR
2500 SCAR 94070 769-F5
NANTUCKET DR
800 RDWC 94065 750-C6
NANTUCKET ST
400 FCTY 94404 749-F5
NAOMI AV
100 PCFA 94044 727-A2
NAOMI CT
1600 RDWC 94061 790-A1
NAPLES AV
2800 HMBY 94019 767-D4
NAPLES ST
300 SF 94112 687-G1
NARANJA WY
- PTLV 94028 810-A5
NASH AV
600 MLPK 94025 790-H2
NASH DR
1700 SMTO 94401 749-C1
NASSAU DR
2000 SMCo 94061 790-B4
NASTURTIUM RD
- SMCo 94019 787-G5
NATAQUA AV
100 PCFA 94044 727-B2
NATHAN CT
3700 PA 94303 791-F7
NATHAN WY
3700 PA 94303 791-F7
NATHAN ABBOTT WY
- SCIC 94305 790-H7
NATHHORST AV
100 PTLV 94028 810-C7
NATIONAL DR
1100 SBRN 94066 707-H5
NATIVE SONS RD
500 SMCo 94060 868-F2

NATIVE SONS OF THE GOLDEN WEST
1400 SMCo 94062 808-E3
NATOMA RD
13100 LAH 94022 810-J7
27200 LAH 94022 830-J1
NATURE LN
- RDWC 94065 750-B4
NAUGHTON AV
3800 BLMT 94002 769-A2
W NAUGHTON AV
3700 BLMT 94002 768-J2
3700 BLMT 94002 769-A2
NAVAJO AV
- SF 94112 687-F1
NAVAJO PL
- PTLV 94028 810-B5
NAVARRA AV
100 SMCo 94019 767-A1
NAVARRE DR
500 PCFA 94044 726-H4
NAYLOR ST
- SF 94112 687-G2
NEAL AV
700 SCAR 94070 769-G5
NEEDLERIDGE CT
- SMTO 94402 748-C7
NELSON AV
100 PCFA 94044 707-A3
NELSON CT
- DALY 94015 707-C3
NELSON RD
- SCIC 94305 790-J6
NEPTUNE CT
800 SMTO 94404 749-D2
NEPTUNE DR
400 RDWC 94065 749-H7
NEPTUNE LN
700 FCTY 94404 749-E4
NERLI LN
1200 BURL 94010 728-E5
NEUCHATEL AV
700 BURL 94010 728-F6
NEUMAN LN
- WDSD 94062 789-G6
NEVADA AV
100 PA 94301 791-B6
200 SMCo 94038 746-F7
400 SMTO 94402 748-H4
NEVADA ST
- RDWC 94062 769-H6
600 RDWC 94061 769-J7
700 RDWC 94061 789-J1
NEWBRIDGE AV
1200 SMTO 94401 749-B1
1900 SMTO 94401 729-C7
NEWBRIDGE ST
100 MLPK 94025 770-J7
600 MLPK 94025 790-J1
800 MLPK 94025 791-A1
900 EPA 94303 791-A1
NEW BRUNSWICK DR
2000 SMCo 94402 768-G1
NEWCASTLE CT
200 RDWC 94061 790-B2
NEWCASTLE DR
300 RDWC 94061 790-B2
NEWCASTLE LN
100 BLMT 94002 749-F6
NEWELL PL
800 PA 94303 791-B4
NEWELL RD
- EPA 94303 791-B3
400 PA 94303 791-B5
400 PA 94301 791-B4
NEWHALL RD
700 BURL 94010 728-E6
700 HIL 94010 728-E6
NEWLANDS AV
600 SMTO 94403 749-B7
1500 BURL 94010 728-G7
2500 BLMT 94002 769-B1
NEWMAN DR
300 SSF 94080 707-D1
NEW MAYFIELD LN
200 PA 94306 791-A7
NEW PLACE RD
- HIL 94010 748-D1
NEWPORT AV
- SMCo 94038 746-F7
NEWPORT CIR
700 RDWC 94065 749-H6
NEWPORT CT
500 FCTY 94404 749-F5
NEWPORT ST
2300 SMCo 94402 748-F7
NEWTON DR
100 SMCo 94010 728-B6
NEWTON ST
- SF 94112 687-F2
NIAGARA AV
- SF 94112 687-E1
NIAGRA AV
- SMCo 94038 746-F5
NIANTIC AV
- SF 94132 687-C2
400 DALY 94014 687-C3
NIANTIC DR
700 FCTY 94404 749-G2
NIBBI CT
- SF 94134 688-B2
NICE CT
500 RDWC 94065 749-J5
NICHOLS WY
- SF 94124 688-C1
NICK GUST WY
400 PCFA 94044 726-H2
NILES AV
1300 SBRN 94066 727-H1
NIMITZ AV
- RDWC 94061 790-B3
- SMCo 94061 790-B3
NIMITZ DR
1000 SMCo 94015 687-A4
NIMITZ LN
1100 FCTY 94404 749-G4
NINA LN
700 FCTY 94404 749-G2
NIZHONI RD
100 SMCo 94037 746-G5
NOB HILL RD
900 RDWC 94061 789-H2
NOE AV
1500 SMTO 94401 749-C2

NOEL DR
1000 MLPK 94025 790-G3
NOEL RD
- WDSD 94062 789-F7
- WDSD 94062 809-F1
NOOR AV
400 SSF 94080 707-H5
NORA WY
- ATN 94027 790-D2
900 SSF 94080 707-G2
NORBURT LN
2800 SCAR 94070 769-G6
NORFOLK DR
300 PCFA 94044 707-A3
N NORFOLK ST
1200 SMTO 94401 729-A7
S NORFOLK ST
1200 SMTO 94401 729-A7
1300 SMTO 94401 749-B1
1500 SMTO 94403 749-D4
NORIEGA WY
700 PCFA 94044 726-H4
NORMA LN
800 FCTY 94404 749-H1
NORMAN ST
1300 RDWC 94061 790-A1
NORMANDY CT
- HIL 94010 748-H2
100 SCAR 94070 769-D5
NORMANDY LN
100 ATN 94027 790-D2
100 WDSD 94062 789-J3
NORTH CT
- SBRN 94066 727-G2
1100 BLMT 94002 749-D7
NORTH LN
1000 BURL 94010 728-G6
NORTH PZ
- MLPK 94025 790-J1
NORTH RD
800 SMTO 94403 749-D7
800 BLMT 94002 749-D7
1400 BLMT 94002 769-D1
NORTH ST
- SMCo 94060 868-B2
NORTHAM AV
- SCAR 94070 769-E2
NORTHAMPTON DR
700 PA 94303 791-B5
NORTHAVEN DR
300 DALY 94015 687-A7
NORTHCREST DR
1200 SSF 94080 707-H1
NORTH FORK LN
13400 LAH 94022 810-J7
NORTHGATE AV
- DALY 94015 687-A3
200 DALY 94015 686-J3
NORTHGATE CT
- DALY 94015 687-A3
NORTHGATE DR
100 WDSD 94062 790-A5
NORTHGATE ST
100 ATN 94027 790-D2
NORTHHAMPTON LN
100 BLMT 94002 749-F6
NORTH HILL DR
- BSBN 94005 687-J5
- BSBN 94005 688-A5
NORTHRIDGE DR
- DALY 94015 686-J6
NORTHRIDGE LN
100 WDSD 94062 789-J3
NORTHUMBERLAND AV
- RDWC 94063 770-C7
- SMCo 94063 770-C7
300 RDWC 94061 790-B1
NORTH VIEW WY
- SMCo 94062 789-F1
NORTHWOOD DR
100 SSF 94080 707-F5
1000 SCAR 94070 769-G2
NORTON ST
900 SMTO 94401 749-B1
1600 SMTO 94403 749-B1
NORWICH DR
200 SSF 94080 707-D2
NORWOOD AV
- DALY 94015 707-C2
NOTRE DAME AV
- SMTO 94402 748-J3
900 BLMT 94002 769-D1
1600 EPA 94303 771-B7
1600 BLMT 94002 749-C7
NOTRE DAME PL
- BLMT 94002 769-D1
NOTTINGHAM AV
- SMCo 94063 770-C7
- SMCo 94063 790-C1
NOTTINGHAM LN
500 FCTY 94404 749-G5
NOVA LN
300 MLPK 94025 790-J3
NUEVA AV
100 SF 94134 688-B2
NUEVA ST
- RDWC 94061 790-B1
NURSERY WY
900 SSF 94080 707-G2
NYLA AV
100 SSF 94080 707-E3

O

OAK AV
- HMBY 94019 787-F1
- RDWC 94061 789-J1
- SSF 94080 707-G2
300 SBRN 94066 727-H1
300 SMCo 94062 788-H5
300 RDWC 94061 790-A1
500 SBRN 94066 707-H7
1000 RDWC 94061 770-B7
1000 SMCo 94038 746-G7
1600 MLPK 94025 790-J2
1600 MLPK 94025 790-F6
1900 SMCo 94025 790-F6
OAK CT
- DALY 94014 687-G3
100 MLPK 94025 791-A3
3200 BLMT 94002 749-A7
OAK DR
3400 SMCo 94025 770-E7
3500 SMCo 94025 790-E1
3600 ATN 94027 790-E1

STREET	Block	City	ZIP	Pg-Grid
OAK LN	900	MLPK	94025	790-F4
OAK RD	-	SCIC	94305	790-F6
OAK ST	-	MLBR	94030	728-A2
	1200	SCAR	94070	769-G2
	1200	SMTO	94402	749-A3
	1300	SMTO	94402	748-J3
OAK CREEK DR	1300	PA	94304	790-F6
OAK CREEK LN	-	SCAR	94070	769-F6
OAKCREST AV	200	SSF	94080	707-F1
OAKDALE AV	400	EPA	94303	791-B1
OAKDALE RD	2200	HIL	94010	728-D7
OAKDALE ST	-	RDWC	94062	769-J5
OAKDELL DR	1600	MLPK	94025	790-E6
OAKES ST	-	EPA	94303	791-C3
OAKFIELD AV	100	RDWC	94061	790-B2
OAKFIELD LN	500	MLPK	94025	790-E6
OAKFORD RD	100	WDSD	94062	789-J4
OAK FOREST CT	-	PTLV	94028	830-D2
OAK GROVE AV	-	ATN	94027	790-G2
	100	MLPK	94025	790-F3
	500	BURL	94010	728-F6
OAK GROVE PZ	700	MLPK	94025	790-F4
OAKHAVEN WY	-	WDSD	94062	789-J5
OAKHILL CT	3400	SMTO	94403	748-J7
OAKHILL DR	-	WDSD	94062	809-F1
OAK HILL LN	100	SMCo	94010	728-B7
OAK HOLLOW WY	-	MLPK	94025	790-E7
OAKHURST AV	1300	SCAR	94070	769-G4
OAKHURST PL	200	MLPK	94025	770-G7
OAK KNOLL DR	1200	RDWC	94062	769-C1
	1200	SMCo	94062	769-C1
	1700	BLMT	94002	749-D7
	1700	BLMT	94002	769-C1
	3200	RDWC	94062	789-G1
	3200	SMCo	94062	789-G1
OAK KNOLL LN	500	MLPK	94025	790-E6
OAKLAND AV	1000	MLPK	94025	770-H7
	1000	MLPK	94025	790-H1
OAKLAWN DR	-	DALY	94015	687-A3
OAKLEY AV	200	SCAR	94070	769-D4
	200	SMCo	94070	769-D4
	2000	SMCo	94025	790-D6
OAKMONT DR	-	DALY	94015	686-J4
	1800	SBRN	94066	707-D5
	3100	SSF	94080	707-D5
OAK PARK WY	500	SMCo	94062	789-E2
S OAK PARK WY	500	SMCo	94062	789-F2
OAKRIDGE DR	-	DALY	94014	687-G3
	200	SMCo	94014	687-G3
	400	RDWC	94062	789-H1
	600	RDWC	94061	789-H1
OAK RIM DR	1400	HIL	94010	748-E5
OAKS DR	2100	HIL	94010	728-D7
OAKSIDE AV	500	SMCo	94063	770-D7
OAK TREE LN	-	BLMT	94002	769-E2
OAK TREE PL	-	HIL	94010	728-C7
OAK VALLEY RD	-	SMTO	94402	748-H4
OAKVIEW DR	100	SCAR	94070	769-G5
OAKVIEW WY	600	SMCo	94062	789-G1
	700	RDWC	94062	789-G1
OAKWOOD BLVD	-	RDWC	94061	790-C1
	-	ATN	94027	790-C1
E OAKWOOD BLVD	200	RDWC	94061	790-C1
W OAKWOOD BLVD	200	RDWC	94061	790-C1
OAKWOOD CT	1200	PCFA	94044	726-J6
OAKWOOD DR	-	RDWC	94061	790-C1
	1100	MLBR	94030	727-H3
	1600	SMTO	94403	748-H7
	2000	EPA	94303	791-A2
OAKWOOD PL	300	MLPK	94025	770-H7
	300	MLPK	94025	790-H1
OBERLIN ST	1900	SCIC	94305	791-A7
OBISPO RD	500	SMCo	94019	767-B3
OBRIEN DR	900	MLPK	94025	771-A7
	1400	EPA	94303	771-B7
O BRINE LN	-	PA	94303	791-D4
OCCIDENTAL AV	100	BURL	94010	728-F7
	100	BURL	94010	748-G1
	400	SMTO	94402	748-G1
	400	HIL	94010	728-F7
OCCIDENTAL WY	800	SMCo	94062	789-F2
OCEAN AV	-	SMCo	94019	766-J3
	500	HMBY	94019	787-E1
OCEAN BLVD	200	SMCo	94038	746-F7
	300	SMCo	94038	766-F1
OCEANA BLVD	300	PCFA	94044	706-J4
OCEAN GROVE AV	-	DALY	94015	687-A5
OCEANSIDE DR	-	DALY	94015	686-J7
	-	DALY	94015	687-A7
OCEANSIDE WY	-	RDWC	94065	749-J5
OCEAN VIEW AV	500	SMTO	94401	729-B7
	500	SMTO	94401	749-B1
OCEANVIEW AV	-	HMBY	94019	787-G5
OCEAN VIEW DR	-	SMCo	-	768-C3
O CONNOR ST	900	EPA	94303	791-C2
OCONNOR ST	100	MLPK	94025	791-A2
	500	EPA	94303	791-A2
W OCONNOR ST	100	MLPK	94025	791-A2
	300	MLPK	94025	790-J2
ODDSTAD BLVD	600	PCFA	94044	727-C5
ODDSTAD DR	1100	RDWC	94063	770-B5
ODDSTAD WY	600	PCFA	94044	726-J2
ODELL PL	-	ATN	94027	790-E2
ODESSA CT	-	RDWC	94063	770-F6
OFARRELL ST	1900	SMTO	94403	749-A4
OGDEN DR	1800	BURL	94010	728-B4
OHIO AV	2400	RDWC	94061	790-A3
OHLONE	-	PTLV	94028	830-C2
OHLONE WY	-	SMCo	94020	850-F6
OKEEFE ST	100	MLPK	94025	791-A2
	300	MLPK	94025	790-J2
E OKEEFE ST	100	EPA	94303	791-A2
	100	MLPK	94025	791-A2
OLCESE CT	-	DALY	94015	687-B6
OLD CANADA RD	-	SMCo	94062	768-F3
	-	SMCo	94062	769-A7
OLD COUNTY RD	-	BLMT	94002	749-D7
	-	BSBN	94005	688-A6
	100	SCAR	94070	769-G3
	400	PCFA	94044	726-J2
	700	BLMT	94002	769-F1
	1300	SMCo	94002	769-F1
	4100	SMTO	94403	749-D7
OLD LA HONDA RD	-	PTLV	94028	809-H7
	-	PTLV	94062	809-G6
	-	WDSD	94062	809-H5
	1300	SMCo	94020	809-G6
	1300	SMCo	94020	829-F2
OLD PAGE MILL LN	28000	LAH	94304	810-H4
OLD PAGE MILL RD	2000	LAH	94304	810-J4
	2000	SCIC	94304	810-J4
	2200	PA	94304	810-J4
	2300	LAH	94022	810-J4
OLD PAGE MILL TR	20800	SMCo	94020	850-E2
OLD RANCH RD	100	SMCo	94062	788-H4
OLD SPANISH TR	-	SMCo	94028	830-D4
	100	PTLV	94028	830-D4
OLD STAGE RD	1400	SMCo	94060	848-B5
	1400	SMCo	94074	848-B5
OLD STAGE COACH RD	-	SMCo	94062	769-E7
OLD STATE HWY	200	SMCo	94037	746-F5
OLD WOMANS CREEK RD	-	SCrC	95017	888-J5
	-	SMCo	94060	888-G7
OLEANDER WY	-	SMCo	94019	787-H5
OLIVE AV	300	PA	94306	791-B7
	600	SSF	94080	707-J2
OLIVE CT	-	SMTO	94401	729-B7
	700	SBRN	94066	707-H7
OLIVE LN	-	PCFA	94044	706-J6
OLIVE ST	300	MLPK	94025	790-E5
	1100	SCAR	94070	769-G3
OLIVE HILL LN	100	WDSD	94062	789-F5
OLIVER CT	-	MLPK	94025	790-C6
OLIVER ST	-	DALY	94014	687-E3
	-	SF	94112	687-E3
	1100	RDWC	94061	790-A1
OLIVET PKWY	400	CLMA	94014	687-D6
OLMO FIRE RD	-	SMCo	94060	888-H2
OLMSTEAD CT	2500	SSF	94080	707-C4
OLMSTEAD ST	-	SF	94134	688-A1
	700	SF	94134	687-J1
OLMSTED RD	-	SCIC	94305	791-A7
	-	SCIC	94305	810-J1
	-	SCIC	94305	790-J7
OLYMPIAN WY	100	PCFA	94044	726-G4
OLYMPIC AV	2300	MLPK	94025	790-D7
	4200	SMTO	94403	749-D6
OLYMPIC CT	100	SBRN	94066	707-D5
OLYMPIC DR	2300	SSF	94080	707-D5
	2500	SBRN	94066	707-D5
OLYMPIC WY	2100	SMCo	94015	686-J3
	2200	DALY	94015	686-J3
ONEIDA AV	-	SF	94112	687-F1
ONEILL AV	-	BLMT	94002	749-F7
	-	SMCo	94002	749-F7
	200	BLMT	94002	769-E1
	200	SMCo	94002	769-F1
ONEILL DR	3900	SMTO	94403	749-D5
ONEONTA AV	500	PCFA	94044	727-A1
ONONDAGA AV	-	SF	94112	687-F1
ONTARIO ST	-	SMTO	94401	729-B7
OPAL AV	100	RDWC	94062	769-H7
ORACLE PKWY	100	RDWC	94065	749-F6
ORANGE AV	-	SSF	94080	707-H3
	700	SCAR	94070	769-G3
	1100	MLPK	94025	790-D5
	1100	SMCo	94025	790-D5
W ORANGE AV	-	SSF	94080	707-F3
ORANGE CT	-	DALY	94014	687-D5
	-	HIL	94010	748-D1
ORANGE ST	500	DALY	94014	687-D5
ORCHARD AV	-	RDWC	94061	790-B1
ORCHARD HILL LN	-	WDSD	94062	809-H6
ORCHARD HILLS ST	-	ATN	94027	790-B4
ORCHID DR	-	SSF	94080	707-E2
ORDWAY ST	-	SF	94134	688-A1
OREGON AV	100	PA	94301	791-B6
	200	SMTO	94402	748-H4
	700	PA	94303	791-B6
	2100	RDWC	94061	789-J2
	2100	RDWC	94061	790-A2
OREGON EXWY Rt#-G3	-	PA	94301	791-C6
	-	PA	94306	791-C6
	2500	PA	94303	791-C6
ORIENTE ST	-	DALY	94014	687-J4
	-	SF	94134	687-J4
ORINDA AV	-	PCFA	94044	727-A2
ORINDA DR	3500	SMTO	94403	749-D5
ORION LN	700	FCTY	94404	749-F4
ORISKANY DR	-	SMCo	94402	748-G7
ORIZABA AV	100	SF	94132	687-D2
	100	SF	94112	687-D2
ORREY WY	-	SSF	94080	707-E5
ORTEGA CT	-	PCFA	94044	726-J4
	3700	PA	94303	791-F7
ORVAL AV	100	SMCo	94038	746-G7
OSBORN AV	1100	SMCo	94061	790-B3
OSO ST	3600	SMTO	94403	749-D5
OSPREY CT	-	RDWC	94065	750-A5
OSPREY DR	-	RDWC	94065	750-A5
OTAY AV	-	SMTO	94403	749-C5
OTEGA AV	-	SF	94112	687-E1
OTIS AV	100	WDSD	94062	789-G5
OTSEGO AV	300	SF	94112	687-F1
OTTAWA AV	-	SF	94112	687-E1
OTTAWA ST	-	SMTO	94401	729-A6
OTTERSON CT	2900	PA	94303	791-D5
OTTILIA ST	300	DALY	94014	687-J3
OUR HILL LN	2900	WDSD	94062	789-H6
OUTER CIR	200	RDWC	94062	769-H7
OUTLOOK CIR	1000	PCFA	94044	707-B6
OUTLOOK DR	-	SBRN	94066	707-B6
	1100	PCFA	94044	707-B6
OUTLOOK HEIGHTS CT	-	PCFA	94044	707-B6
OUTLOOK HEIGHTS DR	-	PCFA	94044	707-B6
OUTRIGGER LN	1100	FCTY	94404	749-H4
OVERLAND DR	1300	SMTO	94403	748-J7
OVERLOOK CT	800	SMTO	94403	749-A7
OVIEDO CT	-	PCFA	94044	726-J4
OXFORD AV	200	PA	94306	791-A7
	1500	SMTO	94403	749-C3
OXFORD CT N	-	BLMT	94002	749-F7
OXFORD CT S	-	BLMT	94002	749-F7
OXFORD LN	100	SBRN	94066	727-G2
OXFORD PL	-	BLMT	94002	749-E7
OXFORD RD	1100	BURL	94010	728-D5
OXFORD ST	500	SF	94134	687-J1
	1300	RDWC	94061	790-A1
OXFORD WY	100	BLMT	94002	749-F7
OYSTER CT	500	FCTY	94404	749-F5
OYSTER POINT BLVD	100	SSF	94080	708-B2
P				
PABLO CT	100	HMBY	94019	787-G2
PACIFIC AV	-	SBRN	94066	707-J5
	100	PCFA	94044	706-J6
	200	PCFA	94044	707-A6
	200	SMCo	94063	770-C7
	900	HMBY	94019	767-E6
PACIFIC BLVD	1800	SMTO	94402	749-B3
	1800	SMTO	94403	749-B3
PACIFIC CREST DR	-	SMCo	-	768-D3
PACIFIC HEIGHTS BLVD	3700	SBRN	94066	707-C5
PACIFICO AV	-	DALY	94015	687-A7
PACIFIC VIEW DR	-	PCFA	94044	707-B6
	-	SBRN	94066	707-B6
	-	SMCo	-	768-D4
PACIFIC VIEW LN	-	SMCo	94060	868-F3
PADDINGTON CT	-	BLMT	94002	769-B3
PAGE ST	3000	RDWC	94063	770-E6
PAGE MILL RD	100	PA	94306	791-B7
	600	PA	94304	791-B7
	1000	PA	94304	830-G2
	1000	SCIC	95014	830-G2
	1800	PA	94304	810-H7
	1800	SCIC	94305	810-H7
	4100	SCIC	94028	830-F7
	4100	SCIC	94028	850-E1
	11400	LAH	94022	830-G2
	11900	SCIC	94022	830-G2
	12700	LAH	94022	810-H7
	20600	SMCo	94020	850-E1
	20800	SMCo	94028	830-F7
PAGE MILL RD Rt#-G3	1800	SCIC	94305	810-J4
	1800	PA	94304	810-J4
	1900	SCIC	94304	810-J4
	2100	LAH	94022	810-J4
PALISADES DR	-	DALY	94015	686-J5
PALM AV	-	MLBR	94030	728-A3
	100	SCAR	94070	769-F3
	500	SSF	94080	707-H2
	700	RDWC	94061	790-A1
	800	RDWC	94061	789-J2
	900	SMTO	94401	749-A2
	1200	SMTO	94402	749-A2
	2000	SMTO	94403	749-B4
PALM CT	-	MLPK	94025	790-E5
	100	SBRN	94066	707-E7
PALM DR	100	PA	94305	790-H6
	100	SCIC	94305	790-H6
	1100	BURL	94010	728-E6
PALM PL	1900	SMTO	94403	749-B4
PALM ST	400	PA	94301	791-A3
PALMA ST	100	SMCo	94019	767-B2
PALM BEACH AV	100	SMCo	94019	766-J2
	100	SMCo	94019	767-A1
PALM CIRCLE CT	-	SMCo	94062	789-E3
	-	WDSD	94062	789-E3
PALMCREST DR	100	DALY	94015	687-B4
PALMDALE AV	-	DALY	94015	687-A5
PALMER AV	2400	BLMT	94002	769-B1
PALMER LN	-	PTLV	94028	810-C6
	200	SMCo	94025	790-E1
	200	ATN	94027	790-E1
	400	SMCo	94025	770-E7
PALMETTO AV	300	SF	94132	687-C2
	500	PCFA	94044	706-J2
	4400	PCFA	94044	707-A2
PALMETTO CT	5000	PCFA	94044	707-A2
PALMITO DR	900	MLBR	94030	728-A2
PALO DR	-	PA	94304	790-H5
	-	SCIC	94305	790-H5
PALO ALTO AV	100	PA	94301	790-J3
	1000	PA	94301	791-A3
PALO ALTO WY	1900	SMCo	94025	790-E7
PALOMA AV	-	PCFA	94044	706-J5
	100	SMCo	94019	767-A2
	200	PCFA	94044	707-A5
	700	BURL	94010	728-D5
	1300	BLMT	94002	769-E1
PALOMA RD	-	PTLV	94028	810-B5
PALOMAR CT	300	SBRN	94066	727-H1
PALOMAR DR	300	DALY	94015	687-A7
	700	SMCo	94062	769-E6
S PALOMAR DR	-	SMCo	94062	769-F6
PALOMAR OAKS LN	-	SMCo	94062	769-F7
PALOS VERDES CT	3200	SMTO	94403	748-J6
PALOS VERDES DR	1300	SMTO	94403	748-J6
PALOS VERDES WY	3700	SSF	94080	707-C4
PALOU DR	1100	PCFA	94044	726-J6
PALO VERDE AV	2300	EPA	94303	791-A1
PAMELA CT	-	DALY	94015	687-B6
PAMPAS LN	300	SCIC	94305	790-J7
PANAMA ST	100	SCIC	94305	790-G7
	100	SF	94132	687-C2
PANORAMA CT	-	PCFA	94044	707-C5
	-	HIL	94010	748-B1
PARADISE CT	-	HIL	94010	748-G6
PARADISE DR	100	PCFA	94044	707-A2
PARADISE WY	700	SMCo	94062	789-F2
PARAMOUNT DR	200	MLBR	94030	728-A2
	300	MLBR	94030	727-J3
PARIS ST	300	SF	94112	687-F1
PARK AV	100	PA	94306	791-A7
	100	SCAR	94070	769-H5
	100	SMCo	94038	746-G7
	300	SMCo	94038	766-G1
	700	BURL	94010	728-F6
	1200	SBRN	94066	707-H7
PARK BLVD	100	MLBR	94030	728-A2
	100	MLBR	94030	727-J2
	200	SBRN	94066	727-J2
	200	PA	94306	791-A6
PARK DR	-	ATN	94027	790-D2
PARK LN	-	MLPK	94025	790-J1
	100	ATN	94027	790-D4
	100	BSBN	94005	688-A6
	400	SMTO	94402	748-G1
PARK PL	-	SMTO	94403	749-D4
	-	RDWC	94065	749-J2
	100	MLBR	94030	727-J2
	100	MLBR	94030	728-A2
	100	SBRN	94066	727-J2
	100	SBRN	94066	728-A2
	100	BSBN	94005	688-A6
PARK RD	-	BURL	94010	728-G7
	600	SMCo	94062	789-F1
	3000	SMCo	94063	770-D7
	3200	SMCo	94025	770-D7
PARK ST	100	RDWC	94061	770-C7
	100	RDWC	94061	790-B1
	800	SMCo	94037	746-J5
PARK WY	100	SSF	94080	707-H2
	1000	SMCo	94038	746-G7
PARKDALE WY	3100	RDWC	94061	789-H2
PARKER AV	-	ATN	94027	790-B4
PARKGROVE DR	-	SSF	94014	707-H1
PARKINSON AV	1000	PA	94301	791-A4
PARK MANOR DR	-	DALY	94015	686-J4
PARK PACIFICA AV	900	PCFA	94044	727-B5
PARK PLAZA DR	-	DALY	94015	687-B3
	200	SMCo	94015	687-B4
PARKRIDGE CIR	-	SSF	94014	687-H7
	-	SSF	94014	707-H1
PARKRIDGE CT	-	BLMT	94002	769-C3
PARKROSE AV	-	DALY	94015	707-B2
PARKSIDE AV	-	DALY	94015	687-A3
	1900	HIL	94010	748-F1
PARKSIDE WY	500	SMTO	94403	749-A5
PARKVIEW AV	-	DALY	94014	687-C3
N PARKVIEW AV	200	DALY	94014	687-C3
S PARKVIEW AV	-	DALY	94014	687-C3
PARKVIEW CIR	600	PCFA	94044	707-B2
PARKVIEW CT	100	SBRN	94066	727-H2
	600	PCFA	94044	707-B2
PARKVIEW DR	100	SBRN	94066	727-H2
PARKVIEW WY	2700	SMTO	94403	749-A5
W PARKWAY LN	500	FCTY	94404	749-E3
PARKWOOD DR	-	ATN	94027	790-H1
	-	DALY	94015	687-B3
	1400	SMTO	94403	748-H7
	1800	SMTO	94403	768-H1
PARKWOOD WY	1000	RDWC	94061	790-B2
PARMA ST	-	DALY	94014	687-D4
PARNELL AV	-	DALY	94015	707-C2
PARQUE DR	100	SF	94134	687-H2
PARROTT CT	-	SMTO	94402	748-H7
PARROTT DR	200	SMTO	94402	748-H3
	900	HIL	94010	748-G5
	1100	SMCo	94402	748-G5
PARTITION RD	3500	WDSD	94062	789-E7
	3500	WDSD	94062	809-F1
PARTRIDGE AV	100	DALY	94014	687-J3
	600	MLPK	94025	790-G4
PARTRIDGE LN	-	DALY	94014	687-E3
PASADENA DR	3500	SMTO	94403	749-D5
PASADENA ST	-	DALY	94014	687-H2
	-	SF	94134	687-H2
PASEITO TER	900	PCFA	94044	706-J5
PASEO DEL ROBLE	13500	LAH	94022	810-H6
PASEO DEL ROBLE CT	13600	LAH	94022	810-H6
PASO DEL ARROYO	-	PTLV	94028	810-D7
PASSAGE LN	-	RDWC	94065	750-C4
PASTEUR DR	100	PA	94304	790-G6
	100	SCIC	94305	790-G6
	200	PA	94305	790-G6
PATRICIA AV	400	SMTO	94401	749-B1
PATRICIA DR	-	ATN	94027	790-C2
PATRICIA LN	500	PA	94303	791-C4
PATRICIA PL	-	MLPK	94025	790-F5
PATRICK WY	-	HMBY	94019	787-G1
PATROL CT	-	WDSD	94062	789-D6
PATROL RD	500	WDSD	94062	789-D6
PATTERSON AV	-	SMCo	94025	790-D5
PATTON PL	-	HIL	94010	728-C7
	-	HIL	94010	748-C1
PAUL AV	-	BSBN	94005	688-A7
	-	SF	94124	688-B1
PAUL ST	-	DALY	94014	687-D4
PAUL ROBESON CT	800	EPA	94303	791-B1
PAUL SCANNELL DR	-	SMCo	94402	768-H2
PAULSEN LN	200	PA	94301	790-J4
PAULSON CT	-	SMTO	94403	749-B4
PAVO LN	600	FCTY	94404	749-E4
PAYSON ST	-	SF	94132	687-C2
PEABODY ST	-	SF	94134	688-A2
PEACHWOOD CT	1200	SBRN	94066	707-H7
PEAK LN	-	PTLV	94028	810-D5
PEAR CT	-	HIL	94010	748-D2
PEARCE MITCHELL PL	-	SCIC	94305	810-H1
PEARL AV	100	SCAR	94070	769-H5
	1000	SMCo	94038	746-G6
PEARL ST	700	SMCo	94038	746-F6
PEAR ORCHARD WY	-	SMCo	94019	787-G5
PEARY LN	800	FCTY	94404	749-F4
PEBBLE DR	1300	SCAR	94070	769-E6
	1300	SMCo	94062	769-E6
PEBBLEWOOD WY	1100	SMTO	94403	749-E6
PECAN CT	1600	RDWC	94061	790-A2
PECK ST	1600	SMTO	94401	729-B7
PECKS LN	100	SSF	94080	708-A2
PECORA WY	100	SMCo	94028	810-D4
PEGASUS LN	600	FCTY	94404	749-E3
PEGGY LN	900	MLPK	94025	770-G7
PELICAN CIR	-	HMBY	94019	787-G5
PELICAN CT	200	FCTY	94404	749-H1
PELICAN LN	-	RDWC	94065	749-H6
PEMBROKE CT	-	HMBY	94019	787-F5
PEMBROKE PL	-	MLPK	94025	790-F6
PENHURST AV	-	DALY	94015	707-B2
PENHURST CT	100	DALY	94015	707-B2
PENINSULA AV	-	BURL	94010	728-H7
	-	SMTO	94401	728-H7
	200	SF	94134	688-A2
PENINSULA WY	900	SMCo	94025	790-H1
PENNANT CT	500	RDWC	94065	749-H7
PENNSYLVANIA AV	100	RDWC	94063	770-B6
PENOBSCOT DR	200	RDWC	94063	770-C4
PENSACOLA ST	1000	FCTY	94404	749-F5
PEORIA ST	-	DALY	94014	687-D3
PEPPER AV	100	BURL	94010	728-F7
	100	BURL	94010	748-F1
	200	HIL	94010	728-F7
	400	PA	94306	791-B7
PEPPER DR	600	SBRN	94066	707-G7
PEPPER LN	-	SCAR	94070	769-E2
PEPPERTREE CT	3900	RDWC	94061	789-G3
PEPPERWOOD CT	-	MLPK	94025	790-H2
PERALTA RD	100	PCFA	94044	726-H5
	900	SMCo	-	726-H5
PERCHERON PL	-	HIL	94010	748-H4
	900	SMTO	94402	748-H4
PEREZ DR	1400	PCFA	94044	726-J6
PERIMETER RD	-	SMTO	94402	748-H5
N PERIMETER RD	-	MLPK	94025	790-J1
S PERIMETER RD	600	MLPK	94025	790-J2
W PERIMETER RD	600	MLPK	94025	790-J1
	600	SMCo	94025	790-J1
PERITA DR	-	DALY	94015	687-A7
PERRY AV	400	PCFA	94044	707-A4
	1900	SMCo	94025	790-E7
PERRY ST	-	RDWC	94063	770-A5
PERSEUS LN	800	FCTY	94404	749-F4
PERSHING AV	1200	SMTO	94403	749-C2
PERSIA AV	100	SF	94112	687-G1
	900	SF	94134	687-G1
PERSIMMON CT	-	HIL	94010	748-C1
PESCADERO CREEK RD	-	SMCo	94060	867-H2
	1700	SMCo	94060	868-B2
	4900	SMCo	94021	868-F2
	5100	SMCo	94021	848-J7
	5200	SMCo	94021	849-B7
	9500	SMCo	94020	849-E2
PETER ST	-	DALY	94014	687-C4
PETER COUTTS RD	-	SCIC	94305	810-J1
PETRINI CT	-	MLBR	94030	728-A5
PHELPS RD	300	SCAR	94070	769-F3
PHILIP DR	200	DALY	94015	707-C1
PHILIP LN	-	SCAR	94070	769-F3
PHILLIP RD	-	WDSD	94062	809-H3
PHILLIPS RD	-	PA	94303	791-B3
PHLEGER RD	-	SMCo	94062	789-B2
PHOENIX LN	800	FCTY	94404	749-H1
PHYLLIS CT	-	BLMT	94002	769-D1
PICARDO AV	-	PCFA	94044	727-B4
PICARDO CT	-	PCFA	94044	727-B4
PICCADILLY CT	-	SCAR	94070	769-E5
PICCADILLY LN	4100	SMTO	94403	749-D6
PICCADILLY PL	100	SBRN	94066	707-G6
PICO AV	600	SMTO	94403	749-A5
PICO BLVD	600	RDWC	94065	769-H1
	600	SCAR	94070	769-H1
PICO TER	800	PCFA	94044	707-A5
PIEDMONT AV	100	SBRN	94066	727-G2
	200	PCFA	94044	727-A2
PIEDMONT WY	800	RDWC	94062	789-H1
PIERCE RD	100	MLPK	94025	770-H7
	400	MLPK	94025	790-J1
PIERCE ST	100	DALY	94015	687-B5
	1700	SMTO	94403	749-C3
PIER POINT LN	-	RDWC	94065	749-H5
PIERS CT	900	PA	94303	791-D6
PIERS LN	-	SMCo	94025	810-E2
	900	SCIC	94304	810-E2
PIGEON POINT RD	-	SMCo	94060	888-B4
PIKE LN	-	SMTO	94403	749-D5
PILAR PL	-	PCFA	94044	727-A3
PILARCITOS AV	-	HMBY	94019	767-E6
	-	HMBY	94019	787-F1
PILARCITOS CT	100	HIL	94010	748-E6
PILARCITOS RD	-	SMCo	-	727-G6
	-	SMCo	-	747-G1
PILARCITOS CREEK RD	-	SMCo	-	768-B4
PILGRIM DR	500	FCTY	94404	749-G2
PILOT CIR	-	RDWC	94065	749-J5
	-	RDWC	94065	750-C4
PINE AV	-	SCAR	94070	769-F3
	100	SSF	94080	708-A2

STREET	Block	City	ZIP	Pg-Grid
PINE AV				
	100	SMCo	94038	746-G7
	200	SSF	94080	707-J2
	400	HMBY	94019	787-F1
PINE CT				
	-	HIL	94010	748-D2
	1000	DALY	94014	687-H3
PINE LN				
	-	SMCo	94060	868-H5
PINE ST				
	-	RDWC	94063	770-B7
	200	SBRN	94066	707-J7
	300	MLBR	94030	728-B2
	600	SBRN	94066	708-A6
	1000	MLPK	94025	790-G3
	1200	PA	94301	791-B5
PINE TER				
	500	SSF	94080	707-J2
PINECREST DR				
	1900	SBRN	94066	707-E6
PINECREST TER				
	-	SMTO	94402	748-G1
PINEHAVEN DR				
	-	DALY	94015	687-A4
PINEHAVEN WY				
	200	PCFA	94044	707-A7
PINE HILL RD				
	800	SCIC	94305	810-J1
PINEHILL RD				
	100	HIL	94010	748-E2
PINEHURST CT				
	1000	MLBR	94030	727-H3
PINEHURST LN				
	-	HMBY	94019	787-F5
PINEHURST WY				
	100	SSF	94080	707-G5
PINE KNOLL DR				
	1500	BLMT	94002	769-D1
	1700	BLMT	94002	749-D7
PINE RIDGE DR				
	100	SMCo	-	768-D4
PINE RIDGE WY				
	-	PTLV	94028	810-D5
PINEVIEW LN				
	100	MLPK	94025	790-D5
PINEWOOD CT				
	-	SMTO	94403	748-H7
PINNACLE ST				
	-	SSF	94014	707-J1
PINON AV				
	800	MLBR	94030	728-B5
	800	BURL	94010	728-B5
PINON DR				
	100	PTLV	94028	810-B4
PINRAIL LN				
	600	FCTY	94404	749-J1
PINTA LN				
	700	FCTY	94404	749-G2
PINTO AV				
	-	SF	94132	687-A1
PINTO WY				
	-	WDSD	94062	789-D6
PIONEER CT				
	2000	SMTO	94403	749-A4
PIO PICO WY				
	-	PCFA	94044	727-C5
PIRATE CV				
	-	DALY	94014	687-E5
PISA CT				
	-	SSF	94080	707-G4
PISCES LN				
	500	FCTY	94404	749-E4
PITCAIRN DR				
	500	FCTY	94404	749-G5
PITMAN AV				
	1200	PA	94301	791-A3
	1300	PA	94303	791-A3
PIXIE LN				
	-	SCAR	94070	769-C4
PIZARRO LN				
	900	FCTY	94404	749-F3
PLACER WY				
	-	BSBN	94005	688-A7
PLACITAS AV				
	-	ATN	94027	790-E1
	500	SMCo	94025	770-E7
	500	SMCo	94025	790-E1
PLAID PL				
	-	HIL	94010	748-E4
PLATEAU DR				
	3300	BLMT	94002	769-A1
PLAYA				
	1900	SMTO	94403	749-E5
PLAY BOWL DR				
	-	SMCo	94020	849-E1
PLAZA LN				
	900	FCTY	94404	749-E3
	1500	BURL	94010	728-C4
PLAZA ALHAMBRA				
	500	SMCo	94019	767-B3
PLAZA CABRILLO				
	1200	SMCo	94019	767-C3
PLEASANT ST				
	-	FCTY	94404	749-E6
PLEASANT HILL RD				
	900	RDWC	94061	789-H2
PLOVER ST				
	800	FCTY	94404	749-H2
PLUMAS AV				
	1400	MLPK	94025	770-H7
PLUMAS CT				
	100	SBRN	94066	707-D7
PLUMAS ST				
	-	BSBN	94005	688-A6
PLUMWOOD PL				
	1400	SBRN	94066	707-H7
PLYMOUTH AV				
	-	SCAR	94070	769-E4
	100	SF	94112	687-D2
PLYMOUTH CIR				
	-	DALY	94015	707-D3
PLYMOUTH LN				
	600	FCTY	94404	749-F4
PLYMOUTH WY				
	600	BURL	94010	728-G6
	2600	SBRN	94066	707-E7
POE ST				
	300	PA	94301	790-H4
POETT RD				
	300	HIL	94010	748-H2
POINSETTIA AV				
	-	SMTO	94403	749-C5
POINTE PACIFIC DR				
	700	DALY	94014	687-D3
POINTE VIEW PL				
	-	SSF	94014	708-A1
POINT REYES WY				
	-	PCFA	94044	727-B5
POINT SAN BRUNO BLVD				
	300	SSF	94080	708-C3
POLARIS AV				
	600	FCTY	94404	749-F4
POLARIS WY				
	200	DALY	94014	687-F2
	300	SF	94112	687-F2
POLHEMUS AV				
	200	ATN	94027	790-C4
POLHEMUS RD				
	-	SMTO	94402	748-G7
	200	SMCo	94402	748-G7
	700	SMCo	94402	768-H1
	700	SMTO	94402	768-H1
POLITZER DR				
	-	MLPK	94025	790-E5
POLK AV				
	2000	SMTO	94403	749-C2
POLLUX CT				
	800	FCTY	94404	749-F4
POLO CT				
	1900	SMTO	94403	749-A4
POLYNESIA DR				
	1100	FCTY	94404	749-G2
POMEROY CT				
	2500	SSF	94080	707-C4
POMPANO CIR				
	300	FCTY	94404	749-H2
POMPEIIAN WY				
	-	PCFA	94044	726-G4
POMPONIO				
	-	PTLV	94028	830-C1
POMPONIO TKTR				
	-	SMCo	94021	848-G6
	-	SMCo	94021	849-A5
	-	SMCo	94060	848-G6
	-	SMCo	94060	868-D2
POMPONIO CREEK RD				
	-	SMCo	94074	848-B2
	100	SMCo	94021	848-F3
	100	SMCo	94021	849-A5
PONCE AV				
	2600	BLMT	94002	769-B1
PONCETTA DR				
	-	DALY	94015	687-B3
PONDEROSA RD				
	-	SSF	94080	707-F4
	200	SMCo	94080	707-F4
POPE RD				
	-	SMCo	94020	849-E2
POPE ST				
	-	DALY	94014	687-F2
	-	SF	94112	687-F2
	100	MLPK	94025	791-A3
	200	MLPK	94025	790-J2
POPLAR AV				
	-	MLBR	94030	728-B4
	100	SBRN	94066	727-J1
	100	RDWC	94061	790-B1
	300	SBRN	94066	707-J7
	500	SSF	94080	707-H2
	1100	RDWC	94061	789-J2
	1300	PCFA	94044	727-B5
	1800	RDWC	94061	770-B7
	2000	EPA	94303	791-A1
E POPLAR AV				
	-	SMTO	94401	748-H1
	100	SMTO	94401	728-J6
	1100	SMTO	94401	729-A6
W POPLAR AV				
	-	SMTO	94402	748-G1
POPLAR ST				
	100	HMBY	94019	787-F2
POPPY AV				
	1700	MLPK	94025	790-E6
POPPY DR				
	2100	BURL	94010	728-C6
POPPY LN				
	-	SMCo	94019	787-G5
	-	SCAR	94070	769-C4
PORT DR				
	600	SMTO	94404	749-D1
PORTAL LN				
	500	FCTY	94404	749-F3
PORTAL PL				
	700	PA	94303	791-B5
PORTIFINO CIR				
	-	RDWC	94065	749-J6
PORTMAN DR				
	800	RDWC	94065	750-C6
PORTOFINO CT				
	-	SCAR	94070	769-E4
PORTOFINO DR				
	300	SCAR	94070	769-E5
PORTO FINO LN				
	600	FCTY	94404	749-F3
PORTOLA AV				
	-	SMCo	94037	746-G5
	-	DALY	94015	687-A7
	-	SSF	94080	707-G4
	1500	PA	94306	791-A6
PORTOLA DR				
	200	SMTO	94403	749-B5
PORTOLA RD				
	-	SMCo	-	727-F5
	-	SMCo	-	747-H1
	-	SMCo	-	748-A3
	-	PTLV	94028	810-A6
	1000	PTLV	94028	809-J4
	1000	WDSD	94062	809-G2
	1700	SMCo	94025	809-H4
PORTOLA WY				
	100	SBRN	94066	727-J2
PORTOLA GREEN CIR				
	-	PTLV	94028	810-C7
PORTOLA HEIGHTS RD				
	-	SMCo	94020	850-H4
PORTOLA STATE PARK RD				
	-	SMCo	94020	850-B7
PORTO MARINO DR				
	1000	SCAR	94070	769-E5
PORTO MARINO LN				
	-	SCAR	94070	769-E5
PORTO MARINO WY				
	-	SCAR	94070	769-E5
PORTO ROSA WY				
	2800	SCAR	94070	769-F5
PORT ROYAL AV				
	-	FCTY	94404	749-E5
PORTSMOUTH LN				
	600	FCTY	94404	749-F5
PORTSMOUTH WY				
	2200	SMTO	94403	749-D4
PORT WALK PL				
	700	RDWC	94065	749-H6
POSEIDON LN				
	200	RDWC	94065	749-J4
POSITANO CIR				
	400	RDWC	94065	749-J4
POSITANO WY				
	400	RDWC	94065	749-J4
POSSUM LN				
	-	PTLV	94028	810-A6
POTOMAC WY				
	2000	SMTO	94403	749-C4
POTTER AV				
	500	HMBY	94019	787-E2
POWELL ST				
	-	SMTO	94401	729-B7
POWHATAN PL				
	-	SMCo	94402	768-G1
PRADO CT				
	-	PTLV	94028	810-C7
PRADO SECOYA				
	-	ATN	94027	790-E4
PRAGUE ST				
	-	SMTO	94401	729-A6
	-	SF	94112	687-G1
PRAIRIE CREEK DR				
	700	PCFA	94044	727-C5
PRECITA AV				
	100	SMCo	94038	766-G1
PRESCOTT LN				
	700	FCTY	94404	749-G5
PRESERVE LN				
	-	RDWC	94065	750-A4
PRESIDIO AV				
	100	SMCo	94019	767-A2
PRESTON RD				
	-	WDSD	94062	809-H4
PRETOR WY				
	-	SF	94112	687-F2
PREUSS RD				
	-	SMCo	94060	868-J2
PRICE AV				
	500	RDWC	94063	770-A4
PRICE CT				
	3000	PA	94303	791-D6
PRICE ST				
	-	DALY	94014	687-C4
PRIMROSE LN				
	-	SCAR	94070	769-E2
PRIMROSE RD				
	100	BURL	94010	728-G7
PRIMROSE WY				
	-	PA	94303	791-C4
PRINCETON AV				
	-	SMCo	94019	766-H3
PRINCETON DR				
	2200	SBRN	94066	727-F1
PRINCETON RD				
	-	MLPK	94025	790-G5
	400	SMTO	94402	748-H3
PRINCETON ST				
	2000	PA	94306	791-A7
PRINDLE RD				
	2600	BLMT	94002	769-B2
PRIOR LN				
	200	ATN	94027	790-F2
PRISM LN				
	-	RDWC	94065	750-B3
PRIVET DR				
	2900	HIL	94010	748-B1
PRODUCE AV				
	100	SSF	94080	707-J4
	100	SSF	94080	708-A4
PROMENADE LN				
	-	RDWC	94065	750-B3
PROMONTORY CT				
	500	RDWC	94065	749-H6
PROMONTORY POINT LN				
	700	FCTY	94404	749-E4
PROSPECT RW				
	600	SMTO	94401	728-G7
PROSPECT ST				
	-	WDSD	94062	789-G6
	500	SCAR	94070	769-F3
	1600	BLMT	94002	769-F2
	2100	MLPK	94025	790-D7
	2100	SMCo	94025	790-D7
PROSPECT WY				
	400	SMCo	94019	766-J2
PROVIDENT DR				
	-	HIL	94010	748-D2
PROWSHEAD LN				
	800	FCTY	94404	749-H5
PUEBLO ST				
	-	DALY	94014	687-J3
	-	SF	94134	687-J3
PUFFIN CT				
	200	FCTY	94404	749-G1
PULGAS AV				
	1800	EPA	94303	791-C1
	2500	EPA	94303	771-C7
PULLMAN AV				
	2100	BLMT	94002	769-C2
	2900	HMBY	94019	767-D4
PULLMAN RD				
	-	HIL	94010	748-D3
PURDUE AV				
	1600	EPA	94303	771-B7
PURISIMA RD				
	100	SMCo	94062	788-G4
PURISIMA WY				
	300	SMCo	94019	767-D3
PURISIMA CREEK RD				
	1200	SMCo	94019	807-J2
	1200	SMCo	94019	808-A1
	1400	SMCo	94019	788-A7
PURISIMA CREEK TR				
	-	SMCo	94062	789-A6
PURISSIMA ST				
	300	HMBY	94019	787-F1
PYROLA LN				
	-	SCAR	94070	769-C5
Q				
QUADRANT LN				
	400	FCTY	94404	749-J1
QUAIL				
	-	PTLV	94028	830-C1
QUAIL CT				
	-	ATN	94027	790-H1
	-	SMCo	-	788-F1
QUAIL LN				
	-	SCAR	94070	769-D5
QUAIL MEADOWS CT				
	-	WDSD	94062	789-J6
QUAIL MEADOWS DR				
	-	WDSD	94062	789-H6
QUAIL POINT CIR				
	2000	SBRN	94066	707-F7
QUARRY RD				
	100	PA	94304	790-H5
	100	SCIC	94305	790-H5
	300	SCAR	94070	769-F1
	500	PA	94305	790-H5
QUARTZ AV				
	500	HMBY	94019	767-F7
QUARTZ ST				
	400	RDWC	94062	769-J7
	400	RDWC	94062	789-J1
	600	RDWC	94061	789-J1
QUAY LN				
	300	RDWC	94065	749-H7
N QUEBEC ST				
	-	SMTO	94401	729-A6
S QUEBEC ST				
	100	SMTO	94401	729-B7
QUEEN ANNE CT				
	-	MLBR	94030	728-A2
QUEENS AV				
	1300	SMTO	94403	749-C3
QUEENS CT				
	-	ATN	94027	790-C4
	200	SCAR	94070	769-D4
QUEENS LN				
	2000	SMCo	94402	768-H1
QUENTIN L KOPP FRWY I-380				
	-	SBRN	-	707-H6
	-	SBRN	-	708-A6
	-	SMCo	-	708-A6
	-	SSF	-	708-A5
QUESADA WY				
	1600	BURL	94010	728-B5
QUILEN CT				
	-	SCIC	94305	790-J7
QUINCE ST				
	1200	SMTO	94402	748-J3
R				
RACINE LN				
	-	SF	94134	688-A2
RADBURN DR				
	3700	SSF	94080	707-D4
RADCLIFF DR				
	28100	LAH	94022	810-H5
RADFORD LN				
	700	FCTY	94404	749-G5
RADIO RD				
	-	RDWC	94065	750-A5
	-	SMCo	94014	687-F4
RAE AV				
	-	SF	94112	687-E2
RAILROAD AV				
	300	SSF	94080	707-H3
	700	HMBY	94019	787-F2
	1000	SMCo	94019	807-J7
	1700	SMTO	94402	749-B3
N RAILROAD AV				
	-	SMTO	94401	748-J1
S RAILROAD AV				
	-	SMTO	94401	748-J1
	100	SMTO	94401	749-A2
	400	SMTO	94402	749-A2
RAILROAD PL				
	1000	SBRN	94066	707-J5
RAILWAY AV				
	1100	SMTO	94401	749-A2
	1100	SMTO	94402	749-A2
RAIMUNDO WY				
	700	SCIC	94305	810-J2
RAINBOW DR				
	1300	SMCo	94402	748-G6
RAINIER AV				
	200	SSF	94080	707-G4
	1000	PCFA	94044	727-C5
RAINSONG LN				
	-	RDWC	94065	750-B4
RALMAR AV				
	2000	EPA	94303	791-A1
	2400	EPA	94303	771-A7
RALSTON AV				
	100	HMBY	94019	767-E7
	100	RDWC	94065	749-F7
	400	BLMT	94002	749-F7
	500	BLMT	94002	769-B2
	1500	BURL	94010	728-F7
	1600	HIL	94010	728-F7
	1700	HIL	94010	748-E1
	2800	SMCo	94070	768-J2
	2900	SMTO	94402	768-J2
	2900	SMCo	94402	768-J2
	2900	BLMT	94002	768-J2
RALSTON CT				
	-	HIL	94010	748-D2
RALSTON RD				
	-	ATN	94027	790-C3
	-	SMCo	94074	828-H3
	-	SMCo	94062	828-H3
RALSTON ST				
	-	SF	94132	687-C1
RALSTON RANCH RD				
	3900	BLMT	94002	768-J2
RAM LN				
	800	FCTY	94404	749-F4
RAMBLEWOOD WY				
	1100	SMTO	94403	749-E6
RAMBOW DR				
	3400	PA	94306	791-D7
RAMONA AV				
	100	PCFA	94044	727-A2
	100	SSF	94080	707-G4
RAMONA RD				
	100	SMCo	94028	830-E3
RAMONA ST				
	200	PA	94301	790-H4
	200	SMTO	94401	728-J7
	300	SMTO	94401	748-J1
	1100	PA	94301	791-B7
	2500	PA	94306	791-B7
RAMOSO RD				
	100	PTLV	94028	810-B4
RAMPART WY				
	-	DALY	94014	687-E3
RAMSELL ST				
	-	SF	94132	687-C2
RANCH RD				
	-	WDSD	94062	809-F4
	-	SMCo	94062	809-F4
S RANCH RD				
	700	SMCo	94060	868-F6
RANCH RD W				
	-	SMCo	94060	868-D3
RANCHO AV				
	-	SMCo	94063	770-F5
RANCHO DE LA BANA				
	-	SMCo	94020	850-A4
RAND ST				
	400	SMTO	94401	729-B7
	500	SMTO	94401	749-B1
RANDALL CT				
	-	SMCo	94015	687-B5
RANDALL PL				
	-	MLPK	94025	790-F6
RANDALL RD				
	1800	SMTO	94402	748-H7
	1800	SMCo	94402	748-H7
RANDERS CT				
	2700	PA	94303	791-C6
RANDOLPH AV				
	-	SSF	94080	708-A2
	200	SSF	94080	707-J1
RANDOLPH PL				
	-	PCFA	94044	727-B6
RANDOLPH ST				
	-	SF	94132	687-C2
RANDY CT				
	-	SMCo	94061	790-A3
RANELAGH RD				
	300	HIL	94010	748-H1
RANGER CIR				
	700	FCTY	94404	749-G2
RAPLEY RD				
	-	WDSD	94062	809-G7
RAVENSCOURT RD				
	500	HIL	94010	748-G2
RAVENSWOOD AV				
	100	ATN	94027	790-G3
	100	MLPK	94025	790-G3
RAVENWOOD WY				
	100	SSF	94080	707-G5
RAVILLA CT				
	-	DALY	94014	687-E2
RAVINE DR				
	100	WDSD	94062	789-G5
RAY CT				
	-	BURL	94010	728-C5
RAY DR				
	1500	BURL	94010	728-C5
RAYMOND AV				
	-	SF	94134	688-A2
	200	SF	94134	687-J2
RAYMOND CT				
	-	SCAR	94070	769-G6
RAYMUNDO DR				
	100	WDSD	94062	789-D4
RAYNOR PL				
	-	SMCo	94060	868-F3
READ AV				
	2400	BLMT	94002	769-B2
REBECCA LN				
	-	ATN	94027	790-G2
RECREATION AV				
	-	MLPK	94025	790-J1
RECREATION DR				
	-	SMCo	94020	849-F1
	100	SMCo	94020	829-F7
RECREATION WY				
	1300	RDWC	94061	789-H3
REDBERRY RDG				
	-	PTLV	94028	830-D2
RED HAWK CT				
	-	BSBN	94005	687-J5
	-	BSBN	94005	688-A5
REDINGTON RD				
	2100	HIL	94010	728-D7
REDLAND RD				
	-	SMCo	94062	809-F5
RED LEAF CT				
	-	DALY	94014	687-G3
RED OAK WY				
	3700	RDWC	94061	789-G2
REDONDO AV				
	-	SMCo	94038	746-F7
REDONDO ST				
	-	SF	94124	688-B1
REDONDO BEACH RD				
	400	HMBY	94019	787-E4
REDROCK RD				
	26600	LAH	94022	830-H2
REDWOOD AV				
	-	MLPK	94025	790-J2
	-	SMCo	94060	868-H5
	-	RDWC	94061	770-B7
	400	SBRN	94066	727-H1
	500	SSF	94080	707-H3
	2000	RDWC	94061	790-A1
	2000	RDWC	94061	789-J2
REDWOOD DR				
	-	SMCo	94021	849-A7
	-	HIL	94010	748-H2
	-	SMCo	94020	849-E1
REDWOOD RD				
	-	SMCo	94062	788-H5
REDWOOD TER				
	-	SMCo	94062	788-J4
REDWOOD WY				
	-	ATN	94027	790-E2
	1200	MLBR	94030	727-H3
	1200	PCFA	94044	727-A5
REDWOOD SHORES PKWY				
	100	RDWC	94065	749-H7
	100	RDWC	94065	769-H1
	600	RDWC	94065	750-A5
REDWOOD SPRING RD				
	-	SMCo	94062	788-J5
REEF DR				
	400	SMTO	94404	749-E1
	400	FCTY	94404	749-E1
REEF POINT RD				
	-	SMCo	94038	746-F6
REESE ST				
	1200	RDWC	94061	790-A1
REFLECTION CIRCLE DR				
	-	SMCo	-	768-C3
REGAL CT				
	700	MLPK	94025	790-J2
REGAN DR				
	3900	SMTO	94403	749-D6
REGENT CT				
	800	SCAR	94070	769-D5
	900	RDWC	94061	790-B1
REGENT PL				
	-	PA	94301	791-A4
REGENT ST				
	-	SMCo	94019	766-J2
	-	SF	94112	687-D2
	1300	RDWC	94061	790-A1
REGINA WY				
	900	PCFA	94044	726-J4
REGULUS ST				
	700	FCTY	94404	749-F4
REICHLING AV				
	100	PCFA	94044	727-A2
REID AV				
	800	SBRN	94066	707-H7
REIDS ROOST				
	-	SMCo	94062	809-C3
REINA DEL MAR AV				
	100	PCFA	94044	727-A1
REINER ST				
	-	DALY	94014	687-C5
	-	SMCo	94014	687-C5
REMILLARD DR				
	400	HIL	94010	748-D3
RENATO CT				
	-	RDWC	94061	790-C1
REPOSA WY				
	3600	BLMT	94002	769-A2
RESERVOIR RD				
	-	SMCo	94037	746-H3
	-	ATN	94027	790-B6
	100	HIL	94010	748-G3
	1000	SMCo	94060	867-H2
RESERVOIR HILL DR				
	-	DALY	94014	687-D4
RESIDENT LN				
	-	MLPK	94025	790-J2
RESSA RD				
	300	PCFA	94044	707-A6
RESTANI WY				
	-	SF	94112	687-F1
RESTON CT				
	3900	SSF	94080	707-D4
RETIRO LN				
	100	SMCo	94038	766-H2
REVERE WY				
	800	SMCo	94062	789-F2
REX ST				
	1700	SMTO	94403	749-C3
REY ST				
	-	SF	94134	687-J2
REYNA PL				
	-	MLPK	94025	790-F5
REYNOLDS CT				
	-	HIL	94010	728-D7
RHINE ST				
	-	SF	94112	687-D2
	200	DALY	94014	687-D2
RHINETTE AV				
	1100	BURL	94010	728-E6
RHODES DR				
	500	PA	94303	791-C4
RHUS RD				
	-	SMCo	94020	850-E7
RHUS ST				
	1200	SMTO	94402	748-J3
RIBBON ST				
	1300	FCTY	94404	749-H2
RICE ST				
	-	DALY	94014	687-D2
	-	SF	94112	687-D2
RICHARDSON CT				
	800	PA	94303	791-D7
RICHLAND CT				
	-	SCAR	94070	769-H4
RICHMOND DR				
	200	MLBR	94030	728-A4
	400	MLBR	94030	727-J4
RICHMOND RD				
	200	HIL	94010	748-G2
RICKOVER LN				
	1100	FCTY	94404	749-G5
RIDGE CT				
	-	WDSD	94062	789-G5
	800	SSF	94080	707-G1
	1200	SF	94134	687-H3
RIDGE LN				
	-	SF	94112	687-E1
RIDGE RD				
	-	SMCo	94062	788-J6
	300	SCAR	94070	769-G5
	1500	BLMT	94002	749-D7
RIDGECREST TER				
	-	SMTO	94402	748-H7
RIDGEFIELD AV				
	-	DALY	94015	687-A7
RIDGEVIEW CT				
	800	SSF	94080	707-G1
RIDGEVIEW DR				
	-	ATN	94027	790-A5
RIDGEWAY AV				
	2600	SBRN	94066	727-F1
RIDGEWAY DR				
	500	PCFA	94044	707-A7
RIDGEWAY RD				
	-	HIL	94010	748-G3
	100	WDSD	94062	789-H4
RIDGEWOOD CT				
	-	BLMT	94002	769-C3
RIDGEWOOD DR				
	1000	MLBR	94030	727-H3
RIDGEWOOD RD				
	-	SMCo	94060	868-G4
RIFLE RANGE RD				
	-	PCFA	94044	707-A7
RIGEL LN				
	800	FCTY	94404	749-E3
RILEY WY				
	800	RDWC	94061	790-C2
RINCONADA AV				
	100	PA	94301	791-A6
RINCONADA CIR				
	-	BLMT	94002	768-J3
	-	BLMT	94002	769-A3
	-	SMCo	94070	768-J3
RINGWOOD AV				
	-	SMCo	94025	790-H2
	-	ATN	94027	790-H1
	800	MLPK	94025	790-H1
	1000	MLPK	94025	770-H7
RIO CT				
	-	BURL	94010	728-B5
RIORDAN PL				
	-	MLPK	94025	790-H2
RIO VERDE ST				
	-	SF	94134	687-H3
	-	DALY	94014	687-H3
RIO VISTA DR				
	900	PCFA	94044	726-J5
RISEL AV				
	-	DALY	94014	687-E3
RITTENHOUSE AV				
	-	ATN	94027	790-D2
RIVAS AV				
	-	SF	94132	687-B1
RIVERA DR				
	2800	BURL	94010	728-A6
RIVERMIST LN				
	500	RDWC	94065	749-J3
RIVER OAKS RD				
	-	HMBY	94019	787-F5
RIVERSIDE DR				
	-	SBRN	94066	707-D6
RIVERTON DR				
	700	MLBR	94030	727-J4
	900	SCAR	94070	769-G2
RIVIERA CIR				
	-	RDWC	94065	749-J7
RIVIERA CT				
	100	SBRN	94066	707-D5
RIVIERA RD				
	600	SMCo	94037	746-H4
RIX LN				
	-	WDSD	94062	809-J5
RIZAL DR				
	100	HIL	94010	748-F5
ROAN PL				
	-	WDSD	94062	789-D6
ROBERT AV				
	-	BLMT	94002	768-J1
ROBERT PL				
	-	MLBR	94030	728-A3
ROBERTA DR				
	-	WDSD	94062	809-G1
	1400	SMTO	94403	749-D3
ROBERT S DR				
	-	MLPK	94025	790-E4
ROBERTS RD				
	200	PCFA	94044	726-H3
ROBERTS WY				
	-	HIL	94010	748-E4
ROBERTSON WY				
	500	RDWC	94062	789-E2
	500	SMCo	94062	789-E2
ROBIN CT				
	700	EPA	94303	791-B1
ROBIN LN				
	800	MLBR	94030	727-H3
ROBIN RD				
	-	HIL	94010	748-E2
ROBIN WY				
	-	SCAR	94070	769-G6
	200	MLPK	94025	790-J3
ROBINSON DR				
	-	SF	94112	687-G2
	-	DALY	94014	687-G2
ROBIN WHIPPLE WY				
	1600	BLMT	94002	769-D1
ROBINWOOD LN				
	200	HIL	94010	748-E3
ROBLAR AV				
	100	HIL	94010	748-H1
	300	MLBR	94030	728-C3
ROBLE AV				
	200	RDWC	94061	790-C1
	600	MLPK	94025	790-F4
ROBLE DR				
	500	SCIC	94305	790-G7
ROBLE PL				
	100	SMCo	94020	829-F7
ROBLE RD				
	1200	MLBR	94030	728-A5
ROBLE ALTO				
	27900	LAH	94022	810-H7
ROBLE ALTO CT				
	13600	LAH	94022	810-H6
ROBLE BLANCO				
	27900	LAH	94022	810-H7
ROBLEDA DR				
	-	ATN	94027	790-C2
ROBLES DR				
	-	WDSD	94062	809-G1
ROCCA AV				
	500	SSF	94080	707-H2
ROCCA CT				
	-	SSF	94080	707-J2
N ROCHESTER ST				
	-	SMTO	94401	729-A6
S ROCHESTER ST				
	-	SMTO	94401	729-B7
ROCKAWAY BEACH AV				
	100	PCFA	94044	726-H2
	700	PCFA	94044	727-A3
ROCK CREEK CT				
	-	SMCo	94062	789-F2
ROCKFORD AV				
	-	DALY	94015	706-J1
	-	DALY	94015	707-A1
ROCK HARBOR LN				
	-	FCTY	94404	749-E6
ROCKINGHAM LN				
	-	RDWC	94065	750-B3
ROCKPORT AV				
	-	RDWC	94065	750-A4
ROCKRIDGE AV				
	-	DALY	94015	687-A6
ROCKRIDGE RD				
	-	HIL	94010	748-G2
	100	SCAR	94070	769-F4
ROCKWOOD CT				
	-	SMTO	94403	748-J6
ROCKWOOD DR				
	100	SSF	94080	707-G5
ROCK WREN LN				
	-	BSBN	94005	687-J5
ROCKY WY				
	500	WDSD	94062	789-E2
RODRIQUES RD				
	-	SMCo	94060	868-F3
ROEBLING RD				
	300	SSF	94080	708-B3
ROEHAMPTON RD				
	400	HIL	94010	748-G2

STREET Block City ZIP Pg-Grid

ROEMER WY
- SF 94112 687-E2
ROGELL AV
1200 SMTO 94401 729-A7
ROGELL CT
400 SMTO 94401 729-A6
ROGERS AV
100 SCAR 94070 769-F5
ROGGE RD
100 EPA 94303 791-C1
ROLAND AV
2800 SCAR 94070 769-F6
ROLISON RD
3000 MLPK 94025 770-E6
3000 RDWC 94063 770-E6
ROLLING HILLS AV
- SMTO 94403 749-B7
ROLLINGWOOD DR
2000 SBRN 94066 707-E6
ROLLINS RD
- BURL 94010 728-D4
- MLBR 94030 728-D4
ROLPH ST
- SF 94112 687-F2
ROME ST
- SF 94112 687-E1
ROMERO RD
100 WDSD 94062 789-G6
ROMNEY AV
100 SSF 94080 707-E2
RONALD CT
900 HMBY 94019 787-G2
RONDO WY
- SMCo 94025 790-D5
ROOSEVELT AV
- DALY 94014 687-E3
100 RDWC 94061 789-J2
1400 RDWC 94061 790-A1
2100 BURL 94010 728-D7
2200 RDWC 94061 770-A7
ROOSEVELT BLVD
100 HMBY 94019 767-D5
ROQUENA DR
100 SMCo 94020 829-E7
RORKE WY
800 PA 94303 791-E6
ROSA FLORA CIR
100 SSF 94080 707-G4
ROSALITA LN
- MLBR 94030 727-J2
ROSE AV
800 SMCo 94063 770-F7
900 MLPK 94025 770-F4
900 RDWC 94063 770-F7
ROSE CT
900 BURL 94010 728-F5
ROSE LN
100 BLMT 94002 769-E2
ROSE RD
- SMCo 94019 787-G6
ROSEDALE AV
1100 BURL 94010 728-D5
ROSEFIELD WY
1100 MLPK 94025 790-E5
ROSELLA CT
- SF 94112 687-F1
ROSEMARY LN
1700 RDWC 94061 790-A2
ROSEMARY ST
- MLPK 94025 770-J7
ROSEWOOD AV
900 SCAR 94070 769-G3
ROSEWOOD DR
- ATN 94027 790-G1
- ATN 94027 770-G7
700 PA 94303 791-C6
900 SMTO 94401 749-A2
2100 SBRN 94066 727-F1
ROSEWOOD WY
100 SSF 94080 707-G5
ROSILIE ST
100 SMTO 94403 749-E6
ROSITA CT N
1000 PCFA 94044 726-J5
ROSITA CT S
1000 PCFA 94044 726-J5
ROSITA RD
700 PCFA 94044 726-H5
1100 PCFA 94044 727-A6
ROSLYN AV
- SCAR 94070 769-E4
- SMCo 94070 769-E4
ROSLYN CT
- DALY 94015 686-J4
ROSS CT
800 PA 94303 791-D6
ROSS LN
200 FCTY 94404 749-F5
ROSS RD
2300 PA 94303 791-C5
ROSS ST
1100 BLMT 94002 749-D7
ROSS WY
- BSBN 94005 688-A7
- SBRN 94066 707-D6
ROSSI WY
1000 SMTO 94403 749-C4
ROTH WY
100 SCIC 94305 790-G6
ROUND HILL RD
800 RDWC 94061 789-H2
ROURKE RD
- SMCo 94060 868-H2
ROWAN TREE LN
- HIL 94010 748-C2
ROWNTREE WY
2400 SSF 94080 707-D4
ROXBURY LN
- SMCo 94402 748-F6
ROXBURY WY
500 BLMT 94002 749-E7
ROYAL AV
1300 SMTO 94401 749-B2
ROYAL LN
- SF 94112 687-F2
1100 SCAR 94070 769-D6
ROYAL PALM AV
200 SMCo 94019 766-J1
ROYCE WY
- DALY 94014 687-D5
ROZZI PL
400 SSF 94080 708-B2
RUBY AV
100 SCAR 94070 769-G5
RUBY ST
400 RDWC 94062 769-J7
400 RDWC 94062 789-J1
600 RDWC 94061 789-J1
1200 RDWC 94061 790-A1
RUDDER LN
1000 FCTY 94404 749-H4
RUISSEAU FRANCAIS AV
500 HMBY 94019 767-E5
RUNNING FARM LN
- SCIC 94305 790-J7
- SCIC 94305 810-J1
RUNNYMEDE RD
800 WDSD 94062 789-E4
RUNNYMEDE ST
400 EPA 94303 791-C1
RURAL LN
300 MLPK 94025 810-E1
300 SMCo 94025 810-E1
RUSSELL AV
- PTLV 94028 809-J6
RUSSELL CT
- MLPK 94025 790-J3
RUSSIA AV
- SF 94112 687-G1
RUTGERS ST
1600 EPA 94303 771-C6
RUTH AV
800 BLMT 94002 749-D7
RUTH CT
1000 EPA 94303 791-C1
RUTHERDALE AV
800 SCAR 94070 769-F4
RUTHERFORD AV
100 SMCo 94061 790-B2
RUTHVEN AV
400 PA 94301 790-H4
RUTLAND DR
500 PCFA 94044 707-A2
RUTLAND ST
- SF 94134 688-A2
RYAN CT
- SCIC 94305 810-J2
RYAN WY
100 SSF 94080 707-H4
RYANS AL
700 MLPK 94025 790-F4
RYDER ST
200 SMTO 94401 729-B7

S

SABRINA CT
1200 RDWC 94061 790-A1
SACRAMENTO ST
500 EPA 94303 791-B1
SACRAMENTO TER
900 PCFA 94044 707-A5
SADDLE CT
27800 LAH 94022 810-J6
SADDLEBACK
- PTLV 94028 830-C1
SADDLEBACK DR
- DALY 94014 687-G2
- SF 94134 687-G2
SADDLE MOUNTAIN DR
14300 LAH 94022 810-J6
SADOWA ST
- SF 94112 687-D2
SAGA LN
- MLPK 94025 790-D7
- MLPK 94025 810-D1
SAGAMORE ST
100 SF 94112 687-D2
SAGE ST
- MLPK 94025 770-J7
1100 EPA 94303 791-C2
SAGINAW DR
100 RDWC 94063 770-C3
SAILFISH
- HMBY 94019 787-F6
SAILFISH ISL
300 FCTY 94404 749-H3
SAINT ANDREWS LN
300 HMBY 94019 787-F4
SAINT ANDREWS RD
2100 HMBY 94019 787-F5
SAINT CATHERINE DR
200 DALY 94015 687-A7
SAINT CHARLES AV
- SF 94132 687-C2
SAINT CHRISTOPHER CT
- SMTO 94403 748-J5
SAINT CLAIRE DR
500 PA 94306 791-D7
SAINT CLOUD DR
2500 SSF 94080 707-D5
2500 SBRN 94066 707-D5
SAINT CROIX LN
600 FCTY 94404 749-J1
SAINT FRANCIS BLVD
- DALY 94015 687-B7
600 DALY 94015 707-B1
SAINT FRANCIS CT
500 MLPK 94025 790-F6
SAINT FRANCIS DR
2100 PA 94303 791-D4
SAINT FRANCIS PL
500 MLPK 94025 790-F6
SAINT FRANCIS RD
- HIL 94010 748-H2
SAINT FRANCIS ST
300 RDWC 94062 769-H7
600 RDWC 94061 790-A1
1100 RDWC 94061 789-J1
SAINT FRANCIS WY
100 RDWC 94062 769-H5
600 RDWC 94061 769-H5
700 RDWC 94061 789-J1
1100 SCAR 94070 769-H5
SAINT JAMES AV
500 HMBY 94019 767-E7
SAINT JAMES CT
- DALY 94015 687-B6
SAINT JAMES RD
2700 BLMT 94002 769-A3
2900 BLMT 94002 768-J2
2900 SMCo 94070 768-J2
SAINT JOHN AV
400 HMBY 94019 767-E7
SAINT JOHN CT
- SMTO 94403 748-J5
- SMTO 94401 728-H7
SAINT JOSEPH AV
400 HMBY 94019 767-E6
SAINT KITTS LN
1400 FCTY 94404 749-G5
SAINT LAWRENCE CT
700 PCFA 94044 727-C4
SAINT LAWRENCE DR
800 PCFA 94044 727-C4
SAINT LUCIA DR
- RDWC 94065 749-J5
SAINT MARKS CT
- DALY 94015 687-B6
SAINT MARTIN DR
- RDWC 94065 749-J5
- RDWC 94065 750-A5
SAINT MARYS CT
- SMTO 94401 728-J7
SAINT MARYS PL
- RDWC 94063 770-F7
SAINT MATTHEWS AV
- SMTO 94401 748-J1
SAINT MICHAEL CT
3300 PA 94306 791-D7
SAINT MICHAEL DR
- SMCo 94403 748-J5
- SMTO 94403 748-J5
3300 PA 94306 791-D7
SAINT MICHAELS CT
- DALY 94015 687-A6
SAINT PATRICK CT
- SSF 94080 707-D5
SAINT THOMAS LN
500 FCTY 94404 749-G5
SAINT VINCENT LN
500 FCTY 94404 749-J2
SALA TER
- SF 94112 687-E2
SALADA AV
100 PCFA 94044 706-J5
SALADO DR
1500 MTVW 94043 791-G7
SALAL RD
- SMCo 94019 787-H5
SALAS CT
2100 EPA 94303 791-C2
SALINAS AV
100 SF 94124 688-B1
SALISBURY WY
2200 SMTO 94403 749-C4
SALMARK CT
- HIL 94010 748-G5
SALT CT
700 RDWC 94065 749-H5
SALVADOR ST
- SMCo 94019 767-C3
SALVATIERRA ST
500 SCIC 94305 810-H1
SAM MCDONALD RD
- SCIC 94305 790-J6
SAMSON ST
200 RDWC 94063 770-A5
SAN ANDREAS AV
- HMBY 94019 767-C4
SAN ANDREAS DR
100 MLPK 94025 790-H3
SAN ANSELMO AV
200 SBRN 94066 727-J1
200 SBRN 94066 728-A1
S SAN ANSELMO AV
100 SBRN 94066 727-J1
300 SBRN 94066 728-A1
1000 MLBR 94030 728-A1
SAN ANSELMO AV N
200 SBRN 94066 727-J1
400 SBRN 94066 707-J7
SAN ANTONIO AV
100 SBRN 94066 728-A1
100 SMCo 94128 728-A1
300 SMTO 94401 728-J7
1400 MLPK 94025 790-F3
SAN ANTONIO CIR
- DALY 94014 687-F3
SAN ANTONIO RD
800 PA 94303 791-F6
1000 MTVW 94043 791-F6
1100 MTVW 94303 791-F6
SAN ARDO WY
2800 BLMT 94002 769-B1
SAN BENITO AV
- ATN 94027 790-E1
100 SBRN 94066 728-A1
500 SMCo 94025 770-E7
500 SMCo 94025 790-E1
SAN BENITO RD
- BSBN 94005 688-A6
SAN BENITO ST
400 HMBY 94019 787-G1
3600 SMTO 94403 749-D6
SAN BRUNO AV
- BSBN 94005 688-A6
3000 SF 94134 688-A1
SAN BRUNO AV E
- SMCo 94128 708-A6
100 SBRN 94066 707-J6
100 SBRN 94066 708-A6
SAN BRUNO AV W
- SBRN 94066 707-G7
2000 SBRN 94066 727-F1
SAN CARLOS AV
100 SMCo 94061 790-B3
200 SMCo 94070 767-A1
1100 SCAR 94070 769-D2
E SAN CARLOS AV
900 SCAR 94070 769-G2
SAN CARLOS CT
700 PA 94303 791-C6
E SAN CARLOS LN
700 SCAR 94070 769-H2
SANCHEZ AV
100 BURL 94010 728-E6
1700 HIL 94010 728-E6
SANCHEZ WY
1100 RDWC 94061 790-A1
SAN CLEMENTE DR
200 MLPK 94025 790-H3
SAN CLEMENTE LN
600 FCTY 94404 749-G5
SAN CLEMENTE RD
- SMCo 94019 767-B2
SANCTUARY WY
- SMCo - 768-D4
SANDALWOOD CT
2000 PA 94303 791-D4
SAND DOLLAR CT
- HMBY 94019 787-G5
SAND DUNES CT
- HMBY 94019 787-G5
SANDERLING ST
1000 FCTY 94404 749-H1
SAND HILL CIR
100 MLPK 94025 790-B7
SAND HILL CT
- WDSD 94062 809-H2
SAND HILL RD
- CLMA 94014 687-E7
100 MLPK 94025 790-E7
900 PA 94304 790-F6
1100 SMCo 94025 810-A1
1300 SCIC 94305 790-F6
2000 SMCo 94025 790-F6
2400 MLPK 94025 810-C1
3000 SMCo 94025 809-J2
3600 WDSD 94062 809-H3
SANDHURST ST
- RDWC 94065 750-A4
SAN DIEGO AV
- SF 94112 687-C3
100 DALY 94014 687-C3
100 SBRN 94066 728-A2
SANDLEWOOD LN
500 RDWC 94065 749-J3
SANDLEWOOD ST
- MLPK 94025 770-J7
SANDPIPER CT
200 FCTY 94404 749-G1
SANDPIPER LN
- RDWC 94065 749-G6
SANDRA CT
900 SSF 94080 707-G2
SANDRA LN
- MLBR 94030 728-A3
SANDRA PL
2900 PA 94303 791-D6
SANDRA RD
- HIL 94010 748-E3
SANDSTONE
- PTLV 94028 830-C1
SANDY HOOK CT
600 FCTY 94404 749-F5
SAN FELIPE AV
- SSF 94080 707-E3
100 SBRN 94066 728-A1
200 SBRN 94066 727-J1
SAN FERNANDO WY
600 FCTY 94404 749-G5
- DALY 94015 687-B6
SAN FRANCISCO AV
- BSBN 94005 688-A6
SAN FRANCISCO CT
800 SCIC 94305 810-J1
SAN FRANCISCO TER
800 SCIC 94305 810-J1
SAN GABRIEL CIR
- DALY 94014 687-F3
SAN GABRIEL CT
- DALY 94014 687-F3
SAN JOAQUIN CT
100 SBRN 94066 707-D7
SAN JOSE AV
100 PCFA 94044 706-J5
300 MLBR 94030 728-B2
400 SF 94112 687-E2
SAN JOSE AV Rt#-82
100 SF 94112 687-D3
3200 DALY 94014 687-D3
SAN JUAN AV
- DALY 94015 687-A7
- SMCo 94025 790-D5
1000 MLBR 94030 728-A1
SAN JUAN BLVD
2800 BLMT 94002 769-A1
SAN JUAN CT
300 SMTO 94402 748-G1
SAN JUAN ST
500 SCIC 94305 810-H1
SAN LUCAS AV
- SMCo 94038 766-F1
SAN LUIS AV
100 SBRN 94066 727-J1
100 SBRN 94066 728-A1
100 SMCo 94019 767-B2
SAN LUIS CIR
- DALY 94014 687-F3
SAN LUIS CT
- DALY 94014 687-F3
SAN LUIS DR
200 MLPK 94025 790-H2
SAN MARCO AV
100 SBRN 94066 728-A1
100 SBRN 94066 727-J1
SAN MARLO WY
400 PCFA 94044 726-J2
SAN MATEO AV
400 SBRN 94066 707-J5
400 SBRN 94066 727-J1
700 BURL 94010 728-F6
1000 SSF 94066 707-J5
1300 SSF 94080 707-J5
2600 SMCo 94063 770-C7
SAN MATEO DR
- MLPK 94025 790-E4
N SAN MATEO DR
- SMTO 94401 748-J1
300 SMTO 94401 728-H7
S SAN MATEO DR
- SMTO 94401 748-J1
SAN MATEO LN
400 BSBN 94005 688-A7
SAN MATEO RD Rt#-92
100 HMBY 94019 767-G7
100 HMBY 94019 787-G1
300 SMCo - 767-G7
1700 SMCo 94019 766-A5
SAN MATEO-HAYWARD BRDG Rt#-92
- FCTY - 729-H6
SAN MIGUEL AV
- DALY 94015 687-A7
SAN MIGUEL LN
700 FCTY 94404 749-G5
SAN MIGUEL ST
300 SF 94112 687-E1
SAN MIGUEL WY
- SMTO 94403 749-D5
2700 SCAR 94070 769-F5
SAN NICHOLAS LN
600 FCTY 94404 749-G5
SAN PABLO AV
- HMBY 94019 767-D4
300 MLBR 94030 728-B2
SAN PABLO TER
300 PCFA 94044 707-A5
SAN PEDRO AV
200 PCFA 94044 726-G4
SAN PEDRO RD
- DALY 94014 687-C5
- SMCo 94014 687-C5
- SMCo 94019 767-B2
300 DALY 94015 687-C5
SAN PEDRO MOUNTAIN RD
- SMCo - 726-H6
700 SMCo 94037 746-H3
1600 PCFA 94044 726-H6
SAN PEDRO TERRACE RD
700 PCFA 94044 726-G4
700 SMCo - 726-H4
SAN RAFAEL PL
700 SCIC 94305 810-H1
SAN RAMON AV
800 SMCo 94038 766-G1
SAN RAYMUNDO RD
1000 HIL 94010 748-F2
N SAN RAYMUNDO RD
400 HIL 94010 748-F2
SAN REMOS WY
1000 SCAR 94070 769-F5
SAN REY AV
300 MLBR 94030 728-B2
SAN SIMEON WY
2800 SCAR 94070 769-F5
SANTA ANA AV
- DALY 94015 687-A7
SANTA ANA ST
2200 PA 94303 791-C4
SANTA ANNA ST
100 SMCo 94019 767-B3
SANTA BARBARA AV
- SF 94112 687-C2
- DALY 94014 687-C2
600 MLBR 94030 727-H2
SANTA BARBARA PL
100 SBRN 94066 707-D6
SANTA CATALINA LN
600 FCTY 94404 749-G5
SANTA CATALINA ST
2300 PA 94303 791-D4
SANTA CLARA AV
- BSBN 94005 688-A6
100 SBRN 94066 728-A2
100 SMCo 94061 790-B3
100 RDWC 94061 790-B3
SANTA CLARA CT
- DALY 94014 687-F3
SANTA CLARA ST
- BSBN 94005 688-A6
SANTA CLARA WY
200 SMTO 94403 749-D5
SANTA CRUZ AV
- DALY 94014 687-C2
- SF 94112 687-C2
500 MLPK 94025 790-F3
2000 SMCo 94025 790-E6
SANTA CRUZ LN
600 FCTY 94404 749-G5
SANTA CRUZ TER
- PCFA 94044 726-J2
SANTA DOMINGA AV
100 SBRN 94066 727-J1
100 SBRN 94066 728-A1
SANTA ELENA AV
- DALY 94015 687-B7
SANTA FE AV
800 SCIC 94305 810-J1
SANTA FELICIA CT
- HIL 94010 748-H4
SANTA FLORITA AV
400 MLBR 94030 727-J2
SANTA GINA CT
- HIL 94010 748-H4
SANTA HELENA AV
100 SBRN 94066 728-A2
200 MLBR 94030 728-A2
SANTA INEZ AV
100 SBRN 94066 728-A2
E SANTA INEZ AV
- SMTO 94401 748-H1
400 SMTO 94401 728-J7
1000 SMTO 94401 729-A7
W SANTA INEZ AV
- SMTO 94402 748-G2
100 HIL 94010 748-G2
SANTA LUCIA AV
100 SBRN 94066 727-H2
100 SBRN 94066 728-A1
900 MLBR 94030 727-H2
SANTA MARGARITA AV
100 MLPK 94025 790-H3
700 MLBR 94030 727-J2
SANTA MARIA AV
- PTLV 94028 809-J6
- PCFA 94044 706-J5
100 SBRN 94066 728-A2
200 SMCo 94019 767-C3
700 SCIC 94305 810-H2
SANTA MARIA LN
- HIL 94010 748-G1
700 FCTY 94404 749-G5
SANTA MONICA AV
- SMCo 94038 746-F7
100 MLPK 94025 790-H3
SANTA PAULA AV
- MLBR 94030 728-B2
SANTA PAULA DR
100 DALY 94015 687-B6
SANTA RITA AV
- DALY 94015 707-A1
100 PA 94301 791-B6
300 MLPK 94025 790-F5
SANTA ROSA AV
- HMBY 94019 767-C4
100 PCFA 94044 706-J6
SANTA ROSA LN
700 FCTY 94404 749-G5
SANTA SUSANA AV
600 MLBR 94030 727-J2
SANTA TERESA ST
100 SCIC 94305 790-G7
SANTA TERESA WY
500 MLBR 94030 727-J2
SANTA YNEZ ST
600 SCIC 94305 810-H1
SANTIAGO AV
- ATN 94027 790-D4
100 SMCo 94061 790-A3
200 SMCo 94019 767-C3
SANTIAGO ST
3600 SMTO 94403 749-D5
SANTOS ST
- SF 94134 687-H2
200 DALY 94014 687-H2
SAPPHIRE ST
300 RDWC 94062 769-H7
400 RDWC 94062 789-J1
600 RDWC 94061 789-J1
SARA LN
- SCAR 94070 769-F5
SARATOGA AV
1100 EPA 94303 791-A1
1200 EPA 94303 771-A7
SARATOGA DR
3200 SMTO 94403 749-B4
SARGENT RD
- ATN 94027 790-B7
SARGENT ST
- SF 94132 687-C1
SATURN CT
600 FCTY 94404 749-E3
SAUSAL DR
- PTLV 94028 810-C6
SAVAGE WY
- DALY 94015 687-B7
SAVANNAH CT
3900 SSF 94080 707-C4
SAVONA WY
400 RDWC 94065 749-J5
SAWYER ST
200 SF 94134 687-J2
SAXON WY
1100 MLPK 94025 790-F4
SCENIC CT
100 SBRN 94066 727-H2
SCENIC DR
- SMCo 94020 829-E7
- SMCo 94020 849-F1
100 SMCo 94062 769-G6
SCENIC WY
- DALY 94014 687-E3
- SMTO 94403 748-J6
200 PCFA 94044 707-A6
SCHEMBRI LN
700 EPA 94303 791-B1
SCHOOL ST
- DALY 94014 687-C4
- SSF 94080 707-J2
200 DALY 94015 687-C4
1500 SCAR 94070 769-G3
SCHOONER ST
800 FCTY 94404 749-G4
SCHOONER BAY DR
800 RDWC 94065 750-C6
SCHWERIN ST
- SF 94134 687-J3
300 DALY 94014 687-J3
SCHWIE AL
- MLPK 94025 790-E6
SCOFIELD ST
600 EPA 94303 791-B3
SCORPIO LN
600 FCTY 94404 749-E4
SCOTT AV
500 RDWC 94063 770-C6
SCOTT CT
3000 HIL 94010 748-B1
SCOTT DR
- MLPK 94025 770-G6
SCOTT ST
- SBRN 94066 707-J5
900 PA 94301 790-J5
1600 SMTO 94403 749-D1
SEABREEZE CT
- PCFA 94044 707-A1
SEA BREEZE DR
- HMBY 94019 787-G5
SEABRIGHT CT
100 SMCo 94038 746-G6
SEABROOK CT
- RDWC 94065 749-J4
- RDWC 94065 750-A4
SEABROOK LN
- RDWC 94065 750-A4
SEABURY RD
700 HIL 94010 748-F1
SEA CHASE DR
800 RDWC 94065 750-C6
SEACLIFF AV
- DALY 94015 686-J5
SEACLIFF CT
- SMCo 94037 746-F4
SEA CLIFF LN
300 RDWC 94065 749-J2
SEA CLIFF WY
2000 SBRN 94066 707-C5
SEA CLOUD DR
700 FCTY 94404 749-G5
SEA COVE BLVD
- SMCo 94038 746-F7
SEA CREST CT
- SMCo 94019 766-J1
SEACREST CT
- DALY 94015 706-J1
SEAFORTH CT
300 PCFA 94044 707-A7
300 PCFA 94044 727-A1
SEAGATE CT
- RDWC 94065 749-J2
SEAGATE DR
100 SMTO 94403 749-E6
SEAGATE PL
- BLMT 94002 749-E7
SEAGATE WY
500 BLMT 94002 749-E6
SEAGULL LN
- HMBY 94019 787-G5
SEA HAVEN CT
- PCFA 94044 707-A1
SEA HORSE CT
300 FCTY 94404 749-H3
SEAHORSE LN
500 RDWC 94065 749-J6
SEA ISLAND LN
900 FCTY 94404 749-H1
SEAL ST
- SMTO 94403 749-D2
SEALE AV
100 PA 94301 791-A6
600 PA 94303 791-A6
SEALIGHT LN
- RDWC 94065 750-B3
SEAL POINTE DR
800 RDWC 94065 750-A6
SEAN CT
2600 SSF 94080 707-C4
SEAPORT BLVD
- RDWC 94063 770-D2
SEAPORT CT
400 RDWC 94063 770-C3
SEA RANCH AV
100 SMCo 94019 766-J1
SEARS ST
- SF 94112 687-D2
SEARS RANCH RD
- SMCo 94062 829-D5
SEARSVILLE CT
- HIL 94010 748-F6
SEARSVILLE RD
- SCIC 94305 790-F7
SEARVILLE RD
1500 PA 94304 810-G5
1700 SCIC 94304 810-F6
28000 LAH 94022 810-G5
SEASCAPE DR
- HMBY 94019 787-F6
SEA SHELL CIR
- HMBY 94019 787-G5
SEASHORE DR
- DALY 94014 687-E5
SEASIDE DR
200 PCFA 94044 706-J7
200 PCFA 94044 707-A7
SEASIDE SCHOOL RD
1000 SMCo 94074 828-B7
SEASONS LN
- RDWC 94065 750-A5
SEA SPRAY CT
- PCFA 94044 707-C5
SEA SPRAY LN
700 FCTY 94404 749-E3
SEASTORM CT
- RDWC 94065 750-A5
SEASTORM DR
- RDWC 94065 750-A5
SEAVIEW DR
- DALY 94015 686-J5
SEBASTIAN DR
200 MLBR 94030 728-A5
1600 BURL 94010 728-A5
SECLUDED AV
- SMCo 94063 770-F5
SECOND AV
700 HMBY 94019 787-E2
SEKI CT
- SMCo 94062 789-G2
SELBY LN
- ATN 94027 790-C2
- SMCo 94063 790-C1
1100 SMCo 94061 790-B3
W SELBY LN
1100 ATN 94027 790-C2
1400 SMCo 94061 790-B3
SEM LN
- BLMT 94002 749-F7
SEMERIA AV
2200 BLMT 94002 769-C1
SEMICIRCULAR RD
100 SMCo 94063 790-D1
100 SMCo 94025 790-D1
SEMINARY DR
300 MLPK 94025 790-H2
SEMINOLE AV
- SF 94112 687-F1
SEMINOLE WY
800 RDWC 94062 789-G2
SENECA AV
- SF 94112 687-F1
SENECA LN
1500 SMCo 94402 748-F6
SENECA ST
400 PA 94301 790-J3
400 PA 94301 791-A3
SEQUOIA AV
100 SMCo 94061 790-A3
200 PA 94306 791-A6
200 SSF 94080 707-F2
600 MLBR 94030 728-B4
700 SMTO 94403 749-A5
700 SMTO 94403 748-J5
800 BURL 94010 728-B4
1300 SBRN 94066 707-E6
SEQUOIA CT
- SMCo 94061 790-B3
- SCAR 94070 769-D3
SEQUOIA DR
- SMCo 94020 829-F1
- SMCo 94020 849-F1
1700 SMCo 94062 829-F1
SEQUOIA LN
400 SCIC 94305 790-G7
SEQUOIA WY
- PCFA 94044 727-B5
- SMCo 94061 790-B4
- SMCo 94062 809-F6
2600 BLMT 94002 749-B7
2600 BLMT 94002 769-B1
SERANA CT
- SSF 94080 707-E3
SERENA DR
700 PCFA 94044 726-J4
SERENITY CIRCLE DR
- SMCo - 768-C3
SERENITY VALLEY DR
- SMCo 94060 868-F3
SERRA AV
- MLBR 94030 728-B3
SERRA CT
- SMTO 94401 729-A7
100 SBRN 94066 727-H2
SERRA DR
300 SSF 94080 707-E2
1400 PCFA 94044 726-J5
SERRA LN
- DALY 94015 707-C2
SERRA ST
500 SCIC 94305 790-H7
700 SCIC 94305 791-A7
SERRAMONTE BLVD
- DALY 94015 707-B1
400 CLMA 94014 687-C7
500 CLMA 94014 707-B1
SERRANO DR
- ATN 94027 790-C2
- SF 94132 687-B1

STREET Block City ZIP Pg-Grid

SERRAVISTA AV
100 DALY 94015 707-C2
SEVERN LN
400 HIL 94010 748-H1
SEVIER AV
1000 MLPK 94025 790-J1
1100 MLPK 94025 770-J7
1300 MLPK 94025 771-A7
SEVILLA AV
- SMCo 94019 767-A1
SEVILLE CT
- MLBR 94030 728-A2
SEVILLE DR
1100 PCFA 94044 726-J5
SEVILLE ST
- SF 94112 687-F2
SEVILLE WY
- SMTO 94402 748-J3
- SMTO 94402 749-A3
- SSF 94080 707-E6
SEVYSON CT
2900 PA 94303 791-D6
SEXTANT CT
800 SMTO 94404 749-D2
SEYMOUR LN
1000 MLPK 94025 790-E5
SEYMOUR ST
200 HMBY 94019 787-E3
SHAD CT
300 FCTY 94404 749-H2
SHADOW BROOK LN
- WDSD 94062 809-H2
SHADY LN
- HIL 94010 748-E4
SHAFTER ST
1200 SMTO 94402 748-J3
SHAKESPEARE ST
- DALY 94014 687-C2
100 SF 94112 687-C2
SHAMROCK CT
- MLBR 94030 728-A3
3800 SSF 94080 707-C4
SHAMROCK RANCH RD
- SMCo - 726-G5
SHANNON DR
2200 SSF 94080 707-D5
SHANNON WY
500 RDWC 94065 749-J6
SHANNON PARK CT
- SSF 94080 707-C5
SHARON AV
600 HIL 94010 728-E7
2000 BLMT 94002 769-C1
SHARON CT
- DALY 94014 687-H4
- MLPK 94025 790-D7
800 PA 94303 791-B4
SHARON PL
1500 SMTO 94401 729-A7
SHARON RD
2000 MLPK 94025 790-D7
2000 SMCo 94025 790-D7
SHARON WY
- PCFA 94044 706-J4
SHARON OAKS DR
2300 MLPK 94025 790-E7
SHARON PARK DR
100 MLPK 94025 790-C7
SHARP PARK RD
- PCFA 94044 707-A7
700 SBRN 94066 707-A7
SHASTA CT
- SSF 94080 707-F4
SHASTA DR
3300 SMTO 94403 748-J6
SHASTA LN
- MLPK 94025 790-C7
- PCFA 94044 707-A3
SHASTA ST
700 RDWC 94063 770-B7
SHAW CT
- RDWC 94061 789-J1
SHAW RD
200 SBRN 94066 708-A5
200 SSF 94066 707-J5
200 SSF 94080 707-J5
200 SSF 94066 708-A5
200 SSF 94080 708-A5
SHAWNEE AV
- SF 94112 687-E1
SHAWNEE PASS
100 PTLV 94028 810-B6
SHEARER DR
- ATN 94027 790-C1
SHEARWATER ISL
200 FCTY 94404 749-G2
SHEARWATER PKWY
- RDWC 94065 749-J5
400 RDWC 94065 750-A5
SHEFFIELD DR
- DALY 94015 687-B3
SHEFFIELD LN
200 RDWC 94061 790-B2
SHEILA LN
1100 PCFA 94044 727-A5
1200 PCFA 94044 726-J5
SHELBOURNE AV
- DALY 94015 687-A7
SHELBOURNE PL
- SMCo 94402 768-G1
SHELDEN DR
- SMCo 94020 849-E2
SHELDON AV
- SCAR 94070 769-E3
SHELDON WY
- HIL 94010 728-D6
SHELFORD AV
- SCAR 94070 769-E2
SHELL BLVD
500 FCTY 94404 749-F2
SHELL PKWY
400 RDWC 94065 749-H6
SHELL ST
100 PCFA 94044 706-J5
SHELTER LN
- DALY 94014 687-E6
SHELTER COVE DR
100 SMCo 94019 766-J1
SHELTER COVE RD
- PCFA 94044 726-G4
SHELTER CREEK LN
- SBRN 94066 727-G1
100 SBRN 94066 707-G7
SHENANDOAH WY
- PCFA 94044 727-C4
SHEPARD WY
800 RDWC 94062 789-G2
SHERATON PL
2200 SMCo 94402 768-G1
SHERBORNE DR
2500 BLMT 94002 769-B3
SHERIDAN AV
100 PA 94306 791-B7
SHERIDAN DR
300 MLPK 94025 770-H7
SHERIDAN PL
- PCFA 94044 727-B6
SHERIDAN WY
100 WDSD 94062 789-J4
SHERLOCK CT
27300 LAH 94022 830-H2
SHERLOCK RD
27300 LAH 94022 830-H2
SHERMAN AV
100 PA 94306 791-B7
800 MLPK 94025 790-D6
1100 SMCo 94025 790-D6
1500 BURL 94010 728-D6
SHERMAN RD
- SMCo 94037 746-H5
SHERWOOD CT
- HIL 94010 748-H1
- MLBR 94030 727-J5
SHERWOOD DR
2500 SBRN 94066 707-E6
2900 SCAR 94070 769-F5
SHERWOOD WY
100 SSF 94080 707-G5
300 MLPK 94025 790-G4
SHERYL DR
100 SBRN 94066 707-D6
SHIELDS ST
- SF 94132 687-C1
SHIPLEY AV
- DALY 94015 707-C2
SHIRLEY RD
2100 BLMT 94002 749-C7
2100 BLMT 94002 769-B1
SHIRLEY WY
400 MLPK 94025 790-J2
SHOAL CIR
- RDWC 94065 750-A5
SHOAL DR
- DALY 94014 687-E5
900 SMTO 94404 749-D2
SHOOTING STAR ISL
100 FCTY 94404 749-H3
SHOPPE LN
- MLPK 94025 790-J2
SHOREBIRD CIR
100 RDWC 94065 749-H6
SHOREBREEZE CT
- EPA 94303 791-C2
N SHORELINE BLVD
1900 MTVW 94043 791-J7
SHORELINE CT
- BSBN 94005 688-C7
- SSF 94080 708-C1
SHORELINE DR
100 RDWC 94065 749-G7
100 RDWC 94065 769-G1
900 SMTO 94404 749-D3
SHORESIDE DR
- PCFA 94044 726-G4
SHOREVIEW AV
100 PCFA 94044 706-J5
1500 SMTO 94401 729-B7
1500 SMTO 94401 749-B1
2000 SMTO 94404 749-C1
2000 SMTO 94403 749-C1
SHOREWAY RD
- RDWC 94065 749-F7
- RDWC 94065 769-G1
- SCAR 94070 769-F2
1000 BLMT 94002 749-F7
1100 BLMT 94002 769-G1
SHORT ST
- PCFA 94044 707-A3
SHOSHONE PL
- PTLV 94028 810-B6
SHRATTON AV
- SMCo 94002 769-D4
- SMCo 94070 769-D4
- SCAR 94070 769-D4
SICKLES AV
- SF 94112 687-E2
N SIDE AV
2700 SMCo 94063 770-D7
W SIDE AV
2800 SMCo 94063 770-C7
2900 SMCo 94063 790-D1
SIENNA CT
- SMCo 94062 769-G7
SIERRA AV
500 PCFA 94044 727-A1
SIERRA CT
2300 PA 94303 791-D4
SIERRA DR
200 HIL 94010 748-G2
1000 MLPK 94025 790-C6
SIERRA LN
- PTLV 94028 810-C5
SIERRA ST
400 SMCo 94038 746-F5
1200 RDWC 94061 790-A1
SIERRA TER
900 PCFA 94044 707-A5
SIERRA MORENA RD
- SMCo 94062 788-J7
SIERRA POINT PKWY
1000 BSBN 94005 688-B5
SIERRA POINT RD
- BSBN 94005 688-A6
SIESTA CT
- SMCo 94028 810-D4
SILKTREE CT
- HIL 94010 748-C2
SILVA AV
- MLBR 94030 728-B3
SILVER AV
500 HMBY 94019 767-F7
1600 RDWC 94061 790-A1
SILVER HILL RD
1000 RDWC 94061 789-G3
SILVER SKY WY
- SMCo 94062 788-J5
SILVERSPOT DR
- BSBN 94005 687-H5
SILVIA CT
800 PCFA 94044 726-H5
SIMKINS CT
2900 PA 94303 791-D5
SIMON LN
13300 LAH 94022 810-J7
SIMPSON DR
- DALY 94015 707-C2
SIOUX WY
- PTLV 94028 810-C6
SISKIYOU CT
100 SBRN 94066 707-D7
SISKIYOU DR
900 MLPK 94025 790-C7
SISKIYOU PL
- MLPK 94025 790-C7
SISTER CITIES BLVD
- SSF 94080 707-J1
- SSF 94080 708-A1
SKIFF CIR
500 RDWC 94065 749-H7
SKIPJACK LN
100 FCTY 94404 749-J1
SKY CT
3700 SMTO 94403 749-B6
SKYCREST DR
- SBRN 94066 727-F1
SKYFARM DR
2100 HIL 94010 728-D7
2100 HIL 94010 748-D2
SKYLAWN DR
- SMCo - 768-D4
SKYLINE BLVD
100 MLBR 94030 727-H4
500 SBRN 94066 727-F1
1600 BURL 94010 728-A6
1600 SMCo 94010 728-A6
3300 SMCo - 748-D4
5800 SMCo 94010 748-D4
6000 BURL 94010 748-B1
6000 HIL 94010 748-B1
SKYLINE BLVD Rt#-35
- SMCo 94030 727-F2
- SF 94132 686-J3
500 SMCo - 727-E1
500 SBRN 94066 727-F2
900 SBRN 94066 707-D5
900 SMCo - 707-D5
1100 DALY 94015 707-B1
1200 PCFA 94044 707-B1
1200 DALY 94015 687-A5
1900 SMCo - 768-F1
1900 DALY 94015 686-J3
1900 SMCo - 748-E6
2100 DALY 94015 686-J3
2700 SSF 94080 707-D5
7500 SMCo 94062 768-D4
11400 SMCo - 788-G3
11400 SMCo 94062 788-G3
11600 SCIC 95030 850-J5
13800 SMCo 94062 789-A7
14600 SMCo 94062 808-J1
14600 SMCo 94062 809-A1
17100 WDSD 94062 809-G7
17300 SMCo 94020 809-G7
17300 WDSD 94020 809-D4
18000 PTLV 94028 809-G7
18000 PTLV 94062 809-G7
18100 SMCo 94020 829-H1
18100 PTLV 94028 829-H1
18600 SMCo 94020 830-A4
18600 PTLV 94028 830-A4
19800 SMCo 94028 830-C7
20800 SMCo 94020 850-E1
20800 SMCo 94028 850-D1
21100 SCIC 94028 850-E1
21200 PA 94304 850-H2
SKYLINE DR
- DALY 94015 686-J4
- SMCo 94062 809-F7
300 DALY 94015 687-A5
900 DALY 94015 707-A1
1200 DALY 94015 706-J1
SKYLINE FRONTAGE RD
1900 HIL 94010 748-B1
1900 SMCo 94010 748-B1
SKYLONDA DR
- SMCo 94020 809-F5
SKYMONT CT
- BLMT 94002 768-J1
SKYMONT DR
4100 BLMT 94002 768-J1
SKYPARK CIR
- SSF 94014 687-J7
- SSF 94014 707-J1
SKYRIDGE DR
- PCFA 94044 707-C5
SKYVIEW DR
1300 BURL 94010 748-B1
SKYWAY RD
600 SCAR 94070 769-H1
SKYWOOD WY
- WDSD 94062 809-F5
SLEEPY HOLLOW AV
- SMCo 94063 770-F5
SLEEPY HOLLOW LN
1100 MLBR 94030 727-H4
SLOOP CT
100 FCTY 94404 749-H4
SMOKE TREE LN
- WDSD 94062 809-F1
SNEATH LN
- PCFA 94044 727-D1
800 SBRN 94066 707-G6
3600 SBRN 94066 727-D1
3600 SMCo 94044 727-D1
SNECKNER CT
- SMCo 94025 810-F1
SNOWDEN AV
- ATN 94027 790-D1
SOHO CIR
- BLMT 94002 769-A3
SOLANA CT
- BLMT 94002 769-E2
SOLANA DR
1400 BLMT 94002 769-D2
SOLANA RD
100 PTLV 94028 810-B5
SOLANO AV
300 SMCo 94019 767-A2
SOLANO DR
1300 PCFA 94044 726-J5
SOLANO ST
- BSBN 94005 688-A6
SOLSTICE LN
- RDWC 94065 750-A4
SOMERSET CT
- BLMT 94002 769-B3
800 SCAR 94070 769-E5
SOMERSET DR
2500 BLMT 94002 769-B3
SOMERSET LN
- ATN 94027 790-D4
600 FCTY 94404 749-G5
SOMERSET PL
- PA 94301 791-A4
- WDSD 94062 789-F4
SOMERSET ST
100 RDWC 94062 769-H5
200 SF 94134 688-A1
SONJA RD
100 SSF 94080 707-H1
SONOMA AV
- ATN 94027 790-H1
1000 MLPK 94025 790-H1
1000 MLPK 94025 770-H7
SONOMA CT
100 SBRN 94066 707-D6
SONOMA PL
1000 MLPK 94025 770-H7
SONOMA TER
800 SCIC 94305 810-J1
SONORA AV
- SMCo 94019 767-A2
- SSF 94080 707-H4
600 SMCo 94019 766-J1
SONORA DR
200 SMTO 94402 748-J3
SORICH RD
- SCrC 95033 850-J6
- SMCo 94020 850-G5
SORREL LN
- SCAR 94070 769-C4
SOTOCASTLE LN
100 BLMT 94002 749-F6
SOUTH BLVD
100 SMTO 94402 749-A3
SOUTH CT
2200 PA 94301 791-C7
2500 PA 94306 791-C7
SOUTH LN
1000 BURL 94010 728-G6
SOUTH PL
400 RDWC 94062 769-J7
SOUTH PZ
- MLPK 94025 790-J2
SOUTH RD
300 BLMT 94002 749-D7
300 BLMT 94002 769-E1
SOUTHAMPTON DR
700 PA 94303 791-C5
SOUTHAMPTON WY
2200 SMTO 94403 749-C4
SOUTHCLIFF AV
100 SSF 94080 707-E3
SOUTHDALE AV
- DALY 94015 687-A7
SOUTHDALE WY
500 WDSD 94062 789-E3
SOUTHDOWN CT
- HIL 94010 748-F4
SOUTHDOWN RD
1100 HIL 94010 748-F4
SOUTHERN FRWY I-280
- DALY - 687-C4
- SF - 687-D2
SOUTH FORK LN
13400 LAH 94022 810-J7
SOUTHGATE AV
- DALY 94015 687-A4
400 DALY 94015 686-J4
SOUTHGATE DR
- WDSD 94062 789-J5
- WDSD 94062 790-A5
SOUTHGATE ST
- ATN 94027 790-D2
SOUTH HILL CT
200 DALY 94014 687-F3
SOUTH HILL DR
100 BSBN 94005 687-H5
SOUTHMOOR DR
600 PCFA 94044 707-B4
SOUTHPORT DR
800 RDWC 94065 750-A6
SOUTHRIDGE CT
- SMTO 94402 748-H6
SOUTHRIDGE WY
- DALY 94014 687-G3
SOUTH SAN FRANCISCO DR
100 SSF 94080 707-H1
100 SSF 94080 708-A1
100 SSF 94014 707-H1
100 SSF 94014 708-A1
SOUTHVIEW CT
600 BLMT 94002 769-E1
SOUTHVIEW WY
700 WDSD 94062 789-F3
SOUTHWOOD AV
3600 SMTO 94403 749-B6
SOUTHWOOD CTR
100 SSF 94080 707-G4
SOUTHWOOD DR
100 PA 94301 791-B3
600 SSF 94080 707-F3
SOVEREIGN WY
800 RDWC 94065 750-C6
SPAR DR
600 RDWC 94065 749-H7
800 SMTO 94404 749-D2
SPARROW CT
- EPA 94303 791-C2
SPARTA ST
- SF 94134 688-A1
SPEAR AV
1000 SF 94124 688-D1
SPEERS AV
1300 SMTO 94403 749-C2
SPENCER LN
- ATN 94027 790-E3
SPICE RD
- SMCo 94062 788-F2
SPINDRIFT WY
500 HMBY 94019 767-E6
SPINNAKER CT
200 FCTY 94404 749-H4
SPINNAKER LN
1500 HMBY 94019 767-E6
SPINNAKER PL
- RDWC 94065 749-H6
SPINNAKER ST
100 FCTY 94404 749-H4
SPIROS WY
- SMCo 94025 790-D5
SPRAGUE LN
1100 FCTY 94404 749-G4
SPRING LN
- BLMT 94002 769-E2
SPRING ST
- SMCo 94038 746-F7
- PCFA 94044 727-A3
- RDWC 94063 770-B5
1200 SCAR 94070 769-F2
2200 SMCo 94063 770-D6
SPRINGDALE DR
200 PCFA 94044 707-A2
SPRINGDALE WY
- SMCo 94062 769-E7
SPRINGFIELD DR
900 MLBR 94030 727-H4
900 SCAR 94070 769-G2
SPRINGFIELD WY
2200 SMTO 94403 749-C4
SPRING VALLEY LN
- MLBR 94030 728-A5
SPRING VALLEY WY
- SCAR 94070 769-F3
SPRINGWOOD WY
100 SSF 94080 707-G5
1200 PCFA 94044 726-J6
SPRUANCE LN
700 FCTY 94404 749-G4
SPRUCE AV
- ATN 94025 790-E2
- SSF 94080 707-J2
- MLPK 94025 790-E2
N SPRUCE AV
- SSF 94080 707-J2
400 SSF 94080 708-A1
S SPRUCE AV
- SSF 94080 707-H4
SPRUCE CT
- PCFA 94044 727-A4
SPRUCE LN
- SMCo 94060 868-H6
SPRUCE ST
- MLBR 94030 728-B2
- RDWC 94063 770-B7
200 HMBY 94019 787-F2
SPURAWAY DR
100 SMTO 94403 749-A4
SPYGLASS CT
- HMBY 94019 787-E5
SPYGLASS DR
1900 SBRN 94066 707-B5
3400 SMTO 94403 749-A6
SPYGLASS LN
- HMBY 94019 787-E5
STACEY CT
- HIL 94010 728-E7
STADLER DR
- WDSD 94062 809-F5
STAFFORD ST
- DALY 94015 707-C3
1400 SCAR 94070 769-J4
1400 RDWC 94063 769-J4
STAG AV
2000 SMCo 94402 768-H1
STAGE RD
- SMCo 94060 868-B2
700 SMCo 94060 848-A7
1600 SMCo 94074 848-B1
7500 SMCo 94074 828-A5
STAMBAUGH ST
- RDWC 94063 770-B6
STAMFORD CT
2600 SSF 94080 707-C4
STANCHION LN
700 FCTY 94404 749-J1
STANDISH CT
800 PCFA 94044 726-J5
STANDISH RD
800 PCFA 94044 726-H5
STANDISH ST
200 RDWC 94063 770-A5
STANFORD AV
- SCIC 94304 810-J2
100 SMCo 94019 766-H3
100 SMCo 94025 790-E6
200 PA 94306 791-A7
300 MLPK 94025 790-E6
400 SMCo 94063 770-D7
500 SCIC 94305 791-A7
1100 PA 94306 810-J2
1100 SCIC 94305 810-J2
1500 SMTO 94403 749-C3
STANFORD CT
900 MLPK 94025 790-E5
14100 LAH 94022 810-H5
STANFORD LN
- SCAR 94070 769-H5
STANISLAUS CT
100 SBRN 94066 707-D7
STANLEY AV
100 PCFA 94044 726-G4
STANLEY RD
- BURL 94010 728-H6
STANLEY ST
- SF 94132 687-D2
100 RDWC 94062 769-H7
STANLEY WY
900 PA 94303 791-B4
STANTON RD
800 BURL 94010 728-D4
STAR WY
- BURL 94010 728-E5
STARBOARD DR
400 RDWC 94065 749-H7
500 SMTO 94404 749-D1
STARFISH CT
- HMBY 94019 787-G5
STARFISH LN
300 RDWC 94065 749-J2
STAR HILL RD
- SMCo 94074 828-E2
300 SMCo 94062 828-E2
300 SMCo 94062 808-H2
900 SMCo 94062 788-H7
STARLITE DR
100 SMCo 94402 748-G6
STARLITE ST
100 SSF 94080 707-H4
STARWOOD DR
400 SMCo 94062 809-E6
STATE ST
- SMTO 94401 728-J6
STATION AV
- DALY 94014 687-C5
STAUNTON CT
2100 PA 94306 791-A7
STAYSAIL CT
200 FCTY 94404 749-H4
STEIN CT
3900 SSF 94080 707-C3
STEIN AM RHEIN CT
- RDWC 94063 770-C5
STELLING CT
3000 PA 94303 791-D6
STELLING DR
3000 PA 94303 791-D6
STEPHEN RD
400 SMTO 94403 749-B6
STERLING AV
200 PCFA 94044 726-G4
2000 SMCo 94025 790-D6
STERLING WY
3000 RDWC 94061 789-J3
STERLING VIEW AV
500 BLMT 94002 749-D6
STERN AV
700 PA 94303 791-D6
STERN LN
- ATN 94027 790-C4
1000 FCTY 94404 749-H4
STETSON ST
400 SMCo 94038 746-F6
STEVE COURTER WY
- DALY 94014 687-H3
STEVENS AV
1700 EPA 94303 771-C7
STEVENS CT
200 SCAR 94070 769-E6
STEVENSON LN
- ATN 94027 790-D3
STEVICK DR
300 ATN 94027 790-B5
STEWART AV
700 SMCo 94015 687-A4
STILL CREEK RD
- WDSD 94062 809-F4
STILT CT
200 FCTY 94404 749-G1
STIRRUP WY
27600 LAH 94022 810-J5
STOCKBRIDGE AV
- ATN 94027 790-C3
- SMCo 94061 790-C3
2100 WDSD 94062 790-A5
2100 WDSD 94027 790-C3
STOCK FARM RD
- SCIC 94305 790-F6
STOCKTON PL
3100 PA 94303 791-E6
STONE LN
700 PA 94303 791-E7
STONEGATE DR
600 SSF 94080 707-G1
STONEGATE RD
- PTLV 94028 810-B6
STONEHEDGE RD
- HIL 94010 748-H2
STONEPINE CT
- HIL 94010 748-E1
STONE PINE LN
100 MLPK 94025 790-E2
STONE PINE RD
500 HMBY 94019 787-G1
STONEPINE RD
- HIL 94010 748-E2
STONERIDGE LN
- SF 94134 687-H2
STONEY CT
900 MLBR 94030 727-H4
STONEYFORD DR
600 SMCo 94015 687-A5
700 DALY 94015 687-A5
STONEY POINT PL
- SMCo 94402 768-G2
STONY HILL RD
900 RDWC 94061 789-H2
STORY HILL LN
28100 LAH 94022 810-H7
STOWA WY
- DALY 94014 687-D5
STOWE CT
- SMCo 94025 810-F1
STOWE LN
- SMCo 94025 810-E1
STRATFORD DR
100 SF 94132 687-B1
STRATFORD ST
100 RDWC 94062 769-J5
STRATFORD WY
2000 SMTO 94403 749-A4
STUDIO CIR
400 SMTO 94401 728-H7
SUDAN LN
- SCAR 94070 769-D5
SUENO CAMINO
100 SMCo 94020 829-F7
SUGAR HILL DR
- HIL 94010 748-G5
SUGARLOAF DR
1600 SMTO 94403 748-H7
1600 SMTO 94403 768-J1
SULLIVAN AV
- DALY 94015 687-B5
100 SMCo 94015 687-B5
SULLIVAN ST
2000 SMTO 94403 749-C4
SUMAC WY
- SMCo 94019 787-H5
SUMMER AV
1100 BURL 94010 728-E5
SUMMERHILL LN
100 WDSD 94062 789-J3
SUMMER HOLM PL
- HIL 94010 728-F7
SUMMERRAIN DR
100 SSF 94080 707-G2
SUMMIT CT
- SMCo 94062 789-F1
- SSF 94080 707-E5
SUMMIT DR
200 SMCo 94062 789-F1
2100 BURL 94010 728-C7
2100 SMCo 94010 728-B7
SUMMIT DR
2200 HIL 94010 728-C7
2800 SMCo 94010 748-B1
2800 HIL 94010 748-B1
W SUMMIT DR
- SMCo 94062 789-F1
SUMMIT RD
- SMCo 94037 746-H4
- SMCo 94062 788-H6
- WDSD 94062 809-G6
3100 SBRN 94066 707-C5
SUMMIT ST
100 SF 94112 687-E1
SUMMIT WY
500 RDWC 94062 789-F3
500 SMCo 94062 789-F3
SUMMIT RIDGE PL
- SMCo 94062 789-F1
SUMMIT SPRINGS RD
400 WDSD 94062 789-E7
SUNBEAM LN
- SF 94112 687-F1
SUN BLOSSOM LN
- RDWC 94065 750-B3
SUNFISH CT
300 FCTY 94404 749-H3
SUNHILL
- PTLV 94028 830-C2
SUNNYBRAE BLVD
500 SMTO 94402 749-B2
SUNNYDALE AV
- SCAR 94070 769-H5
300 SF 94134 688-A2
700 SF 94134 687-H2
SUNNY HILL RD
- SMCo 94062 789-E1
SUNNYSIDE DR
1000 SSF 94080 707-F2
SUNNYSLOPE AV
1300 BLMT 94002 769-E1
SUNRISE CT
- MLPK 94025 790-E7
- SMCo 94019 766-J1
- SSF 94080 707-E5
SUNRISE DR
- WDSD 94062 809-G4
SUNRISE WY
300 SF 94134 687-J2
SUNRISE FARM RD
27400 LAH 94022 830-J1
SUNSET AV
600 SSF 94080 707-G2
SUNSET CT
- PCFA 94044 707-C5
- MLPK 94025 790-D7
SUNSET DR
- DALY 94015 706-J2
700 SCAR 94070 769-F5
3500 SBRN 94066 707-B6
SUNSET LN
- MLPK 94025 790-D7
SUNSET TER
- HMBY 94019 787-G5
2600 SMTO 94403 748-J6
2600 SMTO 94403 749-A6
SUNSET WY
500 SMCo 94062 789-E2
SUNSET CIRCLE DR
- SMCo - 768-C3
SUNSHINE DR
100 PCFA 94044 707-A1
SUNSHINE VALLEY RD
1100 SMCo 94038 746-G6
1600 SMCo 94037 746-G6
SURF ST
100 PCFA 94044 706-J5
SURF BIRD ISL
200 FCTY 94404 749-G1
SURFPERCH ST
800 FCTY 94404 749-H2
SURREY CT
- DALY 94015 707-C2
SURREY LN
- ATN 94027 790-F2
SUSAN CT
1500 SMTO 94403 749-D3
SUSAN DR
3000 SBRN 94066 707-C5
SUSAN GALE CT
- MLPK 94025 790-C6
SUSIE LN
2800 SCAR 94070 769-G6
SUSIE WY
300 SSF 94080 707-G2
SUSSEX CT
300 BLMT 94002 749-E7
SUSSEX PL
1800 MLPK 94025 790-F2
SUSSEX WY
200 PCFA 94044 726-G4
2700 RDWC 94061 789-J3
2700 RDWC 94061 790-A3
SUTHERLAND DR
- ATN 94027 790-B5
SUTTER AV
700 PA 94303 791-C6
SUTTON AV
- SSF 94080 707-D1
SUZANNE CT
1000 HMBY 94019 787-G2
SUZIE ST
4100 SMTO 94403 749-E6
SWAIN WY
- PA 94304 790-G6
SWALLOWTAIL CT
- BSBN 94005 687-H5
SWAN ST
900 FCTY 94404 749-H1
SWEENEY AV
800 SMCo 94063 770-C6
SWEET WILLIAM LN
- SMCo 94025 770-E7
SWEETWOOD DR
1300 SMCo 94015 687-B5
1300 DALY 94015 687-B5
SWETT RD
200 SMCo 94062 788-J7
200 SMCo 94062 808-H1
SWIFT AV
300 SSF 94080 708-B4
SWORDFISH ST
1200 FCTY 94404 749-H3
SYCAMORE AV
100 SMTO 94402 728-G7
100 SMTO 94402 748-G1

SYCAMORE AV
SAN MATEO COUNTY STREET INDEX
VINE ST 906

© 2008 Rand McNally & Company

SAN MATEO CO.

STREET
Block City ZIP Pg-Grid
SYCAMORE AV
100 SSF 94080 707-H4
700 SBRN 94066 707-H7
SYCAMORE CT
- RDWC 94061 790-A2
SYCAMORE DR
800 PA 94303 791-D6
1000 MLBR 94030 727-H3
SYCAMORE ST
100 SCAR 94070 769-F3
SYDNEY LN
- RDWC 94063 770-B4
SYLVAN AV
100 SBRN 94066 707-J7
100 SMTO 94403 749-A6
SYLVAN CT
- MLBR 94030 728-A4
SYLVAN DR
900 SCAR 94070 769-G2
SYLVAN ST
500 SMCo 94014 687-D5
500 DALY 94014 687-D5
SYLVAN WY
- SMCo 94021 849-A7
- SMCo 94074 849-B1
200 SMCo 94062 769-E7
200 SMCo 94062 789-E1
SYLVESTER RD
100 SSF 94080 708-A3

T

TACOMA WY
1500 RDWC 94063 769-J4
1500 RDWC 94063 770-A4
TADIN LN
1500 WDSD 94062 809-H4
TADLEY CT
300 RDWC 94061 790-B1
TAFT ST
900 RDWC 94061 789-J1
TAGUS CT
- PTLV 94028 810-D5
TAHOE CT
- SSF 94080 707-F4
TAHOE DR
1000 BLMT 94002 769-A2
TALBERT CT
- SF 94134 688-A2
TALBERT ST
100 SF 94134 688-A3
200 DALY 94014 688-A3
400 DALY 94014 687-J3
TALBOT AV
300 PCFA 94044 707-A5
TALBRYN DR
1200 BLMT 94002 769-E2
TALBRYN LN
- BLMT 94002 769-E1
TALBRYN PL
- BLMT 94002 769-E2
TALISMAN CT
700 PA 94303 791-E7
TALISMAN DR
800 PA 94303 791-E7
TALLWOOD CT
- ATN 94027 790-C6
TALLWOOD DR
100 DALY 94014 687-D4
TAMARACK AV
700 SCAR 94070 769-F4
TAMARACK DR
- HIL 94010 748-E1
TAMARACK LN
200 SSF 94080 707-G2
TAMARIND ST
1000 SMCo 94037 746-G4
TAMPA CT
300 FCTY 94404 749-F5
TANAGER CT
- BSBN 94005 687-J5
TANAGER LN
- RDWC 94065 750-A5
TANFORAN AV
- SBRN 94066 707-H5
- SSF 94080 707-H5
TANGLEWOOD WY
1100 SMTO 94403 749-E6
TANKLAGE RD
900 SCAR 94070 769-H3
TANLAND DR
1000 PA 94303 791-D5
TAN OAK DR
100 PTLV 94028 830-C1
TAPIA DR
- SF 94132 687-B1
TAPIS WY
1100 PCFA 94044 726-J5
TARA LN
2400 SSF 94080 707-D5
TARA ST
100 EPA 94303 771-C7
100 EPA 94303 791-C1
100 SF 94112 687-E1
TARPON ST
900 FCTY 94404 749-H2
TARRYTOWN RD
1400 SMCo 94402 748-F7
TARTAN TRAIL RD
1000 HIL 94010 748-E4
TASKER LN
- SCAR 94070 769-F5
TASSO ST
100 PA 94301 790-J3
1300 PA 94301 791-A5
TATE ST
- EPA 94303 791-C3
TAURUS DR
800 FCTY 94404 749-E3
TAYLOR AV
300 SBRN 94066 707-J7
300 SBRN 94066 727-J1
TAYLOR BLVD
100 MLBR 94030 728-A4
TAYLOR DR
200 SSF 94080 707-G4
TAYLOR ST
1600 SMTO 94403 749-C2
TAYLOR WY
500 SCAR 94070 769-G2
TEA CT
- EPA 94303 791-C2
TEA RD
- SMCo 94019 787-H5
TEAL ST
600 FCTY 94404 749-G1
TEATREE CT
- HIL 94010 748-C2
TEDDY AV
- SF 94134 688-A2
300 SF 94134 687-J1
TEHAMA AV
1000 MLPK 94025 770-H7
1000 MLPK 94025 790-H1
TEHAMA CT
100 SBRN 94066 727-E1
TELFORD AV
600 SSF 94080 707-J2
TEMESCAL WY
700 SMCo 94062 789-F2
TEMPLE CT
2800 EPA 94303 771-C7
TEMPLE ST
- SMCo 94037 746-H5
TEMPLETON AV
- DALY 94014 687-E3
TENDER LN
700 FCTY 94404 749-G5
TENNIS DR
800 SSF 94080 707-G3
TENNYSON AV
100 PA 94301 791-A6
700 PA 94303 791-A6
TEREDO DR
500 RDWC 94065 749-H7
TERESA ST
- DALY 94014 687-D5
TERMINAL AV
- MLPK 94025 770-H7
TERMINAL BLVD
2500 MTVW 94043 791-G6
TERMINAL CT
- SSF 94080 707-J4
- SSF 94080 708-A4
TERMINAL PL
1200 SMTO 94401 729-A7
TERMINAL WY
900 SCAR 94070 769-G3
TERRACE AV
- DALY 94015 687-A4
200 SBRN 94066 707-J7
200 SBRN 94066 727-J1
400 SMCo 94038 746-G7
400 SMCo 94019 767-D4
500 HMBY 94019 767-F7
TERRACE DR
200 SSF 94080 707-H4
1300 MLBR 94030 727-H2
1700 BLMT 94002 769-C1
TERRACE LN
- SMCo 94038 746-F7
TERRACE RD
600 SCAR 94070 769-F6
TERRACE WY
400 SMTO 94403 749-B5
TERRACE VIEW CT
- DALY 94015 687-A5
TERRA LINDA CT
- MLBR 94030 728-A5
TERRA NOVA BLVD
1000 PCFA 94044 727-A4
TERRA VILLA AV
2200 EPA 94303 791-C2
TERRIER PL
- HIL 94010 748-F5
TERRY LN
1900 SMCo 94061 790-B4
TEVIS PL
- HIL 94010 748-E1
- PA 94301 791-B4
TEXAS PL
300 SBRN 94066 727-J1
TEXAS WY
2000 SMTO 94403 749-B4
THATCHER LN
100 FCTY 94404 749-F5
THE ALAMEDA
100 SMCo 94019 767-B2
THE CROSS WY
500 SMCo 94019 767-D4
THE CROSSWAYS
200 SMCo 94019 767-C3
THE EMBARCADERO
- RDWC 94065 749-J4
500 RDWC 94065 750-A4
THERESA CT
900 MLPK 94025 770-G7
THERESA DR
500 SSF 94080 707-E2
THE STRAND
200 SMCo 94038 746-F7
THETA AV
- DALY 94014 687-C3
THIERS ST
- DALY 94014 687-C4
THIRD AV
600 HMBY 94019 787-F2
THISTLE
- PTLV 94028 830-C1
THOBURN CT
- SCIC 94305 790-J7
THOMAS AV
- BSBN 94005 688-B6
THOMAS CT
- SMTO 94401 728-J7
THOMAS DR
3300 PA 94303 791-E6
THOMAS MELLON DR
- SF 94134 688-B2
THOMAS MORE WY
- SF 94132 687-B2
THORNHILL DR
700 SMCo 94015 687-A5
2600 SCAR 94070 769-F5
THORNWOOD DR
800 PA 94303 791-E7
THREE FORKS LN
13400 LAH 94022 810-H7
THRIFT ST
- SF 94112 687-D1
THURLOW ST
300 MLPK 94025 790-G3
THURM AV
2200 BLMT 94002 749-B7
2200 BLMT 94002 769-B1
2200 SMTO 94403 749-B7
TIARA CT
- SMCo 94010 728-B7
TIBURON WY
2800 BURL 94010 728-B6
TICONDEROGA CT
- SMCo 94402 768-H1
- SMTO 94402 768-H1
TICONDEROGA DR
1900 SMCo 94402 768-G1
TIDEWATER DR
- RDWC 94065 750-A6
TIERRA ALTA ST
700 SMCo 94038 746-G6
TIERRA FUEGO RD
- SMCo 94060 868-E4
TILIA ST
1200 SMTO 94402 748-J3
TILLER CT
100 HMBY 94019 767-E6
TILLER DR
- SMTO 94404 749-D2
TILLER LN
400 RDWC 94065 749-H7
1000 FCTY 94404 749-H4
TILTON AV
- SMTO 94401 748-J1
700 SMTO 94401 728-J7
800 SMTO 94401 729-A7
TILTON TER
- SMTO 94401 748-J1
TIMBERHEAD LN
300 FCTY 94404 749-G6
TIMBERHILL CT
- PCFA 94044 707-B3
TIMBERHILL ST
- PCFA 94044 707-B3
TIMBERLANE RD
1700 SMCo 94402 748-H7
1800 SMTO 94402 748-H7
TIMBERLANE WY
1700 SMTO 94402 768-H1
1700 SMCo 94402 768-H1
TIMOR CT
- SBRN 94066 707-C6
TIMOTHY LN
200 RDWC 94070 769-G6
200 SCAR 94070 769-G6
900 MLPK 94025 770-G7
TINSLEY ST
- EPA 94303 791-C3
TINTERN LN
- PTLV 94028 810-B6
TIOGA AV
- SF 94134 688-A1
TIOGA DR
700 MLBR 94030 727-J4
2200 MLPK 94025 790-C6
TIOGA WY
- BLMT 94002 769-A2
- PCFA 94044 727-B5
TIPPERARY AV
2300 SSF 94080 707-D5
TIPTOE LN
- HIL 94010 748-B1
- SMCo 94010 748-B1
100 SMCo 94010 728-B7
100 HIL 94010 728-B7
TOBIN CLARK DR
- HIL 94010 748-H4
TOCOLOMA AV
200 SF 94134 688-B2
TODO EL MUNDO
100 WDSD 94062 789-J5
TOLEDO AV
1600 BURL 94010 728-B6
TOLEDO CT
- BURL 94010 728-B6
1600 PCFA 94044 727-B6
TOLLRIDGE CT
- SMTO 94402 748-C7
TOLMAN DR
700 SCIC 94305 810-J2
TOMASO CT
- SF 94134 687-J2
TOPAZ ST
300 RDWC 94062 769-H7
500 RDWC 94062 789-J1
600 RDWC 94061 789-J1
TOPSAIL CT
200 FCTY 94404 749-G4
TORINO DR
300 SCAR 94070 769-E4
300 SMCo 94070 769-E4
TORINO KNOLLS
- SCAR 94070 769-E5
TORO CT
- PTLV 94028 810-D6
TORREYA CT
700 PA 94303 791-D7
TOULOUSE CT
- HMBY 94019 767-E5
TOURAINE LN
2000 HMBY 94019 767-E5
TOURNAMENT DR
700 HIL 94010 748-H4
TOURNAMENT WY
- HIL 94010 748-G5
TOWER LN
900 FCTY 94404 749-E3
TOWER RD
800 SMCo 94402 768-H1
TOWLE PL
600 PA 94306 791-C7
TOWLE WY
600 PA 94306 791-C7
TOWNE FIRE TR
- SMCo 94020 849-E3
TOWN GREEN LN
- FCTY 94404 749-F3
TOYON AV
100 SSF 94080 707-H3
TOYON CT
100 WDSD 94062 789-G5
1600 SMTO 94403 768-J1
TOYON DR
900 BURL 94010 728-F6
1200 MLBR 94030 728-A5
TOYON LN
- SF 94112 687-G2
TOYON PL
600 PA 94306 791-D7
TOYON RD
- ATN 94027 790-G1
TOYON WY
800 RDWC 94062 789-G1
2300 SBRN 94066 707-F6
TRACE LN
- HMBY 94019 787-F5
TRACY CT
14000 LAH 94022 810-H6
14000 PA 94304 810-H6
TRADER LN
2200 SMTO 94404 749-E2
TRAEGER AV
- SBRN 94066 707-H7
TRAIL LN
- WDSD 94062 810-A5
TRAMANTO DR
2800 SCAR 94070 769-F5
TRANSOM LN
400 FCTY 94404 749-G6
TRANSPORT ST
4000 PA 94303 791-F7
TRAPPERS TR
- PA 94304 830-E2
TREASURE ISLAND DR
100 BLMT 94002 749-F6
TREEDUST ST
300 RDWC 94065 749-J3
TREESIDE CT
- SSF 94080 707-G2
TREETOP LN
- SMTO 94402 748-H4
TREE TOPS CIR
3000 SBRN 94066 707-C5
TREE VIEW DR
200 DALY 94014 687-E3
TRENTON DR
2200 SBRN 94066 707-G7
2400 SBRN 94066 727-F1
TRENTON PL
- SMCo 94402 748-F7
TRENTON WY
300 MLPK 94025 790-J3
600 BURL 94010 728-G6
TRIDENT DR
400 RDWC 94065 749-H7
TRILLIUM CT
- SCAR 94070 769-C4
TRIMARAN CT
100 FCTY 94404 749-H4
TRINIDAD LN
400 FCTY 94404 749-F5
TRINITY CT
- MLPK 94025 790-C7
100 SBRN 94066 707-D7
TRINITY DR
1000 MLPK 94025 790-C7
TRINITY LN
- PTLV 94028 809-J6
TRINITY RD
- BSBN 94005 688-A6
TRINITY ST
2000 SMTO 94403 749-C4
TRIPOLI CT
12900 LAH 94022 830-J1
TRIPP CT
- WDSD 94062 789-E7
TRIPP RD
3300 WDSD 94062 789-E6
3500 WDSD 94062 809-F1
TRITON DR
1100 FCTY 94404 749-F2
TROGLIA TER
100 PCFA 94044 727-A3
TROLLMAN AV
1400 SMTO 94401 729-A7
TROON RD
100 HMBY 94019 787-F5
TROPHY CT
- HIL 94010 748-H4
TROUSDALE DR
- SMCo - 728-B6
- SMCo 94010 728-B6
1100 BURL 94010 728-B6
TROUT FARM RD
- SMCo - 727-B7
TRUDY LN
- SMCo 94025 790-D6
TRUMAN ST
1100 RDWC 94061 789-J1
TRYSAIL CT
200 FCTY 94404 749-G4
TUCKER AV
- SF 94134 688-A1
TUDOR DR
1600 MLPK 94025 790-F2
TULANE AV
1600 EPA 94303 771-B6
TULANE CT
700 SMTO 94402 748-H3
TULANE RD
200 SMTO 94402 748-H3
TULARE DR
100 SBRN 94066 707-E7
TULARE ST
- BSBN 94005 688-B6
TULIP CT
- SMCo 94010 748-B1
TULIP LN
- SCAR 94070 769-D4
- PA 94303 791-C4
100 MLBR 94030 727-H4
TUM SUDEN WY
- RDWC 94062 789-F3
- SMCo 94062 789-F3
- WDSD 94062 789-F3
TUNITAS LN
- SSF 94080 707-E3
TUNITAS CREEK RD
- SMCo 94062 789-A7
100 SMCo 94019 828-A1
300 SMCo 94074 828-B1
400 SMCo 94074 808-B7
2000 SMCo 94062 808-F2
2000 SMCo 94019 808-F2
4000 SMCo 94062 788-G7
TUNNEL AV
100 SF 94134 688-A4
400 BSBN 94005 688-A4
TUOLUMNE CT
100 MLBR 94030 727-J4
TUOLUMNE RD
1100 MLBR 94030 727-H4
TURKEY FARM LN
- WDSD 94062 809-G1
TURKS HEAD CT
- RDWC 94065 749-H7
TURKS HEAD LN
- RDWC 94065 749-H7
TURNBERRY DR
2500 SSF 94080 707-D5
2500 SBRN 94066 707-D5
TURNBERRY RD
- HMBY 94019 787-F5
TURNER TER
400 SMTO 94401 728-H7
400 SMTO 94401 748-H1
TURNSTONE CT
200 FCTY 94404 749-H2
TURNSWORTH AV
- RDWC 94062 769-H6
TURTLE BAY PL
- SMCo 94402 768-G1
TUSCALOOSA AV
- ATN 94027 790-C3
TWIN DOLPHIN DR
- RDWC 94065 749-G7
200 RDWC 94065 769-G1
TWIN OAK CT
- LAH 94022 810-J6
1000 RDWC 94061 789-G3
TWIN PINES LN
- BLMT 94002 769-E1
TYNAN WY
- PTLV 94028 809-J6
TYRONE CT
2600 SSF 94080 707-C4

U

UCCELLI BLVD
- RDWC 94063 770-B4
ULMER CT
300 RDWC 94061 790-C1
ULSTER WY
- SSF 94080 707-E5
UNION AV
1500 RDWC 94061 790-A1
UNIVERSITY AV
- PA 94301 790-J4
600 EPA 94303 791-B2
700 PA 94301 791-A3
2500 EPA 94303 771-B7
UNIVERSITY AV Rt#-109
2600 EPA 94303 771-B6
2700 MLPK 94303 771-B6
2800 MLPK 94025 771-B6
UNIVERSITY DR
- MLPK 94025 790-F3
UNIVERSITY ST
500 SF 94134 687-J1
UNWIN CT
2400 SSF 94080 707-D4
UPENUF RD
- PTLV 94028 809-H6
- WDSD 94062 809-H6
UPLAND AV
- DALY 94015 686-J5
- DALY 94015 687-A5
- SCAR 94070 769-F3
UPLAND CT
200 RDWC 94062 769-G7
UPLAND DR
- SSF 94014 707-J1
UPLAND RD
200 RDWC 94062 769-G7
400 SMCo 94062 769-G7
700 RDWC 94062 789-H1
700 SMCo 94062 789-H1
UPLANDS DR
200 HIL 94010 748-H2
UPPER LAKE RD
- WDSD 94062 809-H5
UPPER LOCK AV
3200 BLMT 94002 769-A2
UPTON ST
400 SMCo 94062 769-H7
400 SMCo 94062 789-J1
500 RDWC 94062 789-J1
600 RDWC 94061 789-J1
URBAN LN
600 PA 94301 790-H5
URSA LN
800 FCTY 94404 749-F4
URSULA AV
700 PCFA 94044 727-A2
URSULA LN
27200 LAH 94022 830-J1
URSULA WY
1300 EPA 94303 791-B1
UTAH AV
100 SSF 94080 708-A4
UTAH WY
- RDWC 94062 789-H1

V

VAILWOOD PL
100 SMTO 94403 749-E6
VAILWOOD WY
1100 SMTO 94403 749-E6
VALDEFLORES DR
100 SMCo 94010 728-B7
VALDEZ AV
200 HMBY 94019 787-E1
1800 BLMT 94002 769-D2
VALDEZ PL
900 SCIC 94305 810-J2
VALDEZ WY
1500 PCFA 94044 727-A6
VALDIVIA CT
- BURL 94010 728-C6
VALDIVIA WY
2300 BURL 94010 728-B6
VALE ST
- DALY 94014 687-C5
VALENCIA AV
100 SMCo 94019 767-A2
VALENCIA CT
- PTLV 94028 810-D6
VALENCIA DR
200 MLBR 94030 727-J5
200 MLBR 94030 728-A5
300 SSF 94080 707-F5
VALENCIA ST
- HMBY 94019 767-D4
VALENCIA WY
1000 PCFA 94044 726-J4
1000 PCFA 94044 727-A4
VALERGA DR
2100 BLMT 94002 769-D3
VALLECITO LN
100 PCFA 94044 727-B2
VALLECITOS RD
- SMCo 94037 746-H4
VALLEJO CT
200 MLBR 94030 727-J5
VALLEJO DR
- MLBR 94030 727-J5
200 MLBR 94030 728-A6
VALLEJO ST
100 SMCo 94019 767-A2
VALLEJO TER
700 PCFA 94044 707-A5
VALLEMAR ST
300 SMCo 94038 746-F5
VALLE VISTA RD
- SMCo 94037 746-H3
VALLEY CT
- ATN 94027 790-A7
- WDSD 94062 790-A7
VALLEY DR
100 BSBN 94005 688-A5
300 BSBN 94005 687-J5
VALLEY RD
- ATN 94027 790-A7
- SCAR 94070 769-F3
VALLEY ST
- DALY 94014 687-C5
100 SMCo 94014 687-C5
VALLEY OAK
- PTLV 94028 830-C2
VALLEY VIEW AV
1600 BLMT 94002 749-D7
1600 BLMT 94002 769-D1
VALLEY VIEW CT
- SMCo 94402 748-G6
VALLEYVIEW WY
100 SSF 94080 707-E5
VALLEYWOOD DR
- PCFA 94044 726-J6
2000 SBRN 94066 707-E6
VALMAR PL
- SCAR 94070 769-F5
VALOTA RD
600 RDWC 94061 789-J1
900 RDWC 94061 790-A2
VALPARAISO AV
- ATN 94027 790-E4
- MLPK 94025 790-C6
700 MLPK 94027 790-E4
1800 SMCo 94025 790-D5
VALPARAISO ST
600 SCIC 94305 810-H1
VALVERDE DR
300 SSF 94080 707-F5
VAL VERDE RD
- SMCo 94037 746-J5
VAN AUKEN CIR
900 PA 94303 791-D5
VAN BUREN RD
100 MLPK 94025 770-H7
400 MLPK 94025 790-J1
VAN BUREN ST
1600 SMTO 94403 749-C2
VANCE LN
- EPA 94303 791-C2
VANCOUVER AV
1100 BURL 94010 728-D6
VAN NESS AV
- HMBY 94019 787-F4
VANNESSA DR
600 SMTO 94402 749-B3
VANNIER DR
500 BLMT 94002 749-E7
500 BLMT 94002 769-E1
VAN WATERS & RODGERS RD
- BSBN 94005 688-B6
VAQUERO WY
100 SMCo 94062 789-G1
VARELA AV
- SF 94132 687-B1
VARIAN ST
1000 SCAR 94070 769-J4
VARIAN WY
- PA 94304 790-G5
VASCO DA GAMA
900 FCTY 94404 749-G4
VASILAKOS CT
- SMCo 94025 790-C5
VASILAKOS WY
- SMCo 94025 790-D5
VASSAR ST
100 SMCo 94019 766-J2
VAZQUES DR
700 HMBY 94019 787-G2
VEGA CIR
700 FCTY 94404 749-E4
VEGA CT
- PCFA 94044 727-B3
VELASCO AV
- DALY 94014 687-H2
- SF 94134 687-H2
VELOCITY WY
- FCTY 94404 749-E1
VENDOME AV
- DALY 94014 687-C3
VENICE BLVD
400 HMBY 94019 767-D6
VENTANA CT
- SMCo 94062 789-G2
VENTURA AV
- SMCo 94020 829-E7
500 SMTO 94403 749-A6
VENTURA CT
- PCFA 94044 727-A6
VENTURA ST
- HMBY 94019 767-D4
900 SMCo 94019 767-C3
VENUS CT
600 FCTY 94404 749-E3
VERA AV
100 RDWC 94061 770-A7
1600 RDWC 94061 789-H1
VERA CT
- RDWC 94061 770-A6
VERANO CT
500 HIL 94010 748-H4
500 SMTO 94402 748-H4
VERANO DR
- SSF 94080 707-E3
200 DALY 94015 687-B7
VERBALEE LN
- HIL 94010 748-H4
VERBENA DR
100 EPA 94303 791-C3
VERDE RD
- SMCo 94019 807-G2
VERDUCCI CT
400 DALY 94015 707-D3
VERDUCCI DR
400 DALY 94015 707-C3
VERDUN AV
3100 SMTO 94403 748-J6
3100 SMTO 94403 749-A6
VERITAS WK
300 PCFA 94044 727-A1
VERMONT AV
200 SMCo 94038 746-F6
VERMONT ST
600 SMCo 94038 746-G6
VERMONT WY
1100 SBRN 94066 707-E7
VERNAL WY
700 SMCo 94062 789-F2
VERNIER PL
1000 SCIC 94305 810-J2
VERNON ST
- SF 94132 687-C1
VERNON TER
1100 SMTO 94402 748-J4
3300 PA 94303 791-E6
VERNON WY
600 BURL 94010 728-G6
VERONA AV
100 PCFA 94044 727-A2
VERONICA CT
1000 EPA 94303 791-C1
VERONICA PL
- PTLV 94028 810-C7
VERSAILLES DR
- MLPK 94025 790-F3
VESPERO AV
- PCFA 94044 727-B1
VESPUCCI LN
700 FCTY 94404 749-F4
VETERANS BLVD
- SSF 94080 708-B2
500 RDWC 94063 770-A4
VIA CANON
- MLBR 94030 728-A4
VIA CERRO GORDO
27600 LAH 94022 830-H1
VIA CORITA
27800 LAH 94022 830-J1
VIA CRESPI
400 SCIC 94305 790-G7
VIA DELIZIA
- HIL 94010 748-G3
VIA FELIZ
27800 LAH 94022 810-J7
VIA LAGUNA
1600 SMTO 94404 749-H1
VIA ORTEGA
400 SCIC 94305 790-G7
VIA PALOU
400 SCIC 94305 790-G7
VIA PUEBLO LN
200 SCIC 94305 790-G6
VIA VENTANA
27900 LAH 94022 830-H1
VIA VISTA
1400 SMTO 94404 749-H1
VICTORIA AV
- MLBR 94030 728-B4
VICTORIA DR
- ATN 94027 790-F3
VICTORIA MNR
2700 SCAR 94070 769-G6
VICTORIA RD
- BURL 94010 728-H6
VICTORIA ST
- DALY 94015 707-C2
- SF 94132 687-C2
600 SF 94127 687-C2
VICTORIA WY
1500 PCFA 94044 727-A4
VICTOR PARK LN
- HIL 94010 748-F2
VICTORY AV
300 SSF 94080 707-H4
VIDAL DR
200 SF 94132 687-A1
VIENNA ST
300 SF 94112 687-G1
VIEW AV
- SMCo 94038 746-F7
VIEW TR
- MLBR 94030 728-A4
VIEW WY
1000 PCFA 94044 727-A5
VIEWCREST CIR
- SSF 94080 707-H1
VIEW HAVEN RD
1200 HIL 94010 748-F4
VIEWMONT TER
- SSF 94080 707-H2
VIEW POINT CT
- PCFA 94044 707-C5
VIEW RIDGE CT
- PCFA 94044 707-C5
VIEWRIDGE DR
800 SMTO 94403 749-A7
VILLA AV
- CLMA 94014 687-D7
900 BLMT 94002 769-C1
VILLA CT
- SSF 94080 707-F2
VILLA LN
- MLBR 94030 728-A5
VILLA ST
500 SMCo 94014 687-D5
600 DALY 94014 687-D5
VILLA TER
200 SMTO 94401 728-H7
VILLAGE CT
2200 BLMT 94002 769-C2
VILLAGE DR
1100 BLMT 94002 769-C2
VILLAGE LN
- SMCo 94015 687-B4
VILLAGE WY
200 SSF 94080 707-J3
VILLA VISTA
800 SMCo 94062 789-G1
VINE AV
300 SMCo 94062 788-H5
VINE CT
800 SMTO 94401 749-C1
VINE ST
- SCAR 94070 769-F2

STREET
Block City ZIP Pg-Grid

VINE ST
100 MLPK 94025 790-E6
100 SMCo 94025 790-E6
1500 BLMT 94002 769-F2
VINES CT
- EPA 94303 791-C1
VINEYARD DR
3800 RDWC 94061 789-G3
VINEYARD LN
- PA 94304 790-G5
VINEYARD HILL RD
- WDSD 94062 809-H2
VINTAGE CT
- WDSD 94062 809-H2
VINTAGE PARK DR
300 FCTY 94404 749-E2
VIOLA ST
- SSF 94014 707-J1
VIOLA WY
- SMCo 94074 849-C1
VIOLET LN
- SCAR 94070 769-C4
VIRGINIA AV
- SMCo 94038 746-F7
100 BLMT 94002 749-E7
100 BLMT 94002 769-E1
200 SMTO 94402 748-H3
1100 RDWC 94061 789-J1
1200 RDWC 94061 790-A2
VIRGINIA LN
- ATN 94027 790-E1
VIRGO LN
900 FCTY 94404 749-E5
VISITACION AV
- BSBN 94005 688-A6
200 SF 94134 687-J2
500 SF 94134 688-A2
VISTA AV
- SMTO 94403 749-D6
400 SCAR 94070 769-F3
E VISTA AV
100 DALY 94014 687-D3
VISTA CIR
- SMCo - 768-D4
VISTA CT
- SSF 94080 707-E5
500 MLBR 94030 727-J2
700 SMCo 94062 789-G1
VISTA DR
- SMCo - 768-D4
600 SMCo 94062 789-G1
800 RDWC 94062 789-G1
VISTA LN
- SCIC 94304 810-F1
- SMCo 94010 728-B6
VISTA RD
800 HIL 94010 748-G3
VISTA CAY
1900 SMTO 94404 749-H1
VISTA DEL GRANDE
- SCAR 94070 769-F4
VISTA DEL MAR
1500 SMTO 94404 749-E3
VISTA DEL SOL
1500 SMTO 94404 749-H1
VISTA GRANDE
700 MLBR 94030 727-J4
VISTA GRANDE AV
- DALY 94014 687-C3
VISTA MAR AV
400 PCFA 94044 707 A4
VISTA MONTARA CIR
800 PCFA 94044 726-H5
VISTA VERDE WY
200 SMCo 94028 830-E5
VOELKER DR
400 SMTO 94403 749-B6
VOLANS LN
800 FCTY 94404 749-H1
VUE DE MAR AV
600 SMCo 94038 746-G6

W

WABASH TER
- SF 94134 688-A2
WAKEFIELD AV
- DALY 94015 707-C2
WAKEFIELD CT
- BLMT 94002 769-B3
WAKEFIELD DR
2600 BLMT 94002 769-B3
WALBRIDGE AV
- SF 94134 687-H2
WALLEA DR
500 MLPK 94025 790-F4
WALNUT AV
- ATN 94027 790-E2
300 SSF 94080 707-J3
700 HIL 94010 728-E6
700 BURL 94010 728-E6
WALNUT DR
1500 PA 94303 791-B4
WALNUT ST
- SBRN 94066 707-J6
200 RDWC 94063 770-B5
400 SCAR 94070 769-G3
700 SBRN 94066 708-A6
WALSH RD
300 ATN 94027 790-C6
WALTER HAYS DR
100 PA 94303 791-B4
WALTERMIRE ST
600 BLMT 94002 769-E1
WALTHAM CROSS ST
2700 BLMT 94002 769-A3
WALTON ST
- SCAR 94070 769-F2
WARBLER LN
- BSBN 94005 687-J4
WARD CT
- DALY 94015 707-B1
WARD RD
- SCrC 95033 850-J7
WARD ST
100 SF 94134 688-A1
WARD WY
2100 SMCo 94062 790-A4
2100 WDSD 94062 790-A4
WARE RD
- SMCo 94062 788-H4
WAREHOUSE RD
- MLPK 94025 790-J1
WARM CANYON WY
- HIL 94010 748-D3
WARMWOOD WY
- HIL 94010 748-D3
WARNER RANGE AV
2300 MLPK 94025 790-D7
WARREN RD
- SMTO 94402 748-F1
100 SMTO 94402 728-G7
WARREN ST
400 RDWC 94063 770-A5
WARREN WY
800 PA 94303 791-C5
WARRINGTON AV
400 SMCo 94063 770-D7
WARWICK ST
- DALY 94015 707-C3
100 RDWC 94062 769-H5
300 SCAR 94070 769-H5
WASHINGTON AV
100 PA 94301 791-B6
2000 RDWC 94061 789-J3
2300 RDWC 94061 790-A2
WASHINGTON BLVD
100 HMBY 94019 767-D5
WASHINGTON ST
- DALY 94014 687-B5
- DALY 94015 687-B5
600 SMCo 94015 687-B5
800 SCAR 94070 769-J4
1600 SMTO 94403 749-C2
WATER LN
- SMCo 94060 867-J1
- SMCo 94060 868-A2
WATERBURY LN
600 FCTY 94404 749-F5
WATERFORD CT
- RDWC 94065 749-H5
WATERFORD ST
200 PCFA 94044 706-J3
300 PCFA 94044 707-A3
WATERLILY LN
- RDWC 94065 750-B4
WATERLOO CT
- BLMT 94002 769-A3
WATERMAN AV
- SMCo 94060 868-F3
WATERSIDE CIR
- RDWC 94065 750-A6
WATERS PARK BLVD
- SMTO 94403 749-D3
WATKINS AV
- ATN 94027 790-E2
WATSON CT
2400 PA 94303 791-D4
WATT AV
- SF 94112 687-F2
WATTIS WY
200 SSF 94080 708-A4
WAVE AV
400 HMBY 94019 767-E6
900 SMCo 94038 746-G6
WAVECREST DR
- DALY 94015 686-J7
WAVECREST RD
300 HMBY 94019 787-E4
WAVERLEY CT
- MLPK 94025 790-G3
WAVERLEY ST
100 PA 94301 790-J4
200 MLPK 94025 790-G4
900 PA 94301 791-A5
2600 PA 94306 791-C7
WAVERLEY OAKS
100 PA 94301 791-B6
WAVERLY AV
3000 SMCo 94063 790-D1
WAVERLY CT
- SSF 94080 707-F5
WAVERLY PL
- HIL 94010 748-H1
500 PCFA 94044 707-B3
WAVERLY WY
- DALY 94014 687-F2
- SF 94112 687-F2
WAYLAND ST
1500 SF 94134 687-J1
WAYNE CT
- RDWC 94063 770-F6
WAYNE WY
- SMTO 94403 749-C4
WAYSIDE RD
- PTLV 94028 809-J6
WEBSTER CT
2500 PA 94306 791-C6
2500 PA 94301 791-C6
WEBSTER ST
100 PA 94301 790-J3
700 PA 94301 791-A4
2500 PA 94306 791-C6
WEDGEWOOD DR
1500 HIL 94010 748-E5
WEEKS ST
300 EPA 94303 791-B1
WEEPINGRIDGE CT
- SMTO 94402 748-C7
WELCH RD
700 PA 94304 790-G6
700 PA 94305 790-G6
1000 SCIC 94305 790-G6
WELLER RANCH RD
- SMCo - 727-B6
WELLESLEY AV
1600 SMTO 94403 749-C2
WELLESLEY CRES
100 RDWC 94062 769-J5
WELLESLEY ST
1900 SCIC 94305 791-A7
2100 PA 94306 791-A7
WELLINGTON AV
- DALY 94014 687-D3
WELLINGTON DR
100 SCAR 94070 769-E2
WELLS AV
- PA 94301 790-J5
WELLS ST
800 RDWC 94061 790-B1
WELLSBURY CT
- PA 94306 791-C7
WELLSBURY WY
600 PA 94306 791-D7
WEMBERLY DR
2700 BLMT 94002 769-A3
WEMBLEY CT
400 RDWC 94061 790-B2
WEMBLEY DR
- DALY 94015 707-B2
WENDY WY
1400 SMCo 94025 790-D5
WENTWORTH DR
2500 SSF 94080 707-D5
2500 SBRN 94066 707-D5
WERNER AV
- DALY 94014 687-C5
WERTH AV
1100 MLPK 94025 790-F5
WESSEX WY
- SCAR 94070 769-E3
400 BLMT 94002 749-E7
3100 RDWC 94061 789-H1
WESSIX CT
- DALY 94015 707-C3
WEST WY
- SSF 94014 707-J1
WESTBOROUGH BLVD
- SSF 94080 707-C5
400 SMCo 94080 707-E4
2900 SBRN 94066 707-C5
WESTBRAE DR
- DALY 94015 686-J7
WESTBROOK AV
- DALY 94015 687-A4
100 DALY 94015 686-J4
WESTCHESTER CT
2400 SSF 94080 707-D4
WESTCLIFF CT
- PCFA 94044 707-A1
WESTDALE AV
- DALY 94015 687-A3
WESTFIELD AV
- DALY 94015 687-A5
WESTFIELD DR
1100 MLPK 94025 790-F5
WESTGATE ST
- RDWC 94062 769-H7
WESTHAVEN DR
- DALY 94015 687-A3
WESTHILL DR
300 BSBN 94005 687-H5
WESTHILL PL
100 BSBN 94005 687-H5
WESTLAKE AV
- DALY 94014 687-C4
WESTLAWN AV
- DALY 94015 687-A3
WESTLINE DR
- DALY 94015 706-J1
- DALY 94015 707-A1
100 PCFA 94044 706-J2
WESTMINSTER AV
1100 EPA 94303 791-A1
1200 EPA 94303 771-A7
WESTMONT DR
- DALY 94015 686-J3
- DALY 94015 687-A3
WESTMOOR AV
- DALY 94015 687-A6
300 DALY 94015 686-J5
WESTMOOR RD
1500 BURL 94010 728-C5
WESTMORELAND AV
2600 RDWC 94063 770-C7
2600 SMCo 94063 770-C7
2900 SMCo 94063 790-C1
WESTMORLAND AV
400 SMTO 94402 748-G1
WESTON DR
- DALY 94015 686-J3
WESTPARK DR
- DALY 94015 687-A3
WEST POINT AV
100 SMCo 94019 766-H2
WESTPOINT PL
- SMCo 94402 748-F6
WESTPORT DR
400 PCFA 94044 707-A7
WESTRIDGE AV
- DALY 94015 686-J5
WESTRIDGE CT
27800 LAH 94022 830-H1
WESTRIDGE DR
100 PTLV 94028 810-B5
WESTVIEW DR
200 SSF 94080 707-F2
WESTWIND LN
- RDWC 94065 750-A4
WESTWOOD CT
3400 SMTO 94403 748-J7
WESTWOOD ST
1100 RDWC 94061 789-J2
WEXFORD AV
2200 SSF 94080 707-E5
WHARF RW
- RDWC 94065 749-H5
WHARFSIDE RD
800 SMTO 94404 749-D2
WHEAT ST
- SF 94124 688-B1
WHEELER AV
- RDWC 94061 790-B2
200 SF 94134 688-A2
WHEEL HOUSE LN
900 FCTY 94404 749-H4
WHIPPLE AV
- SF 94112 687-E2
400 RDWC 94063 770-A5
800 RDWC 94063 769-H6
1000 RDWC 94062 769-H6
WHISKEY HILL RD
100 WDSD 94062 789-H7
100 WDSD 94062 809-J1
100 SMCo 94025 789-H7
100 SMCo 94025 809-J1
WHISPER LN
- RDWC 94065 750-B4
WHISPERWAVE CIR
3000 RDWC 94065 749-J4
WHITAKER WY
1200 MLPK 94025 790-E5
WHITE ST
700 SMCo 94015 687-B4
WHITE WY
600 SBRN 94066 707-H7
WHITECLIFF CT
- SMTO 94402 748-H7
WHITECLIFF WY
1800 SMTO 94402 748-H7
2200 SBRN 94066 707-G7
WHITEHALL LN
200 RDWC 94061 790-B2
WHITEHOUSE CREEK RD
- SCrC 95017 888-J7
- SMCo 94060 888-H7
WHITE OAK CT
- MLPK 94025 790-E6
WHITE OAK DR
1800 MLPK 94025 790-E6
WHITE OAK WY
1100 SCAR 94070 769-G5
WHITE PLAINS CT
- SMCo 94402 768-G2
WHITETHORNE WY
1200 BURL 94010 728-E5
WHITMAN CT
- SCAR 94070 769-E6
300 PA 94301 791-A5
WHITMAN WY
2000 SBRN 94066 727-F1
WHITNEY CT
- MLPK 94025 790-C7
WHITNEY DR
1000 MLPK 94025 790-C7
WHITTIER ST
- SF 94112 687-E2
100 DALY 94014 687-E2
WHITWELL RD
1000 HIL 94010 748-F3
WHY WORRY LN
- WDSD 94062 789-F7
- WDSD 94062 809-F1
WICKHAM PL
- HIL 94010 748-H2
WICKLOW DR
200 SSF 94080 707-D2
WIDEVIEW CT
100 SMCo 94062 789-F1
WIDGEON ST
700 FCTY 94404 749-G1
WIENKE WY
100 SMCo 94038 746-F6
WILBURN AV
- ATN 94027 790-D1
WILDE AV
- SF 94134 688-A1
WILDFLOWER CT
- DALY 94014 687-H3
WILD OAK CT
- SMCo 94062 769-F7
WILDWOOD AV
- SCAR 94070 769-G5
800 SMCo 94015 687-A4
900 DALY 94015 687-A4
900 DALY 94015 686-J4
WILDWOOD CT
- SMCo 94015 687-A4
WILDWOOD DR
- SMTO 94402 748-H4
200 SSF 94080 707-F5
WILDWOOD LN
- SMCo 94025 810-E1
600 PA 94303 791-C4
WILDWOOD WY
100 WDSD 94062 789-H4
WILKS ST
- EPA 94303 791-C2
WILLARD LN
- HIL 94010 748-F3
WILLBOROUGH PL
700 BURL 94010 728-F6
WILLIAM AV
3000 SMCo 94063 790-D1
WILLIAM CT
- MLPK 94025 790-E5
WILLIAMS AV
1200 SBRN 94066 707-H7
1500 BLMT 94002 749-D7
WILLIAMS CT
2400 SSF 94080 707-D4
WILLIAMS LN
- FCTY 94404 749-F6
- SCAR 94070 769-E3
WILLIAMS PL
400 SMTO 94401 728-H7
WILLIAMS ST
2000 PA 94306 791-A7
WILLIAMSBURG CT
2400 SSF 94080 707-D4
WILLIAR AV
- SF 94112 687-E1
WILLITS ST
- DALY 94014 687-C3
WILLOW AV
- MLBR 94030 728-B4
200 SSF 94080 707-G2
400 HMBY 94019 787-F1
1500 BURL 94010 728-E6
WILLOW CT
- HIL 94010 728-E7
WILLOW LN
- BLMT 94002 769-D1
WILLOW PL
- MLPK 94025 790-H3
WILLOW RD
- MLPK 94025 790-J1
1000 MLPK 94025 791-A1
1200 MLPK 94025 771-A7
1700 HIL 94010 728-E7
WILLOW RD Rt#-114
- EPA 94303 790-J1
1000 MLPK 94025 790-J1
1100 EPA 94303 791-A1
1100 MLPK 94025 791-A1
1200 EPA 94303 771-A7
1200 MLPK 94025 771-A7
WILLOW ST
400 RDWC 94063 770-C6
800 SMCo 94063 770-C6
WILLOW WY
1700 SBRN 94066 707-E6
WILLOWBROOK DR
100 PTLV 94028 830-B1
200 PTLV 94028 810-B7
WILLOW GLEN WY
- SCAR 94070 769-E4
WILLOWSIDE RANCH RD
- SMCo 94074 848-B3
WILLOW SPRING RD
- SMCo 94060 868-E3
WILMINGTON RD
800 SMTO 94402 748-H4
WILMINGTON WY
900 SMCo 94062 789-F3
900 SMCo 94061 789-F3
WILMINGTON ACRES CT
- SMCo 94062 789-G3
WILMS AV
- SSF 94080 707-G4
WILSHIRE AV
- DALY 94015 687-A2
3600 SMTO 94403 749-B6
WILSHIRE CT
- DALY 94015 687-B3
100 SCAR 94070 769-F5
WILSON ST
- DALY 94014 687-D2
- RDWC 94063 770-A6
100 SF 94112 687-D2
1200 PA 94301 791-B4
WINCHESTER CT
- FCTY 94404 749-E5
WINCHESTER DR
- ATN 94027 790-E2
700 BURL 94010 728-G6
WINCHESTER PL
- BURL 94010 728-G6
WINCHESTER ST
100 DALY 94014 687-D3
WINDBLOWN LN
- RDWC 94065 750-B3
WINDCREST LN
- SSF 94080 707-H1
WINDEMERE RD
- HIL 94010 748-E5
WINDERMERE AV
1000 MLPK 94025 790-J1
1100 MLPK 94025 770-J7
WINDFIELD LN
400 RDWC 94065 749-J3
WINDFIELD ST
- RDWC 94065 750-B4
WINDING WY
- SF 94112 687-F2
- SMCo 94070 769-E5
200 SCAR 94070 769-E5
200 WDSD 94062 809-H1
200 WDSD 94062 789-H7
1500 BLMT 94002 749-D7
WINDJAMMER CIR
1000 FCTY 94404 749-G4
WINDJAMMER PL
- DALY 94014 687-E5
WINDLASS LN
500 FCTY 94404 749-J1
WINDLEA LN
100 RDWC 94065 749-J4
WINDROSE LN
- RDWC 94065 750-B4
WINDSOR CT
100 SBRN 94066 707-E7
100 SCAR 94070 769-E4
12200 LAH 94022 830-J1
WINDSOR DR
- HIL 94010 728-E7
- SCAR 94070 769-E4
- DALY 94015 687-A3
200 SMCo 94070 769-E4
500 MLPK 94025 790-F4
WINDSOR WY
700 RDWC 94061 789-J1
1100 MLPK 94025 790-F4
WINDWARD WY
2000 SMTO 94404 749-E3
WING PL
900 SCIC 94305 810-J2
WINGATE AV
400 SMCo 94070 769-E4
WINGED FOOT RD
- HMBY 94019 787-F5
WINKLEBLECK ST
- RDWC 94063 770-A6
WINONA AV
100 PCFA 94044 727-A2
WINSLOW ST
- RDWC 94063 770-A5
WINSTON WY
- SMCo 94061 790-B3
WINTERCREEK
- PTLV 94028 830-C2
WINTERGREEN WY
800 PA 94303 791-D6
WINWAY
3500 SMTO 94403 749-C6
WINWAY CIR
3500 SMTO 94403 749-B6
WINWOOD AV
200 PCFA 94044 706-J3
200 PCFA 94044 707-A3
WISNOM AV
400 SMTO 94401 748-H1
WISTERIA DR
100 EPA 94303 791-C2
WISTERIA WY
- ATN 94027 790-G1
WITHERIDGE RD
- SCAR 94070 769-C3
- SMCo 94002 769-C3
2700 BLMT 94002 769-C3
WOLFE DR
1600 SMTO 94402 749-B2
WONDERCOLOR LN
100 SSF 94080 708-A4
WONG WY
100 SBRN 94066 707-G6
WOOD LN
- MLPK 94025 790-E5
WOODBERRY AV
1300 SMTO 94403 748-J7
WOODBRIDGE CIR
100 SMTO 94403 749-E6
WOODCREEK CT
- SMCo 94402 768-H1
WOODCREST CT
- HIL 94010 748-F4
WOODFERN
- PTLV 94028 830-C2
WOODGATE CT
- HIL 94010 748-C1
WOODHILL DR
- RDWC 94061 789-G4
- RDWC 94062 789-G4
- WDSD 94062 789-G4
WOODHUE CT
- SMCo 94062 769-G7
WOODLAND AV
- DALY 94015 687-A7
500 MLPK 94025 790-J3
800 SCAR 94070 769-G4
900 MLPK 94025 791-A3
1500 EPA 94303 791-B3
WOODLAND CT
800 MLPK 94025 790-J3
WOODLAND DR
900 SMTO 94402 748-H4
900 SMTO 94010 748-H4
1000 HIL 94010 748-H4
WOODLAND PL
2500 SMCo 94062 789-F1
WOODLAND WY
3800 SMCo 94062 789-G2
3800 RDWC 94062 789-G2
WOODLAND VISTA
100 SMCo 94020 849-F1
200 SMCo 94020 829-F7
WOODLEAF AV
- RDWC 94061 789-G3
WOODRIDGE CT
- RDWC 94061 789-G4
WOODRIDGE RD
- HIL 94010 748-F4
WOODROW PL
- PCFA 94044 727-B5
WOODROW ST
- DALY 94014 687-C3
1100 RDWC 94061 770-B7
WOODS CIR
- SSF 94014 707-J1
WOODS ST
- SSF 94014 707-J1
WOODSIDE AV
- DALY 94015 687-A7
WOODSIDE CT
500 SSF 94080 707-G2
WOODSIDE DR
- RDWC 94061 789-J4
- WDSD 94062 789-J4
WOODSIDE EXWY
- RDWC 94063 770-C6
WOODSIDE EXWY Rt#-84
200 RDWC 94061 770-B7
WOODSIDE RD Rt#-84
400 RDWC 94061 770-C6
400 RDWC 94061 790-B2
700 RDWC 94063 770-C6
1200 SMCo 94061 790-B2
2100 WDSD 94062 790-B2
2100 SMCo 94062 790-B2
2300 WDSD 94062 789-J5
3500 WDSD 94062 809-F1
WOODSIDE WY
600 SMTO 94401 728-H7
600 WDSD 94062 789-E3
WOODSTOCK PL
- RDWC 94062 769-H6
WOODSTOCK RD
600 HIL 94010 748-F2
WOODSWORTH AV
- RDWC 94062 769-H6
WOODVIEW LN
- WDSD 94062 810-A6
WOOLSEY ST
900 SF 94134 687-J1
WOOSTER AV
2300 BLMT 94002 749-B7
2300 BLMT 94002 769-B1
4200 SMTO 94403 749-B7
WORCESTER AV
- SF 94132 687-C2
WREN CT
2400 SSF 94080 707-D4
WRIGHT CT
2400 SSF 94080 707-D4
WRIGHT WY
- SMCo 94021 849-D7
WURR RD
1400 SMCo 94021 849-C6
WYANDOTTE AV
800 DALY 94014 687-D5
WYCOMBE AV
100 SCAR 94070 769-E2
WYLVALE AV
- SMCo 94038 746-F6
WYNDHAM DR
- PTLV 94028 810-A6

X

XAVIER ST
1600 EPA 94303 771-B7

Y

YACHT LN
- DALY 94014 687-E6
YALE AV
100 SMCo 94019 766-J2
YALE CT
14500 LAH 94022 810-H5
YALE DR
400 SMTO 94402 748-H3
700 HIL 94010 748-H3
YALE RD
- MLPK 94025 790-G4
YALE ST
500 SF 94134 687-J1
1900 SCIC 94305 791-A7
2000 PA 94306 791-A7
YANEZ CT
- SMCo 94062 789-F2
YARBOROUGH LN
200 RDWC 94061 790-B2
YARNALL PL
- RDWC 94063 770-F6
YATES WY
900 SMTO 94403 749-D4
YAWL CT
100 FCTY 94404 749-G4
YELLOWSTONE DR
400 SSF 94080 707-F4
YELLOWSTONE WY
- PCFA 94044 727-B5
YEW ST
1300 SMTO 94402 748-J4
YOLO CT
100 SBRN 94066 707-D6
YORK AV
1500 SMTO 94401 729-A7
YORK ST
- DALY 94015 707-C3
YORKSHIRE CT
100 SBRN 94066 727-F1
YORKSHIRE LN
- SMCo 94062 769-G6
YORKSHIRE WY
400 BLMT 94002 749-E7
YORKTOWN RD
1600 SMCo 94402 748-F7
1600 SMCo 94402 768-G1
YOSEMITE AV
1200 SF 94124 688-C1
YOSEMITE CT
600 WDSD 94062 789-E3
YOSEMITE DR
500 SSF 94080 707-F4
900 PCFA 94044 727-B5
2600 BLMT 94002 769-A2
YOUNG AV
100 HMBY 94019 767-D5
YOUNG ST
1400 SMTO 94401 749-B1
YSABEL DR
3600 SBRN 94066 707-B6
YUBA CT
100 SBRN 94066 707-D6
YUBA LN
27800 LAH 94022 810-J7
27800 LAH 94022 830-J1

Z

ZACHARY CT
- MLPK 94025 790-D7
ZAMORA DR
300 SSF 94080 707-F5
900 PCFA 94044 727-A4
ZAPATA WY
- PTLV 94028 810-A5
ZAPPETTINI CT
12600 LAH 94022 830-H2
ZITA DR
500 SSF 94080 707-E2
ZITA MNR
- DALY 94015 687-B5
ZUMWALT LN
700 FCTY 94404 749-G5

#

1ST AV
- DALY 94014 687-C5
100 PCFA 94044 706-J5
200 SMCo 94063 770-D7
200 SMCo 94063 790-D1
200 SMTO 94401 748-J1
400 SMCo 94019 767-C4
400 SMTO 94401 749-A1
500 SBRN 94066 707-J6
500 SBRN 94066 708-A7
1ST LN
300 SSF 94080 707-H3
1ST ST
- SSF 94080 707-G3
100 SMCo 94037 746-F4
W 1ST ST
900 MLPK 94025 790-G2
1ST ST W
1100 SBRN 94066 707-H5
2ND AV
- DALY 94014 687-C5
- SMTO 94401 748-J2
200 PCFA 94044 706-J5
200 RDWC 94063 770-E6
200 SMCo 94063 770-D7
200 SMCo 94063 790-D1
300 SMCo 94014 687-C5
400 SBRN 94066 707-J6
400 SMCo 94019 767-C4
400 SMTO 94401 749-A1
1200 SMTO 94401 729-B7
2ND LN
200 SSF 94080 707-G2
2ND ST
- SSF 94080 707-G3
100 SMCo 94037 746-G4
E 2ND ST
100 MLPK 94025 790-G3
3RD AV
- DALY 94014 687-D5
200 RDWC 94063 770-D7
200 SMCo 94063 770-D7
200 SMCo 94063 790-D1
300 PCFA 94044 706-J5
300 SMCo 94014 687-D5
400 SBRN 94066 707-J6
400 SMCo 94019 767-C4
700 SF 94124 688-E1
E 3RD AV
- SMTO 94401 748-J2
300 SMTO 94401 749-A1
1300 SMTO 94401 729-B7
2000 FCTY 94404 749-E1
W 3RD AV
- SMTO 94402 748-J2
3RD LN
200 SSF 94080 707-G2
3RD ST
100 SMCo 94037 746-F4
1800 SF 94134 688-B1
2000 SF 94124 688-B1
E 3RD ST
400 MLPK 94025 790-H3
W 3RD ST
600 MLPK 94025 790-G3
4TH AV
200 SMCo 94063 790-D1
300 SMCo 94019 767-C3
400 PCFA 94044 706-J5
400 SMCo 94063 770-D7
500 SBRN 94066 707-J6
500 SBRN 94066 708-A7
700 RDWC 94063 770-E6
E 4TH AV
- SMTO 94401 748-J2
100 SMTO 94401 749-A1
400 SMTO 94402 749-A1
W 4TH AV
- SMTO 94402 748-J2
4TH LN
200 SSF 94080 707-G2
4TH ST
100 SMCo 94037 746-G4
E 4TH ST
800 MLPK 94025 790-G3
W 4TH ST
600 MLPK 94025 790-G3

STREET Block	City	ZIP	Pg-Grid
5TH AV			
-	RDWC	94063	770-E6
-	SMCo	94063	790-D1
400	SMCo	94019	767-C3
400	SMCo	94063	770-D7
500	PCFA	94044	706-J4
500	SBRN	94066	708-A7
600	SBRN	94066	707-J6
1200	BLMT	94002	769-F1
E 5TH AV			
200	SMTO	94401	748-J2
200	SMTO	94402	748-J2
300	SMTO	94401	749-A1
400	SMTO	94402	749-A1
W 5TH AV			
-	SMTO	94402	748-J2
5TH ST			
100	SMCo	94037	746-F4
6TH AV			
200	SMTO	94401	749-A2
300	SMCo	94025	790-D1
300	SMCo	94019	767-D3
400	SMCo	94025	770-D7
600	PCFA	94044	706-J5
600	SBRN	94066	708-A6
600	SMCo	94063	770-D7
700	SBRN	94066	707-J6
900	RDWC	94063	770-D7
1000	BLMT	94002	769-E1
1300	SF	94124	688-D1
6TH LN			
100	SSF	94080	707-J2
6TH ST			
100	SMCo	94037	746-F4
7TH AV			
200	SMTO	94401	749-A2
400	SMCo	94025	770-E7
400	SMCo	94025	790-D1
500	SBRN	94066	708-A6
500	SMTO	94402	749-A1
700	SMCo	94063	770-E7
900	RDWC	94063	770-E7
7TH LN			
200	SSF	94080	707-J2
200	SSF	94080	708-A2
7TH ST			
100	SMCo	94037	746-F4
8TH AV			
200	SMTO	94401	749-A2
300	SMCo	94025	770-E7
300	SMCo	94025	790-D1
700	SMCo	94063	770-E6
900	RDWC	94063	770-E6
8TH LN			
200	SSF	94080	707-J2
200	SSF	94080	708-A2
8TH ST			
-	SMCo	94037	746-F4
9TH AV			
-	SMTO	94401	749-A2
-	SMTO	94402	749-A2
300	SMCo	94025	770-E7
300	SMCo	94025	790-E1
700	SMCo	94063	770-E7
9TH LN			
200	SSF	94080	707-J2
200	SSF	94080	708-A2
9TH ST			
100	SMCo	94037	746-F4
10TH AV			
-	SMTO	94401	749-A2
-	SMTO	94402	749-A2
600	SMCo	94025	770-E7
800	RDWC	94063	770-E6
800	SMCo	94063	770-E7
10TH ST			
200	SMCo	94037	746-F4
11TH AV			
-	SMTO	94401	749-A2
-	SMTO	94402	749-A2
600	SMCo	94025	770-E7
800	SMCo	94063	770-E7
11TH ST			
-	SMCo	94037	746-F4
12TH AV			
-	SMTO	94402	749-A3
600	SMCo	94025	770-E7
800	SMCo	94063	770-E7
12TH ST			
100	SMCo	94037	746-F5
13TH AV			
-	SMTO	94402	749-A3
13TH ST			
200	SMCo	94037	746-F5
14TH AV			
-	SMTO	94402	749-A3
600	SMCo	94025	770-E7
14TH ST			
200	SMCo	94037	746-F5
15TH AV			
-	SMTO	94402	749-A3
700	SMCo	94025	770-E7
900	RDWC	94063	770-F7
15TH ST			
-	SMCo	94037	746-F5
16TH AV			
-	SMTO	94402	749-A3
500	SMCo	94025	770-E7
500	SMCo	94025	790-E1
1000	RDWC	94063	770-F6
16TH ST			
200	SMCo	94038	746-F5
17TH AV			
-	SMTO	94402	749-A3
500	SMCo	94025	770-F7
500	SMCo	94025	790-F1
1000	RDWC	94063	770-F7
18TH AV			
-	SMTO	94402	749-B3
600	SMCo	94025	770-F7
600	SMCo	94025	790-F1
1100	RDWC	94063	770-F6
19TH AV			
-	SMTO	94403	749-B3
1000	SF	94132	687-C1
19TH AV Rt#-1			
3600	SF	94132	687-B1
E 20TH AV			
-	SMTO	94402	749-B4
-	SMTO	94403	749-B4
W 20TH AV			
-	SMTO	94402	749-A4
-	SMTO	94403	749-A4
21ST AV			
-	SMTO	94403	749-B4
22ND RD			
-	SMTO	94403	749-A4
23RD AV			
-	SMTO	94403	749-A4
24TH AV			
-	SMTO	94403	749-A5
E 25TH AV			
-	SMTO	94403	749-B4
W 25TH AV			
-	SMTO	94403	749-B5
26TH AV			
200	SMTO	94403	749-A5
700	SMTO	94403	748-J5
26TH PL			
-	SMTO	94403	749-B5
27TH AV			
-	SMTO	94403	749-A5
28TH AV			
-	SMTO	94403	749-B5
29TH AV			
-	SMTO	94403	749-B5
30TH AV			
-	SMTO	94403	749-B5
31ST AV			
-	SMTO	94403	749-A6
900	SMTO	94403	748-J6
36TH AV			
-	SMTO	94403	749-B6
37TH AV			
-	SMTO	94403	749-B6
38TH AV			
400	SMTO	94403	749-B7
E 38TH AV			
-	SMTO	94403	749-D6
W 38TH AV			
-	SMTO	94403	749-C6
E 39TH AV			
-	SMTO	94403	749-D6
W 39TH AV			
-	SMTO	94403	749-C6
E 40TH AV			
-	SMTO	94403	749-D6
W 40TH AV			
-	SMTO	94403	749-C7
W 41ST AV			
-	SMTO	94403	749-C7
E 41ST PL			
-	SMTO	94403	749-D6
42ND AV			
-	SMTO	94403	749-B7
43RD AV			
-	SMTO	94403	749-C7
44TH AV			
100	SMTO	94403	749-D7
87TH ST			
-	DALY	94015	687-A4
-	SMCo	94015	687-A4
1000	DALY	94015	686-J4
88TH ST			
-	DALY	94015	687-B4
-	SMCo	94015	687-B4
89TH ST			
-	DALY	94015	687-B5
400	SMCo	94015	687-B5
90TH ST			
-	DALY	94015	687-B5
300	SMCo	94015	687-B5
91ST ST			
-	DALY	94015	687-B5
92ND ST			
100	DALY	94015	687-B5
100	SMCo	94015	687-B5
I-280 JOHN F FORAN FRWY			
-	SF	-	687-E2
I-280 JUNIPERO SERRA FRWY			
-	DALY	-	687-C7
-	DALY	-	707-C2
-	HIL	-	748-D4
-	LAH	-	810-F3
-	MLBR	-	727-G3
-	MLBR	-	728-A7
-	MLPK	-	810-C1
-	PA	-	810-F3
-	SBRN	-	707-C2
-	SBRN	-	727-G3
-	PA	-	810-F3
-	SMCo	-	727-G3
-	SMCo	-	728-A7
-	SMCo	-	748-D4
-	SMCo	-	768-F1
-	SMCo	-	769-A4
-	SMCo	-	789-C1
-	SMCo	-	790-A6
-	SMCo	-	810-C1
-	SSF	-	707-C2
-	WDSD	-	789-G4
-	WDSD	-	790-A6
I-280 SOUTHERN FRWY			
-	DALY	-	687-C4
-	SF	-	687-D2
I-380 QUENTIN L KOPP FRWY			
-	SBRN	-	707-H6
-	SBRN	-	708-A6
-	SMCo	-	708-A6
-	SSF	-	708-A5
Rt#-G3 OREGON EXWY			
-	PA	94301	791-C6
-	PA	94306	791-C6
2500	PA	94303	791-C6
Rt#-G3 PAGE MILL RD			
1800	SCIC	94305	810-J4
1800	PA	94304	810-J4
1900	SCIC	94304	810-J4
2100	LAH	94022	810-J4
Rt#-G5 FOOTHILL EXWY			
2600	SCIC	94304	810-J3
2600	PA	94304	810-J3
Rt#-G5 JUNIPERO SERRA BLVD			
-	MLPK	94025	790-F7
100	SCIC	94305	790-F7
100	SCIC	94304	790-F7
100	SCIC	94305	810-G1
100	SCIC	94304	810-G1
Rt#-1 19TH AV			
3600	SF	94132	687-B1
Rt#-1 CABRILLO FRWY			
-	DALY	-	687-B7
-	DALY	-	707-A2
-	PCFA	-	707-A2
-	PCFA	-	706-J5
Rt#-1 CABRILLO HWY			
-	PCFA	94044	707-A7
-	HMBY	94019	767-D4
-	HMBY	94019	787-G7
-	SMCo	94019	767-D4
-	SMCo	94038	746-G7
300	PCFA	94044	726-H3
300	PCFA	94044	727-A1
300	SMCo	94037	746-F1
600	SMCo	-	746-F1
2000	SMCo	-	726-F6
2100	SMCo	94038	766-H1
2100	SMCo	-	766-H1
2400	SMCo	94019	787-G7
4000	SMCo	94060	888-B5
9000	SMCo	94060	867-G4
9500	SMCo	94019	766-H1
9600	SMCo	94019	807-G1
9600	SMCo	94019	828-A4
20000	SMCo	94074	828-A4
Rt#-1 JUNIPERO SERRA BLVD			
1100	SF	94132	687-C1
Rt#-1 JUNIPERO SERRA FRWY			
-	DALY	-	687-B3
-	SF	-	687-B3
Rt#-35 SKYLINE BLVD			
-	SMCo	94030	727-F2
-	SF	94132	686-J3
500	SMCo	-	727-E1
500	SBRN	94066	727-F2
900	SBRN	94066	707-D5
900	SMCo	-	707-D5
1100	DALY	94015	707-B1
1200	PCFA	94044	707-B1
1200	DALY	94015	687-A5
1900	SMCo	-	768-F1
1900	DALY	94015	686-J3
1900	SMCo	-	748-E6
2100	SMCo	94015	686-J3
2700	SSF	94080	707-D5
7500	SMCo	94062	768-D4
11400	SMCo	-	788-G3
11400	SMCo	94062	788-G3
11600	SCIC	95030	850-J5
13800	SMCo	94062	789-A7
14600	SMCo	94062	808-J1
14600	SMCo	94062	809-A1
17100	WDSD	94062	809-G7
17300	SMCo	94020	809-G7
17300	WDSD	94020	809-D4
18000	PTLV	94028	809-G7
18000	PTLV	94062	809-G7
18100	SMCo	94020	829-H1
18100	PTLV	94028	829-H1
18600	SMCo	94020	830-A4
18600	PTLV	94028	830-A4
19800	SMCo	94028	830-C7
20800	SMCo	94020	850-E1
20800	SMCo	94028	850-D1
21100	SCIC	94028	850-E1
21200	PA	94304	850-H2
Rt#-82 EL CAMINO REAL			
-	BURL	94010	728-E6
-	CLMA	94014	687-C5
-	MLBR	94030	728-A2
-	MLPK	94025	790-F3
-	PA	94301	790-F3
-	SCAR	94070	769-F2
-	PA	94304	790-F3
100	ATN	94027	790-C1
100	BLMT	94002	749-D7
100	SBRN	94066	727-J1
100	SSF	94080	707-G4
100	SBRN	94066	707-G4
100	SMCo	94025	790-C1
200	DALY	94014	687-C5
200	SMCo	94014	687-C5
200	SCIC	94305	790-F3
200	PA	94305	790-F3
500	BLMT	94002	769-F2
500	HIL	94010	728-E6
700	CLMA	94014	707-E1
800	SMTO	94402	749-D7
1000	ATN	94025	790-F3
1200	RDWC	94062	769-H3
1200	RDWC	94063	769-H3
1300	SBRN	94066	728-A2
1400	MLPK	94027	790-F3
1400	RDWC	94062	770-A6
1400	RDWC	94063	770-A6
1500	PA	94306	790-F3
1500	PA	94306	791-A6
1500	SCIC	94305	791-A6
1700	MLBR	94030	727-J1
1800	RDWC	94061	770-A6
2300	PA	94304	791-A7
2600	RDWC	94061	790-C1
2600	SMCo	94063	770-A6
2600	SMCo	94063	790-C1
Rt#-82 N EL CAMINO REAL			
-	SMTO	94401	728-G7
-	SMTO	94402	728-G7
100	SMTO	94402	748-H1
100	SMTO	94401	748-H1
800	BURL	94010	728-G7
Rt#-82 S EL CAMINO REAL			
100	SMTO	94403	749-A2
100	BLMT	94002	749-A2
400	SMTO	94402	748-J2
500	SMTO	94402	749-A2
500	SMTO	94401	749-A2
500	SMTO	94401	748-J2
Rt#-82 MISSION ST			
6300	DALY	94014	687-C4
Rt#-82 SAN JOSE AV			
100	SF	94112	687-D3
3200	DALY	94014	687-D3
Rt#-84 BAYFRONT EXWY			
-	MLPK	94025	770-G6
-	MLPK	94025	771-A6
Rt#-84 DUMBARTON BRDG			
-	FRMT	-	771-D4
-	MLPK	-	771-D4
Rt#-84 HIGHWAY			
-	FRMT	94555	771-G1
-	MLPK	94025	771-B5
-	MLPK	94303	771-D4
Rt#-84 LA HONDA RD			
-	SMCo	94074	828-A6
300	WDSD	94062	809-F5
400	SMCo	94062	809-F5
1600	SMCo	94062	829-F3
1700	SMCo	94020	829-F3
1700	SMCo	94020	809-F7
1700	WDSD	94020	809-F5
4100	SMCo	94074	848-H1
4300	SMCo	94020	849-A1
4300	SMCo	94062	849-A1
4500	SMCo	94074	849-A1
5200	SMCo	94074	829-E7
Rt#-84 MARSH RD			
2300	MLPK	94025	770-F7
Rt#-84 WOODSIDE EXWY			
200	RDWC	94061	770-B7
Rt#-84 WOODSIDE RD			
400	RDWC	94061	770-C6
400	RDWC	94061	790-B2
700	RDWC	94063	770-C6
1200	SMCo	94061	790-B2
2100	WDSD	94062	790-B2
2100	SMCo	94062	790-B2
2300	WDSD	94062	789-J5
3500	WDSD	94062	809-F1
Rt#-92 CANADA RD			
-	SMCo	-	768-G2
-	SMCo	94062	768-G2
-	SMCo	94402	768-G2
Rt#-92 HALF MOON BAY RD			
2900	SMCo	-	768-E3
2900	SMCo	94062	768-E3
Rt#-92 J ARTHUR YOUNGER FRWY			
-	BLMT	-	768-H2
-	FCTY	-	729-G7
-	FCTY	-	749-F2
-	HIL	-	748-J5
-	SMCo	-	748-J5
-	SMCo	-	768-H2
-	SMTO	-	748-J5
-	SMTO	-	749-A4
-	SMTO	-	768-H2
Rt#-92 SAN MATEO RD			
100	HMBY	94019	767-G7
100	HMBY	94019	787-G1
300	SMCo	-	767-G7
1700	SMCo	-	768-A5
Rt#-92 SAN MATEO-HAYWARD BRDG			
-	FCTY	-	729-H6
Rt#-109 UNIVERSITY AV			
2600	EPA	94303	771-B6
2700	MLPK	94303	771-B6
2800	MLPK	94025	771-B6
Rt#-114 WILLOW RD			
-	EPA	94303	790-J1
1000	MLPK	94025	790-J1
1100	EPA	94303	791-A1
1100	MLPK	94025	791-A1
1200	EPA	94303	771-A7
1200	MLPK	94025	771-A7
U.S.-101 BAYSHORE FRWY			
-	BLMT	-	749-B1
-	BLMT	-	769-G1
-	BSBN	-	688-B4
-	BSBN	-	708-B1
-	BURL	-	728-F5
-	EPA	-	790-J1
-	EPA	-	791-E5
-	MLBR	-	728-B2
-	MLPK	-	770-C5
-	MLPK	-	790-J1
-	MLPK	-	791-E5
-	MTVW	-	791-E5
-	PA	-	791-E5
-	RDWC	-	769-G1
-	RDWC	-	770-C5
-	SCAR	-	769-G1
-	SF	-	688-B4
-	SMCo	-	708-A6
-	SMCo	-	728-B2
-	SMTO	-	728-F5
-	SMTO	-	729-A7
-	SMTO	-	749-B1
-	SSF	-	708-B1

FEATURE NAME PAGE-GRID
Address City, ZIP Code

AIRPORTS

HALF MOON BAY, SMCo 746 - G7
PALO ALTO, PA 791 - E2
SAN CARLOS, SCAR 769 - H2
SAN FRANCISCO INTL, SMCo 708 - C6

BEACHES, HARBORS & WATER REC

BEAN HOLLOW ST BCH, SMCo 867 - G6
DUNES BEACH, HMBY 767 - C5
EL GRANADA BEACH, HMBY 767 - A3
ELMAR BEACH, HMBY 767 - D7
ESPLANADE BEACH, SMCo 706 - J3
FRANCIS BEACH, HMBY 787 - D1
GAZOS CREEK ANGLING ACCESS, SMCo 888 - D7
GRAYWHALE COVE ST BCH, SMCo 746 - F1
HALF MOON BAY ST BCHES, HMBY 767 - B3
MARTINS BEACH, SMCo 807 - G6
MIRAMAR BEACH, HMBY 767 - C4
MONTARA ST BCH, SMCo 746 - F3
NAPLES BEACH, HMBY 767 - C5
PACIFICA ST BCH, PCFA 726 - H2
PEBBLE BEACH, SMCo 867 - G4
PENINSULA BEACH, SMTO 728 - J5
PESCADERO ST BCH, SMCo 868 - A2
POMPONIO ST BCH, SMCo 848 - A2
ROCKAWAY BEACH, PCFA 726 - H2
ROOSEVELT BEACH, HMBY 767 - C5
SAN GREGORIO ST BCH, SMCo 828 - A7
SHARP PARK BEACH, PCFA 706 - J6
SURFERS BEACH, HMBY 767 - B3
THORNTON ST BCH, DALY 686 - J3
VENICE BEACH, HMBY 767 - D6

BUILDINGS

ANZA CORPORATE CTR 728 - G5
433 AIRPORT BLVD, BURL, 94010
CENTRUM III 749 - G6
300 ORACLE PKWY, RDWC, 94065
COUNTY FAIR BLDG 749 - C4
2495 S DELAWARE ST, SMTO, 94403
ELKS LODGE 789 - F3
1059 WILMINGTON WY, RDWC, 94061
FOURTEEN NINETY-NINE BLDG 728 - E4
1499 BAYSHORE HWY, BURL, 94010
GATEWAY, THE 708 - A2
651 GATEWAY BLVD, SSF, 94080
HILLCREST JUVENILE HOME 768 - H2
TOWER RD, SMCo, 94402
MAPLES PAVILION 790 - J7
CAMPUS DR, SCIC, 94305
STANFORD LINEAR ACCELERATOR CTR 810 - D1
2575 SAND HILL RD, SMCo, 94025

BUILDINGS - GOVERNMENTAL

ATHERTON CITY HALL 790 - E2
91 ASHFIELD RD, ATN, 94027
BELMONT CITY HALL 769 - E1
1070 6TH AV, BLMT, 94002
BRISBANE CITY HALL 688 - A5
50 PARK PL, BSBN, 94005
BURLINGAME CITY HALL 728 - F6
501 PRIMROSE RD, BURL, 94010
COLMA CITY HALL 687 - D7
235 EL CAMINO REAL, CLMA, 94014
DALY CITY HALL 687 - B5
333 90TH ST, DALY, 94015
EAST PALO ALTO CITY HALL 791 - B1
2415 UNIVERSITY AV, EPA, 94303
FOSTER CITY CITY HALL 749 - F2
610 FOSTER CITY BLVD, FCTY, 94404
HALF MOON BAY CITY HALL 787 - F1
510 MAIN ST, HMBY, 94019
HALL OF JUSTICE 770 - A5
400 COUNTY CIR, RDWC, 94063
HILLSBOROUGH CITY HALL 728 - F7
1600 FLORIBUNDA AV, HIL, 94010
MENLO PARK CITY HALL 790 - G3
701 LAUREL ST, MLPK, 94025
MILLBRAE CITY HALL 728 - B3
621 MAGNOLIA AV, MLBR, 94030
PACIFICA CITY HALL 706 - J5
170 SANTA MARIA AV, PCFA, 94044
PALO ALTO CITY HALL 790 - J4
250 HAMILTON AV, PA, 94301
PALO ALTO COURTHOUSE 791 - B7
270 GRANT AV, PA, 94306
PORTOLA VALLEY TOWN HALL 810 - A6
765 PORTOLA RD, PTLV, 94028
REDWOOD CITY HALL 770 - B6
1017 MIDDLEFIELD RD, RDWC, 94063
SAN BRUNO CITY HALL 707 - J7
567 EL CAMINO REAL, SBRN, 94066
SAN CARLOS CITY HALL 769 - G3
600 ELM ST, SCAR, 94070
SAN FRANCISCO JAIL 707 - D7
COUNTY JAIL RD, SMCo, 94044
SAN MATEO CITY HALL 749 - A4
330 W 20TH AV, SMTO, 94403
SAN MATEO COUNTY COURT BLDG 707 - F2
1050 MISSION RD, SSF, 94080
SAN MATEO COUNTY GOVERNMENT CTR 770 - A5
455 COUNTY CIR, RDWC, 94063
SAN MATEO COUNTY HEALTH CTR 707 - G2
OAK AV, SSF, 94080
SOUTH SAN FRANCISCO CITY HALL 707 - J3
400 GRAND AV, SSF, 94080
WOODSIDE TOWN HALL 789 - H6
2955 WOODSIDE RD, WDSD, 94062

CEMETERIES

CATHOLIC CEM, HMBY 767 - F7
CEMETERY, SMCo 789 - A1
CHINESE CEM, DALY 707 - B1
CHINESE CHRISTIAN CEM, DALY 707 - C1
CYPRESS LAWN CEM, CLMA 687 - E7
CYPRESS LAWN MEM PK, CLMA 687 - E6
ETERNAL HOME CEM, CLMA 687 - D6
GOLDEN GATE NATL CEM, SBRN 707 - G5
GOLDEN HILLS MEM PK, CLMA 687 - E6
GREEK ORTHODOX MEM PK, CLMA 687 - D7
GREENLAWN MEM PK, CLMA 687 - C7
HILLS OF ETERNITY MEM PK, CLMA 687 - D7
HOLY CROSS CEM, CLMA 687 - E7
HOME OF PEACE CEM, CLMA 687 - D6
HOY SUN MEM CEM, CLMA 687 - E6
HOY SUN NING YUNG CEM, DALY 707 - C1
ITALIAN CEM, CLMA 687 - D6
JAPANESE CEM, CLMA 687 - D6
OLIVET MEM PK, CLMA 687 - D5
PILARCITOS CEM, HMBY 767 - F7
SAINT JOHNS CEM, SMTO 748 - H4
SALEM MEM PK, CLMA 687 - D6
SERBIAN CEM, CLMA 687 - E6
SKYLAWN MEM PK CEM, SMCo 768 - C3
TUNG SEN CEM, DALY 707 - C1
UNION CEM, RDWC 770 - B7
WOODLAWN MEM PK, CLMA 687 - C6

COLLEGES & UNIVERSITIES

CANADA COLLEGE 789 - G4
4200 FARM HILL BLVD, WDSD, 94062
CITY COLLEGE OF SF CAMPUS 708 - C5
N ACCESS RD, SSF, 94080
COLLEGE OF SAN MATEO 748 - G6
1700 W HILLSDALE BLVD, SMTO, 94402
MENLO COLLEGE 790 - E3
1000 EL CAMINO REAL, ATN, 94027
NOTRE DAME DE NAMUR UNIV 769 - E1
1500 RALSTON AV, BLMT, 94002
SAINT PATRICKS SEMINARY & UNIV 790 - H2
320 MIDDLEFIELD RD, MLPK, 94025
SAN FRANCISCO STATE UNIV 687 - B1
1600 HOLLOWAY AV, SF, 94132
SKYLINE COLLEGE 707 - C6
3300 COLLEGE DR, SBRN, 94066
STANFORD UNIV 790 - J6
JUNIPERO SERRA BLVD, SCIC, 94305

ENTERTAINMENT & SPORTS

BAY MEADOWS RACETRACK 749 - C4
2600 S DELAWARE ST, SMTO, 94403
COW PALACE 687 - H3
GENEVA & RIO VERDE, DALY, 94014
MONSTER PK (CANDLESTICK PARK) 688 - C2
GIANTS DR, SF, 94124
SAN MATEO PERF ARTS CTR 728 - J7
600 N DELAWARE ST, SMTO, 94401
SHORELINE AMPHITHEATRE AT MTN VIEW 791 - H7
1 AMPHITHEATRE PKWY, MTVW, 94043
STANFORD STADIUM 790 - J6
NELSON RD & SAM MCDONALD RD, SCIC, 94305

GOLF COURSES

BURLINGAME CC, HIL 728 - E7
CALIFORNIA GC OF SAN FRANCISCO, SMCo 707 - F4
CRYSTAL SPRINGS GC, SMCo 748 - C3
CYPRESS HILLS GC, CLMA 687 - E6
EMERALD HILLS GC, RDWC 789 - F3
GLENEAGLES INTL GC, SF 687 - H2
GREEN HILLS CC, MLBR 727 - J3
HALF MOON BAY GOLF LINKS, HMBY 787 - E5
HARDING PK MUNICIPAL GC, SF 686 - J1
LAKE MERCED GOLF & CC, DALY 687 - B3
MARINERS POINT GOLF LINKS, FCTY 729 - E7
MENLO CC, WDSD 789 - J4
OLYMPIC CC, THE, SF 686 - J3
PALO ALTO HILLS GOLF & CC, PA 810 - G7
PALO ALTO MUNICIPAL GC, PA 791 - D2
PENINSULA GOLF & CC, SMCo 748 - J5
POPLAR CREEK GC, SMTO 728 - J6
SAN FRANCISCO GC, SF 687 - B2
SHARON HEIGHTS GOLF & CC, MLPK 790 - B7
SHARP PK GC, PCFA 706 - J7
SHORELINE GOLF LINKS, MTVW 791 - G7
STANFORD UNIV DRIVING RANGE, SCIC 790 - G7
STANFORD UNIV GC, SCIC 810 - F1

HISTORIC SITES

FILOLI HOUSE & GARDENS 769 - A7
CANADA RD, SMCo, 94062
SF BAY DISCOVERY CO HIST SITE 727 - D3
SWEENEY RIDGE TR, PCFA, 94044
WAR MEM 687 - D3
6655 MISSION ST, DALY, 94014
WOODSIDE COUNTRY STORE HIST SITE 789 - E6
471 KINGS MOUNTAIN RD, WDSD, 94062

HOSPITALS

CRYSTAL SPRINGS REHABILITATION CTR 768 - H2
35 TOWER RD, SMCo, 94402
KAISER FOUNDATION HOSP 770 - B5
1150 VETERANS BLVD, RDWC, 94063
KAISER FOUNDATION HOSP 707 - F2
1200 EL CAMINO REAL, SSF, 94080
MILLS HOSP 748 - J2
100 S SAN MATEO DR, SMTO, 94401
PACKARD, LUCILLE CHILDRENS HOSP STA 790 - H6
725 WELCH RD, PA, 94305
PALO ALTO MED FOUNDATION 790 - J5
795 EL CAMINO REAL, PA, 94301
PENINSULA HOSP 728 - C5
1783 EL CAMINO REAL, BURL, 94010
SAN MATEO COUNTY GENERAL HOSP 749 - C6
222 W 39TH AV, SMTO, 94403
SAN MATEO MED CTR 749 - C6
222 W 39TH AV, SMTO, 94403
SEQUOIA HOSP 769 - H6
170 ALAMEDA DE LAS PULGAS, RDWC, 94062
SETON MED CTR 687 - B6
1900 SULLIVAN AV, DALY, 94015
SETON MED CTR COASTSIDE 746 - G6
600 MARINE BLVD, SMCo, 94038
STANFORD HOSP & CLINICS 790 - G6
300 PASTEUR DR, PA, 94305
VETERANS ADMIN HOSP MENLO PK 790 - J2
795 WILLOW RD, MLPK, 94025

HOTELS

BEST WESTERN GROSVENOR HOTEL 708 - A4
380 S AIRPORT BLVD, SSF, 94080
CLARION HOTEL 728 - C3
401 E MILLBRAE AV, MLBR, 94030
COURTYARD BY MARRIOTT 707 - H6
1050 BAYHILL DR, SBRN, 94066
COURTYARD BY MARRIOTT 749 - F2
550 SHELL BLVD, FCTY, 94404
CROWNE PLAZA-FOSTER CITY 749 - E2
1221 CHESS DR, FCTY, 94404
DOUBLETREE HOTEL 728 - F5
835 AIRPORT BLVD, BURL, 94010
EMBASSY SUITES-SFO BURLINGAME 728 - G5
150 ANZA BLVD, BURL, 94010
EMBASSY SUITES SOUTH SAN FRANCISCO 708 - A3
250 GATEWAY BLVD, SSF, 94080
HOLIDAY INN SAN FRANCISCO INTL 708 - A4
275 S AIRPORT BLVD, SSF, 94080
HOTEL SOFITEL 749 - G7
223 TWIN DOLPHIN DR, RDWC, 94065
HYATT REGENCY SF 728 - E4
1333 BAYSHORE HWY, BURL, 94010
PARK PLAZA 728 - E5
1177 AIRPORT BLVD, BURL, 94010
RAMADA INN 728 - E4
1250 BAYSHORE HWY, BURL, 94010
RAMADA INN SAN FRANCISCO NORTH 708 - A4
245 S AIRPORT BLVD, SSF, 94080
RESIDENCE INN 749 - E3
2000 WINDWARD WY, SMTO, 94404
RITZ-CARLTON HOTEL HALF MOON BAY 787 - E5
1 MIRAMONTES POINT RD, HMBY, 94019
SF HILTON 728 - B2
S MCDONNELL RD, SMCo, 94128
SF MARRIOTT 728 - D3
1800 BAYSHORE HWY, BURL, 94010
SAN MATEO MARRIOTT 749 - C3
1770 S AMPHLETT BLVD, SMTO, 94402
SHERATON GATEWAY 728 - G5
600 AIRPORT BLVD, BURL, 94010
SHERATON PALO ALTO 790 - H5
625 EL CAMINO REAL, PA, 94301
STANFORD PARK HOTEL 790 - H4
100 EL CAMINO REAL, MLPK, 94025
WESTIN HOTEL - PALO ALTO 790 - H5
675 EL CAMINO REAL, PA, 94301
WESTIN - SF 728 - D3
1 BAYSHORE HWY, MLBR, 94030

LAW ENFORCEMENT

ATHERTON POLICE DEPARTMENT 790 - E2
83 ASHFIELD RD, ATN, 94027
BELMONT POLICE STA 769 - E1
1070 6TH AV, BLMT, 94002
BRISBANE POLICE DEPARTMENT 688 - A5
50 PARK LN, BSBN, 94005
BROADMOOR POLICE DEPARTMENT 687 - B4
388 88TH ST, DALY, 94015
BURLINGAME POLICE STA 728 - C4
1111 TROUSDALE DR, BURL, 94010
CALIF HIGHWAY PATROL-REDWOOD CITY 770 - A5
355 CONVENTION WY, RDWC, 94063
COLMA POLICE STA 687 - D7
1199 EL CAMINO REAL, CLMA, 94014
DALY CITY POLICE DEPARTMENT 687 - B5
333 90TH ST, DALY, 94015
EAST PALO ALTO POLICE STA 791 - B1
2415 UNIVERSITY AV, EPA, 94303
FOSTER CITY POLICE DEPARTMENT 749 - F2
1030 E HILLSIDE BLVD, FCTY, 94404
HALF MOON BAY POLICE DEPARTMENT 787 - F1
537 KELLY ST, HMBY, 94019
HILLSBOROUGH POLICE STA 728 - F7
1600 FLORIBUNDA AV, HIL, 94010
MENLO PARK POLICE DEPARTMENT 790 - G3
801 LAUREL ST, MLPK, 94025
MILLBRAE POLICE DEPARTMENT 728 - B3
581 MAGNOLIA AV, MLBR, 94030
PACIFICA POLICE DEPARTMENT 727 - A1
2075 CABRILLO HWY, PCFA, 94044
PACIFICA POLICE STA 706 - J5
1850 FRANCISCO BLVD, PCFA, 94044
PALO ALTO POLICE DEPARTMENT 790 - J5
275 FOREST AV, PA, 94301
REDWOOD CITY POLICE DEPARTMENT 770 - B5
1301 MAPLE ST, RDWC, 94063
SAN BRUNO POLICE DEPARTMENT 707 - H5
1177 HUNTINGTON AV, SBRN, 94066
SAN CARLOS POLICE STA 769 - G3
600 ELM ST, SCAR, 94070
SAN MATEO POLICE STA 749 - B3
2000 S DELAWARE ST, SMTO, 94403
SOUTH SAN FRANCISCO POLICE DEPARTMENT 707 - F3
36 ARROYO DR, SSF, 94080

LIBRARIES

ATHERTON 790 - E2
2 DINKLESPIEL STATION LN, ATN, 94027
BAYSHORE 687 - H3
460 MARTIN ST, DALY, 94014
BELMONT 769 - C2
1110 ALAMEDA DE LAS PULGAS, BLMT, 94002
BRISBANE 688 - A6
250 VISITACION AV, BSBN, 94005
BURLINGAME 728 - G6
480 PRIMROSE RD, BURL, 94010

FEATURE NAME Address City, ZIP Code	PAGE-GRID
COLLEGE TERRACE BRANCH 2300 WELLESLEY ST, PA, 94306	791 - A7
DALY CITY 40 WEMBLEY DR, DALY, 94015	707 - C2
DALY, JOHN D 6351 MISSION ST, DALY, 94014	687 - D3
DOWNTOWN BRANCH 270 FOREST AV, PA, 94301	790 - J5
EASTON BRANCH 1800 EASTON DR, BURL, 94010	728 - D6
EAST PALO ALTO BRANCH 2415 UNIVERSITY AV, EPA, 94303	791 - B1
FAIR OAKS BRANCH 2600 MIDDLEFIELD, RDWC, 94063	770 - C7
FOSTER CITY 1000 E HILLSDALE BLVD, FCTY, 94404	749 - F2
GRAND AVENUE 306 WALNUT AV, SSF, 94080	707 - J3
HALF MOON BAY 620 CORREAS ST, HMBY, 94019	787 - F1
HILLSDALE BRANCH 205 W HILLSDALE BLVD, SMTO, 94403	749 - B6
MARINA BRANCH 1530 SUSAN CT, SMTO, 94403	749 - D3
MENLO PARK BRANCH 800 ALMA ST, MLPK, 94025	790 - G3
MILLBRAE 1 LIBRARY AV, MLBR, 94030	728 - A3
OCEAN VIEW 345 RANDOLPH ST, SF, 94132	687 - C2
PACIFICA BRANCH 104 HILTON WY, PCFA, 94044	706 - J6
PALO ALTO CHILDRENS 1276 HARRIET ST, PA, 94301	791 - B4
PALO ALTO MAIN 1213 NEWELL RD, PA, 94303	791 - B4
PORTOLA VALLEY BRANCH 765 PORTOLA RD, PTLV, 94028	810 - A6
REDWOOD CITY BRANCH 1044 MIDDLEFIELD RD, RDWC, 94063	770 - B6
SAN BRUNO 701 ANGUS AV W, SBRN, 94066	707 - J7
SAN CARLOS 610 ELM ST, SCAR, 94070	769 - G3
SANCHEZ 1111 TERRA NOVA BLVD, PCFA, 94044	727 - B5
SAN MATEO COUNTY 25 TOWER RD, SMCo, 94402	768 - H2
SAN MATEO 55 W 3RD AV, SMTO, 94402	748 - J2
SCHABERG, H W 2140 EUCLID AV, RDWC, 94061	789 - J1
SOUTH SAN FRANCISCO 840 W ORANGE AV, SSF, 94080	707 - F3
VISITACION VALLEY 45 LELAND AV, SF, 94134	688 - A2
WESTLAKE BRANCH 275 SOUTHGATE AV, DALY, 94015	687 - A4
WOODSIDE 3140 WOODSIDE RD, WDSD, 94062	789 - G6

MUSEUMS

FEATURE NAME Address City, ZIP Code	PAGE-GRID
BAYLANDS NATURE INTERPRETIVE CTR 2775 EMBARCADERO RD, PA, 94303	791 - F2
CANTOR ARTS CTR AT STANFORD UNIV 328 LOMITA DR, SCIC, 94305	790 - G6
COYOTE POINT MUS 1651 COYOTE POINT DR, SMTO, 94401	729 - A5
HILLER AVIATION MUS 601 SKYWAY RD, SCAR, 94070	769 - H2
MUS OF AMERICAN HERITAGE 351 HOMER AV, PA, 94301	790 - J5
PALO ALTO JUNIOR MUS & ZOO 1451 MIDDLEFIELD RD, PA, 94301	791 - B5
SANCHEZ ADOBE MUS 1000 LINDA MAR BLVD, PCFA, 94044	726 - J5
SAN MATEO COUNTY HIST MUS 777 HAMILTON ST, RDWC, 94063	770 - A5

OPEN SPACE

FEATURE NAME	PAGE-GRID
ARASTRADERO PRESERVE, PA	810 - E7
BAYLANDS NATURE PRESERVE, EPA	771 - D7
BYRNE PRESERVE, LAH	830 - J2
COAL CREEK OPEN SPACE, SMCo	830 - C5
EDWARDS, DON SF BAY NATL FOREST, RDWC	770 - C1
EL CORTE DE MADERA OPEN SPACE, SMCo	808 - H2
FITZGERALD MARINE RESERVE, SMCo	746 - E6
FOOTHILLS OPEN SPACE, PA	830 - G3
LA HONDA CREEK OPEN SPACE, SMCo	809 - E7
LONG RIDGE OPEN SPACE, SMCo	850 - J6
LOS TRANCOS OPEN SPACE, PA	830 - F6
MILLS CREEK OPEN SPACE, SMCo	768 - D7
MONTE BELLO OPEN SPACE, PA	830 - F7
PULGAS RIDGE OPEN SPACE, SMCo	769 - C6
PURISIMA CK REDWOODS OPEN SPACE, SMCo	808 - D2
RANCHO SAN ANTONIO OPEN SPACE, PA	830 - J7
RAVENSWOOD OPEN SPACE PRESERVE, MLPK	771 - D4
RUSSIAN RIDGE OPEN SPACE, SMCo	830 - C7
SAN FRANCISCO STATE FISH & GAME REFUGE, - SMCo	768 - F6
SKYLINE RIDGE OPEN SPACE, SMCo	850 - F3
TEAGUE HILL OPEN SPACE, WDSD	789 - C7
THORNEWOOD OPEN SPACE, WDSD	809 - G4
TIMBERLAND OPEN SPACE, SMTO	768 - H1
WINDY HILL OPEN SPACE, PTLV	809 - J7

OTHER

FEATURE NAME Address City, ZIP Code	PAGE-GRID
ALLIED ARTS GUILD 75 ARBOR RD, MLPK, 94025	790 - G5
ALPINE HILLS CLUB 4139 ALPINE RD, PTLV, 94028	810 - D7
BAYLANDS ATHLETIC CTR 1900 GENG RD, PA, 94303	791 - D3
HOOVER PAVILION 211 QUARRY RD, PA, 94304	790 - H5
MAUSOLEUM LOMITA DR & CAMPUS DR, SCIC, 94305	790 - H6
PALO ALTO ART CTR 1313 NEWELL RD, PA, 94303	791 - B5
PORT OF RDWC ADMINISTRATIVE OFFICE 675 SEAPORT BLVD, RDWC, 94063	770 - D3
RONALD MCDONALD HOUSE 520 SAND HILL RD, PA, 94304	790 - G5
SAN FRANCISCO LOG CABIN BOYS LOG CABIN RANCH RD, SMCo, 94020	849 - G2
SUNSET MAGAZINE CTR MIDDLEFIELD RD & WILLOW RD, MLPK, 94025	790 - H3
US LIGHTHOUSE RESERVE CABRILLO HWY, SMCo, 94038	746 - F5

PARK & RIDE

FEATURE NAME	PAGE-GRID
101/92, SMTO	749 - C3
3RD AV, SMTO	729 - A7
CALIFORNIA AVE CALTRAIN STA, PA	791 - B7
CRESPI, PCFA	726 - H3
EDGEWOOD, SMCo	789 - D1
HAYNE RD, SMCo	748 - D4
MENLO PK CALTRAIN STA, MLPK	790 - G3
PAGE MILL & EL CAMINO REAL, PA	791 - B7
PAGE MILL & HWY 280, LAH	810 - H5
PARK & RIDE, BSBN	688 - B6
PARK & RIDE, DALY	687 - C6
RALSTON, SMCo	768 - J2
SAMTRANS, SMTO	748 - J1
SAMTRANS, PCFA	726 - H4
SAMTRANS, RDWC	770 - A6
SAMTRANS, SSF	707 - E4
SAMTRANS TRANSIT TRANSFER POINT, PA	790 - H5
UNIV AVE CALTRAIN STA, PA	790 - H5
WOODSIDE, WDSD	789 - J6

PARKS & RECREATION

FEATURE NAME	PAGE-GRID
7TH & WALNUT PK, SBRN	708 - A6
7TH AV PK, SBRN	708 - A6
ALEXANDER PK, BLMT	749 - E7
ANO NUEVO STATE PK, SMCo	888 - G6
ANO NUEVO STATE RESERVE, SMCo	888 - D7
ARCTURUS PK, FCTY	749 - E4
ARDEN PK, DALY	687 - G3
ARGUELLO PK, SCAR	769 - E3
BARKLEY FIELDS AND PK, WDSD	789 - G4
BARRETT PK, BLMT	769 - D2
BAYFRONT PK, MLBR	728 - D3
BAYFRONT PK, MLPK	770 - H5
BAYSHORE CIRCLE PK, SBRN	707 - J5
BAYSHORE HEIGHTS PK, DALY	687 - H3
BAYSHORE PK, DALY	687 - J3
BAYSIDEPARK, BURL	728 - F5
BAYSIDE PK, SMTO	749 - C1
BAYSIDE PK, MLBR	728 - C3
BAYVIEW PK, SF	688 - B2
BEEGER, DOVE PK, RDWC	769 - H7
BELAMEDA PK, BLMT	769 - C2
BELL STREET PK, EPA	791 - B2
BELMONT SPORTS COMPLEX, BLMT	749 - F6
BERESFORD PK, SMTO	749 - A5
BIG CANYON PK, SCAR	769 - D5
BOAT PK, FCTY	749 - G3
BOOTHBAY PK, FCTY	749 - F5
BOREL PK, SMTO	748 - J4
BOWDEN PK, PA	791 - B7
BOWLING GREEN PK, PA	791 - A5
BRENTWOOD PK, SSF	707 - F5
BRIGHTON SCENIC MINI PK, PCFA	707 - A6
BROOKS PK, SF	687 - C1
BUCKEYE PK, SBRN	727 - G1
BURGESS PK, MLPK	790 - G3
BURI BURI PK, SSF	707 - F3
BURLEIGH-MURRAY RANCH STATE PK, SMCo	787 - J3
BURTON PK, SCAR	769 - G4
BUTANO STATE PK, SMCo	888 - G3
BYXBEE REC AREA, PA	791 - F3
CALLAN PK, SSF	707 - C4
CAMERON PK, PA	791 - A7
CAMPBELL-RUTLAND PLGD, SF	688 - A2
CANDLESTICK POINT STATE REC AREA, SF	688 - D2
CARTER, JOHN L MEM PK, HMBY	787 - G1
CASANOVA PK, SMTO	749 - E6
CATAMARAN PK, FCTY	749 - G3
CAYUGA PLGD, SF	687 - E2
CEDAR STREET PK, SCAR	769 - F2
CENTRAL PK, SMTO	748 - J2
CENTRAL PK, MLBR	728 - A3
CHALMERS, ALICE PLGD, SF	687 - E2
CIPRIANI FIELD, BLMT	769 - B1
CITY HALL PK, SCAR	769 - G3
CITY PK, SBRN	727 - J1
CLAY AVENUE PK, SSF	707 - C2
COGSWELL PLAZA, PA	790 - H4
COLMA HIST PK, CLMA	687 - D6
COMMODORE PK, SBRN	707 - G6
CONNIE PK, SMTO	749 - B3
COYOTE POINT COUNTY REC AREA, SMTO	728 - J5
CRESTVIEW PK, SCAR	769 - D6
CROCKER AMAZON PLGD, SF	687 - G2
CROSSROADS PK, HIL	748 - F3
CUERNAVACA PK, BURL	728 - A6
DE ANZA HIST PK, SMTO	748 - J2
DOG PK, MTVW	791 - J7
DOG PK, RDWC	750 - B5
DOLPHIN PK, RDWC	749 - G7
DUNCAN PK, RDWC	769 - J7
EASTER BOWL, RDWC	789 - F2
EATON PK, SCAR	769 - E6
EDGEMAR PK, PCFA	707 - A3
EDGEWATER PK, FCTY	749 - E4
EDGEWOOD COUNTY PK, RDWC	769 - D7
E HILLSDALE PK, SMTO	749 - B6
EL CAMINO PK, PA	790 - H4
EL PALO ALTO PK, PA	790 - H4
ERCKENBRACK PK, FCTY	749 - G2
EXCELSIOR PLGD, SF	687 - G1
FAIRMONT PK, PCFA	707 - A2
FAIRMONT WEST PK, PCFA	707 - A2
FAIRWAY PK, PCFA	707 - A7
FARELL, JACK PK, EPA	771 - C7
FARRAGUT PK, FCTY	749 - F4
FASSLER PK, PCFA	727 - A4
FERNANDEZ, ELBERT KITTY PK, HMBY	787 - F2
FIESTA MEADOWS PK, SMTO	749 - C4
FIRTH PK, BSBN	688 - A7
FLEETWOOD PK, SBRN	707 - E7
FLEISHMAN PK, RDWC	770 - B7
FLOOD COUNTY PK, MLPK	770 - H7
FOREST LANE PK, SBRN	707 - H6
FREMONT, MLPK	790 - F4
FRENCHMANS CREEK COMMON PK, HMBY	767 - E5
FRONTIERLAND PK, PCFA	727 - C5
GARRETT PK, RDWC	789 - G1
GATEWAY PK, SMTO	749 - A1
GELLERT PK, DALY	707 - B1
GILBRECH, DAN PK, DALY	687 - E3
GILMAN PLGD, SF	688 - C1
GLENVIEW PK, SBRN	707 - F7
GOLDEN GATE NATL REC AREA, PCFA	727 - C1
GREEN HILLS PK, MLBR	728 - A3
GREER PK, PA	791 - D5
GRUNDY PK, SBRN	707 - H7
GULL PK, FCTY	749 - G1
HALLMARK PK, BLMT	769 - B3
HARBOR VIEW PK, SMTO	729 - A6
HAWES PK, RDWC	770 - A7
HEATHER PK, SCAR	769 - E5
HERITAGE GROVE, SMCo	849 - H4
HERITAGE PK, PA	790 - J5
HERMAN STREET PK, SBRN	707 - J6
HIGHLANDS PK, SCAR	769 - E4
HILLCREST CIRCLE PK, SCAR	769 - F3
HILLSIDE PK, DALY	687 - D4
HOOVER PK, PA	791 - C7
HOOVER PK, RDWC	770 - C6
HOPKINS CREEKSIDE PK, PA	790 - H4
HUDDART COUNTY PK, SMCo	789 - B5
INDIAN SPRINGS PK, SMTO	749 - B7
JARDIN DE NINOS PK, RDWC	770 - B6
JOHNSON PK, PA	790 - H4
JOINVILLE PK, SMTO	749 - D1
JUNIPERO SERRA COUNTY PK, SBRN	727 - H2
KEHOE PK, HMBY	767 - E6
KELLOCH-VELASCO PK, SF	687 - J2
KELLOGG PK, PA	791 - A5
KELLY PK, MLPK	770 - H7
KETCH PK, FCTY	749 - G4
KILLDEER PK, FCTY	749 - G1
KING, MARTIN LUTHER PK, EPA	791 - D2
KING, M L PK, SMTO	728 - J7
LAGUNA PK, BURL	728 - D5
LAKESHORE PK, SMTO	749 - D4
LAUREL ST PK, SCAR	769 - G3
LAURELWOOD PK, SMTO	748 - J7
LAUREOLA PK, SCAR	769 - G2
LESSING & SEARS MINI PK, SF	687 - D2
LINCOLN PK, DALY	687 - E3
LINDEN PK, RDWC	770 - C7
LIONS FIELD PK, SBRN	707 - J7
LIONS PK, MLBR	727 - J4
LITTLE HOLLYWOOD PK, SF	688 - B2
LOMITA PK, SBRN	728 - A1
LONGVIEW PK, DALY	706 - J1
LOS PRADOS PK, SMTO	749 - E5
LYLE, JACK PK, MLPK	790 - F4
MADDUX PK, RDWC	790 - A3
MARCHBANK PK, DALY	687 - C3
MARINA ISLAND PK, SMTO	749 - D2
MARINA VISTA PK, SMCo	728 - A2
MARINER PK, RDWC	749 - H7
MARKETPLACE PK, MLPK	770 - H7
MARLIN PK, FCTY	749 - H2
MARLIN PK, RDWC	749 - H6
MAYFIELD PK, PA	791 - A7
MCDOUGAL PK, BLMT	769 - D2
MCLAREN, JOHN PK, SF	687 - H1
MCNEE RANCH STATE PK, SMCo	726 - H7
MEADOWS, LAURIE PK, SMTO	749 - E6
MERCED HEIGHTS PLGD, SF	687 - C1
MEZES PK, RDWC	770 - A5
MILL ESTATE PK, MLBR	728 - A5
MILLS CANYON PK, BURL	728 - B6
MIRADA SURF, SMCo	767 - C3
MISSION HILLS PK, DALY	687 - F3
MONTE VERDE PK, SBRN	707 - E5
MORTON, RED COMM PK, RDWC	769 - J7
NEALON PK, MLPK	790 - G4
NORTHRIDGE PK, DALY	686 - J6
OCEAN VIEW PK, HMBY	787 - F1
OCEAN VIEW PLGD & REC CTR, SF	687 - D1
ODDSTAD PK, PCFA	726 - J4
ORANGE MEM PK, SSF	707 - G3
OVAL PARK, THE, SCIC	790 - H6
OYSTER POINT PK, SSF	708 - C2
PACIFIC HEIGHTS PK, SBRN	707 - D6
PALISADES PK, DALY	686 - J5
PALMER, HOLBOOK PK, ATN	790 - E2
PALMETTO MINI PK, PCFA	706 - J6
PALM PK, RDWC	790 - B1
PARADISE VALLEY PK, SSF	707 - J2
PARDEE, ELEANOR PK, PA	791 - B4
PARKSIDE AQUATIC PARK, SMTO	749 - D2
PEERS PK, PA	791 - A6
PERSHING PK, BURL	728 - G7
PESCADERO CREEK COUNTY PK, SMCo	849 - G6
PESCADERO CREEK COUNTY PK, SMCo	850 - A6
POINT SAN BRUNO PK, SSF	708 - D3
POLARIS PK, DALY	687 - F3
POMO PK, PCFA	707 - A5
PONDEROSA PK, SBRN	707 - C5
POPLAR BEACH PK, HMBY	787 - E1
PORTOLA HIGHLANDS PK, SBRN	707 - D7
PORTOLA REDWOODS STATE PK, SMCo	850 - D7
PORT ROYAL PK, FCTY	749 - F6
PORTSIDE PK, RDWC	749 - H7
POSEY PK, SBRN	707 - J6
PULGAS WATER TEMPLE, SMCo	769 - A6
RAMOS PK, PA	791 - E7
RAY PK, BURL	728 - C5

FEATURE NAME	PAGE-GRID
RINCONADA PK, PA	791 - B5
ROTARY PK, MLBR	728 - A4
RYAN, LEO J MEM PK, FCTY	749 - F3
RYDER COURT PK, SMTO	729 - B7
SAM MCDONALD COUNTY PK, SMCo	849 - F4
SAN BRUNO MTN STATE AND CO PARK, SMCo	687 - F5
SAN CARLOS NEIGHBORHOOD PK, SCAR	769 - E3
SANDPIPER PK, RDWC	750 - A5
SAN MATEO COUNTY MEM PK, SMCo	849 - B6
SAN PEDRO VALLEY COUNTY PK, PCFA	747 - C1
SCHULTZ PK, MLBR	728 - A4
SCOTT PK, PA	790 - J5
SEA CLOUD PK, FCTY	749 - G4
SEALE PK, PA	791 - D6
SELLICK PK, SSF	707 - E4
SEMINARY OAKS PK, MLPK	790 - H3
SHAD PK, FCTY	749 - H2
SHANNON PK, RDWC	749 - J6
SHARON HILLS PK, MLPK	790 - C6
SHARON PK, MLPK	790 - C7
SHARP PK, PCFA	707 - B7
SHOREBIRD PK, RDWC	749 - H6
SHORELINE AT MTN VIEW, MTVW	791 - H7
SHOREVIEW PK, SMTO	749 - C1
SIGN HILL PK, SSF	707 - H2
SISTERS CITIES PK, SSF	707 - H3
SMITH FIELD PK, HMBY	787 - F3
SPINAS, ANDREW PK, RDWC	770 - D6
SPUR TRAIL PK, MLBR	728 - B4
STAFFORD PK, RDWC	769 - J6
STANFORD HILLS PK, MLPK	790 - E7
STANFORD/PALO ALTO PLAYING FIELDS, PA	791 - A7
STULSAFT PK, RDWC	789 - H3
SUNFISH PK, FCTY	749 - H3
SUNNYBRAE PK, SMTO	749 - B2
TIDELANDS PK, SMTO	749 - D1
TINKER PK, MLPK	790 - E5
TRAP & SKEET RANGE, SF	686 - J1
TRINTA PK, SMTO	749 - B4
TURNSTONE PK, FCTY	749 - H2
TWIN PINES PK, BLMT	769 - E1
UNIV SQUARE, EPA	791 - C3
UPPER STEVENS CREEK COUNTY PK, PA	850 - J4
VICTORIA PK, BURL	728 - H6
VILLAGE PK, BURL	728 - D5
VISITACION VALLEY PLGD, SF	687 - J2
VISTA PK, SCAR	769 - C4
VISTA PK, HIL	748 - G3
WALLIS PK, PA	791 - B7
WASHINGTON PK, BURL	728 - G6
WATER DOG LAKE PK, BLMT	769 - B2
WAUGH PK, MLBR	728 - A4
WELLESLEY CRESCENT PK, RDWC	769 - J5
WERRY PK, PA	810 - J1
WESTBOROUGH PK, SSF	707 - D4
WESTLAKE PK, DALY	687 - A3
WESTMOOR PK, DALY	687 - A6
WESTWOOD PK, RDWC	789 - J2
W HILLSDALE PK, SMTO	749 - B6
WHITE FIELD, PCFA	726 - J5
WILLOW OAKS PK, MLPK	790 - J2
WINSTON MANOR PK, SSF	707 - D1
WUNDERLICH COUNTY PK, SMCo	809 - F2

POST OFFICES

FEATURE NAME	Address City, ZIP Code	PAGE-GRID
25TH AVENUE	135 W 25TH AV, SMTO, 94403	749 - B5
BRANCH	SF INTERNATIONAL AIRPORT, SMCo, 94128	728 - C2
BELMONT	640 MASONIC WY, BLMT, 94002	769 - E1
BRISBANE	280 OLD COUNTY RD, BSBN, 94005	688 - A6
BURLINGAME ANNEX	820 STANTON RD, BURL, 94010	728 - D4
BURLINGAME	220 PARK RD, BURL, 94010	728 - G7
CAMBRIDGE	265 CAMBRIDGE AV, PA, 94306	791 - B7
CAPUCHINO	1141 CAPUCHINO AV, BURL, 94010	728 - E6
CHESTNUT	36 CHESTNUT AV, SSF, 94080	707 - G3
COLMA	7373 MISSION ST, DALY, 94014	687 - C5
DALY CITY	1100 SULLIVAN AV, DALY, 94015	687 - B5
DOWNTOWN REDWOOD CITY	855 JEFFERSON AV, RDWC, 94063	770 - B6
EAST PALO ALTO	1600 BAY RD, EPA, 94303	791 - B1
EL GRANADA	20 AVE PORTOLA, SMCo, 94019	767 - B3
EXCELSIOR	15 ONONDAGA AV, SF, 94112	687 - F1
FOSTER CITY	1050 SHELL BLVD, FCTY, 94404	749 - G4
HALF MOON BAY	500 STONE PINE RD, HMBY, 94019	787 - G1
HAMILTON	380 HAMILTON AV, PA, 94301	790 - J4
LA HONDA	8865 LA HONDA RD, SMCo, 94062	849 - E1
LINDA MAR	690 ROBERTS RD, PCFA, 94044	726 - H3
LINDEN AVENUE	322 LINDEN AV, SSF, 94080	707 - J3
LOMA MAR	8150 PESCADERO CREEK RD, SMCo, 94021	849 - A7
MENLO PARK	3875 BOHANNON DR, MLPK, 94025	770 - F7
MILLBRAE	501 BROADWAY, MLBR, 94030	728 - B3
MONTARA	215 7TH ST, SMCo, 94037	746 - F4
MOSS BEACH	2315 CARLOS ST, SMCo, 94038	746 - F6
OAK GROVE	655 OAK GROVE AV, MLPK, 94025	790 - F3
PACIFICA	50 W MANOR DR, PCFA, 94044	706 - J3
PALO ALTO	2085 E BAYSHORE RD, PA, 94303	791 - D4
PESCADERO	2020 PESCADERO CREEK RD, SMCo, 94060	868 - B3
REDWOOD CITY	1100 BROADWAY, RDWC, 94063	770 - C5
SAINT MATTHEWS	210 S ELLSWORTH AV, SMTO, 94401	748 - J1
SAN BRUNO	1300 HUNTINGTON AV, SBRN, 94066	707 - H5
SAN CARLOS	809 LAUREL ST, SCAR, 94070	769 - G3
SAN GREGORIO	7615 STAGE RD, SMCo, 94074	828 - B6
SAN MATEO	1630 S DELAWARE ST, SMTO, 94402	749 - B3
SOUTH SAN FRANCISCO POSTAL RETAIL	844 DUBUQUE AV, SSF, 94080	708 - A2
SOUTH SAN FRANCISCO	1070 SAN MATEO AV, SSF, 94066	707 - J5
STANFORD	531 LASUEN MALL, SCIC, 94305	790 - H6
STANFORD UNIV BRANCH	LAGUNITA DR & LANE W, SCIC, 94305	790 - H7
VISITACION	68 LELAND AV, SF, 94134	688 - A2
VISTA GRANDE	6025 MISSION ST, DALY, 94014	687 - D2
WESTLAKE	199 SOUTHGATE AV, DALY, 94015	687 - A4
WEST MENLO PARK BRANCH	2120 AVY AV, SMCo, 94025	790 - D6
WOODSIDE PLAZA	364 WOODSIDE PZ, RDWC, 94061	790 - A3
WOODSIDE	2995 WOODSIDE RD, WDSD, 94062	789 - H6

SCHOOLS

FEATURE NAME	Address City, ZIP Code	PAGE-GRID
ABBOTT MID	600 36TH AV, SMTO, 94403	749 - B6
ADDISON ELEM	650 ADDISON AV, PA, 94301	791 - A4
ADELANTE SPANISH IMMERSION ELEM	3150 GRANGER WY, RDWC, 94061	789 - J3
ALLEN, DECIMA M ELEM	875 ANGUS AV W, SBRN, 94066	707 - H7
ALL SOULS ELEM	479 MILLER AV, SSF, 94080	707 - J3
ALMA HEIGHTS ACADEMY HIGH	1030 LINDA MAR BLVD, PCFA, 94044	726 - J5
ALMA HEIGHTS CHRISTIAN ELEM	1295 SEVILLE DR, PCFA, 94044	726 - J5
ALPHA BEACON CHRISTIAN	1950 ELKHORN CT, SMTO, 94403	749 - B7
ALTA LOMA MID	116 ROMNEY AV, SSF, 94080	707 - E2
ANTHONY, SUSAN B ELEM	575 ABBOT AV, DALY, 94014	687 - D5
ARAGON HIGH	900 ALAMEDA DE LAS PULGAS, SMTO, 94402	748 - J4
ARMSTRONG, CHARLES ELEM	1405 SOLANA DR, BLMT, 94002	769 - E2
ARUNDEL ELEM	200 ARUNDEL RD, SCAR, 94070	769 - E3
AUDUBON ELEM	841 GULL AV, FCTY, 94404	749 - H1
BADEN HIGH	825 SOUTHWOOD DR, SSF, 94080	707 - F4
BALBOA HIGH	1000 CAYUGA AV, SF, 94112	687 - F1
BAYSHORE ELEM	155 ORIENTE ST, DALY, 94014	687 - J3
BAYSIDE MID	2025 KEHOE AV, SMTO, 94403	749 - C1
BAYWOOD ELEM	600 ALAMEDA DE LAS PULGAS, SMTO, 94402	748 - H3
BEECHWOOD ELEM	50 TERMINAL AV, MLPK, 94025	770 - H7
BELLE AIR ELEM	450 3RD AV, SBRN, 94066	708 - A7
BELLE HAVEN ELEM	415 IVY DR, MLPK, 94025	770 - J7
BELMONT OAKS ACADEMY	2200 CARLMONT DR, BLMT, 94002	769 - C2
BERESFORD ELEM	300 28TH AV, SMTO, 94403	749 - B5
BOREL MID	425 BARNESON AV, SMTO, 94402	749 - A4
BOWDITCH MID	1450 TARPON ST, FCTY, 94404	749 - J2
BREWER ISLAND ELEM	1151 POLYNESIA DR, FCTY, 94404	749 - G2
BRIDGEMONT HIGH	777 BROTHERHOOD WY, SF, 94132	687 - B2
BRISBANE ELEM	550 SAN BRUNO AV, BSBN, 94005	688 - A6
BRITTAN ACRES ELEM	2000 BELLE AV, SCAR, 94070	769 - G4
BROOKS, PHILLIPS ELEM	2245 AVY AV, MLPK, 94025	790 - D7
BROWN, MARGARET PAULINE ELEM	305 EASTMOOR AV, DALY, 94015	687 - B6
BURBANK, LUTHER MID	325 LA GRANDE AV, SF, 94112	687 - H1
BURI BURI ELEM	120 EL CAMPO DR, SSF, 94080	707 - E3
BURLINGAME HIGH	400 CAROLAN AV, BURL, 94010	728 - G6
BURLINGAME INTERMED	1715 QUESADA WY, BURL, 94010	728 - C5
BURTON, PHILLIP & SALA HIGH	400 MANSELL ST, SF, 94134	688 - A1
CABRILLO ELEM	601 CRESPI DR, PCFA, 94044	726 - J3
CAPUCHINO HIGH	1501 MAGNOLIA AV, SBRN, 94066	727 - J2
CAREY ELEM	1 CAREY SCHOOL LN, SMTO, 94403	749 - A4
CARLMONT HIGH	1400 ALAMEDA DE LAS PULGAS, BLMT, 94002	769 - D3
CASTILLEJA HIGH	1310 BRYANT ST, PA, 94301	791 - A5
CASTILLEJA MID	1310 BRYANT ST, PA, 94301	791 - A5
CENTRAL ELEM	525 MIDDLE RD, BLMT, 94002	749 - E7
CENTRAL MID	828 CHESTNUT ST, SCAR, 94070	769 - G3
CHARTER LEARNING CTR	750 DARTMOUTH AV, SCAR, 94070	769 - D2
CHAVEZ, CESAR ELEM	2450 RALMAR AV, EPA, 94303	791 - A1
CIPRIANI ELEM	2525 BUENA VISTA AV, BLMT, 94002	769 - B1
CLEVELAND ELEM	455 ATHENS ST, SF, 94112	687 - G1
CLIFFORD ELEM	225 CLIFFORD AV, SMCo, 94062	769 - G6
CLOUD, ROY ELEM	3790 RED OAK WY, RDWC, 94061	789 - G2
COLMA ELEM	444 E MARKET ST, DALY, 94014	687 - D5
COLUMBUS, CHRISTOPHER ELEM	60 CHRISTOPHER CT, DALY, 94015	707 - A1
CORTE MADERA MID	4575 ALPINE RD, PTLV, 94028	830 - C1
COSTANO ELEM	2695 FORDHAM ST, EPA, 94303	771 - B7
CRESTMOOR ELEM	2322 CRESTMOOR DR, SBRN, 94066	707 - F7
CROCKER, WILLIAM H MID	2600 RALSTON AV, HIL, 94010	748 - E1
CRYSTAL SPRINGS AND UPLANDS HIGH	400 UPLANDS DR, HIL, 94010	748 - H2
CUNHA, MANUEL F INTERMED	KELLY AND CHURCH ST, HMBY, 94019	787 - F1
DAY, BRANDEIS HILLEL ELEM	655 BROTHERHOOD WY, SF, 94132	687 - B2
DENMAN, JAMES MID	241 ONEIDA AV, SF, 94112	687 - F1
DUVENECK ELEM	705 ALESTER AV, PA, 94303	791 - C4
EAST PALO ALTO CHARTER	1286 RUNNYMEADE ST, EPA, 94303	791 - C1
EAST PALO ALTO CHARTER HIGH	475 POPE ST, MLPK, 94025	790 - J2
EDISON-BRENTWOOD ELEM	2086 CLARKE AV, EPA, 94303	791 - C2
EDISON-MCNAIR CHARTER	2033 PULGAS AV, EPA, 94303	791 - C2
EDISON, THOMAS ELEM	1267 SOUTHGATE AV, DALY, 94015	687 - A7
EL CAMINO HIGH	1320 MISSION RD, SSF, 94080	707 - F1
EL CARMELO ELEM	3024 BRYANT ST, PA, 94306	791 - C7
EL CRYSTAL ELEM	201 BALBOA WY, SBRN, 94066	727 - J1
EL DORADO ELEM	70 DELTA ST, SF, 94134	688 - A1
EL GRANADA ELEM	400 SANTIAGO ST, SMCo, 94019	767 - C3
ENCINAL ELEM	195 ENCINAL AV, ATN, 94027	790 - F2
EPIPHANY ELEM	600 ITALY AV, SF, 94112	687 - G1
ESCONDIDO ELEM	890 ESCONDIDO RD, SCIC, 94305	810 - J1
FAIR OAKS ELEM	2950 FAIR OAKS AV, SMCo, 94063	770 - D7
FARALLONE VIEW ELEM	LE CONTE AV & 3RD ST, SMCo, 94037	746 - G4
FIESTA GARDENS INTL ELEM	1001 BERMUDA DR, SMTO, 94403	749 - C3
FLOOD, JAMES ELEM	320 SHERIDAN DR, MLPK, 94025	770 - H7
FORD, HENRY ELEM	2498 MASSACHUSETTS AV, RDWC, 94061	790 - A3
FOSTER CITY ELEM	461 BEACH PARK BLVD, FCTY, 94404	749 - F4
FOX ELEM	3100 ST JAMES RD, BLMT, 94002	768 - J2
FRANKLIN, BENJAMIN INTERMED	700 STEWART AV, SMCo, 94015	687 - A4
FRANKLIN ELEM	2385 TROUSDALE DR, BURL, 94010	728 - B5
GARDEN VILLAGE ELEM	208 GARDEN LN, SMCo, 94015	687 - B4
GARFIELD CHARTER ELEM	3600 MIDDLEFIELD RD, SMCo, 94025	790 - D1
GERMAN-AMERICAN OF SAN FRANCISCO	275 ELLIOT DR, MLPK, 94025	791 - A2
GILL, JOHN ELEM	555 AVE DEL ORA, RDWC, 94062	769 - J7
GOOD SHEPHERD ELEM	909 OCEANA BLVD, PCFA, 94044	706 - J4
GREEN HILLS ELEM	401 LUDEMAN LN, MLBR, 94030	728 - A3
GREEN OAKS ELEM	2450 RALMAR AV, EPA, 94303	791 - A1
GUADALUPE ELEM	859 PRAGUE ST, SF, 94112	687 - G2
HALF MOON BAY HIGH	LEWIS FOSTER DR, HMBY, 94019	767 - F7
HALL, GEORGE ELEM	130 SAN MIGUEL WY, SMTO, 94403	749 - D5
HARTE, BRET ELEM	1035 GILMAN AV, SF, 94124	688 - C1
HATCH, ALVIN S ELEM	490 MIRAMONTES AV, HMBY, 94019	787 - F1
HAWES ELEM	909 ROOSEVELT AV, RDWC, 94061	770 - A7
HAYS, WALTER ELEM	1525 MIDDLEFIELD RD, PA, 94301	791 - B5
HEATHER CHARTER ELEM	2757 MELENDY DR, SCAR, 94070	769 - E5

FEATURE NAME	Address City, ZIP Code	PAGE-GRID
HEATHER ELEM	2757 MELENDY DR, SCAR, 94070	769 - E5
HERITAGE CHRISTIAN ACADEMY	1305 MIDDLEFIELD RD, RDWC, 94063	770 - B6
HIGHLANDS CHRISTIAN ELEM	1900 MONTEREY DR, SBRN, 94066	707 - E7
HIGHLANDS CHRISTIAN HIGH	1900 MONTEREY DR, SBRN, 94066	707 - E7
HIGHLANDS ELEM	2320 NEWPORT ST, SMCo, 94402	748 - F7
HILLDALE	79 FLORENCE ST, DALY, 94014	687 - D4
HILLSDALE HIGH	3115 DEL MONTE ST, SMTO, 94403	749 - A6
HILLSIDE ELEM	1400 HILLSIDE BLVD, SSF, 94080	707 - H1
HILLVIEW MID	1100 ELDER AV, MLPK, 94025	790 - E5
HOLY ANGELS ELEM	20 REINER ST, SMCo, 94014	687 - C5
HOOVER ELEM	701 CHARTER ST, RDWC, 94063	770 - C6
HORRALL, ALBION H. ELEM	949 OCEAN VIEW AV, SMTO, 94401	749 - C1
IMMACULATE HEART OF MARY	1000 ALAMEDA DE LAS PULGAS, BLMT, 94002	769 - C2
INTL SCH OF THE PENINSULA COHN CAMPUS	151 LAURA LN, PA, 94303	791 - D3
INTL SCH OF THE PENINSULA COWPER-CAMPUS	3233 COWPER ST, PA, 94306	791 - D7
JEFFERSON HIGH	6996 MISSION ST, DALY, 94014	687 - C4
JEWISH DAY	800 FOSTER CITY BLVD, FCTY, 94404	749 - G3
JORDAN, DAVID STARR MID	750 N CALIFORNIA AV, PA, 94303	791 - C5
KENNEDY, JOHN F ELEM	785 PRICE ST, DALY, 94014	687 - D4
KENNEDY, JOHN F MID	2521 GOODWIN AV, RDWC, 94061	789 - J2
KEYS	2890 MIDDLEFIELD RD, PA, 94306	791 - C6
KIDS CONNECTION	1998 BEACH PARK BLVD, FCTY, 94404	749 - G1
KINGS MOUNTAIN ELEM	211 SWETT RD, SMCo, 94062	788 - J7
KROUZIAN-ZEKARIAN ST GREGORY ARMENIAN	825 BROTHERHOOD WY, SF, 94132	687 - B2
LACY, INGRID B MID	1427 PALMETTO AV, PCFA, 94044	706 - J5
LA ENTRADA MID	2200 SHARON RD, MLPK, 94025	790 - D7
LA HONDA ELEM	SEARS RANCH RD, SMCo, 94062	829 - E7
LAS LOMITAS ELEM	299 ALAMEDA DE LAS PULGAS, ATN, 94027	790 - C5
LAUREL ELEM	316 36TH AV, SMTO, 94403	749 - B6
LAUREL ELEM	95 EDGE RD, ATN, 94027	790 - H1
LEADERSHIP HIGH	300 SENECA AV, SF, 94112	687 - F1
LINCOLN ELEM	1801 DEVEREUX DR, BURL, 94010	728 - C5
LINDA MAR ELEM	830 ROSITA RD, PCFA, 94044	726 - H5
LIPMAN, NATALIE MID	1 SOLANO ST, BSBN, 94005	688 - A6
LOMITA PK ELEM	200 SANTA HELENA AV, MLBR, 94030	728 - A2
LONGFELLOW ELEM	755 MORSE ST, SF, 94112	687 - E2
LOS CERRITOS ELEM	210 W ORANGE AV, SSF, 94080	707 - G3
MARTIN ELEM	35 SCHOOL ST, SSF, 94080	707 - J2
MATER DOLOROSA ELEM	1040 MILLER AV, SSF, 94080	707 - G2
MCKINLEY ELEM	701 PALOMA AV, BURL, 94010	728 - F6
MCKINLEY INTERMED	400 DUANE ST, RDWC, 94062	770 - A6
MEADOW HEIGHTS ELEM	2619 DOLORES ST, SMTO, 94403	749 - A5
MEADOWS ELEM	1101 HELEN DR, MLBR, 94030	727 - H3
MENLO-ATHERTON HIGH	555 MIDDLEFIELD RD, ATN, 94027	790 - G2
MENLO HIGH	50 VALPARAISO AV, ATN, 94027	790 - F3
MENLO MID	50 VALPARAISO AV, ATN, 94027	790 - E3
MERCY HIGH	2750 ADELINE DR, BURL, 94010	728 - C6
MID-PENINSULA HIGH	1340 WILLOW RD, MLPK, 94025	771 - A7
MILLS HIGH	400 MURCHISON DR, MLBR, 94030	728 - B4
MONTE VERDE ELEM	2551 SAINT CLOUD DR, SBRN, 94066	707 - E5
MUIR, JOHN ELEM	130 CAMBRIDGE LN, SBRN, 94066	727 - F1
NATIVITY ELEM	1250 LAUREL ST, MLPK, 94025	790 - F3
NESBIT ELEM	500 BIDDULPH WY, BLMT, 94002	749 - E7
NIXON, LUCILLE M ELEM	1711 STANFORD AV, SCIC, 94305	810 - J2
NORTH HILLSBOROUGH ELEM	545 EUCALYPTUS AV, HIL, 94010	748 - E1
NORTH SHOREVIEW ELEM	1301 CYPRESS AV, SMTO, 94401	729 - A7
NORTH STAR ACADEMY	400 DUANE ST, RDWC, 94062	770 - A6
NOTRE DAME ELEM	1500 RALSTON AV, BLMT, 94002	769 - E1
NOTRE DAME HIGH	1540 RALSTON AV, BLMT, 94002	769 - D1
NUEVA CTR FOR LEARNING	6565 SKYLINE FRONTAGE BLVD, HIL, 94010	748 - C2
OAK KNOLL ELEM	1895 OAK KNOLL LN, MLPK, 94025	790 - E6
OCEANA HIGH	401 PALOMA AV, PCFA, 94044	707 - A5
OCEAN SHORE ELEM	411 OCEANA BLVD, PCFA, 94044	707 - A3
ODDSTAD ELEM	930 ODDSTAD BLVD, PCFA, 94044	727 - C5
OHLONE ELEM	950 AMARILLO AV, PA, 94303	791 - D5
ORION	815 ALLERTON ST, RDWC, 94063	770 - A5
ORMONDALE ELEM	200 SHAWNEE PASS, PTLV, 94028	810 - B6
ORTEGA ELEM	1283 TERRA NOVA BLVD, PCFA, 94044	727 - A5
ORTEGA, JOSE ELEM	400 SARGENT ST, SF, 94132	687 - C1
OUR LADY OF ANGELS ELEM	1328 CABRILLO AV, BURL, 94010	728 - D6
OUR LADY OF MERCY ELEM	7 ELMWOOD DR, DALY, 94015	687 - A4
OUR LADY OF MOUNT CARMEL ELEM	301 GRAND ST, RDWC, 94062	769 - J6
OUR LADY OF PERPETUAL HELP ELEM	80 WELLINGTON AV, DALY, 94014	687 - D3
OUR LADY OF THE VISITACION ELEM	785 SUNNYDALE AV, SF, 94134	687 - J2
PALO ALTO HIGH	50 EMBARCADERO RD, PA, 94301	790 - J6
PALO VERDE ELEM	3450 LOUIS RD, PA, 94303	791 - E7
PANORAMA ELEM	25 BELLEVUE AV, DALY, 94014	687 - F3
PARK ELEM	161 CLARK DR, SMTO, 94402	748 - G1
PARKSIDE ELEM	1685 EISENHOWER ST, SMTO, 94403	749 - C2
PARKSIDE INTERMED	1801 NILES AV, SBRN, 94066	727 - H1
PARKWAY HEIGHTS MID	825 PARK WY, SSF, 94080	707 - G2
PENINSULA HIGH	300 PIEDMONT AV, SBRN, 94066	727 - G2
PENINSULA LTD	920 PENINSULA WY, SMCo, 94025	790 - H1
PESCADERO ELEM	620 NORTH ST, SMCo, 94060	868 - B2
PESCADERO HIGH	350 BUTANO CTO, SMCo, 94060	868 - C3
POLLICITA, THOMAS R MID	550 E MARKET ST, DALY, 94014	687 - D5
PONDEROSA ELEM	295 PONDEROSA RD, SMCo, 94080	707 - G4
PORTOLA ELEM	300 AMADOR AV, SBRN, 94066	707 - D7
RALSTON MID	2675 RALSTON AV, BLMT, 94002	769 - A2
REDEEMER LUTHERAN ELEM	468 GRAND ST, RDWC, 94062	769 - J6
REDWOOD HIGH	1968 OLD COUNTY RD, RDWC, 94063	769 - J4
RIVERA, FERNANDO INTERMED	1255 SOUTHGATE AV, DALY, 94015	687 - A7
ROBERTSON, GARNET J INTERMED	1 MARTIN ST, DALY, 94014	687 - J4
ROLLINGWOOD ELEM	2500 COTTONWOOD DR, SBRN, 94066	707 - E6
ROOSEVELT ELEM	1151 VANCOUVER AV, BURL, 94010	728 - D6
ROOSEVELT ELEM	2223 VERA AV, RDWC, 94061	789 - J1
ROOSEVELT, FRANKLIN D ELEM	1200 SKYLINE DR, DALY, 94015	707 - A2
SACRED HEART PREP HIGH	150 VALPARAISO AV, ATN, 94027	790 - E4
SAINT CATHERINE OF SIENA ELEM	1300 BAYSWATER AV, BURL, 94010	728 - G7
SAINT CHARLES ELEM	850 TAMARACK AV, SCAR, 94070	769 - F4
SAINT DUNSTANS ELEM	1150 MAGNOLIA AV, MLBR, 94030	728 - A3
SAINT ELIZABETH SETON CATHOLIC COMM	1095 CHANNING AV, PA, 94301	791 - B4
SAINT GREGORY ELEM	2701 HACIENDA ST, SMTO, 94403	749 - B5
SAINT JOSEPHS ELEM	50 EMILIE AV, ATN, 94027	790 - E4
SAINT MATTHEWS EPISCOPAL	16 BALDWIN AV, SMTO, 94401	748 - J1
SAINT PAUL OF THE SHIPWRECK ACADEMY	1060 KEY AV, SF, 94124	688 - B1
SAINT PIUS ELEM	1100 WOODSIDE RD, RDWC, 94061	790 - B2
SAINT RAYMOND ELEM	1211 ARBOR RD, MLPK, 94025	790 - F4
SAINT ROBERTS CATHOLIC ELEM	345 OAK AV, SBRN, 94066	727 - H1
SAINT THOMAS MORE ELEM	50 THOMAS MORE WY, SF, 94132	687 - C2
SAINT TIMOTHY ELEM	1515 DOLAN AV, SMTO, 94401	729 - B7
SAINT VERONICA ELEM	434 ALIDA WY, SSF, 94080	707 - G4
SANDPIPER ELEM	801 REDWOOD SHORES PKWY, RDWC, 94065	750 - A5
SAN FRANCISCO CHRISTIAN ELEM	25 WHITTIER ST, SF, 94112	687 - E2
SAN FRANCISCO JUNIOR ACADEMY ELEM	66 GENEVA AV, SF, 94112	687 - F1
SAN MATEO HIGH	506 N DELAWARE ST, SMTO, 94401	728 - J7
SEA CREST	901 ARNOLD WY, HMBY, 94019	787 - G2
SELBY LANE ELEM	170 SELBY LN, ATN, 94027	790 - B3
SEQUOIA HIGH	1201 BREWSTER AV, RDWC, 94062	770 - A6
SERRA, JUNIPERO ELEM	151 VICTORIA ST, DALY, 94015	707 - C2
SERRA, JUNIPERO HIGH	451 W 20TH AV, SMTO, 94403	749 - A4
SHERIDAN ELEM	431 CAPITOL AV, SF, 94112	687 - D2
SKYLINE ELEM	55 CHRISTEN AV, DALY, 94015	707 - C3
SOUTH HILLSBOROUGH ELEM	303 EL CERRITO AV, HIL, 94010	748 - H2
SOUTH SAN FRANCISCO HIGH	400 B ST, SSF, 94080	707 - G4
SPRING VALLEY ELEM	817 MURCHISON DR, MLBR, 94030	728 - B5
SPRUCE ELEM	501 SPRUCE AV, SSF, 94080	707 - J2
SUNNYBRAE ELEM	1031 S DELAWARE ST, SMTO, 94402	749 - B2
SUNSET RIDGE ELEM	340 INVERNESS DR, PCFA, 94044	707 - B3
SUNSHINE GARDENS ELEM	1200 MILLER AV, SSF, 94080	707 - F1
TAFT ELEM	903 10TH AV, RDWC, 94063	770 - E6
TAYLOR MID	850 TAYLOR BLVD, MLBR, 94030	728 - A4
TERRA NOVA HIGH	1450 TERRA NOVA BLVD, PCFA, 94044	727 - B4
THORNTON HIGH	115 1ST AV, DALY, 94014	687 - C5
TIERRA LINDA MID	750 DARTMOUTH AV, SCAR, 94070	769 - D2
TOBIAS, MARJORIE H ELEM	725 SOUTHGATE AV, DALY, 94015	687 - A5
TRINITY EPISCOPAL ELEM	2650 SAND HILL RD, MLPK, 94025	810 - D1
TURNBULL LEARNING ACADEMY	715 INDIAN AV, SMTO, 94401	728 - J7
VALLEMAR ELEM	377 REINA DEL MAR AV, PCFA, 94044	727 - A1
VISITACION VALLEY ELEM	55 SCHWERIN ST, SF, 94134	687 - J2
VISITACION VALLEY MID	450 RAYMOND AV, SF, 94134	687 - J2
WASHINGTON ELEM	801 HOWARD AV, BURL, 94010	728 - H6
WASHINGTON, GEORGE ELEM	251 WHITTIER ST, DALY, 94014	687 - E2
WEBSTER, DANIEL ELEM	425 EL DORADO DR, DALY, 94015	687 - B7
WEST BAY CHRISTIAN ACADEMY	233 TOPAZ ST, RDWC, 94062	769 - H7
WESTBOROUGH MID	2570 WESTBOROUGH BLVD, SSF, 94080	707 - D4
WEST HILLSBOROUGH ELEM	376 BARBARA WY, HIL, 94010	748 - D3
WESTLAKE ELEM	80 FIELDCREST DR, DALY, 94015	687 - B3
WESTMOOR HIGH	131 WESTMOOR AV, DALY, 94015	687 - A6
WHITE OAKS ELEM	1901 WHITE OAK WY, SCAR, 94070	769 - H5
WILLIAMS, ROGER PRIVATE ELEM	600 GRAND AV, SSF, 94080	707 - H2
WILLOW OAKS ELEM	620 WILLOW RD, MLPK, 94025	790 - J2
WILSON, WOODROW ELEM	43 MIRIAM ST, DALY, 94014	687 - C3
WOODLAND ELEM	360 LA CUESTA DR, SMCo, 94028	810 - E3
WOODSIDE ELEM	3195 WOODSIDE RD, WDSD, 94062	789 - G7
WOODSIDE HIGH	199 CHURCHILL AV, SMCo, 94062	790 - A4
WOODSIDE PRIORY	302 PORTOLA RD, PTLV, 94028	810 - C7

SHOPPING CENTERS

FEATURE NAME	Address City, ZIP Code	PAGE-GRID
280 METRO CTR	1 COLMA BLVD, CLMA, 94014	687 - C7
BRIDGEPOINTE SHOPPING CTR	3010 BRIDGEPOINTE PKWY, SMTO, 94404	749 - E2
HILLSDALE CTR	60 HILLSDALE BLVD, SMTO, 94403	749 - B5
MERVYNS PLAZA	250 WALNUT, RDWC, 94063	770 - B5
SAN BRUNO TOWNE CTR	EL CAMINO REAL & NOOR AV, SBRN, 94066	707 - H5
SERRAMONTE CTR	SERRAMONTE BLVD & CALLAN BLVD, DALY, 94015	707 - C1
SHOPS AT TANFORAN, THE	EL CAMINO REAL & SNEATH LN, SBRN, 94066	707 - H5
STANFORD SHOPPING CTR	180 EL CAMINO REAL, PA, 94304	790 - G5
WESTLAKE CTR	285 LAKE MERCED BLVD, DALY, 94015	687 - A4

TRANSPORTATION

FEATURE NAME	PAGE-GRID
BART/CALTRAIN MILLBRAE STA, MLBR	728 - C3
BART COLMA STA, SMCo	687 - C6
BART DALY CITY STA, DALY	687 - C3
BART SAN BRUNO STA, SBRN	707 - H5
BART SFO TRANSIT STA, SMCo	728 - B1
BART SOUTH SAN FRANCISCO STA, SSF	707 - F1
CALTRAIN ATHERTON STA, ATN	790 - E2
CALTRAIN BAYSHORE STA, BSBN	688 - A3
CALTRAIN BELMONT STA, BLMT	769 - E1
CALTRAIN BROADWAY STA, BURL	728 - E5
CALTRAIN BURLINGAME STA, BURL	728 - G6
CALTRAIN CALIFORNIA AV STA, PA	791 - B7
CALTRAIN HAYWARD PK STA, SMTO	749 - B3
CALTRAIN HILLSDALE STA, SMTO	749 - C5
CALTRAIN MENLO PK STA, MLPK	790 - F3
CALTRAIN PALO ALTO STA, PA	790 - H5
CALTRAIN REDWOOD CITY STA, RDWC	770 - A6
CALTRAIN SAN BRUNO STA, SBRN	707 - J7
CALTRAIN SAN CARLOS STA, SCAR	769 - G3
CALTRAIN SAN MATEO STA, SMTO	748 - J1

FEATURE NAME Address City, ZIP Code	PAGE-GRID
CALTRAIN S SAN FRANCISCO STA, SSF	708 - A3
CALTRAIN STANFORD STA, PA	790 - J5
MUNI METRO BROAD & PLYMOUTH STA, SF	687 - D2
MUNI METRO GENEVA & SAN JOSE STA, SF	687 - E1
MUNI METRO GILMAN AV STA, SF	688 - B1
MUNI METRO LE CONTE AV STA, SF	688 - B1
MUNI METRO RANDOLPH & ARCH STA, SF	687 - C2
MUNI METRO SF STATE STA, SF	687 - B1
MUNI METRO STA, SF	688 - A2
SAMTRANS TRANSFER POINT, SMCo	728 - B1
SAMTRANS TRANSIT TRANSFER POINT, SMTO	748 - J1
SAMTRANS TRANSIT TRANSFER POINT, SSF	708 - A2
SAMTRANS TRANSIT TRANSFER POINT, SSF	707 - F3
SAMTRANS TRANSIT TRANSFER POINT, BSBN	688 - B6
SAMTRANS TRANSIT TRANSFER POINT, PCFA	726 - H3
SAMTRANS TRANSIT TRANSFER POINT, SMTO	749 - C5
SAMTRANS TRANSIT TRANSFER POINT, RDWC	770 - A6
SAMTRANS TRANSIT TRANSFER POINT, MLPK	790 - F3
SAMTRANS TRANSIT TRANSFER POINT, SBRN	707 - H5
SAMTRANS TRANSIT TRANSFER POINT, SMTO	749 - C6
SAMTRANS TRANSIT TRANSFER POINT, SMTO	749 - C3
SAMTRANS TRANSIT TRANSFER POINT, DALY	687 - C3
SAMTRANS TRANSIT TRANSFER POINT, DALY	687 - C6
SAMTRANS TRANSIT TRANSFER POINT, PCFA	726 - H4
SAMTRANS TRANSIT TRANSFER POINT, MLBR	728 - C4
SAMTRANS TRANSIT TRANSFER POINT, PCFA	706 - J3
SAMTRANS TRANSIT TRANSFER POINT, SCAR	769 - G3
SAMTRANS TRANSIT TRANSFER POINT, DALY	707 - C1
SAMTRANS TRANSIT TRANSFER POINT, RDWC	770 - A4
SAMTRANS TRANSIT TRANSFER POINT, SSF	707 - E4
SAMTRANS TRANSIT TRANSFER POINT, PCFA	706 - J3

VISITOR INFORMATION

FEATURE NAME Address City, ZIP Code	PAGE-GRID
SAN MATEO COUNTY CONV & VIS BUR 111 ANZA BLVD, BURL, 94010	728 - G5

Note Page

Note Page

Note Page

Note Page

CUT ALONG DOTTED LINE

The Thomas Guide®

Thank you for purchasing this Rand McNally Thomas Guide! We value your comments and suggestions.

Please help us serve you better by completing this postage-paid reply card.
This information is for internal use ONLY and will not be distributed or sold to any external third party.

Missing pages? Maybe not... Please refer to the "Using Your Street Guide" page for further explanation.

Thomas Guide Title: San Mateo County **MKT: SFB**

Today's Date: ____________ Gender: ☐M ☐F Age Group: ☐18-24 ☐25-31 ☐32-40 ☐41-50 ☐51-64 ☐65+

1. What type of industry do you work in?
   ☐Real Estate ☐Trucking ☐Delivery ☐Construction ☐Utilities ☐Government
   ☐Retail ☐Sales ☐Transportation ☐Landscape ☐Service & Repair
   ☐Courier ☐Automotive ☐Insurance ☐Medical ☐Police/Fire/First Response
   ☐Other, please specify: ____________
2. What type of job do you have in this industry? ____________
3. Where did you purchase this Thomas Guide? (store name & city) ____________
4. Why did you purchase this Thomas Guide? ____________
5. How often do you purchase an updated Thomas Guide? ☐Annually ☐2 yrs. ☐3-5 yrs. ☐Other: ____________
6. Where do you use it? ☐Primarily in the car ☐Primarily in the office ☐Primarily at home ☐Other: ____________
7. How do you use it? ☐Exclusively for business ☐Primarily for business but also for personal or leisure use
   ☐Both work and personal evenly ☐Primarily for personal use ☐Exclusively for personal use
8. What do you use your Thomas Guide for?
   ☐Find Addresses ☐In-route navigation ☐Planning routes ☐Other: ____________
   Find points of interest: ☐Schools ☐Parks ☐Buildings ☐Shopping Centers ☐Other: ____________
9. How often do you use it? ☐Daily ☐Weekly ☐Monthly ☐Other: ____________
10. Do you use the internet for maps and/or directions? ☐Yes ☐No
11. How often do you use the internet for directions? ☐Daily ☐Weekly ☐Monthly ☐Other: ____________
12. Do you use any of the following mapping products in addition to your Thomas Guide?
    ☐Folded paper maps ☐Folded laminated maps ☐Wall maps ☐GPS ☐PDA ☐In-car navigation ☐Phone maps
13. What features, if any, would you like to see added to your Thomas Guide? ____________
14. What features or information do you find most useful in your Rand McNally Thomas Guide? (please specify)
15. Please provide any additional comments or suggestions you have. ____________

We strive to provide you with the most current updated information available if you know of a map correction, please notify us here.

Where is the correction? Map Page #: ____________ Grid #: ____________ Index Page #: ____________

Nature of the correction: ☐Street name missing ☐Street name misspelled ☐Street information incorrect
☐Incorrect location for point of interest ☐Index error ☐Other: ____________

Detail: ____________

CUT ALONG DOTTED LINE

I would like to receive information about updated editions and special offers from Rand McNally

☐via e-mail E-mail address: ____________

☐via postal mail

Your Name: ____________ Company (if used for work): ____________

Address: ____________ City/State/ZIP: ____________

Thank you for your time and help. We are working to serve you better.

TAPE SHUT

TAPE SHUT

get directions at

randmcnally.com

CUT ALONG DOTTED LINE

2ND FOLD LINE

NO POSTAGE
NECESSARY
IF MAILED
IN THE
UNITED STATES

BUSINESS REPLY MAIL

FIRST-CLASS MAIL PERMIT NO. 388 CHICAGO IL

POSTAGE WILL BE PAID BY ADDRESSEE

RAND MCNALLY
CONSUMER AFFAIRS
PO BOX 7600
CHICAGO IL 60680-9915

1ST FOLD LINE

RAND McNALLY

The most trusted name on the map.

You'll never need to ask for directions again with these Rand McNally products!

- EasyFinder® Laminated Maps
- Folded Maps
- Street Guides
- Wall Maps
- CustomView Wall Maps
- Road Atlases
- Motor Carriers' Road Atlases

CUT ALONG DOTTED LINE

SGTG_07